HANDBOOK OF DEVELOPMENT ECONOMICS
VOLUME II

HANDBOOKS IN ECONOMICS

9

Series Editors

KENNETH J. ARROW

MICHAEL D. INTRILIGATOR

NORTH-HOLLAND
AMSTERDAM • LONDON • NEW YORK • TOKYO

HANDBOOK OF DEVELOPMENT ECONOMICS

VOLUME II

Edited by

HOLLIS CHENERY
Harvard University

and

T.N. SRINIVASAN
Yale University

NORTH-HOLLAND
AMSTERDAM • LONDON • NEW YORK • TOKYO

ELSEVIER SCIENCE PUBLISHERS B.V.
Sara Burgerhartstraat 25
P.O. Box 211, 1000 AE Amsterdam, The Netherlands

Distributors for the United States and Canada
ELSEVIER SCIENCE PUBLISHING COMPANY INC.
655 Avenue of the Americas
New York, N.Y. 10010, U.S.A.

First printing: 1989
Second impression: 1992

Library of Congress Cataloging-in-Publication Data
(Revised for vol. 2)

Handbook of development economics.

   (Handbooks in economics: 9)
   Includes bibliographies and indexes
   1. Economic development – Handbooks, manuals, etc
I. Chenery, Hollis Burnley.   II. Srinivasan, T. N.
1933–   III. Series: Handbooks in economics;
bk. 9.
HD82 H275   1988   338.9   87-34960
ISBN 0-444-70339-X (U.S.: set: jacket)
ISBN 0-444-70337-3 (U.S.: v. 1: jacket)
ISBN 0-444-70338-1 (U.S.: v. 2)

ISBN North-Holland for this set   0 444 70339 X
ISBN North-Holland for this volume   0 444 70338 1

PRINTED IN THE NETHERLANDS

INTRODUCTION TO THE SERIES

The aim of the *Handbooks in Economics* series is to produce Handbooks for various branches of economics, each of which is a definitive source, reference, and teaching supplement for use by professional researchers and advanced graduate students. Each Handbook provides self-contained surveys of the current state of a branch of economics in the form of chapters prepared by leading specialists on various aspects of this branch of economics. These surveys summarize not only received results but also newer developments, from recent journal articles and discussion papers. Some original material is also included, but the main goal is to provide comprehensive and accessible surveys. The Handbooks are intended to provide not only useful reference volumes for professional collections but also possible supplementary readings for advanced courses for graduate students in economics.

CONTENTS OF THE HANDBOOK

PREFACE TO THE HANDBOOK

The scope of the Handbook

Development economics has been defined as the study of the economic structure and behavior of poor (or less developed) countries [W.A. Lewis (1984)]. It is generally agreed that "development" encompasses the reduction of poverty, improvements in the health and education of the population, and an increase in productive capacity as well as rising per capita income. Although the core concerns of development economics are clear enough, its outer boundaries are difficult to establish and essentially arbitrary.

Earlier empirical work in this field focused on changes in the composition of demand, production, employment, and international trade that were observed in the comparative studies done by Kuznets and others. This led to a description of development issues in structural terms, such as the transformation of a poor, stagnant rural society into a more diversified, urbanizing economy capable of sustained growth. The processes associated with this transformation include capital accumulation, human resource development, and the evolution of political and economic institutions, including markets.

In approaching the study of development, it is natural to examine the applicability of conventional analytical tools of economics to the features characteristic of less developed economies. Although the salient problems of a traditional peasant society, a rapidly industrializing economy and a mature nation may be quite different, and countries enter their development stage in varying historical contexts, these differences may not have much impact on the choice of analytical concepts. In its extreme form, this hypothesis is tantamount to a denial of the usefulness of a separate economics of development. Whether neoclassical economics can serve this unifying role is one of the central issues discussed in this Handbook.

Since development economics is explicitly characterized by competing paradigms, rather than by a dominant orthodoxy, we have organized the Handbook around the implications of different sets of assumptions and their associated research programs. While we follow Lewis in identifying the field of development with the problems and behavior of poor countries, we leave open the question of the extent to which this implies a need for a distinctive analytical framework. Exploration of this issue has been ensured by selecting authors known to have different views.

The focus of development economics on problems of poverty and growth makes some branches of conventional economics more relevant than others. Explaining the stylized facts of development involves both the microeconomic behavior of households and production units and the macroeconomics of saving, investment, and financial development. Sectors of the economy that undergo substantial changes during the transformation – such as agriculture, manufacturing, and infrastructure – require particular attention. Perhaps most important of all is the changing international economy within which national development takes place. Indeed, international trade is often described as an engine of growth and development.

Finally, the role of the state is at least as important in the early stages of development as it is later on. Although governments have chosen to intervene in the mobilization and allocation of resources in a variety of ways, their performance of these functions is one of the crucial aspects of a development strategy. We have therefore included in Part 6 a comparison of the experience of countries following different strategies.

Organization

The simplest way to organize the Handbook would be to adopt the traditional division of economics, devoting a chapter to each of the more relevant branches. While we have followed this pattern to a considerable extent, it had to be supplemented to give a more integrated view of related development processes. Thus, we have divided the Handbook into two volumes, each with three parts which focus on the broad processes of development. Each part has an introduction, describing its unifying themes and summarizing its contents.

Volume I starts with a part of six chapters dealing with the concept of development, its historical antecedents, and alternative approaches to the study of development broadly construed.

Part 2 of Volume I is devoted to the structural transformation of economies as they develop over time. Chapter 7 introduces the overall patterns of structural change. Subsequent chapters in Part 2 cover the major development processes: agricultural transformation, industrialization and trade, saving, migration, and urbanization. The main themes of Part 2 are the relations among these development processes and the ways in which they vary from country to country.

The role that human resources play in economic development is the theme of Part 3. As development gains momentum, the quality of the labor force improves through accumulation of human capital in terms of better health, nutrition, and education. The efficiency with which labor markets function in allocating various (skill) categories of labor across sectors and occupations is an important aspect of development. At the early stages, agriculture is the major sector of employment.

The tenurial arrangements under which land is cultivated, and the functioning of credit markets influence resource allocation as well as the pace of technical progress in agriculture. Among other related topics, the five chapters in Part 3 cover the determinants and consequences of population growth, the process of human capital formation (education, health, and nutrition), and labor and credit markets.

In Volume II, the emphasis shifts toward policy issues. Part 4 examines techniques of resource allocation and policy planning at both macro and micro levels. The use of multisectoral models for development policy is first surveyed in general terms and then applied to problems of income distribution. Separate chapters are devoted to macroeconomic management, taxation, and the micro-economics of project selection.

Part 5 consists of seven chapters dealing with the international aspects of development and their effects on policy. Policy issues are introduced in a chapter on international cooperation, which discusses the global institutions needed to integrate developing economies into the world economy. Neoclassical and alternative approaches to studying the role of international trade in the development process are each the subject of a chapter. The role of international capital flows is discussed, with separate chapters devoted to public lending, private lending, and transnational corporations. Since smooth adjustment to shocks is important if development is not to be jeopardized, a separate chapter is devoted to the process of adjustment by which economies handle the experience of unanticipated shocks.

The final part of Volume II looks at the experience of countries pursuing different development strategies and draws lessons for policy. One strategic choice concerns the orientation towards the outside world. An outward-oriented strategy is neutral between production for home use and for export, and between earning foreign exchange through exports and saving foreign exchange through import substitution. An inward-oriented strategy emphasizes production for home use and import substitution. The four chapters of part 6 deal in turn with the experience of primary product exporters, the contrast between countries that have followed an import substitution strategy and those that have had an outward orientation and the special features of large countries.

Acknowledgements

We owe a deep debt of gratitude to the authors of the two volumes for their diligence in preparing their chapters, and in particular for revising them to take account of comments received from other authors and the editors. We thank them for commenting on each others' chapters and on our introductions. Thanks are also due to the Harvard Institute for International Development for sponsoring the conference where authors discussed their preliminary drafts, and to its editor, James Ito-Adler. Our assistants, Melissa Davy at Harvard and Louise Danishevsky at Yale, bore the brunt of keeping various drafts of each chapter in order, typing comments, and generally seeing to it that the preparation of the volumes was kept on an even keel.

HOLLIS CHENERY
Harvard University

T.N. SRINIVASAN
Yale University

Reference

Lewis, W.A. (1984) 'The state of development theory', *American Economic Review*, March: 1–10.

CONTENTS OF VOLUME II

Chapter 19

Income Distribution and Development

IRMA ADELMAN and SHERMAN ROBINSON

Chapter 21
Project Evaluation in Theory and Practice
LYN SQUIRE   1093

PART 5: INTERNATIONAL ASPECTS

PART 6: COUNTRY EXPERIENCE WITH DEVELOPMENT

Introduction
HOLLIS CHENERY

Chapter 29
Primary Exporting Countries
STEPHEN R. LEWIS, JR.

PART 4

PLANNING AND RESOURCE ALLOCATION

INTRODUCTION TO PART 4

HOLLIS B. CHENERY

Harvard University

Introduction

This part of the Handbook places greater emphasis on normative aspects of development. Although policy implications have not been neglected in Parts 2 and 3, they have been treated in the context of individual sectors and markets. Part 4 concentrates more broadly on economy-wide analysis and on the general instruments of development policy.

Since development economics evolved in a period of rapid political and economic change, it has always been heavily policy oriented. In the fifties this typically meant combining macro and micro analysis to produce a set of projections of a country's economic structure that was euphemistically called a national "plan". Its purpose was rarely the detailed control of resources, but rather the exploration of alternative macro-economic approaches or strategies. This approach is largely due to Tinbergen (1956). Its focus was on the relationship between economic objectives (or targets) and the policy instruments available to achieve them. Although his terminology can be subject to misinterpretation, Tinbergen (1956, p. 10) stressed that "this use of the word 'planning' has nothing to do with the type of policy involved". In the Tinbergen tradition, the design of policy and use of planning models are means of testing the feasibility – and in particular the mutual consistency – of various policy alternatives.

The great increase in empirical knowledge, together with changing views of the social objectives to be served by development, have led to some divergence in approaches to development policy. At one extreme is the study of the efficiency of market mechanisms in LDCs with the implication that they have less need for macro economic projections. This trend has led to more sophisticated forms of partial analysis in fields such as project evaluation and taxation.

At the other extreme, analytical advances in multisectoral modeling and the development of efficient computational algorithms have fomented other tendencies, notably the construction of computable general equilibrium (CGE) models. These models are direct descendants of the Leontief input–output system, which was the predominant approach to policy analysis in the fifties – and which is still the technique of choice for simpler economies.

Handbook of Development Economics, Volume II, Edited by H. Chenery and T.N. Srinivasan
© *Elsevier Science Publishers B.V., 1989*

Scope

The five chapters of this part of the Handbook are designed to illustrate techniques for policy planning and resource allocation as these have developed in practice:

Chapter 17 by Arida and Taylor, "Short-Run Macroeconomics", arises out of the experience of the past fifteen years, which has been dominated by issues of inflation, unemployment, and balance of payments disequilibrium, all stemming from external shocks since the early seventies. Their central theme is the need to reformulate the tools of macroeconomics to fit the structural characteristics and periodic disequilibria of LDCs.

Chapters 18 and 19 by Robinson, and Adelman and Robinson, respectively, are devoted to the design of long-term strategies. They incorporate many of the stylized facts of structural change from Volume I in their specification of initial conditions. Chapter 18 traces the evolution of multisectoral analysis from Leontief and Johansen to the current generation of CGE models. Chapter 19 assesses the use of these models for analyzing distributional objectives, which has proved to be one of the most difficult problems in the field of development studies.

Chapters 20 by Ahmad and Stern, and 21 by Squire, evaluate the techniques currently used in designing two of the most important approaches to resource allocation: taxation and the choice of public investments. The two chapters demonstrate how current techniques have emerged from several decades of empirical and theoretical analysis.

Neo-classical vs. structural approaches

The conceptual issues that were discussed in Volume I of this Handbook arise even more acutely in the design and use of policy models. There are two major distinctions in Part 4; one, between general and partial equilibrium analysis, and the other between neo-classical and structural assumptions (see Bardhan, Chapter 3). In the present context, it is not so much a question of the logic of the several approaches as of the usefulness of the empirical research programs based on them. Four logical possibilities result from these distinctions.

The oldest and most widely used planning technique is almost certainly *project evaluation*, using a partial equilibrium framework and neo-classical assumptions. The fact that it has been subject to almost continuous application and refinement over the past thirty years has produced a number of empirical generalizations and rules of thumb, such as those illustrated by Squire (Chapter 21). These lead to the identification of several different kinds of project derived from the experience of the lending agencies.

Input–output, the oldest technique of applied general equilibrium analysis, has also benefited from over thirty years of testing and refinement. Although its theoretical potential is much more limited than the computable general equilibrium approach, this disadvantage is partly offset by the extensive statistical comparisons that have been made of the results of I–O systems in different countries. However, the family of CGE models described by Robinson (Chapter 18) is producing a rapidly growing body of applications that should offset this advantage of the older system.

The research frontier

Although it is hard to predict the movements of the research frontier, there is something to be learned from considering past shifts. At the moment, two of the five chapters listed under Part 4 – *Short-Run Macroeconomics* and *Income Distribution and Development* – are recognized as promising fields, but lack a theoretical framework for organizing research. A more adequate framework will almost certainly require a broader range of hypotheses than has been common in mainstream economics and may involve formal modeling of the political economy of policy choice. This may turn out to be one of the features that distinguish the analysis of developing countries from comparable studies of advanced countries.

Reference

Tinbergen, J. (1956) *Economic policy: Principles and design*. Amsterdam: North-Holland.

Chapter 17

SHORT-RUN MACROECONOMICS

PERSIO ARIDA

Pontifical Catholic University of Rio de Janeiro

LANCE TAYLOR*

Massachusetts Institute of Technology

Contents

*Research support from the Ford Foundation is gratefully acknowledged.

Handbook of Development Economics, Volume II, Edited by H. Chenery and T.N. Srinivasan
© *Elsevier Science Publishers B.V., 1989*

1. Introduction

In this chapter we take up macroeconomic questions arising in the short run, principally regarding stabilization broadly construed. The implicit time frame is one to several quarters. Long-run issues of income distribution and growth are discussed on their own terms in Chapter 6 of this Handbook. For the most part, longer term implications of short-run actions are left unexamined here for want of a framework. Filling this gap is a major task of development macroeconomics – possible approaches are suggested in the conclusion to this chapter and Arida (1986). The reader should also be warned that we concentrate on recent work. Most of the papers cited were written in the 1980s. By our choice of coverage, we do not mean to imply that older contributions are obsolete. To the contrary, the institutional richness of earlier papers – many of them country studies – exceeds that of their successors. However, being more analytical, recent work is easier to survey.

2. Exchange rate management

The possible contractionary effects of devaluation on output are an *ostinato* theme in structuralist macroeconomics. Hirschman (1949) pointed out that if a country devalues from an initial trade deficit, aggregate demand reduction is a likely result. The devaluation gives with one hand, increasing local currency export receipts, but takes more with the other in higher import costs. Lower internal demand is the result. Diaz-Alejandro (1963) further pointed out that by driving up internal prices (for example, through a mark-up over intermediate import costs), devaluation will reduce demand by cutting the real wage. These and other effects were pulled together by Krugman and Taylor (1978) in a static Kaleckian model. They suggested that contractionary devaluation is the likely case in the developing world.

Dynamic processes involving the exchange rate are often important, and two affect these demand-driven results. First, export volume may gradually respond to a higher real exchange rate along a "J-curve". Devaluation is immediately contractionary, but expansionary from the lagged export response. On the other hand, with intermediate goods a large share of prime costs, real devaluations are always less (say by a third) than their nominal counterparts. Real depreciation is further eroded (in the absence of an aggressive crawling peg) by inevitable nominal wage increases in the wake of the exchange rate shift. Which effect – expansion from exports rising along the J-curve or contraction as the profitability of exports or import substitution is reduced by wage inflation – wins the race in a given economy depends intimately on its institutional and techno-logical characteristics. Empirical work is just beginning along these lines [e.g. Solimano (1986) finds several quarters of initial contraction in Chile] and should be aggressively pursued.

Devaluation is inflationary in these demand-driven models – it typically is assumed to drive up prices through intermediate import costs. Recent orthodox pronouncements in Africa (especially from the IMF) seem to assert that exchange depreciation will make prices go down. One story is that with "correct" prices based on a revised real exchange rate, aggregate supply will increase dramatically, with anti-inflationary effects. This argument resembles other neoclassical jumps from low- to high-level circular flow discussed in Chapter 6, and can safely be dismissed. A second line is that devaluation may reduce "rents" accruing to import quota-holders by driving up their import costs. Their reduced spending might bid down internal prices, but if so there would be domestic contraction as well. The price-deflationary effect occurs only when overall activity declines [Taylor (1987)] – the gain on the inflation front does not obviously offset the GNP cost.

Other work has brought supply effects into the picture. Devaluation can be contractionary via intermediate imports [Buffie (1986)], via imported consumer goods and via reduced real credit volume [van Wijnbergen (1986)]. In spite of the already vast literature on the subject, it still forms a promising research topic, particularly from the viewpoint of the financial consequences of devaluation.

In the classical regime model of Buffie (1984), devaluation could be expansion-ary in two circumstances. First, if it alters the real wage. Second, and more interesting, if it decreases the curb market rate of interest. The degree of wage indexation governs the increase in the demand for loans caused by the devalua-tion; the increase in loan supply depends on foreign bonds (or, more generally, on dollar-denominated bonds). If the share of dollar-indexed assets in financial wealth exceeds the degree of wage indexation, the fall in curb market rates stimulates output.

In the classical regime model of van Wijnbergen (1986), dollar-denominated bonds appear in contrast as liabilities of domestic firms. Private wealth holders do not own foreign assets. A devaluation is contractionary because it increases the debt burden; interest on foreign borrowing increases while disposable income falls. Of particular interest is van Wijnbergen's solution to the Argentinean riddle of the late 1970s as to why inflation accelerated in the face of a preannounced slowdown in the rate of devaluation of the nominal exchange rate. Demand expansion caused by the reduction in debt servicing spurred faster inflation.

Like van Wijnbergen, Arida and Lara-Resende (1983) disregard dollar-denominated assets in portfolios. Dollar-denominated debt is invoked to explain the acceleration of inflation. The Central Bank pegs the real interest rate; by

Fisherian arbitrage, the profit rate is therefore given. A devaluation decreases total profits. The same volume of profit can either be obtained through a devaluation of capital stock or through an acceleration of inflation that diminishes real wages and magnifies subsidies. In the face of an increased debt burden, inflation is a mechanism for the defense of the firms' net worth at the expense of workers and public budget equilibrium.

The macro model of Easterly (1985) combines the two strands of financial effects. Portfolios of wealth holders include dollar-denominated assets; dollar-denominated debt occupies a central role in firms' liabilities. As in Arida and Lara-Resende (1983), interest rate pegging occurs. (For more on this see Section 4, below.) Easterly maintains that in Mexico, firms' net worth declined as the upward revaluation of capital stock was insufficient to compensate the increase in dollar-denominated liabilities due to devaluation. The leverage ratio for firms increased accordingly. Since credit risk is based on leverage, investment fell because of the ensuing credit rationing. The fall in consumption, however, was less severe. The wealth effect of devaluation led to an increase in the consumption of the profit-earning class who hold the bulk of financial wealth. Easterly is thus able to explain the common observation that investment is much more affected by devaluation than consumption.

This leads to an interesting conjecture. Suppose that expenditure switches are important. Investment is crucial to the structural adjustment towards an increasingly open economy. But unless countered by Central Bank intervention, capital losses on foreign liabilities after the devaluation can crowd out domestic capital formation [see Taylor and Rosensweig (1984) on Thailand]. In heavily indebted countries, the negative effect of devaluation on investment could in principle be counteracted by a decline in interest rates, as argued by Arida and Lara-Resende (1983). But for heavily indebted countries, the external real interest rate is the lower possible limit for the real domestic interest rate, as will be argued in Section 4 below. If the external interest rate is too high, the country cannot take advantage of the expenditure-switch effect because of bottlenecks in the production of tradables.

A still unexplored financial repercussion of devaluation follows from foreign property. Discussing the case of an exporting sector owned by foreigners, Barbone (1985) showed that devaluation has another contractionary effect. Because of profit remittances, the only component of value added contributing to national income in this sector is the wage bill. The fall in real wages caused by the devaluation reduces aggregate demand. The elasticity conditions in the domestically-owned export sector needed to prevent output contraction are more stringent. A tax on profit remittances is thus justified.

Apart from the financial aspects of devaluation, exchange rate management involves other issues worth pursuing. In the disequilibrium model proposed by Arida and Bacha (1987), optimal exchange rate management depends on the goods markets. In the basic case, devaluation lowers the dollar price of exports and therefore enhances potential demand. If the initial condition is excess demand in the goods markets, devaluation worsens the trade balance by reducing the purchasing power of exports. The quantity exported does not adjust, making the excess demand situation more acute. Even if there is excess supply in goods markets, devaluation may fail to improve the trade balance. The reason is that export demand needs to be more than unit price elastic to offset the import content of export production. Since external disequilibrium may occur under either excess supply or excess demand in goods markets, the habit of prescribing without hesitation a devaluation to correct balance of payments problems is again hardly justifiable. The novelty of Arida and Bacha in that regard is to explore the significance of goods market disequilibrium for exchange rate management.

The Arida and Bacha model allows a reinterpretation of an old development theme: surplus labor. [See also Bacha (1984).] Suppose there is a critical value e^* of the exchange rate e beyond which devaluations fail to increase the dollar value of export receipts. A Walrasian equilibrium may not exist even if $e = e^*$. In this case, one cannot reconcile full employment with external balance by "getting the prices right". The optimal exchange rate e^* is to be supplemented by structurally oriented policies to suppress surplus labor.

In contrast to these limiting results, the Arida and Bacha model enlarged in one significant respect the scope of exchange rate management. In contrast to the case of decreasing returns, a successful devaluation under increasing returns need not necessarily lower real wages. The larger the price elasticity of exports and the degree of increasing returns, the more likely it is that a devaluation may increase real wages. The result is crucially dependent upon the assumption that firms are constrained to zero profit positions. Yet it illustrates the advantages of introducing increasing returns into the discussion of LDC problems as many authors reviewed in Chapter 6 have attempted.

In Arida and Bacha, the exchange rate is set by government fiat. Financial institutions in most LDCs are insufficiently developed to make floating exchange rate regimes viable. A common arrangement involves dual exchange regimes in which the black market rate floats to equilibrate transactions ruled out from the official market by capital controls. Advocates of floating exchange rates frequently look at black-to-official market differentials as revealing the feasibility or not of abandoning fixed exchange rate regimes. But black market differentials respond to several factors – and particularly to domestic interest rates. With floating likely to be infeasible, current dual exchange regimes pose at least two interesting issues.

First, there is the issue of the optimal real exchange rate in the official market over time. Although capital controls give the Central Bank considerable leeway to maintain an overvalued or undervalued exchange rate for long periods, the optimal rate is not likely to be stable. Blind processes of trial and error have characterized policy practice; the magnitudes of the devaluations undertaken after the Mexican Moratorium of 1982 were arbitrary. The widely shared belief that PPP-oriented exchange rate policy is good policy advice has no firm basis [Dornbusch (1982)]. An interesting conjecture is that, in an uncertain environment and leaving aside the financial aspects just discussed, the optimal path would exhibit a severely˜devalued exchange rate after an external credit shock such as the one Mexico suffered in 1982. The initial overshooting would be corrected over time: as reserves build up, the exchange rate would appreciate. The updating rule could be preannounced, making appreciation a known function of the reserves to debt ratio. Contingent rules for the exchange rate in fixed exchange rate regimes are a pressing issue for LDCs.

Three different considerations give plausibility to this conjecture. First, a very large initial depreciation following a very large credit shock is the result to be expected in a floating exchange rate regime; the conjecture amounts to replicating it in the context of fixed rates and capital controls. Second, the effectiveness of devaluation in increasing official reserves may be undermined when black market perceptions differ from the government's. The advantages in timing and scope of a surprisingly large, and consensually definitive, devaluation under uncertainty are underlined by Collins (1983). Her argument, however, is crucially dependent upon the hypothesis that illegally acquired foreign asset holdings constitute an important share of domestic wealth. Third, in an uncertain environment, a very large devaluation is needed to overcome the problems posed by investment irreversibility. A relatively small devaluation leaves in suspense the future course of the exchange rate, increasing the returns to waiting for information. Since the structural adjustment to a credit shock does require sizeable fresh investment, a large devaluation increases the returns to early investment commitment against the benefits of waiting. The bearing of investment irreversibility [see Bernanke (1983a)] on the optimal path of the exchange rate is a wide open research area.

Another aspect of exchange rate policy – the appropriateness of a dollar peg – was recently discussed by Rosensweig (1985). His actors are a pegging country (a LDC), pegged to a pivot country (the United States) and the floating rest of the world. The United States follows a mix of tight money and loose fiscal policy. Consider the case of fiscal policy: U.S. income rises; the dollar appreciates (but not relative to LDC currency); interest rates increase. The trade surplus in the LDC that adheres to the dollar tends to increase because of the income spillover. But it tends to decrease because of both trade diversion out of the dollar area towards exports of the countries that have floating currencies and the adverse direct effect of dollar appreciation on trade with non-dollar-area countries. The net result may be negative under plausible specification of relevant parameters. In the case of tight money in the United States the outcome is certainly negative as the spillover effect turns from positive to negative.

In Rosensweig's model, LDCs willing to stay in the dollar area should adopt expansionary fiscal policy. But while the United States has no problem in financing its deficits, underdeveloped domestic capital markets and rationing in external credit markets render it impossible for LDCs to follow its fiscal lead. As a consequence, the LDC has no choice but to decouple from the dollar area by depreciating its currency. Rosensweig is thus able to explain the decline of the dollar area in the face of present U.S. policies, a finding not obtainable in the usual two-country float model.

The second interesting issue posed by dual exchange rate regimes is the optimal allocation of transactions between the two markets. Continuous financial speculation on black markets can lead to a smaller surplus in the trade balance as the large premiums stimulate over- and under-invoicing. Developing countries often maintain an official peg as a way of preventing the negative financial effects of devaluations discussed above, since it is the official rate that governs financial liabilities. Although experiments with double official markets have not been successful, the issue of insulation between real and financial aspects of devaluations through exchange markets deserves more study. The creation of futures markets on dollar-denominated assets may be a way out. In other cases, the official rate works as a subsidy to essential imports or tax on inelastic exports. These complications lead to the use of taxes and subsidies in exchange rate management.

In Islam (1984) a tax and export-subsidy mix is shown to be preferable to exchange devaluation. The economy produces a tradable export good X and a non-tradable consumption good Q out of labor and an essential imported input N. Imports also include a competitive consumption good M. Wages are indexed to both consumption goods.

In the Islam model, a devaluation increases prices of X, N and M. The output of X increases although it is restrained to some extent by higher N prices and by wage indexation. The demand for Q increases by the income effect derived from sector X. The supply of Q decreases because of higher N prices and wage indexation. The net effect of the devaluation on Q is therefore ambiguous. In contrast, a tax/subsidy policy that spares the imported input while penalizing M and enhancing profitability in X has better results. The adverse supply effect is confined to wage indexation; and demand increases more than in the case of devaluation because the income effect derived from exports is stronger. The tax/subsidy scheme is to be combined with restrictive monetary policy to achieve desired trade balance objectives.

In policy practice the replacement of a quota system in which quotas are tradable by an equivalent system of tariffs on imports is again often seen as a first but necessary step towards a free trade system. The effect of the shift to a tariff system in goods markets depends on whether tariff revenues are rebated or not; in the negative case, the resulting budget surplus is of course contractionary.

More interestingly, quota liberalization decreases wealth by imposing a capital loss on holders of quota rights, as shown by Barbone (1985). If demand deposits are better substitutes for quotas than loans, trade liberalization leads to higher interest rates on loans with ensuing contraction of output.

Ocampo (1987) sets up a full macro model to analyze the effects of changes in pre-existing import quotas. Usually, a quota reduction will shift the national IS curve to the right, by stimulating domestic demand in the short run. Liquidity within the country will also increase if international reserves go up from the trade balance improvement brought about by tighter quotas. If not sterilized, the reserve increase will lead interest rates to fall and output to rise further. If there is a black market in foreign exchange, the reserves may leak back out, and in addition dynamic effects may be important. But, on balance, quotas appear to be a policy instrument well worth considering.

The results of Islam, Barbone, and Ocampo do not relate to trade liberalization as a long-run *desideratum*. Even if freer trade is desirable (recall the doubts of Section 5 of Chapter 6), that happenstance provides no guidance about the problems likely to be encountered during any liberalization attempt. In an economy where trade restrictions are a deepseated feature, the above results indicate that naive trade liberalization may be detrimental to welfare.

Edwards (1984) surveyed the literature on one aspect of trade liberalization dynamics: the current account versus trade account order of liberalization problem. If the current account is opened at a stage where the domestic capital market is repressed, with internal interest rates below external levels, massive capital outflows will take place. In these circumstances, betting against the Central Bank becomes a self-fulfilling prophecy: the probability of regime switch depends on the degree of belief in the capacity of the Central Bank to abort speculative runs by, in fact, switching the regime before they get momentum. If the capital account is opened with domestic interest rates above external rates, appreciation of the real exchange rate due to capital inflows follows. But successful liberalization of the trade account requires a real devaluation of the domestic currency. The conflicting movements of the real exchange rate create the order problem. Given the differential speeds at which goods and capital markets adjust, it seems preferable to open the current account first. Again, the initial depreciation of the exchange rate would be followed by an appreciation in the future.

The relationship between liberalization and debt forms yet another policy puzzle for LDCs. On the one hand, liberalization of the trade account may lead the private sector to overborrow, as argued in Section 5, below. The probability of a debt crisis increases with liberalization. On the other hand, trade liberalization is frequently implemented in the face of foreign borrowing constraints. Since the real interest rate is positive, liberalization in these circumstances is costly if it increases the burden of debt by reducing the trade surplus in the short run. The reluctance of heavily indebted countries to undertake cold-turkey liberalization may be rationally justified, since it increases the probability of either occurrence or persistence of debt crises.

Summarizing these contributions to the devaluation/commercial policy literature is not feasible, since so many "effects" are involved. The initial demand contraction line has been supplemented by financial and supply-side channels which may be more important in practice. Black markets and dual rates raise interesting problems, as do combinations of simultaneous or phased changes in the exchange rate and commercial policy. Numerical model simulations, e.g. Taylor, Yurukoglu and Chaudhry (1986) for Nigeria, suggest that there may be substantial gains from imaginative policy design along the lines suggested by Islam (1984). However, policies must be unique to each economy, since institutions and policy flexibility vary enormously in the Third World. In Nigeria, for example, Barbone's (1985) contractionary effect of devaluation via foreign ownership of export industries is reversed, since proceeds from oil extraction are directed to state and local governments which spend freely on non-traded goods.

A final point is that dynamics of exchange adjustment are crucial. Because it is inflationary, may be contractionary, and creates risk of bankruptcy (Section 5), devaluation may be rationally eschewed in any short run. But as noted in Section 3 of Chapter 6, progressive real appreciation may result, imperiling the current account. As discussed in the following section, speculation against the pegged rate is the usual outcome. It creates pressure for a maxi-devaluation with resultant real side shocks. After the maxi, lags in export response and the erosion of the initial real depreciation by wage increases vie as the dominant effects. A crawling peg policy [Williamson (1981), Bacha (1978)] is one way to smooth such dynamics, creating difficulties in accommodation to indexation in its own turn. Macro adjustment problems in developing economies are intriguing, precisely because they never disappear.

3. Speculation

Speculation is frequently blamed in LDCs for being inflationary and detrimental to growth. Analytical representations of policy-makers' anxieties usually take the form of changes in price expectations or asset preferences. Prime areas for speculation are in land, food, and foreign exchange markets.

Land is a non-produced asset. Keynes' strictures of Chapter 17 apply: speculation shifts demand from assets with positive to zero employment elasticity – unemployment will thereby rise [Drazen (1980)]. An accelerator in investment demand means that linkage land speculation may lead to an inferior growth trajectory as well. This argument has to be qualified, however, by technical change which increases the relevant concept of land supply. Two lines of research are of interest. First, since housing is an important item in workers' consumption basket, a demand shift toward urban land is inflationary for the usual reasons stressed in core theories of inflation. Note, however, that this characteristic is not unique to land; food speculation would provoke the same consequences. Second, rural land speculation may hasten the demise of traditional agriculture, creating a powerful incentive towards the capitalistic organization of production. To the extent to which capitalism proves to be more efficient, land speculation may actually enhance growth. The introduction of land speculation into the terms of trade models discussed in Section 3 of Chapter 6 is an open area for research, especially if capitalistic industry seems blocked by traditional arrangements of agricultural production.

In contrast, food is a produced good. If food can be both stored as an item of wealth and currently produced, food speculation can be better dealt with by a redefined Tobin's q concept. In Dutt (1986), however, agricultural output does not react to stock prices. The analysis is interesting when speculation is construed as a response to an exogenous and temporary shock such as a bad harvest. Dutt provides an analytical basis for the intuitive argument that price increases following a bad harvest may last longer with than without food speculation. While the result gives support to the claim that speculation plays an important role in famines, the absence of effects of stock prices on output inevitably leads to the conclusion that food speculation does not matter in the long run. There is obvious interest in finding out conditions under which a Tobin's q analysis of food speculation may not generate the normal result, namely that food speculation enhances food output. Under diminishing returns and fixed working capital, it may be conjectured that speculation may actually decrease production if the change in the rate of return on stocks brought by the speculative price increase exceeds the change in the rate of return on production at current output levels.

The case of exchange speculation is somewhat more complicated. Consider an active fixed real exchange rate regime. Capital controls permit the Central Bank to peg the official exchange rate. If substitution between domestic and foreign imports is imperfect, exchange speculation as reflected in the black market premium is inflationary to the extent to which imported raw materials are priced in the assessment of costs by black market quotations. Under these circumstances, exchange speculation is equivalent to a supply shock. It may be stagflationary when the Central Bank faces an acute shortage of foreign reserves. When the black market premium increases, official exports are postponed and imports anticipated. As a result, the trade surplus decreases and reserves are depleted. Under- and over-invoicing of items in the current account may dampen to some extent the speculative increase in the black market premium. But as noted in Section 4, the final outcome is most often a discrete devaluation with the usual stagflationary shocks. Exchange speculation becomes a self-fulfilling prophecy, as Frenkel (1983) shows in a neat model. Attempts at credit creation to offset an external shock may reduce confidence in domestic assets by holding internal interest rates down. Capital flight may ensue, perhaps not easily reversed by subsequent credit restriction, as Arida (1985) argues in the institutional context of Brazil. By driving up internal interest rates, capital flight ensures its own ends.

This sad history repeats itself every few months in some corner of the Third World. Is there any way it can be avoided? The crawling peg, as pointed out above, is one partial solution. Another is interest rate management. The higher the domestic rate of interest (or, more generally, the tighter domestic credit controls), the more costly speculation becomes even for holders of foreign bonds. The danger lies in throwing out the domestic activity baby with the black market speculation bath. Speculation may indeed by effectively repressed by pegging internal interest rates at high positive real levels. But the policy constrains output by cutting investment while accelerating inflation via the Cavallo/Wright Patman effect. The problems of exchange rate speculation under a foreign exchange constraint form a research area extending beyond the consequences of foreign exchange being a non-produced asset.

Finally, one has to deal with the frequently heard arguments against speculation on the grounds that it "dries up" credit. Field (1984) rediscusses the old theme of speculation as "draining" funds from the rest of the economy. The characteristics of the speculative asset scarcely matter; what is relevant is heavy trading. High trading volumes can persist without necessarily giving rise to changes in asset prices; conversely, asset prices may rise or fall on very low levels of trading. As a consequence, the actual price of the speculative asset also matters little. The "draining" effect occurs when expectations change rapidly in different ways for different individuals. The transactions demand for money increases for given real income and interest rates, giving rise to potential macro instability as analyzed by Minsky (1975) and Taylor and O'Connell (1985). Because of the dependency of transactions demand on volatility of trading volumes, a speculative spurt can increase interest rates, therefore substantiating the impressionistic arguments so common in LDCs. Note, however, that speculation in this sense takes place only to the extent to which information is differentially available or differently interpreted; the expectations that can lead to the "draining" effect are not rational in the established sense (as consensually based on a proper grasp of the true structure of the economy) but are Keynesian as expounded in Chapter 12 of *General Theory*. In light of the historical experience recounted by Kindleberger (1978), the Keynesian approach makes more practical sense than rational expectations.

4. Interest rate management

As noted in Section 6 of Chapter 6, interest rate determination in many developing countries which have gone through a process of dollarization of asset markets can hardly be described by closed economy models in which the short-term real interest rate may deviate from the long-run equilibrium by the liquidity effect. True, open economy determination by the arbitrage condition does not exactly apply in most cases. Exchange and capital controls blur the equalization of the domestic rate to the external rate plus expected depreciation. Yet two factors have rendered the open economy model increasingly appropriate. The first is dollarization itself. To the extent to which dollar holdings form a sizeable proportion of financial wealth, unstable movements in black market premium tend to validate the arbitrage condition. The second factor is the presence of dollar-denominated liabilities. Heavy foreign borrowing causes the external interest rate to govern a substantial part of domestic liabilities. Arbitrage occurs between domestic currency and dollar-denominated liabilities; the functioning of the economy resembles a fully open system's except that no transactions in real dollars take place. The first factor pertains to domestic wealth holders; the second, to indebted domestic firms.

Under external credit rationing, the arbitrage condition should be replaced by an inequality. We will label the sum of the external rate and expected depreciation premium the "natural" interest rate. If the domestic rate is below the natural rate, both domestic firms and wealth holders borrow on domestic capital markets. The former borrow to prepay dollar-denominated debt; the latter to invest abroad. The excess demand on domestic capital markets increases the interest rate until equalization to the natural rate obtains. If the domestic rate is above the natural rate, however, neither domestic firms nor domestic wealth holders can borrow abroad because of credit rationing. External rationing reconciles financial openness with the widely observed practice of pegging the domestic interest rate by monetary policy: interest rate pegging is possible above, but not below, the natural rate.

The first conjecture here is that there is no justification on normative grounds to peg the interest rate above the natural rate. For a situation in which the external credit constraint is binding is of necessity inferior to a situation in which credit markets operate normally. A second conjecture is that it is costly to run against market expectations. The advantage of the optimal exchange rate path sketched in Section 2 is that along this path the devaluation premium is either nil or transformed into an appreciation premium; as a consequence, along this path equalization with the natural rate leads to lower interest rates than along paths characterized by timid devaluations that perpetuate the devaluation premium. Optimum exchange rate management gives the maximum rate of investment because it minimizes the domestic interest rate without violating the natural rate lower limit.

A promising research field is the optimal strategy of equalization to the natural rate. One obvious candidate is interest rate pegging. In favour of it lies the common belief that interest rate floating to clear domestic capital markets is as undesirable as exchange rate floating to clear exchange markets. Yet this apparent isomorphism lacks theoretical justification; its claim to truth deserves further investigation. Against interest rate pegging is the fact that the natural rate depends on the expectation premium, a variable that cannot be observed directly. Under interest rate pegging, fluctuations in the premium can only be observed through unexpected variations in the quantitative accommodating variable (typically money).

Another strategy that may lead to the natural rate is market determination. With some modifications to eliminate transaction costs, the Brazilian case [Dornbusch and da Silva (1984)], might provide a model for this alternative mode of equalization. Firms indebted in dollars are allowed to prepay the debt at any given moment by making a deposit of the corresponding amount at the Central Bank at the ruling exchange rate. If the domestic interest rate is lower than the natural rate, indebted firms borrow on domestic capital markets, thus driving the domestic interest rate to equalization with the natural rate. The interesting part of the arrangement is that it works the other way around. If domestic interest rates are too high, firms can draw on dollar-denominated deposits. The corresponding inflow of money drives interest rates down. It is thus possible to assure equalization by market forces without having to open the capital account. Two arguments can be made against this mode of equalization. First, it implies that exchange risk is borne by the Central Bank on the total amount of prepaid foreign debt. A correction for this distortion is suggested in Section 5. Second, it holds for economies in which financial openness manifests itself through dollar-denominated debt. For truly dollarized LDCs, interest rate pegging may be only feasible alternative since most of dollar assets are illegally acquired.

5. Government behavior

The conservatism of present times has replaced the Keynesian emphasis on market failures by a growing concern over public failures. Policy misbehavior is seen at the heart of inflation, balance of payments and unemployment problems. Instead of benignly operating to eliminate imperfections and to articulate citizens' demand for public services, government is perceived as operated by utility-maximizing individuals whose budget constraints are given by the particular cost–reward structure they confront. The problem of how to design government systems and policy rules to prevent bureaucrats and politicians from inflating or indebting the economy is the order of the day.

Interest groups, however, ought not be ignored. Much of current theory is cast in atomistic terms. But, however abstract government may be portrayed, it is backed by, and responds to, specific interest groups. There is no reason to expect interest groups endowed with political leverage not to act rationally to increase their share in income. Market failures may provoke public policy failures.

Unsustainable attempts at exchange rate appreciation or pursuing explosive paths of indebtedness are phenomena that cannot be understood without reference to the political economy of government behavior. We can illustrate the possibilities with one more dynamic exchange rate example. Devaluation may be expansionary or contractionary in the short run. The government may respond to an increased level of activity by gradual appreciation (to reduce inflation to protect holders of non-indexed assets) or depreciation (to improve the trade balance). The contractionary devaluation/gradual depreciation and expansionary devaluation/gradual appreciation combinations correspond to cases A and B in the model of Taylor (1985) described in Section 2 of Chapter 6; they are dynamically stable. Other combinations of macro and government policy responses diverge from the steady state, but in practice could well be pursued. Such instabilities may be exacerbated by widespread indexing which precludes the distributional changes necessary for exchange rate modifications to be effective, or by supply shocks.

Winograd (1987) and Taylor (1988) elaborate the details of these trade-offs. Winograd argues that money wage increases may be expansionary. But then if there is a Phillips type dynamic response of wages to higher output, a destabilizing inflation/output spiral may ensue which must be braked by monetary or other policies. Taylor shows that money wage increases are expansionary under the same conditions in which devaluation is contractionary in a simple Kaleckian model. If these conditions apply, macro stabilization in semi-industrialized countries is a correspondingly difficult exercise. These distributional responses played a role in upsetting recent heterodox shock inflation stabilizations of the type discussed in Section 6.

Leaving aside interest groups, there are some lines of research which can be followed up without having to specify the social matrix. The first is given by the bankruptcy constraint. It seems useful to model government behavior in LDCs (and probably in developed countries, too) under the assumption that it will not allow widespread bankruptcies to develop. An economy-wide level of bankruptcy risk, as expressed by the inability to meet current cash transactions and rising intermediation costs, may worsen recessions. This point was raised by Fisher (1933); see also Bernanke (1981, 1983b). Net social costs caused by bankruptcies are augmented by their disastrous consequences for the ruling group or party. The bankruptcy constraint in LDCs affects state actions regarding exchange risk, inertial inflation, and financial instability.

An exchange rate devaluation poses a bankruptcy risk for private firms indebted in dollars. Both the fear of internal disarray and political pressure exerted by foreign banks curiously oblivious to local free market ideologies (as in Chile in recent years) force government explicitly to absorb exchange risk [see Diaz-Alejandro (1985)]. Alternatively, the state may buy assets of indebted firms at favorable prices; or it can sell to indebted firms (and multinationals) a hedge against exchange risk (typically, a government bond with exchange indexation clauses). Regardless of the form, the exchange rate subsidy increases the budget deficit. Given the burden of external debt, the larger the probability that the government finds it necessary to devalue, the stronger the latent tendencies towards budget disequilibrium. This suggests that the assessment of intertemporal budget deficits in heavily indebted LDCs requires allowance for the bankruptcy constraint; the larger the private non-insured debt outstanding, the more important this allowance becomes. The reverse argument also holds. Aware of the bankruptcy constraint, government will seek overvaluation or will push to its extreme the chance of succeeding in adjusting to an external crisis without depreciating the exchange rate. All external shocks are assumed to be temporary unless their persistance makes it impossible not to recognize their permanent character.

This suggests an interesting conjecture. Without the exchange subsidy, private borrowing in dollars would be smaller. To the extent to which the private sector anticipates that it will be bailed out by government, moral hazard sets in. Moreover, an exchange rate subsidy permits government to meet obligations in foreign exchange for a longer period than without the subsidy because private borrowing cannot be perfectly replaced by public borrowing. The capacity to postpone the collapse by exchange subsidies adds another aspect of the over-borrowing effect. Finally, because of the subsidy, the government tends to delay the adjustment and continues to borrow until facing a foreign credit constraint. The conjecture is that exchange subsidies have a crucial role in the phenomena of over-indebtedness in LDCs. A crucial difficulty in proving this conjecture lies in the absence of a theory of optimal external indebtedness. Given the uncertainty in external environment, apparent incapacity to pay is no proof of over-indebtedness – because of unforeseen circumstances, even sensible policies pursued in the past might have gone away.

Turning to inflation, it stands to reason that either in a flex-price world or in a world where contracts are perfectly price-level or inflation-contingent, demand policies to reduce inflation are almost costless. But inflation in several LDCs does not unfold in these ideal worlds. Legal or informal indexed contracts staggered over time impart inertia to inflation (see Section 6 below). A liquidity squeeze would be translated into bankruptcies as the lack of demand prevents firms from meeting contractual obligations. Bankruptcies become more acute the more successful the liquidity squeeze. An abrupt decline of inflation from 200 percent to 0 percent in one year leads to an increase in real wages of approximately 30 percent under 100 percent wage indexation every six months. When the inertial component of inflation is large, active monetary policy violates the bankruptcy constraint. This explains why LDC governments committed to, or forced to comply with, tight money targets defined over the stock of high powered money, or M_1, eventually grant liquidity status to a more inclusive aggregate. The awareness of the bankruptcy constraint also explains the diffusion of indexed contracts; it lies at the root of the inflexibility of inflationary expectations observed in chronic processes of inflation in several LDCs. Indexation is a natural response once inflation is perceived to reach a chronic stage. If there are costs in indexing, as experience suggests, the incentive towards indexation depends on the belief that money will accommodate. Awareness of the bankruptcy constraint reinforces this belief, causing over-indexation.

The bankruptcy constraint operates more visibly still in connection with financial instability [Diaz-Alejandro (1985)]. LDC experiences with financial deregulation show a recurrent pattern. Easy access to financial intermediation and less controls on the asset side led to increasing levels of risk. When bankruptcies developed, government was forced to insure demand and time deposits. In the extreme case of Chile the needed rescue operations rendered government directly responsible for more than 75 percent of the entire banking system. The conjecture here is that the awareness of the bankruptcy constraint induces financial intermediaries to overexposure on the asset side. Since the probability of government underwriting the intermediaries' portfolio risk is perceived as being high, the adoption of prudent standards is not rational. In historical experiences of de-regulation in financial markets, the distinction between the lender of last resort and the socializer of private losses was artificial. Irrespective of written rules, government realized that it was politically impossible not to honor the implicit 100 percent insurance on deposits of financial intermediaries.

We have three cases in which private awareness of the bankruptcy constraint leads to public excesses – over-indebtedness, over-indexation, and over-exposure. Moreover, private losses seem only to be socialized when the losers are firms as opposed to individuals. Workers may not be fully compensated for lower real wages, nor profit-recipients for losses in stock markets, black markets, or land markets. Aside from inequalities in access to and power over decision-makers, the phenomenon may be attributed to organizational capital [Arida and Lara-Resende (1983)]. Models that do not recognize firms as more than bundles of workers and fixed capital cannot distinguish between the bankruptcy and unemployment constraints. In recent experience in troubled developing countries, dramatic declines in employment have not been followed by waves of bankruptcy of the same extent.

Apart from the bankruptcy constraint, government behavior in LDCs is subject to political constraints on expenditures and taxes. These constraints account for the discrepancy between actual government behavior and the optimal behavior prescribed by Barro (1983). In Barro's model, a permanent loss in revenues would be immediately and fully offset by higher taxes and reduced outlays, leaving debt unchanged. In the face of a transitory shock, debt finance would bridge the budget gap in the short term; small taxes and outlay changes would assure in this case the intertemporal solvency of government.

Actual government behavior in LDCs seems to be the opposite: government accommodates permanent shocks while responding in the short run to transitory shocks. Political constraints on the rate of expenditures or the rate of increase in taxes explain partially (at least) the failure in following tax-smoothing behavior. Dornbusch (1984) gives additional reasons for departing from the Barro model: the difficulties of separating out transitory from permanent disturbances, discount rates in excess of market rates because of the government's budget constraint, and the necessity (particularly for LDCs) of supporting minimum standards of living for the maximum time possible. The rapid growth of indebtedness of many raw materials exporting countries after the terms of trade shocks of the late 1970s can be rationalized along such lines [Eaton and Taylor (1986)]. Another open research field refers to dynamically inconsistent policies. Debt repudiation and taxation on interest or debt are examples of outcomes which, if socially desirable under certain circumstances, may provide a rationale for accommodating large shocks through explosive debt trajectories. Calvo (1978) has shown that governments maximizing inflation tax revenue have an incentive to be dynamically inconsistent. Accommodation of large shocks through debt may provide another case of an incentive for inconsistent behavior. As a conjecture, the adaptation of the problems of regime switching such as discussed in Flood and Garber (1980) may provide an interesting framework for dynamic inconsistency. Because of uncertainty, in some circumstances reconsideration of obligations incurred in the past may be inevitable [Fischer (1983)]; the conditions for repudiation of the old money as discussed by Flood and Garber in hyperinflations may be replicated, mutatis mutandis, for the debt repudiation problem in hyperindebtedness processes.

Another solution to the failure in following Barro's tax-smoothing prescription may be obtained by specifying the social matrix. Going beyond atomistic models is essential in connection with this problem. Consider the following setting. Workers do not hold government debt. Because of effective demand, employment is sensitive to government outlays. In the face of a permanent budget shock, workers' first choice would be equilibrating the budget via taxes on capital. The second choice would be additional finance through debt. Profit recipients' preferred solution differs. Under mark-up pricing and a fixed labor-to-output ratio, a cut in government outlays would jeopardize profits by reducing demand. Ideally, budget equilibrium would be restored by taxes on wages or, if public servants form a sizeable proportion of total employment, by lower wages. The second choice of profit recipients is debt finance.

The conjecture is that debt finance emerges initially as a social compromise. In non-Marxian theories, a game theoretical approach should be used; in Marxian theories, Elster's (1983) variational rationality would account for this strategic class behavior. Each class holds the hope of winning in the future. Debt finance is more likely to emerge in contexts in which the result of social conflicts on how to equilibrate the budget is unclear. The more permanent the shock is perceived to be, the stronger the incentive to compromise on a second choice. Hirschman (1981) describes these dramas in a political economy with characteristic flair.

This conjecture about the origin of debt generates a result opposite to Barro's. It also helps explain why the fiscal deficit is not fully matched by private saving. Since holders of debt believe that workers will bear the future tax increase, they do not offset deficits by increasing either current or future savings. If true, the conjecture would give additional support for an endogenous wealth concept. In the defense of endogeneity of wealth by Taylor and O'Connell (1985), the state of confidence plays a crucial role. Here, endogeneity follows from uncertainty on the resolution of social conflicts. Since no social class anticipates that it will have to absorb the debt burden, perceived social wealth is greater then wealth that would result from a perfectly forseeable future. As the problem of assuring government solvency becomes acute, two conflicting solutions emerge. Workers favor debt default or wealth taxes to alleviate the debt burden; profit recipients prefer taxes on wages or at least cutting expenditures to government not honoring its obligations. The similarities between this "core" theory of government debt to core theories of inflation should be explored.

Indeed, the exploration can go further to take up issues of public enterprise finance. In several corners of the Third World, the budget for entrepreneurial activities of the state is several times the traditional treasury budget. Private interests cluster around state enterprises because investment of the latter is effective demand for the former. The implications in terms of political economy cannot be overstated, but even standard analytical tools can be used to address the impact on the public deficit of state enterprise activity, as in the innovative computable general equilibrium simulations of Sarkar and Panda (1986).

Increases in regulated state enterprise prices are frequently viewed· as a politically attractive alternative to tighter fiscal policy. Even in countries with a well-established fiscal apparatus, political costs of raising regulated prices may be smaller (or at least are levied by different groups) than those of increasing taxes. For countries with large external debts, higher state enterprise prices seem to be the obvious response to the fact that much of the debt is owed directly by such firms. However, depending on the institutional arrangement that regulates financial flows between publicly controlled firms and the treasury, only part of the proceeds from regulated price increases goes to the fiscal accounts; the remainder may finance investment or other outlays. The net effect on aggregate demand cannot be predicted a priori – even the net effect on the fiscal deficit is subject to doubt. The point is that a real increase in regulated prices acts as a supply shock which tends to accelerate inflation, reducing the real value of tax collection.

Moreover, high regulated prices may worsen the trade balance because the outputs of state enterprises enter as inputs into tradables. Given the devastating effects of exchange devaluation on the public budget, it may be rational from a deficit-reducing viewpoint to increase the trade surplus by subsidizing regulated prices than by increasing them and depreciating the exchange rate.

A final question regards the distribution of wealth. In several LDCs the capacity of shifting away the inflation tax on liquid assets is affected by class status. Workers do not typically own equity; their transactions demand for money is relatively large; changes in the interest rate affect their wealth since housing represents, by and large, the bulk of accumulated savings. The list of class differences that affect the allocation of wealth could be easily expanded. In models like Taylor's (1985), classes are crucial to the dynamics of the real side and to income determination; but asset markets and wealth decisions are based on "the public". Correcting this omission may add policy insight. For example, suppose that wage earners hold a higher share of their wealth in the form of money than do profit recipients. A shift in the wealth distribution away from workers will reduce money demand and lead interest rates to fall, raising output. Across steady states in which the degree of capacity utilization is held constant, a more expansionary fiscal stance will be offset by *less* concentration in wealth. The trade-off might be important in practice.

6. Inertial inflation

The critique of naive prescription of tight money as a strategy to curb inflation (noted in Section 6 of Chapter 6) is already vast and still expanding. Arguments come from the most diverse models. As an example, consider Taylor's (1985) and Liviatan's (1984) standard monetary-growth model of the Sidrauski–Brock type. In Taylor, long-run neutrality does not obtain. Expansionary monetary policy leads to higher steady-state inflation in case A but to *lower* inflation in case B. In Liviatan, the tightening of monetary policy leads to a uniformly *higher* rate of inflation under a sensible (although certainly not unique) definition of the constant budget deficit condition.

Common criticism in LDCs, however, is less sophisticated. The dismal record of tight money (and exchange appreciation) strategies to curb inflation is attributed not to theoretical pitfalls but rather to the inertial component of inflation. Inertia, of course, is not unique to LDCs [see Gordon (1982)]. The recognition inertia poses the quest for its understanding. The problem has been amply debated in Argentina and Brazil, e.g. Lopes (1984) and Arida and Lara-Resende (1985). These authors ascribe inertia to a salient characteristic of entrenched inflation: contract indexation.

Consider the following abstract setting. Both labor and non-labor contracts are indexed to the general price level. Contracts are endowed with backward-looking 100 percent plus indexation clauses. The average length of contracts is six months, say. Readjustment of nominal values takes place at the end of the six-month indexation period. Not honoring the indexation clause is very costly. Contracts are staggered over time; money accommodates.

In this setting, the on-going rate of inflation perpetuates itself even if the real fiscal budget is in equilibrium and no supply shocks are under way. Inflation is inertial under these circumstances: the best predictor for future inflation is past inflation. Inertial inflation occurs because of indexation. At every point in time the nominal value of a contract is revised upwards; events that happened up to six months in the past are brought to bear to current inflation. Six months becomes the extent of the past kept in the memory of the economic system. A success in bringing down inflation in period t, say, is undermined by the fact that contracts revised in period $t + 1$ still reflect the higher inflation rates that prevailed from $t - 5$ to t. Eliminating the memory of the economic system altogether is one possible way of breaking down inflation inertia.

Three strategies have been suggested. The first consists in removing the frictions that account for the sluggishness in reducing the indexation period. The argument is that the smaller the transaction costs involved in recasting contracts, the smaller the inflation rate needed to obtain a given contraction in the memory of the economic system. The danger of this strategy is that more perfect indexation increases the vulnerability of the economy to supply shocks.

The second strategy, most widely applied in practice, is a wage and price freeze. A key question is the impact of the freeze on aggregate demand. The efficiency of tax collection is likely to improve and investment may fall if real interest rates rise when inflation is slowed. These contractionary effects may be offset, on the other hand, by a reduction in forced saving and removal of the inflation tax, as well as by progressive redistributional policies pursued along with the freeze.

The outcome in several recent "heterodox shock" stabilizations of the type proposed by Lopes (1984) was that demand held stable or rose – getting rid of forced saving and the inflation tax had visible expansionary effects. But then demand pressure on flex-price markets set off renewed price inflation which fed back into wages and exchange rate à la Winograd (1987).

Further problems in heterodox shocks stem from the volatility of relative prices at high inflation caused by indexed contracts. Since contracts are staggered, it is only through time that relative prices achieve equilibrium. To freeze nominal prices at any given day by legislative fiat would in all probability freeze inconsistent relative prices. Inconsistency as well as any shocks to supply and demand would be absorbed by rationing devices. The lifting of the freeze in this case is likely to be followed by pressures to restore previous relatives which would revive inflation. A successful freeze depends on solving the nearly unsurmountable practical problem of adjusting freeze prices to the time elapsed since the last pre-freeze increase. Another complication derives from betting against the freeze. If agents believe that the freeze will not last, velocity increases; unless the Central Bank reduces money supply adequately, the expectation of a collapse of price controls becomes self-fulfilling [Solimano (1984)].

The third strategy to eliminate inertial inflation was put forward by Arida and Lara-Resende (1985). It is the Pareto-superior dual to the freeze: instead of stopping prices by legislative fiat, it gives agents the option of switching to indexed money. The Monetary Reform strategy has three elements. The first element is the introduction of new money (NM). On a pre-announced date, the NM will be put into circulation. During the transition period, NM and old money circulate side by side. The rate of exchange between old and NM is revised daily. The NM appreciates daily in accordance with the general price index in the old money. Agents are free to convert old for NM or vice versa. The Central Bank accommodates the demand for NM.

The second component is a conversion rule for contracts indexed in the old money. Full indexation clauses in the old money will not be abolished. It will be possible, however, to opt for a conversion of both labor and non-labor contracts in NM in accordance with a definite formula. The conversion formula would calculate the average real value of the contract over the previous period and transform it into NM. The conversion formula is not intended to give gains or losses to those switching to NM contracts; it replaces the peak-and-valley pattern of real contract values which cause inflation inertia by constant real values. As an incentive towards shifting to NM contracts, the depreciation of old money can be set at a rate slightly above inflation.

The third element of the Monetary Reform is the solution to the anchor problem. How can agents be assured that government will not reinflate the economy? Reputational reasons alone can hardly be sufficient. A possible solution is to impose tight limits on the supply of NM. But because the fall in velocity is probably large, tight supply of NM forces the government to choose between violating the limits or permitting massive over-contraction.

Another solution is to anchor the NM on the exchange rate. Pegging the exchange rate in the passive sense, however, is not feasible for LDCs subject to external credit rationing. The third aspect of the Monetary Reform put forward Arida and Lara-Resende is a Wicksellian solution to the anchor problem. As discussed in Section 4 above, LDCs with large stocks of dollar-denominated liabilities may promote interest rate arbitrage without having to switch to passive pegging of the exchange rate. To appreciate the Wicksellian solution, consider an unexpected increase in money demand. Domestic interest rates increase. If the

NM is anchored to the exchange rate, an inflow of foreign capital occurs. The expansion of monetary base accommodates demand and brings the domestic interest rate down to the natural level r^*. In the Wicksellian solution, no inflow of foreign capital occurs. But domestic firms would increase their indebtedness in dollar-denominated assets. If Central Bank accommodates the larger demand for these assets, monetary base expands until the domestic interest rate is again equal to r^*.

There are two unsettled issues posed by the Monetary Reform strategy which deserve emphasis. One is the feasibility of extending it to dollarized LDCs. In dollarized economies, the NM would have to compete with the dollar. Another issue is the proper timing of Monetary Reform. Low, one-digit inflation may be inertial but hardly seems a candidate for Monetary Reform as designed in Arida-Resende; hyperinflations, on the other hand, may impose some form of monetary reform as the old money fulfills neither of the three traditional functions of money. The proper range of inflation is that, being inertial, would call forth Monetary Reforms is an open question.

Leaving aside the Monetary Reform, there are several issues of inertial inflation itself that deserve further investigation. First, there is the problem of the proper measurement of inflation. Suppose inflation accelerates, but that the indexation period is reduced in such an extent that the real average value of both labor and non-labor contracts is unchanged. Moreover, suppose that agents are able to economize on money holdings either because the economy is dollarized or because Central Bank allows interest or indexation on bank deposits. A concept of "adjusted for indexation effects" inflation would exhibit little sensitivity to the acceleration of inflation under these circumstances. The acceleration would impose a tax on holdings; but cash holdings decrease very fast with indexation of bank deposits and inflation. The conjecture here is that, because of indexation, the normal measure of inflation over-estimates the relevant inflation. A constant inflation accompanied with by lower transaction costs in indexing bank deposits would mean a reduced inflation in the adjusted concept.

Second, there is the problem of understanding imperfect indexation. Why would agents, and particularly workers, adhere to fixed length 100 percent plus indexation if the indexation clause fails to provide constancy of the real contract value? In Arida and Lara-Resende (1985), two explanations are offered. First, that by sticking to fixed length contracts workers succeed in keeping the relative wage structure constant. The parallel to Keynes' argument on the downward rigidity of nominal wages is evident. Second, that the alternative arrangement which assures constancy of contract values is unstable. Trigger-point indexation induces running every specific product controlled by the firm ahead of the general price index based on which wages and raw-material prices are readjusted. As a consequence, inflation tends to accelerate. Research on alternative indexation schemes is a promising research field. Apart from trigger-point schemes, forward-looking indexation and futures markets as hedge against unexpected fluctuations in inflation rates are alternative candidates worth investigating.

Full backward-looking indexation clauses do not prevent adjustment of relative prices. Rigidity of relative prices, the topic of the next section, derives from other causes.

7. Disequilibrium

Some key prices in LDCs – the exchange rate and minimum wages – are set by government fiat. The fixed-price assumption of disequilibrium macroeconomics à la Malinvaud (1977) and Grandmont (1983) is rendered literally true because of government regulation. Moreover, as noted in Chapter 6, policy discussions in LDCs are frequently centered on "getting prices right" to eliminate unemployment and deficits. But one can only determine how to adjust prices properly based on the understanding of how the economy functions under "wrong" relative prices. This task falls naturally within the scope of disequilibrium macroeconomics. Finally, the awkward problems or modelling spill-over effects that have hampered the disequilibrium approach do not result from needlessly complicating disequilibrium models. They do capture and reflect actual policy dilemmas. As examples, consider an oil or an external credit shock. No universal characterization of their effects can be given by disequilibrium macroeconomics because they depend on the initial disequilibrium regime and on cross-restrictions between agents and markets. But this is no defect of disequilibrium theory; the reality of LDCs has already exhibited a wide range of responses to these disturbances.

The most interesting disequilibrium models for LDCs are two-sector open economy models. In Solimano (1984), a cut in tariffs increases unemployment in both Classical and Keynesian regimes. (The positive effect under Repressed Inflation is trivial.) The case against the liberalization of trade in heavily indebted LDCs could be made even stronger in terms of this line of analysis by introducing intertemporal debt effects. To the extent to which it alters trade surplus, trade liberalization increases the present value of the burden of debt (assuming away repudiation). The larger debt burden in turn reinforces the tendencies driving the economy towards Keynesian unemployment.

In Esfahani (1983), the common export-first rationing rule in case of excess demand for goods is shown to be destabilizing if the foreign exchange constraint is not binding. Adjustment is analyzed under an endogenous rationing rule: maximize domestic absorption. The frequently altered priorities given to exports in LDCs may be rationalized not as testifying to political pressures but as responses to different disequilibrium regimes.

In Arida and Bacha (1987), the tools of disequilibrium macroeconomics illuminate the long-standing debate on stabilization policies between IMF medicine and the structural approach launched at ECLA and reflected in the two-gap model of Section 3 of Chapter 6. It is shown that observation of unemployment and diminishing reserves is not sufficient to determine the applicability of competing stabilization policies. Central to the debate is the state of the market for goods. IMF prescriptions make sense if the goods market is in excess demand. In this case, lower real wages and domestic absorption lead to external equilibrium and more employment; a Classical deficit obtains. In contrast, the Structural deficit occurs when the goods market is in excess supply. In this opposite case, a wage squeeze only worsens the income distribution; a domestic demand contraction can only reach external equilibrium at the cost of increased employment.

In Arida and Bacha, the scope for a satisfactory application of IMF doctrine turns out to be much more limited than claimed by orthodoxy. Similarly, the ECLA doctrine needs to be rectified. The structuralist viewpoint correctly describes the nature of disequilibria when the goods market is in excess supply. But the economy can present unemployment, external deficit and excess supply of goods – apparently confirming the ECLA diagnosis – and yet, a Walrasian equilibrium may exist. If this is the case, exchange rate devaluations are recommended. The conditions for truly structural deficits that emerge from Arida and Bacha model are shown to be more stringent than claimed by the ECLA doctrine.

One crucial limitation of existing two-sector open-economy models is worth emphasizing. Both assets and domestic credit markets are missing. As to credit markets, the integration of the credit rationing literature with disequilibrium macroeconomics forms an obvious research topic. Of interest in this connection is the still unexplored experience of quantitative credit controls in LDCs. The increase in interest rates led to declines in output and larger default risks. Increasing default risk in turn launched spontaneous credit rationing. The adverse impacts of credit controls were therefore magnified. The integration mentioned above would cast light on the failure of quantitative credit controls. The pegging of interest rates, discussed in Section 4 above, is another feature that reinforces the attractiveness of disequilibrium tools.

As to asset markets, the alleged reason for their absence is that price stickiness is deemed to be reasonable only for goods markets. Asset prices can jump at any point in time. Yet this feature hardly justifies the exclusion of asset markets. Because of the faster adjustment speed, they accommodate otherwise restricted demands deriving from rationing in goods markets. In populistic Repressed Inflation regimes, the conjecture would imply that assets are hedges against latent inflation. In Keynesian excess supply regimes, the conjecture would predict depressed asset prices.

8. Policy conclusions in the short run

To tie the foregoing discussion together, it helps to recall from Section 6 of Chapter 6 that a full short-run macro model must incorporate theories of (1) inflation from the side of costs, (2) determination of real demand–supply equilibrium in one or more sectors, and (3) functioning of financial markets. The models discussed herein emphasize one or another aspect of this overall structure.

Regarding devaluation, the earlier structuralist models emphasized inflationary and demand linkages. Depreciation drives up prices through costs (despite orthodox arguments in the African context to the contrary), and may lead thereby to demand contraction. Later models brought in supply-side and (with greater interest) financial effects. By altering relative wealth positions in the short run, exchange rate changes can have effects throughout the real and financial systems. As practical policy matters, alternatives to full-blown depreciation or appreciation have recently been discussed. Import controls and similar sectorally-directed interventions, if administratively feasible, avoid many of the undesirable economy-wide repercussions of full-scale devaluation. On the financial side, capital controls and the hazards of exchange rate speculation are topics of current research interest.

During the 1970s, debates about interest rate policy focused on its potential for raising the economy to a higher level of circular flow. The argument was that changes in the financial market could lead to better performance on inflation and growth. This hope was frustrated – experiments in Latin America's Southern Cone and elsewhere had disastrous results, because they failed to take into account the direct effects of interest rate increases on aggregate demand and the inflationary process. At about the same time, with the expansion of external debt, Latin American economies (especially) increased their use of financial instruments either indexed to the inflation rate or tied closely to the world market in a process of dollarization. Is the world market rate (plus inflation) a "natural" interest rate under such circumstances? If so, how does one use the natural rate as a lodestar for the macro system? These are unavoidable questions in economies that have gone through indexation or dollarization. More traditional, though not necessarily easily resolvable, problems of management of domestic fiscal and inflation tax policies remain of interest in other parts of the world.

Recent macroeconomic work in both poor and rich countries has emphasized that the government cannot avoid affecting, and reacting to, all parts of the economy – the benign tutelary state of the neoclassical synthesis does not exist. In developing countries, the government seems driven into counter-productive policy action. Reducing the risk of widescale bankruptcy of domestic firms in the external indebtedness process, for example, is an unenviable state task – it leads to excessive external debt via exchange rate subsidies to firms, over-exposure of national intermediaries due to the moral hazard of state guarantees for financially troubled firms, and over-indexation of contracts to protect all parties against inflation risk. Inflation in capitalist economies has been the traditional means for blunting conflicting income claims. Socialization of debt and other contracts is the more recent manifestation, with perverse feedbacks to the inflationary process. How the vicious circle can be surmounted is by no means clear. Both inflation and socialization affect flow income claims (forced saving and output adjustments) and wealth positions (the real interest rate and revaluation of liabilities and assets). Who gains and loses is intimately related to the institutions and class structure in each economy. In many countries, economic stalemate is not an easily avoidable result. One example may be inertial inflation in Latin America; another is stasis around the agricultural terms of trade. Solutions through new money or heterodox shocks on the one hand, or rigging prices on the other, cannot have assured success.

As noted in Taylor (1983) orthodox stabilization policy usually features monetary contraction, fiscal restraint, devaluation, trade liberalization, and increases in the interest rate. Recent work by structuralist economists shows that this package makes no sense. It fails to take into account interactions among inflation, real equilibrium, and financial balance, and elides consideration of the role of the state. How to design a rational alternatives appropriate to the diverse objective circumstances of developing countries is a goal toward which progress is slowly being made.

9. Final thoughts

The short and long run have always avoided integration. The dilemma is most poignant in the Third World, where there is no agreement about an adequate vision of long-run circular flow, and short-run stabilization problems lead through orthodox policy into contractionary solutions. One way of posing the question about how short-run decisions and long-run outcomes hang together is to ask about "irreversibilities" caused by large recessive shocks. The argument is that large shocks and long and severe recessions alter the structure of the economy. There is no guarantee that it will ever return spontaneously to the pre-recession equilibrium. Technical backwardness, industrial concentration, wealth concentration, and sectoral imbalances are three consequences of deep recessions which imprint their mark on economic structure. The intuitive argument frequently heard is that a moderate recession caused by moderately restrictive policies can be undone by moderately expansionist policies; but a large recession would change the catalog of options available to society. Time can be run backwards from the viewpoint of small shocks; irreversibility would be felt from the viewpoint of large shocks. As a consequence, policies that promote growth after long depressions are not given by reversing the policies that launched the recession.

This intuitive and vague argument can easily be cast in terms of multiple stable real equilibria or configurations of circular flow. It amounts to the argument that small shocks have transitory effects if the economy still gravitates around the same long-run equilibrium. But large shocks succeed in displacing the economy toward a different and possibly inferior stable equilibrium.

With regard to monetary policy, for example, the long-run Phillips curve could be vertical around each real equilibrium, but a policy change could be effective in a fundamental sense by inducing a transverse from one long-run equilibrium to another. Fiscal policy would be more needed to support some real equilibrium that another. The formalization of policy discussions in these terms, however, requires a discussion of the reasons for multiple equilibria. In the history of economic thought, Myrdal (1934) in his predevelopment years is the obvious reading. For in full contrast with modern theories, he argued that, whereas the monetary equilibrium is unique, several real equilibrium positions for an economy exist. Two aspects of the existence of multiple equilibria are worth mentioning: hysteresis and increasing returns.

Hysteresis is the property of dynamic systems that the stationary equilibrium is a function of the initial conditions and/or the transition trajectory towards the steady state. Hysteresis in the natural unemployment rate occurs when unemployment destroys human capital by having a negative effect on attitudes and aptitudes. A long recession may increase the natural rate. Hysteresis may occur because of external credit shocks that impose on the country the generation of excessive trade surpluses. If to produce at full capacity in the engineering concept violates the target surplus negotiated with lenders, capacity in the economic concept of the term is destroyed. LDCs that experienced credit shocks in 1982 are much closer to full capacity than is commonly recognized. Hysteresis seems to be the proper way of conceptualizing the shifting or moving long-run equilibrium argument.

The insight that increasing returns lie at the heart of processes of development is a profound one, as development economists since Adam Smith have pointed out. The interest of increasing return models for LDCs is, of course, somewhat diminished by the importance of agriculture and mineral sectors; but even in little industrialized countries declining average total costs may obtain because of heavy investment in fixed capital. Increasing returns are also of interest from the viewpoint of inflation; restrictive fiscal policies then equivalent to an adverse supply shock as less demand is translated into higher average costs.

Finally, note that multiple equilibria can provide an analytical framework for revisiting the wisdom of unbalanced growth theories. For if the current equilibrium is stable, one has to put the economy out of balance to enable it to reach a more satisfactory real equilibrium. The art lies in bringing the economy from an old to a new, perhaps less oppressive, pattern of circular flow.

References

Arida, P. (1985) 'Recesao e pago de juros: A economia Brasileira no inicio dos anos 80', *Revista de Economia Politica*, 5:5–20.

Arida, P. (1986) 'Macroeconomic issues for Latin America', *Journal of Development Economics*, 22:171–208.

Arida, P. and E.L. Bacha (1987) 'Balance of payments: A disequilibrium approach for developing countries', *Journal of Development Economics*, 27:85–108.

Arida, P. and A. Lara-Resende (1983) 'Recession and interest rates: A note on the Brazillian Economy in the 1980's', Departamento de Economia, Pontifical Catholic University, Rio de Janeiro.

Arida, P. and A. Lara-Resende (1985) 'Inertial inflation and monetary reform', in: John Williamson, ed., *Inflation and indexation: Argentina, Brazil, and Israel*. Washington, D.C.: Institute of International Economics.

Bacha, E.L. (1978) 'Notes on the Brazilian experience with mini-devaluations, 1968–76', *Journal of Development Economics*, 6:463–481.

Bacha, E.L. (1984) 'Growth with limited supplies of foreign exchange: A reappraisal of the two-gap model', in: M. Syrquin, L. Taylor and L. Westphal, eds., *Economic structure and performance: Essays in Honor of Hollis B. Chenery*. New York: Academic Press.

Barbone, L. (1985) 'Essays on trade and macro policies in developing countries,' Ph.D. dissertation, Department of Economics, Massachusetts Institute of Technology, Cambridge, MA, unpublished.

Barro, R. (1983) *Macroeconomics*. New York: Wiley.

Bernanke, B.S. (1981) 'Bankruptcy, liquidity, and recession', *American Economic Review*, 71:155–159.

Bernanke, B.S. (1983a) 'Irreversibility, uncertainty, and cyclical investment', *Quarterly Journal of Economics*, 98:85–106.

Bernanke, B.S. (1983b) 'Nonmonetary effects of the financial crisis in the propagation of the Great Depression', *American Economic Review*, 73:257–276.

Buffie, E. (1984) 'Financial repression, the new structuralists, and stabilization policy in semi-industrialized countries', *Journal of Development Economics*, 14:305–322.

Buffie, E. (1986) 'Devaluation, investment, and growth in LDC's', *Journal of Development Economics*, 20:361–380.

Calvo, G. (1978) 'On the time consistency of optimal policy in a monetary economy', *Econometrica*, 46:1411–1128.

Collins, S. (1983) 'Expected devaluation with capital market restrictions: The role of black markets', Department of Economics, Harvard University, Cambridge, MA.

Diaz-Alejandro, C.F. (1963) 'A note on the impact of devaluation and distributive effect', *Journal of Political Economy*, 71:577–580.

Diaz-Alejandro, C.F. (1984) 'Some aspects of the 1982–83 Brazilian payments crisis', Brookings Papers on Economic Activity, 2:515–552.

Diaz-Alejandro, C.F. (1985) 'Good-bye financial repression, hello financial crash', *Journal of Development Economics*, 19:1–24.

Dornbusch, R. (1982) 'PPP exchange rate rules and macroeconomic stability', *Journal of Political Economy*, 90:158–165.

Dornbusch, R. (1984) 'External debt, budget deficits, and disequilibrium exchange rates', Department of Economics, Massachusetts Institute of Technology, Cambridge, MA.

Dornbusch, R. and A. Da Silva (1984) 'Taxa de juros e depositos em moeda no Brasil', *Revista Brasileira de Economia*, 38:39–52.

Drazen, A. (1980) 'Recent developments in macroeconomic distribution theory', *Econometrica*, 48:283–305.

Dutt, A. (1986) 'Stock equilibrium in flexprice markets in macromodels for less developed countries: The case of food speculation', *Journal of Development Economics*, 21:89–110.

Easterly, W. (1985) 'A computable general equilibrium model of Mexico with portfolio balances: With application to devaluation', Ph.D. dissertation, Department of Economics, Massachusetts Institute of Technology, Cambridge, MA, unpublished.

Eaton, J. and L. Taylor (1986) 'Developing country finance and debt', *Journal of Development Economics*, 22:209–265.

Edwards, S. (1984) 'The order of liberalization of the external sector in developing countries', World Bank, Washington, D.C.

Elster, J. (1983) *Sour grapes*. New York: Cambridge University Press.

Esfahani, H.S. (1983) 'Foreign exchange constraint and macroeconomic adjustment in developing economies', mimeo.

Field, A.J. (1984) 'Asset exchange and the transactions demand for money, 1919–1929', *American Economic Review*, 74:43–59.

Fischer, S. (1983) 'Comments', *Journal of Monetary Economics*, 12:95–99.

Fisher, I. (1933) 'The debt-deflation theory of great depressions', *Econometrica*, 1:337–357.

Flood, R. and P. Garber (1980) 'An economic theory of monetary reform', *Journal of Political Economy*, 88:24–58.

Frenkel, R. (1983) 'Mercado financiero, expectativas cambiarias y movimientos de capital', *El Trimestre Economico*, 50:2041–2076.

Gordon, R.J. (1982) 'Price inertia and policy ineffectiveness in the United States, 1890–1980', *Journal of Political Economy*, 90:1087–1117.

Grandmont, J.-M. (1983) *Money and value*. New York: Cambridge University Press.

Hirschman, A.O. (1949) 'Devaluation and the Trade Balance: A note', *Review of Economic and Statistics*, 31:50–53.

Hirschman, A.O. (1981) 'The social and political matrix of inflation: Elaborations on the Latin American experience', in: *Essays in trespassing: Economics to politics and beyond*. Cambridge, MA: Cambridge University Press.

Islam, S. (1984) 'Devaluation, stabilization policies, and the developing countries', *Journal of Development Economics*, 14:37–60.

Kindleberger, C.P. (1978) *Manias, panics, and crashes: A history of financial crises*. New York: Basic Books.

Krugman, P. and L. Taylor (1978) 'Contractionary effects of devaluation', *Journal of International Economics*, 8:445–456.

Liviatan, N. (1984) 'Tight money and inflation', *Journal of Monetary Economics*, 13:5–16.

Lopes, F.L. (1984) 'Inflacao inercial, hiperinflacao e disinflacao: Notas e conjecturas', *Revista da ANPEC*, 8:55–71.

Malinvaud, E. (1977) *The theory of unemployment reconsidered*. Oxford: Basil Blackwell.

Minsky, H.P. (1975) *John Maynard Keynes*. New York: Columbia University Press.

Myrdal, G. (1934) *Monetary equilibrium*. London: Hodge.

Ocampo, J.A. (1987) 'The macroeconomic effect of import controls: A Keynesian analysis', *Journal of Development Economics*, 27:285–306.

Rosensweig, J. (1985) 'Empirical essays on the dollar area', Ph.D. dissertation, Department of Economics, Massachusetts Institute of Technology, Cambridge, MA, unpublished.

Sarkar, H. and M. Panda (1986) 'Administered prices, inflation, and growth: Some results for Indian economy', National Council of Applied Economic Research, New Delhi.

Solimano, A. (1984) 'Devaluation, unemployment, and inflation: Essays on macroeconomic adjustment', Ph.D. dissertation, Department of Economics, Massachusetts Institute of Technology Cambridge, MA, unpublished.

Solimano, A. (1986) 'Contractionary devaluation in the Southern cone: Chile', *Journal of Development Economics*, 23:135–152.

Taylor, L. (1983) *Structuralist macroeconomics*. New York: Basic Books.

Taylor, L. (1985) 'A stagnationist model of economic growth', *Cambridge Journal of Economics*, 9:383–403.

Taylor, L. (1987) 'Macro policy in the tropics: How sensible people stand', *World Development*, 15:1407–1435.

Taylor, L. (1988) 'The real wage, output, and inflation in the semi-industrialized world', Department of Economics, Massachusetts Institute of Technology, Cambridge, MA.

Taylor, L. and S.A. O'Connell (1985) 'A Minsky crisis', *Quarterly Journal of Economics*, 100:871–885.

Taylor, L. and J.A. Rosensweig (1984) 'Devaluation, capital flows and crowding-out: A computable general equilibrium model with portfolio choice for Thailand', Department of Economics, Massachusetts Institute of Technology, Cambridge, MA.

Taylor, L., K.T. Yurukoglu, and S.A. Chaudhry (1986) 'A macro model of an oil exporter: Nigeria', in: J.P. Neary and S. van Wijnbergen, eds., *Natural resources and the macroeconomy*. Oxford: Basil Blackwell.

van Wijnbergen, S. (1986) 'Exchange rate management and stabilization policies in developing countries', *Journal of Development Economics*, 23:227–248.

Williamson, J. ed. (1981) *Exchange rate rules: The theory, performance, and prospects of the crawling peg*. London: Macmillan.

Winograd, C. (1987) *Active crawling peg, disinflation, and macroeconomic stability*. Paris: Ecole Normale Superieure.

Chapter 18

MULTISECTORAL MODELS

SHERMAN ROBINSON*

University of California, Berkeley

Contents

*My thanks to Irma Adelman, Hollis Chenery, Shanta Devarajan, Mark Gersovitz, Victor Ginsburgh, Kenneth Hanson, Jeffrey Lewis, Jaime de Melo, T.N. Srinivasan, and Lance Taylor for very helpful comments on an earlier draft. Participants at various seminars and classes at the University of California, Berkeley; Harvard University; the International Institute for Applied Systems Analysis; and the Economic Research Service, U.S. Department of Agriculture, also contributed numerous helpful reactions and comments. Of course, any remaining errors or omissions are my responsibility.

Handbook of Development Economics, Volume II, Edited by H. Chenery and T.N. Srinivasan
© *Elsevier Science Publishers B.V., 1989*

1. Introduction and scope

Multisectoral models appear in economics whenever questions of economic structure are at issue. While they have long been used to provide the analytic and empirical underpinnings of comprehensive economic planning in socialist countries, they have also been widely used in non-socialist settings. In developing countries, they have been used to analyze issues including long-term growth and structural change, investment allocation, choice of development strategy, income distribution, trade policy, and structural adjustment to external shocks. Given that changes in economic structure largely define the process of development, multisector models – where multi might be as few as two – have always been among the indispensable tools of a development economist.

There have been a number of surveys of multisectoral models applied to developing countries up to the early 1970s.[1] Since that time, there has been a major shift both in the questions to which models have been addressed and in the types of models used. This survey focuses on multisectoral, economywide models developed in the last ten to fifteen years. There is no coverage of models of individual sectors, or of multi-country models. At the other end of the aggregation spectrum, short-run macro models also will not be considered.[2] There is, however, consideration of multisectoral models which seek to explore the medium-term impact of short-run stabilization policies.

2. Typologies of models

There are a number of different ways to classify models. One approach is by mathematical structure or methodology: optimization or simulation, static or dynamic, and linear or non-linear. Another is according to policy focus. Models can also be classified by theoretical type or by the nature of the underlying theoretical paradigm.

---

[1]See Taylor (1975), other chapters in Blitzer, Clark and Taylor (1975), and also Manne (1974).
[2]They are the subject of a separate survey by Arida and Taylor in Chapter 17 of this Handbook.

2.1. Mathematical structure

In the 1950s, the linear input–output model was the only technology available. Static "multiplier" models were used a great deal and there was active work on linear dynamic models.[3] Dynamic input–output models have been a mainstay of development planning and are still in use in various forms today.[4] Their technological and demand assumptions are simple, but such linear models are very useful because they capture major elements of interdependence in an economy. In the past decade, there has been a great deal of new work on multiplier models in the framework of an extended input–output model based on a Social Accounting Matrix (SAM). The SAM provides an excellent framework for exploring both macroeconomic and multisectoral issues and is a useful starting point for more complex models.

In the 1960s, the development of efficient computer programs for solving linear programming (LP) models provided a way to introduce choice and optimization into policy models and also offered the possibility of introducing prices explicitly into the analysis. While widely used in academic exercises, economywide LP models never really caught on among policy-makers in developing countries. There are serious theoretical and practical difficulties in using economywide LP models, which have led to a relative decline in their use in the past decade.[5]

The problems fall into three categories. First, the linearity assumptions tend to lead to unrealistic specialization and extreme behavior, especially in dynamic models. Modellers sought to control this tendency by adding ad hoc constraints, but these made the models more difficult to interpret. Second, in dynamic models, there is a problem in specifying appropriate terminal constraints. The model's dynamic behavior in later periods is sensitive to assumptions made about the post-plan period, especially the role of sectoral capital stocks in the terminal year. While a difficult problem in any dynamic model, optimizing models are especially sensitive to variations in assumptions concerning terminal conditions. Third, there are problems with the interpretation of shadow prices generated by programming models.

A correctly formulated non-linear programming model will generate shadow prices which can be interpreted as competitive market prices. In particular, a single-consumer model in which the maximand is utility and the constraint set reflects the production technology will generate shadow prices which can be

[3] There was also a great deal of theoretical and practical concern about the stability properties of the linear dynamic model. See Dervis, de Melo and Robinson (1982, ch. 2), for a discussion of the dynamic input–output model.

[4] Albeit in more sophisticated forms than the original models. These models are discussed further below.

[5] These problems have been discussed in detail in other surveys. See Taylor (1975), Manne (1974), and Dervis, de Melo and Robinson (1982, ch. 3).

interpreted as market prices, with the consumer satisfying his budget constraint and producers maximizing profits. Multi-consumer models will also work, but only with appropriate weights for the objective function, and the determination of those weights becomes part of the problem.[6] In practice, modellers specified many demanders and imposed a number of constraints designed to make the primal behave realistically, capturing structuralist rigidities that characterize developing countries.[7] They did not worry much about the behavior of the dual price system.

In the later work with linear programming models, modellers sought to improve the treatment of prices in such models. The goal of this work, however, was not explicitly to simulate market prices, but rather to be able to use the shadow prices for policy analysis (for example, to generate shadow prices for project analysis).[8] Two economywide applied models represent the high point of this literature and reflect major advances in the art of multisectoral modelling: the Evans (1972) model of Australia and the Goreux (1977) model of the Ivory Coast.[9] The Evans model has perhaps the most careful treatment of foreign trade of any linear programming model and the Goreux model incorporates features of multilevel planning in which price signals play a crucial role for planners. In neither model, however, can the shadow prices be interpreted as market prices. Both have multiple demanders and, in order to prevent unrealistic behavior, imposed many ad hoc constraints which cannot be interpreted as representing constraints facing actors in a market economy.

In the early 1970s, work was started on a new type of non-linear, multisectoral model which sought to simulate the workings of a market economy, solving for both market prices and quantities simultaneously. These computable general equilibrium (CGE) models can be seen as a natural outgrowth of input–output and LP models, adding neoclassical substitutability in production and demand, as well as an explicit system of market prices and a complete specification of the income flows in the economy. The first developing country application was Adelman and Robinson (1978), which started an extensive literature.[10]

---

[6] For a discussion of the theoretical issues, see Ginsburgh and Robinson (1984).

[7] See, for example, Chenery (1971) and Adelman and Thorbecke (1966) for examples of such economywide LP models.

[8] Bruno (1975) provides an excellent statement of this approach. See also Taylor (1975).

[9] There was also work to integrate programming models of individual sectors in a consistent multi-level framework that sought to compute shadow prices in a way that could be seen as reflecting market prices. The work on Mexico described in Goreux and Manne (1973) is an excellent example of this strand. See also Westphal (1975).

[10] At about the same time, starting from the theoretical work of Scarf on fixed-point algorithms, CGE models were also being built for developed countries. These models concentrated primarily on issues of tax incidence and had a very different focus from the models of developing countries. See Scarf and Shoven (1983) and Shoven and Whalley (1984).

In the 1970s, major advances were made in solution techniques that permitted the implementation of CGE models. There are four different approaches that were pursued. First, the solution of a CGE model can be formulated as a problem in finding a fixed point in a mapping of prices to prices through excess demand equations. This approach was pioneered by Herbert Scarf, and variations on his fixed-point algorithm have been used to solve a number of CGE models of developed countries.[11] A second approach involves treating a CGE model as just a collection of non-linear algebraic equations and attacking them directly with numerical solution techniques. This approach was used by Adelman and Robinson (1978) and a number of others since then.[12] A third approach involves first linearizing all the equations of the CGE model and then solving the linear approximation by simple matrix inversion. This approach was used in the first applied CGE model formulated by Johansen (1960) and has been used in a number of applications since then.[13] Finally, as noted above, it is possible to construct a non-linear programming model whose solution yields shadow prices that can be interpreted as market prices. The general approach of using programming techniques to solve CGE models is described in detail in Ginsburgh and Waelbroeck (1981), who also survey the other techniques.[14]

All of these techniques work. At this time, CGE models can be solved routinely and cheaply. Implementing a CGE model now is significantly easier than developing an economywide LP model was in the 1970s.[15] In fact, with the further development of non-linear programming methods, many of the shortcomings of LP models have been overcome, and it is now possible to integrate optimization with a more complete specification of market systems, including endogenously determined prices.[16]

[11]See Scarf and Hansen (1973).

[12]Dervis, de Melo and Robinson (1982, appendix B), describe the approach in detail. Within this framework, there are variations depending on how one chooses to attack the system of equations.

[13]See Dixon et al. (1982) who apply this technique in an enormous CGE model of Australia. They extend the method considerably and show how approximation errors arising from the linearization can be eliminated.

[14]For discussions of computation techniques, see, for example, Takayama and Judge (1971) and Dixon (1975). Manne, Chao and Wilson (1980) simultaneously developed an approach very close to that of Ginsburgh and Waelbroeck (1981). Chenery and Raduchel (1979) use non-linear programming to solve a stylized model that is almost, but not quite, a CGE model. Norton and Scandizzo (1981) suggest a way of using a piecewise linear programming formulation to solve a CGE model, but their approach can only work for a one-consumer economy, an overly restrictive specification.

[15]The World Bank has developed three different approaches to providing solution packages for CGE models. One package starts from models developed by Dervis, de Melo and Robinson (1982) and has been used in a number of applied models. Another, the "transactions value" (TV) method, starts from a social accounting matrix presentation of a CGE model and is described in Drud, Grais and Pyatt (1984). A third starts from a general non-linear programming package called GAMS and is described in Meeraus (1983).

[16]Some work in this vein is described at the end of the survey in the section on directions for future research.

2.2. Policy issues

Another way of classifying models is according to the issues that they seek to address. The early work with input–output and LP models was largely concerned with questions of sectoral allocation of investment, international trade, and the implications of different development strategies in the medium to long run. The main focus was on growth and structural change in production and foreign trade, and on the size and timing of the required domestic and foreign investment.[17] However, these models are not well suited to analyze mixed market economies in which autonomous decision-making by various economic actors and market mechanisms largely determine resource allocation. Linear programming and input–output models do not capture market mechanisms through which incentive instruments such as taxes and subsidies affect the economy. While they do provide a consistent economywide framework, which is very valuable in itself, they do not provide a way to relate solution variables to actual policy decisions.[18]

In the early 1970s, international attention shifted to a concern about income distribution.[19] Although there was some imaginative work using input–output models to analyze distributional issues, the shift in policy interest generated further pressure to include prices and incomes directly in models.[20] The focus on income distribution arose from a growing concern that rapid growth and structural change did not suffice to reduce poverty and that large groups of poor people were not benefiting from growth.[21] Two broad questions provided the focus of modelling work: (1) What were the distributional implications of different development strategies? (2) How could one design policy packages that would reduce the incidence of poverty and ameliorate the worsening of the distribution that seemed inevitably to accompany industrialization? It was to address these questions that the first CGE models were built for developing countries: the model of Korea by Adelman and Robinson (1978) and, later, the model of Brazil by Lysy and Taylor (1980).[22]

The work on income distribution proceeded throughout the 1970s. However, the first oil crisis again focused attention on foreign borrowing so that by the

---

[17]See Kornai's chapter in Blitzer, Clark and Taylor (1975). He discusses the adequacy of the then existing planning methodologies for examining these questions.

[18]Taylor (1975) provides a good survey. See also Blitzer, Clark and Taylor (1975), Adelman and Thorbecke (1966), and Chenery (1971).

[19]In some countries, such as India and Brazil, there was serious policy concern about distributional issues much earlier.

[20]See Weisskoff (1970) and Cline (1972) for input–output models with a distributional focus. Chenery and Duloy (1974) discuss the problems of integrating distribution into the "standard" planning models.

[21]The seminal international comparative work espousing this view was Adelman and Morris (1973), which led to a continuing controversy about who benefits from growth.

[22]Work on these models was started in the early 1970s, and the Korea model is discussed in the Taylor (1975) survey and in Chenery et al. (1974).

time of the second crisis in 1977–78, policy-makers both in developing countries and in international agencies were preoccupied with issues of foreign debt. Policy analysis focused on questions of "structural adjustment". How could countries bring about the changes in the structure of production and trade required to adapt to lower levels of foreign resources? What macroeconomic adjustments were required, and what was their impact on medium to long-run growth and structural change? The term "structural adjustment" has become something of a catch-all, and will be used here to mean an adjustment to some shock that requires not only compositional changes in production, resource allocation, demand, and relative prices, but also changes in macroeconomic aggregates such as income, investment, absorption, consumption, and government expenditure.

In the face of a foreign exchange crisis leading to a complete halt in growth, issues of income distribution and poverty alleviation faded into the background. Policy-modellers also reacted to the shift in priorities and turned their attention to improving the treatment of foreign trade in multisectoral models, particularly CGE models. Most of the multisector models built in the last decade have been concerned with such trade issues, and they will provide a major focus of this survey.

2.3. Analytic, stylized, and applied models

In developing countries, most of the work on empirical multisector models has been driven by policy concerns. In all policy analysis, there is a tension between theoretical simplification and empirical realism. In judging empirical models, it is necessary to keep this tension in mind. One can classify models along a continuum running from analytic to applied. Analytic models are designed to explore the implications of various sets of theoretical postulates, with as few assumptions as possible about the magnitudes of parameters. The principle of Occam's Razor in science holds that simplification in theoretical work is a virtue, and an important part of analytic model-building is to find the sparsest set of assumptions required to explain a set of stylized facts. Thus, analytic models are deliberately simplified to focus attention on important assumptions and causal mechanisms. In this process, the stylized facts are often exaggerated, which simplifies an analytic model and allows mathematical analysis of its properties.

In evaluating analytic models which focus on the logical implications of different sets of assumptions, empirical realism is not the most relevant criterion. An analytic model is useful if it isolates important effects while retaining a reasonable specification or some heuristic validity. There is clearly a tradeoff between empirical relevance (i.e. the range and complexity of issues that can be considered in a model) and analytic tractability. Analytic models are usually narrowly focused with, whenever possible, a preference for a partial rather than a general equilibrium approach. The application of Occam's Razor strongly favors smaller models.[23]

By their nature, analytic models will be limited in their applicability. Many economic phenomena that can be isolated in particular analytic models work in contradictory directions, and the net effects in a real economy depend on the values of various parameters. When an analytical model does not suffice, the next line of attack is to draw on empirical work and to build a stylized numerical model. Stylized numerical models have two main uses: (1) to analyze problems that are too difficult to solve analytically or that have ambiguous implications that depend on particular parameter values, and (2) to illustrate the numerical order of magnitude of various effects whose analytic properties are well understood.

Typically, stylized numerical models are more complex than analytic models, since wider applicability is desired and simplicity is no longer required. Stylized numerical models nonetheless tend to stay close to their underlying analytic models. Since the goal is to explore particular causal mechanisms, simplicity is desirable. Stylized models are still a long way from models which seek to capture in a realistic way the variety of important effects that might impinge on a particular policy problem facing a particular country.

Applied models differ from stylized models in two important ways. First, they broaden further the range of stylized facts that are incorporated. Second, they seek to capture important features of a particular economy or situation. For example, while a stylized model can represent a number of similar countries (e.g. oil-importing, semi-industrial countries), an applied model would be built for a particular country. By including more institutional detail, applied models are more specific and narrow.

Moving from analytic to stylized to applied models allows increased institutional specificity, as well as the inclusion of a wider range of economic phenomena. The tradeoff, of course, is that the additional detail and size may obscure the major causal mechanisms that drive the model, without adding any empirically significant effects. Since different types of models permit different insights, it is often desirable when analyzing various problems to move back and forth between analytic, stylized, and applied models. There are costs and benefits to operating at each level that must always be balanced, and it is generally true that the analysis of any particular problem will be improved by using more than one kind of model.

The advantages and disadvantages of using models at different levels are clearly evident in analyzing the impact of different policies on the economy. In such analysis, one can distinguish between strategic planning and policy analysis.

---

[23]Although one should not confuse size and complexity. Small models can be quite complex, and large models can be quite simple theoretically.

Strategic planning, for example, might involve the choice of an appropriate medium to long-term development strategy. Should a country follow an inward-looking, import-substitution strategy or an outward-looking strategy that relies more on export-led growth? Policy analysis would then concern the appropriate choice of policies to support the strategy. For an inward-looking strategy, should one rely on tariffs or quantity restrictions? What levels of tariffs or restrictions? At what level should the exchange rate be pegged, and for how long? The distinction is analogous to the difference between strategy and tactics. Policy analysis must involve detailed analysis and careful consideration of the special circumstances of a particular economy, while questions of strategic planning can be more widely applied and generalized.

In general, analytic models do not yield specific policy recommendations. At that level, the stylized facts being considered are usually too stylized to be realistic enough for policy analysis. The policy conclusions that can be derived from analytic models tend to be general statements such as: "free trade is good", "price distortions are bad and attempts to fix prices are terrible", "quantity restrictions on imports are worse than tariffs", or "do not ignore market mechanisms". And even in these cases, there is an active industry among economists who delight in thinking up counterexamples. For similar reasons, a stylized numerical model can only rarely be used for policy analysis, since it is usually too simplified to capture the institutional and country detail required to provide good numerical estimates of the impact of various specific policies.

While the three types of models are different, the boundaries between them are often fuzzy. They really represent different points along a continuum of models that differ in size, scope, and focus. The differences are, however, significant and much of the criticism of particular models often amounts to taking a stylized numerical model to task for not being an applied model, or vice versa.

The multisector models applied to developing countries that are discussed in this survey all fall in the continuum from stylized to applied. Their location on this continuum affects the standards by which they should be judged. All models should be transparent in the sense that the modeller should be able to trace any effect the model produces back to features of its theoretical structure or to particular parameter values. With their focus on the institutional details of a particular economy, applied models will be inherently more difficult to interpret. The test is whether the gain in institutional detail generates more realistic empirical results. Stylized models, on the other hand, are often designed to reflect common features of a class of countries. While the models are often easier to handle, the question is whether country-specific effects are empirically important enough to offset the commonalities that the models are designed to explore.

It is also often possible to simplify an applied model after the fact. Experimentation often leads to insights about the empirical importance of model specifications that could not be determined a priori. Given the results, one can then move toward a more stylized numerical model which still captures the major mechanisms that turned out to be empirically important in the applied model.

2.4. Theoretical paradigms

All multisector models start with the input–output model, which captures sectoral interdependence arising from the flow of intermediate goods among sectors. Even with its strong linearity assumptions, input–output models and their extensions into social accounting represent powerful tools for applied general equilibrium analysis. The later computable general equilibrium (CGE) models build on the input–output core, adding non-linear equations and endogenous prices. All these models are essentially structural, with explicit specification of supply and demand behavior. The extensions to non-linear models incorporating substitution possibilities and prices only reinforce the essential microeconomic spirit of the models. As Dervis, de Melo and Robinson (1982, p. 6) state: "Walras rather than Keynes is the patron saint of multisector analysis".

While multisector models applied to developing countries are Walrasian and neoclassical in spirit, most modellers quickly abandoned many of the strong assumptions of neoclassical theory when faced with the problem of capturing the stylized facts characterizing these economies. The assumptions of perfect competition, perfectly functioning markets with flexible prices, and free mobility of products and factors are not sustainable in actual economies. Instead, modellers have incorporated a variety of "structuralist" rigidities into their models that seek to capture non-neoclassical behavioral relations, macro imbalances, and institutional rigidities characteristic of developing countries. Such deviations from the Walrasian paradigm lead to methodological problems that have concerned some writers. For example, Bell and Srinivasan (1984), Srinivasan (1982), and Shoven and Whalley (1984) all express concern about models which incorporate what they consider to be ad hoc features not rooted in traditional theory. Shoven and Whalley (1984, p. 1046) put the problem well:

> Unfortunately, the problem is, the models that make major departures from known theoretical structures can become difficult to interpret. The conflict between modellers' desire to build realistic models which seek to capture real features of the policy issue at hand, and to stay within the realm of developed economic theory is something that seems to be increasingly apparent in some of the more recent models.

While the conflict is real, using a model with clean theoretical roots in a situation where its assumptions are not satisfied will not yield valid empirical results or aid in policy analysis. And while deviations from the standard neoclassical paradigm certainly do give rise to problems of interpretation, such problems can also be seen as a challenge to theorists.

One problem is that applied modellers often seek to draw on strands of theory outside the paradigm of Arrow–Debreu general equilibrium theory. The concept of equilibrium imbedded in the neoclassical general equilibrium model underlying all multisector models is that of flow equilibrium in product and factor markets. There are additional equilibrium concepts that one might want to capture in a model, reflecting different underlying analytical theories. A second concept is that of equilibrium in aggregate "financial" or "nominal" flows, which defines a notion of macro equilibrium – the heart of Keynesian macroeconomics. A third concept is that of equilibrium in asset markets, defining another form of macro equilibrium. Fourth, there is intertemporal equilibrium involving expectations – adaptive, rational, consistent, or whatever – in an explicitly dynamic framework. The four equilibrium concepts are not independent, and it is an open question how adequate are theoretical and empirical models that only include one or two of them.

In applications to developing countries, modellers have often justified the imposition of "structuralist" constraints on their flow-equilibrium models by citing theoretical literature on macro adjustment, political economy, uncertainty, incomplete markets, temporary equilibrium, implicit contracts, and the like. The typical approach is not to incorporate such theoretical features directly into the empirical model, but instead to impose constraints on the model which are essentially ad hoc in that they are not related to any endogenous rational behavior of agents. The justification for this approach is the current inadequate state of theory.

For example, many modellers have persuasively argued for the need to incorporate notions of macro equilibrium into multisector models. However, the theoretical literature on the micro foundations of macroeconomics, while suggestive, gives little concrete guidance to the empirical modeller.[24] There is as yet no acceptable reconciliation of micro and macro theory, and the Walrasian model is an uneasy host for incorporating macro phenomena. Thus, while there are many multisector models with macro features, they all have an ad hoc flavor reflecting this theoretical tension. The open question, which will be discussed further below, is whether the tradeoff between empirical relevance and theoretical purity implicit in the marriage of Walras and Keynes in an empirical model is justified by the results.

It is important to note, however, that moving beyond the Walrasian paradigm in multisector models does not mean abandoning all notions of equilibrium. In a

---

[24] Discussion of this literature is beyond the scope of this survey. For an entry point, see Hahn (1978) and Weintraub (1979). Some of the issues are discussed further below in the context of stylized and applied models.

transparent model, it is feasible to sort out the effects of non-neoclassical specifications on the results and so clarify the limits of "standard" theory in explaining model behavior. While the definitions of equilibrium are not the same as in a neoclassical model, they are no less rigorous. Malinvaud (1977) has put the general point very well:

> The type of consistency that is assumed to exist between individual decisions is specific to each equilibrium theory. For the study of (Keynesian) employment it can only be a short-run consistency which will be quite different from the long-run consistency that one will want to consider when studying, for instance, industrial structure.

As we shall see, structuralist models have a lot of structure.

3. Input–output and social accounting

Just as the national income and product accounts (or NIPA) provide the statistical foundation for macro models, the input–output accounts underlie multisector models. There are many good treatments of the input–output accounts, so they will not be covered here.[25] However, issues such as income distribution and structural adjustment require analysis that goes beyond the sectoral production accounts to include income and expenditure flows that are captured in the national income and product accounts. The development of social accounting matrices (SAMs) was motivated by the need to reconcile the NIPA and input–output accounts within a unified statistical framework. The work was greatly influenced by Sir Richard Stone, who was the major architect of the United Nations System of National Accounts (SNA).[26]

3.1. Social accounting matrices

Figure 18.1 provides a representative SAM that forms the underlying statistical basis for a number of models of developing countries. The "activities" account includes the sectors as defined in input–output tables and the matrix of intermediate flows (or "use" matrix) appears as cell (2, 1) in the SAM. The "commodity" account can be seen as representing the domestic product market, buying domestic goods from activities and imports from the rest of the world, and selling

---

[25]See, for example, Chenery and Clark (1959), Bulmer-Thomas (1982), United Nations (1973), and Miller and Blair (1985).

[26]See United Nations (1968, 1975), Stone (1966), and Stone and Stone (1977). Pyatt and Round (1985) provide an excellent introduction to SAMs and their uses, especially the chapter by King (1985).

Receipts: \ Expenditures:	1 Activities	2 Commodities	3 Factors	4 Enterprises	5 Households	6 Government	7 Capital acct.	8 World	9 Total
1 Activities		domestic sales				export subsidies		exports	total sales
2 Commodities	intermediate demand				household consumption	government consumption	investment		total demand
3 Factors	factor payments								value added
4 Enterprises			gross profits			transfers			enterprise income
5 Households			wages	distributed profits		transfers		foreign remittances	household income
6 Government	indirect taxes	tariffs	factor taxes	enterprise taxes	direct taxes				government receipts
7 Capital acct.				retained earnings	household savings	government savings		net capital inflow	total saving
8 Rest of world		imports							imports
9 Total	total payments	total absorption	value added	enterprise expenditure	household expenditure	government expenditure	total investment	foreign exchange	

Figure 18.1. A representative social accounting matrix.

the goods to all domestic purchasers. In this definition, exports are assumed to be sold directly to the rest of the world by activities. The commodity account so defined is especially useful in models that focus on international trade, since the column sum of commodities equals total absorption (including intermediate inputs).[27] Note that since the commodity account is defined separately from activities, they need not have the same sectoral definitions. Entry $(1, 2)$ in the SAM provides the mapping from activities to commodities, and is sometimes called the "make" matrix.[28]

The rest of the SAM traces the flow of income from producing sectors to factors of production – entry $(3, 1)$ – and then on to "institutions", which represent the various economic actors in the economy. The SAM provides a complete account of the circular flow in the economy. Depending on the problem at hand, the various accounts can be specified at different levels of aggregation. For example, if the focus is on the distribution of income, it would be important to disaggregate the household accounts. If the focus is on tax incidence, it would be important to provide details of the tax flows, perhaps creating separate tax accounts differentiated by type of tax.

The point is that the definition of the SAM should be tailored to the problem being analyzed, and there is no standard SAM that can serve all purposes. For example, some analysts who wish to focus on distributional questions reorder the accounts, starting with the factor accounts at the upper left and moving the activity and commodity accounts to the lower right.[29]

While the definitions of the accounts in a SAM will vary, all SAMs satisfy certain conventions. The rows and columns represent the income and expenditure accounts of the various actors, and must always balance. A SAM is thus defined as a square matrix, with the totals of corresponding rows and columns always being equal. The conventions of double-entry bookkeeping guarantee that there will be no leakages or injections into the system and every flow must go from some actor to some other actor.

There are two different kinds of entries in a SAM. First, there are entries which reflect flows across markets, with payment moving in one direction (from column account to row account) and some commodity moving in the opposite direction. Accounts 1 to 3 in Figure 18.1 are of this type, representing the flow of goods and

---

[27]Another definition is often used which includes exports in the commodity account. In this case, the account defines total supply, not just domestic supply.

[28]"Use" and "make" matrices are also sometimes provided as part of the input–output accounts, with the same sectoral definitions. The approach allows for the possibility that a particular activity may produce more than one commodity.

[29]See King (1985). Pyatt and Round (1977) discuss a number of SAMs and motivate the shift in the order of the accounts depending on the focus of the analysis, although changing the order is somewhat confusing for those used to starting from an input–output matrix.

services across product markets and of factors across factor markets.[30] Second, there are entries which represent nominal flows that have no real counterpart, i.e. no transaction across a product or factor market. In terms of the national income and product accounts, all such flows represent "transfers", since no productive activity or real exchange occurs – no value added is produced or new product sold. However, with an eye toward macro theory, one can distinguish between pure transfers and financial transactions that involve the sale of assets.

For the purpose of this survey, I shall use the term "nominal flow" to describe all entries in the SAM denominated in currency units, whether or not the transaction can be seen as a price times a commodity flow. "Financial flows" are nominal flows which involve the exchange of assets (that is, the entries in the capital account) even though the table does not keep track of asset balances. These financial flows summarize the workings of the financial system, collecting savings from various actors (along the row) and using the funds to purchase new capital goods (investment) in the column. "Transfers" include all other non-market nominal flows among agents, including pure transfers such as welfare payments and involuntary transfers such as tax payments. While financial flows and transfers have no real counterparts, they nonetheless represent important economic transactions, reflecting the institutional structure of the economy and assumptions about the behavior of various actors. These flows largely define the macroeconomic structure of the economy and must be captured in any model that is concerned with distributional issues or macro adjustment.

Figure 18.2 presents an aggregated macroeconomic SAM, which should provide a convenient starting point for economists more familiar with the NIPA than with input–output tables. All entries represent macro aggregates and the factor, household, and enterprise accounts have been aggregated into a single household account. Consistent with the NIPA, intermediate flows have been assumed away or netted out. Activities produce GDP (X) along the first row and pay out gross domestic income (Y) down the first column. In contrast to the SAM in Figure 18.1, the commodity account includes exports, so the row sum equals aggregate demand while the column sum reflects aggregate supply. The standard macro identities are set out in Figure 18.2 below the SAM. They follow immediately from the defining assumption of the SAM that corresponding row and column sums must be equal.

As in the SAM in Figure 18.1, the first two rows and columns reflect transactions across product and factor markets, while the remaining accounts include financial flows and transfers of the sort captured in macro models. This

---

[30] For purposes of economic analysis, it is very convenient to define the accounts such that the price at which a commodity or factor is exchanged is the same in every entry along a given row. While easy to do in theory, this principle is difficult to achieve in practice.

Expenditures:

Receipts:	Activities	Commodities	Households	Government	Capital account	World	Total
Activities		X					GDP
Commodities			C	G	Z	E	demand
Households	Y						income
Government			T^h				taxes
Capital acct.			S^h	S^g		B	savings
Rest of world		M					imports
Total	domestic income	supply	←—— expenditure ——→			foreign exchange	

Variables:

X = output (GDP)   Domestic income = domestic product
C = household consumption   Aggregate supply = aggregate demand
G = government consumption Household income = expenditure
Z = investment   Government savings = taxes minus expenditure
E = exports   Investment = savings
Y = income (value added)   Balance of trade (= foreign savings)

T^h = taxes
S^h = household savings
S^g = government savings
B = balance of trade
M = imports

Macroeconomic identities:

(1) $Y = X$
(2) $X + M = C + G + Z + E + T^h$
(3) $Y = C + S^h + T^h$
(4) $S^g = T^h - G$
(5) $Z = S^h + S^g + B$
(6) $B = M - E$

Figure 18.2. A macroeconomic SAM.

SAM does not include assets or, indeed, distinguish investment by sector of destination, and so cannot portray the workings of financial markets. Disaggregation to include investment by sector of destination is relatively easy and is standard in many models. There has also been work to extend the SAM accounting framework to include assets, but there are few multisectoral models that attempt to include asset markets explicitly.[31]

3.2. Linear models in a SAM framework

To go from a set of accounts to a model requires more assumptions. The simplest way is to divide the columns of the input–output accounts by their sums and assume that the resulting coefficients are fixed over time. The result is the static input–output model, which is probably the most widely used tool in the world for analyzing issues in which the structure of production is a major focus. The model is solved to yield multipliers through which changes in final demand are translated into changes in sectoral output. These multipliers provide a way to do comparative statics analysis of the impact of exogenous changes in various coefficients, or in the size and composition of final demand (including, for example, foreign trade), on sectoral production and, perhaps, employment.[32]

The essence of an input–output model, and of its SAM extensions, is to capture linkages in a general equilibrium framework that allows the computation of indirect as well as direct effects of an exogenous shock. One strand of work has sought to measure the linkages and define indicators of the degree of complexity of an economy.[33] Some of this work was motivated by Hirschman's notion that one should invest in sectors with very strong forward and backward linkages, and so take advantage of the "pull" and "push" the investment would have in promoting the growth of linked sectors.[34] More recently, measures have been developed which decompose input–output and SAM multipliers into direct and indirect effects.[35] These decomposition measures indicate how important empiri-

---

[31]See United Nations (1975) for a description of SAMs which include assets. Models that explicitly include asset markets are discussed below.

[32]Static input–output models and their uses are surveyed in Blitzer, Clark and Taylor (1975) and Dervis, de Melo and Robinson (1982). Chenery, Robinson and Syrquin (1986) discuss and apply various comparative statics decomposition procedures with input–output models. See also Stone (1984).

[33]See, for example, Rasmussen (1965) and Robinson and Markandya (1973).

[34]See Hirschman (1958). Measures of sectoral linkages are discussed by Chenery and Clark (1959), Yotopoulos and Nugent (1976, chs. 15 and 16), Torii and Fukasaku (1984), and Kubo, Robinson and Syrquin (1986).

[35]The original inspiration for this work was provided by Richard Stone. See Stone (1985). Various decompositions are discussed by Pyatt and Round (1979) and Robinson and Roland-Holst (1987). Defourny and Thorbecke (1984) present generalized SAM decompositions which include the others as special cases.

cally are the indirect linkages, and how different are SAM-based multipliers compared to simple input–output multipliers.

Decomposition measures can be used to address questions such as: "When is it feasible to ignore indirect linkages and stay with partial-equilibrium analysis?" and "When is it important to consider the institutional linkages incorporated in a SAM, rather than capture only the linkages embodied in intermediate flows in an input–output table?" The answer to both questions appears to be "often". Simply arraying national data in a SAM framework provides a lot of information about the structure of an economy. The decomposition measures indicate both qualitative information about the main causal linkages at work and quantitative information about the magnitudes of the indirect and direct effects.

Within the SAM framework, one simple way to create a model is to assume the various column coefficients are all constant. However, since the matrix is square and the coefficients in every column will sum to one, there are no exogenous elements and hence no multipliers. One approach is to specify one or more accounts – columns and rows in the SAM – as being exogenous. For example, the standard input–output model can be derived from the SAM by combining the activity and commodity accounts and specifying all other accounts exogenously. The final demands become exogenous, and the value-added coefficients are no longer in the square matrix of coefficients to be inverted.

Extending the input–output model to include more accounts in the SAM requires that we assume that various expenditure coefficients are fixed. It thus becomes important to define accounts so as to make this interpretation reasonable. For example, in the SAM in Figure 18.1, the distribution of nominal income between wages and profits would be assumed fixed, as would be the average tax and savings rates of enterprises and households. Also, the sectoral composition of nominal consumption, government, and investment expenditure would be assumed fixed. Such assumptions represent a considerable extension of the fixed-coefficients technology in the standard input–output model.

In models based on the SAM, an important question is which accounts are to be assumed exogenous. Standard practice is to pick one or more of the government, capital, and rest of the world accounts, justifying the choice on the basis of macroeconomic theory.[36] The resulting multiplier models are completely demand driven, since no constraints on supply are specified, and are thus Keynesian in spirit. For example, assume that only the investment account is exogenous and solve for the resulting multipliers. Changes in investment provide the "injection" that drives the model and the various savings rates provide the "leakages" that permit the model to be solved. For a given change in investment (perhaps sectorally differentiated), the model will solve for the equilibrium levels of all

---

[36]See Pyatt and Round (1979) and Stone (1985) for a general discussion of multipliers in a SAM framework and the choice of exogenous accounts.

endogenous accounts such that the change in nominal savings equals the nominal value of the change in investment.

Given that we are choosing among three accounts (capital, government, and the rest of the world), there are seven different combinations of exogenous accounts – each one singly, three pairwise combinations, plus all three together. Each of these choices defines a different macro "closure" to the SAM model. In each case, a shock is defined as a change in elements of the exogenous columns. The nature of the adjustment will depend on the size and structure of the coefficients in the endogenous accounts and of those in the excluded rows (which define the leakages). Of course, the computed multipliers will be sensitive to the choice, and the resulting model must be defended in terms of theory and empirical realism for the particular problem under study.

The choice of macro closure in the SAM framework serves to open the model. If a single account is taken as exogenous, the fact that the endogenous accounts all will balance at a new equilibrium guarantees that the exogenous account will also balance since the SAM as a whole must balance. Any SAM-multiplier model satisfies a variant of Walras' Law – if all accounts but one balance, then the last must also balance. If two or more accounts are set exogenously, then only their sum must balance, given a solution for the endogenous accounts.

This issue of macro closure appears again in the context of CGE models. It is useful to see the problem first in the SAM framework, since the macro issues are very similar and can easily be obscured in the additional detail of non-linear functions, many sectors, and various choices of equilibrating mechanisms. Another point to note is that any model in the SAM framework, or any model that provides a complete account of the circular flow, will have financial and transfer accounts for which there are no corresponding real flows. Such a model thus has an implicit macro structure, no matter how well hidden. The problem of macro closure cannot be avoided.

One major use of multiplier models in the SAM framework has been to explore issues of income distribution. Two early models in this tradition are Cline (1972) and Weisskoff (1970). They sought to explore the linkages from the distribution of income to the structure of demand to the structure of production and hence back to employment and income distribution. Both authors extended the standard input–output model in order to trace the links from value added to demand, but without explicitly using the SAM framework.[37] During the 1970s, a number of more ambitious and complete SAM-multiplier models designed to explore issues of income distribution were built. See Pyatt and Thorbecke (1976) and Thorbecke (1985) for surveys of this work.[38]

---

[37] In a later extension of his model, Weisskoff (1985) recognized that he had implicitly been working with a SAM, and discusses his new model in the SAM framework.

[38] This work is also discussed in Chapter 17 by Adelman and Robinson in this Handbook.

3.3. Prices and static SAM models

Any input–output model has a dual price system, which can be seen as a set of cost prices in a linear framework. There is an extensive literature which uses input–output models to trace out cost linkages as an element in benefit–cost analysis. For example, the literature on effective protection and domestic resource costs is largely based on the static input–output model.[39] In an economy where domestic tradables are perfect substitutes for goods traded on the world market, the domestic price of every tradable good will equal its world price. In addition, subject to an aggregate balance of trade constraint, net exports or imports should provide the mechanism by which supply and demand are equated for tradable sectors. Jan Tinbergen suggested an extension of the input–output model to capture this phenomenon. The resulting "semi-input–output" model has been used for a variety of purposes in a number of countries.[40] One important application has been to generate shadow prices for the purposes of cost–benefit analysis.[41]

The semi-input–output model has also been extended in the SAM framework. For example, Bell and various coauthors have developed a multiplier model using a regional SAM with links to the rest of the economy to explore the impact of a large agricultural project on its surrounding region. Their technique shares with the semi-input–output model the assumption that tradable goods should be valued at world prices, but also considers expenditure multipliers in the SAM framework.[42] These models represent an elegant marriage of benefit–cost analysis with SAM-based multiplier analysis. The framework permits the analysis of the impact of large projects, while standard benefit–cost methods usually must assume that all projects are marginal.

3.4. Linear dynamic models

The dynamic input–output model provided the first approach to endogenizing investment in the input–output model. Using a vector of fixed capital–output ratios, the model links changes in investment by sector of destination to changes in sectoral output. Then, using a matrix of capital coefficients, the model translates demand for investment by sector of destination into demands for

---

[39] The literature on DRCs and ERPs is beyond the scope of this survey. See Corden (1974), Bhagwati and Srinivasan (1978), and Balassa and Associates (1971) for discussions of the concepts and their uses.

[40] See Tinbergen (1966). Kuyvenhoven (1978) provides extensive discussion of the method, with applications to Nigeria.

[41] In a series of articles, Bell and Devarajan (1980, 1983, 1985) have explored the use of the semi-input–output model as a framework for project evaluation.

[42] See Bell and Hazell (1980), Bell, Hazell and Slade (1982), and Bell and Devarajan (1985). See also Greenfeld and Fell (1979).

investment goods by sector of origin – the investment column in the input–output table or SAM. While the model includes a theoretically clean definition of dynamic equilibrium, it shares with its one-sector cousin, the Harrod–Domar model, a distressing tendency toward instability.[43] However, patched up in various ways, applied models based on the dynamic input–output model have been widely used in developing countries.

Dynamic input–output models have been extended in a number of ways designed to make them more useful in an applied setting. These applied models stay relatively close to their input–output antecedents, adding features such as gestation lags and constraints on aggregate investment, employment, or the balance of trade. Models in this tradition, however, do not seek to include nominal flows or prices. The intent is to stay within the input–output framework, but to move beyond the demand-driven input–output model, where final demand is exogenous, to models incorporating various constraints on supply as well. Such models have been used by the planning agencies of a number of developing countries, and variants were also developed for some developed countries.[44] More recently, dynamic input–output models have been developed which incorporate macro constraints in a non-linear framework, but still avoid any consideration of prices.[45]

In the past decade, a number of dynamic simulation models have been developed which start from a core dynamic input–output model, but which then include macro aggregates and a number of relationships derived from macro models. Such models often start from an explicit SAM framework and may focus on distributional as well as macro issues. Some include a few non-linear equations. Some also use cost prices to calculate nominal flows endogenously, but they do not specify any price adjustment mechanism to equilibrate supply and demand.[46] Thorbecke (1985) describes such models focused on distributional issues as "first generation" models, in contrast to "second generation" CGE

---

[43]See Dervis, de Melo and Robinson (1982, ch. 2), for an extensive discussion of the dynamic input–output model and its mathematical structure. Note that while the model is a multisector analogue to the Harrod–Domar model, the nature and sources of its unstable growth are more complex. The early applications are surveyed by Taylor (1975).

[44]Typical applications of such extended models include Sri Lanka, Colombia, Korea, India, Chile, and Turkey. These models are surveyed by Clark (1975). Applied dynamic input–output models of developed countries include the model of the United States by Almon et al. (1974) and the Cambridge model of the United Kingdom developed under the direction of Richard Stone, described in Stone (1981). See Tsukui and Murakami (1979) for a general theoretical discussion and a model of Japan.

[45]See, for example, Kubo, Robinson and Urata (1986) who use a stylized dynamic input–output model applied to Korea and Turkey that incorporates non-linear constraints on cumulative investment and foreign capital inflows. The model is used to explore the implications of pursuing an outward-looking versus an inward-looking development strategy.

[46]Examples of such models include: Korea, Gupta (1977a); Indonesia, Gupta (1977b); Iran, Pyatt et al. (1972); Colombia, Thorbecke and Sengupta (1972); Thailand, Grais (1981); Egypt, World Bank (1983); Dominican Republic, McCarthy (1984); and China, World Bank (1985). A number of these models start from the World Bank's Revised Minimum Standard Model (RMSM), which is essentially a two-gap macro model that can be applied to almost any country.

models, and surveys a few using the underlying SAM to provide a framework for comparison.

All of these are applied models and focus on policy concerns in particular country settings. To an academic reader, these models seem cluttered with ad hoc specifications designed to capture institutional features of the particular countries. In some cases, the clutter makes it difficult to see exactly what is driving the models. They all include a number of strong linearity assumptions but, in the dynamic models, it is difficult to tell if such assumptions lead to instabilities since there is in no case any discussion of steady-state properties. In the models that stay close to the SAM framework – for example, the Iran, Colombia, and Thailand models – it is relatively easy to sort out the causal linkages at work. The SAM framework imposes a structure that helps achieve the goal of transparency in an applied model.

Assumptions about fixed coefficients and cost prices limit the applicability of all linear input–output and SAM-based models, static and dynamic. These models reveal much about the structure of the economy and focus on important indirect as well as direct causal linkages. However, they are inherently limited in their ability to reflect the workings of a multi-market economy in which price adjustments play an important role and in which there are important substitution possibilities in both production and demand. Supply and demand interactions are largely beyond their scope, and they cannot capture policy choices that work through price incentives. To capture such features, non-linear models are required. Such computable general equilibrium models emerged in the early 1970s, along with the required computer software needed to solve them.

4. Computable general equilibrium models

In the literature on developing countries, computable general equilibrium (CGE) models represent an incremental step in a long tradition of work with multisector programming models.[47] A CGE model works by simulating the interaction of various economic actors across markets. Optimizing behavior of individual actors is assumed and is incorporated in equations describing their behavior, which essentially describe various first-order conditions for profit and utility maximization. The CGE framework requires a complete specification of both the supply and demand sides of all markets, including all the nominal magnitudes in the circular flow. The models are thus structural in spirit, capturing market mechanisms explicitly.

---

[47]See Devarajan, Lewis and Robinson (1986) for an extensive bibliography of work dealing with CGE models of developing countries.

The SAM accounts provide the underlying data framework for CGE models, with an income–expenditure account for each actor in the model. Neoclassical general equilibrium theory provides the analytical underpinnings. The body of mainstream neoclassical theory provides a powerful framework of analysis, with its systematic accumulation of useful taxonomies and formal analytical results. In many applications to developing countries, however, the framework has been stretched to accommodate a variety of structuralist features. In trying to judge the validity and applicability of the many non-neoclassical specifications that have been incorporated into CGE models, it is useful to start from the neoclassical paradigm and to establish a standard approach to describing the features of a general equilibrium model.

4.1. The structure of a CGE model

A general equilibrium model can be usefully described in terms of the following components.[48] First, one must specify the economic actors or agents whose behavior is to be analyzed. A simple Walrasian model would include only producers and households. Most CGE models add other actors such as government and the rest of the world – additional institutions in the SAM framework. Second, behavioral rules must be specified for these actors that reflect their assumed motivation. For example, producers are typically assumed to maximize profits subject to technological constraints and households to maximize utility subject to income constraints. Third, agents make their decisions based on signals they observe. For example, in a Walrasian model, prices are the only signals agents need to know. Fourth, one must specify the "rules of the game" according to which agents interact – the institutional structure of the economy. For example, assuming perfect competition implies that each agent is a price taker and that prices are flexible – markets exist and work perfectly.

The specification of the institutional structure and of the signals agents observe and react to are, of course, closely related. For example, under perfect competition, actors need only know prices. Alternatively, if some market is monopolistic, then one must specify that the monopolist makes supply decisions based on information about the demand functions of the demanders, not just the market price. In a model with some fixed prices, agents will be subject to rationing and one must specify their behavior in this situation – for example, what are the rationing rules and resulting spillover effects.

With the specification of the agents, their motivation, and the institutional constraints under which they interact, a general equilibrium model is still not completely determined. One must also define "equilibrium conditions" which are

---

[48] This description draws on Ginsburgh and Robinson (1984).

"system constraints" that must be satisfied, but that are not taken into account by any agent in making his decisions.[49] Formally, an equilibrium can be defined as a set of signals such that the resulting decisions of all agents jointly satisfy the system constraints. The signals represent the equilibrating variables of the model. For example, a market equilibrium in a competitive model is defined as a set of prices and associated quantities such that all excess demands are zero. In a market economy, prices are the equilibrating variables that vary to achieve market clearing.

As discussed earlier, the definition of equilibrium conditions is a fundamental property of a model. The specification of equilibrating variables and of system constraints that characterize an equilibrium can be seen as a simplifying device that provides a way to describe the results of the workings of an actual economy. For example, instead of specifying prices as equilibrating variables to achieve market clearing, one could instead try to model price determination explicitly, specifying "disequilibrium" price adjustment rules to describe how prices change over time. Such a specification is theoretically very difficult to implement – indeed, even to define – and completely unnecessary if one is willing to accept the market-clearing system constraints under flexible prices as a reasonable description of the final result of such a process within the time period described by the model.

There are, however, times when certain market-clearing assumptions are not reasonable. In CGE models of developed countries, for example, it is usually assumed that capital is mobile across sectors and is allocated so as to equate sectoral (after-tax) rental rates – an equilibrium condition that is consistent with an assumption of perfect capital markets.[50] Such a specification obviates the need to describe exactly how the capital market functions – we are only interested in the result. In models of developing countries, the assumption of sectoral capital mobility is rarely if ever reasonable. Instead, modellers have tended to assume that sectoral capital stocks are fixed within a period and, since sectoral rental rates are not equal across sectors, they have had to specify explicitly how the sectoral allocation of investment is determined from period to period.

4.2. A neoclassical, closed-economy, CGE model

Table 18.1 presents a stylized neoclassical CGE model of a closed economy and Figure 18.3 presents the associated SAM. Equations (1) to (5) in Table 18.1 describe the behavior of the various actors. There are n sectors, m factors of

---

[49] The term "system constraint" is due to Ginsburgh and Waelbroeck (1981) who provide a formal definition in the context of optimizing models.

[50] For examples of such models, see Scarf and Shoven (1983).

Table 18.1
A neoclassical closed-economy CGE model

Real flows

(1) $X_i^S(F_{i\cdot}^D)$ production (n)

(2) $C_i^D(P, \tilde{C})$ consumption demand (n)

(3) $Z_i^D(P, \tilde{Z})$ investment demand (n)

(4) $F_k^S(W_k, P)$ factor supply (m)

(5) $F_{ik}^D(W_k, P_i)$ factor demand $(n \cdot m)$

Real system constraints

(6) $C_i^D + Z_i^D - X_i^S = 0$ products (n)

(7) $\sum_i F_{ik}^D - F_k^S = 0$ factors (m)

Nominal flows

(8) $\tilde{Y} = W \cdot F^S$ nominal income

(9) $\tilde{C}(\tilde{Y})$ consumption function

(10) $\tilde{S} = \tilde{Y} - \tilde{C}$ nominal savings

Nominal system constraints

(11) $\tilde{S} - \tilde{Z} = 0$ savings-investment

(12) $f(P, W) = \bar{P}$ price index (scalar)

Accounting identities

(13) $\sum_i \sum_k W_k \cdot F_{ik}^D = P \cdot X^S$ factor payments = total sales

(14) $P \cdot C^D = \tilde{C}$ consumption demand = expenditure

(15) $P \cdot Z^D = \tilde{Z}$ investment demand = expenditure

Equilibrating price variables

P = vector of product prices (n)

W = vector of factor prices (m)

Notes: X^S, C^D, Z^D, and P are all vectors with n elements, using subscript i. F^S and W are vectors with m elements, using subscript k. F^D is a matrix with $m \cdot n$ elements. In equation (1), the F^D with a subscript $i \cdot$ is a vector of k factor inputs into sector i. Nominal variables, all scalars, are denoted by a tilde. A dot $(\cdot)$ indicates either an inner product of two vectors or multiplication. The $f(-)$ in equation (12) denotes a function that defines the numeraire price index, which is fixed exogenously. There are $4n + 2m + n \cdot m + 4$ endogenous variables and the same number of independent equations.

Receipts:	Expenditures: Activities	Commodities	Factors	Households	Capital	Total
Activities		$P \cdot X^S$				$P \cdot X^S$
Commodities				$P \cdot C^D$	$P \cdot Z^D$	$\tilde{C} + \tilde{Z}$
Factors	$W \cdot F^D$					$W \cdot F^D$
Households			$\tilde{Y}$			$\tilde{Y}$
Capital acct.				$\tilde{S}$		$\tilde{S}$
Total	$W \cdot F^D$	$P \cdot X^S$	$W \cdot F^S$	$\tilde{Y}$	$\tilde{Z}$	

Figure 18.3. Social accounting matrix for a neoclassical CGE model. *Note*: Variables are defined in Table 18.1.

production, and one household. Equation (1) describes the production possibility frontier for the economy, given the set of sectoral production functions. In this simple model, intermediate goods have been netted out. In almost all applied CGE models, input–output coefficients are used to determine the demand for intermediate goods, while primary factors – capital and various kinds of labor – are assumed to be inputs in a neoclassical production function.[51] Given the production technology, profit-maximizing behavior, and the existence of competitive factor and product markets, equation (5) describes the demand for factors by sectors. Equation (4) describes aggregate factor supplies, which are usually just fixed exogenously in most CGE models applied to developing countries.[52]

Equations (2) and (3) describe the demand for products. Equation (2) is an expenditure function for the single household describing how total consumption expenditure is allocated among goods. Various expenditure systems have been used, usually assuming that some utility function is being maximized.[53] While this model has only one consumer, it is possible to specify any number of households in the model, each with its own sources of income and separate expenditure function.[54]

Equation (3) converts aggregate investment into demands for investment goods by sector of origin. In most applied models in developing countries, the sectoral allocation of aggregate investment is explicitly modelled and equation (3) then serves to translate investment by sector of destination into demand for investment goods by sector of origin. The standard technique follows that used in dynamic input–output models, with fixed capital-share coefficients describing different compositions of capital across sectors. The assumption of heterogeneous sectoral capital is empirically important in developing countries, where the agriculture and service sectors are large and use quite different kinds of capital goods than do the manufacturing sectors.[55]

---

[51]A variety of functional forms have been used, including, Cobb–Douglas, CES, generalized Leontief, translog, and various multi-level versions of these forms. See Dervis, de Melo and Robinson (1982, ch. 5), for a discussion of different specifications.

[52]CGE models applied to developed countries often have more elaborate factor supply equations incorporating the labor–leisure choice of workers. See, for example, Ballard, Fullerton, Shoven and Whalley (1985).

[53]The linear expenditure system is probably the most popular in models of developing countries, but others have been used. Dervis, de Melo and Robinson (1982) describe some of the choices.

[54]The one-consumer model, of course, is easier to solve. As noted above, it can be solved as a straightforward one-step non-linear programming problem.

[55]Most models of developed countries do not allow for heterogeneous capital across sectors. It is difficult to tell how important is the omission, but it might well be significant, especially in models where investment allocation is computed in some optimal fashion. See Dervis (1975) for an analysis of the importance of heterogeneous capital in a dynamic CGE model which includes intertemporal equilibrium.

Equations (8), (9), and (10) map the distribution of income from the factor accounts in the SAM to institutions. In this case, the SAM shown in Figure 18.3 is very simple, with only one aggregate household and a consolidated capital account. The household receives income, saving some and using the rest for consumption. The capital account serves the function of the financial sector, collecting savings and allocating it to investment, leading to demands for investment goods. Equation (11) specifies that aggregate nominal savings equal investment, or that the model be in macroeconomic equilibrium. Since the model has no independent investment function, the system constraint that investment equals savings [equation (11)] serves to determine aggregate investment. The model is "savings driven" and has no place for any interesting macroeconomic adjustment mechanisms and additional equilibrating variables.

Equations (6) and (7) represent the excess demand equations for the product and factor markets and provide the system constraints defining equilibrium in these markets. The equilibrating variables are product and factor prices, which serve as signals to producers and households in determining supply and demand behavior. Equations (13), (14), and (15) are accounting identities that the model must satisfy. They are not independent equations, but instead are implied from the factor and product demand equations.[56] Given these identities, the excess-demand equations satisfy Walras' Law – the sum of the nominal excess demands across all product and factor markets is zero. In the SAM in Figure 18.3, the identities guarantee that the "total" row and column have the same sum. In this case, the $n + m$ system constraints are not independent and will not suffice to determine $n + m$ product and factor prices. However, the behavioral assumptions are such that typically all the supply and demand functions are homogeneous of degree zero in all prices. Thus, one is free to add an additional equation defining a numeraire price index, equation (12), which defines a unit of account and has no effect on the equilibrium value of any real variable.[57]

Given the definition of the numeraire, the non-linear system has at least one solution endogenously determining relative prices and all real flows.[58] A fair amount of mathematical rigor is being finessed here. The supply and demand

---

[56] For example, homogeneous production functions yield factor demand equations which satisfy equation (13). If production functions were not homogeneous, then some factor return (such as profits) would have to be defined residually. Any expenditure functions arising from utility maximization will satisfy equation (14). Equation (15) is certainly a reasonable requirement to impose on investment demand.

[57] The "numeraire" is a good, or aggregation of goods, whose price is set to one (or any exogenous value) in order to define the units of all relative prices in the system. I will often use the term "numeraire price index" to refer to the price of this numeraire good.

[58] Problems of existence have been much studied and will not concern us here. See Ginsburgh and Waelbroeck (1981) and Scarf and Hansen (1973) for further discussion in the context of empirical models. Arrow and Hahn (1971) and Mas-Colell (1985) provide excellent textbook treatments of general equilibrium theory.

equations are specified as functions, not correspondences, and the equilibrium conditions as equalities, which is typical of CGE models. All prices will be strictly positive, with correspondingly strong assumptions about the nature of production technology and utility functions. While a CGE model with many consumers potentially might have multiple solutions, no one has ever reported such a problem with an applied model.[59]

It is possible, given the numeraire, to view producers as maximizing nominal profits and consumers as maximizing utility subject to nominal budget constraints. Such an interpretation is not necessary and the system can also be seen as representing a barter economy with relative prices indicating exchange values. For the neoclassical, savings-driven model, the choice of numeraire is purely a matter of convenience, essentially only setting the units in which nominal magnitudes are measured. The nominal variables – the ones with a tilde in Table 18.1 and Figure 18.3 – represent macro aggregates in the national income and product accounts. It is useful to define these macro aggregates for later use, but they could easily be substituted out in this model.[60]

While useful for exposition, the neoclassical CGE model has had very limited application in developing countries. The simplifications are too confining for applied work, and it has usually been used to analyze questions where a stylized model is appropriate. The original CGE model of Norway by Johansen (1960) stays close to the neoclassical paradigm and essentially the same model was also applied to Chile by Taylor and Black (1974).[61] In these cases, the scope of the analysis is carefully restricted, and the authors recognize the limitations of the stylization.[62] The neoclassical model seems to have had a longer life in developed countries; only very recently have models of these countries started to reflect any structuralist features.[63]

Over long time horizons, the assumptions of the neoclassical model are more appropriate. For example, stylized, long-run CGE models have been used fruitfully to examine determinants of long-run urbanization and structural change.

---

[59] See Mas-Colell (1985) and Kehoe (1980) for discussions of uniqueness of equilibria in general equilibrium models. It is evidently much more of a problem for theorists than for applied models.

[60] In standard textbook treatments of general equilibrium models, the expenditure function [equation (2)] has as arguments product prices, factor prices, and initial endowments. Nominal magnitudes are just side equations.

[61] These models have a different specification of aggregate investment than the neoclassical CGE model in table 18.1, which will be discussed below.

[62] Serra-Puche (1983) and Kehoe and Serra-Puche (1983), on the other hand, have constructed a stylized, neoclassical CGE model of Mexico and attempt to use it for policy analysis. Their use of such a stylized model for policy analysis is criticized by Robinson (1983) on the grounds that the model does not adequately reflect the structure of the Mexican economy, given their policy focus.

[63] For a survey of these models, see Shoven and Whalley (1984). See also the survey by Manne (1985).

These stylized historical models illuminate basic dynamic forces in development and give the economic historian a simulation laboratory for doing controlled experiments. They provide an excellent framework for sorting out historical trends and for doing experiments in counterfactual history. Such models have been constructed by Jeffrey Williamson, with various coauthors, for Japan, England, the United States, and India.[64]

One also might argue that a neoclassical model provides an appropriate framework for doing shadow pricing exercises for project analysis. Shadow prices used for large projects should reflect long-run scarcities, as well as take into account general equilibrium interactions. The work using SAMs to generate shadow prices can easily be extended to the framework provided by the neoclassical CGE model, and there is some work in this vein.[65]

Similarly, CGE models have been used to generate general equilibrium variants of measures such as effective rates of protection (ERPs) which have been developed to measure the impact of the tariff structure on value added, and hence resource allocation, in the economy. Empirical work with CGE models indicates that general equilibrium effects may matter a lot, changing the ranking of sectoral protection measures based on partial equilibrium assumptions. The standard partial equilibrium measures do especially badly when assumptions of imperfect substitutability between domestic and imported goods are introduced, as is done in the model described below.[66]

4.3. Extending the neoclassical CGE model

Modellers working on developing countries, however, have not stayed long with the neoclassical model. As discussed above, they have sought to extend the models in a variety of directions in order to capture "structuralist" features of developing countries. Within the framework of the CGE model, one can distinguish three kinds of structuralist models. First, one can stay within the theoretical structure of the neoclassical model, but specify limited substitution elasticities in a variety of important relationships. This type of model might be termed

[64]See Kelley, Williamson and Cheetham (1972), Kelley and Williamson (1974, 1984), Williamson and Lindert (1980).

[65]See, for example, Bell and Devarajan (1983). Bell and Srinivasan (1984) suggest that such an approach should be productive.

[66]Balassa (1982) discusses conditions under which the general equilibrium results from CGE models assuming perfect substitutability will be consistent with partial equilibrium measures. See also de Melo (1980). For comparisons of partial and general equilibrium measures in models assuming imperfect substitutability, see de Melo and Robinson (1981) and Devarajan (1987).

"elasticity structuralist". A second type, which can be called "micro structuralist", assumes that various markets do not work properly or are not present at all. Instead, there are assumed to be restrictions on factor mobility, rigid prices, rationing, and neoclassical disequilibrium in one or more important markets. "Macro structuralist" models represent a third type and focus on questions of achieving equilibrium among various macro aggregates; in particular, savings and investment, exports and imports, and government expenditure and revenue. While there has been some work to extend the macro structuralist models to include asset markets, virtually all of the applied models have incorporated constraints and equilibrium conditions on nominal flows representing macro aggregates.

There are various schools of thought in development economics that argue for models with differing mixes of structuralist features. For example, Hollis Chenery has argued that developing countries are characterized by a mix of elasticity and micro structuralist features. This school, which might be described as "neoclassical structuralist", accepts the neoclassical model of resource allocation and the importance of the operation of markets, but argues that substitution possibilities are more limited in developing countries than is usually assumed in neoclassical models, especially in foreign trade and production. In addition to low response elasticities, neoclassical structuralists also argue that there are important imperfect or incomplete markets, especially for factors of production and foreign exchange, in which prices do not respond properly to market forces. These imperfections may arise either from institutional sources or from policy choices. Another strand of this school's view is that rapid structural changes characteristic of the process of industrialization lead to continuing dynamic micro and macro disequilibria as market adjustments try to catch up with the dynamic processes. Chenery (1975) provides a succinct statement of the major arguments.[67] While there are many disagreements among neoclassical structuralists, they have in common an eclectic theoretical approach and probably share with most development economists the feeling that an uncritical application of the textbook neoclassical model to developing countries will lead to serious errors of analysis and policy advice.

A second school emphasizes the disequilibria that work through macroeconomic mechanisms, but whose roots lie in political and social conflict. The intellectual lineage of this school can be traced from Marx through Cambridge,

---

[67]See, for example, Chenery and Strout (1966), Chenery (1979), Chenery and Raduchel (1979), and Eckaus (1955). See also Chenery (1971, 1984), Chenery, Robinson and Syrquin (1986), and Adelman and Thorbecke (1966) for further elaboration of the approach and examples of models in this tradition.

England, to Latin America. Lance Taylor and his coauthors are prominent in this tradition.[68] While the term "Latin American structuralists" is sometimes used, it is more descriptive to view these models as examples of "macro structuralist" models in order to emphasize the mechanisms by which the disequilibrium adjustments are assumed to operate. This approach seeks to integrate macro models with multisector models, and so blend Keynes and Walras.

The attempt to force a macro framework onto a multisector model leads to many problems, including the need to add a number of micro structuralist features in order to capture the desired impact of macro adjustment on the economy. While the Latin American structuralists represent one school of thought, there are other macro structuralist approaches that mix macro adjustment and micro structuralist features. A variety of approaches will be discussed below in the context of alternative "macro closures" of a CGE model.

There are difficulties in extending the CGE model to incorporate these different structuralist features. As discussed above, the Walrasian model provides an uneasy host for macro models, and mixes of CGE and macro models all have an ad hoc flavor that arises from the fact that there is as yet no acceptable reconciliation of their different underlying theories. While the macro structuralist models probably place the greatest strain on existing theory, imposing micro structuralist features also has theoretical problems in that the structuralist rigidity often cannot be justified within the structure of the model.

The usual approach is to impose a rigidity on the model from outside, and then examine how the resulting mixed model performs. In many cases, it is possible to view the rigidity as arising from technological or institutional constraints that prevent maximizers from interacting across markets, even if they are not explicitly included in the model. For example, there is now a large body of theoretical literature indicating that there are many circumstances under which it is reasonable to assume that prices will not adjust as needed in the neoclassical model, and such frictions are widely observed in both developed and less developed countries. Models with price rigidities and "fixprice" adjustment mechanisms are now common in the theoretical as well as applied literature.[69]

The extension of a neoclassical CGE model to include micro and macro structuralist features raises two major complications in sorting out equilibrating mechanisms in the resulting hybrid model. First, is the model still homogeneous, i.e. is the real side "neutral" to the choice of numeraire? Many micro structuralist

---

[68]See Taylor (1979, 1983). Diamand (1978) provides an excellent discussion of the Latin American school.

[69]See, for example, Benassy (1982) for a discussion of fixprice general equilibrium models which exhibit Keynesian features. Waelbroeck (1986) discusses the problems and benefits of incorporating such features into CGE models.

Table 18.2
An elasticity structuralist CGE model

Real flows

(1) $X(L^D, V^D, K^D)$ production
(2) $X(E, D^S)$ export transformation
(3) $Q^D(M, D^D)$ import aggregation

(4) $M/D^D = f_1(P^m, P^d)$
      import demand
(5) $E/D^S = f_2(P^e, P^d)$ export supply
(6) $C^D(P^q, \tilde{C})$ consumption demand
(7) $Z^D(P^q, \tilde{Z})$ investment demand
(8) $V^D(R, W, P^q, P^x)$
      intermediate demand

(9) $Q^D = C^D + Z^D + V^D + \overline{G}^D$ total
(10) $L^S(W, P^q)$ labor supply
(11) $L^D(R, W, P^q, P^x)$ labor demand
(12) $K^D(R, W, P^q, P^x)$ capital demand

Real system constraints
(13) $D^D - D^S = 0$ product market

(14) $L^D - L^S = 0$ labor market

(15) $K^D - \overline{K}^S = 0$ capital market

Nominal flows

(16) $\tilde{Y}^L = W \cdot L^S \cdot (1 - \overline{T}^L)$ labor income
(17) $\tilde{Y}^K = R \cdot \overline{K}^S \cdot (1 - \overline{T}^K)$ capital income
(18) $\tilde{Y}^G = \overline{T}^L \cdot W \cdot L^S + \overline{T}^K \cdot R \cdot \overline{K}^S$
      government income
(19) $\tilde{C}(\tilde{Y}^L, \tilde{Y}^K)$ consumption function

(20) $\tilde{S}^P = \tilde{Y}^L + \tilde{Y}^K - \tilde{C}$ private saving
(21) $\tilde{M} = \overline{P}^{\$m} \cdot M$ dollar imports
(22) $\tilde{E} = \overline{P}^{\$e} \cdot E$ dollar exports

Price equations
(23) $P^m = r \cdot \overline{P}^{\$m}$ import price
(24) $P^e = r \cdot \overline{P}^{\$e}$ export price
(25) $P^q(P^m, P^d)$ composite price
(26) $P^x(P^e, P^d)$ output price

Nominal system constaints
(27) $\tilde{S}^P + \tilde{S}^G + r \cdot \overline{B} - \tilde{Z} = 0$
      savings-investment
(28) $\tilde{Y}^G - P^q \cdot \overline{G}^D - \tilde{S}^G = 0$
      government balance
(29) $\tilde{M} - \tilde{E} = \overline{B}$ balance of trade
(30) $f_3(P^d, P^m, P^e, W) = \overline{P}$ numeraire

Accounting identities
(31) $P^x \cdot X = P^e \cdot E + P^d \cdot D^S$ value of output = value of sales
(32) $P^q \cdot Q^D = P^m \cdot M + P^d \cdot D^D$ value of composite goods = absorption
(33) $P^x X = W \cdot L^D + R \cdot K^D + p^q \cdot V^D$ value of sales = value of inputs
(34) $P^q \cdot C^D = \tilde{C}$ consumption demand = expenditure
(35) $P^q \cdot Z^D = \tilde{Z}$ investment demand = expenditure

---

Endogenous variables
X = aggregate output
D^S = supply of domestic output
D^D = demand for domestic output
E = exports
M = imports
Q^D = composite good demand
V^D = intermediate demand
L^S = labor supply
L^D = labor demand
K^D = capital demand
C^D = real consumption
Z^D = real investment
$\tilde{Y}^L$ = nominal income
$\tilde{Y}^K$ = capital income

Endogenous variables, cont.
$\tilde{M}$ = dollar value of imports
$\tilde{E}$ = dollar value of exports
P^m = domestic price of imports
P^e = domestic price of exports
P^x = price of aggregate output
P^d = price of domestic sales
P^q = price of composite good
W = wage of labor
R = rental rate of capital
r = exchange rate
$\tilde{Y}^G$ = government income
$\tilde{S}^P$ = private savings
$\tilde{S}^G$ = government savings
$\tilde{C}$ = nominal consumption
$\tilde{Z}$ = nominal investment

Table 18.2 Continued

Exogenous variables	
$\overline{G}^D$ = real government demand	$\overline{B}$ = balance of trade (in dollars)
$\overline{K}^S$ = aggregate capital supply	$\overline{P}^{\$m}$ = world price of imports
$\overline{T}^L$ = tax rate on labor income	$\overline{P}^{\$e}$ = world price of exports
$\overline{T}^K$ = tax rate on capital income	$\overline{P}$ = numeraire price index

Notes: Variables with a tilde denote nominal magnitudes. Variables with a bar are exogenous. The superscripts d, m, e, x, and q refer to the domestic good, imports, exports, output, and the composite good, respectively (D, M, E, X, and Q). The superscripts D and S refer to demand and supply. The superscripts L and K refer to labor and capital. Superscripts P and G refer to private and government. A dot denotes multiplication. There are 29 endogenous variables and 30 equations. The equations, however, are functionally dependent and represent 29 independent equations.

The production function and import aggregation function [equations (1) and (3)] are CES functions [equation (1) is often a two-level nested function]. The export transformation function [equation (2)] is a CET function. Equations (4), (5), (8), (11), and (12) are the corresponding demand equations based on first-order conditions for profit maximization or cost minimization. In many models, intermediate demand is assumed to be given by fixed input–output coefficients, in which case equation (8) is a function only of output. Equations (25) and (26) are the cost function duals to the import aggregation and export transformation functions. Equation (30) defines the numeraire price index.

features can be captured by specifying various fixed relative prices, with the resulting model still neutral to the choice of numeraire. If not, however, then the numeraire price normalization must be interpreted as an aggregate price index which serves as an important signal to some actors; an exogenous variable whose changes will affect real behavior.

A second issue concerns the interpretation of the nominal flows, including financial flows (in the capital account) and transfers. Extending the CGE model to include macro flow equilibrium conditions does require that the model be seen as reflecting a monetized economy in which nominal aggregates play an important role. However, the model need not include assets and money explicitly. It is an open question whether macro structuralist models can be truly convincing without explicitly including assets and asset markets, but it is certainly possible to capture a number of interesting macro stories in such models.

While the theoretical difficulties in extending the CGE model are great, the potential payoff in developing useful policy models is also great. But it is important to proceed with caution, adding at each step only as much complication as is needed, and retaining a clear view of the causal mechanisms at work.

4.4. An elasticity structuralist CGE model

Table 18.2 sets out the equations of a simplified version of a stylized elasticity structuralist model of an open economy that also includes a government account. The associated SAM is given in Figure 18.4. The model is representative of a

Expenditures:			Factors:					Capital account	World	Total
Receipts:	Activities	Commodities	Labor	Capital	Households	Government				
Activities	$P^Q \cdot V^D$									$P^x \cdot X$
Commodities		$P^d \cdot D^S$			$P^q \cdot C^D$	$P^q \cdot G^D$	$P^q \cdot Z^D$		$p^e \cdot E$	$P^q \cdot Q^D$
Factors:										
Labor	$W \cdot L^D$									$W \cdot L^D$
Capital	$R \cdot K^D$									$R \cdot K^D$
Households			$\tilde{Y}^L$ $\bar{T}^L \cdot W \cdot L^S$	$\tilde{Y}^K$ $\bar{T}^K \cdot R \cdot \bar{K}^S$	$\tilde{S}^P$	$\tilde{S}^G$			$r \cdot \bar{B}$	$\tilde{Y}^L + \tilde{Y}^K$
Government										$\tilde{Y}^G$
Capital acct.										saving
Rest of world		$P^m \cdot M$								$P^m \cdot M$
Total	$P^x \cdot X$	supply	$W \cdot L^S$	$R \cdot \bar{K}^S$	$\tilde{Y}^K + \tilde{Y}^L$	$\tilde{Y}^G$	$\tilde{Z}$		foreign exchange	

Figure 18.4. Social accounting matrix for an elasticity structuralist CGE model. *Note*: Variables are defined in Table 18.2.

class of CGE models that have been widely used to analyze issues of structural adjustment in developing countries. With some variations, a number of applied models developed over the past ten years are based on this essential structure.[70] Many of the features of the model are described in detail in Dervis, de Melo and Robinson (1982, ch. 6 and 7).[71]

To save on notation, the simplified model has one sector producing a single commodity (X) which is then transformed into an export good (E) and a good for the domestic market (D). Equation (1) is the production function, using labor, an intermediate input, and capital.[72] In this case, the factor demand equations [(11) and (12)] involve no summing over sectors. Expanding to a multisector model involves: (1) adding sectoral subscripts to equations (1)–(9), (13), and (23)–(26); (2) differentiating demand for intermediate inputs by sector of origin and destination; and (3) summing over sectors where required [e.g. equations (11), (12), (21), (22), (28), and (31)–(35)]. In many models, labor is also disaggregated by skill category and/or the labor markets are segmented across broad sectors (agriculture, industry, and services). Thus, average wages may differ between agricultural, industrial, and service sectors. Also, capital is often assumed to be sectorally immobile, so that capital rental rates (R) will differ across sectors.

Equation (2) gives the function for transforming output into different goods for export and domestic sales, which is usually a constant elasticity of transformation (CET) function. In a multisector model, the assumption is that domestic sales and exports with the same sectoral classification represent goods of different qualities or, perhaps, subsector composition. The CET function describes the ease with which it is possible to shift the composition of sectoral production between the domestic and foreign markets.

On the import side, domestic goods sold on the domestic market are assumed to be imperfect substitutes for imports. What demanders want is a composite commodity, which is a CES aggregation of imported and domestic goods. Equation (3) is the CES import aggregation function.[73] Given equation (2) and

---

[70] For examples of applications in this tradition, see Dervis and Robinson (1978, 1982); Dervis, de Melo, and Robinson (1981); Lewis and Urata (1984); Robinson and Tyson (1985); Grais, de Melo, and Urata (1986); Condon, Corbo, and de Melo (1985a,b); Drud and Grais (1983); Benjamin and Devarajan (1985); and Michel and Noel (1984). Sanderson and Williamson (1985) provide a survey of some of these applications. Decaluwe and Martens (1987) survey over 40 CGE models of 20 countries, of which something over half are applied models. Devarajan, Lewis, and Robinson (1986) list some 40 references describing applied models of around 30 countries.

[71] See also Condon, Robinson, and Urata (1985), who describe an updated version of the core model, including some new features included in the model in Table 2 such as the CET export transformation function.

[72] Often, a two-level CES function is used. One can also work directly with cost functions. Intermediate inputs are usually assumed to be given according to fixed input-output coefficients.

[73] The import aggregation function is sometimes called the Armington function, after Armington (1969) who used this formulation to derive import demand functions. Dervis, de Melo and Robinson (1982) call it the trade aggregation function.

(3), plus standard assumptions about profit maximization and cost minimization, it follows that desired import and export ratios are functions of relative domestic and foreign prices. These functions are given by equations (4) and (5).[74] Equations (25) and (26) define the prices of the two composites, X and Q, and correspond to cost function duals to equations (2) and (3). Homogeneity of the CES and CET functions guarantees the satisfaction of the accounting identities given in equations (31) and (32).

In contrast to the standard trade theory model in which all goods are tradable and all tradables are perfect substitutes, this specification endows the domestic price system with a significant degree of autonomy. There are seven prices associated with the single sector: P^x, P^q, P^d, P^m, P^e, $P^{\$m}$, and $P^{\$E}$. This represents quite a lot of structure for a one-sector model! The model can, however, be seen as a three-sector model, with a domestic non-tradable (D), an exportable (E), and a non-produced import (M). Equation (2) can be viewed as a production possibility frontier, and equation (3) becomes part of a two-level utility function. In a multisector model, the interpretation here of imperfect substitutability and transformability of goods within the same sector classification is more appealing. The model retains the standard "small country" assumption in that the world prices of imports and exports are assumed fixed.[75] However, trade policy, which puts a wedge between the world price and domestic price of imports and exports, will have much less effect on domestic prices than in the standard model.

In the past few years, the properties of models in which there is imperfect substitutability in trade have been analyzed in detail.[76] To summarize the results, the model is still very neoclassical in spirit and presents no problems theoretically. Compared to the neoclassical, closed-economy model in Table 18.1, there are additional system constraints involving the balance of trade, equation (29), and the government account, equation (28). There is also an additional price, the exchange rate, which serves as the equilibrating variable to ensure equilibrium in the balance of trade. Since there are no assets in the model and the amount of the balance of trade in equation (27) is exogenous, the exchange rate will vary to achieve a flow equilibrium. The equilibrating mechanism works through changes

---

[74] Dervis, de Melo and Robinson (1982, ch. 7), present a model in which equation (5) is a logistic function, while equation (2) is a simple linear aggregation. Empirically, their model behaves almost exactly like the model in Table 18.2.

[75] Some CGE models assume instead that there is a downward-sloping world demand function for the country's exports. Such a specification does not change the essential nature of the model. For example, see Dervis and Robinson (1978).

[76] See, for example, de Melo and Robinson (1981, 1985, 1989), Dervis, de Melo and Robinson (1982, chs. 6 and 7), Bergman (1982), and Whalley and Yeung (1984). In particular, de Melo and Robinson (1989) discuss the role of the exchange rate under different choices of numeraire in a simplified version of the model presented in Table 18.2.

in the real exchange rate, which in this model is the ratio of the price of the domestic non-tradable, D to the prices of tradables, E and M.

If the domestic good is chosen as numeraire (setting P^d to one), then the nominal exchange rate in the model, r, will correspond to the real exchange rate. If some other price index is chosen to define the numeraire, which is common in applied models, then changes in the real exchange rate will be a monotonic function of changes in the nominal exchange rate. In analytic models, it is usually convenient to pick the foreign good as numeraire (setting r to one), which means that P^d then serves the role of the real exchange rate.

There appears to be some confusion about this specification in the literature.[77] One problem seems to lie in the interpretation of the behavior of the rest of the world in this single-country model. One view is that, in effect, we really have a two-country model, and the balance of payments constraint should be seen as the budget constraint of the rest of the world. In this view, the model requires an equilibrating mechanism to ensure that the foreign actor is content to be on his budget constraint. However, such an interpretation really strains the single-country model in which the rest of the world is assumed to supply unlimited imports and demand unlimited exports at fixed world prices. In this case, the behavior of the rest of the world is summarized by a straight-line offer curve.[78] The exchange rate in the model is not a signal that affects the behavior of the rest of the world, which passively buys and sells whatever is supplied or demanded. It is probably better to view these equations as providing an empirical description of the operation of international markets, with no assumptions about optimizing behavior on the part of foreigners.

A second problem concerns the interpretation of the exchange rate variable in the model. What the CGE model determines is a stable relationship between the balance of trade and the real exchange rate. Given this relationship, a macro model is needed to determine any two, but no more than two, of the following variables: the domestic aggregate price level, the balance of trade, and the nominal exchange rate. Given fixed value of two of these variables, the CGE model will determine the equilibrium values of the third, given the flow system constraints. In the model in Table 18.2, and in many applied models, the aggregate price level and the balance of trade are set exogenously, and the model solves for the exchange rate. Fixing the nominal exchange rate, the model will solve for the domestic price level. In both of these cases, the model solves for a single equilibrium real exchange rate. Alternatively, fixing the exchange rate and the aggregate price level, the model will solve endogenously for the balance of

[77]See, for example, Srinivasan (1982) and Whalley and Yeung (1984). They criticize applied CGE models for including the exchange rate as a "financial" variable.

[78]Assuming a downward-sloping world demand curve for exports does not change the essential nature of the model, but only adds some curvature to the foreign offer curve. The foreigner is still assumed to be a price taker. See de Melo and Robinson (1989) for a discussion of this point.

trade. In a more complete macro model, one which includes assets, there are undoubtedly additional relationships among these variables, but they are outside of the CGE model.[79]

There are a few studies which use a CGE model of this type to analyze the impact of various exogenous price and policy shocks on the equilibrium exchange rate. In these studies, the CGE model is used as a laboratory for doing counterfactual experiments to sort out the relative importance of factors such as: (1) the maintenance of a fixed exchange rate in the face of differential domestic and world inflation rates, (2) changes in world prices of goods such as oil, (3) changes in capital inflows and remittance flows, (4) changes in export demand, and (5) changes in the structure of trade. The results from studies of Turkey and Yugoslavia indicate that the calculation of price level deflated exchange rates to measure changes in the equilibrium exchange rate – a common practice in the IMF and World Bank – can be badly off the mark.[80] In a world of changing relative prices and world market conditions, a partial equilibrium analysis appears to do very badly compared to a CGE model.

The open-economy CGE model in Table 18.2 has a set of nominal flows similar to those in the earlier neoclassical model, with some additional macro aggregates. The SAM in Figure 18.4 lays out the various accounts. Factor income is separated into two types, labor and capital, and the capital account has new sources of savings: the balance of trade in domestic currency (foreign savings) and the balance on the government account (government savings). As in the earlier model, investment is assumed to be savings-driven; aggregate consumption is given by equation (19), government saving is determined residually in equation (28), and equation (27) serves to determine aggregate investment. Also, as in the earlier model, the accounting identities [equations (31)–(35)] are implied by the behavioral equations.[81] They ensure that the model satisfies Walras' Law; the sum of the nominal values of equations (13)–(15) and (27)–(29) equals zero.

With the addition of foreign trade and the government, and more substitution possibilities, the elasticity structuralist model can serve as a richer framework for policy analysis. Many of the applications explore the structural impact of changes in the composition of the macro aggregates (balance of trade, government deficit, and savings–investment balance). With both foreign and domestic savings identified, and assuming low substitution elasticities for imports, the model also

---

[79] Keeping these macro relationships outside of the CGE model assumes a certain separability between the models. For example, one might argue that macro forces affect the parameters of the CES and CET functions determining the real demand for imports and supply of exports in the CGE model.

[80] See, for example, Dervis and Robinson (1982), Lewis and Urata (1984), and Robinson and Tyson (1985). These and other related studies are surveyed in Sanderson and Williamson (1985).

[81] Equation (33) requires an assumption of homogeneity of the production function, or else the rental rate on capital must be defined residually.

captures elements of the Chenery and Strout (1966) two-gap model, which is evident in a number of applications. The basic model structure can also be used to analyze the implications of different choices of development strategy (such applications will be discussed below).

4.5. Micro structuralist models

While a considerable advance, the assumptions of the elasticity structuralist model of an open economy are still quite stylized. All prices are assumed to be flexible and all markets are assumed to clear. The model is still fundamentally neoclassical, with some limitations on the ease with which factors and products are substituted. Relative prices are the equilibrating variables and are the only signals actors need to see.

Most applied models, while largely staying within this framework, have also added some structuralist constraints on the ability of markets to function. First, most models of developing countries assume that capital is sectorally fixed. In equilibrium, rental rates will thus differ across sectors. Two additional common micro structuralist constraints are to assume that wages and/or the exchange rate are fixed. In a general equilibrium model, when an equilibrating variable such as a price is fixed, then some other equilibrating mechanism must be specified that includes a rationing mechanism by which the "excess" supply or demand is allocated in the system. For the labor market, a common assumption is to assume that firms are always on their demand curves for labor and that all unemployment is borne by the suppliers of labor. In this case, the labor supply equation is dropped from the system and the labor market equilibrium equation states that labor demand is always met by supply.[82] A different mechanism would be required if the wage were fixed too low (i.e. excess demand for labor).

Similarly, a model with a fixed exchange rate requires the specification of a rationing rule and equilibrating mechanism. One approach, which was used in many earlier linear programming models, is to assume that the net foreign capital inflow becomes the equilibrating variable. In Table 18.2, with a fixed exchange rate, the balance of trade (B) simply becomes endogenous. While perhaps reasonable in models built during the 1960s, such a specification, which implies unlimited borrowing capacity, is clearly inappropriate for models used in the last decade.

---

[82] This rationing rule assumes that there will be unemployment, or that suppliers will freely supply all labor demanded at the fixed wage. The labor supply function can be used as a side equation to compute involuntary unemployment. The unemployed, however, are assumed to receive no income, do not consume, and effectively disappear from the system.

With a fixed exchange rate and a fixed balance of trade, some new equilibrating mechanism must be specified which involves rationing of imports.[83] Dervis,
de Melo and Robinson (1982) explore two mechanisms: a fixprice and a flexprice
rationing system. In the fixprice system, the equilibrating variable is an average
quantity rationing rate, and all demanders are assumed to be forced off their
import demand functions so as to achieve equilibrium in the balance of trade.[84]
In the flexprice system, in which there is an open market in import licenses, the
average import premium rate becomes the equilibrating variable and serves as a
uniform tariff to raise domestic prices of imports and so achieve equilibrium. In
the flexprice system, it is necessary to model explicitly who receives the value of
the import licenses, which represents the rents generated by import rationing.

A number of stylized and applied models have been built which incorporate
one or both of these import rationing mechanisms.[85] One theme of some of these
models is to assume that there is rent-seeking behavior arising from the import
rationing that leads to waste of resources and, hence, efficiency losses.[86] An
important stylized fact coming out of this work is that, in many countries, the
value of the "chaseable rents" generated by import rationing is a very large
number. Chaseable rents arising from even a relatively mild import rationing
scheme can easily amount to 10–15 percent of GDP in a semi-industrial country
with a significant trade share.[87]

The existence of rents does not necessarily imply that there will be rent
seeking, with concomitant waste of resources. Indeed, in a system in which
distortions have long been institutionalized, one would expect that the allocation
of the resulting rents would also have been settled, with little scope for further
rent-seeking activity. However, in a period in which new distortions are introduced that generate major rents, there would likely be major disruptions in the
system as agents adjust to the new situation. An element adding to this disruption is the fact that the chaseable rents are not reflected in standard national
income statistics, adding to the difficulties facing policy-makers trying to figure
out what is going on in the economy. In addition, since it is usually illegal to

---

[83] The assumption is that the real exchange rate is set at an overvalued level, given the numeraire,
thus requiring import rationing. An excess supply of foreign exchange would require a quite different
rationing mechanism.

[84] The question of spillovers in this quantity rationing mechanism is important, and has been dealt
with in a variety of ways in existing models. See, for example, Dervis, de Melo and Robinson (1982
ch. 9) and Dewatripont and Robinson (1985).

[85] See, for example, World Bank (1980, 1983), Robinson and Tyson (1985), Kis, Robinson and
Tysin (1985), Robinson, Tyson and Dewatripont (1986), Dervis and Robinson (1978); de Melo and
Robinson (1980), Drud, Grais and Vujovic (1982), Lewis and Urata (1983, 1984), and Condon, Corbo
and de Melo (1985a, 1985b).

[86] The seminal theoretical article is Krueger (1974). See also Bhagwati and Srinivasan (1980).

[87] Condon, Robinson and Urata (1985) present a stylized model of Turkey which explores these
costs. The effect on income distribution of different adjustment mechanisms in explored in a stylized
model by de Melo and Robinson (1982). See also references to applied models cited earlier.

monetize the value of import rationing, its imposition adds to incentives to cheat and to report data inaccurately.

In an economy with reasonable consumption and factor substitution possibilities, dead-weight efficiency losses arising from price distortions seldom amount to more than 1–2 percent of GDP. During the adjustment period, the potential disruption costs arising from the generation of chaseable rents is a much larger number. In the short to medium run, implementing policies designed to improve allocative efficiency by "getting the prices right" may well be less important than implementing policies designed to reduce chaseable rents or to control rent seeking, although the two goals are probably often interdependent.

While a fixed exchange rate and fixed wages are the most common features of micro structuralist models, there are also some models which specify fixed product prices for various sectors. A common feature of Latin American macro structuralist models is to assume that manufacturing firms set prices by imposing fixed markups over prime costs in order to ensure an acceptable profit. In a CGE model, this pricing rule amounts to fixing some sectoral prices relative to non-capital input costs. In these sectors, a quantity adjustment mechanism, often Keynesian in nature, is specified to clear the product markets, dropping the assumption of profit-maximizing supply behavior and replacing it with an assumption of excess capacity.

Whenever a modeller chooses to fix some prices, it is necessary to explain exactly what is being fixed and to specify the alternative adjustment mechanisms and equilibrating variables. In a CGE model, a fixed price is always a fixed relative price, and the modeller must specify relative to what. For example, fixing the real wage involves fixing the ratio of the nominal wage to an appropriate price index.[88] In this case, the solution values of real variables will still be unaffected by the choice of numeraire. However, some modellers choose to fix the nominal wage.[89] In this case, what is being fixed is the wage relative to the numeraire price index, and the real wage will not be fixed unless the appropriate consumption bundle was chosen as numeraire. Similarly, a fixed exchange rate is usually set in nominal terms, and hence must be interpreted as fixed relative to the numeraire price index. In this case, the real exchange rate – the relative price of tradables to non-tradables – is not fixed unless the appropriate domestic price index is chosen to define the numeraire.

Even though some relative prices are fixed in a micro structuralist CGE model, the system constraint equations are still part of the model. Equilibrium is still well defined but, since prices no longer serve as the equilibrating variables for

---

[88] In a model with many labor categories and many sectors, the definition of the appropriate real wage is not trivial. For example, is it the sectoral marginal revenue product or the supply price of labor of a given skill category?

[89] See, for example, Lysy and Taylor (1980) and Ahluwalia and Lysy (1979). This specification is common in macro structuralist models.

these markets, some other mechanism must be specified. In addition, since prices no longer serve their proper signalling function, it is necessary to reconsider the behavioral equations of the various actors. What is their new, constrained optimization problem? What are the spillover effects when there is quantity rationing? The gains in realism from extending the neoclassical model are not bought cheaply, but instead impose new theoretical and expositional burdens on the modeller.

The justification for fixing various prices must come from theoretical considerations outside of the Walrasian paradigm. There is now a large and growing literature justifying fixprice assumptions, most of it in the context of macro models. In the development literature, there are models in which the real urban or industrial wage is fixed, with the corresponding labor supply assumed to be infinitely elastic at the exogenous wage.[90] In CGE models, this formulation is easily accommodated, without any need to worry about the choice of numeraire. However, fixed nominal wages or a fixed nominal exchange rate, which are common assumptions in macro models, require justification in macro theory and must, in a CGE model, be viewed as fixed relative to the choice of numeraire. The numeraire defines a price index that is to be set exogenously in the CGE model. In this case, the definition of this index matters, affecting real variables, and must be part of the underlying macro model. While exogenous to the CGE model, it is an active variable in a macro model that is, in a sense, being imposed from outside the CGE model.

For example, in Table 18.2 there are three prices that might be set exogenously, depending on the underlying macro theory: the domestic price, the output price, or the composite price. These correspond to a domestic wholesale price index, a GDP deflator, and a retail price index, respectively. Which of these indices one would wish to assume fixed, along with the nominal wage and/or the exchange rate, depends on one's view about the nature of monetary policy and price level determination in the particular economy.

Macro problems have insidiously crept into the micro structuralist model. Note that, given the aggregate price index defining the numeraire, there are no theoretical problems concerning the functioning of the CGE model. It is now a less well-behaved general equilibrium model with some fixed relative prices.[91] What is at issue is the rationale for the choice of relative prices to fix. In the CGE model, the clear dichotomy between the real and nominal sides is no longer sustainable. Indeed, interaction between the nominal and real sides is a crucial part of any interesting macro model. If money were always neutral and relative

---

[90] The Lewis model, with its many variants. See Fei and Ranis (1964).

[91] With some relative prices fixed, existence proofs are harder. However, there are existence theorems for some fixprice models, and no one has reported any difficulties finding solutions to empirical models.

prices always free to vary to clear product and factor markets, there would be little for macro economists to do.

4.6. Macro structuralist models

Controversies about the macroeconomic properties of CGE models have been intense since the first such models were constructed for developing countries. The debate started with the distribution-focused models of Korea by Adelman and Robinson (1978) and Brazil by Lysy and Taylor (1980), but quickly moved beyond particular multisector models.[92] The discussion has focused on what has come to be called the macro "closure" of economywide models, be they one-sector or CGE models.

The early work on macro closure was concerned only with how equilibrium was achieved between aggregate savings and investment and largely ignored the macroeconomic impact of both the government and the foreign accounts. A variety of savings–investment closure rules have been specified in CGE models, which illustrate the different macro theories at issue.[93] In comparing alternative macro specifications, it is important to distinguish between the macro equilibrating mechanisms at work and the equilibrating variables in the models.

The two CGE models given in Tables 18.1 and 18.2 both exhibit "neoclassical closure." They are savings-driven, with no special equilibrating variable required to achieve savings–investment equilibrium. In his model of Norway, Johansen (1960) replaces the aggregate savings function – equation (20) in Table 18.2 and equation (10) in Table 18.1 – with an aggregate investment function. In this "Johansen closure," aggregate consumption is determined residually, and again no additional equilibrating variable is required. The macro story, however, is quite different. The Johansen model is investment-driven, which implies that some unspecified macro mechanism outside of the model, presumably involving government expenditure policy, works to make aggregate consumption adjust residually.[94]

---

[92] The controversy with regard to those two models is discussed in Taylor and Lysy (1979) and Adelman and Robinson (1988). For a review of the early debate, see Bruno (1979) and Dervis, de Melo and Robinson (1982, ch. 12). These two models are also discussed in surveys by Bigsten (1983), Sanderson (1980), and Thorbecke (1985). Distribution models in general are surveyed in Chapter 17 by Adelman and Robinson in this Handbook.

[93] The seminal work on macro closure is Sen (1963). Rattso (1982) and Lysy (1983) provide surveys. See also Dewatripont and Michel (1987) and Robinson and Tyson (1984) for different approaches to the macro closure issue.

[94] Johansen (1960) justifies his specification on the basis of explicit government tax and expenditure policies designed to maintain a target level of aggregate investment. All this is implicit, however, since his model does not include government as an actor.

If one wished to have a model with both an aggregate consumption or savings function and an aggregate investment function, then some new equilibrating variable would be required to achieve macro equilibrium. One approach, which might be termed "Fisherian closure," would be to include a loanable funds market in the model, with both savings and investment depending on a new equilibrating variable, the interest rate.[95] While the model would not need to include any assets explicitly, it certainly begins to strain the Walrasian paradigm.

The three macro closures discussed so far are all similar in that they view the macro problem as one of achieving the proper composition or balance among macro aggregates. Disturbances in nominal macro balances in the model may affect the sectoral composition of demand, and hence production, but will have little or no effect on aggregate output. The models all assume full employment and, with reasonable substitution possibilities, empirical models adjust to compositional changes with little change in aggregate production and real income. Minor variations on these themes have been used in a number of CGE models of developing countries designed to analyze medium-term development strategies. The time horizon is long enough in these models so that exogenous projections of aggregate employment are reasonable.

In contrast to these essentially neoclassical models, structuralist macro models postulate strong links between the real and macro sides of the model. That is, changes in the composition of the nominal macro aggregates affect both the level of aggregate output and employment as well as their sectoral structure. Drawing on Keynes, Kalecki, and Kaldor for intellectual inspiration, Lance Taylor and various associates argue that the macro specification drives the model, determining both aggregate and distributional outcomes.[96] In these Latin American macro structuralist models, relative prices do not work as in the neoclassical paradigm and quite different mechanisms come into play in order to achieve macro equilibrium. Two equilibrating mechanisms common to most such models are: (1) Keynesian multiplier effects by which changes in aggregate demand lead to changes in aggregate supply, and (2) Kaldorian distributional effects by which changes in the distribution of income lead to changes in aggregate savings.

The CGE model of Brazil by Lysy and Taylor (1980) is an early example of models in the Taylor tradition, and its major features can be seen by starting from the neoclassical structuralist model in Table 18.2. First, an aggregate investment function is added to the system, usually by making aggregate real investment an exogenous variable. The model now needs a macro equilibrating variable to balance aggregate savings and investment. Second, the labor supply

---

[95]One should probably be careful with names. Lance Taylor noted that this closure could be attributed to J.S. Mill.

[96]See Taylor (1979, 1983). An excellent discussion of this literature is provided by Buffie (1984). See de Janvry and Sadoulet (1985) for a survey of macro structuralist CGE models of six countries: India, Peru, Mexico, Egypt, Korea, and Sri Lanka. These models display a wide variety of structuralist features. See also Taylor (1989).

function is dropped from the system and firms are assumed always to be on their demand curves for labor. The wage no longer serves as the equilibrating variable for the labor market, since labor supply is always assumed to meet demand. Third, the nominal wage is chosen as numeraire [equation (30)] and the aggregate output price level is no longer assumed fixed. Finally, the model also specifies different savings rates out of capital and labor income, so changes in the functional distribution will affect aggregate savings.

This model displays what Taylor and Lysy (1979) call "Keynesian closure". Assume an increase in exogenous investment. With fixed savings rates, the levels of income and real output increase through a Keynesian multiplier process, and so generate the increased savings necessary to match the higher level of investment. Since firms are assumed to be on their demand curves for labor, they must be induced to hire the required additional labor. The real wage must therefore fall and provides the driving variable by which the multiplier process operates. Given that the nominal wage is fixed, the macro equilibrating variable is the aggregate price level. An increase in the aggregate price level lowers the real wage, inducing firms to hire more labor and increase output, which leads to higher income and hence savings.

Note that if the aggregate price level were chosen to define the numeraire, then the nominal wage would serve as the equilibrating variable to achieve balance between aggregate savings and investment. The mechanism is exactly the same in the CGE model – changes in the real wage serve to drive the multiplier process. In either case, the underlying macro story justifying the process lies outside of the CGE model. In neither case is it possible to view the equilibrating variable as a signal entering decision functions of actors in the system. Certainly, neither the nominal wage nor the aggregate price level can serve as a signal in the loanable funds market, even if the CGE model had such a market! The price-level adjustment story sounds more plausible, especially in Latin American countries, although either will give the same result for all real variables in the CGE model.[97]

One important feature of the CGE model with Keynesian closure is that any increase in aggregate output is always associated with a decrease in real wages. This property leads to unfortunate distributional effects – any Keynesian expansion cuts wages as it increases employment.[98] In a different version of Keynesian closure, Dewatripont and Robinson (1985) specify a macro structuralist CGE

---

[97]In fact, in the Brazil model, the story is a bit more complex. Some nominal flows, including categories of government expenditure, are fixed, so changes in the aggregate price level have real effects in addition to driving the multiplier process. There is also a fixed exchange rate, so variations in foreign capital inflows potentially may affect savings–investment equilibrium.

[98]Lysy and Taylor recognize this property of their Brazil model. See Lysy and Taylor (1980, p. 161). In a model with markup pricing, one can potentially break this link since firms are no longer assumed to be on their demand curves for labor.

model with simultaneous rationing in the product and labor markets.[99] In their model, the Keynesian multiplier also drives the macro equilibrating mechanism, but – given spillover effects from the product market to the labor market – increases in demand lead to a relaxation of rationing in the product market and are associated with rises in the real wage. Which of these Keynesian closures better reflects the views of J.M. Keynes is a debate I leave to others.

Given that different actors have different savings rates, macro structuralist models have potentially important links between the functional distribution of income and macro equilibrium.[100] In some CGE models, these distributional effects are enhanced by assuming markup pricing rules for some sectors, usually manufacturing. In this case, as noted above, output prices relative to non-capital input prices are fixed, and the assumption that firms maximize profits is dropped. Output supply is assumed to adjust to demand, with employment linked to output by fixed coefficients. After capacity output is achieved, the regime shifts and the markups adjust. The underlying story is that capitalists attempt to maintain their profit share through the fixed markups, nominal wages are fixed, and the aggregate price level is again the macro equilibrating variable.[101]

In an open economy, the balance of trade provides another potential equilibrating mechanism for achieving savings–investment balance. Even assuming a fixed balance of trade in dollars, changes in the exchange rate will lead to changes in the value of the trade balance in domestic currency, and so affect aggregate savings. If the balance of trade is assumed to adjust, there is an even stronger link. At one extreme, Ahluwalia and Lysy (1981) built a model of Malaysia in which the balance of trade adjusts to achieve equilibrium between savings and investment, with the real exchange rate thus serving as the macro equilibrating variable.[102] Models in which foreign borrowing adjusts to changes in macro variables seem especially important for Latin American countries. There are a number of examples, although none with such extreme behavior as specified in the Malaysia model.[103]

[99] Their model is in the tradition of macro models analyzed by Malinvaud (1977) and Muellbauer and Portes (1978).

[100] Lysy and Taylor (1980) assert that these Kaldorian linkages are very important in their Brazil model, but Adelman and Robinson (1988) find that, in a stylized version of their model, the Keynesian multiplier is empirically far more important. In most of their experiments, distributional effects on aggregate savings are insignificant. For a different approach to capturing macro distributional effects in a CGE model, see Bourguignon, Michel and Miqueu (1983).

[101] See, for example, Taylor, Sarkar and Rattso (1984). In this model, applied to India, there is a mix of fixprice and flexprice sectors. See also Gibson (1985) and Gibson, Lustig and Taylor (1985) for similar CGE models of Nicaragua and Mexico.

[102] In this model, the nominal exchange rate is fixed, so variations in the domestic price level serve as the equilibrating variable. The equilibrating mechanism, however, works entirely through changes in the real exchange rate, which cause changes in the trade balance.

[103] See, for example, Condon, Corbo and de Melo (1985a, 1985b), Feltenstein (1980), and Levy (1987). Adelman and Robinson (1988) consider how the Keynesian multiplier is weakened in models with a fixed exchange rate. See also Devarajan and de Melo (1987).

Macro structuralist CGE models are based on a variety of assumptions that lead to adjustment problems and links between changes in nominal macro aggregates and real aggregate output and employment. These include: (1) markup pricing rules, resulting in rationing in the product markets, (2) working capital financing requirements, (3) segmented credit markets, (4) financial repression leading to low savings levels and investment rationing, (5) fixed exchange rates, leading to import rationing, (6) fixed nominal wages, leading to unemployment, (7) fixed aggregate real investment, (8) non-competitive imports of intermediate inputs, and (8) immobile sectoral capital.

Empirical support for a number of these specifications is weak, and some of them are better suited for a stylized rather than an applied model. For example, assuming that aggregate real investment is fixed is theoretically convenient when tracing out the analytic implications of some structuralist specifications. In an applied model, however, it is empirically untenable to assume that real investment does not change as part of a process of macro structural adjustment. Similarly, it is common in some analytic macro structuralist models to assume all intermediate inputs are imported, which serves to focus attention on the effect of devaluation on costs. In applied models, the assumption would be empirically inappropriate. In evaluating these different specifications, it is important to keep in mind the purpose of the model. Strong assumptions that are reasonable and useful for an analytic or stylized model must be qualified in an applied model and countervailing linkages must be taken into account.

Macro structuralist models strain received theory. Questions of macro closure in a model that incorporates only flow equilibria can take us only so far. Further progress probably requires the explicit inclusion of assets and asset markets in the model. There has been some work in this direction.[104] A good example of such a model is Lewis (1985), who has built a stylized CGE model of Turkey that incorporates money and bonds, as well as a segmented loanable funds market that can capture elements of financial repression.[105] The model is able to incorporate a variety of structuralist features and is used to explore the empirical implications of various combinations of macro specifications, including markup pricing. Lewis finds that dividing sectors into two types, markup and flexprice, leads to unstable dynamic behavior in the flexprice sectors as they are forced to take the residual adjustment burden. He argues that this empirical result brings the basic assumption into question, and should lead to further work on ways to

---

[104] Dewatripont and Michel (1987) argue persuasively that further progress on macro closure issues must involve explicit incorporation of assets in a dynamic model with expectations. Adelman and Robinson (1978) included money in their model and also had an elaborate specification of the loanable funds market, but no explicit asset markets. Taylor and Rosensweig (1984) present an initial version of a stylized structuralist CGE model of Thailand with asset markets, portfolio choice, and endogenous determination of interest rates. See also Feltenstein (1984).

[105] Along the lines suggested by McKinnon (1973).

incorporate the stylized fact that some prices do not adjust to changes in market conditions as fast as others.

Neoclassical CGE models are best suited for looking at medium-run issues. The longer the time horizon, the more appropriate are the assumptions of the neoclassical paradigm, with prices adjusting to clear markets in an environment of mobile factors and reasonable substitution possibilities in demand and supply. Macro structuralist models often justify some of their structural rigidities (e.g. assuming a fixed nominal wage, markup pricing, or lack of supply constraints) on the basis of short-run considerations, but then are applied to analyze the impact of shocks over the medium run. The view that the medium run is a sequence of short runs is a temporal tautology but a theoretical error. The types of assumptions and equilibrium specifications appropriate for a short-run analytic model are quite different from those appropriate for a medium-run model, and it is difficult to mix the two types of models. While the payoffs from a successful mixing are potentially great, more care and diffidence seem called for than is evident in a number of the macro structuralist models built to date.

5. Structural adjustment and alternative development strategies

Since the initial work on income distribution, macro structuralist models have been mostly used to analyze questions of structural adjustment – how an economy adjusts to some shock emanating from the world economy such as an exogenous decline in foreign capital inflows or an increase in import prices of commodities such as oil or capital goods. Neoclassical and micro structuralist CGE models have also been used for such analysis, and there is an active debate about the appropriateness of different specifications. While it is premature to judge the outcome of these debates, there is wide agreement of the need to use multisectoral models to analyze the issues. Structural adjustment involves shifts in the sectoral structure of demand, trade, resource allocation, and production, as well as in the magnitudes of macro aggregates.

Even given the difficulties in using CGE models for analyzing macro issues, they nonetheless provide the best framework available for analyzing issues of structural adjustment. Unlike any macro model, CGE models incorporate sectoral detail that permits a richer analysis of changes in the structure as well as the volume of production and trade. The CGE framework is all the more important in a situation in which relative world prices have changed, and they have been widely used to analyze the impact on the structure of production and trade arising from changes in the price of oil.[106] Under suitable assumptions, as noted

[106]See, for example, Gelb (1985) and Mitra (1984) for comparative studies of structural adjustment when oil prices change. Many of the applications to individual countries cited earlier also analyze this issue. See also Dick et al. (1983) who look at the impact of changes in the prices of primary commodities in a stylized CGE model.

above, they also provide a better framework for analyzing changes in the equilibrium exchange rate after an external shock than a macro model or computations based on price-level-deflated exchange reates. These specifically trade-focused CGE models have been recently surveyed by de Melo (1988) and Devarajan (1987).

Empirically, the models to date have indicated the importance of considering structural rigidities when analyzing structural adjustment. The neoclassical, full-employment model adjusts to shocks with relative ease and little cost – a result confirmed in many empirical exercises. Actual economies are clearly less flexible, and a model must capture the important rigidities if it is to provide a useful framework for policy analysis. Where on the continuum from elasticity structuralist to macro structuralist one must be is still an open and controversial question, but that one cannot remain at the neoclassical end of the spectrum is widely understood.

Another use of structuralist CGE models has been the analysis of the implications of alternative choices of development strategy. In this use, the models follow in a long tradition of dynamic input–output and LP models. More recent applications have tended to mix questions of structural adjustment with choice of development strategy, which is reasonable given the international environment in the past decade. The concept of development strategy has narrowed in many applications to include only trade strategy, and most of the applications cited earlier also consider issues of the best choice of trade policies.

The debate in the 1960s on the choice of appropriate development strategy asked whether a country should follow an open, outward-looking development strategy based largely on manufacturing exports, or should it pursue an inward-looking strategy in which industrialization is largely based on encouraging import substitution? The recent discussion is more careful, identifying an "open" strategy with neutral trade incentives leading to investment, production, and trade consistent with comparative advantage, with no particular bias toward the industrial sectors.[107] The general consensus, at least in international institutions such as the World Bank and the IMF, is that an open development strategy emphasizing neutral trade incentives is best, even given the uncertainties of the world economy in the last decade. However, analysis with multisector models has turned up some worries that lead one to question the unqualified promotion of policies designed simply to get the prices right.

An open development strategy involving significant expansion of manufacturing exports, if it is to be successful, involves a balancing and a sequencing of

---

[107]See Balassa (1985) for a consistent statement of this approach. Also see, for example, Adelman (1984) who argues, using a stylized CGE model, that the changes in world conditions now favor an open strategy of what she calls "agricultural development led industrialization", or ADLI, which emphasizes agricultural exports.

three related processes.[108] First, there must evolve an industrial base sufficient to support significant manufacturing exports. The required industrial base involves a level of technology as well as composition of output, including some complexity in interindustry relations as well as productivity of primary inputs. Second, the country must be able to achieve and maintain significant sectoral rates of total factor productivity growth. Third, the country must be able to finance significant balance of trade deficits in the early phase of the process. After the process has succeeded, the export base will be large enough to generate trade surpluses without hindering further growth.

It may be that these processes are causally related, but not a lot is known about some of the linkages. Operating on the assumption that simply adopting a policy of neutral trade incentives would necessarily start up these processes requires a serious leap of faith. There are a number of success stories among the semi-industrial countries, but they all involved activist governments which certainly did a lot more than adopt policies designed to get the prices right.

Furthermore, there are a number of assumptions about the economic environment that appear necessary for the successful working out of these processes. The world economy must be able to absorb the country's exports without major changes in the terms of trade. The domestic economy must be flexible enough so that the required structural changes, which involve major and relatively rapid changes in sectoral resource allocation, can take place. These structural changes, and the underlying trade policies, may involve major shifts in the distribution of income, which may, in turn, have implications for the ease or feasibility of implementing the strategy.[109]

While the benefits of achieving a successful, export-led development strategy are great, the risks are also significant. If, for example, a country borrows heavily on the assumption that export growth will suffice to generate sufficient surpluses in the future, and the export growth aborts for some reason, then the country is left with a debilitating debt overhang. If the required growth of total factor productivity is not achieved – a process about which very little is known – then the strategy will fail. If factor and product markets do not work properly, then there will be strains on the economy's ability to achieve the necessary structural changes. All of these questions are largely assumed away in the standard neoclassical model. Multisectoral models and analysis that focuses on structural issues are required to illuminate such problems.

---

[108] The analysis on which this paragraph is based is brought together in Chenery, Robinson and Syrquin (1986). Chapter 11 of that book [by Chenery, Lewis, de Melo and Robinson (1986)] uses a dynamic CGE model to analyze issues of choice of trade strategy. See also Kubo, Robinson and Urata (1986) who use a dynamic input–output model to analyze some of the same issues. For related studies, see Westphal (1981) and Nishimizu and Robinson (1984).

[109] See, for example, de Melo and Robinson (1982) for a CGE model analyzing the impact of different trade policies on the distribution of income.

6. Directions for future research

Multisector models have come a long way since the early input–output models. A combination of advances in economic theory, numerical methods, and computer technology have made a reality of Oscar Lange's dream of computing equilibrium quantities and prices for a multi-market economy. Of course, as soon as we can solve a general equilibrium model, we then see a myriad of new problems. The theoretical limitations of general equilibrium simulation models which only capture flow equilibria across markets become evident. Of the many directions in which new theoretical and applied work are needed, four appear to be commanding the most attention: micro–macro interactions, dynamics, uncertainty, and optimization.

6.1. Micro–macro interactions

The problems of incorporating macro features into multisector models have been discussed extensively above. At this point, given the extensive work on macro closure, the behavior of CGE models when different macro models are imposed on them is fairly well understood. The most active research direction is to extend the notion of macro equilibrium beyond that of nominal aggregate flows and to incorporate asset markets explicitly into the CGE model.[110] Just adding asset markets, however, will do little if the assumptions of full employment and neoclassical equilibrium are maintained. In such a model, macro adjustments only involve changes in the composition of aggregate GDP, but have no effect on its magnitude. An interesting micro–macro model must involve micro structuralist features if it is to be at all realistic. The analysis of links between micro markets and macro signals is an area of active research in macroeconomics, drawing heavily on notions of uncertainty and expectations in a dynamic framework. It is challenging to incorporate such theory directly into a multisector model, and research in this direction with analytic and stylized models is clearly worthwhile. It is, however, easier to build stylized and applied multisector models that include asset markets and micro structuralist features, and so reflect the stylized facts emerging from the new macro work.[111]

6.2. Dynamics

The dynamic behavior of multisector models has been a central concern from the time it was realized that the dynamic input–output model tended to be unstable.

---

[110] Initial work in this direction was discussed above.
[111] Waelbroeck (1986) is a strong proponent of research is this direction.

The general problem with dynamics is that existing theory is inadequate to give the applied modeller much guidance. Theorists tend to analyze dynamics in terms of intertemporal optimality and steady states, and to avoid discussing how long it takes to achieve the steady state, if it is possible at all. Forward-looking models embodying notions of intertemporal equilibrium based on consistent or rational expectations are theoretically interesting and analytically manageable, but do not seem very realistic.

Applied modellers have tended to respond by building adaptive dynamic models which are recursive in time, with current behavior depending only on solutions from previous periods. While it is important to check the model for stability, and it is sometimes reassuring to show that there is a steady state which the model will approach, its behavior in the relevant time period will be dominated by the dynamic adjustment mechanisms specified. The approach is justifiable in theoretical terms as representing a sequence of temporary equilibria, but there is little theoretical guidance about adjustment speeds and the notions of intertemporal equilibrium such models embody seem unsatisfactory.[112]

The issue of dynamics is certainly not confined to multisector models and has long been recognized as a major problem in macroeconometric models as well. There are numerous theoretical issues involved, including questions of micro–macro linkages and short-run versus long-run adjustment mechanisms. Criticizing applied models because they do not reflect what is acknowledged to be unrealistic theory dealing with long-run steady states and expectations is neither illuminating nor helpful.[113] The challenge is as much to theorists as it is to applied modellers.

6.3. Uncertainty

It is a sign of how far multisector models have come in terms of ease of implementation that one can now seriously contemplate trying to incorporate stochastic elements into the models. Certainly, the last decade has demonstrated the importance of uncertainty, especially about price variations, to policy-makers. For example, a variety of schemes have been proposed to dampen international price variations in primary commodities and uncertainties in export markets have often been cited as reasons for avoiding an open development strategy. The theoretical literature has also advanced and it is evident that optimal policy rules in an environment of uncertainty may differ significantly from those derived in a

[112] On the theory of temporary equilibrium, see Grandmont (1977). Richard Day is a strong proponent of adaptive dynamic models. See Day and Cigno (1978).

[113] See, for example, Bell and Srinivasan (1984).

deterministic model.[114] There is some work underway to incorporate uncertainty in CGE models.[115] The results so far are suggestive and indicate that there are potential payoffs to further research.

6.4. Optimization

The decade from about 1965 to 1975 saw a steady stream of multisector optimizing models, mostly based on linear programming. After 1975, the stream slowed to a trickle as simulation models became more popular. The reasons for the decline of optimizing models were discussed above. Essentially, they were difficult to build and tended to generate unrealistic behavior both because of strong linearity assumptions and because of weaknesses in their theoretical underpinnings. They were never able to provide a reasonable representation of an actual market economy, and so had to be used with considerable care and artful interpretation.

The last decade has seen a growing torrent of simulation models. Now, however, it is time to reappraise the role of optimizing models. There have been major advances in computational algorithms so that now it is easy to solve very large LP problems and relatively easy to solve moderately large, non-linear programming problems. As noted earlier, it is feasible to solve CGE models using non-linear programming and such models have been implemented. For the correct choice of maximand, the shadow prices from a properly specified non-linear program are equivalent to the market prices solved in a CGE simulation model. However, one can get more out of optimization than just another solution technique.

One approach that looks fruitful is to extend to multisector models the methods that have been used for some time to explore questions of optimal policy choice in macro models.[116] For example, one could embed a CGE model as the constraint set in an optimizing model in which one sought to maximize a planner's objective function.[117] The objective function might include macro variables such as aggregate employment, the price level, government balance, and the balance of trade. Policy instruments might include variables such as the exchange rate, taxes, subsidies, and government expenditure. The policy question

---

[114] For a short review of the relevant theoretical issues, see Arrow (1986). See also Newbery and Stiglitz (1981) and Schmitz (1984).

[115] See Adelman and Serris (1982) and Adelman, Roland-Holst and Sarris (1986). These papers propose models incorporating both uncertainty and optimization, and are discussed below.

[116] For surveys, see Chow (1975) and Kendrick (1981).

[117] Existing CGE models that use such an approach are Zonnoor (1983) for Iran and Martin and van Vijnbergen (1986) for Egypt.

is: What is the best choice of policy instruments to achieve various macro goals, given the workings of the market economy as captured by the CGE model?

An optimization model might also be used to explore "second best" policy questions. For example, Dahl, Devarajan and Van Wijnbergen (1986) use a CGE model of Cameroon imbedded within an optimization framework to ask: What is the best choice of sectoral tariff rates, given that the goverment must achieve some target level of revenue? Their results indicate that the common rule of thumb that countries should seek to equalize tariffs across sectors may often be incorrect. With a government revenue constraint, and especially in the face of existing distorting indirect taxes, optimal tariffs vary widely across sectors. In addition, they find that even a movement from the initial differentiated rate structure toward sectoral equality of rates is not necessarily welfare improving. Such a model might also be used to explore the appropriate choice of shadow prices given the existence of various distortions in the economy, either policy induced or institutional. Again, the constraint set includes the CGE simulation model, so the policy-maker takes as given the institutional structure of the economy.

Finally, it is also empirically feasible to combine optimization and uncertainty in the framework of a stochastic control problem. In their preliminary empirical work, Adelman, Roland-Holst and Sarris (1986) use a linearized version of a stylized CGE model in the constraint set and explore the optimal choice of policies in a dynamic setting given uncertainty about world prices of crucial traded goods. Their objective function is to minimize the deviation over time of a number of macro variables from a target path. The model generates policy rules that differ significantly from those that would be optimal in a deterministic or certainty-equivalent model.

7. Conclusion

Lance Taylor, in his 1975 survey of multisector models, concluded with the question that must face a policy-maker contemplating devoting major resources to building any multisector model beyond the simplest input–output model: "Do they provide enough illumination to justify their own construction?"[118] Based on work with applied models in the past decade, the answer is a clear "yes." Of the twenty-five or so countries for which applied CGE models have been built in the past few years, a number have been collaborative efforts with government ministries.[119] Countries for which such collaborative projects have been done, or are currently underway, include: Bangladesh, Bolivia, Cameroon, Colombia,

---

[118] Taylor (1975, p. 104).

[119] The number of stylized models is, of course, much greater, See Devarajan, Lewis and Robinson (1986) for a bibliography of work on CGE models applied to developing countries. They also list applications separately, arranged by country. See also Decaluwe and Martens (1987).

Egypt, Hungary, India, Indonesia, Ivory Coast, Malaysia, Mexico, Morocco, Thailand, Turkey, and Yugoslavia. In addition, various static and dynamic SAM-based applied models have been built for a number of countries. While not all equally successful, these exercises indicate that the potential usefulness of multisector models is widely recognized.

At this time, the level of resources required to build a CGE model is little more than would be required for a careful SAM-based analysis. The decision about which tool to use is now less constrained by available computing technology. The modeller can concentrate on matching issues with the appropriate methodology, rather than be forced to pick a simpler methodology because available solution algorithms limit his ability to formulate more realistic models. Indeed, the gap between the formulation of new theory and its implementation in empirical models has shortened considerably in the past decade.

Over the past decade, multisectoral models have been used in a variety of settings and have demonstrated that, for a variety of issues, intersectoral linkages and general equilibrium effects matter. In the past few years, the literature has moved away from large, general purpose models and has focused more on smaller stylized numerical models that illustrate a few important linkages. In analyzing issues such as structural adjustment, income distribution, investment allocation, trade policy, tax policy, choice of development strategy, and the structural impact of macro stabilization policies, stylized multisectoral general equilibrium models have been used to test the validity of insights and policy "rules of thumb" arising from partial equilibrium analysis or macro models. The debate in these areas is still active, but it is certainly possible to conclude from the work surveyed here that it is often misleading to ignore general equilibrium linkages. Indirect effects working through both product and factor markets can often vitiate or reverse the impact effects of some policy change.

The science of economics advances through an interplay among new theory, statistical estimation, and empirical modelling. There is a healthy tension among these three strands that is evident in the work with multisector models. In the last decade, empirical implementation has pushed the limits of available theory and has moved significantly ahead of econometric estimation. In the last few years, there has been work to advance the theoretical underpinnings of CGE models, especially in the areas of trade and macro, and also to improve the statistical base for parameter estimation. It is worth emphasizing, however, that no single strand has monopoly on "correct" analysis – it is through an interplay among all three that progress is made.

References

Adelman, I. (1984) 'Beyond export-led growth', *World Development*, 12, no. 9:937–950.
Adelman, I. and C.T. Morris (1973) *Economic growth and social equity in developing countries.* Stanford, CA: Stanford University Press.

Adelman, I. and S. Robinson (1978) *Income distribution policy in developing countries: A case study of Korea.* Stanford, CA: Stanford University Press.

Adelman, I. and S. Robinson (1988) 'Macroeconomic adjustment and income distribution: Alternative models in two economies', *Journal of Development Economics*, 29:1–22.

Adelman, I. and A. Sarris (1982) 'Incorporating uncertainty into planning of industrialization strategies for developing countries', World Bank Staff Working Paper no. 503. Washington, DC: World Bank.

Adelman, I. and E. Thorbecke, eds. (1966) *The theory and design of economic development.* Baltimore, MD: Johns Hopkins University Press.

Adelman, I., D.W. Roland-Holst, and A.H. Sarris (1986) 'Modelling uncertainty with computable general equilibrium models', Working Paper no. 405, Department of Agricultural and Resource Economics, University of California, Berkeley.

Ahluwalia, M.S. and F.J. Lysy (1979) 'Welfare effects of demand management policies: Impact multipliers under alternative model structures', *Journal of Policy Modeling*, 1, no. 3:317–342.

Ahluwalia, M.S. and F.J. Lysy (1981) 'Employment, income distribution, and programs to remedy balance-of-payments difficulties', in: W.R. Cline and S. Weintraub, eds., *Economic stabilization in developing countries.* Washington, DC: Brookings Institution.

Almon, C., Jr., M.B. Buckler, L.M. Horwitz, and T.C. Reimbold (1974) *1985: Interindustry forecasts of the American economy.* Lexington, MA: D.C. Heath and Company.

Armington, P.S. (1969) 'A theory of demand for products distinguished by place of production', *IMF Staff Papers.* 16, no. 1:159–178.

Arrow, K.J. (1986) 'Plannings under uncertainty', in: I. Adelman and J.E. Taylor, eds., *The design of alternative development strategies.* Rohtak, India: Jan Tinbergen Institute of Development Planning.

Arrow, K. and F. Hahn (1971) *General competitive analysis.* San Francisco, CA: Holden-Day.

Balassa, B. (1982) 'Incentive measures: Concepts and estimation', in B. Balassa and associates, eds., *Development strategies in semi-industrial countries.* Baltimore, MD: Johns Hopkins University Press.

Balassa, B. (1985) *Change and challenge in the world economy.* London: MacMillan Press.

Balassa, B. and associates (1971) *Structure of protection in developing countries.* Baltimore, MD: Johns Hopkins University Press.

Ballard, C.L., D. Fullerton, J.B. Shoven, and J. Whalley (1985) *A general equilibrium model for tax policy evaluation.* Chicago, IL: University of Chicago Press.

Bell, C.L.G. and S. Devarajan (1980) 'Semi-input–output and shadow prices: A critical note', *Bulletin of the Oxford Institute of Economics and Statistics*, 42, no. 3:251–256

Bell, C.L.G. and S. Devarajan (1983) 'Shadow prices for project evaluation under alternative macroeconomic regimes', *Quarterly Journal of Economics*, 98, no. 3:457–478.

Bell, C.L.G. and S. Devarajan (1985) 'Social cost-benefit analysis in a semi-input–output framework: An application to the Muda irrigation project', in: G. Pyatt and J.I. Round, eds., *Social accounting matrices: A basis for planning.* Washington, DC: World Bank.

Bell, C.L.G. and P.B.R. Hazell (1980) 'Measuring the indirect effects of an agricultural investment project on its surrounding region', *American Journal of Agricultural Economics*, 62, no. 1:75–86.

Bell, C.L.G. and T.N. Srinivasan (1984) 'On the uses and abuses of economy-wide models in development policy analysis', in: M. Syrquin, L. Taylor, and L.E. Westphal, eds., *Economic structure and performance.* New York: Academic.

Bell, C.L.G., P.B.R. Hazell, and R. Slade (1982) *Project evaluation in regional perspective.* Baltimore, MD: Johns Hopkins University Press.

Benassy, J.P. (1982) *The economics of market disequilibrium.* New York: Academic.

Benjamin, N.C. and S. Devarajan (1985) 'Oil revenues and economic policy in Cameroon: Results from a computable general equilibrium model', World Bank Staff Working Paper no. 745. Washington, DC: The World Bank.

Bergman, L. (1982) 'A system of computable general equilibrium models for a small open economy', *Mathematical Modelling*, 3:421–435.

Bhagwati, J. and T.N. Srinivasan (1978) 'Shadow prices for project selection in the presence of distortions: Effective rates of protection and domestic resource costs', *Journal of Political Economy*, 86, no. 1:97–116.

Bhagwati, J. and T.N. Srinivasan (1980) 'Revenue seeking: A generalization of the theory of tariffs', *Journal of Political Economy*, 88:1069–1087.

Bigsten, A. (1983) *Income distribution and development: Theory, evidence, and policy*. London: Heinemann.

Blitzer, C.R., P.B. Clark, and L. Taylor, eds. (1975) *Economy-wide models and development planning*. Oxford: Oxford University Press.

Bourguignon, F., G. Michel, and D. Miqueu (1983) 'Short-run rigidities and long-run adjustments in a computable general equilibrium model of income distribution and development', *Journal of Development Economics*, 13:21–43.

Bruno, M. (1975) 'Planning models, shadow prices, and project evaluation', in: C.R. Blitzer, P.B. Clark, and L. Taylor, eds., *Economy-wide models and development planning*. London: Oxford University Press.

Bruno, M. (1979) 'Income distribution and the neoclassical paradigm', *Journal of Development Economics*, 6, no. 1:3–10.

Buffie, E. (1984) 'Financial repression, the new structuralists, and stabilization policy in semi-industrial economies', *Journal of Development Economics*, 14:305–322.

Bulmer-Thomas, V. (1982) *Input–output analysis in developing countries: Sources, methods, and applications*. New York: Wiley.

Chenery, H.B., ed. (1971) *Studies in development planning*. Cambridge, MA: Harvard University Press.

Chenery, H.B. (1975) 'The structuralist approach to development policy', *American Economic Review*, 65, no. 2:310–316.

Chenery, H.B. (1979) *Structural change and development policy*. London: Oxford University Press.

Chenery, H.B. (1984) 'The evolution of development planning', *Journal of Policy Modeling*, 6, no. 2:159–174.

Chenery, H.B. and P.G. Clark (1959) *Interindustry economics*. New York: Wiley.

Chenery, H.B. and J.H. Duloy (1974) 'Research Directions', in: Chenery et al., *Redistribution with growth*. London: Oxford University Press.

Chenery, H.B. and W. Raduchel (1979) 'Substitution and structural change', in: H.B. Chenery, *Structural change and development policy*. London: Oxford University Press.

Chenery, H.B. and A. Strout (1966) 'Foreign assistance and economic development', *American Economic Review*, 56:679–733.

Chenery, H.B., M.S. Ahluwalia, C.L.G. Bell, J.H. Duloy, and R. Jolly (1974) *Redistribution with growth*. London: Oxford University Press.

Chenery, H.B., J.D. Lewis, J. de Melo, and S. Robinson (1986) 'Alternative routes to development', in: H.B. Chenery, S. Robinson, and M. Syrquin, *Industrialization and growth: A comparative study*. London: Oxford University Press.

Chenery, H.B., S. Robinson, and M. Syrquin (1986) *Industrialization and growth: A comparative study*. London: Oxford University Press.

Chow, G.C. (1975) *Analysis and control of dynamic economic systems*. New York: Wiley.

Clark, P.B. (1975) 'Intersectoral consistency and macroeconomic planning', in: C.R. Blitzer, P.B. Clark, and L. Taylor, eds., *Economy-wide models and development planning*. Oxford: Oxford University Press.

Cline, W.R. (1972) *Potential effects of income redistribution on economic growth: Latin American cases*. New York: Praeger.

Condon, T., V. Corbo, and J. de Melo (1985a) 'Productivity growth, external shocks, and capital inflows in Chile: A general equilibrium analysis', *Journal of Policy Modeling*, 7, no. 3:379–405.

Condon, T., V. Corbo, and J. de Melo (1985b) 'Capital inflows, the current account, and the real exchange rate: Tradeoffs for Chile 1977–81', mimeo, Development Research Department. Washington, DC: World Bank.

Condon, T., S. Robinson, and S. Urata (1985) 'Coping with a foreign exchage crisis: A general equilibrium model of alternative adjustment mechanisms', *Mathematical Programming Study*, no. 23. Issue edited by A.S. Manne under the title *Economic equilibrium: Model formulation and solution*. Amsterdam: North-Holland.

Corden, W.M. (1974) *Trade policy and economic welfare*. London: Oxford University Press.

Dahl, H., S. Devarajan, and S. van Wijnbergen (1986) 'Revenue-neutral tariff reform: Theory and an application to Cameroon', Discussion Paper no. 1986-25, Country Policy Department, World Bank.

Day, R. and A. Cigno, eds. (178) *Modelling economic change: The recursive programming approach.* Amsterdam: North-Holland.

Decaluwe, B. and A. Martens (1987) 'Developing countries and general equilibrium models: A review of the empirical literature', IDRC Report no. IDRC-MR155e, International Development Research Center, Ottawa, Canada.

Defourny, J. and E. Thorbecke (1984) 'Structural path analysis and multiplier decomposition within a social accounting matrix framework', *Economic Journal*, 94:111–136.

de Janvry, A. and E. Sadoulet (1985) 'Agricultural price policy in general equilibrium frameworks: A comparative analysis', Department of Agricultural and Resource Economics, Working Paper no. 342, University of California, Berkeley.

de Melo, J. (1980) 'Tariffs and resource allocation in partial and general equilibrium', *Weltwirtschaftliches Archiv*, 116:114–130.

de Melo, J. (1988) 'Computable general equilibrium models for trade policy analysis in developing countries: A survey', *Journal of Policy Modeling*, forthcoming.

de Melo, J. and S. Robinson (1980) 'The impact of trade policies on income distribution in a planning model for Colombia', *Journal of Policy Modeling*, 2, no. 1:81–100.

de Melo, J. and S. Robinson (1981) 'Trade policy and resource allocation in the presence of product differentiation', *Review of Economics and Statistics*, 63, no. 2:169–177.

de Melo, J. and S. Robinson (1982) 'Trade adjustment policies and income distribution in three archetype developing countries', *Journal of Development Economics*, 10, no. 1:67–92.

de Melo, J. and S. Robinson (1985) 'Product differentiation and trade dependence of the domestic price system in computable general equilibrium trade models', in: T. Peeters, P. Praet, and P. Reding, eds., *International trade and exchange rates in the late eighties.* Amsterdam: North-Holland.

de Melo, J. and S. Robinson (1989) 'Product differentiation and foreign trade in CGE models of small economies', Working Paper WPS-144, Country Economics Department, The World Bank. *Journal of International Economics*, forthcoming.

Dervis, K. (1975) 'Substitution, employment, and intertemporal equilibrium in a non-linear multi-sector planning model for Turkey', *European Economic Review*, 6:77–96.

Dervis, K. and S. Robinson (1978) 'The foreign exchange gap, growth and industrial strategy in Turkey: 1973–1983', World Bank Staff Working Paper no. 306. Washington, DC: World Bank.

Dervis, K. and S. Robinson (1982) 'A general equilibrium analysis of the causes of a foreign exchange crisis: The case of Turkey', *Weltwirtschaftliches Archiv*, 118, no. 2:259–280.

Dervis, K., J. de Melo, and S. Robinson (1981) 'A general equilibrium analysis of foreign exchange shortages in a developing country', *Economic Journal*, 91, no. 364:891–906.

Dervis, K., J. de Melo, and S. Robinson (1982) *General equilibrium models for development policy.* Cambridge: Cambridge University Press.

Devarajan, S. (1987) 'Models of adjustment and growth in developing countries', mimeo, John F. Kennedy School of Government, Harvard University.

Devarajan, S. and J. de Melo (1987) 'Adjustment with a fixed exchange rate: Cameroon, Cote d'Ivoire, and Senegal', *The World Bank Economic Review*, 1, no. 3:447–487.

Devarajan, S., J. D. Lewis, and S. Robinson (1986) 'A bibliography of computable general equilibrium (CGE) models applied to developing countries', Working Paper no. 400, Department of Agricultural and Resource Economics, University of California, Berkeley.

Dewatripont, M. and G. Michel (1987) 'On closure rules, homogeneity, and dynamics in applied general equilibrium models', *Journal of Development Economics*, 26, no. 1:65–76.

Dewatripont, M. and S. Robinson (1985) 'The impact of price rigidities: A computable general equilibrium analysis', Giannini Foundation Working Paper no. 375, University of California, Berkeley.

Diamand, M. (1978) 'Towards a change in the economic paradigm through the experience of developing countries', *Journal of Development Economics*, 5:19–53.

Dick, H., S. Gupta, T. Mayer, and D. Vincent (1983) 'The short-run impact of fluctuating primary commodity prices on three developing countries: Colombia, Ivory Coast, and Kenya', *World Development*, 11, no. 5:405–416.

Dixon, P.B. (1975) *The theory of joint maximization.* Amsterdam: North-Holland.

Dixon, P.B., B.R. Parmenter, J. Sutton, and D.P. Vincent (1982) *Orani: A multisectoral model of the Australian economy.* Amsterdam: North-Holland.

Drud, A. and W. Grais (1983) 'Macroeconomic adjustment in Thailand: Demand management and supply conditions', *Journal of Policy Modeling*, 5, no. 2:207–232.

Drud, A., W. Grais, and G. Pyatt (1984) 'The TV-approach: A systematic method of defining economywide models based on social accounting matrices', in: T. Basar and L. Pau, eds., *Proceedings of the 4th IFAC/IFORS conference on the modelling and control of national economies*. London: Pergamon.

Drud, A., W. Grais, and D. Vujovic (1982) 'Thailand: An analysis of structural and non-structural adjustments', World Bank Staff Working Paper No. 513. Washington, DC: World Bank.

Eckaus, R.S. (1955) 'The factor proportions problem in underdeveloped areas', *American Economic Review*, 45:539–565.

Evans, H.D. (1972) *A general equilibrium analysis of protection: The effects of protection in Australia*. Amsterdam: North-Holland.

Fei, J.C.H. and G. Ranis (1964) *Development of the labor surplus economy: Theory and policy*. Homewood, IL: Richard D. Irwin.

Feltenstein, A. (1980) 'A general equilibrium approach to the analysis of trade restrictions, with an application to Argentina', *IMF Staff Papers*, 27, no. 4:749–784.

Feltenstein, A. (1984) 'Money and bonds in a disaggregated open economy', in: H. Scarf and J.B. Shoven, eds., *Applied general equilibrium analysis*. Cambridge: Cambridge University Press.

Gelb, A. (1985) 'Are oil windfalls a blessing or a curse? Policy exercises with an Indonesia-like model', mimeo, Development Research Department, World Bank, Washington, DC.

Gibson, B. (1985) 'A structuralist macromodel for post-revolutionary Nicaragua', *Cambridge Journal of Economics*, 9, no. 4:347–369.

Gibson, B., N. Lusting, and L. Taylor (1985) 'Terms of trade and class conflict in a Marxian computable general equilibrium model for Mexico', *Journal of Development Studies*, forthcoming.

Ginsburgh, V. and S. Robinson (1984) 'Equilibrium and prices in multisector models', in: M. Syrquin, L. Taylor, and L.E. Westphal, eds., *Economic structure and performance*. New York: Academic.

Ginsburgh, V. and J. Waelbroeck (1981) *Activity analysis and general equilibrium modelling*. Amsterdam: North-Holland.

Goreux, L.M. (1977) *Interdependence in planning: Multilevel programming studies of the Ivory Coast*. Baltimore, MD: Johns Hopkins University Press.

Goreux, L.M. and A.S. Manne, eds. (1973) *Multi-level planning: Case studies in Mexico*. Amsterdam: North-Holland.

Grais, W. (1981) 'Aggregate demand and macroeconomic imbalances in Thailand: Experiments with the SIAM1 model', World Bank Staff Working Paper No. 448. Washington, DC: World Bank.

Grais, W., J. de Melo, and S. Urata (1986) 'A general equilibrium estimation of the effects of reductions in tariffs and quantitative restrictions in Turkey in 1978', in: T.N. Srinivasan and J. Whalley, eds., *General equilibrium trade policy modelling*. Cambridge, MA: MIT Press, 61–88.

Grandmont, J.M. (1977) 'Temporary general equilibrium theory', *Econometrica*, 45, no. 3:535–572.

Greenfeld, C.C. and H. Fell (1979) 'The estimation of price effects in a social accounting matrix', *Review of Income and Wealth*, 25, no. 1:65–81.

Gupta, S. (1977a) *A model for income distribution, employment, and growth: A case study of Indonesia*, World Bank Staff Occasional Papers no. 24. Baltimore, MD: Johns Hopkins University Press.

Gupta, S. (1977b) 'Alternative development strategies of korea (1976–1990) in an input–output dynamic simulation model', World Bank Staff Working Paper no. 154. Washington, DC: World Bank.

Hahn, F. (1978) 'On non-Walrasian equilibria', *Review of Economic Studies*, 45, no. 1.

Hirschman, A.O. (1958) *The strategy of economic development*. New Haven, CT: Yale University Press.

Johansen, L. (1960) *A multi-sectoral study of economic growth*. Amsterdam: North-Holland.

Kehoe, T. (1980) 'An index theorem for general equilibrium models with production', *Econometrica*, 48, no. 5:1211–1232.

Kehoe, T.J. and J. Serra-Puche (1983) 'A computational general equilibrium model with endogenous unemployment: An analysis of the 1980 fiscal reform in Mexico', *Journal of Public Economics*, 22, no. 1:1–26.

Kelley, A.C. and J.G. Williamson (1974) *Lessons from Japanese development: An analytical economic history*. Chicago, IL: University of Chicago Press.

Kelley, A.C. and J.G. Williamson (1984) *What drives third world city growth? A dynamic general equilibrium approach*. Princeton, NJ: Princeton University Press.

Kelley, A.C., J.G. Williamson, and R.J. Cheetham (1972) *Dualistic economic development: Theory and history*. Chicago, IL: University of Chicago Press.

Kendrick, D. (1981) 'Control theory with applications to economics', in: K.J. Arrow and M.D. Intriligator, eds., *Handbook of mathematical economics*. Amsterdam: North-Holland.

King, B.B. (1985) 'What is a SAM?', in: G. Pyatt and J.I. Round, eds., *Social accounting matrices: A basis for planning*. Washington, DC: World Bank.

Kis, P., S. Robinson, and L.D. Tyson (1985) 'Computable general equilibrium models for socialist economies', Working Paper no. 394, Department of Agricultural and Resource Economics, University of California, Berkeley. Forthcoming in L. Bergman, D.W. Jorgenson, and E. Zalai, eds., *Proceedings of an IIASA conference on applied general equilibrium models*.

Krueger, A.O. (1974) 'The political economy of the rent-seeking society', *American Economic Review*, 64, no. 3:293–303.

Kubo, Y., S. Robinson, and M. Syrquin (1986) 'The methodology of multisector comparative analysis', in: H.B. Chenery, S. Robinson, and M. Syrquin, *Industrialization and growth: A comparative study*. London: Oxford University Press.

Kubo, Y., S. Robinson, and S. Urata (1986) 'The impact of alternative development strategies: simulations with a dynamic input–output model', *Journal of Policy Modeling*, 8, no. 4:503–529.

Kuyvenhoven, A. (1978) *Planning with the semi-input–output method: With empirical applications to Nigeria*. Leiden: Martinus Nijhoff.

Levy, S. (1987) 'A short-run general equilibrium model for a small, open economy', *Journal of Development Economics*, 25, no. 1:63–88.

Lewis, J.D. (1985) 'Financial liberalization and price rigidities in a general equilibrium model with financial markets', Development Discussion Paper no. 211, Harvard Institute for International Development, Harvard University, Cambridge, MA.

Lewis, J.D. and S. Urata (1983) 'Turkey: Recent economic performance and medium-term prospects, 1978–1990', World Bank Staff Working Paper no. 602. Washington, DC: World Bank.

Lewis J.D. and S. Urata (1984) 'Anatomy of a balance-of-payments crisis: Application of a computable general equilibrium model to Turkey, 1978–1980', *Economic Modelling*, 1, no. 3:281–303.

Lysy, F.J. (1983) 'The character of general equilibrium models under alternative closures', mimeo, Department of Economics, Johns Hopkins University.

Lysy, F.J. and L. Taylor (1980) 'The general equilibrium income distribution model', in: L. Taylor, E. Bacha, E. Cardoso, and F.J. Lysy, *Models of growth and distribution for Brazil*. London: Oxford University Press.

Malinvaud, E. (1977) *The theory of unemployment reconsidered*. Oxford: Basil Blackwell.

Manne, A.S. (1974) 'Multi-sector models for development planning: A survey', *Journal of Development Economics*, 1, no. 1:43–69.

Manne, A.S. (1985) 'On the formulation and solution of economic equilibrium models', in: A.S. Manne, ed., *Economic equilibrium: Model formulation and solution*, Mathematical Programming Study no. 23. Amsterdam: North-Holland.

Manne, A.S., H.-P. Chao, and R. Wilson (1980) 'Computation of competitive equilibria by a sequence of linear programs', *Econometrica*, 48:1595–1615.

Martin, R. and S. van Wijnbergen (1986) 'Shadow prices and the intertemporal aspects of remittances and oil revenues in Egypt', in: J. Peter Neary and S. van Wijnbergen, eds., *Natural resources and the macro economy*, Ch. 4. London: Basil-Blackwell.

Mas-Colell, A. (1985) *General equilibrium analysis: A differential approach*. Cambridge: Cambridge University Press.

McCarthy, F.D. (1984) 'Macroeconomic policy alternatives in the Dominican Republic: An analytical framework', World Bank Staff Working Paper no. 649. Washington, DC: World Bank.

McKinnon, R.I. (1973) *Money and capital in economic development*. Washington, DC: Brookings Institution.

Meeraus, A. (1983) 'An algebraic approach to modelling', *Journal of Economic Dynamics and Control*, 5:81–108.

Michel, G. and M. Noel (1984) 'Short-term responses to trade and incentive policies in the Ivory Coast: Comparative static simulations in a computable general equilibrium model', World Bank Staff Working Paper no. 647. Washington, DC: World Bank.

Miller, R.E. and P. Blair (1985) *Input–output analysis: Foundations and extensions*. Englewood Cliffs, NJ: Prentice-Hall.

Mitra, P. (1984) 'Adjustments to external shocks in selected semi-industrial countries: 1974–81', Discussion Paper no. 114, Development Research Department. Washington, DC: World Bank.

Muellbauer, J. and R. Portes (1978) 'Macroeconomic models with quantity rationing', *Economic Journal*, 88, no. 352:788–821.

Newbery, D.N.G. and J.E. Stiglitz (1981) *The theory of commodity price stabilization: A study in the economics of risk*. Oxford: Clarendon Press.

Nishimizu, M. and S. Robinson (1984) 'Trade policies and productivity change in semi-industrialized countries', *Journal of Development Economics*, 16, no. 1–2:177–206.

Norton, R.D. and P.L. Scandizzo (1981) 'Market equilibrium computations in activity analysis models', *Operations Research*, 29, no. 2:243–262.

Pyatt, G. and J.I. Round (1977) 'Social accounting matrices for development planning', *Review of Income and Wealth*, 23, no. 4:339–364.

Pyatt, G. and J.I. Round (1979) 'Accounting and fixed-price multipliers in a social accounting matrix framework', *Economic Journal*, 89, no. 356:850–873.

Pyatt, G. and J.I. Round, eds. (1985) *Social accounting matrices: A basis for planning*. Washington, DC: World Bank.

Pyatt, G. and E. Thorbecke (1976) *Planning techniques for a better future*. Geneva: International Labour Office.

Pyatt, G. et al. (1972) *Employment and income policies for Iran: Methodology for macroeconomic projections*. Geneva: International Labour Office.

Rasmussen, P.N. (1965) *Studies in intersectoral relations*. Amsterdam: North-Holland.

Rattso, J. (1982) 'Different macroclosures of the original Johansen model and their impact on policy evaluation', *Journal of Policy Modeling*, 4, no. 1:85–97.

Robinson, S. (1983) 'Comments on "The impact of the 1980 fiscal reform on unemployment in Mexico" by Jaime Serra-Puche,' in: H. Scarf and J. Shoven, eds., *Applied general equilibrium analysis*. Cambridge: Cambridge University Press.

Robinson, S. and A. Markandya (1973) 'Complexity and adjustment in input–output systems', *Oxford Bulleting of Economics and Statistics*, 35, no. 2:119–134.

Robinson, S. and D.W. Roland-Holst (1987) 'Modelling structural adjustment in the U.S. Economy: Macroeconomics in a social accounting framework', Working Paper no. 440, Department of Agricultural and Resource Economics, University of California, Berkeley.

Robinson, S. and L.D. Tyson (1984) 'Modelling structural adjustment: Micro and macro elements in a general equilibrium framework', in: H. Scarf and J.B. Shoven, eds., *Applied general equilibrium analysis*. Cambridge: Cambridge University Press.

Robinson, S. and L.D. Tyson (1985) 'Foreing trade, resource allocation, and structural adjustment in Yugoslavia: 1976–1980', *Journal of Comparative Economics*, 9:46–70.

Robinson, S., L.D. Tyson, and M. Dewatripont (1986) 'Yugoslav economic performance in the 1980's: Alternative scenarios', in Joint Economic Committee, U.S. Congress. *East European Economies: Slow growth in the 1980's*. Volume 2: *Country studies*. Washington, DC: U.S. Government Printing Office.

Sanderson, W.C. (1980) *Economic-demographic simulation models: A review of their usefulness for policy analysis*. Laxenburg, Austria: International Institute for Applied Systems Analysis (IIASA), RM-80-14.

Sanderson, W.C. and J.G. Williamson (1985) 'How should developing countries adjust to external shocks in the 1980s? An examination of some World Bank macroeconomic models', World Bank Staff Working Paper no. 708. Washington, DC: World Bank.

Scarf, H.E. and T. Hansen (1973) *The computation of economic equilibria*. New Haven, CT: Yale University Press.

Scarf, H. and J.B. Shoven, eds. (1983) *Applied general equilibrium analysis*. Cambridge: Cambridge University Press.

Schmitz, A. (1984) 'Commodity price stabilization: The theory and its applications', World Bank Staff Working Paper no. 668. Washington, DC: World Bank.

Sen, A.K. (1963) 'Neo-classical and neo-Keynesian theories of distribution', *Economic Record*, 39:53–66.

Serra-Puche, J. (1983) 'A general equilibrium model for the Mexican economy', in: H. Scarf and J.B. Shoven, eds., *Applied general equilibrium analysis*. Cambridge: Cambridge University Press.

Shoven, J.B. and J. Whalley (1984) 'Applied general-equilibrium models of taxation and international trade', *Journal of Economic Literature*, 22, no. 3:1007–1051.

Srinivasan, T.N. (1982) 'General equilibrium theory, project evaluation and economic development', in: M. Gersovitz, et al., eds., *The theory and experience of economic development: Essays in honor of Sir W. Arthur Lewis*. London: George Allen and Unwin, 229–251.

Stone, J.R.N. (1966) 'The social accounts from a consumer point of view', *Review of Income and Wealth*, 12, no. 1:1–33.

Stone, J.R.N. (1981) *Aspects of economic and social modelling*. Geneva: Librairie Droz.

Stone, J.R.N. (1984) 'Where are we now? A short account of the development of input–output studies and their present trends', in: United Nations Industrial Development Organization. *Proceedings of the seventh international conference on input–output techniques*. New York: United Nations.

Stone, J.R.N. (1985) 'The disaggregation of the household sector in the national accounts', in: G. Pyatt and J.I. Round, eds., *Social accounting matrices: A basis for planning*. Washington, DC: World Bank.

Stone, J.R.N. and G. Stone (1977) *National income and expenditure*, 10th ed. London: Bowes and Bowes.

Takayama, T. and G.C. Judge (1971) *Spatial and temporal price and allocation models*. Amsterdam: North-Holland.

Taylor, L. (1975) 'Theoretical foundations and technical implications', in: C.R. Blitzer, P.B. Clark, and L. Taylor, eds., *Economy-wide models and development planning*. London: Oxford University Press.

Taylor, L. (1979) *Macro models for developing countries*. New York: McGraw-Hill.

Taylor, L. (1983) *Structuralist macroeconomics: Applicable models for the third world*. New York: Basic Books.

Taylor, L., ed. (1989) *Structuralist computable general equilibrium models: Socially relevant policy analysis for the developing world*, forthcoming.

Taylor, L. and S.L. Black (1974) 'Practical general equilibrium estimation of resource pulls under trade liberalization', *Journal of International Economics*, 4, no. 1:37–58.

Taylor, L. and F.J. Lysy (1979) 'Vanishing income redistributions: Keynesian clues about model surprises in the short run', *Journal of Development Economics*, 6, no. 1:11–30.

Taylor, L. and J.A. Rosensweig (1984) 'Devaluation, capital flows and crowding-out: A computable general equilibrium model with portfolio choice for Thailand', mimeo, Department of Economics, MIT.

Taylor, L., H. Sarkar, and J. Rattso (1984) 'Macroeconomic adjustment in a computable general equilibrium model for India', in: M. Syrquin, L. Taylor, and L.E. Westphal, eds., *Economic structure and performance*. New York: Academic.

Thorbecke, E. (1985) 'The social accounting matrix and consistency-type planning models', in: G. Pyatt and J.I. Round, eds., *Social accounting matrices: A basis for planning*. Washington, DC: World Bank.

Thorbecke, E. and J. Sengupta (1972) 'A consistency framework for employment, output, and income distribution projections applied to Colombia', mimeo, Development Research Center, World Bank.

Tinbergen, J. (1966) 'Some refinements of the semi-input–output method', *Pakistan Development Review*, 6:243–247.

Torii, Y. and K. Fukasaku (1984) 'Economic development and changes in linkage structure: an input–output analysis of the Republic of Korea and Japan', in: United Nations Industrial Development Organization, *Proceedings of the seventh international conference on input–output techniques*. New York: United Nations.

Tsukui, J. and Y. Murakami (1979) *Turnpike optimality in input–output systems: Theory and application for planning*. Amsterdam: North-Holland.

United Nations (1968) *A system of national accounts*, series F, no. 2, rev. 3. New York: United Nations.

United Nations (1973) *Input–output tables and analysis*, Document ST/STAT/SER.F/14/Rev. 1. New York: United Nations.

United Nations (1975) *Towards a system of social and demographic statistics*, Series F, no. 18. New York: United Nations.

Waelbroeck, J. (1986) 'Some pitfalls in applied general equilibrium modelling', Discussion Paper no. 86-01, Department of Economics, University of British Columbia, Vancouver, Canada.

Weintraub, E. R. (1979) *Microfundation: The compatibility of microeconomics and macroeconomics*. Cambridge: Cambridge University Press.

Weisskoff, R. (1970) 'Income distribution and economic growth in Puerto Rico, Argentina and Mexico', *Review of Income and Wealth*, 16:303–332.

Weisskoff, R. (1985). *Factories and food stamps: The Puerto Rico model of development*. Baltimore, MD: Johns Hopkins University Press.

Westphal, L. (1975) 'Planning with economies of scale', in: C.R. Blitzer, P.B. Clark, and L. Taylor, eds., *Economy-wide models and development planning*. London: Oxford University Press.

Westphal, L.E. (1981) 'Empirical justification for infant industry protection', World Bank Staff Working Paper no. 445. Washington, DC: World Bank.

Whalley, J. and B. Yeung (1984) 'External sector "Closing" Rules in Applied General Equilibrium Models', *Journal of International Economics*, 16, no. 1/2:123–138.

Williamson, J.G. and P. Lindert (1980) *American inequality: A macroeconomic history*. New York: Academic.

World Bank (1980) *Turkey: Policies and prospects for growth*. Washington, DC: World Bank.

World Bank (1983) *Arab Republic of Egypt: Issues of trade strategy and investment planning*. Washington, DC: World Bank.

World Bank (1985) 'China: Economic model and projections', in: *China: Long term development issues and options*, Annex 4. Washington, DC: World Bank.

Yotopoulos, P.A. and J.B. Nugent (1976) *Economics of development: Empirical investigations*. New York: Harper and Row.

Zonnoor, S.H. (1983) 'Maximization over a set of competitive equilibria', *Journal of Economic Dynamics and Control*, 6:351–369.

Chapter 19

INCOME DISTRIBUTION AND DEVELOPMENT

IRMA ADELMAN and SHERMAN ROBINSON*

University of California, Berkeley

Contents

*We would like to thank Hollis Chenery, T.N. Srinivasan, and Paul Streeten for their careful reading of earlier drafts. We also thank students in our course in economic development at the University of California who commented on various presentations of the material.

Handbook of Development Economics, Volume II, Edited by H. Chenery and T.N. Srinivasan
© *Elsevier Science Publishers B.V., 1989*

1. Societal tolerance for inequality

Even with unchanging values, one would expect the social priority accorded to distributional concerns to change over time. Social tolerance of inequality is determined on the one hand by societal values and attitudes and, on the other, by perceptions of what can be feasibly achieved by economic policy. One can make a few generalizations about how and why societies differ in their attitudes about inequality, and the evolution of these attitudes over time. Our discussion below draws on the extensive political science literature on the subject but is not meant to be a survey.[1] The literature suggests the following propositions.

Changes in relative inequality are more tolerable if a process of change involves absolute gains for all. This argues for Pareto improving changes, provided they do not preclude future, more desirable distributional changes. Of course, opportunities for such Pareto improvements are rare and not characteristic of the process of industrialization.[2] However, if the economy is in the initial stages of a development process, actual improvements in the income of richer groups could signal impending improvement for poorer groups. Initially, expectations about one's own prospects in a society may be tied to the rate of growth of incomes in some reference group. The poor, in effect, may feel better off in anticipation of later improvement.[3] If aspirations run ahead of achievements or if the improvement fails to materialize, however, their patience wears thin. The resulting "revolution of unfulfilled rising expectations" is a force to be reckoned with in developing countries.

In times of crisis, societal tolerance of hardship and inequality increases, provided the crisis is perceived as due to exogenous events. War, pestilence, drought, and other plagues such as a foreign debt crisis can elicit a national response which, for a time, legitimates personal hardship and sacrifice. Political leaders, alas, are not above manufacturing such crises.

---

[1] A good entry point into this literature is Nelson (1979) and Huntington and Nelson (1976).
[2] See the discussion of stylized facts below.
[3] This proposition is put forward by Hirschman and Rothschild (1973).

If there are opportunities for "exit", either through rural–urban or international migration, greater inequality is more tolerable.[4] Even apart from income transfers to be obtained through migrant remittances, exit opportunities provide a social "safety valve" through which potential political tensions can be relieved. There are many examples, including Turkey, Mexico, and the opening up of the west in the United States during the nineteenth century. In a growing economy, high social, geographic, and economic mobility imply an equalizing trend in lifetime (or perhaps intergenerational) income and status. High income inequality at a point in time is therefore more tolerable in a mobile society. The converse also holds.

Another dynamic argument is that inequality is more tolerable if it is widely perceived to be a necessary precondition for eventual improvement in everyone's income. For example, it has been argued that inequality is necessary for accumulation, and that it therefore contains the seeds of eventual increases in everyone's income.[5] Stiglitz (1986) illustrates this view, arguing that there is a bargaining game between workers and capitalists underlying distributional allocations. They negotiate over the division of the current pie, each with a view to raising their own future income. Rawls (1971) reflects a similar, although normative, approach, arguing that societies should tolerate only that degree of inequality which is necessary to raise the income of the poorest over time.

Tolerance of inequality, of course, depends on perceptions of income differences. Such perceptions, in turn, depend on what is visible. For example, inter-regional and/or inter-group inequalities are more tolerable if the within-region or within-group distributions are relatively unchanged. A corollary is that ostentatious display of wealth differentials invites lower tolerance. The discreet rich are more secure. By contrast, modern communications and education broaden horizons, facilitate comparisons with more distant groups, and make the rich more visible.

Finally, social attitudes about the incidence of absolute and relative wealth and poverty are influenced by religion, culture, and history. In Western thought, various arguments have been advanced to justify the continued tolerance of extensive poverty. For example, at different times, the poor have been assumed to be lacking in virtue, thrift, enterprise, or abstinence. Christian religious arguments have been used on both sides: to justify acceptance of the existing order, as well as to support some ameliorative, essentially charity-based, programs. On the other hand, it is asserted that Confucianism does not tolerate large inequalities. The influence of this philosophy may be partly responsible for some of the policy

---

[4] This is the equivalent of the opportunity for "exit" in Hirschman's terminology. See Hirschman (1978).

[5] The view goes back to Marx and Schumpeter. Bauer (1981) is a modern proponent.

choices underlying the good distributional performance of the East Asian economies.[6] In addition to ethical arguments, analogies have been drawn from biology to support a policy of ignoring distributional issues by arguing that survival of the fittest is the mechanism underlying social evolution, and being rich is therefore evidence of desirable survival characteristics.

It is evident from the above discussion of tolerance of inequality that, in practice, one would expect the weight placed on distributional concerns to vary over time. Fundamentally, however, the concern never disappears and there are definite limits, varying from society to society and over time, on the extent of inequality which is socially tolerable. In the next section, we consider the evolution of such concerns in development policy in the period since World War II.

2. Values and policy concerns since 1950

One can discern at least three different subperiods from 1950 to the present in the priority accorded to poverty and income distribution as an independent goal of development policy.

2.1. Phase I: 1950–1970

In the West, the period immediately following World War II was one of great optimism about economic aid and growth. The high rates of economic growth were unprecedented in both developing and developed countries and flows of foreign assistance from developed to developing countries were large and un-grudging. The dominant development models at the time were all capital constrained; that is, growth was assumed to be limited only by accumulation.[7] These models all suggested that the growth of the modern sector, if sustained, would eventually result in spreading the benefits of that growth across the economy – the "trickle down" hypothesis. In policy debate, some advocated corrective action by the state to ensure that the poor did not fall below a certain level of basic needs (e.g. India in the early 1960s). Others argued that, in the long period required for accumulation, concern about equality and poverty was premature since it is only the rich that save. In fact, industrialization proceeded rapidly, at first stimulated by import substitution policies. In the early 1960s, a few countries, mainly in East Asia, achieved rapid growth through labor-intensive, export-oriented industrialization.

[6]See, for example, Nakamura (1966).
[7]Major figures in this tradition were Lewis (1954), Fei and Ranis (1964), and Chenery and Strout (1966).

The trickle-down hypothesis was based on a misreading of history by Western economists, who ignored the increasing inequality characteristic of the Industrial Revolution in the nineteenth century.[8] It was assumed that growth would affect the poorest in contemporary developing countries as it affected those in developed countries during the twentieth century, when conditions of the poor did improve. This assumption implicitly ignored the major institutional reforms (e.g. development of labor unions and welfare legislation) introduced at great social cost in developed countries since the turn of the century. At the time, no data on income distribution, poverty, or unemployment in developing countries existed to test the then accepted view that the benefits of growth were trickling down to the poor.

There were some critics of the prevalent optimistic view of the development process. Baran (1957) argued that the nature of capitalist industrial development fostered an alliance between domestic and international elites against the economic interests of the domestic majority. The dependency school, of which Prebisch (1959) was an initiator, argued that the world economy operated to turn the international terms of trade against developing counties. Observers of the Indian subcontinent, such as Myrdal (1968), argued that the combination of locally corrupt governments and a dualistic economic structure impeded the spread of the benefits of industrialization outside the enclave economy. The socialist government of India was concerned with distributional issues quite early [see Government of India (1964)]. In the absence of general data, the failures of the development process analyzed by these critics were considered by mainstream development economists to be either not central or very special cases of an otherwise beneficial process. During the 1960s, the principal debates were not about distributional consequences but rather about the relative benefits of import substitution versus export promotion, or about fostering primary versus manufacturing exports.

2.2. Phase II: 1970–1975

The first identification of development failures by mainstream Western economists came at the end of the 1960s, when it was realized that rapid aggregate growth had been accompanied by deteriorating employment opportunities. The development models of the 1950s and 1960s were based on the classical model of rapid industrialization achieved by syphoning labor and economic surplus for capital accumulation from the traditional agricultural sector. The first attempts to

---

[8] There is a long debate on this subject in economic history. Recent work by Adelman and Morris (1983), Morris and Adelman (1987), Williamson (1985), Williamson and Lindert (1980), and Lindert and Williamson (1985) indicates that the early phases of the industrial revolution led to increasing inequality.

explain the failures of this development model pointed to inappropriate factor prices. In contrast to the assumptions of the Lewis model, wages in the modern sector were rising rather than remaining constant, despite the continued existence of surplus labor in the traditional sector. Efforts to accelerate the growth of the modern industrial sector had led to subsidization of investment in physical capital, thus increasing the wage–rental ratio. The result was encouragement of capital-intensive technology; the remedy would be to increase the price of capital.

Several other arguments were put forth to explain the employment problem. Stewart and Streeten (1972) argued that the employment problem was only the result of inappropriate factor prices, but also due to lack of appropriate labor-intensive technologies. Industrial technologies available for use by developing countries originated in developed countries where wage–interest ratios are high and most goods are consumed by the middle class and rich. In addition to correcting factor price distortions, there was a need for developing appropriate technologies centered on wage goods that would be consumed by the bulk of the populations of developing countries.[9]

Another villain was demographic: the combination of rapid population growth with heavy rural–urban migration. The model by Harris and Todaro (1970) was used to explain why migration could sensibly coexist with urban unemployment. Such migration constituted a gamble on finding an urban job and would continue as long as the expected value of playing the urban job lottery exceeded average earnings in the rural sector. Since urban wages are typically at least twice rural per capita incomes, continued migration is compatible with urban unemployment rates of up to 50 percent, assuming that all urban workers have an equal probability of finding a job.[10] The remedy would be population control activities and reductions in rural–urban income gaps and in social amenity differentials.

Another demographic argument focused on the role of education. In many developing countries, an education explosion at the secondary and university levels had created a mismatch between the educational profile of the labor force and the structure of employment opportunities generated by rapid industrial growth. The result was high unemployment rates among graduates, with consequent economic and social tensions.[11] The obvious remedy would be a shift towards primary education, emphasizing numeracy and literacy for the masses, and away from academic and classical education. The opposite argument was made in Brazil. Part of the explanation for Brazil's worsening distribution of income was that the high growth rate had caused a shortage of educated

---

[9]A related argument by Pack (1971) linked unemployment to low capacity utilization arising from foreign exchange shortages.

[10]See the survey by Todaro (1980) which covers a number of variations of the standard Harris–Todaro model.

[11]For a study of graduate unemployment in India that was influential in the development of this argument, see Blaug (1973).

manpower, leading to increased wages for skilled labor and a consequent widening gap in wages between skilled and unskilled labor. The Brazil debate was quite heated, with much discussion about the data and the relative importance of the different trends.[12]

The combination of trends such as slow labor absorption in the modern sector, rapid population increase, education explosion, and exploitation of agriculture transformed disguised rural underemployment into urban underemployment in a large "informal sector" consisting of low-income, self-employed and casually-employed people. The problem was not one of open unemployment with zero wages, but rather one of low productivity and low-income employment [Turnham (1971)]. The underemployed work long hours but earn only a poverty income since they are employed in low-productivity jobs in which they are underutilized. At this point, the employment problem and the poverty problem merge.

Independently of the employment problem, research into the distribution of benefits of growth was initiated.[13] Empirical work indicated that the development programs of the previous two decades had gone seriously wrong. For most countries, the distribution of income had deteriorated as a consequence of growth, and social and political participation bore little relationship to economic growth [Adelman and Morris (1973), Paukert (1973), Ahluwalia (1976a)]. These findings altered both the research and the policy agenda in the latter part of the 1970s, and led to a search for development policies, strategies, and programs that would result in a more egalitarian distribution of development benefits.

2.3. Phase III: 1975–present

In the 1980s, distributional and poverty issues were again pushed off the research and policy agenda. The combination of policies in the developing countries aimed at maintaining growth in the face of declining exports and rising oil prices after 1973 with policies in developed countries aimed at fighting inflation through monetary restraint generated both supply and demand pressures to increase lending to developing countries. In the 1970s, oil-importing developing countries borrowed massively from commercial banks in the OECD countries, and at variable interest rates. When real interest rates rose, problems of insolvency, potential default, and debt refinancing became acute and came to dominate development policy.

Short-term problems of structural adjustment to current and capital account imbalances in the balance of payments of developing countries took priority over

---

[12] See Taylor et al. (1980), Morley and Williamson (1974), Langoni (1975), and Fishlow (1972, 1973).

[13] This literature is reviewed in more detail below.

more fundamental problems of designing development strategies that could generate economic growth and structural change while benefiting the poorer members of society. Also, disenchantment with income transfer programs in developed countries and an ideological turn to the right among policy-makers in the OECD countries legitimized a shift away from direct concerns with the poor in formulating economic policy.

Along with this shift in policy concern went a shift in underlying theoretical focus. The tenets of neoclassical economics stress the role of market prices as signals for Pareto optimal static resource allocation. False analogies with the growth process in the successful Gang of Four countries have been used by some to buttress a Candide-like faith that free markets will generate the best outcomes in the best of all possible worlds. This faith underlies arguments that polices to make prices flexible, privatize, and downgrade the role of government policy are all that is required to achieve successful development.[14] At a theoretical level, these arguments ignore the many qualifications which severely limit the applicability of the standard proof of static optimality: e.g. external economies, uncertainty, intertemporal inefficiencies when private and social discount rates diverge, and the theory of the second best. At an empirical level, the applicability of the neoclassical model to developing countries must also be qualified by the absence of some markets, the incompleteness of others, and the mixed nature of property rights, all of which tend to blunt and circumscribe the transmission of market incentives to individual economic actors.

In any case, even within its own theoretical confines, the neoclassical model cannot provide an answer to distributional concerns. Any judgment of optimality of relative prices must necessarily entail a judgment about the optimality of the wealth distribution or, alternatively, a positive welfare judgment about the distributional outcome.[15] Prices not only allocate resources between economic actors, but also economic welfare between people.

The period since 1973 has been dominated by exogenous shocks and crisis responses. As discussed earlier, initially, crisis response leads to tolerance of increasing inequality during a recovery period. However, this tolerance erodes over time, especially if, as happened, absolute real incomes fall. Distributional concerns therefore cannot be ignored indefinitely. Poverty in developing countries is still massive. At the same time, the decline in inflation and interest rates, the resumption of OECD growth, and various debt reschedulings (including writedowns and swaps) are making the debt problems less acute. Economic and

[14] This sentence covers a lot of welfare economics beyond the scope of this survey. See Rawls (1971), Sen (1982), and Nozick (1981).

[15] Extreme examples of this view are provided by Bauer (1981) and Lal (1985). More reasoned arguments along these lines can be found in Little (1982), Balassa and Associates (1982), and Krueger (1978).

political considerations render the resumption of growth in developing countries imperative.

There is a dawning realization that the poor and near poor have borne the brunt of many IMF-inspired structural adjustment programs. A number of international institutions have started analyzing the distributional implications of alternative macroeconomic stabilization policies.[16] The concern now is on the impacts of policies designed to achieve stabilization and structural adjustment on malnutrition and poverty in one to five years. The focus of our survey, following the concerns of past work, is on the distributional implications of different choices of development strategy in the medium to long term.

While the analytic framework required to analyze structural change is not the same as that required to analyze stabilization and structural adjustment, there are lessons that carry over from the research program of the seventies on distribution and development. It is important to pull these together. We start by reviewing the empirical patterns and trends characterizing the relation between inequality and development. We then consider diverse theoretical paradigms yielding alternative forecasts of the course of inequality. Policy models, some based on competing theoretical underpinnings, are examined next. Finally, we conclude with an examination of policy options in structuring programs and strategies yielding "equitable" growth in the medium to long term.[17]

3. Stylized facts

In his famous article "Economic Growth and Income Equality", Kuznets (1955) posed the research agenda for studies of the relationship between income distribution and development. He asked two questions, which subsequent analyses have tried to address: "What is the systematic long term relationship between the shape of the overall size distribution of income and economic growth?" and "What factors determine the secular level and trends of income inequality?"

3.1. The U-hypothesis

Using data on long-term growth in developed countries and drawing on his earlier studies, Kuznets (1966) showed that after 1930 the size distribution of income in developed countries narrowed. Based on an analytic model discussed below, he also hypothesized that early economic growth produced increasing

---

[16]See, for example, IMF (1986) and Addison and Demery (1986). Thorbecke (1987) and Pinstrup–Anderson (1986) discuss current work and propose a research agenda.
[17]For two good recent surveys, see Bigsten (1983) and Lecaillon et al. (1984).

inequality. The combination constitutes the U-hypothesis. To explore this hypothesis in contemporary developing countries, Adelman and Morris (1973) used a particular type of analysis of variance (the analysis of hierarchic interactions) with data they developed on the size distribution of income by quintiles for 44 less developed countries.[18] They found that: (1) all less developed countries experience a significant decrease in the share of income accruing to the poorest when development starts; (2) the share of income accruing to the poorest 60 percent of the population continues to decline, albeit more slowly, for a substantial portion of the development process; and (3) in the phase of development represented by the most developed third of developing countries, policy choices determine whether an improvement in the share of income accruing to the poorest does or does not occur. The cross-country relationship can be either U-shaped or J-shaped.

Their analysis was followed by cross-country regression studies of the inequality–development relationship based on somewhat more refined, but still quite heterogeneous, data. The samples varied and often included developed countries [Paukert (1973), Chenery et al. (1974), Ahluwalia (1976a, 1976b), Ahluwalia, Carter and Chenery (1979), Bacha (1979), Papanek and Kyn (1986)]. These studies generally assumed that the relationship between the income share of the poorest 40 percent and per capita GNP is quadratic in the log of per capita GNP and may be conditioned by a set of dummy variables capturing characteristics such as whether the country is socialist or not, dualistic or not, or rich in resources. These studies generally support the U-hypothesis. Anand and Kanbur (1986) argue that the location of the minimum of the U is sensitive to the sample composition and to the specific functional form. Such sensitivity is to be expected if the underlying relationship is either U- or J-shaped in specific countries, depending on their policy choices. Papanek and Kyn (1986), on the contrary, argue that the relationship is stable and robust to the inclusion of additional explanatory variables, which may have captured some features of different policy choices. The mixed and sometimes contradictory results from these regression studies tend to confirm the early skepticism about this approach expressed by Adelman and Morris.

All these studies agree on one descriptive result: the initial phase of the development process, during which a mostly agrarian economy starts industrialization, is necessarily marked by substantial increases in the inequality of the distribution of income, with a sharply reduced share of income going to the poorest 20, 40, and 60 percent of the population. But there is controversy whether

---

[18] They argued that neither the quality of the data, which is quite heterogeneous, nor the state of a priori knowledge, which at the time was scant, permitted the use of regression analysis with a priori specification of functional forms. Their particular approach is robust to data quality, imposes no a priori constraints on the functional shape of the relationship, and permits highly non-linear relationships to become manifest.

a decrease in inequality with development is inevitable (the U-hypothesis) or a matter of policy choice (the J-hypothesis). There is also controversy about whether the real incomes of significant groups of the poverty population actually fall during the early stages of the transition.

3.2. Analytics of the U-hypothesis

To study what factors affect how income distribution changes with development, we require some analytic apparatus. A simple conceptual framework is provided by variance decomposition. National inequality can be decomposed into the weighted sum of sectoral (or regional, group, or class) inequality. If the decomposition is performed on an aggregate index and the index is statistically decomposable, then the decomposition is strictly the weighted sum of within and between-sector inequalities, with population shares as weights. Otherwise, the decomposition must take account of the covariance between within-sector inequalities as well [see Fields (1980) and Pyatt (1976)].

The earliest two-sector decomposition is due to Kuznets (1955). Using a hypothetical numerical example for a two-sector economy, Kuznets showed that, even if within-sector inequality is constant and the ratio of mean sectoral incomes is also constant, the shift of population between sectors at first produces a widening in inequality and then a narrowing. In his model, the U arises because the sector with the higher mean income into which population is shifting (non-agriculture) is also the sector with the higher internal inequality. Varying numerical assumptions concerning intrasectoral inequalities and sectoral income ratios place the maximum inequality at a proportion of population anywhere from 0.6 in agriculture to 0.8. Robinson (1976) demonstrates that the existence of a U does not depend on whether the expanding sector has higher income or higher inequality, but only on the presence of intersectoral differences.[19]

Fields (1980) divides the economy into *n* sectors and decomposes the increase in aggregate income into three components, which he terms: the sector enlargement effect, the sector enrichment effect, and an interaction term. He then applies this decomposition to a two-sector Lewis model and categorizes different phases of growth in that model by different combinations of "modern sector enlargement", "modern sector enrichment", or "traditional sector enrichment". He argues that modern sector enrichment results in an increase in inequality in the relative distribution, which is tolerable because average incomes are rising even though there is no change in the poverty population. Modern sector enlargement

---

[19]Robinson decomposed the variance of income in a two-sector model. See Fields (1980) who derives a similar result for the Gini coefficient. See also Lewis (1972) who argues that his dualistic model generates increasing inequality for the same reasons that Kuznets notes.

leads to a U-path for relative inequality, but an increase in average income and a decline in absolute poverty.[20] Traditional sector enrichment results in decreases in inequality and less poverty.

We now use the decomposition of variance approach as a framework for analyzing both the initial worsening of the distribution and the existence of the turning point in the U or J.

3.3. Factors determining distributional trends

The initial decline in the share of income of the poor is inevitable and arises through the introduction of a small high-income island in a large low-income sea. Avoiding the initial increase in relative inequality with development would require that there be a narrowing of the income gap between the two sectors and/or that the distribution of income within the sectors become more equal. Neither process is likely without specific policy interventions. In developing countries, increases in agricultural productivity lag increases in non-agricultural productivity and convergence in productivity between sectors occurs quite late in the development process. Initially, the average income gap between sectors therefore increases.[21]

The second factor is the within-sector variances. The typical developing country experiences an initial widening in the distribution of income within agriculture. Avoiding such widening requires one or more of the following: (1) policies targeted at increasing productivity in small farms; (2) agrarian reforms that redistribute land (either access or ownership); or (3) increases in non-agricultural employment opportunities in rural areas. None of these occurs automatically. The first two depend on policy choices and the third is unlikely since industrialization destroys cottage industry and so reduces rather than increase non-agricultural rural employment opportunities. The only non-socialist countries (other than city states) that have avoided this initial widening have been Korea and Taiwan, where initial land reforms redistributed land to the tillers and substantial increases in agricultural productivity occurred early in the industrialization process.[22]

Within the urban sector, growth is also unequalizing. Industrialization starts from reliance on import substitution, usually with extensive subsidization of

---

[20] In this case, welfare judgments about the results depend on the particular welfare function chosen. See Fields (1980, pp. 54–55).

[21] See Kuznets (1966) and Chenery and Syrquin (1975).

[22] See Adelman (1978) and Fei, Ranis and Kuo (1979).

capital accumulation and tolerance, if not active fostering, of oligopolies. This type of industrialization leads to dualistic development patterns within the urban sector, with increasing relative income inequality.

In summary, economic development in the early phase is characterized by: an increase in the share of the population involved in the modern high-income (and usually high variance) sector of the economy; an increase in the income gap between the high-income and the low-income sectors of the economy; and increases in inequality within both the high-income and the low-income sectors. Overall, the tendency is for inequality to increase for a considerable time. Simulations with simple models that incorporate a turning point indicate that inequality increases until at least more than half the population is in the high income sector.[23] The existence of such a turning point in more complex models is not guaranteed.

As the process of industrialization unfolds, there is no automatic tendency for the distribution of income to improve. Brazil, for example, experienced a J-shaped transition in the period of rapid growth in the late 1960s and early 1970s. Korea, Taiwan, and Japan (in the post Meiji period) followed the U-shaped pattern. Whether inequality does or does not decrease in the late stage of the transition depends upon the policies which countries follow. In particular, it depends upon the extent to which the policies adopted narrow the mean income gap between sectors; decrease the dispersion of income within the modern sector; and affect the relative speed of absorption of labor into the modern sector.

Policies aimed at achieving convergence between rural and urban incomes necessarily entail increasing the rate of growth of agricultural incomes above those of urban incomes. This, in turn, requires raising the productivity of agriculture in order to achieve convergence in productivity between the two sectors while allowing the transfer of resources from agriculture to industry required for industrialization. Reduction of inequality within urban areas, the second possible source of reduced inequality, requires fostering labor-intensive growth and stressing human-resource-investment policies which widen access to education. The combination of these policies will raise non-agricultural wages and equalize the distribution of urban wage income. The contrast between Taiwan and Korea, on the one hand, and countries such as Brazil and Turkey, can in part be explained by their differences in policy choices along these lines.[24]

---

[23]See the models of Kuznets, Robinson and Fields cited earlier. See also Frank and Webb (1977) and Adelman and Morris (1973).

[24]Differences in initial conditions are also important. Dervis and Robinson (1980) use various decomposition techniques to analyze the role of between-group and within-group differences in "explaining" overall inequality in Turkey, using a variety of definitions of "groups", including socioeconomic status, region, and sector. See also other articles in Ozbudun and Ulusan (1981). For the Brazil case, see Bergsman (1979) and Taylor et al. (1980).

Table 19.1
Trends in income distribution and poverty, 1960–1980

	Overall		Eliminating inter-country inequality[a]		Eliminating within-country inequality[a]	
	1960	1980	1960	1980	1960	1980
Income distribution (Gini coefficient[b])						
All non-communist						
developing countries	0.544	0.602	0.450	0.468	0.333	0.404
Low-income	0.407	0.450	0.383	0.427	0.113	0.118
Middle-income, non-oil	0.603	0.569	0.548	0.514	0.267	0.251
Oil-exporting	0.575	0.612	0.491	0.503	0.328	0.375
Poverty (poverty ratio[c] – percentages)						
All non-communist						
developing countries	46.8	30.1	5.2	0.9	8.8	3.5
World	39.8	22.4	9.9	1.6	6.3	2.0

[a] The sum of the only-within and only-between country inequalities does not add up to the overall total because of inter-correlations between the two.

[b] The numbers labeled Gini coefficients are measures of the degree of concentration of the size distribution of income. A higher figure indicates greater inequality.

[c] Percentage of population falling below the poverty level (held fixed in real purchasing power). The definition of absolute poverty adopted for these calculations is that of the World Bank: an annual per capita income of less than U.S. $50 (1960). National currencies were converted into dollars using the Kravis purchasing power parity index for 1975.

Source: Irma Adelman (1985).

3.4. Postwar trends

The trends in inequality during the last two decades are consistent with the stylized facts described above. Table 19.1 presents summary data on income concentration and on the poverty ratio from 1960 to 1980 in groups of non-socialist developing countries. The figures in the table were calculated by estimating the size distribution of income in each country by regressing the parameters of rural and urban Pareto distributions against various economic characteristics of the two sectors in individual countries. The estimated rural and urban frequency distributions were aggregated numerically in each country to generate national distributions. The national distributions were then aggregated numerically into regional distributions distinguished by levels of development.[25]

[25] The method is explained in Adelman (1985).

The figures in the Table 19.1 indicate that, between 1960 and 1980, income inequality in the group of non-communist developing countries increased substantially. But separate groups of developing countries were subject to different trends in income concentration. Concentration increased quite markedly in the group of low-income non-socialist countries and in the group of oil-exporting countries, and decreased significantly in the middle-income non-oil-exporting countries. Nevertheless, despite the overall increase in inequality, the percentage of the population with income falling below a poverty level defined as a fixed level of real purchasing power declined by a third during this period.

To sort out the relative contributions to these trends of "within-country" and "between-country" inequality, two experiments were performed. In columns 3 and 4 of Table 19.1, per capita income in each country was set equal to the worldwide average income; the only source of inequality in these columns is inequality within each country. In columns 5 and 6, the opposite experiment was performed; all individuals in each country were assumed to have a per capita income equal to the country average. The only source of inequality in columns 5 and 6 is therefore inequality among countries.

It is clear from these experiments that both within-country inequality and among-country inequality increased between 1960 and 1980. The growth process inside the non-socialist developing countries has generated greater income disparities within countries. The dispersion of growth rates among these countries has also increased since the middle-income countries grew considerably more rapidly than the poorest non-socialist developing countries, and the dispersion in growth rates among the oil-exporting countries increased as well.

The experiments also indicate that both within-country and among-country inequality are important contributors to overall inequality in the non-socialist developing countries as a group. Within-country inequality is the more important in explaining total inequality, but reductions in either source of inequality can make important contributions to reducing poverty in these countries. Either, admittedly extreme, Gedanken experiment would result in the virtual elimination of poverty. In order to reduce poverty in developing countries, therefore, one must both foster more participatory growth processes and accelerate their growth rates.

4. Theoretical paradigms

There has been continuing controversy about alternative theoretical explanations for the stylized facts described above. Part of the theoretical controversy about the determinants of the dynamics of the distribution of income arises from the use of different concepts of "the distribution of income". Before discussing alternative theoretical paradigms, one must therefore sort out the different concepts of distribution in common use.

4.1. Concepts of income distribution

At least three different concepts of income distribution can be distinguished: (1) the functional distribution, (2) the extended functional distribution, and (3) the size distribution. The functional distribution refers to the shares of the national income accruing to the primary factors of production – land, labor, and capital. The extended functional distribution disaggregates the functional distribution by sector and mode of production.[26] The appropriate disaggregation depends on the country and the problem under study. In most developing counties, for example, extended functional distributions which are of interest would differentiate: capitalists and workers in both rural and urban areas; subsistence and commercial farmers; different tenancy forms in agriculture; and self-employed and other workers in the urban sector. Finally, the size distribution of income looks at the society disaggregated by income level. It describes the shares of national income accruing to each quantile (e.g. decile, quintile, or vintile) of recipients. "Recipients" can be defined in a number of ways: households, total population, economically active population, or households per capita. Conceptually, the latter is probably the most appropriate for welfare analysis. The size distribution includes all sources of income, including transfers.[27] A separate issue relates to the time period to which the data refer (e.g. current income, "permanent income", or lifetime income).

Most economic theory relates to the dynamics of the functional distribution of income, but, in many ways, this is the least interesting concept for either political or welfare analysis. The functional distribution would be of political interest if the major political conflicts were defined only by the nature of the primary assets owned. This is the orthodox Marxian view. Contemporary Marxists, however, consider various extended functional distributions and argue about which version is appropriate.[28] In developing countries, the major interest-group cleavages include: urban and rural groups; major industrial categories; and importers (including those who import intermediate and capital goods) and exporters

---

[26]Our specification of the extended functional distribution is closely related to the "institutional distribution" specified in a social accounting matrix (SAM). Using a SAM framework, Dervis, de Melo and Robinson (1982, ch. 12), distinguish five types of income distributions. The approach is described in more detail below in the survey of policy models.

[27]There are lingering conceptual and empirical problems concerning the treatment of government expenditures (expenditure incidence), taxes, and undistributed profits. Also, there is no uniform convention used in empirical measurement concerning the appropriate choice of the unit of analysis (e.g. workers, individuals, households, or "adult equivalents").

[28]For a discussion of modern Marxist approaches, see de Janvry (1981) and Brenner (1977).

(including those of primary commodities).[29] The simple functional distribution does not incorporate these distinctions and therefore cannot be used to portray the economic pressures operating on the policy process in a typical developing country. The extended functional distribution provides a better framework for analyzing these policy conflicts and is therefore the distributional concept that is the most useful for understanding interactions between economics and politics in developing countries. By contrast, the size distribution of income is the distributional concept most relevant to welfare analysis if one believes that people in similar economic circumstances (including stage in life cycle) ought to be valued similarly.[30]

One way to distinguish among theories is by indicating the kind of distribution they treat. As noted above, most theoretical work has been concerned with the functional distribution. While there is a significant literature on models of the size distribution, only a small body of theoretical work seeks to explain the size distribution by taking an integrated view of the demand and supply of income-generating attributes.

4.2. Models of the functional distribution

Concern with the functional distribution has been a part of economics since its earliest beginnings. For our purposes we need only consider a few strands of the literature. We start from the classical economists and trace out two modern approaches, one through Marx and Cambridge, England, and the other through the development of neoclassical general equilibrium theory.

4.2.1. The classical view

In the time of Ricardo and Mill, the primary distributional issues were the distribution of power and income among classes defined by their ownership of the major factor of production in the rural and urban sectors: the landed elites, on the one hand, and the rising manufacturing groups, on the other. It is these distributional issues which the classical models sought to illuminate.

Rather than attributing the dynamics of relative class shares to political forces, the classical models of distribution were based on the characteristics of the production system and how it changes over time. Of the classical economists, Ricardo has had the greatest influence on modern development theory. Ricardo's

---

[29]For discussion of these political cleavages by political scientists, see Nelson (1979), Huntington and Nelson (1976), Bienen and Diejomaoh (1981), and Danielson and Keles (1981). For discussions by economists, see Lipton (1977), Adelman and Morris (1973), and Chenery et al. (1974).

[30]In interpreting aggregate inequality indicators, one must thus also take into account population characteristics such as age structure, family size, and so forth.

theory of distribution attributes long-run variations in the functional distribution to systematic changes in returns to factors at the margin. He distinguished between the market wage rate, which varies with the demand and supply of labor, and the natural wage rate, which is the long-run equilibrium rate around which the market rate fluctuates. The natural rate tends towards subsistence, but subsistence is a relative concept. The cost of the subsistence bundle is set by the marginal productivity of land, and its content is determined by socio-cultural norms and customs. Population growth, responding to the margin between the market and the natural wage rate, serves to keep market wages close to the natural wage rate.

The employment of labor depends upon the rate of capital accumulation. Accumulation, in turn, is a function of the surplus over wage payments ("net income" in Ricardo's definition) and of the difference between the actual rate of profit and the socio-culturally determined minimal rate of compensation for risk-bearing.[31] The rate of profit in Ricardo is also set by the natural wage rate and varies inversely with it. Diminishing returns in agriculture lead to a natural tendency for profits to decline. The decline can be checked periodically by technological innovations in agriculture and in wage-goods industries, but, since Ricardo believed that these innovations are also subject to diminishing returns, this is a temporary phenomenon.

Total land is fixed, varies in quality, and is cultivated so that, at the margin, the last unit yields no rent. Furthermore, in Ricardo, wage payments above the natural wage are also part of profit. The share of profits is therefore determined as a residual over and above natural wages on that portion of land which yields no rent. In a stationary state, profits go to zero, the wage stays at subsistence, and the residual goes to rent – the fixed factor captures the entire surplus. However, in their dynamics, the classical economists argued that the speed of approaching the stationary state involved a tradeoff between growth and distribution, given that the subsistence level is determined by cultural and political factors and accumulation is out of profits alone.[32]

There is no feedback in the classical system between the functional distribution of income and demand for commodities. Distribution is purely a technological and socio-cultural phenomenon. In an economy in which all goods are internationally traded and in which there is always full employment, this view of the functional distribution is theoretically consistent. But these assumptions are not applicable to the typical developing country in which there is both open and disguised unemployment, and in which non-traded goods are extremely important. Furthermore, in the medium run, political forces influence both the choice

---

[31] There are many expositions of Ricardo that make this argument, if not always using this terminology. See, for example, Blaug (1962) and Adelman (1961).

[32] This point is nicely made in Lindert and Williamson (1985).

of development strategy and the evolution of the institutional structure of the economy. Rates of return to factors, accumulation patterns, and hence functional shares thus depend on political as well as economic choices and not just on technology and tastes.[33]

4.2.2. Dual economy models

In his famous article on the labor-surplus economy, Lewis (1954) saw himself as just updating the classical model. The major difference between Lewis and Ricardo arises from Lewis's assumption that there exists a quasi-permanent supply of surplus labor in agriculture in a developing country. As a result, the market wage and the natural wage are always equal and industrial labor is always paid a wage which is a constant multiple of the agricultural subsistence wage. Furthermore, the subsistence wage is fixed over time in real terms. Employment in the modern sector is determined by the marginal productivity of labor, which in turn is a function of the capital stock in the modern sector. Thus, the share of wages in national income is determined by agricultural productivity and by the accumulation of capital in industry. Since unlimited supplies of labor are available at a constant wage, the reinvestment of any part of profits will increase the share of profits in national income. The functional distribution of income therefore moves against wage earners. The distributional path is set in a "U" from the beginning, and there is no tradeoff between growth and distribution. Growth only determines how fast a country traverses the "U".

What happens to rent as a share of the national product depends on the ratio of population to land and on agricultural technology. In overpopulated countries, competition for land among cultivators sets the level of rent equal to the surplus over subsistence in agriculture. As long as there continues to be surplus labor in agriculture, the benefits of technical progress in agriculture accrue to the landlords and to the profit earners in the industrial sector. It is therefore puzzling that Lewis argues that the owners of plantations have no interest in land-augmenting technical progress [Lewis (1954, p. 410)]. He also argues that, since capitalists have an interest in keeping the level of subsistence in agriculture low, they are against technical progress in agriculture. But this conflicts with his argument that technical progress does not increase the subsistence level of the farmer and that the cost of the subsistence bundle drops with technical progress.

Fei and Ranis (1964) considered themselves to be providing a mathematical implementation of the Lewis model. In fact, while starting from Lewis, their model is quite neoclassical in spirit.[34] While Lewis emphasized the role of profits

---

[33] For an exposition of theories of the state and their relevance to development, see Chapter 3 by Bardhan in Volume I of this Handbook, and de Janvry (1981).

[34] Lewis also has some disagreements with the characterization of his model by Fei and Ranis. See Lewis (1972).

in determining the size of the investment effort and hence the rate of growth, Fei and Ranis focused on the issue of labor absorption and the "turning point" when the surplus agricultural labor has all migrated and the urban wage starts to rise. At that point, they argue, the functional distribution will also start to improve. Theirs is an optimistic view of the development process, with no groups losing absolutely as development unfolds and with the upturn of the "U" roughly corresponding with the labor-absorption turning point. The distributional implications of this model have been sorted out by Fields (1980, ch. 3).[35]

4.2.3. The Marxian model

Marx was the first classical economist to introduce an explicit ethical judgment into a theory of the functional distribution. His ethical judgment was the same as that of the neoclassical economists who followed: each factor of production is entitled to the value of its product, although they differed in their definition of "product". For Marx, as for the other classical economists, capital is just congealed labor. Based on his value judgment that labor ought to retain ownership of the fruits of its labor, Marx argued that the return to capital as well as wages should belong to labor.[36]

In Marx's theory of the operation of the capitalist economy, labor is not paid a wage which reflects its marginal product. Instead, labor is paid a wage that varies cyclically around a socio-culturally defined subsistence level. The rest accrues to owners of capital. The difference between the wage bill and total income constitutes "surplus value". The ratio of surplus value to the wage bill is the "rate of exploitation of labor".

The long-run dynamics of capitalist development, according to Marx, are dismally unjust to workers. In the long run, there is a tendency for the productivity of capital to rise and for the capital–labor ratio to increase. Since, unlike Ricardo, Marx believed that population growth is exogenous, there is a secularly rising excess supply of labor (the "reserve army") with a declining per capita income for workers at a secularly varying subsistence wage.[37]

In the Marxian model, the rate of accumulation depends upon the distribution of income between wage earners and profit takers, since wage earners do not save. In turn, the rate of accumulation determines the rate of technical change, the employment of labor, and hence the functional shares in the next period. The evolution of the Marxian economy is thus uniquely determined by the initial

[35]See also Fei, Ranis and Kuo (1979) and Ranis (1978).Fields' models have been discussed above.
[36]The Marxian view also treats labor's claim collectively rather than individually. This class view enables him to argue that the returns to past congealed labor should accrue to current workers.
[37]He also argued that there is a secular tendency for the rate of profit to decline, a proposition that has since been argued is inconsistent with his other assumptions. See Adelman (1961) and Morishima (1985).

conditions of the system (primary endowments, technology, and institutions) and by its structural parameters reflecting technology and tastes.

4.2.4. Neo-Keynesian models

Kaldor combines the Marxian assumption that all saving is out of profits with a Harrod–Domar dynamization of the Keynesian model. In a two-class society, the choice of growth rate determines the functional distribution of income. The causal chain goes from fixed growth rate to required fixed investment rate, to which the economy adjusts by changing the distribution of income between savers and non-savers. When the society is disaggregated into an extended functional distribution, the Kaldorian specification is not sufficient to derive a unique functional distribution. Furthermore, it is not obvious that, in practice, investment drives savings in this manner. There tends to be a mutual adjustment between savings and investment in mixed economies. In this case, there is no unique link between macro adjustment and the functional distribution, even in a two-class society.

Kalecki's theory of economic development and income distribution is more subtle than Kaldor's. Like Kaldor, Kalecki (1971) posited that development is capital constrained.[38] Investment, however, is constrained not only by the supply of savings, but also by an absorptive-capacity constraint imposed by limitations of skills and natural resources and by a shortage of wage goods. The latter two constraints on investment arise from the need to engage in a non-inflationary growth process. Inflation must be avoided in order to prevent falls in the real incomes of the poor and of wage earners whose nominal incomes are sticky. Accordingly, development of the industrial sector is constrained by the rate of growth of agricultural output, a theme which was later taken up by Fellner and sounds very modern indeed. In Kalecki's view, the natural tendency is for development to worsen the distribution of income and reduce the incomes of the poor. He argued that, in a mixed economy, investment is financed partially from private and government savings and partially through inflation. The major burden of inflation-financed investment is borne by the poor since the rich have sufficient political and market power to shift the incidence of taxation and rising production costs to the poor.

The theoretical strand that runs from Marx through Kaldor and Kalecki has been used by Lance Taylor and others to build a family of models that link the macroeconomic behavior of the economy to distributional outcomes. In its recent incarnation, this approach is often referred to as the "Latin American Structuralist School". We will discuss these models below in the section on economywide

---

[38] For an exposition of Kalecki's views on economic development, see Feiwel and Klein (1975, ch. 16), and Kalecki (1966).

policy models and compare them with alternative approaches to linking macro and distributional processes.[39]

4.2.5. The neoclassical approach

Partly in response to Marx, the Austrian School (e.g. Menger, Boehm-Bawerk) focused on the role of capital as a true factor of production, emphasizing the role of time. Schumpeter, in turn, added the role of entrepreneurship, including risk-bearing, as a factor of production deserving remuneration. They argue that, at the margin, each factor should be paid its marginal product, with thrift and risk-bearing deserving an appropriate return. This school provided a legitimation of Marxian "exploitation" and a transition to the neoclassical "marginalist revolution".

In the final fruition of the neoclassical model, provided by the Walrasian model of competitive equilibrium, all factors are paid the value of their marginal products, all markets clear, and the result is a Pareto optimum in which no one can be made better off without making someone else worse off. The notion of a Pareto optimum defines an "efficient" equilibrium which is consistent with any distribution of initial endowments and, hence, of income. Negishi (1960) proved that a competitive equilibrium can be described as the result of maximizing a "Paretian" social welfare function consisting of the weighted sum of individual utilities. The weights in the "Paretian" welfare function are determined endogenously and depend on the initial distribution of endowments.[40]

Thus, even if one accepts fully the apparatus of neoclassical general equilibrium theory, one need not accept the distributional implications of a purely competitive equilibrium as either optimal or even desirable. If the static distribution of income generated by a particular structure of endowments in a competitive market economy is considered undesirable, there are a number of policy choices available for altering distributional outcomes: (1) a one-time change in the distribution of initial endowments; (2) post-equilibrium transfers of income; or (3) either pre- or post-equilibrium adjustments to market prices through taxes and subsidies. In theory, in a static world, the first should engender no efficiency costs, the second may (if lump-sum transfers are impossible), and the third will definitely lead to incentive distortions and hence an efficiency–equity tradeoff. In a dynamic setting, if the asset transfers must be repeated, there will be incentive effects as agents anticipate the policy.

---

[39] This approach is also discussed in Chapter 17 by Arida and Taylor and in Chapter 18 by Robinson in this Handbook.

[40] Given these endowments, the social welfare function whose maximum yields a competitive equilibrium has welfare weights that are inversely proportional to the marginal utilities of individual incomes. For a discussion of the Negishi theorem in the context of planning models, see Ginsburgh and Waelbroeck (1981).

We shall discuss each of these approaches to inequality in the policy sections below. In general, based on the empirical and theoretical evidence, we tend to favor primary reliance on asset-oriented approaches, using a broad notion of assets that includes human and physical assets, as well as access to institutions for accumulation, access to jobs, and rights to the use of assets in the productive process. Research to date indicates that pure transfers, while potentially beneficial, must be maintained indefinitely and are too expensive for the typical developing country. Direct adjustments to market prices are usually less effective and have efficiency consequences (including strains and growth costs) which must be balanced against their distributive benefits.

Implicit in the concern with the functional distribution, reflected in the theories discussed above, is the assumption that a stable relationship exists between the functional and size distributions. The literature on distribution is full of statements linking a higher wage share with increases in relative equality. Empirical evidence for such a link is tenuous, at best. Indeed, empirical models that explicitly derive the size distribution from the extended functional distribution find no stable relationship.[41] Therefore, if one is concerned with the size distribution, one must analyze it directly.

4.3. Models of the size distribution

Theories of the size distribution start at the individual level and are micro in nature.[42] They attempt to describe the course of the size distribution of income by looking at dynamic changes in the distribution of the supply side of factors. They take as given the economically, socially, and institutionally determined dynamics of the rates of remuneration of factors and the configuration of the overall supply of jobs and opportunities in the economy. These givens are the very factors stressed by the classical economists when discussing the long-run dynamics of the functional distribution of income.

4.3.1. Supply models

Meade (1964) and Champernowne (1953) are good starting points for theories of the size distribution. They start from the basic definition of personal income as the market value of "sales" of services from human and non-human capital. Taking the distribution of rates of return to human and non-human wealth as given, changes over time in the size distribution of income are, as Fisher (1912,

---

[41]See Adelman and Robinson (1978, 1987) and Lysy and Taylor (1980). These studies are discussed further below.

[42]Sahota (1978, 1986) has done two surveys of this literature.

p. 513) pointed out, due to "inheritance, constantly modified by thrift, ability, industry, luck, and fraud". Inherited fortunes, both human and non-human, play a central role and determine the distribution of initial endowments among households. The sale of services from these endowments (affected by market conditions and "industry") and the prices at which they are sold (affected by ability, luck, inherited opportunities, and choice of strategies, policies, and institutions at the macro level) set the gross incomes of households.[43] Accumulation and decumulation (affected by thrift, inheritance laws, and marriage patterns) determine the changes in individual endowments over time.

There are good reasons to presume that the rich get systematically higher rates of return on their assets, both human and non-human, and that the rate of saving from profit income is higher than from non-profit income. These stylized facts give rise to unequalizing tendencies which, if not combatted by social policy (e.g. inheritance laws, equal opportunity legislation, tax policy, and compensatory social programs), lead the size distribution to worsen over time. But even if one were to start from a completely equal distribution of wealth and assume only that there is a stochastic distribution of luck and that the rate of accumulation is proportional to endowments, these assumptions suffice to generate a lognormal distribution of wealth and income in the long run.[44]

In the literature, there are different schools of thought about the relative weight of human and non-human capital in determining the dynamics of distributional changes. The Chicago school posits an explicit intertemporal optimizing model of intra-generational accumulation and inter-generational transfers that is used to explain investment and inheritance patterns over time.[45] The Cambridge school, represented by Meade and Champernowne, uses reduced-form models that do not explicitly specify the behavior of agents.

Empirical tests of these theories [Pryor (1973) and Clague (1974)] demonstrate that no more than 50 percent of household income changes can be explained by systematic forces; the rest is in the stochastic term. In addition, the direct policy implications of the analysis are meager. In effect, according to these models, the poor are poor because they are born of poor parents, marry other poor folk, and/or are unlucky. We will consider such "micro based" policies, in the context of developing countries, in more detail in a separate policy section below. The theories of the personal distribution impound macro processes in their ceteris paribus conditions. Unfortunately, relatively little can be accomplished to make the distribution of income more equal without affecting the macro environment in which micro actors operate.

[43] For consideration of human capital, see Becker (1967). Meade (1964) and Champernowne (1953) consider the role of non-human capital.
[44] See Wold and Whittle (1957).
[45] See Becker (1967, 1983) and Chiswick (1974). In this area, one can also include Blinder (1974) as part of the Chicago tradition. See the survey by Sahota (1978).

4.3.2. Supply–demand models

There are a few models in the micro tradition that attempt to capture demand–supply interactions. Beginning with Tinbergen (1956), a class of models of the size distribution has been based on the notion that an individual's income is determined by the sale of a variety of personal attributes.[46] The vector of attributes includes not only ownership of factors of production, but also such characteristics as race, sex, social status, geographic location, and aptitudes. These represent the supply side.

The demand for these attributes is generated by the production profile of the economy, as well as by social, cultural, and political institutions. The "price" associated with each attribute is thus determined by the interaction of supply and demand forces that extend beyond traditional markets, deep into the structure of society. This framework is useful, for example, for studying the social and private costs of barriers to mobility inherent in such institutions and attitudes as: discrimination, caste, social stratification, and segmented labor markets. There are no models that implement this approach fully.[47] The applied general equilibrium models discussed below are also in this spirit, although they do not disaggregate by attributes and do not have sophisticated models of the supply of factors.

5. Economywide policy models

The theories summarized in the previous section provide us with alternative perspectives on the long-run determinants of the functional and size distributions of income. These perspectives suggest different approaches to policy intervention, including choice of instruments and time horizon. Theories focusing on the functional distribution suggest that economywide interventions are required. By contrast, the theories of the size distribution suggest that micro based interventions focusing on the characteristics of households represent the best approach. Our approach to policy is eclectic, drawing from both strands.

For any policy analysis, however, the underlying theories and theoretical models need to be given empirical content. Starting around 1970 (earlier in India), efforts were begun to incorporate distributional concerns in empirical models. These models have been applied in a number of countries to evaluate the distributional implications of alternative choices of development strategies. We

---

[46]See Ritzen (1977) and Adelman and Levy (1984) for applications of such models to developing countries.
[47]A model of the U.S. labor market by Bennett and Bergmann (1986) comes close. See also Robinson and Dervis (1977) who use a dynamic model based on transition matrices to explore the distributional impact of socioeconomic mobility in developing countries.

review these economywide models below and then review the policy findings in a separate section.

5.1. Linear multiplier models

Initial attempts to introduce distribution into linear multisector models involved closing the input–output models on the demand side by modelling the links between production, factor incomes, and consumption. The first approaches assumed an exogenously given distribution of income, calculated the corresponding consumption patterns, incorporated the sectoral consumptions into the final demand vector of the input–output tables, and then used the Leontief inverse to calculate the implied changes in production and employment.[48] These models did not specify how the poor would get the income to purchase the basic needs bundle, nor did they worry about the consistency between the income distribution induced by the structure of production and that required to generate the assumed demand vector. Contrary to expectations, major changes in the distribution of income were found to have only minor impact on the consumption vector (about 1 to 2 percent, at most, in a few sectors) and hence only minor effects on the patterns of production and employment.

Subsequent approaches made changes in distribution consistent with the patterns of production through the factor income side as well as through the demand side. They were implemented first by iterating between the initially assumed distribution of income and the distribution of income derived from the pattern of consumption and employment until the two became mutually consistent.[49]

Later, the input–output accounting framework was enlarged into a Social Accounting Matrix (SAM) in order to maintain accounting consistency between the patterns of production, the institutional and household distributions of income, and the patterns of consumption.[50] The earlier linear models can now be seen as special cases within the SAM framework.[51]

In the SAM, value added is distributed first to factors of production to generate the functional distribution of income. Functional income is, in turn, distributed to "institutions" which include categories such as government, enterprises, households, investment (the capital account), and the rest of the world.

---

[48]See, for example, the Indian Third Five Year Plan, Cline (1972); and Weisskoff (1970, 1985). The Indian Third Five Year Plan is described in Srinivasan and Bardhan (1974).

[49]Thorbecke and Sengupta (1972) apply such an approach to Colombia.

[50]Further discussion of SAMs is provided in Chapter 18 by Robinson in this Handbook. Pyatt and Round (1985) collect a number of studies which include examples of SAMs focused on distributional issues. See, especially, the survey chapters by Thorbecke (1985) and Stone (1985).

[51]Weisskoff (1985), in his updating of his earlier work, notes that his model can be recast into a SAM framework.

These categories, suitably disaggregated, can be used to generate the "extended functional" distribution described earlier. Finally, the household accounts are disaggregated by income ranges (and, perhaps, by socioeconomic groups as well) to generate the overall size distribution.[52]

These SAMs can be converted into linear models by assuming constant distribution and expenditure coefficients, in addition to the standard Leontief constant production coefficients. The linear model enables the use of multiplier analysis to trace through the effects of changes in some exogenous variables on income distribution. However, unlike the input–output table, all SAMs are square, with column and row sums equal by accounting convention. Hence, the coefficients in every column of the full SAM sum to one and there is no inverse. In order to construct a multiplier model, one or more accounts in the SAM must be specified as being exogenous. The result is a partitioned SAM, with some columns exogenous and some rows excluded. Such a SAM coefficient matrix is given below, with the partitioned structure of non-zero coefficient matrices indicating the circular flow of income from activities to value added (V) to endogenous institutional incomes (Y), and finally back as final demand for goods (F).

$$
A^* = \begin{bmatrix} A & 0 & F \\ V & 0 & 0 \\ 0 & Y & T \end{bmatrix},
\tag{1}
$$

with the following matrices:

A^* = SAM coefficients ($n + m + k, n + m + k$),
A = input–output coefficients (n, n),
V = value added coefficients (m, n),
Y = income distribution coefficients (k, n),
F = expenditure coefficients (n, k),
T = inter-institutional transfer coefficients (k, k),

and where:

n = number of sectors,
m = number of value added categories, and
k = number of endogenous institutions.

Given the choice of exogenous accounts, the balance equations can be written:

$$
A^* \begin{bmatrix} x \\ v \\ y \end{bmatrix} = \begin{bmatrix} e^x \\ e^v \\ e^y \end{bmatrix},
\tag{2}
$$

---

[52] See Dervis, de Melo and Robinson (1982), Pyatt and Thorbecke (1976), and Thorbecke (1985) for a discussion of this mapping process in SAM-based models.

with the following vectors:

x = sectoral supply $(n, 1)$,
v = value added by categories $(m, 1)$,
y = institutional incomes $(k, 1)$,
e^x = exogenous sectoral demand $(n, 1)$,
e^v = exogenous value added $(m, 1)$, and
e^y = exogenous institutional incomes $(k, 1)$.

Inverting A^*, we can write the multiplier matrix equation relating changes in sectoral supply, valued added, and institutional income to changes in the exogenous variables:

$$\begin{bmatrix} x \\ v \\ y \end{bmatrix} = M \begin{bmatrix} e^x \\ e^v \\ e^y \end{bmatrix}, \tag{3}$$

where $M = (I - A^*)^{-1}$.

Such multiplier models have been used to analyze the distributional impacts of large investment projects, of changes in government expenditure patterns, and of changes in development strategy.[53] Given the special structure of the circular flow captured in the SAM, it is also possible to decompose the multiplier matrix into terms that trace the direct or impact effects of a change in exogenous variables, the within-block effects, and the between-block effects.[54] Such a decomposition is very useful for determining the importance of indirect or "net SAM linkages" that capture how policies and programs affect the extended functional and size distributions of income.

The choice of which accounts to specify as being exogenous is important. Standard practice is to pick one or more of the capital, government, and rest-of-the-world accounts, justifying the choice on the basis of macroeconomic theory. The resulting multiplier model is completely demand driven, since no constraints on supply are specified, and is thus very Keynesian in spirit. In each case, a shock is defined as a change in some elements of the exogenous columns. The computed multipliers are sensitive to the initial choice of exogenous ac-

[53]See, for example, Bell and Devarajan (1985), Grais (1981), Pyatt, Roe and Associates (1977), and Pyatt and Round (1979). Thorbecke (1986) has developed a linear optimizing model that uses the SAM as a constraint set. In his model, a poverty measure based on the incomes of socioeconomic groups is the maximand. The model is used to explore how different degrees of societal aversion to poverty affect the optimal structure of the economy.
[54]Versions of this decomposition approach are described in Stone (1985) and Pyatt and Round (1979).

counts, and the realism of the resulting model must be judged on the basis of the particular question under study.[55]

The multipliers computed from a SAM overstate the adjustment to exogenous shocks. First, they do not allow for substitution effects in production, consumption, and international trade. Second, there are no resource constraints on the adjustment. Finally, the linear model derived from the SAM has no room for price effects and assumes that marginal and average coefficients are the same. It does, however, correctly portray the interdependence between production and the primary and secondary distributions of income.

5.2. Non-linear, non-market models

There are a few examples of models incorporating income distribution developed during the 1970s which went beyond the linear framework, but did not seek to incorporate market interactions endogenously. A number of models were developed at the World Bank which incorporated distributional phenomena into an essentially dynamic input–output framework. For example, Gupta (1977a, 1977b) built models of Indonesia and Korea which were very close to standard dynamic input–output models in that they incorporated demand-driven growth paths constrained by sectoral investment allocation. However, he also incorporated various income flows and income distribution in the models, ending up with a mix of a SAM-based model including various macro, income–expenditure constraints, and a dynamic input–output model constrained by capital stock growth. These models have non-linear elements and incorporate wage and price equations, but do not seek to model market interactions.

Another class of non-linear models is represented by the long-run, economic-demographic, BACHUE models.[56] These models were developed at the International Labour Organization (ILO) and were intended to provide a modelling framework that could be applied to a number of countries. They explicitly incorporate the extended functional and size distributions of income, as well as functional relations between economic and demographic variables. While the BACHUE models are non-linear, they have a nearly-recursive structure that made them feasible to solve. They solved for wages and prices endogenously and also achieved balance between supply and demand, but not through endogenous

[55]Cardoso and Taylor (1979), for example, use the term "identity based" model to describe their Sraffian, fixed-coefficient model of distribution in Brazil. The issue of macro closure of the model, which is implicit in the choice of exogenous accounts in the SAM, carries over to the more elaborate CGE models. The question is discussed in detail in Chapter 18 by Robinson in this Handbook.
[56]The BACHUE model of the Phillippines by Rodgers et al. (1977) is perhaps the best example of this family of models. The BACHUE models are surveyed by Sanderson (1980), who compares them with CGE models. See also the critical review of BACHUE by Arthur and McNicholl (1975) and the response by Rodgers, Hopkins and Wery (1978).

price variation. The models focus on demographic variables and the labor market, with a much sketchier treatment of production and structural change.

5.3. Computable general equilibrium (CGE) models

The theoretical roots of CGE models are diverse. Their structure is sufficiently flexible to portray, at one extreme, a purely neoclassical paradigm of complete, competitive markets with perfect price flexibility and, at the other extreme, an economy characterized by a number of "structuralist" features, as in the classical and neo-Keynesian paradigms. For example, some models that are neoclassical in spirit specify perfectly mobile capital and labor, and also have all prices flexible.[57] Most development economists, however, do not believe that such a specification offers a reasonable description of a developing country. Realistic models of developing countries usually combine structuralist features with some standard, neoclassical, general equilibrium features.

The derivation of CGE models from SAMs is discussed in Chapter 18 by Robinson in this Handbook. We focus here only on the modifications of the basic CGE model needed to capture distributional phenomena.[58]

5.3.1. Incorporating income distribution into CGE models

Starting from standard CGE models, both the institutional structure and the household accounts need to be disaggregated. This requires several steps. First, the endogenous institutions need to be defined so that they are both consistent with the extended functional distribution and adequate for mapping income flows to the classification of households by major socioeconomic groups. One must also move from the simpler one-consumer model to a model with many households. The institutional and household classification should delineate socioeconomic groups that are both economically and politically relevant. Second, given the partitioning of the society, a mapping of income sources of endogenous institutions is required. This mapping will consist of both flows from value added and inter-institutional transfers. Third, the mapping from institutions to households, including inter-household transfers, must be specified. Fourth, one must go from the distribution of income to categories of households to the overall size distribution. One way is to specify the distribution of income within each

---

[57]See Shoven and Whalley (1974).
[58]The Adelman and Robinson (1978) CGE model was developed specifically to analyze distributional policy. Dervis, de Melo and Robinson (1982, ch. 12), also discusses in detail how distributional phenomena can be captured in CGE models.

category by a distribution function whose parameters (mean, variance, or log variance) can be estimated from the CGE model itself. The typical CGE model generates not only mean incomes for each functional category but also some income dispersion endogenously, since, for example, both wages and profits can vary by sector of activity. The overall distribution is then generated by aggregating the collection of within-group distributions.[59]

The process described above yields the size distribution by economically-active individuals. Finally, the distribution of income to households can then be derived from the distribution by individual recipients. To achieve this mapping, individual income earners must be grouped into households. One approach is to use a household composition matrix (based on survey data) which describes how individuals in different occupations (including dependents and unemployed) combine into households. This household composition matrix enables one to trace the percolation of a shock from the production side onto household incomes through the employment of economically active members of the households. It is not a decision model portraying occupational choices, labor force participation, or household formation, though it can be seen as a linear reduced form approximation of some elaborate household models. In the short to medium term, it is reasonable to assume that the occupational structure of the labor force and household composition are exogenous.

5.3.2. Macro closure and income distribution

There are three macro balances involved in any SAM-based model: the government deficit, the balance of trade, and the savings–investment balance. In all three, there is a potential for ex ante disequilibrium, which must be reconciled ex post. The manner in which this reconciliation is achieved defines the model's "macro closure" rules.[60] The CGE models built to examine issues of income distribution fall into two broad strands distinguished by their treatment of macro closure, especially with regard to the savings–investment balance. Both strands are "structuralist" in that the models incorporate many rigidities in various markets, include some magnitudes fixed in nominal terms, and/or some fixed relative prices. Where they differ is in the specifics.

One strand achieves savings–investment equilibrium either by having investment adjust to savings [M. de Melo (1979) and de Melo and Robinson (1980, 1982a, 1982b)] or by incorporating price-level adjustments which affect both real savings and real investment [Adelman and Robinson (1978)].

---

[59] The details of this procedure are described in Adelman and Robinson (1978) and Dervis, de Melo and Robinson (1982, ch. 12).

[60] The general issue of macro closure in CGE models is discussed in more detail in Chapter 18 by Robinson in this Handbook.

The second strand draws on Kaldor in specifying fixed aggregate real investment, to which savings must adjust [Lysy and Taylor (1980) and Ahluwalia and Lysy (1979)]. In this second, Latin American structuralist strand, two mechanisms are specified to generate the savings required to match the fixed real investment. The first mechanism relies on a Keynesian multiplier in which real wages adjust, changing employment, aggregate real output, aggregate real income, and hence aggregate savings. The model specifies a fixed nominal wage, with changes in the aggregate price level generating the required changes in the real wage. In addition, markup pricing is commonly assumed in a number of sectors, with supply adjusting passively to meet demand. The second mechanism is Kaldorian. It relies on changes in real wages that shift income between low and high savers to achieve a level of savings that matches the exogenously specified level of investment.

Given their Keynesian flavor, the Latin American structuralist models appear best suited for examining short run adjustment issues. It appears to us unrealistic to assume that nominal wages are fixed over a number of years or that fixed markup rates can be sustained very long. By contrast, models in the first strand were designed for examining the impact of alternative development strategies in the medium run. In the medium run, it seems more likely that there will be mutual adjustment in real savings and investment and that real wages and markup rates will vary to clear markets.

Current work on the impact of stabilization packages on the distribution of income and poverty should draw on both strands. The impact of a stabilization package is felt in the short run. However, devising "structural adjustment" programs to reduce the negative impact of stabilization policies on the poor requires reconciling short-run stabilization policies with medium-term development strategies.

5.4. Models and policy

In empirical applications, we find that the implications for the size distribution are largely unaffected by the significant differences in theoretical specification. Adelman and Robinson (1987) compare the effect of specifying a variety of macro closures from the two strands in a CGE model framework applied to Korea and Brazil. They find the impact of shocks on the size distribution to be virtually identical, and small, under all macro closures. This insensitivity to specification also carries across models not in the CGE family. Comparison of results from a BACHUE model of the Philippines with a CGE model of Korea indicates that the implications for policies aimed at changing the size distribution are very similar, notwithstanding the vast differences in theoretical specification.[61]

---

[61] See Adelman et al. (1979).

There was some sensitivity to differences in initial conditions, especially with regard to land tenure and resource endowments.

Empirical work with all these economywide models has yielded a few robust results:

(1) The extended functional distribution is very sensitive to exogenous and policy shocks.

(2) The size distribution is very insensitive to exogenous and policy shocks. Trends in the size distribution seem to be rooted in initial conditions, including resource endowments, asset distribution, and institutions, all of which are specified exogenously in these models.

(3) The initial effects of policy interventions rapidly dissipate throughout the economy. Programs targeted at specific groups or sectors tend to be very expensive or unsuccessful.

(4) Price changes which have a significant impact on the extended functional distribution are the agricultural terms of trade and the real exchange rate. The latter is especially significant in models that include trade restrictions and import rationing.

(5) Quantity adjustments that have a significant impact on the extended functional distribution relate to structural changes in employment, including population growth, aggregate employment, rural–urban migration, skill composition, and education.

(6) Alternative macro-adjustment mechanisms can have significantly different effects on the extended functional distribution. In particular, Keynesian, Kaldorian, and neoclassical macro models adjust factor shares and/or aggregate employment, and hence the extended functional distribution, differently, given the same exogenous macro shock.

(7) The size distribution is minimally affected by price, quantity, and macro interventions.

(8) The size of the poverty population is more sensitive to policy than the overall size distribution. The trick is to combine growth with little change in the size distribution – a combination that appears to make "trickle down" work.

The robustness in a variety of applied models of the above empirical results to variations in the underlying paradigms, theoretical specification, and functional forms is striking. There are two possible explanations, which are not mutually exclusive. One is that the course of income distribution is determined by factors not included as endogenous in the models such as the distribution of assets, institutional structure of the economy, and the dynamics of technical change. Second, the feasible space circumscribed by the accounting constraints, technology, tastes, and institutions is so small that it allows little room for policy impact, once the economy's basic course is set. We believe that both explanations are true and that the models correctly reflect the great distributional inertia that characterizes the functioning of economic and social systems in non-revolutionary settings in which the scope for institutional reform is limited.

Under either explanation, the modelling results in applied settings suggest that, if the object of income distribution theory is to shed light on policy in practical settings, the theoretical fights among competing paradigms about macro adjustment through changes in the functional distribution are of little practical significance. This is a heartening conclusion since it suggests that discussions of anti-poverty policy need not be dependent on particular macro paradigms and tend to be robust with respect to specific modelling choices. There are two basic reasons for this result. First, households reduce income risk by diversifying their sectoral, occupational, and geographic sources of income, thus decreasing their exposure to market-induced price and wage fluctuations.[62] The result, which the multisectoral models capture, is that the link between the functional and size distributions is diffused. Second, the differing theories of macro adjustment focus on institutional differences in the urban labor market. The agricultural sector is seen as adjusting to macro shocks only by altering its marketable surplus without changes in institutions and technology. The major links to the rest of the economy are through the agricultural terms of trade, migration, and exports. In these models, macro shocks affect the rural distribution only indirectly. Third, substitution possibilities greatly dampen the income and price effects of shocks on the economy so that the ultimate impact of differences in their shock behavior on the distribution of income is small.[63] These results are relevant to those currently interested in studying the impact of stabilization policies on poverty.

6. Micro based policy interventions

In the previous sections we argued that the evidence indicates that it is necessary to be concerned with distributional outcomes in the design of medium-term development policy. We also provided different theoretical vantage points from which to view the design of such policy interventions. In this section we consider policies based on theories of the size distribution, starting from households as the basic unit of analysis. In the next section, we widen our scope to include economywide policies.[64]

6.1. Policy focus

The general reformist approach to improving the distribution of income focuses on raising the absolute incomes of the poor rather than on cutting the incomes of the rich. A policy focus on raising incomes of the poor leads to a more equal

---

[62] Taylor (1984) and Adelman, Taylor and Vogel (1987) explore this issue in a village setting.

[63] For example, Adelman and Berck (1987) find that a CGE model of the Adelman–Robinson type translates a standard error of unity in the world price of grains into a standard error of 0.36 in the domestic price of grains and a standard error of 0.24 in the income of farmers.

[64] This discussion of alternative policies draws heavily on Adelman (1986).

relative distribution if the rate of growth of the real income of the poor exceeds the average rate of growth of total household income and the rate of growth of the upper tail is less than the average. Substantial increases in the incomes of the poor thus improve the relative distribution as well, provided that the middle class does not lose ground. In their cross-section study, Adelman and Morris (1973) found that the middle 40 percent gain consistently from development. As an empirical fact, then, a long-run focus on poverty reduction as a policy goal in development will subsume the goal of improving the relative distribution.

Our discussion of policy will thus concentrate on poverty reduction as a means of improving the distribution. The emphasis on the poorer groups in society is consistent with any utilitarian social welfare function. Bentham defined a good society as one that achieves the greatest happiness for the greatest number. From a utilitarian vantage point, one can justify a more direct policy focus on the relative distribution than is adopted in the rest of this survey by noting that "deprivation" is both an absolute and relative concept. People at both ends of the distribution care about the incomes received by others.

The relationship between the relative distribution and poverty is thus complex, both factually and in terms of normative welfare theory. The relevant concept is "deprivation", a multi-faceted, multi-dimensional notion that combines both relative and absolute poverty. Most of the classical economists made "subsistence" a socioeconomic (i.e. relative) concept. Surveys of welfare evaluation in OECD countries indicate that people's self-evaluation of satisfaction and deprivation are based on their perceptions of where they are located relative to the mean [Van Praag et al. (1978)]. Self-evaluation of future prospects – dynamics – also matter [Gutkind (1986)]. Recent work on "basic needs" recognizes these complexities [see Streeten and Associates (1981)].

In developing countries, poverty is overwhelmingly rural. Usually, 80–100 percent of the population in the poorest first to fourth deciles is engaged in agricultural pursuits. The landless and the near landless are the poorest of the poor. In urban areas, the majority of the poor are unskilled workers in the service sector, but even they are generally richer than the rural poor. In developing countries, workers in the manufacturing sector, whether skilled or unskilled, are part of the richest 20–40 percent of the population. Unskilled labor is the major asset owned by the poor.

The design of anti-poverty strategies at the micro level starts from the observation that the income of the poor consists of the value of the services of the assets owned by them which are sold on the market. In a very basic sense, then, the poverty problem is one of too few assets, not enough market sales, and too low a price.

All effective approaches to anti-poverty policy must therefore accomplish one or more of the following: (1) increase the quantity and productivity of assets owned by the poor; (2) increase the sale price of the services of the assets sold by the poor, and/or (3) increase the volume of market sales by the poor. A fourth approach, pursued successfully in socialist countries, is to subsidize the prices of goods and services comprising the "basic needs" basket – food, housing, medical care, education, and public transport. We discuss this approach under the heading of programs to improve the human capital of the poor, though the rationale of such programs is not limited to human-capital productivity-improving investments. The general approaches which have been advocated to achieve a non-immiserizing growth process can be grouped under these headings.

6.2. Asset-oriented strategies

The quantity of assets owned by the poor can be increased either by redistribution policies (e.g. land reform) or by creating institutions for preferential access by the poor to asset-accumulation opportunities, or both. The approaches can be summarized in two slogans: "redistribution before growth" and "redistribution with growth". Adelman (1978) argues for the former approach for land and the second approach for education, while Chenery et al. (1974) argue for the latter approach for both types of assets.

Adelman (1978, 1980, 1986) examines the experience of the non-communist, newly industrializing countries that have successfully combined improvement in (or at least maintenance of) the relative incomes of the poor with accelerated growth and argues for: (1) tenurial reform in agriculture before implementation of policies designed to improve the productivity of agriculture, and (2) massive investments in education before rapid industrialization. Her rationale for the proposed sequence, which she calls "redistribution before growth", is twofold. First, with a better distribution of the major asset whose productivity is about to be improved and with more equal access to markets and to opportunities for improving the productivity of the major asset, most of the negative effects of change upon the asset-poor can be avoided. Second, before improvements in productivity, the redistributed asset is not as valuable as it is thereafter. Redistribution with full compensation would therefore be possible, at least in principle.[65] Third, once the redistribution has taken place, the same policies will promote both growth and equality.

Chenery's recommendations are more modest. In an approach he calls "redistribution with growth" he advocates differentially allocating a larger share of the proceeds of economic growth to asset accumulation by the poor. If, for example, the rate of growth is 6 percent per year, a third of the growth (or 2 percent of

---

[65]Adelman (1980) argues for the establishment of an internationally financed Land Reform Fund to help countries interested in implementing land reform to design the reforms and to provide international guarantees for the nationally-issued industrial and commodity bonds used to compensate the landlords whose lands are redistributed. Montgomery (1984), in a review of land reform, supports the Adelman proposal.

GNP) should be devoted to investment in assets owned by the poor or in assets which are complementary to assets owned by the poor. Examples of such investments include: nutrition, health, and education programs for the poor; investment in irrigation facilities for land owned by the poor; and investment in credit programs or input subsidies aimed at subsistence farmers.

6.3. Productivity-increasing strategies

Another way to increase the price of the services of the major assets owned by the poor is to increase their productivity. This can be done through: (1) upgrading the quality of the asset owned by the poor (e.g. investment in their human capital); (2) increasing the access of the poor to complementary assets whose productivities are interrelated; and (3) productivity-enhancing technical change (e.g. land augmenting innovations in agriculture or innovations to improve total factor productivity in labor-intensive enterprises).

The effectiveness of these programs in enhancing the incomes of the poor, depends, of course, on the elasticity of demand for the goods and services they produce. The more price-inelastic the demand, the less the poor will gain from any increases in supply; indeed, they may actually lose. Similarly, to the extent that the poor produce goods for which the income elasticity of demand is low, they will lose relatively from any increase in average income; for inferior goods, they will lose absolutely. Under either of these circumstances, the long-run adjustment will involve displacing labor from these sectors and absorbing them elsewhere. This process generates adjustment costs, takes time, and imposes burdens on the poor in the short to medium run.

6.3.1. Human capital investments

Direct investments in the poor are desirable in and of themselves, as part of providing the poor with the minimal bundle of goods necessary to allow them access to opportunities for a full life. In contrast to the previous section, we are here viewing education as enhancing the quality of labor, rather than as increasing the stock of assets they own. The discussion which follows will focus only on how such investments can affect the productivity of the poor thereby enabling them to earn higher incomes which, in turn, would permit them to purchase the "basic needs" basket on the market by themselves at some future date. This represents one strand of the "basic needs" development strategy [Streeten and Associates (1981), Streeten (1986)].

Investments in the nutrition, education, and health of the poor not only increase their welfare directly, but also enhance their capacities for productive labor. Much of the labor of the poor is physical. A study of food-for-work programs found that the wage which the poor were paid was not even sufficient to allow them to purchase enough food to replace the calories used up in earning that wage [Rodgers (1975)]. In this case, wage labor resulted in exposing the poor to higher morbidity and mortality rates and to higher health hazards than they would have had, had they remained unemployed. It is not surprising, therefore, that the productivity of the poor when employed remains low. In these circumstances, nutrition supplements or higher wages can raise the productivity of the poor.[66]

Investments in the education of the poor, through adult literacy campaigns and through increases in primary education facilities wherever the poor reside, spread the ownership of human capital. They qualify the poor for more productive jobs and narrow the distribution of wage income. They may also increase the rate of rural–urban migration, thereby allowing the poor access to higher-income employment opportunities and improving the agricultural terms of trade. Primary education of females also tends to reduce population growth.[67]

Improving the basic health status of the poor in developing countries can be achieved by investing in mobile clinics, "barefoot doctors", environmental sanitation, potable water, and training in food preparation practices and in elementary hygiene. Such investment raises the well-being of the poor, but there is little evidence of significant direct links with productivity. From a productivity point of view, the contributions of investments in better health are mostly indirect, raising the effectiveness of other productivity-enhancing investments. Better health increases school attendance and learning while in school. It also raises the efficiency of transforming nutritional intake into caloric output and therefore substantially reduces malnutrition.

These productivity-enhancing programs are designed to supply "basic needs" to the poor at subsidized prices and require special administrative actions by governments. Insofar as they involve targeting of special poverty populations, they require setting up special distribution channels and rationing mechanisms,

---

[66] Benefit–cost studies of nutrition supplement programs indicate their cost-effectiveness. See, for example, Reutlinger and Selowsky (1976) and Dasgupta and Rey (1984). Leibenstein (1957) argued for an efficiency-wage approach that, by paying higher-than-market wages to the poor, would raise their productivity.

[67] The relationship between population growth and poverty is complex and depends on the time horizon. The most important effects of population growth are its impact on the demand and supply of food, and on the evolution of the age structure of the population in urban and rural areas. These affect the agricultural terms of trade, the dependency ratios, and the demographic demands on the government budget. Experiments with the BACHUE models indicate that, in the first period (up to 15 years) after a decline in birth rate, food supply and demand effects predominate, with a greater decline in demand than in the supply of food. Food prices drop, there is a fall in the incomes of the food producing poor, and hence a deterioration in the household size distribution of income. Over 20–30 years, dependency rate changes become important and lead to some deterioration in the household size distribution. Wage rates improve, but there are fewer, less productive, earners per household as the ratio of old to young rises. It is only in the long run, with the achievement of a new steady state age structure, that the distribution improves.

and are vulnerable to abuse. Such programs may strain the administrative capacities of the poor countries which can least afford the programs and hence most need to target them efficiently.

6.3.2. Complementary resources

The poverty of the rural poor is largely due to the meager amount of land they have to till, combined with a low demand for hired labor by large cultivators. The most effective productivity improvements for raising the incomes of the rural poor are therefore land-augmenting investments and innovations, which stretch the yields from whatever land the poor cultivate and significantly raise demand for hired labor by larger farmers.[68] Investment in irrigation and drainage facilities, for example, induces better water control and permits multiple cropping. Improvements in seeds through the "green revolution" can triple the yield per acre and require considerably more labor-intensive cultivation methods.

To be most effective, these innovations and investments require making complementary resources available to the poor. For example, even when, as with high-yielding varieties of wheat and rice, the more productive technologies are scale-neutral, the poor are not able to take advantage of the yield-enhancing innovations because they do not have access to water, improved seed, credit to buy fertilizer, and the technological know-how disseminated by agricultural extension services. At least in the early stages of the diffusion of such innovations, productivity-increasing innovations tend to have two opposite effects on the rural poor. They increase the demand for wage labor since the land-augmenting innovations are all quite labor-intensive. But they also reduce the price of the marketable surplus of small cultivators since the increase in output from the larger farms generates an increase in overall supply in the face of inelastic demand. Large farmers benefit since they can increase their sales volume. But small farmers lose since they are not able to take advantage of the yield-increasing innovations. The initial net impact of agricultural innovations upon the rural poor therefore depends on the share of their income which they derive from farming as opposed to wage labor.

The backwash effects of the yield-enhancing innovations upon the near landless could be avoided if institutions were developed to provide them with access to the complementary resources needed to shift to more productive technologies. In order of decreasing importance, the necessary resources appear to be: credit, irrigation and drainage facilities, improved seed and fertilizer, and agricultural extension.

---

[68] If the goods are tradeable and the country is a "small" supplier on world markets, all farmers will gain.

7. Economywide policy interventions

In this section we consider policies aimed at changing the economic environment in which actors operate. We consider three broad types of economywide policy interventions. First, there are market interventions designed to change relative prices in ways favorable to the poor. Second, there are institutional reforms designed to change the "rules of the game" by which factor markets operate. Finally, we consider the distributional implications of different choices of development strategy.

7.1. Price-increasing strategies

Policies designed to benefit the poor can operate not only by increasing the quantity and quality of resources to which the poor have access, but also by increasing the prices of the services and commodities sold by the poor or by lowering the prices they pay for goods and services they consume. Price strategies can operate through factor markets or commodity markets.

A price-increasing strategy that operates through commodity markets must raise the prices of the goods produced with the labor of the poor. An increase in the agricultural terms of trade, for example, will benefit all farmers, including subsistence farmers (to the extent that they have a marketable surplus). An increase in the agricultural terms of trade will also benefit landless workers, even though they are net buyers of agricultural produce, by increasing the demand for their labor. Given the usual employment elasticities in agriculture in developing countries, the employment effect raises the nominal income of landless labor roughly in proportion to the increase in agricultural prices, while the food-price effect reduces only that fraction of their income which the landless spend on purchased food. In the case of the urban poor, unless counteracted by price subsidies, an increase in the agricultural terms of trade will reduce their real wages. However, the urban poor, poor as they are, are richer than the rural poor. The net effect of improving the agricultural terms of trade will be a reduction in overall poverty.

One approach to a "basic needs" strategy involves subsidization of the prices of goods and services consumed by the poor (including food, housing, medical care, education, and public transportation). In the case of food, such a strategy pits urban consumers against rural producers and may actually increase economywide poverty. The strategy has been successfully implemented in socialist economies where governments have direct control over rural as well as urban incomes. However, in market economies, it is probably a bad idea.

Price-increasing strategies which operate through factor markets must raise the wages of the poor. Labor-intensive growth strategies (discussed below) can raise average real wages since they involve an increase in the demand for labor. Success in raising average real wages depends on: (1) how quickly the supply of surplus labor is depleted (the Fei–Ranis turning point), and (2) whether the government supports or directly engages in general wage-repression policies.

Even if average wages rise, the wages of the poor may not. The result for the poor depends critically on how the labor market operates. If barriers to access to jobs by the poor are low and the amount of unemployment and underemployment is small, an increase in the demand for labor will raise the wage rate of the poor. On the other hand, if there are institutional or economic barriers to an increase in the quantity of labor which can be sold by the poor (for example through interlinking, obstacles to migration, or large transactions costs), the increase in total labor demand engendered by the strategy will augment the wage rate of the non-poor, while leaving the wage rate of the poor largely unchanged. The poor may benefit some through a second-round multiplier effect on their employment. The effects of demand-increasing strategies on the price of labor therefore critically depend on the institutional organization of the labor market.

7.2. Institutional reform

Structural change associated with development simultaneously increases the absorption of some factors, displaces other factors, and generates geographic and sectoral reallocations of all factors. The net effect on the poor of these processes of displacement, absorption, and labor force redistribution depends upon institutions in factor and product markets. Segmentation of factor markets prevents the evening out of unemployment in some regions and sectors with labor shortages in others. Socially induced rigidities, lack of adaptability of skills, or absence of capital and information may prevent the poor from counterbalancing the contractionary influences to which they may be exposed with expansionary ones elsewhere, in either the short or medium run.

7.2.1. Labor and credit markets

Studies of the structure of labor markets in developing countries indicate that they do not function in a neoclassical manner.[69] For example, Bardhan (1980) argues that labor markets are interlinked with credit markets and that the wage rate is lower than the undistorted market-clearing wage would be.[70] The inter-

---

[69]See, for example, Newbery (1977), Cheung (1969), Bell and Zusman (1976), and Stiglitz (1974). A recent survey of a number of these issues is provided by Binswanger and Rosenzweig (1981).

[70]Much of this work draws on the theory of implicit contracts to establish the nature of the equilibrium in agricultural labor and land markets. See also Braverman and Srinivasan (1981), and Braverman and Stiglitz (1986).

linked contracts reduce transactions and enforcement costs, circumvent incomplete markets, and reduce moral hazard with respect to work-monitoring [Bardhan (1989)]. However, the interlinking also poses barriers to mobility by making both entry and exit from the interlinked contracts more difficult. Interlinking also increases the power of the landlord vis-à-vis the peasant, and operates to segment the labor market. Institutional reforms to unbundle labor markets by making sources of rural consumption and production credit available to farmers on reasonable terms therefore appear essential for allowing the poor to benefit from employment opportunities which open up as a result of growth and structural change. Hayami and Ruttan (1971) and Hayami and Kikuchi (1982) find that in periods of substantial structural and technological change, contracts are changed in a manner which works against the weak and poor, minimizing the benefits they reap from development.

7.2.2. Land markets

There are two aspects of land tenure which are relevant for our purposes: the size of land holdings and the extent to which the cultivator reaps the benefits from his actions. Agrarian reforms that increase subsistence holdings and strengthen the link between cultivator choices and their net incomes can be powerful instruments to reduce rural poverty.[71] The recent success of the Chinese institutional reforms in agriculture shows the power of market incentives upon farmers.

Agrarian reform may be defined as a rapid change in one or more aspects of agrarian structure: land title; manner and scale of operation; relations between the cultivator, landowner, supplier of critical inputs, and marketing institutions; and the nature of the interlinking of all these characteristics [World Bank (1975)]. Actual agrarian reforms have been of many different types, as have the economic and political goals they were intended to serve. Some land reforms have guaranteed security of tenure to the cultivator without affecting the vesting of land titles or the scale of operation. Others have involved land redistribution without directly changing the relations between the land operator and suppliers of inputs, while still others have altered relations between suppliers of inputs and farm operators without directly modifying land titles and scale of operation. Changes in any feature affect other features, and may either strengthen the reform or nullify it.

Virtually every recent study of Third World agriculture stresses the economic superiority of agricultural development based on small owner-operated farms [Ladejinsky (1977), World Bank (1982)]. The most comprehensive study of land tenure to date is that of Berry and Cline (1979). They used aggregate cross-coun-

---

[71] There is a vast literature on land reform in less developed countries. See surveys by Dorner (1971), Barrachlough (1973), de Janvry (1981), and Montgomery (1984).

try data for different samples of 20, 30, and 40 developing countries and farm-level studies in six countries to conclude that: (1) there is no evidence that farming is subject to increasing returns to scale; (2) both total factor productivity and the productivity of land are higher on small farms than on large ones; and (3) there is no evidence in favor of the common assertion that large farm size increases agricultural dynamism. They conclude that land redistribution into family farms is an attractive policy instrument for increasing output, enhancing employment, and reducing rural inequality.

The East Asian land reforms of the 1950s increased the productivity of agriculture, enabled the acceleration of economic growth without a concomitant deterioration in the distribution of income, enhanced rural political stability, and generated fairly high rates of rural savings. The Latin American agrarian reforms in Bolivia, Chile, Mexico, Peru, and Venezuela had more varied economic outcomes. However, after an in-depth study, Eckstein et al. (1978) concluded that, with the possible exception of Peru, the effects of these reforms on agricultural production were generally positive, and that they uniformly improved the distribution of income despite the fact that none of the reforms extended to all of the rural landless. The critical variables explaining the economic impact of land reform were the post-reform public support policies, the post-reform tenurial arrangements, the type of pre-reform lands redistributed, and the socioeconomic characteristics of the beneficiaries. Experience with land reform indicates that "land to the tiller" programs, complemented by appropriate infrastructural, institutional, and financial follow-up, are likely to contribute significantly to both efficiency and equity.

The case for land reform is thus quite strong on both productivity and equity grounds. Many of the obstacles to implementation could be overcome by the creation of an internationally funded land reform fund that could help with the design of the reform, provide guarantees of compensation to landowners, and provide funds for follow-up programs [Adelman (1980)]. In the early 1970s, there were examples of several regional agricultural projects funded by the World Bank that did just that.

7.3. Alternative development strategies

In the absence of major asset redistribution and institutional change, the choice of development strategy becomes the principal means for raising the relative incomes of the poor. With this restricted view of policy options, once the course of the economy has been set by the choice of development strategy, including the aggregate growth rate, policies and programs aimed at changing the primary distribution of income can accomplish very little. As discussed earlier, work with CGE models indicates that the size distribution of income tends to be quite stable around the trend established by the basic choice of development strategy. This result applies to both transfer programs and poverty-oriented investment projects. After any intervention, even when sustained over time, the size distribution of income tends to return to the pre-intervention distribution. Only large, well-designed, complementary packages of anti-poverty policies and programs can change the primary distribution of income significantly. But, to be effective, they must essentially amount to a gradual change in development strategy. Any changes in strategy that increase the growth rate without worsening the relative distribution will, of course, decrease poverty.

The strategy choice governs the speed of absorption of labor into the modern sector, the extent of the income gap which develops between the modern and the traditional sectors, and the degree of income inequality within sectors. The major policies which foster absorption into the modern sectors are reliance upon more labor-intensive growth in the modern sectors. The labor intensity of growth can, in principle, be changed either by expanding the share of labor-intensive products and sectors in total employment or by increasing the labor intensity of production of a given output mix (i.e. by appropriate technology). Of the two, the first process appears to be the most effective. Artificial shifts away from best-practice technology for a given factor mix reduce the amount of output obtainable from a given amount of resources. This approach is therefore less effective than shifting the mix of output towards sectors requiring a mix of resources which corresponds more closely to the basic factor endowments of the labor-abundant economies of developing countries.

Since the assets owned by the poor consist largely of unskilled labor, development strategies that increase the absolute and relative demand for unskilled labor, coupled with institutions which enhance labor mobility and access to jobs by the poor, will benefit the poor most. Once institutional conditions have been established that permit access by the poor to high-productivity jobs, equitable growth requires strategies that stress rapid growth in high-productivity, labor-intensive sectors and activities. The most labor-intensive sectors in any economy are agriculture, light manufacturing, and some types of services, particularly construction.[72] But these are not necessarily high-productivity sectors. Generally, in developing countries, labor-intensive manufacturing is a (relatively) high-productivity sector, while agriculture and labor-intensive services are low-productivity sectors. The policies required to foster high-productivity, labor-intensive growth are therefore quite different in different sectors.

Strategies that stress employment growth in manufacturing must focus primarily on generating demand for the output of the labor-intensive industries. In

---

[72] Many services, such as banking and insurance, are skill-intensive rather than labor-intensive.

smaller countries, this implies that development will have to be oriented towards export markets. The small countries that follow this approach must therefore adopt a strategy of export-led growth and tailor their incentive policies to be compatible with such a strategy. In large countries, industrialization can be oriented towards the domestic market, particularly when the distribution of income is not too skewed [de Janvry (1984)].

By contrast, strategies that focus on agriculture or on services can appeal to existing demand, but must concentrate on increasing the productivity of labor in these sectors. There are no known technologies for increasing the productivity of purely labor-intensive services nor are there any developing countries in which the service sector has been a leading sector.[73] The choice therefore is between a labor-intensive manufacturing strategy, on the one hand, and an agricultural strategy, on the other.

More specifically, the promising strategies entail either: (1) reliance upon export-oriented growth in labor-intensive manufactures; or (2) reliance upon agricultural development led industrialization (ADLI) in an outward-looking trade policy regime.[74] The choice between the two strategies depends on two factors: (1) the size of the direct and indirect employment multipliers from expanding either labor-intensive manufactures or agriculture; and (2) the cost and feasibility of entering export markets, on the one hand, versus the cost and feasibility of increasing agricultural productivity, on the other.[75]

Simulations with the two alternative strategies in a CGE model of South Korea by Adelman (1984) and in a global, multi-regional, CGE model by Adelman, Bournieux and Waelbroeck (1986) indicate that both strategies can be effective in achieving higher growth rates and better distributions of income. However, they also indicate that, during a period of low growth in world demand for labor-intensive manufacturing exports (which is likely to be typical of the rest of the 1980s), the agricultural strategy is more effective. It results in less inequality and poverty, as well as in a higher rate of growth and a better balance of payments. During the coming decade, these results indicate that the agricultural strategy looks more promising for most developing countries which do not yet have an established position in markets for manufacturing exports.

---

[73] Historically, Holland is about the only example of a country which pursued a service-led growth strategy. For a discussion of leading sectors in contemporary semi-industrial countries that supports the generalization made in the text, see Chenery, Robinson and Syrquin (1986).

[74] See Adelman (1984), Mellor (1976), and Singer (1979). In a sense, the arguments for an ADLI strategy are similar to those put forward in the 1960s in favor of balanced growth. For a review of the earlier debate, see Scitovsky (1959) and Streeten (1963).

[75] Little, Scitovsky and Scott (1970), Bhagwati (1978), Krueger (1978), Balassa (1985), Balassa and Associates (1982) espouse the manufacturing strategy, while Mellor (1976), Adelman (1984), and Singer (1979) advocate the agricultural strategy.

The basic reasons for the superiority of the agricultural strategy are: (1) agriculture is much more labor-intensive than is even labor-intensive manufacturing; (2) increases in agricultural productivity generate increases in demand for the labor of the poorest of the poor, agricultural landless labor; (3) increases in agricultural incomes generate high leakages into demand for labor-intensive manufactures on the consumption side and for manufactured inputs on the production side; (4) expansion in agricultural production is less import intensive than is an equivalent increase in manufacturing production; (5) increases in agricultural output with good-practice, developing-country technology are less capital-intensive than increases in manufacturing; and finally (6) the agricultural infrastructure required to increase agricultural productivity (roads, irrigation, and drainage facilities) has a high employment effect.[76]

It should be noted, however, that the success of both strategies depends on certain institutional and asset distribution prerequisites. The labor-intensive growth strategy in manufacturing requires a wide distribution of education and low barriers to access to jobs by the poor. The agricultural strategy requires that tenurial conditions in agriculture be favorable enough so that small farmers have both incentives to improve productivity and access to the necessary complementary resources, particularly credit and water. Both strategies will fail if rapid productivity growth in the leading sector is not achieved.[77]

Both strategies also have implications for price policies. The trade-oriented strategy requires a price policy that does not discriminate against exports by means of an overvalued exchange rate and tariffs.[78] The agricultural strategy requires a price policy that allows farmers to capture some of the benefits from improvements in agricultural productivity. It therefore implies an agricultural terms-of-trade policy which shares the income benefits of increased output between urban and rural groups.[79] An international trade policy which is neutral between exports and import substitution is consistent with the agricultural strategy, since manufactures now tend to be excessively protected and agriculture suffers from negative effective protection.

---

[76]See Lewis (1977) who is a strong proponent of a rural-public-works approach to poverty alleviation. To the extent that improving agricultural productivity requires infrastructure such as roads and irrigation facilities, it is dependent on a rural public works program. Such a program then becomes a necessary part of the agricultural strategy.

[77]For a discussion of the productivity requirements for successful manufacturing export-led growth, see Chenery, Robinson and Syrquin (1986) and Kubo, Robinson and Urata (1987). The institutional implications of manufacturing export-led growth are discussed in Balassa (1985).

[78]Indeed, the definition of outward-led growth is that incentives for domestic sales and foreign sales are neutral. See, for example, Balassa and Associates (1982), Krueger (1978), and Srinivasan (1983).

[79]Terms-of-trade problems have, of course, haunted agricultural policy in all countries. For a discussion in the context of developing countries, see Krishna (1982) and de Janvry and Sadoulet (1985).

8. Policy summary

This review of policy approaches to improving the distribution of income through poverty alleviation suggests a number of lessons.

First, successful strategies, policies, and programs for poverty alleviation exist. Indeed, between 1960 and 1980 there has been substantial progress in reducing the share of the population living in poverty in the non-socialist developing countries as a group, despite the fact that the distribution of income has also become substantially less equal.

Second, approaches to poverty alleviation require the implementation of mutually consistent, mutually reinforcing, multifaceted packages of programs and strategies. The most effective approaches entail a combination of several elements: asset-oriented programs, institutional reforms to encourage access of the poor to jobs and resources that enhance the productivity of their assets, and development strategies which generate high total factor productivity growth and a rapid increase in the demand for unskilled labor.

Third, approaches to poverty alleviation are not unique. More than one method exists to achieve each element of the packages described above. The choice among instruments needs to be tailored to each country's particular initial conditions, its resource base, size, asset distribution, institutional structure, and socio-political configuration, as well as to the external conditions and trends which the country faces. Choices among packages and programs for rapid progress towards poverty alleviation entail political choices among competing goals and instrumentalities. A critical element in the political choice is the speed and time phasing of progress towards this goal. The most effective strategies are likely to vary over time as both the initial conditions within the country and the economic and political environment in which the country operates change dynamically.

Fourth, the sequence in which different policy interventions are taken up is important. The most effective approach to poverty alleviation entails implementing asset-oriented policies and institutional changes designed to give the poor access to high productivity jobs before, not after, shifting development strategies. If that is done, there is no tradeoff between growth promotion and poverty alleviation. The same development strategy is optimal for both goals.

Finally, strategies for poverty alleviation are not compatible with just any kind of economic growth. While all successful strategies require growth, it must be particular kinds of growth. Two development strategies appear to promise the poor the most: (1) reliance upon export-oriented growth in labor-intensive manufactures, and (2) reliance upon agricultural-development-led industrialization. Adelman (1984) argues that the coming decade is likely to involve low growth in world demand for labor-intensive manufactured exports. In this case, the ADLI strategy is likely to be superior on both growth and distribution grounds.

9. Conclusion

In this survey, we have indicated how concern with distributional issues involves an interweaving of empirical work, theoretical paradigms, experience with applied models and policies, and societal concerns expressed through political processes. Whatever ethical judgments one might have about social welfare, distributional impacts are central to the political decision-making process in all systems. In policy analysis, economists cannot ignore distribution. Indeed, it seems odd even to have to make the point!

There are a few lessons from the postwar experience of developing countries. First, there is an inevitable initial deterioration in the distribution of income which reflects the uneven, disequilibrium nature of the initial phase of the development process. Second, the persistence of this deterioration into the middle and later phases of development is more a matter of policy choice. There is a variety of country experience, some quite successful in marrying rapid industrialization with at least no deterioration in the relative distribution and with rapid reduction in poverty. There are also a number of spectacular failures, some combining successful growth with substantial increases in inequality, and others failing on both fronts.

There are several distinct strands of theoretical analysis of distributional issues. The neoclassical model, the most thoroughly developed theoretical framework, has the least to say about distributional concerns. In their grand dynamics, the classical economists, whether Marxian or Ricardian, provide a better framework for analyzing distributional issues. However, they limited themselves to the functional distribution. If one is concerned both with welfare and with providing analysis that reflects political reality, one must go beyond the classical analysis and incorporate both the size and extended functional distributions into an integrated framework.

The theoretical debates have been very heated. When it comes to policy analysis that is anchored in empirical economywide models, however, it turns out that differences in the policy implications of alternative paradigms are far less striking than one would have thought from theoretical analysis. Models in different paradigms yield similar results for the impact of typical policy interventions on the overall size distribution. The different underlying economywide models all focus on the impact of shocks and policies on the extended functional distribution. Empirical models in each of the paradigms indicate that the extended functional distribution is indeed sensitive to such shocks and changes. These models, however, also indicate that the overall size distribution is insensitive to shocks. The empirical fact is that the link between changes in the extended functional distribution and changes in the size distribution is diffused. The differences between the way the models incorporate the extended functional distribution are not translated into differences in size distribution, and the policy results with regard to the size distribution are, in fact, similar.

The fact that the size distribution is relatively insensitive to shocks under a variety of theoretical specifications does not mean, however, that policy does not matter. To the contrary, our review indicates that the extent and incidence of poverty are strongly affected by policy choices with regard to: asset-oriented policies, productivity-enhancing policies, institutional reform in factor markets, and overall development strategy. The impact of policy choice on the relative size distribution is considerably weaker, but potentially significant.

Much has been learned about the interactions between income distribution and development. Advances have been made through an interplay among three strands of analysis: investigation of the stylized facts, theoretical explanations, and empirical modelling. It has also been an area where policy concerns have been a major driving force behind the analysis, and one which has strained the boundaries of "standard" economics. As interest in distributional questions waxes again, we hope that future work will further strain those boundaries, providing a vehicle for bringing back into economics the sorts of institutional, social, and political concerns that preoccupied the classical economists.

References

Addison, T. and L. Demery (1986) *The consequences for income distribution and poverty of macroeconomic stabilization*. London: Overseas Development Institute.

Adelman, I. (1961) *Theories of economic growth and development*. Stanford, CA: Stanford University Press.

Adelman, I. (1978) 'Redistribution before growth – a strategy for developing countries', Inaugural Lectural for the Cleveringa Chair, Leiden University. The Hague: Martinus Nijhof.

Adelman, I. (1980) 'Income distribution, economic development, and land reform', *American Behavioral Scientist*, 23:437–456.

Adelman, I. (1984) 'Beyond export-led growth', *World Development*, 12:937–950.

Adelman, I. (1985) 'The world distribution of income', *Weltwirtschaftliches Archiv*, 121:110–120.

Adelman, I. (1986) 'A poverty-focused approach to development policy', in: J. Lewis and V. Kallab, eds., *Development strategies reconsidered*. Washington, DC: Overseas Development Council.

Adelman, I. and P. Berck (1987) 'Food security in a stochastic world,' Giannini Foundation Working Paper no. 445. University of California, Berkeley.

Adelman, I. and A. Levy (1984) 'The equalizing role of human resource intensive growth strategies: A theoretical model', *Journal of Policy Modeling*, 6:271–287.

Adelman, I. and C.T. Morris (1973) *Economic growth and social equity in developing countries*. Stanford, CA: Stanford University Press.

Adelman, I. and C.T. Morris (1983) 'Institutional influences on poverty in the nineteenth century: A quantitative comparative study', *Journal of Economic History*, 43:43–55.

Adelman, I. and S. Robinson (1978) *Income distribution policy in developing countries: A case study of Korea*. Stanford, CA: Stanford University Press.

Adelman, I. and S. Robinson (1987) 'Macroeconomic adjustment and income distribution: Alternative models applied to two economies', Giannini Foundation Working Paper no. 85, University of California, Berkeley. *Journal of Development Economics*, 29(1988):23–44.

Adelman, I., J.M. Bournieux, and J. Waelbroeck (1986) 'Agricultural development led industrialization in a global perspective', Paper presented at Eighth International Economic Association World Congress, New Delhi.

Adelman, I., M.J.D. Hopkins, S. Robinson, G.B. Rogers, and R. Wery (1979) 'A comparison of two models for income distribution planning', *Journal of Policy Modeling*, 1, no. 1:37–82.

Adelman, I., J.E. Taylor, and S. Vogel (1987) 'Life in a Mexican village: A SAM perspective', Giannini Foundation Working Paper 443. University of California, Berkeley.

Ahluwalia, M. (1976a) 'Inequality, poverty, and development', *Journal of Development Economics*, 6:307–342.

Ahluwalia, M. (1976b) 'Income distribution and development: Some stylized facts', *American Economic Review*, 66:128–135.

Ahluwalia, M.S. and F.J. Lysy (1979) 'Welfare effects of demand management policies: Impact multipliers under alternative model structures', *Journal of Policy Modeling*, 1, no. 3:317–342.

Ahluwalia, M.S., N.G. Carter, and H.B. Chenery (1979) 'Growth and poverty in developing countries', *Journal of Development Economics*, 6:299–341.

Anand, S. and S.M.R. Kanbur (1986) 'Inequality and development: A critique', Paper Presented to the 25th Anniversary Symposium, Yale Growth Center, April 11–13, 1986.

Arthur, W.B. and G. McNicholl (1975) 'Large scale simulation models in population and development: What use to planners', *Population and Development Review*, 1, no. 2:251–265.

Bacha, E. (1979) 'The Kuznets curve and beyond: Growth and change in inequalities', in: E. Malinvaud, ed., *Economic growth and resources*. New York: St. Martins Press, 52–73.

Balassa, B. (1985) *Changes and challenges in the world economy*. London: Macmillan.

Balassa, B. and associates (1982) *Development strategies in semi-industrial economies*. Baltimore, MD: Johns Hopkins University Press.

Baran, P. (1957) *The political economy of growth*. New York: Monthly Review Press.

Bardhan, P. (1980) 'Interlocking factor markets and agrarian development: A review of issues', *Oxford Economic Papers*, 32, no. 1:82–98.

Bardhan, P. (1989) 'Interlinked transactions and the theory of rural institutions: A critical note', *World Development*, forthcoming.

Barrachlough, S. (1973) *Agrarian structure in Latin America*. Boston, MA: Lexington Books.

Bauer, P.T. (1981) *Equality, the Third World, and economic delusion*. Cambridge, MA: Harvard University Press.

Becker, G.S. (1967) *Human capital and the personal distribution of income: An analytical approach*. Ann Arbor, MI: Institute of Public Administration.

Becker, G.S. (1983) *Human capital: A theoretical and empirical analysis, with special reference to education*. Chicago, IL: University of Chicago Press.

Bell, C. and S. Devarajan (1985) 'Intertemporally consistent shadow prices in an open economy: Estimates for Cyprus', mimeo, World Bank, Washington, DC.

Bell, C.L.G. and P. Zusman (1976) 'A bargaining theoretic approach to cropsharing contracts', *American Economic Review*, 66:578–588.

Bennett, R.L. and B. Bergmann (1986) *A microsimulated transactions model of the United States economy*. Baltimore, MD: Johns Hopkins University Press.

Bergsman, J. (1979) *Growth and equity in semi-industrialized countries*. World Bank Staff Working Paper no. 351. Washington, DC: World Bank.

Berry, R.A. and W.R. Cline (1979) *Agrarian structure and productivity in developing countries*. Baltimore, MD: Johns Hopkins University Press.

Bhagwati, J.N. (1978) *Anatomy and consequences of exchange control regimes*. Cambridge: Ballinger Press.

Bienen, H. and V.P. Diejomaoh, eds. (1981) *The political economy of income distribution in Nigeria*. New York: Holmes & Meier.

Bigsten, A. (1983) *Income distribution and development: Theory, evidence, and policy*. London: Heinemann.

Binswanger, H.P. and M.R. Rosenzweig (1981) *Contractual arrangements, employment, and wages in rural labor markets: A critical review.* New York: Agricultural Development Council.

Blaug, M. (1962) *Economic theory in retrospect.* Homewood, IL: Richard D. Irwin.

Blaug, M. (1973) *Education and the employment problem in developing countries.* Geneva: International Labour Organization.

Blinder, A.S. (1974) *Toward an economic theory of income distribution.* Cambridge, MA: MIT Press.

Braverman, A. and T.N. Srinivasan (1981) 'Credit and sharecropping in agrarian societies', *Journal of Development Economics*, 9, no. 3:289–312.

Braverman, A. and J.E. Stiglitz (1986) 'Landlords, tenants, and technical innovations', *Journal of Development Economics*, 23:313–354.

Brenner, R. (1977) 'The origins of capitalist development: A critique of neo-Sraffian Marxism', *New Left Review*, 104:25–92.

Cardoso, E.A. and L. Taylor (1979) 'Identity-based planning of prices and quantities: Cambridge and neoclassical models for Brazil', *Journal of Policy Modeling*, 1:83–111.

Champernowne, D.G. (1953) 'A model of income distribution', *Economic Journal*, 63:318–351.

Chenery, H. and A.S. Strout (1966) 'Foreign assistance and economic development', *American Economic Review*, 56:679–733.

Chenery, H.B. and M. Syrquin (1975) *Patterns of development 1950–70.* London: Oxford University Press.

Chenery, H. et al. (1974) *Redistribution with growth.* London: Oxford University Press.

Chenery, H.B., S. Robinson, and M. Syrquin (1986) *Industrialization and growth: A comparative study.* London: Oxford University Press.

Cheung, S.N.S. (1969) *The theory of share tenancy.* Chicago, IL: University of Chicago Press.

Chiswick, B.S. (1974) *Income inequality: Regional analyses within a human capital framework.* New York: National Bureau of Economic Research.

Clague, C. (1974) 'The effects of marriage and fertility patterns on the transmission of distribution of status', mimeo, University of Maryland reprint series.

Cline, W.R. (1972) *Potential effects of income redistribution on economic growth: Latin American cases.* New York: Praeger.

Danielson, M.N. and R. Keles (1981) 'Urbanization and income distribution in Turkey', in: E. Ozbudun and A. Ulusan, eds., *The political economy of income distribution in Turkey.* New York: Holmes and Meier, 269–309.

Dasgupta, P. and D. Rey (1984) 'Inequality, malnutrition, and unemployment: A critique of the competitive market mechanism', Technical Report no. 454, Stanford University.

de Janvry, A. (1981) *The agrarian question and reformism in Latin America.* Baltimore, MD: Johns Hopkins University Press.

de Janvry, A. (1984) 'The search for styles of development: Lessons from Latin America and implications for India', mimeo, Department of Agricultural and Resource Economics, University of California, Berkeley.

de Janvry, A. and E. Sadoulet (1985) 'Agricultural price policy in general equilibrium frameworks: A comparative analysis', Department of Agricultural and Resource Economics, Working Paper no. 342, University of California, Berkeley.

de Melo, M.H. (1979) 'Agricultural policies and development: A socioeconomic investigation applied to Sri Lanka', *Journal of Policy Modeling*, 1, no. 2:217–234.

de Melo, J. and S. Robinson (1980) 'The impact of trade policies on income distribution in a planning model for Columbia', *Journal of Policy Modeling*, 2, no. 1:81–100.

de Melo, J. and S. Robinson (1982a) 'Trade adjustment policies and income distribution in three archetype developing countries', *Journal of Development Economics*, 10, no. 1:67–92.

de Melo, J. and S. Robinson (1982b) 'Trade policy, employment, and income distribution in a small, open, developing economy', in: S.B. Dahiya, ed., *Development planning models.* New Delhi: Inter-India Publications.

Dervis, K. and S. Robinson (1980) 'The structure of income inequality in Turkey (1950–1973)', in: E. Ozbudun and A. Ulusan, eds., *The political economy of income distribution in Turkey.* New York: Holmes and Meier.

Dervis, K., J. de Melo, and S. Robinson (1982) *General equilibrium models for development policy.* Cambridge: Cambridge University Press.

Dorner, P. (1971) 'Land reform in Latin America', *Land economics, monograph no. 3, Issues and cases.*

Eckstein, S. et al. (1978) 'Land reform in Latin America: Bolivia, Chile, Mexico, Peru, Venezuela', World Bank Staff Working Paper no. 275. Washington, DC: World Bank.

Fei, J.C.H. and G. Ranis (1964) *Development of the labor surplus economy: Theory and policy.* Homewood, IL: Richard D. Irwin.

Fei, J.C., G. Ranis, and S.W.Y. Kuo (1979) *Growth with equity: The Taiwan case.* New York: Oxford University Press.

Feiwel, G. and L.R. Klein (1975) *The intellectual capital of Michal Kalecki: A study in economic theory and policy.* Knoxville, TN: University of Tennessee Press.

Fields, G.S. (1980) *Poverty, inequality, and development.* New York: Cambridge University Press.

Fisher, I. (1912) *Elementary principles of economics.* New York: MacMillan.

Fishlow, A. (1972) 'Brazilian size distribution of income', *American Economic Review*, 62:391–402.

Fishlow, A. (1973) 'Some reflections on post-1964 Brazilian economic policy', in: A. Stepan, ed., *Authoritarian Brazil.* New Haven, CT: Yale University Press, 69–118.

Frank, C.R. and R. Webb, eds. (1977) *Income distribution: Policy alternatives in developing countries.* Washington, DC: Brookings Institution.

Ginsburgh, V. and J. Waelbroeck (1981) *Activity analysis and general equilibrium modelling.* Amsterdam: North-Holland.

Government of India, Planning Commission (1964) 'Report of the committee on distribution of income and levels of living', New Delhi: Government of India.

Grais, W. (1981) 'Aggregate demand and macroeconomic imbalances in Thailand: Experiments with the SIAM1 model', World Bank Staff Working Paper no. 448. Washington, DC: World Bank.

Gupta, S. (1977a) *A model for income distribution, employment, and growth: A case study of Indonesia.* World Bank Staff Occasional Papers no. 24. Baltimore, MD: Johns Hopkins University Press.

Gupta, S. (1977b) 'Alternative development strategies of Korea (1976–1990) in an input–output dynamic simulation model', World Bank Staff Working Paper no. 154. Washington, DC: World Bank.

Gutkind, E. (1986) *Patterns of economic behavior among the American poor.* New York: St. Martin's Press.

Harris, J. and M. Todaro (1970) 'Migration, unemployment and development: A two sector analysis', *American Economic Review*, 60:126–142.

Hayami, Y. and M. Kikuchi (1982) *Asian village economy at the crossroads: An economic approach to institutional change.* Baltimore, MD: Johns Hopkins University Press.

Hayami, Y. and V. Ruttan (1971) *Agricultural development: An international perspective.* Baltimore, MD: Johns Hopkins University Press.

Hirschman, A.O. (1978) *Exit, voice, and loyalty.* Cambridge, MA: Harvard University Press.

Hirschman, A.O. and M. Rothschild (1973) 'The changing tolerance for income inequality in the course of economic development', *Quarterly Journal of Economics*, 87, no. 4:544–566.

Huntington, S. and J. Nelson (1976) *No easy choice: Political participation in developing countries.* Cambridge, MA: Harvard University Press.

International Monetary Fund (1986) 'Food support programs, fiscal policy and income distribution', Occasional Paper no. 46. Washington, DC: International Monetary Fund.

Kalecki, M. (1966) 'Highly developed and backward capitalist economies: Differences between the crucial economic problems', *EK*, 5:971–977.

Kalecki, M. (1971) *Selected essays on the dynamics of the capitalist economy.* Cambridge: Cambridge University Press.

Krishna, R. (1982) 'Some aspects of agricultural growth, price policy, and equity in developing countries', Paper AAEA-82-174, Food Research Institute, Stanford University.

Krueger, A.O. (1978) *Foreign trade regimes and economic development: The liberalization attempts and consequences.* Cambridge: Ballinger Press.

Kubo, Y., S. Robinson, and S. Urata (1987) 'The impact of alternative development strategies: Simulations with a dynamic input–output model', *Journal of Policy Modeling*, forthcoming.

Kuznets, S. (1955) 'Economic growth and income inequality', *American Economic Review*, 65:1–28.

Kuznets, S. (1966) *Modern economic growth: Rate, structure, and spread.* New Haven, CT: Yale University Press.

Ladejinsky, W.I. (1977) *Agrarian reform as unfinished business: The selected papers of W.I. Ladejinsky.* New York: Oxford University Press.

Lal, D.K. (1985) *The poverty of "development economics".* Cambridge, MA: Harvard University Press.

Langoni, C.G. (1975) 'Income distribution and economic development: The Brazilian case', paper presented at the World Econometric Society Congress, Toronto.

Lecaillon, J., F. Paukert, C. Morrisson, and D. Germidis (1984) *Income distribution and development: An analytic survey.* Geneva: International Labour Office.

Leibenstein, H.S. (1957) *Economic backwardness and economic growth.* New York: Wiley.

Lewis, W.A. (1954) 'Economic development with unlimited supplies of labour', *Manchester school of economic and social studies*, 22:139–191.

Lewis, W.A. (1972) 'Reflections on unlimited labor', in: L.E. Marco, ed., *International economics and economic development.* New York: Academic.

Lewis, J.P. (1977) 'Designing the public works mode of anti-poverty policy', in: C.R. Frank and R. Webb, eds., *Income distribution and growth in the less-developed countries.* 337–379. Washington, DC: Brookings Institution.

Lindert, P.H. and J.G. Williamson (1985) 'Growth, equality, and history', *Explorations in Economic History*, 22:341–377.

Lipton, M. (1977) *Why poor people stay poor.* Cambridge, MA: Harvard University Press.

Little, I.M.D. (1982) *Economic development: Theory, policy, and international relations.* New York: Basic Books.

Little, I.M.D., T. Scitovsky and M. Scott (1970) *Industry and trade in some developing countries: A comparative study.* London: Oxford University Press.

Lysy, F.J. and L. Taylor (1980) 'The general equilibrium distribution model', in: L. Taylor et al., *Models of growth and distribution for Brazil.* London: Oxford University Press.

Meade, J.E. (1964) *Efficiency, equality, and the ownership of property.* London: Allen and Unwin.

Mellor, J.W. (1976) *The new economics of growth: A strategy for India and the developing world.* Ithaca, NY: Cornell University Press.

Montgomery, J., ed. (1984) *International dimensions of land reform.* Boulder, CO: Westview Press.

Morishima, M. (1985) *Marx's economics: A dual theory of value and growth.* Cambridge: Cambridge University Press.

Morley, S. and J.G. Williamson (1974) 'Demand, distribution, and employment: The case of Brazil', *Economic Development and Cultural Change*, 23:33–60.

Morris, C.T. and I. Adelman (1987) *Comparative patterns of economic growth: 1850–1914.* Baltimore, MD: Johns Hopkins University Press.

Myrdal, G. (1968) *Asian drama.* New York: Pantheon Press.

Nakamura, J.I. (1966) *Agricultural production and the economic development of Japan, 1873–1922.* Princeton, NJ: Princeton University Press.

Negishi, T. (1960) 'Welfare economics and the existence of an equilibrium for a competitive economy', *Metroeconomica*, 12:92–97.

Nelson, J. (1979) *Access to power: Politics and the urban poor in developing nations.* Princeton, NJ: Princeton University Press.

Newbery, D.M.D. (1977) 'Risk sharing, share-cropping, and uncertain labor markets', *Review of Economic Studies*, 44:585–594.

Nozick, R. (1981) *Anarchy, state, and utopia.* Totowa, NJ: Rowman and Littlefield.

Ozbudun, E. and A. Ulusan, eds. (1981) *The political economy of income distribution in Turkey.* New York: Holmes and Meier.

Pack, H. (1971) *Structural change and economic policy in Israel.* New Haven, CT: Yale University Press.

Papanek, G.S. and O. Kyn (1986) 'The effect of income distribution on development, the growth rate, and economic strategy', *Journal of Development Economics*, 23:55–66.

Paukert, F. (1973) 'Income distribution at different levels of development: A survey of evidence', *International Labour Review*, 108:97–125.

Pinstrup-Anderson, P. (1986) 'Macroeconomic adjustment policies and human nutrition: Available evidence and research needs', mimeo, Washington. International Food Policy Research Institute.

Prebisch, R. (1959) 'Commercial policy in the underdeveloped countries', *American Economic Review*, 49:251–273.

Pryor, F. (1973) 'Simulation of the impact of social and economic institutions on the size distribution of income and wealth', *American Economic Review*, 63, no. 1:50–72.

Pyatt, G. (1976) 'On the interpretation and disaggregation of Gini coefficients', *Economic Journal*, 76:243–255.

Pyatt, G. and J.I. Round (1979) 'Accounting and fixed-price multipliers in a social accounting matrix framework', *Economic Journal*, 89, no. 356:850–873.

Pyatt, G. and J.I. Round, eds. (1985) *Social accounting matrices: A basis for planning*. Washington, DC: World Bank.

Pyatt, G. and E. Thorbecke (1976) *Planning techniques for a better future*. Geneva: International Labour Organization.

Pyatt, G., A.R. Roe, and Associates (1977) *Social accounting for development planning with special reference to Sri Lanka*. Cambridge: Cambridge University Press.

Ranis, G. (1978) 'Equity and growth in Taiwan: How "special" is the "special case"?', *World Development*, vol. 6, no. 3:397–409.

Rawls, J. (1971) *A theory of justice*. Cambridge: Belknap Press.

Reutlinger, S. and M. Selowsky (1976) *Malnutrition and poverty*. World Bank Staff Occasional Paper no. 23. Baltimore, MD: Johns Hopkins University Press.

Ritzen, J.M. (1977) *Education, economic growth, and income distribution*. Amsterdam: North-Holland.

Robinson, S. (1976) 'A note on the U hypothesis relating income inequality and economic develop-ment', *American Economic Review*, 66, no. 3:437–440.

Robinson, S. and K. Dervis (1977) 'Income distribution and socioeconomic mobility: A framework for analysis and planning', *Journal of Development Studies*, 13, no. 4:347–364.

Rodgers, G.B. (1975) 'Nutritionally based wage determinations in the low income labor markets', *Oxford Economic Papers*, 27, no. 1:61–81.

Rodgers, G.B. et al. (1977) *Economic-demographic modeling for development planning: Bachue–Philip-pines*. Geneva: International Labour Organization.

Rodgers, G.B., M.J. Hopkins, and R. Wery (1978) 'The myth of the cavern revisited: Are large-scale behavioral models useful?', *Population and Development Review*, 2, no. 3/4.

Sahota, G. (1978) 'Theories of personal income distribution: A survey', *Journal of Economic Literature*, 16:1–55.

Sahota, G. (1986) 'Theory of personal income distribution – A consummative survey', presented at the meetings of the American Economic Association, December 28, 1986.

Sanderson, W.C. (1980) *Economic–demographic simulation models: A review of their usefulness for policy analysis*. Laxenburg, Austria: International Institute for Applied Systems Analysis (IIASA), RM-80-14.

Scitovsky, T. (1959) 'Growth: Balanced or unbalanced', in: M. Abramovitz, ed., *The allocation of economic resources: Essays in honor of Bernard Francis Haley*. Stanford, CA: Stanford University Press.

Sen, A.K. (1982) *Choice, welfare, and measurement*. Cambridge, MA: MIT Press.

Shoven, J.B. and J. Whalley (1974) 'On the computation of competitive equilibria in international markets with tariffs', *Journal of International Economics*, 4, no. 4:341–354.

Singer, H.B. (1979) 'Policy implications of the Lima target', *Industry and Development*, 3:17–32.

Srinivasan, T.N. (1983) 'International factor movements, commodity trade, and commercial policy in a specific factor model', *Journal of International Economics*, 14:289–312.

Srinivasan, T.N. and P. Bardhan, eds. (1974) *Poverty and income distribution in India*. Calcutta: Statistical Publishing Society.

Stewart, F. and P. Streeten (1972) 'Conflicts between output and employment', in: P. Streeten, ed., *The frontiers of development studies*. London: Macmillan, ch. 19.

Stiglitz, J.E. (1974) 'Incentives and risk sharing in agriculture', *Review of Economic Studies*, 41:209–256.

Stiglitz, J.E. (1986) *Economics of the public sector*. New York: Norton.

Stone, J.R.N. (1985) 'The disaggregation of the household sector in the national accounts', in: G. Pyatt and J.I. Round, eds., *Social accounting matrices: A basis for planning*. Washington, DC: World Bank.

Streeten, P. (1963) 'Balanced vs. unbalanced growth', *The Economic Weekly*, 20 April, 669–671.

Streeten, P. (1986) 'Basic needs: The lessons', in: I. Adelman, ed., *The design of alternative development strategies*. Rohtak: Jan Tinbergen Institute of Development Planning.

Streeten, P. and associates (1981) *First things first: Meeting basic needs in developing countries*. London: Oxford University Press.

Taylor, L., E. Bacha, E. Cardoso, and F.J. Lysy (1980) *Models of growth and distribution for Brazil*. London: Oxford University Press.

Taylor, J.E. (1984) 'Migration networks and risk in household labor decisions: A study of migration from two Mexican villages', Ph.D. Dissertation, University of California, Berkeley.

Thorbecke, E. (1985) 'The social accounting matrix and consistency-type planning models', in: G. Pyatt and J.I. Round, eds., *Social accounting matrices: A basis for planning*. Washington, DC: World Bank.

Thorbecke, E. (1986) 'Planning techniques for social justice', paper presented at the Eighth International Economic Association World Congress.

Thorbecke, E. (1987) 'Impact of stabilization and structural adjustment measures and reforms on agriculture and equity', paper presented for the Sequoia Institute's Conference on Policy Reform and Equity in LDCs, May 20, 1987, Washington, DC.

Thorbecke, E. and J. Sengupta (1972) 'A consistency framework for employment, output, and income distribution projections applied to Colombia', mimeo, Development Research Center, World Bank.

Tinbergen, J. (1956) 'On the theory of income distribution', *Weltwirtschaftliches Archiv*, 77, no. 2:155–173.

Todaro, M.S. (1980) 'International migration in developing countries: A survey', in: P.A. Easterlin, ed., *Population and economic change in developing countries*. Chicago, IL: University of Chicago Press.

Turnham, D. (1971) *The employment problem in less developed countries*. Paris: OECD.

Van Praag, B., T. Goedhart and A. Kapteyn (1978) 'The poverty line: A pilot survey in Europe', Center for Research in Public Economics, Leiden University, Leiden.

Weisskoff, R. (1970) 'Income distribution and economic growth in Puerto Rico, Argentina and Mexico', *Review of Income and Wealth*, 16:303–332.

Weisskoff, R. (1985) *Factories and food stamps: The Puerto Rico model of development*. Baltimore, MD: Johns Hopkins University Press.

Williamson, J.G. (1985) *Did British capitalism breed inequality?* Boston, MA: Allen and Unwin.

Williamson, J.G. and P.H. Lindert (1980) *American inequality: A macroeconomic history*. New York: Academic.

Wold, H. and P. Whittle (1957) 'A model explaining the Pareto distribution of wealth', *Econometrica*, 25:591–595.

World Bank (1975) *The assault on world poverty*. Baltimore, MD: Johns Hopkins University Press.

World Bank (1982) *World development report: 1982*. London: Oxford University Press.

Chapter 20

TAXATION FOR DEVELOPING COUNTRIES

EHTISHAM AHMAD and NICHOLAS STERN*

The London School of Economics

Contents

*We are grateful to A.B. Atkinson, W. Buiter, D. Coady, J.P. Drèze, J. Eaton, N. Jetha, M. King, S. Ludlow, D.M.G. Newbery, G. Sicat, L. Squire, T.N. Srinivasan, V. Tanzi and participants at the 1985 Harvard meeting of authors of the Handbook for helpful comments. Errors are ours.

Handbook of Development Economics, Volume II, Edited by H. Chenery and T.N. Srinivasan
© *Elsevier Science Publishers B.V., 1989*

1. Introduction

1.1. Scope and structure of the chapter

Public economics is about the application of economic analysis to the problems of public policy. As such its scope is obviously vast, including, inter alia, the role and objectives of government, taxation, planning, project appraisal, control of demand and inflation, public enterprises, regulation of private activities and so on. One cannot hope to cover all these topics in one chapter, and our focus here will be on taxation. This is justified in part by the concentration of recent research in public economics, but also by the discussion of, for example, cost–benefit analysis and planning in other chapters in this Handbook. We shall, however, emphasise the close relationship between the many parts of public economics.

Division of the subject into topics, which is understandable in terms of a desire to keep analysis manageable, has often had unfortunate consequences in that basic underlying principles and themes have been neglected or overlooked. Hence, we place our discussion of taxation firmly in the context of public economics. The term public economics is now generally used in contrast to "public finance". This is to emphasise that the subject is much more than the way in which public expenditure is financed but concerns the effects of government actions on resource use and income distribution throughout the economy [and the attraction of the wider term has been stressed by many writers, e.g. Johansen (1965) and Musgrave (1959, Preface)].

Our concentration will be on methods and principles to bring out what can be done together with the basic ideas which should guide research and policy, rather than on providing an exhaustive survey of what has been done. Our emphasis on taxation has implied that a number of interesting topics on the expenditure side are not covered here, including the allocation of public expenditure between consumption and investment and the analysis of public goods. The reader who wishes to pursue the broad area of public economics in more detail should consult the two-volume *Handbook of Public Economics* edited by Auerbach and Feldstein (1985, 1987).

Questions and issues in public economics in general, and taxation in particular, are both positive and normative. Examples of the former are: "What are the effects of tariffs on the prices of other goods?" "How does the corporation tax affect incomes and the allocation of investment?" "What features of the economy influence the potential and actual revenue from different sorts of taxes?" Amongst the normative questions are: "What should be the balance between direct and indirect taxation?" "Should indirect taxes be uniform?" "What is the appropriate price for electricity?" And so on. All of these will be discussed (at varying levels of detail) in this chapter but it should be immediately clear that the positive questions are logically prior. We cannot examine the normative questions until we know what taxes are available and what are their effects.

The issues we shall raise, for example those just mentioned, are relevant for both developed and developing countries and the application of many of the approaches and principles we shall examine is certainly not confined to developing countries. As with a number of other aspects of development economics conceptual advances motivated by the study of poor countries have been most fruitful for the analysis of the economies of more advanced countries. Nevertheless there are important features of the fiscal systems and economies of developing countries which require particular attention and make some of the analysis distinctive. Amongst these we would emphasise the enforcement costs or administrative difficulties which may limit the choice of tax instruments, partial coverage of various taxes in that certain sectors or types of firm may escape the tax net, legally or otherwise, the central role of the agricultural sector which is usually poor, fragmented and backward, the structure of the labour market, the poor quality of information, and the variety of objectives, structures and powers of governments.

The plan of the chapter is as follows. In the remainder of this section we explain the broad outlines of our approach and point to lines of enquiry which, whilst in many respects important and interesting, do not receive close attention in the rest of the chapter.

In Section 2 we examine the sources of government revenue in different countries, including which taxes are used and how much they provide, and the incidence of taxation on different groups. We discuss also the administrative problems with enforcement and evasion which often lie behind the choice of taxes and exercise strong influences on the revenue they raise. In Section 3 we consider the appraisal of different taxes, the central issues there being incentives, distribution and the structure of production. These are examined in relation to government objectives, which may be articulated in a range of concerns, such as growth and employment, together with the many constraints which the government may face. We pay particular attention to indirect taxes (tariffs, excise taxes, sales taxes, VAT and the like) which provide a far higher fraction of revenue in developing than developed countries, although corporate income, personal income, land and other direct taxes are also examined. Agriculture is the subject of Section 4. A brief discussion of examples of tax reform in practice, which reflects the application of the principles we have described in relation to the particular difficulties and problems facing specific countries is in Section 5. Concluding remarks and directions for further research are offered in Section 6.

It should be clear from this description of the chapter that our emphasis is on microeconomics and the medium or longer run. Macroeconomic modelling and its use in economic policy are discussed in other chapters of this Handbook, although again we suspect that something is lost in the separation in that one should consider consistency of the models underlying different topics and the policies which emerge, as well as recognising the similarities of questions and techniques. Nevertheless our analytical capabilities are such that full and explicit integration of macro and micro and short-run and long-run analyses is not possible and, at present, we should look for the complementarities. Thus, one would not wish, if possible, short-run policies to run directly counter to medium-term directions of reform.

Even though this is a long chapter there are a number of important issues within taxation that are omitted or mentioned only briefly. Significant examples concern fiscal relations in a federal structure (a proper analysis would have to include a full discussion of expenditure) and the effects of taxation on risk-taking (see Subsection 1.5).

1.2. The role of government

An examination of the role of government will enter directly into both positive and normative analyses. Thus, in the former one may ask how the limitations on government affect the taxes which may be considered and their impact on the economy. For example, the constitution may rule out some taxes, the administration may not be willing or able to collect others, and certain tools may be politically unacceptable. On the normative side one must ask what the government objectives are. Indeed, logically prior is the question of whether it is reasonable to describe its actions in terms of consistent objectives. Thus, one must ask how government actions are determined.

The positive aspects of government powers and limitations appear implicitly throughout in terms of the taxes discussed and will in a number of cases be explicit as, for example, when we discuss enforcement. On the normative side we shall for the most part adopt one particular approach. We shall see the normative problem as choosing instruments to try to improve the welfare of the different households in the population subject to whichever constraints on the economy and government action are present.

The normative analysis therefore proceeds by first pursuing the positive analysis in a particular direction, i.e. looking at the effects of a policy change, and then evaluating those consequences using explicit criteria. It should be obvious immediately that this approach does not involve the assertion that this is the way governments do in fact behave. One is using economic analysis to work out the consequences, for example, for different households or groups, in a systematic way so that informed and consistent normative judgements of governmental economic actions are possible. Those judgements themselves can then be made by commentators, governments, aid-givers, members of the community or whoever wishes to make them. The presentation of the consequences in a manner which allows the application of systematic values would seem to be an essential part of reasonable discussion of policy.

Our emphasis here, therefore, is on the analysis of judgements concerning possible public policies. This is in contrast to alternative approaches which see policies as determined within a system by the participating individuals or agents. Important and interesting examples concern voting models where public choices are determined by votes of individuals, models of bureaucracy where those who administer the organs of state determine outcomes, and models of interest groups where different classes compete against others for group gains and for control. A leading figure in this literature has been James Buchanan and many of these positive theories are included under the heading "public choice" [see Buchanan and Tollison (1972) and for a survey see Mueller (1976)]. It must be recognised, however, that a systematic analysis of policies in terms of their consequences is necessary for this approach also.

Recently there has been particular attention in the study of public policy in developing countries to "rent-seeking". Government policy, such as tariffs or quotas on particular goods, raises the incomes of certain individuals or groups. Those individuals or groups seek the rents which might be conferred by such policies by expending resources on trying to get them implemented. Those who decide or administer the policies can thereby gain substantially and favour systems which allow themselves to benefit from the exercise of their discretion. For further discussion of "rent-seeking" and "neoclassical political economy", see Krueger (1974), Buchanan, Tollison and Tullock (1980), Colander (1984), Srinivasan (1985) and Bhagwati (1987).

Most theories, however, whether or not policy is determined within the system, share the requirement that the effects of policy have to be calculated explicitly. This is the first, and often most difficult, part of any analysis of policy in terms of its consequences. Thus, for example, the normative approach to a change in the income tax should calculate who gains and who loses in a similar manner to a model where changes take place according to whether particular interest groups would benefit. Insofar as constraints on government actions and the effects of changes for households are central to this chapter it has much in common with the positive theories of policy determination. We shall not, however, examine in detail the models of endogenous public choice. This is not because we believe these approaches to be misguided and neither do we think the results are unimportant. Nevertheless the applied literature is less extensive, particularly for developing countries, and it is often not easy to provide empirical hypotheses in a way that allows one to test between competing theories. And whether or not the policy is determined within the system it remains interesting to ask how external commentators with prescribed sets of values might judge between different policies in terms of their effects on different households or groups.

Given that the approach here is normative one must ask whether the criteria applied by governments in developing countries are likely to be or should be very different from those of developed countries. It would often seem that the differences in objectives are substantial and some writers [e.g. Prest (1972) and Musgrave and Musgrave (1984)] have emphasised this aspect as a main distinctive feature of public economics for developing countries. Thus, for example, governments in developing countries have often seen themselves as having particular responsibilities to promote growth and one finds that capital formation often forms a higher proportion of government budgets than for developed countries. Other commonly articulated concerns are the relief of poverty, the promotion of employment and the encouragement of self-sufficiency. One may see all of these, however, as relating in large part to the material well-being of households, present and future. As such they can to a substantial extent be analysed in terms of a model where the welfare of households is the central policy criterion. Other objectives, such as changing the values of participants in society (e.g. at times China and Tanzania) are less easily incorporated into the analysis.

1.3. Other public activities

Many government actions, other than those involving taxation, affect government revenue, prices, incomes, welfare and the allocation of resources. These include: subsidies, rations and transfer payments, which are usually classified under expenditure; expenditure on health, education, defence and so on; pricing and investment policies of publicly owned companies; and laws and regulations imposing constraints on the actions of private companies and households. Many of these can be analysed in a similar fashion to taxation. For example, subsidies and transfer payments (including subsidised rations) are negative taxes and the difference between price and social marginal cost of public enterprises are analogous to taxes. And the pricing of and expenditure on education and health raise similar problems to those involved in taxation as well as involving aspects of social cost–benefit analysis. We shall argue both that the interdependence of these topics is crucial to policy for any one of them and that their analysis can be integrated in a systematic way using shadow prices. Furthermore, many of the principles which we shall describe for taxation can and should be applied to, for example, public-sector pricing, subsidies and transfer payments. Those government actions which are closely related to taxation are, in developing countries, often different from those in developed countries. An important example concerns transfer payments. In many developing countries transfer payments frequently take the form of subsidised rations whilst extensive social security systems rarely exist. Rations are less important in developed countries but public provisions for unemployment and social security benefits and pensions are common.

1.4. Stabilisation

Musgrave's third "branch of government activity", together with revenue and distribution, was stabilisation [see, for example, Musgrave (1959)]. By this he meant the design of fiscal policy to counter unemployment during downturns in the cycle and to help control inflation. Whilst revenue and distribution are now seen as inseparable issues in many models of public economics, the analysis of stabilisation in the sense described has tended to be split off and treated separately. Partly this is because the time scale for stabilisation discussions is much shorter but also because macro-economic models have often looked very different from those used for micro-economic analysis. Short-run macro-economic models are now, however, increasingly based on firmer micro-economic foundations so that it is possible that the incentive and distribution issues may play a more prominent role. There is also some integration in certain computable general equilibrium models [see, for example, Kehoe and Serra-Puche (1983)]. We shall not, however, focus on stabilisation in this chapter and for further discussion of macroeconomics and the shorter run the reader should consult other chapters in this Handbook.

Stabilisation in public policy analysis has also taken on a broader meaning than simply counter-cyclic policy of the Keynesian kind in that major problems in some developing countries have been associated with chronic government and balance of payments deficits and inflation which appear not to be temporary and which cannot easily be seen in terms of oscillating cycles. Stabilisation is sometimes viewed as the correction of a chronic deficit or an adjustment to a change that may seem non-cyclical, e.g. adverse changes in the dollar exchange rate, interest rates or export/import prices. The perennial feeling of the Finance Minister that he has too few sources of revenue and too many demands for expenditure may seem particularly acute in poor countries so that the temptation

to run deficits is very strong or that adjustment to a permanent adverse movement may be very difficult. It is important, therefore, that both the debtor and
creditor countries come to a sober and balanced view of what is possible for a
particular country in terms of revenue raising. In this context the discussion of
"tax effort" in Section 2 can be useful. It should be recognised, however, that
whilst the structure of the economy exerts an important influence on tax as a
proportion of GNP it is not immutable and can be raised quite sharply over
relatively short periods (see Section 2).

1.5. Other issues

It should be emphasised that our concentration on micro-economics in this
chapter does not rule out the treatment of issues such as unemployment, savings
and investment. They play a central role in the determination of shadow prices
which in turn influence one's view of tax reform. Furthermore, the microeconomic models can be adapted to examine intertemporal tax issues, in particular the treatment of savings and investment.

The impact of alternative taxes on risk-taking and risk-sharing is discussed
theoretically in Atkinson and Stiglitz (1980, lecture 4). This has not figured
prominently in the applied literature relating to taxation in developing countries
and is an area for further research.

It is possible that the issue is of relatively greater importance for developing
countries since the potential role of government in using the tax system to share
risk is less the more the private market provides for risk-sharing and, for
developing countries, risk and capital markets are considerably less sophisticated.
Thus corporation tax, for example, can provide risk-sharing with the government
taking a fraction of the positive profits and, with loss off-set, taking the same
fraction of the losses. In many countries, however, the problems with the
corporation tax lie less in fine tuning for risk than in collecting taxes in the face
of effective concealment of profits. Similarly, there is substantial potential for
influencing risk through price support policies and buffer stocks.

Issues of fiscal-federalism are important for some developing countries like
India, as for other "federal" states such as Canada, Australia and the United
States. In India the Constitution lays down a requirement for a Finance Commission to meet periodically to review the sharing of revenues between the States and
the Federal Government, and a compromise is generally produced in terms of
balancing revenue transfers according to needs (however defined) and collections.
There are also different formulae regarding the division of some of the major
taxes, and this often forms the subject of "revenue seeking" by the players
concerned. Many countries are less fortunate than India in that the divisions of
taxation and expenditure powers between different levels of government are

ill-defined. We do not treat this subject in any great detail in this chapter, although we show briefly in Section 3 and Ahmad and Stern (1987) how revenue from State and Central taxes may be evaluated if a clear distinction can be made between the tax instruments associated with different levels of government.

2. The choice of revenue instruments

Resources are needed by governments in developing countries, as in advanced nations, for a wide variety of expenditures, ranging from public administration and defence to the maintenance and provision of social services and infrastructure. While there is considerable debate in many Western countries concerning which services should be provided by the state (and these arguments are also reflected in some developing countries), raising the level of government expenditure and particularly of public investment in key areas of the economy has often been seen as a necessary ingredient of the development process.

The costs of these expenditures are usually only partly met through taxation and profits of government undertakings, and the discrepancy between revenues and expenditures is often substantial. In India the combined expenditures of central and state governments increased from 10 percent of GNP in 1950/51 to over 30 percent in 1980/81, and 35 percent in 1983/84 [see Ahmad and Stern (1987)]. The 1982 figures for other low-income countries such as Sri Lanka, Pakistan, Tanzania and Kenya were 34, 16, 32 and 30 percent, respectively; and for Latin American countries such as Mexico, Chile, Argentina and Brazil, 32, 38, 22 and 22 percent, respectively. In developed countries, government expenditure ranged from 18 percent of GNP for Japan to 25 percent of GNP for the United States, 42 percent for the United Kingdom, to 45 percent for Sweden and 58 percent for Belgium and the Netherlands [World Bank (1985)]. On the other hand, around 1982, tax revenues in poorer developing countries were generally under 20 percent of GNP: India 18 percent; Sri Lanka 20 percent; Pakistan 13 percent; Tanzania 18 percent; Kenya 21 percent; with Mexico 17 percent; Chile 25 percent; Argentina 20 percent; and Brazil 23 percent. The "shortfall" was thus often substantial.

It should be remembered that there are serious problems in defining the government deficit or borrowing requirement. Some of these arise from different classifications of profits and losses of public corporations. Others are associated with inflation when it is usual to classify *nominal* interest on outstanding public debt as government expenditure. Thus comparing two countries which were identical in every respect other than the inflation rate one would be forced to say that the one with the higher inflation rate (and thus nominal interest rate) had the bigger deficit.

One should also bear in mind that success in raising revenue may well increase expenditure [the Please (1971) hypothesis]. This tendency may be particularly problematic if the effect works quickly since then short-run revenue increases may lead to rapid expenditure increases which can be cut back only slowly. Thus, public finance difficulties of countries such as Mexico and Nigeria can in part be traced to the expenditure expansions following revenue booms associated with the oil price increases of the 1970s.

In this section we examine the alternatives facing a government with a given revenue requirement, however this might arise. A major option is taxation where the tools adopted and the revenue obtained will be a function of the pattern and organisation of production activities and the administrative capabilities of the tax authorities as well as the bases defined for taxation and the selected rates. Here cross-country comparisons can suggest the sorts of taxes that are possible, particularly with respect to administration, and may provide guidance as to how revenue flows might change in the course of time.

Various "tax handles" are discussed in Subsection 2.1 along with the evolution of tax structure and the incidence of taxes. Non-tax issues and the financing of deficits are addressed in Subsection 2.2 with a consideration of domestic non-bank borrowing in Subsection 2.2.1 and money creation in Subsection 2.2.3. Although these tools may be outside the remit of tax reform, some discussion cannot be avoided since the extent to which they are available or desirable will influence directly total tax revenue requirements. The balance between tax and non-tax revenue is a central policy choice that faces most governments. Foreign resources have been treated extensively in chapters by Eaton (Chapter 25) and Cardoso and Dornbusch (Chapter 26) in this Handbook and are not examined here. Administrative considerations and implementation are considered in Subsection 2.3.

2.1. Taxation

2.1.1. Tax handles

Relationships between the "level of development" and the structure of taxation were examined by Hinrichs (1966) and Musgrave (1969). Since then there have been a large number of studies which have concentrated on cross-section international comparisons of "tax capacity" and "effort" carried out primarily by staff members of the IMF's Fiscal Affairs Department [see, for example, Lotz and Morss (1967), Bahl (1971), Chelliah, Baas and Kelly (1975), Tait, Gratz and Eichengreen (1979)]. These are discussed in Subsection 2.2.2.

Using international cross-section comparisons, both Hinrichs and Musgrave stress that the scarcity of simple ways of collecting revenue, or "tax handles", characterise early stages of development. Hinrichs uses an "ideal-type" classification to describe the pattern of change in tax structure during development. A four-fold classification of stages is proposed: traditional; transitional – incorporating "breakaway" from old; "adoption" of new; and modern. Traditional societies appear to rely on a combination of direct taxes on agriculture (land, output, livestock, and water rates, for example), poll taxes and non-tax revenue. These sources become less prominent in "later stages". In the "breakaway" period, indirect taxation becomes more important, and in particular trade taxes dominate, depending on the degree of "openness" of the economy. The foreign trade sector provides a convenient handle, as it is possible to monitor flows of goods at a "bottleneck", and also because in a dualistic framework, the degree of monetization is likely to be high in such activities. The domestic indirect taxes – excises, sales and transaction taxes and profits of government enterprises – become important with the increase in domestic production capability, monetization and the volume of internal transactions. Older forms of direct taxation become less important relative to the taxation of *net* income of individuals and businesses. Thus the classification suggested is one where taxation varies from (i) agriculture, to (ii) foreign trade, to (iii) consumption, to (iv) income.

Hinrichs is careful to caution against determinism and the pattern described "does not necessarily mean that all countries have traced or will follow such a sequence at all times" (p. 106). Moreover, averaging over the tax structures of low-income countries might be misleading, since in some the ratio of direct to indirect taxation might be increasing whilst in others it might be decreasing. The simple averages might suggest a "generalised half truth that development brings with it a steady trend towards more direct taxation" (p. 108). The pattern of change in tax structure for India illustrates the danger of resorting to simple averages. The Indian tax revenue/GNP ratio averaged under 8 percent during the 1950s. By 1963/64 this had increased to over 14 percent and it fluctuated around that level to the mid-seventies. Since 1977, total tax revenue has averaged over 18 percent of GNP. Although "traditional" taxes (on property and property transactions) fell from 13 percent of total tax revenue in 1950/51 to under 4 percent by 1979/80, taxes on income also declined from 28 percent of total tax revenue to under 16 percent during the same period. On the other hand, indirect taxes increased from 58 percent of tax revenue during 1950/51 to around 80 percent thirty years later. With indirect taxes, the major structural change occurred during the 1950s with the increase in domestic productive capacity. In 1950/51 customs formed the most important indirect "tax handle" and accounted for 43 percent of commodity tax revenue; Union excises (on domestic production) were 18 percent, sales taxes 16 percent and state excises (largely on liquor) 14 percent of indirect tax revenue. By 1959/60, the Union excise had become the most important indirect tax (45 percent of commodity tax revenue), and customs had fallen to under 20 percent, ahead of sales taxes (18 percent) and state excises (6 percent). This pattern was maintained over the next twenty years, with sales taxes stabilising on a par with customs at around 20 percent of commodity tax revenue, and the predominance of the Union excise tax being maintained [see Ahmad and Stern (forthcoming), for further details].

The Indian example highlights some of the major policy issues and paradoxes indicated above. First, the move to direct taxes may be associated with a desire to link taxation to ability to pay and it is often claimed that indirect taxes are inegalitarian. The validity of this claim depends on the context, and the Indian Indirect Taxation Enquiry Committee (1978) found the incidence of Indian indirect taxes during the mid-seventies to be quite progressive [see also Chelliah and Lal (1978)]. If such progression is desired there is the further question of how this might best be combined with simplicity and administrative feasibility.

Second, it might be more appropriate for less-developed countries to learn from the recent experiences of other low-income developing countries than to imitate more developed societies, leading, possibly, to an emphasis on indirect taxes at least in the medium term. This does not mean that direct taxes are unimportant, simply that to be effective they require proper design, administration and implementation, and need to be incorporated into a changing mix of taxes over time. Thus, with limited administrative capabilities, it may be unwise for many countries to expect them to provide substantial revenue in the short or medium term.

A third consideration arises concerning the possible policy conflict between ease of collection and administrative expediency on the one hand and disincentive effects on the other. Growing sectors provide convenient tax handles which are often eagerly grasped by governments, even though this might impair the long-run development of such sectors and consequently reduce the growth of revenue in the future. Argentina is an example of excessive taxation of the export sector "one can milk only so much out of the export sector without drying up the cow" (Hinrichs, p. 116). Similarly in Africa, export taxes have been used extensively, often as a means of taxing agricultural income, e.g. cocoa in Ghana and groundnuts in Malawi [World Bank (1981)]. In India, the very extensive reliance on taxation of domestic production causes distortion through the taxation of inputs and discrimination against exports (since rebating indirect taxes is difficult) and against the large-scale sector (small-scale production is often exempt and is difficult to tax). [See Section 3 below, Ahmad and Stern (1987) and Ahmad and Stern (1986a) for an example from Pakistan.] Influenced in part by these problems the Indian Indirect Taxation Enquiry Committee [Government of India (1978)] recommended a shift from excises to a system of value-added taxation restricted to the manufacturing sector. Eventually (in the 1986 Budget) a system of rebating excises on inputs was introduced, known as MODVAT. And a growing number of developing countries now have experience with variants of the VAT [Tanzi (1987)].

The personal income tax raises similar difficulties. It is least likely to be evaded by employees in the modern sector and the more productive whose success is difficult to conceal. It is most likely to be evaded by certain established groups with influence, landlords and farmers, shopkeepers and small-scale businessmen or traders, speculators and the like. In the sub-continent despite an elaborate legal system very little is collected through the income tax.

In an analysis of the tax structure of 86 countries around 1981, Tanzi (1987) found a weak correlation of personal income taxes and GDP/head, and personal income taxes were on average less than 2 percent of GDP in developing countries, and less than 5 percent of GDP in all but three LDCs. Corporate income taxes were relatively more important than the personal income tax and accounted for some 3 percent of GDP on average. In many mineral-exporting countries, the corporate income tax appeared to be a useful tax handle in that production and export were carried out by a few large corporations. Thus, it provided a means of taxing the exportable good as well as the (usually foreign) corporation. However, production of agricultural commodities, carried out by many heterogeneous agriculturalists, is easier to tax through export taxes than through direct taxation. (See Section 4 below for a further discussion of agricultural taxation.)

More fruitful bases of direct taxation, that would require less administrative costs and bear less heavily on incentives, such as urban property, and land values may often not be politically acceptable. Indeed, the difficulties they raise for avoidance and evasion may be precisely the reason that those who might have to pay them create such powerful political objections to their introduction or successful administration.

2.1.2. Taxable capacity, elasticity and buoyancy

2.1.2.1. Taxable capacity. Goode (1984) defines taxable capacity as the ability of people to pay tax and the ability of the government to collect; the tax effort reflects the degree to which taxable capacity is used. The tax ratio (of total tax revenue to GNP, discussed above) reflects, however, both tax capacity and effort, the latter influenced by the level of government expenditure and availability and use of non-tax resources. The IMF studies mentioned above explore the cross-country relationships between identifiable tax handles and the tax ratio. These "handles" are taken as a proxy for taxable capacity, and the residual between *estimated* taxable capacity and the tax ratio is taken to measure tax effort. Thus, taxable capacity is given by the tax ratio which would arise if a country used its tax handles to the average extent used by countries in the sample (and we see that under this definition the tax ratio will be above capacity for many countries – a slightly curious use of language).

The procedure is to specify a single-equation model with tax as a proportion of GNP being the dependent variable and to include as explanatory variables measures of factors which might be seen as representing elements of taxable capacity. Examples of the latter include the share of mining, which is often found to have a positive contribution, and that of agriculture which generally has a negative one; see, for example, Chelliah, Baas and Kelly (1975) who found that the equation that gave the "best fit" was one which included only these variables [see also Chelliah (1971)]. Tait, Gratz and Eichengreen (1979) carried out "international tax comparisons" rather than tax effort estimates for developed countries and less developed countries considered together and separately, over 1972–76.

The cross-country comparisons have been subjected to a number of criticisms. Bird (1976) pointed out that one of the most damaging is that there is inadequate a priori justification for the use of the selected variables as measures of taxable capacity. For instance, the omission of the share of agriculture on the grounds that it reflects not only capacity but "willingness" to tax [a step eventually taken by Chelliah, Baas and Kelly (1975)] should also lead to the exclusion of the mining share "on equally firm (or infirm) grounds". The distinction between "capacity" and "willingness" is a very fuzzy one: indeed, one might say that "capacity" without "willingness" is not really "capacity" – or "effective capacity" – at all. Similarly, per capita income "is presumably included because it is a proxy for a potentially higher tax base, or a larger 'taxable surplus'. But in fact income is surely as much a 'demand' as it is a 'supply' factor: the identification problem seems insuperable in this respect" [Bird (1976, p. 43)]. Furthermore, the errors in variables problem may be serious and the approach obscures the complex interrelationship between government revenue and other factors such as expenditures.

A major danger with the international tax comparisons is that they are often used (or misused) for normative policy issues. Even if the question of taxable capacity could be correctly identified, taxable effort, or the residual between fitted and actual tax ratios, may indicate little of value for policy since the "average" may have no relevance at all for a given country. A tax effort ratio less than 1.0 may mean that a country has a preference for a lower than "average" level of taxation, or that a higher ratio is, for some reason, unnecessary. However, one should not view this analysis with excessive rigidity and one may simply view a low index as suggestive of the feasibility of raising additional taxes.

A rigidly deterministic interpretation of cross-country studies is made still less attractive by the patchy quality of data. Quite often national aggregates, such as per capita incomes are crude guesses and tax information is often suspect with sharply differing definitions and practices across countries which cannot satisfactorily be placed on a comparable basis. And there are the usual objections to using results from international cross-sections as a guide to policy-making for a particular country over time (one must ask whether the underlying model is really the same). Bird (1976, pp. 49–50) concludes that "the effort which has gone into 'effort studies' would contribute more to both knowledge and policy formulation if it were redirected to perhaps less glamorous but surely more rewarding studies of particular problems in particular countries", although most protagonists would probably agree that such "effort studies" should be seen as suggestive only and not as a substitute for the detailed analysis of individual countries.

2.1.2.2. Tax elasticity and buoyancy. The "built-in tax elasticity" relates to the ability of the tax structure to generate growth in revenue through changes in gross income or output levels – one contemplates the growth of revenue in the absence of "discretionary actions" which might affect the tax base or rates. Thus, revenue series are put together which have discretionary changes "netted out", to separate the "automatic" from the "discretionary" elements in taxation. This modified time series for revenue is regressed on income or output, to yield the built-in tax elasticity.

The overall elasticity of the tax system may be decomposed into elasticities for the various taxes constituting the system, and each may be written as an elasticity of the base with respect to income together with the elasticity of the yield with respect to the base [see, for example, Goode (1984, pp. 93–95)]. A major problem in this type of analysis is to put together data on the bases of the major taxes and on "estimated" yields at constant rates. And it is not clear whether applying rates to the base is a particularly good way of forecasting, assuming of course that information on "bases" is known. In practice the elasticity of a tax will depend not only on its design, including exemptions and "hypothetical" coverage, but also on its administration, enforcement and evasion. It is also difficult to correct for inflation. There is no reason to suspect that the latter set of factors will remain constant over time and it would not be easy to disentangle in a series separate effects of changes in policy, income, compliance, administration and so on particularly where enforcement and administration are in part matters of policy.

"Tax buoyancy" studies, on the other hand, simply relate total revenue to income or output, without making any such adjustment to revenue. This is "analogous to separating 'capacity' from residual (in tax effort studies) and consequently subject to the same objections" [Bird (1976, p. 52)]. However, overall measures of elasticity and buoyancy may be useful as a descriptive tool, and may lead to further questions (particularly concerning future financing difficulties) and point to a more detailed examination of particular taxes in certain countries.

There have been many tax elasticity and buoyancy studies, for various individual countries [see, for instance, Mansfield (1972), Levin (1968) and Wilford and Wilford (1978) for studies of Latin American countries; and Dwivedi (1981a), Purohit (1981) and Bagchi and Govinda Rao (1982) for examples from India] and some broad conclusions appear to emerge. First, general sales taxes, excises and consumption taxes seem to have elasticities in excess of unity. Second, whilst in several cases income taxes are found to be an elastic source of revenue other studies point in the opposite direction. Customs duties and stamp duties seem to be relatively inelastic [see Goode (1984)].

Although these studies, which are often carefully conducted, provide a useful commentary on particular taxes, they do not provide a very sound basis for policy, despite the presumption in "resource mobilisation" studies that there should be a greater reliance on "more elastic" taxes. The low elasticity of a particular tax relates only to the actual revenue collections during the period under consideration. Elasticities can change and in any case do not tell us whether it is desirable or undesirable to increase yields from that tax in the future. For example, the Indian income tax was apparently inelastic during earlier periods, but was seen to have an elasticity of 1.1 between 1965/66 and 1978/79 [Bagchi and Govinda Rao (1982)]. There may also be arguments for a greater reliance on a "better designed" land tax (see Section below), although estimates may show that such taxes have been the most inelastic [e.g. Purohit (1981) on India]. In some poor countries, the majority of government revenues come from (inelastic) customs duties and (hypothetically elastic) income taxes may exist only in spirit and provide only a small fraction of government revenue [see Tanzi (1987)]. An attempted switch from customs (through lower rates or more exemptions) to income taxes (higher rates, greater coverage and enforcement) may not be advisable on revenue grounds and could be administratively infeasible.

The conclusion is that estimates of tax elasticity and buoyancy do not provide direct guidance for policy and are not a substitute for a careful analysis of the consequences of particular policy changes. They may nevertheless be of assistance in anticipating revenue problems and suggesting areas of focus for specific studies.

2.1.3. Tax incidence

A common and voluminous strand in the literature relating to taxation and development concerns the "incidence" of particular taxes on various household groups (for example on deciles of the income distribution, with respect to rural and urban sectors, regions and so on). The concept is intended to reflect the degree to which the real income of households is reduced by taxation and how this varies across households. It should be clear that a thorough implementation of the idea requires the modelling of the full general equilibrium impact of taxes and a measure or measures of how household welfare is affected by price, tax and other changes (taking into account behavioural responses). There is no doubt that the modelling problems are severe [see, for example, Shoven (1983)] but the assumptions and definitions lying behind an incidence calculation should be carefully scrutinized since usually crude short cuts are taken. Sometimes "benefits" of government expenditure are included and quite often incidence refers to the taxes and benefits taken together. Explicit criteria are then applied, for instance to discuss the equity of "tax burdens" and to comment on the "degree of progression". These studies are used, then, in arguments for or against certain types of taxes or policies.

Goode (1984) reflects a common sentiment that "indirect taxes, which are a major revenue source in developing countries, tend to be regressive with respect to income... however, careful selection of objects of indirect taxation and tax rates can result in a distribution of indirect taxes that is broadly proportional or progressive with respect to income or total consumption" (p. 79). Contrast this with the review of tax incidence studies until the mid-seventies by de Wulf (1975, p. 71): "the general impression... is that the tax systems in developing countries tend to burden the incomes of rich families relatively more than the incomes of the poor... this finding is interesting in the light of the prevailing view that the tax structures are regressive in developing countries, since they rely heavily on indirect taxes". A study prepared for the Indian Indirect Taxation Enquiry Committee [Government of India (1978)] in the late seventies remarked on the progressivity of Indian indirect taxes [also see Chelliah and Lal (1978)]. It has been argued that in practice the degree of progression that could be achieved through the sales tax, for example, is at the expense of complicated rate structures and exemptions, leading to revenue losses with little impact on "progressivity". Gandhi (1979) argues for a low, uniform rate sales tax for revenue purposes, supplemented by other indirect taxes for equity considerations. In practice, we would suggest, an important degree of progression can be achieved whilst retaining simplicity, with a system which exempts many foods, has a low uniform rate for most goods and a luxury rate for certain other goods (see Section 5 below).

Similarly, the relative burden of taxation on the rural or agricultural sector vis-à-vis the urban sector is an emotive issue that has been fuelled (inconclusively) by tax incidence analyses. Gandhi (1966), for instance, found that the rural sector in India paid "too small a share of tax". Lipton (1978, pp. 201–203) criticised some of Gandhi's assumptions and argued that the taxation of Indian agriculture *exceeds the ability to pay* (as measured by mean income levels and estimates of minimum subsistence) of agriculturalists, although agricultural incomes in most Indian states and Pakistan do not attract the personal income tax. The analysis of price levels for inputs and outputs and the implicit taxes they embody should play a crucial role in such comparisons and the results are likely to vary both with the method by which these are treated and across countries. Furthermore, one should not forget that ultimately one's distributional values relate to individuals and households rather than to sectors and that within sectors there are generally very large variations in individual incomes.

Following Musgrave et al. (1951) a distinction has been made between "absolute incidence" and "differential incidence". The purpose of incidence is to compare distributions of tax burdens under two different systems. The absolute incidence approach compares the actual with the "hypothetical" situation in which there are assumed to be no taxes (or expenditures). However, with differential incidence one assumes that a specific tax (or expenditure) is replaced by a different tax (or expenditure) of the same revenue magnitude. When absolute incidence estimates are invoked, the implication is that the extent to which a given sub-group could be made better off (worse off) by the removal of a tax or all taxes (expenditures) has been shown. The relevance of the no-tax base line is obscure and this is what motivates the analysis of differential incidence. However, whichever approach is used, a basic assumption usually remains that the *existing* pre-tax income distribution would *continue to exist*, under an alternative tax system in the case of differential incidence, and in the absence of a tax system in the case of absolute incidence [see de Wulf (1975) and Bird and de Wulf (1983)].

A variant of incidence analysis has also been used in recent years to work through the consequences of various policy changes for households in different circumstances. This involves an identification of gainers and losers and a measure of the money loss or gain associated with given policy changes. If small changes are considered, actual expenditures or incomes provide an accurate first approximation. However, for larger policy changes, demand and labour supply responses become important. These issues are discussed further in Section 3 [and for empirical estimations see, for example, Ahmad and Stern (1987) for India, and Ahmad and Stern (1986a) for Pakistan].

There are many further problems associated with incidence studies, several of which may generate considerable additional work. One set of questions concerns the shifting of taxes. This is, in part, an issue of market structure [see Seade (forthcoming) and Stern (1987b) for a theoretical analysis]. The solution generally adopted in applied work has been to assume the full forward shifting of indirect taxes, and complete non-shifting of personal income taxes. When the effects of different taxes are spliced together for overall incidence calculations one should check for consistency of models although this consistency may be difficult to achieve whilst retaining the relevant empirical detail. Additional problems are created with the taxation of intermediate goods and raw materials [see Ahmad and Stern (1987) and Section 3 below], the analysis of which in principle requires full information on the input–output structure of the economy. Other problems relate to the lumping together of disparate households with varying characteristics into aggregated income categories. For example, a single-person household with Rs. 1000 per month is not "equivalent" in welfare terms to a ten-person household with the same income, though they may be classified in the same group. Some data sources might allow correction for this aspect but many others, such as age, housing and health would usually remain. Aggregating into income or other classes may be inappropriate for the tax questions at issue, and one might miss the result that there would be many gainers of a certain type simply because the particular features of gainers and losers are not closely related to the categories used for incidence analysis. In the Indian context, income tax laws apply to individuals except for Hindu undivided families (HUFs) where the taxable unit is the family. Mappings from HUFs and individuals to households can be quite difficult [but see Chelliah and Lal (1978)]. A household survey with data at the household level is invaluable in this respect although many problems remain. For example, the particular concept of income used could greatly influence results and transitory but large factors, e.g. poor harvests, may affect different households to varying extents. Furthermore, as in several African countries, nomadic or transitory populations add further constraints to the efficacy of household surveys.

2.2. The financing of deficits

In this subsection we discuss, briefly, possible non-tax measures used to finance the gap between government revenues and expenditures. Three main sources are commonly used, to varying degrees in different countries: non-bank borrowing, money creation, and external borrowing or aid. Each alternative has an attendant profile of costs and benefits that must be considered by the government, in relation to raising additional revenue through taxation. In Subsection 2.2.1 we examine non-bank domestic borrowing, the constraints on this option and possibility of equivalence with taxation. In Subsection 2.2.2 we discuss borrowing from the banking system or money creation. The inflation tax is also discussed in that subsection.

Some of the principles that govern the choice of financing deficits through external capital mirror the discussion relating to domestic borrowing. However, foreign capital flows are treated in detail elsewhere in this Handbook: foreign private flows in Chapter 26 and foreign public capital flows in Chapter 25, and will not be discussed in detail here.

2.2.1. Domestic non-bank borrowing

In this subsection we are concerned primarily with borrowing from domestic sources other than central banks. Domestic borrowing often arises with an unexpected shortfall in revenues, or to cover emergencies such as floods or defence requirements. Thus, borrowing often substitutes for increases in taxation which would otherwise have to be of considerable magnitude to meet the "one-off" requirements [see Goode (1984, p. 197)]. Unlike taxation borrowing is usually voluntary (although there are examples of compulsory borrowing). The differences between, and possible "equivalence" of, domestic borrowing and taxation are discussed below.

A major constraint to the overall level of domestic borrowing is the degree of monetisation in the economy and the sophistication of the financial markets. However, the experience of low-income countries in South Asia has shown that relatively complex financial markets have developed within a short period and that this has had an impact on the composition and generation of savings. In India, the rate of gross saving has increased from 10 percent of GDP in 1950/51 to over 20 percent in 1975/76 and has been maintained above that level since. The household sector has provided around 75 percent of total gross savings and around 90 percent of total private sector savings throughout the period. However, the composition of household savings has changed dramatically: physical assets provided over 96 percent of household savings in 1951/52 and financial assets 3.9 percent but since the mid-1970s on, financial assets have accounted for around 50 percent on average of household savings [see Government of India (1982), Raj Committee]. There has been a corresponding change in the pattern of financing of total government expenditure in India; tax revenues declined from 70 percent of expenditure in 1950/51 to 61 percent in 1979/80, and domestic borrowing (in terms of net market loans and small savings increased from 4 percent of expenditure in 1950/51 to over 10 percent in 1979/80 [see Ahmad and Stern (forthcoming)]. Thus, provided financial markets exist, as they do to an increasing extent, "tapping" the resources of the "household" sector through domestic borrowing may be seen as a "supplement" or an alternative to tax revenues. Given that tax revenue involves collection costs and generates consumer resistance, which may be substantial in developing countries, and that the purchase of government securities is more or less voluntary, governments may well be tempted to make more use of the latter if financial markets and institutions permit.

There is a contention that the impact of domestic borrowing is equivalent in terms of behaviour and welfare to that of taxation, since individuals would realise that debt servicing and repayment entails taxation in the future. Rational individuals with perfect foresight would then adjust their behaviour accordingly and under certain assumptions borrowing would have exactly the same effect on consumption and savings decisions as taxation [see Barro (1974)]. It should be clear that key assumptions in addition to perfect foresight are perfect capital markets, proportional taxation and that bequests, in present value terms are positive and valued at par with current consumption. This "equivalence theorem" has been attributed to Ricardo. Musgrave (1985) suggests that though Ricardo accepted the possibility of equivalence, he rejected it as unrealistic. Tax finance has an immediate impact on consumption and saving behaviour, whilst "loan finance is a system which tends to make us less thrifty – to blind us to our real situation" [Ricardo (1817, p. 247)]. Thus, on the Ricardian view loan and tax finance differ with respect to their impact on capital formation; saving and capital formulation being reduced by a switch towards domestic borrowing.

The assumptions required for "equivalence" involving not only the correct perception of future tax liabilities from debt creation but also that present generations see the present value of the future liabilities in the same terms as a tax liability now, are unlikely to be acceptable in the context of developing countries. The theoretical literature shows that complete "Ricardian" equivalence could prevail under very special circumstances. Thus, liquidity constraints, imperfect capital markets with divergence of personal and government interest rates, myopic consumers and distortionary effects of taxation inter alia could cause divergence from Ricardian equivalence. Since it could be argued that although the stringent theoretical conditions required do not hold, the actual behaviour of economies nonetheless approximately follows the predictions of Ricardian equivalence, a final evaluation is essentially an empirical matter [see Poterba and Summers (1987)].

There are few satisfactory tests for Ricardian equivalence for developing countries. The most forceful confirmation of the proposition is for the United States, by Kormendi (1983), who shows that over the period 1930–76 increases in government spending on goods and services depress consumer spending, while changes in taxation have no effect on private sector consumption. However, Feldstein and Elmendorf (1987) using alternative functional forms and with more recent data show that Kormendi's result is reversed if the period of the Second World War (with its appeal for self-restraint, rationing and shortages) is excluded. Poterba and Summers (1987) argue that recent U.S. deficits present a natural experiment for testing equivalence, since the increasing deficits have not been caused by wars or natural emergencies. They show that increasing deficits have been accompanied by a decline in national savings and unprecedentedly high levels of real interest rates, in contrast to Ricardian theory. Furthermore, the evidence that pre-announced tax policies have affected private consumption provides a refutation of the equivalence proposition in the U.S. context.

The comparison between debt and tax finance will also depend on whether or not there are underemployed resources. Thus, a fiscal expansion through debt creation (rather than taxation) may lead to greater effective demand and higher incomes in the short run if Ricardian equivalence does not apply. In less-developed countries debt finance could be a mechanism for activating unproductively used funds in that government borrowing may lead to better developed capital markets (e.g. by introducing new "instruments" for savings) so that there might also be some beneficial long-term effects.

Simple rules of thumb in relation to domestic borrowing have occasionally been used to guide policy, and some have various shortcomings [see Goode (1984, pp. 197–198)]. One view is that it is appropriate to use borrowing to finance investment outlays on the grounds that returns to finance the debt service and repayment will be generated. This rule fails to distinguish between the relative costs and benefits that accrue from financing "the project" from alternative sources. Another related maxim is to "avoid borrowing to pay for government consumption expenditures", on the grounds that such borrowing would reduce aggregate savings, and thus government investment. However, as well as making the previous mistake, this further ignores the possibility that some government consumption may in fact be more conducive to growth than particular forms of government investment.

Whether or not to use loan finance, could be treated as a particular project or programme and subject to the same principles of social cost–benefit analysis as enunciated in Section 3 and other chapters of this Handbook. A government, in deciding on the question of loan versus other finance for a given activity, would need to compare the present value of the loan, given the time pattern of resultant government revenues and the accounting rate of interest, with the costs of servicing the debt. The latter would be a function of the maturity of the loan and the interest paid, and would include considerations such as whether or not the debt is index linked. The decision whether the activity ought to be loan financed can be treated formally as follows in such a way that the comparison with tax finance is integrated into the analysis.

As a simple example we suppose that the government is considering raising a loan of one unit this year (year 0) from consumers and repaying $(1 + j)$ next year. We suppose that the shadow value of a unit of income to consumers this year and next year is μ_0 and μ_1 (this should take full account of the way in which consumers dispose of their income) and for the government ν_0 and ν_1, all items being expressed as present values (i.e. in terms of a given unit of account this year). The net benefit of the loan (NPV) is then

$$NPV = -\mu_0 + \nu_0 - \nu_1(1 + j) + \mu_1(1 + j). \tag{1}$$

This is positive where ρ is the accounting rate of interest, if

$$\lambda_0 \equiv \frac{\nu_0}{\mu_0} > \frac{1 + \rho}{1 + r} \frac{r - j}{\rho - j}, \tag{2}$$

where r is the consumption rate of discount, defined as $r \equiv (\mu_0 - \mu_1)/\mu_1$ the rate at which the present value of consumption is falling, and by definition when government revenue is numeraire for each period, $\rho \equiv (\nu_0 - \nu_1)/\nu_1$; we have assumed $\rho > j$. The quantity λ_0 is the value of a unit of public funds relative to a unit of private funds or the social marginal cost of public funds that we shall examine in Section 3. Hence, if the alternative to loan finance is indirect taxation of a particular good, then λ_0 would be measured through the social marginal cost for that particular good (see Section 3 for a discussion of its measurement). Thus, the comparison with tax finance is built into the analysis and we would prefer loan to tax finance if condition (2) holds. One could define the r.h.s. of (2) as the social marginal cost, $\hat{\lambda}$, of raising a current unit of revenue by loan finance and say that loan finance is preferred if $\hat{\lambda} < \lambda_0$.

The interpretation of the condition is aided by the consideration of a special case. Suppose that ρ is equal to r so that λ_0 is equal to λ_1, and the social marginal cost of funds is constant over time (where λ_1 is ν_1/μ_1). This is a possibility that has been stressed by Arrow (1966) – it amounts to the assertion that, loosely speaking, the costs and difficulties of raising revenue will not increase or decrease over time. Condition (2) then becomes $\lambda_0 > 1$, where $\rho > j$ (with $\lambda_0 < 1$ for $\rho < j$). This is intuitively very obvious since the gain from the loan in the first period is simply $(\nu_0 - \mu_0)$ the difference between the value of a unit to the government and that to the individual; the present value of the next period's loss is $[(\nu_0 - \mu_0)/(1 + \rho)](1 + j)$ and then $\nu_0 > \mu_0$ tells us that the net gain is positive. Clearly, if $\rho > r$ so that λ falls over time ($\lambda_0 > \lambda_1$), then the argument is reinforced since the loan is repaid out of government funds next period which are less costly to raise. So the rule tells us that if revenue-raising is expected to become easier and the loan is at an interest rate below the accounting rate of interest, then it will be attractive relative to tax finance.

A note of caution is in order lest this is treated as an argument which it is always in favour of a loan relative to tax finance. It is very tempting for a short-sighted government to believe that difficulties in raising revenue will be less next year and thus to borrow. Following the principles embodied in (1) and (2) the optimum balance between loan and tax finance is when we have equality in those expressions. It is quite possible that a government with a limited time horizon may push borrowing beyond this point making revenue-raising in future that much more difficult on the margin and implying that tax finance is preferable. Furthermore, once a tax system is in place it will generate a stream of revenues in the future, whereas loans have to be raised on a year-by-year basis.

The same type of analysis can be extended to foreign borrowing where the shadow prices would have to take account of movements of the shadow value of foreign exchange over time. Similarly, the shadow prices should take full account of the shadow value of factors and any associated multiplier effects within the economy. The argument shows that the same principles as used for the analysis of investment projects and tax reform can be used for the question of borrowing versus taxation. Again it is quite possible that the short-sighted government will see tax-raising in the future as easier than now and borrow excessively. The procedure described would require fairly extensive further development to be applied to a particular economy. The integration of macro and micro analyses to provide more unified principles is a promising and important topic for both theoretical and applied work.

As we have just seen, foreign resource flows could be treated as a marginal "project" and the relative social costs and benefits evaluated using the methods described in this chapter. Rather than pursuing this formally, in this subsection we examine some of the distinguishing features of "foreign borrowing". Foreign public capital flows have been treated by Eaton in Chapter 25 and foreign private capital flows by Cardoso and Dornbusch in Chapter 26 of this Handbook.

Foreign borrowing differs from domestic in that it enables a country to command current goods and services in addition to those arising from domestic resources. Furthermore, the possible displacement of finance for private investment may be less likely to be a serious problem (although public foreign indebtedness may make finance more difficult for private borrowers). Over time, debt servicing and repayment entail a reverse transfer of resources abroad. The principal methods for dealing with debt servicing or repayment include new loans or grants, domestic production in excess of consumption or investment (which would be converted into foreign exchange through international trade), or repudiation. Despite the severe debt crises for developing countries in recent years which have led to "rescheduling of debt" there has been no widespread formal repudiation of debt since the 1930s.

2.2.2. Money creation

Money creation is another instrument that governments often use to pay for expenditures. This generally takes the form of borrowing from the central banks which leads to an addition to deposits and currency. Government borrowing from commercial banks also has the effect of money creation if the commercial banks are not fully "loaned up" and have excess reserves. If loans to commercial banks' customers are not affected, there is a net addition to money stock. The immediate impact of the deficit financing of government expenditure (as opposed to loan or tax finance) is to increase aggregate spending. In this subsection we examine some of the implications of such expenditures on output, balance of payments, inflation and other government revenues.

Central bank borrowing which generates output expansion may or may not be accompanied by inflation – this would depend on the specifics of the model, for example the structure of the labour market, the extent of underutilised capacity and resources, the foreign exchange regime, the demand for money and so on. Balance of payments difficulties could result if output expansion leads to an increase in imports.

If government spending through money creation leads to inflation, holders of money face a reduction in their purchasing power, thus involuntarily transferring resources to the government through the *inflation tax* [see Bailey (1956)]. The impact of this tax depends on the effects of changing prices on real incomes, money holdings and the velocity of money circulation. A decline in real cash balances resulting from inflation may decrease the resource transfer that governments might expect with further deficit financing. However, even with hyperinflation, demand for money persists to a small degree. With steady inflation, individuals are more easily able to adjust their expectations of price changes to reduce real cash balances, hence limiting the usefulness of the inflation tax as a tool at the disposal of the government. Thus, Johnson (1977) argued that "revenue" from the inflation tax arising from irregular doses of (continuing) inflation would be greater than that from inflation at a constant rate.

The effects of inflation on real government revenues (excluding the inflation tax) depend on collection lags and the elasticity of tax revenue with respect to income changes [see Tanzi (1977, 1978)]. In general, the longer the collection lags, the lower the real revenue. Furthermore, revenue from specific taxes – which require frequent rate changes to adjust to inflation – tends to lag behind price changes. Aghevli and Khan (1978) express a similar idea in terms of a "two-way causality" between money and prices in the inflationary context: inflation causes government expenditure to rise, but revenues do not rise proportionately because of collection lags. Financing the inflation-induced deficits would increase money supply and thus inflation would be boosted further. Aghevli and Khan recommend the reduction of inflation through indexing taxes with long collection lags – and in particular income, corporation and property taxes. Without such indexing there may be some tendency for deficit finance to be self-perpetuating.

The financing of a government deficit through money creation (either borrowing directly from the central bank or indirectly through commercial banks as described above) for 64 developing countries [see Tanzi (1986)] suggests that in the early 1980s only five countries raised more than 10 percent of GDP in this fashion [Zambia 13 percent, Trinidad and Tobago 12 percent, Portugal and Sierra Leone 11 percent and Zaire 10 percent]. A further ten countries raised between 5 percent and 10 percent of GDP [Brazil 9.5 percent, Greece 8 percent, Nigeria 7.5 percent, Tanzania 7.2 percent, Mauritius 6.5 percent, Uruguay 6.4 percent, W. Samoa 5.6 percent, Mexico 5.7 percent, Israel 5.5 percent and Argentina 5 percent].

The effects of inflation on real balances, the base of the inflation tax, were illustrated by Tanzi (1986) with reference to Argentina. In 1970, a 14 percent inflation rate (with reference to the wholesale price index) was associated with ratios of M1/GDP of 0.15 percent. In 1983, with 430 percent inflation, the M1/GDP ratio had fallen to 0.038. Tanzi with a number of simulations suggested that there was a maximum level of financing that could be generated by central bank borrowing, given the ratio, a, of money to GDP (at zero expected inflation) and an estimate of the sensitivity, b, of the demand for money with respect to the rate of inflation, π. Thus, if $a = 0.10$ and $b = 0.5$ the ratio of money to GDP is $a \exp(-b\pi)$, a maximum of 7.4 percent of GDP could be achieved through central bank borrowing at 200 percent inflation (given by the maximum of $a\pi \exp(-b\pi)$) [see Tanzi (1986, p. 145)].

A full analysis of the costs of inflation is beyond the scope of this chapter, but the interested reader is referred to Fischer and Modigliani (1978) for a general discussion in the U.S. context, and Fischer (1982) for a discussion of the use of a foreign currency and the inflation tax.

2.3. Administration and evasion

2.3.1. Administration

The choice of tax-tools in a particular country should be strongly influenced by the government's perception of the costs of collection relative to the revenue yield. Thus, we have an emphasis on convenient "tax handles" in low-income countries, usually indirect taxes, such as trade taxes, or production excises in countries with substantial domestic manufacturing bases. In this section we point to examples of some of the common administrative problems that may arise in developing countries with respect to the operation of existing taxes and proposed reforms. Of course there is considerable diversity and some countries may be more successful in overcoming particular problems than others. The problems we shall consider are (i) obscurities and complexities of the tax laws; (ii) definitions of income; and (iii) corruption or incompetence of staff. These problems are set in the context of the structure of the economy and the monetization, accounting practices, literacy and so on of the potential tax payers.

An indication of the potential severity of the first problem is that quite often it is not clear what law the "administrators" are supposed to administer, even in countries with a fairly sophisticated system of laws and a highly developed bar, judiciary and administration, such as in South Asia. The tax structure has evolved as a result of an ad hoc series of legislations in response to varying problems and government circumstances over the years. For instance, a Government of India Committee on Controls and Subsidies [Government of India (1979)] found over a hundred notifications with respect to the textile industry, some of them dormant, and that even the Office of the Textile Commissioner did not have a full version of the control laws. The result was a "framework which is perhaps being violated unwittingly almost daily by most people in the textile industry and trade, which is in theory punishable" [Government of India (1979, p. 193)]. There is thus a need for a periodic review of the legal stipulations to weed out laws that are no longer applicable and discover those that are contradictory to others or to their stated intentions.

An attempt to obtain greater precision can help in reducing the scope for misinterpretation (deliberate or otherwise), corruption and evasion. Often, however, the attempt at greater precision results in contortions which conflict with the aim of greater simplicity and clarity and may add to rather than reduce difficulties of administration and evasion. For example, one can find a differential, complex and very tightly defined rate structure on goods that are close substitutes, or sold through the same outlets or produced in the same enterprise. This provides considerable scope for "interpretation" as to which rates should be applicable (since detailed verification is difficult), encourages evasion, and can lead to an excessive call on the resources of the tax administrators and the book-keeping of the manufacturers or sellers. Consequently, it becomes difficult or impractical to extend coverage to the small-scale sector. A case in point is cloth in India. For distributional and political reasons, hand-made cotton and silk fabrics received a nominal subsidy in 1979 (on the grounds, for example, that handloom cloth is an item of mass consumption – though much to the taste of the well-heeled in India and other countries – and is produced by relatively poor, often rural, artisans). On the other hand, mill-made cloth was subject to excises, the rates of which were an increasing function of the "count" of the cloth, and the extent of man-made fibres used. Small-scale producers were exempt, partly because of the difficulty in implementation and partly because it was deliberate policy to encourage them.

In some countries there is a curious admixture of excises, various surcharges levied for different emergencies in the past and not removed (no one knowing why or the present rationale), and cesses, with often a combination of specific and ad valorem rates on a particular commodity. Such structures are needlessly complex and often restrict the base to large-scale manufacturers who keep accountants (who usually devote considerable wit and ingenuity to grappling with the provisions and often maintain alternative sets of accounts).

A second major problem in administration is the definition of "income" used, particularly with reference to the income tax as it relates to those with independent sources such as professionals, agriculturalists, and small-scale producers. For instance, in agriculture income is a fairly nebulous concept. Typically only a proportion of the produce (of food crops in particular) is marketed, and the prices received are subject to considerable variability. This causes difficulties with the determination of gross sale receipts, in addition to those associated with the valuation of consumption out of home-grown stock, and lost output due, for instance, to rodents and the weather. If a "gross" value of output could be arrived at, costs of production would have to be calculated to derive "taxable income". This would involve payments for capital and material inputs, land rental and labour. The last two items are particularly difficult to evaluate, given that different land tenure and labour-use systems coexist in poor countries.

One way to tax incomes that are ill-defined or for which there are few records is to use *forfait* [Goode (1981, 1984)] or the presumptive tax [Musgrave (1987)] which determines income by external or indirect indicators. A fairly elaborate *forfait* system exists in France and has also been adapted to a number of francophone countries in Africa. In France, *forfaits* are used to assess taxes on farmers' incomes, unincorporated business incomes and professional incomes. For other activities, manuals are prepared in consultation with representatives of professions or business organisations which provide information on gross profit margins for various products or activities. In addition, the tax administration has the statutory power to assess income with reference to indicators of the tax payer's lifestyle, each being assigned a specific value including rental values of homes, ownership of cars, racehorses, etc. and employment of servants. Such powers are common (although often defined in less detail) to a number of countries. Land revenue assessed on the basis of a cadastral survey is a particularly simple form of *forfait* that used to be an important source of revenue in the sub-continent. For a further discussion of the taxation of agriculture, see Section 4 below.

Ambiguity in valuations could be reduced by using *forfait*. Systematic indicators of activity levels such as consumption of electricity or floor space may be available. Coupled with estimated profit margins they could form the basis of income taxation. Similar indicators may also be used for the sales tax. Similar or further forms may be devised to circumvent the problem of transfer-pricing by multinationals. The availability of computers in most developing countries now permits the extensive collection and processing of information that would help in cross-checking records and returns in support of such a system. On the introduction of *forfait* the assessee might, in certain circumstances, be given the option of being assessed under the existing law provided appropriate information is supplied. Whilst the ingenious evader will no doubt find some ways of reducing liability, the *forfait* system can provide a considerable expansion in the effective base.

A third major problem in administration is the corruption or incompetence of revenue staff. Often such officials are poorly paid, and being in a position to monitor very large sums of money are subject to monetary inducements and temptations. Whilst "adequate" salary structures and a close watch on the life-style of revenue officials and their families would help, it may be somewhat more difficult to root out corruption once it has become an accepted way of life. Quite often, as in South Asia, tax cases for the administration are prepared and argued by ill-paid, over-worked and, at best, mediocre officials, while the really big fish are represented by the best legal brains and chartered accountants. In major cases, governments may well be advised to turn the tables on "evaders", and avoid stress on administrative personnel by hiring the best legal and financial help for the prosecution. Substantial penalties may provide a deterrent although they can provide their own incentives for further corruption.

It is important in empirical investigations of reform to work as far as possible with actual revenue collections [see, for example, Ahmad and Stern (forthcoming)] rather than some notional expected revenue on the basis of statutory rates. Whilst this method circumvents some of the problems of analysing systems where there is inefficiency of collection and significant evasion, it does require considerable work to translate data on tax collection into implicit rates on different types of goods and incomes. Tax authorities should be encouraged to keep data in a form which is designed to facilitate the economic analysis of possible reforms as well as meeting statutory requirements and the organisational and management needs of the administration.

2.3.2. Evasion

Evasion is a major preoccupation of tax designers, administrators, tax payers and the general public and the term "black economy" has been coined to describe those economic activities which are illegally concealed from the tax authorities. It is a subject which is important and universal but where there is a great deal in the way of anecdotes and little in terms of hard information.

Legally the distinction between evasion and avoidance is that the former activity "breaks the law" in some sense and the latter does not. From the point of view of positive economic analysis, if the legal position is clear and the tax authorities are reliable, "avoidance" implies certainty on the part of the tax payer with respect to tax payments (if any) and his consequent decisions concerning his activities, whereas evasion involves uncertainty as to punishment and liabilities. Models of evasion and estimations of its importance have been used for both developing and developed countries. For an excellent recent survey of the theory and applications to developed countries see Cowell (1985).

One simple model of behaviour is that of "portfolio selection" and the results are often based on the assumption of a risk-averse individual who maximises expected utility and makes a free choice of evasion activities subject to an exogenous linear budget constraint (thus marginal penalties are constant). The major results are that increasing the penalty must reduce tax evasion, as does increasing the probability of detection [Allingham and Sandmo (1972)]. Mean-preserving increases in risk, so that the expected returns per unit of tax evasion remain constant, also lead to less evasion – for instance reduced tax rates with increased penalty but unchanged probability of detection. Restrictions on the structure of preferences lead to additional results. With decreasing absolute risk aversion, increases in income (caused for instance by a cut in tax rates., with a given probability of detection and unchanged penalty) will increase the absolute amount of tax evasion [Yitzhaki (1974)] but evasion as a proportion of taxable income may go either way. Decreasing, constant or increasing relative risk aversion will lead to an increasing, constant or decreasing evasion as a proportion of income with a tax cut.

The simple model has been refined in a number of ways. Srinivasan (1973) considers a progressive tax system and progressive penalties. Although the model becomes more complicated than the linear case, increases in the marginal penalty and probability of detection are shown to reduce evasion. Koskela (1983) shows, with decreasing absolute risk aversion, that increases in marginal tax rates together with the minimum income guarantee will reduce evasion (assuming a given probability of detection and surcharge, such that either expected revenue or expected utility are constant). Other potential, useful extensions in the models include (a) making investigation rules dependent on the "signal" provided by the returns; (b) introducing a game-theoretic framework to discuss the tax payer–revenue authority interrelationships: (c) incorporating the interactions between the tax payer and the rest of the community (introducing the prevalent degree of tax evasion by others in the community); (d) making income endogenous [see Cowell (1985) for further references]. The models have made a beginning towards the analysis of a complex and difficult phenomenon. Cowell (1985) is of the view they show how "intelligent use of information can play a central role" in combatting evasion.

Optimum policy towards evasion has been considered by a number of authors where the criterion, for example, is the maximisation of expected social welfare for given expected revenue. It is common to find extreme results of the kind that penalties should be infinite together with zero probability of application – essentially in the model such policies can eliminate evasion. There are a number of reasons one can advance which would, if included in the model, avoid this extreme solution. An example might be perceived social loss from punishing the innocent. The precise status of such arguments needs careful thought and if they are examined closely it is difficult to avoid the conclusion that the simple economic calculus leaves out central elements of what is commonly understood as justice [see, for example, Hart (1968) and Stern (1978)]. This is not an argument in favour of "irrationality" but simply an acknowledgement that there is more to the philosophical basis of punishment than is generally captured in standard economic models.

The models discussed above indicate an a priori possibility of increasing evasion by a cut in tax rate with given expected revenue. On the other hand there is a general belief, as shown in several tax commission reports and rate changes in various countries, that high tax rates are the main cause of tax evasion. For instance, Kaldor (1956) argued this case for India, and found very substantial evasion of income tax[1] for the year 1953/54. The Indian Central Board of Revenue disputed this figure and estimated evasion to be a tenth of that calculated by Kaldor. The Direct Taxes Enquiry Committee [Government of India (1971)] recommended a reduction of marginal income tax rates (which effectively exceeded 100 percent when income and wealth taxes were considered together in some cases) from 97.75 percent for the highest bracket to 75 percent. During the period 1971 to 1978 marginal tax rates were reduced as recommended, and there were no substantial increases in the proportion of income tax collections in GNP. Marginal income tax rates have been reduced again in the recent past, along with other measures designed to reduce evasion and the laundering of "black" money, and there has been some increase in income tax revenue. This may be construed as lending support for the conclusion that reduction in marginal tax rates can lead to a decrease in evasion. However, this increase may also be due to more efficient administration, more severe penalties

---

[1] Kaldor estimated that income tax evaded in 1953/54 was of the order of Rs. 200–Rs. 300 crore [Kaldor (1956, p. 105)]. Collections for that year were Rs. 123 crore.

for default or evasion, and amnesties for past concealments if declarations are made before a deadline. It would be very difficult empirically to disentangle these effects from the adjustment in the marginal rate.

Whilst high tax rates might well be one of the causes for the existence of a "black" or underground sector, they are probably not the only reason. There is first an overlap between evasion and the existence of criminal activities, such as narcotics, extortion and bootlegging (in countries with prohibition) and other illicit trades. It is unlikely that a reduction in income tax rates would have much of an impact on these activities. Moreover, as noted in the previous section, developing countries are likely to have considerable small-scale or cottage production and services in the informal sector which are difficult to monitor and consequently to tax, as are household production and barter, particularly in agriculture. The cost of enforcing tax laws in less formal sectors can be high. Tanzi (1983) listed, in addition to taxes, regulation, prohibition and bureaucratic corruption as likely causes of the "black" economy [see also Tanzi (1982)].

There have been a number of methods proposed for the measurement of the size of the black economy or the extent of evasion: although some (or most) of them are rather dubious.

(a) The *expenditure–income gap approach* assumes that whilst incomes may be concealed, expenditures will show up say, in National Accounts data, and since the two should be of equal magnitude, the gap represents the "black" economy. This was the method used by Kaldor (1956) (see above), and the Direct Taxes Enquiry Committee [see Government of India (1971, p. 8)] which estimated income tax evasion in 1968/69 to be Rs. 470 crores (as against collections of Rs. 378 crore in that year). The major limitation of this approach is that the measurement of both income and expenditure is subject to error, and the "gap" may be more reflective of this "noise" than evasion.

(b) The *labour-market approach*, which originated in Italy [Contini (1981)] compares crude employment projections from labour force participation rates with reported employment; it also surveys firms and workers on secondary employment or moonlighting. The black economy is given by the difference between projected and reported employment; the surveys also reveal concealed secondary employment. Problems with employment projections are that these are also liable to be subject to errors, which may be large relative to the difference between projected and reported magnitudes. The survey estimates are discussed below (see direct methods).

(c) The *monetary-aggregate approach*, in one of its forms, assumes that increases in the number of large denomination banknotes reflects increases in the underground economy, or its change over time. It is generally impossible to disentangle the effects on the demand and supply of large banknotes of factors such as inflation, interest rates, money substitutes, expectations, policies of central and commercial banks and so on. In such circumstances the practice of ascribing the unexplained residual in the calculations to the "black economy" (rather than inadequacies of theory, of statistical technique, of data, and of the researcher) is unattractive. This criticism applies also to other variants of the monetary-aggregates approach. Guttmann (1977) assumes a stable relationship between cash held by the private sector and the total monetary base, and provided one could fix a base-year when the underground economy is assumed not to exist, or be negligible, this yields an "estimate" of the underground economy – 10 percent of GNP for the United States in 1976. Feige (1979) relies on the quantity theory to project the total transactions or true GNP, assuming that money stock is known and the velocity of circulation is understood. The difference between the predicted and measured GNP then reflects the underground economy – 13 percent of GNP for the United States in 1976. The base year is of crucial importance in this exercise, as are the assumption of constancy of the velocity estimates and the measures of stock. Gupta and Gupta (1982) estimate the underground economy to be 49 percent of the Indian GNP for 1978/79. Acharya (1983) has criticised this approach since there are good reasons to believe (i) that the ratio of transactions to income would change over time in a developing country like India – because of increasing monetisation, increasing density of input–output transactions, and the disproportionate growth of purely financial transactions from the growing sophistication of the financial and capital market; (ii) the proxy values for the life-time transactions of currency notes – borrowed from U.S. estimates – might not be appropriate for India; (iii) constant currency turnover rates are inappropriate, and (iv) the results are implausible – since over half of measured GNP was in sectors such as agriculture, banking and insurance, railways, public administration and defence, for which there would be little under-reporting, with the implication that if the estimates are correct, official figures would measure less than half of the value-added in the remaining sectors.

(d) The "*soft-modelling*" *approach* seeks indicators (other than GDP) of general activity levels. Gupta and Mehta (1982) assume a stable relationship between the use of electricity and GDP, and estimate the black economy at over 19 percent of GDP in India in 1978/79 [for a detailed critique see Acharya (1983)]. The specification of such models is likely to be the main problem with this approach, as are the correspondence between the economy under consideration and that for which the parameters were estimated.

(e) An *intensive audit* of a sample of tax payers by the tax authority is one of the main direct methods of estimating under-reporting, and requires the "grossing-up" of the results from the survey to get to aggregate figures for the economy as a whole. This method has been used by the U.S. Internal Revenue Service (IRS) since 1961 [see U.S. IRS (1979)] and gives conservative estimates in the sense that non-filers are excluded altogether.

(f) A *survey* of economic activities and attitudes is another direct form of investigating underground activities independently of tax returns, and we can compare results with the actual returns. This method is likely to have severe problems of non-response, evasiveness and misrepresentation, which may be mitigated somewhat if the main focus of the survey is on other activities and evasion is estimated by inference. This method was used by the Musgrave Reform Commission for Columbia in 1971 and estimates of non-reporting ranged from 22 percent for clothing manufacturers, to 36 percent for restaurants. Under-reporting of income ranged from 95 percent for lawyers, 76 percent for dentists and 28 percent for physicians [see Herschel (1971)].

Notwithstanding the problems associated with a particular method for the measurement of the underground economy, it is apparent that such activities exist and should be taken seriously in both theoretical and empirical research. And a central question for any proposed reform must be how far the proposed taxes can be collected.

3. The appraisal of taxes

3.1. Introduction

If one asks how the tax system could be improved, or how extra revenue should be raised, then one must consider, in relation to objectives, the effects of possible tax changes on revenue, on incentives, on the distribution of welfare, and on the pattern of production. These effects will be closely linked through the behaviour and objectives of participants in the economy. One should also ask how the changes are to be enforced and at what cost. Thus, any proposal under study should be examined systematically in relation to criteria which embody these considerations. The links between the four issues described are illustrated, for example, if one considers the effects of a tax change on the incentive to save. One is then concerned with the distribution of consumption across individuals at different points of time, and must ask what happens to revenue in each period (which will depend on behaviour). One must also examine how the pattern of production will change to meet the changed demands. Similarly, a discussion on the progressivity of the income tax will involve possible effects on incentives to work, and thus revenue and production, together with concern for the distribution of disposable income. The main body of the theory in this section will be directed towards developing principles and methods for the simultaneous treatment of these issues. Administration has been treated (less formally) above and plays an important role in the theory in terms of the taxes to be examined, their relative prominence and their coverage, i.e. it usually enters through the constraints rather than in terms of explicit cost calculations, although as we shall see such costs can be made explicit in the theory of reform. Our main concern is with the medium or long term and the concentration is on indirect taxes, excises, tariffs, sales taxes, VAT and the like, although personal and corporate income taxes will also be considered.

The theory plays two related roles. First, we can use it without numbers to develop principles, train our intuition, sort out coherent from incoherent arguments, and to help identify the important assumptions or parameters. In this attempt to aid our understanding it is important to keep the models as simple as possible consistent with capturing the essentials of the problem in hand. Subsection 3.2 contains this type of theoretical discussion. The second role of theory is in the organisation and direction of empirical analysis and it is important to develop theory in such a way that it can be integrated explicitly into methods for applied work. Thus, it should tell us what data are required and provide an analytic basis for the empirical calculations. The development of the theory in this way involves not only analytical skills but an appreciation of the demands and difficulties of empirical work; it provides part of the subject matter of Subsection 3.3 in which we discuss applied policy models. An important element in that analysis will be the calculation of the effect of tax changes on price, or tax shifting.

There are difficulties and dangers associated with each role for theory. In the first role clear results are an advantage in showing where different assumptions lead but we should not let their definiteness cloud our judgement of the relevance of the assumptions. This danger is particularly severe where there are strong preconceived views on what policy should be (e.g. the uniformity of indirect taxation, see below). And we should not be deluded into thinking that the presence of numbers indicates a serious applied study. For example, in models which are too complicated to yield clear results the numbers may be used simply to illustrate possible theoretical outcomes.

In Subsection 3.4 we set the methods in context by showing how they form part of the general theory of tax reform using shadow prices. This not only provides a considerable extension of their applicability but also provides a link with other chapters on policy, particularly cost–benefit analysis, in that we see how policy problems of different kinds have a similar underlying structure. Extensions of the models to deal explicitly with dynamic issues are described in Subsection 3.5. Taxes and production are discussed in Subsection 3.6.

The final three parts of this section move closer to practical policy. In Subsection 3.7 we look at the taxation of income and profits and in Subsection 3.8 some problems of indirect taxation. In the final subsection we summarise by formulating some simple practical guidelines from the theory.

3.2. Theory

The development of basic principles requires an analytical foundation so that we can understand the circumstances in which they apply and the critical assumptions in their justification. In this subsection we shall, therefore, sketch the outline of the standard models of normative tax theory and then ask what lessons they offer for taxation in developing countries. Those who wish to avoid the technical detail can examine the principles themselves set out in Subsection 3.8 where we draw together the main lessons in the form of simple and intuitive rules.

As a benchmark and to keep things simple at the beginning we take two of the standard frameworks in the theory of taxation, first where revenue can be raised in a lump-sum manner directly from households, and second where revenue has to be raised by the taxation of transactions between consumers and producers. In the former case if there are no externalities, and indifference curves and isoquants have the usual convex shape, then any Pareto efficient outcome can be achieved as a competitive equilibrium in which the government raises revenue and redistributes purchasing power using the appropriate set of lump-sum taxes. The policy is clear: there are no taxes of any kind (neither on commodities nor income) except those which are lump sum. Whilst the model is presented mainly as a benchmark it does immediately generate a general principle which is of value in guiding policy: revenue should be raised and redistributed in ways, which as far as possible, are lump sum. There are examples such as land or poll taxes which are relevant but generally governments will also have to consider taxes which are not lump sum.

In the second case we retain the competitive framework and the assumption of no externalities but now revenue has to be raised by the taxation of commodities bought and services supplied. The standard theory in the tradition of Pigou, Ramsey, Samuelson, Boiteux, and Diamond and Mirrlees is to formulate the problem as one of the choice of the indirect taxes to maximise a Bergson–Samuelson social welfare function whilst raising a given revenue. The use of a Bergson–Samuelson welfare function is not per se restrictive since it simply says that our judgements of welfare are conducted basically in terms of the living standards of the households in the community (current and future). Neither does it presuppose a benevolent all-knowing government. We ask simply how a commentator interested in raising living standards and in the distribution of welfare would evaluate policy in this simple framework. An absence of understanding of the logic of policy in this simple example would preclude us from generalising to more complicated worlds. The problem is to raise a given level of revenue using commodity taxes whilst lowering the welfare of households as little as possible. Formally we choose a tax vector t to

$$\text{maximise } V(q) \tag{3}$$

subject to

$$R(t) = t \cdot X(q) \geq \bar{R}, \tag{4}$$

where p are the prices faced by producers; q, equal to ($p + t$), are the consumer prices; the level of household welfare corresponding to q is $v^h(q)$ and household demands are $x(q)$; $X(q)$ is the aggregate demand vector, and $V(q)$ is social welfare arising from those prices; $R(t)$ is indirect tax revenue and $\bar{R}$ the required revenue. Notice that we are assuming that there are no lump-sum incomes so that the demands and welfare of households (and thus social welfare) depend only on the prices which they face for the goods and services which they buy and sell. The assumptions on production are essentially that all production is either by the government or by competitive private firms, with constant returns to scale, all trading at the same prices. We are assuming that there is no taxation on transactions between producers but that all final sales to the consumer can be taxed. One can show that these assumptions allow us to conduct the analysis as if producer prices are fixed.

The formulation of the problem should make it clear that the same model applies to public-sector pricing of good i where we interpret p_i as the marginal cost (assumed constant for simplicity although this is not essential) and t_i as the excess over marginal cost. Thus, it is immediately obvious that the final price of a good sold directly to the final consumer by the public sector should *not* be marginal cost since optimal t_i would only exceptionally be zero. Public-sector prices should include an element of taxation for goods sold to the final consumer, i.e. there should be a contribution to resource mobilisation or revenue-raising.

The solution to problem (3)–(4) gives us the many-person Ramsey rule for optimal commodity taxation. It is useful to have this in front of us since it is the simplest embodiment of the basic trade-off between equity and efficiency in taxation. The rule is derived straightforwardly from the first-order conditions for the Lagrangian, $V + \lambda R$, for the above maximisation problem; λ is the Lagrange multiplier on the revenue constraint, i.e. the social marginal utility of government income. We have:

$$\frac{\partial V}{\partial t_i} + \lambda \frac{\partial R}{\partial t_i} = 0. \tag{5}$$

We then substitute

$$\partial V/\partial t_i = -\sum_h \beta^h x_i^h \quad \text{and} \quad \partial R/\partial t_i = X_i + t \cdot \partial X/\partial t_i,$$

and we use the Slutsky decomposition of demand derivatives to yield:

$$\frac{\sum_k t_k \sum_h s_{ik}^h}{X_i} = -\sigma_i \tag{6}$$

$$\sigma_i = 1 - \sum_h \frac{x_i^h}{X_i} \frac{b^h}{\bar{b}}, \tag{7}$$

where s_{ik}^h is the compensated (Slutsky) demand derivative for household h (the relevant utility level is at the post-tax equilibrium) and σ_i is negatively related to the covariance between the (net) social marginal utility of income, b^h, of household h (where the "net" means there is an adjustment to the social marginal utility, β^h, for the marginal propensity to spend on taxes out of extra income, and $\bar{b}$ is the average of b^h) and the consumption of good i by household h, (x_i^h). Thus, σ_i is higher the more the good is consumed by those who have a low social marginal utility of income (e.g. the rich).

We may now interpret (5) in terms of a trade-off between efficiency and equity. If there is a single household, then we may think of the problem as one of efficiency – raising a given revenue from the household at minimum cost. Of course in that case a poll-tax might well be an option and, if it is, it provides the best way of raising revenue. If, however, we are confined to commodity taxes, then the equality of the r.h.s. of (6) for all i gives us the familiar Ramsey rule that the l.h.s. is independent of i: this is often interpreted as saying that (for small taxes) the proportional reduction in compensated demand arising from taxes should be the same for all goods (t_k measures the price change and the Slutsky terms the compensated response in demand to the price change). The same result holds if we are not concerned with distribution in the sense that b^h is independent of h. Crudely speaking, the efficiency result is to tax goods which are in inelastic demand, although as we have seen the correct expression is in terms of quantity reductions and compensated demands. This may seem inegalitarian in that it would lead to taxation of necessities but then we have explicitly ignored distribution.

Where we *are* concerned with distribution, then (5), (6) and (7) tell us that the reduction in compensated demand should be more for goods consumed relatively more by those with low net social marginal utility of income (b^h). We might think of those with low b^h as the rich and it is in this sense that we orient taxes towards the consumption of the better-off. Thus, (5)–(7) capture the essential elements of the trade-off between equity and efficiency in the standard analysis of optimal commodity taxation.

The expression (6) is known as the many-person Ramsey rule and also allows us to investigate the relationship between indirect taxation and other tax or subsidy instruments and the appropriate balance between them. Suppose, for example, we can make lump-sum transfers which depend on the demographic characteristics of the household. An example would be a subsidised rice ration where the amount depends on household composition. The model of (3) and (4) is then augmented to include the influence of the grants on household welfare and demands and we take off their costs from $t \cdot X$ in (4). The optimality condition for the transfers can then be combined with (5)–(7) to analyse the appropriate construction of policies. One can then show [see Deaton and Stern (1986)] that if the Engel curves are linear and parallel but where the intercepts can vary with household composition, factors supplied are separable in the utility function from consumption goods, and if the grants are set optimally then commodity taxes should be at the same proportional rate. Intuitively, all the redistribution that is desirable is carried out through the lump-sum grants which are financed by uniform commodity taxation, and there is no justification for further redistribution through differentiation of commodity taxes since everyone has the same marginal propensity to spend on each good. To put it another way, efficiency points us to taxing necessities and distribution towards luxuries; under special assumptions about the shape of preferences and the setting of direct taxes the two effects cancel and the role of indirect taxes is simply to raise revenue for the grants which act as a basic income guarantee related to household composition.

The above uniformity result was first stated by Atkinson (1977) for the linear expenditure system and then generalised by Deaton (1979, 1981) to linear Engel curves although in these models households are identical except for differences in wages. Atkinson and Stiglitz (1976) analysed the case of non-linear income taxation (again where individuals differ only in the wage) and one finds that the more subtle form of income taxation allows one to dispose of the assumption concerning the linearity of the Engel curves (whilst retaining separability). We have focused on the Deaton and Stern (1986) treatment since it allows demands to vary with household composition and deals with direct tax tools of some empirical relevance for developing countries – we do see transfers related to household composition but not workable sophisticated non-linear income taxes.

The formal results of the last few years have allowed a better understanding of both indirect taxation and of the balance between direct and indirect taxation than was possible from previous discussions which simply listed some of the things to be borne in mind. Having seen the assumptions which are used in establishing the results we are in a position to see how far they help in analysing the problems of developing countries. In our judgement they are valuable in three ways. First, they train the intuition to understand what is important in an argument about the structure of taxes and thus help in organising practical enquiry and in using empirical results. Second, they help in further research because in modifying the models to be more appropriate for developing countries one has a baseline for building new models and judging results. Third, they lead rather naturally to the theory of reform which allows one to devise practical checks on optimality conditions and on desirable directions of movement. There is no suggestion, here, that formula (5) provides a practical basis for calculating what taxes should be. The model is a benchmark, not a workable description, and the amount of information on the demand structure which would be required could not be available [see Deaton (1987)].

An example of the first concerns the level of the lump-sum grant which emerged in the special model considered by Deaton and Stern as the central redistributive tool. This leads us to ask whether a system of lump-sum grants related to household structure is possible. In many developing countries one does find some transfers through rationing systems (particularly for food) which are rather like lump-sum grants, the rations being often related to family structure. Where rations are re-saleable, then from the formal point of view they are just like lump-sum transfers (and even if they are not re-saleable they are like lump-sum transfers if the level is lower than total purchases of the commodity). Thus, a prominent feature of an argument concerning whether indirect taxes should be uniform is a judgement concerning the optimality or otherwise of the rations. This judgement can itself be structured since we have an explicit condition for their optimality in terms of the net social marginal utilities of income, the b^h; the average value of these net social marginal utilities in terms of public income should be one (if the average value were greater, for example, the transfer should be increased). With explicit value judgements (the welfare weights β^h), a knowledge of taxes t, and an estimate of the demand system this can be checked [see, for example, the Ahmad and Stern analysis of reform in India, Subsection 3.3]. More generally the results tell us that the inter-relations between different parts of a tax system will be crucial in that the design of one part depends sensitively on the existence of options and the choice of policy elsewhere. Thus, it is of special importance in developing countries to scrutinise carefully the availability of a wide range of instruments and to ask whether those that are used have been appropriately adjusted.

The second class of lessons involves the relaxation of some of the assumptions of the simple model to better describe developing countries. There should be no delusion that one can specify a single model for all developing countries – see Newbery and Stern (1987a) for a collection of models. There are, however, at least two common features of poor countries which should be accommodated. Production often takes place in units which cannot be described adequately by (competitive) firms facing prices distinct from those of consumers and producing under constant returns to scale. Peasant agriculture is an obvious and central example. Furthermore, one cannot reasonably assume that all goods can be taxed. Whilst models which deal with these features in a direct way can be, and have been constructed, it is important to recognise that they do not require us to jettison immediately all of the standard model and its lessons. Thus, for example, if production goes on in the peasant household which faces consumer prices for its purchases and sales then the model is formally unaffected and one simply interprets demands and demand responses as being net of household production. And the optimal tax rules (5), (6) and (7) are first-order conditions for those taxes which can be chosen and thus apply for the subset of taxes which are set optimally.

What does change if either production takes place in households, or there is a restriction on those goods which can be taxed, are the production efficiency theorems. Diamond and Mirrlees (1971) showed that if private production takes place under perfect competition and constant returns to scale (one need not assume that producer prices are fixed) then aggregate production should be efficient so that marginal rates of transformation should be the same for public and private sectors and public sector shadow prices and private market prices should coincide. One can allow diminishing returns to scale if profits are optimally taxed. If some production is conducted by households facing consumer prices q, whilst firms transact at prices p, then clearly overall production will not be efficient, although the Diamond–Mirrlees analysis shows that production in the public sector and private firms taken together should be efficient. When some goods cannot be taxed then one would want to consider taxing inputs into those goods as a surrogate for taxing final goods [see Stern (1984) and Newbery (1986)]. This would violate efficiency. Where aggregate efficiency is desirable, then goods sold by the public to the private sector should be priced at marginal cost. Notice the difference here between private producers and consumers; for the latter the appropriate price will generally include a tax element over and above marginal cost.

There has been some analysis of restricted taxation in models of the Arrow–Debreu and Diamond–Mirrlees variety, with n goods which are numbered $1, 2, \ldots, n$ and not immediately associated with certain commodities such as corn or manufactures [see, for example, Stiglitz and Dasgupta (1971), or Drèze and Stern (1987) who, in addition, consider rationing and non-market clearing]. However, for the most part studies which attempt to take account of peasant production and restricted taxation deal with models which have an explicit distinction between agricultural and other sectors. Then particular relative prices such as the terms of trade between agriculture and industry and the structure of certain markets, especially that for labour, take a central place. Examples of public policy analysis in such models (often of the dual economy variety) include Dixit (1971), Dixit and Stern (1974), Newbery (1974), Srinivasan and Bhagwati (1975), and a number of chapters in the 1987 volume edited by Newbery and Stern (e.g. Chapters 7 and 13, Newbery; Chapter 15, Heady and Mitra; and Chapter 16, Sah and Stiglitz) which may also be consulted for further references.

The main results from these models continue to have the general form of a trade-off between efficiency and equity [such as (5), (6) and (7)]. For example, the appropriate price for an agricultural input will depend on its marginal social cost of production, the elasticity of net demand and the pattern of use by different types of farmer. Broadly speaking the higher the social cost, the less elastic the demand and the richer the users, the higher should be the price. There are two further specific features which often play a role: the structure of labour markets and any premium on government revenue. Thus, if a tax reduces the rural demand for labour it may have the deleterious effect of increasing migration, where urban wages are fixed. Or it may reduce both urban and rural wages where these are endogenous. Clearly, the calculation of the effects and their welfare consequences are going to depend on the precise structure of the labour market (see Chapter 11 by Williamson in this Handbook, for some discussion of the evidence).

The shadow value, λ, of government revenue is endogenous in the model of (3) and (4) and does not need separate specification. It will depend, however, inter alia on the revenue requirement $\bar{R}$. In terms of the Lagrangian for the problem $\bar{R}$ plays no explicit role (it comes into the solution, of course, since the constraint must be satisfied) but we can think of a desire for extra revenue being reflected in a higher λ. Thus, one can write government objectives to include a term for government revenue, suppress the constraint containing $\bar{R}$, specify λ and then think of the eventual revenue as being endogenous. Then the weight on revenue can be discussed in terms of λ, and, for example, a government that attached a high value to public investment would have a high λ. In the dynamic context the value of investment is itself endogenous and this is discussed in Subsection 3.5. Generally, as should be obvious, the higher is λ the higher are taxes and the lower subsidies.

The third class of lessons from the standard optimisation models concern their extension to reform. Suppose we start from a given status quo which is not an optimum and try to identify improving directions of reform. We show how such an investigation may be usefully structured. We retain the notation and model of (3) and (4) but no longer assume optimisation. We define:

$$\lambda_i = -\frac{\partial V}{\partial t_i} \bigg/ \frac{\partial R}{\partial t_i}. \tag{8}$$

We can interpret λ_i as the marginal cost in terms of social welfare of raising an extra unit of revenue from increasing the taxation of good i; $-\partial V/\partial t_i$ represents the welfare cost of a unit change, and the inverse of $\partial R/\partial t_i$ tells us the magnitude of the change in t_i required to raise one rupee. What matters for policy then is the relative size of the λ_i, i.e. if $\lambda_i > \lambda_j$, then we increase welfare at constant revenue by increasing the tax on good i and decreasing it on good j (optimality would require λ_i to be independent of i). The analysis places the status quo in a central position and asks: "Given where we are, in what direction should we move?" It seems quite likely (and it is confirmed by our experience) that the type of language involved is more easily understood by the policy-maker than the notion of a large move towards some optimum which may emerge from a model of which he is suspicious. This may be an advantage for the applied worker who is collecting data, although much of his underlying model is the same (but he can assume rather less, see next subsection). We assume here that producer prices are fixed. The assumptions are examined further in Subsection 3.4.

As we shall see (Subsection 3.3) an advantage of this approach is that it uses less information than is required for optimality – essentially we need only "local" information (demand responses around the status quo), rather than the "global" information (a full description of demand functions for all price vectors) required for the analysis of optimality. Furthermore, it allows considerations which are not captured in the model to be set alongside the calculated welfare increase in an appraisal of the costs and benefits of change. This type of discussion is less straightforward when the full optimum is computed since they are not easily integrated into a calculation whose output is a specific set of optimal rates. A disadvantage is that directions only and not step-size are identified. And there will usually be a choice between many welfare-improving directions which, like that for step size, must be taken using criteria outside the model. Examples of relevant considerations might be (i) administrative convenience, e.g. which directions are easily achievable using existing tools or (ii) political acceptability which may limit how far one can go, or (iii) confidence in estimates of the critical parameters working in favour of a particular direction. Such questions are typically ignored in the optimality calculation. The use of expression (8) requires the simple assumptions about production used in the model of (3) and (4) and is discussed further in Subsections 3.4 and 3.6.

The potential from using the simple λ_i notation is illustrated in Ahmad and Stern (1984). We show, for example, how it can be related in practice to Pareto improvements and the calculation of welfare weights, β^h. Thus, either a Pareto improvement is possible or there exists a non-negative set of welfare weights with respect to which the current state of affairs is optimal [see also Guesnerie (1977)]. One can use these welfare weights as a commentary on the status quo (e.g. it could only be considered optimal with respect to an unattractive set of weights), or for use in other policy problems.

The basic theories of public economics can then take us quite a long way in thinking about the problems of developing countries. In the remainder of this section we shall discuss some of the complications and difficulties of extending and applying the theory, before putting together some simple principles and lessons.

3.3. Applied policy models

Applied policy models can have many sectors or just a few and they can be used to study both marginal and non-marginal reform. Each of the four possible cases which arise has its uses and examples are available in the literature. We discuss them briefly in turn.

Policy models with many sectors and for the study of non-marginal changes are often grouped under the heading of computable general equilibrium models (CGEs). It is unnecessary to review these in detail because there are excellent surveys [see, for instance, Shoven (1983) and Shoven and Whalley (1984)], and Chapter 18 by Robinson in this Handbook is devoted to this type of model [for applications see, for example, Dervis, de Melo and Robinson (1982), or for a country case study, Mexico, Kehoe and Serra-Puche (1983)]. Typically production functions are constant elasticity of substitution (CES), factor markets are perfect and preferences are of a fairly standard type (often also CES). The free parameters in the model are chosen so that the national accounts structure fits for a particular base year. Policy variables are then changed and the new equilibrium is re-computed. Household utilities can be compared before and after the change to come to a judgement as to whether the change is beneficial.

This is not the place to discuss these models at length and we shall confine ourselves to some brief comments concerning their use in policy discussion. First, they require a very large number of parameters many or most of which are essentially imposed exogenously. Second, the scope for sensitivity analysis is rather narrow. Thus, one can vary an elasticity of substitution fairly easily but it would generally require a great deal of work to change the structure of a market. Third, and related to the first two points, it is not easy to make an intuitive assessment of the role of crucial assumptions in determining the answers. Thus, they often have a tendency to be used as black boxes with few questions asked as to where answers are coming from. Fourth, the detail they provide on the consumption side is generally rather less than would be required in coming to a judgement about the different types of gainers and losers – typically there may be twenty or so household groups compared with a household survey of five or ten thousand households. Frequently it is the fate of different types of households which is crucial in determining the attractiveness or otherwise of a reform and one cannot characterise in advance just who those households will be. Increasingly the appraisal of taxes is being influenced by analyses utilising the detail at the household level [see Atkinson and Sutherland (1987)].

On the more positive side the models are explicit and they do allow some flexibility. The greater detail in production may pick up important points which might be missed in a more aggregated framework. And the models allow estimation of changes in factor prices. However, some of the detail in the results is spurious in the sense that it is the consequence of fairly arbitrary assumptions and the calculations for a particular industry would be unlikely to substitute for an industry study if some special sectors were at issue.

There are two main advantages of using more aggregated computable applied models. First, it is often possible to gain a good intuitive understanding of how the model works. Second, they can allow optimisation. There are a number of recent examples of the study of non-marginal changes in such policy models [e.g. Braverman, Hammer and Ahn (1987)]. Heady and Mitra (1987) provide in addition some optimisation. They also show how the model's simple structure can be used to discuss the analytical framework before embarking on computations.

The marginal approach, as described briefly at the end of Subsection 3.2 can be followed in both multi-sectoral and more aggregated models. Its first detailed application was by Ahmad and Stern [e.g. (1984), (1987), and (forthcoming)] in the study of Indian indirect taxes. In order to see what is involved we write out (8), the expression for the marginal social cost of revenue arising from an adjustment of the ith tax (8), more fully:

$$\lambda_i = \frac{\displaystyle\sum_h \beta^h x_i^h}{X_i + t \cdot \dfrac{\partial X}{\partial q_i}}. \tag{9}$$

Intuitively the numerator represents the money cost (x_i^h) to households of a unit price change weighted by the welfare weight β^h and aggregated across households. The denominator measures the response of revenue to the tax change and involves the vector of demand responses $\partial X / \partial q_i$. Note that only the *aggregate* demands and demand responses appear in the denominator. An alternative way of writing (9) is as the distributional characteristic D_i divided by a tax elasticity:

$$\lambda_i = \frac{\rho_i D_i}{\eta_i}, \tag{10}$$

where

$$D_i = \frac{\displaystyle\sum_i \beta^h x_i^h}{X_i}, \quad \rho_i = \frac{t_i X_i}{R} \quad \text{and} \quad \eta_i = \frac{t_i}{R} \frac{\partial R}{\partial t_i}. \tag{11}$$

The distributional characteristic is the sum of the x_i^h weighted by the β^h divided by the unweighted sum, ρ_i is the share of the ith good in tax revenue and η_i is the elasticity of tax revenue w.r.t. the ith specific tax. One may see λ_i therefore as the product of a distributional term and an "efficiency" term since distributional judgements do not enter ρ_i and η_i.

Expression (9) tells us about the data requirements: we need the welfare weights β^h, the consumptions x_i^h, the tax rates t, and the aggregate demand responses. The β^h are the value judgements which can be discussed directly and can be varied to allow for more or less egalitarian viewpoints. The x_i^h come from household surveys, the demand responses from estimates of consumer demand systems and t is the vector of taxes on final goods (effective taxes). Where the tax data are scattered, classified differently from national accounts commodity categories, and there are many taxes on inputs, then the calculation of the tax rates t can be a major task. For calculations of λ_i see Ahmad and Stern (1984, 1987) on India, and Section 5 below for a discussion of Pakistan.

We now discuss briefly some of the problems of applying and extending the method focusing on demand responses, administration and tax rates. Usually it will be very difficult to estimate cross-price elasticities in any detail in demand analysis. The number of cross-price terms goes up as the square of the number of goods and the number of observations on each price is often small (for example one per year or quarter). Thus, many of the cross-price effects may be imposed by the demand structure selected for estimation. We saw that this can have an important effect in optimality calculations and similar considerations apply to the analysis of reform [see Deaton (1987)]. In the case of reform, sensitivity may be qualitatively less since if we use observed (rather than fitted) values in the numerator of (9) (and for X_i in the denominator) the demand system comes only into the aggregate response terms in the denominator. On the other hand, estimated demand responses for each separate household come into optimising methods since we have to work out consumer demands at a position different from the status quo.

The costs of administration may be formally incorporated into the reform analysis as follows. Suppose that an extra rupee collected via the ith good costs γ_i in administration so that, net $1 - \gamma_i$ is raised. Then to raise one rupee net we have to collect $1/(1 - \gamma_i)$ gross so that the marginal social loss from one rupee net is $\lambda_i/(1 - \gamma_i)$. We would switch a net rupee on the margin from tax i to tax j if

$$\frac{1}{(1 - \gamma_i)}\lambda_i > \frac{1}{(1 - \gamma_j)}\lambda_j \tag{12}$$

or

$$\frac{\lambda_i}{\lambda_j} > \frac{1 - \gamma_i}{1 - \gamma_j}. \tag{13}$$

Although estimates of γ_i and γ_j may not be easy (for example allocation of tax authority expenditures is not straightforward), it may be possible once estimates of λ_i and λ_j have been obtained to come to a judgement as to which side of (13) is the larger. For example, if λ_i/λ_j is 1.5, then if we guess that γ_i is around 0.25 rupees per rupee of gross revenue, then provided γ_j is less than 0.50 we would want to switch on the margin from i to j.

The calculation of the tax element in the price of final goods involves the modelling of tax shifting. This will depend on the detailed structure of the model and we merely indicate some of the considerations which arise. To keep things simple we examine a model with no joint production and constant returns to scale. We suppose now that factors are not subject to indirect taxes and denote their price vector by w. Consider first a closed-economy model. Then under competitive conditions, where $c(\cdot)$ is the unit cost of production,

$$p = c(p, w), \tag{14}$$

where we suppose producers have taxes on inputs rebated (as with VAT). Differentiating we find:

$$\frac{\partial p}{\partial t} = \frac{\partial w}{\partial t} B(I - A)^{-1}, \tag{15}$$

where $\partial p/\partial t$ and $\partial w/\partial t$ are the matrices of price and wage responses to taxes, B is the matrix of factor requirements and A the input–output matrix for goods. Where taxes are not rebated on inputs, so that producers buy at q, then (14) and (15) become:

$$p = c(q, w), \tag{16}$$

$$\frac{\partial p}{\partial t} = A(I - A)^{-1} + \frac{\partial w}{\partial t} B(I - A)^{-1}, \tag{17}$$

$$\frac{\partial q}{\partial t} = (I - A)^{-1} + \frac{\partial w}{\partial t} B(I - A)^{-1}. \tag{18}$$

These equations may readily be extended to the open economy where we have to consider both the matrix of domestic inputs into domestic production, and the matrix of foreign inputs, in the calculation of the effects on domestic prices of a tax change.

Hence, in the competitive model, crucial elements are the rebating or otherwise of taxes on inputs, the openness of the economy and the relations between domestic and foreign commodities (e.g. the patterns of substitutes and complements in production and consumption) and the general equilibrium effects operating through factor prices. For this last aspect CGEs may be useful. For examples of calculations of the tax element in price in simple input–output models for India and Pakistan, see Ahmad and Stern (1986a, 1987).

In the non-competitive model a very broad range of outcomes is possible. This has been studied in the conjectural variations model by Seade (forthcoming) and

Stern (1987b). The results depend critically on the elasticity (F) of the elasticity of demand. If this is high, then tax-shifting is low because a price increase resulting from a cost increase gives a big increase in the elasticity thus dampening the effect of the cost increase. It is easy to produce examples (the case of linear demand) where tax-shifting is less than 100 percent and examples where it is greater (isoelastic demand) – it is above or below 100 percent as F is below or above one. Whilst it may not be practicable, or desirable, to use the conjectural variations model in direct applications, it does illustrate that the range of possibilities can be very wide.

The marginal method is now being applied to some of the more aggregated models [see, for example, Newbery (1987b)]. This allows one to avoid some of the more unsatisfactory assumptions about production and factor markets made in the more detailed framework (although it allows less detail on the consumption side). These assumptions can also be relaxed by using shadow prices, the subject of the next subsection.

3.4. The general theory of reform and shadow prices

The reform analysis discussed in the previous subsection forms part of the more general theory of shadow prices. This has been examined at length in Drèze and Stern (1987) and a detailed discussion will not be provided here (and there is a separate chapter in this Handbook on cost–benefit analysis). Our aim here is to bring out the general principles and show how they provide a unifying framework for much of policy analysis. The treatment is based on Drèze and Stern (1987).

The government is concerned with the selection of certain policy variables, for example, taxes, quotas, or rations. At the initial position some are chosen optimally and the remainder are fixed at predetermined positions – the vector describing the former group is s and the latter group ω. The choice of the (s) for given ω may then be described by the solution of the problem (19):

$$\underset{s}{\text{maximise }} V(s, \omega)$$

subject to $\hspace{10cm}$ (19)

$$E(s, \omega) = z,$$

where V is the social welfare function, E net excess demands and z public supply (many components of which may be zero). We suppose the problem is feasible so that the dimension of s is at least as great as that of z. When the two dimensions are exactly equal, then if $E(\cdot)$ is invertible (given ω), s is defined as a function of z and there will essentially be no choice. Thus, the situation where the policy variables are fully determined and there is no scope for optimisation is a special case of the model. The equality in the constraint in (19) and the assumption that the dimension of s is at least as great as z are not strong assumptions but involve merely the assertion that there is a process by which equilibrium is established and goods are allocated in the economy (it may well be of the non-competitive variety with fixed prices, rationing and so on).

The Lagrangian for (19) is

$$L(s, \omega) = V(s, \omega) - \nu[E(s, \omega) - z],\qquad(20)$$

where ν is the vector of shadow prices. The shadow price of a good is *defined* as the increase in the value of the social welfare function when an extra unit of public supplies becomes available, and it is a standard result that it will equal ν in (20) (whether or not the model is fully determined). Thus, the increment in social welfare from a given project dz (at constant ω but with s endogenous), from the definition of ν, is $\nu\, dz$.

The first-order conditions for a maximum in (19) are

$$\frac{\partial V}{\partial s} - \nu \frac{\partial E}{\partial s} = 0.\qquad(21)$$

A reform is a change $d\omega$ in the variables ω which had previously been seen as predetermined. In order to satisfy the constraints we must have:

$$\frac{\partial E}{\partial \omega} d\omega - \frac{\partial E}{\partial s} ds = 0.\qquad(22)$$

Using (21) and (22) we have:

$$dV = \left(\frac{\partial V}{\partial \omega} - \nu \frac{\partial E}{\partial \omega} \right) d\omega.\qquad(23)$$

This is the general result on policy reform. It tells us that the welfare impact of a reform is given by the direct effect on social welfare less the cost of the extra net demands at shadow prices $\nu\, \partial E/\partial \omega$. This is a unifying principle which underlies very many discussions of policy change. It is at one level simple and obvious but it often seems to be imperfectly understood.

The model (19) and the derivation of (23) we have used makes it very clear that the shadow prices will depend critically on how equilibrium is re-established after a change in z or ω, i.e. they will be different for different specifications of the endogenous variables s. For example, we can think of a change in net demands of an imported good (whose world price is fixed) from a parameter change being satisfied by extra imports with no price change or by rationed imports with an increase in the domestic price. In the former case it is the net imports that form part of s and in the latter case the price. The general equilibrium effect on social welfare will be different, and thus so too will be the shadow prices.

The marginal analysis of the preceding section can readily be seen as a special case of (23). The details are not provided here [see Stern (1987a)] but one way of expressing the generalisation provided by (23) for the case where indirect taxes are to be reformed is through

$$\lambda_i^{\nu} = - \frac{\partial V}{\partial t_i} \bigg/ \frac{\partial R_{\nu}}{\partial t_i} , \tag{24}$$

where R_{ν} is *shadow* revenue, i.e. government revenue where we treat $q - \nu$ as shadow consumption taxes and $(\nu - p)$ as shadow production taxes. When $\nu = p$, shadow and producer prices coincide, and we are back with λ_i and (10). One can also write

$$dV = \left[\frac{\partial V}{\partial t} + \frac{\partial}{\partial t}(t \cdot X) + (p - \nu)\frac{\partial X}{\partial t} \right] dt \tag{25}$$

(where the derivatives are taken for constant p) so that in addition to the welfare and revenue effects [the first two terms on the r.h.s. of (25)] we have an additional shadow revenue term arising from the difference between shadow and producer prices.

There are many economies where shadow prices have been calculated. We have seen here that their use is not confined to project appraisal but applies also to the analysis of policy reform in general. Care should be taken, however, to ensure consistency of the models used in the reform discussion and those used to calculate shadow prices.

The shadow prices capture a great deal of information, essentially the full general equilibrium effects on welfare of a policy change. In principle they should be derived from a fully articulated general equilibrium model and one could argue that if such a model is available then welfare effects of policy changes can be calculated directly. However, in many cases the set of shadow prices will be a tool which is more flexible, reliable, less demanding and more easily understood than the full model. They provide sufficient statistics for policy from the full model and can be discussed directly. And one supposes that corresponding to any plausible set of shadow prices one could construct a general equilibrium model and welfare judgements which would be consistent with the shadow prices. Hence, for example, if one argued that population growth, and better labour market policies were likely to bring about a substantial reduction in the shadow wage, one could then examine fairly rapidly the consequences for tax policy. On the other hand it may involve a great deal of effort to redesign a large model (if such already exists) to take account of the changed assumptions. At the same time one hopes that (or should try to check that) variations of assumptions in one area do not produce huge changes in the whole shadow price vector otherwise the credibility of the approach would be undermined (although such a situation would be likely to make any approach perilous).

3.5. Dynamic assumptions

The theories described so far have had n goods and time has not appeared explicitly. We now ask how they can be reinterpreted in a dynamic context and what extensions or modifications would be desirable [for a more detailed discussion of the issues raised see Newbery and Stern (1987b)]. The familiar Arrow–Debreu model of general equilibrium which underlies the standard models presented in Subsection 3.2 can be interpreted in the usual way as a full intertemporal model provided all goods are distinguished by their date of availability. Thus, if there are N physically different goods and T periods, there will be NT markets (a similar interpretation in terms of uncertainty and different states of nature is also possible). The standard results in welfare economics relating competitive equilibrium to Pareto efficiency then apply (and one can extend this to infinite horizons provided one adds an assumption about asymptotic behaviour to rule out over-saving). Similarly, the Diamond and Mirrlees taxation model can be applied to this framework too. Thus, consumers maximise utility, defined over the indefinite future, with knowledge of future consumer prices and incomes and make commitments for supplies of services and purchase of goods. Producers maximise the present value of profits at the producer prices which they face. The Ramsey taxes which are the difference between consumer and producer prices then define a tax system over the indefinite future. All producers face the same interest rates, profits taxation applies to present values and is not based on period-by-period returns, and savings would in general be taxed (producer and consumer prices will differ) to raise revenue and improve the intertemporal and interpersonal distribution of income.

The model is a useful point of reference but raises a number of basic difficulties for applied policy analysis for developing countries, many of which apply to analyses for developed countries also, and examples of which follow. First, many of the postulated markets do not exist. Second, it is difficult to separate savings and investment decisions (and thus consumer and producer intertemporal prices) for a large fraction of the private sector. For example, many or most business startups are financed out of individual savings [see Little, Mazumdar and Page (1984)]. This problem arises in part from lack of markets but also has to do with the poor development of financial intermediaries, asymmetric perceptions or information (the bank may not share my view of my chances of success) and costs of enforcing arrangements in an informal sector. Third, the kind of dynamic optimisation by individuals and firms which is assumed is implausible for individuals who may have a hazy vision of the future and ill-formed and complex preferences over future outcomes. This is not to say that they are irrational but that the detailed dynamic optimisation model with unrestricted trading possibilities may not have an overwhelming claim as the appropriate representation of their behaviour. There is no doubt that all these problems arise in some shape or form in the static model but they are particularly pervasive and severe in the dynamic context. There has not in our judgement been great success in the literature in integrating these features into a dynamic tax analysis, but we shall discuss below some models which are specifically designed for a dynamic context.

Furthermore, there are particular features and difficulties which arise when we move to dynamic problems. For example, there may be incentives to renege on previous commitments or announced policies (sometimes called "dynamic inconsistency"). Second, the open-endedness of the economy can lead to problems of dynamic inefficiency of the kind which do not arise in a static economy (e.g. it is easy to write down growth problems where no optimum exists, essentially because there appear to be grounds in the model for postponing consumption indefinitely). Third, there are problems associated with how individuals are forced to observe budget constraints (there have to be mechanisms to prevent build-up of debt in circumstances where individuals can promise to pay later). Fourth, in models of overlapping generations transfers between generations can produce types of inefficiency which do not arise in static problems (e.g. if each generation is endowed with a chocolate then the first generation can be made better off by each generation passing a chocolate forward whilst none of the others is worse off). One has to look carefully at how resources can be transferred.

Of the problems special to dynamic economics perhaps the one which has received most attention in the policy literature is that of "dynamic consistency". The issue was raised by Kydland and Prescott (1977) and a clear description in the tax policy context is provided in Fischer (1980). The idea is that the future tax policy announced by the government last period will no longer be optimal when it comes to implementation this period not because the future has developed in an unexpected way, but because the passage of time makes certain disincentives now irrelevant. Thus, last period the government may have announced that capital taxation in the second (now current) period would be low in order to encourage accumulation. In the second period the government may then simply announce a capital levy. This is a lump-sum tax with no distortionary implications and, ex post, is the best way to raise second-period revenue. The argument is persuasive if the second period is the last one. However, things are more complicated if the economy is open-ended, for then government which has made a capital levy in the past may not be believed if it promises not to do it again in the future, so that the second period capital levy ceases to be lump-sum and has its own distortionary aspect.

Examples of the problem arise with amnesties for tax evaders. These are sometimes announced as one-off chances to "come clean" with very lenient penalties if evasion is revealed before a certain date but very severe penalties if evasion is subsequently discovered. If the evader believes this then he may be tempted to reveal, and the subsequent very severe penalties will become redundant and need not be used. However, if the taxpayers see this happen once they may be very tempted to evade subsequently.

The discussion of practical policy towards taxation in developing countries has avoided the more esoteric modelling problems and has expressed the dynamic issues in terms of broader or more aggregated concepts such as savings, investment and growth. Much of the early post-war literature on development [see, for example, Lewis (1954)] placed the rate of growth at the centre of the stage and many authors have singled out government concern, and perceived responsibility, for raising the rate of growth as a major distinguishing feature of public finance in developing countries [e.g. Prest (1972), Eshag (1983) and Goode (1984)]. Developed countries may worry about the growth rate too but often greater emphasis is placed on the rate of technical progress than on savings and investment per se. And the experience of developing countries in the 30 years since Lewis was writing tells us that raising the savings rate is not necessarily a sufficient condition for rapid growth [for example, India and many other developing countries have savings and investment rates between 18 and 25 percent in common with most of the industrial market economies – see World Bank (1984)].

If the growth objective is firmly adopted then governments should take careful account of the effects of its policies on saving and the level and productivity of investment. Policies for the encouragement of savings and investment include favourable tax treatment of saving, promotion of financial institutions and interest rate policy. One would like to examine these policies in the consequentialist manner by first predicting their outcomes and then evaluating the changes. A major problem is that the elasticities of response are very hard to judge. This applies to both savings and investment.

There has been a considerable recent literature on modelling and estimating savings responses in developed countries. A useful survey is provided by King (1985) who argues that one often finds that life-cycle models are consistent with behaviour for 70–75 percent of the population but not for the remaining 20–25 percent, and one may suggest that for this minority credit constraints may be important. Whilst the data underlying these studies are very rich compared to those available for developing countries, the researchers have not found it easy to pick up the response of savings to post-tax returns, an aspect which is crucial for the design of tax policy. The lessons for developing countries of these studies may be as follows. First, the 20–25 percent for whom life-cycle models are inappropriate may be much larger in developing countries where financial markets are less well-developed. Second, it is unlikely to be possible given current data to establish an interest elasticity of saving for developing countries. In the meantime policy has to be formulated and it seems sensible to avoid losing substantial amounts of tax revenue in schemes for the promotion of savings whose net effect may be very obscure. Furthermore, one should try to avoid creating tax anomalies which may arise from special treatment of different kinds of savings since they can lose tax revenue and redistribute income in favour of the more rich and knowledgeable, and may have little further effect other than the rearrangement of some portfolios.

There have been a number of applied policy models focused on taxation and savings for developed countries but they will not be reviewed in detail here [for recent discussions see Chamley (1983), Kotlikoff (1984) and Newbery and Stern (1987b)]. In most of the models, however detailed, the interest elasticity is a crucial variable yet it is one on which we have little reliable in the way of estimates [see, for example, Gersovitz's chapter on savings in this Handbook (Chapter 10) or Giovannini (1985)]. The policy simulations have often been concerned with switches from income to consumption-based taxes and a central issue has been the effect on capital accumulation via saving.

The base of taxation has also been discussed in overlapping generations models which are in the same spirit as the Diamond–Mirrlees standard model of taxation in Subsection 3.2 [see Atkinson and Sandmo (1980) and King (1980)]. The relevant goods in the utility function are, for example, consumption in two periods and labour supply in one (if the second period is retirement). With separability of consumption from labour one can show (analogous to the results in the static model of Subsection 3.1) that taxation of consumption in the two periods should be uniform and one can interpret this as a proportional expenditure tax in the two periods. However, with labour supply in more than one period, or without separability, the result does not hold and thus one can conclude that there is no strong theoretical argument for an expenditure tax. More recent advocacy of such taxes has been on practical grounds and, in particular, that it removes the distinction between capital and income, a common basis of tax dodges and anomalies [see, for example, Meade (1978) and Kay and King (1986)]. These suggested practical advantages have not impressed themselves on many governments, at least not to the point of actually introducing it. An unfortunate example which still reinforces such hesitancy was the Indian experience when in the 1950s an expenditure tax was introduced on the advice of Kaldor, but raised negligible revenue and much protest and was very quickly withdrawn.

Our conclusion from this brief discussion of dynamic issues is that similar principles to the static analysis can be applied but that our present state of knowledge of response is not firmly based. Nevertheless, a concern to promote saving and growth can be embodied in the techniques which we used to guide public policy. Thus, for example, a premium on savings can be incorporated in shadow prices [see, for example, Little and Mirrlees (1974) and Drèze and Stern (1987)]. One should try to discover the consequences of proposed reforms for savings but be circumspect about confident claims for the likely effects of special tax concessions. There is no convincing theoretical argument in favour of expenditure rather than income taxes, although one should be aware of revenue losses associated with separate treatment of capital and income. On the investment side promising areas for study of the dynamic effects of public policy are the potential of financial markets in supplying credit more easily, constraints on investment associated with infrastructure such as water and electricity supplies, and the pricing of public sector enterprises. Thus, there may well be substantial scope for promoting the profitability of investments in ways which do not involve big tax concessions. Arguments for tax concessions should be examined rather carefully to check that any claimed response is likely to be present. Otherwise the concessions may simply act as a transfer payment. It should be emphasised that there is no assertion here that we should assume from our lack of knowledge that savings and investment actually are inelastic. Our ignorance should make us cautious and we should not therefore tax investment heavily on the dubious grounds that we "may as well assume" it is interest inelastic. At the same time the static analysis of taxes implicitly assumes that there are no strong intertemporal linkages particular to certain goods which are sufficiently large to change the whole picture.

3.6. Taxes and production

One of the most striking contrasts between discussions of public economics for developed and for developing countries lies in the treatment of taxes and production. The concentration in the theory for developed countries has been on government revenue, on the allocation of consumption and on factor supply, issues which are within the spirit of the standard model of Subsection 3.2. The assumption of fixed producer prices is common. On the other hand, in the study of developing countries great attention has been focused on the incentives facing producers in terms of the effects of government policies on the prices they face – these considerations lie at the heart of discussions of effective protection, shadow prices and so on. Thus, many have argued that the consequences of government policy, particularly concerning taxes, in developing countries have been the wrong pattern of outputs, whereas in developed countries criticism is often focussed on the alleged curtailment of incentives for factor supply and on the distributive effects on different types of household.

The basic principles of the normative analysis of policy reform when shadow prices are not equal to producer prices are provided in Subsection 3.4. One calculates the direct effect on households of a policy change and then adjusts this for the value at shadow prices of the net changes in excess demand associated with the direct effects in order to pick up the general equilibrium repercussions of the change. It is interesting to contrast this approach with discussions based on effective protection, a very popular applied tool used in discussions of tariffs and the pattern of production [see the *Journal of International Economics* symposium (1983), where a number of aspects of effective protection are examined]. The first point to note is that the rate of effective protection, defined as the value added at domestic prices less that at world prices (as a proportion of value added at world prices) is not a normative concept but an attempt to describe what happens to value added in different industries as a result of tariffs. It is often rapidly transformed into a normative statement with the suggestion that resources should be transferred to sectors with a lower effective rate of protection from those with a higher.

As a normative suggestion concerning resource movements the argument is unsatisfactory. First, it takes no account of possible divergences between market prices and social opportunity costs (or shadow prices) for non-traded and factor inputs. Once proper account is taken of the former we have domestic resource cost (or DRC) calculations and the further step of treating the social opportunity cost of factors carefully takes us to a system of shadow prices. Second, the adjustment prescription based on effective protection takes no account of the scale of movement. If coefficients for non-factor inputs are fixed it would appear to tell us to transfer an indefinite amount into the activity with the lowest effective protective rate. Third, one cannot in general argue that when there is substitution amongst inputs and factors that resource flows follow the direction indicated by rates of effective protection; thus the effect of a tariff structure may be to direct resources to an industry with a lower rate of effective protection [see Dixit and Norman (1980, ch. 5)]. Fourth, the question as to why one might want to protect is not put. Whilst the arguments for protection are often spurious one should not assume that they always are.

Effective protection calculations are also often used in discussions of tariff reform in that it is suggested that tariffs should be adjusted to make lower the effective protection rates for industries with higher rates of protection. Again this is unsatisfactory. There is nothing to suggest that uniform effective protection rates have any general optimality properties. As we argued in the previous section, in the absence of lump-sum taxes a government concerned with incentives and distribution should in an open-economy competitive world have taxes on final sales only, irrespective of origin. Thus, there would be no tariffs or any other taxes affecting relative producer prices. And the taxes on final sales would not usually be uniform. One would require an articulated model with a careful statement concerning constraints on policies to justify any assertion that uniform effective rates of protection are optimal and it is very unclear how such an argument could be constructed.

The main advantage of calculations of effective rates of protection lies in reminding policy-makers that their actions affect not only output prices but also input costs and in making some of these effects explicit. As we have argued, however, they are unreliable guides to policy reform. The central notion in the area is that of shadow prices and greater use of this concept outside the area of project appraisal could be valuable.

The analysis of tax reform which incorporates an account of production and general equilibrium when producer prices and shadow prices are unequal would essentially add an extra term to an analysis of costs and benefits of tax reform as we saw in eq. (25). Thus, in addition to revenue and direct effects on household welfare one takes account of the losses associated with any shift in demand towards industries with shadow prices higher than producer prices, i.e. one subtracts $(\nu - p)\Delta X$ corresponding to a demand shift ΔX arising from the tax reform. This is a suggestion which should apply to policy reform for both developed and less developed countries. We find the general assumption that producer prices are equal to shadow prices for developed countries a little surprising. Is it true, for example, that the labour market clears under conditions of perfect competition? Are there tariffs? Does the pricing policy for major inputs to production such as electricity, oil, transport and so on, avoid either implicit taxes or subsidies and reflect social marginal costs? Are all final goods taxed and are the rates optimally set? If the answer to such questions is negative, then one must take seriously the possibility that producer and shadow prices do not coincide.

3.7. The taxation of income and profits

The analysis of Section 3 has, to this point, been mainly theoretical. We have been trying to assemble what theory has to offer in the provision of methods of applied policy analysis and in the formulation of principles for the setting of policy and by which it may be judged. In the remainder of Section 3 we shall draw this analysis together in a discussion of particular taxes and in a set of guidelines or principles which summarise some of the lessons of the theory. In so doing we must bring to the centre of the stage some of the practical difficulties which governments and tax authorities face, some of which have been discussed at the end of Section 2. We begin with income and profits taxes. From the point of view of a theory which sees changes in welfare in terms of effects on households the corporation tax has a limited role. In the class of models considered in Subsection 3.1 the pure profits tax should in general be used where possible (assuming owners of firms do not have very high net social marginal utilities of income) but a corporation tax does not otherwise appear in the models unless one considers it as, in part, a tax on entrepreneurial or capital services provided by households. In answering the question, however, why there should be a corporation tax within the type of theory we have been examining one can point to four possible responses. First, it acts in part as a tax on monopoly rents or pure profits. Second, it provides a way of taxing foreign owners. Third, it may help in policies designed to promote savings or investment. Fourth, because it is already there in the sense that its removal would provide a windfall gain to groups which are far from impoverished. All of these arguments apply to both developed and developing countries but they may well be stronger in the latter case. Hence, the more prominent role of the corporation tax, relative to the personal income tax, in developing countries is not without foundation in the principles we have been discussing. Perhaps the most important reason, however, for taxing corporations is as a means of collection of taxes on personal incomes. As we have already noted, this applies to foreign owners but it applies to domestic owners too where the system of domestic personal income taxation is weak and easily evaded, particularly by the owners of corporations who, we suppose, are not usually amongst the poorest of the population.

The form of the corporation tax can vary greatly depending on its treatment of distributed and undistributed profits, depreciation allowances, inflation, interest payments, and so on. Profits can also be manipulated by multi-nationals through transfer-pricing, e.g. inflating the costs of certain inputs, or deflating output prices to depress measured profits in countries where profits taxation is high. These complications require careful scrutiny in the examination of policy for a particular country.

Theoretical and empirical research on the corporation tax is even less easy to present in a coherent and integrated form than it is for other taxes, partly because it sits somewhat unhappily in the economic theory of tax policy. Discussion has focused on a number of issues concerning the possible effects of the tax rather than on attempting to construct a theory of policy design. Furthermore, the effects of the tax are rather difficult to quantify both theoretically and empirically. Thus, concentration has often been on the incentives and disincentives associated with different systems rather than the explicit modelling of the full effects of these incentives. Most of the work has been for developed countries although, as ever, the issues apply to developing countries too. However, in the latter case one suspects that the immediate problems are more in devising ways to actually collect revenue rather than fine tuning. This should not, however, lead us to ignore the possible effects on the level and allocation of investment and saving. The revenue from the corporation tax is likely to grow over time as more advanced sectors develop and it is important to have a sensible system in advance. It is surely possible to learn from the experience of developed countries where, for example in the United Kingdom the corporate tax system has grown as a series of rather ad hoc responses to short-term pressures [see Kay and King (1986)].

We shall describe very briefly some of the prominent issues in the literature on the corporation tax and then point to possible lessons for tax design. One of the major themes has been the differential treatment of distributed and undistributed profits together with the returns to and choices between different forms of finance. With the *classical* system, for example, the corporation tax applies (usually at a flat proportional rate) on all profits whether distributed or undistributed, together with a personal income tax on the dividends. Thus, dividends are taxed at a higher rate than undistributed profits. In this sense there is a "discrimination" in favour of retentions. Undistributed profits, it is true, may be taxed via a capital gains tax, if it exists, but this is usually at a lower rate than personal income taxes. Furthermore, it is often haphazardly collected, raising very little revenue.

Under this classical system there is a bias in favour of loan finance as against raising money from new share issues. Interest payments are deductible for corporation tax purposes so that a project which yields a return above the rate of interest will generate a surplus for the shareholders if it is financed by a loan (assuming all costs are properly charged including depreciation). In this sense the corporation tax treats loan-financed investment in a neutral way. On the other hand, a project financed out of a new share issue is financed by a promise to pay dividends (as opposed to interest). Dividends are not an allowable cost for corporation tax purposes so that the required return on the company's investment now exceeds the rate of interest.

Finance out of retained profits is more complicated. If a firm retains profits rather than paying out dividends, then the shareholder forgoes the net-of-tax dividends. The company invests this amount gross-of-tax. If it retains the proceeds from the investment, then from the point of view of the net returns to the individual shareholder, these are taxed at the corporation tax rate plus the capital gains tax rate. If this latter combined rate exceeds the personal income tax rate, then the required rate of return again exceeds the rate of interest. Thus, whether there is also a bias against retained earnings (relative to loan finance) depends on the personal tax position of the shareholder. If corporate taxes are collected more effectively than the personal income tax we would indeed expect this bias to be present.

The other major form of the corporate income tax in practice is the *imputation* system. Tax withheld on dividends is credited against the corporate tax at a rate known as the *imputation* rate. If the imputation rate is equal to the individual shareholder's personal marginal rate then that is the end of the matter. Otherwise there will be extra tax to pay by the individual if the imputation rate is lower than the marginal rate (and a refund if higher). This system reduces the bias in favour of loan versus equity finance but it is still present provided the imputation rate is lower than the corporate rate (if the former is 30 percent and the latter 50 percent, then £100 in gross dividends reduces corporate tax liability by £30, whereas £100 in interest by £50). The classical system operates in the United States and several other developed and developing countries, whereas the imputation system applies in the United Kingdom and several Commonwealth countries.

The discussion makes it clear that the relation between the rate of return on an investment gross-of-tax and the return to savers will be a very intricate one depending on many things, including the form of finance, the corporate tax system, the personal income tax system, the tax status of the saver, the tax treatment of the particular kind of asset, and so on. In these circumstances the task of describing the tax system in terms of the "wedge" placed between the gross and net-of-tax rate of return is formidable, leaving aside any attempt to work out the allocative consequences of such wedges in terms of the response by individuals to the different incentives and the general equilibrium ramifications of these responses. For further discussion of the implications of different forms of corporation tax, along the lines presented above, see, for example, Kay and King (1986) and King (1977). Calculations of the different tax wedges for different forms of asset, finance, and individual for the United States, the United Kingdom, Sweden and West Germany are presented in King and Fullerton (1984). They show that within a country the range of tax wedges is very large. It also varies considerably across countries with pre- and post-tax rates of return being on average very close for the United Kingdom, and the latter being half the former, an average, for West Germany.

Notwithstanding the difficulties of describing the system, there have been a number of calculations of the welfare losses associated with the tax wedge following the work of Harberger in 1962 [reprinted in Harberger (1974)] – see, for example, McLure (1975) and Shoven and Whalley (1972). The assumptions involved are highly restrictive even for developed countries and according to Goode (1984, p. 116), have little influence or relevance for developing countries. It is nevertheless important to try to understand the likely important determinants of the incidence of corporation tax. This is often referred to as "the shifting of the corporation tax", although the term is ambiguous as it is sometimes taken to mean the effect on prices and sometimes the ultimate incidence in terms of its effect on households [see King (1977, p. 248)]. In particular, Diamond (1970) has looked at the incidence of property taxes in a growth model. Perhaps the most important influence on incidence, however, is the openness of the economy as Goode (1984), King (1977) and Gil Diaz (1987) all emphasise. Gil Diaz (1987) in particular provides a valuable practical example in his evaluation of Mexico's recent tax reform (1978–82) where he argues that post-tax rates of return in Mexico cannot fall below the pre-tax rates in the United States for those Mexicans who cannot be prevented from having access to these U.S. investment opportunities. Hence, taxes on capital income are borne in large part by those credit users without access to international markets.

Another interesting recent discussion of the role of corporation tax has been Gersovitz (1987), who examined the effects of such taxes on foreign private investment. These effects turn out to be very complex depending on many factors including the tax agreements and treatments of host and home countries, the likelihood of expropriation, the potential for transfer pricing, and so on.

In such an intricate, and rather messy, problem one cannot expect to be able to provide a synthesis of the basic determinants of optimal policy in the manner attempted for indirect taxes. King's response (1977, p. 249), is to seek criteria of neutrality or ask that the system be non-distortionary. Thus, for example, it is suggested that, unless there is special reason it should not distinguish amongst different forms of finance or amongst different forms of assets. Possibilities are (i) a classical system without deductibility of interest payments, together with capital gains taxed at full personal rates; (ii) full integration of corporate and personal income taxation (with deductibility of interest); or (iii) a cash flow corporation tax (where the flow excludes financial transactions). Space limitations prevent further detail here but it should be clear that the merits of any particular system will depend on what is possible in practice in the country under study.

A corporate tax system which does not distort will, in general, act like a government shareholding in the firm, if losses are fully off-set, since the government takes a given fraction (the tax rate) of the gains and losses from any project. This sharing of risks between public and private sector may encourage risk-taking.

Special incentives for investment are very popular in developing countries. Amongst these, tax holidays are particularly popular [see, for example, Shah and Toye (1979)]. However, as Gersovitz (1987) points out, there are a number of problems and abuses which may lead simply to a loss of tax revenue without any corresponding increase in investment. And any tax bonus for investment should be very carefully justified. Are there externalities to investment which are not reflected in market prices? If so, perhaps taxation or subsidy policy should be focused directly on those prices which are supposed to be wrong. Is the tax incentive proposed compensating for some alleged disincentive elsewhere in the tax system of the kind we have been discussing? If so, then perhaps it is the disincentive which should be tackled directly. Or is it being argued that for reasons of inter-temporal allocation (e.g. future generations being under-represented) the tax wedge should be negative rather than positive? Again, the position is unclear. Too often, it is taken as obvious that special tax incentives for investment are needed. The evidence that they have much incentive effect is scanty and it is likely that revenue losses are substantial.

Our conclusions from the somewhat messy state of the subject are that the guiding principles should probably be simplicity, practicality and neutrality. Complex provisions without clear rationale should be discarded, particularly where they lose revenue. Special treatment for particular industries should be viewed with suspicion. Allowable deductions should be scrutinised very carefully. Finally, we would suggest that the withholding of tax on dividends is likely to be a practical way of actually collecting the revenue.

As we have seen, the theory of the optimal personal income tax is rather better developed than that of the optimal corporate tax. However, it probably has limited applicability to developing countries where the coverage of the income tax is usually limited. Nevertheless, like the corporate income tax, it has potential for the future and one should think ahead. Again it is sensible to focus on simplicity and practicality in designing policy.

One area where theory and practicality come together concerns transfers where distributive objectives can be effectively pursued by direct transfers to the poorest. The personal income tax is not a useful tool for protecting the poorest. How far it is a useful tool for redistribution by taxing the rich is largely a question of coverage and enforcement. Here, as broad a base as possible, together with moderate marginal rates, probably provides the best marriage between theoretical and administrative considerations. There is no general theoretical argument for anything other than a broad base. Permissible allowances should be confined to aspects of horizontal equity, principally concerned with family structure. Non-cash fringe benefits such as housing, cars and education should, as far as possible, be included. A broad base provides scope for lower rates and we find that calculations of optimal taxes in which redistribution and incentives are traded off do not provide arguments for very high rates [see, for example, Mirrlees (1971) and Stern (1976)]. It is often argued that very high rates encourage evasion so that theory and administration, in this case, point the same way. As with the taxation of dividends, the withholding of tax at source for all types of income is an important tool for collection.

The exemption level for the personal income tax involves balancing redistribution, revenue and administration. A low exemption level is likely to bring more potential taxpayers into the tax net than might be managed by the revenue authorities. On the other hand, high exemption levels lose revenue and may be seen as unfair. There is no general rule but often governments in developing countries seem to err on the side of generosity. This may be understandable where administrative resources are scarce but it may be desirable in some cases to let these exemption levels increase less fast than money GNP per capita so that over time a greater proportion of the population is brought into the income tax net. In this way one can provide for a growing role of the personal income tax.

We have seen in Section 3 that theory has quite a lot to say about the optimal balance between income and indirect taxes. The crucial elements are (i) the sources of differences between households, (ii) the structure of preferences, and (iii) the form of the available income tax. We saw, in particular, how one could check the requirement in this theory that an optimal uniform lump-sum transfer was in operation – one compares the social marginal cost of a rupee of revenue spent on such a transfer with the social marginal cost of raising it through indirect taxes. If the former is higher, then indirect taxes should be increased to finance an increase in the transfer. In Ahmad and Stern (1987) we carry out such a calculation for India and find that for most reasonable value judgements the lump-sum transfer would appear to be too low. This is hardly surprising since the element of transfer for many households would be negligible. We also carry out a comparison between the welfare costs of raising revenue from higher income tax payers and from indirect taxes and find that the former is preferable under most value judgements.

There are, however, major problems with this type of calculation. First, one would normally be forced to leave out of account factor supply responses. These are imperfectly understood for developed countries notwithstanding the great amount of econometric work on rich data sets [see, for example, Hausman (1981)]. There are few data sets in developing countries which would permit such exercises, and even those that exist might not provide answers. Second, they require an assessment of the incidence of changes in the income taxes or transfers. If the food-ration system were to be expanded, would this really be a transfer to each household or would just a few benefit? If so, whom? Similarly we have to ask about the pattern of extra payments if rates for upper income groups are changed. Third, one has to consider administration costs. It should be emphasised, however, that these are not problems special to the marginal or non-marginal techniques we have been examining. They would arise in any serious attempt to examine possible changes.

It is probably reasonable to suggest that the relatively small role for the income tax in developing countries can be attributed to costs of administration rather than judgements about items (i)–(iii) listed above. Nevertheless as the economies grow, the population becomes better educated, and accounting more widespread, one may suppose that the income tax will play an increasing role and one should think carefully how to structure the tax system to take advantage of the potential for growth. An advantage of the theory is that it points to tax tools and to comparisons which might otherwise be missed – for example, the central role of lump-sum transfers or taxes linked to household characteristics.

3.8. Indirect taxation

Indirect taxation can take a number of different forms. We briefly discuss three here: tariffs (and quotas), domestic excises, sales taxes and VAT. In general, trade quotas are inferior to tariffs. One could improve on a quota/licence system by auctioning the licences and the auction price is then the equivalent of a tariff – the value of the quota licence goes to the government rather than the firm getting the licence. Furthermore, one can argue that tariffs are inferior to taxes (sales taxes or VAT) on final consumption goods, whether domestically produced or imported, since tariffs distort the allocation of resources in favour of the domestic production of the good under tariff [see Dixit (1985)]. More formally one can show that if lump-sum taxes are impossible, then the optimal indirect tax system (with respect to a welfare function embodying both incentives and distribution) in an open economy is to have taxes on final sales, a sales tax for short – this is essentially an application of the Diamond and Mirrlees (1971) efficiency theorem, and see Dixit and Norman (1980, ch. 6), for an explicit formal argument. A tariff plus an equal excise on domestic production would have the same effect as a sales tax, for goods which are for final consumption only.

Arguments in favour of tariffs as against sales taxes would then be associated with administration or with the desire to protect a particular domestic industry. No doubt the administrative considerations are of substance but it is important for revenue growth over time to build up an efficient internal tax administration and to encourage formal accounting, so that one would not want to hold fast to an administrative argument in favour of tariffs over the indefinite future. The protection argument would have to be examined directly in terms of the particular industry, whether it was likely to grow or whether it should grow, whether or not there were better ways of encouragement than the tariff and so on. It seems that some of the more recent theories of international trade without the (perfectly) competitive assumption have added arguments for protection although not all the theorists would want to emphasise this point [see, for example, Dixit (1984) and Helpman and Krugman (1985)]. For example, as Dixit (1984, p. 14) puts it, there is the "possibility that a partly countervailing duty may be desirable when a foreign country subsidises exports". On the other hand, if oligopoly is associated with increasing returns to scale, then there are potential gains from specialisation which are not included in the standard model of gains from trade.

Our last comparisons will be amongst domestic excises, sales taxes and the VAT. Excises on domestically produced goods distort production in an analogous manner to tariffs – this time in the opposite direction. If coupled with a tariff they have the effect of a sales tax if the good is for final consumption. Distortions arise, however, if the good concerned is also an input into production. Domestic excises, as with tariffs, may lead to unintended consequences. For example, in our calculation of effective taxes in India we found [see Ahmad and Stern (1987)] that some goods for which the government offered subsidies (e.g. khadi and handloom cloth) were in fact taxed if one took into account taxes on inputs, and the particular culprit was domestic excises. As with tariffs the main argument for domestic excises would appear to be administration. It is interesting to note that in India the revenue from domestic excises has overtaken that from tariffs as the productive base of the economy has expanded (see Section 2) as in the story told by Hinrichs (1966). In the Indian case an important element is also the federal structure. Excises on production are the preserve of the centre whereas sales taxes are generally in the hands of the states.

The most attractive taxes from the point of view of theory are the final point sales tax and the VAT. The former has the advantage that it need involve only the final sale. Thus, firms throughout the economy are not involved as they are with VAT. A disadvantage with this sales tax is that the final stage has to be identified and this can lead to much evasion. However, many countries, e.g. India, have had some success in levying a sales tax at the wholesale stage. The VAT has been introduced in a number of countries in recent years, Tanzi (1987) noted 22 developing countries, stimulated in part perhaps by its extensive use in the European Community. It has the advantage of the in-built checking system whereby buyers have an incentive to reveal the purchase (in order to get credit for tax paid on inputs) thus discouraging concealment by a seller. Furthermore, VAT can be applied to services as well as goods since it does not require the specification of a unit of output (although a sales tax could be extended in this way too). It is also straightforward to rebate VAT on exports. A major disadvantage is that it involves everyone in the production chain thus imposing a substantial administrative cost both on the authorities and the enterprises.

One advantage that should *not* be claimed for the VAT is uniformity. There is nothing in the logic of a VAT to require uniformity and neither, as we have seen, is uniformity generally a desirable property of an indirect tax system.

This discussion therefore suggests a fairly clear strategy for indirect taxes. This consists of a replacement of trade taxes by taxes on final goods. These taxes should be differentiated to take account of the distributional pattern of consumption with such differentiation being less important the more successful is the direct income support system. Whilst this advice is useful as a description of a long-term goal, the strategy is not something that most developing countries could introduce very quickly. Administration is a central problem and many developing countries would have difficulty in levying taxes at the retail stage. This would appear to be true, for example, for much of Africa and Bangladesh. On the other hand, many other countries do levy taxes at the retail stage with some success. For example, in 1985, Turkey introduced a full-scale VAT including the retail stage which with a 12 percent rate now raises around 3 percent of GDP. Thus, the coverage is one quarter of GDP (with a notional legal coverage estimated around 50 percent of GDP). The Mexican VAT is also collected with some success, as is sales tax in a number of Indian states. The appropriate sequencing of an introduction of a consumption tax through to the final stage will depend on the circumstances of the country concerned. Most countries should be capable of handling the import and manufacturers stage and many could include wholesale. Probably the majority could not go directly to the retail stage although one should not assume it is impossible without careful scrutiny. It is an advantage of the VAT that it can be introduced incrementally through the system gradually increasing coverage and revenue. Thus if a stage is lost it does not imply that a good escapes tax altogether, whereas with a final stage tax (such as the old U.K. purchase tax) all revenue is lost if evasion takes place at the final stage. There is a great advantage of the VAT over other types of indirect taxation where introduction has to be gradual.

Where an indirect tax is not at the final stage then retail and/or wholesale margins will influence the proportion of tax in the price. In these circumstances an "effective tax" calculation of the type described in Ahmad and Stern (1986a) would be necessary and input–output information including retail and wholesale margins would be necessary.

We shall not discuss in detail here the precise form of a VAT. One has to define the base for taxation and how the taxes are to be calculated and administered. The "consumption base" allows the deduction of capital inputs in computing value added but the "income base" does not. The most common method of administration is the "subtraction" method whereby the taxpayer levies taxes on all output and subtracts from this tax collection the taxes paid on his inputs to compute the tax he must transmit to the authorities. This appears to allow the most satisfactory administration. An excellent recent discussion of experience and problems with VAT is provided in Tait (1988).

The basic theories of public finance do then provide help in judging the balance of taxes of different types. Furthermore, if developed, and with enough data and assumptions, they can be constructively applied to guide decisions on possible reforms. Examples of explicit calculations comparing the impacts of different types of tax increases, domestic excises, tariffs, sales taxes and so on are contained in Ahmad and Stern (1987).

3.9. Some simple guiding principles

As a partial summary for this long section we shall draw out some simple guiding principles from the analysis. We shall attempt to keep the statements short and direct and as such the many qualifications which would be necessary are omitted. We have discussed the relevant assumptions and the underlying logic in the preceding subsections.

(i) Where possible lump-sum taxes and transfers, or close approximations, should be used to raise revenue and transfer resources. Examples are land taxes and subsidised rations. It is not easy to find other examples where the lump-sum taxation can be appropriately linked to a relevant criterion (particularly wealth or poverty) without the tax or transfer ceasing to be lump-sum. See Subsection 3.2 for further discussion.

(ii) It can be very misleading to look at one set of tax tools in isolation from what is happening elsewhere in the tax system. For example, we should not allocate redistribution to the income tax and revenue-raising to indirect taxes. Both taxes affect distribution, affect resource allocation, *and* raise revenue; furthermore, the presence and role of the one set of taxes strongly influences the appraisal of the other. In particular the desirability of the differentiation in commodity taxes on distributional grounds is closely related to other policies towards distribution. The stronger are the other tools the smaller is the redistributive role for commodity taxes. See Subsection 3.2.

(iii) The focus of indirect taxation should be final consumption. This means that intermediate goods should not be taxed unless there is difficulty in the way of taxing final goods or there are special distributional reasons for taxing these intermediates. This applies also to tariffs, which should be rebated on intermediate goods and linked to other taxes on final goods. They should be used for protection only when the case for supporting a particular domestic industry (and penalising its users) is very strong and where other means of stimulating the industry are less satisfactory. It must be recognised that the elimination of tariffs except for protection is a long-term goal which for revenue reasons could not be achieved in the short or medium term in countries with very few tax handles. But it should be pursued in the sense that tariffs should be reduced as and when the revenue from final goods taxation can be built up. Again in the short term, it is generally preferable to replace quotas by tariffs so that the rent from the quota flows directly to the government rather than to those agents who allocate or receive the quota. See Subsections 3.6 and 3.8.

(iv) Public-sector prices should be set according to the same principles as indirect taxes: price equal to marginal social cost for intermediate goods (except for the cases noted in (iii) above) and marginal social cost plus an element for taxation for final goods. See Subsection 3.2.

(v) The appropriate microeconomic criterion for the expansion of industries is profitability at shadow prices of the incremental output. Other indicators (such as effective protection rates or domestic resource costs) are reliable only where they coincide with shadow prices. Similarly, a reform rule based on the other indicators, such as adjusting tariffs to move towards uniform effective protection is incorrect. See Subsections 3.4, 3.6, and 3.8.

(vi) Indirect taxes should be guided by a trade-off between efficiency and equity and in the absence of well-functioning schemes for income support there is no prescription for uniformity of indirect taxation. See Subsection 3.2.

(vii) A central argument for a corporate income tax is as a means for taxing personal incomes and thus an analysis of the tax should be closely linked to the personal income tax. See Subsection 3.7.

4. The taxation of agriculture

4.1. Distinctive features for taxation

There are many reasons why the taxation of agriculture deserves special study in developing countries and cannot be treated as just another example of a production activity in the standard competitive model. First, it is of central importance in both employment and output, the contributions often being in the region of one-half to three-quarters and one-quarter to one-half, respectively. Second, there are strong limitations on the tax tools available to the government, in particular it is often impossible to tax transactions between producers and consumers, the difficulty arising both when the "transaction" is within the household and when sales are between households or in informal markets. Third, the rural labour market and working arrangements dominated by agriculture, interact directly and indirectly with labour markets throughout the economy with important repercussions for all households and production activities. Fourth, land is a crucial input so that the problems with taxing rents must play a role. Fifth, the government is often the main or only supplier of vital inputs such as water and electricity so that its pricing policy must be integrated into the taxation of production. Sixth, food, its availability, distribution and price is of such importance to welfare that all governments have to take some responsibility for its price, quality and security.

The subject is clearly a major one and we do not have the space to go into details of data, arguments and models. In this section we shall simply try to bring out some of the major issues; we draw on the introductory chapter (Newbery) to Part V of Newbery and Stern (1987a). In Subsection 4.2 we look at some of the main influences on the incidence of agricultural taxes. We discuss briefly in Subsection 4.3 the question of the extent of taxation of agriculture as a whole, and the allocation of resources between agriculture and industry. Finally, in Subsection 4.4 we examine the availability and use of different kinds of tax instruments towards agriculture.

4.2. Some influences on tax incidence

With agriculture playing such an important role in output and labour markets it is clear that one has to take a general equilibrium view and, therefore, there will be many influences on the incidence of taxes. In this subsection we focus on four of these: the difficulty of taxing food transactions within the country, the elasticities of supplies and demands, effects operating through the labour market, and the variety in technological choice by farmers.

If transactions between producers and consumers of a food commodity cannot be taxed, then the price for producers and consumers (apart from selling and transport costs) will be the same. Let us suppose, for example, that the good (rice, say) is imported (without quantity restrictions and from a competitive world market) and subsidised. This will act as a tax on producers, as well as a subsidy to the domestic price (the domestic price is the world price less the subsidy). This means that the (marginal) incidence of the subsidy is as an imposition on producers related to their production and as a benefit to consumers related to their consumption. The policy analysis of the subsidy must therefore take account of the welfare weights on incomes of both consumers and producers. The revenue cost will be given by net imports in equilibrium (times the subsidy) and this will depend on net supply elasticities by producers and demand elasticities of consumers. An import tariff can be analysed in an analogous manner with the signs reversed. Pricing policies of marketing boards raise similar issues. Notice that the difference between world and domestic prices for producers involves a basic inefficiency in production.

Where the good is non-traded, the incidence of a tax will depend on supply and demand elasticities. Consider, for example, a tax on an input such as water. The effect on food prices will depend on the elasticity of net supply of foods with respect to input and output prices and the elasticity of demand. Generally, it should be clear that the overall effects on prices and incomes of any tax will depend sensitively on whether or not the good is traded, supply and demand elasticities, and the extent to which the government can tax transactions, for example, how far it can separate urban and rural markets.

Taxes on agriculture would in general affect the wages and real incomes of both urban and rural workers. They will affect different kinds of workers in different ways. If the price to producers of food is lowered then the agricultural labourer will be worse off to the extent that the real wage in agriculture would be expected to fall – for example, less inputs complementary with labour may be used thus lowering the marginal product. This is an argument sometimes used against food aid. Furthermore, any reduction in agricultural wages may also have an affect on urban wages although urban workers would benefit from the reduction in food prices. And a reduction in urban wages might increase investible surpluses. One has to ask again whether urban and rural labour and food markets can be separated, whether the food is imported (lower prices then implying an import subsidy) or produced domestically and so on. A number of models can be constructed and we shall not go into details, but it should be clear that the consequences flowing through the labour market may be of importance for the incomes of the poor, for profits and for government revenue.

Finally, on judging incidence one must remember the very broad range of production techniques one finds within agriculture, indeed within a single village. Thus, some farmers will use electrically powered tubewells, others bullock-driven

Persian wheels, and some land will not be irrigated. Some will use a combination of chemical fertilisers, some farmyard manure and others no fertiliser at all. Cropping pattern and thus input choice will vary considerably. The reasons for these differences may be many, including differences in knowledge, attitude to risk, access to credit, influence over government suppliers, position and quality of land and so on. One cannot assume that techniques are homogeneous and thus the pricing and taxing of inputs and the relation of input patterns to outputs should take account of these differences in practices amongst peasant householders and other producers. Such differences would not matter for the consideration of incidence if they were uncorrelated with social marginal utilities of income. Prima facie this is unlikely and should at least be investigated. For further discussion of some of these issues see Part V of Newbery and Stern (1987a).

4.3. The balance between agriculture and other sectors

The terms of trade between agriculture and industry and the allocation of resources between agricultural and non-agricultural sectors has long been a central topic in discussions of development [see, for example, the early Indian five year plans, Dixit (1973), Lipton (1977)]. We examine briefly here the influences of some of the issues raised for the analysis of tax policy. There are a number of arguments which have been advanced for turning the terms of trade against agriculture. Given that the discussion is often in terms of a single price and we are looking at the agricultural sector as a whole the discussion is at a fairly aggregated level. First, it may be suggested that aggregate agricultural supply is relatively inelastic. Second, one might argue that investible surplus should be extracted from agriculture to finance growth elsewhere. Third, it might be argued that food producers are relatively well off, whereas consumers, rural or urban, are not. We examine these suggestions briefly.

Given that food is such a high proportion of output and budgets it may well be necessary to spread the tax net to include it if sufficient revenue is to be raised. It may also be true that the taxation will fall in large part on production since the opportunities for taxing consumption and production separately are limited. The size of supply elasticities will then be an important element in the analysis. The magnitude of the aggregate elasticity is an empirical issue. A recent survey by Binswanger et al. (1985) has suggested rather low aggregate own-price elasticities (between 0.1 and 0.3). Individual crop elasticities will, of course, be higher [see, for example, Askari and Cummings (1976) and Timmer, Falcon and Pearson (1983)].

The second argument which concentrates on dynamic aspects is less well-founded. The allocation of investment is related to but distinct from its source of finance. If the marginal investment has high social productivity in a certain sector this does not tell us that the revenue should come from that sector or some other. And there should be no presumption that investment in agriculture is less productive than elsewhere, often the opposite will be true [see, for example, Schultz (1978)].

The third suggestion relates to the incidence of taxes. It is not obviously correct that food producers are relatively well off, and incidence may not only be on landowners or producers. As we saw in the previous section incidence is sensitive to a number of questions concerning the structure of the labour market (e.g. what happens to agricultural workers and the rural and urban wage) and the government's ability to control prices in different sectors of the economy.

Overall we would suggest that there are no strong and general arguments one way or another. The appropriate terms of trade and their control by government policy would depend on the structure of the economy, investment possibilities, and the availability of tax tools in a particular context. And it should be remembered that agriculture versus industry may not be a very useful way of putting any question. Welfare does not reside in industries or sectors but in households. We should be asking about the distribution and incentive effects of combinations of taxes and of investment policies in different parts of agriculture and industry.

4.4. The use of individual tax instruments

4.4.1. The land tax

As we have emphasised, the appropriate policy for any particular tax instrument will depend on the availability and levels of other taxes and policies. We shall therefore examine briefly some of the instruments that exist for the taxation of agriculture and how they might interact. An obvious and important example is the *land tax*. Land is in inelastic supply and its distribution is unequal. From the viewpoint of both efficiency and equity it would seem the natural base for taxation and has been seen as such by economists from David Ricardo and Henry George. And historically [see, for example, Bird (1974)] the land tax seems to have been of substantial or dominant importance in many countries (for example in India under Moghul and British Rule). Now, however, land taxes seem to be a negligible source of revenue. One of the main reasons for this would seem to be that the rich and powerful have been particularly successful in resisting the tax [see Bird (1974) and Wald (1959)]. Land taxation would require careful land records but this is not in principle so difficult (compared to measuring the base for other taxes) when landowners have a strong incentive to establish the legal title to their lands. One can adjust for the quality of the land by basing the tax on its presumptive value. And it can be made progressive by taxing only holdings above a certain level.

The reason land taxation becomes difficult is that resistance to proper valuation and collection can be fierce and effective. Apart from possible disincentives to the improvement of land this resistance to effective implementation seems the crucial argument against land taxation. There are two possible reactions. One can either advise governments to attempt to force measures through or take the absence of land taxation as a constraint and devise other taxes. The former course can be perilous for the government, possibly also for the economist, and may damage his credibility as an adviser. We shall discuss some of the alternatives, but, the possible political difficulties notwithstanding, one should not remove land taxation from the agenda without careful discussion and thought concerning the circumstances in the particular country under examination.

4.4.2. Taxation of inputs and outputs

It is interesting to ask how far taxes on inputs and outputs substitute for a land tax. Clearly, if the prices of all outputs and inputs are reduced in the same proportion, then this is equivalent to a proportional tax on land. This would involve an output tax and an input subsidy. Such a combination is clearly impossible, however, since labour could not be subsidised in this way. An attempt at such a system would therefore distort incentives towards purchased inputs. The example does show, however, that one must examine carefully the effects of combinations of taxes.

A tax on marketed surplus, for example, is equivalent to a tax on the purchases by the agricultural sector of non-agricultural goods. This latter method is perhaps the most common form of taxation of the agricultural sector in developing countries.

Water and electricity are important examples of publicly provided services to agriculture. The basic principles of second-best pricing would seem to suggest prices at least as high as marginal cost, for reasons of revenue and of distribution. Similar second-best analysis can be applied to the other main inputs, fertilisers and draught power. Bullock power, however, would not easily be taxed, and such a tax is likely to be undesirable for distributional reasons (at least relative to tractors) since it is the richer farmers who own the tractors (although poorer farmers may rent their use, so the issue is not clear-cut). One would also want to take into account the extent to which governments wanted to encourage technical change based on water and/or electricity. If there were benefits which were underestimated by households or considered too risky then there may be an argument for subsidy. Insofar as the underestimation is based on ignorance and will diminish over time then this element of subsidy should be gradually removed. It is unlikely, however, that adequate insurance for risk in agriculture will emerge quickly and it is possible that some subsidy might be justified on these grounds. The argument would have to be developed rather carefully and in our judgement it is far from obvious that this would be the best vehicle for dealing with the problem.

4.4.3. Agricultural income tax

An agricultural income tax is, in principle, equivalent to a tax on income from land and household labour. A major problem concerns the definition and measurement of the value of inputs and outputs. And there are a vast number of small producers and limited resources of the tax authorities. A partial solution would be to use *forfaits* or taxes on presumptive income, and a land tax is an example. A challenge of an assessment of forfait should then require production of accounts. An alternative would be to have an output levy, with some standard adjustment for inputs. This would be made progressive and would reduce administration costs if it were limited to larger farmers.

4.4.4. Export duties

In practice certain crops are often singled out for special treatment. Often these are export crops such as cocoa in Ghana or cotton in Pakistan. And in many cases such taxation occurs through marketing boards. Given that supply elasticities for individual crops (see Subsection 4.3) are likely to be much higher than for agriculture as a whole, considerable distortions are possible through substitution between taxed and untaxed crops. Smuggling can also become a major problem.

The different possible methods we have indicated suggest that a careful study of the potential for reforming different combinations of the taxation of outputs, the pricing for publicly supplied inputs and the taxation of purchased inputs may well yield substantial improvements for revenue, efficiency and distribution. It is an area where it can be very misleading to look at one agricultural tax in isolation and for which a general equilibrium framework will be important. For examples of empirical work of this kind, see the chapters by Braverman, Ahn and Hammer, Heady and Mitra, and by Newbery, in Newbery and Stern (1987a).

5. Tax reform in practice

5.1. Some experience since the Second World War

Tax reform has been an important item in the agenda of most governments in developing countries, faced with an increasing need for revenues. In Subsection

5.1 we review some of the major reform enquiries or missions that have been conducted since the War. And in Subsection 5.2 we illustrate proposals for reform for India and Pakistan based on our own work, which attempts to apply some of the unifying principles described in Section 3 above, and which is influenced by the experience of the earlier enquiries [see Ahmad and Stern (1986b)].

There have been a number of comprehensive studies or proposals for tax reform for developing countries in the post-war (and for some countries, post-colonial) years. The fashion seems to have been set by the Shoup mission to Japan in 1949 [see Shoup et al. (1949)], if post-war Japan may be considered to be less-developed. The Shoup mission was the first time that the reform of taxation was considered as a comprehensive exercise to cover all aspects of the tax system. The Shoup report also contained the first detailed proposal for the introduction of a VAT in such a context. Although a number of the Shoup proposals were accepted by the Japanese, then under U.S. administration, the VAT was not and a further attempt to introduce a VAT bill was defeated in the Japanese Parliament in 1978. However, the eventual introduction of a VAT in Japan is considered inevitable by some legal experts [see Kaneko (1985)]. Other missions also led by Shoup include Cuba, before the War, and Liberia and Venezuela since. The 1958 Shoup Venezuela mission included some of the leading public finance specialists of the time and was influential in moulding other missions. However "what it did not do is reform the tax system of Venezuela...many of the Report's recommendations were not followed and, what is more important some of the subsequent changes went against the spirit of the Shoup report" [Tanzi (1985)].

Musgrave has also been associated with a number of important tax reform studies, two of the best known being those in Colombia [see Musgrave and Gillis (1971)] and the 1977 Bolivia report [Musgrave (1981)]. While the recommendations of the Bolivia report were not implemented, possibly due to a change in the government, a number of influential Colombians were on the Musgrave Colombia Commission, which subsequently greatly influenced the 1974 reform.

In addition to a large number of proposals for comprehensive tax reform, there have been several attempts to reform or introduce given taxes in particular less-developed countries. Perhaps the best known such example is the "expenditure tax" recommended by Kaldor in reports for India and Sri Lanka. Both countries unsuccessfully experimented twice with the tax. Whilst the theoretical justification for the expenditure tax is not overwhelming (see Section 3 above), it has been advocated in the United Kingdom [see Meade Report (1978) or Kay and King (1986)] on administrative grounds, in terms of removing the distinction between capital and income and thus simplifying the tax base. However, practical difficulties with the administration of such a tax make it unlikely that the expenditure tax experiment will be repeated in another developing country before convincing workable examples have been provided in countries with more administrative resources and skills.

The VAT is an example of a tax that has a number of theoretical advantages (particularly the avoidance of the taxation of intermediates and exports, see Section 3) and has gradually come into use in a number of countries, where it has been shown that the administrative difficulties are not insuperable. Moreover, accumulated experience helps in avoiding pitfalls, drafting laws and polishing administrative procedures. Over 20 LDCs now have a variant of the VAT [Tanzi (1987)], and it has most recently been introduced in Indonesia [see Gillis (1985)]. India, through its MODVAT introduced in 1986, has initiated systematic rebating or crediting of excise taxes paid on inputs. For an excellent recent review of experience and discussion of problems, see Tait (1988).

The land tax is another theoretically superior tax (see Section 4) which has been recommended in a number of contexts [see, for example, Herschel (1971), which formed part of the Musgrave Colombia Report]. However, not all countries have the administrative capability to conduct cadastral surveys and administer the tax, which is often opposed by powerful interest groups. Furthermore, where there are migratory or transient populations, or where property rights are not well defined, as in parts of Africa, the land tax may not be a viable option. However, a land tax was recently proposed for Zimbabwe with the tax to be levied as a percentage of the "rate value" of output [for details see Government of Zimbabwe (1986)]. A flat rate for land tax was also suggested for communal areas, with a charge per unit of livestock in lieu of a land tax on pastures, although this recommendation was rejected by the government.

Tanzi (1985) has criticised expatriate advice on tax reform for often reflecting cultural biases of the experts rather than conditions and attitudes in the countries receiving the advice. This is partly associated with the emphasis on income and capital gains taxes relative to, for example, taxes on foreign trade that are so important in terms of contributions to revenue. There is also a tendency, particularly on the part of lawyers, to dwell at length on the direct taxes.

Yet another criticism of the expatriate adviser faced with an apparently open brief is that it is difficult to resist the temptation to experiment. In this respect, Shoup's recommendation for a VAT for Japan after the War was somewhat before its time, as the administrative and legal framework for a VAT was then, it seems, inadequate. On the other hand, many reports today recommend the VAT. Tanzi (1985) also cautioned against "intellectual fashions", pointing to the popularity of the VAT today, as against the unification of schedular income tax schedules which predominated in most reports in the 1950s and 1960s. However, the more recent recommendations may genuinely reflect cumulative learning experience and the relative unimportance of the income tax in most developing countries.

5.2. *Some recent recommendations for India and Pakistan*

In this subsection we highlight some of the main recommendations made during the course of studies on Pakistan and India conducted by the authors, although it should be emphasised that these were research programmes rather than tax missions and were much concerned with method. Indirect taxes account for around three-quarters of government revenue in Pakistan, as in India; consequently, the reform of the indirect tax system formed a major concern of our work. Much of our research on India (which preceded that for Pakistan) consisted of describing tax collections by commodity group and working through the effects of the taxation of intermediate goods and raw materials to the tax element in the price of final goods. This we called the "effective tax" and was calculated with the help of input–output information. Organisation of the data in this way was very useful to policy-makers in both Pakistan and India, showing the consequences of a complicated system operated by a number of different authorities and applied at different stages in the production and distribution processes. In both India and Pakistan there is a heavy reliance on the taxation of intermediate goods and raw materials, often imported. This has had effects which often diverged sharply from the expressed intentions of the policy-makers. Thus, the tool of "effective taxes" provided the policy-makers with a method of assessing the consequences of their proposed past actions.

The effective taxes were also a central element in evaluating the balance of taxation across commodity groups in terms of the marginal social cost of an extra rupee of government revenue. These methods, described in Section 3, involved the use of data on household consumption bundles and aggregate demand responses, in addition to the effective taxes. They also allow an evaluation of the balance across different types of taxes, say customs duties and excises, and between central and provincial taxes, such as sales taxes and excises which are the responsibility of the State and Central Governments respectively in India.

As well as looking at the consequences, problems and adjustment of the existing system, we also considered the possibilities of major reform [Ahmad and Stern (1984)]. Indeed, the approaches are complementary since the identification of difficulties with the existing system leads one to look at alternative methods of taxation which might avoid or ameliorate the problems. With respect to the taxation of inputs, an obvious candidate is the VAT, thus avoiding the cascading effects of the tax systems of India and Pakistan. We were able to examine the consequences of the introduction of major reforms, such as the VAT, by describing gainers and losers for different policy packages and looking at problems of introduction, administration and coverage. The distributive implications of a VAT are rather sensitive to the use of exemptions, particularly on food items. Whilst there will always be some losers and some gainers, a reasonably progressive VAT package can be designed using appropriate exemptions and only one or two rates.

In the course of our research on Pakistan we were requested by the Pakistani authorities to formulate some specific suggestions arising from our work. Our main recommendations for Pakistan included, inter alia, a rationalisation of the indirect tax structure, particularly of the tariff structure, the introduction of a VAT with two rates; appropriate user charges; greater use of presumptive methods and deduction at source for corporate dividends; and a land tax. Since the Pakistan study provides an example of the economy-wide application of the principles and methods developed in this chapter, we provide a sketch of some of the proposals, analysis and arguments.

5.2.1. Indirect taxes

We envisage the VAT as eventually the major source of indirect tax revenue in Pakistan gradually replacing many customs and excise taxes, covering the intermediate goods early on but extending to final goods also. We emphasised that some customs and excise taxes should remain, for example on tobacco and certain imported luxuries, for revenue, distributional and social reasons. Rationalisation of the rate structure of tariffs would involve a reduction in the number of rates, a reduction of extreme import duties (say, those in excess of 100 percent) and a shift from quantitative restrictions to tariffs.

The current sales tax falls mainly on large- and medium-scale manufacturing and on imports. There is in place a system for deducting sales tax on inputs which appears to operate fairly successfully. This provides very useful experience for the introduction of a VAT.

As well as providing a more flexible, efficient, buoyant and productive base, the introduction of the VAT in this way would be a major step towards dismantling the haphazard and arbitrary structure of protection. Since the VAT treats imports and domestic goods symmetrically, it is a tax on final consumption which discriminates neither for nor against domestic production. This is what one would wish, given a realistic exchange rate. The promotion of specific domestic industries would then be carried out with much greater clarity and rigour than is possible at present where the current system makes the existing structure of protection very opaque and one suspects, unlikely to be consistent with government objectives. Thus, the protection of particular industries, e.g. heavy goods and chemicals, goes with the discouragement of industries which use these goods as inputs. If there are clear arguments for promoting particular industries (and thus implicitly discouraging others) then there may be a number of methods for carrying this out, including protective tariffs. The adoption of protective tariffs on the argument that other satisfactory methods are not available, would require careful justification.

Finally, on the VAT we should note how the rates may be calculated. Essentially, one examines the revenue from the replaced taxes, assesses the likely base of the VAT to be introduced and divides the former by the latter to obtain the rate which would give constant revenue. Note that this would provide guidelines for the basic rate and there would be a luxury rate for certain items. The design of the balance between basic and luxury rates and the goods to which they apply should take account of the distribution of the consumption of the goods in the population and the pattern of demand responses to changing prices.

5.2.2. User charges and public sector pricing

As seen in Section 3, user charges and public-sector prices should be set on the same principles as indirect taxes. Thus, for intermediate goods a guideline is social marginal cost, and for final goods, social marginal cost plus an element for taxation (e.g. the VAT at a basic or luxury rate). The application of these principles could yield considerable benefits for efficiency, equity and revenue. Examples would include domestic electricity and heavy road transport. Domestic electricity is a good consumed primarily by the better off in Pakistan and with very high social opportunity costs in terms of generation, and often of disruption caused by load-shedding arising from the excess demand associated with prices being too low. The social costs of heavy road transport are very high in terms of damage done to roads (the damage, it is estimated, increases as the fourth power of the axle weight, so that if a lorry is 10 times as heavy as a car, the damage to the roads is 10 000 times as great [see Newbery (1986), Hughes (1987)]. We would argue that there is great scope in public-sector pricing and user charges for simultaneously raising more revenue and improving the allocation of resources.

5.2.3. Personal income tax and corporate tax

In this, as in other areas, particularly of direct taxation, we found in our discussions great emphasis on the importance of reducing the discretion of income tax collectors. We argued that more codified and publicly announced methods of presumptive taxation would help in this objective. We suggested a withholding tax on dividends as a means of collecting the corporation tax. This would yield revenue sooner than collecting through the personal income tax or corporation tax and dividends may be less easy to conceal than profits.

5.2.4. Land taxation

Our proposal for a land tax in Pakistan with a generous exemption limit (ownership above 12.5 acres) should be seen in the context of pricing policy for agriculture and industry (and of the already existing wealth tax on non-agricultural property). It is much more efficient and open to raise the taxation directly on land rather than implicitly through increases of prices of goods bought by the agricultural sector and decreases in the prices of goods that are sold by the sector. Thus, we argued that a land tax coupled with appropriate pricing policy could yield a major stimulus to agriculture – the taxation would be on a fixed input and not on production.

The monitoring of the required collection in a given area by the tax authorities would be much easier than for other taxes since the amount of land eligible would not be difficult to identify and is public knowledge. We estimate from data on the distribution of land that the exemptions would apply to 75 percent of the holdings. The tax as a percentage of gross output would rise with farm size and the maximum rate suggested, would we estimate for the (relatively few) largest farmers represent approximately 7.50 percent of output. If successfully collected the revenue would be substantial (more than the tax revenues collected by the Provinces put together). This source of revenue could (for political and constitutional reasons) be earmarked for the Provinces and would save resources for the Centre in reduced transfers.

5.2.5. Data and estimation

The central question we have sought to address is how best to raise additional revenue. The methods we have described in the theory of Section 3 and put into practice for India and Pakistan examine reform in terms of its effects on households, revenue and production. The analysis of the consequences for households involves certain basic data requirements including (i) revenue collections, by commodity group for indirect taxes, and by income group for income taxes; (ii) household income and expenditure information; and (iii) inter-industry transactions data or an input–output table. Some estimates of aggregate demand responses are also necessary if one is to make a judgement concerning the effects of reforms of indirect taxes on revenue. And a system of shadow prices is required to analyse the effects of reform on the production side. These sets of information are also potentially useful for other analyses, and accumulating a systematic set has had several externalities for other studies.

6. Concluding comments and further research

In describing our subject we have tried to focus on a simple unifying principle: in considering a proposed reform or designing a tax system we first analyse its consequences and then evaluate them. This is, at one level, banal but it does lead to a structuring of theoretical and empirical enquiry in a systematic way in a subject which has sometimes seemed to consist of rather disparate elements. The implementation of this general principle could lead to an investigation of possible reforms as follows. First, we have to ask which policy tools are possible and how they will work. Second, we have to consider the effect of using these tools in a general equilibrium framework which reflects the major aspects of the economy under study. Third, the inter-relationships between the various policies should be examined carefully since they may, in principle, play a crucial role. Thus, the list of possible policies should be kept open and their connections examined closely.

This approach to analysis is reflected in the structure and content of the chapter. We have not attempted an exhaustive account of the literature, although we have tried to give some picture of the most important areas. Rather, we have tried to describe what is possible in a systematic way. This has led us to concentrate on some of the more developed avenues of research. At the same time we have tried to show how the methods we have described can be extended to other problems of public policy and thus seek a greater coherence in the subject. Some of the possibilities will be emphasised in this concluding section.

The organisation of the chapter followed from the approach we have described. Thus, in Section 2 we examined the relationship between the structure of the economy, the balance between public expenditure and different forms of finance, administration and evasion, and the availability or importance of different tax tools. The appraisal of taxes formed the subject matter of Section 3 concentrating particularly on theory but also on empirical methods. We commented on the extension of the analysis to other areas of public decision-making such as public-sector pricing and rationing and controls in production and consumption. Agriculture plays a central role in the economies of developing countries and raises particular problems, for taxation and it was therefore given special attention in Section 4. And in Section 5 we described the experience of attempts to apply the principles described to practical problems of reform. Our concentration has, for the most part, been on micro-economic and medium-term issues.

Our description of the subject underlines the close inter-twining of theory and applied work. The tax tools to be analysed in the theory and the structure of the models should be influenced by close knowledge of the economy at hand. And the theoretical analysis will point to possible reforms, raise practical questions, show what data should be collected and influence how they should be used. The interaction of theory and applied work and of public and development economics make this a particularly rewarding and fascinating subject for research.

We shall not attempt an overall summary of the contents of this chapter but shall try to draw out some of the main lessons and possibilities for further work. Theoretical lessons and research avenues are considered first, and then the applied, although as we have emphasised they cannot and should not be disentangled.

6.1. Theoretical lessons and research

The first of the themes which we shall emphasise for further theoretical research concerns coherence in the analysis of different aspects of government policy: notably taxation, public-sector pricing, public expenditure, planning and regulation, trading policies and borrowing. The application of a single set of principles can point to inconsistencies. For example, the marginal-cost pricing rule for public enterprises is not appropriate in a world where revenue is raised by indirect taxes and the prices of public firms should be set according to the same principles as those used in taxation, taking account of revenue requirements, income distribution, elasticities of demand, marginal cost, shadow prices and so on.

This procedure should also bring out interrelationships between different aspects of policy. Thus, the role of indirect taxes for improving income distribution will depend on the availability of other tools. For example, increasing a uniform lump-sum transfer may be a more attractive way of spending extra resources on the poor than reducing some indirect taxes and one may want to increase indirect taxes in order to raise revenue to finance the uniform benefit. This broad view of policies and their connections should always lead us to ask whether the particular tool under discussion may not be the best way of achieving the results which are claimed for it. And it means that revenue and expenditure cannot be separated. This is not only because the structure of taxes will depend on the total level of expenditure one is trying to finance but also that the type of expenditure being proposed (e.g. food rations, which are a type of lump-sum subsidy) will have a critical influence on the appropriate choice of tax tools.

In looking for this consistency across areas of policy we have emphasised marginal techniques, the use of household data, and a disaggregated approach. And shadow prices will play a key unifying role. The formal discussion of shadow prices was set out in Section 3 where we saw that, on the one hand, shadow prices could and should be brought into tax analysis and, on the other, the correct shadow prices depend critically on the way in which government policies are determined. Project appraisal and tax policy are inseparable topics.

We have, however, gone further than describing techniques, methods and interrelationships arising from theory and have tried to distil the basic lessons arising from existing theory into the simple practical rules and guidelines which were described in Subsection 3.9. These guidelines show, we would argue, that careful but simple theoretical analysis can be of substantial practical value in designing and evaluating tax policy.

The second theme concerns the use of non-marginal techniques as complements to the marginal analysis. Here an important tool will be the applied general equilibrium modelling of the type discussed, for example, in Shoven (1983) and in Chapter 18 by Robinson in this Handbook. We emphasised that marginal analysis makes less severe demands on data and on modelling assumptions than the computable general equilibrium (CGE) model. On the other hand, the CGE model does allow the analysis of large changes (although results can follow mainly from particular structures chosen for convenience and from untested assumptions). Furthermore, they do allow the examination of the shadow price of factors: thus they are complementary to marginal analysis in the additional sense of allowing checks on some of the more "macro" shadow prices such as shadow wage rates.

Third, both the multisectoral marginal analysis and the CGE models can and should be supplemented by smaller scale theorical general equilibrium models which allow one to focus more easily on the functioning of the economy than large models. And they should also be cast in a form which brings out the numerical role of crucial parameters.

The three themes above concern methods of approach and are equally applicable for developed and developing countries. The same applies to two problems which we would recommend for closer attention by theorists. The first concerns dynamic aspects of taxes. Some of these we examined in Section 3 and we showed that similar techniques to those used in the static analysis could be utilised and some progress had been made. There is no doubt, however, that the characterisation of dynamic behaviour by agents and the effect of taxes and government policies requires intensive theoretical investigation. Furthermore, one would like to see more careful integration of the long-run and short-run analyses through these dynamic models. Short-run stabilisation problems, for example, have been examined using models which are rather different from those used in medium- or long-run discussions. Different forms should not necessarily be based on or lead to different principles.

A similar requirement for intensive theoretical research applies to the welfare economics of policy with non-competitive markets and imperfect information. Again, this is beginning although much of the positive theory is still at an early stage, for example, of establishing the existence of equilibrium.

We have intentionally discussed theory in a way which applies to both developed and developing countries. The structure of the economies of developing countries and their limited tax tools bring out clearly the importance of using the techniques of second-best welfare economics, or to put it in language that some might find more palatable, the study of policy where governments have a variety of objectives and face many constraints. In developing countries those constraints are particularly important in relation to the availability and coverage of tax tools. Here policies have to take account, for example, of the fact that income taxes will have a limited role and that many food transactions may not be directly taxed or subsidised. Other taxes may be applicable to some sectors, or types of enterprise, only. We have emphasised the limitations on tools and coverage as a crucial aspect of public policy in developing countries and they should be a central feature of any research which attempts to adapt and construct the tools of public policy analysis for application to models of developing countries.

6.2. Applied research

Many of our recommendations for applied research arise from the same considerations as those which generate our suggestions for theoretical work. Thus, we need to know more about the supply response of, for example, savings, entrepreneurial effort and factors to tax changes. These are not simple applied questions that one could expect to have answered by a single research project. Rather, we should work for a gradual and systematic accumulation of evidence.

The investigation of the coverage of different taxes and subsidies in practice would be of substantial value in considering reforms. Thus, for example, one would be greatly assisted by simple descriptions of which groups do and do not pay income tax, which type of establishments collect sales taxes, what sorts of household actually receive food and other subsidies and so on. These affect not only the models we should be building but would directly influence the appraisal of particular reforms.

One should encourage the collection of data by national and regional agencies in a form which allows tax analysis. For example, where possible indirect taxes should be attributed to goods which are described in a similar manner to other economic data such as national accounts classifications. Household income and expenditure surveys should be made available to Finance Ministries and academic researchers to enable the study of the distributional effects of proposed reforms. Indeed, the calculation of these effects should be a responsibility of the Finance Ministry when it prepares changes for discussion or enactment.

The interrelationship between taxes and other policies could be a most fruitful area for analysis. One could investigate, for example, the relationship between pricing rules for public enterprises and tax policy; or food subsidies and tax policy. A systematic analysis of agricultural taxation and the pricing and supply of inputs would be likely, in many countries, to produce striking results, both in terms of inconsistencies and the effect of the policies as a whole on incomes and incentives.

Detailed case studies of actual reforms would be very desirable [a notable and valuable example is Gil Diaz (1987) on Mexico]. A systematic description of effects and pitfalls that occurred in practice could provide real guidance to those embarking (or thinking of so doing) on substantial changes.

All these recommendations refer to analyses which involve detailed investigation of the circumstances of particular countries. Comparisons between countries can be instructive and useful but they are no substitute, and should not supplant, the close examination of the country at hand. Thus, we should be suspicious of simple formulae of the type that say country A has the following five simple characteristics and therefore should follow tax policy B. Accumulated experience, clear theory, and empirical research no doubt have systematic lessons but these should be in terms of simple principles, areas for study, warnings and so on rather than in packaged policy prescriptions.

The agenda is clearly long and daunting. However, much real progress has been made in recent years and we would suggest that many of the lines of enquiry proposed could be very fruitful, both for practical policy and in advancing our conceptual understanding. There have been many theoretical advances in both public economics and development economics and the availability of and facilities for use of data have expanded very rapidly. The further integration of the two areas provides fascinating possibilities.

References

Acharya, S. (1983) 'Unaccounted economy in India: A critical review of some recent estimates', *Economic and Political Weekly*, 18:2057–2068.

Aghevli, B.B. and M.S. Khan (1978) 'Government deficits and the inflationary process in developing countries', *IMF Staff Papers*, 25:383–416.

Ahmad, S.E. and N.H. Stern (1984) 'The theory of reform and Indian indirect taxes', *Journal of Public Economics*, 25:259–295.

Ahmad, S.E. and N.H. Stern (1986a) 'Tax reform for Pakistan: Overview and effective taxes for 1975/76', *Pakistan Development Review*, Spring: 43–72.

Ahmad, S.E. and N.H. Stern (1986b) 'The analysis of tax reform for developing countries: Lessons from India and Pakistan', Discussion Paper no. 2, Development Economics Research Programme, London School of Economics.

Ahmad, S.E. and N.H. Stern (1987) 'Alternative sources of government revenue: Illustrations from India for 1979/80', in: D.M.G. Newbery and N.H. Stern, eds., *The theory of taxation for developing countries*. New York: Oxford University Press and World Bank.

Ahmad, S.E. and N.H. Stern (forthcoming) *Tax reform and development*.

Allingham, M. and A. Sandmo (1972) 'Income tax evasion: A theoretical analysis', *Journal of Public Economics*, 1:323–338.

Arrow, K.J. (1966) 'Discounting and public investment criteria', in: A.V. Kneese and S.C. Smith, eds., *Water research*. Baltimore, MD: Johns Hopkins.

Askari, H. and J.T. Cummings (1976) *Agricultural supply response: A survey of the econometric evidence*, New York: Praeger.

Atkinson, A.B. (1977) 'Optimal taxation and the direct versus indirect tax controversy', *Canadian Journal of Economics*, 10:590–606.

Atkinson, A.B. and A. Sandmo (1980) 'Welfare implications of the taxation of savings', *Economic Journal*, 90, no. 359:529–549.

Atkinson, A.B. and J.E. Stiglitz (1976) 'Design of tax structure: Direct versus indirect taxation', *Journal of Public Economics*, 6:55–75.

Atkinson, A.B. and J.E. Stiglitz (1980) *Lectures on public economics*. New York: McGraw-Hill.

Atkinson, A.B. and H. Sutherland, eds. (1987) 'Tax-benefit models', Suntory–Toyota International Centre for Economics and Related Disciplines, London School of Economics.

Auerbach, A.J. and Feldstein, M.S. eds. (1985) *Handbook of public economics*, Vol. I. Amsterdam: North-Holland.

Auerbach, A.J, and Feldstein, M.S. eds. (1987) *Handbook of Public Economics*, Vol. II. Amsterdam: North-Holland.

Bagchi, A. and M. Govinda Rao (1982) 'Elasticity of non-corporate tax in India', *Economic and Political Weekly*, 17:1452–1458.

Bahl, R.W. (1971) 'A regression approach to tax effort and tax ratio analysis', *IMF Staff Papers*, 18:570–612.

Bailey, M.J. (1956) 'The welfare costs of inflationary finance', *Journal of Political Economy*, 64:93–100.

Barro, R.J. (1974) 'Are government bonds net wealth?', *Journal of Political Economy*, 82:1095–1117.

Bhagwati, J. (1978) 'Anatomy and consequences of exchange control regimes', National Bureau of Economic Research, Cambridge, MA.

Bhagwati, J. (1987) 'Directly-unproductive-profit-seeking activities', in: J. Eatwell, M. Milgate and P. Newman, eds., *The new Palgrave*. London: Macmillan.

Binswanger, H., Y. Mundlak, Maw-cheng Yang and A. Bowers (1985) 'Estimation of aggregate agricultural supply response from time-series of cross-country data', mimeo, Working Paper no. 1985-3, World Bank, Commodity Studies and Project Division.

Bird, R.M. (1974) *Taxing agricultural land in developing countries*. Cambridge, MA: Harvard University Press.

Bird, R.M. (1976) 'Assessing tax performance in developing countries: A critical review of the literature', *Finanzarchiv*, 34:244–265. Reprinted in: J.F.J. Toye, ed., *Taxation and economic development*. London: Frank Cass.

Bird, R. and L. de Wulf (1983) 'Taxation and income distribution in Latin America. A critical review of empirical studies', *IMF Staff Papers*, 20:639–682.

Braverman, A., J. Hammer and C.Y. Ahn (1987) 'Multi-market analysis of agricultural pricing policies in Korea', in: D.M.G. Newbery and N.H. Stern, eds., The theory of taxation for developing countries. New York: Oxford University Press and World Bank.

Buchanan, J.M. and R.D. Tollison (1972) *Theory of public choice*. Ann Arbor, MI: University of Michigan Press.

Buchanan, J.M., R.D. Tollison and G. Tullock, eds. (1980) Towards a theory of the rent-seeking society. College Station, TX: Texas A & M University Press.

Chamley, C. (1983) 'Taxation in dynamic economies: Some problems and methods', mimeo, World Bank.

Chelliah, R.J. (1971) 'Trends in taxation in developing countries', *IMF Staff Papers*, 18:292–293.

Chelliah, R.J. and R.N. Lal (1978) Incidence of indirect taxation in India 1973–74, National Institute of Public Finance and Policy, New Delhi.

Chelliah, R.J., H. Baas and M.R. Kelly (1975) 'Tax ratios and tax effort in developing countries, 1969–71', *IMF Staff Papers*, 22:187–205.

Colander, D., ed. (1984) *Neoclassical political economy*. Cambridge, MA: Ballinger Press.

Contini, B. (1981) 'The second economy of Italy', *Journal of Contemporary Studies* 4: No. 3. Reprinted in: V. Tanzi, The underground economy in the United States and abroad. Lexington, MA: D.C. Heath, 1982.

Cowell, F.A. (1985) 'The economics of tax evasion: A survey', Discussion Paper no. 80, ESRC Programme on Taxation, Incentives and the Distribution of Income, London School of Economics.

de Wulf, L. (1975) 'Fiscal incidence studies in developing countries: Survey and critique', *IMF Staff Papers*, 22:61–131.

Deaton, A.S. (1979) 'Optimally uniform commodity taxes', *Economics Letters*, 2, no. 4:357–361.

Deaton, A.S. (1981) 'Optimal taxes and the structure of preferences', *Econometrica*, 49:1245–1260.

Deaton, A.S. (1987) 'Econometric issues for tax design in developing countries', in: D.M.G. Newbery and N.H. Stern, eds., The theory of taxation for developing countries. New York: Oxford University Press and World Bank.

Deaton, A.S. and N.H. Stern (1986) 'Optimally uniform commodity taxes, taste differences, and lump-sum grants', *Economics Letters*, 20:263–266.

Dervis, K., J. De Melo and S. Robinson (1982) *General equilibrium models for development policy*. London: Cambridge University Press for the World Bank.

Diamond, P.A. (1970) 'Incidence of an interest income tax', *Journal of Economic Theory*, 2:211–224.

Diamond, P.A. and J.A. Mirrlees (1971) 'Optimal taxation and public production I: Production efficiency and II: Tax rules', *American Economic Review*, 61:8–27 and 261–278.

Dixit, A.K. (1971) 'Short-run equilibrium and shadow prices in the dual economy', *Oxford Economic Papers*, 23:384–400.

Dixit, A.K. (1973) 'Models of dual economies', in: J.A. Mirrlees and N.H. Stern, eds., *Models of Economic Growth*. New York: Macmillan.

Dixit, A.K. (1984) 'International trade policy for oligopolistic industries', *Economic Journal, Supplement*, 94:1–16.

Dixit, A.K. (1985) 'Tax policy in open economies', in: A. Auerbach and M. Feldstein, eds., *Handbook of public economics, I*. Amsterdam: North-Holland.

Dixit, A.K. and N.H. Stern (1974) 'Determinants of shadow prices in open dual economies', *Oxford Economic Papers*, 26:42–54.

Dixit, A.K. and V. Norman (1980) *Theory of international trade*. London: Cambridge University Press.

Drèze, J.P. and N.H. Stern (1987) 'The theory of cost-benefit analysis', in: A. Auerbach and M. Feldstein, eds., *Handbook of public economics*. Amsterdam: North-Holland.

Dwivedi, D.N., ed. (1981a) *Readings in Indian public finance*. Delhi: Chanakya Publications.

Dwivedi, D.N. (1981b) 'A buoyancy approach to evaluation of excise taxation', in D.N. Dwivedi, ed., *Readings in Indian Public Finance*. Delhi: Chanakya Publications.

Eshag, E. (1983) *Fiscal and monetary problems in developing countries*. London: Cambridge University Press.

Feder, G. and R.E. Just (1977) 'An analysis of credit terms in the Eurodollar market', *European Economic Review*, 9:651–659.

Feige, E.L. (1979) 'How big is the irregular economy?', *Challenge*, 22:5–13.

Feldstein, M. and D.W. Elmendorf (1987) 'Taxes, budget deficits and consumer spending: Some new evidence', Working Paper no. 2355, National Bureau of Economic Research, Washington.

Fischer, S. (1980) 'Dynamic inconsistency, cooperation and the benevolent dissembling government', *Journal of Economic Dynamics and Control*, 2:93–107.

Fischer, S. (1982) 'Seigniorage and the case for a national money', *Journal of Political Economy*, 90:295–313.

Fischer, S. and F. Modigliani (1978) 'Towards an understanding of the real effects and costs of inflation', *Weltwirtschaftliches Arciv*, 114:810–833.

Gandhi, V.P. (1966) 'Tax burden on Indian agriculture', Harvard Law School.

Gandhi, V.P. (1979) 'Vertical equity of general sales taxation in developing countries', mimeo, IMF.

Gersovitz, M. (1987) 'The effects of domestic taxes on foreign private investment', in: D.M.G. Newbery and N.H. Stern, eds., *The theory of taxation for developing countries*. New York: Oxford University Press and World Bank, Ch. 23.

Gil Diaz, F. (1987) 'Some lessons from Mexico's tax reform', in: D.M.G. Newbery and N.H. Stern, eds., *The theory of taxation for developing countries*. New York: Oxford University Press and World Bank.

Gillis, M. (1985) 'Micro and macroeconomics for tax reform: Indonesia', *Journal of Development Economics*, 19:221–254.

Giovannini, A. (1985) 'Saving and the real interest rate in LDCS', *Journal of Development Economics*, 18, nos. 2–3:197–218.

Goode, R. (1981) 'Some economic aspects of tax administration', *IMF Staff Papers* 28:249–274.

Goode, R. (1984) *Government finance in developing countries*. Washington, DC: The Brookings Institution.

Government of India, Ministry of Finance, Wanchoo Committee (1971) 'Final report: Direct taxes enquiry committee', New Delhi.

Government of India, Ministry of Finance, Jha Committee (1978) 'Report of the indirect taxation enquiry committee', New Delhi.

Government of India, Ministry of Finance, Dagli Committee (1979) 'Report of the committee on controls and subsidies', New Delhi.

Government of India, Ministry of Planning, Department of Statistics, Raj Committee (1982) 'Capital formation and saving in India 1950–51 to 1979–80', Reserve Bank, Bombay.

Government of Zimbabwe (1986) 'Report of the commission of inquiry into taxation' (under the Chairmanship of Dr. R.J. Chelliah), Harare.

Guesnerie, R. (1977) 'On the direction of tax reform', *Journal of Public Economics*, 7:179–202.

Gupta, S. and S. Gupta (1982) 'Estimates of the unreported economy in India', *Economic and Political Weekly*.

Gupta, S. and R. Mehta (1982) 'An estimate of underreported national income', *Journal of Income and Wealth*, 5, no. 2.

Guttmann, P.M. (1977) 'The subterranean economy', *Financial Analysts Journal*, 34:24–27.

Harberger, A.C. (1974) *Taxation and welfare*. Boston, MA: Little, Brown.

Hart, H.L.A. (1968) Punishment and responsibility: Essays in the philosophy of law. New York: Oxford University Press.

Hausman, J.A. (1981) 'Labour supply', in: H.J. Aaron and J.A. Pechman, eds., *How taxes affect economic behaviour*. Washington, DC: Brookings Institution.

Heady, C. and P. Mitra (1987) 'Optimal taxation and shadow pricing in a developing economy', in: D.M.G. Newbery and N.H. Stern, eds., *The theory of taxation for developing countries*. New York: Oxford University Press and World Bank.

Helpman, E. and P.R. Krugman (1985) *Market structure and foreign track*. Wheatsheaf Books.

Herschel, F.J. (1971) 'Taxation of agriculture and hard-to-tax groups', in: R.A. Musgrave and M. Gillis, eds., *Fiscal reform for Colombia*. Cambridge, MA: Harvard Law School.

Hinrichs, H.H. (1966) 'A general theory of tax structure change during economic development', Harvard Law School International Tax Programme.

Hughes, G.M. (1987) 'The incidence of fuel taxes: A comparative study of three countries', in: D.M.G. Newbery and N.H. Stern, eds., *The theory of taxation for developing countries*. New York: Oxford University Press and World Bank.

Johansen, L. (1965) *Public economics*. Amsterdam: North-Holland.

Johnson, H.G. (1977) 'A note on the dishonest government and the inflation tax', *Journal of Monetary Economics*, 3:375–377.

Kaldor, N. (1956) 'Indian tax reform: Report of a survey', Ministry of Finance, New Delhi.

Kaneko, H. (1985) 'Public finance in Japan today: Current issues in domestic taxation', mimeo, University of Tokyo.

Kay, J.A. and M.A. King (1986) *The British tax system*, 4th ed. London: Oxford University Press.

Kehoe, T.J. and J. Serra-Puche (1983) 'A computational general equilibrium model with endogenous unemployment: An analysis of the 1980 fiscal reform in Mexico', *Journal of Public Economics*, 22, no. 1:1–26.

King, M.A. (1977) *Public policy and the corporation*. London: Chapman and Hall.

King, M.A. (1980) 'Savings and taxation', in: G.M. Heal and G.A. Hughes, eds., *Public policy and the tax system*. London: Allen and Unwin.

King, M.A. (1985) 'The economics of savings: A survey of recent contributions', in: K.J. Arrow and S. Honkapohja, eds., *Frontiers of economics*. London: Blackwell.

King, M.A. and D. Fullerton (1984) *The taxation of income from capital*. Chicago, IL: The University of Chicago Press.

Kormendi, R.C. (1983) 'Government debt, government spending and private sector behaviour', *American Economic Review*, 73:994–1010.

Koskela, E. (1983) 'A note on progression, penalty schemes and tax evasion', *Journal of Public Economics*, 22:127–133.

Kotlikoff, L.J. (1984) 'Taxation and savings—A neoclassical perspective', Working Paper no. 1302, National Bureau of Economic Research.

Krueger, A.O. (1974) 'The political economy of the rent-seeking society', *American Economic Review*, 64:291–303.

Kydland, F.E. and E.C. Prescott (1977) 'Rules rather than discretion: The inconsistency of optimal plans', *Journal of Political Economy*, 5:473–492.

Levin, J. (1968) 'The effects of economic development on the base of a sales tax: A case study of Colombia', *IMF Staff Papers*, 15:30–99.

Lewis, W.A. (1954) 'Economic development with unlimited supplies of labour', *Manchester School*, 22, no. 2:139–191.

Lipton, M. (1977) *Why poor people stay poor: Urban bias in world development*. London: Temple Smith.

Lipton, M. (1978) 'Transfer of resources from agriculture to non-agricultural activities: The case of India', in: J.F.J. Toye, ed., *Taxation and economic development*. London: Frank Cass.

Little, I.M.D. and J.A. Mirrlees (1974) *Project appraisal and planning for developing countries*. London: Heinemann.

Little, I.M.D., D. Mazumdar and J. Page (1984) 'Small manufacturing enterprises: A comparative study of India and other countries', mimeo, World Bank.

Lotz, J.R. and E.R. Morss (1967) "Measuring 'tax effort' in developing countries", *IMF Staff Papers*, 14:478–499.

Mansfield, C.Y. (1972) 'Elasticity and buoyancy of a tax system: A method applied to Paraguay', *IMF Staff Papers*, 19:425–443.

McDonald, D.C. (1982) 'Debt capacity and development country borrowing: A survey of the literature', *IMF Staff Papers*, 29:603–646.

McLure, C.I. (1975) 'General equilibrium incidence analysis: The Harberger model after 10 years', *Journal of Public Economics*, 4:125–162.

Meade, J.E. (1978) *The structure and reform of direct taxation: a report of a committee for the Institute of Fiscal Studies*, chaired by J.E. Meade. London: Allen and Unwin.

Mirrlees, J.A. (1971) 'An exploration in the theory of optimum income taxation', *Review of Economic Studies*, 38, no. 114:175–208.

Mueller, D.C. (1976) 'Public choice: A survey', *Journal of Economic Literature*, 14:396–433.

Musgrave, R.A. (1959) *The theory of public finance*. New York: McGraw-Hill.

Musgrave, R.A. (1969) *Fiscal systems*. New Haven, CT: Yale University Press.

Musgrave, R.A. (1981) 'Fiscal reform in Bolivia', Harvard Law School.

Musgrave, R.A. (1985) 'A brief history of fiscal doctrine', in: A. Auerbach and M. Feldstein, eds., *Handbook of public economics*. Amsterdam: North-Holland, Vol. 1, Ch. 1.

Musgrave, R.A. (1987) 'Tax reform in developing countries', in: D.M.G. Newbery and N.H. Stern, eds., *The theory of taxation for developing countries*. New York: Oxford University Press and World Bank.

Musgrave, R.A. and M. Gillis (1971) 'Fiscal reform in Colombia', Harvard Law School.

Musgrave, R.A. and P.B. Musgrave (1984) *Public finance in theory and practice*. New York: McGraw-Hill.

Musgrave, R.A., J.J. Carroll, L.D. Cooke and L. Frane (1951) 'Distribution of tax payments by income groups: A case study for 1948', *National Tax Journal*, 4:1–53.

Newbery, D.M.G. (1974) 'The robustness of equilibrium analysis in the dual economy', *Oxford Economic Papers*, 26, no. 1:32–41.

Newbery, D.M.G. (1986) 'On the desirability of input taxes', *Economics Letters*, 20, no. 3:267–270.

Newbery, D.M.G. (1987a) 'Agricultural taxation—The main issues', in: D.M.G. Newbery and N.H. Stern, eds., *The theory of taxation for developing countries*. New York: Oxford University Press and World Bank.

Newbery, D.M.G. (1987b) 'Identifying desirable direction of agricultural price reform in Korea', in: D.M.G. Newbery and N.H. Stern, eds., *The theory of taxation for developing countries*. New York: Oxford University Press and World Bank.

Newbery, D.M.G. and N.H. Stern, eds. (1987a) *The theory of taxation for developing countries*. New York: Oxford University Press and World Bank.

Newbery, D.M.G. and N.H. Stern (1987b) 'Dynamic tax issues', in: D.M.G. Newbery and N.H. Stern, eds., *The theory of taxation for developing countries*. New York: Oxford University Press and World Bank.

Please, S. (1971) 'Mobilising internal resources through taxation', in: R.E. Robinson, ed., *Developing the third world: Experience of the 1960s*. London: Cambridge University Press.

Poterba, J.M. and L.H. Summers (1987) 'Finite lifetimes and the effects of budget deficits on national saving', *Journal of Monetary Economics*, 20:369–391.

Prest, A.R. (1972) *Public finance in under-developed countries*. Weidenfeld and Nicholson.

Purohit, M.C. (1981) 'Buoyancy and income-elasticity of state taxes', in: D.N. Dwivedi, ed., *Readings in Indian public finance*. Delhi: Chanakya Publications.

Ricardo, D. (1817) 'The principles of political economy and taxation', in: P. Sraffa, ed. (1962), *The works and correspondence of David Ricardo*. London: Cambridge University Press. Vol. 1.

Sah, R.K. and J.E. Stiglitz (1987) 'The taxation and pricing of agricultural and industrial goods in developing countries', in: D.M.G. Newbery and N.H. Stern, eds., *The theory of taxation for developing countries*. New York: Oxford University Press and World Bank.

Schultz, T.W., ed. (1978) *Distortions of agricultural incentives*. Bloomington, IN: Indiana University Press.

Seade, J. (forthcoming) 'Profitable cost increases and the shifting of taxation: Equilibrium responses of markets in oligopoly', *Journal of Public Economics*.

Shah, S.M.S. and J.F.J. Toye (1979) 'Fiscal incentives for firms in some developing countries: Surveys and critique', in: J.F.J. Toye, ed., *Taxation and economic development*. London: Frank Cass.

Shoup et al. (1949) 'Report on Japanese taxation', General Headquarters, Supreme Commander for the Allied Powers, Tokyo.

Shoven, J.B. (1983) 'Applied general equilibrium tax modelling', *IMF Staff Papers*, 30:350–393.

Shoven, J.B. and J. Whalley (1972) 'A general equilibrium calculation of the effects of differential taxation of income from capital in the U.S.', *Journal of Public Economics*, 1:281–321.

Shoven, J.B. and J. Whalley (1984) 'Applied general equilibrium models of taxation and international trade', *Journal of Economic Literature*, 22:1007–1051.

Srinivasan, T.N. (1973) 'Tax evasion: A model', *Journal of Public Economics*, 526–536.

Srinivasan, T.N. (1985) 'Neo-classical political economy, the state and economic development', Lecture to Asian Development Bank, mimeo.

Srinivasan, T.N. and J.N. Bhagwati (1975) 'Alternative policy rankings in a large, open economy with sector-specific minimum wages', *Journal of Economic Theory*, 11:356–371.

Stern, N.H. (1976) 'On the specification of models of optimum income taxation', *Journal of Public Economics*, 6, no. 1–2:123–162.

Stern, N.H. (1978) 'On the economic theory of policy towards crime', in: J. Heineke, ed., *Economic models of criminal behaviour*. Amsterdam: North-Holland, Ch. 4.

Stern, N.H. (1984) 'Optimum taxation and tax policy', *IMF Staff Papers*, 31:339–378.

Stern, N.H. (1987a) 'Aspects of the general theory of tax reform', in: D.M.G. Newbery and N.H. Stern, eds., *The theory of taxation for developing countries*. New York: Oxford University Press and World Bank.

Stern, N.H. (1987b) 'The effects of taxation, price control and government contracts in oligopoly and monopolistic competition', *Journal of Public Economics*, 32, no. 2:133–158.

Stiglitz, J.E. and P.S. Dasgupta (1971) 'Differential taxation, public goods and economic efficiency', *Review of Economic Studies*, 38:151–174.

Tait, A.A. (1988) *Value added tax: International practice and problems*. Washington, DC: International Monetary Fund.

Tait, A.A., W. Gratz and B.J. Eichengreen (1979) 'International comparisons of taxation for selected developing countries 1972–76', *IMF Staff Papers*, 26:123–156.

Tanzi, V. (1977) 'Inflation, lags in collection, and the real value of tax revenue', *IMF Staff Papers*, 24:154–167.

Tanzi, V. (1978) 'Inflation, real tax revenue and the case for inflationary finance: Theory with an application for Argentina', *IMF Staff Papers*, 25:417–451.

Tanzi, V. (1982) *The underground economy in the United States and abroad*. Lexington, MA: D.C. Heath.

Tanzi, V. (1983) 'The underground economy', *Finance and Development*, 10–13.

Tanzi, V. (1985) 'A review of major tax policy missions in developing countries', paper presented to the Congress of the International Institute of Public Finance, Athens.

Tanzi, V. (1986) 'Is there a limit to the size of fiscal deficits in developing countries?', in: B.P. Herber, ed., *Public finance and public debt*. Detroit, MI: Wayne University Press.

Tanzi, V. (1987) 'Quantitative characteristics of the tax systems of developing countries', in: D.M.G. Newbery and N.H. Stern, eds., *The theory of taxation for developing countries*. New York: Oxford University Press and World Bank.

Timmer, C.P., W.P. Falcon and S.R. Pearson (1983) *Food policy analysis*. Baltimore, MD: Johns Hopkins and World Bank.

Toye, J.F.J., ed. (1978) *Taxation and economic development*. London: Frank Cass.

U.S. International Revenue Service (IRS) (1979) 'Estimates of income unreported on individual income tax returns', Department of Treasury, #1104, (9-79), Washington, DC.

Wald, H.P. (1959) *Taxation of agricultural land in underdeveloped countries*. Cambridge, MA: Harvard University Press.

Wilford, D.S. and W. Wilford (1978) 'Estimates of revenue elasticity and buoyancy in Central America, 1955–74', in: J.F.J. Toye, ed., *Taxation and economic development*. London: Frank Cass.

World Bank (1981) *Accelerated development in sub-Saharan Africa: An agenda for action*. Washington: World Bank.

World Bank (1984) *World development report*. Oxford: Oxford University Press.

World Bank (1985) *World development report*. Oxford: Oxford University Press.

Yitzhaki, S. (1974) 'Income tax evasion: A note', *Journal of Public Economics*, 3:201–202.

Chapter 21

PROJECT EVALUATION IN THEORY AND PRACTICE

LYN SQUIRE*

World Bank

Contents

*Comments on an earlier version from Trent Bertrand, Shanta Devarajan, Hafez Ghanem, Homi Kharas, Pradeep Mitra, T.N. Srinivasan and Nick Stern are gratefully acknowledged.

Handbook of Development Economics, Volume II, Edited by H. Chenery and T.N. Srinivasan
© *Elsevier Science Publishers B.V., 1989*

1. Introduction

Project evaluation is a means of choosing among alternative investment options. Selection is based on profitability measured at "shadow" prices. If shadow prices are consistently defined as the ultimate effect on society's welfare of a change in the net supply of a particular input or output, then a project that shows a profit at these prices will also make a positive contribution to society's welfare.

The above characterization is perfectly general and applies equally to the selection of public and private projects in developed and developing countries.[1] During the last fifteen years, however, the evaluation of public sector projects in developing countries has received special attention.[2] The motivation for this interest presumably lies in the view that the level and composition of investment is critically important to the process of development; the rate and style of future development are a direct consequence of past and present investment decisions. That portion of total investment which is under government control should, therefore, be subject to careful scrutiny.[3]

Apart from this basic point, other arguments can be advanced to explain the interest in project evaluation in developing countries. For example, it is generally accepted that market imperfections are more significant in developing countries. As a result, the prices relevant to the evaluation of projects may depart further from prevailing market prices than is the case in developed countries. This has, indeed, been fully recognized in the literature. An extreme example is the view of some early contributors that the shadow cost of unskilled labor is zero.[4] Although this particular view is not prevalent today, it illustrates the degree to which market imperfections have been an important element of project evaluation in developing countries. A second argument concerns the role of the public sector in these countries. The literature focusing on developed countries has frequently been concerned with the evaluation of traditional public sector projects especially roads and water supply.[5] In developing countries, however, the public sector is often engaged directly in production. This, too, has been recognized in the literature.[6]

---

[1]Several surveys are available at this level. Early reviews are provided by Eckstein (1961), Henderson (1968), and Prest and Turvey (1965). A much more recent one is that of Drèze and Stern (1987).

[2]The major contributions are UNIDO (1972) and Little and Mirrlees (1974).

[3]Note that this includes both public projects and private sector projects that require clearance from a licensing or other public agency.

[4]See Khan (1951).

[5]See, for example, Foster and Beesley (1963) and Krutilla and Eckstein (1958).

[6]The first version of the Little–Mirrlees approach [Little and Mirrlees (1969)] was specifically concerned with industrial projects. See also UNIDO (1972).

Another factor that distinguishes project evaluation in developed and developing countries is the scarcity of skilled manpower. Agencies concerned with the appraisal of investment options in developing countries invariably face tight deadlines, suffer from inadequate data bases and experience severe shortages of appropriately skilled manpower. Despite its importance in practice, this argument has not attracted the attention of those engaged in the theoretical derivation of shadow prices.[7] It, nevertheless, points to a natural tension between the heavy demands on time and information implied by the more sophisticated approaches to shadow pricing and the urgent need of practitioners for simple, easily applied shadow pricing rules.

The existing literature bears on these points to differing degrees. For example, the derivation of shadow prices in particular markets – labor, foreign exchange, capital – is treated extensively. On the other hand, the significance of inadequate staff and time for the appraisal of projects has received much less attention. In this review, the balance is reversed. In particular, a very preliminary attempt is made to assess the benefits of increasingly sophisticated approaches to the evaluation of projects. In principle, if such information were available on a more general basis, one could weigh the benefits of increased precision against the costs arising from additional requirements of manpower and time. This more ambitious task, however, is not undertaken here.

The three levels of sophistication that are identified in this chapter can be equated loosely with the historical development of the subject. The first, and simplest, involves the use of partial equilibrium techniques. These are well known, easily implemented and usually transparent.[8] They are, however, subject to obvious criticism and much of the recent literature, therefore, has been concerned with the general equilibrium derivation of shadow prices.[9] This, the second level of sophistication, has its own strengths and weaknesses. On the one hand, important repercussions which may otherwise be omitted can now be incorporated in the derivation of shadow prices. On the other hand, the degree of detail that can be achieved is limited by the difficulties of solving analytically complex models. A further weakness concerns the assumption regarding the manner in which the government restores economy-wide equilibrium following the introduction of a project. Traditionally, both partial and general equilibrium approaches have assumed that any project-induced impact on the budget can be offset by lump-sum transfers. Since developing countries are not able to implement such transfers, the third level of sophistication allows explicitly for the use of distortionary taxation as the mechanism for restoring fiscal balance.[10]

---

[7]Harberger is an exception. He has consistently advocated the merits of simplicity.

[8]Many of the manuals on cost–benefit analysis for practitioners are cast in partial equilibrium terms. See, for example, Mishan (1976) or UNIDO (1972).

[9]For a discussion of general equilibrium theory and project evaluation, see Srinivasan (1982).

[10]The general point that shadow pricing rules depend on existing policies is developed in Drèze and Stern (1987). In fact, they demonstrate that the choice of projects and the choice of policies can, and should, be examined within the same framework.

Although the emphasis of this review is on the issue just noted, some of the more general matters relating to project evaluation are also treated. In Section 2 the basic rationale of project evaluation is outlined and the criterion for the acceptance of a project is defined. Since this criterion is not based on the concept of welfare improvements associated with Pareto, the discussion leads naturally to the treatment of equity in project evaluation. Projects may imply losers as well as gainers and the manner in which gains and losses are to be aggregated must be addressed. Subsequent discussion abstracts from matters of income distribution by assuming a single-consumer economy.[11] Within this framework, a general definition of shadow prices is provided and a particular expression for shadow prices – in relation to consumer prices – is also derived. This derivation of shadow prices, although perfectly general, does not yield a set of rules that are easy to apply in practice and thus motivates the discussion in Section 3 of alternative means of deriving rules that are easy to implement.

Section 3 uses a simple, general equilibrium model of a tax-distorted, open economy to explore the three approaches to the derivation of shadow prices noted above and, in particular, to identify the nature of the approximations involved in successive stages of simplification. The first two approaches derive shadow prices on the assumption that any budget imbalance is corrected by means of lump-sum transfers. In a general equilibrium framework this yields shadow prices equal to border prices for tradables. For nontradables and primary factors, shadow prices equal producer prices plus a term measuring direct and indirect effects on the budget. If the indirect effects on the budget are ignored, a partial equilibrium rule is obtained that equates the shadow prices of nontradables and factors of production with consumer prices. These indirect budget effects, therefore, provide a measure of the approximation implied by the use of partial equilibrium techniques.

As mentioned above, the shadow pricing rules obtained with both these approaches have been questioned on the grounds that lump-sum transfers are not a feasible policy instrument in developing countries and that, therefore, the budget must be balanced by some other means which may, in turn, influence the shadow pricing rules. The third approach addresses this issue directly by deriving general equilibrium shadow prices for an economy in which lump-sum transfers are not available. These shadow prices can be written as the sum of the shadow prices relevant for an economy in which such transfers are feasible plus a term reflecting the cost or benefit of adjusting the budget by some means other than lump-sum transfers. This term is a measure of the approximation resulting from an inappropriate reliance on the assumption concerning the availability of lump-sum transfers.

---

[11] Most agencies practicing project evaluation ignore the project's impact on income distribution or else treat it qualitatively (see Section 5).

Section 3, therefore, examines the approximation involved in the use of progressively simpler approaches within a standard, open-economy model. The analysis reveals that, within this framework, *border prices remain the appropriate shadow prices for tradable commodities at all three levels of sophistication.* This is the single most important result to emerge from recent work, not only because of its relevance in a wide range of circumstances, but also because it is easy to use in practice. A second point worth noting is that *relative shadow prices for non-tradables and factors depend on the method of closing the budget whenever a change in the net supply of the commodity being shadow priced causes a direct change in private welfare.* This observation provides a basis on which to judge the adequacy of the simpler approaches and hence the need for more complex procedures.

Section 4 accomplishes two tasks. First, it uses the framework of Section 3 to examine the assumptions underlying several well-known results for particular shadow prices. Although not a full review of the extensive literature on these matters, it does cover, among other things, the Little–Mirrlees technique of decomposition for shadow-pricing nontradables, a common formula for the shadow wage rate, the role of conversion factors and shadow exchange rates and the choice of discount rate. Second, and simultaneously, Section 4 examines the consequences for shadow pricing of complications to the simple model of Section 3. In particular, it explores the significance of markets that fail to clear. For example, tradables may be subject to binding quotas or labor markets to minimum wage legislation. Both examples illustrate situations in which private welfare is affected directly and, as expected from the results of Section 3, this complicates the derivation of shadow prices.

In Section 5 the emphasis switches from theory to practice. The section begins with an assessment of practice in selected developing countries. It then turns to an examination of the likely errors introduced by the observed gap between theory and practice. In particular, it explores the possibility of quantifying the errors involved in the use of, say, partial equilibrium techniques or reliance on the assumption that lump-sum transfers are available. Since a general approach to this issue is not feasible, Section 5 employs the notion of representative projects. Drawing on the results of Section 3, project types were identified according to the importance of tradables in costs and benefits and according to the size of the project's direct impact on private welfare. This procedure led to the selection of three basic types of project.

The first type of project is termed an "industrial project" and is characterized by public production of a tradable output. Projects of this type have a large tradable component and have very little direct effect on private welfare. Virtually the entire return accrues to the public sector, the only leakage, if any, to the private sector being through factor payments. As a result, the simple methods currently used in many countries and by international institutions such as the World Bank are probably adequate. The second type of project is described as an "infrastructural project". In this case, the public sector provides certain infrastructure (a nontradable) which results in increased private sector profits. This type of project usually has a significant impact on private sector income and raises important questions regarding cost recovery. The evaluation of these projects is likely to be sensitive to the method of budget closure so that the simple shadow pricing rules currently used are likely to be misleading. In particular, it appears that these methods *systematically overestimate the net benefits of infrastructural projects*. The final type of project is called a "utility project". This type of project provides a nontradable service – electric power, for example – to the private sector. Again, one can expect a significant impact on private sector incomes if appropriate pricing policy for the output is not followed. This, in turn, can lead to an incorrect assessment of net benefits. Although this often happens in practice, the pricing recommendations that usually emerge from the appraisal of utility projects effectively eliminate the factor – a price that fails to clear the market – causing the problem.

In Section 6 some concluding remarks are offered on areas where additional work seems to be most needed.

2. Fundamentals of project evaluation

2.1. Coverage

This section is concerned with several basic issues: definitions of a project and a shadow price are presented, the criterion for choosing among projects is established, and the treatment of project-induced changes in the distribution of income is examined. Two other important issues – the treatment of uncertainty and the implications of nonmarginal projects – are not discussed. The former has generated a substantial body of literature, most of which is concerned with the specification of states of the world by means of probability distributions and the evaluation of those states through some preference function. Major theoretical contributions to the subject include Hirschleifer (1965), Arrow and Lind (1970) Henry (1974) and Graham (1981). Reutlinger (1970) shows how, in practice, a probability distribution can be developed for a project's net present value and case studies incorporating aspects of uncertainty are reported in Pouliquen (1970), Stern (1972a) and Anand (1976). In practice, however, most appraisals limit their examination of uncertainty to sensitivity analysis. On the latter, the available literature is scant. Harris (1978) derives rules for the evaluation of nonmarginal projects which require information on pre-project and post-project equilibrium prices. The estimation of post-project prices, however, is itself extremely difficult. Hammond (1983) suggests a procedure that leads to approximately correct results which require information only on pre-project prices, incomes and quantities. For the remainder of this review, it is assumed that project costs and benefits are known with certainty and that the projects being evaluated can truly be considered marginal. This focus is consistent with the mainstream of literature on project evaluation.

2.2. Project definition and the role of the evaluator

A project may be defined as a combination of inputs and outputs. While this definition is obvious and straightforward, further details are required to define the nature of evaluation. In particular, one needs to know the extent of the evaluator's authority.[12] For example, the evaluation of a nonmarginal project may involve elements of macroeconomic policy. Evaluation may also extend to private sector projects. Clearly, different specifications will be appropriate in different countries and at different times. For the purpose of this review, it is assumed that the projects being evaluated are in the public sector and that the evaluator's role is relatively limited. That is, we have in mind an official located in a sectoral or possibly central department who takes the general policy environment as given. Apart from the accept/reject decision, therefore, his focus is on project-specific matters such as design, timing and size. In addition, certain sectoral pricing decisions – for example, output prices in the case of nontradable services or cost recovery policy in the case of infrastructure – may be subject to his control. This description is probably a reasonable reflection of practice in most countries (see Section 5).

The assumption of a relatively passive project evaluator is far from innocuous. It allows, for example, the acceptance of a project that may be profitable solely as a result of some highly inappropriate policy imposed by some other branch of the government. The standard example of this possibility is a project designed to produce an import substitute when actual imports are prohibited. Although the project may be welfare-improving given the ban on imports, it may not be internationally competitive and may, therefore, be a source of pressure for the retention of the ban. When the continuation of such policies is critical to the success of a project, one is well advised to examine the project's merit with and without the questionable policy and to alert the appropriate decision-makers to the consequences of accepting such projects. While the ability of the project evaluator to secure policy changes may often be limited, this need not always be the case. International agencies, for example, may be able to secure such changes in conjunction with project lending.

---

[12] This point is discussed in Sen (1972) and made a central feature of cost–benefit analysis in Drèze and Stern (1987).

2.3. Selection criterion

One wants a selection criterion that allows public sector resources to be allocated in such a way that aggregate welfare is as large as possible. Furthermore, since many agencies and individuals are usually involved in the allocation of public resources, the criterion must allow easy decentralization. Project evaluation is one method that is commonly used to achieve this purpose, its means of decentralization being the provision of shadow prices to those responsible for project selection. These shadow prices must satisfy the condition that the project's net profits at shadow prices be positive if, and only if, the project increases aggregate welfare. If such prices could be identified, this rule would lead to welfare maximization provided there were no mutually exclusive projects.[13] To allow for such projects, the shadow prices must also satisfy the condition that, for any set of mutually exclusive projects, the project yielding the greatest increase in aggregate welfare also earn the largest "shadow" profits. In addition, one would like shadow prices to be independent of any particular project and, for ease of implementation, adjustments from market prices to arrive at shadow prices should be as simple as possible.

2.4. Income distribution

The focus on changes in aggregate welfare as a selection device raises an important issue concerning the distribution of net benefits. If aggregate welfare (W) is a function of individual utilities (U) which are, in turn, functions of commodities consumed (c), then a project-induced change in welfare is given by:

$$dW = \sum_h \frac{\partial W}{\partial U^h} \sum_i \frac{\partial U^h}{\partial c_i^h} \, dc_i^h, \tag{1}$$

where the h superscripts denote households or individuals, the i subscripts denote commodities and the dc_i^h represent the effects of a project on the consumption of commodities by household. Since dW can be positive even though some households may experience a decrease in utility, exclusive focus on the change in aggregate welfare (dW) implies that projects can be accepted that do not satisfy the Pareto condition.

This observation notwithstanding, most texts on projects evaluation accept the change in aggregate welfare as a satisfactory criterion for project selection. This,

---

[13] The importance of mutually exclusive projects is often overlooked. Such projects are, in fact, very common since alternative designs, sizes or timings of what is essentially the same project are mutually exclusive.

however, leads to a further question: How are losses and benefits accruing to different households to be aggregated? This is a much more contentious issue. Some authors, especially Harberger (1971a) and Mishan (1976), argue that, for purposes of cost–benefit analysis, all losses and benefits should receive equal weight regardless of the personal circumstances of the individual losers and gainers. Others, among them UNIDO (1972), Little and Mirrlees (1974) and Squire and van der Tak (1975), argue in favor of differential treatment for those whose incomes are changed by the project, the basis of differentiation being the individual's pre-project income. In this way, a concern with equity can be introduced into the selection criterion.

Much has been written on this issue and a blow-by-blow account would quickly become overwhelming.[14] Rather than stress the differences, it may be more fruitful to identify areas of agreement. This can be done by expressing the change in aggregate welfare as the sum of the project's effect on total consumption and its effect on the distribution of consumption. If consumers allocate their expenditure in order to maximize utility, then the marginal utility of consuming the ith commodity $(\partial U^h / \partial c_i^h)$ is equated with the prices (q_i) of that commodity multiplied by the marginal utility of income (λ^h) for the hth household. Using this information, equation (1) can be written as:

$$dW/\lambda = \sum_i q_i \, dc_i - \sum_h (1 - \omega) \sum_i q_i \, dc_i^h, \qquad (2)$$

where $\lambda = \lambda^H \, \partial W / \partial U^H$, H being the income group or household whose increase in income receives a weight of one, and $\omega^h = (\partial W / \partial U^h)(\lambda^h / \lambda)$ and is known as a welfare weight [see Stern (1977)].

Compared with equation (1), equation (2) accomplishes two things. First, division by λ allows the change in welfare to be expressed in terms of prices and changes in quantities consumed rather than in terms of marginal utilities. Second, the change in aggregate welfare now comprises two terms, the first of which is independent of the distribution of gains and losses among households, the distributive impact of the project being captured exclusively in the second term. The first term is an essential ingredient in the derivation of shadow prices in virtually all texts on project evaluation and is simply the value at consumer prices of the total increase in consumption generated by that project. In some circumstances, exclusive focus on this term would be appropriate. If costless income transfers were available, the effect of a project on income distribution could always be neutralized by transfers of income and the second term could be omitted. Since such transfers are not usually assumed to be available, various

---

[14] For a discussion of these issues, see Ray (1984).

authors have explored the possibility of retaining the exclusive focus on the first term by relying on hypothetical transfers or potential compensation.[15]

It is now generally accepted that the second term cannot be ignored. Different authors, however, choose to handle this term in different ways. Some, such as Mishan, argue that the project analyst should focus on the first term of equation (2) but should also provide the decision-maker with information on the distribution of net gains (i.e. $\sum_i q_i \, dc_i^h$ by household).[16] The decision-maker may wish to incorporate this information in accepting or rejecting a project, but the system of welfare weights remains implicit. Others, such as Little and Mirrlees, prefer to make the welfare weights explicit and to incorporate them in the formal analysis on the grounds that this will contribute to the consistency of decision-making.

The differences between the protagonists, therefore, are rather minor compared with the similarities. The major task of the project evaluator that is common to both approaches is the calculation of the changes in consumption by household following the introduction of a project. This task is extremely difficult to accomplish for a project that may last 20 or 30 years. As a result, most practitioners either ignore or, at best, provide only a qualitative assessment of the distribution of project benefits.[17] Further difficulties are encountered if one wishes to use explicit welfare weights. While alternative specifications can be used, arriving at a consensus has proved difficult.[18] Practitioners have been reluctant, therefore, to incorporate welfare weights in their formal analysis.

In the remainder of this chapter the treatment of the interpersonal distribution of project benefits is ignored. This is accomplished by using the notion of a single-consumer economy. This allows attention to be focused exclusively on the first term of equation (2) which, as noted above, is common to all methods of project evaluation. This is not to deny the potential importance of specific projects on the distribution of income. Section 5, therefore, offers some observations on when such effects may be especially significant.

2.5. Shadow prices

While equation (2) provides a theoretically correct measure of a project's worth, it does not relate immediately to most practical methods of project evaluation.

[15] See Kaldor (1939), Hicks (1940), and Scitovsky (1941) and the discussion of hypothetical compensation in Little (1950). Boadway (1974), provides a valuable clarification of the validity of potential compensation as a measure of welfare change.

[16] "The least he (the project analyst) should do is point up the distributional implications wherever they appear significant" [Mishan (1976, p. 405)].

[17] For attempts to include income distribution effects in a fairly systematic way, see Scott, McArthur and Newberry (1976), Little and Scott (1976), McArthur (1978) and Porter and Walsh (1978).

[18] For more discussion of the use of welfare weights and their derivation, see Ray (1984) and Stern (1977).

Equation (2) views a project from the perspective of the (net) beneficiaries. It is based on the effect of the project on consumption, this being the primary determinant of individual welfare. In practice, however, one usually examines the inputs and outputs of a project and assigns values to them. Using vector notation, these values, known as shadow prices, can then be used to express the project-induced change in aggregate welfare as:

$$dW/\lambda = \pi \cdot dx, \tag{3}$$

where $\pi = (\partial W/\partial x)/\lambda$ is a vector of shadow prices and dx is a vector of changes in the net supplies from the public sector occasioned by a new project. Thus, the appropriate definition of the shadow price of a commodity is the *change in aggregate welfare following a marginal increase in the net supply of that commodity by the public sector*.[19] If this definition is applied consistently, then the shadow profits of a project will be positive if, and only if, welfare is increased.

Since equations (2) and (3) both measure the effect on welfare of a new project, a simple expression for shadow prices can be derived immediately. Assuming a single consumer, these equations imply that:

$$\pi = q \cdot \partial c/\partial x, \tag{4}$$

where $\partial c/\partial x$ are the partial derivatives associated with a return to a full equilibrium following the introduction of the project denoted by dx. That is to say, the shadow price for a particular commodity equals all changes, valued at consumer prices, in the consumption of commodities induced by the change in the net supply of that commodity. Consumer prices are, therefore, a perfectly acceptable vehicle for deriving shadow prices.

Provided the changes in consumption ($\partial c/\partial x$) are those resulting from a return to a full equilibrium, the shadow prices defined by equation (4) capture all general equilibrium effects. While clearly an attractive feature of this definition, it, nevertheless, raises some difficult problems for the practitioner. This occurs because the changes in consumption and the associated consumer prices may be for commodities which, on the surface, have little direct interaction with the commodity being shadow priced. The commodity in question may, for example, be an intermediate with no consumer price of its own. Nevertheless, its use in a public sector project may lead to all kinds of changes in consumption before full equilibrium is restored. Thus, although shadow prices can be expressed in terms of consumer prices, the relevant consumer prices may have little to do with the commodity actually being demanded or supplied by the public sector. It is not

---

[19] This definition is implicit in most texts on project evaluation. More recently, it has been made very explicit in papers by Bell and Devarajan (1983), Blitzer, Dasgupta and Stiglitz (1981) Drèze and Stern (1987) and Sieper (1981).

immediately obvious, therefore, how one can conveniently derive a link between the relevant consumer prices and the producer price of the commodity being shadow priced. This difficulty has led to a search for alternative expressions for shadow prices that relate directly to the market price of project inputs and outputs. This search is the subject matter of the next section.

3. Shadow pricing: An overview

Alternative shadow pricing rules can be derived by specifying an economic structure and identifying the links between the market price of the commodity being shadow priced and the ultimate effect on aggregate welfare. The choice of structure and the assumptions made about prevailing policies will influence the resulting shadow prices. The structure used here corresponds to a simple, tax-distorted, open economy and, as noted above, assumes a fairly limited role for the project evaluator so that distortions are expected to persist.[20] Although this model does not allow the treatment of all possible sources of distortion, the difference between partial and general equilibrium results and the significance of the assumption regarding lump-sum transfers can be demonstrated and a basic formula useful for subsequent analysis can be derived.

3.1. Model structure

The model used in this section describes a small, tax-distorted, open economy.[21] It incorporates private consumption and production, public production and international trade. As discussed in Section 2, the model uses the notion of a single consumer in order to avoid complications arising from the possible impact of a project on the distribution of income. The budget constraints for the private sector and the public sector are:

$$q \cdot c = q \cdot e + p \cdot y + L \tag{5}$$

and

$$Z = R + p \cdot x - L, \tag{6}$$

[20] That is, we are concerned with second-best shadow prices. While some early contributors such as Tinbergen (1958) advocated the use of prices that would prevail in a distortion-free economy, this first-best approach has been generally rejected. Nevertheless, changes in the policy environment may occur in the future and should be incorporated into the analysis. The evaluator may even be able to influence the general direction of policy change and, where possible, should do so. An integrated approach to policy reform and project evaluation is presented in Drèze and Stern (1987).

[21] The model is similar to that described by Dixit (1987). Applications of similar models to shadow pricing include Dasgupta and Stiglitz (1974), Boadway (1975a), Bertrand (1979) and Srinivasan and Bhagwati (1978).

where q and p represent vectors of consumer and producer prices, respectively; c, e and y are vectors of private sector consumption, initial endowment of primary factors and net outputs, respectively; L represents lump-sum transfers; Z and R are the government's budget surplus and net revenue, respectively; and x is a vector of net outputs from the public sector. The vector, c, includes consumption of the private sector's factor endowment so that $q \cdot c$ measures "full" expenditure. The terms $p \cdot y$ and $p \cdot x$ measure private sector and public sector profits, respectively, both valued at producer prices.

Note that the model includes lump-sum transfers between the public sector and the single consumer. In principle, therefore, one could easily handle a multi-consumer economy and allow the government to offset project-induced effects on the distribution of income by means of costless transfers. The purpose of this section, however, is to examine the significance of lump-sum transfers, not for the distribution of income among households, but for that between the private and public sectors. Accordingly, we retain the single-consumer assumption and, initially, allow transfers.

Government revenue (R) derives from net taxes (t) on the consumption of tradables and net subsidies (s) to domestic producers. That is,

$$R = t \cdot c - s \cdot (y + x). \tag{7}$$

This implies that consumer prices (q) for tradables equal $(r + t)$, where r is the relevant border price and that producer prices (p) for tradables equal $(r + s)$. Thus, the link between consumer and producer prices is $q = p - s + t$. If s and t are equal, the consumer tax and producer subsidy are the same as an import tariff. Trade tariffs, therefore, are fully consistent with this approach. For nontradables and primary factors, the link between consumer and producer prices is simply $q = p - s$.

The behavioral assumptions of the model are standard. Consumers maximize utility subject to full expenditure and take prices as given. Private sector producers maximize profits subject to their constant-returns-to-scale technology and also take prices as given. In the absence of a full model of government behavior, public sector production, however, is assumed to be exogenous. The markets for tradables clear by means of changes in net imports, whereas those for nontradables and primary factors clear by means of price adjustments. Thus, in general:

$$c = y + x + e + m. \tag{8}$$

For tradables, $e = 0$. For nontradables, $m = e = 0$. For primary factors, $x = m = 0$. International prices are assumed to be given – that is, the "small country" assumption is adopted.

This completes the description of the model. Before proceeding, however, we can check that if the government's budget is balanced ($Z = 0$) and if equation (5) (the private sector's budget constraint) and (8) (the market-clearing conditions) are met, a full equilibrium is achieved and the economy's transactions ($r \cdot m$) with the rest of the world are in balance. First, note that $r \cdot m = r \cdot (c - x - y)$. Using the relationship between border prices and domestic prices, and the market-clearing conditions for nontradables and primary factors, this may be written as $r \cdot m = q \cdot c - q \cdot e - p \cdot y - t \cdot c + s \cdot (y + x) - p \cdot x$. Finally, using equations (5) and (7), this simplifies to $r \cdot m = L - p \cdot x - R = -Z$. That is, a negative trade balance ($r \cdot m > 0$) corresponds to a negative surplus in the government's budget. If the government balances its budget ($Z = 0$), then full equilibrium is achieved and $r \cdot m = 0$. It is unnecessary, therefore, to treat both the government budget constraint and the balance-of-payments constraint and, in the remainder of the chapter, we focus on the former.

3.2. Full and compensated shadow prices

The analysis in this subsection employs a decomposition technique introduced by Sieper (1981). He notes that, in a full equilibrium, welfare is determined by the set of exogenous variables – endowments and border prices – and by the government's policy instruments. Not all of the government's policy instruments, however, can be determined independently. If, for example, the government sets net output levels (x) for the public sector and its desired budget surplus (Z), then equation (6) reveals that the government can set either its net revenue (R) from commodity taxation or its lump-sum transfers (L), but not both.[22] Leaving aside the choice between these two alternatives for the moment, aggregate welfare can be expressed as a function of net output from the public sector and the government's desired budget surplus ($W = W(x, Z)$). In a full equilibrium, Z equals zero.

Starting from a full equilibrium, a change in the net supply of any commodity produced by the public sector (x) will leave welfare unchanged if the budget surplus (Z) is changed such that the following equation is satisfied:

$$dW(x, Z) = \frac{\partial W}{\partial x} \cdot dx + \frac{\partial W}{\partial Z} \cdot dZ = 0,$$

or, dividing through by λ, and using the definition of shadow prices, if:

$$\pi \cdot dx - \pi_Z \cdot dZ = 0, \tag{9}$$

---

[22] Boadway (1975b, p. 364) develops the same point in a closed-economy model.

where $\pi_Z = [-\partial W(x, Z)/\partial Z]/\lambda$ and is the marginal social cost of increasing the budget surplus. It follows from equation (9) that shadow prices are given by:

$$\pi = \pi_Z \pi^*, \tag{10}$$

where $\pi^* = dZ/dx|_{dW=0}$ and is a vector of *compensated* shadow prices.[23]

The significance of this decomposition is examined in detail later in this subsection. Here we simply note three points. First, the method of increasing the budget surplus implicit in π_Z has not been specified. It could be distortionary taxation (R) or lump-sum transfers (L). This observation plays an important role in our subsequent discussion of the error implied by incorrectly assuming the existence of lump-sum transfers. Second, since π_Z is independent of the commodity being shadow priced, it is a scalar which has no influence on the project accept/reject decision and may, therefore, be omitted. That is, if $\pi\,dx \geq 0$, then, provided $\pi_Z > 0$, $\pi^*\,dx \geq 0$. Compensated shadow prices are all that is required for the consistent selection of projects and they are, therefore, the focus for the remainder of this analysis.[24] And third, the focus on compensated shadow prices amounts to the use of public income as numeraire. [That is, one can divide both sides of equation (10) by π_Z, the marginal social cost of additional government revenue.] Compensated shadow prices, therefore, define the shadow prices implied by the Little–Mirrlees approach to project evaluation.

To derive an expression for a compensated shadow price in full equilibrium, Sieper proceeds in two steps. He first calculates the compensated shadow price on the assumption that compensation is achieved by means of lump-sum transfers. He then introduces an adjustment to allow for the fact that compensation may be by means of a change in distortionary taxation. We follow this procedure. This allows us to explore the differences between partial and general equilibrium shadow prices given the standard assumption that lump-sum transfers are available. We then examine the adjustment factor to establish the consequences of abandoning this assumption.

3.3. Partial versus general equilibrium

Allowing the existence of lump-sum transfers, π^* can be derived immediately from equation (6):

$$\pi^* = \frac{\partial Z}{\partial x}\bigg|_{\partial W=0} = p + \frac{\partial R(x, W)}{\partial x} + \frac{\partial p(x, W)}{\partial x}x - \frac{\partial L(x, W)}{\partial x}, \tag{11}$$

---

[23]See Sieper (1981, pp. 21). He describes π^* as "compensated" since private welfare is held constant.
[24]Some possible exceptions to this statement are explored later in this section.

where the functions denoted (x, W) are evaluated at the compensated equilibrium. Equation (11) shows π_k^* to be dependent on the effect of the increase in net supply of the kth commodity on the government's budget surplus when private welfare is held constant.

This equation can be further simplified by examining the condition for constant welfare. By adding equations (5) and (6) and taking the total differential of the result, one obtains:

$$q \cdot dc = p \cdot dx + dR - dZ. \tag{12}$$

In arriving at equation (12), use has been made of the following facts:
- endowments are fixed ($de = 0$);
- the private sector maximizes profits ($p \cdot dy = 0$);
- all taxes and subsidies are specific ($dp = dq$);
- markets clear for nontradables and factors of production ($e + y + x = c$);
- prices for tradables are fixed ($dp = dq = 0$).

Substituting for dZ from equation (6) into equation (12) yields:

$$q \cdot dc = dL - x \cdot dp. \tag{13}$$

Since $q\,dc = dW/\lambda$ [see equation (2)], welfare is constant ($dW/\lambda = 0$), if the lump-sum transfer $\partial L/\partial x = \partial p/\partial x\, x$ which is the change in profits of public sector production resulting from induced price changes. That is, lump-sum transfers are required to offset the loss or gain to the private sector resulting from the payment of higher or lower prices for publicly produced goods. This term is important because in Sieper's model it is the only way in which a change in the net supply of a public sector commodity affects private welfare directly.[25]

Using this result in equation (11) yields:

$$\pi^* = p + \partial R(x, W)/\partial x, \tag{14}$$

which shows π^* to be equal to its producer price plus any induced change in net government revenue.[26] Equation (14), therefore, provides the required link between producer prices and shadow prices.

The induced effect on government revenue can be analyzed further. From the definition of government revenue [equation (7)]:

$$\frac{\partial R(x, W)}{\partial x_k} = -s_k + \phi_c - \phi_p, \tag{15}$$

---

[25]Other ways in which net public production affects private welfare are examined in Sections 4 and 5.

[26]Boadway (1978, 1975a) expresses shadow prices in this form for a simpler version of the model presented here. See also Boadway (1975b) for a closed-economy version.

where $-s_k$ is the direct effect on the budget and ϕ_c and ϕ_p are indirect effects involving consumption taxes and production subsidies, respectively (see below). Using equations (14) and (15), one can arrive at some very simple partial equilibrium results. If one is prepared to ignore effects in other markets – $\phi_c = \phi_p = 0$ – the shadow pricing rules become:

$$\pi_k^* = r_k, \quad k \in T,$$

$$\pi_k^* = q_k, \quad k \in H,$$

(16)

where T denotes tradables and H denotes nontradables and primary factors. These results suggest that, if induced price changes are negligible, or if distortions – taxes and subsidies – in affected markets are negligible or offsetting, shadow prices equal boarder prices for tradables and consumer prices for all other commodities and factors.

Rules as simple as these have an excellent chance of being used in practice on a regular basis. Moreover, they can be modified to approximate the shadow prices associated with a full equilibrium by judicious inclusion of selected indirect effects.[27] The shadow pricing rules defined by equation (16) should be interpreted, therefore, as only one example of the many different approaches that are possible in a partial equilibrium framework.[28] The essential point is not that partial equilibrium approaches are undesirable, but that one should be aware of the assumptions implicit in one's approach.

The approximation implicit in equation (16) can be analyzed further by examining the indirect effects, ϕ_c and ϕ_p. Since private welfare is held constant the indirect effects involve price changes only. Moreover, since the domestic prices of tradables are fixed, these effects can only arise from induced changes in the prices of nontradables and factors of production. Thus:

$$\phi_c = \sum_{i \in T} t_i \sum_{j \in H} \frac{\partial c_i(q \cdot W)}{\partial q_j} \frac{\partial q_j(x \cdot W)}{\partial x_k},$$

(17)

$$\phi_p = \sum_i s_i \sum_{j \in H} \frac{\partial y_i(p)}{\partial p_j} \frac{\partial p_j(x, W)}{\partial x_k}.$$

That is to say, ϕ_c shows the effect on revenue arising from changes in the consumption of tradables as the prices of nontradables and primary factors adjust to the increased supply of the kth public sector output. And ϕ_p performs a

---

[27] In fact, Section 4 examines a specific instance when equation (16) would yield the correct general equilibrium shadow prices.
[28] A common formula used in partial equilibrium analysis is developed below.

similar function for the subsidies to domestic production of both tradables and nontradables.

Since the markets for nontradables and factors of production must clear in full equilibrium, it is possible to derive an explicit expression for the price changes of these goods. Market clearing requires that $c_i(q, W) = y_i(p) + x_i + e_i$ so that the price changes must satisfy the following system of equations:

$$\left[\frac{\partial c_i(q, W)}{\partial q_j} - \frac{\partial y_i(p)}{\partial p_j} \right] \left[\frac{\partial p_i(x, W)}{\partial x_k} \right] = [\varepsilon_i] \quad i, j \in H, \tag{18}$$

where $\varepsilon_i = 1$ if $i = k$ *and* $i \in H$ (that is, if i is the commodity being shadow priced and if i is a nontradable or factor of production). If $i = k$ and $i \in T$ (that is, if the commodity being shadow priced is a tradable), then $\varepsilon_i = 0$ indicating that the prices of nontradables and primary factors remain constant. This result arises because a change in the net supply of a tradable does not cause an immediate change in price and because any direct income effects are offset by lump-sum transfers. Thus, no impulse is transmitted to the markets for tradables and primary factors. This conclusion, i.e. that *changes in the net supply of tradables do not influence the prices of nontradables or factors of production*, allows equation (14) to be rewritten as:

$$\pi_k = r_k, \qquad\qquad\qquad k \in T,$$

$$\pi_k = p_k + \partial R(x, W)/\partial x_k, \quad k \in H, \tag{19}$$

which establishes that the compensated shadow prices for tradables are equal to border prices if lump-sum transfers are available. The degree of approximation implicit in the use of the partial equilibrium rules defined by equation (16) depends, therefore, on the importance of nontradables and primary factors in project costs and benefits.

As shown in Boadway (1975a), a standard partial equilibrium formula for nontradables and primary factors can be derived from equations (14), (15), (17) and (18). If all cross-price effects on both supply and demand are omitted, these equations yield:

$$\pi_k^* = \frac{q_r \, \partial c_r/\partial q_r - p_r \, \partial y_r/\partial p_k}{\partial c_r/\partial q_r - \partial y_r/\partial p_r}, \quad k \in H.$$

That is to say, shadow prices for nontradables and primary factors are given by a weighted average of demand and supply price, the weights being the proportions in which increased public sector demand is met by reduced private sector demand and increased private sector supply. This is a standard, partial equilibrium formula associated with, among others, Harberger (1971a), and illustrates the general point that different partial equilibrium rules can be derived depending on the particular set of assumptions that are chosen. In this case, the accuracy of the partial equilibrium rules depends on the importance of cross-price effects and the degree of distortion in the affected markets.

3.4. *Lump-sum transfers versus distortionary taxation*[29]

The preceding discussion focused on the consequences of using partial rather than general equilibrium analysis given that the government could maintain fiscal balance by means of lump-sum transfers. This, a standard assumption in much of the literature, raises serious questions of internal consistency. If governments have the ability to implement lump-sum transfers, why do they also use trade taxes, production taxes and consumption taxes that distort markets? Since it is the presence of such taxes that has, in part, led to the development of shadow pricing as a topic, it is awkward to maintain the assumption that governments have recourse to lump-sum transfers. But, if the budget is balanced by means of policy instruments that introduce or eliminate distortions, their social cost or benefit ought to enter in the calculation of shadow prices.

Several sets of authors have addressed this issue:

Accounting prices of goods and services appear not to be insensitive to the equilibriating mechanisms that are pursued by a government [Blitzer, Dasgupta and Stiglitz, (1981, p. 73)].

The manner in which the government attempts to restore balance of payments equilibrium determines the appropriate set of shadow prices [Bell and Devarajan (1983, p. 475)].

These two quotes capture the essence of the modern approach to shadow pricing – since projects can be expected to disrupt the existing equilibrium, and since lump-sum transfers are not generally available, the manner in which the economy is restored to equilibrium should matter in the determination of shadow prices. This issue is of considerable practical importance in that it reduces the likelihood that one can arrive at a set of easily implemented shadow prices. It is of interest, therefore, to examine the nature of the difference between general equilibrium shadow prices with lump-sum transfers and those without such transfers.

---

[29] Boadway (1975b) conducts a similar analysis in the context of a closed-economy model.

Recall Sieper's decomposition of a full shadow price into the marginal social cost of increasing the budget surplus and a compensated shadow price ($\pi = \pi_Z \pi^*$). The significance of this is that it apparently isolates the welfare effect of an adjustment to the budget surplus. Moreover, since the mode of adjustment is unspecified, it suggests that, whatever method – lump-sum transfer (L) or commodity taxation (R) – is used to balance the budget, relative shadow prices are adequately represented by relative compensated shadow prices (π^*), the marginal social cost of public revenue (π_Z) being a scalar that cancels out. Sieper, in fact, makes precisely this argument: a budget surplus arising from a slight expansion in the net supply of the kth commodity produced by the public sector will result in the same adjustment to fiscal policy (and hence the same effect on welfare) as the budget surplus arising from a slight expansion in the net supply of the ith commodity produced by the public sector. In a sense, the budget surplus can be thought of as a pool into which the net profits of many projects flow. Once in the pool, funds become indistinguishable. Every so often, the conventions of accounting require that the "pool" be balanced. Regardless of the method or methods of achieving balance, it will be impossible to derive a link between the net profits of any project, or between any shadow price, and the equilibriating mechanism(s) provided all funds are indeed indistinguishable. In this case, relative shadow prices are independent of the budget-balancing procedures. Alternatively, if the method of budget balancing is unique, then, whether or not funds are indistinguishable, the welfare effect of closing the budget is the same for all shadow prices and can, once again, be ignored. Thus, it appears that whatever the method of budget closure – lump-sum transfers or distortionary taxation – relative shadow prices remain immune.

Although fundamentally correct, this argument must be qualified in two respects precisely because funds from different projects may not be indistinguishable and the budget-balancing mechanism may not be unique. The most obvious cause of such a situation is the passage of time. Since most accounts are closed annually, it should be possible to identify flows of net profits from projects by accounting period. Also, one might expect the equilibriating mechanism to change through time. In particular, as administrative capacity improves, one would expect the shadow cost of raising revenue to decline. Thus, while shadow prices and the selection of projects could well be considered independent of this year's shadow cost of public revenue, they would depend on the change in this shadow cost through time since the time profile of net benefits will differ among projects.[30]

The second qualification is similar but arises within an accounting period. Some sectors and even some projects are required to maintain balanced budgets. For example, road projects are often financed by an earmarked fuel tax such that the sector is financially self-sufficient. Similarly, individual agricultural projects

---

[30] In Section 4 it is shown that his difficulty is handled through the choice of discount rate.

can be self-financing through special cesses. In these cases the social cost of public revenue is sector or project specific and may well differ from the economy-wide cost of raising revenue. This, however, is probably not a very serious problem since one needs only to know that the net profits at shadow prices of a project are positive. Only in the event that the selection involves mutually exclusive projects and those projects have different project-specific or sector-specific social costs of revenue would it be necessary to treat explicitly the welfare effects associated with the different methods of raising revenue in the calculation of shadow prices.

Apart from these two qualifications, it appears that Sieper's observation is correct. π_Z is a scalar in equation (10); it can be cancelled out and compensated shadow prices are a perfectly adequate basis on which to select projects. It does not necessarily follow, however, that project evaluation is *independent* of the marginal social cost of public revenue. If lump-sum transfers are not available, the compensated shadow price (π^*) may be dependent on the marginal social cost of public revenue (π_Z). Recall that π_k^* measures the effect of an increase in the supply of the kth commodity with private welfare held constant. It follows that, if the increased supply of the kth commodity affects private welfare *directly*, some adjustment must be made to restore private welfare to its original level. In the derivation of equation (19) this was achieved by a lump-sum transfer. If such transfers are not available, the compensated shadow price may have to be adjusted to allow for the additional costs implicit in the use of distortionary taxation. This does indeed turn out to be the case.

To explore this issue further, one must examine the adjustment to equation (19) required to capture the possibility that budget balancing may be by means of distortionary taxation (R) rather than lump-sum transfers (L). The intuition of this step may be explained as follows. Recall that equation (19) is derived on the assumption that any change in private welfare is offset by lump-sum transfers. It is necessary, therefore, to calculate the change in welfare that is offset by these transfers and then calculate the net cost to the budget if this change in welfare is offset by distortionary taxation rather than lump-sum transfers.

From equation (13) we know that the lump-sum transfer required to keep private welfare constant equals the change in profit $(\partial p/\partial x\, x)$ of public sector production arising from changes in the prices of nontradables and primary factors. A lump-sum transfer of one unit, however, does not result in a unit increase in private welfare because, as that unit is spent, the prices of publicly produced nontradables and primary factors increase further. Assume, therefore, that a unit increase in private welfare is achieved by means of a lump-sum transfer of $1 + \gamma$.[31] The lump-sum transfers underlying equation (19), therefore, are associated with a change in private welfare of $\partial p/\partial x\, x$ deflated by $(1 + \gamma)$.

---

[31] Sieper shows that $\gamma = \sum_{i \in H} x_i \beta_i$, where $\beta_i = -\sum_{j \in H} \delta_{ij} \partial c_i/\partial E$ and is the change in the price of the ith commodity per unit increase in real private spending. Note that δ_{ij} is the inverse of the net demand/supply substitution matrix defined by equation (18).

Having calculated the change in private welfare, it remains to calculate the cost to the budget if this change in private welfare is offset by distortionary taxation rather than lump-sum transfers. Let π_L measure the marginal welfare cost of increasing the budget surplus by lump-sum transfers, so that $1/\pi_L$ measures the effect on the budget of reducing private welfare by one unit by this means. Similarly, if the fiscal compensation is achieved by distortionary taxation, the effect on the budget can be expressed analogously as $1/\pi_R$, where π_R is the marginal social cost of increasing revenue by means of distortionary taxation. It follows that the net budgetary cost per unit of private welfare resulting from a switch from lump-sum transfers to distortionary taxation is given by $\alpha = (1/\pi_L - 1/\pi_R)$. Because π_R generates distortions, whereas π_L does not, $1/\pi_R < 1/\pi_L$ so that the effect on the budget is smaller per unit of private welfare when distortionary taxation is used rather than lump-sum transfers (that is, $\alpha > 0$).[32]

Recalling that changes in prices will occur only if the commodity being shadow priced is a nontradable or factor of production, substitution of the above results in equation (19) yields:

$$\pi_k^* = r_k, \qquad\qquad\qquad\qquad k \in T,$$

$$\pi_k^* = p_k + \frac{\partial R(x, W)}{\partial x_k} + \frac{\alpha}{(1 + \gamma)} \Sigma x_i \frac{\partial p_i}{\partial x_k}, \quad k \in H. \qquad (20)$$

Compared with the simple, partial equilibrium results of equation (16), equation (20) reveals two differences. First, the presence of distortions in other affected markets is captured through the second term $(\partial R(x, W)/\partial x_k)$. Second, the likelihood that budget balancing is by means other than lump-sum transfers is captured by the third term of equation (20). This term disappears if indeed lump-sum transfers are the mechanisms actually used.[33] Finally, note that these adjustments occur only in the shadow prices for nontradables and factors of production; *the shadow prices for tradables remain equal to border prices.* While the possible importance of the second term has long been recognized by practitioners,[34] the third term is rarely treated in practice. This term becomes more important as the change in private sector welfare increases and as the distortionary cost of taxation increases. If the increase in private welfare is positive,

[32]Although Sieper does not express the adjustment factor in this manner – and hence its dependence on π_L and π_R remains obscure – he does provide explicit expressions for π_L and π_R. See his Propositions 8 and 17.

[33]Boadway (1975b) shows that, even if lump-sum transfers are unavailable, shadow prices should equal producer prices provided the government can set every tax optimally. This is the famous Diamond–Mirrlees result. See Diamond and Mirrlees (1971).

[34]cf. Harberger's exhortation that the change in welfare following a policy change be measured by the sum of all induced changes multiplied by the degree of distortion (tax or subsidy) in each market [Harberger (1971a)].

then omission of the third term results in an overestimation of the true shadow price. The practical consequences of this are examined in Section 5.

Sieper's decomposition, therefore, does not demonstrate that project evaluation is independent of the marginal social cost of public revenue. Nevertheless, it does clarify the manner in which this shadow price enters cost–benefit analysis. Consider the following three examples. First, imagine a project that uses non-taxed, tradable inputs and produces nontaxed, tradable outputs so that its entire net profit at market prices accrues directly to the budget. Assume, furthermore, that this project shows a profit at market prices which results in a fiscal surplus. As long as the eventual distribution of this surplus to the private sector results in an increase in welfare, the precise mechanism – lump-sum transfers or reductions in taxation – is irrelevant to the accept/reject decision for the project. All that one needs to know is that the project's impact on the budget is positive. The shadow price of public revenue, therefore, is not required in this case even though the project disturbs the fiscal equilibrium. This is the point of Sieper's decomposition.

The preceding example is straightforward. Most analysts, however, have been concerned with the situation in which a project that is marginally acceptable at shadow prices shows a loss at market prices. Corden, for example, argues that the method used to finance such a loss may "create by-product distortions that must be taken into account" [Corden (1974, p. 391)]. For the second example, therefore, imagine a project that uses one, untaxed, tradable input and produces one, taxed, tradable output. Assume further that the project is just profitable at shadow prices so that, by assumption, it shows a loss at market prices. In this case, however, the difference between shadow profits and market profits is offset exactly in the government's accounts by the increased tax revenue resulting from the difference between the shadow price and market price of the output. This point, first elaborated by Warr (1977), can also be deduced from Sieper's analysis since the compensated shadow prices for tradables equal border prices even if lump-sum transfers are not available.

In the above examples the entire impact of the project falls directly on the budget. The third example is quite different in that the project affects private welfare directly. Imagine a public sector project that produces an untaxed tradable with the use of labor hired at a fixed wage. Assume further that at this wage the labor market fails to clear and that, in particular, the labor used in the project is drawn from an unemployed pool. Finally, assume that the project has no direct effect on the budget and that expenditure out of wage income is entirely on untaxed, tradable goods so that there are no indirect effects on the budget. This project is clearly very profitable to the economy in that the budget has not changed and yet private consumption (welfare) has increased significantly. How is this reflected in cost–benefit analysis? The answer is that one needs a price to convert private welfare into units of public income. This is, of course, accomplished by application of the shadow price of public revenue [see equation (9)]. Thus, even though the fiscal equilibrium of the economy has not been affected, the shadow price for public funds is still required.[35] Thus, in Sieper's model, when lump-sum transfers are not feasible, the marginal social cost of raising revenue does enter the compensated shadow price for nontradables and primary factors because changes in the net supplies of these items lead to immediate changes in private welfare.[36]

The significance of the above analysis, therefore, is that it directs attention away from an unnecessary focus on the project's fiscal impact per se – a project can lead to a fiscal surplus or deficit and yet not require an estimate of the shadow price of public revenue in its evaluation even if lump-sum transfers are not available. Instead, attention is directed towards the project's immediate effect on private welfare. Since the availability of lump-sum transfers is not a reasonable expectation, the extent to which shadow-pricing procedures are influenced by the method used to adjust the budget depends in practice on the extent to which a change in the supply of the kth commodity affects private welfare. Several alternative examples are examined in Sections 4 and 5.

4. Shadow pricing: Market-specific results

Equation (20) is used in this section to review several results in the literature concerning the derivation of shadow pricing in the context of specific market structures. As noted in the Introduction, the literature on this topic is extensive and no attempt will be made to be comprehensive. Where possible, however, additional references are provided for the reader. In addition, the significance of several complications – especially nonclearing markets – to the simple model of Section 3 are also explored.

4.1. Tradables

Equation (20) confirms the validity of the border price rule in a tax-distorted, open economy. The use of border prices in project selection owes much to the influence of Little and Mirrlees. Most subsequent writers reproduce this result in

---

[35] This particular example and the role of the shadow price of public revenue in the definition of the shadow wage rate is discussed further in Section 4 in the context of a model analysed by Bell and Devarajan (1983).

[36] This is also a feature of the Little–Mirrlees approach in which projects are evaluated in terms of their impact on public income. If private income is affected, some "price" must be used to arrive at its value in terms of public income.

models of varying degrees of complexity.[37] A major exception is the analysis of Blitzer, Dasgupta and Stiglitz (1981). This is especially surprising because they examine an economy comprising only two tradables, a project being defined as a marginal change in the net supply of both commodities. It is, therefore, worth examining in more detail. If commodity taxation is the equilibrating device, the authors claim that the ratio of shadow prices for the two tradables "lies between the international price ratio and the domestic producer price ratio" [Blitzer, Dasgupta and Stiglitz (1981, p. 67)]. In a variation of the same model, foreign borrowing is used as the equilibrating device. In this case the authors conclude that the ratio of shadow prices for tradables equals the ratio of their international prices if "the government has optimised its level of borrowing" [Blitzer, Dasgupta and Stiglitz (1981, p. 68)].

Both of these results conflict with the general conclusion of the previous section where it was argued that relative shadow prices for tradables equal relative border prices regardless of the method used to increase the net budget surplus. To explore this further, the Sieper decomposition is used to derive shadow prices for the simple model considered by Blitzer, Dasgupta and Stiglitz. Recall that the compensated price for the kth commodity equals the effect on the budget surplus $(\mathrm{d}Z/\mathrm{d}x_k)$ computed at a constant level of welfare [see equation (10)]. The budget surplus for this particular model equals that defined by equation (6) with the exception that lump-sum transfers are not available $(L = 0)$. It follows that $\mathrm{d}Z = \mathrm{d}R + p \cdot \mathrm{d}x$; that is, the change in the budget surplus is the sum of the change in net revenue and the change in public sector profits.

If the commodities involved in the project (the $\mathrm{d}x$) are indeed tradable, changes in their net supply can be accommodated by changes in imports and exports. From the definition of net revenue, this implies that $\mathrm{d}R = -s \cdot \mathrm{d}x$, where s is the difference between producer prices and border prices for the project's net outputs. Moreover, since this will have no effect on domestic prices, on private consumption or on private production, private welfare remains unchanged. Hence, $\pi_k^* = p_k - s_k = r_k$, thus confirming that compensated shadow prices do indeed equal border prices and that, therefore, the ratio of full shadow prices equals the ratio of border prices. Shadow prices of tradables are independent of the method of macroeconomic adjustment whether it be accomplished by means of a change in tariff policy or a change in foreign borrowing.

How do Blitzer, Dasgupta and Stiglitz arrive at their results? They calculate the change in *total welfare* when private income is increased by $p \cdot \mathrm{d}x$ – that is, by the net profit at market prices of the public sector project – and the government restores equilibrium by means of a tariff change or by resorting to foreign

---

[37]See, for example, Bell and Devarajan (1983), Warr (1979), Boadway (1975a), Dasgupta and Stiglitz (1974), and Drèze and Stern (1987).

borrowing [see their equations (9) and (17)]. Their procedure is open to two interpretations. One possibility is that the project is located in the private sector. In this case, the net profits at market prices from the project do indeed accrue immediately to the private sector. The change in welfare associated with such a project and the implied need to restore equilibrium may be an interesting number of calculate for some purposes – when granting an investment license, for example – but it does not shed light on the appropriate shadow prices for public sector projects. The second possibility is that the project is located in the public sector, the resulting profits at market prices are distributed to the private sector by means of lump-sum transfers and a change in tariffs or foreign borrowing is then used to restore equilibrium. Under this interpretation, they calculate, first, the effect of the project on the budget and, second, the effect on welfare of distributing the project's net profits to the private sector while simultaneously maintaining fiscal equilibrium. As long as the second effect is positive, one only needs to calculate the first effect to decide whether or not to proceed with the project.

Lump-sum transfers, tariff changes and foreign borrowing are only relevant for calculating the shadow price of public finance. Note, however, that only one instrument is, in general, required to balance the budget, whereas the Blitzer–Dasgupta–Stiglitz example uses two. This occurs because the distribution of lump-sum transfers equal to the project's net benefits at market prices ($p \cdot dx$) will balance the budget only if the project's inputs and outputs are not taxed and if consumer expenditure out of the lump-sum transfer is on untaxed items. Since this is not the case in the Blitzer–Dasgupta–Stiglitz example, a second fiscal instrument – a tariff change or foreign borrowing – is required. Obviously, however, there is some level of transfer which would obviate the need for a second instrument.[38]

While the border price rule clearly survives the case in which lump-sum transfers are not available there are two instances where the rule does break down [Bhagwati and Srinivasan (1981)]. The first arises when trade is quota-restricted and the second when the border price depends on the quantity traded. Both of these cases can result in changes in domestic prices so that the basic conclusion of equation (18) no longer holds: that is, domestic price changes will occur that will have ramifications elsewhere in the economy and will require explicit treatment of effects in other markets and changes in private welfare [cf. the second and third terms in equation (20)].

Although the project evaluator cannot assume that other policies will be adjusted to accommodate his project, it is worth noting that compensating policy changes can resurrect the border price rule even in the presence of quotas and

---

[38] If this procedure were followed, the shadow prices are those defined by equation (19), i.e. with the lump-sum transfer.

monopoly power in trade. For example, if the quota is chosen optimally to offset some externality or if, in the case of monopoly power, an optimal tariff is applied, the rule still holds. Alternatively, if adjustments are made to the quota or tariff such that domestic prices remain unchanged, then again the rule is valid.[39] In practice, optimality of other policies or appropriate compensating adjustments should not be assumed too readily. The presence of quotas and the existence of monopoly power can be expected, therefore, to limit the applicability of the border price rule.

4.2. Nontradables and labor

Equation (20) demonstrates that relative shadow prices for tradables equal relative border prices. This is, of course, the most fundamental element of the Little–Mirrlees approach to shadow pricing. Does the equivalence between compensated shadow prices and Little–Mirrlees shadow prices extend to non-tradables and labor?

Under certain circumstances it is possible to derive very simple rules for shadow pricing nontradables and primary factors within the traditional tariff-distorted, constant-returns-to-scale, general equilibrium model of trade theory. In particular, if the number of primary factors equals the number of tradables, then *all* domestic prices are determined by the initial input–output structure and (fixed) border prices.[40] This can be readily seen as follows. First note that the domestic prices of tradables are determined by border prices and tariffs. This leaves the domestic prices of nontradables and factors. To determine these prices, note that if production is subject to constant returns to scale, then the costs of production equal domestic prices for each produced good. That is, one can write equations such as:

$$p_j = \sum_i p_i a_{ij} + \sum_k p_k l_{kj}, \tag{21}$$

where p denotes domestic prices, and a_{ij} and l_{kj} are the average input of good i and primary factor k needed to produce a unit of good j. Since there is one such equation for each produced good (tradable and nontradable) and since the p_j for tradables have already been determined, then if the number of tradables equals the number of primary factors, equation (21) provides enough relationships to

---

[39] The basic reference for these issues is Bhagwati and Srinivasan (1981). Drèze and Stern (1987) provide a general model that incorporates both policy reform and project selection and allows an exploration of the particular issue addressed here.

[40] Models along these lines are explored in Findlay and Wellisz (1976), Bhagwati and Srinivasan (1981), Srinivasan and Bhagwati (1978) and Bhagwati and Wan (1979).

solve for all prices of nontradables and primary factors in terms of initial technical coefficients and the prices of tradables.

The significance of this result – that all domestic prices are determined by technical factors and world prices – can be seen from equation (17). If domestic prices are fixed, the terms ϕ_c and ϕ_p capturing indirect effects on government revenue are zero. It follows from equation (20) that shadow prices are given by:

$$\pi_k^* = p_k - s_k, \tag{22}$$

that is, by the sum of the producer price and the direct effect on the government budget.

Apart from providing a general equilibrium justification for the "partial equilibrium" shadow prices described by equation (16), this result provides a rationale for the Little–Mirrlees recommendations concerning the shadow pricing of nontradables and primary factors. Consider primary factors first. Little and Mirrlees recommend that the shadow price of, say, labor be equated with its forgone marginal product valued at shadow prices.[41] The solution to equation (21) yields the result that the market wage equals labor's forgone marginal product at market prices.[42] The purpose of equation (21), in fact, is to identify the sectors from which labor is withdrawn. Thus, p_k in equation (22) equals labor's marginal product at market prices. But, if labor is withdrawn from a sector that is subject to a tariff on its output, government revenue is also affected. This is captured in the term s_k in equation (22). It is the sum of the net subsidies to all commodities whose output is reduced as a result of the withdrawal of one unit of labor.[43] Adding the net subsidies to labor's marginal product at market prices yields labor's marginal product at border prices as recommended by Little and Mirrlees.

The same result applies even if labor is withdrawn from a nontradable sector. By essentially the same argument, π_k^* in equation (22) equals the cost of production at market prices [see equation (21)] and s_k equals the sum of all net tax revenue on inputs.[44] Adding the former to the latter yields the cost of production at shadow prices. This is the well-known Little–Mirrlees recommen-

---

[41] This assumes that the labor market clears. The consequences of a nonclearing labor market are discussed below.

[42] See, for example, Srinivasan and Bhagwati (1978).

[43] This may be regarded as an indirect rather than direct effect on the government budget. The relevant point in eliminating the indirect effects denoted by ϕ_c and ϕ_p in equation (17), however, is that they involve price changes. The term s_k does not.

[44] Labor may, of course, be one of the inputs. In this event, the equations for labor and nontradables have to be solved jointly. This procedure is described in Bell and Devarajan (1980). For examples of the approach, see Powers (1981), Schohl (1979), Sott, MacArthur and Newberry (1976) and the case studies in Little and Scott (1976).

dation to decompose nontradables into their constituent inputs and value each input at its relevant shadow price.

As pointed out by Bertrand (1979), these simple results for nontradables and primary factors depend crucially on the assumption that the number of tradables equals the number of primary factors. This condition is essential since it ensures that all domestic prices are fixed. In general, however, Bertrand shows that increased demand for a nontradable or primary factor can be expected to result in price changes in which case induced effects on production and consumption must be treated explicitly and one is back to equation (20). Since it is unlikely that primary factors and tradables are of equal number, the simple results derived above should be regarded as the product of partial equilibrium analysis [see equation (16)] rather than that of a (very special) general equilibrium.

Before leaving this class of models, one other result can be demonstrated. Bell and Devarajan (1983) introduce a labor market distortion that results in an increase in private sector income in response to increased demand for labor. The significance of this distortion is that it is not the result of a tax subsidy. If the private sector supplies a commodity to a public sector project and that commodity is taxed, the market is distorted but the transaction does not result in an increase in private sector income. If, however, the private sector supplies labor to a public sector project that pays wages above the going rate, again the market is distorted but, in this instance, hiring one more laborer results in an increase in private sector income. As a result, at least in the specification used by Bell and Devarajan, the public sector's failure to pay a wage that clears the market results in an income transfer to the private sector. This suggests that the shadow prices for nontradables and factors of production calculated by Bell and Devarajan should incorporate the shadow price of public finance in the adjustment term of equation (20).[45]

The Bell–Devarajan model includes an input–output structure, two tradables, a nontradable and labor. To illustrate the link between the shadow pricing rules developed in Section 3 and the Little–Mirrlees shadow wage rate, the nontradable is excluded. As expected, the shadow wage for the Bell–Devarajan model is given by:

$$w^* = m + \alpha\,\Delta w, \tag{23}$$

where m is labor's forgone marginal product measured at border prices and Δw is the difference between the wage paid by the project and the going wage in the source sector.[46]

---

[45] Drèze and Stern (1987) examine the failure of markets to clear in a more general model.

[46] See equation (25) in Bell and Devarajan (1983). Note that, since there are no price changes, the deflator, $(1 + \gamma)$, is not required; see equation (20) above.

As before, $\alpha = (1/\pi_L - 1/\pi_Z)$, where π_L^* is the shadow price of public revenue when lump-sum transfers are available and π_Z is the shadow price when some other means of generating revenue is used. Since $1/\pi_L$ can be interpreted as the effect on the budget of reducing private welfare by one unit, it can be equated with the consumption conversion factor of the Little–Mirrlees approach. This is shown very clearly in the Bell–Devarajan result where $(1/\pi_L)$ equals a weighted sum of the ratios of border prices to market prices, the weights being the marginal consumption shares out of project-induced additional expenditure.[47] Furthermore, the actual means of generating revenue in the Bell–Devarajan model is through foreign borrowing so that π_Z measures the welfare value of uncommitted foreign exchange in the hands of the public sector relative to the welfare value of private sector income and is, therefore, equivalent to the famous, Little–Mirrlees $\underline{s}$ factor. Accordingly, $\alpha = (CFF - 1/s)$ which, upon substitution into equation (23), yields a common version of the Little–Mirrlees shadow wage rate.[48]

The Bell–Devarajan derivation illustrates an additional point concerning the method of revenue generation. In addition to foreign borrowing, they examine the case in which revenue is generated by means of a change in tariff rates. Although this results in a change in market prices, the formula for the compensated shadow wage rate remains unchanged.[49] The shadow price of public finance used in the formula, however, will be different. In calculating this price, all the consequences of changed tariff rates must be incorporated.[50] This demonstrates the basic point that, while the manner in which the shadow price of public finance enters other shadow pricing formulae does not depend on the way in which revenue is actually generated [that is, their shadow wage rate still takes the general form show in equation (23)], the price itself is dependent on the method of generation. A further interpretation of this price is provided below in the section on foreign exchange and the shadow exchange rate.

Labor market distortions have played an important role in the literature on shadow pricing. Much of the work has used Lewis's notion of the dual economy [Lewis (1954)]. The Bell–Devarajan model illustrates the various elements usually studied but is a relatively simple version. Intertemporal versions are available that focus on the consequences of employment-induced increases in consumption that detract from the national savings effort.[51] Static versions are available which elaborate the process of intersectoral migration.[52] Empirical studies include Seton (1972), Scott (1976) and Scott, MacArthur and Newbery (1976).

---

[47]Again, see equation (25) in Bell and Devarajan. Recall that the nontradable is omitted.
[48]See Squire and van der Tak (1975, p. 84).
[49]See their equations (25) and (36).
[50]Their derivation is shown on p. 474.
[51]Among others, see Newbery (1972), Stern (1972b) and Lal and Squire (1980).
[52]See, for example, Harberger (1971b), Lal (1973) and Mazumdar (1976).

4.3. Foreign exchange

The literature on shadow wage rates is matched in volume by the literature on shadow exchange rates. Two broad strands may be identified. The first investigates the change in welfare resulting from an increase in the net supply of foreign exchange. This is a legitimate interpretation of the shadow exchange rate and corresponds exactly to the general definition of any shadow price. The second involves an averaging concept. That is, the "shadow exchange rate" can be thought of as some average of the ratios of shadow prices to market prices for a collection of nontradables. These concepts are quite different in principle but can overlap significantly in practice.

Consider the first approach. What is the effect on welfare of an additional unit of foreign exchange obtained by borrowing abroad? Recall that in the discussion of shadow wage rates, the shadow price of public finance was equated with the welfare value of foreign borrowing. Several authors – see, for example, Sieper (1981), Bell and Devarajan (1983), Warr (1977) and Bhagwati and Srinivasan (1981) – have, in fact, made this identification of the shadow exchange rate with the shadow price of public finance. This conclusion essentially reflects the observation that, if the private sector budget constraint is met, then achievement of balance-of-payments equilibrium implies fiscal equilibrium and vice versa. It follows that, if this interpretation is correct, the shadow exchange rate appears as a scalar in the derivation of full shadow prices [see equation (10)] and as an important element in compensated shadow prices whenever there is a change in private welfare [see equation (20)].

It follows from the above discussion that the shadow price of public revenue derived from the model of Section 3 should correspond to the standard formulae for shadow exchange rates available in the literature. These formulae usually take the form of a weighted sum of tariffs, the weights being marginal propensities to import or export.[53] Although the derivation is not presented here, Sieper shows that such formulae are correct if lump-sum transfers are available, if tradables are subject to trade tariffs only, and if the markets for nontradables and primary factors are either undistorted or else unaffected by the acquisition of an additional unit of foreign exchange.[54] These qualifications reflect the emphasis in most discussions of shadow exchange rates on distortions that affect international trade directly.

The alternative procedure of interpreting the shadow exchange rate (or standard conversion factor as it is known) as a weighted average of the ratios of shadow prices to market prices for a bundle of nontradables raises no new conceptual issues. The only issue here is that of accuracy in practice. If such a

---

[53]See, for example, Bacha and Taylor (1971), Balassa (1974) and Bertrand (1974).
[54]See Sieper (1981, pp. 37–38). Also see Boadway (1978).

weighted average is calculated for some "typical" collection of nontradables and then applied in several different projects, it is unlikely that the weights used in the average will correspond to the weights implicit in each of the projects. Some studies have indicated a rather narrow, unimodal distribution for individual conversion factors which suggests that, in practice, averaging may not be seriously misleading.[55]

As noted above, the overlap between these two concepts can be substantial in practice. One instance has already been discussed: the case of the consumption conversion factor. On the one hand, it can be viewed as the weighted average of shadow prices to market prices for consumption goods. At the same time, it can be viewed as the inverse of the shadow price of public finance when lump-sum transfers are the means of generating revenue. In both cases, the weights are the marginal propensities to consume out of additional income. While the equivalence is exact in this case, in general it would be inappropriate to equate standard conversion factors with the shadow price of public finance (that is, the shadow price of foreign exchange).

4.4. Discount rates

Since projects usually last for several years, some method of aggregating net benefits accruing in different periods is required. If net benefits in each period are expressed in terms of the value, in that period, of a common numeraire, then net benefits can be expressed in terms of the numeraire in a given period by allowing for changes in the value of the numeraire between periods. If the present period is chosen, then the discount rate depends on the rate of change in the numeraire through time. Although there is no reason to presume that this rate of change will remain the same from period to period, the discount rate for project selection has usually been assumed to remain constant throughout the life of the project.

The choice of numeraire is, of course, a matter of indifference as far as the evaluation of projects is concerned. Different authors have at various times recommended different numeraires on grounds of ease of implementation. UNIDO, for example, uses consumption as numeraire, whereas Little and Mirrlees prefer public income. The relationship between these alternatives can be explored by examining the change through time in the shadow price of public income. Recall that in Section 3 it was argued that changes in this shadow price – due possibly to improved tax administration – had to be incorporated in the shadow pricing rules. From the discussion of equation (10), the shadow price of public finance is:

$$\pi_Z = - \left. \frac{\partial W}{\partial Z} \right/ \lambda , \qquad (24)$$

[55]See, for example, Scott (1974).

where λ is the welfare value of private sector consumption. Taking the differential of equation (24) with respect to time yields:

$$-\dot{\pi}_Z/\pi_Z = ARI - CRI,$$

that is, the rate of fall in the shadow price of public income equals the difference between the accounting rate of interest (ARI) and the consumption rate of interest (CRI).

If, as in UNIDO, consumption is chosen as the numeraire, then the appropriate discount rate is the CRI and public income in each period must be expressed in units of consumption by application of the shadow price of public revenue (π_Z) relevant to that period. Alternatively, if, as in Little and Mirrlees, public income is chosen as numeraire, the relevant discount rate is the ARI and consumption is translated into public income by multiplying by $1/\pi_Z$. Either way, the information content is the same. Unfortunately, however, efforts to estimate these discount rates have invariably faced severe difficulties arising from data deficiencies.[56]

5. Implementing project evaluation

Insufficient skilled manpower, inadequate data and lack of time are common features of investment planning in developing countries. The resources engaged in the selection of investment projects must, like any other resource, be used as efficiently as possible. This is interpreted to mean that procedures for project evaluation be designed such that a given input on the part of the evaluator results in the greatest benefit possible. That is, it is much more important to use a unit of "evaluation resources" to avoid a large mistake then to fine tune the appraisal of a marginal project. If a project will a small negative net present value is mistakenly accepted, the cost to society is small. On the other hand, if a project with a large positive net present value is rejected, or if a project with a large negative net present value is accepted, the costs to society are substantial.

The above argument is an application of the rule for choosing among mutually exclusive projects. In this case, however, mutual exclusivity arises from the fact that the resources available for evaluating projects are limited – use of these resources on one project precludes their use on another one. It follows that one wants some means of anticipating where additional refinements are likely to have a big payoff. That is, one wants to identify situations where the product of the difference between a shadow price and a market price and the size of an input or

---

[56] For an approach to the estimation of the CRI, see Scott (1977). Efforts to estimate the ARI are usually based on the observed returns at shadow prices to public sector investment. See, for example, Squire, Little and Durdag (1979). Others, such as, Scott, MacArthur and Newberry (1976) equate the ARI with the cost of foreign borrowing.

output is a "large number". In this context, the number should be expressed in net present values and "large" should be interpreted in the light of the scarcity of evaluation resources. Can one identify such situations? The procedure adopted here is, first, to compare existing practice in selected developing countries and international institutions with the theoretical results of Sections 3 and 4 to establish the areas in which improvement may yield the greatest benefit. Second, an attempt is made to identify types of projects where, once again, improvement in appraisal methods may yield a substantial gain. This notion is explored for three types of projects – an "industrial" project, an "infrastructural" project and a "utility" project – each of which has different, shadow-pricing requirements.

5.1. Current practice

To what extent are countries or international agencies presently undertaking project evaluation on a routine basis? According to information obtained from the staff of the World Bank, most countries have an office or offices charged with the evaluation of projects. This was the case in all but three of the 27 countries surveyed.[57] All the major international agencies and the larger bilateral lenders also undertake some form of project evaluation.

Certain features are common to the techniques employed by these countries and agencies. First, the effects of a project on the distribution of income are not included in the formal analysis. That is, all those engaged in the practice of project evaluation have chosen to examine project-induced changes in the distribution of income qualitatively, if at all. Second, the same point applies to the third term of equation (20). Neither the international agencies nor individual countries allow for the costs associated with efforts to generate government resources through means other than lump-sum transfers. The effect of this on project selection is examined below. And third, no attempt is made to incorporate indirect effects on the budget arising from changes in the prices of nontradables and primary factors. That is, the terms ϕ_c and ϕ_p in equation (15) are neglected. In the main, therefore, practitioners are, at best, operating with the partial equilibrium rules of equation (16).

Apart from these basic similarities, the approach to project evaluation differs significantly among practitioners. At one extreme, a group of countries including Cyprus, Dominican Republic, Guatemala, Nigeria, Senegal, Somalia and Zimbabwe do not discount net benefits or do not use border prices for tradables or do neither. For several other countries, information was not available concerning

---

[57]The countries included in the survey are Brazil, China, Cyprus, Dominican Republic, Ethiopia, Fiji, Guatemala, Indonesia, India, Ivory Coast, Korea, Malaysia, Malawi, Nigeria, Oman, Pakistan, Papua New Guinea, Peru, Philippines, Senegal, Sierra Leone, Sri lanka, Somalia, Thailand, Yugoslavia, Zambia, and Zimbabwe.

their use of discounting procedures and border prices. There is, therefore, a substantial number of countries which fail to meet even minimally acceptable standards of evaluation.

At the other extreme, countries such as Ethiopia, Ivory Coast, Korea, Pakistan, Philippines, Sierra Leone, Thailand and Yugoslavia discount net benefits, use border prices more or less regularly and, where necessary, use other shadow prices especially for labor. This characterization also applies to the international agencies. The World Bank, for example, has estimated shadow prices for non-tradables using the Little–Mirrlees decomposition technique for several countries and has also estimated shadow wage rates in selected cases. Procedures in the World Bank, therefore, are broadly consistent with the class of models in which the number of tradables equals the number of primary factors (see Section 4).

5.2. Project types

The discussion reveals clearly that practice departs significantly from the recommendations emerging from theory. Are these failures to apply theory resulting in serious misallocations of resources? To approach this question, we examine three different types of projects – industrial projects, infrastructural projects, utility projects – that rely on tradables and that effect private welfare to different degrees. This allows at least some assessment of the cost implied by the failure to use border prices for tradables and that implied by the neglect of the distortionary costs of taxation.

Industrial projects are characterized by relatively minor interactions with the private sector. All production is within the public sector and the main outputs and inputs are tradable. Purchases of nontradable inputs and factors of production represent the only interaction with the private sector and these may be relatively small. Table 21.1 presents the cost and benefit structure of a typical industrial project. The data are, in fact, from an actual project supported by the World Bank. The entries in column 1 show the net present value at market prices of each input or output expressed as a percentage of the net present value of total benefits at market prices, and reveal that tradables do indeed dominate both the benefit stream and the cost stream. Labor, for example, accounts for only 5 percent of the net present value of benefits. On the other hand, coal, a tradable output, accounts for 100 percent of the net present value of benefits. Moreover, in this particular case, the price of the output is highly distorted (see column 2 of table). It is much more important, therefore, to focus on this item than to worry about fine tuning the shadow wage rate. Column 3 shows that the effort to shadow price coal increased the net present value of the project by 116 percent. In fact, the project has a negative net present value without this adjustment. For the other items, efforts to shadow price have only a small impact.

Table 21.1
Structure of an industrial project

Item	Costs and benefits at market prices[a] (%)	Distortion[b]	Costs and benefits at shadow prices[c] (%)
Capital costs			
Foreign component	39	1.0	39
Local construction	21	1.1	22
Local equipment	9	1.3	12
Land	1	1.0	1
Other	4	1.0	4
Operating costs			
Administration	2	1.0	2
Wages	5	1.2	6
Electricity	5	1.5	8
Maintenance	9	1.3	12
Materials	14	1.3	19
Total costs	108		
Benefits			
Coal	100		216

[a] The entries show costs and benefits expressed as a percentage of the net present value of total benefits at market prices. All items are discounted to the present by application of an interest rate of 10 percent.
[b] The items in this column are the ratios of shadow price to market price.
[c] As a percentage of the net present value of total project benefits at market prices.

The example shown in Table 21.1 may be extreme but it does, nevertheless, indicate the general characteristic of industrial projects. Thus, although indirect effects on revenue and adjustments for alternative means of raising revenue are not incorporated in the formal analysis undertaken by the World Bank, this may not lead to serious errors and the use of simple shadow pricing rules is probably acceptable and efficient at least in the case of industrial projects.[58] The evidence of Table 21.1 also suggests that the failure to treat explicitly the effect of projects on income distribution is probably also of minor consequence in the case of industrial projects.

Infrastructural projects have quite different characteristics from industrial projects. For these projects the costs are borne by the public sector but the benefits accrue directly to the private sector. Examples of such projects are roads, irrigation facilities and basic research. The cost and benefit structure (again expressed in ratios of the net present value of total benefits) of a typical infrastructural project is displayed in Table 21.2. In this project the World Bank

---

[58] This point was also recognized in the original version of Little and Mirrlees (1969).

Table 21.2
Structure of an infrastructural project

Item	Costs and benefits at market prices (%)[a]	Distortion[b]	Costs and benefits at shadow prices (%)[c]
Public costs			
Capital costs	5	0.8	4
Operating costs	10	0.7	7
Private costs			
Fertilizer	11	1.0	11
Farm equipment	1	0.8	1
Farm labor	24	0.9	22
Total costs	51		46
Private benefits			
Sorghum	18	0.5	9
Maize	34	0.5	18
Rice	11	0.3	3
Cowpeas	1	0.5	–
Groundnuts	7	0.7	5
Rootcrops	2	0.4	1
Cotton	3	1.1	4
Vegetables	23	0.4	9
Total benefits	100		50

[a] The entries show costs and benefits expressed as a percentage of the net present value of total benefits at market prices. All items are discounted to the present by application of an interest rate of 10 percent.

[b] The items in this column are the ratios of shadow price to market price.

[c] As a percentage of the net present value of total project benefits at market prices.

provided a loan to finance agricultural input distribution, research, seed multiplication, extension services, feeder roads, dams and civil works. These "infrastructural" improvements are expected to lead to increased output of several crops (see Table 21.2) all of which are produced by private operators. The transfer to the private sector in this case, therefore, does not occur through a factor payment, which may be small in relation to total costs, but through the provision of infrastructure at zero cost to the private sector. In some projects, the transfer implied by this operation could approach the value of total costs. In the particular project depicted in Table 21.2, publicly-borne costs amount to less than 30 percent of total costs. Nevertheless, this is more than twice the value of net project benefits. Clearly, such transfers can often be very large in absolute terms and will nearly always be large relative to net benefits from the project. Infrastructural projects, therefore, tend to provide large increases in private sector incomes which point to the potential importance of the adjustment factor capturing the method of revenue generation. Moreover, note that this may occur even if most inputs and outputs are tradable.

Of course, the transfer to the private sector can be offset by an appropriate policy of cost recovery. While it is implicit in the present categorization of projects that direct charges for use are infeasible in the case of infrastructural projects, there may be other indirect methods of recovering cost.[59] This then raises a second issue in that the method of balancing the budget may now be project specific. As noted in Section 3, this is of importance only to the extent that the project being appraised is one of several mutually exclusive projects, at least some of which are associated with different procedures for balancing the budget.

The shadow pricing rules for infrastructural projects can be analyzed more formally as follows. Assume that a public sector project results in an output – infrastructure – that moves the private sector production possibility frontier outwards. Assume, in particular, that this results in an increase in private sector net output of dy. If lump-sum transfers are not available to offset the transfer to the private sector occurring through the project, and if all private sector net outputs are tradables so that there are no induced price changes, then the shadow price of the project's output – infrastructure – can be derived from equation (20):

$$\pi^* = (r - \alpha p)\, \partial y/\partial x, \tag{25}$$

where $p\, \partial y/\partial x$ is the increase in private sector income following the improvement in infrastructure and $\alpha = (1/\pi_L - 1/\pi_R)$ as before.

Equation (25) shows that the shadow price of public sector infrastructure equals the value at border prices of the induced private sector output less the "cost" of offsetting the increase in private sector incomes. In appraising infrastructural projects, agencies such as the World Bank do not use the approach implicit in equation (25). Instead, the project is treated as though both inputs and outputs were part of a public sector project. Border prices are then applied throughout. This approach captures the first term $(r\, \partial y/\partial x)$ on the right-hand side of equation (25); the second term $(\alpha p\, \partial y/\partial x)$ is omitted.

As Table 21.2 suggests, incorporating the first term at border prices may be an important factor in the appraisal of projects and should be encouraged. It is difficult, however, to assess the seriousness of omitting the second term. Because π_R involves use of a mechanism that distorts the economy whereas π_L does not, one can conclude that $1/\pi_R < 1/\pi_L$ which, in turn, implies that this procedure *systematically overestimates the net benefits of infrastructural projects.*

[59] For some of the items provided by this project – for example, agricultural inputs – direct charging is, of course, possible. This issue is ignored here but is addressed in the discussion of utility projects.

The magnitude of the overestimation is extremely difficult to quantify. Estimates of the welfare cost of different fiscal instruments are extremely difficult to accomplish with any degree of certainty. Several estimates, however, are available for developed countries. Using computable, general equilibrium models,[60] Ballard, Shoven and Whalley (1985) suggest that, for the U.S. tax system, an additional $1 of revenue results in a welfare loss of $0.33. Stuart (1984) reports a loss of $0.21 to $0.24 for an additional unit of revenue from labor taxation in the United States. For a much higher marginal tax rate (around 70 percent), Hansson and Stuart, however, report a welfare loss of $0.69 to $1.29 in the case of Sweden.[61] Similar exercises for developing countries have yet to be undertaken. On the assumption that producer prices remain fixed, Ahmad and Stern have developed a relatively simple procedure for assessing the welfare cost of commodity taxation. Since this form of taxation is a major source of revenue in most developing countries, their approach is highly relevant to the present discussion. In a series of papers, they conduct an extensive analysis of the Indian indirect tax system and conclude that the welfare loss associated with a unit increase in revenue ranges up to $0.24 for the nine commodities examined [Ahmad and Stern (1984)].[62] Since this approach rules out the possibility of distortions in production, their analysis results in an underestimate of the true welfare loss. Moreover, the underestimation could be quite large.

The available empirical evidence, therefore, does not provide clear indication of the likely magnitude of π_R. An alternative procedure involves calculating the value of π_R required to eliminate the net benefits of the project shown in Table 22.2. For example, if the marginal social cost of raising revenue through lump-sum transfers (π_L) equals 1.2,[63] net benefits of the project are completely eliminated only if π_R is 2.7. While values for π_R as high as this are unlikely, they are not impossible. Moreover, the required value of π_R falls as the share of publicly borne costs increases and as the project's net present value decreases. The quantitative significance of omitting the third term of equation (20), therefore, remains an open question.

This discussion suggests that, at a minimum, those in charge of the appraisal of infrastructural projects should be instructed to use border prices for tradable inputs and outputs regardless of their location in the private or public sector. Moreover, if the appropriate shadow prices of public revenue are provided to the project evaluator, there is no reason why a proper analysis cannot be undertaken

---

[60] These models are discussed by Sherman Robinson in Chapter 18 of this Handbook.
[61] Reported in Ballard, Shoven and Whalley (1985, p. 137).
[62] For further details on this approach, see Stern and Ahmad, Chapter 20 in this Handbook.
[63] Assuming no changes in prices ($\gamma = 0$), a unit reduction in welfare achieved by a unit reduction in lump-sum transfers results in less than a unit increase in the budget surplus because the reduction in private expenditure implies a tax loss; therefore, $\pi_L > 1$. Recall that $1/\pi_L$ can be interpreted as a consumption conversion factor, for which a value of 0.8 is not unreasonable [see Scott (1974)].

Table 21.3
Structure of a utility project

Item	Cost and benefits at market prices (%)[a]	Distortion[b]	Costs and benefits at shadow prices (%)[c]
Costs			
Capital cost	5	1.0	5
Coal	20	1.1	22
Oil	27	0.4	10
Unskilled labor	1	0.7	–
Other labor	8	0.8	7
Gas	18	0.5	9
Total	79		53
Benefits			
Industrial output	100	0.9	90

[a] The entries show costs and benefits expressed as a percentage of the net present value of total benefits at market prices. All items are discounted to the present by application of an interest rate of 10 percent.

[b] The items in this column are the ratios of shadow price to market price.

[c] As a percentage of the net present value of total project benefits at market prices.

when the distribution of project net benefits is known. For the project shown in Table 21.2, all the required information on the induced outputs in the private sector is already available. This may not always be the case, however, especially where the project's benefits are widely dispersed. This information on private sector beneficiaries would also be required if the analysis were to deal explicitly with income distribution.

A particular advantage of the present analysis is that the treatment of cost recovery policy becomes part of the evaluation process. While π_R could be the social cost of raising revenue by some economy-wide means, it could also be project-specific. Land taxes or output taxes are often used as a means of partial cost recovery in situations where direct changes for use are infeasible. The significance of this point is that, whereas decisions regarding the physical design of the project are usually made early in the project cycle and often before the project has been exposed to economic analysis, decisions regarding the financial design of the project are usually made quite late in the cycle. The economist can, therefore, play a potentially important role in this decision.

Utility projects are characterized by the public provision of a nontradable service – electricity, for example – to the private sector. The structure of such a project is shown in Table 21.3. Often such projects are provided in markets where prices are fixed by the government below the level required to clear the market. These projects, therefore, illustrate in the output market the kind of situation analyzed by Bell and Devarajan in an input market. Recall that in their case the distortion in the labor market resulted in an increase in private sector incomes. In the case of utility projects, a failure to clear the market by price adjustments also results in a transfer to the private sector. Moreover, since the distortion applies to the project's entire output, the likelihood of a large transfer is much greater than if the distortion occurs in a single input market.

This case can be analyzed in a similar manner to that for infrastructural projects. If dy is the private sector increase in tradable net output following the expansion in the supply of the utility (x), and if there is no impact on nontradables, the compensated shadow price for the utility's output is:

$$\pi^* = r \, \partial y / \partial x - \alpha (p \, \partial y / \partial x - \bar{p}), \tag{26}$$

where $\bar{p}$ is the fixed price charged for the service. This result parallels that for an infrastructural project [equation (25)] with the exception that equation (26) allows for the fixed charge for the service. Utility projects have traditionally been an important part of the World Bank's portfolio and methods of appraising these projects are relatively well established. The standard approach equates the value of the output produced by the utility with its market price multiplied by a conversion factor.[64] Application of a general conversion factor to $\bar{p}$ is supposed to capture the difference between market prices and shadow prices for the mixture of net outputs induced by the increased provision of dx. The appropriate estimate for the conversion factor (CF) in this case, therefore, is $(r \, \partial y / \partial x)/(p \, \partial y / \partial x)$. Obviously, in practical applications one can only hope to approximate this value.

Abstracting from this difficulty, this approach introduces two errors. First, the second term of equation (26) – the adjustment factor – is omitted. Second, the first term of equation (26) is misspecified. The conversion factor should be applied to private sector net output at market prices and not the price paid for the output of the public utility. Given that the transfer ($p \cdot dy/dx - \bar{p}$) to the private sector is positive, the sign of the net error introduced into the calculation of net project benefits by this method depends on the sign of CF $- \alpha$. If this term is positive, net benefits are underestimated. Conversion factors, especially for groups of commodities, usually have values of about 0.8.[65] If, as before, π_L is assumed to be about 1.2, the sign of the term is positive (and the term itself is equal, more or less, to $1/\pi_R$) so that in this case net benefits are probably underestimated. It can be concluded, therefore, that standard appraisal methods cause net benefits to be underestimated for utility-type projects, more or less

[64] Thus, the gross benefits at market prices shown in Table 21.3 represent the gross revenue earned by the project and the conversion factor is 0.9.
[65] See Scott (1974).

accurately estimated for industrial-type projects, and overestimated for infrastructure-type projects.

The underestimation of net benefits associated with utility projects is probably not a serious problem in practice, however, since the issue is partially recognized by practitioners and appropriate rectifying steps are taken. Thus, the World Bank, for example, usually recommends that prices, if they are below long-run marginal (shadow) costs, be increased to that level. This is, in fact, often a formal condition of project loans. This, of course, need not necessarily eliminate all excess demand. Nevertheless, if excess demand is identified, it is often used as the basis for recommending further expansion of the system. Thus, even though project benefits may have been underestimated, the correct investment decision – a further expansion – is usually made. Ambiguity arises only in cases in which the underestimation of benefits causes a project to be rejected even if its true benefits exceed costs. Even this problem, however, is recognized and dealt with in a qualitative manner – some judgment is made regarding the additional benefits associated with excess demand.

Assuming that the underestimation resulting from the misspecification of the first term in equation (26) is recognized and, where necessary, compensated for, the overestimation resulting from the omission of the second term implies that net benefits for the whole project are overestimated. This error, however, would not lead to overinvestment because, as capacity approaches its optimal level, so the extra profits accruing to the private sector tend to zero. Calculation of the social cost of public revenue can, therefore, be ignored for the purposes of appraising utility projects. These projects do, however, affect the distribution of income in ways which might be quite difficult to estimate in practice.

This brief evaluation of current practice suggests that the complications introduced by the absence of lump-sum transfers may not be too serious for some projects but could be critical for others. Current methods seem reasonably adequate for industrial projects and utility projects but potentially seriously deficient for infrastructure projects. This, however, depends on the difference between the shadow price of raising revenue by means of different instruments. This difference is not presently well quantified. Note, however, that in each of the three projects reviewed here corrections to tradable inputs and outputs have been quantitatively significant. The border price rule, therefore, has the merit of being both simple to use and important in practice.

6. Conclusion

This review of the theory and practice of project evaluation leads to two major conclusions regarding the direction of future work.

First, agencies such as the World Bank should make every effort possible to encourage developing countries to discount future net benefits and use border prices for tradables. These measures are relatively simple to implement and yield potentially significant benefits. Moreover, border prices remain the relevant shadow prices in the face of a wide range of policy changes and are equally appropriate for marginal and nonmarginal projects.

Second, further empirical research should be undertaken to provide better and more estimates of the welfare loss associated with the generation of additional tax revenue. The use of computable general equilibrium models or less formal methods to arrive at estimates of the shadow price of public finance would be of value not only for project evaluation but also for tax reform and other issues of public policy.

References

Ahmad, E. and N. Stern (1984) 'The theory of reform and Indian indirect taxes', *Journal of Public Economics*, 25:259–298.

Anand, S. (1976) 'Little–Mirrlees appraisal of a highway project', *Journal of Transport Economics and Policy*, X:199–218.

Arrow, K.J. and R.C. Lind (1970) 'Uncertainty and the evaluation of public investment decisions', *American Economic Review*, 60:364–378.

Bacha, E. and L. Taylor (1971) 'Foreign exchange shadow prices: A critical review of current theories', *Quarterly Journal of Economics*, May:197–224.

Balassa, B. (1974) 'Estimating the shadow price of foreign exchange in project appraisal', *Oxford Economic Papers*, 26:147–168.

Ballard, C.L., J.B. Shoven, and J. Whalley (1985) 'General equilibrium computations of the marginal welfare costs of taxes in the United States', *The American Economic Review*, 75:128–138.

Bell, C. and S. Devarajan (1980) 'Shadow prices and semi-input–output: A critical note', Oxford Bulletin of Economics and Statistics, *XLII*:251–256.

Bell, C. and S. Devarajan (1983) 'Shadow prices for project evaluation under alternative macroeconomic specifications', *Quarterly Journal of Economics*, 97:457–477.

Bertrand, T. (1974) 'The shadow exchange rate in an economy with trade restrictions', *Oxford Economic Papers*, 26:185–191.

Bertrand, T. (1979) 'Shadow pricing in distorted economies', *The American Economic Review*, 69:903–914.

Bhagwati, J.N. and H. Wan, Jr., 'The "stationarity" of shadow prices of factors in project evaluation', *The American Economic Review*, 69:261–273.

Bhagwati, N.J. and T.N. Srinivasan (1981) 'The evaluation of projects at world prices under trade distortions: Quantitative restrictions, monopoly power in trade and nontraded goods', *International Economic Review*, 22:385–399.

Blitzer, C., P. Dasgupta, and J. Stiglitz (1981) 'Project appraisal and foreign exchange constraints', *The Economic Journal*, 91:58–74.

Boadway, R.W. (1974) 'The welfare foundation of cost–benefit analysis', *Economic Journal*, 84:926–939.

Boadway, R.W. (1975a) 'Benefit–cost shadow pricing in open economies: An alternative approach', *Journal of Political Economy*, 83:419–430.

Boadway, R.W. (1975b) 'Cost–benefit rules in general equilibrium', *Review of Economic Studies*, 42:361–373.

Boadway, R.W. (1978) 'A note on the treatment of foreign exchange in project evaluation', *Economica*, 45:391–399.

Corden, W.M. (1974) *Trade policy and economic welfare*. London: Oxford.

Dasgupta, P. and J.E. Stiglitz (1974) 'Benefit–cost analysis and trade policies', *Journal of Political Economy*, 82:1–23.

Diamond, P. and J.A. Mirrlees (1971) 'Optimal taxation and public production, I: Production efficiency and II: Tax rules', *American Economic Review*, 61:8–27 and 261–278.

Dixit, A. (1987) 'Tax policy in open economies', in: A. Auerbach and M. Feldstein, eds., *Handbook of public economics*. Amsterdam: North-Holland.

Drèze, J., and N. Stern (1987) 'The theory of cost–benefit analysis', in: A. Auerbach and M. Feldstein, eds., *Handbook of public economics*. Amsterdam: North-Holland.

Eckstein, O. (1961) 'A survey of the theory of public expenditure criteria', in: *Public finances: Needs, sources and utilisation*, Princeton, NJ: National Board of Economic Resources, Princeton University Press.

Findlay, R. and S. Wellisz (1976) 'Project evaluation, shadow prices, and trade policy', *Journal of Political Economy*, 84:543–552.

Foster, C.D. and M.E. Beesley (1963) 'Estimating the social benefit of constructing an underground railway in London', *Journal of the Royal Statistical Society*, 126, Part 1.

Graham, D.A. (1981) 'Cost–benefit analysis under uncertainty', *The American Economic Review*, 71:715–725.

Hammond, P. (1983) 'Approximate measures of the social welfare benefits of large projects', Technical Report no. 410, Institute for Mathematical Studies in the Social Sciences, Stanford, California.

Harberger, A.C. (1971a) 'Three basis postulates for applied welfare economics: An interpretive essay', *Journal of Economic Literature*, 9:785–797.

Harberger, A.C. (1971b) 'On measuring the social opportunity cost of labor', *International Labor Review*, 103:559–579.

Harris, R. (1978) 'On the choice of large projects', *Canadian Journal of Economics*, X1:404–423.

Henderson, P.D. (1968) 'Investment criteria for public enterprises', in: R. Turvey, ed., *Public Enterprise: Penguin Modern Economics*. Harmondsworth: Penguin books.

Henry, C. (1974) 'Investment decisions under uncertainty: The "irreversibility effect"', *American Economic Review*, 64:1006–1012.

Hicks, J.R. (1940) 'The valuation of social income', *Economica*, 7:105–124.

Hirshleifer, J. (1965) 'Investment decisions under uncertainty: Choice-theoretic approaches', *The Quarterly Journal of Economics*, LXXIX.

Kaldor, N. (1939) 'Welfare propositions and interpersonal comparisons of utility', *Economic Journal*, 49:549–552.

Khan, A.E. (1951) 'Investment criteria in development programmes', *Quarterly Journal of Economics*, LXV.

Krutilla, I.V. and O. Eckstein (1958) *Multiple purpose river basin development*. Baltimore, MD: Johns Hopkins Press.

Lal, D. (1973) 'Disutility of effort, migration and the shadow wage rate', *Oxford Economic Papers*, 25:112–126.

Lal, D. and M.C. Jain (1976) 'Shadow prices for non-traded goods: India – 1973', *The Indian Journal of Statistics* (*Sankhya*), Series C, 38, Part 4:127–148.

Lal, D. and L. Squire (1980) 'The Little–Mirrlees shadow wage rate: A comment on Sjaastad and Wisecarver', *Journal of Political Economy*, 88:1237–1241.

Lewis, W.A. (1954) 'Economic development with unlimited supplies of labor', *Manchester School*, XXI.

Little, I.M.D. (1950) *A critique of welfare economics*. London: Oxford University Press.

Little, I.M.D. and J.A. Mirrlees, (1969) *Manual of industrial analysis in developing countries*, *II*, *Social Cost Benefit Analysis*. Paris: OECD.

Little, I.M.D. and J.A. Mirrlees (1974) 'Project appraisal and planning for developing countries'. London: Heinemann.

Little, I.M.D., and M.FG. Scott (1976) 'Using shadow prices'. London: Heinemann Educational Books Ltd.

Mazumdar, D. (1976) 'Rural–urban wage gap migration and the shadow wage', *Oxford Economic Papers*, 28:406–425.

McArthur, J.D. (1978) 'Appraising the distribution aspects of rural development projects: A Kenyan cast study', *World Development*, 6:167–194.

Mishan, E.J. (1976) *Cost–benefit analysis*. New York: Praeger.

Newbery, D.M.G. (1972) 'Public policy in the dual economy', *The Economic Journal*, 82:567–590.

Porter, R.S. and M.R. Walsh (1978) 'Cost–effectiveness analysis in practice: A case study of domestic water supplies in an African country', *World Development*, 6:195–208.

Pouliquen, L.Y. (1970) 'Risk analysis in project appraisal', International Bank for Reconstruction and Development, World Bank Staff Occasional Papers.

Powers, T.A. (1981) 'Estimating accounting prices for project appraisal', Inter-American Development Bank, Washington, DC.

Prest, A.R. and R. Turvey (1965) 'Cost–benefit analysis: A survey', *Economic Journal*, 75:683–735.

Ray, A. (1984) 'Cost–benefit analysis, issues and methodologies', Baltimore, MD: The Johns Hopkins University Press.

Reutlinger, S. (1970) 'Techniques for project appraisal under uncertainty', International Bank for Reconstruction and Development, World Bank Staff Occasional Papers No. 10.

Schohl, W.W. (1979) 'Estimating the shadow prices for Colombia in an input–output table framework', Bank Staff Working Paper no. 357. Washington, DC: World Bank.

Scott, M.FG. (1974) 'How to use and estimate shadow exchange rates', *Oxford Economic Papers*, 26:169–184.

Scott, M.FG. (1976) 'Shadow wages in Mauritius', in I.M.D. Little and M.FG. Scott, eds., *Using shadow prices*. London: Heinemann Educational Books.

Scott, M.FG. (1977) 'The test rate of discount and changes in base-level income in the United Kingdom', *The Economic Journal*, 87:219–241.

Scott, M.FG., J.D. MacArthur, and D.M.G. Newbery (1976) 'Project appraisal in practice: The Little–Mirrlees method applied in Kenya'. London: Heinemann Educational Books Ltd.

Scitovsky, T. (1941) 'A note on welfare propositions in economics', *Review of Economic studies*, 9:77–88.

Sen, A.K. (1972) 'Control areas and accounting prices: An approach to economic evaluation', *Economic Journal*, 82: 486–501.

Seton, F. (1972) 'Shadow wages in the Chilean economy', Paris: OECD.

Sieper, E. (1981) 'The structure of general equilibrium shadow pricing rules for a tax-distorted economy', Department of Economics, Australian National University.

Squire, L. and H.G. van der Tak (1975) 'Economic analysis of projects', Baltimore, MD: The Johns Hopkins University Press.

Squire, L., I.M.D. Little, and M. Durdag (1979) 'Shadow pricing and macroeconomic analysis: Some illustrations from Pakistan', *The Pakistan Development Review*, XVIII:90–112.

Srinivasan, T.N. (1982) 'General equilibrium theory, project evaluation, and economic development', in: M. Gersovitz, C.F. Diaz-Alejandro, G. Ravis and M.R. Rosenzweiq, eds. *The Theory and Experience of Economic Development*, London: George Allen and Unwin.

Srinivasan, T.N. and J.N. Bhagwati (1978) 'Shadow prices for project selection in the presence of distortions: Effective rates of protection and domestic resource costs', *Journal of Political Economy*, 86:97–116.

Stern, N.H. (1972a) 'An appraisal of tea production in small-holdings in Kenya', Paris: OECD.

Stern, N.H. (1972b) 'Optimum development in a dual economy, *Review of Economic Studies*, 39:171–184.

Stern, N.H. (1977) 'Welfare weights and the elasticity of the marginal valuation of income', in: M. Artis and R. Nobay, eds. *Studies in modern economic analysis*. Oxford: Blackwell.

Stuart, C. (1984) 'Welfare costs per dollar of additional tax revenue in the United States', *The American Economic Review*, 74:352–362.

Tinbergen, J. (1958) *The design of development*. Baltimore, MD: Johns Hopkins.

UNIDO (1972) *Guidelines for project evaluation*, Project Formulation and Evaluation Series, No. 2. New York: United Nations.

Warr, P.G. (1977) 'On the shadow pricing of traded commodities', *Journal of Political Economy*, 85:865–872.

PART 5

INTERNATIONAL ASPECTS

INTRODUCTION TO PART 5

T.N. SRINIVASAN*

Yale University

The interaction between international trade and national development has attracted the creative attention of economists virtually from the earliest days of economics as an intellectual discipline. It has continued to generate lively controversies to which some of the best minds of each generation of economists have contributed, dating early on from Adam Smith, David Ricardo, John Stuart Mill, Alfred Marshall and in this century to Bertil Ohlin, J. Maynard Keynes, Dennis Robertson, Raul Prebisch, Ragnar Nurkse, Jacob Viner, Arthur Lewis, and Paul Samuelson. Whether international trade promotes development as an "engine of growth", as argued by Dennis Robertson (1940), or merely accompanies growth as a "handmaiden", as suggested by Irving Kravis (1970), still evokes fierce debates.

The principle of comparative advantage, namely that both parties to a voluntary trade could gain and do so even when one country is absolutely more productive in every commodity, is the most celebrated and best known proposition in the theory of international trade. Yet, despite two centuries of writings by eminent economists, it does not sound convincing to policymakers in most countries (developed and developing), to laymen and even to some economists. Once Paul Samuelson was asked by the mathematician Stanislaw Ulam "to name one proposition in all of the social sciences which is both true and non-trivial" [Samuelson (1969)]. A suitable answer did not suggest itself to him immediately but, thirty years later, he thought of comparative advantage as the appropriate response. Apparently the truth of the principle of comparative advantage is at once easy to forget and extremely difficult to grasp intuitively.

Mercantilism, against which Adam Smith so forcefully argued two centuries ago, has survived to this day in the advocacy of extreme forms of import substitution or export promotion as development strategies. Indeed, paradoxical as it may seem, the sacred notion of reciprocity in the General Agreement on Tariffs and Trade (GATT), an organization devoted to the promotion of liberal

*I thank Jonathan Eaton, David Evans and Hollis Chenery for their comments. I am indebted to James Ito-Adler for his comments and for patiently reading and editing several drafts.

international trade, is mercantilist at its core. After all, only a mercantilist would view a reduction in a country's import tariffs as a "concession" to be offered in GATT negotiations in return for reciprocal "concessions" via tariff reductions on its exports by its trading partners.

The macroeconomic counterpart of the microeconomic theory of international trade is the theory of international finance dealing with exchange rates between national currencies and flows of funds between countries. This too has a long history dating back to David Hume. It has also been a fertile field of ideas and controversies with its own share of cranks and prophets. In addition to the flow of goods and of funds, this theory deals with international factor flows (labor, capital, and technical knowledge) that also influence the course of development. In the past, for example, permanent international migration played an important role in the development of newly settled areas, such as the Americas, Australia, and New Zealand. More recently, remittances from temporary migrants to areas experiencing an economic boom, such as West Asia[1] in the recent post-oil shock era, have been an important source of external finance to many labor exporting developing countries.

Part 5 of the Handbook contains discussion of alternative theoretical perspectives and empirical assessments of evidence on the role of international trade, finance, and factor movements and of the institutional framework governing these flows. While no consensus has emerged as yet, one could say without fear of contradiction that the divergence of views has narrowed and, more important, an impressive accumulation of analytical and empirical studies as well as experience with alternative policies in many developing countries has enabled proponents to support their points of view by drawing, albeit selectively, upon these studies.

It is worth recalling that development economics emerged as a subdiscipline within economics only in the early postwar years. It is natural that the pioneers of development economics with very few exceptions viewed problems of international trade from the perspective of the disastrous interwar period of a deep depression, defaults on international debt, "beggar-thy-neighbor" trade policies and the consequent collapse of trade volumes. This led them to believe that prospects for substantial growth in world trade and for international flows of investment capital from financial centers were dim. Although the actual course of events in the next four decades were to prove them wrong, it is clear that this pessimism about world trade and capital flows led to the identification of a shortage of foreign exchange as one of the two *key* constraints of economic development–the other being domestic savings. Cairncross (1962, p. 208) puts the

---

[1] Though common usage would label this region the Middle East, logic and a non-Eurocentric perspective would categorize Asian countries west of Afghanistan as being West Asia.

dominant view succinctly:

> At the end of it all, the reader may still feel that neither Nurkse nor Haberler has settled the primary issue: how far a shortage of foreign exchange (contrasted with capital, skilled labour, land, etc.) is a limiting factor in economic development. The majority of the under-developed countries are monocultures, dependent for their earnings of foreign exchange on a single commodity (or at most two or three). These earnings are highly inelastic except when exports of the principal commodity form a small fraction of the world's consumption. At the same time, nearly all the plant and machinery that they require has to be imported, so that the scale of industrial investment is limited by the foreign exchange available to pay for it. In those circumstances, what should be the policy of a country seeking to accelerate its development? We know what most countries have done; it would be interesting if we could be told by an economist of the standing of Nurkse or Haberler, what the results have been and what they should have done.

This view was formalized in the very influential two-gap development model of Chenery and Bruno (1962). In this model external resources filled two gaps. One gap, referred to as the *savings gap*, was between aggregate investment for achieving a growth target and domestic savings. The other, referred to as the *foreign exchange gap*, was between foreign exchange expenditure on imports needed for growth and foreign exchange earnings from exports of goods and services. This model, in conjunction with the Harrod-Domar growth model with capital as the only factor of production, was widely used as a development planning tool to arrive at consistent projections of domestic savings and foreign aid needed to sustain a targeted growth of income. It is a testimony to the influence of this model that interest in it has revived in the context of structural adjustment in the eighties after a hiatus in the seventies when the serious constraints on development appeared to be neither inadequate domestic savings nor foreign exchange, but, rather inappropriate foreign-trade and exchange-rate policies. Almost all the chapters in Part 5 discuss some variant of this model.

The chaos of international economic relations in the interwar period also led to the initiatives taken by Great Britain, the United States and others to devise an institutional framework which would not only avoid the disasters of the interwar era, but also promote orderly growth of trade, facilitate the reconstruction of war-damaged economies, and help in the economic development of poor countries. Three institutions were originally conceived at a conference held in Bretton Woods, New Hampshire: The International Monetary Fund (IMF); the International Bank for Reconstruction and Development (IBRD) – more popularly known as the World Bank; and the International Trade Organisation (ITO). The importance of the roles played and policies espoused by the IMF and the World

Bank to the development of most developing countries cannot be exaggerated. All the chapters of Part 5 discuss some aspect or other of these institutions and their policies.

The ITO did not get off the ground because of protectionist opposition in the United States, particularly in the Senate. The GATT, originally intended to be another in a series of reciprocal trade agreements into which The United States entered under the 1934 Reciprocal Trade Agreements Act and its extensions, took ITO's place. From early on, developing countries were not convinced that subscribing to the liberal trading order being promoted under GATT rules would be consistent with their objective of rapid industrialization. Eventually an explicit exemption for developing countries from some of the GATT rules was incorporated into GATT. Also the United Nations Conference on Trade and Development (UNCTAD) was established in the sixties to deal specifically with trade issues in the context of development. Still, the feeling that the existing world economic order was not fair led a number of developing countries to propose a New International Economic Order (NIEO) in the early seventies. Although there has been a spate of writing on the economic merits (or more precisely the lack thereof) in NIEO, there has been no movement to negotiate such an order.

The rapid advances in the technology of transport, communications, and information exchange and processing since the seventies have integrated the world commodity and capital markets to a significant extent. This growing interdependence and the consequent gap between technological and institutional change is a major theme in Paul Streeten's chapter (Chapter 22). After analyzing the causes of a partial breakdown of the old order, he points to the opportunities to build a genuinely pluralistic one and offers some specific suggestions for institutional reform. Streeten candidly admits that his suggestions, such as the creation of a global central bank, an international income tax to be levied at marginal rates increasing with consumption per head for generating resources for assistance to developing countries, the establishment of international bodies that will ensure coordination of lumpy investment in long gestation industry and recycle surpluses from developed countries to investment in developing countries by providing investment guarantees, to mention only a few, are Utopian. While his argument that a vision (even if Utopian) can provide a sense of direction and offset biases in favor of the *status quo* has considerable merit, one cannot assume that the benefits that might accrue to the developing countries were the proposed institutions to function effectively would in fact be realized in practice. The information requirements for effective functioning in themselves appear to be formidable let alone incentive problems that will surely arise.

In the conventional theory of trade, the patterns of trade among countries are largely driven by patterns of comparative advantage. In the classical Ricardian system, differences in the pattern of comparative advantage among countries arose from technological differences that led to differential labor productivity patterns (across commodities) among countries. In the neoclassical theory associated with the names of Hecksher, Ohlin, and Samuelson (H–O–S) all countries were assumed to have access to the same technology. Returns to scale were constant and the ratios in which different factors are combined to minimize unit costs of production vary across commodities. An explanation for differences in comparative advantage patterns according to this approach is found in the differences in factor endowments among countries. H–O–S theory has the strong implication that under certain conditions trade in commodities alone will be sufficient to equalize factor returns across countries as long as their factor endowment patterns are not too different. Although this implication does not find much empirical support, the association between patterns of trade and factor endowments does [Leamer (1984)].

The relevance of classical and neoclassical theories of international trade for developing countries is a major theme in Chapter 23 by Christopher Bliss. He also addresses the broader issues of the role of trade in the process of economic development and, in particular, the normative question of determining which pattern of international exchange best serves certain commonly agreed upon objectives of economic development. These include a rapid rate of capital accumulation and a more equitable pattern of income distribution among socio-economic groups within a country. He explores the positive question of the implications for these objectives of alternative trade policies pursued by governments. Bliss finds that theoretical developments in the last four decades have greatly clarified optimal policy interventions in an open economy and more important, pinpointed the negative effects of certain misguided but all-too-prevalent policies.[2] The relationship between economic policy including trade policy and economic performance is obviously quite subtle, and Bliss correctly cautions against hasty attribution of success or failure to trade policy alone.

In Chapter 24 David Evans looks to trade theory for an explanation of the historically rapid, but uneven rate of growth of real income in the developing countries in the postwar period. In particular he looks at the relationship between changes in economic structure and growth in the volume of trade. He contrasts the neoclassical, Marxian, and structuralist-institutionalist schools identified by Bardhan (Chapter 3, Volume I of this Handbook). His analysis starts with a basic two-commodity circulating capital model with two non-produced factors, labor and a natural resource. Besides fitting well with some important stylized facts about capitalist national economies, this model of dynamic comparative advan-

---

[2] Detailed analysis of the different trade strategies pursued by developing countries can be found in Part 6. The development performance of countries that followed an outward-oriented development strategy is discussed by Bela Balassa (Chapter 31). Henry Bruton (Chapter 30) evaluates import substitution as development strategy. The experience of exporters of primary products is described by Stephen Lewis (Chapter 29). Dwight Perkins and Moshe Syrquin (Chapter 32) focus their attention on the experience of large countries.

tage can be linked to H–O–S theory and includes the two-gap model as a special case.

Evans then discusses models which focus on international exploitation, class, and international inequality, concentrating on unequal exchange. In contrast to the view that commodity exchange between countries with widely different real wages is inherently unequal, Evans' primary emphasis is on the theory of class dominance and exploitation of which unequal exchange of labor is a special case. It turns out that the unequal exchange of labor may not be a good proxy for either international class relationships or inequality. Exploitation by a class or group of another is defined as the exercise of dominance by the former to prevent a change from the status quo to another social state in which the latter will be better off and the former will be worse off. Integral to this definition is some extra-economic force that enforces the dominance of one class or group in the status quo. As such, as Evans suggests, analytical attention should be devoted to this force rather than to its economic manifestation.

Evans examines the role of transnational corporations and the state in the development process within a framework in which organization and location of production (nationally and internationally) and state power are used to sustain the domination of one group or class over another. He is rightly critical of the naive anthropomorphic interpretation of nations as individuals and unrealistic prescriptions of international redistribution present in the extensive literature on the NIEO. Like Bliss, he is also critical of simplistic attempts to attribute spectacularly good or bad economic growth performance of countries, respectively, solely to their outward orientation (i.e. neutral stance between export promotion and import substitution) or inward orientation (i.e. tilt in favor of import substitution). This criticism is well taken since it is clearly possible to achieve spectacular rates of growth simply by putting massive resources into growth regardless of the efficiency of their use or their opportunity costs as has happened in Soviet industrialization. Evans rightly points out the more tenable arguments such as in Bhagwati (1977, 1978) in favor of some components of the NIEO and the reasons why outward orientation tends to promote *efficient* growth. His conclusion that there are lessons to be learned from both the orthodox and the less orthodox literature on outward-oriented strategies is perhaps more controversial.

Historically, external capital played a vital role in the growth of some of the contemporary developed countries such as Australia, Canada, New Zealand, and the United States. However, with the virtual collapse of the capital market in the interwar period and the radically different political framework in many of the newly independent developing countries, a significant flow of private capital to these countries was not to be expected. As a partial response to this market failure, governments of industrialized countries offered foreign aid in the form of loans on concessional terms as well as outright grants to governments in developing countries. Also as part of the cold war competition for the political support of the developing world, foreign aid became an instrumental means to an end other than economic development per se. Finally, in addition to bilateral aid between governments, there was lending by the multilateral lending institutions, such as the World Bank and the regional development banks. Since the major shareholders of these institutions were governments of industrialized countries, they were able to borrow from the world capital markets at modest rates of interest and lend these funds on terms which the developing countries could not get on their own from the markets.

In order to enable the poorest among developing countries to invest in infrastructural projects of long gestation period and in human capital, the returns from which cannot be easily mobilized for servicing loans, a soft loan window, called the International Development Association (IDA), was opened in the World Bank in the sixties entirely financed by subscriptions by member governments. Until the emergence of surpluses in oil exporting countries after the first oil shock, such public capital was the major source of funds for developing countries. Since the oil shock and prior to the onset of the debt crises in the early eighties, lending by private commercial banks was substantial. Indeed, the ease with which such loans could be obtained, often at negative real rates of interest, led to a rapid increase in the private debt of a number of countries. When the environment shifted in the eighties to one of moderately high and variable real rates of interest, while at the same time the flow of funds was drastically reduced by the banks, these countries faced extremely serious adjustment problems.

Jonathan Eaton's chapter (Chapter 25), although principally devoted to foreign public capital flows, also provides a detailed analytical discussion of the role and impact of capital flows in general. Static models of capital flow in terms of transfers of purchasing power between countries and in terms of factor movements are explicated. In models of purchasing power transfers, with outputs given, the focus is on the impact of the transfer on terms of trade and distribution of welfare. It is well known from general equilibrium theory that, in an exchange economy with more agents than commodities, the only properties of *aggregate* excess demand functions that can be derived from the postulate that individual agents maximize well-behaved utility functions in deriving their demands other are that such functions satisfy Walras' Law and are homogeneous of degree zero in prices. Since the effect of the transfer of purchasing power is mediated essentially through changes in global excess demand functions, it is not surprising that the effects of transfers on equilibrium terms of trade and distribution of welfare are ambiguous. In models of factor movements, the pattern of outputs, and not just consumption, also change. The focus then is on the impact of factor movements on factor rewards and functional distribution of income. As can be expected from the theory of the second best, if there are distortions present, then factor movements can have impacts opposite in direction to what they would have had, in the absence of distortions.

Eaton then provides a dynamic analysis of external finance for capital accumulation and growth, first considering descriptive models in which savings rates are exogenously fixed and then models in which savings rates are derived from intertemporal optimizing behavior. Included among the models in the first category are the Harrod–Domar fixed coefficients model, the Chenery–Bruno two-gap model and the Solow–Swan neoclassical model. The growth rate of borrower's income derived from the Harrod–Domar model can be compared with the interest rate on foreign debt to analyze the solvency of the borrower. However, the assumption that the parameters of this model, including the interest rate, are exogenously fixed makes such a use rather problematic. The Solow model is more realistic in allowing factor substitutability, but still assumes a fixed savings rate. It provides a simple analytical basis for the stages through which a country may go in its balance of payments from being an immature debtor–borrower at the early stages of development, passing successively to the states of mature debtor–borrower, debtor–repayer, immature creditor–lender, and finally to the state of mature creditor–lender once development is complete.

Eaton then considers issues relating to public capital inflow proper, such as sovereign risk and potential repudiation, foreign aid, and lending by multilateral organizations, such as the World Bank and the IMF. Problems arising from lack of credibility of announced policies or strategies, difficulty of pre-commitment to a course of action, moral hazard and so on, some of which are consequences of information relevant to the fulfillment of a contract being available to one and not the other of the two parties to a contract, have been the focus of recent research in other areas. These are also relevant to the analysis of sovereign debt as Eaton demonstrates. Yet the sensitivity of the results to particular assumptions about the distribution of information, length of the time horizon etc. calls for some caution in their use for policy purposes. There will be widespread agreement with Eaton's conclusions that not enough is known about the determinants of supply and demand for international capital. He also points out there are few econometrically sound empirical studies of the role of foreign capital in financing investment and growth.

Eliana Cardoso and Rudiger Dornbusch (Chapter 26) deal with the role of private external capital in development. They start with the historical experience in the nineteenth and early twentieth centuries. This experience is very interesting in the context of the debt crisis of the 1980s. Default on debt was not infrequent then and a default did not mean that the defaulting country was shut out of the capital market ever after. Countries were indeed able to borrow after a decent time interval had elapsed after default, although it was sometimes necessary to settle defaulted debt at a value far less than the capital and accumulated interest.

What distinguishes the debt of the eighties is the prominence of governments and multilateral lending institutions in the debt collection business. The availability of standby credits from the IMF and structural adjustment assistance from the World Bank facilitated rescheduling of debt rather than suspension of debt service as in the 1930s. Furthermore, there was virtually no disruption of trade in the 1980s as contrasted with the depression-induced collapse of trade in the 1930s. These two authors, and Eaton, also discuss some welfare aspects of foreign capital inflow (private or public) into a distorted economy.

Many believe that the flight of private capital from some of the Latin American countries to safe havens abroad has not only been quantitatively significant but also may have added to debt problem of these countries. Cardoso and Dornbusch analyze the incentives for capital to flee and the role of government policy (taxes, tariffs, etc.) in creating such incentives. Whether a government can credibly change its policies to create the incentives for a return of private capital invested abroad is also discussed. The proposed solutions to the debt problem and the innovations in financial market instruments that have come about in the wake of the debt crisis are discussed as well. Cardoso and Dornbusch conclude that until the problem of debt overhang is resolved one way or another, fresh resources will not flow to the developing countries.

Gerald Helleiner's chapter (Chapter 27) discusses transnational corporations (TNCs), direct foreign investment, and economic development. The role of TNCs in economic development has been very controversial. The debate has generated a lot of heat and very little light, since as Helleiner points out, the critics of TNCs are in fact opposed to foreign culture, or large firms, or the market system, or some combination of the three at the same time. Helleiner carefully reviews the historical evolution of TNC activities in the developing countries. He then examines some of the theoretical models of direct foreign investment. Empirical results as well as a priori arguments relating to the possible benefits and costs to host countries of their interaction with TNCs are then considered in some detail. The relative bargaining strengths of host governments and TNCs with respect to rent sharing, transfer pricing, and investment are compared. A major rationale for host governments to invite TNCs is their potential role in technology transfer and export markets. Helleiner assesses this role from available evidence. The emergence of TNCs from the developing countries themselves is also briefly discussed.

Helleiner sees the frontier of theoretical research on TNCs in the application of game theory to the analysis of host government/TNC relationships and the use of industrial organization theory to modelling global markets of interest to developing countries. However, given the lack of robustness of results with respect to the way a game is modelled and the concept of equilibrium used, his enthusiasm for application of game theory has to be tempered. The plea for better analytical understanding and collection of empirical evidence on the determinants and effects on host countries' development of alternative forms of TNC involvement, however, will be widely echoed. He is surely right in suggesting that the most needed research is likely to be country-specific and only disaggregated data at country and industry levels will further such research. After all, as Helleiner points out, variables such as the sources of TNCs oligopolistic advantages in specific industries and markets, the precise nature of barriers to entry into these industries, and the overall global structure of such industries are bound to influence TNC performance in particular countries.

The present decade has been a period in which many developing countries faced a particularly adverse external environment with a downward shift in their terms of trade, slow growth in export demand because of relative stagnation in the developed countries, a drying up of private external capital flow, and high real interest on part of their external debt, and so on. They were forced to adjust to these external shocks as well as to any pre-existing unsustainable disequilibria (actual or incipient) arising from inconsistent policies. Sebastian Edwards and Sweder van Wijnbergen (Chapter 28) discuss the analytics of structural adjustment programs meant either to stabilize an economy facing macroeconomic disequilibria arising from unanticipated permanent external shocks or as a set of reforms enacted to eliminate distortions and inconsistencies in past policies that led to unsustainable disequilibria in the medium to long run. Most often these programs are undertaken with the financial support and policy advice of the IMF and World Bank.

A major element of many such programs is a nominal devaluation, which is viewed as the most direct means of achieving an increase in the domestic price of tradables relative to non-tradables, i.e. a real devaluation. Edwards and Wijnbergen evaluate the efficacy of exchange rate policy in the context of structural adjustment. Given the diversity of structural adjustment programs as well as of the macroeconomic problems that necessitated them, they have chosen to concentrate on certain important analytical and empirical issues, placing special emphasis on the interaction between disequilibrium situations, relative price changes, and structural adjustment programs. The issues covered include exogenous shocks (e.g. shocks to the interest paid on external debt and changes in domestic trade policies), and changes in capital market interventions. The Salter model of a dependent economy producing two tradables (an exportable and an importable) and a non-tradable with two factors of production is used very effectively to analyze the impact on output, employment, and factor prices of various shocks under different assumptions about flexibility of price changes and resource movements. They report an empirical finding of Edwards (1986) that nominal devaluations have a contractionary effect in the short run, while in the long run this effect is completely reversed. This result is particularly interesting since one of the major criticisms of the IMF-supported adjustment programs is that the devaluation recommended in such programs is contractionary.

The chapters in Part 5 make brief references to some recent contributions to the theory of international trade [Helpman and Krugman (1985), Krugman (1986)]. These involve significant departures from the two strong assumptions of the dominant H–O–S theory, namely constant returns to scale in production and pure competition in international and national markets. Contributors to this literature draw their analytical tools from game theory and the theory of industrial organization, and explicitly model increasing returns to scale in production technology at the level of the firm and imperfect (e.g. monopolistic and oligopolistic) competition between firms located in different countries. In these models firms engage in strategic behavior since they perceive their market power and recognize the influence of the action of competitors on their own profits. The information structure (i.e., what is common knowledge among all firms and what is private information known only to a particular firm), the strategies available to the participant firms, and the particular concept of equilibrium used, all influence the outcome of imperfect competition. In such an environment government interventions cannot only influence the final outcome but, more important, enable firms to adopt strategies, which in the absence of such intervention, would not be credible to its competitors. Protection from competition from foreign firms through a tariff can, in some of these models, increase the share of domestic firms in rents generated by the oligopoly.

Development economists who view international markets as an oligopoly in which transnationals from developed countries dominate may find a rationale for protection in the recent contributions. However, since this literature is still dominated by theory and very few empirical studies are available, it is too early to assess the relevance of this literature to trade policy. Even the theoretical results are far from "robust", that is, they are extremely sensitive to the assumptions made about information structures, rules of the game, and the particular equilibrium concept used. At any rate, whatever be the relevance of such models for policy making in industrialized countries, their relevance for developing countries is likely to be considerably less [Srinivasan (1989)].

References

Bhagwati, J.N., ed. (1977) *The new international economic order: The north–south debate*. Cambridge, MA: MIT Press.

Bhagwati, J.N. (1978) *Anatomy and consequences of exchange control regimes*. Cambridge, MA: Ballinger.

Cairncross, A. (1962) *Factors in economic development*. London: Allen and Unwin.

Chenery, H.B. and M. Bruno (1962) 'Development alternatives in an open economy', *Economic Journal*, 72:79–103.

Edwards, S. (1986) 'Are devaluations contractionary?', *Review of Economics and Statistics* 68(3):501–508.

Helpman, E. and P. Krugman (1985) *Market structure and foreign trade*. Cambridge, MA:MIT Press.
Kravis, I. (1970) 'Trade as a handmaiden of growth: Similarities between the nineteenth and twentieth centuries', *Economic Journal*, 80(320):850–872.
Krugman, P., ed. (1986) *Strategic trade policy and the new international economics*. Cambridge, MA: MIT Press.
Leamer, E. (1984) *Sources of international comparative advantage: Theory and evidence*. Cambridge, MA: MIT Press.
Robertson, D. (1940) *Essays in monetary theory*. London: P.S. King and Son.
Samuelson, P.A. (1969) 'The way of an economist', in: P.A. Samuelson, ed., *International economic relations: Proceedings of the third congress of the International Economic Association*. London: Macmillan.
Srinivasan, T.N. (1989) 'Recent theories of imperfect competition and international trade: Any implications for development strategy?', *Indian Economic Review*, 24(1):January–June.

Chapter 22

INTERNATIONAL COOPERATION

PAUL P. STREETEN*

Boston University

Contents

*I am indebted to Henry Bruton, Hollis Chenery, T.N. Srinivasan, and Frances Stewart for helpful comments.

Handbook of Development Economics, Volume II, Edited by H. Chenery and T.N. Srinivasan
© *Elsevier Science Publishers B.V., 1989*

1. Introduction

It has been said that the nation state has become too small for the big things, and too big for the small things. In the course of national integration, the state has increasingly assumed new functions and responsibilities. To the watchman's duty of maintaining law and order have been added such responsibilities as maintaining price stability, ensuring high levels of employment and high growth rates; devising a population policy, regional policy, industrial policy and agricultural policy; responsibility for redistributing incomes and alleviating poverty through social services; protection of the environment, physical and human resources, and energy policy; as well as numerous others. As a result, some of these functions have not been carried out satisfactorily, while others have been neglected. The need for a greater degree of decentralization, delegation downwards, including delegation to market forces, and increased participation, while part of the basic needs approach to development, is not the subject of this chapter. Rather, the need to delegate some functions upwards, to temper the claims of national sovereignty in order to pursue the national interest more effectively, is at its heart.

A major theme of this chapter is that we are suffering from a lag of institutional adjustment behind technological advance. Technologically, the world has shrunk, but our social and political arrangements have not caught up with this advance. The result has been threats of mutual impoverishment and even mutual destruction.

In analysing the direction of needed reforms, a distinction is drawn, following Boulding, between three systems: the exchange system, the threat system, and the integrative or love system. The bulk of the economic development literature is concerned with the exchange system, in which transactions between the North and South yield mutual benefits. Discussion of the threat system is largely confined to experts on military matters, but should also cover economic threats such as competitive protectionism, competitive devaluation, investment wars, or R&D wars. The integrative system, in which sacrifices by the North in the spirit of human solidarity are called for, is not fashionable, but in this chapter I argue that without it, little progress can be made. The implications of heeding the principles of the integrative system embrace not only more and better development aid, but also changes in the rules, procedures, and institutions that are now biased in favor of the North (such as cascading tariffs that discriminate against processing in developing countries, or discriminatory rules about immigration by the industrialized countries), and more " voice" in the councils of nations, for the developing countries.

Section 2 of the chapter analyses briefly the causes of the partial breakdown of the old world order, and points to the opportunity to build a genuinely pluralistic new one. Section 3 describes the existing order as it grew out the post-war agreements and institutions. Section 4 analyses the concept of international interdependence, some of its implications and qualifications. We proceed to a discussion of the gap between institutions and technology, and then of the three systems that may contribute to bridging this gap. Finally, some specific suggestions for institutional reform are made. We move from the past, through the present to the future, and from mutual benefits and the way to avoid mutual harm to the moral basis of a global community.

2. Causes of the disorder

In order to understand the present international economic disorder, it is useful to remember some of the functions that any international order must fulfill if there is to be equitable economic development.[1] There must be, first, a source for the generation of balance of payments surpluses. Second, there must be institutions that fulfill three financial functions: (1) financial institutions that convert these surpluses into long-term development loans on commercial terms; (2) a lender of last resort to provide liquidity should confidence collapse; and (3) a supplier and withdrawer of international liquidity, to meet the requirements of international trade and capital flows: a lender or a borrower of last resort, analogous to a national Central Bank at the global level. It is also a help to have a country that keeps access to its markets open and provides the function of buying distress commodities when their prices fall. Third, there must be the industrial and commercial capacity to produce and sell the capital goods needed for development. Fourth, there must be military power to back the economic power, to see that contracts are enforced, property rights observed, and peace kept.

These four functions had been combined until about 1970 by a single dominant power, with the rest of the world dependent on the coordination by the center. Until 1914 this power was Great Britain, which established an international order and developed the areas of recent settlement in Canada, the United States, Australia, New Zealand, South Africa, and Latin America under the *Pax Britannica*. Current account surpluses were generated by Britain, the financial institutions had grown in the City of London, gold or sterling provided the reserve currency for international monetary transactions, free trade kept up demand and employment in periods of recession, the industrial capacity of the

---

[1] See Stewart and Sengupta (1982, p. 3).

North of England provided the iron, steel and capital goods, and the British navy kept world order.

There was not much of an order between the two world wars, when a domestic recession led to reduced, instead of increased foreign lending, and the United States put on tariffs as soon as demand for agricultural products declined, instead of being a buyer of distress goods. But for a quarter of a century after the end of the Second World War, the *Pax Americana* established an international order centered on the dollar. Current account surpluses originated from the United States and for a time people worried about a chronic dollar shortage; New York became a rival center to London for financial transactions; the dollar replaced sterling as the world's reserve currency; the industrial capacity grew strong in the United States; and the American army enforced the peace. But since 1970 these functions have been fragmented, split up between different centers, without coordination. For a period the surpluses were generated by a few desert sheikhdoms in the Gulf, joined by Germany and, most conspicuously, and recently, by Japan. As the capital surpluses of the OPEC countries dwindled away and turned into deficits with the drop in the price of oil, Germany and Japan continued to run surpluses, $100 billion of surpluses were unaccounted for, presumably largely unrecorded capital flight from some of the developing debtor countries, and the United States had become the giant borrower of last resort.

The concentration in the financial centers of London and New York was diluted by the mushrooming of banks in Singapore, Hong Kong, Japan, Germany, and their affiliates in the Cayman Islands, the Bahamas, and other tax havens. International liquid reserves were either too plentiful or too scarce and ill distributed, in spite of the creation of Special Drawing Rights. The industrial capacity had increasingly shifted to Germany and Japan, and to the newly industrializing countries. One of the most striking structural changes in the world economy has been the growth of manufacturing production and trade in a growing number of developing countries. And the military pigmies are the economic giants, whereas the military superpowers are economically weakened by their military expenditure. The four functions are dispersed among different groups of countries. And the coordination arising from dominance by one country has been replaced by more or less successful forms of cooperation between countries with different degrees of power.

But this break-up and dispersal of the previously coordinated functions also provides us with the opportunity for a constructive institutional response, and for the replacement of the past international orders based on dominance and dependence, and on the needs of a superpower, by a pluralistic and more egalitarian order of interdependence. International liquidity could be created according to global requirements of trade and capital flows, not according to the need to run deficits in the balance of payments of a capital-rich reserve currency country. Financial institutions and multinational corporations would compete with one another on equal terms, and everyone would be free to buy in the cheapest and sell in the dearest markets. Many would say that such an order, even if it were desirable (which some doubt) would not be feasible. Richard Cooper for example has pointed out that it took fifty years for international cooperation in such an obvious area as health to be achieved.[2]

On the other hand, Robert Keohane has shown that it is easier to maintain international regimes than to bring them into being. Their continued momentum, after the power that has set them up has declined, depends on their economizing in transaction costs, on inertia, sunk costs, and absence of alternatives. This explains to some extent the continued existence of the rules and procedures set up after the war even after American power had ebbed away.[3]

3. The post-war economic order

The post-war world economic order of convertibility, non-discrimination, and multilateralism expressed the interests of the United States as the dominant world power. Just as Britain as the strongest power in the nineteenth century advocated and practised free trade, so the United States after having emerged from the Second World War as the dominant world power, persuaded the other capitalist countries to subscribe to a multilateral, liberal economic order. Liberal trade and open markets are in the interest of the economically most advanced power, because it can win in competitive bidding, and its domestic flexibility and mobility permits easier adjustment to external change. The era was initiated by the Truman doctrine and Marshall Aid, acts of enlightened long-term national self-interest. And the departure of the dollar from gold in 1971 rang down the curtain.

The main economic areas to which the rules applied were money, capital flows, trade in manufactured goods and, in the initial intention, trade in primary products. Energy, and specifically petroleum, multinational corporations, private foreign investment, trade between government enterprises, and trade in services were issues that arose later, but did not play an important part in the original design of the post-war order. The principles of the liberal order were non-discrimination in trade with few barriers, currency convertibility at fixed exchange rates, and, at least in the intentions of the Havana Charter, commodity price

---

[2] Cooper (1985).

[3] Keohane (1984, pp. 100–103). The key question discussed in the book *After Hegemony* is "how international cooperation can be maintained among the advanced capitalist states in the absence of American hegemony" (p. 43). From that point of view the normative position taken in this paper is naively institutionalist, but the positive position is realist, for I believe that the post-war international regimes are best explained in terms of U.S. hegemony. Nevertheless, Keohane comes to the same conclusion, namely that continuing cooperation is possible if built on the interests of the leading capitalist states.

stabilization. The encouragement, in the early post-war years, of European cooperation and even discrimination against the United States, may appear to conflict with these principles. The Marshall Plan (1947–48), the encouragement of the Organization for European Economic Cooperation (OEEC), of the European Payments Union (EPU, 1950), of the European Coal and Steel Community, and of the European Economic Community (1957) appear to have been inconsistent with multilateralism, convertibility, and non-discrimination. The explanation of this apparent contradiction is partly that strategic, military, and political considerations (i.e. strengthening Western Europe in resisting communism) were regarded as worth a short-term economic sacrifice by the United States, and partly that these discriminatory arrangements were regarded as steps toward multilateralism and liberalism. The European Payments Union, for example, strongly supported by the United States, discriminated against American trade, but was a step toward more multilateral arrangements than the previous bilateral trade and payments arrangements. It is one of the very few institutions that actually was dissolved.

Marshall Aid, the EPU, and the encouragement of European integration are examples of farsighted American self-interest. They illustrate that the United States then was clearly aware of the distinction between uniform and universal rules (discussed below in Section 6), which later got lost sight of. Insistence on reciprocity and non-discrimination were sacrificed for the sake of long-term moves toward a liberal international order. The formation of the European Common Market had trade-creating effects, insofar as lower cost sources of supply within a European country replaced higher cost domestic sources of another member country, but also trade-diverting ones, as a result of higher cost intra-European sources replacing lower cost ones outside, including the United States. And since the trade-creating effects hurt some vocal and possibly powerful interests, while the inside beneficiaries (consumers) are dispersed and inarticulate, whereas the losers from trade-diverting ones are outside, it was to be expected that for these political reasons the Community would not be very "outward-looking".

The three pillars of the post-war economic order are the two Bretton Woods institutions, the International Monetary Fund (the IMF or the Fund) and the International Bank for Reconstruction and Development (the IBRD or The World Bank), and the General Agreement on Tariffs and Trade (GATT). At San Francisco other United Nations Agencies concerned with development were set up, such as the United Nations Educational, Scientific and Cultural Organization (UNESCO) and the World Health Organization (WHO). There was also the much older International Labour Organization (ILO). In later years the United Nations Industrial Development Organization (UNIDO) and the United Nations Conference on Trade and Development (UNCTAD, 1964) were set up. But the role of these specialized agencies, in technical assistance, standard setting, and information gathering, has been small compared with that of the two Bretton Woods institutions which had money, and GATT which had bargaining power. It was the IMF and the Bank in which weighted votes corresponded to financial contributions, and GATT in which concessions were matched by counter-concessions.

A conference of the United Nations at Bretton Woods in New Hampshire in 1944 agreed upon the formation of the Fund and the World Bank, which opened for business in 1946. The Fund, which has 151 members, encourages international cooperation on monetary matters and makes short-term loans for balance of payments support and corrections.[4] The member governments of the IMF were required to maintain official par values for their currencies, which could be changed only to correct a "fundamental disequilibrium", and (at least in principle) in consultation with the Fund.

All member countries subscribe, according to their quotas, their currencies to the Fund. The borrowers then draw on these. The degree of conditionality with respect to monetary and fiscal policy increases with higher proportions of these quotas being drawn. In the course of time, the Fund has created a number of additional "facilities". One is the Compensatory Financing Facility (1963) which provides compensation for a shortfall in export earnings beyond the control of the country, and, in 1981, for rises in the costs of imported cereals; to this were added in 1969 the Buffer Stock Financing Facility, in 1974–75 the Oil Facility, in 1974 the Extended Fund Facility, in 1974 the Supplementary Financing Facility, and in 1986 the Structural Adjustment Facility. This facility provides assistance to low-income countries on concessional terms. It is financed partly by the Trust Fund, which uses gold sales to make loans with few conditions at low interest rates.

The breakdown of the Bretton Woods system in 1971 led to a period of floating exchange rates, with several countries pegging their rates to a major trading country. Multilateral surveillance replaced fixity of rates, and rates were quite volatile. Increasingly they were determined by capital flows which are now a large multiple of trade flows, perhaps forty times as much.

The World Bank, the other institution founded at Bretton Woods in 1944, lends primarily on long term for specific projects, such as highways and power plants.[5] Its annual lending now amounts to about $15 billion. But the distinctions between Fund and World Bank lending have become blurred as the Fund's loans have become longer term, and as the Bank has moved into program lending and structural and sectoral adjustment loans conditional on reforms in policies for

---

[4]A good description of the Fund is to be found in Chandavarkar (1984). The full history of the Fund is recorded by de Vries (1985).
[5]For a detailed history, see Mason and Asher (1975).

stimulating growth. The rationale for this is that these reforms in policies make the project loans more effective.

The Havana Charter attempted to set up an International Trade Organization (ITO) and agreement was reached in March 1948. But the U.S. Senate rejected it.[6] It contained some of the provisions for which the developing countries asked in their call for a New International Economic Order nearly thirty years later, such as commodity price stabilization,[7] new preferences, quantitative restrictions in some conditions, and provisions for planning and state trading. At the time, however, this was too much for American business interests. The trade objectives were then implemented through the General Agreement on Tariffs and Trade (GATT) which had been set up in 1947 as a provisional agreement, until the ratification of the ITO. As so often happens, the provisional proved more permanent than what was intended to be permanent. The GATT is built on the principles of reciprocity, liberalization, and non-discrimination. Its 90 members include both advanced and developing countries. Although the Soviet Union is not a member, they nevertheless represent about four-fifths of world trade. One of the current controversial issues is whether services should be covered (the United States being particularly interested in free trade in telecommunications, insurance, and banking in many developing countries). Areas still excluded from GATT are intra-firm trade, important for the growing number of multi- and transnational companies; trade between state enterprises; much of trade in primary products; and rules about private foreign investment.

Seven rounds of tariff negotiations, including the Kennedy Round, concluded in 1967, and the Tokyo Round, concluded in 1979, greatly reduced tariffs. But at the same time various more or less concealed weapons of trade policy sprang up in the 1970s and 1980s. These included subsidies, government trading or government pressures on private companies, procurement practices, quantitative restrictions, and voluntary export restraints. The Multifiber Agreement was particularly restrictive for many items produced by developing countries. Fairly early on, exceptions to some of the general rules were made, such as the Generalized System of Preferences, by which developing countries were given non-reciprocal trade preferences.

GATT has to some extent been guilty of the confusion between uniformity and universality discussed below,[8] though the need for differential treatment for countries at different stages of development and for the same country in different conditions has come to be accepted. Thus in 1964 a chapter (Part IV) on "Trade and Development" was added to the General Agreement. It released developing countries from the obligation of reciprocity in trade negotiations and in 1971 it

---

[6] Keynes protested against the obstruction of two British negotiating nay-sayers who were called Shackle and Fetter: "we shall not be shackled or fettered".

[7] Keynes' memorandum on commodity price stabilization was reprinted in Keynes (1974).

[8] See Section 6.

accommodated generalized preferences. But it does not, for example, permit multi-tier discrimination, which may be necessary for integrating developing countries at different stages of development.

In addition to these institutions a number of regular groups have met to discuss and coordinate action in the economic sphere. The Group of Five meets informally to discuss international monetary problems. The Finance Ministers of the United States, Britain, France, West Germany and Japan are members. It sets the agenda for the Group of Ten. The Group of Ten, established in 1982, discusses the same issues as the Group of Five, and has in addition Canada, Belgium, Italy, The Netherlands, and Sweden. Switzerland joined later, making eleven. The Group of 24 represents the developing countries on international monetary and trade matters. It consists of eight developing countries each from Asia, Africa and Latin America.

The post-war economic order, though not designed with development in mind, did have provisions for the developing countries. The World Bank soon became an agency for concessional project lending to low-income countries. An attempt to set up a Special United Nations Fund for Economic Development (SUNFED), was defeated,[9] but the United Nations Development Programme emerged as an agency for technical assistance. The International Development Association (IDA, 1960), an affiliate and integral part of the World Bank, took over the function of lending on soft terms, which initially met with strong opposition, especially by the United States and Britain.

We have seen that GATT accommodated some of the demands of the developing countries to be exempted from most favored nations obligations and reciprocity, though it has been questioned whether this has been in their interest. Some have argued that these concessions have sprung from the desire of the dominant powers to find legitimacy, others from the growth of greater international interdependence and power of some of the developing countries.

The desire on the part of the developing countries to change the international power distribution was articulated in the demand for a New International Economic Order from 1974 onwards. Among the motivations for this call were, of course, the successful oil price hike, which gave rise to hopes of "commodity power" in other areas, and also the disappointment with political independence and with the volume and quality of development aid. The call for a new international economic order was regarded by most observers as a challenge to the liberal order from the point of view of anti-market, regulatory economic planners and bureaucrats. But the threats to the liberal order in the later 1970s and 1980s came not from the barbarians outside the gate, but from within the

---

[9]Originally it was called the United Nations Fund for Economic Development. But "when it was realized... that the initials of this new animal would read UNFED, [t]hat was too close to the truth and would no doubt be used by critics (including the World Bank) to discredit and ridicule the whole idea" [Singer (1984, p. 301)].

citadel of the liberal order. The growth of protectionism and of various devices to regulate and organize international trade sprang from the United States, Europe, and Japan.

4. Interdependence

The period of post-war U.S. dominance was one of comparative calm, economic expansion, and commitment to development on the part of the rich countries. The retreat from Third World commitments started in the 1970s. The two oil shocks, the election of Mrs. Thatcher in Britain and Mr. Reagan in the United States, the turning of attention to East–West issues abroad and to fighting inflation and unemployment at home, and the dominance of the international debt problem all contributed to this. At the same time the old doctrinal wisdom on economic policy was overturned, partly as a result of what was happening in the world and partly as a result of internal theoretical strains. The emphasis, at least in the rhetoric, shifted from fiscal to monetary policy, from demand mangement to supply management, from the accelerator to interest rates as investment determinants, from public interventions to reliance on the private sector and market forces, and, somewhat earlier, from fixed to flexible exchange rates. In the same vein, there was a turn from concern for development to domestic issues.

Before embarking upon an outline of a framework for more positive and constructive international responses to the needs of the Third World, let us draw some conceptual distinctions. International *interdependence* should be distinguished from *integration*, which in turn is not the same as *common* or *mutual* interests. *Integration* implies policy behavior on the part of separate countries as if they were a single country. Integration can be defined without value premises. If the omitted value premiss is that all members of the integrated area should be treated as equals with respect to achievements as well as with respect to opportunities, i.e. that they should not only have equal access to trade, capital flows and migration, but should also be subject to a system of taxation and enjoy social services and other benefits of the welfare state, the world was more integrated in the nineteenth century than it is today. By imposing fewer objectives on government policy, and by accepting what later, in retrospect, appeared to be irrational constraints, such as the gold standard, fixed exchange rates and balanced budgets, different countries were unwittingly integrated into a single world economy, dominated by one power. Domestic policies were constrained by the need to adhere to fixed exchange rates. The later addition of numerous objectives, apart from keeping law and order, to government policy, such as full employment, economic growth, income distribution, price stability, regional balance, protection of the natural environment, etc. and the rejection of constraints on policy such as fixed exchange rates and limits on the discretion of fiscal and monetary policy, while leading to greater integration of national economies, has led to the disintegration of the international economy. Such disintegration is, however, consistent with a high degree of interdependence. For *interdependence* can exist when one country by unilateral action can inflict harm on other countries. Competitive protectionism, devaluation, deflation, or global pollution of the air or oceans beyond national boundaries are instances. A nuclear war would be the ultimate form of interdependence resulting from international disintegration.

Interdependence is measured by the costs of severing the relationship. The higher these costs to one partner, the greater the degree of dependence of that partner. If a small country benefits more from the international division of labor, its dependence is greater. If high costs from severing economic links were to be incurred by both partners to a transaction, there would be interdependence. It is quite possible to have intensive and rapidly growing international *relations*, without a high degree of interdependence, if the relations can be abandoned at low costs. There is a (different) sense of "interdependence", according to which "dependence" means only "influenced by", without great benefits from maintaining or costs from severing the relationship. In this attenuated sense there can be interdependence, even though the costs of severing it are low or even negative. But this is not the sense in which the concept will be used in this essay.

Sometimes *mutual interests* are confused with interdependence. Yet, mutual interests can exist without any interdependence. Two countries may be wholly autarkic in their trade policies and therefore completely independent of one another, yet it may be in their mutual interest to open up foreign trade or capital flows with each other. While interests can refer to potential relations, interdependence is always actual.

Mutual interests are sometimes confused with *common interests*. Mutual interests imply that actions on the part of one agent are reciprocated by different actions on the part of the other agent, such as trade. Common interests refer to shared areas of interest, such as the preservation of the stock of fish in the sea or of trees in the forests, or clean air, or a stable monetary system, or free access to markets, or peace. Mutual interests apply to transactions in private goods; common interests to public goods.

Interdependence is often said to be strong and to have increased. International trade is taken to be an indicator of interdependence, and its high and, with some interruptions, growing values are accepted as evidence. Yet three important qualifications are necessary.

First, if we take the ratio of international trade to national income, the rapid growth in the post-war decades until 1976 can be taken to be a return to pre-1914 values. For the major countries, trade as a proportion of GNP has just about caught up with what it had been before the damage done by two world wars and the great depression. The ratio of world exports to world GNP was nearly 14 percent in 1960 and over 22 percent at the end of the 1970s, but it was about that before 1914.[10] In 1980, when the ratio of exports to GNP had reached the 1913 figure, exports ceased to grow. World exports fell in 1981, 1982 and 1983, went up moderately in 1984 and barely held even in 1985. (A lot of this is due to the fall in the price of oil.) If, however, we allow the fact that the public sector has greatly increased, and that the prices of non-tradable services in this sector have risen more than the average price level, trade as a ratio of private tradable goods has indeed increased since 1914 and continues to grow.[11]

The second qualification is that the countries, and (in some cases) the groups within countries that have participated in the benefits from the growing trade, have been confined to a few, though their number has grown. The large, poor masses of the Indian subcontinent and of Sub-Saharan Africa have not participated substantially in the growth of international trade.

The third qualification is that it is not the volume of trade or its rate of growth that should be accepted as an indicator of economic interdependence, but the damage that would be done by its elimination, i.e. consumers' and producers' surpluses. Much trade is conducted in slightly differentiated consumers' goods, which could readily be replaced by domestic production without great loss to consumers, judged by consumers' surpluses. This would have to be qualified only if the product differentiation is based on substantial economies of scale and yields great benefits to consumers, so that the elimination of these lines and their replacement by domestic production would be very costly or would reduce consumers' satisfactions greatly.

There may even be an excess of international trade beyond the optimum indicated by trade theory because of cross-hauling at prices that are below total unit cost for foreign sales of, say, motor cars. On the other hand, small volume and slowly growing items of trade could be of great importance and lead to substantial losses if they were cut out. The United States, for instance, depends strongly on imports of manganese, tin, and chromium.

Trade is, of course, only one, and not the most important, among many manifestations of economic interdependence. Others comprise the flow of factors of production, capital, enterprise and labor, across frontiers; there is the exchange of assets, the acquisition of legal rights, of information and knowledge. In addition to economic interdependence, there are educational and cultural, as well

---

[10] The ratio of exports to GNP was for the United Kingdom: 19.3 percent in 1913, 20.7 percent in 1976, and 21.7 percent in 1984 (28.4 percent including services); for the United States: 6.5 percent in 1913, 6.8 percent in 1976, and 6 percent in 1984 (7.4 percent including services); and for Germany: 20.5 percent in 1913, 22.3 percent in 1976, and 26.5 percent in 1984 (33.5 percent including services). In 1984 the ratio of merchandise trade to GNP for the advanced industrial countries was 29.9 percent.

[11] It is, of course, obvious that trade cannot grow indefinitely faster than national income. Its rate of growth has, in fact, slowed down considerably in the four years after 1980.

as military, strategic and political impulses that are rapidly propagated throughout the world.

Sir Arthur Lewis, when he invited us to imagine that all the developed countries were to sink under the sea,[12] suggested that, after an unspecified period of adjustment, it would not make much difference to the developing world. The same might be said about the developed countries, if the developing countries were to sink under the sea.

Yet, with these qualifications, there is no doubt that interdependence has increased. Richard N. Cooper has drawn a useful distinction between four effects which he calls the trampoline effect, the ricochet effect, the erosion of policy, and the transformation of the impact of policy.[13] To these I would add the interdependence of government policies.

The trampoline effect derives from the analogy that a major impact in one place has a consequential, though a smaller impact on all other places of the area. Sir Dennis Robertson used to say in the early post-war period that when America sneezes the rest of the world catches pneumonia. This is no longer so, but the rest of the world still catches cold. But interdependence (as opposed to dependence) has led to reciprocity. As Richard Cooper has reminded us, if the rest of the world sneezes, America also catches a cold. Shortages of a particular commodity, such as that of sugar some years ago, spread rapidly throughout the world. This is a very different mechanism from the monetary mechanism described by David Hume, in which the outflow of gold spells deflation in the specie-losing country and inflation in the gaining country. To change the metaphor – the world is no longer a seesaw (and perhaps has never been one outside some theories) but a rollercoaster, in which we all go up and down together; or at least down. Since 1970 there have been two world-wide, coordinated slumps: 1973–75 and 1979–82. The rollercoaster mechanism may work less well in the upswing, when an American recovery left the rest of the world with high levels of unemployment.

The exception to the rollercoaster mechanism occurs when a combination of fiscal expansion with monetary restriction in the United States raises the value of the dollar as a result of capital inflows and forces other countries to follow suit in adopting a tight monetary policy. Then an expansion in the United States is combined with recession abroad, with a detrimental impact on the developing countries. The contraction from high interest rates in a country like Britain outweighs any expansion from cheap exports. Tight fiscal and loose monetary policy in the United States is more consistent with a joint world-wide expansion, better export prospects for the developing countries and a lower debt burden.

But while the degree of dominance of the United States has diminished compared with the early post-war years, a country running a $200 billion budget

---

[12] Lewis (1970, p. 12).
[13] Cooper (1985).

deficit and a \$160 billion trade deficit, that has by historical standards still very high interest rates, cannot be said to pay much attention to the impact of its policies on other nations. Interdependence was probably greater in 1979 than it was in 1985. Both American autonomy in policy-making and her comparative independence of other countries' policies again seem to have increased. She has once again become more of an "unmoved mover", even while she pleads with Japan and Germany to expand their economies. This situation may, however, be only temporary and dominance, in the long run, may again be reduced.

The second form of interdependence takes the form of the ricochet (or boomerang) effect. The United States restricts steel imports from Europe, Europe then restricts steel imports from Brazil, South Africa and Korea, and, as a result, more Brazilian, South African and Korean steel comes into the United States. (Some extra Brazilian imports into the United States would have been caused even without European restrictions.) The United States now has to impose restrictions on steel imports from Brazil, etc. Restriction of grain sales to Russia led the Russians to substitute purchases from Argentina. Chile, Peru, Japan, Spain and Italy, no longer able to buy from Argentina, shift their purchases to the United States. But the target of depriving the Soviet Union of grain has not been hit.

The erosion of policy, the third effect, means that the old methods of economic control have become much less effective because of the internationalization of many transactions. The multiplier of fiscal stimulation has been reduced because a higher proportion of extra income is spent on imports. Therefore, fiscal policies of expansion are less effective. If a larger proportion of the extra income resulting from tax reductions had been spent on U.S. goods, the budget deficit would have been much smaller. Thus, the tax reduction in the United States ultimately added to the coffers of the treasuries of other countries. But this has to be qualified. In a world of flexible exchange rates, governments can to some extent insulate themselves against the foreign multiplier effects by exchange-rate variations. In the terminology used below, the efficacy of a given instrument (tax policy) has declined, while the number of instruments has increased (foreign exchange-rate policy). Not only fiscal but also monetary policy is less effective because capital can easily flow abroad, or a restrictive monetary policy can be frustrated by capital inflows. When people can lend and borrow anywhere in the world, the national money supply and its control become meaningless concepts.[14] Even microeconomic policies aiming at industrial regulation have become eroded. Transnational corporations can escape regulation by moving to tax havens in

---

[14]A report of a group of senior Central Bank officials of the Group of Ten, *Recent Innovations in International Banking* [Bank of International Settlements (1986)] shows that financial innovation and deregulation have made it harder for monetary authorities to use policy tools effectively. One of the conclusions of the report is that policy responses "may call for closer cooperation between banking authorities and those responsible for capital market regulation at national and international levels".

Switzerland or to regulatory havens in Luxembourg. As a result of this partial paralysis of economic policy the call has arisen for stronger international coordination.

The question of the erosion of policies should be analyzed in three steps. First, is the disease greater? Second, do we have more or fewer medicines to cure the disease? And, third, is the efficacy of any given medicine increased or reduced? It may well be that the internationalization of transactions reduces the need of policy actions for intervention, because it permits, for example, disturbances originating at home to be absorbed through foreign trade. A domestic inflationary impulse will spill over into imports and thereby reduce the need to take anti-inflationary action. Whether we have more or fewer medicines depends upon the degree of international cooperation, and the commitments under international agreements. Membership of the IMF, of GATT, of the European Community, and other institutions prohibits certain unilateral interventions, such as tariff increases, and to that extent reduces the number of medicines that a fully sovereign country would have in its cupboard. And so do current efforts to reduce exchange-rate flexibility and return to a system of stabler exchange rates. Finally, the efficacy of any given medicine is affected by the internationalization. We have seen that multiplier effects of fiscal policy are reduced because of leakages into imports. On the other hand, a small devaluation may show a greater response because of the large volume of foreign trade and its higher elasticities of demand and supply.

Fourthly, the impact of policy has been transformed. We have to take new consequences into account that arise from international transactions. When countries were more isolated a rise in the rate of interest affected mainly construction of long lasting assets such as houses, investment in stocks, and consumption through changes in the stock exchange valuation of financial assets. Today, a rise in the U.S. interest rate leads to an inflow of capital, if the expected depreciation of the dollar over the period of the loan is less than the interest differential between foreign and American real interest rates (i.e. nominal rates minus expected rates of inflation) and if other things, such as expectations of other currency values, relative rates of inflation, expectations about the U.S. economy, and political conditions, remain the same. For short-term loans it is possible to buy forward exchange, in which case the cost of the forward exchange has to be deducted from the interest differential. High real interest rates attract capital inflows and lead to an appreciation of the dollar which makes imports from Britain and Japan cheaper.[15] If workers in Caterpillar Tractors become unemployed, they blame the Japanese tractor industry, not the restrictive monetary policy of the United States, or the large budget deficit caused by military expenditure, which has contributed to high interest rates. In the United States

[15]See previous footnote.

there is conflict between the financial and banking interests that benefit from a high (and stable) dollar and from the resulting capital inflow, because they raise the profits in international banking, and the industrial interests that want a low value of the dollar for exports, for import substitutes, and for employment.

Or, to take another example, the IMF imposes austerity measures on a given debtor country so as to create the capacity to repay debt. As a result, that country cuts imports not only from the advanced industrial countries, but also from other developing countries, with which trade has grown rapidly in the past. Not only may Northern growth rates be reduced, but the debt-paying capacities of the other countries whose exports have been cut are also reduced and the debt crisis is aggravated. Mexico, Chile, Venezuela, Argentina, and Mexico are among the principal customers for Brazil's exports and as these countries obey the IMF and cut their imports from Brazil, its ability to service debt is reduced. The outcome depends, of course, on what we assume the alternative situation would have been. Contraction in the absence of an IMF loan may have been even greater, but restrictions with an IMF loan provided under different conditions less so.

Finally, there is much greater interdependence of government policies. According to what Paul Krugman calls the "new view",[16] the crucial channel of interdependence "is not via the direct impacts of one country's policies on the economies of other countries, [communicated through the foreign multiplier], but indirectly, via the induced changes in the *policies* of these countries' governments". An example would be the way in which U.S. tight monetary policy communicates itself to the rest of the world. Higher U.S. interest rates attracted capital from abroad and raised the value of the dollar. Britain, while welcoming the boost this gave to her exports, attempted to stem the flight of capital and the decline in the pound by also raising her interest rates.

The United States has, of course, combined a restrictive monetary policy with a very expansionist fiscal policy. This reinforces the rise in interest rates and therefore in the dollar. If other countries resist the fall in the value of their currencies, the U.S. fiscal expansion can lead to a deeper recession abroad. We are back at the seesaw mechanism, this time not the result of the impersonal impact of the flow of specie, but of responses by government policies. Had the United States followed an expansionary monetary policy, this expansion would have communicated itself to the rest of the world and the recovery would have been world-wide.

The interdependence of policies is reinforced, for the developing countries, by IMF conditionality. When the balance of payments of a developing country suffers, deflation is imposed upon it if it wants to borrow from the Fund. The current recessions in many developing countries are less the direct effect of

[16]Krugman (1985).

reduced demand from the OECD countries than the indirect effect of Fund-imposed austerity. This, in turn, is the result of the debt burden, aggravated by high interest rates and reduced confidence of the banks. In spite of all the talk of growing interdependence, the United States through its monetary policy, directly and indirectly, continues to influence the fate of the developing countries, without being much influenced by them.

But while the ability to control policy instruments has been weakened as a result of international interdependence and the risk of retaliation, the demands on the government have increased. People demand protection against not only potential enemies, but also unemployment, especially of the young, the disabilities of the old, the impact of imports from abroad, of inflation at home, and of environmental pollution. Gunnar Myrdal pointed out that national integration has led to international disintegration. But international interdependence has also weakened the power to meet these demands. The international integration that has resulted from the technical revolutions in communications, information, travel, and transport has led to a loss of national power for integration.

From the point of view of the developing countries, an easing of U.S. monetary policy accompanied by a more expansionary policy of other OECD countries, a fall in the value of the dollar, and a return to world recovery would be best. The developing countries would benefit from lower interest rates on their debt and expanding demand for their exports. The worst outcome would be a return to tight monetary policy in the United States to combat renewed inflation, a rising value of the dollar, and continuing restrictions of other OECD countries. Demand for the exports of the developing countries would be low, interest payments would be high, and the dollar-nominated value of the debt would rise. In such conditions we may face debtors' cartels, debt repudiation, and threats to the financial system.

5. Technology and institutions

The gap between the rapid advances in technical knowledge, resulting in the revolutions in transport, travel, information, and communications, which have shrunk distances, on the one hand, and the political institution of the nation state, with its claims to sovereign authority and its attempts to regulate the lives of its citizens and respond to their clamor for protection and insurance against the impact of interdependence, was vividly symbolized by such events as the shooting down of the Korean commercial airliner over Soviet territory, or by the Iranian revolution, or by the large sums of money moving across the world in response to instant information, and determining exchange and interest rates. As Stanley Hoffman has said, the nation state has remained more obstinate than obsolete.[17] The tensions and contradictions created by this gap are at the root of the negative sum games, the mutual infliction of damage in an interdependent, though far from integrated, and in some respects, disintegrating, world.

The main conclusion to be drawn from this argument is that we are suffering from a lag of institutional adaptation to the technological and political reality of the end of the twentieth century. One institution, the nation state, is still rooted in a soil 350 years old. In 1648 the Peace of Westphalia ended the Holy Roman Empire and codified the triumph of national sovereignty as the constitutive principle of the international system. Since then modern science and technology have moved ahead rapidly. The dispersal and fragmentation of the four development functions discussed above has meant that opportunities have been missed, and damage has been inflicted by the uncoordinated actions of these nation states. What is needed is institutional innovation.

Clarity on this point is critical. By "institutional innovation" I do not mean additional international bureaucracies; clearly new bodies, organizations, and forums have mushroomed. But international bureaucrats have often been an obstacle rather than a help to progress and reform and have increased the resistance to change.[18] Sir Hermann Bondi has said that the stupidity of an organization is proportional to the cube of the number of its members. And one can imagine the size or number of global institutions were they allowed to proliferate. What I have in mind by institutional innovation is rules, procedures, and organizations that: (1) have precise technical functions (such as the successful Universal Postal Union, the International Telecommunication Union, the International Civil Aviation Organization or the World Meteorological Organization), (2) are immune from politicization, and (3) are publicly accountable. I view institutions "not simply as formal organizations with headquarter buildings and organized staffs, but more broadly as 'recognized patterns of practice around which expectations converge'".[19]

It is worth noting that these institutional responses have occurred in the private sector. The multinational corporations, the Eurocurrency market, and the transnational banks are responses to the revolution in information, communications, travel, and transport. The equivalent response in the public sector can be achieved, as is shown by some successful international bodies mentioned in the previous paragraph. We should aim at functional solutions at the global level.

Many of the problems in the international relations of interdependence arise from a combination of the free-rider problem, Olson's problem,[20] and the

---

[17]Stanley Hoffman "Obstinate or obsolete? The fate of the nation-state and the case of Western Europe", *Daedalus*, vol. 95 (Summer): 862–915; quoted in Keohane (1984, p. 238).

[18]See Streeten (1986).

[19]Keohane (1984, p. 8). The quotation is from Young (1980, p. 337).

[20]See below.

prisoners' dilemma. The free-rider problem exists because some of the solutions of international difficulties consist in the provision of public goods.[21] A public good is one from whose supply all those who value the good benefit, irrespective of whether they have contributed to its costs. The concept can readily be extended to cover common goals or common interests, the achievement of which benefits all, irrespective of whether they have contributed to the costs of achieving these goals or interests. The enjoyment of the good or service by one person does not detract from the enjoyment by others. In this sense international cooperation and the prevention of international wars are public goods. So are functioning markets and a working international monetary order with an international central bank as a lender of last resort and as a provider of liquidity,[22] and scientific research.

An international income tax or the coordination of international fixed investment decisions fall under the same heading. But these public goods will be systematically undersupplied, because any one country will not find it worthwhile to take the appropriate action, and will rely on others to do so, even though the benefits would exceed the costs, were all to contribute. And each country knowing that others will act that way will not have an incentive to be the only one which contributes to something that benefits others. As a result, international cooperation, peace, research, international monetary stability, market access, and world development will be undersupplied. No one contributes and everyone is worse off.

The Invisible Hand, which, according to Adam Smith, coordinates the independent decisions of a multitude of individuals, could also be applied, and has been applied to the unintended coordination of the actions of nation states. But this Invisible Hand that is supposed to guide the self-interest of each agent, whether individual or country, to the common good is not to be seen in the cases discussed above.[23] Everyone's attempt to free ride has led to the disappearance of the horse.

---

[21] Kindleberger (1978, 1986a, 1986b). The free-rider problem is a special case of a more general problem, when agreement on cooperative action that would promote everybody's interest cannot be reached because of disagreement over the distribution of benefits or costs. Each partner wishes to minimize his contribution to the joint costs, in the case of the free rider to zero, or maximize his share of the benefits.

[22] Some might regard the current position of the United States as a borrower of last resort as an example of a public bad.

[23] Related problems have also been discussed under the concepts of "tragedy of the commons" (each agent, acting in his self-interest, contributes to social losses, such as overgrazing on a common pasture or overpopulating the globe), and "social traps" (no driver has an incentive to install a gadget that reduces pollution). These, as well as prisoners' dilemma, "collective action", and Olson's problem, are special instances of "market failure".

It is true that free-rider problems are not ubiquitous. Individuals may be afraid of the sanctions attached to such behavior. Or they may avoid free riding because they believe that their contributions will make others contribute. Individuals sometimes do behave according to Kant's categorical imperative, in a manner that can be universalized. Otherwise, why should anybody clap after a theatre performance (assuming you do not get pleasure from clapping), or vote in a democratic election? But Kant's categorical imperative, or the notion that we should behave in the way we should want others to behave, may apply less to the actions of nation states than to those of individuals. Leadership, and even hegemony, particularly by a strong superpower, and enlightened self-interest can contribute to such Kantian behavior by nation states.

The prisoners' dilemma arises because each country, in promoting its own national interest rationally, contributes to a situation in which all countries are worse off. Just as public goods are undersupplied, public bads are oversupplied. No single actor has an adequate incentive to remove them. This applies to competitive protectionism, beggar-my-neighbor devaluations or deflations, the spread of inflation, investment wars, the arms race, global pollution of the air and the sea, overfishing and excessive exploitation of exhaustible resources to which no property rights are attached, and similar situations.

The same competitive infliction of damage occurs in government policies toward multinational enterprises. Each government insists that they should export more and import less, or create more jobs, or use more local inputs, but as more and more governments impose these performance criteria, they become self-defeating. The same applies to competitive attempts to attract footloose labor-intensive multinationals by tax holidays and subsidies to various inputs. The elasticity of supply to any given country in response to these incentives is rather high, but the total elasticity of supply is low. In the game of these competitive blandishments, the countries lose tax revenue, without reaping corresponding benefits. Ronald Dore has argued that the competitive research race in technological innovation also falls into this category, because it is faster than the evolution of social institutions.[24]

Richard Cooper has likened the situation to a crowd in which each member, wishing to see a passing parade better, rises to his tiptoes, with the result that no one sees better but everyone is more uncomfortable.[25] What is needed is either coordination and cooperation or supra-national sanctions that force all countries to act in what will amount to their self-interest. Without such coordinated or enforced action, the outcome of nationally rational actions will be irrational

[24]See Dore (1988). A pace of technical progress much in advance of the progress of institutions, can, like the arms race, lead to mutual harm. But the solution may lie just as much in speeding up institutional change as in slowing down technological change. Indeed, this is one of the main arguments of this chapter.

[25]Copper (1986, pp. 160–173).

damage and mutual impoverishment. For the damaging course of action is the best, whether other nations act similarly or not.[26]

On the other hand, according to Coase's theorem, if, in the absence of transaction costs, and in the presence of a legal framework and full information, one country inflicts damages on another which are greater than the benefits to the first country, the injured country can enter into a contract and compensate the injuring country for not inflicting the injury and be better off than it would be with the injury, or the injuring country can compensate the injured country for the damage, and still be better off than it would be if it had to forgo the injury. Such international compensations or bribes are in fact not common but they point, in principle, to the other extreme from that of the prisoners' dilemma. In a world of Coase's outcomes Pareto optimal allocations would be achieved, for any deviation would give rise to potential joint gains, out of which losers could be compensated for accepting moves toward the Pareto optimum.[27]

The difficulties of reaching Coase-type agreements and the dangers of ending in prisoners' dilemma situations are aggravated by four factors. First, there is no longer a hegemonic power, such as Britain before the First World War and the United States for a quarter of a century after the Second World War, which is prepared to carry a large part of the cost of the public goods and to exercise leadership to make others contribute. Second, the proliferation of independent nation states to about 160 makes agreements more difficult than previously when fewer governments could establish a system of mutual trust or enforcement (Olson's problem). It is, however, true that most of these are quite small and that coordination by a few large ones is what ultimately matters. Third, the rapid pace of social and technical change makes it more difficult to evolve the stability on which trust can be built. It has been shown that repeated games of prisoners' dilemma in similar situations tend to lead to cooperative solutions. Rapid change of the conditions on which cooperation is based prevents this.[28] Finally, the absence of world government and world courts makes it impossible to establish property rights, to enforce contracts, and to set the sanctions for failing to abide by agreements.

---

[26] The case against international cooperation between governments has been based on the view that uncoordinated, competitive actions by national governments give better results than global coordination, in analogy to Adam Smith's Invisible Hand. But the assumptions required to make such a position true are too unrealistic to be seriously considered. Nation states are not in atomistic relations to one another, and there is a particular need for the provision of public goods. More serious is the objection that coordinated international action can give rise to countervailing power by private agents, destroying the benefits. It would also have to be assumed that the cooperative action is based on a fairly accurate prognosis and diagnosis of the economic situation, and an approximately correct understanding of the causal relations between policies and results.

[27] Lipton (1985).

[28] Axelrod (1984).

As Michael Lipton has said,[29] if all outcomes were non-cooperative prisoners' dilemmas, no government would be possible. (But one important reason for establishing government is to avoid prisoners' dilemmas.) If Coase's theorem held universally, no government would be needed (except for income redistribution). The actual world is between the two extremes. But the relations of nation states are nearer the prisoners' dilemma end of the spectrum, for the four reasons given above.

In current economic controversies there has been a repeated call for stronger microfoundations of macroeconomics and macropolicies. But we hear much less of the need for the macrofoundations of micropolicies. The policies of national governments in isolation can be destructive and self-defeating, unless they are conducted in a framework of cooperation and obey the rules of global institutions. We need a set of global norms, rules and procedures that prevent national policies from becoming counter-productive.

6. Three systems

In order to set up a framework for a more constructive response to the call of the South for a better world order Kenneth Boulding's distinction between the exchange system, the threat system, and the integrative system is useful. The exchange system is based on the principle: "I do something good for you if you do something good for me." It covers the area of mutual interests. The threat system is based on the principle: "unless you do something good for me I shall do something horrid to you". In the integrative or love system the principles of love and duty applied to ourselves and our family are extended to other members of a wider community. We do good neither in the expectation of good in return nor under the threat of harm, but from a sense of unity or solidarity or obligation. This sense can derive from a common ideology or from a sense of community. These not only reduce the danger of too many free riders, so that every one contributes voluntarily to the common good that also benefits them, but also lead to some sacrifice for the benefit of others: genuine altruism. The three systems correspond roughly to positive sum games, in which all participants benefit; avoiding negative sum games, in which all would lose in the absence of coordinated action; and zero sum games, in which one side has to make concessions for the benefit of others.

Systems can, of course, be mixed. What appears to be a genuine sacrifice in the short run may turn out to be beneficial to the sacrificer in the long run. Or the removal of the benefit (such as access to markets) can constitute a threat. Or the division of the joint gains can give rise to conflicts. This, in practice, is a

---

[29]Lipton (1985).

particularly important obstacle to the pursuit of positive sum games. The gains come to be accepted and only the wrangles over their division remain.

In distinguishing between the integrative system and the exchange system it is important to distinguish between doing what is right and wishing to be seen to be doing right because this is in the nation's self-interest. The United States is dedicated to a value system, characterized by Myrdal as the American Creed. It adds cohesion to American society and strength to its foreign policy. But it is an entirely different thing to say, as a paragraph in the Kissinger Commission Report on Central America does, that it is in the American national self-interest *to be seen* to be acting right. "To preserve the moral authority of the United States. To be perceived by others as a nation that does what is right *because* it is right is one of this country's principal assets." There is all the difference in the world between doing what is right because it is right, and doing it because the United States must be seen to do what is right because it is right. It is in the U.S. national interest to be seen to act in a moral way. The first action is moral, disinterested; the second self-interested.[30]

The distinction between the three systems is useful for a clear analysis, but should not be proclaimed too clearly for negotiations. There we have an interest in pretending that what is truly a benefit to us is a sacrifice, so that we may get concessions on other fronts.

The exchange system of mutual interests has been much promoted, especially by the Brandt Commission, the OECD, and the Overseas Development Council. Trade liberalization is the most frequently advocated policy. It is, of course, a modern version of the doctrine of the harmony of interests. Each participant in free international trade is thought to benefit from the international division of labor. Rousseau said: "Man was born free, and everywhere he is in chains." Similarly, all economists recommend free(r) trade, but everywhere there is protection.

The most powerful argument for international trade is, however, not the one based on the theory of comparative advantage, which assumes either constant costs (Ricardo) or increasing costs (Heckscher–Ohlin), but one based on economies of scale, increasing returns, learning-by-doing and decreasing unit costs, as elaborated by Allyn Young. Adam Smith already had pointed out that "the division of labour is limited by the extent of the market". He thought mainly of the geographical extent. Allyn Young added the reverse propostion, that the extent of the market, not only in the geographic sense, but also in the sense of the size and number of incomes, depended on the division of labor. Production, productivity, and incomes rise as specialization proceeds. It is on the interaction between these two – the division of labor and the extent of the market – that economic progress depends. To widen the market, to raise incomes

---

[30] The point is made and the quotation cited in an article by Ash (1984).

in the South, makes greater international specialization possible, which in turn contributes to raising productivity and incomes. But this avenue to reaping mutual benefits has not been much explored by economists, partly because it conflicts with the general equilibrium model which must assume increasing costs, and partly perhaps because some object to the style of development that relies on large-scale production and increasing specialization as inconsistent with the desire for diversity, human dignity, self-reliance, and respect for the environment.

It might be thought that, by and large, people, groups, and nations are very good in detecting and pursuing their self-interest and that not much exhortation is needed. Neither teaching nor preaching is needed to make people pursue their self-interest. But, as we have seen, there can be important divergencies between reaching for and achieving what is in one's interest. In some cases the self-interested action leads to damage to oneself. We have already discussed the prisoners' dilemma and the free-rider problem. The former leads to the infliction of mutual harm, and the latter to the undersupply of public goods and the oversupply of public bads.

In addition, the national self-interest may fail to be pursued by the government for several reasons. There can be conflict between groups with different power, articulateness, and influence, so that the more powerful influence policy more strongly, even if their gains are smaller than the losses of the less powerful, the less articulate, and the less influential. Or there may be conflict between dispersed larger and concentrated smaller gains, or between uncertain larger and certain smaller gains, or between larger future and smaller present gains, or between perceived larger but effectively smaller gains. The last may be one of the reasons why both the general public and policy-makers are not prepared to surrender national sovereignty, even though its surrender might lead to a more effective achievement of self-interested objectives than adherence to full sovereignty, autonomy, and control, in the same way in which the acceptance of traffic regulations enlarges our freedom to drive accident-free, while restricting our freedom of choice.

Finally, the gains to some may be much larger than the gains to others, who, though gaining a little, resent this. In any case, the distribution of gains presents quite different problems at the international level from those at the national. For any national community, a central government can tax and redistribute gains if this is deemed desirable. But without a world government, this cannot be done at the international level.

In all these cases, selfish action may not lead to the achievement of the self-interest, and the achievement of self-interested objectives may involve some sacrifice in unconstrained and uncoordinated selfishness. Moreover, it would be only a coincidence if the actions dictated by the national self-interest of advanced countries were to coincide with the development objectives, whether these are accelerated growth, growth with equity, redistribution with growth, or basic needs. In particular, the poorest groups and the poorest countries will tend to be left out in a strategy based on national self-interest.

There are further problems in postulating a national self-interest. On the one hand, in a divided society in which interests clash deeply, there is little or no meaning in the concept "national interest". On the other hand, interest alignments may run across national boundaries. The European farm lobby campaigns against the European industrialists; the textile manufacturers organize themselves against consumers in the Multifiber Arrangement. The internationalization of transactions that has resulted from the revolution in communications, information, travel, and transport has strengthened these interest alignments across frontiers and weakened the notion of a national self-interest. Moreover, national governments may pursue objectives that have nothing to do with the interest of the national community, even where such a community and such common interests exist.

Removal of dangers of the threat system and the avoidance of negative-sum games, should have a high priority, for it can lead to mutual impoverishment and even destruction. Disarmament, removal of the threat of protection, an end to beggar-my-neighbor deflation, devaluation or inflation, and of "voluntary" export restraints, and agreement on policies toward multinational corporations, are all clearly lines of action worth pursuing. They call for international coordination and institutional responses of the kind discussed here.

It may be thought that all agreements entered into voluntarily between states must amount to positive-sum games, in which each is better off. But this is not so. Some alliances may be formed with either the specific purpose or with the unintended result of inflicting costs on outsiders. In this case alliances or pacts can lead to negative-sum games.

One of the reasons why agreements on avoiding negative-sum games, on reducing bads, and creating anti-bads, are so difficult, is to be found in the logic of collective action, so well analysed by Mancur Olson.[31] The larger the group, the weaker the incentive for any one member to contribute to the action that benefits all. And we now have about 160 countries in the world. As a result, the public goods are not produced, or are underproduced, even though their value is greater than their costs to the group of countries as a whole. It is true that some smaller subset of countries, the Group of Five or the Group of Seven, may take responsibility for the rest, but they may also act in a way that imposes costs on others.

We can build on areas of common national interests, emphasizing mutual benefits to be derived from such things as resumption of orderly and equitable growth in the world economy, forswearing self-defeating protectionism, exploring ways of increasing the resources in globally scarce supply, and, while scarcity

---

[31] Olson (1971).

exists, sharing them out equitably, etc. But while there is considerable scope for positive-sum games in exploring areas of common and mutual interests, and of avoiding self-defeating, mutually destructive policies of the prisoners' dilemma type, there is also a "higher" interest in a world order that both is, and is seen to be, equitable, that is acceptable and therefore accepted, and that reduces conflict and confrontation.

All societies need a basis of moral principles for their self-regulation and for social control. Individuals are ready to make sacrifices for the communities they live in. This forms the basis of the integrative system. Can this principle stop at the nation state? A belief in the harmony between self-interest and altruism is deep-seated in Anglo-Saxon thought and action. One is reminded of the eighteenth-century bishop Joseph Butler: "when we sit down in a cool hour, we can neither justify to ourselves this or any other pursuit, till we are convinced that it will be for our happiness...".[32] The only question is why it appears to be easier to identify, or at least harmonize, individual happiness with the national interest than with that of the world community. It is odd that a moral, disinterested concern by rich countries with the development of the poor is hardly ever conceded. As hypocrisy is the tribute vice pays to virtue, so professions of national self-interest in the development of poor countries may be the tribute that virtue has to pay to vice.

In the present fashion of stressing common and mutual interests, we run the danger of underestimating the power of moral or humanitarian appeals. Holland, Sweden, and Norway, which have put international cooperation squarely on a moral basis, have hit the 0.7 percent aid target. It is the countries in which aid has been sold to the public as in the national self-interest where the effort is lagging.

The common interest must also be defined in terms of different time horizons: the next year, the next five years, the next twenty years. There may be conflicts and trade-offs between these different time spans. For example, concessionary aid to the poorest may involve economic sacrifices in the near future but, by laying the foundations for a world in which all human beings born can fully develop their potential, it contributes to the long-term interest of mankind.

One difficulty is that in democracies adults have votes, but children and the unborn have no votes. The fight is not only against powerfully organized vested interests, but also against all our own short-term interests that neglect the interests of future generations.

Any attempt to build cooperation for development on moral principles has to answer three questions. First, do the rich in a community have an obligation on the ground of social justice (not only of charity) to the poor and do the poor have a just claim on the rich? Second, does mankind constitute a community in the

[32] Butler (1950, Sermon 11, para. 20).

relevant sense or do communities stop at national boundaries? Third, does the existence of national governments not interfere with the discharge of the obligations of the rich, if such obligations exist, to the poor in the world community, if there is such a community?

The first question may be answered by an analysis of various theories of moral philosophy, although it is doubtful that actual action is guided by the answer. Utilitarianism, Rawls' approach, and various types of entitlement theory would provide a basis for an obligation of the rich to contribute to improving the lot of the poor in a community. The utilitarian argument is that a dollar redistributed from a rich to a poor man adds more utility than it detracts, and therefore increases the sum total of utility. The Rawlsian argument, according to which our concern should be the relief of the poorest people, is more appealing than utilitarian arguments, partly because the relief of absolute poverty is a more widely accepted objective than abstract egalitarianism, and partly because it justifies enriching some rich individuals – almost inevitably the result of aid – if this is a condition for improving the fate of the poorest.

Entitlement theories might claim that differential rules guiding immigration, encouraging the immigration of professionals while discouraging that of unskilled workers, provide a basis for a claim to compensation. More common is the claim that past colonial exploitation entitles ex-colonies to compensation. But there are the questions whether in fact our ancestors had been guilty of exploitation; whether, even if they were, the present generation has a right to compensation for ills done by our ancestors; and, if they have, whether development aid is the correct form of compensation. Arguments for the need to develop human potential of people born into the world, are more convincing. Even without a theoretical basis for moral obligations, the moral obligation of the rich to the poor may be part of people's intuition, on which greater agreement exists than on the philosophical basis of this intuition.

Perhaps more difficult is the case for saying that mankind does constitute a community in the relevant sense. Social contract theories might say that we need not do anything for the world community because the world community does not do anything for us, whereas the state provides protection, security, and certain other services. But even if the first two questions were answered in the affirmative, the third question presents the difficulty that the discharge of the obligation may take the form of what opponents of aid-giving have called, "a redistribution of resources from the poor in rich countries to the rich in poor countries". To meet this difficulty we have to exercise our institutional imagination in finding procedures and institutions that avoid, or at least minimize, this possibility.

The "higher" interest in an acceptable world order can be defined either in moral terms or in terms of the desire to avoid negative-sum games, breakdown, and wars. Whatever the definition and justification, its aim is to transform adversary relationships into cooperation. When interests diverge or conflict, the task of statesmanship is to reconcile them. This is a task quite distinct from, and more important than, that of exploring areas of common or mutual interest. It is in this light that cooperative action to eradicate world poverty and to restructure the international economic order has to be seen.

What, then, are the requirements of a sensible international order? It will consist of negative rules of what national governments must not do, and agreements on certain positive cooperative actions. The rules of abstention will be intended to prevent negative-sum games, and the rules of action to create some public goods and avoid public bads. Ralph Bryant has called these rules "supranational traffic regulations".[33] Some critics have accused the developing countries of requesting exemption from some general rules (such as reciprocity in tariff reductions or the banning of preferential trading arrangements) to which the developed countries should adhere. The discussion about appropriate rules for international economic relations has suffered from a long-standing confusion between *uniform* (sometimes also called *general*) principles or rules (the opposite of specific ones, and therefore necessarily simple) and *universal* principles or rules (which may be highly specific and complicated, provided that they contain no uneliminable reference to individual cases). Further confusion is caused if a third characteristic of rules is added: *inflexibility* over time, and confused with either uniformity or universality. A rule is capable of being *altered*, though it remains either uniform, i.e. simple, or universal, i.e. may have a lot of "exceptions" written into it. The "equal" treatment of unequals is not a principle of justice, and a general rule commanding it is an unjust rule. In order to prevent partiality and partisanship, rules have to be universal, i.e. not contain references to individual cases. They may not, and indeed should not, be uniform. They should pay attention to the varying characteristics and circumstances of different countries.

Those who charge the developing countries with asking for exemptions from rules are guilty of this confusion between *uniform* and *universal* rules. Thus, a differentiated system of multi-tier preferences according to the level of development of the exporting countries, may be best and most just for a group of trading countries at different stages of development. A fair system of rules also points to the differentiation in responsibilities and rights according to circumstances. Middle-income countries would not have the responsibility to give aid, but neither would they receive it. They would not have to give trade preferences, but neither would they receive them. Even finer differentiation would be possible. A country with a large balance of payments surplus might be asked to contribute to loans because of its foreign-exchange earnings, and, if its citizens enjoy high incomes, to aid because of its income per head, but might receive trade preferences if its level of industrialization is low. The 0.7 percent aid target would be

---

[33] Bryant (1980, p. 470).

replaced by a system in which those below a certain income per head are exempted, and the percentage target rises with income per head.

There is, of course, a practical and tactical case for *simple* rules, which might overrule the case in fairness for universal (though complex) rules: they are less open to abuse and easier to police. And there may be a tactical case for uniform rules: they may be easier to negotiate. It is for such pragmatic reasons rather than on theoretical grounds that one may advocate that rules should not be too complex, and should not be changed too often.[34]

Any specific proposal, such as non-reciprocity on trade concessions by advanced countries or the granting of trade preferences would, of course, have to be examined on its merits. But the distinction between "exemption from rules" and "drawing up new rules" is logically untenable, to the extent to which the call for exemption is really a call for a set of universal rules that pays attention to the different characteristics and circumstances of different countries, just as income tax allowances for dependents or lower rates on earned than on unearned income are not "exceptions" but reflect our notions of fairness.

Those who are concerned with changing the rules of international relations are aiming partly at removing biases in the present rules, partly at the exercise of countervailing power where at present the distribution of power is felt to be unequal, and partly at counteracting biases that arise not from rules but from the nature of economic processes. In the latter category are such processes as the cumulative nature of gains accruing to those who already have more resources, and the cumulative damage inflicted on those who have initially had relatively little.

Insofar as the call for new rules is about strictly economic relations, there is scope for positive-sum games. But insofar as it is about national power relations

---

[34]Of this long-standing confusion between universal and uniform, or general rules even such a clear-headed thinker as David Hume is guilty. Hume contrasts the highly specific reactions when we are seeking our own self-interest with the "universal and perfectly inflexible" laws of justice. He seems, like many others (including GATT), not to make a necessary distinction between general principles (the opposite of specific ones and therefore necessarily simple) and universal principles (which may be highly specific and highly complicated, provided that they contain no uneliminable reference to individual cases). Thus, Hume says, in one place "universal and perfectly inflexible", but lower down "general and inflexible". And the use of the word "inflexible" conceals a confusion between a principle being able to be altered (which has nothing to do with its universality or generality) and its having a lot of exceptions written into it (which is consistent with universality but not with generality). Hume evidently thinks that the rules of justice have to be simple, general ones. He argues that unless the rules are general, people will be partial in their application of them and "would take into consideration the characters and circumstances of the persons, as well as the general nature of the question... the avidity and partiality of men would quickly bring disorder into the world, if not restrained by some general and inflexible principles". But this is fallacious. In order to prevent people from being partial, the principles have to be universal, i.e. not contain references to individuals; they may, and indeed should, not be general; surely our judgements based on them ought to "take into consideration the characters and circumstances of the persons as well as the general nature of the question" [Hume (1978, pp. 581–587 and 602–603)].

between sovereign states with different and conflicting aims, power is by its very nature a relative concept, and what is at stake are zero-sum games. The demand for greater participation in the councils of the world and for corrections by the developing countries in the biases of the international power distribution are bound to diminish the power of the industrialized countries in conditions of conflict.

7. Institutional innovations

In addition to rules there is a need for institutions. Let me give six illustrations of the kind of institutional reform I have in mind. First, there is the creation of an International Central Bank that would be able to create (and withdraw) international liquidity, both for transactions and for precautionary reasons. A panic run on the banks would cause an international financial breakdown unless an institutional arrangement existed that provided the liquidity. The General Arrangements to Borrow do this now to some extent, but an international central bank would do this on a more solid and reliable basis.

The new type of central bank would also be responsible for the growth of global reserves at a pace which gives neither an inflationary nor a deflationary bias to the world economy. In the absence of such a global authority, the competitive actions of nation states will tend to be either too restrictive, transmitting unemployment and unused industrial capacity, as each country scrambles to accumulate scarce reserves, or too expansionary, transmitting inflation throughout the world, as the reserve currency country incurs large balance of payments deficits to pay for economic or military ventures abroad.

Second, there is the institution of an international income tax, levied progressively on GNP according to incomes per head, or, better yet, according to consumption per head so as to encourage saving. It would have a lower exemption limit. It would be collected automatically, but disbursed to developing countries according to agreed criteria. The monitoring of the fulfillment of the criteria should be done either by the developing countries themselves or by a mutually accepted transnational body.

Third, there is an international body to provide information on decisions for fixed, durable investment with long construction periods and long lasting plant and equipment, so that both entry and exit are slow. The purpose is to avoid the lurches from scarcity to excess capacity in steel, shipbuilding, and fertilizers that we are suffering now. It should obviously not be a super-cartel that goes in for market-sharing agreements, but a method of coordinating investment decisions.

Fourth, there is an international investment trust that channels the surpluses of the surplus countries in a multilaterally guaranteed scheme to the developing countries. It would have guarantees against inflation and exchange-rate losses for the lenders, and the loans would be on commercial terms to middle-income countries. By 1987 Japan had become the largest lending country with a large surplus in its balance of payments on current account. This surplus is in search of good and safe investment opportunities which call for the creation of appropriate institutions that convert a part of it into long-term loans to the developing countries. This would be in the interest of Japan, which could continue its export-led growth without having either to reduce its rate of savings or find domestic, lower-yielding alternatives. It would also be in the interest of other OECD countries on whose exports some of the loans will be spent. And it would certainly be in the interest of the capital-hungry developing countries, whose resources are waiting to be mobilized by such capital flows. Finally, it would be in the interest of the world economy which could resume its expansionary momentum. An interest-subsidization scheme could be grafted onto this for the low-income countries.

If this argument is accepted, the general call for Japan to raise its level of consumption or divert investment to the domestic market to the full extent of the current account surplus is seen to be misplaced. Higher consumption in a rich country should not be applauded in a world that is short of savings and in need of capital. And higher domestic Japanese investment (apart from housing and some infrastructure) is not desirable if it is subject to declining returns. Instead of calling on the Japanese to reflate, we should encourage Japan to mobilize its excess savings and channel them on acceptable terms, by long-term lending or equity capital, through either the private or the public capital markets to the developing countries. For this to occur, financial innovation is necessary.

Fifth, there should be a better way of dealing with the oil price problem than the erratic zig-zag movements that we have experienced since 1973. Oil-producing and oil-consuming countries would get together and agree on a small, annual increase in the real price of oil, say 2 percent. This assumes agreement on the best guess as to the real price of oil in twenty years' time. The balance of payments surpluses generated by such an increase could be channeled into the investment trust proposed above. The incentives to oil exploration, to the search for alternatives to oil, and to conservation would be gradual but steady. The incentives for the oil-exporting countries to use their revenue for investment in alternative productive assets would also be gradual and steady. And incentives to consumers of oil would permit a foreseeable and gradual adaptation. There would be neither debt crises nor the volatile movement of large funds in search of speculative gains, which would spare the world economy at least one major source of shocks and instability. Both inflation and unemployment rates would be reduced.

Sixth, it would also be worth re-examining the macroeconomic case for commodity price stabilization that has been argued mainly by the late Professor

Nicholas Kaldor.[35] The stabilization of the prices of primary commodity inputs into manufactured goods would reduce the fluctuations in prices, which have contributed to both inflation and unemployment in the advanced countries, and to losses and reduced investment incentives in the developing primary exporting countries. The collapse of primary product prices has been a major contributory cause of the debt crisis. In spite of all the objections to price stabilization that have been made on microeconomic grounds, the macroeconomic case has been less carefully explored.

There is also a need for reforming the institutions charged with North–South cooperation. What has the Marshall Plan experience to teach us for current relations with the South? It is now generally agreed that the Marshall Plan loans to Europe were given on too soft terms, perhaps in too large amounts, but they achieved their objective of rapid European reconstruction. It has also become a platitude to say that the lessons are not applicable to the developing countries because in Europe the human capital existed and to reconstruct with a skilled and well motivated labor force is a much easier task than developing an underdeveloped society. But one important lesson can still be learned. Critics of both the Left and Right have pointed to numerous faults of aid, and in particular that it has not achieved its intended objectives, whether they are poverty alleviation, redistribution, or economic growth. They conclude that we should get rid of aid. A better conclusion might be to get rid of the faults and to evolve mechanisms that ensure that the objectives of the aid donors are achieved.

The intervention of donor governments for the purpose of applying performance criteria to development aid has been regarded as inconsistent with national sovereignty, has been dismissed as intrusive, and has bred acrimony. It has also been difficult to separate objectives of accelerating development from objectives in the narrow national interest such as export promotion, gaining votes in the United Nations, forming political alliances, or getting strategic support. Performance criteria imposed in bilateral relations by donor governments have therefore been suspect and often counter-productive.

The task is then to evolve institutions that achieve the objectives of the donors and the recipients and are trusted by both sides. These must resolve the dilemma between avoiding intrusiveness and paying respect to national sovereignty on the one hand, and responsible accounting for taxpayers' money on the other. Here the Marshall Plan has still something to teach. It is not about the speed of development which, for European reconstruction, was much faster than for the structural changes needed for development; nor about the terms of the aid, which were too soft compared with today's terms for development aid, but about monitoring procedures. In a generous and imaginative gesture the European powers were encouraged to monitor one another's performance, and the heavy

---

[35] Kaldor (1987).

hand of the U.S. government was kept out of it. Each government submitted a plan which was inspected, vetted, and monitored by other European governments in the Organization for European Economic Cooperation (OEEC). Control by peers rather than supervisors is also a principle advocated in business mangement. A similar procedure could be adopted for groups of developing countries.

There are at least two other options. It would be desirable to create a genuine transnational secretariat whose loyalty would be only to the international community; that would be trusted by both donors and recipients. The staff of the present multilateral agencies do not quite achieve this, partly because the system of country quotas emphasizes national origins rather than merit, partly because the organizations are intergovernmental institutions, and partly because the recruitment, training, location, etc. of the staff of these organizations is to some extent in conflict with the ethos of a staff serving only the global community. In addition to having technical competence, the staff would be trained to be sensitive to social and political factors.

Finally, we might consider setting up a council of wise men and women whose task it would be to monitor the performance of both donors and recipients, and who again would be trusted by both sides. The existence of national governments that insist on the exercise of their full sovereignty interferes with the moral concern and enlightened self-interest in development cooperation. Until this obstacle is overcome, we can make no progress.

These proposals may be regarded as unrealistic and Utopian. There are three defenses against this criticism. First, the Utopian vision gives a sense of direction, which can get lost in approaches that take into account only what is feasible. Second, excessive preoccupation with the feasible tends to reinforce the status quo. In negotiations, for example, it strengthens the hand of those opposed to change, or even those favoring reaction, and attempts at reform are then liable to be frustrated. Third, it is sometimes the case that the conjuncture of circumstances changes, and that the constellation of forces, quite unexpectedly turns out to be favorable for even quite radical innovation. Unless one is prepared with a carefully worked out, detailed plan, reforms will lose out by default. It is for these three reasons that Utopians should not be discouraged to formulate their proposals in considerable detail.

References

Ash, T.G. (1984) 'Back yards', in: *The New York review of books*. New York: Rea S. Hederman.
Axelrod, R. (1984) *The evolution of cooperation*. New York: Basic Books.
Bank of International Settlements (1986) *Recent innovations in international banking*, Report of a Group of Senior Central Bank Officials. Basel.
Bryant, R. (1980) *Money and monetary policy in interdependent nations*. Washington, DC: The Brookings Institution.

Butler, J. 1692–1752 (1950) *Five sermons preached at the Rolls Chapel*. New York: Liberal Arts Press.

Chandavarkar, A.C. (1984) *The International Monetary Fund: Its financial organization and activities*, Pamphlet Series No. 42. Washington, DC: International Monetary Fund.

Cooper, R.N. (1985) 'International economic cooperation: Is it desirable? Is it likely?', *Bulletin of the American Academy of Arts and Sciences*, XXXIX(2):November.

Cooper, R.N. (1986) *The economics of interdependence: Economic policy in the Atlantic community*. New York: McGraw-Hill for the Council on Foreign Relations.

Dore, R. (1988) 'Technology in a world of national frontiers', *World Development*. Oxford: Pergamon Press.

Hume, D. 1711–1776 (1978) *A treatise of human nature*, edited by Selby-Bigge. Oxford: Oxford University Press.

Kaldor, N. (1987) 'The role of commodity prices in economic recovery'. *World Development*, 15:551–558.

Keohane, R.O. (1984) *After hegemony, cooperation and discord in the world economy*. Princeton, NJ: Princeton University Press.

Keynes, J.M. (1974) 'Memorandum on commodity price stabilization', *Journal of International Economics*, 4.

Kindleberger, C.P. (1978) *Government and international trade*, Essays in international finance, 129. Princeton, NJ: Princeton University Press.

Kindleberger, C.P. (1986a) 'International public goods without international government', Presidential Address to the Ninety-Eighth Meeting of the American Economic Association, December 29, 1985. *American Economic Review*, March.

Kindleberger, C.P. (1986b) 'Hierarchies versus inertial cooperation', *International Organization*, 40.

Krugman, P. (1985) 'U.S. macroeconomic policy and the developing countries', in: J.W. Sewell, R.E. Feinberg, and V. Kallab, eds., *U.S. foreign policy and the third world: Agenda 1985–86*. Washington, DC: Overseas Development Council.

Lewis, W.A. (1970) *The development process*. New York: United Nations.

Lipton, M. (1985) 'Prisoners' dilemma and Coase's theorem: A case for democracy in less developed countries?' in: R.C.O. Matthews, ed., *Economy and democracy*. New York: Macmillan.

Mason, E.A. and R.E. Asher (1975) *The World Bank since Bretton Woods*. Washington, DC: The Brookings Institution.

Olson, M. (1971) *The logic of collective action*, 2nd ed. Cambridge, MA: Harvard University Press.

Singer, H.W. (1984) 'The terms of trade controversy and the evolution of soft financing: Early years in the U.N.', in: G.M. Meier and D. Seers, eds., *Pioneers in development*. Oxford: Oxford University Press.

Stewart, F. and A. Sengupta, eds. (1982) *International financial cooperation: A framework for change*. London: Frances Pinter; Boulder, CO: Westview Press.

Streeten, P. (1986) 'The United Nations: Unhappy family', in: D. Pitt and T.G. Weiss, eds., *The nature of United Nations bureaucracies*. London: Croom Helm.

de Vries, M.G. (1985) *The International Monetary Fund, 1972–1978*. Washington, DC.

Young, O.R. (1980) 'International regimes: Problems of concept formation', *World Politics*, 32.

Chapter 23

TRADE AND DEVELOPMENT

CHRISTOPHER BLISS*

Nuffield College, Oxford

Contents

*Helpful comments and advice from too many people to mention individually are gratefully acknowledged, and in particular from the editors, Jon Eaton, David Evans, Lyn Squire, Nicholas Stern and Lance Taylor.

Handbook of Development Economics, Volume II, Edited by H. Chenery and T.N. Srinivasan
© Elsevier Science Publishers B.V., 1989

1. Introduction

Economic development is a wide-ranging field. Indeed, some have questioned whether there is such a field, whether the economics of development amounts to more than the application of a number of branches of economic theory and applied economics to the problems of developing countries. Even if correct, this argument is unimportant. In an ultimate sense biology may be reducible to physics, physics applied to the collections of molecules that constitute living organisms. Physics, however, embraces statements too general to give us biological insights unless it is adapted to biological applications.

This analogy is valid within its limits. Those parts of economic theory and method which apply more or less universally (such as the notion of opportunity cost) are among the most useful tools in the subject. However, alone they tell us less then we need in a particular application. To give them life they have to be enlarged and translated. When this is done a specialty is created. Development economics consists in part of the refinement of general economics to deal with questions which arise in the context of development, and partly of certain special ideas which have proved useful in studying developing countries.

The theory of international trade is another large field and a great deal of it applies to developing countries. In this way a truly enormous field might be created. Much of this programme has yet to be initiated but enough has been to provide the theory of trade and development with an extensive literature. A concentration on policy narrows the scope of the subject only a little, as a policy orientation is natural to the economics of development.

Despite the diversity of the subject, certain questions recur so frequently that it is natural to consider them as central and basic. Among them are the following:

(1) What is the role of trade in the process of economic development?

(2) Given certain objectives which most developing countries have chosen to pursue (a rapid rate of capital accumulation, improved income distribution, etc.), which type or pattern of international exchange has in practice best served those objectives?

(3) The authorities in developing countries have made use of various instruments to affect the trade pattern. What are the consequences of these instruments and which if any achieve the trade pattern of (2) above?

The above list overlaps with the list included in the survey by Diaz-Alejandro (1975) which also provides extensive references up to the early 1970s. These are fairly practical questions, but their answers naturally depend on the answer to another and more theoretical question:

(4) Are classical and neoclassical theories of international trade suitable for application to the situation of developing countries?

It can hardly be claimed that our knowledge includes definite answers to any of these questions, and there is no reason to suppose that there are universal answers good for all countries at all times. However, granted an affirmative answer to question (4), it is not too much to claim that the best work in the field of trade and development has greatly advanced our understanding of the problems defined by questions (1) to (3).

Our material could be arranged in more than one way. The chosen arrangement follows a somewhat historical principle. Early wide-ranging models which rather neglected trade are followed by more detailed models from the "fixed price" or structuralist family. Next comes a discussion of the application of the comparative cost principle and of other models of trade to development. We consider the theory of project evaluation in the same section as tariffs because the question of how to assess projects in a tariff-bound economy is a leading issue of the theory of project evaluation. Policies to influence the terms of trade and growth form independent sections.

A different approach would arrange matter according to the nature of the questions considered. We might distinguish the long and the short run. Or we might consider all policy reform questions together. Finally, one could explicitly separate static models from dynamic models. Unfortunately, such neat classifications are difficult to apply. For example, should structuralist models be classified as short-run static? Many would say that they should be, but certainly not all will agree. Again, is the abolition of a tariff just one change in an economy which should be considered in exactly the same way as we consider a public investment project? Ideally yes, but such a powerful synthetic approach would not make for easy reading.

The chapter is arranged as follows. In Subsection 2.1 some rather broad issues are lightly reviewed. These include the relation between the wide angle or "development strategy" approach to development planning and the microscopic or decision formula approach which includes project evaluation. The view of trade that was reflected in the writings of the founding fathers of development economics is considered in Subsection 2.2. These ideas are further developed in Subsection 3.1 where the implications for trade of a particular assessment of the role of prices in the developing economy, known as "structuralism", is discussed. The most notable contribution of the structuralist approach to the theory of the open economy was the "two-gap" model and this is investigated in Subsection 3.2. In Subsection 3.3 we consider a different kind of failure of the price system, that induced by a distortion or an externality.

Comparative costs is the subject of Section 4. The meaning of comparative costs in the developing economy is discussed in Subsection 4.1. Perhaps the best-known trade model of all is the Heckscher–Ohlin model. The question of whether this model has any relevance to the trade of a developing economy is considered in Subsection 4.2. Subsection 4.3 examines various extensions of the comparative advantage model which make the model more "dynamic". The new trade theories may be loosely defined as models of trade which borrow ideas from industrial economics and dispense with the assumption of perfect competition. In Subsection 4.4 their importance for development theory is assessed.

Most of the subject-matter of Section 5 finds its application when there are tariffs and other so-called "distortions". In Subsection 5.1 the problems of assessing the effects of a tariff regime, by means of effective protection indices or other tests, is reviewed. The consequences for policy of distortions and external economies are examined in Subsection 5.2. The use of border prices in project evaluation is investigated in Subsection 5.3. Section 6 is concerned with policies designed to influence the prices which a country's producers receive. Subsection 6.1 lightly reviews the general issues, while Subsection 6.2 concentrates on commodity price stabilization. The relationship between trade and economic growth is reviewed in Section 7. A general overview is provided in Subsection 7.1 and in Subsection 7.2 the turnpike model of economic growth is applied to analyze the effect of trade on growth. Some concluding remarks are assembled in Section 8.

There is no generic description of the countries whose economic problems form the subject-matter of this chapter which cannot plausibly be convicted of inaccuracy, condescension, unrealism or equally serious shortcomings. However, it is almost impossible to proceed without a term. I have preferred less developed country, shortened to LDC, to the various even more unsatisfactory possibilities. There is of course no implication that development is one-dimensional or that all countries are at different stages on a road to the same destination.

2. Development planning and international trade

2.1. The strategy of economic development

The question of the role of trade in development presented itself at the very beginning. Most LDCs were already engaged in international exchange during the colonial period. They started from a base line involving a certain international division of labour. However, plans for a quickened rate of capital accumulation were seen to imply the need for increased imports of capital goods and other items not producible in the home economy, and adapting trading patterns was judged to be a necessary component of the movement towards a more desired performance. Later new dissatisfactions with trading role of the LDCs emerged in the form of demands for a New International Economic Order.

It does not follow from a dissatisfaction with a trading pattern that trade policy should be used. One could imagine, for example, increasing the national saving rate through the use of non-trade policies, and thus raising the rate of growth, lowering imports and releasing resources for exports. However, policy in practice was seldom as sophisticated as this argument implies. It is too easy to feel that because imports are currently higher than they must be with successful development direct restrictions of imports should be applied.

In any case, given that a high level of imports is required, an attempt to accelerate growth requires either that less non-development goods be imported, that exports be increased, or that there be increased borrowing during a transition period to finance a trade deficit. Some policy changes must somehow achieve at least one of these outcomes. Combinations of these types of outcome may be called a "development strategy" [see, for example, Blitzer (1975)]. Such a strategy may or may not determine which instruments will be used, and so does not necessarily determine exactly which goods will be traded within the broad categories concerned. The decision may favour import substitution, for example. However, unless all non-development goods are to be substituted by domestic production, it remains to select precisely which goods are to be favoured by the strategy of import substitution.

Thus, trade questions, along with other questions in development design, may be decided by means of broad strategies or decided by detailed rules. Both approaches are encountered but the relation between them has never been theoretically clarified.[1] On the one hand, broad strategies demand formulae for their implementation. On the other hand, rules consistently and globally applied entail strategies, but strategies whose character may not be obvious in advance. In the first country to develop, Britain, for example, the policy was laissez-faire and the eventual emergence of export-orientated growth was not the result of a conscious policy to promote growth of that kind.

One might instead reserve the term "strategy" for the choice of variables which have an economy wide impact (such as the interest rate) as against local decisions such as favouring the production of one type of steel over the production of another. Yet sometimes when many instruments are applied to one end it is easiest to characterize the policy by the end rather than the means adopted.

The issue of trade policy for a developing country is an old one. However, each period demands new answers to fit new circumstances and to reflect experience. So with trade and development there has been a reaction against the import-substituting export-pessimistic type of policy usually favoured in the first generation of development plans. It may be that the consensus to which this reaction has given rise will itself eventually need modification. However, it is unlikely that the simple import substitution strategy will ever be rehabilitated.

[1] Heal (1973), for example, in one of the most authoritative general treatments of the mathematical theory of planning offers no discussion relevant to this issue. Janos Kornai has proposed the concept of "multilevel planning" [see, for example, Kornai (1973)] but this again does not capture what is involved in the concept of a development strategy.

2.2. Trade and balanced growth

The early attempts to formulate models of development in the 1940s and 1950s demanded the construction of new theory. True, ideas about growth had been proposed in the past, especially by the classical writers,[2] but these ideas were usually too general and vague to serve as guides to specific policy recommendations. In reviewing this pioneering work we concentrate upon the treatment of international trade.

Rosenstein–Rodan (1943, 1961) proposed the theory of the Big Push. Widespread development affecting a large number of sectors of the economy will be self-reinforcing, where the attempt to develop too narrowly would run into a problem of inadequate demand. The model is not entirely consistent in its treatment of trade. Thus, an example of the (1943) paper, which not surprisingly became famous, is of a shoe factory employing 20 000 previously unemployed workers. By generating an excess supply of shoes and an excess demand for foodstuffs (because the workers will require more than subsistence in their new employment) the example is intended to illustrate pointedly the problems of unbalanced growth.

Little (1982 pp. 38–39) criticizes Rosenstein–Rodan for assuming that the economy can import development goods in the production of which it lacks comparative advantage, while neglecting the possibility that export markets might allow for a more uneven pattern of development. Shoes, after all, are tradable goods. This point is not answered by the claim that a country may face absolute limits on the quantities that it can export. For the model assumes that the developing country will be able to export enough to repay its loans. If opportunities to export are good enough to permit a big push but are more restricted in some branches than in others, it is the pattern of export opportunities that development must respect and not the requirements of balance as that is normally understood.

The requirements that a development plan should respect the balance between supply and demand, that it should avoid burdening one sector with shortages imposed by another, and that enterprises should be large enough to give them the benefit of economies of scale, are more readily satisfied in an open economy. Shoes are rather easily tradable, as the shoemaking industries of rich countries have discovered.

A concept which leads to similar conclusions is provided by Leibenstein (1957) who proposes the idea of the "minimum critical effort". The chief mechanism which enables rapid economic development to take place where a slower rate would be infeasible is that the supply of saving expressed as a share of income is

---

[2] Findlay (1984) argues cogently that Ricardo's advocacy of free trade was based as much on its efficacy in promoting rapid economic development as on its static benefits.

related to the rate of growth in a nonlinear manner. This is best seen as a complication, albeit it an important one, of the two-gap model discussed in Subsection 3.2 below.

The idea of the "big push" is not identical to the concept of "balanced growth" but the two are connected. Put simply, balanced growth plus economies of scale equals the big push. Hence, the advocacy of balanced growth employs many of the same arguments as were employed by Rosenstein–Rodan. Lewis (1955) and Nurkse (1953) provide the best-known accounts and Hirschman (1958) the most pointed counter arguments. See also Fleming (1955), Scitovsky (1959), Streeten (1959), Lipton (1962), and Sutcliffe (1964).

Lewis (1955) argued that "... various sectors must grow in the right relationship to each other or they cannot grow at all". This again applies with less force to the open economy. Also, even where non-tradables are concerned the market system may ensure that sectors grow in balance. It may be argued that the market system does not work well in the typical LDC but even if true this need not imply a lack of balance. The efficiency of domestic markets has important implications for trade theory and this question will be touched on in Subsections 3.1 and 5.2. The argument for balanced growth mainly amounts to an emphasis on the importance of external economies in LDCs. The self-reinforcing nature of these external economies requires that many sectors should expand together and gives rise to what Nurkse (1953) calls the "simultaneity problem".

The problem of balance is relatively less serious for the open economy and this leads Nurkse to ask explicitly why poor small countries should not push exports of goods in which they enjoy a comparative advantage (which Nurkse took to be primary products) and to import to obtain what he called the "balanced diet" (meaning the satisfaction of demands). His answer is interesting for he points out that "... balance applies on a global scale". The policy would be self-defeating if generally adopted, as it would create a world excess supply of primary products and drive the terms of trade sharply against the countries which had adopted the strategy. This is an example of "immizerizing growth", which Bhagwati (1958) applied to the output from a group of countries. The argument applies when producers are large enough individually, or in like-minded blocks, to affect the prices at which they sell. If these same producers have irrational expectations, and in the absence of efficient forward markets, an inefficient outcome is to be expected.

Hirschman (1958) offers trenchant criticisms of the balanced growth doctrine and argues that it is impossible for a truly underdeveloped economy to leap forward on all fronts simultaneously. Rather, development should be seen as "a chain of disequilibria". Hirschman's unbalanced growth works through the well-known "backward and forward linkages". This idea is further developed in Hirschman (1977). For a development of the linkage hypothesis without unbalanced growth, see Riedel (1976). For Hirschman an underdeveloped economy is a mass of potential initiative and economic activity waiting to be prodded into life. Hence, the stronger the linkages associated with an investment the better. Discussing this idea, Little (1982, pp. 43–44) remarks acidly that administratively created linkages have been one of the main causes of misallocation.

How are linkages affected by international trade, particularly imports? Assume a new industry established in a developing country and consider the backward and forward linkages that will result. The backward linkage will be a new and expanded market for the inputs used by the industry. The forward linkage arises when the availability of the product produced by the industry encourages new uses and generates new demands. These linkages are clearly relevant to the cost–benefit analysis of a project. Both linkage effects need to be considered in an open economy. Local producers will already have a market for a tradable good and domestic availability will not make much difference where the good could have been imported.

Hirschman, interestingly, argues that domestic production does make an important difference. He points to the shortage of skills required for importing, uncertainties of the balance of payments and the exchange rate, and claims that domestic production is more effective in promoting local use of a product than is its import. Today one more often encounters the claim that importers, particularly in the shape of transnational companies, promote imports effectively against local competition than the view that the domestic producer has an important natural advantage.

While early writers on development all conceded some validity to the principle of comparative advantage (sometimes conceived in simplistic terms), they mostly underestimated the enormous potential which trade was to offer in the post-war world. Some of them, notably Hirschman, realized that imports were more than just a necessary evil, but the idea that there were great opportunities to export for countries able to take advantage of them was only weakly perceived. It is not always clearly seen even today.

3. Structuralism, gap models, and distortions

3.1. Structuralism and international trade

"An economy has structure", writes Taylor (1983, p. 3), "if its institutions and the behaviour of its members make some patterns of resource allocation and evolution substantially more likely than others. Economic analysis is structuralist when it takes these factors as foundation stones for its theories." This quotation illustrates the breadth and ambition of the structuralist programme. However, as it stands, the definition is too general to give us much purchase on trade and trade policy. To achieve that we need to consider specific examples of institutions and behaviour. Probably it is not an excessive simplification to say that where international trade is concerned the chief import of the structuralist message is that prices are poor and unreliable allocators, either because they are not flexible enough, or because, even when they do change, the quantity responses that they elicit are too small in extent or undesirable in kind. For a less cursory exposition of structuralist ideas, see Taylor (1983, ch. 1).

It is important to distinguish cases which are quite different in kind and implication. If agents behave conventionally or irrationally, then the operation of the price system, whether they respond to it strongly or weakly, lacks desirable properties. It is when agents maximize subject to the prices that they face that a price system functions as an efficient allocator. However, even if agents do maximize, their quantitative responses to price changes, at least over a certain range, may be small. This point is sometimes overlooked. It is no part of neoclassical doctrine, whatever some of its adherents may believe, that elasticities are high, in trade or elsewhere.

Neoclassical theory, properly understood, is silent on the question of whether elasticity, or any other pessimism, characterizes the world. Such pessimism is perfectly consistent with a model in which prices do change and agents do maximize. Sometimes large changes in prices may make little difference to patterns of production and international exchange but may largely affect distribution and the welfare of vulnerable groups. Less price variation and even quantitative controls might in principal be preferable. Some people who believe this will be surprised to have it pointed out that it is perfectly consistent with neoclassical theory.

While it can easily embrace certain kinds of structural rigidity, neoclassical theory as usually understood is based on the idea that prices clear markets. If they do not, the result may be a fix-price economy with quantity rationing. The implications for balance of payments adjustment of a fix-price model were first examined in the context of aid and LDCs, and the model that resulted is the subject of the next subsection.

3.2. Closure rules and two-gap models

The terminology "closure rule" is due to Sen (1963) who demonstrated how various growth models could be generated from a common set of specifications which by themselves were insufficient to close the model. By selecting among various extra conditions several models were related to each other in an illuminating manner. Harrod (1939), for example, did not impose a full-employment condition, where Kaldor (1956) did. Income distribution adjusts in Kaldor's model to bring about full employment and it has to be free of the marginal productivity conditions.

Two types of closure appear at first to be different, although from the mathematical point of view they are the same. Conditions may be imposed upon the solution, or adjustment mechanisms admitted to the model. The reason why they are formally the same is that they both have the effect of adding an extra equation to those already present. The closure issue is not in itself a fundamental problem. We are ultimately dealing with the question of which model is best, where a model is a complete and consistent set of equations. Dividing the equations into those about which most agree and those concerning which there is debate is a handy expository device but it is not more than that.

Models of economic growth in closed economies may seem remote from the problem of planning economic development in an open economy. However, the issues that arose in the growth models are echoed in the problem of formulating an aggregate model of economic development. It is not surprising therefore that the problem of "closure" is encountered in the development literature [see, for example, Bell (1979)] and that development economists in the 1960s formulated models which were essentially open versions of Harrod's growth model.[3]

Closure is closely related to the idea of "gaps". If the model does not necessarily have a full-employment solution we could say that it may have a "labour demand gap". This gap, however, did not greatly interest the early development theorists. It was taken for granted that full employment in the modern sector would not be achieved for a long time. In the meantime development was seen as proceeding with "unlimited supplies of labour" [Lewis (1954)]. Attention was directed instead to other gaps.

Most influential has been the so-called "two-gap" model of an open developing economy, see Little (1960), Chenery and Bruno (1962), McKinnon (1964), Chenery and Strout (1966), and Williamson (1983, Section 12.3). The idea behind the two-gap model is apparently simple and highly appealing.[4] However, it can involve quite intricate problems of interpretation. We first present an uncritical account and then turn to the arguments that have been advanced against the simple two-gap model. It is easiest to understand the concepts from an aggregated model of an open economy subject to various rigidities. The aim is to elucidate what role foreign aid can play in assisting an economy of that type.

Foreign aid plays two apparently distinct roles. First, it enables the LDC to accumulate goods without its own residents doing the saving necessary to finance that accumulation. Secondly, as aid takes the form of a transfer of foreign exchange to the LDC, it relaxes the balance of payments constraint and makes it

[3]Some of the pioneering models followed Harrod, or the model associated with Feldman (1957), so closely that they were not even open. These include the influential Mahalanobis model, on which see Bhagwati and Chakravarty (1969).
[4]Little (1982, p. 147) reports "a very high United Nations official" in the 1970s saying that "there had been just two very important ideas in development economics". One of these was the two-gap idea.

possible for the country to import more. While aid achieves both these objectives, one may be more important than the other. It seems therefore that a country may be constrained from achieving a faster rate of development either by a shortage of saving, or by a shortage of foreign exchange, and that according to which regime applies the effectiveness of aid will differ.

In the model to be explained we employ the following notation.

$$
\begin{aligned}
Y_0 &= \text{capacity domestic output,} \\
E &= \text{demand for exports,} \\
A &= \text{foreign aid,} \\
s &= \text{propensity to save,} \\
u(v) &= \text{investment–output ratio for domestic (foreign) goods,} \\
g &= \text{growth rate,} \\
a &= A/Y_0, \quad \text{and} \\
e &= E/Y_0.
\end{aligned} \tag{1}
$$

All absolute quantities are measured in domestic prices which may be thought of as constant. We assume, for the sake of simplicity, that it is only for investment that imports are required. It is helpful to think of the growth rate g as a target the feasibility of which is to be determined. We try for a solution in which domestic production will be at a full capacity level defined by the availability of plant and equipment. The availability of labour will not impose a constraint.

Investment must not exceed the sum of domestic and foreign saving:

$$
(u+v)gY_0 \le sY_0 + A. \tag{2}
$$

Dividing both sides of (2) by Y_0, and rearranging, we obtain:

$$
g \le (s+a)/(u+v). \tag{3}
$$

Next note that imports should not exceed exports plus foreign aid:

$$
vgY_0 \le E + A. \tag{4}
$$

Dividing by Y_0 and rearranging yields:

$$
g \le (e+a)/v. \tag{5}
$$

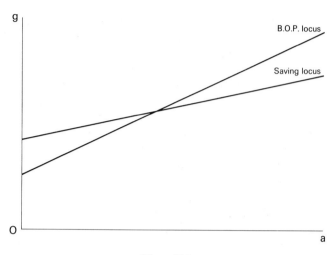

Figure 23.1

Bringing together (3) and (5), we have two independent restrictions on the growth rate, one from the consideration of the adequacy of saving, the other from the balance of payments. According therefore as our target g violates one or other of these constraints, and supposing it not to violate both, we may speak of a savings gap or a foreign exchange gap.

For there to exist positive values of a and g at which the economy will grow with saving equal to investment and the balance of payments in equilibrium we must have:

$$\frac{s}{u+v} > \frac{e}{v}. \tag{6}$$

For this we require that the saving–investment locus has the larger intercept but the smaller slope (see Figure 23.1). If the economy grows at the smaller of the two growth rates defined by substituting equalities into (3) and (5), it follows that aid is more effective in raising growth rates at low levels, when it relaxes the foreign exchange gap, then at higher levels when it serves to augment domestic saving. This was the lesson generally drawn from two-gap theory.

Taylor (1975, Section 1.2) emphasizes the "mechanistic" nature of this model with its many fixed ratios and parameters. However when the model is used to check the consistency of a forecast, the fixity of parameters will not be a weakness. In fact, later work within the two-gap approach was more concerned with optimal borrowing and adjustment mechanisms that would equate the two gaps. See, for example, Bruno (1966) and Chenery and MacEwan (1966).

It is often assumed that the economy will grow at the smaller of the two growth rates defined by substituting equalities for the inequalities in (3) and (5). However the outcome depends on the closure rule adopted. Suppose, for example, that (3) with equality defines the lower value of g, and (5) is slack at that growth rate. This corresponds to a relatively high level of a. If the economy grows at this rate it will tend to run a balance of payments surplus and we could close the model by allowing it to do so. This means that the amount of aid that is being transferred to the country cannot all be absorbed. The aid is boosting domestic capital accumulation and increasing growth, but it is increasing domestic saving more than it is increasing investment, with the consequence that some of the domestic saving is used to acquire foreign assets. Part of the aid flows abroad or is absorbed by the accumulation of foreign reserves.

Alternatively, consider that the balance of payments constraint, (5), with an equality in place of the inequality, defines the lower value of g. This corresponds to a lower level of a. Now, with full capacity utilization, there is a tendency to an excess of saving over investment. The authorities, given the balance of payments constraint, find it impossible to generate enough effective demand to fully employ capacity. A possible closure rule for this case would be the Keynesian adjustment mechanism under which domestic income falls below the capacity level Y_0 until the gap is closed. Now (2) and (4) with equalities in place of the inequalities, and with a now meaning the ratio of aid to actual as opposed to potential domestic production, provide two equations in g and Y:

$$(u + v)gY = sY + A, \tag{7}$$

$$vgY = E + A. \tag{8}$$

If we suppose the availability of aid and opportunities to export to be related to potential domestic product rather than to their actual levels, $A = aY_0$ and $E = eY_0$ and we may solve (7) and (8) for g and Y. Together these equations give a unique value for the growth rate which will typically not equal either of the rates defined by the saving and balance of payments constraints. It may exceed both.

To see this, let $Y_0 = 500$; $a = e = 0.1$; $u = 1$, $v = 3$; and $s = 0.2$. Then the largest value of g consistent with the saving constraint (3) is 7.5 percent, and the largest consistent with the payments constraint (5) is 6.7 percent. However, A and $E = 50$, and (7) and (8) are satisfied by $g = 8$ percent and $Y = 416.7$.

This model can be criticized. It assumes, for example, that the accelerator principle operates even when Y is below full capacity, and the assumption that aid and exports are related to potential rather than actual product is not obviously appropriate. However, it serves to illustrate an important asymmetry between the balance of payments constraint and the saving constraint and suggests that arguments which treat them as two like constraints can be misleading.

This conclusion is similar to that of Joshi (1970), although his model is different as it is concerned with two-gap problems in the context of an optimizing model. The type of two-gap model discussed above owes its rigidities to the fact that prices do not take the values most appropriate to a rapid rate of growth. Thus, for example, the relative fixity of export demand might be attributed to an inappropriate exchange rate, or a shortage of saving to poor incentives to private saving. In Joshi's model, however, constraints are real. Saving is bounded above by the impossibility of pushing consumption below a floor determined presumably by political-economic facts. Where export constraints are concerned, on the other hand, a real constraint is less plausible. So if domestic saving can be increased, extra foreign exchange can be made available at some cost. The mechanism will be the adjustment of domestic prices. The conclusion is that the saving constraint tends to rule.

Nelson (1970) has similar orientation to that of Joshi in that he is concerned with how an open economy can best adapt to its situation and he sees the adoption of optimal prices as playing an essential role in that adjustment mechanism. These papers reflect the gradual movement of interest away from the structuralist rigid-price model towards the idea of optimal prices for economic development which has dominated the recent literature.

The model of Findlay (1971) is different again. The rigidity in this case is an immovable upper bound on the exports that must be used to purchase the investment goods without which growth is impossible. The propensity to save out of income is also fixed. When the export constraint is binding, extra saving is ineffective as a means of raising the rate of growth. Notice that what is presented as a quantitative constraint in fact entails a price rigidity. If investors could bid competitively for foreign exchange they would drive up its price. More saving would not mean more growth but there would be full equilibrium and no gap. Alternatively, as discussed by Findlay, if imports are consumed as well as invested the rigidities may be overcome. In the second half of his paper Findlay demonstrates that the complexities of the relation between saving and growth can be illuminated without assuming extreme rigidities.

The early models of the two gaps were most readily interpreted as fixed price models. Also, by employing export constraints, these models created a category of non-tradable goods, even where the demand and supply for these was not considered explicitly. The link between fixed-price theory, non-traded goods, and the balance of trade is explored by Neary (1980), and van Wijnbergen (1986) investigates the effects of foreign aid in an open economy disequilibrium model. For another example of the fixed price approach, see Standaert (1985).

In van Wijnbergen's model the exchange rate is flexible while domestic nominal prices are fixed. Hence, an inflow of foreign aid leads to exchange rate appreciation and discourages exports. This argument provides a link between the effects of foreign aid on the one hand, and the "Dutch disease" effects of resource discoveries on the other. As the author points out, it is the level of non-tradables' prices which, failing to clear that market, account for the possibility of an ex ante distinction between domestic net saving and the trade gap. Without non-tradables, Walras's Law would ensure the equality of these two magnitudes. The van Wijnbergen model, like other gap models, is founded in a assumption of fixed prices. Some will argue that this assumption is illegitimate unless the fixity of prices can be explained by a model. However, even those who are not willing to go that far must wonder what period is appropriate for the application of a fixed-price model.

The early papers on the two-gap model would not have been so influential had they not captured an idea that rang true for many development specialists. If today they seem somewhat dated, the reasons are partly a change in the style of economic theory, with greater emphasis today on precise general equilibrium models, and partly institutional changes. On the one hand, longer experience of development has made some of the rigidities which were taken for granted by early writers seem less plausible. On the other hand, with the growing access of many LDCs to highly flexible and fluid private capital markets, the treatment of aid as quantity rationed official aid came to seem less compelling.

3.3. Distortions and external economies

The idea that markets in LDCs operate in a less than ideal manner, so that total reliance on them as allocators of resources is not to be recommended, is one that unites structuralists and the great majority of "neoclassical" writers. As is often the case, it was in the context of international trade that the issues to which this gives rise were first explored. The problem of distortions applies as much to advanced countries as to LDCs. Advanced countries are strangers neither to segmented labour markets nor to highly distortionary protection, to cite but two examples.

It is clear that the term "distortions" is a catch-all name for problems which are different in kind as well as in their particularities. The following list, which lays no claim to completeness, serves to illustrate the diversity involved.[5] Distortions include:

(i) Market imperfections of various kinds. Examples would be monopoly or externalities. These will produce the result that, without intervention, the market,

[5]On distortions see also Srinivasan (1987).

although it may clear, will not allocate optimally. This is termed *market distortion* for short.[6]

(ii) Divergence between the solution at which even an ideal market system would arrive and the social welfare criterion which takes account of income distribution. This is a *distribution distortion*.

(iii) The effect on the economy of one or more policy instruments, such as tariffs, which do not serve one of the objectives of the government. This is a *policy distortion*.[7]

(iv) The pursuit by the government of certain objectives which have an overriding importance compared to economic considerations. These are known as *non-economic objectives*.

Externalities are a case of the linkages discussed in Subsection 2.2 above but clearly they range over other possibilities. Furthermore, not all linkages are externalities, for some are no more than input–output relationships. See Scitovsky (1954) and Little (1982, pp. 38–44) who provide further references. Market imperfection must be carefully distinguished from policy distortion. For the former to prevail some structural feature of the market, rather than a government policy, must account for the failure of the price to clear the market and to equal marginal social cost. An example of market distortion would be a tendency for the supply price of labour from an agricultural sector to exceed the marginal opportunity cost of rural labour because the latter is paid the average product of the rural family [see Sen (1975, Part III)]. Distribution distortion represents a different motive for intervention. That the market system might achieve efficiency in association with a badly unequal distribution of income is a standard observation of welfare economics.

With policy distortion we reach more difficult ground. We are using a welfare function (sometimes called welfare weights) to evaluate states of the economy. It cannot be correct to say that whatever welfare function the government chooses

---

[6] Numerous separate cases are included under this general heading. In one case a market might operate competitively and clear without quantity rationing, yet an external economy or diseconomy, would result in market imperfection. In another case there might be monopoly or imperfect competition, in which case the market clears only in the special sense which includes one or more agents being quantity rationed. Here the sellers are quantity rationed. They would like to sell more at the price at which they are selling but they are constrained by the demand curve.

[7] This use of the term "policy distortion" is different from the one employed by Bhagwati (1971, pp. 72–74). Bhagwati regards any departure from the necessary conditions for efficiency which results from the action of a government as a policy distortion. He then goes on to make the distinction between "policy imposed" and "instrumental policy imposed" distortions according to whether the policy intervention is achieving an objective of the government. Only the former corresponds to what we have called policy distortion. As Bhagwati deals only with efficiency and ignores our distribution distortion, it seems that the only cases in which instrumental policy imposed distortion is genuinely distorting fall under our (iv) non-economic objectives.

will be the right one. However, it is usual to suppose a fairly benign government and to imagine that the welfare function might represent its objectives. Can it be supposed that the same government has imposed, or left in place, policies which interfere with the objectives that are embodied in the welfare function?

While it is difficult to resolve this puzzle in a fully satisfactory manner, the existence of tariffs which apparently serve no clearly identifiable interest suggests that the choice of some policy may be inconsistent with wider objectives of the government. This leads to the positive theory of protection: see Baldwin (1982) and Findlay and Wellisz (1982). See also the discussion of the role of government in Chapter 24 of this Handbook. Finally, non-economic objectives are not strictly distortions at all, but they are included with true distortions as they have been discussed along with them in the literature and because they do represent a case in which the unmodified price system fails to achieve the desired allocation.

4. Comparative costs and development

4.1. The meaning of comparative costs in the LDC

The theory of comparative advantage and the gains from trade has been extensively exposited and surveyed elsewhere [see, for example, Chenery (1961), Bhagwati (1969), Meier (1969, pp. 10–40), and Corden (1984)], and this is not the place to provide another survey. The idea that trade should follow comparative costs has not always proved popular with development economists. Compare the discussion here with that of Chapter 24 in this Handbook.

Sometimes doubts about comparative advantage are due to misunderstanding concerning the theory, and they are accounted for by feeling that the theory is not applicable to developing economies. In fact, the rule that trade should follow comparative costs can be interpreted in more than one way. We would like a definition of the principle of comparative costs which is free of unnecessarily restrictive assumptions and that is general enough to be applicable. It would be helpful also to avoid the battery of special assumptions that have become traditional in the literature. These include: two goods and two factors, constant returns to scale, perfect competition in all markets, the same technical possibilities in all countries, and a rather static treatment of technology. These assumptions have their pedagogic uses but they are not required to elucidate the theory of comparative costs.

In one simple interpretation the costs of the principle of comparative costs are opportunity costs in terms of domestic production defined by the technical production possibilities of the country. When comparative cost is defined in this sense we shall refer to the *technical transformation rate*. Comparative cost according to the technical transformation rate is not always the right guide to trade.[8] This is most easily understood if we start from the assumptions that are standardly employed to demonstrate the superiority of trade according to comparative advantage. Among these is usually included the existence of lump-sum transfers which are used to cancel, if necessary, unfavourable distributional effects of a resource reallocation.

Realistically, lump-sum transfers will not be available, and this is an important consideration, as distortionary taxation, including tariffs, are a vital source of revenue in most developing countries. However, less powerful taxation instruments may suffice. This issue is treated at length in Dixit (1985) which the interested reader should consult. Even so, there are cases in which comparative advantage should be set aside in an optimal solution. One such case would be a model which strongly links income distribution to the allocation of resources. The separation of these two is fundamental to the welfare economic advocacy of free trade.

Anand and Joshi (1979) provide a succinct demonstration of the point that the maximization of the value of domestic production at world prices, equivalent to the comparative advantage criterion, is an inappropriate rule when that separation cannot be achieved. In this model workers in the advanced sector receive a higher wage, due to political or other influences. Maximizing the value of domestic production at world prices in this case leads to an unavoidable distortion of income distribution. Therefore the transfer of labour to the advanced sector should not be pushed as far as comparative advantage alone would dictate.

The Anand–Joshi example serves to underline the complexity of assessing a change in trade when this change affects a distorted economy. The distortion of the example is an unusually immovable one. However, even less intractable distortions need to be taken into account. In particular the effects of taxes on domestic production must be included when trade is considered.

It seems then that the comparative costs of the technical transformation rates are not always a sure guide to trade that will improve welfare as measured by a welfare function, although additional assumptions, particularly the existence of lump-sum transfers, will guarantee that they are. More generally an optimal plan defines shadow prices for goods which are the rates at which the welfare function could be augmented if the constraints on the availability of the goods were relaxed slightly. If comparative costs are defined in terms of these shadow prices the doctrine that trade should follow comparative costs becomes a truism.

---

[8] However, a further important case will be discussed below in which the presumption for the correctness of the narrow interpretation of comparative costs is stronger. This is when the technical transformation rates are those of the public sector.

Nevertheless, this last approach, which leads directly to a cost–benefit analysis in terms of shadow prices, is a helpful one.

The above assumes that comparative advantage can be stated in terms of the relation between transformation rates for the home country, somehow defined, and the transformation rates made available by international exchange. In other words, there is no reference to the transformation possibilities in production of the other countries in the world. In Ricardo's famous discussion, England should produce cloth if it could produce it at a lower cost in terms of wine forgone compared with the same cost in Portugal. However, looked at from the point of view of one developing country, it can reasonably be held to be immaterial whether the prices that international exchange makes available correspond to the costs however defined of the other countries engaged in trade. For the pursuit of its own interest what matters to one country is the opportunities which trade makes available to it. Hence, our restatement of the traditional principle of comparative costs is quite deliberate. A comparison is still involved but now it is between domestic transformation rates, and external transformation rates in international exchange, both appropriately defined.

The extension is important in that it allows, for example, trading with monopolistic sellers[9] or distorted foreign economies to be included within the theory of comparative advantage. What matters is the rates at which goods can actually be transformed into other goods in international exchange. In the competitive economy of the Ricardian example the prices define real trading opportunities and if the country is small they can be taken as given. Suppose in contrast that a country purchases a good from a perfectly informed monopolistic foreign seller. What rate of exchange should it assume for that good? The answer is clearly that the exchange rate will be chosen by the monopolist to maximize his profit, so that it will not be independent of the value of trade to the home country. The separation of trading opportunity and domestic situation breaks down and the principle of comparative advantage must take this into account.[10]

4.2. The Heckscher–Ohlin model and LDCs

So far we have neglected the sources of comparative advantage. This issue gave rise to probably the best-known trade model, the Heckscher–Ohlin model

[9]On monopoly in international trade and its implications for trade theory, see Helpman and Krugman (1985).

[10]A similar point is encountered in the optimal tariff model. There is a difference, however. When the government intervenes to set the best domestic price for a commodity which is traded with a monopolist it enters into a two-player game for which theory cannot pinpoint a unique equilibrium concept. In the optimal tariff case the foreign player acts passively and predictably and a unique equilibrium results.

(henceforth denoted the HO model). In the HO model comparative advantage is based on the relative abundance of factors of production. Surveys which treat the HO model and the substantial literature related to it are provided by, inter alia, Chipman (1965–66), Bhagwati (1969) and Jones and Neary (1984). Empirical aspects of this and other models of comparative advantage are surveyed in Stern (1975). See also Deardorff (1980, 1982), and Leamer (1984).

An obvious problem in applying the HO model in practice is that in its usual exposition it is based on two traded goods and two factors of production. Extensions to many goods and factors, not necessarily equal in number, are available [see Dixit and Norman (1980) and Ethier (1984)], but even these, generally weaker, results depend upon assuming that all countries share the same underlying production functions. This assumption is difficult to reconcile with even casual observation. For example, any of the technologies considered in the literature generates a unique factor-price frontier, i.e. a function relating the return to one factor to the returns to all others. In the two-factor case the factor-price frontier gives the wage rate as a function of the profit rate. However, empirical investigations suggest that rates of return on capital in LDCs are not very different from the returns in advanced countries, while real wages are obviously markedly lower in the former. This point was explicitly noted by Minhas (1963) in connection with his research into the homohyphallagic (CES) production function and factor intensity reversals. Capital intensity reversal might explain the lack of factor-price equalization in the world in terms consistent with the HO model, but similar profit rates and strongly divergent wage rates indicate a more fundamental failure.

One way to explain this observation, while keeping the assumption of common technologies, would be to assume a third factor which would be highly priced in the LDC. However, it is not entirely clear what it would be. One possibility is human capital. The disaggregation of labour which is implied by the human capital model is in line with the general trend in trade theory towards greater disaggregation. On measuring the return to human capital in LDCs, see Krueger (1968). Another possible candidate to be the third factor is land, for which see the argument of Chapter 24 in this Handbook.

An alternative to including human capital or land is to allow that the application of factors may be less productive in LDCs. Perhaps the factors applied are not identical to the same category of factor in advanced countries, but this cannot be taken to be true by definition. This admission, implying as it does factors specific to particular countries, is just as damaging to the HO model as are variations in technology across countries. Next consider the suggestion of Leontief (1954) that labour might be less productive in some countries so that more man-hours of the less productive type are required to do what is done by less in advanced countries (in Leontief's case the United States). Even this ingenious argument, however, fails to explain the relatively high capital–output ratios observed in most LDCs. If in the HO solution factor prices are equalized, low wages would exactly offset the low productivity of labour in the LDC, and capital–output ratios at international prices would be the same in all countries.

A serious attempt to test the predictions of the HO model is unlikely to be satisfied with the simple basic version. Deardorff (1980, 1982) provides a testable formalization of the idea that there may be a connection between an appropriately defined measure of the factor content of goods, factor endowments of countries and trade patterns. Most of the literature which deals with extensions of the HO model and the investigation of its testable implications is not especially concerned with LDCs. Deardorff (1984) provides a survey.

Leaving aside the difficulties of applying HO theory to exchange mainly between advanced countries and the LDCs, we may note that the theory does not imply the traditional patterns of specialization. These were based more on Ricardian comparative advantage than on the HO variety. If the typical LDC is taken to be abundantly supplied with labour and poorly supplied with capital, the theory would predict that LDCs should export labour-intensive products. The primary products which traditionally dominated LDC exports, even when they were labour-intensive, were only incidentally so. What mattered more was that climatic and geological conditions made the cost of producing bananas or copper relatively low in certain LDCs. The same problem arose with Leontief's comparison of the factor intensity of U.S. imports and exports which is affected according to whether natural resource based industries are included in or excluded from the comparison [see Chipman (1965–66)]. Samuelson's parody makes a valid point. Tropical fruit *is* grown in tropical countries because they have a greater abundance of tropical conditions.

The HO model as it is usually presented assumes an undistorted economy. Travis (1972) argues that tariffs make an important difference to the trade flows actually observed. Travis has in mind the protection of the U.S. economy against labour-intensive imports but a similar argument, though based on the opposite tendency, may be applied to LDCs. Measuring the effects of tariff protection on domestic production is a complicated exercise requiring a computable general equilibrium model.

Probably of more relevance than the HO model of factor-price equalization to the case of a small LDC is the Rybczynski (1955) result, according to which an expansion in the supply of a factor will be associated with an expansion in the sector which uses that factor relatively intensively. This result goes beyond the two-good two-factor case. We assume output prices fixed, as would be the case with a small open economy with no tariffs or with given tariffs. With many goods and factors the Rybczynski change in outputs typically involves the expansion of a number of sectors and the contraction of others.

Let p be world goods prices, A the matrix of factor requirements for unit production of the various goods, x the vector of production, and f the vector of domestic factor supplies. The optimal production x solves:[11]

$$\max_{x} \boldsymbol{p} \cdot \boldsymbol{x} \text{ subject to } A \cdot \boldsymbol{x} \leq \boldsymbol{f}. \tag{9}$$

Following a small increase in one component of f, say the labour component, there will be a change in x, Δx, such that $x + \Delta x$ solves the reformulated programme (9). Incidentally, the shadow price of labour will be equal to $\boldsymbol{p} \cdot \Delta x$, which is the increase in the maximal value of production made possible by an extra unit of labour. Let $\boldsymbol{u}_L$ be the vector which has unity in the element corresponding to labour and zeros elsewhere, and assume that all factors are fully employed.[12]

We now have:

$$A \cdot (\boldsymbol{x} + \Delta \boldsymbol{x}) = \boldsymbol{f} + \boldsymbol{u}_L, \tag{10}$$

and as $A \cdot \boldsymbol{x} = \boldsymbol{f}$,

$$A \cdot \Delta \boldsymbol{x} = \boldsymbol{u}_L. \tag{11}$$

If A is square and of full rank, the shadow price of labour is:

$$\boldsymbol{p} \cdot A^{-1} \cdot \boldsymbol{u}_L, \tag{12}$$

which is the value at world prices of a shift towards a more labour-intensive product mix such that one more unit of labour is employed.

We may define the output change Δx as a pure increase in the labour intensity of production.[13] This is a natural generalization of the increase in the output of the labour-intensive sector and the decrease in the output of the other sector which would be observed in the two-good two-factor model. However, if we consider an increase in the supply of labour, the full-employment assumption which underlies the Rybczynski result ensures that the consequent change in production will be a move towards greater labour intensity at the national level. If domestic prices are unchanged and foreign trade takes up the changes in domestic production, more labour will entail exports which are more labour-intensive in this sense.

---

[11] This assumes that p are world prices but the argument is the same even if p is domestic prices which equal world prices plus tariffs.

[12] Underemployed factors are simply dropped from the equations.

[13] This definition side-steps the intricate problem of defining relative factor intensities of production when there are many factors. It must be the case therefore that it is not fully satisfactory as a definition and it will be seen that it classifies only a subset of output changes as corresponding to an increase in the use of one of the factors. More complicated changes can be difficult to classify and the classification may be inconsistent across countries.

The problems with the application of HO theory should not be allowed to obscure the more fundamental consideration that development planning and the institutions and policies under which decision-makers operate should be such that the resources available to the economy are effectively utilized. The excessive capital intensity of production in many LDCs is not a ground for concern because the HO model apparently dictates a low intensity. The real reason for worrying about it is that it plausibly reflects price and other distortions in the domestic economy which lead among other things to a lack of international competitiveness in sectors which should be exporting. However, the way to find out whether a certain sector should be exporting is not to apply the HO model but rather to evaluate the activity at shadow prices (see Subsection 5.3 below).

4.3. Dynamics and comparative advantage

As a reason for the rejecting comparative advantage in the context of planning development the argument that comparative advantage theory is too static predominates over all others. The argument finds its most eloquent expression in the "infant industry" case [see Kemp (1964, ch. 12), Baldwin (1969), and Johnson (1970)]. If we take "static" to be the opposite of "dynamic", and mean by "dynamic" change through time, it is clear that there is nothing inherently static about the idea of comparative advantage. A fundamental insight of modern general equilibrium theory is that goods delivered at different dates can be treated as different goods and that this leaves largely unaffected the formal structure of general equilibrium theory. Of course such an extension will soon take us beyond two goods and two factors, but that is a path which we must take in any case. There is no formal difficulty in imagining that an LDC might have a comparative advantage in *two* goods: a primary product today and a manufactured good tomorrow. Furthermore, interdependence of production constraints is normal and costs may have to be incurred today, even losses run in producing the manufactured good today, to make possible the delivery of the manufactured good tomorrow. This simply reminds us that comparative advantage depends upon the complete structure of international prices, and that the same structure includes their development through time.[14]

These arguments would probably be generally accepted, but many would argue that they are too formal and that they fail to take into account the difference between the idealized intertemporal markets of general equilibrium theory and the extant price systems embodied in the concrete markets of LDCs. That is indeed an important point and much of the discussion of the infant industry case turns on questions of information and the functioning of capital markets. Simple

---

[14]On the intertemporal aspects of trade theory see Smith (1982, 1984).

infancy, it has often been pointed out, does not provide a case for intervention unless either the economies generated in the early stages are external to the individual enterprise (in which case infancy reduces to another case of an externality) or unless the firm is unable to borrow against the profit that will follow as a consequence of early investment.

Different from the infant industry case are simple increasing returns to scale. In that case the optimality of a decentralized market system cannot be presumed, and investment, because it must be on a large scale, is likely to generate external economies and diseconomies which cannot be ignored. Increasing returns to scale are a central component of the new trade theories which are reviewed in the following section.

4.4. The new trade theories

As the theory of international trade has been particularly active in recent years many different models could be described as new trade theory. Kierzkowski (1987), in what he calls a selective survey, includes no less than five distinct models,[15] and the list could easily be extended. Any or all of these new models could be applied to a developing country. Here space only permits brief reference to trade with oligopolistic producers and to trade in services.

References on trade with imperfect competition and an exposition of various leading models are to be found in Kierzkowski (1987); see also Kierzkowski (1984) and Helpman and Krugman (1985). The implications of the new trade theories for policy are discussed in Bliss (1987b). Srinivasan (1989) provides an accessible review of the main ideas as well as discussing the application to development. See also Krugman (1986) and Stewart (1984).

Take the Krugman (1984) model of import protection as export promotion. This model is a prime example of the new approach and captures the spirit with which the new theory is applied to policy. Two firms, each the sole producer in its home market, compete in each others' markets. Marginal costs for each firm decline with the level of production. The firms set delivery levels for their goods to each market and we examine the Nash equilibrium of the resulting game. If one government intervenes say by prohibiting imports, the home firm will then cover the home market rather than sharing it and its production level will increase and marginal cost will be lower. The foreign firm will sell less and its

---

[15]These are: the specific factors model; specialized production models; trade with imperfect competition; gains from variety; and trade in services.

marginal cost will be higher. This will result in the protected firm selling more in the foreign market, hence the title of the paper.

The analysis is strangely silent on home consumers' welfare and alternative policy approaches. In fact, the effect on home consumers is ambiguous. Removing foreign competition is bad for them but lowering the domestic firm's marginal cost is good. The net effect may go either way. In any case protection is not the best intervention. As usual a subsidy of domestic production would be better even if financed by indirect taxation.

That models of international trade with oligopolistic producers provide new theoretical justifications for policy intervention is not to be doubted. Even Srinivasan, who is sceptical concerning the efficacy of such interventions in practice, admits that there is a theoretical case. However, just as in the old policy ranking literature, a tariff, although often better than no intervention, is seldom the best intervention.

Generally the new trade theories do not provide models more applicable to a LDC than to an industrial country. Indeed, some of these models are rather unsuitable for a LDC. The protection as export promotion model, for example, assumes a large domestic market, a property of few LDCs. Similarly, to benefit from strategic behaviour in international markets (e.g. centralized purchase of imports) a country will require an efficient and uncorrupt administration. Even when this exists, employing it in an import board will divert one of the most scarce factors in a LDC and the return may not be worth the price.

Trade in services does concern LDCs as the theory is addressed to the question of the international division of labour between developed and less developed countries. Bhagwati (1984) first posed the question of why services should be cheaper in developing than in developed countries and attributed this fact to the failure of factor-price equalization. Where factor endowments are very different countries specialize in the production of tradables and the prices of non-tradables reflect factor scarcity. This reasonably assumes that services are labour-intensive and suggests that whenever services can be traded LDCs would do well to consider their promotion.

This simple argument needs to be developed to take account of the complexity of the category services [see Bhagwati (1985)]. Sometimes the trade of a service involves factor mobility (as when a Korean contractor builds a hotel in Kuwait and provides labour as well as expertise), or customer mobility (as with tourism). Sometimes no factor mobility is involved (as with insurance). It is a striking fact that only a tiny fraction of the non-urgent type setting of the English speaking world is done in India, which would seem on the face of things to have an overwhelming comparative advantage in that activity. One problem is that services which are readily tradable often employ skilled labour which in turn is scarce in LDCs.

5. Tariffs, shadow prices, and project evaluation

5.1. The evaluation of tariff structures

We shall follow the emphasis of the literature in concentrating on tariffs. While other forms of protection raise similar issues, some important differences should be noted. Take the effective protection rate (EPR) for example. The EPR is defined as the addition to domestic value added due to tariffs, including those on inputs to the activity, as a proportion of value added at international prices. With a quota the measurement of effective protection, except in simple cases, becomes nearly an empty exercise. Assuming the implicit tariff (that would give the same level of imports as the quota allows) and calculating effective protection accordingly, is of no great help. The demand function has to be inverted to obtain the prices at which particular quantities would be demanded and hence, even when the demand function is invertible, one needs to know the answer that the EPR was meant to furnish, changes in activity levels, before one can calculate the EPR itself.[16]

One might ask why, if tariffs capture the essence of trade intervention, quotas are so commonly adopted. Because the shadow price on the quota is in principle unbounded, they can be extremely costly. However, the fact that the cost is not transparent may go some way to explain their popularity.

Two questions may be asked of the tariffs and other forms of protection imposed by LDCs. First, we may ask whether protection constitutes the best policy. Secondly, we may take the tariff structure as given and asks what its effect has been. The first approach is in some sense more fundamental and critical, in that it takes no policy as given. The second, however, has the advantage that it can be more readily applied. Hence, it is not surprising that a large literature has grown up around particularly effective protection or allied concepts applied to LDCs. Ultimately, of course, there is no conflict between the two approaches, since a full evaluation of the effects of tariffs would indicate whether another policy would have been preferable.

We begin with the most influential concept, the rate of effective protection (EPR).[17] The EPR is intended to measure the extent to which resources have been pulled towards (or perhaps driven away from) the activity concerned. This linking of the EPR measure with the direction of resource reallocation lacks a clear and general theoretical justification.[18] However, by providing a concrete measure, which is feasible to compute, and which is at least highly suggestive, the

---

[16] I am grateful to Max Corden for bringing this point to my attention.

[17] There is a large literature. See, in particular, Bhagwati and Srinivasan (1973), Corden (1974), Ethier (1977), and Michaely (1977).

[18] See Ramaswami and Srinivasan (1971).

EPR concept has focused attention on important issues and motivated valuable research.[19]

Consider first the question of validating the concept of effective protection. For the sake of simplicity, take an economy in which there is no fundamental reason why there should be tariffs, but tariffs have been imposed. This implies that the economy is distorted, which means that an alternative set of policies would be better than those in place. We can define "better" according to a welfare function and we can show that an appropriate policy package will be an improvement upon the tariff regime whatever particular welfare function is employed.[20] This is a standard qualitative conclusion of trade theory which serves only to distinguish the undistorted from the distorted: there is no more or less involved. It is true that trade theory admits of policy rankings which state: given a policy of type A some policy of type B will dominate it. However, these results often depend upon A and B being of different type. If both policies are tariff regimes, ranking is usually impossible.

It is not, for example, generally the case that a uniform tariff is better than one with variable rates (whether measured as an effective or a nominal rate) and the same average level.[21] A high tariff on a good supplied completely inelastically in the domestic economy by poor agents and consumed by the rich might well be better than a uniform tariff generating the same revenue.[22]

EPRs are designed to measure the effect of tariffs on activities but activities as such do not enter into the welfare function, although the profits that they generate may do. This constitutes a difficulty in the way of providing a rigorous welfare interpretation of the EPR measure. Thus, we can ask two questions in turn. First, how much have domestic activities been influenced by a particular tariff structure? Secondly, how much does whatever change that has resulted matter for social welfare? EPRs were never intended to answer the second question.

On the first question the presumption was that a greater change in domestic demand prices for value added activities is likely on average to lead to a greater effect on the promotion or inhibition of those activities and the greater the effect the worse. This may well be so but there is no difficulty in the way of

---

[19] For some of these applications, see Balassa (1982) and Little, Scitovsky and Scott (1970).

[20] Assuming of course that the function does not include a feature that might make tariffs optimal, such as non-economic objectives.

[21] If tariffs are raising a given amount of revenue, then they should raise that revenue at least cost. The problem of minimizing that cost is analogous to the problem of optimal indirect taxation. See Dixit (1985, p. 3).

[22] This tariff is equivalent to sales taxation plus a subsidy to the producers of the good concerned. On the production side there is no distortion, by assumption, but this is not necessary to the conclusion. Corden (1984, pp. 93–94) gives references to work concerned with piecemeal tariff reform, including results which show that a reduction of relatively high effective tariff rates while no tariff is increased will be welfare improving. This supposes that such a change would be feasible, an assumption not satisfied if equal revenue-generating tariff structures are compared.

constructing examples in which highly uneven rates of effective protection are fairly innocuous. Corden (1984, p. 102) writes as follows:

> Thus calculations of *rates* of protection and rates of divergence between private and social cost are ingredients in cost of protection calculations, as well as being of interest as guides to understanding resource allocation effects ex-ante and ex-post.

EPRs then are only ingredients. They can, however, be used to measure the cost of tariff-induced distortion under certain precise conditions such as the following. If all activities in a small country employ the same non-tradable inputs in exactly the same proportions, and if there are constant returns to scale, a movement of a unit of those inputs from a high EPR activity to a lower EPR activity increases the international value of domestic production by the difference between the higher and the lower EPR. In this case the EPR measures the absolute gain in international values from a resource reallocation. The assumptions stated are needed, however.

Despite these problems of interpretation, EPRs have attracted a great deal of attention because the strong flavour of what has often emerged goes a long way towards defining how the completed dish, which must be a calculation of the cost of protection, is going to taste. Krueger (1983) provides a recent review of the findings of empirical investigations into rates of effective protection in LDCs. See also Balassa (1971) and Little, Scitovsky and Scott (1970). The striking features that emerge from these studies are, first, how high is the level of effective protection afforded to certain activities in some LDCs; secondly, how high is the average rate of effective protection, particularly for manufacturing, in some but not in all LDCs; and, finally, sometimes, the extreme and apparently capricious variations in the EPRs provided to different activities in the same country. Most striking of all are activities which return negative value added at world prices, a situation most unlikely to be justifiable.[23] These observations provide no measure of the harm done by the distorted price structure but they do suggest that the harm might be considerable.

An approach which comes close to the EPR is the domestic resource cost (DRC) measure, on which see Bhagwati and Srinivasan (1978, 1979). We have seen above how the EPR measure can sometimes be used to measure the cost

---

[23] Within the framework of social cost–benefit analysis, see Subsection 5.3 below, it is not strictly impossible that a project with negative value added at international prices would be accepted. Imagine, for example, that the disabled can only make wooden toys worth less at world prices than the inputs required to produce them but would otherwise starve. In the taxation model of Diamond and Mirrlees (1971) direct transfers to the disabled which are not affected by indirect taxation are not admitted. If the labour of the disabled cannot be directly subsidized it may be necessary to raise the rents that they earn by banning the import of wooden toys. This theoretical curiosum is surely not the explanation of the cases of negative value added which have been uncovered. Non-economic objectives are more likely to account for them.

imposed by the tariff structure on domestic production valued at international prices. However, the conditions required are special. The DRC measure enables these conditions to be considerably relaxed but only at the cost, as would be expected, of requiring more information. The DRC of an activity is the value at shadow prices, that is the social opportunity cost, of the resources used by that activity to generate one unit of international value added. This measure less one is equivalent to the EPR measure when domestic prices equal shadow prices. The DRC approach leads naturally into project evaluation, see Subsection 5.3 below, of which it forms a special case.

We noted earlier the distinction between tariffs and quotas. This is most important where the distribution of income and the private gains from protection are concerned. Much of the trade literature pushes these issues aside by allowing lump-sum transfers as required to override these effects. However, interest in second-best economics, including trade theory, and particularly the need for models applicable to policy decisions for LDCs, has lead to models which focus more attention on the distributional consequences of protection. This approach has given rise to one of the most interesting developments in trade theory of recent years, the idea of rent seeking, which is considered in Subsection 5.2. The theme of the distributional consequences of trade policy also runs through the theory of shadow prices for the developing economy and into project evaluation, which are considered in Subsection 5.3.

5.2. Protection, distortions, and rent-seeking

Consider the best type of intervention to deal with a distortion. When might that intervention be tariff protection? Despite the diversity of types of distortion listed in Subsection 3.3 above, a theory has been developed that embraces them all and what emerges is a unity of conclusion. The underlying theme of work by Bhagwati (alone and with various combinations of Ramaswami and Srinivasan), Johnson, Kemp and Negishi [for references see Bhagwati (1971)] may be stated simply: direct intervention is superior to oblique intervention.

Take beneficial linkages associated with a certain activity. This case has been made the basis of support for protection of the activity concerned against foreign competition. That would constitute an oblique intervention as the beneficial linkage effects are gained only as an indirect consequence of the increase in the domestic price which results from the tariff. Domestic producers would be given an advantage and domestic production encouraged; however, the higher domestic price would discourage demand with the consequence that domestic production would be expanded less than it would be with a subsidy. A subsidy is the direct intervention given beneficial externalities. This type of argument may be and has been replicated through numerous cases.

A natural question to ask is whether there is a distortion for which protection is the best and direct intervention. What is required is that trade as such should matter in a negative sense. The best known case is the optimal tariff in which the negative consequence of trade is a worsening in the terms of international exchange. Other examples would be a desire for self-sufficiency in some or all lines of production, or the wish to avoid the socially contaminating effects of foreign products. These last cases fall under the heading of non-economic objectives.

For the LDCs it is somewhat difficult to believe that the case for protection could be quite so irreducibly narrow and it should be noted that the theory is constructed on optimistic assumptions concerning the fiscal instruments available to the authorities. Tariffs are revenue generating while subsidies demand the disbursement of revenue. What most easily beats a tariff as a low distortion revenue generator is lump-sum taxation, but this is remote from reality. For advanced countries a suitable sales tax or VAT is not an unreal assumption, and when used to support a subsidy on an activity with external economies is likely to be superior to tariff or quota protection of the activity. Where the LDC is concerned the feasibility of additional sales taxation might be questioned. When an industry should be subsidized but the good it sells should attract a high rate of sales tax, a tariff might even come close to achieving the optimum.

While the theory of optimal intervention in distorted economies is useful in clearing up ideas and showing the right directions for policy, it suffers when taken alone from being qualitative when quantitative assessment is vital. The extensive empirical literature on the costs of protection has sometimes suggested that the costs are small in relation to national income. For reviews of this literature see Corden (1975, 1984). For the computable general equilibrium model approach to the costs of protection see de Melo, Grais and Urata (1986). Balassa commenting on Corden (1975) in the same volume cautions against applying this conclusion too freely to LDCs. Balassa's point is that some LDCs have tariffs that are both high and extremely uneven. Still more important are the qualifications implied for the costs of protection argument by "rent-seeking", see below.

It is not strictly a reason for being sceptical about the claim that tariffs are harmful that, while the most rapidly growing LDCs at the present time have low rates of protection, historical example includes successful development with high levels of protection, notably in Japan. It would be perilous to recommend high levels of protection to other countries on the basis of the Japanese example. It is not clear that the success was due to high levels of protection and the unusual ability of Japan to avoid crippling other domestic activities while protecting some does not travel well. However, all this suggests that it is the impact of the totality of policies on development that matters and that the quantitative effect of various measures as well as their qualities must be taken into account.

There is a large literature concerned with the cost of protection. For references see Corden (1984). We have seen above (Subsection 5.1) that in one simple case the cost of protection to the economy, in terms of loss of value at world prices can be estimated using indices of effective protection. The gain from moving a unit of resources from one activity to another can be measured as the difference between the EPRs of these activities. The point that the computation involves differences between EPRs is emphasized by Corden. However, the absolute levels of EPRs matter too on the plausible assumption that tariff protection is not provided for all activities. If protection is given to manufacturing and the resources used in manufacturing are sector specific, there will be no tendency for resources to be pulled into manufacturing, and a uniform rate of effective protection would make no difference to resource allocation. We may reasonably assume that protection will not be provided in this case, as it has no effect. Variable rates of effective protection will, however, affect the allocation of resources within the manufacturing sector and Corden's point applies. It is the dispersion of EPRs that matters.

In the LDCs the anti-protection of, for example, agriculture is such a crucial consideration that the absolute level of effective protection, typically of manufacturing activities, must be considered as important. There remain problems when protection encourages activities that produce tradables at the expense of activities that produce non-tradables. As the non-tradable, by definition, has no world price, the calculation of the resource-pulling consequence of protection is complicated.

A point which has impressed writers concerned with developed economies is that many simple calculations of the cost of protection, which ignore the transfer effects of tariffs and estimate only the deadweight loss, come up with rather modest computations of the costs. For a review of this literature see Corden (1975). The reason for these findings is that the deadweight loss consists of the areas of the usual "triangles", and unless tariffs are extremely high, and demands and supplies highly elastic, these tend not to amount to a large share of total national product.

The same theoretical point which explains the apparent low cost of protection in advanced countries applies to the LDCs. However, certain features of LDC protection need to be taken into account in a final assessment of the costs. Indeed, the consideration of LDC protection provides a useful counterbalance to the "small triangles complacency" of advanced country studies. First, some LDCs exhibit very high and strongly discriminatory tariffs, with the consequence that even the usual partial equilibrium estimate of the deadweight loss may be large. In such cases, however, the partial equilibrium approach is likely to be a bad approximation, and programming models or computable general equilibrium models should be employed. See Taylor and Black (1974), de Melo (1978),

Dervis, de Melo and Robinson (1982), Krueger (1984, section 3.5), and Srinivasan and Whalley (1986). Secondly, it is more common in LDCs to encounter quota restrictions, or features such as costly and time-consuming procedures to obtain import licenses. These may make the true cost to the user of obtaining an input effectively infinite, while the official tariff on the input may not be large, and the calculated EPR for the activity positive. The resource allocation costs of the shortage economy, though difficult to calculate, may be enormous.

The scope for distortion in the system of import licensing is explored by Bhagwati and Desai (1970). An entrepreneur with excess capacity might rationally invest in more plant in the belief that the additional capacity would help to obtain highly valued import licenses. This case provides an example of rent-seeking which is encountered when valuable resources are sucked into the pursuit of the rents created by protection and other intervention. Rent-seeking, and its cousin directly unproductive activities or DUPs, has generated a large literature. Some of this goes outside and beyond economics, and even in economics the concept is not only applicable to international trade. For a broad review, see Buchanan, Tollison and Tullock (1980), and for economic applications Bhagwati (1982) and Collander (1984). On the trade implications of rent-seeking see Krueger (1974), Bhagwati and Srinivasan (1980), and Bhagwati, Brecher and Srinivasan (1984).

The most obvious point is that rent-seeking may greatly increase the cost of protection and other interventions. In the limit the cost may include the whole of the revenue in addition to the triangles. In Krueger's original model revenue-seeking always increases the costs of protection. When one considers, however, that an economy subject to a tariff is distorted it should not be surprising that "paradoxes" may be encountered. These are explored in Bhagwati and Srinivasan (1980). A single example will serve as an illustration. To a standard two-factors two-goods HO model we add a revenue-seeking activity which also employs the two factors. The effect of the activity is to milk the economy of resources which could otherwise produce valued outputs. However, in general it can take away resources in any proportions, according to the revenue-seeking production function and the factor prices, which depend on international prices and the tariff. With a tariff distortion a suitable loss of factors can be welfare improving. Hence, revenue-seeking may be welfare improving.

As LDCs typically protect capital-intensive activities, revenue-seeking would have to be capital intensive for the foregoing paradox to work. In the case of the excess capacity of the Bhagwati–Desai example this condition is satisfied. More generally, revenue-seeking probably uses skilled labour most intensively. If we count skilled labour as a combination of raw labour and human capital, we might again find the condition satisfied. Note, however, that where the

Bhagwati–Srinivasan paradox holds the LDC would benefit if a foreign power destroyed part of its capital stock in a bombing raid. This is not a plausible assumption for most LDCs.

5.3. Shadow prices and project evaluation

As project evaluation is considered in detail in Chapter 21 of this Handbook we confine our discussion to the issue posed for the theory by trade, the use of international values in the calculation of shadow prices. Diamond and Mirrlees (1971) showed that public sector production should be efficient[24] on the assumption that optimal commodity taxation (strictly optimal indirect taxation of all commodities and factor services) could be levied. In other words, they showed that the assumption of lump-sum taxation is more than we need, for one can assume a much less powerful form of taxation and still justify efficiency. This was a great advance on earlier arguments, which still persist in the trade and even in the development literature, based on assuming, whether explicitly or implicitly, lump-sum taxes.[25] However, the assumption of the Diamond–Mirrlees analysis, according to which it is feasible to tax factor services, is not that appealing for the case of an LDC where a sizable part of the labour force is involved in household production using household labour. It is fortunate, therefore, as will be shown below, that a much weaker assumption suffices.

Since international trade can be considered as an extension of the domestic production possibilities of the public sector, it follows that the public sector can only be efficient if it maximizes the value of its production, given its use of non-tradable resources, at world prices. The Diamond–Mirrlees result plus only this simple line of reasoning establishes the optimality of world prices as relative shadow prices for public sector production decisions. The shadow prices support the production set at the optimal point and as exchanges at relative world prices are part of the set it can only be supported by relative tradable prices equal to relative world prices (or border prices as they are usually known).

So far we have considered only relative shadow prices for tradables. This does not determine the *numeraire*, the unit in terms of which social cost–benefit accounting will be conducted. The idea of obtaining as many shadow prices as possible working back from international values is developed in Little and

---

[24] To be precise, Diamond and Mirrlees showed that public sector production should not be in the interior of the production set. This is importantly different from efficiency when there are goods with which the public sector is in no way involved – a situation especially likely to be encountered in a LDC. Imagine, for example, that lowering the prices of other goods raises the demand for household labour services which are not in the public sector production space but do affect the utilities of consumers.

[25] Ignoring income distribution, assuming all households to be the same and assuming the existence of community indifference curves, all amount to the same thing as assuming lump-sum transfers.

Mirrlees (1974). See also Joshi (1972), Dasgupta and Stiglitz (1974), and Lal (1974). Dasgupta, Marglin and Sen (1972) (UNIDO) is similar to Little and Mirrlees (1974) at the theoretical level and shadow prices for traded goods are again proportional to international values. For a comparison of the methods see Dasgupta (1972). However, the emphasis in Little and Mirrlees is strongly towards working from border prices back to non-tradable shadow prices rather than using domestic market valuations directly. Hence, in practice the two systems may well produce significantly different results.

The use by Little and Mirrlees of border prices to calculate shadow prices has come in for criticism. See Stewart and Streeten (1972) and the reply by Little and Mirrlees (1972), also Joshi (1972) and Sen (1972). This debate raises complex issues which need not concern us here, such as how all-pervasive are external effects and how one should measure them. However, we can distinguish two fairly clear issues from this tangled debate. One concerns the validity of using world prices as shadow prices when, as must be the case if one can talk in terms of a world price, a good is tradable, but where a quota inhibits trade. The other has to do with how shadow prices for non-tradables should be calculated.

On the first question, the most pointed argument is due to Sen (1972). A similar argument is put forward by Joshi (1972). Sen considers the case in which a good which might be traded will not be traded because government policy has established a quota which protects domestic production of the good so that additional import is effectively prohibited. We may suppose, to discuss this case, that the project only involves tradable goods, since non-tradables and their shadow-pricing are not relevant to this argument.

The method by which the Diamond–Mirrlees argument demonstrates the improvability of any solution for which public sector production is in the interior of the possibility set is illustrated for a simple two-good case in Figure 23.2. For the sake of simplicity we assume that all production is in the public sector. *PP* is the production possibility surface and we assume that production is efficient in the sense that it is on the frontier of the domestic production possibility set. However, production is not at *A*, which is the point at which the value of domestic production at world prices would be maximized. The line *QA* is the line with slope equal to the negative of world relative prices through *A*. At *A* the EPR is zero for both activities. However, production takes place at *B* and consumption at *C*. *II* is the indifference curve through *C* defined as the boundary of the set of all quantities of the two goods which can make all consumers at least as well off as they are at *C*.[26] To show that the allocation defined by production at *B* and consumption at *C* is inefficient, we lower consumer prices for both goods by a sufficiently small extent that the aggregate consumption does not go

[26]As is well known, this is the type of indifference curve that may cross the indifference curves drawn to pass through different points. However, for the present argument this does not matter.

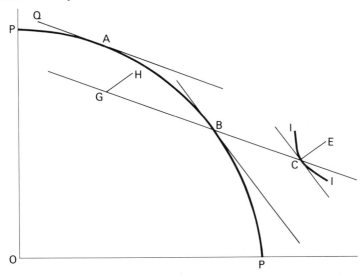

Figure 23.2

above *QA*. This point is shown on the figure as *E*. As the figure shows, it is feasible to deliver *C* to consumers by producing at *G* and exchanging through international trade the segment *GC*. It will then be seen that production at *H*, where *GH* is the same vector as *CE*, must also be feasible. Moreover, producing at *H* and exchanging the equivalent of the vector *AC* in international trade results in *E*. Hence, *C* can be feasibly dominated and the same goes for any initial allocation in which production is not at *A*.

Note how this argument might fail if the public sector production set were to lie in a subspace of the complete goods space. This would happen if, for example, household labour were to play no part in public production activities. In that case within the full space public production is always on a boundary and the result loses its force.[27]

We may now consider the movement from *B* to *A* as a project. Suppose that *B* was domestic production because a quota had been imposed to increase the production of the good whose output is measured along the *y*-axis. The foregoing argument shows that if the project is assessed using border prices then it will pass the test. This implies that if the project is carried out and international exchange allowed to accommodate the resultant changes in overall domestic supply and demand for tradables, the government's objectives, in this case simply private

[27] It might be argued that even if the public sector cannot produce household labour and has no use for it, it could still buy it, so that the public sector production set will have full rank. However, a welfare-improving change might increase the demand for household labour, in which case we rule out the public sector initially having a surplus (i.e. buying more than it needs). Then the result is trivial.

welfare, may be better realized. When applied to public sector projects the Sen argument assumes policy inconsistency on the part of the authorities. Given their objectives the project would be an improvement but a quota which they have put in place debars the improving project. It may, however, be that project evaluation must cover this case. Given the quota there will be no movement from B to A and the project is infeasible. It is possible to devise a system of shadow prices which take certain policies, such as tariffs, as given and immovable. On this see Bliss (1987a).

Sen's point is somewhat different and is most easily illustrated by considering that production was at B in Figure 23.2 in the initial allocation because there was a quantitative target for the export of the y-axis good. If that quantitative target will not be removed, then production at B is optimal and a test of the project B to A using world prices is misleading. This example will be seen to fall into place as a case of non-economic objectives.[28] One might also say that the assumptions of the argument effectively reduce a tradable good to a non-tradable good.

The general point is that the recommendation that a project be adopted is always contingent upon certain assumptions about how it might be implemented within a specific policy framework. One approach would hold that an economist should tailor his recommendations to the policy changes which he believes the government will be willing to allow. So if a quota will not be relaxed the good should be treated as effectively non-tradable. The danger of this approach is that the cost of policies in place is never clearly exposed. On the other hand, if recommendations always assume that widespread reform is on the agenda they may end up in the wastepaper basket.

We have seen that relative shadow prices for public sector project evaluation for genuine tradables should equal relative border prices. There remains the problem of how to convert from shadow prices in terms of tradables to the shadow prices of non-tradables. This involves among other considerations the choice of what Little–Mirrlees call the "conversion factor" and the analogue of the same number in the UNIDO manual (actually its inverse), the shadow price of foreign exchange. Each of these values plays the role of converting international values into units of domestic opportunity cost, or (in the case of Little–Mirrlees) the other way about. We shall use the term "conversion factor" to cover both measures. Despite ambiguities in some discussions, it is clear that when the individual project evaluator comes to look at a project he will need to be told the conversion factor.

Diamond and Mirrlees (1971) presented the result which became central to the modern theory of project evaluation in a paper entitled, "Optimal taxation and public production". It is not surprising therefore that the result became associated in many people's minds with the use of optimal taxation and that this was

---

[28] However, world prices do measure the opportunity cost of the non-economic objective. I am grateful to David Evans for pointing this out to me.

seen to be a limitation. It is clear that if each public sector project recommendation carries with it the assumption that as a result of its implementation a small adjustment will be made to indirect taxes, it depends on an assumption unlikely to be satisfied. It is important to note therefore that the efficiency of public sector production and hence the equality of relative tradables prices to border prices does not require optimal taxation.

Drèze and Stern (1985) show how project evaluation may be considered within a very general framework in which the government sends signals to the private sector (which may be prices, tax rates, quotas, etc.). It only requires that a small change in such a signal should be improving for all agents in the economy to show that optimal production cannot be in the interior of the public sector production set and hence that tradable shadow prices should be proportional to border prices, as above. This is true for any fixed signals not necessarily optimal. Hence, the result that relative border prices define relative tradable goods prices is extremely general [see Hammond (1988)]. However, the Sen argument reminds us that a tradable should be genuinely tradable. Also, we must note for the application of this theory to the case of an LDC, that goods not involved at all in the public sector, such as domestic labour, or even illegal drugs, may render the result empty.

6. Policies to influence the terms of trade

6.1. Objectives and constraints

In Subsection 2.2 above we encountered Nurkse's appeal to the global balance between supply and demand for primary products. LDCs generally cannot expand primary product production without suffering terms of trade losses. This point, which is surely valid, should be distinguished from the much more questionable claim that the terms of trade between manufactures and primary products must inevitably move against the latter, a view associated with the names of Prebisch and Singer [see UNDEA (1949) and Prebisch (1950)]. For a painstaking review of the issues and the evidence which, broadly speaking, finds the view unsupported, see Spraos (1980), and also the extended discussion of this question in Chapter 24 of this Handbook.

The claim that the terms of trade will decline secularly against primary product producers should be distinguished from the conclusions attributed to two controversial North–South models due to Chichilinsky [see Chichilinsky (1980, 1981), and the Chichilinsky and others (1983, 1984) and references therein]. According to the first paper, a transfer from rich to poor countries may cause such a movement in the terms of trade as to make the recipient countries worse off (transfer paradox), while the second paper argues that a shift in the demand curve of the North for South's exports may bring about a worsening in the terms of trade from South's point of view (terms of trade paradox). Since both these papers gave rise to extensive and ill-tempered debates, the reader will have to refer to the references provided and form an independent judgement of the issues. It is worth noting, however, that, on the one hand, there is eventual agreement that a transfer paradox is possible in a simple stable model, and that, on the other hand, Chichilinsky significantly shifted her position with regard to the specification of the terms of trade paradox. The empirical importance of these findings remains an open question.

The focus of the present section is on policies, particularly policies which LDCs might implement alone or in consort, to influence the terms of trade. This section is concerned with general considerations and policies to improve the terms of trade. In Subsection 6.2 we consider commodity price stabilization.

The most basic distinction is between an improvement in the average level of the terms of trade in favour of some or all LDCs, and a reduction in some measure of fluctuation. We shall refer to these different objectives as terms of trade improvement and stabilization. Formally, the distinction is clear. It corresponds roughly to the effects of policy on two statistical measures, the mean and the variance of a distribution. However, these two aspects of the outcome tend to be intimately connected. Stabilization, for example, may alter the average level of prices, a point which we shall discuss in Subsection 6.2 below. Equally, policies to improve the terms of trade may be destabilizing in the long run. This would happen if a cartel were to force up the price of a commodity, resulting eventually in such an increase in the supply that the cartel would break down and the price collapse.

Economic theory provides a number of concepts and models which are relevant to terms of trade improvement. Where a single exporter can influence the terms of trade, optimum tariff theory may be applied. For references see Corden (1984, section 5). Possible problems are retaliation, and an increase in the price elasticity of demand in the long run as the higher price encourages entry to the market. The first difficulty will seldom be the most important. Retaliation is quite hard to organize, harder even than establishing a producers' cartel in the first place. However, influential governments might take punitive actions to try to destroy a cartel at birth. The problem of erosion of market share, however, is crucial, and this has plagued most attempts to take advantage of the short-run inelasiticity of demand for a commodity. The erosion of the share of OPEC in world oil production during the 1970s and 1980s indicates the magnitude of this problem.[29] In theory a difference between the short-run and the long-run value of

---

[29]OPEC was not a single seller but a loose coalition led by a major producer. Some of its difficulties were of policing the productions of its own members, but even if it had been able to act as a unity it would have faced acute problems. This is shown by the fact that the share of total oil production sold by OPEC members declined despite the fact that indiscipline of some members of the cartel tended to push up OPEC production.

the elasticity of demand should lead to a declining time path for the optimum tariff, and a knowledge that the price would decline over time could deter some entry and moderate the decline required. These issues have been explored in connection with the theory of the firm and are formally similar in the optimum tariff case.

In very few cases can one country acting alone significantly improve its terms of trade. More usually concerted action is required involving many producers. Characteristic difficulties are that successful intervention will require control over production, which may be difficult to police. If production is unchecked and the price increased, a conflict arises between the interests of the consortium and the self-interest of the individual member. This is an example of the familiar "free-rider" problem of public goods theory. Similar conclusions are to be found in game theory. If there is no control over production but the price is raised, problems of chronic oversupply will arise. This has been the experience of the Common Agricultural Policy of the European Economic Community.

Various schemes have been put forward for terms of trade improving schemes run by international organizations. The proposal of Kaldor, Hart and Tinbergen (1964) was to increase world demand for commodities by having countries use stockpiled commodities as international reserves. The enormous administrative problems which would have attached to this elegant scheme go some way to explaining its failure to attract official support. More recently UNCTAD has shown an interest in a buffer stock scheme combined with supply management [see UNCTAD (1975)], but without international support such schemes are doomed to failure.

6.2. Commodity price stabilization

This subsection will be concerned with a buffer stock scheme, organized by an official body, which intervenes by buying when the price of a commodity is low and selling when the price is high. Such schemes have been popular both as proposals and in practice. They have to do with development, because instability of primary commodity markets has been held to be a leading problem of economic development. They are not strictly to do with trade, as in principle a single country could organize a buffer stock scheme.

For references and a review of past discussions of commodity price stabilization, see the papers in Adams and Klein (1978), also Lipton (1970). There was not much application of complex economic theory to this problem until recently. Many writers employed a partial equilibrium approach. The influence of uncertainty was examined by Oi (1961) who noted that a competitive firm faced by price uncertainty would enjoy a greater expected value of profit than it would enjoy if the price were invariant and the mean the same. This is a consequence of the convexity of the profit function. Massell (1970) examined a simple partial equilibrium model with supply and demand curves. He noted that there is an optimal degree of price stabilization from the point of view of the producer. The implications of uncertainty and general equilibrium consequences of stabilization are further examined in Newbery and Stiglitz (1981). Goss and Yamey (1976) reprint papers concerned with futures trading. We shall mainly consider the contribution of Newbery and Stiglitz who bring out the possible problems associated with commodity price stabilization in an theoretically ambitious setting. A critical review of this work, which includes an excellent summary, is to be found in Ravi Kanbur (1984). We first examine a simple partial equilbirium model with linear demands and supplies. This model forms the starting point of the programme undertaken by Newbery and Stiglitz.

Consider a single market which is so small that income effects may be neglected. Without intervention the price fluctuates according to disturbances in the supply or the demand conditions (we consider the former as analogous results may be shown for the latter). The outcome may be compared with the state of affairs that would pertain if the price were stabilized so that supply and demand were equal. To keep the argument simple we assume that fluctuations take the form of two states, with equal probability, in one of which supply (or demand) is high while in the other it is low. Suppose that supply fluctuates and consider the implications for the consumer.

Denote demand by $b - c \cdot p$ and supply by $\beta + \gamma \cdot p + z \cdot \sigma$, where z is a random variable which takes the values 1 or -1 with probability 0.5 in each case. Without intervention the price will be:

$$\left[\frac{(b - \beta) - z \cdot \sigma}{c + \gamma} \right]. \tag{13}$$

Assume that the marginal utility of income is constant and equal to 1. By Roy's identity demand is the negative of the derivative of the indirect utility function. Hence, the consumer's utility as a function of price will be:

$$a - b \cdot p + 0.5c \cdot p^2. \tag{14}$$

Substituting (13) into (14) we obtain the consumer's utility as:

$$a - b \left[\frac{(b - \beta) - z \cdot \sigma}{c + \gamma} \right] + 0.5c \left[\frac{(b - \beta) - z \cdot \sigma}{c + \gamma} \right]^2. \tag{15}$$

With intervention price will be:

$$p = \frac{b - \beta}{c + \gamma}, \tag{16}$$

and utility will be:

$$a - b\left[\frac{(b-\beta)}{c+\gamma}\right] + 0.5c\left[\frac{(b-\beta)}{c+\gamma}\right]^2. \tag{17}$$

The difference between the expected value of (15) and (17) is $c \cdot \sigma^2$. Hence, the consumer is worse off with price stabilization, and his loss increases as the square of the variation in supply.

In a similar manner we may examine the outcomes with and without stabilization from the point of view of the producer, assuming profit to be his objective. The profit function will be:

$$\alpha + (\beta + z \cdot \sigma)p + 0.5p^2, \tag{18}$$

which without stabilization will take the value:

$$\alpha + (\beta + z \cdot \sigma)\left[\frac{(b-\beta) - z \cdot \sigma}{c+\gamma}\right] + 0.5\gamma\left[\frac{(b-\beta) - z \cdot \sigma}{c+\gamma}\right]^2, \tag{19}$$

which may be rearranged to yield:

$$\alpha + (\beta + z \cdot \sigma)\left[\frac{b - (\beta + z \cdot \sigma)}{c+\gamma}\right] + 0.5\gamma \cdot \left[\frac{b - (\beta + z \cdot \sigma)}{c+\gamma}\right]^2. \tag{20}$$

With stabilization profit will be:

$$\alpha + \beta \cdot \left[\frac{(b-\beta)}{c+\gamma}\right] + 0.5\gamma\left[\frac{(b-\beta)}{c+\gamma}\right]^2. \tag{21}$$

The difference between expected unstabilized profit and stabilized profit will again involve only terms in σ^2. From (20) this will be seen to be:

$$\sigma^2\left[\frac{\gamma}{(c+\gamma)^2} - \frac{2}{c+\gamma}\right], \tag{22}$$

which is negative. Hence, the supplier is worse off with fluctuations, he gains from stabilization.

Analogous arguments show that if fluctuations originate on the demand side, the consumer gains from stabilization while the producer loses. On the assumption that stabilization is costless, fluctuations serve no useful role and in fact cause harm. Hence, whichever party loses from fluctuation could afford to bribe the other party to accept stabilization and still be better off. Linearity is crucial to all the above results except for the last. If a buffer stock scheme is costless, fluctuations are inefficient regardless of the shape of the supply and demand curves.

In the models examined by Newbery and Stiglitz (1981) a number of influences are taken into account which the foregoing simple model neglects. Of particular importance are the responses of producers to the "policy regime", an issue which has been much investigated by macroeconomic theorists. In the above treatment, for example, supply depends only upon price and a random variable. It is uninfluenced by the fact, or the absence, of stabilization, and the same is true of demand. This is unrealistic. If producers are guaranteed a certain price for a crop, they will tend to prefer to produce it in preference to another crop the price of which fluctuates. A parallel effect operates with consumers. If we stabilize and this encourages production, the average level of the terms of trade will tend to move against producers. If growers know that the price of coffee will not vary, they will plant more trees, and this will eventually result in a larger average supply.

That the manner in which expectations are formed is important for the behaviour of a primary product market is obvious when one considers that static expectations can give rise to the familiar cobweb cycle, which is inconsistent with rational expectations. In the model due to Hazell and Scandizzo (1975) the outcome is inefficient, even with rational expectations, on account of the absence of a complete set of contingency, or insurance, markets. Newbery and Stiglitz point out that as these authors assume risk neutrality on the part of producers, there is no role for insurance markets and the result is efficient after all. This mistake could easily be repaired. Indeed, Newbery and Stiglitz themselves argue that the market solution will be inefficient and their reason is the same as the advanced by Hazell and Scandizzo, namely that there are absent markets.

The conclusion reached by Newbery and Stiglitz concerning the benefits of price stabilization are generally rather negative. One reason is that the effects of stabilization on long-run average supply and demand, the so-called "transfer benefits", are likely to be unfavourable to producers. When these costs are set against relatively modest estimates of the benefits of stabilization as such, the net benefits of a buffer stock scheme are unlikely to exceed the costs.

Any analysis of the consequences of price stabilization must posit a level at which prices are stabilized. Newbery and Stiglitz assume that the price will be stabilized at a level at which buffer stocks will not accumulate when output is unrestricted. Ravi Kanbur (1984) argues that enough restriction of output to make the transfer benefits zero might not call forth from the buyers the resistance which would meet the attempt to create a cartel, and could lead to a different conclusion.[30]

---

[30]Of course another policy mix might obviate the need for output reduction while still ensuring that transfer benefits would be zero.

Another reason for Newbery and Stiglitz's scepticism concerning the benefits of stabilization is an awareness of the numerous alternative means available to the producer or the consumer to spread risk and mitigate its cost. Among these is the use of futures markets.

Ravi Kanbur argues that the Newbery and Stiglitz study neglects the macro-economic aspects of stabilization. He presents a model in which commodity price fluctuations have Keynesian effects on the national economy. In this model the benefits of stabilization are much larger. They depend of course upon assuming that foreign exchange reserves or international borrowing cannot overcome the need for income reduction to stabilize the balance of payments following a fall in foreign currency earnings due to an unfavourable development in the commodity market.

7. Trade and the rate of growth

7.1. Various approaches to growth and trade

The subject of growth and development in trade models already enjoys in Findlay (1984) the benefit of an excellent recent survey. Less recent, but also of great use is Corden (1971). The fact of these surveys permits us to discuss in the present subsection some rather general differences between the various models that have been proposed and to refer the reader to Findlay (1984) and Corden (1971) for more detailed presentation and for further references.

"Growth" can mean more than one thing and a definitional elasticity is to be observed in the literature on trade and growth. Thus, Johnson (1955) in a paper which became well known and led to further work in the same vein was concerned with growth in the sense of "expansion" – a once-for-all improvement in production possibilities or factor availability. Exercises of this type are essentially comparative static. They can usefully show the effects on trade, and particularly on the terms of trade, of differences in productivity or the sizes of economies. They are not suitable, however, for answering questions to do with long-run and continuing differences in rates of growth.

Turning to steady state models, the most striking and fundamental distinction is between those in which the long-run rate of growth is exogenous and those in which it is endogenous. In the neoclassical models of the Solow–Swan variety and their two sector derivatives, the long-run rate of growth is determined by the growth rate of the labour supply and the rate of technical change. It is of course possible to adapt the neoclassical growth model so that these two factors become to some extent variable, and when that has been done there is no difficulty in making trade influence the growth rate. However, where trade is concerned work on these lines has not been extensive. The 1960s, not surprisingly, saw a number of papers written on steady-state growth in the open economy, a natural extension of the closed growth models which were fashionable at the time. Bardhan (1970) provides an example of some of the best work of that period. See also Smith (1977).

Analyzing the effects of growth on trade is different from investigating the effects of trade on growth. The latter is perhaps of more compelling interest to economic development theory and certainly to policy. Distinctly different results emerge according to whether or not the full utilization of labour and other resources is assumed to be assured by the smooth functioning of the market system. Most interesting are models where this is not assumed. In particular the most dramatic role for trade is provided by so-called " vent for surplus" models. Caves (1965), which should be consulted for a detailed exposition of the model, puts the basic idea succinctly when he writes:

> These models share an essential common characteristic in that they depict the effects of trade on growth as involving the exploitation of resources lacking in that place and at that time any alternative uses of significant economic value [Caves (1965, p. 96)].

This is an extreme case. Trade can also promote growth by putting into more productive employment resources which otherwise would have found only less productive employment. In any case this analysis is essentially static. The growth is a gain from opening up trade, not the result of factor accumulation technical progress, etc.

Much of the theory with which this subsection has been briefly concerned was not constructed for the purpose of modelling LDCs. One might add that a good deal of it is not particularly suitable for that purpose. In particular the neoclassical growth models seem ill-designed to treat of economies which are widely agreed to be subject to dual features, even if the unlimited supply of labour assumption might be questioned. Also, the claim that a country cannot accelerate its long-run growth rate because that is determined by exogenous rates of population growth and technical progress is not particularly convincing where development theory is concerned. A great deal of technical progress in LDCs takes the form of moving local practice a little closer to best practice in advanced countries. Technological knowledge is unlikely to be the most important bottleneck.

7.2. A turnpike model for the open economy

We argued in the previous subsection that given the assumptions commonly adopted in theoretical models of development, in particular the Lewis assumption of "unlimited supplies of labour", the neoclassical growth model in which steady state growth is limited by the long-run rate of growth of efficiency units of labour is perhaps not suitable for examining the relationship between trade and growth in the developing economy.

Without any suggestion that it provides a complete model of growth and development, we examine in the present section a model of development based on the von Neumann growth model[31] and show how the solution is affected when the model is opened up to trade. The idea of applying the von Neumann model and the turnpike result to trade and development is due to Findlay (1973, ch. 3) where it was developed in a simple diagrammatic framework. The analysis is loosely related to the model of Deardorff (1973) in that the saving function is the same and the effect of opening up the economy to trade is to increase the rate of accumulation through increasing the investible surplus available. However, Deardorff's model is closer to the neoclassical growth model, because the long-run growth rate is exogenous. There are similarities again to the dynamic Ricardian model of Findlay (1984, pp. 187–191) but neither of these papers develops the general multi-commodity model which the von Neumann framework readily permits. Finally, the choice of technique which emerges from the model, although this point will not be developed explicitly, will reflect the influence of the consideration emphasized by Sen (1960), namely that reinvestible surplus in the hands of the government is not weighted equally with additional consumption.[32]

We consider a small economy which can trade with the rest of the world at prices *p* which are assumed given. Making these prices variable would take us outside the von Neumann framework by introducing non-linear activities. All activities of the economy are linear but as is usual with the von Neumann model we allow any amount of joint production. The matrices A and B represent domestic production possibilities in the formal sector of the economy. A is the input matrix and B is the output matrix and a one-period production lag between an input and an output is assumed. Labour in unlimited supplies is assumed available from the informal sector and to require a given consumption vector to attract it to employment in the formal sector. These consumptions are included in the input requirements of the various activities. Hence, labour is not represented explicitly but the commodity input requirements represent the costs to the formal sector of attracting labour. However, the transformation of un-skilled into skilled labour by education and training can be well represented in the von Neumann model with its unrestricted joint production. We assume that there is no other unaugmentable scarce resource which limits growth.

If the economy were to choose autarky, the domestic production possibilities would represent the entirety of production possibilities. Let *x* be the activity vector in some period. Then input requirements are $A \cdot x$ and output available next period will be $B \cdot x$. We assume that the formal sector can reinvest the

---

[31] See von Neumann (1938).
[32] In the cost–benefit analysis literature the same idea is developed by Little and Mirrlees (1974).

whole of the gross output $B \cdot x$. This is reasonable as wage costs have already been taken into account in the input requirements. The following well-known properties of the von Neumann model[33] now apply to our development model.

(i) There exists a maximum steady-state rate of growth g^* such that for some x^*, $A \cdot x^*(1 + g^*) \leq B \cdot x^*$. An x^* which satisfies this relation will be said to be on the von Neumann ray.

(ii) All sufficiently long developments which are efficient[34] spend most of their time near to the von Neumann ray (the turnpike theorem).

These results are well known when applied to the closed economy. What is the effect of opening up the economy to trade at prices p? This is equivalent to augmenting the linear activities represented by A and B. If, for example, the world price of wheat is 1 and the world price of steel is 10, we may add two activities which transform, respectively, 10 units of wheat into 1 of steel and 1 unit of steel into 10 of wheat. If some goods, such as second-hand capital goods, are not tradable we enter no extra activities transforming them in trade.

The effects on the von Neumann growth rate and on the turnpike result of opening up economy to trade are clear. First, g^* can only be increased, for it is a maximum, and the augmentation of the matrices A and B by extra activities does not require the solution to make use of them.[35] Secondly, the turnpike result will apply to the augmented system and efficient growth in the augmented system will again spend most of a long development close to the turnpike. Trade can only improve the menu of feasible terminal capital stocks at which the economy could arrive. In summary, trade can increase the steady-state rate of growth of the formal sector, and out of steady state it can make possible a higher rate of growth as measured by the final capital stock attained.

Although these are strong and general results, they could be regarded as somewhat obvious. They argue that trade expands production possibilities and note that an expansion of production possibilities is likely to increase the rate of growth. Of course this is particularly likely to be the case in a model such as the von Neumann model with unlimited supplies of labour[36] in which the rate of growth is maximized. Yet this result, which is obvious in the von Neumann

---

[33] For precise and formal statements, see Hahn and Matthews (1964) and Turnovsky (1970).

[34] In the sense that no other development could start with the same capital stock as the efficient plan and arrive at one which dominates the final stock of the said plan.

[35] This argument could be adapted to the case in which the country cannot sell indefinitely growing amounts of exports at fixed terms of trade. It is still the case that allowing a little trade can only increase the rate of growth at least initially.

[36] Notice that should the rate of growth on the von Neumann ray exceed the natural rate of growth of labour, then a time will arrive at which labour will no longer be available in "unlimited" quantity. However, our argument is confined to the period during which the excess labour supply has not yet been mopped up by investment in the formal sector.

model in which the rate of growth is variable and endogenous, cannot hold in a neoclassical growth model in which the long-run rate of growth is exogenous.

It seems at first that the von Neumann model of economic development, despite the richness of the technologies that can be encompassed within its specification, suffers from some deficiencies when it comes to representing economic development. We next examine these deficiencies, some of which turn out not to be too serious.

(i) In maximizing the rate of growth, or taking account only of the final capital stock, the model appears to ignore the important consideration of employment creation in the course of economic development. If the wage rate which the formal sector pays exceeds that which is received in the informal sector, then a positive value attaches to employment which the model seems to ignore.

(ii) The rate of saving in the model, the entire surplus over the supply cost of labour, might be unrealistic.

(iii) The model ignores land and other non-produced resources, excepting labour.

(iv) The von Neumann technology appears to exclude external economies and diseconomies.

(v) The model appears to assume that the formal sector is planned.

We next briefly consider each of these points in turn.

On employment we need only note that the model can take into consideration the creation of employment, both in steady-state and in the turnpike applications. Let an activity which employs h man-hours of labour create a joint output of h units of "new worktime". Next, add to the activities included in A and B notional activities which convert new worktime or old worktime into units of old worktime. In this way all the employment hours ever created can be carried forward to the end of the development to form the integral of employment hours created. This number measures the employment created by a development during its life. In steady state it grows at g^*. In the turnpike application it is one of the components of the terminal capital stock.[37] Thus, the employment creation aspect of development planning can be taken into account within the von Neumann framework.

It is true that the von Neumann model assumes that the entire output vector can be reinvested to provide input requirements for the next period's activities. However, wage costs have been included as part of input requirements, and hence of investment costs, so the model does not imply the unrestricted pursuit of growth.

---

[37]An obvious implication of this approach is that only the integral of employment creation at the end of the development is taken into account. However, as any weighting may be applied to the new worktime values, this is not too restrictive.

The model as formulated assumes that for the time being labor is available in unlimited supply. What about other non-produced inputs, such as land? In most, but not in all, LDCs it would not be reasonable to assume land to be freely available. However land-augmenting technical progress has been one of the most prominent forms of technical progress as it has affected LDCs. Hence, while it would not be correct to assume that raw land is unlimited, it may not be a bad approximation to assume that the land supply can grow.

On external economies and diseconomies, it is true to say that these are not always readily incorporated into the von Neumann framework. We need to distinguish between different types of externality. First, consider *contemporaneous externalities* which comprise the effect of one activity on another during the period in which the first is being carried out. Beekeeping assisting the productivity of apple growing would be a classic example of this type. The trouble which this causes for the von Neumann framework is that it interferes with the simple additivity of activities and their effects. Consider, on the other hand, *sequential externalities*. here one activity does something which will make other, or the same, activities less (or more) productive in the future. Imagine that one activity pollutes a water supply and detracts from the productivity of another activity that will use that supply in the future. Here we can include notional outputs, such as gallons of water polluted in the example just given. However, the von Neumann model allows free disposal of all goods, so we cannot require activities in the future to use the notional outputs which represent today's pollution or other external diseconomy. Plainly some types of externality are difficult to incorporate into the von Neumann framework.

Finally, we consider whether the von Neumann model is essentially a model of planned economic development. While natural exposition of the model invites its interpretation as a model of planned development, it is well known that the solution is accompanied by dual or shadow prices which support it under decentralized profit-maximizing behaviour.

The von Neumann framework of this subsection differs importantly from several of the models of trade and development discussed above in that it makes saving subject to central choice, taking account of course of the need to pay fixed wage rates and any similar constraints. This is different from the given saving propensities of many neoclassical growth models and of Findlay's dynamic Ricardian model. However, the change of assumption that really delivers the different conclusion is that the rate of growth varies with the technology in the von Neumann framework. It is not particularly difficult to construct a model in which the autarkic economy grows faster than the open economy. However, the reasons why trade slows down growth, should it do so, are unlikely to include the effect of trade on the underlying growth possibilities of the economy. Trade should make faster growth possible. Whether faster growth results is governed by institutional and policy arrangements.

8. Concluding remarks

It is impossible to leave a review of the literature on trade and development without the feeling that considerable progress has been made. There has undoubtedly been an increase in rigour and in the care with which models are formulated. It is true that rigour is not an end in itself but only a vehicle to better understanding. Indeed, an excessive reverence for rigour risks giving to the exact banality a hearing which is denied to the inexact but perhaps more searching insight. This may happen, but generally speaking it is a fallacy to suppose that poor models suit poor people, or that the careless argument somehow cuts deeper. Despite greater rigour, the subject still accommodates quite a diversity of ideas.

Alongside the progress of theory, there has been a huge increase in the volume of the empirical data and empirical studies on which the specialist may draw. Today grand theory risks having to answer regression analysis. This is entirely healthy and there is no evidence that it paralyzes thought or debate.

Despite the clear progress that has been made there remain matters on which contemporary opinion is perhaps too complacent. Theory has greatly clarified optimal policy intervention in an open economy and has identified the negative effects of certain misguided but all-too-prevalent policies. These views are supported by empirical studies especially where the harm that bad policy can do is concerned. However, the relationship between economic policy and economic performance is quite subtle and we may expect that it will continue to engage researchers for some time to come.

References

Adams, F.G. and S.A. Klein (1978) *Stabilizing world commodity markets*. Lexington, MA: Heath-Lexington.

Anand, S. and V.R. Joshi (1979) 'Domestic distortions, income distribution and the theory of optimum subsidy', *Economic Journal*, 89:336–352.

Balassa, B. (1971) 'Effective protection in developing countries', in: J.N. Bhagwati and others, eds., *Trade, balance of payments and growth*. Amsterdam: North-Holland.

Balassa, B. (1982) *Development strategies in semi-industrial economies*. Baltimore, MD: Johns Hopkins University Press.

Baldwin, R.E. (1969) 'The case against infant-industry tariff protection', *Journal of Political Economy*, 77:295–305.

Baldwin, R.E. (1982) 'The political economy of protectionism', in: J.N. Bhagwati, ed., *Import competition and response*. Chicago, IL: University of Chicago Press.

Bardhan, P.K. (1970) *Economic growth, development and foreign trade*. New York: Wiley.

Bell, C. (1979) 'The behaviour of a dual economy under different "closing rules"', *Journal of Development Economics*, 6:47–72.

Bhagwati, J.N. (1958) 'Immizerizing growth: A geometrical note', *Review of Economic Studies*, 25:201–205.

Bhagwati, J.N. (1969) 'The pure theory of international trade: A survey', reprinted from the *Economic Journal* 74, March, with an addendum in: J.N. Bhagwati, *Trade, tariffs and growth*, Cambridge, MA: MIT Press.

Bhagwati, J.N. (1971) 'The generalized theory of distortions and welfare', in: J.N. Bhagwati and others, eds., *Trade, balance of payments and growth*. Amsterdam: North-Holland.

Bhagwati, J.N. (1982) 'Directly unproductive profit-seeking (DUP) activities: A welfare-theoretic synthesis and generalization', *Journal of Political Economy*, 90:988–1002.

Bhagwati, J.N. (1984) 'Why are services cheaper in poor countries?', *Economic Journal*, 94:279–86.

Bhagwati, J.N. (1985) 'International trade in services and its relevance for economic development', Xth Annual Lecture of the Geneva Association held at the London School of Economics.

Bhagwati, J.N. and S. Chakravarty (1969) 'Contributions to Indian economic analysis: A survey', *American Economic Review*, supplement, September.

Bhagwati, J.N. and P. Desai (1970) *Planning for industrialization: A study of India's trade and industrial policies since 1950*. Cambridge: Cambridge University Press.

Bhagwati, J.N. and T.N. Srinivasan (1973) 'The general equilibrium theory of effective protection and resource allocation', *Journal of International Economics*, 3:259–281.

Bhagwati, J.N. and T.N. Srinivasan (1978) 'Shadow prices for project selection in the presence of distortions: Effective rates of protection and domestic resource costs', *Journal of Political Economy*, 86:97–116.

Bhagwati, J.N. and T.N. Srinivasan (1979) 'On inferring resource allocational implications from DRC calculations in trade distorted, small open economies', *Indian Economic Review*, 14, April.

Bhagwati, J.N. and T.N. Srinivasan (1980) 'Revenue-seeking: A generalization of the theory of tariffs', *Journal of Politicial Economy*, 88:1069–1087.

Bhagwati, J.N., R.A. Brecher and T.N. Srinivasan (1984) 'DUP activities and economic theory', *European Economic Review*, 24:291–307.

Bliss, C. (1987a) 'Taxation, cost–benefit analysis and effective protection', in: D.M.G. Newbery and N.H. Stern, eds., *The theory of taxation in developing countries*. New York: Oxford University Press.

Bliss, C. (1987b) 'The new trade theory and economic policy', *Oxford Review of Economic Policy*, 3, no. 1:20–36.

Blitzer, C.R. (1975) 'The status of planning: An overview', in: C.R. Blitzer, P.B. Clark, and L. Taylor, eds., *Economy-wide models and development planning*. New York: Oxford University Press.

Bruno, M. (1966) 'A programming model for Israel', in: I. Adelman and E. Thorbecke, eds., *Theory and design of economic development*. Baltimore: MD: Johns Hopkins Press.

Buchanan, J.M., R.D. Tollison, and G. Tullock (1980) *Toward a theory of the rent-seeking society*. College Station, TX: Texas A & M University Press.

Caves, R.E. (1965) ' "Vent for surplus" models of trade and growth', in: R.E. Baldwin et al., eds., *Trade, growth and the balance of payments: Essays in honor of Gottfried Harbeler*. Chicago, IL: University of Chicago Press.

Chenery, H.B. (1961) 'Comparative advantage and development policy', *American Economic Review*, 51:18–51.

Chenery, H.B. and M. Bruno (1962) 'Development alternatives in an open economy: The case of Israel', *Economic Journal*, 72:79–103.

Chenery, H.B. and A. MacEwan, (1966) 'Optimal patterns of growth and aid: The case of Pakistan', in: I. Adelman and E. Thorbecke, eds., *Theory and design of economic development*. Baltimore, MD: Johns Hopkins Press.

Chenery, H.B. and A. Strout (1966) 'Foreign assistance and economic development', *American Economic Review*, 56:679–733.

Chichilinsky, G. (1980) 'Basic goods, the effects of commodity transfers and the international economic order', *Journal of Development Economics*, 7:505–519.

Chichilinsky, G. (1981) 'Terms of trade and domestic distribution: Export-led growth with abundant labour', *Journal of Development Economics*, 8:103–192.

Chichilinsky, G. and others (1983 and 1984) Exchanges concerning the validity of Chichilinsky's ideas in *Journal of Development Economics*, 13:197–252 and 15:131–184.

Chipman, J.S. (1965–66) 'A survey of the theory of international trade', *Econometrica*, 33:477–519, 33:685–760, 34:18–76.

Collander, D. (1984) *Neoclassical political economy: The analysis of rent-seeking and DUP activities*. London: Ballinger Publishing Company.

Corden, W.M. (1971) 'The effects of trade on the rate of growth', in: J.N. Bhagwati and others, eds., *Trade, balance of payments and growth*. Amsterdam: North-Holland.

Corden, W.M. (1974) *Trade policy and economic welfare*. Oxford: Clarendon Press.

Corden, W.M. (1975) 'The costs and consequences of protection: A survey of empirical work', in: P.B. Kenen, ed., *International trade and finance: Frontiers for research*. London: Cambridge University Press.

Cordon, W.M. (1984) 'The normative theory of international trade', in: R.W. Jones and P.B. Kenen, eds., *Handbook of international economics*, Vol. I. North-Holland: Amsterdam, Ch. 2.

Dasgupta, P.S. (1972) 'A comparative analysis of the UNIDO Guidelines and the OECD Manual', *Bulletin of the Oxford University Institute of Economics and Statistics*, 34:33–51.

Dasgupta, P.S. and J.E. Stiglitz (1974) 'Benefit–cost analysis and trade policies', *Journal of Political Economy*, 82:1–33.

Dasgupta, P.S. and S. Marglin, and A.K. Sen (1972) *Guidelines for project evaluation*, for UNIDO. New York: United Nations.

Deardorff, A.V. (1973) 'The gains from trade in and out of steady growth', Oxford Economic Papers, 25:173–191.

Deardorff, A.V. (1980) 'The general validity of the law of comparative advantage', *Journal of Political Economy*, 88:941–957.

Deardorff, A.V. (1982) 'The general validity of the Heckscher–Ohlin theorem', *American Economic Review*, 72:683–694.

Deardorff, A.V. (1984) 'Testing trade theories and predicting trade flows', in: R.W. Jones and P.B. Kenen, eds. *Handbook of international economics*, Vol. I. Amsterdam: North-Holland, Ch. 10.

de Melo, J.A.P. (1978) 'Estimating the costs of protection: A general equilibrium approach', *Quarterly Journal of Economics*, 92:209–226.

de Melo, J.A.P., W. Grais, and S. Urata (1986) 'A general equilibrium estimation of the effects of reductions in tariffs and quantitative restrictions in Turkey in 1978', in: T.N. Srinivasan and J. Whalley, eds., *General equilibrium trade policy modelling*. Cambridge, MA: MIT Press.

Dervis, K., J.A.P. de Melo, and S. Robinson (1982) *General equilibrium models for development policy*. Cambridge: Cambridge University Press.

Diamond, P.A. and J.A. Mirrlees (1971) 'Optimal taxation and public production', *American Economic Review*, 61:8–27, 261–278.

Diaz-Alejandro, C.F. (1975) 'Trade policies and economic development', in: P.B. Kenen, ed., *International trade and finance*. Cambridge: Cambridge University Press.

Dixit, A.K. (1985) 'Tax policy in open economies', in: A.J. Auerbach and M. Feldstein, eds., *Handbook of public economics*, Vol. I. Amsterdam: North-Holland, Ch. 6.

Dixit, A.K. and V.D. Norman (1980) *Theory of international trade*. Cambridge: Cambridge University Press.

Drèze, J. and N.H. Stern (1985) 'The theory of cost–benefit analysis', in: A. Auerbach and M. Feldstein, eds., *Handbook of public economics*. Amsterdam: North-Holland.

Ethier, W. (1977) 'The theory of effective protection in general equilibrium: effective-rate analogues of nominal rates', *Canadian Journal of Economics*, 2:233–245.

Ethier, W. (1984) 'Higher dimensional issues in trade theory', in: R.W. Jones and P.B. Kenen, eds., *Handbook of international economics*, Vol. I. Amsterdam: North-Holland, Ch. 3.

Feldman (1957) 'A Soviet model of growth', translation included in: E. Domar, *Essays in the theory of economic growth*. New York: Oxford University Press.

Findlay, R.E. (1971) 'The "foreign exchange gap" and growth in developing countries', in: J.N. Bhagwati et al., eds., *Trade, growth and the balance of payments*. Amsterdam: North-Holland.

Findlay, R.E. (1973) *International trade and development theory*. New York: Columbia University Press.

Findlay, R.E. (1984) 'Growth and development in trade models', in: R.W. Jones and P. Kenen, eds., *Handbook of international economics*. Amsterdam: North-Holland, Ch. 4.

Findlay, R.E. and S. Wellisz (1982) 'Endogenous tariffs, the political economy of trade restrictions, and welfare', in: J.N. Bhagwati, ed., *Import competition and response*. Chicago, IL: University of Chicago Press.

Fleming, J.M. (1955) 'External economies and the doctrine of balanced growth', *Economic Journal*, 65:241–256.

Goss, B.A. and B.S. Yamey (1976) *The economics of futures trading*. London: Macmillan.

Hahn, F.H. and R.C.O. Matthews (1964) 'The theory of economic growth: A survey', *Economic Journal* 74:779–902.

Hammond, P.J. (1988) 'Principles for evaluating public sector projects', in: P.G. Hare, ed., *Surveys in public sector economics*. Oxford: Blackwell.

Harrod, R.F. (1939) 'An essay in dynamic theory', *Economic Journal*, 49:14–33.

Hazell, P.B.R. and P.L. Scandizzo (1975) 'Market intervention policies when production is risky', *American Journal of Agricultural Economics*, 57:641–649.

Heal, G.M. (1973) *The theory of economic planning*. Amsterdam: North-Holland.

Helpman, E. and P. Krugman (1985) *Increasing returns, imperfect competition and the international economy*. Cambridge, MA: MIT Press.

Hirschman, A.O. (1958) *The strategy of economic development*. New Haven, CT: Yale University Press.

Hirschman, A. O. (1977) 'A generalized linkage approach to development with special reference to staples', *Economic Development and Cultural Change*, 25, supplement: 67–98.

Johnson, H.G. (1955) 'Economic expansion and international trade', *Manchester School*, 23:95–112.

Johnson, H.G. (1970) 'A new view of the infant-industry argument', in: I.A. MacDougall and R.H. Snape, eds., *Studies in international economics: Monash conference papers*. Amsterdam: North-Holland.

Jones, R.W. and J.P. Neary (1984) 'The positive theory of international trade', in: R.W. Jones and P.B. Kenen, eds., *Handbook of international economics*, Vol. I. Amsterdam: North-Holland, Ch. 1.

Joshi, V.R. (1970) 'Saving and foreign exchange constraints', in: P. Streeten, ed., *Unfashionable economics*. London: Weidenfeld and Nicholson.

Joshi, V.R. (1972) 'The rationale and relevance of the Little–Mirrlees criterion', *Bulletin of the Oxford University Institute of Economics and Statistics*, 34:3–32.

Kaldor, N. (1956) 'Alternative theories of distribution', *Review of Economic Studies*, 23–94–100.

Kaldor, N., A.G. Hart, and J. Tinbergen (1964) 'The case for an international commodity reserve currency', reprinted in: N. Kaldor, *Essays on economic policy*, Vol. II. London: Duckworth.

Kemp, M.C. (1964) *The pure theory of international trade*. Englewood Cliffs, NJ: Prentice-Hall.

Kierzkowski, H., ed. (1984) *Monopolistic competition and international trade*. New York: Oxford University Press.

Kierzkowski, H. (1987) 'Recent advances in international trade theory: A selective survey', *Oxford Review of Economic Policy*, 3, no. 1:1–19.

Kornai, J. (1973) "Thoughts on multi-level planning systems', in: L.M. Goreux and A.S. Manne, eds., *Multi-level planning: Case studies in Mexico*. Amsterdam: North-Holland.

Krueger, A.O. (1968) 'Factor endowments with per capita income differences among countries', *Economic Journal*, 78:641–659.

Krueger, A.O. (1974) "The political economy of the rent-seeking society', *American Economic Review*, 64:291–303.

Krueger, A.O. (1983) *Alternative trade strategies and employment*, Vol. 3: *Synthesis and conclusions*. Chicago, IL: Chicago University Press.

Krueger, A.O. (1984) 'Trade policies in developing countries', in: R.W. Jones and P.B. Kenen, eds., *Handbook of international economics*, Vol. I. Amsterdam: North-Holland, Ch. 11.

Krugman, P. (1984) 'Import protection as export promotion: International competition in the presence of oligopoly and economies of scale', in H. Kierzkowski, ed., *Monopolistic competition and international trade*. New York: Oxford University Press.

Krugman, P. (1986) 'New trade theory and the less developed countries', presented at the Carlos Diaz-Alejandro Memorial Conference, WIDER, Helsinki.

Lal, D. (1974) *Methods of project analysis: A review*. Washington, DC: World Bank.

Leamer, E.E. (1984) *Sources of international comparative advantage: Theory and evidence*. Cambridge, MA: M.I.T. Press.

Leibenstein, H. (1957) *Economic backwardness and economic growth*. New York: Wiley.

Leontief, W.W. (1954) 'Domestic production and foreign trade: The American capital position re-examined', *Economica Internazionale*, 7:9–45.

Lewis, W.A. (1954) 'Economic development with unlimited supplies of labour', *The Manchester School of Economic and Social Studies*, 22:139–191.

Lewis, W.A. (1955) *The theory of economic growth*. London: George Allen and Unwin.

Lipton, M. (1962) 'Balanced and unbalanced growth in underdeveloped countries', *Economic Journal*, 72:641–657.

Lipton, M. (1970) 'Farm price stabilization in underdeveloped agricultures: Some effects on income stability and income distribution', in: P. Streeten, ed., *Unfashionable economics*. London: Weidenfeld and Nicholson.

Little, I.M.D. (1960) 'The strategy of Indian development', *National Institute Economic Review*, May, 9:20–29.

Little, I.M.D. (1982) *Economic development: Theory, policy and international relations*. New York: Basic Books.

Little, I.M.D. and J.A. Mirrlees (1972) 'A reply to some criticisms of the OECD Manual', *Bulletin of the Oxford University Institute of Economics and Statistics*, 34:153–168.

Little, I.M.D. and J.A. Mirrlees (1974) *Project appraisal and planning for developing countries*. London: Heinemann educational books.

Little, I.M.D., T. Scitovsky, and M. Scott (1970) *Industry and trade in some developing countries: A comparative study*. New York: Oxford University Press.

McKinnon, R. I. (1964) 'Foreign exchange constraints and economic development', *Economic Journal*, 74:388–409.

Massell, B.F. (1970) 'Some welfare implications of international price stabilization', *Journal of Political Economy*, 78:404–420.

Meier, G.M. (1969) *The international economics of development*. New York: Harper and Row.

Michaely, M. (1977) *Theory of commercial policy*. Oxford: Phillip Alan.

Minhas, B.S. (1963) *An international comparison of factor cost and factor use*. Amsterdam: North-Holland.

Neary, P. (1980) 'Non-traded goods and the balance of trade in a neo-Keynesian temporary equilibrium', *Quarterly Journal of Economics*, 95:403–429.

Nelson, R.R. (1970) 'The effective exchange rate: employment and growth in a foreign exchange constrained economy', *Journal of Political Economy*, 78:546–564.

Newbery, D.M.G., and J.E. Stiglitz (1981) *The theory of commodity price stabilization: A study in the economics of risk*. Oxford: Clarendon Press.

Nurkse, R. (1953) *Problems of capital formation in underdeveloped countries*. New York: Oxford University Press.

Oi, W.Y. (1961) 'The desirability of price instability under perfect competition', *Econometrica*, 29:58–64.

Prebisch, R. (1950) *The economic development of Latin America and its principle problems*.

Ramaswami, V.K. and T.N. Srinivasan (1971) 'Tariff structure and resource allocation in the presence of factor substitution', in: J.N. Bhagwati et al., eds., *Trade, growth and the balance of payments*. Amsterdam: North-Holland.

Ravi Kanbur, S.M. (1984) 'How to analyze commodity price stabilization: A review article', *Oxford Economic Papers*, 36:336–358.

Riedel, J. (1976) 'A balanced growth version of the linkage hypothesis: Comment', *Quarterly Journal of Economics*, 90:319–322.

Rosenstein–Rodan, P. (1943) 'Problems of industrialization in eastern and southeastern Europe', *Economic Journal*, 53:202–211.

Rosenstein–Rodan, P. (1961) 'Notes on the theory of the "big push"', in: H.S. Ellis and H.C. Wallich, eds., *Economic development for Latin America*. New York: St. Martin's Press.

Rybczynski, T.M. (1955) 'Factor endowments and relative commodity prices', *Economica*, 22:336–341.

Scitovsky, T. (1954) 'Two concepts of external economies', *Journal of Political Economy*, 62:143–151.

Scitovsky, T. (1959) 'Growth – balanced or unbalanced', in: M. Abramovitz, et al., *The allocation of economic resources*. Stanford, CA: Stanford, University Press.

Sen, A.K. (1960) *Choice of techniques: An aspect of the theory of planned economic development*. Oxford: Basil Blackwell.

Sen, A.K. (1963) 'Neo-classical and neo-Keynesian theories of distribution', *Economic Record*, 39:46–53.

Sen, A.K. (1972) 'Control areas and accounting prices: An approach to economic evaluation', *Economic Journal*, supplement, 82:486–501.

Sen, A.K. (1975) *Employment technology and development*. Oxford: Clarendon Press.

Smith, M.A.M. (1977) 'Capital accumulation in the open two-sector economy', *Economic Journal*, 87:273–282.

Smith, M.A.M. (1982) 'Intertemporal gains from trade', *Journal of International Economics*, 9:239–48.

Smith, M.A.M. (1984) 'Capital theory and trade theory, in: R.W. Jones and P.B. Kenen, eds., *Handbook of international economics*, Vol. I. Amsterdam: North-Holland, Ch. 6.

Spraos, J. (1980) 'The statistical debate on the net barter terms of trade between primary commodities and manufactures', *Economic Journal*, 90:107–128.

Srinivasan, T.N. (1987) 'Distortions', entry in *The New Palgrave Dictionary of Economics*. London: Macmillan.

Srinivasan, T.N. (1989) 'Recent theories of imperfect competition and international trade: Any implications for development strategy?', *Indian Economic Review*, XXIV(1):January–June.

Srinivasan, T.N. and J. Whalley, eds. (1986) *General equilibrium trade policy modelling*. Cambridge MA: MIT Press.

Standaert, S. (1985) 'The foreign exchange constraint, suppression of the trade deficit and shadow price of foreign exchange in a fixed-price economy', *Journal of Development Economics*, 18:37–50.

Stern, R.M. (1975) 'Testing trade theories', in: P.B. Kenen, ed., *International trade and finance*. Cambridge: Cambridge University Press.

Stewart, F. (1984) 'Recent theories of international trade: Some implications for the south', in H. Kierzkowski, ed., *Monopolistic competition and international trade*. New York: Oxford University Press.

Stewart F. and P. Streeten (1972) 'Little–Mirrlees methods and project appraisal', *Bulletin of the Oxford University Institute of Economics and Statistics*, 34:75–91.

Streeten, P. (1959) 'Unbalanced growth', *Oxford Economic Papers*, 11:167–190.

Sutcliffe, R.B. (1964) 'Balanced and unbalanced growth', *Quarterly Journal of Economics*, 78:621–640.

Taylor, L. (1975) 'Theoretical foundations and technical implications', in: C.R. Blitzer, P.B. Clark, and L. Taylor, eds., *Economy-wide models and development planning*. New York: Oxford University Press.

Taylor, L. (1983) *Structuralist macroeconomics*. New York: Basic Books.

Taylor, L. and S.L. Black (1974) 'Practical general equilibrium estimation of resource pulls under trade liberalization', *Journal of International Economics*, 4:37–58.

Travis, W.P. (1972) 'Production, trade and protection when there are many commodities and two factors', *American Economic Review*, 62:87–106.

Turnovsky, S.J. (1970) "Turnpike theorems and efficient economic growth', in: E. Burmeister and A.R. Dobell, *Mathematical theories of economic growth*. London: Macmillan.

UNCTAD (1975) *Compensatory financing of export fluctuations*. Geneva: United Nations Conference on Trade and Development.

United Nations: Department of Economic Affairs (1949) *Relative prices of exports and imports of under-developed countries*. New York: United Nations.

van Wijnbergen, S.J.G. (1986) 'Macroeconomic aspects of the effectiveness of foreign aid: On two-gap models, home goods disequilibrium and real exchange rate misalignment', *Journal of International Economics*, 21(1/2):123–136.

von Neumann, J. (1938) 'A model of general economic equilibrium', translated by O. Morgenstern in *Review of Economic Studies*, (19456) 13:1–9.

Williamson, J. (1983) *The open economy and the world economy*. New York: Basic Books.

Chapter 24

ALTERNATIVE PERSPECTIVES ON TRADE AND DEVELOPMENT

DAVID EVANS*

Institute of Development Studies
University of Sussex

Contents

*I am grateful to Christopher Bliss, John Eaton, Rob Eastwood, Carlos Fortin, Raphie Kaplinsky, Stephen Lewis, Jean-Phillipe Platteau, Robin Murray, Kunibert Raffer, T.N. Srinivasan, Lance Taylor, John Toye and Adrian Wood for their helpful comments on earlier drafts of this chapter, and particularly to Parvin Alizadeh who assisted in extending our joint work [Evans and Alizadah (1984)] for incorporation in this chapter. I thank them all but implicate none.

Handbook of Development Economics, Volume II, Edited by H. Chenery and T.N. Srinivasan
© *Elsevier Science Publishers B.V., 1989*

1. Introduction

Why an alternative perspective on trade and development? Partly because the mainstream literature does not ask all the right questions, partly because it does not give all the right answers. In both cases, this is because it systematically excludes some important aspects of reality, most notably ownership and class at the macro and micro level.

The four basic questions to be answered by trade and development theory and policy suggested by Christopher Bliss in his Introduction to Chapter 23 of this Handbook can be considered to be common ground between alternative perspectives. The broader approach taken in the present chapter suggests a fifth question which gives the following list:

(i) What is the role of trade in the process of economic development?

(ii) What patterns of international exchange best serve the objectives of developing countries?

(iii) What are the consequences of various instruments used by developed and developing countries aimed at achieving the desired pattern of trade?

(iv) Are the classical and neo-classical theories of international trade suitable for application to the situation of developing countries?

(v) How is trade related to class relationships and to inequalities of income and power, both within and between developed and developing countries?

A survey article must inevitably employ some explict or implicit principle of selection in attempting to address the above questions. Broadly speaking, this chapter draws on three contending approaches to trade and development identified in Chapter 3 of Volume I by Pranab Bardhan, namely neo-classical, Marxian and structuralist-institutionalist. For the most part, the literature covered attempts some sort of formal analytical exposition of the core arguments. To the extent that some of these questions have been answered in Chapter 23 by Christopher Bliss and in other recent survey articles discussed below, they will not be dealt with in this chapter.

The principal organising device used in the chapter is a two-commodity circulating capital model with labour and a resource as the primary non-produced inputs. This model is extended to a dual economy version with specific factors, or is simplified by dropping the resource as a second primary non-produced inputs where appropriate. Some relevant microeconomic behaviour is also analysed. The models considered are both analytically tractable and capture some strategic elements of the role of produced means of production in trade and class structure, and the interplay between endowments and institutional determinants of comparative advantage, growth and international inequality.

The survey aims to make the insights of alternative perspectives on trade and development available to others in the language of standard economics. This aim is not always easily achieved, particularly where the arguments are expressed using classical Marxian value theory. To the extent that there are interesting and/or influential ideas expressed in this mode, I have attempted to discuss them within the analytical framework used in this chapter.

The rationale for selection was strongly influenced by my desire to focus on some of the more fundamental divides between alternative perspectives on trade and development. There are many other issues of obvious interest which could be added to this survey. For example, I will not be able to do justice to the more fully dynamic models of trade, growth and development, some of which are discussed in Findlay (1984), M.A.M. Smith (1984), Ocampo (1986) and in Chapter 23 of this Handbook by Christopher Bliss. Nor have I dealt with the new theories of trade with imperfect competition, economies of scale and technology modelled, covered briefly in Subsection 4.4 of Chapter 23 of this Handbook and also in the recent survey by Greenaway and Milner (1987). As far as possible, other relevant literature is directly or indirectly referenced.

There are no agreed maps for navigating between the shoals of the contending methodologies and assumptions used in the major schools. All too often, when neither theory or empirical evidence are decisive, legitimate differences in judgement become caught up with different values and welfare weights. Nevertheless, I believe that the differences between the major schools are often narrower than perceived, and that all have something to contribute to the themes developed in this chapter.

Section 2 focuses mainly on the suitability of classical, neo-classical and neo-Ricardian theories of international trade for answering the questions raised above. It is argued that the basic two-commodity circulating capital model with two primary non-produced inputs fits with some important stylised facts about trade between capitalist national economies. The model can be extended and developed along well-known lines to explore issues ranging from the concerns of classical Marxian theories of imperialism to contemporary issues in North–South and South–South trade. The two-gap model discussed in the chapters by Bliss (Chapter 23) and Eaton (Chapter 25) is a special case of the basic model. The model also compliments the analysis of long-run capital flows in the chapters by Eaton (Chapter 25) and by Cardoso and Dornbusch (Chapter 26), and the analysis of primary commodity trade in the chapter by Stephen Lewis (Chapter 29). With due care, it can be used for the positive and normative theory of comparative advantage and growth.[1]

The second theme explored in Section 3 of the chapter is the division of labour in the world economy in the context of exploitation, class and international inequalities, often referred to as Unequal Exchange. This section uses the basic

---

[1] Most of the standard literature on positive and normative trade theory is based on a simplification of the circulating capital model to exclude the explicit role of time and produced means of production. To the extent that such simplification does not materially affect the analysis, it should obviously be welcomed by those who find themselves in the "alternative perspectives" camp.

model or special cases of this model. Exploitation theory makes explicit assumptions about the relations of domination and power, but the argument in Section 3 concentrates on the economic aspects. It is argued that the Unequal Exchange of labour fails to capture international differences in the endowments of productive assets in the basic model and may be a poor empirical proxy for measuring international equality. This suggests that the study of the international division of labour should focus on class relations and the direct investigation of the sources of international inequality arising from ownership patterns, institutional differences, technological capacity, power and so on.

The non-market relations including domination and power which play an important role in economic life are often affected by the specific ownership and class relations associated with the models discussed in Sections 2 and 3. These non-market relations are the third theme discussed in Section 4. Ownership and class affect the organisation of production, the extraction of work from labour power or the capacity to work, and the international division of labour. This discussion is developed particularly in relation to some of the literature on the Trans National Corporation (TNC), also discussed in Chapter 27 of this Handbook by Gerald Helleiner. Market and non-market relations, particularly with respect to interest groups and class, affect the way in which governments are organised, how they intervene in the national economies, and the way in which they relate to each other in the world economy. These issues are discussed in relation to the role of the state in development at the national and international level.

The final theme discussed is trade and development strategy, both nationally and for the world economy. In particular, the calls for a New International Economic Order are subject to critical scrutiny, as are the more extreme versions of inward and outward orientation of trade policy at the national level. It is argued that, within these extremes, there is ample scope for a variety of active trade and development strategies, also discussed in Chapter 23 by Christopher Bliss and Chapters 29–31 by Stephen Lewis, Henry Bruton, and Bela Balassa, respectively.

The chapter concludes with a discussion of an agenda for future research.

2. Comparative advantage and growth

The models discussed in this section are intended to provide an analytical bridge between contending schools and a framework for discussing some of the central themes in the Marxian and structuralist-institutionalist trade literature. One entry point into understanding the relevance of trade models, their analytical structure, and the limits to their use, is through a brief discussion of the history of trade theory, taken up in the first subsection. In the second subsection, I set out a circulating capital model with two primary non-produced inputs which can provide a useful starting point for the analysis of many trade and development issues. The model is developed further in the next two subsections. The first is with reference to a stylised analysis of nineteenth-century trade and factor flows between "England" and "America", an example which could also be viewed as clarifying the economic drive toward imperialism based on generalised resource abundance when there is competition in commodity markets. The second example refers to twentieth-century trade between "England" and the "Tropics", including an analysis of some of the determinants of the long-run terms of trade and sources of international inequality. The second example could also be thought of as clarifying the economic drive towards imperialism through the potential outflow of capital when there are specific factors and a dual economy. In the final subsection, I discuss some aspects of historical analysis.

2.1. Smith, Ricardo, Marx and modern trade theory

There is a strong tradition within trade theory to regard movements on given production and consumption possibilities frontiers as providing the most important insights into the sources of gains from trade. Such a procedure understates the often radical nature of the effects of the opening of foreign trade historically.[2] In this regard, the Ricardian tradition is very different from Adam Smith's starting point.

In Smith's view, a trade-induced division of labour is the main underlying condition for modern economic growth. Abstracting from the new institution which gave birth to this new division of labour, the factory, Adam Smith's argument was implicitly based on economies of scale. Another aspect is the "vent for surplus" argument for the opening of trade developed by Smith and elaborated by Myint (1958) which suggests that, in the pre-trade position, the economy may be operating inside the typical production possibilities frontier used to describe the pre-trade position. The opening of trade therefore may lead to two types of irreversible changes: the realisation of scale economies and the utilisation of previously under-utilised resources.[3] Smithian trade-induced growth is "trade as the engine of growth" par excellence.

---

[2]See, for example, the recent historical analysis of the effects of opening Africa to the world economy in Sender and Smith (1986).

[3]Establishing the role of trade as in a "vent for surplus" requires the identification of particular institutional features or domestic preferences which give rise to under-utilisation of resources, which will vary from case to case. S. Smith (1976) discusses some of the pitfalls which arise from the hasty application of the vent for surplus model to the Nigerian colonial experience.

The great strength of the formal analysis of comparative advantage is that it makes more precise some of the consequences of the opening of trade and the characteristics of a trading equilibrium. In classical Ricardian theory the pre-conditions for the establishment of each trading unit were taken for granted – for example the development of a capitalist national economy with complete internal mobility of factors and complete external immobility of factors.[4] It is worth recalling that this procedure does not necessarily conform with the historical conditions under which national economies were formed, as emphasised by the Marxian tradition and also noted by Williams (1929).

The central message of Williams' critique of classical trade theory was that the development of the world economy went hand in hand with the development of the national economy. This meant that there was in fact far more international mobility of commodities and factors than within national economies at an early stage of their development, thus undermining the assumed dichotomy between national mobility and international immobility of capital and labour. Of course, Williams was right for the analysis of the opening of trade, but it is partly possible to take his critique on board, either through the analysis of interregional as well as international trade as in Ohlin (1933), or through the explicit modelling of imperfect mobility as in the Harris and Todaro (1970) tradition. In practice, trade theory is mainly used for the analysis of changes in a with-trade equilibrium position rather than for historical analysis of the opening and development of trading relationships.

As far as possible, the unit of analysis and property relations assumed to be in place will be chosen bearing in mind the Williams critique. These caveats should be kept in mind when using formal models to understand the interrelations between trade, growth and development.

The Marxian tradition has been ambivalent about the role of formal models of trade, not withstanding Marx's own application of Ricardian theory when discussing his counter-tendencies for the rate of profit to fall. This is reflected in the voluminous Marxian literature on imperialism, the expansion of capitalism as a social system.[5] Yet Murray (1978, p. 18) argues that "any general theory of imperalism should be able to explain the motive for expansion, the timing of expansion, the forms of expansion and the mechanisms of expansion" (of capitalism internationally). It would seem that the application of trade theory, by clarifying the economic motives and economic analysis, might help to answer these questions in the historical study of the processes and forms of imperialism.[6]

---

[4]Capitalist property relations are not necessarily implied in Ricardo's example of trade between England and Portugal, but they are in his closed and open growth models.

[5]For an excellent survey of Marxian theories of imperialism, see Brewer (1980).

[6]Not all of the relevant issues are addressed by trade theory, as noted by Robinson (1974). For example, Robinson (1951) clarified the role of trade between capitalist and non-capitalist areas in improving the incentive to invest, the driving mechanism in Luxembourg's theory of imperialism. Barratt-Brown (1974) drew on what he called "ultra Keynesian" theory to shed light on the nature of competition between imperialist nation states.

In fact, this has hardly been done with the exception of the Unequal Exchange literature discussed in Section 3, at least in part because so much of the Marxian theorising uses classical Marxian value theory.[7] There are some notable exceptions outside the Unequal Exchange problematic such as Krugman (1981), who used a model of trade with economies of scale and imperfect competition to analyse the economic drive and mechanisms behind Lenin's theory of imperialism. One of the possible applications of the trade models discussed in Subsections 2.2 and 2.3 and in Section 3 is their potential role in a more general theory of imperialism.

Much of the Marxian and structuralist-institutionalist literature on trade and development is ambivalent about the relationship between trade and growth. This is inspite of the strong empirical association between periods of rapid growth of trade and the rate of growth of GDP over a long historical period, shown in Table 24.1. With the exception of the period between 1870 and 1912, the statistical association between trade and growth is positive. However, the statistical relationship says nothing about the direction of causality, which can only be established with the help of a theoretical model.[8]

Table 24.1
Historical rates of growth (1820–1979),
arithmetic average of 16 countries

| | Average annual change (percent) | |
	GDP	Exports
1820–1870	2.2[a]	4.0[b]
1870–1913	2.5	3.9
1913–1950	1.9	1.0
1950–1973	4.9	8.6
1973–1979	2.5	4.8
1979–1985	1.9	3.5

[a]Average for 13 countries.
[b]Average for 10 countries.
Source: Maddison (1982, table 4.9) and World Bank (1987, figure 3.2).

The theoretical models of trade and growth favoured by the Marxian and structuralist-institutionalist literature often fail to take into account the role of

---

[7]For a discussion of some of the analytical difficulties in using classical Marxian value theory for economic analysis, see Steedman (1977), Morishima and Catephores (1978), and Roemer (1981, 1982a). Recent contributions to the Marxian value debate include Elson (1979), Fine and Harris (1979), Roemer (1986), and Steedman (1981).

[8]There is an extensive literature on the relationship between trade and growth. Some recent examples include Aghazadeh and Evans (1988), Kravis (1970), Lewis (1980), Riedel (1984), Taylor (1986), and World Bank (1987, ch. 3) and the references therein. The aggregate statistical evidence is consistent with the idea that trade is the "handmaiden" rather than the "engine" of growth, although Taylor and Aghazadeh and Evans find no statistical evidence of export-led growth from cross-section or time-series data for the 1960s or 1970s.

Table 24.2

(a) *Shares of manufactures in commodity GDP (percent)*

	Per capita GDP (1970 $)	
	400	1000
Small countries with ample resources, primary orientation	20	39
Small countries with ample resources, industrial orientation	36	56
Large countries	44	58

Source and definitions of standard shares of manufactures: World Bank (1987, p. 55)

(b) *Share of resource based trade in 1980 (percent)*

Intra developed market economies	36
Imports of developed market economies from developing countries	79
Exports of developed market economies to developing countries	23
Total world trade	44

Source: Evans (1989, appendix 9.1).

resource endowments as one of the determinants of comparative advantage and growth. This may be the result of a negative vision of dependent but resource-abundant nations remaining hewers of wood and drawers of water, or because the positive virtues of industrialisation are seen as an end in themselves. Such imagery is not in accord with empirical reality as shown in Table 24.2.

The standard patterns of the manufacturing share of commodity GDP (GDP excluding services) shown in Table 24.2(a) for per capita GDP of $U.S.400(1970) and $U.S.1000(1970) are strongly affected by resource endowments. The full analysis of standard patterns of manufacturing shares of commodity GDP in World Bank (1987, p. 55) shows clearly that small resource-abundant countries have been able to achieve high levels of GDP per capita with significantly smaller shares of manufactures than for larger countries. Moreover, a large amount of world trade is in commodities which require some form of natural resources for their production as can be seen from Table 24.2(b). Thus, in 1980, about 44 percent of total world trade and about 36 percent of intra developed market economy trade was resource based. Trade between developed market and developing countries is still dominated by the exchange of manufactures (77 percent of developed market economy exports) for resource-based commodities (79 percent of developed market economies imports from developing countries). This structural dominance of resource-based trade for developing country exports should not mask the rapidly rising share of manufactured exports in developing countries which has been important since the mid 1960s.

Modern dynamic extensions of static Ricardian models with circulating capital and a single non-produced input, labour,[9] or the H-O-S model with labour and a single capital good[10] do not fit the above stylised facts since there is no resource input.[11] In contrast, the open economy version of Ricardo's dynamic model developed by Findlay (1974) which includes labour, land and a single capital good fits one aspect of the empirical reality to be understood by the inclusion of land.[12] In many ways, the open dynamic Ricardian model is the natural starting point for the analysis of trade and growth. However, the long-run stationary state equilibrium arises from the particular assumptions made about wage determination and population growth which bring the rate of growth of capital and population into equilibrium with the rate of growth of the supply of land.

A more useful starting point is the two-commodity circulating capital model with two primary non-produced inputs developed by Metcalfe and Steedman (1972) and Steedman and Metcalfe (1977).[13] This model is a special case of the more general non-steady-state circulating capital model developed by M.A.M. Smith (1984). A role for both produced means of production and resource-based trade in the analysis of comparative advantage and growth is captured by the Steedman and Metcalfe model whilst leaving open the possible institutional determination of one of the factor prices. It can also be used as the starting point for comparative dynamic analysis.

---

[9] This class of models are often referred to as neo-Ricardian models. The clearest summary statement of the neo-Ricardian approach can be found in the introduction to Steedman (1979c). The most important writings from this school can be found in Steedman (1979c). See also Steedman (1979a), Pasinetti (1981), and Mainwaring (1984). For the formal links between the neo-Ricardian approach and the von Neumann analysis of linear production models, see Steedman (1979b).

[10] The classic H-O-S papers by Stolper and Samuelson (1941) and Samuelson (1948, 1949) refer to the second primary non-produced input as land, whereas most textbook versions call it capital. In the dynamic extensions of the H-O-S model, the second input is a single produced capital good.

[11] See the surveys of dynamic models of trade and growth by Findlay (1984) and M.A.M. Smith (1984).

[12] For a discussion of exhaustible resources in trade models, see Kemp (1984). The known stock of exhaustible resources can be augmented by new discoveries so that, in some cases such as coal in Britain, the measured reserves have hardly changed even during periods of very fast extraction. In this case, exhaustible resources can be treated as if they were non-exhaustible.

[13] Metcalfe and Steedman use their model as a part of their critique of H-O-S theory, arguing that no reliance should be placed on factor proportions theories of comparative advantage. This objection derives from the observation that factor-price ratios may not be governed by relative factor scarcities when there are multiple equilibria as discussed below.

The choice of a model depends on a judgement about the best way to capture some strategic elements of the problem under analysis. As a rough empirical approximation, the period over which the long-run equilibrium is established might be thought of as 15–20 years.[14] There are obvious problems with using a steady-state model to take a "snap-shot" of a long-run non-steady-state equilibrium. First, steady-state equilibrium requires that the exogenously specified rates of growth of the primary non-produced inputs be equal, an uninteresting trivial case. The steady-state model only gives a rough approximation to the long-run non-steady-state equilibrium when the exogenously specified growth rates will not be equal. Second, the comparative dynamic analysis across steady states does not take into account transitional gains or losses and therefore should be used with care when making welfare statements.[15] The choice of a model therefore depends on a judgement about the best way to capture some strategic elements of the problem under analysis whilst retaining analytical tractability. The consequences of excluded factors and simplifying approximations must inevitably be left to more informal theorising and judgement.

2.2. The basic Ricardo–Ohlin–Lewis model of comparative advantage

The two-commodity circulating capital model with two primary non-produced inputs supposes that there are fully developed capitalist relations of production. Circulating capital is advanced for the period of production and wages are not advanced at all. Other assumptions include constant returns to scale (CRS), no externalities, and no joint production. In this case, the price and quantity equations in equilibrium for simple reproduction under perfect competition

---

[14]See Marglin (1984) for further discussion. Where the object of the analysis requires a fully dynamic specification, as in the analysis of intergenerational transfers discussed in M.A.M. Smith (1984), a tractable analysis of non-steady-state growth can be achieved by dropping the resource inputs and the number of circulating capital inputs to one. Alternatively, it is necessary to construct some kind of a computable general equilibrium model to generate the long-run non-steady-state path.

[15]The general case when all of the usual incredible assumptions are made is analysed in M.A.M. Smith (1984). The analysis of the gains from trade (or any other transition) is particularly sensitive to the assumption of perfect knowledge and foresight and the rate of profit being equal to the rate of pure time preference plus the rate of growth of labour, neither of which are likely to pertain under capitalism or existing socialism. See Mainwaring (1979, 1984) and Neary (1985) for further discussion of possible sources of transition costs when some of the incredible assumptions cease to hold. With few notable exceptions such as Bardhan (1970), the Marxian literature has paid very little attention to non-steady-state growth. For example, Roemer (1982a) focuses entirely on models of balanced simple or expanded reproduction in his analysis of exploitation and class. All discussion of the transition between feudalism and capitalism, or capitalism and socialism, is done in a heuristic manner.

(excluding the output disposition and demand conditions) will be as shown in equations (1)–(4):[16]

$$p = (1 + \pi) pA_K + wa_L + ra_R,$$ (1)

$$pA_K X = K,$$ (2)

$$a_L X = L,$$ (3)

$$a_R X = R,$$ (4)

where p is a (1×2) vector of commodity prices, π is the rate of profit (interest), w is the wage rate, r is the rental on land, $A_K = (a_{Kij})$ is the (2×2) matrix of input–output coefficients, a_L is the (1×2) vector of labour input coefficients, a_R is the (1×2) vector of resource input coefficients, X is the (2×1) vector of gross outputs, K is the value of the capital stock, L is the total amount of labour power used during the period of production, and R is the stock of the resource. For any given p, π, w and r, the choice of technique (A_K', a_L', a_R') is the cost-minimising choice from the convex set of techniques (A_K, a_L, a_R).

There are five independent equations and nine relative price, distribution and quantity variables in equations (1)–(4). One of the distribution variables can be exogenously determined, often referred to as the distribution closure, or closure rule.[17] With the remaining two factor supplies and three independent equations

---

[16] Roemer (1981, section 1.2) formalises the equilibrium concept for circulating capital models of a capitalist economy in which time plays an essential role by appealing to the notion of the expansion of a given sum of commodity capital over a finite time period. It turns out that the initial endowment of commodity capital must be suitably close to the proportions required for balanced simple reproduction. Neo-Ricardian trade theory defines the relevant long-period equilibrium as one which requires consistency with a uniform rate of profit [Steedman (1979a, p. 8)]. Walsh and Gram (1980, chs. 11 and 12) and Garegnani (1983) argue that this definition of equilibrium follows the methodology of classical political economy, so that the long-run equilibrium prices are the classical natural prices which act as "centres of gravity" around which actual market prices fluctuate. However, it is neither necessary nor particularly helpful to maintain an equilibrium concept which is given by assumption rather than as the outcome of an economic process.

[17] For further discussion of closure rules, see Subsection 3.2 in Chapter 23 of this Handbook by Bliss. There is, of course, considerable debate in the literature on how the stories behind exogenously determining the wage or the rate of profit are told, and on the cost of separating the determination of key prices from endogenous economic mechanisms. There is wide agreement that social, historical, and institutional processes can override purely economic determination of the wage for long periods of time from Ricardo (1817, chs. 1 and 5) onwards. Contrary to some misconceptions, Ricardo's theory of substance wages included both biological and social determination of the subsistence wage and population growth [see Ricardo (1817, chs. 1 and 5), Kaldor (1955, p. 85, footnote 1), Metcalfe and Steedman (1973) and Steedman (1982)]. For a discussion of the Marxian theory of wages, see Rowthorn (1980), Roemer (1981), and Marglin (1984). The Lewis surplus labour argument can be found in Lewis (1954, 1969, 1973), Marglin (1976), Sen (1966), and Findlay (1982). For recent summaries of the profits closure stories, see Marglin (1984) and Evans (1989). See also Bardhan, Chapter 3, and Taylor and Arida, Chapter 18, in this Handbook. Note that in this literature there is a unique rate of growth of the single primary non-produced input which may enter into an investment

from the output disposition and the demand side, the equilibrium solution with the cost-minimising choice of technique can be obtained for the autarkic economy. To the extent that the stock of circulating capital K is treated as an exogenous endowment when wages are endogenously determined, it is assumed that the initial endowments are measured at prices set arbitrarily close to the equilibrium prices consistent with balanced simple reproduction. Note also that the price of the resource in terms of commodity 1 will be given by $p_R = r/\pi$ and the capital/output ratio is defined by $a_{Kj} = \sum_i p_i a_{Kij}$.

In some important respects, the basic two-commodity circulating capital model has the same properties as the standard Heckscher–Ohlin–Samuelson or H-O-S model without circulating capital.[18] Providing there is no factor intensity reversal, the familiar Stolper–Samuelson relationship will hold between commodity prices and the two endogenously determined factor prices. When the exogenously fixed distribution variable is the same in both countries,[19] there is incomplete specialisation, and when each country has the same homothetic preferences, there will be factor-price equalisation of the endogenously determined factor prices at the common price ratio ($p = p_2/p_1$).

Depending on the closure rule, either the demand for the capital stock or the demand for labour will be endogenously determined at equilibrium prices. Bearing in mind the sense in which the circulating capital stocks can be treated as an exogenously given endowment discussed above, the quantity equations (2)–(4) can be totally differentiated at long-run equilibrium prices and the standard Rybczynski result follows for the two exogenously determined factor supplies when the factor supply ratios lie within the cone of diversification. Note that since the changes specified are across comparative dynamic equilibrium, the composition of K will change for any change in the exogenous factor supplies.[20]

One of the important differences between the standard H-O-S model and the basic circulating capital model arises with the Heckscher–Ohlin (H-O) theorem on the pattern of trade between two economies which are identical in every

---

function. When the circulating capital model is viewed as a snapshot of a long-run non-steady-state equilibrium, the relevant rate of growth for the investment function will be the same weighted average of the growth rate of the two primary non-produced inputs.

[18] See Steedman and Metcalfe (1977), Ethier (1979) and M.A.M. Smith (1984, p. 312).

[19] For the moment, equalising the exogenously fixed distribution variable in both countries is an arbitrary assumption made to facilitate comparison with the standard factor-price equalisation theorem. Whilst the usual behavioural assumption required to bring this about is capital mobility, as will be seen below one of the applications of the model is in situations where there is imperfect factor mobility and no factor-price equalisation.

[20] For a more detailed statement of the standard theorems in the context of circulating capital models, see Ethier (1979) and M.A.M. Smith (1984, p. 313). The results reported here for the basic model with a fixed real wage follow Ethier once the resource replaces labour as the primary non-produced input.

respect except the endowments of the exogenous factors. For example, in the case of the basic model with the same exogenous rate of profit in each country, the H-O theorem holds, but pre-trade factor prices may not reflect relative factor abundance. This is because of the possible existence of multiple equilibrium positions leading to a relative supply curve which is backward bending over some range of relative price changes.[21] When the real wage is exogenously determined and equal in both countries, the H-O theorem holds only if the stocks of circulating capital are measured at common prices in the pre-trade situation and if a further restriction is added to hold the endowments of circulating capital constant across steady states.[22]

The model described by equations (1)–(4) can easily be modified so that the second economy entering trade is a dual economy in which there is a capitalist sector and a subsistence sector under some form of pre-capitalist relations of production.[23] For example, in the Lewis case the number of commodities can be increased to take into account the dual economy with a capitalist sector 3 producing crops for export, or commercials for short, and the subsistence farming sector 4 producing tropical food with individual holdings of land. The dual economy may be modelled with mobile labour between both sectors but no capital or resource mobility.[24]

Thus for the peripheral or tropical economy producing and exporting commercials (sector 3), producing non-traded tropical food (sector 4)[25] and having commodities 1 and 2 produced in England available through trade, the equilib-

---

[21] For a detailed discussion of the derivation of the relative supply curve over the full range of possible endowment ratios, see Metcalfe and Steedman (1972) and Steedman and Metcalfe (1977).

[22] For further discussion, see Ethier (1979, 1981) and Metcalfe and Steedman (1981). Metcalfe and Steedman argue that the theory of comparative advantage as developed by Torrens and Ricardo requires a comparison of independently determined autarky prices between potential trading partners. In contrast, following Ethier (1981), the formulation of the H-O theorems in the basic model are in some cases dependent on a knowledge of common prices in both countries prior to the opening of trade. Metcalfe and Steedman conclude from this observation that the H-O theorems are price-dependent, requiring additional information which fundamentally alters the concept of comparative advantage. However, it is not clear why the altered concept of comparative advantage is unacceptable since in almost all of the relevant applications of the concept of comparative advantage, all that one can observe is the trading equilibrium. Dixit (1981) and M.A.M. Smith (1984) have also paid attention to the distinctive role played by the presence of heterogeneous capital in trade models in contributing the breakdown of the standard trade theorems. With one exception, analysed in Metcalfe and Steedman (1973), their conclusion is that heterogeneous capital per se is not the culprit.

[23] The model described here is very similar to the timeless dual economy specific factors model developed by Bardhan (1982). For a useful survey of dual economy models, see Kanbur and McIntosh (1984).

[24] For the purposes of the argument, all that is required is that there is no equalisation of the rate of profit or resource rents. The lack of mobility of resource use between capitalist and subsistence sectors could flow from different infastructural requirements even when the physical characteristics of the land used in both sectors is the same.

[25] Tropical food can also be treated as tradable and in long-run competition with temperate food produced in England, as in Lewis (1969).

rium price and quantity relations are given by:

$$p^T = (1 + \pi^T)pa_K^T + w^T\hat{\mu}^Ta_L^T + r^Ta_R^T, \tag{5}$$

$$pA_K^TX^T = K^T, \tag{6}$$

$$a_L^TX^T = L^T, \tag{7}$$

$$a_R^TX^T = R^T, \tag{8}$$

where T stands for the Tropics, p^T is a (1×2) vector of prices of commodities produced in the Tropics, π^T is a (2×1) vector of sectoral rates of profit, p is now a (1×3) vector prices of traded commodities produced in both England and the Tropics, A_K^T is now a (3×1) matrix circulating capital coefficients, w^T is the wage rate, $\hat{\mu}^T$ is a (2×2) diagonal matrix of parameters defining the difference between the marginal and average product of labour in the subsistence sector, K^T is a (2×1) vector of sectoral capital stocks, L^T is the total amount of labour power available, R^T is a (2×1) vector of sector specific resources available, and X^T is a (2×1) vector of output from the Tropics, and the parameters follow the previous definitions in an obvious way. Setting the real wage in the capitalist sector to the average net product in the subsistence sector so that $\mu_3^T = (p_4 - pA_{K4}^T)/w^Ta_{L4}^T$ and $\mu_4^T = 1$, with given prices of commodities produced in England $p^E = (p_1, p_2)$, with given endowments R^T and L^T, with the endowment of K^T defined at prices set arbitrarily close to the equilibrium prices for simple reproduction and with the output disposition and demand conditions added, the model for the Tropics can be solved for equilibrium prices and outputs.

In the next two subsections, I describe some applications of the basic Ricardo–Ohlin–Lewis model of comparative advantage and growth.

2.3. Nineteenth-century trade between England and America

There are few examples of attempts to use simple analytical models to analyse the basis of trade and factor movements in the historical context of colonial trade and imperialism under competitive conditions. From a neo-classical perspective, Jones (1971) sets out the typical stylised facts about the pattern of trade and factor movements between England and America in the nineteenth century, namely England exporting manufactures, capital, and labour, and America exporting corn whilst importing capital and labour. The example could be extended to those within the many countries divided into those within the central land peripheral areas of the world economy. Jones argues that the stylised facts cannot be explained within the context of the simplest paradigm[26] $2 \times 2 \times 2$

---

[26] By "paradigm" cases in trade theory, I mean differences in technology in static Ricardian theory and differences in resource endowments in the H-O-S theory as the basis for trade.

H-O-S model, because incompletely specialised trade leads to factor-price equalisation even without factor movements. Instead, he finds that the stylised facts can be explained within the context of a specific factors model where factor-price equalisation does not take place.[27] The basic model described in the previous subsection does not imply factor-price equalisation through trade and does not require the assumption of specific factors to produce results consistent with Jones' stylised facts. Both countries may be assumed to have access to the same technology (on account of trade and factor movements which ensured that the lands of recent settlement had access to the same technology as in England), to have homogeneous endowments of primary non-produced inputs which differ only in their relative supply, to be incompletely specialised with England exporting manufactures in exchange for corn, and with America having both a higher wage and a higher rate of profit.[28]

The equations (1) describing the equilibrium price relations for the basic model can be used to define a three-dimensional factor-price frontier for both England and America. With infinitely many techniques of production the factor-price frontier will be formed by the outer envelopes of the frontier for any given technique of production. For present purposes it is sufficient to consider the factor-price frontier for a single technique of production. This is shown in Figure 24.1 when wages and rent are measured in terms of commodity 1, where sector 1 always has the higher resource/labour ratio and a higher resource/capital ratio, but the ranking of the sectors in terms of their capital/labour ratios may vary.

Some of the important properties of the three-dimensional factor-price frontier shown in Figure 24.1 for a single technique can be readily described. As a consequence of the assumption that sector 1 has the higher resource/labour ratio, a rise in rent relative to wages will raise the relative price of commodity 1 ($p = p_2/p_1$ falls) for any given rate of profit. When the rate of profit is zero, the factor-price frontier is linear in the (r, w) plane as shown in Figure 24.1(a) and (b). As a consequence of the assumption that sector 1 always has the higher

[27]See also Samuelson (1971). The best summary of the early contributions to the specific factors model can be found in Caves (1963). Modifications to the static Ricardian model when specific factors are introduced can be found in Evans (1972, ch. 2, 1989 ch. 2). The specific factors model has been taken up and extended in the development literature by Krueger (1977) and Havrylyshyn (1985). Specific factors in manufacturing industries are treated as capital and in agriculture or mining they are treated as land, whereas in the model developed in Corden and Neary (1982), sector-specific capital stocks become fully mobile in the long run. The model has also been applied to the analysis of the multi-national corporation in Caves (1982).

[28]It may be objected that it is not correct to assume that America had the same institutions as England, namely a class which only owns land, as well as a class which owns circulating capital and a working class. Initially, this may not be the case, as in the example discussed by Marx (1867, ch. 33) in relation to Wakefield's theory of colonisation. When there is abundant land which is freely available for immigrants to take immediate possession, there will be none of the institutional requirements for the operation of a labour market. The present argument requires that capital and labour markets are operating with intersectoral mobility of capital and labour, and that homogeneous land can be used in both sectors. Agents who own both land and circulating capital receive the same rate of profit (interest) when the price of land is the capitalised value of rent.

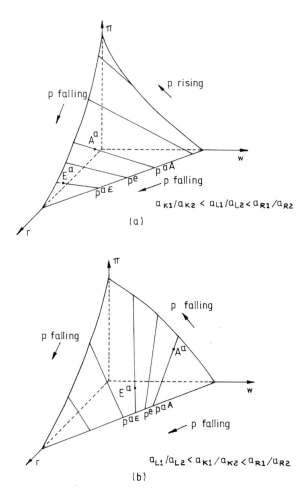

Figure 24.1

resource/capital ratio, a rise in rent relative to profit will raise the relative price of commodity 1 for any given real wage (p falls). When the real wage is equal to zero, the factor-price frontier is convex to the origin, as shown in Figures 24.1(a) and (b) in the (r, π) plane as a consequence of the factor intensity assumptions.

The effect of changing the ratio of profits to wages for any given rent will depend on the capital/labour ratios in sector 1 compared with sector 2. This is shown in Figures 24.1(a) and (b) in the (π, w) plane. Thus, when sector 1 has the lower capital/labour ratio, a rise in the rate of profit relative to wages will lower the relative price of commodity 1 (p rises) and the (π, w) frontier is convex to the origin as in Figure 24.1(a). When sector 1 has the higher capital/labour ratio, a rise in the rate of profit relative to wages will raise the relative price of commodity 1 (p falls) for a given rent and the (π, w) frontier is concave to the origin as in Figure 24.1(b).

An important property of the factor-price frontier for a single technique is that its surface is made up by linear iso-price contours.[29] This follows from the observation that, for constant p, equations (1) are equations of planes in (π, w, r) space which intersect in a straight line which lies on the factor price frontier. Thus, in Figure 24.1(a), the iso-price lines all have a negative but decreasing slope relative to the profit axis as p falls as drawn. Similarly, the iso-price lines all have a positive slope relative to the profit axis in Figure 24.1(b) for low values of (r/w); one of the iso-price curves will lie in the same plane as the profit axis before taking on a negative slope as (r/w) rises.

The above makes possible the analysis of the opening of trade between two economies identical in every respect except the exogenously determined distribution variable and exogenously determined endowments. First, suppose that, compared with England, America has more of the resource relative to labour and a higher exogenously given rate of profit. The capital stocks are those required for simple reproduction in both countries. The autarky positions for England and America, indicated by E^a and A^a in Figures 24.1(a) and (b), respectively, have autarky price ratios p^{aE} and p^{aA}, respectively. Both wages and profits are high at A^a compared with E^a, satisfying Jones' stylised facts in the autarky position. The autarky price ratios are such that England exports commodity 2 (manufactures) and imports commodity 1 (corn). However, in the case shown in Figure 24.1(a), a trading equilibrium when transport costs are zero at price p^e yields $w^A < w^E$ when $\pi^A > \pi^E$, contrary to the stylised facts. Only with transport costs included which prevent the full equalisation of commodity prices through trade could a trading equilibrium be consistent with the stylised facts. However, at the common trading price p^e in Figure 24.1(b), Jones' stylised facts are satisfied.

Second, suppose that wages are exogenously determined and are higher in America than in England. If, in addition, America has the smaller endowment of capital stocks relative to the resource when measured at a common relative price, then the above argument with respect to the pattern of trade and configurations of distribution variables can be repeated. The argument can be extended to the many technique cases in which the iso-cost curves will be made up of piecewise linear segments on the factor-price frontier made up of the outer envelope of the single technique frontiers. The number of countries can also be expanded on the usual lines.

It would therefore appear that the basic model making the H-O-S "paradigm" case assumptions can be used to construct a story of nineteenth-century trade between England and America which satisfies Jones' stylised facts for a more general case than with the specific factors model. Whilst a finer cut with Occam's

---

[29]I am grateful to Ian Steedman for pointing this out to me.

Razor is not everything in model building, the above example suggests that the basic model provides a useful starting point for the analysis of the basis of trade and factor movements between countries with the same or similar techniques but differing endowments and institutional determinants of one of the distribution variables. The circulating capital model has the additional virtue of taking into account the difference between reproducible capital and nonreproducible factors, a source of endless forced assumptions or even confusion when using the timeless H-O-S model or the timeless specific factors model in the analysis of comparative advantage.[30] Furthermore, the circulating capital model is consistent with the approach to testing trade theories developed by Deardorff (1984) based on the average factor intensities of commodities which enter trade. It is also consistent with Leamer (1984), who used the Vanek (1968) formulation of the generalised Heckscher–Ohlin theorem for testing trade theories. The main difference between Leamer's tests of the H-O model and the interpretation offered here is the suppression of the role of the stock of a factor in determining comparative advantage when there is a corresponding institutional determination of its price.

No attempt was made to establish why an exogenously set rate of profit might be higher in America than in England. One route might seek to specify endogenously the reasons for a differential rate of profit from an examination of differences in the financial institutions in England and America.[31] Again, one might consider a wages closure for England along Ricardo–Marx lines, and the rate of profit in America might be determined by the rate of profit in England adjusted for a risk premium plus some differential because of imperfect capital mobility which is not eliminated in equilibrium. Another variant might proceed by noting that, when there is capital export in search of raw materials or land and climate suitable for plantation agriculture, some form of a dual economy model with specific factors may be more appropriate for the second trading economy. This possibility is discussed in the next subsection.

2.4. Trade between England and the Tropics

Ideally, the choice of model for the analysis of trade and growth prospects for developing countries should allow for the analysis of competing hypotheses. In

---

[30] For example, Krueger (1977) and Havrylyshyn (1985) use the specific factors model for the analysis of comparative advantage in which it is necessary to assume that no capital is used in agriculture and mining. Similarly, UNIDO (1986) incorrectly expresses concern over the fact that capital endowments are valued at traded prices rather than autarky prices for the analysis of comparative advantage.

[31] This is in fact the approach adopted by Binswanger and Rosenzweig (1986) and Binswanger and McIntire (1984) in the discussion of financial institutions in land-scarce south-Asian agriculture and land-abundant Africa.

practice, the choice of model reflects the prior position taken on the competing hypotheses. This problem is no more evident that in empirical and policy debates over the long-run terms of trade and the transmission of growth through trade.

Lewis (1969) models trade between "temperate" England and the Tropics in a beautifully simple three-commodity Ricardo–Graham model. England produces temperate food and manufactures whilst the Tropics produces food and "commercials" for export. With all three commodities traded, the fundamental determinant of wage differences in terms of food will be the level of productivity of labour in temperate vs. tropical food production. The relatively faster rate of improvement in labour productivity in temperate compared with tropical agricultural over a long historical period found by Lewis translates in this simple model into declining terms of trade for Tropical exports of commercials compared with England's manufactures. Any productivity improvement in commercials exports from the Tropics will be passed on to England. The only way out of the terms of trade dilemma is by productivity improvement in tropical food production.

The terms of trade in the Lewis model are governed by purely supply side effects. This is in contrast with the supply and demand side considerations which underlie the Prebisch–Singer terms of trade thesis [Prebisch (1950), Singer (1950, 1975, 1984)] and more recent terms of trade models in the Kaldorian tradition by Vines (1984) and Thirlwall (1986). Within the Lewis model there is no scope in the analysis for the changes in labour productivity to be decomposed into technical change and change in the supply of the productive inputs labour, land and capital. Also, the static Ricardian framework does not permit the endogenous analysis of a second traded activity in the Tropics such as manufactures production, initially as an import substituting activity, and possibly as an emerging export activity. Given the very rapid rate of growth of manufactured exports from the so-called Newly Industrialising Countries (NICs) in the 1970s, this is a serious limitation of the static Ricardian framework. These deficiencies can be overcome in the dual economy version of the basic model.

Suppose that the basic model for England [producing temperate food (commodity 1) and manufactures (commodity 2)] described by equations (1)–(4) is modified by adding in the superscript E to all variables and parameters for England. The Tropics are modelled along the lines outlined in equations (5)–(8). Commercials can be imported from the Tropics as intermediate inputs so that A_K^E is now a (3×2) matrix of circulating capital requirements, which is valued by the (3×1) vector of prices of traded commodities, p. A parameter representing the degree of unionisation μ_2^E is introduced into the expression for wage costs in manufactures for $\mu_2^E \geq 1$. England's equilibrium conditions are characterised by either full employment and a rate of profit which is fixed exogenously, or unemployment and an institutional wage set exogenously. As before, it is assumed that temperate agriculture always has the higher resource/labour and resource/capital ratio compared with manufactures.

The behaviour of the model for England follows from a standard analysis of the magnification effects of price and quantity changes in a two-commodity two-factor H-O-S world with wages and rents (or profits and rent) being the endogenously determined factor prices and the rate of profit (or wages), being exogenously determined. As a result of the basic factor intensity condition, any change on the cost side which favours temperate agriculture will increase rent relative to wages (or profit) when the exogenously determined factor price is the rate of profit (or wages); the opposite will be the case if manufactures are favoured relative to temperate agriculture. For the Tropics, the results follow from the typical magnification effects of a two-sector specific factors model. These observations can be made a little more precise.

Suppose for England that the endowments of labour and the resource are given when profits are set exogenously, or the endowments of reproducible capital and the resource are given when the wage is fixed exogenously. In the Tropics, the endowments of labour and sector-specific capital and resources are given. Then, given the demand conditions in both England and the Tropics, the standard Stolper–Samuelson relationship between commodity prices and the endogenously determined factor prices will hold. These are shown in Figures 24.2(a) and (b) for England, and Figure 24.2(c) for the Tropics.

The equilibrium commodity and factor prices are denoted by the superscript e. The equilibrium combinations of the rent/wage ratio in England as the manufactures/temperate food price ratio p_2/p_1 varies (for given Tropical prices p^T and no unionisation so that $\mu_2^E = 1$) are shown in Figure 24.2(a) when the rate of profit is given exogenously. In Figure 24.2(b), the equilibrium combinations of the rent/profit ratio (the price of land) as p_2/p_1 varies (with given Tropical prices and no unionisation) are shown when wages are given exogenously. Similarly, from a straightforward application of the specific factors model, the equilibrium combinations of the rate of profit in commercials (assumed for simplicity to move in proportion to specific factor rent) and the internal Tropical terms of trade p_3/p_4 for given equilibrium prices in England p^{eE} are shown in Figure 24.2(c).

Now consider the effects of technical change or a change in the degree of unionisation in England. Hicks-neutral technical change in temperate agriculture in England will shift the factor-price/commodity-price locus wholly to the right, say to position (ii) in Figures 24.2(a) and (b) whilst Hicks-neutral technical change in manufactures (or an increase in the degree of unionisation) will shift the loci wholly to the left. The Lewis hypothesis of sectorally biased technical change towards agriculture (abstracting from factor bias in technical change) will tend to lead to a net shift in the factor-price/commodity-price loci to the right. Similarly, an improvement in productivity in Tropical agriculture raises the subsistence wage and the commercials profit/price locus will shift to the right whilst Hicks-neutral technical change in commercials will shift the locus upwards. If there is a net bias in Tropical technical change towards commercials as

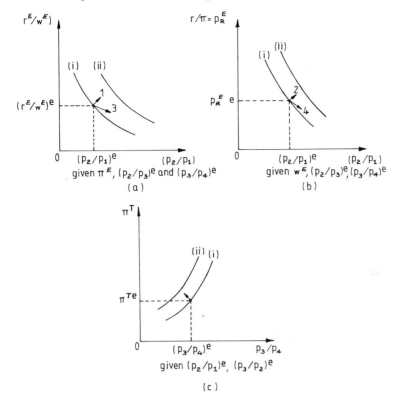

Figure 24.2

hypothesised by Lewis, the profit/price locus for the tropics will shift to the left to, say, (ii) in Figure 24.2(c).

For given average rates of technical change, increasing inequality of wages between England and the Tropics will be more likely when technical change is biased towards manufactures in England combined with a bias towards commercials in the Tropics. The final effects of any technical change, induced factor substitution, change in factor supply or change in institutional arrangements which affect the degree of unionisation, can be analysed by a straightforward application of the output and price magnification effects of the initial change.[32] A flavour of some of the results which can be obtained now follow.

On the output side, technical change or factor supply changes which expand the effective supply of the resource relative to labour when profits are exogenously fixed or the resource relative to capital when wages are exogenously fixed

---

[32] For an analysis in terms of magnification effects, see Evans (1987, appendix). Bardhan (1982), working in the framework of the timeless specific factors model, obtains similar results but does not separate the resource from capital in England or consider intermediate inputs.

will, at constant factor and commodity prices, increase the supply of temperate food and decrease the supply of manufactures. This follows from the application of the Rybczynski theorem when temperate food has the higher resource/labour and resource/capital input ratio compared to manufactures. Technical change or exogenous factor supply changes which directly or indirectly augment the effective supply of the capital (when wages are given exogenously) or labour (when the rate of profit is given exogenously) will have the opposite effects. In the Tropics, technical change biased towards commercials will tend to raise the relative supply of commercials to tropical food. The terms of trade and final distribution effects follow from an analysis of the patterns of excess demand and excess supply created by the technical change or other exogenous shifts.

Consider the Lewis case in which it is hypothesised that technical change in England is sectorally biased toward temperate agriculture and towards commercials in the Tropics. For the moment, suppose that the absolute level of technical change is the same in both England and the Tropics so that attention can be focused on the sectorally biased technical change hypothesis. Sectorally biased technical change in England towards temperate food will tend to raise the supply of temperate agriculture relative to manufactures. It is possible that the supply of manufactures will fall absolutely, but this is less likely the higher the overall rate of technical change in England for any relative degree of sectoral bias in technical change. In the Tropics, biased technical change towards commercials will tend to raise the supply of commercials relative to tropical food. Thus, with a proportional change in income in England and the Tropics, there will tend to be excess supply of temperate food and commercials and excess demand for manufactures and tropical food. Market clearance will require a deterioration in the temperate food/manufactures and the commercials/manufactures terms of trade with indefinite effects on the temperate food/commercials terms of trade. As in the original Lewis model this result is independent of any sectoral bias on the demand side. If the income and price elasticities of demand for temperate food, commercials and tropical food are less than one and for manufactures are greater than one, the temperate agriculture/manufactures and the commercials/manufactures terms of trade will tend to deteriorate rather more than for the case when all of the income elasticities are equal to one. The outcome for the relative wage differentials will be indeterminate.[33] Thus, the Lewis result, that the commercials/manufactures terms of trade will tend to worsen as a result of sectorally biased technical change, will occur within the

---

[33] It is possible that, for a given rate of profit and with biased technical change in England towards temperate food, wages will fall absolutely in terms of all prices. Since biased technical change in the Tropics towards commercials will increase the subsistence wage (albeit by less than the rise in profit and rent), it is possible that international wage inequality will decrease with biased technical change along Lewis lines. This result is in contrast with the result obtained by Bardhan (1982) whereby technical change in temperate agriculture always increases the international wage differential.

model described even without sectoral differences on the demand side. The Engel curve effects on the demand side will tend to reinforce this result.

The above patterns of biased technical change and shifts in the terms of trade will modify the previous analysis of the distribution of income, summarised by the direction of the arrows shown in Figures 24.2(a)–(c). For a given rate of profit and price of commercials in terms of food, the improvement in the terms of trade for manufactures in terms of food in England will tend to offset the initial effects of technical change in shifting the distribution of income away from wages or profit and in favour of rent as shown by the arrows 1 and 2 in Figures 24.2(a) and (b), respectively. If the price effects dominate the initial effects of the biased technical change, it is also possible for the distribution of income to move in favour of wages or profit in each case, shown by the arrows 3 and 4, respectively.

The patterns of biased technical change which induces shifts in the terms of trade and the distribution of income will be further modified when substitution effects in production are taken into account. If the substitution effects dominate the initial effects of the sectorally biased technical change, it is possible for the pattern of supply responses to be reversed. However, given that empirical estimates of the elasticities of substitution in production are almost always less than one, this possibility is unlikely. The analysis will also be modified when North–South differences in the rate of technical change are taken into account, as increasingly emphasised by Singer (1975, 1984). To the extent that the benefits of technical change in the North are captured as Schumpeterian rents, the model would have to be modified to take this into account.

The combined effects of biased technical change and factor supply change in England and the Tropics on both the distribution of income and the terms of trade can only be determined empirically. The empirical evidence summarised in Evans (1987) shows a great variety of experience of terms of trade movement. Whilst there is evidence of an absolute sectoral bias in technical change in developed countries ("England") towards temperate agriculture, the rate of technical change in temperate agriculture is now comparable to that experienced in manufactures. It would therefore seem that Engel curve effects now produce the observed decline in the long-run terms of trade between temperate agricultural commodities and manufactures for a wide variety of commodities, overriding the effects of diminishing returns to natural resources as developed country population expansion and capital accumulation takes place. The empirical evidence on biased technical change in developing countries is much more sketchy and the empirical evidence on the movements in various components of developed–developing country terms of trade is much more varied.

The model of the Tropics can be modified in an obvious way to allow for the production of manufactures. If both capital and the resource are fully mobile between commercials and manufactures, as in England, the capitalistic sector of the Tropics will be the same as in the model for England. If resources remain sectorally specific but capital is mobile, the capitalistic sector will behave as in the specific factors model [for an application to the Dutch Disease in reverse in a small mineral exporting economy, see Evans (1986)]. In both cases, the interaction between the capitalistic (and traded) sectors and the non-traded tropical food will proceed along similar lines to Corden and Neary (1982). The supply of labour to commercials may also be modified if immigrant labour, such as Chinese or Indian coolie labour, is available as in some parts of the Tropics during the nineteenth century. The models of trade and factor flows with general and specific resources also provide a stylised account of the economic drive towards imperialism in the search for general and specific resources discussed by Magdoff (1978, ch. 4) and Murray (1978).

2.5. Some aspects of historical analysis

The exogenous wage determination mechanism along Ricardo–Marx–Lewis lines, or the exogenous determination of the rate of profit described in Subsection 2.2, are often associated with what may be called a historicist position on the process of development and change. Roughly speaking, the historicist argues that the relative power and organisation of contending classes will strongly influence the distribution of income, depending on the particular historical circumstances. The rate of growth will be affected by the indirect effects of the relative power of contending classes on investment working through the distribution of income, and on the direct effects of contending classes in accelerating or resisting change. In this view, trade is of less importance in the process of development and change than the direct effects of class struggle. The economic determinist position roughly argues that the distribution of income is determined entirely by supply and demand once endowments are given. Within this general perspective, trade has a much more powerful transforming role. Roemer (1984) suggests that the two positions may be reconciled, arguing that market forces may be sufficient to explain the basic trends in the distribution of income, but that the relevant choice of equilibrium position may be influenced by particular historical events. These two broadly identified positions also have different perspectives on the transition between one mode of production and another.[34]

The historicist approach, well exemplified by Brenner (1976, 1977, 1986), tends to rely on the intervention of political forces, most notably class struggle, to bring

---

[34]It is not my purpose to discuss the voluminous literature on the transition between modes of production. For a discussion of the concept of mode of production and some of the different ways in which it has been used in the literature, see Brewer (1980, ch. 11) and Foster-Carter (1978) and the references cited therein. Whilst much of this literature remains locked in a definitional and epistemological cul de sac, I use the concept of mode of production only in a broad sense here.

about changes in property relations and the labour process which are more conducive to economic growth. He argues that capitalist growth requires the emergence of free wage labour which sells its labour power competitively on the market, as opposed to a situation where labour remains tied to the land.[35] In other words, he focuses on the relation between direct producers and their exploiters, and thus on the wage relation, as the defining characteristic of capitalist society. In the functionalist case, the particular institutions and relations of production are identified with particular levels of development of the forces of production, which are determinants of the possibility of transition from one form of organisation of production to another [see Cohen (1978, 1986, pp. 16–17)].[36]

Both the historicist and functionalist positions argue that the dynamic of a society is explained either in terms of the development of the forces of production and the associated changes in institutions (Cohen) or in terms of property relations and collective class actions which might change them (Brenner). The insights obtained by stark models need to be supplemented by the qualitative assessment of the historical context of transitions, a process which can be informed from the historicist or functionalist positions.

The primary emphasis in the consideration of the basic model has been the discussion of the proximate basis of trade and factor movements in which the endowments of land, labour and capital played a role in conjunction with the distribution of income. In the next section, the basic model is used to examine some issues which arise from the Marxian discussion of international exploitation and class, and to make some further observations on the question of international inequality.

3. Unequal Exchange and international inequality

3.1. Why Unequal Exchange?

The term Unequal Exchange is sometimes used to describe a trading situation where there is a systematic bias in the movement in the net barter terms of trade. A flavour of some of the results which can be obtained along these lines from the model of trade between England and the Tropics was discussed in Subsection 2.4.

---

[35] This does not mean that any social or institutional ties to land should be automatically assumed to have adverse consequences for growth and welfare. As discussed by Bardhan in Chapter 3, Volume I, of this Handbook in relation to share-cropping arrangements, it is necessary to establish that the observed institutional ties are not a surrogate for a missing market function before the conclusion can be drawn that a pre-capitalist institutional arrangement is both exploitative and growth inhibiting.

[36] There is much in common with the work discussed by Stiglitz in Chapter 5 of this Handbook. See also, Binswanger and Rosenzweig (1986) and Binswanger and McIntire (1984).

Another branch of this literature, recently developed by Spraos (1983) and Raffer (1987, ch. 7) and surveyed by Ocampo (1986), concerns itself with the double factoral terms of trade, the number of units of labour or per worker national incomes exchanged through trade. The Marxian tradition suggests that, behind the veil of the market, there may be Unequal Exchange of labour arising from an unequal distribution of productive assets. This section contrasts the various approaches to Unequal Exchange and examines the usefulness of exploitation theory and the Unequal Exchange of labour for the analysis of international inequality, and for the analysis of international class relationships.

3.2. Exploitation and trade

The Unequal Exchange of labour is a special case of a more general specification of the theory of exploitation developed by Roemer based on the theory of cooperative games.[37] The central idea is to specify the core of a game, that set of income distributions for which no agents participating in an economy are exploited. A coalition of agents is said to be exploited if, under appropriately defined rules of withdrawal from the game, their initial position is worse than that which can be obtained under some hypothetically achievable alternative. In the case of a single closed economy, each state of the economy will differ fundamentally in the institutional arrangements which govern them, but each state must in some sense be hypothetically feasible. In the case of nations which enter into exchange, the fundamental differences refer to alternative endowments of productive assets, or some other form of differentiation between nations. In broad terms, Roemer draws on historical materialism to define such hypothetically feasible states, although his method allows for the construction of any hypothetical alternative in which the defining character of exploitation is removed.

More precisely, if society is made up of P agents in which a coalition of Q agents would be better off under an alternative state, whilst the complimentary coalition $Q' = P - Q$ would be worse off, and if the coalition Q' is in a position of dominance in the original state, then it is said that the coalition Q is exploited by the coalition Q' in the original state.[38] The concept of dominance is discussed further in Section 4. It entails at least two components, the domination of capitalists over workers as required to maintain and enforce private property in the means of production, and as in the hierarchical and autocratic structure of the organisation of production. Inevitably, it is difficult to give precision to the

[37]A comprehensive exposition of exploitation theory can be found in Roemer (1981, 1982a, 1982b, 1983b, 1986). The discussion which follows draws on Roemer's argument.
[38]The dominance condition is discussed in Roemer (1982a, p. 195 and p. 237, 1982b, 1983a, 1986).

dominance condition, but it entails at least that the coalition S' prevents the alternative from being realised, so that S is exploited.[39] This might come about through the operation of relations of domination at the point of production as well as through the enforcement of existing property relations.

This definition of exploitation captures the common sense idea that exploitation takes place when one group of agents, or a class, is better off than another group or class and when the former prevent the alternative from being realised.[40] It is the configuration of market institutions and property relations which are central to the categorisation of relations of exploitation and class. Feudal exploitation occurs when there are unequal endowments of land and no labour market. Surplus labour is provided to the feudal lord under coercive production relations without the operation of a labour market. Capitalist exploitation is defined when there is a labour market but unequal ownership of alienable assets or commodity capital, whilst socialist exploitation arises from unequal endowments of inalienable assets or skills. Marxian exploitation can arise when there is unequal ownership of productive assets and competitive commodity markets but neither capital or labour markets. Neo-classical exploitation, the absence of the freedom of exchange of labour, is equivalent to feudal exploitation. A potentially unending variety of sub-forms of exploitation based on status, need, gender, race and so on can be readily constructed. It should be stressed that the concept of exploitation is quite compatible with gains from trade. In fact, the presence or absence of freedom of exchange will be one of the defining characteristics of the different forms of exploitation considered.

International inequality can be formulated in terms of alternative configurations of endowments of productive assets, of relationships of status and privilege, of needs, of knowledge, or subsistence wages or other distribution relations, and so on.[41] Clearly, each type of exploitation defined in this way implies an ethical judgement which would not be accepted by many neo-classical economists; but more on this in Section 5. A schematic representation of the endowments and other historical or moral attributes of nation q can be set out as follows:

$$\Gamma^q = (K^q, R^q, L^q, T^q, w^q, N^q, D^q, I^q), \tag{9}$$

[39] As has been pointed out to me by the editors, there is no formal discussion of the costs of coalition formation, enforcement costs, or free-rider problems such as discussed in Olsen (1982) in this definition of exploitation, but such a discussion is by no means ruled out.

[40] Forms of inequality such as slavery may have been regarded as just and non-exploitative at the time, but would not now be so regarded. Similarly, whilst Marxists view the inequalities between workers and capitalists under capitalism as being exploitative, the same inequality is not perceived as being exploitative by many. See Roemer (1982a, p. 194).

[41] The neo-classical reader will readily observe that there is no analysis of how the inequalities came about in this definition of exploitation. The definition offered asks questions about exploitation in the context of simple or extended reproduction of the exploitative relations.

where Γ^q is the total vector of endowments and attributes, K^q is the endowment vector of reproducible commodity capital, R^q is the endowment vector of non-reproducible commodity capital, L^q is the endowment vector of labour of different skill types, T^q is the endowment vector of productive knowledge, w^q is the subsistence wage (or other exogenously given return such as the rate of profit π), N^q is the vector of differential needs, D^q is an index of market and non-market forms of domination including monopoly power, and I^q is the set of institutional arrangements designed to distribute the fruits of economies of scale or other externalities.

If there are m nations each with a population P^q, then a coalition of S nations can in principle alter the relations of exploitation or international inequality by adjusting their endowments to the per capita levels based on world averages or through the elimination of some undesired differentiation in their attributes. Some of the processes by which such differentiation might be eliminated are discussed in Section 5. Thus, elimination of international inequality arising from unequal endowments of commodity capital would require a coalition of S nations each of whom altered their stock of K^q, or claims on the world capital stocks, according to the rule:

$$\Gamma^q = \left(K^{qs}, R^q, L^q, T^q, w^a, N^q, D^q, I^q \right), \tag{10}$$

where $K^{qs} = \sum_m K^q \cdot P^q / \sum_m P^q$ is the per capita share of the coalition of S nations in world capital stocks. This concept of exploitation is the Marxian one which parallels the closed economy case in which the counterfactual is socialism. The potential elimination of other forms of international inequality for a subset of S nations follows in an obvious manner.

The more familiar mode of analysis of exploitation in the Marxian tradition is through the Unequal Exchange of labour, and the relationship of this to inequality of asset distribution is pursued in the next subsection.

3.3. Unequal endowments of capital

A special case of the basic model developed in Subsection 2.2 can be used to analyse international inequality of the per capita distribution of reproducible commodity capital. The second primary non-produced input (resource, R) is dropped from equations (1)–(4). It is assumed as before that there is no factor intensity reversal and that commodity 2 is labour intensive.[42] Thus, suppose that there are m nations producing two commodities which have the same technology

---

[42] Roemer (1983b) uses a many-country, many-commodity model with Leontief technology. In the exposition here, I have used the two-commodity framework with choice of technique. The results presented here can readily be extended to a many commodity framework.

set available so that each country can be defined by adding a country superscript to the variables in equations (1)–(4). The net product for country q will be given by:

$$Y^q = p(I - A)X^q, \tag{11}$$

or, in terms of output per worker:

$$y^q = p(I - A)x^{\tau q}$$
$$= px^{\tau q} - k^q, \tag{12}$$

where y^q is the net product per worker in country q, the vector $x^{\tau q}$ is defined by $x^{\tau q} \equiv (x_1^q \tau, x_2^q(1 - \tau))$, where the x^q's are outputs per worker and τ is the share of employment in industry 1 and k^q is the average capital/labour ratio in country q.

As a consequence of the choice of technique (A', a'_L) being the cost-minimising choice from the convex set of techniques (A, a_L) for any given set of prices and endowments, the y's will be an increasing function of the k's or $y = f(k)$. Thus, for a given set of equilibrium prices p, the standard Deardorff (1974) diagram showing the maximal output per worker in the world economy with trade in commodities as the capital/labour ratio varies with and without international factor immobility, as shown in Figure 24.3(a) and (b). The rate of profit will be given by the slope of $OAA'BB'CD$ and $O'BB'CD$ in Figures 24.3(a) and (b), respectively, the real wage in terms of commodity 1 will be given by the height of the intercept of the tangent to the $y = f(k)$ function.

There are five separate segments on $OAA'BB'CD$ in Figure 24.3(a) corresponding to incomplete specialisation and factor-price equalisation when factor endowments lie between (iii) and (iv), the cone of diversification; complete specialisation and no factor-price equalisation when the endowments ratios lie between (i) and (iii), (iv) and (v). When the endowment ratios are less than (i) or greater than (v), one of the factor prices will be zero. In Figure 24.3(b), the cone of diversification lies between (iii) and (iv). For nations with endowment ratios outside the cone of diversification, there will be incomplete specialisation and factor movements are required to achieve international factor-price equalisation.

The Unequal Exchange of labour giving rise to exploitation in the trading relationship between countries can be made more specific.

Roemer (1983b, p. 41) defines exploitation in trade independently of the composition of demand as follows:

A country will be said to be unequal exchange (UE) exploited at equilibrium p if, no matter how it spends is national income on goods, it cannot purchase goods embodying as much labour as it supplied. A country is said to be UE exploiting if, no matter how it chooses to spend its national income on goods, it commands more labour than it supplied.

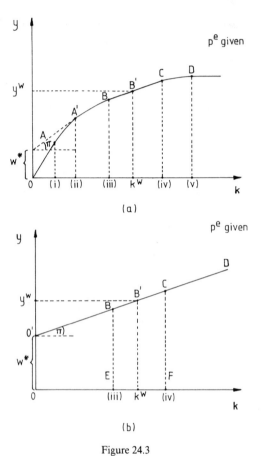

Figure 24.3

Analytically, this can be shown by observing that the best way that a country can use its per worker net product $y^q = (\pi^q k^q + w^q)$ to purchase embodied labour, is to choose

$$\left(a_L^{\#}/p\right)_{\max} = \max_{i,\,q}\left(a_{Li}^{\#q}/p_i\right), \tag{13}$$

where $a_L^{\#}$ are the direct and indirect labour input coefficients given by $a_L^{\#} = (I - A)^{-1}a_L$ and the a_L and A are the cost-minimising choice of technique at the equilibrium commodity prices. Thus, country q is trade (UE) exploited if and only if

$$1/\left(\pi^q k^q + w^q\right) > \left(a_L^{\#}/p\right)_{\max}. \tag{14}$$

That is to say, if the amount of labour embodied in a country's net product is greater than the maximum amount of labour which can be purchased through trade. Similarly, country q is a trade (UE) exploiter if and only if

$$1/(\pi^q k^q + w^q) < \left(a_L^\# /p\right)_{min}. \tag{15}$$

In other words, a country is a trade exploiter when the amount of embodied labour in its net product is less than the minimum amount of labour which can be purchased through trade.

The absence of international factor mobility is equivalent to the closed economy case of no capital or labour markets, so that the form of Unequal Exchange of labour is equivalent to Marxian exploitation defined in Subsection 3.2 above. In this case, it turns out that conditions (14) and (15) will only hold when countries have capital/labour ratios less than (i) and more than (v) shown in Figure 24.3(a). A country will only be exploited in trade independently of demand in the sense defined only when it has excess supply of labour and a zero wage, and all other countries will be exploitation neutral.[43] The reason why there is trade exploitation in the sense defined only in the extreme ranges of the capital/labour endowment ratios follows from the stringency of the definition: exploitation in trade is defined independently of demand and independently of the country with which trade takes place.

With factor mobility, international exploitation is equivalent to the closed economy cases with either a capital or labour market. Using the same definition of exploitation through trade set out in (14) and (15), exploitation through trade is no longer dependent on the excess supply of one of the productive assets. Furthermore, it can be proved that the relationships summarised in Table 24.3 will exist between the individual countries' endowment ratios, their class position or status as exporters or importers of workers (capital), and their exploitation position.[44] That is, the division of nations by their exploitation position corresponds exactly to their class position as exporters or importers of capital and/or

---

[43] The proof of the exploitation theorem can be seen graphically be setting out the dual to Figure 24.3(a), the factor-price frontier. The cost-minimising technique is found when the unit cost function (whose slope is governed by the labour/capital endowment ratio) is tangent to the lowest point of the wage–profit locus (whose slope is governed by the labour/capital ratios in production). When there is an extreme solution with either $w = 0$ or $\pi = 0$, the result follows from a comparison of the two slopes.

[44] The condition (14) that a nation be exploited in trade can be rewritten as $(\pi^q k^q + w^{*q}) < 1/(a_L^\# /p)_{max}$. The left-hand term in the inequality is simply the output per worker, y. The denominator of the right-hand term is embodied labour which can be obtained through trade, in this case through purchasing the labour-intensive commodity 2. The whole of the right-hand term is simply net product per worker from commodity 2 production or EB in Figure 24.3(b). Thus, a country is trade exploited when its net product per worker is less than EB. The reader can check that (15) can be re-written to show that a country is trade exploited when its net product per worker is greater than FC.

Table 24.3

Endowment ratios	Optimising factor movement	Exploitation position	Class position
$a_k/a_L = 0$	L export (K import)	exploited	"proletarian"
$0 \le a_k/a_L <$ (iii)	L export (K import)	exploited	"semi-proletarian"
(iii) $\le a_k/a_L \le$ (iv)	none	neutral	"petty bourgeois"
(iv) $< a_k/a_L$	L import (K export)	exploiter	"capitalist"

labour. This is the application of Roemer's Class Exploitation Correspondence Principle to the case of Unequal Exchange between nations.[45]

The ethical sense in which it can be said that a country is trade exploited or exploiting in terms of the Unequal Exchange of labour is clear from the counterfactual required for the equivalent game theoretic formulation of exploitation described in the previous subsection. The relevant counterfactural for the cases with and without international capital and/or labour mobility is defined by the situation in which all workers have access to their proportionate share of the world's capital stock. In terms of Figures 24.3(a) and (b), if the world endowment ratio is given by k^w, then the world average per capita net product in terms of commodity 1 will be given by y^w in Figures 24.3(a) and (b). This is also the per worker product when all countries have access to their per capita share of the world's capital stock. Countries which are trade exploited all have a per capita product of less than EB (also less than y^w), and countries which are trade exploiting have a per capita product which is higher than FC (also higher than y^w). If a further restriction is made, namely that demand is specified, trade exploitation is now defined in terms of the difference between labour embodied in actual production and consumption. In this case, only countries with the world average capital/labour ratio will be exploitation neutral and all others can be regarded as gainers or losers from exploitation through trade.[46]

The Unequal Exchange of labour in the sense defined above is very different from that arising from adverse net barter terms of trade or adverse double factoral terms of trade. Consider the case where there is either capital or labour mobility and one Unequal Exchange exploiting country accumulates capital for one period before the world economy returns to simple reproduction. Suppose

[45] For a discussion of the Class Exploitation Correspondence Principle, see Roemer (1982a).

[46] Roemer (1982a, appendix 1.1) examines a situation where all nations have the same per capita consumption but exploited nations work longer to achieve this compared with the workers in the exploiting nation.

that the new world equilibrium is within the newly defined cone of diversification, and that no country changes its pattern of trade or exploitation position. In this case, both the net barter and the double factorial terms of trade will turn against the Unequal Exchange exploiting countries and the rate of profit will fall. However, there will be increased Unequal Exchange of labour because all exploited countries will have a smaller share of the world capital stock in the counterfactual situation. This observation makes it clear that the Unequal Exchange of labour as defined so far takes place when there are gains from trade, and emphasises the well-known point that it is impossible to make welfare judgements from changes in any measure of the terms of trade.

In addition to the assumptions of CRS and no externalities, the above story is dependent on the absence of wealth effects which may lead to the conclusion that an asset-poor country is an Unequal Exchange exploiter. Thus, suppose that there are only two nations, one asset-rich and the other asset-poor. If the elasticity of labour supply with respect to wealth is greater than one at higher levels of wealth,[47] then it may be Pareto-efficient for the asset-poor country to lend its capital to the asset-rich country and its agents cease working altogether. In this case, by the Unequal Exchange of labour criterion, the asset-poor country exploits the asset-rich country. A similar problem with the Unequal Exchange of labour theory of exploitation arises when there is a second primary non-produced input.

3.4. Unequal resource endowments

A striking characteristic of the model of trade and exploitation discussed above is the exclusion of land or a resource, violating the stylised facts discussed in Subsection 2.2. The Unequal Exchange of labour version of exploitation theory fails to predict the decomposition of the world economy by exploitation and class position with the inclusion of a second primary non-produced input. This can readily be seen because a country which is trade exploited on the basis of its low endowment of reproducible capital may be trade exploiting on account of its resource endowment. The class position of the country as an exporter (importer) of workers (capital) may not go according to the exploitation position indicated by the Unequal Exchange of labour and the exploitation position may not give a correct indicator of the inequality of distribution of productive assets.

Consider the basic model of trade between England and America discussed in Subsection 2.3 when there is factor mobility so that wages and profits are the

---

[47]This is a modified version of the example described in Roemer (1986). In practice, it may not be possible to distinguish the effects of increased supply of labour due to higher asset ownership from the effects of a higher capital/labour ratio on the intensity of work. The latter effects are discussed in Subsection 4.1.

same in both England and America. As before, America has the higher resource/labour endowment ratio compared with England. When commodity 1 has a high capital/labour ratio and a high resource/capital ratio compared with commodity 2, the Unequal Exchange of labour may go in the wrong direction, as noted by Emmanuel (1975b) in his example of Unequal Exchange between Belgium and Katanga. In terms of Figure 24.3(b), the level of the $y^q = f(k^q)$ function for each country will now be dependent of the endowments of the resource R per worker as well as capital per worker and the intercept will refer to wage and rent per worker. When commodity 1 has the higher capital/labour ratio compared with commodity 2, it is now quite possible for America, with a high endowment of resource R but a low endowment of capital, to import capital and to produce and export commodity 1. In terms of the Unequal Exchange of labour, America is an exploiter producing the capital and resource intensive commodity, yet it may have to import capital in order to achieve this. Alternatively, suppose that commodity 1 now has a lower capital/labour ratio compared with commodity 2. Then England, producing and exporting the capital intensive commodity 2, might have to import capital in order to achieve this. In this case, the Unequal Exchange of labour would show that England is the exploiting country in spite of its import of capital.

Roemer (1986) discusses this logical problem with the Unequal Exchange of labour theory of exploitation, arguing that it is more important to concentrate on the ethical questions concerning the distribution of productive assets where exploitation theory gives a conflicting answer. He then modifies the logical criticism of exploitation theory, arguing that in fact the Unequal Exchange of labour is likely to give a good empirical proxy for the inequality of the distribution of assets. This might be a good proxy for the closed economy case. However, given the important role of natural resources in the analysis of world trade discussed in Subsection 2.2, this empirical argument may not hold up. For this reason, it would seem that the Unequal Exchange of labour as a proxy for international inequality should be subject to empirical examination.[48] This would, in turn, require a direct focus on the sources of inequality identified in equation (9) and the ethical basis for any redistributive argument.

3.5. Unequal endowments of skills and productive knowledge

When a country's level of skills L^q are below the highest levels attainable in the world economy, and when productive knowledge T^q is not sufficient to sustain the world best-practice level of productivity, there will be an additional element of exploitation in the counterfactual against which country q is compared. It is in

---

[48]One of the best empirical studies of international inequality is Griffin (1978).

this sense that Pasinetti (1981, p. 247) refers to Unequal Exchange arising from productivity differentials. If the combined effects of differences in skill and productive knowledge are reflected in Hicks-neutral technical differences between developed and underdeveloped countries, the product of the underdeveloped country will embody more labour than the developed country on this account. These elements of international inequality may offset the "wrong" effects of capital or resource endowments in the Unequal Exchange of labour accounts. This does not alter the logical argument against the use of Unequal Exchange of labour as the indicator of exploitation, but may soften the arguments against the use of Unequal Exchange of labour as an empirical proxy for international inequality.

3.6. International wage differentiation

The dual economy model discussed in Subsection 2.2 provides one possible basis for the analysis of Unequal Exchange in the unequal wages sense based on a Lewis-type dual economy model [see also Bardhan (1982)]. The neo-Marxian theories of unequal wages revolve around some form of exogenously given wage differentiation between the centre and the periphery of the world economy when there is a long-run equalisation of the rate of profit through capital mobility. The central vision of this literature, sparked by the work of Emmanuel (1972),[49] is that the centre workers tend to appropriate the benefits of technical change which takes place both in the centre and the periphery. The centre–periphery wage differential leads to a dynamic relationship in which the total size of the centre market grows faster than in the periphery.[50] The underlying cause for wage differentiation is due to exogenous differences in direct wage bargaining power in Emmanuel, relative worker bargaining power in Delarue (1975), or due

---

[49] For a full discussion of the unequal wages neo-Marxian models of Unequal Exchange, see Evans (1984). For a blow-by-blow account of these theories, see Raffer (1987).

[50] The simple Bacha (1978) wages fund model with complete specialisation in the centre and the periphery sets out the elasticity conditions required for the centre to appropriate the benefits of technical change in the Emmanuel case. Two sets of conditions are required to ensure this result, depending on the relative rates of technical change in the centre and periphery. When technical change is faster in the centre than in the periphery, the centre market will grow faster than the peripheral market if the centre income elasticity of demand for imports is less than 1. This result is not dependent on an adverse movement in the terms of trade. On the other hand, if technical progress in the periphery is faster than in the centre, but all the benefits are appropriated by centre workers as a result of their greater bargaining power, there will be both adverse market size and employment effects in the periphery if the Johnson (1955) impoverishment condition holds. In the model of trade between England and the Tropics discussed in Subsection 2.4, there will be a much more complex relationship between the rate of growth of the market in England and the Tropics and the rate of growth of employment, and the bargaining power of England's workers did not come into the story. However, the rate of growth of markets is likely to be less in the Tropics than in England when the terms of trade move against the Tropics and when the demand for Tropical exports is price and income inelastic.

to centre monopoly power in commodity markets and commercial policy in the case of Braun (1973) and Andersson (1976). In the Emmanuel case, the rising real wages in the centre, rather than being the effect of technical progress and industrialisation, precede and are a cause of development.[51]

The most important objection to the neo-Marxian unequal wages theories of Unequal Exchange follows from the observation that the centre and the periphery are both aggregations of many national units. When there is international capital mobility, it is not possible for an exogenous national money wage bargain to be translated into an aggregate real wage bargain or even a relative wage bargain for the centre or the periphery. Similar objections arise in the case of the centre monopoly power theory of wage differentiation of Braun.[52] The obvious alternative closure from the wages side would be to argue for some kind of surplus labour or reserve army mechanism. However, this would undermine Emmanuel's central political conclusion, namely that the centre country worker aristocrats exploit peripherial workers.

3.7. Dependency, neo-Smithian Marxism, and world systems analysis

An influential variant of the Smithian trade-induced growth perspective discussed in Subsection 2.1, albeit from a very different political perspective, has been associated with what might loosely be called the Dependency tradition and the World Systems approach.[53] Despite the heterogeneity of analytical approaches which are included in these schools, it is possible to discern some common characteristics. The logic of the Frank and Wallerstein position is that "underdevelopment" in the periphery is as much the cause of capitalist development in the centre as is capitalist development the cause of "underdevelopment". It is argued that a more contemporary form of dependency is manifested in neo-colonialism and the domination of the manufacturing sector in the periphery by the TNC, and through dependence on the centre for technology and the means of production. Consequently, peripheral countries are not capable of autonomous self-sustained growth and hence capitalist development is impossible in developing countries. The trade-induced division of labour, the engine of growth in the

---

[51] For a further discussion of Emmanuel's loosely formulated laws of motion, see Evans (1984, pp. 209–210).

[52] For more detailed discussion, see Evans (1980, 1981a, 1981b, 1981c, 1984).

[53] The best surveys of the Dependency tradition can be found in Palma (1978) and Brewer (1980). The links between the World Systems approach of Wallerstein (1974, 1979) and the Dependency approach is made clear in Addo (1984). Both schools see the evolution of the world economy as being associated with the development of commerce and the subsequent rapid growth of world trade. One of the main points in the long line of criticism of these schools is the displacement of property and class relations from the centre of the analysis. The internal structure and development of different economies is primarily determined by their place in global exchange relations and the organisation of production and class relations is secondary [Brewer (1980, p. 181)].

Smithian view, is turned on its head and is the historical cause of global polarity and unequal levels of development.

There is a tension in this literature between defining relations of exploitation between centres and peripheries on the lines of Emmanuel and on the basis of the Unequal Exchange theory of Amin (1973) and Frank (1978, pp. 103–110). Amin argues that Unequal Exchange arises when the wage differentials between the centre and the periphery exceed productivity differentials and where there is full international mobility of capital. A peripheral mode of production is defined as characterised by technologically advanced export sectors (and possibly protected import competing sectors) together with an internal Unequal Exchange relationship with marginalised or non-capitalist modes of production. Amin's distribution closure is to set the profit/wage ratio in the centre exogenously through "class struggle", whilst the peripheral wage is determined by the cost of reproduction of labour power in the non-capitalist areas. This Unequal Exchange is imposed by the imperialist centre on the periphery through a whole armory of extra-market forces.

Formally, Saigal (1973) set out Amin's theory in terms of the simple circulating capital model set out in equation (1) in which the resource R is dropped. In order to capture the idea that wage differences between the centre and periphery exceed the productivity differentials, it is sufficient to consider the case where the peripheral technology differs from the centre in a Hicks-neutral manner. Thus, if $\alpha < 1$ is the productivity differential, the hypothesised Unequal Exchange will take place provided $w^P/w^C < \alpha$. The competitive solution which satisfies these restrictions when wages are measured in terms of commodity 1 and when capital is mobile internationally entail that the centre activities are not utilised and all production will take place in the periphery; hence the role of extra-market force in ensuring that production takes place in both the centre and in the periphery. The Amin–Saigal–Frank policy conclusion, that autarkic or semi-autarkic development is not only feasible but will yield a higher rate of profit, and therefore, at a given rate of savings out of profits, a higher rate of growth, follows as a consequence of their definition of Unequal Exchange.[54] In effect, the Amin–Saigal model of exploitation through trade is equivalent to Roemer's concept of Feudal exploitation or the neo-classical concept of exploitation arising from the lack of freedom of exchange of labour. The criticism of this theory of Unequal Exchange is obvious. It is implausible to assume that peripheral capitalists have been unable to act in their interests because of the domination of an all-powerful anthropomorphic "international capital" as the experience of the Newly Industri-

---

[54]As shown by Mainwaring (1980), it is possible to find a set of unequal production parameters which satisfy the condition that wage differentials exceed the average productivity differentials but also yield equilibrium terms of trade which lie inside the Ricardian limbo region. It is the conclusion that the equilibrium terms of trade will lie outside of the Ricardian limbo region, stressed in all of the numerical examples in Saigal (1973), which produces the strong Amin–Saigal results.

alising Countries (NICs) makes clear. The assumed relationships between wage and productivity differentials must therefore be incorrect.

3.8. Unequal Exchange and classical Marxian value theory

Much of the discussion about Unequal Exchange has been couched in terms of classical Marxian value theory, but those authors who attempted to explicitly model trading relationships inevitably had to face the transformation problem.[55] Nevertheless, there remains a considerable body of what might be called fundamentalist or surplus transfer theories of Unequal Exchange and imperialism. For example, Mandel (1976, ch. 11) and Szentes (1976, pp. 199–212) base their surplus transfer theories on differences in the organic composition of capital[56] without international profit equalisation (Mandel) and with international profit equalisation (Szentes). Kay (1975) bases his theory of Unequal Exchange on the extraction of surplus value from non-capitalist areas by merchant capital, attributing the failure of peripheral countries to develop to the operation of this form of exploitation.

It is clear from the discussion in Subsection 4.2 that the surplus transfer theories can be re-formulated for the cases without factor mobility (Mandel and Kay) or with capital mobility (Szentes), but they still suffer from the difficulties elaborated concerning the usefulness of the Unequal Exchange of labour exploitation theory in providing a measure of the inequality of endowments.[57]

4. Domination, the international division of labour, and the developmental state

The general definition of exploitation discussed in Subsection 3.2 encompassed the concept of domination. Domination at the point of production can be

---

[55] Emmanuel originally presented his theory both in terms of a classical Marxian analysis of surplus transfer and in terms of a Sraffian model [Emmanuel (1972, ch. 2 and appendix 5)). In later elaborations, such as in Emmanuel (1975a, 1977), he made it quite clear that he preferred the Sraffian or neo-Ricardian framework since, as already noted, it is quite consistent with his theory for the surplus transfer to go in either direction. It is not surprising that the classical value representation of his theory led to a great deal of confusion as to what was the consistent essence of Emmanuel's theory [see, for example, Samuelson (1973, 1975, 1976)].

[56] The organic composition of capital is simply the capital/labour ratio or technical composition of capital measured in terms embodied labour [Marx (1867, ch. 25)].

[57] The attempt by Murray (1977, 1978) to base his drive for imperialism on the search for general and specific resources entirely outside the Unequal Exchange problematic avoids this problem and his theory of rent can be reformulated along the lines suggested in Subsection 2.3. When exploitation in trade is related to a commodity theory of money, as in Shaikh (1981, pp. 225–227) and Edwards (1985), fundamentalism cannot be rescued. In this case, the whole edifice breaks down once there is trade and specialisation in the production of the money commodity.

examined through a discussion of the organisation of work and the production process. In particular, no account has been given of how the employer extracts work from the labour power hired. The implications of this exclusion for the trade models discussed in Sections 2 and 3 are examined before looking briefly at the TNC and intra-firm trade from this perspective.

The Marxian and the structuralist-institutionalist literature has many examples of forms of domination. One of the classics in this literature is on trade and power by Sideri (1970).[58] However, this survey is not the place to attempt to give coherence to this wide-ranging literature or the literature on the rule of the military in development [see, for example, Kaldor (1976), Kaldor and Eide (1979) and Luckham (1985, 1987)]. Rather, the final subsection looks at the role of the state in the formulation of development policy and strategy.

4.1. The organisation of work and the production process

The large literature on the internal organisation of the firm and the organisation of work is in agreement on the importance of the conflict between individual and collective rationality at the point of production in any social system.[59] The distinctive Marxian contribution to this literature stresses the importance of class as an economic concept through the essential role of ownership of the means of production and the command over the production process thereby obtained. I will take up five propositions that arise from this literature:

(i) In general there will be a conflict between social welfare and profit maximisation when there are transactions costs and when preferences for work itself enters the individual utility function.

(ii) The organisation of production in the interest of profit acts to de-skill the workforce, reducing complex tasks performed by skilled labour to less complex tasks and less skilled labour, and also acts against social welfare.

(iii) Involuntary unemployment is a permanent feature of capitalism central to its institutional structure and growth process.

---

[58]Other examples include the discussion of the role of force in the development and enforcement of property relations [see, for example, Murray (1977, 1978) and the references cited therein], and more specific case studies such as the discussion of the role of the CIA in developing countries by Seers (1977), or economic and social cost of warfare in Southern Africa in Green (1987). Within the Dependency and World Systems schools, the analytical basis on which the study of domination proceeds is often weak, as in the case of imperialist domination in Braun's theory of market power discussed in Subsection 3.6, or the role of extra-market force in the Amin–Saigal theory of Unequal Exchange discussed earlier in Subsection 3.7.

[59]From a neo-classical perspective, some of the most influential contributions include Williamson (1975, 1985) and Lazear (1981). The most important contributions from a Marxian perspective include the over-all syntheses by Bowles (1985) and Pagano (1985).

(iv) Capitalists will generally select methods of production which forgo productive efficiency in favour of maintaining power over workers in the interests of profit.

(v) It will be in the interests of capitalists to undertake divide-and-rule strategies.

4.1.1. Discussion of propositions (i) and (ii)

The general problem of the divergence between the interests of the firm in cost minimisation and the interest of workers in welfare maximisation has a long literature. Adam Smith argued that specialisation of work increases job-specific skills due to improved dexterity, concentration on a particular task, and invention of machinery by workmen specialised in a particular field, but carried to the extreme would reduce work to soul-destroying repetitive tasks. The extent to which specialisation improves skills has long been debated. Babbage (1832) and Ure (1835) argued that the extreme specialisation is in fact associated with the absence of job-specific skill, the opposite of Smithian view on the division of labour. This is because the division of labour in the factory is associated with the creation of a hierarchy in terms of skill. Although at the top of the hierarchy job-specific skills are required, only some general skills such as particular forms of manual dexterity are required at the bottom of the hierarchy.

Babbage argued that simple cost-minimising behaviour makes the employer divide the work into different tasks, each requiring different degrees of skill and force, assigning them to different workers. A division of labour enables the entrepreneur to separate out the skilled from the unskilled tasks and pay the workers only according to the skills required for the particular tasks to be performed [Babbage (1832, pp. 137–138)]. Ure (1835) extended these ideas to the application of machinery in the factory production, arguing that a workman's job-specific skill, which Smith considers as the main advantage of the division of labour, is not only useless in the factory but also damaging [Ure (1835, p. 19)].[60] Carried to its logical limit, the full de-skilling of the workforce through the division of work into separate tasks lies at the heart of the Marxian argument that capitalism has tended to organise work in a hierarchical and dictatorial

---

[60] There is considerable evidence that the subdivision of the production process into elements and subsequent de-skilling of a large number of tasks has accompanied the evolution of the division of labour in modern industrial organisation. For example, Pratten (1980) argues that the division of labour on the shop floor has been actually abolished since jobs have become so simple that they can be rotated. Another important strand of development in the Marxian labour process literature stems from Taylor's scientific management [Taylor (1947)]. Braverman (1974, p. 119) argues that the essential element in Taylor's principles is "the systematic pre-planning and pre-calculation of all elements of the labour process, which now no longer exists as a process in the imagination of the worker but only as a process in the imagination of a special management staff".

manner, without account for the welfare derived from work itself, reducing complex and skilled labour power to a homogeneous labour power, maximising profit but not social welfare. This problem has been formalised by Pagano (1985, chs. 7–9).

Suppose that social welfare is a function of leisure activity, X_0, of the level of consumption of commodities, X, and of the different tasks, T, which may be required in the production of commodities by the workforce. This contrasts with the standard procedure based on the leisure semantic device, whereby only leisure and the consumption of commodities enter into the social welfare function [Pagano (1985, pp. 116–118)]. The tasks specify the work to be done by each skill category, how it is to be done, and the time allowed, for each commodity produced. When production is decentralised to representative firms, each of which produces one of n commodities produced, social welfare maximisation requires the solution of the following problem:

$$\max U(X_0, X, T)$$

$$\text{s.t. } X_{os} = T_{os},$$

$$X_i = f^i(T_i), \tag{16}$$

$$T_{os} + \sum_i \sum_j T_{ijs} = LP_s,$$

$$i = 1, \ldots, n; \ j = 1, \ldots, t; \ s = 1, \ldots, m,$$

where X_0 is the set of leisure activities by skill type; X is the set of commodity outputs X_i; T is the set of tasks T_{ijs} measured in units of time for each product i, task j and skill s; T_0 is the set of leisure time for each skill type; the function f^i is the production function relating output X_i to the set of tasks T_i required in the production of each commodity; and LP is the vector of supply of labour power. There are n commodities and n representative firms each specialising in one commodity, t tasks, and m skills.

Forming the Lagrangian, the first-order maximisation conditions (ignoring corner solutions) will be:

$$U_{xos} = \lambda_{os},$$

$$\lambda_{os} = \lambda_{ws},$$

$$U_{xis} = \lambda_{is}, \tag{17}$$

$$U_{Tijs} + \lambda_i f^i_{Tijs} = \lambda_{ws},$$

$$i = 1, \ldots, n; \ j = 1, \ldots, t; \ s = 1, \ldots, m,$$

where the λ's are the Lagrangian multipliers which can be interpreted as shadow prices. When each product is produced by many profit-maximising representative firms so that the shadow prices are interpreted as competitive market prices, it is evident from (17) that the competitive wage would have to be given by $w_{js} = \lambda_{ws} - U_{Tijs}$ ($j = 1, \ldots, t$; $s = 1, \ldots, m$). A wage bargain must be struck for every task and every skill category.

The above argument ignores transactions costs, for example costs incurred to achieve labour market mobility and costs to the firm in specifying wage bargains by skill and tasks. To the extent that transactions costs lead to a wage bargain to be struck only for each skill category, there will be a conflict between private profit maximisation and social welfare maximisation. Similar considerations lead to a possible conflict of interest between central planners and social welfare.

It is a straightforward matter to extend Pagano's argument to consider a change in the organisation of work or the matrix of tasks T_{ijs} which allows for some jobs to be redefined so that they can be done with fewer skills. It can be readily shown that such a reorganisation of work will be cost-minimising but not welfare-maximising when worker preferences for tasks are ignored by profit-maximising firms and when these preferences are not taken into account indirectly through the labour market. To the extent that worker preferences are not taken into account and jobs are de-skilled, workers will have an incentive to shirk. This leads directly to the problem of extracting work out of a given amount of labour power.

4.1.2. Discussion of propositions (iii), (iv) and (v)

The above assumes that the amount of work done on any task by a worker of any given skill is always equal to the total amount of labour power available. However, the specification of labour contracts is never, in practice, perfect. Given that worker preferences may not be fully taken into account by a profit-maximising firm and that there is scope for workers to pursue non-work activities whilst on the job, the firm has an incentive to incur a variety of costs directed towards extracting work from labour power. A recent synthesis of Marxian contributions to this problem can be found in Bowles (1985).

The amount of work done per unit of labour power purchased by the representative firm will depend on a variety of factors, including the worker's perception of the cost of pursuing non-work activity (e.g. the loss of the job due to detection), the use of production equipment and raw materials which decrease the opportunity for non-work activities, the extent to which the workforce is unified to resist divide-and-rule strategies of employers, and the general institutional environment surrounding the workforce. Thus, if the representative firm in a given industry j has a production function $X = f(K, L)$, where K is the amount of capital employed measured at a given set of commodity prices and L

is the amount of work required in production, the problem of extracting work out of labour power can be formalised by the work extraction function:

$$l^* = h(o, s, w^-, u, k), \tag{18}$$

where $l^* = L/LP$ is the amount of work obtained per unit of labour power, o is a vector reflecting the the general institutional environment surrounding the organisation of work, s is the amount of factory floor supervision per worker to prevent non-work activities, w^- is the cost to workers of losing their job if non-work activities are detected, u is a variable measuring worker unity, and k is the vector of non-labour inputs per worker.

The worker's perception of the fairness of the institutional environment o and its consistency with self-respect may affect the amount of work done for any given employer strategy. Employer expenditure on surveillance s will increase the probability that non-work activities will be detected. Increased cost of losing a job w^-, whether from the employer raising the worker's wage, a fall in the likelihood of obtaining alternative employment or from a lowering of the amount of income from non-work activities such as social security benefits, will increase the amount of work done. The degree of unity and cooperation in the workforce u (proxied by the degree of wage equality) will lower the probability that non-work activities will be detected, and the probability of termination of work if non-work activities are detected. The use of non-labour material inputs in production k – the factory itself, the assembly line, modern information systems – all increase the probability that non-work activities will be detected. On account of the above, it may be supposed that $h_o \geq 0$, $h_s \geq 0$, $h_{w^-} \geq 0$, $h_u \leq 0$, and $h_k \geq 0$.

The presence of these considerations will significantly affect the profit-maximising strategy of the firm facing competitive product markets. Thus, proposition (iii) will follow because the observed payment of significant surveillance costs by profit-maximising firms implies a positive cost (over and above transfer and relocation costs) to the employee of losing his or her job, since otherwise there could be no sanction for the pursuit of non-work activities. Such a cost would not exist if there was full employment at a competitive wage. Hence, involuntary unemployment will characterise the competitive equilibrium.

Proposition (iv) follows from the conjecture that, by creating divisions and hierarchies with the workforce, and discrimination by sex, race, and religion, the employer can foster envy, competition, and disunity, therefore lowering the capacity of workers to undermine surveillance and take action to protect their fellow workers' interests. This possibility is likely to override any account of individual workers' preferences for tasks discussed under (iii) above.

Proposition (v) follows from the observation that, under normal competitive conditions, the use of non-labour inputs will proceed up to the point where the marginal revenue product of the inputs (excluding any profit or interest paid) equals the price of the inputs. However, by using more non-labour inputs, a joint product of a service output, increased effectiveness of surveillance, takes place. The benefits of this in terms of increased work extraction will also have to be taken into account by the profit-maximising firm. This may lead to a Pareto-inefficient choice of technique which, in comparison with the standard competitive equilibrium, may use both more non-labour inputs and entail more work per unit of output. The relative importance of this under capitalism (and, for that matter, under existing socialism) depends on the class structure and the strength of worker resistance.

In total, the above propositions add a new dimension into the determination of comparative advantage – national differences in the worker extraction functions – as well as the analysis of the international division of labour through the TNC.

Recent literature on the labour process and technical change [see, for example, Schonberger (1982), Kaplinsky (1984, 1988, 1989), Piore and Sabel (1984), and Perez (1985)] suggests that radical changes are now taking place both in the production process and the nature of products produced. In this literature it is argued that the dominant mass production methods of the post-war period using specialised machinery to produce standardised products and the associated organisation of work have become increasingly rigid and inflexible, whereas the micro-electronic revolution allows the use of standardised machinery to produce differentiated products and requires for its effective implementation a far-reaching reorganisation of the social relations at the point of production. This has resulted in a change from de-skilling to multiple tasking of work for producing complex products, leading to cuts in transfer costs between different highly specialised processes, to just in time inventory holding and to a dramatic lowering of the cost of error rectification. In terms of equations (16), the new technologies imply a reorganisation of tasks T in such a way that job definition involves both more tasks and a higher level of skill. In some industries, the application of micro-electronic technologies has gone so far that it has become necessary to return to the worker a degree of control over the production process unthinkable in the era of assembly line production. Some of the implications of this literature on radical technical change and the organisation of work for trade policy will be taken up in Section 5.

4.2. The production process and international location

The above discussion suggests an important role for an additional determinant of comparative advantage – national differentiation of the labour extraction function and the organisation of work, and the capacity to change the organisation of work over time. Another aspect concerns the international location decisions of the TNCs.

The widespread importance of TNCs and intra-firm trade undermines the importance of arm's-length pricing in facilitating international trade. Helleiner (1981, pp. 10–13) summarises the range of empirical estimates for the aggregate importance of intra-firm trade and related party trade.[61] For example, he argues that at least 48 percent of U.S. imports in 1977 were sourced from related parties. Much of the Marxian discussion on the TNC itself has focused on aspects of control – control of resources, control of labour, control of markets, and control of economic policy through connections with the state [see, for example, Radice (1975) and Murray (1972)]. The labour process literature seeks to understand the intra-firm division of labour from the perspective of the organisation of work itself. This literature should be seen as complimentary to the standard literature on the TNC discussed by Helleiner in Chapter 27 of this Handbook.

The analysis of the stratification of industrial organisation in terms of a theory of international location, which might broadly be called the application of the Babbage principle to the understanding of the intra-firm division of labour within the TNC theory of international location, was originally elaborated by Hymer (1972).[62] He argued that the evolution of business enterprise from small work-shop to the Marshallian family firm and later to national and international corporations was accompanied by increasing growth in the horizontal and vertical division of labour within the firm. This evolution of corporate structure has given rise to three levels of business administration which can be located in different geographical regions. Level III, the lowest level concerned with managing the day-to-day operations of the enterprise, spread themselves over the globe according to the pull of labour power, raw materials, and markets. Level II activities, which are responsible for coordinating the managers al level III, tend to concentrate in large cities because of their need for white-collar workers, communications systems, and information. The functions of Level I (top management) are goal determination and planning and must be located close to the capital market, the media, and the government.

A more detailed application of the Babbage principle to the study of the international division of labour, particularly associated with the role of TNCs in relocating certian parts of production processes in developing countries since the

---

[61] For full discussion of this literature and the difficulty in defining intra-firm trade, see Chapter 27 in this Handbook.

[62] This view is broadly similar to Palloix (1973), who posits a dual labour market with a highly skilled, relatively small but well-paid workforce on the one hand, and the great majority of unskilled or semi-skilled, poorly paid workers on the other. He argues that this duality tends to reproduce itself increasingly at the international level and that industries based on large numbers of unskilled workers tend to move to the periphery, while the centre retains for itself the production which requires a highly trained workforce.

1960s, can be found in the work of Palloix (1973), Adam (1975), Froebel, Heinrichs and Kreye (1980), and Schmitz (1985) as the main explanation for what was called the New International Division of Labour (NIDL).[63]

The pattern of international location by the TNCs has not exploited the Babbage principle nearly as far as might have been expected on both theoretical grounds, and on the experience of the late 1960s and early 1970s. In fact, much of the rapid growth of manufactured exports from developing countries has taken place through national firms directly exploiting their comparative advantage, whether it be determined by endowments, institutional determinants of factor prices, technological differences, or differences in the organisation of work. Throughout the 1970s, it remained the case that most TNC involvement in the developing countries was either directly related to production for the domestic market, or for the exploitation of raw materials, rather than for the re-location of the labour-intensive processes either for re-export to their own branches or for export as final products on the world market [see MacEwan (1982)]. More recently, the pattern of comparative advantage may have reversed because of radical technical change arising from the application of the micro-economic revolution to production process and products [Hoffman and Kaplinsky (1984)]. This has reduced the share of labour input in many production processes which were formerly sufficiently labour intensive for TNCs to have located production in the Third World, and has increased the economics of proximity for the sourcing of inputs and final markets. However, it is not clear how much of the shift in location is due to a reversal of comparative advantage rather than the effects of increased non-tariff barriers to trade.

The NIDL literature, and indeed much of the Marxian literature, regards the behaviour of international capital as being relatively unconstrained by the state. Implicitly, it is argued that an all-powerful anthropomorphic "capital" can create the conditions required for its own reproduction through technical change or re-location to lessen its dependence on inputs which it cannot control. This perspective understates the role of the state as the institutional focus for the formulation and execution of development strategy and policy.

---

[63] This case-study literature has concentrated on the worldwide sourcing on TNCs looking for attractive locations for a number of industries which are intensive in use of unskilled labour in developing countries. This has been particularly important for traditional labour-intensive industries such as clothing, labour-intensive portions of technology-based industries such as electronics, and labour-intensive portions of mass consumption industries such as automotive components. There is also a case-study literature of the effects of the capacity of TNCs to organise the labour process in agricultural and raw material production in Third World countries in a way which minimises their dependence on either primary non-produced inputs such as land, or inputs of skilled labour. See the case studies by Cowen (1979, 1982) and Ellis (1978) and the study of the changing patterns of U.S. foreign investment by MacEwan (1982).

4.3. The development state

By now, there is a widespread consensus which recognises the importance of the state in the development process, reflect in the attention given to this issue in recent World Bank World Development Reports. However, there is less agreement on which aspects are most important – its class base, its administrative capacity, or its modes of intervention. Nor is there agreement on the most appropriate methods of analysis.

It appears that England, which up to the middle of the nineteenth century was the only industrial power, achieved the transition to modern economic growth without extensive state intervention except in the formation of economic rights. Nevertheless, this has not been the case for latecomers such as Germany, the United States, Japan, and most recently the Newly Industrialising Countries. The most well-known late eighteenth-century and nineteenth-century argument in favour of pervasive state intervention in the process of industrialisation and the development of a modern nation state is the infant industry and infant nation arguments [Hamilton (1791) and List (1885)]. More recently, Gerschenkron (1966), in analysing the industrialisation experience of the European countries (particularly germany and Russia) in the last century, argued that the more backward the economy, the greater was the part played by the state and other institutions in initiating and promoting industrial development. This view of the state as the main initiator of modern economic growth differs qualitatively from that of most neo-classical and Marxist perspectives.

State intervention from a neo-classical perspective is analysed in the context of market failure and the operation of interest group politics [see, for example, Bates (1981, 1983), Bhagwati (1982), Little (1982), Olsen (1982), and Srinivasen (1986)]. That is to say, in the presence of distortions and imperfections in commodity and factor markets, corrective policies are required for an efficient allocation of resources and the realisation of comparative advantage. In line with the authoritarian implications at the point of production of profit or growth maximisation discussed in the previous subsection, it is sometimes implicitly concluded that it may be in the national interest for the state to have sufficient centralised power to operate against interest group politics which distort the operation of the market.[64] This contradiction may go some way to account for the relative lack of concern of neo-classical commentators over the association of phases of economic "liberalisation" or the freeing of markets with authoritarian governments and the curtailment of political rights in many developing countries. This ignores the historical association of the evolution of economic rights in England required as a prerequisite for the development of civil society and a

---

[64] I am grateful to Theo Mars for making this point to me.

democratic political process to remove the arbitrary power of the monarchy.[65] Indeed, one of the factors inhibiting market-orientated economic reform and participation in world trade in the socialist countries is the slow progress in making the required political reforms.

A preliminary sketch of the role of the Developmental State can be found in Bardhan (1984). Although Bardhan's primary concern is with the Indian state, nevertheless his formulation has wider applicability for other developing countries. He argues that the state elite, with a sufficiently unified sense of ideological purpose about the desirability of national economic development, is the main instigator of development policies. Whilst there is a divergence in views about the extent of the autonomy of the state from class forces, Bardhan argues that in many cases of state-directed industrialisation, the leadership genuinely considers itself as the holder of the nation's deeply held normative aspirations.[66] In a world of international military and economic competition, these aspirations often take the form of striving for industrialisation and rapid economic growth.

The state in many developing countries, in addition to providing the basic infrastructure and institutional framework, has substantial power over control and ownership in circulation (banking, credit, transport, distribution, and foreign trade) and over-production (directly manufacturing much of the basic and capital commodities output). The state also regulates the patterns of private investment direction of resource allocation, choice of technology, and import control. However, while the state from its commanding heights formulates goals and policies, nevertheless it often cannot ignore the serious constraints on effective implementation of policies posed by the articulated interest of the propertied classes. When there is significant conflict of interests among those proprietary classes, there may be serious repercussions for the implementation of development policies.

A similar view of the state is presented by White and Wade (1988). They compare the nation-building strategies of the ruling elites of Taiwan and South Korea with those used in Latin America.[67] They argue that in the former countries the state has pursued a strategy of minimising commitments to existing social groups, particularly as a result of land reform which took place in the early 1950s. Whilst some bureaucratic authoritarian regimes in Latin

---

[65] This contradiction is well exemplified in World Bank (1987). The historical association of the evolution of economic rights with the evolution of democratic rights, is discussed in Box 4.2. The association of policies of market liberalisation in many developing countries with increased authoritarianism and the removal of democratic rights is omitted from the discussion of trade policy reform in Chapter 6 of the same publication.

[66] The relative autonomy argument is discussed by Nordlinger (1981), whilst Skocpol (1980) treats the state as a completely autonomous agent.

[67] Much of the literature on the Developmental State is directed against the prevailing neo-classical perspective, which tends to suggest that it was a combination of good policies and the invisible hand which was primarily responsible for the East Asian success stories. See also Jones and Sarkong (1980), Hamilton (1983, 1986), and Evans and Alizadeh (1984).

America may have wanted to do the same, many existing groups already had a considerable autonomy from the state and a capacity to exert influence against it when they came to power. These groups could only be put down by the exercise of great violence. In contrast, both Taiwan and South Korea experienced about 50 years of a hard, growth-oriented Japanese colonial rule which permitted the non-Japanese inhabitants almost no political activity or autonomous organisation of any kind. Later on, independent channels of interest aggregation and interest articulation were successfully prevented from joining together and acquiring autonomy from the state. As a result, the state managers in both countries have had considerable autonomy to define national goals and unusual powers to get those goals accomplished. It has not been necessary to enter into the bargaining process and shifting alliances which have characterised the policy process even in the more authoritarian regimes of Latin America, or the democratic regimes of India described by Bardhan.

The strength of the state at the national level in the formulation of development policy and strategy contrasts with the weakness of international state power for resolving economic conflict and developing international policies more conducive to development [Brett (1985)]. Rather, domination by states at the international level for the enforcement of property relations and the maintenance of political and military alliances through direct and threatened use of military power is all too evident. More subtly, military expenditure itself may have economic effects which makes the resolution of economic conflict in trade and macro adjustment problems more difficult [see, for example, Smith and Smith (1983) and Kaldor and Walker (1988)].

5. Trade and development strategy

Few would argue with the proposition that trade policy implications must derive from an over-all development strategy. There is less agreement when this general proposition is made more concrete, both in terms of the appropriate theory of trade policy and empirical rules of thumb and judgements which are made when implementing policy recommendations.

There is nothing intrinsic in the values or policy concerns addressed in the alternative perspectives which cannot be accommodated by the theory of trade policy discussed by Bliss in Chapter 23 of this Handbook, a view which is not widely shared within the literature surveyed. For example, the discussion of economic organisation in Subsections 4.2 and 4.3 can be accommodated by appropriate specification of the social welfare function within the general framework outlined by Bliss. For example, it is unlikely that the appropriate policy intervention to deal with any conflict between private profit and social welfare in economic organisations would involve directly limiting international trade. The general principle that the best forms of policy intervention tackle the inefficiency directly applies in this case, so that appropriate policies deal explicitly with the problems of economic organisation.

Some of the policy recommendations advocated within the alternative perspectives discussed derive from a faulty economic analysis. Perhaps the most glaring example is argument for semi-autarkic development based on Amin's theory of Unequal Exchange, but the problem is more pervasive. This is evident from the major area of trade policy initiative in the 1970s embodied in the call for a New International Economic Order (NIEO) and partially incorporated into the Brandt Commission [Brandt (1980, 1983)].

The call for a NIEO stems from the United Nations declaration of May 1974 and a number of related policy proposals by the developing countries calling for a reconstruction of the existing international economic system to improve the development prospects for developing countries, narrowing disparities between rich and poor countries and recognising the sovereign rights of nations, and giving them more control over the shape of their development goals and strategies.[68] It seems to me that there are three basic interrelated reasons why so little came out of the high ideals and hopes of this programme.

First, there was a strong emphasis on redistributive rather than productive strategies for development. This can be illustrated with reference the discussion of international inequality dealt with in Section 3. There is a fundamental tension between the entitlement theories based on labour rights, and on property rights [Sen (1981)]. The only area where the two approaches might coincide would be on the analysis of the processes by which the initial endowments were obtained. Such an audit would not be comfortable for property rights entitlement [see Nozick (1974)] insofar as force or non-competitive markets have been important both historically and in the current period in determining the initial endowments taken for granted prior to making ethical judgements on the justice of the international order. Furthermore, the ethical judgements for a redistributive strategy need to be rescued from naive anthropomorphic interpretations in which sovereign nations are treated as individuals. Consistent application of the labour entitlement basis of international redistributive justice requires that attention be paid not only to the per capita national product, but how this is distributed within each nation. Serious advocacy of such a radical international redistribution would require interference with national sovereignty to ensure that such internal redistributive policies were carried out.

Thus, when the OPEC countries radically increased the price of oil in 1973, many countries within the group of 77 Nations at UNCTAD saw this as showing the way for other redistributive policies such as the stabilisation and indexing of

---

[68] For an overview of the call for a NIEO, see Green and Singer (1975), Bhagwati (1977) and the Reports of the Commonwealth Group of Experts (1975, 1976, 1977).

commodity prices. There was also the feeling amongst many Third World governments that the international equivalent of union threats to strike could bring developed country governments into serious negotiation for a NIEO [see, for example, Green and Singer (1975, pp. 427–428) for a discussion]. The Group of 77 support for OPEC policies was based on the idea that the benefits both to OPEC countries and the redistribution to other developing countries through OPEC aid would far outweigh the costs to non-oil-developing countries through increased energy costs, and the extra strains that OPEC policies would place on the world economy. In effect, it was an attempt by developing countries to form a coalition to redistribute rents from the unequal per capita distribution of world energy resources from the rich to the poor. It was hoped that this could be achieved without off-setting direct costs through higher energy prices or indirect costs such as occurred through the strains in the international financial system which have, in part, been induced by OPEC policies. Judged in these terms, and by the lack of lasting developmental effects of high oil prices on many of the OPEC countries themselves, developing country support for OPEC must surely be judged as misconceived.[69]

Second, one of the key policy instruments designed to give effect to the NIEO, the Integrated Programme on Commodities (IPC) and the associated Common Fund to finance international commodity agreements was inefficient, inequitable, and impractical. It was inefficient because the transfers were to be made indirectly between developed country consumers and developing country producers, thus introducing a market distortion, rather than a direct transfer of resources. It was inequitable because some of the benefits of higher commodity prices would go to developed country consumers, and some of the costs would be borne by poor developing country consumers and marginal producers excluded by quota arrangements. It was impractical since the legitimate commodity price stabilisation component was linked with a commodity price indexing proposal with unpredictably large financing requirements. What hopes remained even for a truncated IPC were scuppered by the collapse of the well-established International Tin Agreement in 1985.[70]

Third, there is a strong tendency within much of the NIEO literature to over-emphasise the importance of the international context and class structure at the expense of national issues. There is much scope for the exploration of policy reform designed to enhance mutually gainful exchange such as advocated by Bhagwati and Ruggie (1984). Less radical redistributive strategies, such as the Rawlsian theory of justice which holds that economic inequalities are only acceptable if they can be shown to benefit the least advantaged in society, are

---

[69] I am grateful to Hans Singer for helpful discussions on these points.

[70] See Evans (1979) for a discussion of the IPC and the link between these proposals and the Unequal Exchange literature. For a recent summary of the objections to the IPC's and the current state of negotiations, see Toye (1987, ch. 7).

potentially much more feasible [see, for example, the Basic Needs approach discussed by Streeten and others (1981) and the discussion of aid and trade policy by Toye (1987, ch. 7)]. Moreover, a development strategy orientated towards productive rather than redistributive policies leading to the rapid accumulation of productive assets, might achieve both national and international distributive justice, as is often argued in the case of South Korea.

If the theory of policy analysis is on the side of orthodoxy, are the empirical rules of thumb and judgements made in the application of that theory adequate? To what extent are the values of policy advocates separated from the positive content of the theoretical and empirical components of policy analysis? The final part of this section looks at four aspects of policy application where there may be some doubts on these issues.

First, as argued in Evans and Alizadeh (1984), the typically applied rules of thumb in evaluating infant industry protection – learning periods of about 5 years and a maximum effective protection of 10–20 percent optimally administered through subsidies rather than tariffs or import controls – would seem to be much too conservative, judging at least from the historical experience of South Korea and Taiwan.[71] Yet there is no well-formulated alternative set of rules of thumb or analysis of incentive structures which opponents of neo-classical orthodoxy are able to cite when using the success stories, such as Japan's successful infant industries of the 1950s, particularly automobiles, steel and electronics, as evidence of the failure of orthodox policy prescriptions.[72]

In a similar vein, the empirical link between price distortions or outward orientation and either growth performance and export performance is not as clear-cut as argued in the conventional literature [see, for example, the critique of Agarwala (1983) and the World Bank (1983, ch. 6) in Aghazadeh and Evans (1988), Griffin (1989) and Evans (1989)]. Moreover, since there is no theoretical reason why higher growth leads to higher social welfare, the link between growth and efficiency is not well established.[73] In the case of the discussion of outward orientation based on a study of a sample of 41 countries [World Bank (1987, ch. 5)], a far less glowing account of the benefits of outward orientation, growth, and efficiency emerges if the extreme observations are eliminated. This might be done

---

[71] I am grateful to David Wall for advice on the prevailing rules of thumb for infant industry protection. Whilst the rule of thumb should be based on empirical experience, this is a typical "grey" area in which some aspects of reality are seen by one school but not by another. For example, neo-classical commentators advocating market selection mechanisms cite the failure of some states to "pick the winners". They seldom point to empirical evidence that market processes can fail to achieve this as well, for example through takeover bids [see Singh (1975)].

[72] This is the story which seems to be behind the Cambridge (England) macro arguments for protection, now exported for developing countries wishing to grow their way out of the current crisis [see, for example, Singh (1984) for the outline of the argument and the response by Balassa (1985)].

[73] Improved price efficiency usually leads to a once-and-for-all shift in the level of income when resources are fully employed. When there is unemployed labour and an institutionally fixed wage, improved price efficiency may lead to higher profits and therefore higher growth.

on the grounds that the successful strongly outward orientated countries (South Korea, Singapore, and Hong Kong) are either city states or exemplary nation states whose experience cannot easily be generalised. Similarly, the strongly inward orientated countries are made up of a rag-bag of countries with a wide variety of special factors which may have operated with inward orientation to produce poor economic performance. It is not possible to reach any strong conclusions based on the comparison of the moderately outward and the moderately inward orientated countries. Whilst such statistical exercises cannot give clear-cut empirical answers about the association growth or efficiency with greater trade or fewer price distortions, they have been widely used in recent years to support the case for outward orientation. There is little doubt that a large number of developing countries which would come under the criterion of "strongly inward orientated" are in urgent need of trade and other policy reform. However, in the present context of an increasingly uncertain and sluggishly growing world economy, it is by no means clear that a shift from moderately inward to moderately outward orientation, or from moderately outward orientated to strongly outward orientated policies, would improve economic performance. Furthermore, increased outward orientation of developing countries may have favourable effects on income distribution, as in the case of South Korea, but the very same success stories are likely to have serious implications for the industrial countries if pursued on a large scale. At a minimum there would be large transitional costs [Beenstock (1984)] and possibly also permanent problems caused by reductions in the demand for unskilled labour relative to capital and skilled labour [Bienefeld and Godfrey (1982), Wood (1986)].

However, given the interests of the international agencies such as UNCTAD, the IMF, and the World Bank in representing the views of the member governments which dominate these institutions, there is too often little space for discussion of the types of coalitions of domestic interest groups and classes which might be able to implement more egalitarian and productively orientated strategies in a hostile world environment.

Second, the discussion of domination at the point of production in Subsection 4.2 suggests the need for a closer examination of what might be called Directly Profit-seeking Control in which the conflict between profit and growth on the one hand, and social welfare and equity on the other, is explored. Such a discussion would provide a useful counterpoint to the well-established literature on Directly-unproductive Profit-seeking Activity, or DUP, which extends and generalises the concept or rent-seeking activity [see Krueger (1974) and Bhagwati (1982)]. Whilst the latter emphasises the expenditure of resources for unproductive lobbying and other such activities, the former emphasises the expenditure of resources for increasing profitable activity. In fact, either type of expenditure may be welfare-reducing under existing institutional and organisational arrangements. This has important implications for both technology and industrial policies, where new institutions and forms of organisation of work may be required to overcome market failure. For example, World Bank (1987, Box 4.4) concludes that the role of government as a coordination and information clearing house had an important productive role in East Asian States, a view resisted by many neo-classical economists who argue that the same East Asian states succeeded because they "got their prices right".

In a similar vein, the organisational considerations and the possibilities for radical technical change discussed in Subsections 4.1 and 4.2 can have important policy implications. In a recent study of the industrial sector in Cyprus, Murray et al. (1987) argue that new institutional arrangements combined with changes in attitudes and the over-all organisation of work will be necessary for a small-firm economy to be able to take advantage of new product and process technology. Many of the policy recommendations follow from standard arguments for market intervention based on imperfect information, scale economies, public goods, learning, and externalities. In practice this means finding the appropriate institutional and organisational innovations to enable the functions of the head office of a large firm to be carried out in a small-firm environment.

Third, the literature on the Developmental State discussed in Subsection 4.4 suggests a considerably greater complexity of interaction between the command economy of the state and the decentralised institutions of the market than is often reflected in the policy statements of the international agencies such as the World Bank, or in the neo-classical literature such as Little (1982). An example of this is discussed in Aghazadeh and Evans (1988) in relation to the contribution of price efficiency, and the effectiveness of state institutions, to growth. Whilst there may now be now widespread agreement on the general problem identified, there is less agreement on the details of how major price policy (including trade policy) reform should be combined with institutional reform, and the class and interest group coalitions which may be able to implement such a package [for a recent discussion of some of these issues in relation to Sub-Saharan Africa, see Bates (1986), Bienefeld (1986), White (1986), and Colclough (1988)].

Finally, the literature on the role of the military in development cited in the brief discussion of international domination at the end of Subsection 4.3, draws attention to the increasingly close interconnections between strategic interests, arms trade, and trade policy in general. However, in the absence of any theory of arms trade in the standard trade literature, it is difficult to move beyond the exogenous treatment of "national" or "strategic" interests in the discussion of this aspect of trade policy discussion.[74]

---

[74] It is difficult to establish accurate measures of the importance of arms trade in total world trade, and no single index captures its importance for developing countries. The best source on arms trade is the SIPRI Year Book, which suggests that about 2.5 percent of developed country exports, and about 6 percent of less developed country imports, is accounted for by arms trade. See also Kaldor (1975).

6. Concluding remarks

To what extent does the literature discussed in this chapter help answer the five questions asked in the Introduction?

(i) Much of the literature discussed in Sections 2 and 4 suggests an alternative to the Smithian view of the institutional and organisational environment influencing the relationship between trade and growth. The central thrust of the argument in these sections is compatible with the idea that trade can be the "handmaiden" of growth. However, it was found in Subsection 3.7 that the Dependency and World Systems view that trade leads to development in the centre and underdevelopment in the periphery was based, at best, on an inconsistent model of trade.

(ii) Carried to its logical limits, the achievement of international distributive justice based on the elimination of all reproducible endowment and wage differences between nations discussed in Sections 3 and 5, would restrict the basis of trade to differences in the per capita endowments of natural resources and differential needs. Such an ideal world would of necessity bring trade based on technology, product, and market structure to the forefront. However, given the disparities in the world distribution of productive assets which will exist for the foreseeable future, it would seem both unwise and unnecessary to ignore a role for resource-based trade as is often done in the alternative perspectives literature on trade and development issues.

(iii) On the positive side, some of the literature discussed in Sections 4 and 5 that there is a more important direct role for the state and other non-market institutions at the national and sectoral level, and for organisational innovation, than is sometimes suggested in the mainstream literature on trade policy instruments. On the negative side, the discussion in Section 5 of the NIEO literature joined the chorus of criticism of the inefficient and impractical policy instruments chosen to the exclusion of policies based on mutal gain.

(iv) It was suggested in Section 2 that a circulating capital model in the Ricardo–Ohlin–Lewis tradition provides a useful starting point for the analysis of many trade and development issues. However, the literature surveyed in this chapter has almost nothing to add to the standard theory of trade policy, but does have some original and important implications (discussed in Section 5) for the role of institutions in the application of trade policy.

(v) A central theme of the chapter has been that systematic consideration of class, inequality, and power can be brought to bear on trade and development issues without loss of analytical rigour, as is all too often the case in the alternative perspectives literature. Class is important for the international and national analysis of distribution and inequality for domination in the maintenance of property relations, in the economic effects of domination at the point of production, and in the analysis of the developmental state. In all of these ways, class has direct and indirect implications for the analysis of trade and development. These considerations in part influenced the choice of model in Section 2, but were more systematically addressed in the discussion of exploitation and domination in Sections 3 and 4.

Some areas where there is scope for additional research have already been identified, ranging from the use of trade models in the study of imperialism to some applied trade policy questions discussed in Section 5. Little has been said about the formal analysis of transitions between modes of production in dynamic models of trade and development, nor about the comparative static analyses of trade between different modes of production. In their different ways, the microeconomic analysis of land-abundant and land-scarce peasant economies in Binswanger and McIntire (1984) and Binswanger and Rosenzweig (1986) beg to be married with some of the more anthropologically orientated literature on exchange in pre-capitalist economies [such as the analysis of gift exchange in Gregory (1982) or the literature on long-distance trade exemplified by Meillassoux (1971) and Terray (1974)]. Last but not least, there is a great deal more to be gained from productive cross-fertilisation of competing perspectives than from some efforts to deliver a knockout blow. Attempts by proponents of orthodoxy to claim a monopoly of the truth are as unhelpful as the purist versions of alternative perspectives which reject or ignore the lessons which orthodox theory can offer.

References

Adam, G. (1975) 'Multinational corporations and world-wide sourcing', in: H. Radice, ed., *International firms and modern imperialism*. Harmondsworth: Penguin.

Addo, H. (ed.) (1984) *Transforming the world economy*. London: Hodder and Stroughton in conjunction with UNU.

Agarwala, R. (1983) 'Price distortions and growth in developing countries', World Bank Staff Working Paper no. 575, Management & Development Series, International Bank for Reconstruction and Development, Washington, DC.

Aghazadeh, E. and H.D. Evans (1988) 'Price distortions, efficiency and growth', mimeo, IDS, University of Sussex.

Amin, S. (1973) L'éxchange inegal et la loi sur la valuer: La fin d'un debat, avec une contribution de J.C. Saigal. Paris: editions Anthrohopos–IDEP. English translation, excluding Saigal's contribution, in Section IV of S. Amin (1977) *Imperialism and unequal development*. Hassocks: Harvester Press.

Andersson, J.O. (1976) *Studies in the theory of unequal exchange between nations*. Abo: Abo Akademi.

Babbage, C. (1832) *On the economy of machinery and manufactures*. London: Charles Knight.

Bacha, E.L. (1978) 'An interpretation of unequal exchange from Prebisch–Singer to Emmanuel', *Journal of Development Economics*, 5, no. 4.

Balassa, R. (1985) 'The Cambridge group and the developing countries', *The World Economy*, 8, no. 3: 201–218.

Bardhan, P.K. (1970) *Economic growth development and foreign trade: A study in pure theory*. New York: Wiley.

Bardhan, P.K. (1982) 'Unequal exchange in a Lewis-type world' in: M. Gersovits and others, eds., *The theory and experience of economic development*. London: George Allen and Unwin.
Bardhan, P.K. (1984) *The political economy of development in India*. Oxford: Basil Blackwell.
Barratt-Brown, M. (1974) *The economics of imperialism*. Harmondsworth: Penguin.
Bates, R.H. (1981) *Markets and states in tropical Africa*. Berkeley: University of California Press.
Bates, R.H. (1983) *Essays on the political economy of rural Africa*. Cambridge: Cambridge University Press.
Bates, R.H. (1986) 'The politics of agricultural policy – A reply', *IDS Bulletin*, January.
Beenstock, M. (1984) *The world economy in transition*. London: Allen and Unwin.
Bhagwati, J.N. ed. (1977) *The new international economic order*: *The north–south dialogue debate*. Cambridge, MA: MIT Press.
Bhagwati, J.N. (1982) 'Directly unproductive, profit-seeking (DUP) activities', *Journal of Political Economy*, 90, no. 5:988–1002.
Bhagwati, J.N. and J.G. Ruggie, eds. (1984) *Power, passions and purpose*: *Prospects for north–south negot*. Cambridge, MA: M.I.T. Press.
Bienefeld, M. (1986) 'Analysing the politics of African state policy: Some thoughts on Robert Bates' work', *IDS Bulletin*, January:5–11.
Bienefeld, M.S. and M. Godfrey, eds. (1982) *The struggle for development*: *National strategies in an international context*. London: Wiley.
Binswanger, H.P. and J. McIntire (1984) 'Behavioural and material determinants of production relations in land abundant tropical agriculture', World Bank Report no. ARU 17, Research Unit, Agricultural and Rural Development Department, Operational Policy Staff, International Bank for Reconstruction and Development, Washington, DC.
Binswanger, H.P. and M.R. Rosenzweig (1986) 'Behavioural and material determinants of production relations in agriculture', *Journal of Development Studies*, 22, no. 3:503–539.
Bowles, S. (1985) 'The production process in a competitive economy: Walrasian, neo-Hobbesian and Marxian models', *American Economic Review*, 75, no. 1:16–36.
Brandt, W. (1980) *North–south*: *A programme for survival*. London: Pan.
Brandt, W. (Brandt Commission) (1983) *Common crisis north–south*: *Co-operation for world recovery*. London: Pan.
Braun, O. (1973) *Commercio internacional e imperialismo*. Buenos: Siglo XXI Argentina Editores SA. English translation *International trade and imperialism*. Atlantic Highlands: Humanities Press, 1984.
Braverman, H. (1974) *Labor and monopoly capital*: *The degradation of work in the twentieth century*. New York: Monthly Review Press.
Brenner, R. (1976) 'Agrarian class structure and economic development in pre-industrial Europe', *Past and present*, 70:30–75.
Brenner, R. (1977) 'The origins of capitalist development: A critique of neo-Smithian Marxism', *New Left Review*, 104, July/August.
Brenner, R. (1986) 'The Social Basis of Development', in: Roemer, J.E., ed., *Analytical Marxism*. Cambridge: Cambridge University Press.
Brett, E.A. (1985) *The world economy since the war*: *The politics of uneven development*, London: MacMillan.
Brewer, A. (1980) *Marxist Theories of Imperialism*: *A Critical Survey*. London: Routledge and Kegan Paul.
Caves, R.E. (1963) *Trade and Economic Structure*. Cambridge, MA: Harvard University Press.
Caves, R.E. (1982) *Multinational Enterprise and Economic Analysis*. Cambridge: Cambridge University Press.
Cohen, G.A. (1978) *Karl Marx's theory of history*: *A defense*. Oxford: Oxford University Press.
Cohen, G.A. (1986) 'Forces and relations of production', in: Roemer, J.E., ed., *Analytical Marxism*. Cambridge: Cambridge University Press.
Colclough, C. (1988) 'Zambian adjustment strategy: With and without the IMF', *IDS Bulletin*, 19, no. 1:51–60.
Commonwealth Secretariat (1975) 'Towards a new international economic order', Report by a Commonwealth Group of Experts, London. Further Report (1976); Final Report (1977).

Corden, W.M. and J.P. Neary (1982) 'Booming sector and de-industrialisation in a small open economy', *Economic Journal*, 92, no. 368.

Cowen, M.P. (1979) 'Capital and household production: The case of Wattle in Kenya's central province 1903–64', Ph.D. thesis, University of Cambridge.

Cowen, M.P. (1982) 'The British state and agrarian accumulation in Kenya', in: M. Fransman, ed., *Industry and accumulation in Africa*. London: Heinemann.

Deardorff, A.V. (1974) A geometry of growth and trade, *Canadian Journal of Economics*, 7, no. 2: 295–306.

Deardorff, A.V. (1984) 'Testing trade theories and predicting trade flows' in: R.W. Jones and P.B. Kenen, eds., *Handbook of international economics*, Vol. 1. Amsterdam: North-Holland.

Delarue, A. (1975) 'Elements d'economie néo-Ricardienne', *Revue Economique*, 2, no. 3.

Dixit, A. (1981) 'The export of capital theory', *Journal of International Economics*, 11, no. 2:279–295.

Edwards, C. (1985) *The fragmented world: Competing perspectives on trade, money and crisis*. London: Methuen.

Ellis, F. (1978) 'The banana export activity in Central America 1967–1976: A case study of plantations by vertically integrated transnational corporations', Ph.D. Thesis, University of Sussex.

Elson, D., ed (1979) *Value: The representation of labour in capitalism*. London: CSE Books.

Emmanuel, A. (1972) *Unequal exchange: a study in the imperialism of trade*. London: New Left Books.

Emmanuel, A. (1975a) 'Unequal exchange revisited', Discussion Paper no. 77, Institute of Development Studies, University of Sussex.

Emmanuel, A. (1975b) 'Unequal exchange (a summary)', paper presented to a conference on new approaches to trade, Institute of Development Studies, Sussex.

Emmanuel, A. (1977) 'Gains and losses from the international division of labour', *Review*, 1, no. 2.

Ethier, W. (1979) 'The theorems of international trade in time phased economies', *Journal of International Economics*, 9:225–238.

Ethier, W. (1981) 'A reply to Professors Metcalfe and Steedman', *Journal of International Economics*, 11:273–277.

Evans, H.D. (1972) *A general equilibrium analysis of protection: The effects of protection in Australia*. Amsterdam: North-Holland.

Evans, H.D. (1979) 'International commodity policy: UNCTAD and NIEO in search of a rationale', *World Development*, 7, no. 3:259–279.

Evans, H.D. (1980) 'Emmanuel's theory of unequal exchange: Critique, counter critique and theoretical contribution', Discussion Paper no. 149, Institute of Development Studies, University of Sussex.

Evans, H.D. (1981a) 'Trade, production and self reliance', in D. Seers, ed., *Dependency theory: A critical assessment*. London: Frances Pinter.

Evans, H.D. (1981b) 'Unequal exchange and economic policies: Some implications of the neo-Ricardian critique of the theory of comparative advantage', in: I. Livingstone, ed., *Development economics and policy: Readings*. London: George Allen and Unwin.

Evans, H.D. (1981c) 'Monopoly power and imperialism: Oscar Braun's theory of unequal exchange', *Development and Change*, 12:601–610.

Evans, H.D. (1984) 'A critical assessment of some neo-Marxian trade theories', *Journal of Development Studies*, 20, no. 2:202–226.

Evans, H.D. (1985), 'Back to Benoit', *IDS Bulletin*, 16, no. 4.

Evans, H.D. (1986) 'Reverse Dutch disease and mineral exporting developing economies', *IDS Bulletin*, 17, no. 4:10–13.

Evans, H.D. (1987) 'The long-run determinants of the north south terms of trade and some recent empirical evidence', special issue on commodities of *World Development*, edited by Alf Maizels, 15, no. 5:657–671

Evans, H.D. (1989) *Comparative advantage and growth: Trade and development in theory and practice*. Hemel Hempstead: Wheatsheaf Press (forthcoming).

Evans, H.D. and P. Alizadeh (1984) 'Trade, industrialisation and the visible hand', *Journal of Development Studies*, 21, no. 1:22–46.

Findlay, R. (1974) 'Relative prices, growth and trade in a simple Ricardian system', *Economica*, 41:1–13.

Findlay, R. (1982) 'On Arthur Lewis's contribution to economics', in M. Gersovitz and others, eds., *The theory and experience of economic development*. London: George Allen and Unwin.

Findlay, R. (1984) 'Growth and development in trade models', in: R.W. Jones and P.P. Kenen, eds., Handbook of international economics, Vol. 1. Amsterdam: North-Holland.

Fine B. and L. Harris (1979) *Re-reading capital*. London: MacMillan.

Foster-Carter, A. (1978) 'The modes of production controversy', *New Left Review*, 107, Jan./Feb.

Frank, A.G. (1978) *Dependent accumulation and under-development*, London: MacMillan.

Froebel, F., J. Heinrichs, and O. Kreye (1980) *The new international division of labour*. Cambridge: Cambridge University Press.

Garegnani, P. (1983) 'The classical theory of wages and the role of demand schedules in the determination of relative prices', *American Economic Review*, 73, no. 2:309–313.

Gerschenkron, A. (1966) *Economic Backwardness in Historical Perspective: A Book of Essays*. Cambridge, MA: The Belknap Press of Harvard University Press.

Gersovitz, M. and others, eds. (1982) *The theory and experience of economic development*. London: George Allen and Unwin.

Green, R.H. (1987) 'Killing the dream: The political and human economy of war in sub-Saharan Africa, IDS Discussion Paper no. 238, University of Sussex.

Green, R.H. and H.W. Singer (1975) 'Towards a rational and equitable new international economic order: A case for negotiated structural changes', *World Development*, 3, no. 6: 427–444.

Greenaway, D. and C. Milner (1987) 'Trade theory and LDC's', in: N. Gemmell, ed., *Surveys in development economics*. Oxford: Blackwell.

Gregory, C.A. (1982) *Gifts and commodities*. London: Academic Press.

Griffin, K. (1978) *International inequality and national poverty*. London: MacMillan.

Griffin, K. (1989) *Alternative strategies for economic development*. London: MacMillan.

Hamilton, A. (1791) 'Encouragement of manufacturers', in: R.B. Morris, ed., *Alexander Hamilton & the Founding of the Nation*. New York: Harper & Row, 1957.

Hamilton, C. (1983) 'Capitalist industrialisation in East Asia's four little tigers, *Journal of Contemporary Asia*, 13, no. 1:35–73.

Hamilton, C. (1986) *Capitalist industrialisation in the third world: Revelations from South Korea*. Boulder: Westview Press.

Harris, J.R. and M.P. Todaro (1970) 'Migration, unemployment and development', *American Economic Review*, 60:126–142.

Havrylyshyn, O. (1985) 'The direction of developing country trade: Empirical evidence of differences between south–south and south–north trade', *Journal of Development Economics*, 19, no. 3:255–281.

Helleiner, G.K. (1981) *Intra-firm trade and the developing countries*. London: MacMillan.

Hymer, S. (1972) 'The multinational corporation and the law of uneven development', in: J. Bhagwati, ed., *Economics and the world order from the 1970s to the 1990s*. New York: Collier-MacMillan. Reprinted in Radice (1975).

Hoffman, K. and R. Kaplinsky (1984) 'Changing patterns of industrial location and international competition: The role of TNCs and the impact of microelectronics', Project prepared for UNCTC. New York 1984.

Johnson, H.G. (1955) 'International expansion and international trade', *Manchester School of Economic and Social Studies*, 23, no. 2. Reproduced in *International trade and economic growth*. Cambridge, MA: Harvard University Press, Ch. 3. 1967.

Jones, R.W. (1971) 'A three-factor model in theory, trade, and history', in J.N. Bhagwati, R.W. Jones, R.A. Mundell, and J. Vanek, eds., *Trade, balance of payments, and growth: Essays in honour of Charles P. Kindleberger*. Amsterdam: North-Holland.

Jones, R.W. and P.B. Kenen, eds. (1984) *Handbook of international economics*, Vol. 1. Amsterdam: North-Holland.

Jones, L.P. and I.L. Sarkong (1980) *Government business and entrepreneurship in economic development: The Korean case*. Cambridge, MA: Harvard University Press.

Kaldor, N. (1955) 'Alternative theories of distribution', *Review of Economic Studies*, 23:83–98.

Kaldor, M. (1975) 'Towards a theory of the arms trade', mimeo, Brighton, IDS, University of Sussex.

Kaldor, M. (1976) 'The military in development', *World Development*, 6:453–482.

Kaldor, M. and A. Eide, eds. (1979) *The world military order*. London: MacMillan.

Kaldor, M. and W. Walker (1988) 'Military technology and the loss of industrial dynamism', mimeo, SPRU, University of Sussex.

Kanbur, R. and J. McIntosh (1984) 'Dual economy models: Retrospect and prospect', Department of Economics, University of Essex.

Kaplinsky, R. (1984) *Automation: The technology and society*. London: Longmans.

Kaplinsky, R. (1989) 'Technology, employment and comparative advantage', in: C. Pratt, ed., *Some western middle powers and global poverty*: Vol. III, *Country Studies*. Kingston: Queens University Press.

Kaplinsky, R. (1988) 'Restructuring the capitalist labour process: Some lessons from the automobile industry', *Cambridge Journal of Economics* 12, no. 4:451–470.

Kay, G. (1975) *Development and underdevelopment: A Marxist analysis*. London: MacMillan.

Kemp, M.C. (1984) 'Natural resources in trade models' in: R.W. Jones and P.B. Kenen, eds., *Handbook of international economics*, Vol. 1. Amsterdam: North-Holland.

Kravis, I.B. (1970) 'Trade as a handmaiden of growth: Similarities between the nineteenth and twentieth centuries', *Economic Journal*, 80:850–872.

Krueger, A.O. (1974) 'The political economy of rent seeking society', *American Economic Review*, 64:291–303.

Krueger, A.O. (1977) 'Growth, distortions and the pattern of trade among many countries', Princeton studies in international finance no. 40, Princeton University.

Krugman, P. (1981) 'Trade, accumulation and uneven development', *Journal of Development Economics*, 8, no. 2:149–161.

Lazear, E. (1981) 'Agency, earnings profiles, productivity, and hours restrictions', *American Economic Review*, 71:606–620.

Leamer, E.E. (1984) *Sources of international comparative advantage: Theory and evidence*. Cambridge, MA: MIT Press.

Lewis, W.A. (1954) 'Economic development with unlimited supplies of labour', *Manchester School*, 22, no. 2: 139–191.

Lewis, W.A. (1969) *Aspects of tropical trade 1883–1965*. Stockholm: Almqvist and Wiksel.

Lewis. W.A. (1973) 'Reflections on unlimited labour', in: L.E. DiMarco, ed., *International economics and development: Essays in honour of Raul Prebisch*. New York: Academic.

Lewis, W.A. (1980) 'The slowing down of the engine of growth' (the Nobel lecture), *American Economic Review*, 70, no. 4:555–564.

List, F. (1885) *The national system of political economy*. London: Longmans, Green & Co.

Little, I.M.D. (1982) *Economics development theory, policy and international relations*. New York: Basic Books.

Luckham, R. (1985) 'Anarchy or transformation? Scenarios for change', *IDS Bulletin*, October.

Luckham, R. (1987) 'Europe, the NATO Alliance and the third world: Can they be Dealigned?' in: M. Kaldor and R. Falk, eds., *Dealignment: A new foreign policy perspective*. Oxford: Blackwell.

MacEwan, A. (1982) 'Slackers, bankers, marketers: Direct investment: A working paper', Department of Economics, University of Massachussetts, Harbour Campus.

Maddison, A. (1982) *Phases of capitalist development*. Oxford: Oxford University Press.

Mainwaring, L. (1979) 'On the transition from autarky to trade', in Steedman (1979c).

Mainwaring, L. (1980) 'International trade and the transfer of labour value', *Journal of Development Studies*, 17, no. 1.

Mainwaring, L. (1984) *Value and distribution in capitalist economics: An introduction to Sraffian Economics*. Cambridge: Cambridge University Press.

Magdoff, H. (1978) *Imperialism: From the colonial age to the present*. New York: Monthly Review Press.

Mandel, E. (1976) *Late Capitalism*. London: New Left Books.

Marglin, S.A. (1976) *Value and price in the labour-surplus economy*. Oxford: Clarendon Press.

Marglin, S.A. (1984) Growth, distribution, and inflation: A centennial synthesis. *Cambridge Journal of Economics*, 8:115–144.

Marx, K. (1867) *Capital*, Vol. 1. Harmondsworth: Penguin Books Edition, 1976.

Meillassoux, C. ed. (1971) 'Introduction', *The Development of Indigenous Trade and Markets in West Africa*. Oxford: Oxford University Press.

Metcalfe, J.S. and I. Steedman (1972) 'Reswitching and primary input use', *Economic Journal*, 82. Reprinted in Steedman (1979c).

Metcalfe, J.S. and I. Steedman (1973) 'Heterogeneous capital and the Heckscher–Ohlin–Samuelson theory of trade', J.M. Parkin, ed., *Essays in Modern Economics*. London: Longmans. Reprinted in Steedman (1979c).

Metcalfe, J.S. and I. Steedman (1981) 'On the transformation of theorems', *Journal of International Economics*, 11:267–271.

Morishima, M. and G. Catephores (1978) *Value, exploitation and growth*. London: McGraw-Hill.

Murray, R. (1972) 'Underdevelopment, international firms and the international division of labour', in: *Towards a new world economy*. Rotterdam: Rotterdam University Press.

Murray, R. (1977, 1978) 'Value and theory of rent: Parts I and II', *Capital and Class*, 3:100–122 and 4:1–33.

Murray, R. et al. (1987) 'Cyprus industrial strategy: Report of the UNDP/UNIDO mission', IDS, University of Sussex.

Myint, H. (1958) 'The "classical theory" of international trade and the underdeveloped countries', *Economic Journal*, 68, no. 270:317–337.

Neary, J.P. (1985) 'Theory and policy of adjustment in an open economy', in: D. Greenaway, ed., *Current issues in international trade: Theory and policy*. London: MacMillan.

Nordlinger, E. (1981) *On the autonomy of the democratic state*. Cambridge, MA: Harvard University Press.

Nozick, R. (1974) *Anarchy, state and utopia*. Oxford: Basil Blackwell.

Ocampo, J.A. (1986) 'New developments in trade theory and LDCs', *Journal of development economics*, 22, no. 1.

Ohlin, B. (1933) *Interregional and international trade*, Harvard Economic Studies, Vol. 36. Cambridge, MA: Harvard University Press.

Olsen, M. (1982) *The rise and decline of nations*. New Haven: Yale University Press.

Pagano, U. (1985) *Work and welfare in economic theory*. Oxford: Basil Blackwell.

Palloix, C. (1973) *Les firmes internationales et le proces d'internationalisation*. Paris: Maspero. English extract printed in: H. Radice, ed., *International firms and modern imperialism*. Harmondsworth: Penguin.

Palma, G. (1978) 'Dependency: A formal theory of underdevelopment, or a theology, for the analysis of situations of underdevelopment', *World Development*, 6, no. 7/8:882–924. Reprinted in: D. Seers, ed., *Dependency theory: A critical assessment*. London: Frances Pinter.

Pasinetti, L.L. (1981) *Structural change and economic growth*. Cambridge: Cambridge University Press.

Perez. C. (1985) 'Microelectronics, long wages and structural change: New perspectives for developing countries', *World Development*, 13, no. 3:441–463.

Piore, M.J. and C.F. Sabel (1984) *The second industrial divide: Possibilities for prosperity*. New York: Basic Books.

Pratten, C.F. (1980) 'The manufacture of pins', *Journal of Economic Literature*, 18:93–96.

Prebisch, R. (1950) *The economic development of Latin America and its principal problems*. New York: United Nations.

Radice, H., ed. (1975) *International firms and modern imperialism*. Harmondsworth: Penguin.

Raffer, K. (1987) *Unequal exchange and the evolution of the world system*. London: MacMillan.

Riedel, J. (1984) 'Trade as the engine of growth in developing countries, revisited', *Economic Journal*.

Ricardo, D. (1817) 'The principles of political economy, and taxation', P. Sraffa, edited with the collaboration of M.H. Dobb, *The works and correspondence of David Ricardo*, Vol. 1. Cambridge: Cambridge University Press, for Royal Economic Society.

Robinson, J.V. (1951) 'Introduction', in: R. Luxembourg, *The accumulation of capital*. London: Routledge and Kegan Paul.

Robinson, J.V. (1974) *Reflections on the theory of international trade*. Manchester: Manchester University Press.

Roemer, J.E. (1981) *Analytical foundations of Marxian economic theory*. New York: Cambridge University Press.

Roemer, J.E. (1982a) *A general theory of exploitation and class*. Cambridge, MA: Harvard University Press.

Roemer, J.E. (1982b) 'New direction in the Marxist theory of exploitation and class', *Politics and Society*, 11, no. 3:253–287. Reprinted in: J.E. Roemer, ed., *Analytical Marxism*. Cambridge: Cambridge University Press.

Roemer, J. E. (1983a) 'Property relations vs. surplus value in Marxian exploitation', *Philosophy and public affairs*, 11, no. 4:281–313.

Roemer, J.E. (1983b) 'Unequal exchange, labour migration and international capital flows: A theoretical synthesis', in: P. Desai, ed. *Marxism, central planning and the Soviet economy, Essays in honor of Paul Erlich*. Cambridge MA: MIT Press.

Roemer, J.E. (1984) 'History's effect on the distribution of income', mineo, Department of Economics, University of California, Davis.

Roemer, J.E., ed., (1986) *Analytical Marxism*. Cambridge: Cambridge University Press. Paris: Editions de la maison des sciences de l'Homme.

Roemer, J.E. (1986) 'Should Marxists be interested in Exploitation?' in J.E. Roemer, ed., *Analytical Marxism*. Cambridge: Cambridge University Press.

Rowthorn, B. (1980) *Capitalism, conflict and inflation: Essays in political economy*. London: Lawrence & Wishart Ltd.

Saigal, J.C. (1973) 'Réflexions sur la théorie de l'échange inégal', Appendix, in: S. Amin, *L'Échange inégal et la loi de la valuer*. paris: Editions Anthropos IDEP.

Samuelson, P.A. (1948) 'International trade and the equalisation of factor prices', *Economic Journal*, 58:163–184.

Samuelson, P.A. (1949) 'International factor–price equalisation once again', *Economic Journal*, 59: 181–197.

Samuelson, P.A. (1971) 'Ohlin was right', *Swedish Journal of Economics*, 73:365–384.

Samuelson, P.A. (1973) 'Deadweight loss in international trade from the profit motive?' in: C.F. Bergsten and W.G. Tyler, eds., *Leading issues in international economic policy: Essays in honour of George N. Halm*. Lexington, MA: D.C. Health.

Samuelson, P.A. (1975) 'Trade pattern reversals in time-phased systems and intertemporal efficiency', *Journal of International Economics*, 5, no. 4.

Samuelson, P.A. (1976) 'Illogic of neo-Marxian doctrine of unequal exchange', in: D.A. Belsley et al., eds., *Inflation, trade and taxes: Essays in honour of Alice Bourneuf*. Columbus, OH: Ohio State University Press.

Schmitz, H. (1985) *Technology and employment practices: Industrial labour processes in developing countries*. London: Croom Helm.

Schonberger, R.J. (1982) *Japanese manufacturing techniques: Nine hidden lessons in simplicity*. New York: The Free Press.

Seers, D. (1977) 'Inside the company: The CIA diary by Philip Agee', *IDS Bulletin*, 8, no. 3.

Seers, D., ed. (1981) *Dependency theory: A critical assessment*. London: Frances Pinter.

Sen, A.K. (1966) 'Peasants and dualism with or without surplus labour', *Journal of Political Economy*, 74:425–450.

Sen, A.K. (1981) 'Ethical issues in income distribution: National and international', in: S. Grassman and E. Lundberg, eds., *The world economic order: Past and prospects*. London: MacMillan, pp. 464–494.

Sender, J. and S. Smith, (1986) *The development of capitalism in Africa*. London: Methuen.

Shaikh, A. (1981) 'The laws of international exchange', in: E.J. Nell, ed., *Growth, profits and property: Essays in the revival of political economy*. Cambridge: Cambridge University Press.

Sideri, S. (1970) *Trade and power: Informal colonialism in Anglo-Portuguese relations*. Rotterdam.

Singer, H.W. (1950) 'The distribution of gains between investing and borrowing countries', *American Economic Review*, 40, no. 2:377–382.

Singer, H.W. (1975) 'The distribution of gains from trade and investment – Revisited', *Journal of Development Studies*, 11, no. 4:377–382.

Singer, H.W. (1984) 'The terms of trade controversy and the evolution of soft financing: The early years in the UN', in: G. Meier and D. Seers, eds., *Pioneers in development*. Oxford: Oxford

University Press.

Singh, A. (1975) 'Natural selection and the theory of the firm', *Economic Journal*, 85, no. 339:497–515.

Singh, A. (1984) 'The interrupted industrial revolution of the third world: Prospects and policies for resumption', *Industry and Development*, 12.

SIPRI (Stockholm International Peace Research Institute), Yearbooks on *World armaments and disarmament*.

Skocpol, T. (1980) 'Political response in capitalist crisis: Neo-Marxist theories of the state and the case of the New Deal', *Politics and Society*, 10:155–201.

Smith, M.A.M. (1984) 'Capital theory and trade theory' in: R.W. Jones and P.B. Kenen, eds. *Handbook of international economics*, vol. 1. Amsterdam: North-Holland.

Smith, S. (1976) 'An extension of the vent-for surplus model in relation to long-run structural change in Nigeria', *Oxford Economic Papers*, 28, no. 3:426–446.

Smith D. and R. Smith (1983) *The economics of militarism*. London: Pluto Press.

Spraos, J. (1983) *Inequalising trade: A study of traditional north south specialisation in the context of terms of trade concepts*. Oxford: Clarendon Press in cooperation with UNCTAD.

Srinivasen, T.N. (1986) 'Neoclassical political economy, the state and economic development', paper no. 375, Economic Growth Center, Yale University.

Steedman, I. (1977) *Marx after Sraffa*. London: New Left Books.

Steedman, I. (1979a) *Trade amongst growing economies*. Cambridge: Cambridge University Press.

Steedman, I. (1979b) 'The von Neumann analysis and the small open economy', in Steedman (1979c).

Steedman, I., ed, (1979c) *Fundamental issues in the trade theory*. London: MacMillan.

Steedman, I., ed. (1981) *The value controversy*. London: Verso.

Steedman, I. (1982) 'Marx on Ricardo', in: I. Bradley and M. Howard, eds., *Classical and Marxian political economy*. London: MacMillan.

Steedman, I. and J.S. Metcalfe (1977) 'Reswitching, primary inputs and the H-O-S Theory of Trade', *Journal of International Economics*, 7:201–208. Reprinted in Steedman (1979c).

Stolper, W.F. and P.A. Samuelson (1941) 'Protection and real wages', *Review of Economic Studies*, 9:58–67. Reprinted in: S. Ellis and L.A. Metzler, eds., *Readings in the Theory of International Trade*. Philadelphia, PA: The Blakiston Co. (1949).

Streeten, P. and others (1981) *First things first: Meeting basic human needs in developing countries*. Oxford: World Bank Publication, Oxford University Press.

Szentes, T. (1976) *The political economy of under-development*, 3rd rev. enlarged edition. Budapest: Akademiac Kiadó.

Taylor, F.W. (1947) *Scientific management*. New York: Harper and Brothers.

Taylor, L. (1986) 'Trade and growth', *The Review of Black Political Economy*, 14, no. 4:17–36.

Terray, E. (1974) 'Long-distance trade and the formation of the state: The case of the Abron Kingdom of Gyaman', *Economy and Society*, 3, no. 3:315–345.

Thirlwall, A.P. (1986) 'A general model of Growth and development on Kaldorian lines', *Oxford Economic Papers*, 38, no. 2:199–219.

Toye, J. (1987) *Dilemmas of development*. Oxford: Basil Blackwell.

UNIDO (1986) *International comparative advantage in manufacturing*. Vienna: United Nations Industrial and Development Organisation.

Ure, A. (1835) *The philosophy of manufactures*. London: Charles Knight.

Vanek, J. (1968) 'The factor proportions theory: The *N*-factor case', *Kyklos*, 21, fasc 4.

Vines, D. (1984) 'A north–south growth model along Kaldorian lines', Centre for Economic Policy Research, Pembroke College and London.

Wallerstein, I. (1974) *The modern world-system 1: Capitalist agriculture and the origins of the European world-economy in the sixteenth century*. New York: Academic Press.

Wallerstein, I. (1979) *The capitalist world economy*. Cambridge: Cambridge University Press. Paris: Editions de la maison des Sciencies de l'Homme.

Walsh, V. and H. Gram (1980) *Classical and neoclassical theories of general equilibrium: Historical origins and mathematical structure*. New York: Oxford University Press.

White, G. (1986) 'Developmental states and African agriculture: An editorial preface', *IDS Bulletin*, January.

White, G. and R. Wade, eds. (1988) *Developmental states and markets in East Asia.* London: MacMillan.

Williams, J.H. (1929) 'Theory of international trade reconsidered', *Economic Journal*, 39:195–209.

Williamson, O.E. (1975) *Markets and Hierarchies: Analysis and anti trust implications.* New York: The Free Press.

Williamson, O.E. (1985) *The economic institutions of capitalism: Firms, markets and rational contracting.* New York. Free Press.

Wood, A. (1986) 'North–South trade: Division of labour or diversion of labour?', mimeo, IDS, University of Sussex.

World Bank (1983, 1987) *World development reports.* Washington DC.

Chapter 25

FOREIGN PUBLIC CAPITAL FLOWS

JONATHAN EATON*

University of Virginia

Contents

*Work on this chapter was done at the Development Research Department, World Bank, and at the Hoover Institution, Stanford University. I gratefully acknowledge support from the National Science Foundation under grant SES 8410613. I thank Bela Balassa, Charles Engel, Shannon Mitchell, and T.N. Srinivasan for comments on an earlier version.

Handbook of Development Economics, Volume II, Edited by H. Chenery and T.N. Srinivasan
© *Elsevier Science Publishers B.V., 1989*

1. Introduction

1.1. Historical background and recent trends

The use of foreign capital by developing countries has varied substantially across countries and between historical periods. There has been variation both in the aggregate amounts of capital supplied and in the form in which it has been provided. In the brief period from 1970 to 1984 the ratio of external debt to gross national product of developing countries rose from 14.1 to 33.8 percent.[1] Among some smaller developing countries (Togo, Mauritania, Nicaragua, and Costa Rica) the ratio exceeded 100 percent in 1983. At the other extreme the figure for India that year was 11.2 percent.

Foreign capital had an important role in pre-World War II periods as well. Simon (1960) estimates that the net foreign liabilities of the United States peaked at $3.3 billion in 1896. Combining this figure with unpublished estimates of U.S. GNP implies a debt/GNP ratio of around 15 percent. In terms of flows, the World Bank reports estimates that foreign investment as a share of GNP peaked at 1 percent for the United States in the pre-World War I period and, as a share of total domestic investment, it peaked at 6 percent. Corresponding figures for Canada and Argentina in that era are much higher: 7.5 percent of GNP and 30–50 percent of domestic investment for Canada and 12–15 percent of GNP and 40 percent of total investment for Argentina. North (1962) presents data indicating that substantial net flows of capital occurred during the 1920s, but that these were largely repatriated during the following decade.

---

[1]Unless otherwise indicated, the figures in this section are taken from the World Bank (1985, 1986, 1987).

The pre and post-World War II periods seem to share a volatility in the amount of capital extended to developing regions by capital exporters. There are major differences in the institutional setting in which flows of capital took place, however. Before World War II most foreign capital came from private sources. Private portfolio investment, in particular, appears to have been significant. According to the World Bank (1985), "Lending terms were long: maturities of up to ninety-nine years were not uncommon" (p. 13). Before World War I investments were concentrated in the form of bonds issued by private railroads and utilities, while government bond issues became prevalent in the interwar period. Recipients were relatively high-income countries. Foreign aid programs barely existed and government-supported multilateral lending agencies had yet to emerge.

In contrast, in 1960 nearly two-thirds of net flows to developing countries were of official origin. In that same year bank lending and portfolio investment constituted less than 10 percent of net flows.

Since 1960 there has been a rapid growth in commercial bank lending to developing countries. But as a share of total net flows to developing countries, bank lending has displaced direct foreign investment more than it has foreign aid and official lending, which still contributed nearly half the total in 1983. Private debt as a share of the total stock of outstanding debt of developing countries rose from 50.9 percent to 65.0 percent between 1970 and 1983, with a wide variety of experience across countries. For low-income Asian and African countries the share of public debt, typically extended at concessional terms, is above 80 percent, and the share for Africa, in particular, has actually risen substantially during the last fifteen years. Consequently, official funds remain a major source of finance for developing countries, and almost the only source for very poor countries.

There is some reason to think that public capital could revert to its role as the major source of external funds for developing countries. For one thing, the share of private debt in the total debt of all developing countries fell slightly between 1983 and 1984. For another, the debt–service problems of the large debtor countries, along with the large current account deficits of the United States, may shift future lending by private sources away from developing countries more substantially.

1.2. Public vs. private sources of capital

The assigned purview of this chapter is the role of public foreign capital in economic development. A natural question that this assignment raises is: What are the relevant distinctions between capital from public and private sources? As indicated, the first barely existed before the post-World War II era, but have been the predominant form of transfer between developed and developing countries since then. Indeed, for many purposes the distinction is irrelevant. Hence, much of the discussion here applies to foreign capital of either type. The related question then arises: What market failure justifies government involvement in transferring resources from developed to developing countries? While answering this question would seem an essential first step in formulating appropriate policy toward providing capital to developing countries, the justification for government involvement has largely been taken for granted.

The concessional element in much capital provided publicly is one obvious difference. Regardless of whether the donor's altruism or its pursuit of national interest are motivating these concessional flows, a public-good element may cause them to be underprovided privately. While private charitable contributions can and do provide a conduit for transferring resources to developing countries, their provision in this form may fall below the level that is socially optimal even from the perspective of the donor country. The reason is that individuals in this country benefit from these transfers regardless of their source. Hence any individual making a transfer serves not only his own altruistic concerns or sense of self-interest, but those of his fellow citizens as well.

Much publicly-provided capital is at least purportedly nonconcessional, however. If funds transferred actually earn a competitive rate of return why are private investors not willing to provide them? The World Bank's *World Development Report* for 1985 attempts to grapple with this question:

> The efficiency argument is based on the view that private markets for capital, technology, and other services do not provide the amount and type of resources most suited for specific economic conditions and potentials of individual developing countries and to the efficient allocation of world savings. Official action and assistance, by complementing the flows from these markets, can improve the worldwide allocation of resources. Rates of return on investment are often higher in developing countries, so providing these resources (concessionally and nonconcessionally) to them can yield higher future income not only for the recipients but also for the world as a whole (p. 99).

The Report offers five reasons for the underprovision of private funds: (a) sovereign risk; (b) capital market regulations in developed countries; (c) investment opportunities in developing countries that "yield high social returns, but may yield benefits that are not readily capturable or in the short run earn little or no foreign exchange with which to service foreign commercial loans"; (d) private lender's lack of information about investment opportunities and the "repayment capacity" of developing countries; and (e) banks' aversion to long-term lending.

These explanations are, at best, incomplete. (a) Are public loans less subject to sovereign risk? If so, why? If not, perhaps the risk premium charged is insufficient to compensate for this risk, in which case there is an element of concession involved, after all. (b) If lending to developing countries is profitable, should not developed countries amend their financial regulatory systems to allow private lending rather than lend publicly? (c) Why is "capturability" not a problem for nonconcessional official loans? (d) Why not provide potential private lenders with the necessary information? (e) What are the reasons for banks' "traditional objections" to long-term lending? Much long-term lending does go on within industrial countries.

Limitations on the enforceability of private loan contracts between agents in different countries, an issue brought up in Section 6 below, may salvage some of this argument, but more needs to be said.

The issue extends beyond the choice between private and official sources of capital. As the *World Development Report* points out, official assistance provides "not only long-term nonconcessional capital, but also technical assistance and policy advice" (p. 100). The question then arises as to why this assistance and advice cannot be provided privately. Much of it is, but the buyer's inability to ascertain its quality may justify its public provision.

1.3. Overview of the chapter

Aside from the introduction, eight sections comprise this chapter. The four that follow survey alternative theoretical approaches to analyzing the role of foreign capital, narrowly defined, in development. I have organized these sections according to methodologies that have been adopted.

Sections 2 and 3 concern work that analyzes capital flows in a static framework. This literature has largely addressed the implications of capital movements for relative commodity prices, factor rewards, and welfare. Section 2 briefly surveys the vast literature on the "transfer problem", which considers the effects of exogenous transfers. In this literature the level of output in different countries is typically treated as given. Capital movements transfer purchasing power over internationally traded consumption goods but do not affect productive resources. The major issue is the consequence of such transfers for the terms of trade and welfare. Early work on this topic was motivated not by foreign aid but by German reparations after World War I, but the analytic issues are the same. One important implication of this literature is that there is no presumption about the relationship between changes in the terms of trade (achieved, say, via devaluation) and the trade balance. Arguments that devaluations should improve trade balances by worsening the terms of trade should be treated with skepticism.

Section 3 surveys static models of transfers that augment the capital stock of the recipient. Such transfers consequently change world patterns of production as well as consumption. The focus here is more on how transfers affect factor rewards and the internal distribution of income. One issue is how foreign investment interacts with domestic market imperfections to affect distribution and welfare.

Sections 4 and 5 turn to dynamic analysis. The implications of external finance for growth and the accumulation of capital are at issue. This analysis endogenizes the recipient's decision to allocate a transfer between consumption and investment. This literature divides naturally into analysis based on descriptive assumptions about the savings behavior of the borrowing country and that which derives savings relationships explicitily from intertemporal optimization.

The work discussed in Sections 2–5 is largely devoid of reference to particular institutional features of international capital markets and of developing countries. In particular, contracts are assumed automatically and costlessly enforceable, and distinctions are not drawn among alternative sources of capital, in particular between private and official sources.

The next three sections turn to work on more institutional aspects of international capital markets. Section 6 surveys recent work analyzing problems that emerge because of the potential for default on international debt contracts. It includes a discussion of the nascent literature on the closely-related phenomenon of capital flight.

Section 7 provides a discussion of the institutional framework in which foreign aid is distributed, some analytical issues that aid raises and empirical work on its allocation. Multilateral organizations involved in the distribution of capital to developing countries are the topic of Section 8. Section 9 provides some concluding remarks.

In attempting to honor constraints on space and the reader's patience I have omitted mention of a number of important topics related to foreign capital in developing countries. In particular, there is little discussion of the interaction of foreign capital with the nominal exchange rate or price level in the borrowing country. I do not address the relationship between foreign capital and monetary or fiscal policy. The interaction of foreign debt with international reserves receives no mention. There is a large literature on each of these topics, but each raises a set of issues very different from those addressed here.

2. Static models of international capital movements: The transfer problem

Economists writing on capital movements have, very naturally, used the pure theory of international trade extensively as a framework for analysis. Consequently, a great deal of what has been said about the causes and consequences of capital flows shares a number of features in common with trade theory in general. A particular feature of this framework is its static nature: issues concerning the transfer of resources across time are not explicitly addressed. Despite this limitation a great deal can be, and has been, said. To what extent the approach is incomplete, or misleading, is the topic of Sections 4 and 5.

The static framework has been used to consider two types of capital flows. One is an unrequited transfer between countries of purchasing power over final products. How the terms of trade of donor and recipient respond, thereby creating additional costs or benefits to each, and possibly to others, is an issue known as "the transfer problem". An implicit assumption in most of this work is that the transfer does not affect factor endowments in either the donor or the recipient.

2.1. The secondary burden

While it may seem a rather arcane issue, the transfer problem has caused several major arguments during the last half century. German World War I reparation payments motivated the first dispute, which concerned whether or not these payments would impose a "secondary burden" on Germany by shifting the terms of trade against that country. The most famous protagonists were Keynes (1920, 1929), who took the view that they would, and Ohlin (1929), who argued that they need not. Other participants included Salvesen (1927), Wilson (1931), Robertson (1931), Harrod (1932), Yntema (1932), Pigou (1932), and Haberler (1936). Viner (1937) and Samuelson (1971a) provide summaries of the debate.

In Viner's interpretation, Keynes' view was that "historically the international movement of long-term capital has adjusted itself to the trade balance rather than the trade balance to capital movements" (Viner, p. 364). Consequently, in order for Germany to *effect* the transfer the terms of trade must turn against that country in order to create the necessary trade surplus. Ohlin argued that the *income* effect of the transfer allowed the terms of trade to turn in either direction. As Viner quotes Salvesen: "If the borrower wants what the lender does without, no change in prices is necessary" (p. 329).

The subsequent literature on this issue resolved things in Ohlin's favor: Whether the donor's terms of trade improve or deteriorate depends upon whether the recipient's marginal propensity to consume the donor's export exceeds or is exceeded by the donor's marginal propensity to consume its own export.[2]

---

[2] What actually happens can be shown in the two-commodity case. Drawing on the succinct discussions of Dixit (1983) and Jones (1985), denote demand for the non-numeraire commodity in country i as $C^i(p, y^i)$, where p is the world price of the non-numeraire commodity and y^i the income of country i in terms of the numeraire. Let supply of that commodity equal $Q^i(p), Q^{i\prime}(p) \geq 0$. World commodity markets are in equilibrium when world net imports are zero or

$$\sum_{i=1}^{n} M^i = \sum_{i=1}^{n} C^i(p, y^i) - Q^i(p) = 0.$$

The issue remains as to whether or not there is a *presumption* that a transfer causes the donor's terms of trade to deteriorate, and the recipient's to improve, what is called the "orthodox" presumption. Samuelson (1952) argued that, with similar tastes in different countries, transport costs would cause countries typically to have higher marginal propensities to consume their own exports. Hence, as long as the donor and recipient export different commodities, as they must in the two-country case, orthodoxy emerges.

Jones (1970) defended the unorthodox view, arguing that one reason for trade is national differences in tastes. A country imports those commodities for which it has an unusually strong preference. Marginal consumption propensities and imports are consequently positively correlated. The transfer recipient will tend to worsen its own terms of trade by driving up the demand for the good that it imports. Donors will tend to improve their terms of trade, since they are the largest marginal demanders of their own imports.

The transfer issue continues to arise (often in a disguised form) in the ongoing debate on the relationship between currency values and the current account. The debate takes place in various contexts. One is the role of currency devaluation as a component of IMF conditionality. The argument is apparently that devaluation is beneficial for the current account, thereby reducing borrowing or facilitating repayment. Another is the relationship between the value of the U.S. dollar and the U.S. trade deficit. Krugman and Baldwin (1987) provide a recent discussion of the second, but what they say has implications for the first as well. Their analysis raises four issues.

One is whether there is any relationship between the nominal exchange rate and the terms of trade. The transfer discussion concerns the second. A change in

---

Walrasian stability requires that

$$\Delta \equiv \sum_{i=1}^{n} C_p^i(p, y^i)\big|_c - Q^{i\prime}(p) - C_y^i(p, y^i) M^i < 0,$$

where the effect of price on demand has been broken into its substitution ($C_p^i|_c$) and income (C_y^i) effects. Consider a transfer of the numeraire commodity from country d to country r. The effect on p is given by:

$$\frac{dp}{dt} = \frac{C_y^r(p, y^r) - C_y^d(p, y^d)}{-\Delta},$$

which is positive or negative as the recipient's marginal propensity to consume the non-numeraire commodity exceeds or is exceeded by the donor's. What happens to the price of a commodity depends simply on whether the transfer raises or lowers demand for it at initial prices.

the nominal exchange rate affects the terms of trade only if there are nominal rigidities in at least one country or if it has a real balance effect on wealth which spills over into demand relationships. Krugman and Baldwin argue that nominal rigidities are pervasive enough to support an assumption that a nominal exchange rate change generates a real change in the same direction.

The second issue is whether or not a reduction in expenditure undertaken in the home country to improve the trade balance requires a worsened terms of trade. The question turns out to be the same as whether or not there is a secondary burden to the home country to making a transfer abroad. Krugman and Baldwin develop a simple two-country model to answer this question.

Let y denote output and a expenditure, each in the home country, in terms of home goods. Corresponding values for the foreign country, in terms of foreign goods, are y^* and a^*; p is the relative price of home goods in terms of foreign goods. The world-wide budget constraint is therefore:

$$pa + a^* = py + y^*. \tag{1}$$

The trade balance in terms of home prices, t, identically equals $y - a$. Preferences are Cobb–Douglas, with the share of the imported good given by m at home and m^* abroad. The relative price of home goods is consequently:

$$p = m^*y^* / [(1 - m^*)y - (1 - m - m^*)a]. \tag{2}$$

Given y, an increase in t requires an offsetting fall in a. Treating a^* as a residual, the effect on p is negative or positive depending on whether $1 - m - m^*$ is positive or negative, which is exactly Ohlin's criterion for the presence or absence of a secondary burden. Krugman and Baldwin argue in favor of the orthodox presumption, involving the importance of nontraded goods. Hence, they conclude that an improvement in the trade balance achieved through expenditure reduction must be accompanied by a deterioration in the terms of trade.

Nontraded goods do not actually appear in their analysis. There is a literature on the secondary burden with nontraded goods, to which Johnson (1955), MacDougall (1965), Chipman (1974), and Jones (1975) have contributed. The last summarizes existing results. The criterion for a secondary burden to arise is quite complicated, as both technology and taste parameters matter. To the extent that trade patterns are explained by international differences in production, some support for orthodoxy emerges, while if taste differences are the reason for trade, there is support for the unorthodox presumption.

The third issue is whether, in an orthodox world, one would expect to observe a stable, negative relationship between the trade balance and the terms of trade, as posited in much empirical work. (Indeed, some of this work often seems to go further, following Keynes, in treating the relationship from the second to the first as causal, and the relationship as a structural one.) Since both the terms of trade and the trade balance are endogenous variables, the answer depends on the source of disturbances. Holding y, y^*, m, and m^* constant and treating a^* as a residual, movements in a do indeed generate a negative relationship under orthodoxy. So do movements in y, holding a, y^*, m, and m^* constant. This is true whether the world is orthodox or not. Given changes in t will be associated with larger movements in p, however, when the cause is movements in y rather than in a. Finally, movements in y^*, m, and m^*, given a and y, generate fluctuations in the real exchange rate unaccompanied by any movement in the trade balance (defined in terms of domestic goods). It is consequently not surprising to observe fluctuations in exchange rates (real or nominal) that are not accompanied or followed by movements in trade balances. More generally, the orthodox presumption does not justify the view that there is any stable, structural relationship between the (real or nominal) exchange rate or the terms of trade and the trade balance.

The fourth issue is whether domestic expenditure, a, is independent of the terms of trade, as Krugman and Baldwin assume. This question was addressed by Harberger (1950) and by Laursen and Metzler (1950). Appealing to Keynesian consumption theory, they argued that a worsening in the terms of trade would reduce domestic saving, and consequently cause the trade balance to deteriorate. With such a relationship, shifts in m or m^* would generate *negatively* correlated movements between the trade balance and terms of trade, further undermining the notion that there is a stable positive relationship between these magnitudes.

Interest in understanding the effect of changes in oil prices on the current account has revived interest in how domestic expenditure responds to shifts in the terms of trade. In Section 5 I discuss recent applications of dynamic optimization to this issue.

2.2. Immiserizing transfers

Since there is at least the possibility, if not the presumption, of a secondary benefit for the donor of a transfer, and a burden for the recipient, is it possible for the secondary effects to outweigh the primary income effect, so that the donor winds up better off, or the recipient worse off, from the transfer? The possibility was raised by Leontief (1937), but Samuelson (1947, p. 29) showed that, with two countries, such a result was inconsistent with Walrasian stability.[3]

With more than one country, however, other results are possible. The donor can possibly benefit if uninvolved countries are net importers (exporters) of the donor's export and have a lower (higher) marginal propensity to consume the donor's export than the recipient. The recipient can lose if uninvolved countries are net importers (exporters) of the recipient's export and have a lower (higher) marginal propensity to consume the recipient's export than the donor.

Discussion of this issue has consumed a great deal of economists' time and journal space in the last five years. Gale (1974) demonstrated the potential for paradox in an example, although Komiya and Shizuki (1967) demonstrated an equivalent result in a slightly different context. Recent contributors to the discussion include Chichilnisky (1980, 1983), Brecher and Bhagwati (1981), de Meza (1983), Dixit (1983), Geanakoplos and Heal (1983), Gunning (1983a), Ravallion (1983), Srinivasan and Bhagwati (1983a, 1983b), Yano (1983), Jones (1984), Postlewaite and Webb (1984), Jones (1985), and Majumdar and Mitra (1985). Bhagwati, Brecher and Hatta (1983, 1984) incorporate the transfer paradox into the general theory of trade and distortions. One result is that any paradoxical outcome is ruled out if the donor and recipient impose a jointly optimal tariff against the rest of the world.[4]

---

[3]Assume that preferences in country i can be expressed in terms of the indirect social welfare function $v^i(y^i, p)$. The effect of the transfer on country j's welfare is consequently:

$$\frac{dv^j}{dt} = v_y^j \frac{dy^j}{dt} + v_p^j \frac{dp}{dt},$$

where $dy^j/dt = 1$ for $j = r$, -1 for $j \neq d$, and 0 for $j \neq r, d$.

Applying Shepherd's Lemma this becomes:

$$\frac{dv^j}{dt} \bigg/ v_y^j = \frac{\frac{dy^j}{dt} \left\{ \left[\sum_{i=1}^{n} C_p^i(p, y^i) \big|_c - Q^{i'}(p) \right] - \sum_{i=1, i \neq d, r}^{n} M^i C_y^i(p, y^i) \right\}}{\Delta}$$

$$+ \frac{\left(M^j - M^r \frac{dy^j}{dt} \right) C_y^r - \left(M^j + M^d \frac{dy^j}{dt} \right) C_y^r}{\Delta}.$$

The denominator and the term in square brackets in the numerator are both negative. If there are no countries other than donor and recipient then, since $M^d = -M^r$, this expression has the sign of dy^j/dt: the recipient must benefit and the donor must lose.

[4]Metzler (1942) and Johnson (1956) examine the transfer problem in the context of Keynesian unemployment.

The importance of the terms-of-trade effects of unilateral transfers to developing countries is unlikely to be proportional to the attention devoted to it by economists. Nevertheless, the discussion does have four important implications.

First, international capital flows can have general equilibrium effects substantially beyond the direct transfer of resources. Countries uninvolved in the transfer are then likely to be affected.

Second, when the transfer generates terms-of-trade effects, the denomination of the transfer should not be a matter of indifference to donor or recipient. Transfers fixed in terms of different commodities that are identical in market value at initial prices are likely to have different values when the transfer occurs. This result may be of particular relevance for the agricultural commodities supplied by the United States under Public Law 480 (PL 480).[5]

Third, some discussions of debt repayment problems have raised the transfer issue. See, for example, Nurkse (1961) and Diaz-Alejandro (1984). Important elements in the analysis of transfers are the income effects associated with them, however. Since the extension and repayment of loans do not directly affect *permanent* income of borrowers and lenders, the application of the transfer literature requires some modification. The problem is that the income effect associated with repaying debt is not equivalent to that of an unrequited transfer. The transfer literature considers only the second. See Ruffin (1984). A full analysis of the first issue requires an explicitly dynamic framework.

The fourth point is most critical. While logic clearly resolved the debate between Ohlin and Keynes in the first's favor, the error in Keynes' thinking survives in attempts to explain the trade balance and current account in terms of the "real exchange rate" [see the survey by Goldstein and Khan (1985)]. The argument is that the appropriate terms of trade, as determined by "trade elasticities", must be realized to ensure that a desired transfer, such as a loan repayment, is effected. Cline's (1983) projections of debt repayment, in which exports and imports are projected on the basis of the real exchange rate, are an example. For one thing, this thinking ignores the income effect of the transfer. For another, it treats the determination of relative prices as logically prior to the determination of quantity flows. As Metzler (1968) pointed out in his classic analysis of the balance-of-payments adjustment mechanism, national savings and investment behavior determine the current account and the aggregate trade balance. It is consequently inappropriate to specify these magnitudes as the

---

[5]De Meza (1983) has shown that transfers of the donor's export do not necessarily improve the donor's terms of trade, as was suggested by Mundell (1960). If the transfer is in the form of a commodity that the recipient does not trade internationally, as is frequently the case with agricultural commodities, then there are additional implications for domestic prices that may'be much more important than those for the international terms of trade. Food aid may significantly harm the rural sector and reduce domestic food production, for example. This issue is discussed at greater length in Section 7.

residual of a trade balance relationship specified independently of the underlying determinants of private and public savings and investment.

3. Static models of international capital movements: The factor-endowments approach

Nurkse (1961), writing in 1936, already complained that "the theory of capital movements undoubtedly suffers from the fact that the transfer problem, which arises in capital movements as well as indemnity payments, has taken up far too much room at the center of the stage" (p. 98). He argued that the transfer problem ignored two important features of most capital movements. First was their economic motivation. Foreign investment, unlike an indemnity payment or aid, usually does not involve a transfer of wealth between countries, but arises from the desire on the part of wealth-holders in the country of origin to earn a higher return on their wealth. A capital inflow then creates an offsetting debt obligation for the recipient. Such capital flows should respond to interest differentials. If debt is repaid a capital movement in the other direction will ultimately take place. Second, in contrast to what is assumed in discussion of transfers, capital movements can affect the supply of productive factors, with further implications for welfare.

A theoretical literature on capital movements incorporating these two elements did subsequently emerge, and is now quite vast. Ruffin (1984) surveys it. I will discuss some results that seem particularly relevant in modeling capital flows to developing countries. The relationship between goods trade and factor trade is the topic of Subsection 3.1, Subsection 3.2 surveys the literature on the effects of exogenous capital flows, and Subsection 3.3 that on endogenous flows.

3.1. Capital flows and trade flows

The standard factor-endowments model of the competitive open economy has seen a great deal of service in analyzing foreign investment. The application of computable general equilibrium analysis to modeling policy in developing countries has made this literature more relevant to development economics. An important technical issue turns out to be the relationship between the number of traded commodities and the number of nontraded factors. If a general equilibrium model specifies too few nontraded factors relative to the number of traded commodities produced domestically, it either overdetermines factor rewards or else production patterns are indeterminate.

In general, let $X = \{X_1, \ldots, X_n\}$ denote a vector of outputs that can be produced with factor inputs A_j^i according to the processes:

$$x^i = f^i\big(A_1^i, \ldots, A_m^i\big), \quad i = 1, \ldots, n, \tag{3}$$

where $f^i(\cdot)$ are homogeneous-of-degree-one functions. The vector $\bar{A} = \{\bar{A}1, \ldots, \bar{A}_m\}$ denotes fixed *national* endowments of factors. Assume that all commodities are traded at world prices $p = \{p^1, \ldots, p^n\}$. Factors $1, \ldots, m'$ are internationally immobile while factors $m' + 1, \ldots, m$ are supplied at world prices $\{w_{m'+1}^*, \ldots, w_m^*\}$.

Perfect competition ensures that there are no excess profits, or that:

$$p^i \le \sum_{j=1}^{m} a_j^i(\bar{w}) w_j; \; (= \text{if } X^i > 0), \quad i = 1, \ldots, n, \tag{4}$$

where $a_j^i(\bar{w}) = A^i/X^i$ and $\bar{w} = \{w_1, \ldots, w_{m'}, w_{m'+1}^*, \ldots, w_m^*\}$. Conditions for cost minimization determine the functions $a_j^i(\bar{w})$, the amount of factor j used to produce one unit of commodity i as a function of the vector of factor prices. Factor-market equilibrium requires that:

$$\sum_{i=1}^{n} X^i a_j^i(\bar{w}) = \bar{A}_j + A_j^f, \quad j = 1, \ldots, m, \tag{5}$$

where $A_j^f = 0$, $j \le m'$; A_j^f is foreign supply of factor j. If (4) holds as an equality, then equations (4) and (5) are a system of $n + m$ equations with unknowns $X^i, w_1, \ldots, w_{m'}$, and $A_{m'+1}^f, \ldots, A_m^f$. Thus, the level of domestic outputs, the rewards of nontraded factors, and the level of imports of traded factors are all determined by technology and the world prices of commodities and traded factors.

Assuming that the matrix consisting of $a_j^i(\bar{w})$ is of full rank, a condition ensured by the absence of factor-intensity reversals, three situations can emerge depending upon whether the number of nontraded factors is strictly less than, equal to, or greater than the number of traded commodities ($m' < n$, $m' = n$, or $m' > n$). First, if $m' < n$, then equations (4) overdetermine $\{w_1, \ldots, w_{m'}\}$ if $X^i > 0$ for more than m' commodities. Unless world commodity prices happen to take on particular values, $n - m'$ outputs must equal 0. Producing these commodities domestically must yield strictly negative profits. The remaining system is equivalent to one in which $m' = n$.

If $m' = n$, referred to as the "even" case, then equations (4) uniquely determine $\{w_1, \ldots, w_{m'}\}$ independently of factor endowments $\bar{A}$. Equations (5) then determine X_i and A_j^f given $\bar{w}$ and $\bar{A}$. Changes in $\bar{A}$ will then have no effect on $\bar{w}$

unless they cause the set of commodities actually produced to change. The range of factor endowments consistent with production at non-negative profits of a given set of commodities is sometimes referred to as the "Chipman diversification cone". See Chang (1979) and Ethier (1985) for further discussion.

Finally, if $m' > n$, referred to as the "odd" case, (4) does not determine a unique $\{w_1, \ldots, w_{m'}\}$. Factor endowments, technology, and world prices of commodities and traded factors mutually determine factor rewards and factor use in production. A change in factor endowments will then typically affect domestic factor rewards even when the set of commodities produced domestically does not change.

Consider odd cases first. Introducing trade in a factor that was previously not traded causes the factor to be imported or exported depending upon whether its pretrade reward domestically exceeded or was exceeded by its international price. The set of commodities produced domestically need not change. If the factor is imported its domestic reward falls, but the reward of at least one other factor must rise. If the domestic reward before trade equals the world price, then no trade in the factor is the locally unique equilibrium outcome.

In the even case, however, if the world and domestic rewards coincide before trade, then once trade is introduced the pattern of trade in commodities and factors is indeterminate. The initial factor rewards satisfy (4) but (5) has an additional unknown; m equations now determine $n + m' + 1$ unknowns. There may be no trade, but any factor allocation that falls within the Chipman diversification cone is a possibility.

If, in the even case, the pretrade domestic and international rewards do *not* coincide, then, given the initial set of commodities that are produced, (4) now overdetermines factor rewards. The number of products produced in strictly positive amounts must fall to $n - 1$.

At first it may seem coincidental that, in the even case, the reward of a nontraded factor would coincide with its reward elsewhere. But if the initial n products are produced elsewhere with the same technologies, then equations (4) apply there as well. The existing trade in commodities and factors has already established factor-price equalization (FPE). If two economies satisfy conditions for FPE, then additional factor trade is redundant, and the consequent allocation of factors is indeterminate.[6]

---

[6] Nontraded final goods can be introduced into the analysis very straightforwardly. What matters for evenness is now that the number of *traded* commodities equals the number of nontraded factors. In this case technology and international prices continue to determine all factor rewards independently of factor endowments or domestic tastes. Through the zero-profit conditions, the prices of nontraded commodities are determined independently of these magnitudes as well. In odd cases technology, world prices, domestic factor endowments and, now, domestic taste patterns all interact to determine factor rewards.

To summarize, factor trade has very different implications in even and in odd cases. Factor-endowments models of international investment have focused on both. I discuss examples of each in turn, and the questions that they raise.

3.1.1. Capital flows in even cases

A classic paper by Mundell (1957) considers the two-factor, two-commodity, two-country case. This framework has been used to address several issues:

3.1.1.1. Commodity trade and factor flows: Substitutes or complements? Mundell assumes that technologies are identical in the two countries. Free trade consequently ensures FPE. He then considers the effect of an import tariff imposed by one of the two countries. If the tariff falls on the capital-intensive commodity, then, at the initial allocation of capital, the tariff raises the return to capital in that country relative to its return elsewhere. The higher return attracts capital until interest rates are again equal. The tariff is, at that point, prohibitive. Rybczynski effects associated with the movement of capital ensure that the production patterns change to replicate the free-trade consumption patterns. Factor trade has substituted perfectly for commodity trade, which the tariff has eliminated.

In Mundell's model, a tariff is the cause of the initial differential in rates of return on capital. Purvis (1972) examines the relationship between commodity trade and capital flows where differences in technology rather than a tariff create the initial divergence in returns. If two economies are identical except that one country, A, can produce one commodity, X, more efficiently, then country A will export X in exchange for the other commodity, Y. At the initial allocation of capital, the return on capital in A exceeds or is exceeded by that abroad depending upon whether X is capital- or labor-intensive relative to Y [see Findlay and Grubert (1959)]. If capital becomes mobile, whichever way it flows its movement will engender Rybczynski effects in both countries that raise the output of X in country A, which already exports it, and lower its output abroad, with the reverse consequences for Y. The capital flow consequently *expands* trade. This result emerges where other impediments to FPE are the reason for commodity trade as well.[7]

These results have three implications of general interest. First, factor trade does not necessarily substitute for goods trade, as Mundell's result with tariffs would suggest, but may expand it. Second, they serve as a reminder that, even

---

[7]Markusen (1983) extends Purvis's analysis to consider taxes, external economies of scale, and factor market distortions as additional reasons for FPE to fail. Svensson (1984a) examines the issue of whether factor movements substitute for or complement commodity trade in a general factor-endowments context.

within the context of the factor-endowments model, capital movements may occur for many reasons other than differences in endowments per worker. There is consequently no strong presumption that capital seeking its highest return will flow from capital-abundant to capital-scarce countries. Finally, an implication of Mundell's analysis is that protectionist policies, both in developing and in developed countries, have probably increased the flow of capital from developed to developing countries substantially.

3.1.1.2. Capital flows and specialization. Say that cross-country differences in technology are the cause for commodity trade. Will trade in capital then lead to incomplete specialization in production across countries, or result in factor-endowment ratios that imply complete specialization in some countries?

Jones (1967) argued that, since only a finite number of commodity-price ratios can sustain incomplete specialization everywhere, it was the unlikely outcome. The position was challenged by Kemp and Inada (1969), Chipman (1971), and Uekawa (1971). Chipman showed that, with perfect capital mobility, the world production possibility frontier contains a flat segment along which countries specialize incompletely. A continuum of output levels is consequently consistent with this price ratio. Perfect capital mobility and incomplete specialization in production can consequently occur simultaneously as long as at this price ratio demand corresponds to at least one point in this continuum. This outcome is not a fluke.[8]

3.1.2. Capital flows in odd cases

MacDougall (1960) models the simplest odd case, an economy that produces a single output with two factors, called capital and labor. Labor is immobile while capital is not. For a net importer of capital, an increase in foreign capital raises both domestic and national income, as well as the return to labor. The income of nationally-owned capital falls. If foreign capital takes the form of direct investment, so that it earns the domestic marginal product of capital, the return on existing foreign investment falls as well.[9]

---

[8]Ethier and Ross (1971) analyze the issue in a specifically dynamic framework. They argue that with intertemporal optimizing behavior incomplete specialization in the steady state requires the coincidental equality of the discount rates in both countries with the interest rate compatible with incomplete specialization. Their result assumes a constant discount rate, however. Other specifications of intertemporal preferences, such as overlapping generations and Uzawa (1968) utility functions, do not require this coincidence. More on this in Section 5 below. Jones (1985) and Ferguson (1978) also analyze trade patterns in the two-factor, two-commodity case with capital mobility. Ohyama (1984) discusses the relationship between trade flows and endowment patterns in higher dimensions.

[9]MacDougall extends the analysis to include taxes, an endogenous national capital supply, external economies, economies of scale, and different sorts of monopoly.

A one-sector model cannot, of course, provide answers to questions about the intersectoral effects of foreign investment. Expanding the number of sectors requires, to maintain oddity, expanding the number of factors. Even in low dimensions, general cases are complicated. An assumption sometimes used in computable general equilibrium models is that the number of factors exceeds the number of sectors by exactly one, and that only one factor is productive in all sectors, while the rest are productive in only one. Each sector thus produces output with the single nonspecific factor and its unique specific factor. The simplest version, with two commodities and three factors, is also known as the Ricardo–Viner model because of its antecedents in Ricardo's theory of accumulation and Viner's writing on trade with increasing costs. Jones (1971) and Samuelson (1971a) describe the essential features of the model with factor immobility. Unless two economies by coincidence have proportional endowments of factors as well as identical technologies, commodity trade with no factor trade does not imply FPE. An incentive remains for factors to move. If technologies across countries are identical, however, commodity trade plus perfect capital mobility ensures FPE. Introducing further factor trade results in indeterminacy.[10]

Caves (1971), Ikemoto (1975), Amano (1977), Burgess (1978), Brecher and Findlay (1983), and Srinivasan (1983) have used the model to analyze capital flows. If capital is a factor specific to production in one sector then its inflow raises the return to the general factor, but lowers the return to all specific factors. Output of the capital-using industry expands while all other industries contract. If capital is the general factor, however, capital inflow raises the return to all specific factors and raises the output of all commodities.[11]

The factor-endowments model of the small open economy, by itself, of course, provides little insight into how foreign capital inflows affect small open economies. It does provide a structure for empirical analysis, however. A crucial issue for the specification of empirical models are the definitions of factors and commodities. Theory at this stage provides little insight into the appropriate level of aggregation for either. An unfortunate message of this literature for empirical work is

---

[10]Caves (1971) argued that mobility of all factors makes complete specialization likely. Amano (1977) pointed out that with identical technologies, complete factor mobility implies an indeterminacy in the allocation of factors, but with incomplete specialization the likely outcome. This disagreement parallels that between Jones (1967) and Chipman (1971) and others for the two-factor case discussed above.

[11]Ruffin (1984) has shown that these results extend beyond the specific-factors model for the three-factor, two-commodity case. Jones, Neary and Ruane (1983) use the three-factor, two-commodity model to illustrate the possibility for two-way factor flows. To make the direction of factor flows determinate, they assume that only one commodity is traded. Consequently, even though the economy they consider is small in that it does not affect the world prices of traded factors, one commodity price is endogenous.

that different specifications will yield very different sorts of conclusions regardless of the data brought to bear.

3.2. Exogenous capital movements

One approach is to assume that capital is not normally traded, and to consider the effect of an exogenous movement of capital between countries.[12] As with transfers of final commodities, the possibility arises that an inflow of capital lowers the welfare of the recipient. This is possible even when the inflow is unrequited, imposing no repayment burden on the recipient.

3.2.1. Immiserizing growth: The terms of trade

At initial commodity prices an injection of additional capital into a country will typically affect the amount of trade that the country engages in. If the amount of trade changes sufficiently, then world prices will respond. As with transfers of final commodities, a country will experience a secondary burden or benefit through a deterioration or improvement in its terms of trade. In a classic paper Bhagwati (1958) shows that a reduction in income from worsened terms of trade can exceed income generated by an augmented capital stock, so that growth "immiserizes". The benefit of the added resource is not lost, but transferred to the rest of the world. Obviously, this result requires that the injection of capital makes exports grow and that the foreign demand for exports be relatively inelastic. In the two-factor, two-commodity case with incomplete specialization, the result requires a capital-intensive export sector, so that an increase in capital is "ultra pro-trade biased".[13]

An additional result is that, regardless of demand conditions, if the country experiencing the increase in resources imposes the optimal tariff, its real income must rise [see Bhagwati (1969)]. Nevertheless, if the increase in capital actually occurs simultaneously in a number of countries, their collective imposition of such a tariff is unlikely.

The literature on immiserizing growth does not specifically address increases in the capital stock that arise from foreign capital inflows. When foregin capital is the source of such growth, however, then there is a parallel shrinkage of the capital stock abroad. Unless the source and recipient countries are highly asymmetric, the effect of the resource loss on the source country's trade position

---

[12]An equivalent assumption is that capital is traded, but rationed. Section 6 addresses the issue of why rationing might occur in lending to less-developed countries.

[13]See Johnson (1959). Bhagwati (1958), Mantel (1984), and Hatta (1984) provide various conditions that preclude immiserization.

is likely to mitigate the terms-of-trade effect of the transfer. In the two-factor model with identical technologies and incomplete specialization, the case considered by Mundell (1957), such transfers are completely neutral for this reason.[14]

Ranney (1984) provides an example of an exogenous immiserizing transfer of capital in an explicit North–South setting. The North and the South both produce two goods with capital and labor using fixed-coefficient technologies. The South exports the labor-intensive good. The capital-intensive good in the South is produced both by an indigenous sector with Southern capital and Southern labor and by an enclave sector with Northern capital and Southern labor. The conditions (i) that the enclave sector is more efficient and capital-intensive than its indigenous counterpart, and (ii) that the rate of return on capital in the enclave sector exceeds that in the North ensure that a transfer of capital from the North to the Southern enclave immiserizes the South.

3.2.2. Immiserizing growth: Domestic distortions

Another reason why capital inflows can reduce welfare is that they exacerbate an existing domestic distortion. Consider first the case in which foreign capital arrives simply as a transfer, with no implied debt obligation. Johnson (1967) showed, for the two-factor, two-commodity case, that if the import-competing sector is capital-intensive and protected by a tariff, then an exogenous increase in the capital stock could lower welfare. It generates a Rybczynski effect that increases output of the protected sector. Tan (1969), Melvin (1969), Bertrand and Flatters (1971), Brecher and Diaz-Alejandro (1977), and Martin (1977) provide criteria for immiserization to result.

Other distortions, such as those arising from non lump-sum taxes, variable returns to scale external to the firm, factor-market distortions, and monopolistic competition, can lead to immiserization from an increase in capital. Ohyama (1972), Smith (1982), Eaton and Panagariya (1982), and Helpman and Razin (1983) provide necessary conditions for immiserization in various cases. Again, immiserization requires that the quantity subject to the distortion increases when the capital stock increases.

A related issue is the shadow pricing of capital in a distorted economy. See Bhagwati and Srinivasan (1983a, ch. 32) for a brief discussion and references to the literature. If growth in the capital stock immiserizes, its shadow price is negative.

---

[14]Markusen and Melvin (1979) consider the welfare effects of exogenous capital movements in a more general two-country, two-commodity, two-factor setting. Brecher and Choudhri (183) show the potential for such transfers to immiserize when the export sector in the recipient is capital-intensive, an argument that goes back to Singer's (1950) hypothesis of a secular decline in a developing country's terms of trade.

An interesting possibility is that the transfer itself creates a distortion in the economy. Schultz (1960) suggested this possibility for the case of PL 480 food aid. Brecher and Bhagwati (1982) consider transfers of final products with such effects. The literature on rent-seeking or directly-unproductive-profit-seeking activities may have relevance for unrequited transfers: competition for the transfer among domestic agents in the recipient may undo the gains [see Krueger (1974) or Bhagwati (1982)].

3.2.3. Foreign-owned capital

Brecher and Diaz-Alejandro (1977), Bhagwati and Brecher (1980, 1981), and Bhagwati and Tironi (1980) consider the implications of a given, exogenous foreign investment position for national welfare in a two-factor, two-sector model. The presence of foreign-owned capital can reverse a number of the standard propositions. An improvement in a country's terms of trade, for example, can reduce welfare if capital is largely foreign-owned and the export is capital-intensive: through Stolper-Samuelson effects foreign capitalists appropriate the gains, leaving domestic wage-earners with losses.

These models assume that foreign capital earns the domestic marginal product of capital both before and after the changes under consideration. The results consequently apply only to foreign capital in the form of direct foreign investment. In the case of portfolio investment, which is the typical form of investment from public sources, the interest rate is set ex ante.

3.3. Endogenous capital movements

Another literature assumes an international capital market that, in the absence of legal restrictions, allocates capital across borders to equate after-tax returns. Several issues have been analyzed in such contexts.

3.3.1. Nationally-optimal tariffs

One issue is the optimal taxation of foreign capital. MacDougall (1960), Jasay (1960), and Kemp (1962a, 1962b) extend Mill's argument for the nationally-optimal tariff to borrowing in international capital markets. A large borrower can exploit monopoly power in such a market by restricting its borrowing. With more than one commodity, policies toward capital importation and commodity trade interact. Kemp (1966, 1969), Jones (1967), Brecher (1983), and Brecher and Feenstra (1983) provide results for the two-factor, two-commodity case, as do Brecher and Findlay (1983) and Srinivasan (1983) for the three-factor, two-commodity specific-factors model. A popular exercise is to assume that the government pursues suboptimal policies with respect to one type of trade, and to derive "second-best" policies for other types of trade.

For a country that influences the world interest rate, standard arguments for the nationally-optimal tariff apply. However, because lenders may perceive that the risk of default rises with the total amount borrowed, they may charge even a small borrower a higher nominal rate as its indebtedness rises. If lenders are risk-neutral and correctly calculate the probability of default, then the optimal tariff argument for intervention does not apply. If the probability of default is independent of the amount borrowed, then the risk-free world interest rate corresponds to the *expected* payment, and therefore constitutes the marginal cost of capital to the borrower.

The possibility of default does provide reasons why borrowing to the point at which the marginal product of capital equals the world interest rate is unwise, but these differ from the standard optimal tariff argument. These issues are the topic of Section 6.

3.3.2. Capital autarky vs. free trade in capital

Another issue is whether a country benefits from trade in capital at all. Such trade cannot harm a small undistorted economy, and in "odd cases" will benefit it. Grossman (1984) shows that capital autarky can be a first-best policy for a country that has market power in commodity markets, even when the country taxes commodity trade optimally. For the two-sector, two-commodity case with identical technologies between countries, the result follows from the Mundell (1957) analysis discussed above: factor trade restores free-trade factor prices and consequently free-trade commodity prices. It undoes the nationally-optimal tariff.

Jones (1984a) has made a similar argument in the presence of domestic distortions. In odd cases, a distortion such as a (nonoptimal) tariff typically has an effect on factor prices that generates a capital flow that exacerbates the distortion. For example, if the import-competing sector is capital-intensive then a tariff raises the return to capital, which attracts capital and further raises the output of the protected sector.

3.3.3. Capital flows vs. migration

Ramaswami (1968) provides a result on the choice between trade in capital and trade in labor that has recently received a flurry of attention. Consider the two-factor, one-commodity MacDougall (1960) framework in a two-country setting with fixed world endowments of the two factors, capital and labor. With identical technologies either migration of labor from the capital-poor to the capital-abundant country, or a movement of capital in the opposite direction equates all factor rewards. Nationally-optimal policies of the capital-abundant country might involve (i) prohibiting immigration and restricting capital exports or (ii) taxing immigrants and prohibiting capital exports. From a national perspective the second is preferable.

To see this, consider an equilibrium in which the capital-abundant country pursues the first policy. Allow it to repatriate its capital from abroad and allow the immigration of workers working with that capital. National income is unaffected if the factor proportions in the repatriated and in the original domestic sector are not changed. But if capital and labor are then reallocated to equate marginal products between these sectors, income rises.[15]

Static models, by their very nature, ignore too many fundamental aspects of economic development to provide an adequate foundation for understanding the effect of foreign capital on economic growth. In particular, they ignore its effect on domestic saving. The traditional identification of transfers with consumption of final commodities and of lending with investment in capital is arbitrary. Recipients can invest transfers and borrowing can finance consumption. To understand the effect of foreign capital on investment requires an explicit formulation of resource allocation over time.

4. Dynamic models of international capital movements: Descriptive approaches

Explicitly dynamic models of investment and growth with foreign capital fall into two general categories, with some rather disturbingly different implications for a number of important issues. The first incorporates what are sometimes called "descriptive" or, less charitably, "ad hoc" assumptions about behavior, in particular, that a mechanical linear function of some definition of income (and, in rare cases, some definition of wealth as well) determines savings. The second derives savings behavior explicitly from the maximization of intertemporal utility functions defined over consumption in different periods. Within the first category, one type of analysis follows the tradition of the Harrod–Domar growth model in positing a constant, exogenous incremental capital–output ratio. Another, in the tradition of the Solow growth model, incorporates more neoclassical assumptions about technology, with marginal productivity conditions determining factor rewards. This section concerns nonoptimizing models; Section 5 considers optimizing approaches.

---

[15]Calvo and Wellisz (1983), Bhagwati and Srinivasan (1983b), Wong (1983), and Jones and Coelho (1985) provide recent discussions and extensions of this result.

4.1. Harrod–Domar models: The savings constraint

Consider first the growth models of Harrod (1939) and, more relevantly, Domar (1946) as they apply to a closed economy. There is a constant savings ratio out of income, denoted here by s. A constant incremental capital–output ratio κ describes technology.[16] Saving equals investment which provides new capital to support additional income. The growth rate sustainable by saving is consequently:

$$g^{w} = s/\kappa, \tag{6}$$

what Harrod called the "warranted" rate of growth.

4.1.1. Aid requirements

Rosenstein-Rodan (1968) applies the model to determine "aid requirements". He posits a "target" growth rate, which could correspond to the growth rate of the effective labor force, what Harrod called the "natural" rate of growth. Assuming that all aid is invested, he calculates the aid flow required to achieve the target growth rate. Aid will eventually be required whenever the target growth rate exceeds the warranted rate. The rate of growth in the required amount of aid then converges to the target growth rate.

Fei and Paauw (1965) use this approach to calculate aid requirements for 31 countries. They find that only for 9 is the warranted rate in excess of their target rate.

4.1.2. Foreign debt and solvency

Now assume that the country can borrow at a fixed world interest rate, r. The issue now arises as to the appropriate specification of the savings function. Models differ in what they assume about the propensity to save out of borrowing, interest payments, and output.

Solomon (1977), for example, assumes that domestic saving is a fixed proportion of domestic output and that all foreign borrowing is invested. A condition for the radio of debt to output to remain bounded is that $n \geq r$, or that the target growth rate exceed the interest rate. The asymptotic debt–output ratio is then equal to $(kn - s)/(n - r)$, which is positive or negative depending upon whether the target growth rate exceeds or is exceed by the warranted rate. Solomon

---

[16]One justification for this assumption is a zero elasticity of substitution between capital and labor in the aggregate production function, with the supply of capital the binding constraint. Another is that labor is in perfectly elastic supply at an exogenous real wage.

interprets this ratio as a "debt limit". Based on 1974 data he observes that none of ten major borrowing countries was near this limit.

A comparison of a borrower's growth rate with the interest rate has occasionally been suggested as a measure of its solvency. The assumptions of the Harrod–Domar model are too simplistic for this analysis to support this criterion. It is unreasonable, for example, to treat the interest rate, the capital–output ratio, and the savings ratio as exogenous, time-invariant parameters. The differences between the 1970s and 1980s have made this point painfully obvious.

Even within the context of the Harrod–Domar framework, however, a problem emerges with this treatment of debt dynamics. If, in fact, a country's debt limit is positive, an implication of this analysis is that it will eventually run a trade deficit in perpetuity. Such a situation is incompatible with rational behavior on the part of lenders.[17]

4.2. Two-gap models

The Harrod–Domar model posits a homogeneous output that can either be consumed or invested. The capital–labor ratio and the savings ratio consequently constrain the growth rate. Foreign capital can raise the growth rate by raising the availability of this output, and thereby resources available for investment. In this way aid contributes to growth.

The two-gap approach introduces the assumption that an imported commodity not produced domestically is essential for the production of investment goods. The availability of foreign exchange to purchase these imported capital goods, rather than the supply of domestic saving, can then constrain the growth of the economy. In these circumstances foreign capital raises growth not by raising resources available for saving, but by increasing the availability of foreign exchange to import capital goods.

4.2.1. The basic structure

McKinnon (1964) provides a simple formulation of the model. Capacity P_t is given by:

$$P_t = \min(\alpha K_d, \beta K_f), \quad \alpha > 0, \beta > 0, \tag{7}$$

where K_d and K_f are domestically-produced and imported capital, respectively.

---

[17]Domar (1950) is an early extension of the Harrod–Domar growth model to analyze foreign debt. Avramovic (1958), Avramovic et al. (1964), Gulhati (1967), and King (1968) provide further analysis. The last, in particular, gives formulae for many variations on the basic problem. Grinols and Bhagwati (1976, 1979) and Wasow (1979) use the model to examine the effect of aid and lending on savings behavior and various measures of "dependency" on foreign capital. Kharas (1984) applies the framework to recent debt problems of developing countries. Glick and Kharas (1984) analyze debt dynamics under very general assumptions about propensities to save out of various types of income.

Savings S_t is a proportion s of income Y_t, and exports E_t a proportion ε of capacity. Assume that income is constrained by capacity, so that $Y_t = P_t$. If foreign capital were exchangeable for domestic output, then the warranted rate of growth would equal s/κ, as before, where now

$$\kappa = 1 \bigg/ \left(\frac{1}{\alpha} + \frac{1}{\beta} \right). \tag{8}$$

Each increment to capacity requires $1/\beta$ units of foreign capital, however. To achieve the warranted growth rate requires investment of foreign capital in amount

$$I_t^f = \frac{s}{\beta\kappa} P_t, \tag{9}$$

which is not attainable if $\varepsilon\beta < s/\kappa$. In this case the availability of imports constrains growth. Here one may think of $g^e = \varepsilon\beta$ as the growth rate "warranted" by the availability of foreign exchange, and $g^w = s/\kappa$ as the growth rate "warranted" by savings. The actual growth rate will be no larger than the smaller of these.

This model has been used to argue that the contribution of foreign capital to growth is greater in a situation where growth is constrained by the availability of foreign exchange. Consider the availability of foreign aid in amount a as a share of income. If no aid is consumed, then the two warranted growth rates become:

$$g^w = (s + a)/\kappa, \tag{10}$$

$$g^e = (\varepsilon + a)\beta. \tag{11}$$

Since

$$\frac{dg^w}{da} = \frac{1}{\kappa} < \frac{dg^e}{da} = \beta,$$

an increase in foreign aid raises the growth rate warranted by foreign exchange more than the growth rate warranted by domestic savings. If the foreign exchange constraint is binding, then the apparent rate of saving of the economy is $\varepsilon\beta\kappa < s$. The economy desires to save more but additional investment is unproductive. In this case foreign aid actually *augments* domestic saving and reduces consumption.[18]

---

[18]Sengupta (1965), Chenery (1967), and Bacha (1984) provide alternative analytic descriptions of the model. The phenomenon of a foreign exchange gap and its implications for the effect of aid on growth was observed in numerical planning models by Chenery and Bruno (1962) and Manne (1963). Chenery and MacEwan (1966) and Chenery and Strout (1966) provide subsequent numerical applications. Bruno (1967) introduces the concept into a general activity-analysis problem where maximizing the growth rate is the objective. Simonsen (1985) provides a recent version of the model in which foreign exchange is the sole constraint on growth.

4.2.2. A neoclassical interpretation and critique

Bhagwati (1966), Findlay (1971), and Desai and Bhagwati (1979) reformulate the two-gap model in terms of a static equilibrium model of a trading economy. The notion that foreign exchange is in limited supply makes sense in this framework if the country under consideration faces a world demand for exports that become unit elastic (or less) above some finite quantity. The assumptions of the two-gap model are met exactly if export demand is perfectly elastic up to some level εP_t, and thereafter is unit elastic; εP_t is then the maximum level of imports available through international trade.

The appropriate policy response is an optimal tariff or export tax which, in this case, restricts exports to their maximum level on the elastic portion of the demand curve. Without such a tariff an increase in the country's desire to grow, as manifested by a higher propensity to save, leads not to more investment but simply bids up the relative price of imported capital goods. The optimal tariff can prevent this adverse effect on its terms of trade, but cannot increase the rate of growth.

Interpreted in a neoclassical light, other results of the two-gap model presuppose very special assumptions as well. Domestic output cannot substitute for imports in production of capital beyond some maximum level. The assumptions of a fixed savings rate and a target growth rate imply an unusual specification of intertemporal preferences.

The neoclassical interpretation of the two-gap model highlights the special assumptions required for it to hold in equilibrium situations. Nevertheless, one point suggested by the model holds more generally. Given its terms of trade, a capital-goods importer will benefit more from receiving a given increment of foreign exchange when demand for its exports is more inelastic. The shadow price of foreign exchange for such a country is higher. This is true regardless of whether the country pursues laissez-faire or nationally-optimal trade policies.

4.2.3. A disequilibrium interpretation: A rehabilitation?

The neoclassic critique of the two-gap model emerges from an attempt to translate its assumptions into an explicit market-clearing framework. In his exchange with Bruton (1969), Chenery (1969) defends the approach on the basis of the "structural disequilibrium" that he believes characterizes the developing countries for which the theory was intended. He dismisses the criticism that such disequilibrium might be the consequence of previous (bad) policy as "not particularly relevant to a description of actual policy alternatives" (p. 477).

In the intervening years a substantial amount of research (primarily emanating from Europe or from European economists) has appeared on "disequilibrium macroeconomics". This work has introduced into the standard general equilibrium model the assumption of explicit price rigidities in some or all markets.

Recent extensions of this work have considered the case of disequilibrium in a small, open economy and four, by Gunning (1983b), Waelbroeck (1984), Standaert (1985), and Van Wijnbergen (1985), have shown how a disequilibrium specification can yield a structure with "two-gap" properties. Van Wijnbergen (1985) demonstrates in a two-sector model with traded and nontraded goods that the ex ante difference between the "savings gap" (income minus expenditure) and the "trade gap" (exports less imports) must equal the ex ante difference between demand and supply of nontraded goods.

Gunning (1983b) and Standaert (1985) provide typologies of disequilibrium allocations that can emerge in open-economy models. The second paper derives expressions for the shadow price of foreign exchange in different regimes. The case of classical unemployment (with an excess supply of labor and an excess demand for goods) corresponds most closely to a situation in which the trade gap is binding. Here the shadow price of foreign exchange is high. With Keynesian unemployment (both labor and goods in excess supply) the shadow price of foreign exchange can be negative, however. The reason is that the increased availability of the imported good reduces demand for the domestically-produced good, which reduces output and employment.

Interpreting the two-gap model in this disequilibrium light has done little to raise its standing among its neoclassical critics. It does illustrate a way of making the model consistent with more general assumptions about tastes and technology.

4.2.4. Estimating the two-gap model

The two-gap model poses a problem for empirical implementation in that data could be generated by either of two regimes. Chenery and Strout (1966) address this problem by implicitly assuming that the two gaps always coincide.[19] Weisskopf (1972a) and Blomquist (1976) ran each regime (import-constrained and savings-constrained) for a set of countries, and use a goodness-of-fit criterion to assign countries to one regime or another.[20]

Gersovitz (1982) develops an econometric methodology that explicitly takes into account the inequality constraint relating the two regimes. His approach does not require the assumption that each country was subject only to one constraint or the other over the entire period of estimation. He applies this methodology to annual data from 1950 to 1978 from Argentina, Colombia, Ecuador, Guatemala, and Peru. For 55 percent of the observations the probabil-

---

[19]See the comment by Fei and Paauw (1965).

[20]Weisskopf actually includes a third capacity-constrained regime that Blomquist argues is redundant.

ity that savings is the operative constraint exceeds 0.5. Ecuador and Guatemala exhibit the longest periods of apparently import-constrained growth. Gersovitz also indicates how the basic framework can be extended to incorporate an arbitrary number of gaps, suggesting, for example, the possibility of a "skilled-labor gap".

4.3. Solow growth models

Solow's (1956) contribution to closed-economy growth theory has been used extensively to analyze international capital flows. Solow modifies the Harrod–Domar model by replacing the assumption of a fixed capital–output ratio with a standard neoclassical production function and allows competitive conditions in factor markets to determine factor rewards. Adjustment in the capital–output ratio brings the warranted growth rate into equality with the natural growth rate. An advantage to this approach is that the capital–labor ratio is now endogenous. The analysis continues to assume a fixed savings ratio.

Early applications of the Solow model to the theory of international capital movements were by Borts (1964), Oniki and Uzawa (1965), Negishi (1965), and Kemp (1968). I present a simple, one-sector, small open-economy version of the model to illustrate some basic results. Output per worker as a function of capital per worker k is given by $q = f(k)$, $f' > 0$, $f'' < 0$. If competitive conditions continuously allocate world capital to equate the domestic marginal product of capital to the world interest rate, r, then the relationship,

$$f'(k^d) = r, \tag{12}$$

determines *domestic* capital per worker as a function of r. Domestic capital and foreign assets (which may be negative) are assumed to be the only forms of national wealth. Denote wealth per worker by k^n. Savings is a fixed share s of national income. Hence, the differential equation,

$$\dot{k}^n = s\left[f(k^d) - r(k^d - k^n)\right] - nk^n, \tag{13}$$

describes the evolution of national wealth.

A steady state is a situation in which wealth per worker and the world interest rate are constant. Defining $\bar{x}$ as the steady-state value of variable x, steady-state wealth per worker is:

$$\bar{k}^n = s\left[f(\bar{k}^d) - r\bar{k}^d\right] \big/ (n - s\bar{r}), \tag{14}$$

with k^d determined by condition (12). Stability requires that $sr - n < 0$. Euler's equation, along with stability, guarantees that $\bar{k}^n > 0$, that in the steady state, wealth is positive.

In the steady state, indebtedness per worker d equals $\bar{k}^d - \bar{k}^n$. The country must run a steady-state current account deficit of nd to maintain d at a constant level. The steady-state trade deficit is therefore $(n - r)\bar{d}$. As long as the interest rate exceeds the growth rate, in the steady state net debtors run trade surpluses with net creditors. They do so to service their debt.

Out of the steady state the current-account surplus per worker is:

$$CA_t = sf - nk^d - srd_t, \tag{15}$$

while the per-worker trade balance is:

$$TB_t = sf - nk^d + r(1 - s)d_t. \tag{16}$$

Debt per worker evolves according to the differential equation:

$$\dot{d} = nk^d - sf + (sr - n)d. \tag{17}$$

4.3.1. Stages in the balance of payments

These differential equations have served as the basis for a theory of "stages" in the balance of payments. Consider the case of a primordial country characterized by (i) an initial capital stock below the level which equates the domestic marginal product to the world interest rate (i.e. for which $k_0 < \bar{k}^d$); (ii) which initially has no debt; but (iii) where in the steady state wealth per worker exceeds the capital stock (i.e. $\bar{k}^n > \bar{k}^d$). Given the interest rate, the transition from the initial situation to steady state can be divided into five stages:

(i) Immature debtor–borrower. Both the current and trade balances are negative as the country borrows to acquire the capital to achieve a domestic capital stock $\bar{k}^d$. Per worker indebtedness jumps from 0 to $\bar{k}^d - k_0$.

(ii) Mature debtor–borrower $(d_t > [sf(k^d) - nk^d]/sr)$. Since by assumption $\bar{d} < 0$, $sf(k^d) > nk^d$. But since $d_t > 0$ the country now runs a trade-account surplus. Debt-service obligations initially exceed the trade surplus, so that net indebtedness grows, even though debt per worker is falling. The current account is thus in deficit.

(iii) Debtor–repayer $(0 < d_t < [sf(k^d) - nk^d]/sr)$. As k_t^n grows (and d_t falls) the current account turns positive, but the country remains a net debtor.

(iv) Immature creditor–lender $([nk^d - sf(k^d)]/r(1 - s) < d_t < 0)$. Debt turns negative, but interest income remains less than new lending. The trade balance is positive.

(v) Mature creditor–lender ($d_t < [nk^d - sf(k^d)]/r(1 - s)$). The country now runs a trade deficit, earning resources from the rest of the world.

Note that if the initial level of debt is small enough, the country can skip the second stage.

The notion that a country passes through such stages during the process of development appears in Cairnes (1874). The classification here is taken from Crowther (1957).[21] Papers that have identified such stages in the Solow model are by Fischer and Frenkel (1974a, 1974b), Onitsuka (1974), Hori and Stein (1977), and Ruffin (1979).

Halevi (1971) tests the stages theory with cross-country data. He finds no systematic relationship between per capita income and balance-of-payments positions.

4.3.2. Other applications

Takagi (1981) and Katz (1982) consider the case of a country that can affect the terms on which loans are available.[22] They assume that the cost of loans rises with the ratio of debt to domestic capital. This is meant to capture default risk considerations rather than large country effects.[23]

Takagi's model distinguishes between loans from public and from private sources. The first are available at lower rates and slower amortization schedules than the second. They are in restricted supply, and the supply falls with per capita income. The availability of loans from private sources, in contrast, rises with per capita income.

Saavedra–Sivano and Wooton (1983) look at the choice between labor and capital mobility in a large, open Solow economy (the Ramaswami issue discussed in Section 3). Ruffin (1985) has analyzed the optimal taxation of foreign capital income in a Solow economy.

The Solow model improves upon Harrod–Domar and two-gap analyses in providing a more realistic treatment of the interaction between foreign debt, domestic saving, and capital intensity. Nevertheless, the assumption that saving remains a fixed share of national income regardless of net indebtedness is obviously unrealistic and inconsistent with standard assumptions about intertemporal behavior.

---

[21] Crowther (1957) includes a sixth stage, the creditor–borrower, which begins to draw down its assets abroad, running a current deficit. While recent U.S. experience suggests that this category has empirical relevance, it does not emerge naturally from the analysis here. It can in more elaborate models with large countries. See Fischer and Frenkel (1974a, 1974b) and Ruffin (1979).

[22] Katz (1982) relates savings not to disposable income but to total wealth.

[23] The problem with this interpretation was mentioned in Subsection 3.3.

5. Dynamic models of international capital movements: Optimizing approaches

Understanding the impact of foreign aid and investment on growth requires understanding how domestic saving will respond. Another literature has attempted to derive savings behavior from the intertemporal choices of agents in the economy. An objective function is posited that relates agents' utilities to their consumption levels in different periods. Savings behavior emerges from individuals' efforts to attain their objectives.

Differences emerge according to the nature of the objective function. A major distinction is between the representative consumer approach, on the one hand, and the overlapping generations or life-cycle approach, on the other. The first postulates a single intertemporal objective function for the whole country, which could represent the outcome of social decision making, or if all individuals are identical, simply the aggregate of their preferences. The second approach postulates a series of heterogeneous individuals who differ in the timing of their births and deaths. These individuals derive utility only from consumption in periods in which they are alive. These preferences cannot be aggregated into a social welfare objective without attaching weights to the welfare of different individuals, but observed country behavior can be predicted on the basis of different individuals' attempts to maximize their objective functions.[24]

5.1. Representative-agent models

The larger part of the literature posits a representative agent. The economy can be treated like a single individual.

5.1.1. Two-period models

The simplest class of models posits that the utility of the representative agent is a function of consumption over two periods. As in Solow's analysis, a production technology converts capital and labor into output. In the initial period output is given by available factors of production and the production technology. Current output can be consumed or invested in capital. Borrowing from abroad increases

---

[24] The difference between the representative-consumer and life-cycle approaches is at the heart of the controversy over the effect of government budget deficits on saving, the Ricardian neutrality issue. The representative-consumer approach implies that, given a profile of government spending, the timing of lump-sum taxes to finance that spending is irrelevant for the real allocation of resources. In a life-cycle model, however, the timing affects the distribution of income across generations, and consequently has real effects. The two approaches turn out to have drastically different implications for the welfare consequences of capital movements and foreign aid as well.

resources available for either use in the first period, and any borrowing is repaid in the second period.

One application of this framework has been to analyze the effect of a change in the terms of trade on borrowing, the Harberger (1950) and Laursen and Metzler (1950) question discussed in Section 2. A result is that temporary and permanent terms-of-trade changes have different effects. Sachs (1981), Svensson and Razin (1983), and Svensson (1984a) show that the Harberger–Laursen–Metzler presumption, that a worsened terms of trade increases foreign borrowing, extends to a two-period situation when there is a *temporary* decline in the terms of trade in the first period. The effect of a permanent (i.e. for both periods) decline is ambiguous. For a temporary decline, borrowing provides a means of transferring consumption from the second period to the now less-well-endowed first period. In the case of a permanent decline, real resources in both periods fall. There is no presumption that borrowing should shift resources from the second to the first period. Other models can imply different conclusions, however, as discussed below.

5.1.2. Infinite-horizon models: The constant discounting case

Other models assume optimization over an infinite horizon. The typical approach has been to consider the problem in continuous time, positing explicitly an objective function of the form:

$$W_t = \int_t^T u(c_\tau) e^{-\rho(t-t)} d\tau, \quad u' > 0, u'' < 0, \tag{18}$$

where c_τ denotes period τ per capita consumption, $u(c_\tau)$ the flow of utility derived from that consumption, and ρ is a positive discount factor.[25]

With the linear-homogeneous technology of the Solow model, the flow *budget constraint* implies that per capita consumption is:

$$c_t = f(k^d) - nk^d + (n-r)d - \dot{k}^d + \dot{d}. \tag{19}$$

With perfect capital mobility and a permanent world interest rate r the optimal value of the domestic capital stock, k^d, is again that which equates the domestic return to the world rate. The maximization problem is consequently one

---

[25] In principle ρ can be either zero or strictly positive. In the first case W is unbounded and standard optimization procedures fail. Here von Weizsacker's (1965) overtaking criterion implies that at the optimum steady-state utility is maximized. Early papers by Bardhan (1967), Bade (1972), Hanson (1974), and Feder and Regev (1975) derive borrowing policies that maximize utility in the steady state. The more common approach has been to assume that ρ is strictly positive, so that the objective function is bounded.

of choosing consumption each period to maximize (18) subject to the equation of motion for *d* given by (19).

"Ponzi schemes" and intertemporal solvency. If there is no upper bound on the eventual level of debt, arbitrarily high levels of consumption and utility can be achieved by perpetually borrowing more than current debt–service obligations. The constraint that debt cannot exceed the present discounted value of future output is typically imposed to keep a country from running such a "Ponzi scheme". The *balance sheet* or solvency constraint is consequently that:

$$\frac{f(k^{\mathrm{d}})}{r-n} \le d_\tau, \quad \text{for } r > n. \tag{20}$$

If $r \le n$ the discounted value of future income is infinite. The country has infinite net worth and can consequently borrow as much as it wants and remain solvent. Since such a country does not pose very interesting economic problems and presumably does not warrant the attention of development economists, the restriction $r > n$ is typically imposed. Note the contrast with the analysis of debt in the Harrod–Domar model discussed in Section 4, where the condition $n > r$ emerges as a criterion for creditworthiness.

The optimal consumption path, which defines optimal borrowing and indebtedness through the budget constraint, is the stream c_t that maximizes (18) subject to (19) and (20). It can be characterized by standard dynamic optimization techniques.

The discounted Hamiltonian is:

$$H(d_t, t) = \mathrm{e}^{-\rho t}\big\{ u(c_\tau) + \lambda_\tau \big[c_\tau - f(k^{\mathrm{d}}) + (r-n)d_\tau + nk^{\mathrm{d}} \big] \big\}, \tag{21}$$

where λ_τ is the shadow price of debt in period τ. The first-order condition for a maximum is:

$$u'(c_\tau) = \lambda_t. \tag{22}$$

The dynamic price equation is:

$$\frac{\mathrm{d}(\mathrm{e}^{-\rho\tau}\lambda_\tau)}{\mathrm{d}\tau} = -\frac{\mathrm{d}H}{\mathrm{d}\tau} = \mathrm{e}^{-\rho\tau}\lambda_\tau(r-n), \tag{23}$$

which implies an equation of motion for the shadow price of

$$-\frac{\dot{\lambda}_\tau}{\lambda_\tau} = r - n - \rho. \tag{24}$$

Differentiating (22) and substituting the result into (24) gives:

$$\eta_\tau \frac{\dot{c}_\tau}{c_\tau} = r - n - \rho, \tag{25}$$

where

$$\eta_\tau \equiv -\frac{u''(c_\tau)c_\tau}{u'(c_\tau)},$$

the elasticity of the marginal utility of consumption.

The transversality condition requires that the discounted value of debt remain bounded, or that:

$$\lim_{\tau \to \infty} e^{-\rho\tau} \lambda_\tau d_\tau = 0 \tag{26}$$

which, solving (25), is satisfied if and only if $n \le r$ if $d_\tau = 0$. Thus, the transversality condition is implied by a (nontrivial) solvency requirement.

Assuming, then, that $r \ge n$, three situations are possible:

(i) $r > n + \rho$, in which consumption steadily increases over time. For this to be consistent with (25) (an asymptotically bounded level of debt per capita and $r > n$) requires that d_τ fall over time. The country's wealth per capita steadily rises.

(ii) $r < n + \rho$, in which case consumption per capita steadily falls, asymptotically approaching zero. This requires a steadily increasing debt level up to the point at which the solvency constraint (20) is binding. Asymptotically, all output is used to pay interest.

(iii) $r = n + \rho$, in which case consumption per capita is constant. Whatever the initial level of debt per capita, consumption behavior maintains that level of debt. Since, by assumption, $r \ge n$, countries with an initially high level of debt experience lower per capita income in the steady state than those with an initially low level.

These implications of the analysis are not appealing. In case (i) there is no steady state; national wealth is forever increasing. In case (ii) consumption falls toward zero. In case (iii) there is a continuum of steady states with the choice among them determined by initial conditions.

Extending the analysis to a multi-country situation does not provide implications that are more attractive. If all countries grow at the same rate n, then the country with the lowest discount rate eventually owns all the world's capital. The world interest rate tends toward the discount rate of that country. If all countries have the same discount rate, then the marginal product of capital in all countries converges to that rate. The ultimate distribution of claims depends upon the initial distribution.[26]

The failure of the intertemporal optimizing model to generate an interesting steady state for a small open economy (if $\rho \neq r - n$) or to determine its steady-state wealth level (if $\rho = r - n$) can be remedied by endogenizing the discount rate, ρ, the interest rate, r, or the growth rate, n. For instance, one or more of these magnitudes might depend on wealth or net indebtedness. A recent literature in which the discount rate is endogenized is discussed below.

Another strategy is to assume that r, the interest rate, rises as indebtedness rises. In one of the earliest papers on optimal borrowing, Bardhan (1967) introduces this assumption in two ways. First, he simply assumes that foreign debt generates disutility for the borrower at the margin. As debt grows so does the shadow cost of additional borrowing, even if the interest rate itself is unchanged. Second, as debt grows so does the risk of default. To compensate for this risk lenders charge a risk premium that is an increasing function of indebtedness, since the risk of default grows with indebtedness.[27]

Two papers that develop explicitly stochastic versions of Bardhan's model illustrate the role of foreign borrowing to smooth consumption when domestic output is variable. There is assumed to be no international contingent claims market in which countries can insure against variation in their output. Borrowing in international capital markets provides a second-best means of pooling risk internationally.

McCabe and Sibley (1976) model optimal borrowing for a country with stochastic export revenue. They assume an upward-sloping supply curve of funds

---

[26] Bazdarich (1978) exposits the model for a small economy. He makes the point that if there is a steady state, i.e. if $r \leq n + \rho$, then the model fails to predict anything like Cairnes' stages in the balance of payments discussed in Subsection 4.3. Wan (1971) develops a two-country version with a finite horizon, and Lipton and Sachs (1983) an infinite horizon, two-country version. Martin and Selowski (1984) and Dornbusch (1983) introduce nontraded goods, which break the link between perfect capital mobility and real interest rate equalization: differential changes in the relative price of nontraded goods across countries imply different real returns even when nominal returns are equal.

[27] The problem with this second rationale for an upward-sloping supply curve was mentioned in Subsection 3.3 above and is discussed at greater length in Section 6, which treats default. Papers that have followed Bardhan in positing an interest cost that rises with indebtedness are by Hamada (1969), Hanson (1974), Feder and Regev (1975), and Bruno (1976). Feder and Regev distinguish between foreign direct investment and portfolio borrowing. The first is threatened by expropriation and the second by default. In a steady-state optimum, per capita levels of debt, direct investment, and total capital equate the marginal cost of funds from alternative sources (domestic savings, foreign direct investment, and foreign loans). Foreign investors perceive the risk of expropriation and default as increasing functions of the ratio of foreign direct investment or of portfolio indebtedness to national wealth. A consequence is that in the steady state domestic investment proceeds beyond the point at which the marginal product of capital equals the growth rate plus the discount rate. The reason is that more domestic capital improves the terms on which foreign capital of either type is available. A recent series of papers applies a multi-sectoral version of the constant discount rate model to analyze numerically optimal borrowing in several developing countries. See Kharas and Shishido (1985) and Ghanem (1985).

and a finite horizon. One result is that saving and borrowing will be negatively correlated along an optimal path, since borrowing occurs when income, and hence saving, is low.

Clarida (1985) develops a multi-country model in which individual countries receive random endowments of output. (There is no productive capital.) Debtors repay as long as they are solvent. Loans are available up to a ceiling set to ensure that the borrower is solvent in all states of nature. Hence, default never occurs. He demonstrates the existence of an equilibrium under these assumptions. It is characterized by (i) a market interest rate below any country's discount rate and (ii) the presence of credit rationing.

5.1.3. Infinite horizon models with variable discounting

Another response to the awkward steady-state implications of the optimal borrowing model is to assume that the discount rate, as opposed to the interest rate, responds to the level of indebtedness. Uzawa (1968) provides a specification of preferences in which the discount rate depends on previous consumption.[28] Obstfeld (1982) and Engel and Kletzer (1986a, 1986b) have adopted his formulation. It can be solved with the same Hamiltonian technique applied to the constant discount case by redefining time units appropriately.

The behavior of the model is very much driven by the assumption that the discount rate increases with past consumption.[29]

5.1.3.1. The steady state. In the steady state the level of consumption is that which implies that the discount rate equal the world interest rate less the growth rate. For a net debtor, then, steady-state consumption rises with the world interest rate and falls with the growth rate.

5.1.3.2. Transitional dynamics. Obstfeld (1982) and Engel and Kletzer (1986a) provide a formal analysis of the dynamic adjustment path. A country with an initial level of indebtedness below the steady-state level will first consume more than its steady-state consumption level since it pays less in interest. Consequently it accumulates debt. Consumption declines as debt grows, causing the discount rate to fall, reducing the rate at which debt accumulates.

---

[28] Uzawa's is a special case of a more general specification of preferences provided by Diamond, Koopmans and Williamson (1964).

[29] While this assumption may seem arbitrary it is necessary for stability. To see this consider two endowment economies with the same preferences, one with an income stream y^A and one with an income stream y^B, $y^A > y^B$. With trade in debt, the debt level must equate the two discount rates. Establishing this equality requires that the consumption levels be the same in the two countries, or that country A be in debt to country B. But country A will have a higher autarky interest rate only if discount factors fall with consumption. Otherwise, the opening of trade in debt will result in A lending to B.

A permanent increase in the world interest rate implies an initial drop in consumption to repay debt. Consumption gradually rises again, eventually exceeding its previous steady-state level.

An implication of this result is that, comparing two countries that differ only in the size of their endowments of internationally immobile income-generating resources (such as land), the resource-rich country will be the *debtor*. The reason is that in the steady state the two countries must have the same discount factors and hence the same consumption levels. This is only possible if the resource-rich country makes transfers to the resource-poor country, which requires that the second have net claims on the first.

5.1.3.3. The Harberger–Laursen–Metzler effect. Obstfeld (1982) uses the variable discount factor model to consider the effect of a permanent deterioration in the terms of trade on optimal borrowing in an endowment economy, assuming that there is no change in the world interest rate. If the initial level of debt is zero, a decline in the terms of trade leads to net *lending* on impact and the accumulation of net claims on the rest of the world. This result is in contrast with the standard Harberger–Laursen–Metzler presumption, and with the ambiguous prediction of the two-period model already discussed.

The reason is that a deterioration in the terms of trade reduces the value of the endowment. If debt is unchanged, then consumption falls. This causes the discount rate to fall, and results in an accumulation of foreign assets. This process continues until the equality of the discount rate with the world interest rate is restored.

5.1.3.4. Tariffs and the current account. Engel and Kletzer (1986b) use the model to consider the effect of the imposition of a tariff on the current account. Since a tariff imposes a deadweight loss, the effect is similar to that of a decline in the terms of trade. There is an initial current account surplus to acquire claims on the rest of the world that restores consumption to its initial level. The tariff temporarily improves the current account.

5.1.3.5. Stages in the balance of payments. Engel and Kletzer (1986a) develop a two-sector model with (traded) capital goods and (nontraded) consumption goods. A general issue is the implication of a shift in preferences toward future consumption on optimal borrowing. In the other models discussed so far, such a shift will always reduce optimal indebtedness both on impact and in the steady state. That is not the case here. If the capital good is capital-intensive, a shift in preferences toward future consumption can lead to more *borrowing* on impact as the country expands its output of traded goods to run a trade surplus. Over time it reduces its debt and may acquire net claims on the rest of the world. This specification consequently rehabilitates the notion that a country may pass through "stages" in its balance-of-payments history.

In summary, the representative consumer approach to characterizing optimal borrowing to finance development runs into serious technical difficulties with the standard constant-discount-factor specification. The implications for steady-state behavior are highly unsatisfactory, and policy conclusions based on them should be regarded with caution. The application of preferences embodying a variable discount rate overcomes these technical difficulties. Despite the possibly counter-intuitive implications of this specification, it seems the most promising of the representative agent approaches.

5.2. Life-cycle models

5.2.1. Capital models

Diamond (1965) provides a framework for modeling optimal capital accumulation and borrowing in an economy with an infinite series of finite-lived individuals. Individuals live two periods and their lifetime utility is a function of their consumption in those two periods. In the first period they earn a wage which they can consume or save. In the second period they consume the amount that they invested and any interest that it earns.

As in the Solow model, capital and labor produce output at constant returns to scale. Output is homogeneous and serves either for consumption or for investment in capital. Marginal productivity conditions determine factor rewards.

In a closed economy, the savings of the older generation provide the capital stock with which the younger generation works. Per worker savings as a function of the wage rate, w, and the anticipated interest rate, r, may be expressed as $s(w,r)$. In the steady state the capital–labor ratio, k, must satisfy the condition that

$$s(w, r) = k(1 + n),\qquad(27)$$

where the marginal productivities of capital and labor implied by the production technology and the capital–labor ratio, k, determine r and w.

The capital stock that maximizes the welfare of the typical generation in the steady state equates the marginal product of capital, and hence the interest rate, to the population growth rate. This is known as the Golden Rule capital–labor ratio. If k exceeds this level, then welfare of *all* generations can be raised by perpetually transferring resources from working to retired generations. Such a steady state is consequently inefficient. If k is less than this level, raising steady-state welfare requires a transfer in the opposite direction. At least one generation, the older generation when the transfers begin, suffers. Hence a steady state in which k is less than its Golden Rule is efficient.

The effect of a permanent increase in the level of foreign investment depends on whether the initial equilibrium is efficient or not.

5.2.1.1. Efficient equilibria. Say that the domestic interest rate, r, initially exceeds the growth rate, n, and there is a permanent increase in foreign indebtedness, possibly because the world interest rate is lower than the initial domestic interest rate. The effect is to raise the wage and to lower r. As long as r remains greater than n, the effect on steady-state welfare is positive, but the generation that enters retirement when investment initially occurs earns the lower world interest rate without the benefit of the higher wage. It loses. For a potential borrower, then, foreign borrowing benefits the young at the expense of the old.

5.2.1.2. Inefficient equilibria. If n initially exceeds r, however, not only is the impact effect of a permanent increase in foreign investment negative, but so is the steady-state effect. Foreign investment has a Pareto-worsening effect.

Two differences with the representative-agent model warrant mention. First, since individuals optimize only over a *finite* horizon, a steady state with $r < n$ can arise without violating any transversality condition. If $r < n$, the present discounted value of future national income is infinite, but in a life-cycle model any individual's wealth remains finite.

Second, a constant discount rate poses no problem, as it does in the representative-agent case. Individuals can adjust their own consumption profiles to equate the marginal rate of substitution between periods to the world interest rate, with *aggregate* consumption per worker remaining constant.[30]

5.2.2. The role of land

All the discussion up to this point has treated capital as the sole store of value. The assumption that this asset is reproducible and in perfectly elastic supply rules out the possibility of capital gains or losses. In fact, the presence of nonreproducible assets in fixed supply can modify substantially how foreign borrowing affects the economy. A change in foreign indebtedness can permanently affect the value of such assets in terms of consumption goods, and these asset price changes affect the welfare of different generations.

---

[30] Diamond's (1965) exposition of the overlapping generations model discusses the implications of foreign investment for a single country. Buiter (1981) extends his analysis to two countries. Persson and Svensson (1985) and Dornbusch (1985) develop two-sector versions of the model with nontraded goods. Persson and Svensson examine the Harberger–Laursen–Metzler proposition. They note the importance of distinguishing between unanticipated and anticipated changes, as well as between temporary and permanent ones. They find no presumption about the current account response to a terms-of-trade change, but observe that the interaction of price changes and investment can yield cyclical responses.

Kareken and Wallace (1977) develop a model that demonstrates how foreign borrowing can have diametrically opposite results in the presence of a fixed asset. They consider a two-sector model in which land, rather than reproducible capital, serves as the only store of value and factor of production alternative to labor. The supplies of land and labor in any country are fixed, and all output is consumed.

As long as land is positively valued, inefficiency of the type that arises in the Diamond model is ruled out. In the steady state the price of land is constant, so it offers a return at least as great as the population growth rate of zero. If π_τ denotes the marginal product of land in period τ, then the price of a unit of land in the steady state is π/r.

Consider an economy with one worker each period and T units of land. Output is $f(T)$ and, with perfectly competitive factor markets, $\pi = f'(T)$ and $w = f(T) - \pi T$. In an autarkic steady state the interest rate, r, solves:

$$T\pi/r = s(w, r), \tag{28}$$

if land is the only store of value.

Productive resources, and hence π and w, are now unaffected by foreign investment. If the world interest rate is r, then the price of land becomes π/r and the level of indebtedness d satisfies:

$$T\pi/r - d = s(w, r). \tag{29}$$

The effect of a permanent increase in foreign borrowing on steady-state welfare is now negative, which is Diamond's result *exactly reversed*. With only land present as a domestic asset foreign investment does not add to the productive resources of the economy. It only bids up the price of assets in fixed supply. The wage earned by the young is unchanged, but the return on savings is lower.

The impact effect of foreign investment is also reversed. The initial expectation of future investment generates a capital gain on land enjoyed by the retired generation. Foreign investment does not mean the arrival of additional units of the store of value to compete with those owned by the currently retired. Rather, it means that foreigners will compete with the working generation to purchase the fixed supply of what is now owned by the retired.

If there are both land (in fixed supply) and (reproducible) capital to serve as stores of value as well as factors of production along with labor, then the effect of foreign investment is more complicated. A negative effect on steady-state welfare is more likely the larger the proportion of land in wealth and the lower the interest rate initially.

The model can also be used to consider the implications of land endowments (or other durable resource in fixed supply) for borrowing when the supply of foreign capital is perfectly elastic. Debt equals the domestic capital stock plus the value of land (total domestic wealth) less national wealth. Variation in the land–labor ratio has three effects. First, at the initial capital stock an increase in

T raises domestic wealth. Hence, given savings, foreign indebtedness must rise. Second, an increase in T raises the real wage, which raises national savings. This effect reduces indebtedness. Third, the marginal product of capital rises or falls depending upon whether capital and land are complements or substitutes. In the first case domestic capital rises, increasing indebtedness, with the opposite occurring in the second case [see Eaton (1988)].

To summarize, in a life-cycle model, assets in fixed supply have important implications for understanding the effects of capital inflow. There is no longer such a strong presumption that capital inflow benefits future generations at the expense of current wealth holders. If the primary effect is to create capital gains the opposite is true. Whether resource-rich or resource-poor countries are most likely to be international borrowers depends upon aspects of technology. Unfortunately, there is little empirical evidence as to which effects are most likely. Goldsmith's (1985) data on land as a share of tangible assets in 20 countries indicate that in a recent year the ratio lies between 12 and 27 percent (with Japan an outlier at 50 percent). His data for 1850 have most observations at around 50 percent. More research into the role of land as an asset in the process of development is needed.

5.2.3. Stochastic death models

Diamond's (1965) overlapping generations model provides a useful framework for analyzing theoretically the implications of foreign borrowing for capital accumulation in a life-cycle model. A drawback is that its assumptions about timing are sufficiently stylized to render its empirical application difficult. Yaari (1965) provides a specification of preferences that Blanchard (1985) has adapted to model an aggregate economy that shares many features with the Diamond model but is more realistic in its assumptions about timing.

The model is usually formulated in continuous time. Rather than living a fixed period, individuals face a constant probability of death λ. To maintain a constant population a birth rate equal to this probability of death is also assumed. Individuals are expected-utility maximizers with a constant discount rate.

Individuals invest their nonhuman wealth in an annuities market. If the rate of return on investment is r, then perfect competition in the annuities market ensures that individual investors earn a return $r + \lambda$ if they live.[31]

Engel and Kletzer (1986b) apply this model to analyze foreign borrowing. One issue that they consider is the effect of a tariff on net indebtedness. The answer is sensitive to how the revenue from the tariff is distributed.

---

[31] Weil (1985) provides a variant of the Yaari–Blanchard framework that allows for population growth. Individuals are immortal but their supply increases. Obstfeld (1987) applies this framework to analyzing the effects of fiscal policy on indebtedness.

A related implication of the life-cycle approach is that policies that generate domestic rents (that are not entirely dissipated by contemporaneous rent-seeking activities) affect net foreign indebtedness. The direction of the effect depends on whether they are capitalized or not. Capitalization will occur if access to the rent is attached to some form of nonhuman wealth, such as a firm with a long-term claim on the rent. In this case the capitalized value of rents adds to total domestic nonhuman wealth. If the rent-creating policies have no effect on national wealth at world prices then net indebtedness is greater. Eaton (1987b) models this effect.

In view of the huge variety of dynamic specifications that have been used, insisting that dynamic behavior derive from individual intertemporal optimization is a useful way to restrict the set of possible approaches. Given this restriction, the choice between the representative-agent and life-cycle approaches is partially one of strategy. Empirical evidence from developed countries has not led the original proponents of either view to shift ground substantially, but the life-cycle view seems to have marshalled more support. Consequently, this approach may have greater predictive power. Formulating *optimal policy*, however, then requires weighting the welfare of different generations to form a social welfare function, and then acting on behalf of that representative composite. Hence, the representative-agent approach may prove more useful here.

In terms of their usefulness in illuminating the contribution of foreign capital to the growth of poor countries, a defect of both the descriptive and the optimizing approaches is their emphasis on capital accumulation as a source of growth. Analysis of the sources of growth in both developing and in developed countries indicates that the contribution of investment to income growth is overwhelmed by residual effects.[32] Since economists are hard-pressed to explain the determinants of the residual, their modeling efforts have focused primarily on the role of capital.

This problem is not a justification for static or for ad hoc analysis of the effect of foreign capital on development, but indicates the need for further research on the determinants of economic growth. Recent papers by Lucas (1985) and Romer (1986) suggest a framework for analyzing the contribution of "residual" factors to growth.

6. Foreign borrowing with potential repudiation

This section discusses the role of the solvency constraint in international capital markets in greater detail. In a domestic context this constraint has a straightfor-

---

[32] This finding suggests why direct investment, which transfers technology as well as capital, may contribute much more to growth than portfolio investment.

ward justification. The income of the borrower places an upper bound on the resources available for payment. In principle the legal system forces the borrower to turn over these resources to service debt until debt obligations are fulfilled. If he cannot, then the borrower's assets are transferred to the lender, who can then receive the income that they generate. A solvent borrower consequently has an incentive to service debt, and the value of the debtor's assets provides a lower bound on the return on a loan.

The prospective income of a borrower may vastly overstate the resources that a lender may hope to recover, even in a domestic setting, however. The context of international capital markets exacerbates forces that reduce the lender's probable receipts from borrowers. This issue is one that has received a great deal of attention recently, and has been surveyed at length.[33] This section states some basic points, drawing heavily on Gersovitz (1985) and Eaton, Gersovitz and Stiglitz (1986).

6.1. Solvency

Assume that a lender *could* force a sovereign borrower to relinquish all available current and future resources to service its debt. Resources available for repayment may fall substantially short of the value of domestic resources for several reasons.

6.1.1. Nontraded assets and goods

Unless the lender relocates to the borrowing country, only the borrower's internationally mobile assets and the current and future outputs of traded goods can be transferred. Assets that are immobile and output of nontraded goods do not provide a basis for repayment.

6.1.2. The government fiscal constraint

To the extent that debt is owed by the government of a country, its maximal tax revenue constrains resources available for payment. Even if total domestic output is available as a tax base, the administrative cost and excess burden of taxation reduce maximal tax receipts below total income.

6.1.3. Moral hazard

The lender cannot easily control the allocation of resources within the borrowing country. Once a loan contract has been struck, the interests of the borrower and

[33]See, for example, Eaton and Gersovitz (1981b, 1983), Sachs (1984), Crawford (1987), Gersovitz (1985), Glick (1986), Eaton, Gersovitz and Stiglitz (1986), and Eaton and Taylor (1986).

lender do not necessarily coincide. The borrower, for example, may find a risky investment more attractive, even if it yields a lower expected return than another, safer project. The borrower receives all of the proceeds if the return is high, but the lender bears the downside risk if the borrower goes bankrupt. See Stiglitz and Weiss (1981).

One particular decision made by the borrower that affects the likelihood of repayment is investment. By consuming more in early periods the borrower has less to turn over to the lender when payment is due. Another is the allocation of investment between production of traded and nontraded goods. As mentioned, only the first add to resources for repayment.

Some analysts have attempted to gauge the solvency of a borrowing country by forecasting components of its current account. If the discounted value of projected surpluses exceeds the value of outstanding loans, then the borrowing country is deemed solvent. Cline (1983) adopts this approach. He forecasts the exports and imports of several major borrowers on the basis of posited export and import demand functions and forecasts of income growth and commodity price movements. Since loans are largely provided on a floating rate basis he also forecasts interest payments. Under the assumption that world growth rates would be sufficiently high and interest rates sufficiently low, he concluded that the repayment prospects of most debtors in his sample would improve between 1983 and 1987.

An objection to this approach is the same one that Ohlin raised to Keynes' statement of the transfer problem. It treats the current account as having primacy over the capital account. But the magnitudes being forecast are not independent of the repayment itself.

6.2. The incentive to repay

For the borrower's solvency to indicate the prospects for repayment of a loan requires that nonpayment result in a transfer of assets from borrower to lender. In the context of international loan markets no mechanism enforces such a transfer, except to the extent that the borrower has offsetting claims against the lender, or property in the lending country. (To the extent that it does, no net intertemporal transfer of resources from lender to borrower has occurred.) Whatever incentive the borrower *does* have to repay is unlikely to cause him to transfer total assets or output (or even total tradable assets or total tax revenue) to the lender. Consequently, the incentive to repay will limit what the lender can expect to recover, not the resources of the economy.

Identifying and quantifying these incentives is difficult. Historically, countries and other entities in default on foreign loans have lost access to international capital markets for substantial periods. An exclusion from further lending is also consistent with an equilibrium notion in which failure to cooperate (by repaying) is punished by reverting to a noncooperative equilibrium (not lending). The incentive to repay is consequently governed by the cost of losing access to future borrowing. This exclusion affects the borrowing country's ability to smooth consumption if domestic output is uneven, to fund new investment, and to finance trade. Eaton and Gersovitz (1981a) focus on the cost of consumption-smoothing.

The problem of moral hazard re-emerges in the borrower's ability to reduce the impact of any penalty. Cohen and Sachs (1986) postulate that the harm from any penalty increases with income. Investing less reduces income in the repayment period, and hence the cost of default. It is in the interest of the lender that the borrower invest more in periods prior to repayment. Gersovitz (1983) and Alexander (1987) focus on the allocation of investment between export, import-substitute, and nontraded goods production. The borrower can reduce the impact of a *trade* cut-off by biasing investment decisions away from production of exports toward that of import substitutes.

To the extent that the incentive to repay affects the terms on which loans are provided, the moral hazard problem acts ultimately to the borrower's disadvantage by reducing his access to credit. If the borrowing country can precommit itself to a particular investment program, for example, more credit will be available.

A problem of commitment arises from the lender's side as well. In the case of domestic default, initiating a bankruptcy proceeding is typically in the lender's interest, since it is likely to culminate in a receipt of the borrower's assets. With an international loan, implementing a penalty such as a credit or trade embargo imposes a burden on the lender as well as on the borrower. In the simplest context the threat even to impose a penalty will not be a credible one. Consequently, no lending can ever occur. Lending channeled through a financial intermediary that is expected to make foreign loans into the indefinite future might be viable where loans from individuals are not. If the intermediary fails to penalize a default, future lending would be jeopardized, reducing the equity value of the intermediary. If the loss in equity value exceeds the cost of implementing the penalty, then the threat to invoke the penalty is credible. See Eaton (1986a).

Bulow and Rogoff (1986) assume that debt repudiation forces the country to trade at more unfavorable terms. This cost determines the outcome of the bargaining game that would occur between a borrower and a lender over debt–service payments in event of nonpayment, and consequently affects the maximal payment that a lender could hope to extract from the borrower.

Enders and Mattione (1984) attempt to calculate the implications of a hypothetical repudiation of debt by a set of Latin American lenders on 31 December 1983. They assume that the consequences of this act are (i) no longer paying interest, (ii) a loss of current reserves, but not reserves earned subsequently, (iii) a loss of 5 or 10 percent of export revenue, and (iv) no further credit. Except for

Mexico and Venezuela, the projected effect in the first year is very negative. By 1987, however, income is higher in Argentina, Brazil, and Venezuela, and lower in Chile, Colombia, and Peru under either default scenario as compared with not repudiating. The longer-term implications for Mexico are positive under the assumption of a 5 percent deterioration in export revenues, but negative under the 10 percent assumption. While this calculation is heroic, it does suggest that the debt–service burden for a number of debtors reached a point at which even reasonably tough penalties might not impose greater costs than paying interest.

6.3. Liquidity and rescheduling

In addition to insolvency and an insufficient incentive to repay, some observers [e.g. Cline (1983)] suggest illiquidity as a third reason for nonpayment. The borrower eventually will have resources with value in excess of outstanding debt, and has the incentive ultimately to make payment, but *current* resources fall short of *current* debt–service obligations.

The question arises as to why, if this is the case, lenders do not extend credit until the time when resources for repayment are available. In most specifications of the problem they would. Some insight into how a pure liquidity problem might arise may be provided in a paper by Diamond and Dybvig (1983). They model a domestic bank in which the potential for a "panic" causes all depositors to withdraw funds even though, if all kept funds on deposit, they would realize a higher return. Cooper and Sachs (1985) and Krugman (1985) apply similar reasoning to the problem of international lending. In their models a liquidity crisis appears as a form of coordination failure among lenders. For a liquidity crisis to occur, the amount of lending required to avoid the crisis must exceed the resources that any single lender can extend to the borrower in question.

Ozler (1984) explains liquidity crises in terms of the change in a lender's market power over an individual borrower once an initial loan is made. She assumes that before borrowing, a country faces a competitive set of lenders. The initial loan contract rules out subsequent borrowing from other sources, however. If an (imperfectly anticipated) liquidity problem arises, then the lender and borrower confront each other as bilateral monopolists. The loan is extended, but at terms more adverse to the borrower than the initial loan.[34]

Identifying the cause of a country's payments problems is important in designing the appropriate response. Rescheduling of public debt has been a

---

[34]She also suggests how rescheduling can arise because of a fall in the perceived cost of default. Then rescheduling occurs on terms more favorable to the borrower. She studies the effect of news of rescheduling on the equity values of lending banks, finding a typically positive effect in the 1970s, supporting a liquidity interpretation for rescheduling in that period, but a negative effect in the 1980s, suggesting that a reduction in repayment incentives in this decade was the cause.

regular occurrence for a number of countries under the Paris Club agreements during much of the post-World War II era [World Bank (1985)]. Since 1982, a number of the large debtor countries, in particular in Latin America, have negotiated rescheduling agreements with both public and private lenders. Public institutions like the International Monetary Fund (IMF) and the U.S. Treasury have provided funds to alleviate payments problems. They have also marshalled private lenders to extend new loans and urged them to lengthen the terms of existing loans. A consequence of these episodes has often been an increase in exposure by both public and private sources to the borrowing country.[35]

A question that these episodes raise is whether the payments problem is indeed the consequence of illiquidity, justifying the commitment of additional resources, or signals insolvency or ultimate unwillingness to pay, in which case lenders should cut their losses. In the first case the additional loans facilitate the repayment of the initial loans, and should themselves be repaid. In the second, lenders are simply augmenting the extent of their ultimate losses. Increased IMF and Treasury lending has been conditioned upon participation of original private lenders in providing additional resources, to avoid the appearance of a "bailout". This suggests that these public institutions were not totally confident that the problem is purely one of liquidity.

As mentioned, Cline (1983) and other observers argued for a liquidity interpretation, supporting further lending. Enders and Mattione (1984) were more pessimistic about long-term prospects, although in retrospect even their views appear optimistic: "Sustained increases in output per capita can confidently be expected only in the second half of the decade, so that growth could be restored to the 3.3 percent level for 1986 and 1987" (p. 50). Nevertheless, they also argue in favor of additional commitments of funds from public sources. Simulating the Data Resources, Inc., model for some of these countries they conclude, perhaps not surprisingly, that postponing payment does indeed improve economic conditions in early years, but worsens them in the years when the debt is ultimately due.

6.4. Capital flight

Most analysis of foreign capital in developing countries has addressed the causes and consequences of *net* capital movements between countries. It does not explain the composition of gross flows that yield any given net transfer, nor does the composition have any real consequences.

---

[35] Kraft (1984) provides a vivid account of the Mexican rescheduling in 1983.

Table 25.1
Estimated capital flight[a] and gross capital inflows in selected countries, 1979–82

Country	Capital flight (billions of dollars)	Gross capital inflows (billions of dollars)	Capital flight as a percentage of gross capital inflows
Venezuela	22.0	16.1	136.6
Argentina	19.2	16.1	65.1
Mexico	26.5	55.4	47.8
Uruguay	0.6	2.2	27.3
Portugal	1.8	8.6	20.9
Brazil	3.5	43.9	8.0
Turkey	0.4	7.9	5.1
Korea	0.9	18.7	4.8

Source: The World Bank (1985, table 4.4).
[a] Capital flight is defined as the sum of gross capital inflows and the current account deficit, less increases in official foreign reserves.

There is evidence that a number of large debtor countries also have substantial claims abroad.[36] Table 25.1 presents World Bank estimates for 1979–82 for some major debtors. Because these capital outflows are often interpreted as an escape from the tax base of the source country, particularly the base for the inflation tax, the phenomenon is frequently called "capital flight". While capital flight itself is typically a private phenomenon, it seems often to occur in conjunction with public capital flows in the opposite direction.

One explanation of two-way flows is simply that they result from diversification of exogenous risks associated with national rates of return. To the extent that this is in fact their cause, these flows are not evidence of market failure justifying concern. To the extent that flight capital evades taxation by the country of origin, it may, however, be harmful, as several explanations would imply.

Both macroeconomic and microeconomic interpretations of the phenomenon have been offered, although the two are not mutually inconsistent. Dornbusch (1985) and Ize and Ortiz (1986) are examples of the first type. They attribute flight to exchange-rate overvaluation, and consequent anticipated devaluation. These in turn are related to existing and anticipated fiscal deficits that are expected to be financed by inflation, and to public borrowing that itself is driving up the exchange rate.

Khan and Haque (1985) offer a microeconomic interpretation. They assume that nationals are subject to a greater risk of expropriation on domestic investments than foreigners are. This asymmetry generates two-way flows as each type

---

[36] Dooley, Helkie, Tryon and Underwood (1983), Cuddington (1986), Dooley (1987), and Cumby and Levich (1987) provide estimates and alternative methodologies for arriving at them.

of investor seeks a less risky return. If foreign investors face no risk of expropria-tion at all, then an exogenous gross outflow of local funds is exactly offset by a corresponding inflow of foreign funds that maintains equality of domestic and world returns. There is no welfare cost.

If foreign credit is rationed, however, then outflows are not fully recovered. Flight then lowers the domestic supply of capital. A given exogenous outflow may even lower the probability of repayment perceived by foreigners, reducing the amount of capital they supply as well. In this case the domestic capital stock drops by more than the initial gross outflow.

This explanation can be reconciled with the macroeconomic one discussed earlier. The threat of expropriation perceived by nationals (or, more generally, the threat of high taxation, possibly through inflation, of domestic assets) may derive from anticipated fiscal requirements, which in turn may result from previous or ongoing public borrowing. Hence, public debts can explain the flight of private capital.

As in Diamond and Dybvig's (1983) model of bank runs, there are potentially several equilibria. In one, favorable equilibrium a high level of private investment domestically provides a tax base sufficient to finance repayment of foreign public debt and still provide a competitive after-tax return. If private investment falls below some threshold, however, then the tax on capital income required to finance repayment leaves investors with less than the available foreign return. Capital flight and nonpayment of public debt, much like a bank run in the Diamond–Dybvig analysis, is the consequence. Eaton (1987a) and Eaton and Gersovitz (1986) provide alternative models of this phenomenon.

These models do provide a rationale for capital controls, assuming that they are enforceable. An implication that should probably be given greater weight is that there is a benefit to expanding the tax base of developing countries to include income earned on investment abroad and income earned by immobile domestic factors, like land. To the extent that private investors perceive that income from these sources will provide the revenue base to finance repayment of foreign debt, foreign borrowing is less likely to engender capital flight.

7. Foreign aid

In these last two sections I turn to some specific institutional aspects of the transfer of capital to developing countries. In keeping with the purview of this chapter, I only consider public institutions, but their impact is often through their interaction with private international capital markets, especially when middle-income countries are involved. In this section the topic is foreign aid. The grantor agency is usually a government or government-supported institution, although private sources such as charities also provide funding.

7.1. The historical experience

Mikesell (1968) discusses U.S. and U.K. foreign aid programs before World War II. Formal U.S. Government development assistance began in the late 1930s with government loans to Latin America. These were an outgrowth of President Roosevelt's Good Neighbor Policy. Ohlin (1956) reports that *private* technical assistance to that region dates back to the last century, however.[37] The British government established a foreign aid program for its colonies in 1929.

Only after World War II was foreign aid a quantitatively important component of most national budgets, however. Ohlin (1956) reports that in 1949, 2 percent of U.S. GNP was allocated toward foreign assistance as part of the Marshall Plan. Kennedy and Ruttan (1986) provide a recent account of the political background to the initiation of U.S. official aid programs in that period. Since World War II most developed countries, and, more recently, members of the Organization of Petroleum Exporting Countries (OPEC) have provided official development assistance on a regular basis.

Much official assistance is administered on a bilateral, government-to-government basis. (The Agency for International Development is primarily responsible for administering U.S. aid programs.) Foreign assistance is also channeled through multilateral institutions. The next section examines their role in providing external capital to developing countries. A number of United Nations affiliates, the Food and Agricultural Organization, World Health Organization, World Meteorological Organization, and United Nations Economic, Social and Cultural Organization provide various forms of assistance to developing countries. See Ohlin (1956).[38]

7.2. Types of aid

Development assistance rarely takes the form of a direct transfer of funds from donor to recipient that entail no further obligation on the part of the recipient. In the case of an official loan there is a subsequent debt–service obligation. The donor may tie the aid to the purchase of imports from the donor's country. Aid may take the form of a direct transfer of a particular product or service, such as technical assistance. Funds may be restricted for a particular investment project,

---

[37]Official relief aid, as opposed to development assistance, goes back earlier, as well. During World War I, the U.S. Government provided food aid to Europe under the auspices of the Commission for Relief in Belgium (1914–18), the Food Administration (1917–18), and the Relief Administration (1919–23). The last, with Herbert Hoover as its Director General, was appropriated $100 million to provide food to post-war Europe. Its activities expanded to include the Soviet Union and Middle East. (I am grateful to Ms. Mary Lou Levan for providing this information.)

[38]Cline (1979) provides an overview of trends in official development assistance, and institutions involved in channeling funds toward developing countries.

or for particular uses. Their availability may be conditional upon the recipient's following a particular set of policies. Individual donor countries may make grants through consortia rather than individually. Aid need not involve an explicit transfer, but the cancellation of a debt–service obligation incurred previously. The implications of these alternative forms of aid are now discussed.

7.2.1. Aid vs. credit

Foreign assistance very often takes the form of loans made available on concessional terms. Obviously, if all that is involved is the extension of a loan at market terms, no "foreign aid" occurs at all: official assistance simply displaces private lending with no net benefit to the recipient.

Schmidt (1964) defines the grant element of a loan and provides related formulae. A loan in amount L requiring an annual interest payment p maturing in n years is equivalent to a grant of g per year over n years if $(r - p)L = g$, and is equivalent to a grant in the initial period of G if $(r - p)L = rG/[1 - (1 + r)^{-n}]$. Here r is the *borrower's* discount rate. Proportional terms-of-trade effects associated with current transfers have no impact on these calculations. The net discounted terms-of-trade effect depends only on the grant element itself.[39]

If the lender's discount rate (r') equals the borrower's (r) then the *grant element* corresponds to the *net burden* on the donor, regardless of the form that it takes. A direct grant of g over n years is cheaper for the donor than a loan with the corresponding grant element if $r' > r > p$. If $r > r' > p$, the opposite is true.

A particular problem is assessing r, the borrower's marginal product of capital. Private lenders appear to ration credit to many less-developed countries. The rate on private loans, if there are any at all, will then understate r. In addition, the terms of private loans are often much shorter, and at variable interest rates, making comparison difficult.

Another problem is determining p, the interest obligation. Public loans may allow for repayment in kind or in domestic currency. These elements are likely to reduce the real burden of repayment. The potential for default also reduces the expected burden.

To qualify as "official development assistance" (ODA) under the terms of the Development Assistance Committee (DAC) of the Organization for Economic Cooperation and Development (OECD), a loan must have a grant element of at least 25 percent [see Cassen and Associates (1987)].

---

[39] This result has implications for the secondary burden of debt–service payments discussed in Section 2. If a loan is extended at a market rate there is no net terms-of-trade effect over the horizon of the loan.

7.2.2. Tied aid

Donors have frequently required the recipient to use aid to buy the donor's exports. Export credit agencies such as the Export–Import Bank of the United States (Eximbank) and U.S. Commodity Credit Corporation specifically grant loans at concessional rates to foreign importers.[40]

If the donor sells to the recipient at the world price, and the recipient would either have bought the export anyway or can resell costlessly, then the tying of aid has no consequences for the recipient's welfare. If resale is impossible (as, for example, with an installed nuclear reactor) but exports are priced competitively, then making aid proportional to the amount purchased reduces the implicit cost of buying those exports to the recipient. Because of the price distortion introduced, a comparison of the pre-aid and post-aid consumption points at world prices overstates the grant element involved.

Alternatively, the recipient may be able to resell at the world price p, but receiving aid requires him to buy from the donor at a noncompetitive price $p' > p$. Bhagwati (1967) provides a geometric analysis of this case. Again, the tie reduces the real benefit of the aid transfer.

In their recent examination of the impact of aid, Cassen and Associates (1987) estimate that tying aid to the donor's exports typically reduces its real value to the recipient by at least 20 percent below the value reported by the donor.

7.2.3. Food aid

An extreme form of tied aid takes the form of transfers in kind. An important example is food aid, which has been provided to developing countries in substantial amounts, in particular, under the provisions of the U.S. Public Law 480 (PL 480) administered by the Commodity Credit Corporation (CCC). Food aid accounted for 25 percent of the total U.S. aid budget in 1981, but its importance has since been falling. Total food aid to developing countries totalled US\$ 3 billion that year. The EEC is also a major food donor. Both programs are outgrowths, in part, of government efforts to support high domestic prices for agricultural outputs [see Cassen and Associates (1987)].

To the extent that the food items involved are freely traded at exogenous world prices, transfers in kind have no real implications that differ from a transfer of funds with equal value at world prices. Since most governments intervene heavily in domestic agricultural markets, however, domestic food prices may vary substantially between donor and recipient. The cost to the donor may then differ

---

[40] The extent to which export credit agencies transfer resources to overseas clients or to domestic producers is unclear. Eximbank has, on occasion, provided loans explicitly intended as debt relief. See Feinberg (1982), Baron (1983), Fleisig and Hill (1984), and Eaton (1986b) for a discussion of various aspects of export credit in general and the operation of Eximbank in particular.

significantly from the benefit to the recipient. Assessing the real value of transfers in kind is consequently problematic. Schultz (1960) and Pincus (1963) estimate that the tying of aid substantially reduced the benefit of U.S. aid programs to recipients below their reported costs to the United States.

A criticism of food aid is its potentially depressing effect on agricultural output, and farm income, in recipient countries. In some cases the consequences for the distribution of income internally are possibly highly adverse. Fisher (1963) makes the point that resources earned from the sale of agricultural goods can be used to compensate agricultural households only if the demand elasticity for the products exceeds one. A related criticism is that the availability of food from foreign sources may cause countries to avoid spending resources on agricultural research.[41]

Cassen and Associates (1987) argue that when food aid is successfully transferred to the poorest individuals in the recipient economy its effect is to expand domestic consumption virtually one-for-one. There is consequently little effect on domestic food prices and farm incomes.

Evaluating the contribution of food aid requires assessing not only its "additionality" to food consumption in the recipient country, but its "additionality" to aid contributions. If food aid fully crowds out untied donations, then its existence cannot help the recipient. The recipient would always do just as well or better receiving the cash value of the aid. Because of their interaction with agricultural subsidy programs in donor countries, donors may perceive food donations as nearly costless, however. Hence, the elimination of these programs may not imply much increase in other forms of aid. There is some question, however, in view of the transport costs involved, that the value of a direct transfer of just these costs to the recipients would benefit them more than the food donations themselves. Cassen and Associates (1987) provide further discussion.

7.2.4. Technical cooperation

Kennedy and Ruttan (1986) report that, in its initial years, U.S. aid for economic development was intended primarily to take the form of technical assistance. Cassen and Associates (1987) report that one-fifth of official development assistance takes the form of what is called technical cooperation (TC). This typically involves the provision of skilled personnel to assist with a given aid project or to aid in government administration generally. The personnel need not necessarily work in the recipient country, but work on problems associated with it.

---

[41]Sarris and Taylor (1977) discuss proposals to establish a world stock of food resources to serve as a source of aid for emergency relief.

To some extent, TC may serve the donor's objectives in monitoring the use of funds or in providing data about the recipient's economy to assist in further decisions about granting aid. Indeed, data acquisition has been a major goal of TC, although clearly their acquisition benefits the recipient as well.

For the most part, TC *is* intended to benefit the recipient. Given that capital accumulation fails to explain a major part of growth of per capita income, either in developed or in developing countries, the transfer of technical knowledge from developed to developing countries should be an important source of growth. By facilitating this transfer TC can make an important contribution to development.

The same question arises about TC as about any other transfer in kind. If international markets exist for the technical services transferred, then the donor should be able to provide a greater benefit at the same cost by transferring funds directly to the recipient. The recipient can then purchase these services independently if these do indeed constitute the most efficient use of the foreign exchange.

Two arguments can be made for TC. One is that the recipient may lack the expertise even to hire the appropriate services. To this extent TC is a transfer of government services. Another is that technical expertise is largely an "experience good" whose quality buyers have difficulty ascertaining at the time of purchase. Donor organizations repeatedly involved in employing technical services may be in a better position to elicit satisfactory performance from the personnel involved.

7.2.5. Consortia vs. bilateral aid

Aid may be provided on a bilateral basis or through consortia of donors. Balogh (1967) and Rosenstein-Rodan (1968) have written on this issue. Cassen and Associates (1987) report that lack of coordination among donors is an important reason for aid to fail to achieve its objectives. They cite Haiti as an example where failure to coordinate was especially detrimental. Coordination is sometimes achieved at the initiative of lenders, as through aid consortia or consultative groups, and sometimes at the initiative of the recipient. India provides an example of an aid recipient that actively coordinates the activities of its donors.

7.2.6. Debt relief

One form of aid is excusing debt–resource obligations on previous loans. The United Nations Commission of Trade and Development (UNCTAD) has proposed moratoria on debt–service payments on official bilateral loans for some countries, and alternative proposals abound. The recent decision by the U.S. Treasury Department to guarantee Mexican long-term debt in exchange for a write-down of existing debt by private creditors constitutes aid in the form of debt relief.

Smith (1979) criticizes this approach on the grounds that it allocates aid on criteria that are not (positively) related to the need (based on per capita income) or the economic performance of the beneficiaries. Buiter and Srinivasan (1987) argue that a moratorium on outstanding debt will adversely affect the future loan prospects of all developing countries. The reason is that a moratorium will establish a precedent that reduces the prospect for repayment of future loans. Countries that are not now significantly in debt or are repaying debt without difficulty will suffer at the expense of the profligate.

Sachs (1986), on the other hand, favors partial debt relief for some countries to reduce the disincentive effect of outstanding debt obligations. A premise of the argument is that outstanding loans are not going to be repaid in their entirety regardless of whether or not there is debt relief. Nevertheless, outstanding debt obligations impose a high marginal tax rate on a debtor's foreign exchange earnings, since these will be claimed by creditors. They consequently discourage a debtor from earning foreign exchange revenue at all. By reducing the book value of debt ex ante the creditor may actually increase expected debt–service payments by removing the implicit marginal tax on foreign exchange earnings. The debtor benefits as well.

7.2.7. *Project vs. program aid*

Some aid is intended to fund development expenditures generally (plan or program aid) while at other times it funds a specific project (project aid). Singer (1965) discusses this distinction. To the extent that funds from different sources are fungible the distinction is meaningless.

A justification that has been offered for project aid is that it facilitates the donor's oversight of the use of funds. A problem with this argument is that aid for any particular project frees foreign exchange for other purposes. If the project funded was to have been undertaken anyway, allocating aid for a specific project has no effect on the overall allocation of available resources. Cassen and Associates (1987) argue that funded projects are typically sufficiently large that they would not be undertaken in the absence of the project loan. The counterfactual needs to be specified carefully, however. If the alternative to a project loan were a general loan in the same amount, would the recipient have undertaken the project? If the project is a good one presumably it should have.

Another justification for project lending is that it transfers technical skills to the recipient, since the donor is typically active in the design and implementation of the project. A virtue of project loans may consequently be the transfer of technology embodied in them. Tying loans to particular projects can then be justified on the same grounds offered above to rationalize technical cooperation. The issue again arises as to whether or not the recipient can buy the necessary expertise on its own in world markets.

Plan or program aid or, when it is on a shorter-term basis, balance-of-payments lending, is frequently tied to the recipient's overall development policy or to the achievement of certain objectives specified by the donor. Conditionality, discussed below, raises the question as to why aid is supplied at all, the topic I turn to next.

7.3. The supply of aid

Understanding how aid is distributed and evaluating its success requires first identifying why it is provided at all.

7.3.1. Motivation for aid

The motives of donors in providing aid may be considered ones of self-interest or of altruism.[42] National security and national economic benefit are the two particular objectives that donors have been considered to pursue in providing aid. As the empirical evidence discussed below in Subsection 7.4 indicates, national security interests explain a large amount of aid that is provided, especially what is provided bilaterally by major powers. A small number of "strategic allies" seems to receive a disproportionate share of U.S. aid, for example.

Transfer paradoxes aside, it is hard to see how aid can benefit the donor country economically, at least directly. It may, however, benefit powerful groups within the donor country substantially. Subsidized export credits are an obvious example. Aid may consequently achieve a domestic *political* objective if other forms of internal transfers are precluded. Aid may also be intended to support a government that is pursuing trade and investment policies perceived as beneficial by the donor.

An altruistic concern for the less fortunate is another explanation for aid. A slightly different explanation is that aid derives from the pursuit of an ethical objective. One such objective might be maximization of a utilitarian objective function. Another might derive from the belief that certain countries are entitled to aid on the basis of an unfair distribution of natural resources or as reparations for colonial exploitation. Ruttan (1987) discusses these alternatives.

Jay and Michalopoulos (1987) distinguish between aid intended to promote development from "humanitarian" aid. This distinction is somewhat unclear unless one assumes that the donor has a stronger interest in the development of the recipient country than individuals in that country themselves have. A clearer distinction is between relief aid, intended to maintain current consumption levels

---

[42] My comments draw on the discussion of theories of donor motivation in Mikesell (1968), Riddell (1987), and Ruttan (1987).

during a shortfall in income that is perceived as temporary, and development aid, that is intended to raise investment and future consumption.

7.3.2. The objectives of aid and conditionality

If the objective of aid is to raise the welfare of individuals in the recipient country (whether for selfish or for altruistic reasons) and if the recipient country's government perfectly represents these individuals, then the purpose of aid can be met by an unconditional transfer of resources to the government. Aid typically does take the form of a transfer to the *government* of the recipient country, but it is often made conditional upon the pursuit of particular policies. Possible explanations for conditionality are (i) that the donor has objectives other than raising the welfare of individuals in the recipient country, or (ii) that it believes that the government will not act in those individuals' interest unless it is a condition of aid.

7.3.2.1. Donor vs. recipient objectives. Conditions attached to loans, in particular loans from the International Monetary Fund (IMF), are often quite explicitly intended to enhance the likelihood of repayment. Lenders perceive that the borrower's interest in repayment will be less than their own. The availability of loans is consequently made contingent upon policies by the borrowing government that the lender sees as improving prospects for repayment. Whether lenders have identified the appropriate policies is, of course, another issue.

Donors often evaluate the success of aid in terms of its contribution to growth or to the standard of living of the poorest individuals in the recipient country. One explanation for this focus is that growth and improved living standards for the poor are a concern of the donor not shared equally by the representative individual in the recipient country. Krueger (1981), in fact, argues that aid can contribute more to growth by eliciting appropriate policies through conditionality than by adding to savings or to foreign exchange. For it to be necessary to "buy" these policies implies that recipient governments have other concerns than growth that are not shared by donors.

Donors, for example, may desire growth to reduce the future demand for aid or to improve prospects for repayment of debt. National security considerations may motivate concern about growth or the welfare of the poor. Krueger's (1979) account of Korea's experience with aid indicates that U.S. aid was made conditional upon that country's liberalization of trade regime to enhance prospects for growth. The military security of the country was a concern.

When the donor's altruistic concern about the very poor is the motive for aid, and the representative individual in the recipient country is not believed to share this concern, then aid may be made conditional upon policies that benefit the poor. Cassen and Associates (1987) discuss how donors can design aid projects to ensure that they alleviate poverty. The implicit assumption is that this concern is not equally shared by the recipient government.

7.3.2.2. Governments as imperfect agents. A different reason for a donor to impose conditionality is that it does not expect the government in the recipient country to act in the interest of individuals in the recipient country. This may be because the government has a distinct constituency that acts in opposition to other groups in the economy. Bauer (1981), in particular, has argued that aid has "done much to politicize life in the Third World" (p. 104). By providing resources to the government of a country, aid adds to the power of that constituency, which is to the detriment of other groups in the economy. This criticism is particularly likely to apply to the many developing countries that systematically pursue policies that favor urban groups at the expense of the rural sector. By strengthening the government per se, aid increases its ability to pursue policies that are detrimental to the interests of large groups within the economy.

Cassen and Associates' (1987) discussion of the efficacy of aid indicates that during the last decade major aid donors have indeed become concerned with the potential for aid to encourage a *dirigiste* bias in developing countries. The World Bank's Structural Adjustment Loans (SALs), in particular, have been made contingent upon economic liberalization. Cassen et al. also report techniques whereby donors have attempted to channel aid directly to the private sector. An interpretation of the evidence discussed in their study is that historically aid may have encouraged state involvement in the economy, but that in the last decade donor conditionality has reduced this bias.

A more subtle reason why a government may not act in the interests of its citizens is the problem of time-inconsistency of optimal policy discussed by Kydland and Prescott (1977). Once it is time to implement the optimal policy, the government may have an incentive to do something else. Private citizens recognize this, and behave in response to what they think the government will do, rather than to optimal or announced policy. Imposing a high inflation tax is an example of a policy that may be time consistent but suboptimal.

Aid that is conditional upon optimal policy provides governments a means of committing themselves to this policy. This explanation is consistent with the popular view that recipient governments occasionally welcome conditionality in order to transfer blame for unpopular policies to granting agencies. Interestingly, lower inflation is sometimes a policy upon which aid is made conditional.

7.3.2.3. The experience with conditionality. Krueger and Ruttan (1987a) report that conditionality was an important aspect of USAID activity in the 1960s. Its role in encouraging liberalization in South Korea, for example, appears to have been significant. Since that decade bilateral donor agencies have become more demure in imposing conditionality, while multilateral institutions have taken the lead in this area.

7.3.3. Empirical evidence

Data on recent trends in official development assistance from World Bank members indicates that while the United States remains the largest donor in absolute terms, its official development assistance as a share of GNP is now the lowest among members of the OECD. Overall, official development assistance has grown relatively slowly in real terms since 1965.

Hoadley (1980), Beenstock (1980), and Mosley (1985) have attempted to formulate and to estimate econometric models of aid provision. Using a time series of annual data from nine donor countries for the period 1961–79, Mosley relates net official aid disbursements to lagged commitments, unemployment, and the budget deficit for the donor, and lagged disbursements by the other eight, the donor's relative income among the nine, lagged, and an index of the "quality" of aid. This last measure is based on the grant element, a proportion going to least-developed countries, a proportion going to agriculture and infrastructure, and a proportion untied of the nation's total official development assistance. This index is included on the grounds that the electorate will favor more aid if the aid its government provides is of high quality.[43]

In the pooled sample, only lagged aid by the other donors and lagged commitments of the donor country itself were significant, both with positive signs. For no countries were these variables significantly negative. The analysis thus fails to provide any evidence in support of a free-rider effect among donors in the provision of foreign aid.

7.4. The allocation of aid

Empirical work has attempted to explain the allocation of aid both in terms of donor self-interest and recipient need. The evidence indicates that *bilateral* aid is largely explained by the first. Wittkopf (1972), McKinlay (1978), McKinlay and Little (1977, 1978a, 1978b, 1979), and Maizels and Nissanke (1984) attempt to identify factors associated with donor self-interest and recipient need in the allocation of bilateral aid. In the first category they find strategic, political, and trade interest variables to be significant, and find recipient need variables not to be important.[44] Jay and Michalopoulos (1987) review these studies.

---

[43]According to this index, over the period Norway and Sweden tied in providing aid of highest quality. Japanese aid was the lowest quality, with U.S. aid second lowest.

[44]An exception is that the recipient's balance-of-payments deficit, interpreted as a measure of need, is significant in explaining aid receipts. This interpretation is flawed by the simultaneity between aid flows and the payments deficit.

Once multilateral aid is taken into account, there is more evidence that recipient need is an issue. Several studies have attempted to model aid flows on this basis.

A problem is that, if a given increment of aid transfers the same income to any recipient and if donors' objectives are to maximize a utilitarian social welfare function, then only the very poorest countries would receive what aid is provided, since presumably their marginal utility of income is greatest. Nevertheless, some relatively high-income countries receive aid. One explanation is that this aid serves the donor's perceived national security interest. Another is that the process that transforms aid into income is subject to diminishing returns, and that wealthier countries are more efficient at this transformation.

Edelman and Chenery (1977) analyze econometrically the allocation of aid commitments among developing countries for the periods 1967–69, 1970–72, and 1973–74 among 89 aid recipients.[45] Average per capita commitments (calculated as grant equivalents) are regressed against population, income per capita, income per capita squared (all in logarithms), and the export/GNP ratio. The principal results are that:

(i) Countries with smaller populations receive more aid per capita, although this effect diminishes over the three periods.

(ii) Per capita aid rises with per capita income from the lowest level to about \$200 in 1970–72 prices. It then fails.

Behrman and Sah (1984) develop a model of aid provision based explicitly on the theory of inequality aversion. Two functional forms of the donor's objective function are posited. One is the Kolm–Pollak (K-P) welfare function:

$$W = -\ln\left[\sum_i (a_i N_i / N)\exp(\gamma y_i)\right]\Big/ \gamma,$$

while the other is the CES:

$$W = \sum_i a_i N_i y_i^{1-\varepsilon} / 1 - \varepsilon,$$

where

$$W = \min\{y_i\}, \quad \text{as } \varepsilon \to \infty,$$

$$W = \sum_i a_i N_i \ln y_i, \quad \varepsilon = 1.$$

[45] Earlier econometric studies are by Cline and Sargen (1975) and Dudley and Montmarquette (1976).

Here y_i is per capita income and N_i the population of country i, and a_i a country-specific effect. Behrman and Sah assume that income is a constant elasticity function of aid provided. Thus, there are diminishing returns to additional aid.

If $a_i = a$ for all i (no country-specific effects in preferences) and the elasticity of the marginal product of aid is equal across countries, then the CES function implies that aid per capita is directly proportional to $y_i^{(1-\varepsilon)}$. For $\varepsilon = 0$ aid is independent of income while it increases if $\varepsilon < 1$ and decreases if $\varepsilon > 1$. In the K-P case, aid per capita is proportional to $y_i \exp[k - \gamma y_i]$, where k is a constant. In this case aid increases and then decreases with per capita income (reminiscent of what Edelman and Chenery find). Both forms explain the data quite well without recourse to country-specific effects, although the K-P version provides a better fit.

Estimation of the CES form indicates a value of ε around 1.4. Estimating the K-P formulation gives a value of γ around 0.0015, implying a turning point at $666 per capita.

7.5. The effects of aid

That foreign aid actually benefits the recipient is not universally accepted. Friedman (1958), Bauer (1981), and Griffin (1978) argue, from very different ideological perspectives, that aid has been detrimental to development. That aid can be immiserizing in the presence of distortions was discussed in Subsection 3.2, and the argument that it may encourage government activities that are detrimental to growth and welfare was mentioned in Subsection 7.3. Cassen and Associates (1987) and Krueger et al. (1987) each provide a recent detailed evaluation of aid. The first concludes that overall aid has been successful in achieving standard objectives. The second study concludes more negatively that there is little evidence that aid has been detrimental.

7.5.1. Microeconomic effects: Project aid

Project aid has typically been evaluated in terms of the rate of return on the project funded. The World Bank, for example, insists that projects it funds be projected to yield a 10 percent return [see Krueger et al. (1987)]. The vast literature on project evaluation indicates how hard assessing a rate of return is, ex ante or even ex post. These problems aside, Cassen and Associates (1987) report that a World Bank audit of projects during the 1960s and 1970s reveal an average return of 17 percent.

This return is a high one, but the calculation leaves open the question as to whether or not the projects in question would have been undertaken without aid.

If they would have been, then assessing the return on the aid itself requires identifying the marginal expenditures made possible by the aid, and what the returns on them were.

7.5.2. Macroeconomic effects

An alternative strategy is to assess the aggregate impact of foreign aid. Four questions have received particular attention: To what extent does aid add to domestic investment as opposed to displacing domestic saving? How does aid affect tax revenue? To what extent has aid contributed to growth? Has aid alleviated poverty?

7.5.2.1. Aid and saving. A number of studies, by Griffin and Enos (1970), Rahman (1968), Chenery and Eckstein (1970), and, particularly, Weisskopf (1972b), for example, report econometric analysis suggesting that aid adds little to productive resources because its effects are largely offset by a reduction in domestic saving.

Papanek (1972) criticizes these results for failing to correct for the simultaneity between saving and foreign assistance. Domestic shocks that tend to reduce saving are likely also to attract foreign aid, generating a negative correlation between the two variables with no causal implications.

Chenery and Syrquin (1975) conduct a broad cross-country analysis of the effects of foreign capital inflow on saving, as well as on a number of other variables. They do not address the simultaneity problem raised by Papanek in that they treat capital inflow as exogenous. They find that a dollar increase in capital inflow is associated with a $0.16 increase in investment and a $0.83 drop in domestic saving. They also find that it adds $0.72 to private consumption. Another result is that foreign capital inflow is offset in the balance of payments almost equally by reduced exports and by increased imports.

More recent studies have assessed the impact of aid in different regions and from different donors. It has been found to have a more depressing effect on saving in Latin America than elsewhere. Michalopoulos and Sukhatme (1987) survey this literature.

None of the empirical studies examines the relationship between aid and saving implied by any type of intertemporal maximization. It is useful to consider the effect of aid on saving implied by the various approaches to intertemporal maximization discussed in Section 5. In all these approaches the response does not depend on current aid alone but on anticipated future aid as well. Here I consider the effect of a permanent anticipated stream of aid constant in per capita terms. Hence, there is no conditionality. Since it seems more relevant for most aid recipients, I assume that the country does not have access to private capital at an exogenous interest rate, but is credit rationed for the reasons discussed in Section 6.

(1) *Representative-agent models.* With a constant discount rate *all* aid is consumed. To maintain equality of the marginal product of capital with the discount rate, the capital stock and hence investment do not change. In the case of Uzawa preferences the prospect of a permanent flow of resources from abroad raises permanent consumption, thus raising the steady-state discount rate. Investment actually falls. Hence, foreign aid engenders a *more than offsetting* drop in saving.

Obviously the prospect of termination of aid softens these results. Current aid perceived as temporary will raise current investment to carry over its benefit into future periods.

(2) *Life-cycle models.* A lesson of the life-cycle framework is that the effect of foreign aid on saving depends on how aid is distributed across generations. If aid is dispersed to the older generation, i.e. to individuals who are dissaving, then anticipation of these receipts will depress saving in periods of accumulation. The net effect on investment is negative. If aid is dispersed to the younger generation, i.e. to individuals who are saving, foreign investment will increase investment.

7.5.2.2. The government budget constraint. A closely related issue is how foreign aid affects the government budget.[46] If the excess burden and administrative cost of raising revenue domestically is positive, then the value of aid receipts to the government exceeds their nominal value. The value of aid may therefore differ substantially between countries according to their governments' marginal costs of raising domestic revenue.

7.5.2.3. Aid and growth. Mosley, Hudson and Horrell (1987) recently conducted a cross-section econometric analysis to estimate the effect of aid on growth. They attempt to correct for the identification problem raised by Papanek (1973) by comparing the effect across countries with given saving ratios and export growth rates. They do not find any evidence that aid raises growth rates.

Cassen and Associates (1987) criticize this cross-section methodology on a number of grounds, including its failure to distinguish between food aid and other forms of aid more specifically intended to promote growth. They conclude that nonfood aid has raised growth rates in recipient countries.

7.5.2.4. Aid and poverty. There is less formal analysis of the impact of aid on poverty. Cassen and Associates (1987) discuss some of what evidence there is,

---

[46]Sachs (1984) raises this point as it pertains to public borrowing. Chenery and Syrquin find that a dollar of foreign aid is associated with a $0.15 increase in government consumption and a $0.15 drop in tax revenue. Dacy (1975) argues that even temporary aid will increase the permanent level of government consumption, although why this should be the case is not formally explained.

and conclude that aid programs have been successful in alleviating poverty when properly designed with that intention. Some suggestions they have for directing aid more directly to the poor are: (i) to subsidize goods and services that form a large part of the expenditure of poor people; (ii) to finance current as well as capital costs of projects (to ensure their full utilization); (iii) to reduce capital intensity of projects; and (iv) to promote agricultural research.

8. The multilateral organizations

A particular feature of the post-World War II economic scene has been the presence of a number of government-supported multilateral organizations financing developing countries. These institutions grew partly out of disillusionment with the performance of private international capital markets in the pre-war period.[47] Most important have been the World Bank and the International Monetary Fund (IMF). In addition, there are the regional development banks such as the Asian Development Bank and the Inter-American Development Bank. The literature on these institutions is large. I will briefly mention some key issues regarding the operation of these institutions and their interaction with private markets.

8.1. The World Bank

The International Bank for Reconstruction and Development (IBRD) was founded in 1945 largely to finance investment in countries suffering severe war damage. This job was soon complete, and the Bank reoriented its focus toward lending to less-developed countries. IBRD loans are meant to be at market or near-market rates and require government guarantees. In the 1950s the International Finance Corporation (IFC) and International Development Association (IDA) were added. The first lends to private borrowers in LDCs and does not require guarantees. IDA lends at concessional rates. Eligibility for IDA loans depends upon per capita GNP. At the end of 1984 the IBRD had $94.2 billion in loans outstanding while IDA credits were $33.6 billion.

Bank lending was initially largely on a project basis. Agricultural and rural development projects have been the major category of projects funded. Bank lending has tended to be long term [World Bank (1985)]. More recently, the Bank has emphasized Structural Adjustment Lending that is not project based, and

---

[47]Van Dormael (1978) describes the Bretton Woods agreement of 1944 that established these institutions. Gold (1979) and Maerhage (1980) provide overviews of the operations of these institutions.

more conditional on policy reform. Lending in this category currently constitutes about 10 percent of total Bank lending.[48]

Frey, Horn, Persson and Schneider (1985) model econometrically the Bank's lending activity. They posit a Bank objective function that has as arguments credits outstanding to various countries scaled by their income, and the expected loss from default on outstanding loans. Maximizing this objective function subject to a resource constraint implies a per capita loan supply that depends negatively on per capita GNP and positively on safety. They use the Institutional Investors Credit Ratings to measure the second. Cross-sectional regressions using data from 55 developing countries for 1981 and 1982 yield statistically significant relationships with the anticipated signs for both variables. The relationship explains about 40 percent of the variation in World Bank loans.

8.2. The IMF

The role of the IMF has changed substantially since it was founded. Initially, its primary purpose was to oversee the system of fixed exchange rates envisioned by the Bretton Woods agreement. Its loans were meant largely to allow its members to defend exchange rates in the short run while they undertook fiscal or monetary policies to maintain their currency at par value. The demise of the Bretton Woods exchange rate system as it applied to major industrial countries has shifted the focus of Fund activities more toward developing countries.

The original terms of the Fund charter allowed members to borrow in "tranches" proportional to their initial deposit or quota. Deposits were 25 percent in gold or hard currency. Access to credit in this amount, the "gold tranche", was virtually automatic. Access to further credit was intended to be conditional on specific macroeconomic adjustment policies believed to correct balance-of-payments deficits.

There has been a lot of innovation in the nature of credits that the IMF arranges beyond what is available through standard tranches.[49] Three that have been of particular relevance for developing countries are the Compensatory Financing Faculty (CFF), the Special Drawing Account, and the Extended Funds Facility (EFF). The first was established in 1963 to enable developing countries to smooth out fluctuations in export revenue. Credit available under this facility is available subject to "less exacting tests" than under tranche policies [see Gold (1970, p. 17)].[50]

---

[48] Payer (1982) provides a radical critique of the Bank's operations.
[49] See Gold (1970) for a discussion of "stand-by arrangements".
[50] Diaz-Alejandro (1984) recently called for expansion of this facility.

The Special Drawing Account is the channel through which the IMF allocates Special Drawing Rights (SDRs) to its members. An issue that frequently arises is the creation of new SDRs and their allocation among members. Whether they should be distributed disproportionately to developing countries, establishing a "link" between SDR creation and development assistance, is a topic of debate.[51]

Critics of IMF conditionality have argued that it has failed to elicit the mandated policies, and that if and when it does, these policies are undesirable from the perspectives of lenders, the borrower, or both. The papers in Williamson (1983) provide an extended discussion.[52]

The IMF's outstanding commitments to LDCs were $36 billion at the end of 1984, barely a third those of the IBRD [see the World Bank (1985)]. This comparison may understate the IMF's importance in view of the interaction of its activities with lending by commercial banks.

8.3. The multilateral organizations and private capital

As discussed in Section 1, the share of public capital in the composition of LDC debt fell during the past fifteen years. The importance of the multilateral agencies extends beyond their net contribution of capital, however. They have an important role in sustaining private capital flows. They do so in their roles as monitors of international capital markets, as enforcers of contracts, and as potential lenders of last resort.

8.3.1. Monitoring

Multilateral organizations are the major providers of data on developing countries. These data facilitate capital flows both by providing information on conditions in developing countries themselves and on the overall structure of their debt. With the potential for debt repudiation or insolvency, private competitive lenders can use information on total indebtedness to ascertain the value of a loan.[53] Data on lending to LDCs are provided by the Bank for International

---

[51] Park (1973) discusses alternative "link" proposals and summarizes arguments in favor and against. Williamson (1984) has argued in favor of a substantial increase in SDRs as a means toward resolving the debt problems of developing countries.

[52] Von Furstenberg (1985) formally models IMF conditionality as the consequence of a preference by borrowers to repay debt more slowly than the IMF wants to be repaid. The IMF consequently makes access to funds "conditional" upon repaying more rapidly.

[53] Kletzer (1984) develops a model of repeated borrowing, contrasting situations in which lenders can observe total indebtedness and those in which they cannot. Without observability no equilibrium with positive lending may be possible. If lending does occur credit cannot be rationed. With observability credit rationing may emerge. Less will be lent than in the no observability case (if lending occurs at all in that case), but at a lower interest rate. The borrower's welfare with observability is greater. Borrowing countries consequently benefit from the provision of credible information to potential lenders about their debt.

Settlements (BIS) and OECD as well as by the World Bank and the IMF. The BIS data are on bank lending, and include both long- and short-term loans. They are based on surveys of lending institutions rather than on data from borrowing countries.

As discussed in Section 6, once a loan is extended, the interests of borrower and creditor can diverge. The borrower may find it in its interest to take actions that reduce its solvency or reduce the impact of any penalty incurred by default. Loans may be extended contingent upon the borrowing country pursuing policies deemed in the lender's interest. Another role for multilateral institutions is in monitoring behavior in developing countries to ensure that these policies are pursued. IMF conditionality, in particular, explicitly serves this purpose.

8.3.2. Enforcement

As discussed in Section 6, the enforcement of debt contracts in international capital markets may require the presence of institutions expected to engage in international lending indefinitely. Private banks have many actual or potential loan customers other than developing countries. Their future participation in lending to these countries is in doubt. The futures of the IMF and World Bank, however, are tied to the sustainability of future lending to LDCs. Their commitment to enforcing the terms of loan contracts is consequently greater. Crawford (1987) discusses the possible role of multilateral agencies in enforcing debt contracts.

8.3.3. Lenders of last resort

Guttentag and Herring (1983) and Wellons (1984) have written about the role of lenders of last resort in international capital markets. While the concept of a lender of last resort is a relatively old one, its meaning in terms of a fully-articulated model of borrowing remains vague. The Diamond–Dybvig (1983) model of bank runs, along with the rescheduling models of Sachs (1984) and Krugman (1985), perhaps come closest to providing an explicit framework that points to a role for a lender of last resort.

If there are multiple equilibria generated by interdependence among lenders in affecting the return on a loan, then a lender of last resort can ensure that a more favorable equilibrium emerges. By promising to lend if private capital is not forthcoming, the lender of last resort can guarantee to any private lender that he will not be the victim of a "run" on the country in question.

8.3.4. Evidence of complementarity

The monitoring, enforcement, and lender-of-last-resort functions of multinational institutions suggest a complementarity between the supply of private and public funds. Kraft's (1984) account of the Mexican crisis of 1982 provides anecdotal evidence that public institutions, the IMF, and the U.S. Government, in particular, were instrumental in marshalling private funds to lend to Mexico. Also, Eaton and Gersovitz's (1981a) cross-country econometric analysis of private lending indicates a positive effect of debt to public institutions on private loan supply.

In some cases complementarity is explicit. The World Bank, for example, co-finances project loans with commercial banks [see Cassen and Associates (1987)].

9. Conclusion

The future role of foreign capital in economic development is hard to predict. In the short term, the rapid expansion of net private flows to developing countries that occurred during the previous decade shows signs of reversing, and there is little reason to expect much expansion in concessional aid flows. The multilateral lending organization will probably grow in relative importance as a source of portfolio investment. The experience of individual countries will, of course, vary widely. Some will find access to international capital virtually unfettered; others will find it almost unavailable.

The literature on external capital in economic development is by now very large. An assessment of its contribution is that it has provided methodologies useful for understanding two aspects of the role of foreign capital. One is the static implications of capital movements for relative commodity prices, income distribution, and welfare, the literature discussed in Sections 2 and 3. Another is the dynamic role of foreign capital in a country facing a perfectly elastic supply of external funds, what is surveyed in Sections 4 and 5.

Our understanding of two other, very crucial, issues remains inadequate. One is the determination of supply and demand for capital in international capital markets. Given the absence of supernational institutions to enforce contracts, the mechanisms that support international lending are subtle and imperfectly understood. Improved knowledge about them can provide a basis for identifying how policy in developing countries affects the availability of foreign funds. At this stage most analysis is based on an assumption that developing countries face given conditions in external capital markets. Clearly, their own policies affect how much is available and the terms on which it is lent, but little in the literature indicates the nature of this relationship. Improved understanding of this issue will provide a better basis for predicting what the future role of private capital will be, and for formulating policies for multilateral lending organizations.

A second issue, about which little is known despite a great deal of concern, is the role of foreign capital in financing investment and growth. The discussion in Sections 4 and 5 suggests that there may be too many rather than too few methodologies for analyzing this issue. Those that have been implemented empirically are largely ad hoc. Even if one accepts that developing countries' behavior can be characterized by individual optimization, is a representative-agent approach or a life-cycle approach appropriate? If the second is the case, do assets in fixed supply make up a large share of domestic wealth? What role do these assets play in production and domestic saving?

In turning to the role of public capital flows, a crucial issue is the extent to which governments in developing countries, who normally are the direct recipients, act in the interest of their citizens. An assessment of what publicly-provided capital has contributed and can contribute to development requires a much clearer understanding of the objectives of those providing capital, and determining how these correspond to and diverge from the interests of individuals in capital importers and their governments.

References

Aizenman, J. (1986) 'Country risk, asymmetric information and domestic policies', Working Paper no. 1880, National Bureau of Economic Research.

Alexander, L. (1987) 'Trade and sovereign lending', Ph.D. Dissertation, Yale University, unpublished.

Amano, A. (1977) 'Specific factors, comparative advantage and international investment', *Economica*, 44:131–144.

Auerbach, A. and Kotlikoff, L.J. (1987) *Dynamic fiscal policy*. New York: Cambridge University Press.

Avramovic, D. (1958) *Debt servicing capacity and postwar growth in international indebtedness*. Baltimore, MD: Johns Hopkins Press.

Avramovic, D., et al. (1964) *Economic growth and external debt*. Baltimore, MD: Johns Hopkins Press.

Bacha, E.L. (1984) 'Growth with limited supplies of foreign exchange', in: M. Syrquin, L. Taylor, and L.E. Westphal, eds., *Economic structure and performance*. Orlando, FL: Academic Press, 263–280.

Bade, R. (1972) 'Optimal growth and foreign borrowing with restricted mobility of foreign capital', *International Economic Review*, 13:544–552.

Balogh, Lord T. (1967) 'Multilateral vs. bilateral aid', *Oxford Economic Papers*, new series, 19:332–344. Reprinted in: J. Bhagwati and R.S. Eckaus, eds., *Foreign aid*. Hammondsworth: Penguin, 1970.

Bardhan, P.K. (1967) 'Optimum foreign borrowing', in: K. Shell, ed., *Essays on the theory of optimal economic growth*. Cambridge, MA: MIT Press.

Baron, D.P. (1983) *The export–import bank*. New York: Academic Press.

Bauer, Lord P.T. (1981) *Equality, the third world and economic delusion*. Cambridge: MA: Harvard University Press.

Bazdarich, M.J. (1978) 'Optimal growth and stages in the balance of payments', *Journal of International Economics*, 8:425–443.

Beenstock, M. (1980) 'Political econometry of official development assistance', *World Development*. 8:137–144.

Behrman, J.R. and Sah, R.K. (1984) 'What role does equity play in the international distribution of development aid?', in: M. Syrquin, L. Taylor, and L.E. Westphal, eds., *Economic structure and performance: Essays in honor of Hollis B. Chenery*. Orlando, FL: Academic Press, 295–315.

Bertrand, T.J. and Flatters, F. (1971) 'Tariffs, capital accumulation and immiserizing growth', *Journal of International Economics*, 1:453–460.

Bhagwati, J.N. (1958) 'Immiserizing growth: A geometrical note', *Review of Economic Studies*, 25:201–205.

Bhagwati, J.N. (1966) 'The nature of balance and payments difficulties in developing countries', paper no. 5, in: *Measures of trade expansion of developing countries*. Japan Economic Research Center.

Bhagwati, J.N. (1967) 'The tying of aid', United Nations Committee on Trade and Development, 1-57. Reprinted in: J.N. Bhagwati and R.S. Eckaus, eds., *Foreign aid*. Hammondsworth: Penguin, 1970.

Bhagwati, J.N. (1968) 'Distortions and immiserizing growth: A generalization', *Review of Economic Studies*, 35:481–485.

Bhagwati, J.N. (1969) 'Optimal policies and immiserizing growth', *American Economic Review*, 59:967–970.

Bhagwati, J.N. (1982) 'Directly-unproductive-profit-seeking (DUP) activities', *Journal of Political Economy*, 90:988–1002.

Bhagwati, J.N. and Brecher, R.A. (1980) 'National welfare in an open economy in the presence of foreign-owned factors of production', *Journal of International Economics*, 10:103–115.

Bhagwati, J.N. and Brecher, R.A. (1981) 'Foreign ownership and the theory of trade and welfare', *Journal of Political Economy*, 89:497–511.

Bhagwati, J.N., Brecher, R.A., and Hatta, T. (1983) 'The generalized theory of transfers and welfare (I): Bilateral transfers in a multilateral world', *American Economic Review*, 73:606–618.

Bhagwati, J.N., Brecher, R.A., and Hatta, T. (1984) 'The paradoxes of immiserizing growth and donor-enriching (recipient-immiserizing) transfers: A tale of two literatures', *Weltwirtschaftliches Archiv*, 120:228–243.

Bhagwati, J.N. and Srinivasan, T.N. (1983a) *Lectures on international trade*. Cambridge, MA: MIT Press.

Bhagwati, J.N. and Srinivasan, T.N. (1983b) 'On the choice between capital and labour mobility', *Journal of International Economics*, 14:209–221.

Bhagwati, J.N. and Tironi, E. (1980) 'Tariff changes, foreign capital and immiserization', *Journal of Development Economics*, 7:71–83.

Blanchard, O.J. (1985) 'Debt, Deficits and Finite Horizons', *Journal of Political Economy*, 93:223–247.

Blomquist, A.G. (1976) 'Empirical evidence on the two-gap hypothesis', *Journal of Development Economics*, 3:181–193.

Borts, G.H. (1964) 'A theory of long-run international capital movements', *Journal of Political Economy*, 72:341–359.

Brecher, R.A. (1983) 'Second-best policy for international trade and investment', *Journal of International Economics*, 14:313–320.

Brecher, R.A. and Bhagwati, J.N. (1981) 'Foreign ownership and the theory of trade and welfare', *Journal of Political Economy*, 89:497–511.

Brecher, R.A. and Bhagwati, J.N. (1982) 'Immiserizing transfers from abroad', *Journal of International Economics*, 13:353–364.

Brecher, R.A. and Choudri, E.U. (1983) 'Immiserizing investment from abroad: The Singer–Prebisch thesis reconsidered', *Quarterly Journal of Economics*, 97:181–190.

Brecher, R.A. and Diaz-Alejandro, C.F. (1977) 'Tariffs, foreign capital and immiserizing growth,' *Journal of International Economics*, 14:321–340.

Brecher, R.A. and Feenstra, R.C. (1983) 'International trade and capital mobility between diversified economies', *Journal of International Economics*, 14:321–340.

Brecher, R.A. and Findlay, R. (1983) 'Tariffs, foreign capital and national welfare with specific factors', *Journal of International Economics*, 14:277–288.

Bruno, M. (1967) 'Optimal patterns of trade and development', *Review of Economics and Statistics*, 49:545–554.

Bruno, M. (1976) 'The two-sector open economy and the real exchange rate', *American Economic Review*, 66:566–577.

Bruton, H.J. (1969) 'The two-gap approach to aid and development: Comment', *American Economic Review*, 59:439–446.

Buiter, W.H. (1981) 'Time preference and international lending and borrowing in an overlapping generations model', *Journal of Political Economy*, 89:769–797.

Buiter, W.H. and Srinivasan, T.N. (1987) 'Rewarding the profligate and punishing the prudent: Some recent proposals for debt relief', *World Development*, 15:411–417.

Bulow, J. and Rogoff, K. (1986) 'A constant recontracting model of sovereign debt', NBER Working Paper no. 2088.

Burgess, D.F. (1978) 'On the distributional effects of direct foreign investment', *International Economic Review*, 19:647–664.

Cairnes, J.E. (1874) *Some leading principles of political economy newly expounded*. New York: Harper and Bros.

Calvo, G. (1978) 'On the time consistency of optimal policy in a monetary economy', *Econometrica*, 46:1411–1428.

Calvo, G. and Wellisz, S. (1983) 'International factor mobility and national advantage', *Journal of International Economics*, 14:103–114.

Cassen, R. and Associates (1987) *Does aid work?* Oxford: Oxford University Press.

Caves, R.E. (1971) 'International corporations: The industrial economics of foreign investment', *Economica*, 38:1–27.

Chang, W.W. (1979) 'Some theorems of trade and general equilibrium with many goods and factors', *Econometrica*, 47:709–726.

Chenery, H.B. (1967) 'Foreign assistance and economic development', in J.H. Adler, ed., *Capital movements*. London: MacMillan, 293–325.

Chenery, H.B. (1969) 'The two-gap approach to aid and development: A reply to Bruton', *American Economic Review*, 59:446–449.

Chenery, H.B. and Bruno, M. (1962) 'Development alternatives in an open economy: The case of Israel', *Economic Journal*, 72:79–103.

Chenery, H.B. and Eckstein, P. (1970) 'Development alternatives for Latin America', *Journal of Political Economy*, 78:966–1006.

Chenery, H.B. and MacEwan, A. (1966) 'Optimal patterns of growth and aid', in: I. Adelman and E. Thorbecke, eds., *Theory and design of economic development*. Baltimore, MD: Johns Hopkins University Press.

Chenery, H.B. and Strout, A.M. (1966) 'Foreign assistance and economic development', *American Economic Review*, 56:149–179.

Chenery, H.B. and Syrquin, M. (1975) *Patterns of development*. Oxford: Oxford University Press, published for the World Bank.

Chichilnisky, G. (1980) 'Basic goods, the effects of commodity transfers and the international economic order', *Journal of Development Economics*, 7:505–519.

Chichilnisky, G. (1983) 'The transfer problem with three agents once again: Characterization, uniqueness and stability', *Journal of Development Economics*, 13:237–248.

Chichilnisky, G. (1984) 'The transfer problem in stable markets', *Journal of Development Economics*, 16:319–320.

Chipman, J.S. (1971) 'International trade with capital mobility: A substitution theorem', in: J.N. Bhagwati, R.W. Jones, R. Mundell, and J. Vanek, eds., *Trade, balance of payments and growth*. Amsterdam: North-Holland.

Chipman, J.S. (1974) 'The transfer problem once again', in: G. Horwich and P.A. Samuelson, eds., *Trade, stability and macroeconomics: Essays in honor of Lloyd A. Metzler*. New York: Academic Press, 19–78.

Clarida, R.H. (1985) 'International lending and borrowing in a stochastic sequence economy', Cowles Foundation Discussion Paper no. 771, Yale University.

Cline, W.R. (1979) 'Resource transfers to developing countries: Issues and trends', in: W.R. Cline, ed., *Policy alternatives for a new international economic order*. New York: Praeger, 333–353.

Cline, W.R. (1983) *International debt and the stability of the world economy*. Washington, DC: Institute for International Economics.

Cline, W.R. and Sargen, N.P. (1975) 'Performance criteria and multilateral aid allocation', *World Development*, 3:383–391.

Cohen, D. and Sachs, J.D. (1986) 'LDC borrowing with default risk', *Kredit und kapital*, forthcoming.

Cooper, R.N. and Sachs, J.D. (1985) 'Borrowing abroad: The debtor's perspective', in: G.W. Smith and J.T. Cuddington, eds., *International debt and the developing countries*. Washington, DC: The World Bank, 21–60.

Crawford, V.P. (1987) 'International lending, long-term credit relationships, and dynamic contract theory', Princeton Studies in International Finance no. 59, Princeton University.

Crowther, Sir G. (1957) *Balances and imbalances of payments*. Cambridge, MA: Harvard University Press.

Cuddington, J.T. (1986) 'Capital flight: Issues, estimates and explanations', Princeton Essays in International Finance no. 58, Princeton University.

Cumby, R. and Levich, R. (1987) 'On the definition and magnitude of recent capital flight', in: J. Williamson and D. Lessard, eds., *Capital flight and third world debt*. Washington, D.C.: Institute for International Economics.

Dacy, D.C. (1975) 'Foreign aid and growth in less developed countries', *Economic Journal*, 85:548–561.

de Meza, D. (1983) 'The transfer problem in a many-country world: Is it better to give than receive?' *Manchester School of Economic and Social Studies*, 51:266–275.

Desai, P. and Bhagwati, J.N. (1979) 'Three alternative concepts of foreign exchange difficulties in centrally planned economies', *Oxford Economic Papers*, 31:358–369.

Diamond, D. and Dybvig, P.E. (1983) 'Bank runs, deposit insurance and liquidity', *Journal of Political Economy*, 91:401–409.

Diamond, P.A. (1965) 'National debt in a neoclassical growth model', *American Economic Review*, 55:1126–1150.

Diamond, P.A., Koopmans, T.C., and Williamson, R.E. (1964) 'Stationary utility and time perspective', *Econometrica*, 32:82–100.

Diaz-Alejandro, C.F. (1984) 'Latin American debt: I don't think we are in Kansas anymore', *Brookings papers on economic activity*. Washington, DC: Brookings Institution, 335–403.

Dixit, A. (1983) 'The multi-country transfer problem', *Economic Letters*, 13:49–53.

Domar, E. (1946) 'Capital expansion, rate of growth and employment', *Econometrica*, 14:137–147.

Domar, E. (1950) 'The effect of foreign investment on the balance of payments', *American Economic Review*, 40:805–826.

Dooley, M.P., Helkie, W., Tryon, R., and Underwood, J. (1986) 'An analysis of external debt positions of eight developing countries through 1990', *Journal of Development Economics*, 21:283–318.

Dooley, M.P. (1987) 'Capital flight: A response to differences in financial risks', in: J. Williamson and D. Lessard, eds., *Capital flight and third world debt*. Washington, D.C.: Institute for International Economics.

Dornbusch, R. (1983) 'Real interest rates, home goods and optimal external borrowing', *Journal of Political Economy*, 91:141–153.

Dornbusch, R. (1985) 'External debt, budget deficits, and disequilibrium exchange rates', in: G.W. Smith and J.T. Cuddington, eds., *International debt and the developing countries*. Washington, DC: The World Bank, 213–235.

Dudley, L. and Montmarquette, C. (1976) 'A model of the supply of bilateral foreign aid', *American Economic Review*, 66:132–142.

Eaton, J. (1986a) 'Lending with costly enforcement of repayment and potential fraud', *Journal of Banking and Finance*, 10:281–293.

Eaton, J. (1986b) 'Credit policy and international competition', in: P.R. Krugman, ed., *New directions in trade theory*. Cambridge, MA: MIT Press.

Eaton, J. (1987a) 'Public debt guarantees and private capital flight', *World Bank Economic Review*, 1:377–395.

Eaton, J. (1987b) 'Monopoly wealth and international debt', University of Virginia, unpublished.

Eaton, J. (1988) 'Foreign-owned land', *American Economic Review*, forthcoming.

Eaton, J. and Gersovitz, M. (1981a) 'Debt with potential repudiation: Theoretical and empirical analysis', *Review of Economic Studies*, 48:289–309.

Eaton, J. and Gersovitz, M. (1981b) 'Poor country borrowing and the repudiation issue', Princeton Studies in International Finance no. 47, Princeton University.

Eaton, J. and Gersovitz, M. (1983) 'Country risk: Economic aspects', in: R.J. Herring, ed., *Managing international risk*. New York: Cambridge University Press.

Eaton, J. and Gersovitz, M. (1986) 'Country risk and the organization of international capital transfer', in: G. Calvo, R. Findlay, P.J. Kouri, and J.B. deMacedo, eds., *Debt, stabilization, and development*. Oxford: Basil Blackwell, forthcoming.

Eaton, J. and Panagariya, A. (1982) 'Growth and welfare in a small, open economy', *Economica*, 49:409–419.

Eaton, J. and Taylor, L. (1986) 'Developing country finance and debt', *Journal of Development Economics*, 22:209–265.

Eaton, J., Gersovitz, M., and Stiglitz, J.E. (1986) 'The pure theory of country risk', *European Economic Review*, 30:481–513.

Edelman, J.A. and Chenery, H.B. (1977) 'Aid and income distribution', in: J.N. Bhagwati, ed., *The new international economic order: The north–south debate*. Cambridge, MA: MIT Press, 27–49.

Enders, T.O. and Mattione, R.P. (1984) *Latin America: The crisis of debt and growth*. Washington, DC: Brookings Institution.

Engel, C. and Kletzer, K. (1986a) 'International borrowing to finance investment', Working Paper no. 1865, National Bureau of Economic Research.

Engel, C. and Kletzer, K. (1986b) 'Tariffs, saving and the current account', Working Paper no. 1869, National Bureau of Economic Research.

Ethier, W.J. (1985) 'Higher dimensional issues in trade theory', in: R.W. Jones and P.B. Kenen, eds., *Handbook of international economics*. Amsterdam: North-Holland, 131–184.

Ethier, W. and Ross, S.A. (1971) 'International capital movements and long-run diversification', *Journal of International Economics*, 1:301–314.

Feder, G. and Regev, U. (1975) 'International loans, direct foreign investment, and optimal capital accumulation', *Economic Record*, 51:320–325.

Fei, J.C.H. and Paauw, D.S. (1965) 'Foreign assistance and self-help: A reappraisal of development finance', *Review of Economics and Statistics*, 57:251–267.

Fei, J.C.H. and Ranis, G. (1968) 'Foreign assistance and economic development: Comment', *American Economic Review*, 58:897–912.

Feinberg, R.E. (1982) *Subsidizing success: The export-import bank in the U.S. economy*. New York: Cambridge University Press.

Feltenstein, A. (1980) 'A general equilibrium approach to the analysis of trade restrictions, with an application to Argentina', *International Monetary Fund Staff Papers*, 27:749–784.

Ferguson, D.G. (1978) 'International capital mobility and comparative advantage: The two-country, two-factor case', *Journal of International Economics*, 8:373–396.

Findlay, R. (1971) 'The foreign exchange gap and growth in developing economies', in: J.N. Bhagwati, R.W. Jones, R. Mundell, and J. Vanek, eds., *Trade, balance of payments and growth*. Amsterdam: North-Holland, 168–182.

Findlay, R. and Grubert, H. (1959) 'Factor intensities, technological progress, and the terms of trade', *Oxford Economic Papers*, 11:111–121.

Fischer, S. and Frenkel, J. (1972) 'Investment, the two-sector model and trade in debt and capital goods', *Journal of International Economics*, 2:211–233.

Fischer, S. and Frenkel, J. (1974a) 'Interest rate equalization and patterns of production, trade and consumption in a two-country growth model', *Economic Record*, 50:555–580.

Fischer, S. and Frenkel, J. (1974b) 'Economic growth and stages of the balance of payments', in: G. Horwich and P. Samuelson, eds., *Trade, stability, and macroeconomics*. New York: Academic Press, 503–521.

Fisher, F.M. (1963) 'A theoretical analysis of the impact of food surplus disposal on agricultural production in recipient countries', *Journal of Farm Economics*, 45:863–875. Reprinted in: J.N. Bhagwati and R.S. Eckaus, eds., *Foreign aid*. Hammondsworth: Penguin, 1970.

Fleisig, H. and Hill, C. (1984) 'The benefits and costs of official export credit programs', in: R.E. Baldwin and A.O. Krueger, eds., *The structure and evolution of recent U.S. trade policy*. Chicago, IL: University of Chicago Press, 321–358.

Frey, B., Horn, H., Persson, T., and Schneider, F. (1985) 'A formulation and test of a simple model of world bank behavior', *Weltwirtschaftliches Archiv*, 121:438–447.

Friedman, M. (1958) 'Foreign economic aid: Means and objectives', *Yale Review*, 47:24–38. Reprinted in: J.N. Bhagwati and R.S. Eckaus, eds., *Foreign aid*. Hammondsworth: Penguin, 1970.

Gale, D. (1974) 'Exchange equilibrium and coalitions: An example', *Journal of Mathematical Economics*, 1:63–66.

Geanakoplos, J. and Heal, G. (1983) 'A geometric explanation of the transfer paradox in a stable economy', *Journal of Development Economics*, 13:223–236.

Gersovitz, M. (1982) 'The estimation of the two-gap model', *Journal of International Economics*, 12:111–124.

Gersovitz, M. (1983) 'Trade, capital mobility and sovereign immunity', Research Program in Development Studies Discussion Paper no. 108, Princeton University.

Gersovitz, M. (1985) 'Banks' international lending decisions: What we know and implications for future research', in: G.W. Smith and J.T. Cuddington, eds., *International debt and the developing countries*. Washington, DC: World Bank.

Ghanem, H. (1985) 'Senegal: A study of alternative borrowing strategies', Country Policy Division Discussion Paper no. 1985-7, World Bank.

Glick, R. (1986) 'Economic perspectives on foreign borrowing and debt repudiation: An analytic literature review', Salomon Brothers Center for the Study of Financial Institutions, Monograph Series in Finance and Economics Monograph no. 1986-4, New York University.

Glick, R. and Kharas, H.J. (1984) 'The costs and benefits of foreign borrowing: A survey of multi-period models', unpublished.

Gold, Sir J. (1970) *The stand-by arrangements of the international monetary fund*. Washington, DC: International Monetary Fund.

Gold, Sir J. (1979) 'Legal and institutional aspects of the international monetary system', *Selected essays*. Washington, DC.

Goldsmith, R.W. (1985) *Comparative national balance sheets*. Chicago, IL: University of Chicago Press.

Goldstein, M. and Khan, M.S. (1985) 'Income and price effects in foreign trade', in: R.W. Jones and P.B. Kenen, eds., *Handbook of development economics*. Amsterdam: North-Holland.

Griffin, K.B. (1978) *International inequality and national poverty*. London: Macmillan.

Griffin, K.B. and Enos, J.L. (1970) 'Foreign assistance: Objectives and consequences', *Economic Development and Cultural Change*, 8:313–337.

Grinols, E. and Bhagwati, J.N. (1976) 'Foreign capital, savings and dependence', *Review of Economics and Statistics*, 58:416–424.

Grinols, E. and Bhagwati, J.N. (1979) 'Foreign capital, savings and dependence: A reply to Mr. Wasow', *Review of Economics and Statistics*, 61:154–156.

Grossman, G.M. (1984) 'The gains from international factor movements', *Journal of International Economics*, 17:73–84.

Gulhati, R. (1967) 'The "need" for foreign resources, absorptive capacity and debt-servicing capacity', in: J.H. Adler, ed., *Capital movements and economic development*. London: Macmillan, 240–268.

Gunning, J.W. (1983a) 'The transfer problem, a rejoinder', *Journal of Development Economics*, 13:249–250.

Gunning, J.W. (1983b) 'Rationing in an open economy: Fix price equilibrium and two-gap models', *European Economic Review*, 23:71–98.

Guttentag, J. and Herring, R.J. (1983) 'The lender of last resort function in an international context', Essays in International Finance no. 151, Princeton University.

Haberler, G. (1936) *The theory of international trade*. London: William Hodge.

Halevi, N. (1971) 'An empirical test of the "balance of payments stages" hypothesis', *Journal of International Economics*, 1:103–118.

Halevi, N. (1976) The effects on investment and consumption of import surpluses of developing countries', *Economic Journal*, 86:853–858.

Hamada, K. (1969) 'Optimum capital accumulation by an economy facing an international capital market', *Journal of Political Economy*, 77:684–697.

Hanson, J.A. (1974) 'Optimal international borrowing and lending', *American Economic Review*, 64:616–630.

Harberger, A.C. (1950) 'Currency depreciation, income, and the balance of trade', *Journal of Political Economy*, 58:47–60.

Harrod, Sir R.F. (1932) '"Review" of Roland Wilson, *Capital imports and the terms of trade*', *Economic Journal*, 42:427–431.

Harrod, Sir R.F. (1939) 'An essay in dynamic theory', *Economic Journal*, 49:14–33.

Hatta, T. (1984) 'Immiserizing growth in a many commodity setting', *Journal of International Economics*, 17:335–346.

Heller, P.S. (1975) 'A model of public fiscal behavior in developing countries: Aid, investment and taxation', *American Economic Review*, 65:429–445.

Helpman, E. and Razin, A. (1983) 'Increasing returns, monopolistic competition and factor movements: A welfare analysis', *Journal of International Economics*, 14:263–276.

Hirschman, A.O. and Bird, R.M. (1968) 'Foreign aid – A critique and a proposal', Essays in International Finance no. 69, International Finance Section, Princeton University.

Hoadley, J.S. (1980) 'Small states as aid donors', *International Organization*, 34:121–138.

Hoover, H. (1919) 'Letter to President W. Wilson', 25 January 1919. Hoover Institution Archives.

Hori, H. and Stein, J.L. (1977) 'International growth with free trade in equities and goods', *International Economic Review*, 18:83–100.

Ikemoto, K. (1975) 'Direct foreign investments and the specific factors model', *Kobe University Economic Review*, 29–51.

Ize, A. and Ortiz, G. (1986) 'Fiscal rigidities, public debt, and capital flight', International Monetary Fund, unpublished.

Jasay, A.E. (1960) 'The social choice between home and overseas investment', *Economics Journal*, 70:105–113.

Jay, K. and Michalopoulos, C. (1987) 'Donor policies, donor interests, and aid effectiveness', in: A.O. Krueger, C. Michalopoulos, and V.W. Ruttan, eds., *Aid and development*. Baltimore and London: Johns Hopkins University Press, forthcoming.

Johnson, H.G. (1955) 'The transfer problem: A note on criteria for changes in the terms of trade', *Economica*, 22:113–121.

Johnson, H.G. (1956) 'The transfer problem and exchange stability', *Journal of Political Economy*, 64:212–225.

Johnson, H.G. (1959) 'Economic development and international trade', *Nationalekonomisk Tidsskrift*, 97:253–272.

Johnson, H.G. (1967) 'The possibility of income losses from increased efficiency or factor accumulation in the presence of tariffs', *Economic Journal*, 77:151–154.

Jones, R.W. (1967) 'International capital movements and the theory of tariffs and trade', *Quarterly Journal of Economics*, 81:1–38.

Jones, R.W. (1970) 'The transfer problem revisited', *Economica*, 37:178–184.

Jones, R.W. (1971) 'A three-factor model in theory, trade, and history', in: J.N. Bhagwati, R.W. Jones, R. Mundell, and J. Vanek, eds., *Trade, balance of payments and growth*. Amsterdam: North-Holland, 3–21.

Jones, R.W. (1975) 'Presumption and the transfer problem', *Journal of International Economics*, 5:263–274.

Jones, R.W. (1984a) 'Protection and the harmful effects of endogenous capital flows', unpublished.

Jones, R.W. (1984b) 'The transfer problem in a three agent setting', *Canadian Journal of Economics*, 17:1–14.

Jones, R.W. (1985) 'Income effects and paradoxes in the theory of international trade', *Economic Journal*, 95:330–344.

Jones, R.W. and Coelho, I. (1985) 'Factor movements and the Ramaswami arguments', *Economica*, 52:359–364.

Jones, R.W. and Ruffin, R. (1975) 'Trade patterns with capital mobility', in: M. Parkin and A.R. Nobay, eds., *Current economic problems: The proceedings of the Association of University Teachers in Economics*. London: Cambridge University Press, 307–332.

Jones, R.W., Neary, J.P., and Ruane, F.P. (1983) 'Two-way capital flows: Cross-hauling in a theory of foreign investment', *Journal of International Economics*, 13:357–366.

Kahn, R.B. (1984) 'External borrowing and the common nature of foreign exchange', unpublished.

Kareken, J. and Wallace, N. (1977) 'Portfolio autarky: A welfare analysis', *Journal of International Economics*, 7:19–43.

Katz, M. (1982) 'The cost of borrowing, the terms of trade, and the determinants of external debt', *Oxford Economic Papers*, 34:332–345.

Kemp, M.C. (1962a) 'Foreign investment and national advantage', *Economic Record*, 38:56–62.

Kemp, M.C. (1962b) 'The benefits and costs of private investment from abroad: Comment', *Economic Record*, 38:108–110.

Kemp, M.C. (1965) 'International investment and the long-run national advantage', *Economic Record*, 41:628–633.
Kemp, M.C. (1966) 'Gains from international trade and investment', *American Economic Review*, 56:788–809.
Kemp, M.C. (1968) 'International trade and investment in a context of growth', *Economic Record*, 44:211–223.
Kemp, M.C. (1969) *The pure theory of international trade and investment*. Englewood Cliffs, NJ: Prentice-Hall.
Kemp, M.C. and Inada, M. (1969) 'International capital movements and the theory of international trade', *Quarterly Journal of Economics*, 83:524–528.
Kenen, P.B. (1977) 'Debt relief as development assistance', in: J.N. Bhagwati, ed., *The new international economic order: The north–south debate*. Cambridge, MA: MIT Press, 50–77.
Kennedy, J.V. and Ruttan, V.W. (1986) 'A reexamination of professional and popular thought on assistance for economic development: 1949–1952', *Journal of Developing Areas*, 20:297–326.
Keynes, Lord J.M. (1920) *Economic consequences of the peace*. New York: Harcourt Brace.
Keynes, Lord J.M. (1929) 'I. The German transfer problem, the reparations problem, a discussion', 'II. A rejoinder, and a view of the transfer problem', and 'III. A reply', *Economic Journal*, 30:1–7, 179–182, and 404–408.
Khan, M.S. and Haque, N.U. (1985) 'Foreign borrowing and capital flight', *International Monetary Fund Staff Papers*, 32:606–668.
Kharas, H. (1984) 'The long-run creditworthiness of developing countries: Theory and practice', *Quarterly Journal of Economics*, 99:415–440.
Kharas, H. and Shishido, H. (1985) 'Thailand, an assessment of alternative foreign borrowing strategies', Country Policy Division Discussion Paper no. 1985-29, World Bank.
King, B.B. (1968) 'Notes on the mechanics of growth and debt', World Bank Staff Occasional Paper no. 6, Baltimore, MD: Johns Hopkins University Press.
Kletzer, K. (1984) 'Asymmetries of information and LDC borrowing with sovereign risk', *Economic Journal*, 94:287–307.
Komiya, R. and Shizuki, T. (1967) 'Transfer payments and income distribution', *Manchester School of Economic and Social Studies*, 35:524–528.
Kraft, J. (1984) *The Mexican rescue*. New York: Group of Thirty.
Krueger, A.O. (1974) 'The political economy of the rent-seeking society', *American Economic Review*, 69:291–303.
Krueger, A.O. (1979) *The development role of the foreign sector and aid, studies in the modernization of the republic of Korea: 1945–1975*. Cambridge, MA: Council on East Asian Studies.
Krueger, A.O. (1981) 'Loans to assist the transition to outward-looking policies', *World Economy*, 4:271–281.
Krueger, A.O. and Ruttan, V.W. (1987a) 'Development thought and development assistance', in: A.O. Krueger, C. Michalopoulos, and V.W. Ruttan, eds., *Aid and development*. Baltimore and London: Johns Hopkins University Press, forthcoming.
Krueger, A.O. and Ruttan, V.W. (1987b) 'Toward a theory of development assistance', in: A.O. Krueger, C. Michalopoulos, and V.W. Ruttan, eds., *Aid and development*. Baltimore and London: Johns Hopkins University Press, forthcoming.
Krueger, A.O., Micholopoulos, C. and Ruttan, V.W. (1987) *Aid and development*. Baltimore and London: Johns Hopkins University Press, forthcoming.
Krugman, P.R. (1985) 'International debt problems in an uncertain world', in: G.W. Smith and J.T. Cuddington, eds., *International debt and the developing countries*. Washington, DC: World Bank, 79–100.
Krugman, P.R. and Baldwin, R.E. (1987) 'The persistence of the U.S. trade deficit', *Brookings Papers on Economic Activity*, 1:1–56.
Kydland, F.E. and Prescott, E.C. (1977) 'Rules rather than discretion: The inconsistency of optimal plans', *Journal of Political Economy*, 85:473–491.
Laursen, S. and Metzler, L.A. (1950) 'Flexible exchange rates and the theory of employment', *Review of Economics and Statistics*, 32:281–299.
Leontief, W.W. (1937) 'Note on the pure theory of transfer', in: *Explorations in economics: Notes and essays contributed in honor of F.W. Taussig*. New York: McGraw-Hill, 84–91.

Lipton, D. and Sachs, J. (1983) 'Accumulation and growth in a two-country model: A simulation approach', *Journal of International Economics*, 15:135–160.

Long, N.V. (1974) 'International borrowing for resource extraction', *International Economic Review*, 15:168–183.

Lucas, R.E. (1985) 'On the mechanics of economic development', Marshall Lectures, Cambridge University, unpublished.

MacDougall, G.D.A. (1960) 'The benefits and costs of private investment from abroad', *Economic Record*, 36:13–35.

McCabe, J.L. and Sibley, D. (1976) 'Optimal foreign debt with export revenue uncertainty', *International Economic Review*, 17:675–686.

McDougall, I. (1965) 'Non-traded goods and the transfer problem', *Review of Economic Studies*, 32:67–84.

McKinlay, R.D. (1978) 'The German aid relationship: A test of the recipient need and the donor interest models of the distribution of German bilateral aid 1961–1970', *European Journal of Political Research*, 6:235–257.

McKinlay, R.D. and Little, R. (1977) 'A foreign policy model of U.S. bilateral aid allocation', *World Politics*, 30:58–86.

McKinlay, R.D. and Little, R. (1978a) 'The French aid relationship: A foreign policy model of the distribution of French bilateral aid, 1964–1970', *Development and Change*, 9:457–478.

McKinlay, R.D. and Little, R. (1978b) 'A foreign policy model of the distribution of British bilateral aid, 1960–1970', *British Journal of Political Science*, 8:313–332.

McKinlay, R.D. and Little R. (1979) 'The U.S. aid relationship: A test of the recipient need and the donor-interest model', *Political Studies*, 27:236–250.

McKinnon, R.E. (1964) 'Foreign exchange constraints in economic development and efficient aid allocation', *Economic Journal*, 74:388–409.

Maerhaege, M.A.G. van (1980) *A handbook of international economic institutions.* London.

Maizels, A. and Nissanke, M.K. (1984) 'Motivations for aid to developing countries', *World Development*, 12.

Majumdar, M. and Mitra, T. (1985) 'A result on the transfer problem in international trade theory', *Journal of International Economics*, 19:161–170.

Manne, A.S. (1963) 'Key sectors of the Mexican economy', in: A.S. Manne and H. Markowitz, eds., *Studies in process analysis.* New York: McGraw-Hill.

Mantel, R.R. (1984) 'Substitutability and the welfare effects of endowment increases', *Journal of International Economics*, 17:325–334.

Markusen, J.R. (1983) 'Factor trade and commodity trade as complements', *Journal of International Economics*, 43:341–356.

Markusen, J.R. and Melvin, J.R. (1979) 'Tariffs, capital mobility and foreign ownership', *Journal of International Economics*, 9:395–410.

Martin, R. (1977) 'Immiserizing growth for a tariff-distorted small economy', *Journal of International Economics*, 7:323–328.

Martin, R. and Selowski, M. (1984) 'Energy prices, substitution and optimal borrowing in the short run', *Journal of Development Economics*, 14:331–350.

Melvin, J.R. (1969) 'Demand conditions and immiserizing growth', *American Economic Review*, 59:604–606.

Metzler, L.A. (1942) 'The transfer problem reconsidered', *Journal of Political Economy*, 50:397–414.

Metzler, L.A. (1968) 'The process of international adjustment under conditions of full employment: A Keynesian view', (Delivered before the Econometric Society, December 1960) in: American Economic Association, ed., *Readings in international economics.* Homewood, IL: Richard D. Irwin. Reprinted in: *Collected papers.* Cambridge, MA: Harvard University Press, 1973.

Michalopoulos, C. and Sukhatme, V. (1987) 'The impact of development assistance: Review of the quantitative evidence', in: A.O. Krueger, C. Michalopoulos, and V.W. Ruttan, eds., *Aid and development.* Baltimore and London: Johns Hopkins University Press, forthcoming.

Mikesell, R.F. (1968) *The economics of foreign aid.* Chicago: Aldine.

Mosley, P. (1985) 'The political economy of foreign aid: A model of the market for a public good', *Economic Development and Cultural Change*, 33:373–393.

Mosley, P., Hudson, J., and Horrell, S. (1987) 'Aid, the public sector and the market in less developed countries', *Economic Journal*, 97:616–641.
Mundell, R.A. (1957) 'International trade and factor mobility', *American Economic Review*, 47:321–337.
Mundell, R.A. (1960) 'The pure theory of international trade', *American Economic Review*, 59:14–29.
Negishi, T. (1965) 'Foreign investment and the long-run national advantage', *Economic Record*, 41:628–632.
North, D.C. (1962) 'International capital movements in historical perspective', in: R.F. Mikesill, ed., *U.S. private and government investment abroad*. Eugene, OR: University of Oregon Books.
Nurkse, R. (1961) 'Causes and effects of capital movements', in: G. Haberler and R.M. Stern, eds., *Equilibrium and growth in the world economy: Economic essays by Ragnar Nurkse*. Cambridge, MA: Harvard University Press.
Obstfeld, M. (1982) 'Aggregate spending and the terms of trade: Is there a Laursen–Metzler effect?', *Quarterly Journal of Economics*, 96:251–270.
Obstfeld, M. (1987) 'Fiscal deficits and relative prices in a growing world economy', University of Pennsylvania, unpublished.
Ohlin, G. (1929) 'A discussion: I. Transfer differences, real and imagined, and Mr. Keynes: Views on the transfer problem; II. A reply', *Economic Journal*, 39:179–182 and 400–404.
Ohlin, B. (1956) 'The evolution of aid doctrine', *Foreign aid policies reconsidered* (Organization for Economic Cooperation and Development). Reprinted in: J.N. Bhagwati and R.S. Eckaus, eds., *Foreign aid*. Hammondsworth: Penguin, 1970.
Ohyama, M. (1972) 'Trade and welfare in general equilibrium', *Keio Economic Studies*, 9:37–73.
Ohyama, M. (1984) 'Factor endowments and the pattern of commodity and factor trade', unpublished.
Oniki, H. and Uzawa, H. (1965) 'Patterns of trade and investment in a dynamic model of international trade', *Review of Economic Studies*, 32:15–38.
Onitsuka, Y. (1974) 'International capital movements and the patterns of economic growth', *American Economic Review*, 64:24–36.
Ozler, S. (1984) 'Rescheduling of sovereign government bank debt', unpublished.
Papanek, G.F. (1972) 'The effect of aid and other resource transfers on savings and growth in less developed countries', *Economic Journal*, 82:934–950.
Park, Y.S. (1973) 'The link between special drawing rights and development finance', Princeton Essays in International Finance no. 100, Princeton University.
Payer, C. (1982) *The World Bank: A critical analysis*. New York: Monthly Review Press.
Persson, T. and Svensson, L.E.O. (1985) 'Current account dynamics and the terms of trade: Harberger–Laursen–Metzler two generations later', *Journal of Political Economy*, 93:43–65.
Pigou, A.C. (1932) 'The effects of reparations on the ratio of international exchange', *Economic Journal*, 52:532–542.
Pincus, J.A. (1963) 'The cost of foreign aid', *Review of Economics and Statistics*, 45:360–367. Reprinted in: J.N. Bhagwati and R.S. Eckaus, eds., *Foreign aid*. Hammondsworth: Penguin, 1970.
Postlewaite, A. and Webb, M. (1984) 'The possibility of recipient-harming, donor-benefitting transfers with more than two countries', *Journal of International Economics*, 16:357–364.
Purvis, D.D. (1972) 'Technology, trade and factor mobility', *Economic Journal*, 82:991–999.
Rahman, A. (1968) 'Foreign capital and domestic savings: A test of Haavelmo's hypothesis with cross-country data', *Review of Economics and Statistics*, February.
Ramaswami, V.K. (1968) 'International factor movement and the national advantage', *Economica*, 35:309–310.
Ranney, S.I. (1984) 'International capital transfers and the choice of production technique: A simple two-country model', *Journal of International Economics*, 17:85–100.
Ravallion, M. (1983) 'Commodity transfers and the international economic order: A comment', *Journal of Development Economics*, 13:205–212.
Riddell, R. (1987) *Development assistance reconsidered*. London: James Curry.
Robertson, D.H. (1931) 'The transfer problem', in: A.C. Pigou and D.H. Robertson, eds., *Economic essays and addresses*.
Romer, P.M. (1986) 'Increasing returns, specialization, and external economies: Growth as described by Allyn Young', University of Rochester, unpublished.

Rosenstein-Rodan, P.N. (1961) 'International aid for underdeveloped countries', *Review of Economics and Statistics*, 43:107–138. Reprinted in: J.N. Bhagwati and R.S. Eckaus, eds., *Foreign aid*. Hammondsworth: Penguin, 1970.

Rosenstein-Rodan, P.N. (1968) 'The consortium technique', *International Organization*, 22:223–230. Reprinted in: J.N. Bhagwati and R.S. Eckaus, eds., *Foreign aid*. Hammondsworth: Penguin, 1970.

Rubinstein, A. (1982) 'Perfect equilibrium in a bargaining model', *Econometrica*, 50:97–110.

Ruffin, R.J. (1979) 'Growth and the long-run theory of international capital movements', *American Economic Review*, 69:832–842.

Ruffin, R.J. (1984) 'International factor movements', in: R.W. Jones and P.B. Kenen, eds., *Handbook of international economics*, Vol. 1. Amsterdam: North-Holland, 237–288.

Ruffin, R.J. (1985) 'Taxing international capital movements in a growing world', *Journal of International Economics*, 18:261–280.

Ruttan, V.W. (1987) 'Why foreign economic assistance?', *Economic development and cultural change*, forthcoming.

Saavedra-Rivano, N. and Wooton, I. (1983) 'The choice between international labor and capital mobility in a dynamic model of north–south trade', *Journal of International Economics*, 14:251–262.

Sachs, J.D. (1981) 'The current account and macroeconomic adjustment in the 1970s', *Brookings Papers on Economic Activity*, 1:201–268.

Sachs, J.D. (1984) 'Theoretical issues in international borrowing', Studies in International Finance no. 54, Princeton University.

Sachs, J.D. (1986) 'Conditionality and the debt crisis: Some thoughts for the world bank', unpublished.

Salvesen, H.K. (1927) 'The theory of international trade in the U.S.A.', *Oxford Magazine*, May 19:497–498.

Samuelson, P.A. (1947) *Foundations of economic analysis*. Cambridge, MA: Harvard University Press.

Samuelson, P.A. (1951) 'Abstract of a theorem concerning substitutability in open Leontief models', in: T.C. Koopmans, ed., *Activity analysis of production and allocation*. New York: Wiley.

Samuelson, P.A. (1952) 'The transfer problem and transport costs: The terms of trade when impediments are absent', *Economic Journal*, 59:181–197.

Samuelson, P.A. (1954) 'The transfer problem and transport costs, II: Analysis of effects of trade impediments', *Economic Journal*, 64:264–289.

Samuelson, P.A. (1971a) 'On the trail of conventional beliefs about the transfer problem', in: J.N. Bhagwati, R.W. Jones, R. Mundell, and J. Vanek, eds., *Trade, balance of payments and growth*. Amsterdam: North-Holland, 327–351.

Samuelson, P.A. (1971b) 'Ohlin was right', *Swedish Journal of Economics*, 365–384.

Sarris, A.H. and Taylor, L. (1977) 'Cereal stocks, food aid, and food security for the poor', in: J.N. Bhagwati, eds., *The new international economic order: The north–south debate*. Cambridge, MA: MIT Press, 273–288.

Schmidt, W.E. (1964) 'The economics of charity: Loans vs. grants', *Journal of Political Economy*, 72:387–395. Reprinted in: J.N. Bhagwati and R.S. Eckaus, eds., *Foreign aid*. Hammondsworth: Penguin, 1970.

Schultz, T.W. (1960) 'Value of U.S. farm surpluses to underdeveloped countries', *Journal of Farm Economics*, 42:1019–1030. Reprinted in: J.N. Bhagwati and R.S. Eckaus, eds., *Foreign aid*. Hammondsworth: Penguin, 1970.

Sengupta, A. (1968) 'Foreign capital requirements for economic development', *Oxford Economic Papers*, 20:25–38.

Simon, M. (1960) 'The United States balance of payments, 1861–1900', *Trends in the American economy in the nineteenth century*. Princeton, NJ: National Bureau of Economic Research Studies in Income and Wealth.

Simonsen, M.H. (1985) 'The developing country debt problem', in: G.W. Smith and J.T. Cuddington, eds., *International debt and the developing countries*. Washington, DC: The World Bank, 101–126.

Singer, H.W. (1950) 'The distribution of gains between investing and borrowing countries', *American Economic Review Papers and Proceedings*, 40:473–485.

Singer, H.W. (1965) 'External aid: For plans or projects?', *Economic Journal*, 75:539–545. Reprinted in: J.N. Bhagwati and R.S. Eckaus, eds., *Foreign aid*. Hammondsworth: Penguin, 1970.

Smith, A. (1982) 'Some simple results on the gains from trade, from growth and from public production', *Journal of International Economics*, 13:215–230.

Smith, G.W. (1979) 'The external debt prospects of the non-oil exporting developing countries', in: W.R. Cline, ed., *Policy alternatives for a new international economic order*. New York: Praeger, 287–329.

Solomon, R. (1977) 'A perspective on debt of developing countries', *Brookings Papers on Economic Activity*, 479–510.

Solow, R. (1956) 'A contribution to the theory of economic growth', *Quarterly Journal of Economics*, 70:65–94.

Srinivasan, T.N. (1983) 'International factor movements, commodity trade and commercial policy in a specific factor model', *Journal of International Economics*, 14:289–312.

Srinivasan, T.N. and Bhagwati, J.S. (1981) 'Trade and welfare in a steady-state', in: J.S. Chipman and C.P. Kindleberger, eds., *Flexible exchange rates and the balance of payments*. Amsterdam: North-Holland.

Srinivasan, T.N. and Bhagwati, J.N. (1983a) 'On transfer paradoxes and immiserizing growth: Part I', *Journal of Development Economics*, 13:217–222.

Srinivasan, T.N. and Bhagwati, J.N. (1983b) 'Postscript', *Journal of Development Economics*, 13:251–252.

Srinivasan, T.N. and Walley, J., eds. (1986) *General equilibrium trade and policy modeling*. Cambridge, MA: MIT Press.

Standaert, S. (1985) 'The foreign exchange constraint, suppression of the trade deficit and the shadow price of foreign exchange in a fix-price economy', *Journal of Development Economics*, 18:37–50.

Stiglitz, J.E. and Weiss, A. (1981) 'Credit rationing in markets with imperfect information', *American Economic Review*, 71:393–411.

Svensson, L.E.O. (1984a) 'Factor trade and goods trade', *Journal of International Economics*, 16:365–378.

Svensson, L.E.O. (1984b) 'Oil prices, welfare, and the trade balance', *Quarterly Journal of Economics*, 99:649–672.

Svensson, L.E.O. and Razin, A. (1983) 'The terms of trade and the current account: The Harberger–Laursen–Metzler effect', *Journal of Political Economy*, 91:97–125.

Takagi, Y. (1981) 'Aid and debt problems in less developed countries', *Oxford Economic Papers*, 33:323–337.

Tan, A.H.H. (1969) 'Immiserizing tariff-induced capital accumulation and technical change', *Malayan Economic Review*, 13:1–7.

Uekawa, Y. (1971) 'Generalization of the Stolper–Samuelson theorem', *Econometrica*, 39:197–218.

Uzawa, H. (1968) 'Time preference, the consumption function, and optimal asset holdings', in: J.N. Wolfe, ed., *Value, capital and growth: Papers in honor of Sir John Hicks*. Edinburgh: Edinburgh University Press.

van Dormael, A. (1978) *Bretton Woods: Birth of a monetary system*. New York: Holmes and Meier.

van Wijnbergen, S. (1985) 'Macroeconomic aspects of the effectiveness of foreign aid: On the two-gap model, home goods disequilibrium and real exchange rate misalignment', Center for Economic Policy Research Discussion Paper no. 45.

Viner, J. (1937) *Studies in the theory of international trade*. New York: Harper.

von Furstenberg, G.M. (1985) 'Adjustment with IMF lending', *Journal of International Money and Finance*, 4:209–222.

von Weizsacker, O. (1965) 'Existence of optimal programs of accumulation for an infinite time horizon', *Review of Economic Studies*, 32:85–104.

Waelbroeck, J. (1984) 'Capital, foreign exchange, and growth: The two-gap and labor-income-flow views', in: M. Syrquin, L. Taylor, and L.E. Westphal, eds., *Economic structure and performance*. Orlando: Academic Press, 281–294.

Wan, H.Y. (1971) 'A simultaneous variational model for international capital movement', in: J.N. Bhagwati, R.W. Jones, R.A. Mundell and J. Vanek, eds., *Trade, balance of payments and growth: Essays in honor of Charles P. Kindleberger*. Amsterdam: North-Holland, 261–290.

Wasow, B. (1979) 'Savings and dependence with externally financed growth', *Review of Economics and Statistics*, 61:150–154.

Weil, P. (1985) 'Overlapping families of infinitely-lived agents', Harvard University, unpublished.

Weisskopf, T.E. (1972a) 'An econometric test of alternative constraints on the growth of underdeveloped countries', *Review of Economics and Statistics*, 54:67–78.

Weisskopf, T.E. (1972b) 'The impact of foreign capital inflow on domestic savings in underdeveloped countries', *Journal of International Economics*, 2:25–38.

Wellons, P.A. (1984) 'International institutions in the debt crisis: National interests and long-term consequences', unpublished.

Williamson, J. ed., (1983) *IMF conditionality*. Washington, DC: Institute for International Economics.

Williamson, J. (1984) *A new SDR allocation?*. Washington, DC: Institute for International Economics.

Wilson, R. (1931) *Capital imports and the terms of trade*. Melbourne.

Wittkopf, E.R. (1972) *Western bilateral aid allocation*. London: Sage.

Wong, K.Y. (1983) 'On choosing among trade in goods and international capital and labor mobility: A theoretical analysis', *Journal of International Economics*, 14:223–250.

World Bank (1985, 1986, 1987) *World development reports 1985, 1986, 1987*. Oxford: Oxford University Press.

Yaari, M. (1965) 'Uncertain lifetime, life insurance, and the theory of the consumer', *Review of Economic Studies*, 32:137–150.

Yano, M. (1983) 'Welfare aspects of the transfer problem', *Journal of International Economics*, 15:277–289.

Yntema, T.O. (1932) *A mathematical reformulation of the general theory of international trade*. Chicago: University of Chicago Press.

Chapter 26

FOREIGN PRIVATE CAPITAL FLOWS

ELIANA A. CARDOSO

Tufts University

RUDIGER DORNBUSCH*

Massachusetts Institute of Technology

Contents

*We are indebted to Benjamin Cohen, Jonathan Eaton, Al Fishow, T.N. Srinivasan and Sweder van Wijnbergen for very helpful suggestions.

Handbook of Development Economics, Volume II, Edited by H. Chenery and T.N. Srinivasan
© *Elsevier Science Publishers B.V., 1989*

1. Introduction

Private foreign capital is credited with a major role in the development of the new world in the nineteenth century. It is also held responsible for debt crises and macroeconomic instability in developing countries today. This chapter looks at the role that private capital flows can play in economic development. In this chapter, private capital flows encompass both direct investment as well as portfolio investment, including bonds and bank loans.

The chapter is organized in four parts. We start in Section 2 with a historical overview. From there we proceed to two analytical sections. The first (Section 3) presents models of the role of external finance in economic development. The second (Section 4) focuses on macroeconomic issues associated with overvalued currencies and capital flight. The concluding section (Section 5) reviews the scope for private capital in the aftermath of the present debt crisis.

A brief account of foreign capital in non-oil-developing countries shows that in 1987 the total stock of foreign capital was $1193 billion, or an amount equal to nearly 30 percent of U.S. GNP. Of this total, 15 percent took the form of direct foreign investment and 85 percent corresponded to external debt. Official creditors accounted for 39.4 percent of this debt and private creditors (primarily banks) made up the remainder. These totals include short-term commercial credits, as well as IMF standby credit positions.[1]

The relatively small share of direct investment and the large share of debt to commercial banks were important reasons for the debt crisis of the 1980s. The main question today is how to mobilize a renewed flow of private capital to developing countries.

2. Some history

In this section we review the historical experience of developing countries as borrowers in the world capital market. The review of history is of interest in highlighting the importance of international capital flows as instruments of economic development in the nineteenth and twentieth centuries. But history is also of interest in that it shows previous debt crises and their outcome. Our discussion focuses on three main periods: the nineteenth century, the inter-war period, and the buildup of the present debt crisis in the 1970s.

---

[1] The numbers are obtained by combining the debt data of the IMF *World Economic Outlook* with an update by the authors of the foreign direct investment stock in Goldsbrough (1985, table A2).

2.1. The pre-1914 period

The nineteenth century saw a great expansion of private investment in developing countries, notably in the United States, Canada, Australia and Argentina, as well as in Brazil, Mexico and India. The capital flows to developing countries took two main forms: bond issues by various levels of public administration and direct foreign investment. London was the main financial center, but Germany and France emerged in the later nineteenth century as important rival centers of finance. The United States remained a net debtor until during World War I.[2]

The nineteenth-century experience with international capital flows has given rise to two broad representations of the facts. One is of states with persistently poor public finance defaulting on one loan after another, and of gun boat diplomacy employed for the recovery of debts. The second one is an image of dramatic economic progress in the new world resulting from international lending, together with migration. Both are correct. As Fishlow (1985) points out, lending not only served development purposes as railway construction, for example, but also public revenue needs. The overriding legacy of the period was clearly economic development even though defaults were a recurrent feature, and all modern experiences, including bond-holders protective councils, buy-backs and restructuring were known then. North (1962, p. 14) points out:

> Investors came to recognize that financing revolutions and counterrevolutions was a risky business compared to productive enterprise. Although experience with loans to the United States in 1839–42 shows that the latter was also risky, the idea of investing in productive enterprise became increasingly more popular . . . .
> Certainly the years between 1875 and 1914 witnessed an unprecedented movement of people and capital between countries and an equally striking expansion of international trade. Capital continued to move from western to eastern Europe and to the new regions of the world. This era is marked by the coming of age of the United States, for even while it was absorbing record amounts of capital, it became a capital exporter on a large scale.

Despite major research on investment in the nineteenth century, and comprehensive data on the foreign creditor position of the main lenders, the destination of investment by region and industry remain sketchy. Table 26.1 reports the main gross creditor and debtor countries in 1913. The broad patterns of foreign investment can be discerned. The total stock amounted to $44 billion or some-

---

[2] See Fishlow (1985) for a survey of international capital markets in the nineteenth and twentieth centuries. Other references include North (1962), Thomas (1967), Kenwood and Lougheed (1983) and Edelstein (1982).

Table 26.1
Gross creditor and gross debtor positions: 1914 (percent of total)

Gross creditors	Percent	Gross debtors	Percent
United Kingdom	40.9	Europe	27.3
France	20.4	Latin America	19.3
Germany	13.2	United States	15.5
Benelux	12.5	Canada	8.4
United States	8.0	Asia	13.6
Others	5.0	Africa	10.7
		Oceania	5.2

Source: Thomas (1967) and United Nations (1949).

Table 26.2
Approximate distribution of foreign investment in 1913 (percent)

	United Kingdom	Germany	France
United States and Canada	33.7	15.7	4.4
Europe	5.8	53.2	59.5
Russia	2.9	7.7	25.1
Austria-Hungary	0.2	12.8	4.9
Spain and Portugal		7.2	8.7
Turkey	0.6		7.3
Latin America	20.1	16.2	13.3
Africa		8.5	16.2[a]
South Africa	9.8		
Asia		4.3	4.9
India and Ceylon	10.0		
Australia and New Zealand	11.1		
Others	9.5	2.1	1.7
Total	100.0	100.0	100.0

[a] French Colonies plus Egypt, Suez and South Africa.
Note: Blanks denotes absence of detailed statistics.
Source: Feis (1965) and Thomas (1967).

what more than U.S. GNP at that time.[3] The United Kingdom stands out as the chief creditor; the United States remains a net debtor.

The regional and sectoral distribution of the 1914 stock of foreign investment for the main investing countries is shown in Table 26.2. Both France and Germany show a concentration on lending in Europe. Britain's lending to the empire takes up 47 percent of its total lending.

The stock of *direct* foreign investment in 1914 had the characteristics shown in Table 26.3. Once again the purpose is to give a broad impression of the patterns. Three facts stand out: first, the dominance of the United Kingdom as a source;

[3]See United Nations (1949, p. 2).

Table 26.3
The stock of direct foreign investment in 1914 (percent of total)

By country of origin		By sector		By recipient	
United Kingdom	45.5	Primary	50.0	United States and Canada	45.8
Unites States	16.5	Manufacturing	15.0	Western Europe	7.7
Germany	10.5	Trade	10.0	Other developed countries	9.9
France	12.2	Railroads	20.0	Less developed countries	26.6
Other	13.3	Finance	10.0		

Source: Dunning and Stopford (1983).

second, the financing of primary production (petroleum, mining, smelting, and agriculture); and third, the large share of foreign direct investment in the United States and Canada.

An important feature of debt crises becomes apparent as early as the nineteenth century. This is the waves in lending, followed by a sudden stop to capital flows resulting in distress in the borrowing countries. Taussig (1928, p. 130) points to these waves when he writes:

> The loans from the creditor country...begin with a modest amount, then increase and proceed *crescendo*. They are likely to be made in exceptionally large amounts toward the culminating stage of a period of activity and speculative upswing, and during that stage become larger from month to month so long as the upswing continues. With the advent of crisis, they are at once cut down sharply, even cease entirely. The interest payments on the old loans thereupon are no longer offset by any new loans; they became instantly a net charge to be met by the borrowing country. A sudden reversal takes place in the debtor country's international balance sheet; it feels the consequences abruptly, in an immediate need of increased remittances to the creditor country, in a strain on its banks, high rates of discount, falling prices. And this train of events may ensue not only once.... The final outcome, when this period of irregular movements has run its course, is that the debtor country has more to remit on interest account than to receive on principal account and that the remittance is effected by an excess of merchandise exports over imports. The history of the United States and of Argentina,...shows these successive waves of international borrowing, repeated crises....

Figure 26.1 shows the U.K. net foreign investment, expressed as a fraction of U.K. GNP, as a measure of the gross resource flows. Periods of declining net foreign investment led to major debt problems in the periphery. Debt default was common, and on occasion spectacular. The best known case was the Baring crisis in 1890. The crisis which led to the failure of the banking house Baring arose from Argentina's inability to meet debt service payments.

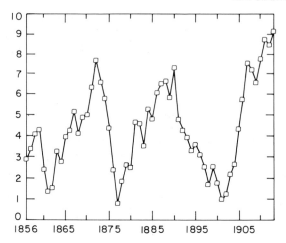

Figure 26.1. U.K. net foreign investment (percent of GDP).

Debt default was common, but in time countries would resume debt service in order to gain renewed access to the credit market. Bond-holders committees negotiated the adjustment of principal, settlement of arrears and the restructuring of debts, on behalf of creditors with the defaulting countries. If debt service was always resumed, the terms were often sharply reduced.

It is interesting to observe the pattern of borrowing and lending of the developing countries of the time. Figure 26.2 shows net capital movements for

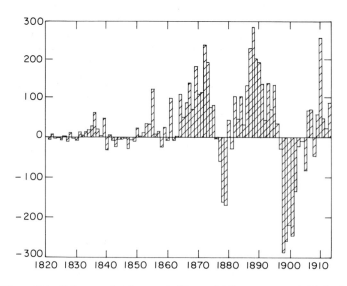

Figure 26.2. U.S. net capital imports (millions of dollars, + = capital inflow).

the United States. The figure does now show what might be expected – a gradual transition from net capital imports to net capital exports. On the contrary, there are spurts of net lending and of net borrowing. Only with the very large net capital exports of World War I did the United States become a net creditor.

2.2. The interwar period

In the 1920s the United States became a lender on a massive scale, and New York the center of the international lending, before the sharp cessation of international lending in the aftermath of the 1929 crash. Lending went to Europe to help pay reparations: it went to Canada and Latin America to finance development and public expenditure; and it went to many countries in South East Europe. Table 26.4 shows the external position of several countries in 1930, at the outbreak of the great crisis in world trade and capital markets.

The great lending spree came to a sharp halt in 1928–29. The sharp decline in commodity prices and in world trade reduced the attractiveness of further loans. Between 1929 and 1933 wool prices declined 65 percent, copper 63 percent, wheat 57 percent and the same pattern prevailed for all primary commodities. U.S. imports declined by 55 percent, and by 1933 Latin American exports had fallen to only 28 percent of their 1928 level. Kindleberger describes the inevitable consequence (1984, p. 317):

> Latin America was hit – especially Argentina, Brazil and Colombia – by the abrupt halt in foreign lending in June 1928 when the New York market started

Table 26.4
Foreign capital in selected countries in 1930 (millions of pound sterling)

	External public debt	Total foreign capital	Total per head
Canada	270	1330	127
Australia	599	817	122
New Zealand	159	197	128
Argentina	240	640	55
Brazil	166	520	13
Chile	80	115	64
Colombia	30	85	9
Peru	22	115	17
Venezuela	0	80	25
China	86	660	2
Japan	192	250	4
India	390	575	2
South Africa	161	260	34

Source: Royal Institute (1937).

Table 26.5
Default status of dollar bonds: 1939
(millions of U.S. dollars and percent)

	Total debt held in the United States	Percent of debt in default
Latin America	1039.6	63.9
West Indies	79.4	14.2
Central America	26.2	82.2
South America	934.0	67.6
Europe	618.7	43.1
Asia	164.6	7.5
Oceania and Africa	97.8	0.0

Source: Feuerlein and Hannan (1940).

its meteoric rise and interest rates tightened on the call money market. On this score a number of Latin American countries date the start of the Depression from the second half of 1928. ... Whatever the merits of U.S. bankers in pushing foreign lending from 1925 to 1928, they were surely at fault in cutting it off abruptly in June of the latter year. Deflation is imposed by the Center on the Periphery, whenever the former suddenly stops lending, as in 1825, 1857, 1866, 1973, 1890, and 1907. First halting lending and then cutting way down on imports is a recipe for disaster.

Lary (1944, p. 6) reports a calculation that dramatizes how the reduction in U.S. lending conflicted with debt service requirements of debtor countries. In 1929 U.S. total external lending amounted to $7.4 billion against a foreign debt service of $900 million, leaving more than $6.5 billion for non-interest deficits of the debtor countries. By 1932 credit rationing was on: U.S. lending had fallen to $2.4 billion, forcing down foreign deficits by 77 percent. Countries with large fixed interest debts could no longer borrow to finance interest, amortization and non-interest deficits. Not only had their terms of trade deteriorated, but in addition, and equally important, there was a massive price deflation in the world economy which increased the real value of debt service payments dramatically.

Without the inflow of new loans, and with reduced export earnings and deflation, many of the debtors could no longer service their debts except at the cost of sharp recession. Many countries, especially in Europe and Latin America, chose not to go that way but rather opted for moratoria and default. Table 26.5 shows the status of debts in 1939.[4]

The immediate effect of the trade and debt crisis was a sharp decline in bond prices for all debtors, especially those in Latin America. Table 26.6 shows the

[4]See, too, the discussion in United Nations (1965) and Gantenbein (1939, ch. 4).

Table 26.6
Latin American gold bond prices in the 1930s

Country (interest, maturity)	1930		1939	
	High	Low	High	Low
Bolivia (8%, 1947)	100.0	35.0	5.0	2.5
Brazil (6.5%, 1957)	88.2	47.5	23.0	9.5
Chile (7%, 1942)	103.3	87.0	18.4	12.0
Colombia (6%, 1961)	83.0	55.0	34.6	19.8
Costa Rica (7%, 1951)	91.0	65.0	30.8	16.5
Guatemala (8%, 1948)	97.0	85.0	39.0	24.0
Mexico (4%, 1934)	17.4	8.0	1.4	0.8
Peru (7%, 1959)	100.0	52.5	13.5	7.5
El Salvador (8%, 1948)	110.2	98.0	21.5	13.5

Note: Mexico had suspended debt service already in 1919.
Source: Feuerlein and Hannan (1941).

extent of decline and Figure 26.3 shows the case of Chile where export losses had been more dramatic than anywhere else.

The recovery of commodity prices in the late 1930s and the increased trade opportunities during World War II sharply improved the trade position of many Latin American countries. In the 1940s, as a result, most debtors worked out resumption of payments on their debts and "repatriation" of their bonds by buying them up at the low prices at which they were trading. The arrangements for resuming debt service differed among countries. Mexico wrote down debts to one-fifth and paid only 1 percent of the accumulated arrears of several decades; Chile earmarked certain revenues for interest payments and buy backs. Brazil

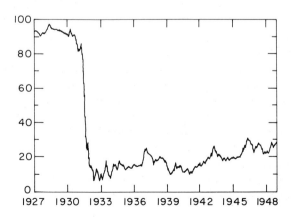

Figure 26.3. Chilean bond prices: 1927–48.

offered creditors no payment for arrears and moderate write downs. As a result, whereas 85 percent of Latin American debt was in default in 1938, by 1945 that number had already declined to only 60 percent. Further adjustment plans came in the late 1940s (Chile, Columbia, Peru) and it took until 1960 to completely clean up the aftermath of this great debt crisis.

An interesting question that remains largely unanswered is the difference in response to the crisis of Latin American debtors compared to countries in the Commonwealth, specifically Australia, Canada and New Zealand. As agricultural exporters they were faced with much the same disturbance as Latin America. The Royal Institute (1937, p. 2) had this explanation:

> Maintenance of debt service upon the foreign capital invested in a country is affected by a number of factors. In the first place, creditors' receipts will be dependent not merely upon the ability but also the willingness of debtors to pay. Many countries have discontinued service payments on their debts even when their financial position was sufficiently sound to enable such payments to be made. Usually, defaults have taken place when the possibility of obtaining fresh supplies of capital seemed remote, and when appearances suggested that there were little to be gained – except in prestige from the fulfillment of obligations.

Part of the reason for their continued debt service was, no doubt, the fact that trade remained open for them under imperial preferences.[5] The League of Nations (1932) has pointed to the trade issue in the following terms:

> When the great creditor countries reduce their export of capital, all their debtors must meet their obligations in gold, instead of by fresh borrowing. Before the extraordinary situation had fully developed, however, a further check was imposed upon the capacity of the debtor countries to pay their external obligations. The increased export surpluses which they placed upon world markets caused concern in the importing countries, which thereupon imposed higher tariffs and supplemented them by additional restrictions on imports. There ensued in consequence an enormous shrinkage in world trade, and the logical consequence of this shrinkage has been a series of moratoria, suspensions of payment, and standstill agreements, as a result of which the credit of many debtor countries has been gravely impaired.

2.3. The postwar experience

Since the interwar period was marked by extensive defaults, it is interesting to ask how the return to the capital market came about. In the immediate postwar

---

[5]Canada's attitude was also influenced by its special relationship with the United States.

Table 26.7
Default status of foreign dollar bonds (billions of dollars and percent)

	1938		1958	
	Amount outstanding	Percent in default	Amount outstanding	Percent in default
Latin America	1.7	75.0	0.6	12.5
Europe	1.9	59.9	1.0	89.6
Far East	0.6	0.1	0.2	1.3
North America	2.2	4.9	1.8	0
International Institute	n.a.		0.8	0
Total	6.3	39.6	4.4	15.1

Source: Gantenbein (1939) and Institute of International Finance (1959).

period and the 1950s there was virtually no borrowing by developing countries in the world capital market. Most of financing took the form of direct investment in developing countries as well as loans from the newly created International Bank for Reconstruction and Development (IBRD) and the U.S. Export–Import Bank. Several developing countries in Latin America during this period "repatriated" bonds still outstanding, or bought up foreign investment as Argentina did in respect to British railroads.[6] Mikesell reports, for the period 1945–53, for Latin America, a total gross capital inflow of $4.7 billion, mostly from official sources. Against this, a gross capital outflow of $2.9 billion, of which 2.0 billion was for repurchases of foreign owned capital.

The reports of the Council of Foreign Bond Holders and of the Institute for International Finance at New York University give a picture of how debts in default were cleaned up in the 1950s. They report the total of dollar bonds outstanding as well as the fraction in default (see Table 26.7).

By the end of the 1950s dollar debts had been significantly reduced and most debts, with the exception of those of Bolivia, were being serviced under new settlements. The cleaning up of debts in Latin America had taken two main forms. One was buy-backs or repatriation, previously mentioned. The other was write-downs of principal in the context of exchange offers or settlements.

This cleaning up of debts was an essential step to prepare the return to the capital market. Mexico, for example, returned to the capital market in 1960. Between 1913 and 1919 Mexican debts went into default. In 1942–46 the International Committee of Bankers accepted a settlement that reduced the debt to 20 percent of the original amount of $350 million. Bond-holders assented to the offer even though the Foreign Bond Holders Protective Council protested the

---

[6]See Weiner and Dalla-Chiesa (1955) and Mikesell (1955) on debt repatriation in Latin America.

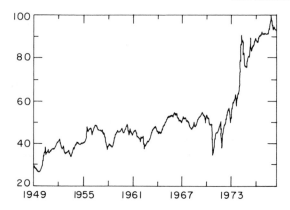

Figure 26.4. Chilean bond price: 1949–78.

plan:[7]

The plan of service offered under this agreement, involving as it does a reduction of principal, cancellation of a very large part of the back interest, payment of the current interest at an exceedingly low rate, and discrimination in favor of certain issues of "secured bonds" involves principles which the Council has not admitted in its principles in its dealings with foreign governments. The Council could not, therefore, accept the plan as a precedent for its negotiations with other countries.

Just at the time of the first new foreign loan of $100 million in 1960, Mexico redeemed the $16 million balance of its outstanding debt.

To the extent that settlements provided for a sinking fund it was often this sinking fund which was the vehicle for buy-backs. Chile's sinking fund, for example, was retiring debt at a discount averaging 55 percent in 1957–60.[8] The ability to buy debt at large discounts reflected the continuing weakness of Latin bonds. Figure 26.4 shows the price of Chilean debt in the period 1949–76. Between 1948 and 1964 half of the dollar debt of $125 million was retired in this fashion.

Although there are differences from country to country, the late 1960s marks the turn from cleaning up debts to renewed commercial borrowing for most countries.

---

[7]Foreign Bond Holders Protective Council *Annual Report* 1962–64, p. 104.

[8]The policy of buying back debt at a discount, rather than using available resources to meet interest liabilities, was sharply attacked by the Foreign Bond Holders Protective Council in the 1936 and 1937 *Annual Reports*. Wallich (1943), however, made a case for such buy-backs.

Table 26.8
Latin America's external payments (percent of exports, averages)

	1946–50	1951–55	1956–60
Current account deficit	3.1	7.2	11.0
Net interest payments	1.5	1.1	2.0
Direct investment income payments	9.8	10.8	11.8
Resource transfers abroad[a]	8.2	4.6	2.8
Gross private capital inflows	5.6	5.6	12.0

[a] Defined as the current account deficit less net investment income payments abroad.
Source: United Nations (1965) and IMF.

2.4. The return to the capital market

After this initial phase of adjustment, which was strongly influenced by the resources Latin America had accumulated during the war, an intermediate phase sets in where official lending (including grants) and direct investment were the main source of finance.

Balance of payments statistics give an idea of the relative size of investment income payments abroad on account of interest and direct investment income. It is clear that interest payments now are only a small portion of external investment income payments. Interestingly, throughout the period to 1960, Latin America was making net resource transfers abroad. The current account averaged deficits, but the deficit adjusted for investment income payments, which is a measure of resource transfers, steadily showed significant surpluses (see Table 26.8).

The return of lending to Latin America was slow. In the period 1946–50 a total of $645 million net inflow was recorded, in 1951–55 it increased to $3.3 billion and increased to $5.7 billion total in 1956–60. Interestingly, most of the net inflow was from private sources in the case of Latin America.

Table 26.9 shows the data for capital flows to all developing countries for the period from the mid-1950s to the 1980s. Note in particular the very large share of direct investment among the sources of finance in the late 1950s.

Return of private portfolio investment and specifically bank lending starts in 1960 and then gathers momentum.[9] Mexico, as noted above, returned to the private capital market in July 1960. From the early 1960s on the share of private financing increases from 34 percent to 60 percent on the eve of the debt crisis. Note that in the 1960–75 period half of private financing was still in the form of direct investment. The dramatic change occurs in 1975–79 when bank financing and bond issues become 41 percent of all financial flows to developing countries. This is the period when the debt crisis was built up.

[9] See Cooper and Truman (1971).

Table 26.9
Capital flows to developing countries, 1956–1985 (annual averages)

Period	Total flows (bill. U.S. $)	Portfolio and direct investment (% of total)	Direct investment (% of total)	Export credits (% of total)
1956–59	7,082	44.2	31.1	5.2
1960–64	9,904	34.1	18.8	7.3
1965–69	11,865	42.9	21.4	11.0
1970–74	20,805	45.9	24.3	9.6
1975–79	55,384	60.5	19.0	13.4
1980–84	80,923	56.8	13.2	9.6
1985	46,325	23.0	16.6	3.3

Source: OECD *Development Assistance Review*, various issues.

Table 26.10
U.S. direct investment stock in Latin America (percent of total)

	1929	1950	1970	1980
Mining and smelting	20.8	14.1	11.4	n.a.
Petroleum	17.5	27.7	25.9	23.3
Manufacturing	6.6	17.5	35.4	59.1
Transport, utilities and communications	25.2	20.9	5.4	n.a.
Other	29.1	19.8	21.9	18.6[a]

[a] Includes mining and smelting as well as transport, utilities and communications.
Source: U.S. *Historical Statistics* and *Survey of Current Business*.

Before looking at the debt crisis, we briefly consider postwar direct foreign investment in developing countries. Table 26.10 draws attention to the changing composition of direct investment. We take as an example U.S. direct investment in Latin America because of the readily available data. The notable fact is the increasing share of manufacturing. Whereas investment, in the interwar period and earlier, concentrated on mining and petroleum, the major share of direct investment stock in 1980 is in manufacturing.

In the 1970s debt became a much more significant source of external capital than direct investment, and the share of concessional debt became relatively small for many of the major debtors in Latin America.[10]

[10]See Goldsbrough (1985).

2.5. The 1980s debt crisis

In August 1982 Mexico was unable to meet scheduled payments and declared a moratorium. In short order many countries followed.[11] These were two reasons for the debt crisis. Economic management in debtor countries had been exceptionally poor. Budget deficits had increased vastly; exchange rates were overvalued; capital flight and excessive consumer imports were the rule. All this was financed by external debt accumulation without much regard for the future cost in terms of debt.

Lenders did not pay much attention to reasons for borrowing and hence made the excessive accumulation of debt possible. But an essential ingredient in the outbreak of the debt crisis was the sharp deterioration in the world economic environment, just as in the 1930s. The U.S. shift to tight money in 1980–1981, together with tighter money in other OECD countries, raised interest rates, and thus led to a recession in the world economy. As a result debt burdens increased and export revenues of debtors fell. In 1981–82 the group of countries which subsequently was to reschedule their debts experienced an 8.5 percent decline in export volume and a 7.6 percent fall in export prices.[12]

Unlike in the 1970s, automatic financing of deficits became unavailable. Debtors could not pay and creditors would not lend: the 1982 debt crisis was ready. Table 26.12 shows some of the relevant data. Before 1982–83 interest payments were automatically borrowed, and non-interest deficits in the current account were also financed. Once commercial lenders rationed credit, this was no longer possible. Now debtors had to run non-interest surpluses to finance at least part of the interest payments. Continued capital flight increased the burden of coping with the debt crisis by trade surpluses.

We conclude this section by offering some remarks, comparing the debt crisis of the 1980s to that of the interwar period. Are the origins much the same? Was the structure of debt much the same? And, how did the post-crisis working of the system compare? We offer here only a few comments and note that a comprehensive evaluation remains to be accomplished.[13] A complete comparison is beyond the scope of this survey, but some points are worth highlighting:
- Debt problems of individual countries are common.[14] But the 1930s, just like the 1980s, presented a situation of simultaneous, widespread debt service

---

[11] There is an extensive literature on the debt crisis. For a discussion and references see Dornbusch (1989).

[12] See IMF *World Economic Outlook*.

[13] See Thorp (1984) for a collection of essays on the 1930s. See, too, United Nations (1965) as well as the annual reports of the Council of Foreign Bond Holders and the Institute of International Finance.

[14] See Winkler (1933), Lewis (1944), Wynne (1951), Imlah (1958), Feis (1965), Bitterman (1973), Landes (1979), Lipson (1985), Cohen (1986) and Stallings (1987).

Table 26.11
Aggregate world macroeconomic indicators

	Real commodity prices (1980 = 100)[a]	Labor (% p.a.)	Inflation[b] (% p.a.)	World activity[c] (% p.a.)
1960–69	115	5.2	1.0	6.2
1970–79	115.	8.0	11.4	3.4
1980	100	14.4	13.0	0.0
1981	96	16.5	−4.1	−7.0
1982	89	13.1	−3.5	−3.3

[a] Measured in terms manufactures export prices of industrial countries.
[b] Rate of increase of industrial countries' unit export values.
[c] Industrial production.
Source: IMF and Economic Commission for Latin America.

Table 26.12
The current account deficit and external debt: Countries with recent debt servicing
difficulties (billions of dollars)

	Non-interest current account (resource transfer)	Interest payments	Current account deficit	External debt
1978	17.1	14.8	31.9	242
1979	10.1	21.8	31.9	292
1980	5.0	34.3	39.6	356
1981	20.2	47.5	67.7	430
1982	5.4	57.5	63.1	494
1983	−30.2	52.1	21.9	514
1984	−48.6	57.2	8.6	534
1985	−50.2	53.6	3.1	553

Source: IMF, *World Economic Outlook*.

difficulties. The world recession and the immediate retrenching of capital flows
are the proximate explanation. The preceding wave of lending provided the
essential vulnerability.

• By comparison with the 1930s the decline in world trade and prices in the 1980s
was very small. Between 1929 and 1932 Latin American exports had declined
by 75 percent. By contrast, between 1979 and 1982 they had increased by 76
percent! But the very sharp increase in interest rates and interest burdens
contributed a disturbance not present in the debt crisis of the 1930s.[15]

• An interesting comparison is shown in Table 26.13. There we compare the debt
service ratios in the interwar period and in the 1980s. The debt service ratios in

[15] Even that argument must be qualified by noting that deflation in the 1930s raised *real* interest
rates on existing debt.

Table 26.13
Ratio of debt service to exports

	Argentina	Bolivia	Brazil	Chile	Colombia	Mexico	Peru
1926–29	9.3	7.4	14.7	8.2	6.8	n.a.	4.8
1930	18.2	13.5	23.5	18.0	14.0		9.5
1931	22.5	24.5	28.4	32.9	15.6		16.3
1932	27.6	50.0	41.0	102.6	21.8		21.4
1933	30.2	38.5	45.1	81.9	29.6		21.7
1980	30	30	56	38	10	38	37
1981	34	30	57	57	17	35	52
1982	38	34	72	62	22	44	44

Note: The data for the interwar period refer to "public" debt service, those for the 1980s to total debt service. Mexico suspended debt service in 1913–19.
Source: Avramovic (1964) and World Bank.

the 1980s were of the same order as those in the 1930s, except in the case of Chile.

- Debt problems of the 1980s were primarily concentrated in Latin America and the Philippines. By contrast, in the 1930s many European countries, including Germany, went into default. Creditor countries themselves in the 1930s experienced widespread domestic defaults of their municipal debts. Bank closings and foreclosures and mass unemployment were the rule worldwide.
- Most debt in the interwar period took the form of bonds. By contrast in the 1980 crisis commercial bank loans and official credits were the major part of the debt. In fact, to the extent that bonds were outstanding, as for example in the case of Brazil or Mexico, their amounts were small and the service has continued unimpaired.
- Investment income accounted for a much more significant share of total investment income payments in the interwar crisis than in the 1980s. For example, in 1935 direct investment income amounted to 70 percent, 35 percent, 53 percent and 50 percent of the total foreign obligations of Argentina, Brazil, Chile and Mexico, respectively. By comparison, in 1983 these shares were 12 percent, 22 percent, 18 percent and 13 percent, respectively.[16]
- Following the abandonment of gunboat diplomacy, in the interwar period bond-holders were primarily represented by protective councils. These negotiated on behalf of the bond-holders and recommended settlements after lengthy periods of suspension of debt service. Their resources and their clout were limited.[17] In the 1980s governments and international institutions have been at the center of the rescheduling process from the very beginning. The existence of

[16]See Buchanan and Lutz (1947) and Goldsbrough (1985).
[17]See Gantenbein (1939). United Nations (1965) notes that the U.S. Foreign Bond Holders Protective Council was working with a budget of $100 000.

standby-credits and the framework of IMF programs facilitated the rescheduling as opposed to 1930s-style suspension of debt service.[18] Debt problems of the developing countries were seen as a threat to the banking system and to the stability of international finance. Political intervention proceeded at the highest level.

- Trade remained relatively open in the 1980s. By comparison, in the 1930s worldwide trade restriction had been the rule.
- A final point: seven years after debt difficulties emerged, Latin America looked better in the interwar period than it does today. After 1933, growth had increased per capita income. Today income per capita has declined sharply. The world economic environment at the time was surely not more favorable. The difference, therefore, must be that policies were better at that time, and that suspension of debt service may have given room for structural adjustment in the 1930s.

3. Models and evaluation of the role of capital inflows

In this section we review the allocation and welfare effects of foreign investment. An extensive review of relevant models is presented by the survey article of Findlay (1984). The analysis here starts from the classical model in the tradition of McDougall (1960), and proceeds to review the issues raised by existing distortions. From there we proceed to a broader examination of the cost–benefit discussion.

It is analytically convenient to discuss the effect of capital inflows under five separate headings. First, the effects of capital inflows on the economy's output potential. Capital inflows add to the economy's productive capacity and thus potentially increase welfare. The supply-side effects of foreign investment raise special questions about sectoral effects and, in special circumstances, they may carry more than the traditional neoclassical benefits by adding to competition or improving technology. But they may also, because of existing distortions, lower welfare.

Second, the scope capital flows provide for intertemporal consumption smoothing. In a context of growth in per capita income over time, or in the case of fluctuations in disposable income, international borrowing may serve to smooth consumption.

Third, the distribution of gains from direct investment flows and the question of debt versus equity must be asked.

Fourth, capital inflows may play a strategic role in circumventing a foreign exchange gap to the growth process.

[18]See Kraft (1984), Portes and Swoboda (1987), Stallings (1987), Frieden (1987) and Cohen (1986) on the financial and political dimensions of the 1980s debt crisis.

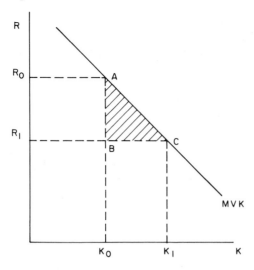

Figure 26.5. The welfare effects of capital inflows.

Fifth, capital flows play an important macroeconomic role in that they help determine the ease or difficulty with which policy-makers can control inflation and economic activity in a context of disturbances. We reserve for a separate section the role of capital flows in a macroeconomic context. We start our discussion with the supply side effects and then discuss consumption smoothing, distribution, and growth.

3.1. Static allocation and welfare effects

The traditional analysis of foreign investment considers a barter economy where capital inflows (direct foreign investment) take the form of an addition to the economy's stock of physical capital.[19] The inflow of productive capital raises the economy's output. In the case of constant returns to scale, the foreign factor earns its marginal product, but also adds to national income, i.e. the income of domestic factors of production. Figure 26.5 shows this kind of analysis for a one-sector economy with the marginal value product of capital schedule (MVK) drawn for a given stock of other factors of production.

Starting from an initial national capital stock, K_0, a capital inflow raises the capital stock to K_1. The capital inflow redistributes income between domestic capital and other factors (the rectangle $R_1 R_0 AB$) and it adds to national

[19] For extensive discussion of capital flows in trade theory see Ruffin (1984), Smith (1984) as well as the symposium in the 1983 *Journal of International Economics*.

income – i.e. income of all domestic factors of production. The increase in the value of gross domestic product (output) is given by the area under the MVK schedule. The rectangle BCK_1K_0 accrues to foreign investors. The triangle ABC represents the increase in national income that arises as a result of the increase in the ratio of capital relative to other factors.

The gain in national income depends on the size of the capital inflow as well as on the elasticity of the derived demand for capital. The steeper the MVP schedule, for a given increase in the capital stock, the larger the gain in national income. Suppose specifically that there is an increase in the capital stock of $x = (K_1 - K_0)/K_0$ percent. The national gain is equal to the triangle ABC and can be expressed as a fraction of national income as follows:

$$(1 - \alpha)\alpha x^2/2\sigma, \tag{1}$$

where α is the distributive share of capital and σ is the elasticity of substitution. Thus, the national gain is larger, the smaller the share of capital, and the smaller the elasticity of substitution between capital and the domestic (composite) factor of production. If all capital is foreign owned, the national gain is larger since the increase in the ratio of capital to other factors redistributes income toward domestic factors by an amount given by the rectangle R_0R_1AB.

The simple analysis can be extended to consider the choice of optimal borrowing. A country facing a perfectly elastic supply of capital should borrow (rent) capital to the point where the MVK is equal to the world cost of capital. But if the supply of capital is upward-sloping, the increasing marginal cost of capital calls for a restriction of capital inflows below the competitive level. Such a restriction could be implemented by a tax on foreign borrowing or by quantitative restrictions.

Much of the discussion about the costs or benefits of foreign capital in developing countries involves departures from the simple neoclassical model analyzed above. These qualifications can be grouped in several categories: extensions of the classical model, market failure or distortions in the host economy, and non-economic arguments against foreign capital. We now present some of these arguments.

3.1.1. Additional benefits

The literature on economic development in the classical vein has emphasized that the gains from foreign capital go beyond the simple factor supply effect shown above. Specifically four additional, positive effects are identified. In each case the emphasis is on foreign firms, as opposed to unembodied or unattached resource flow, as the vehicle for the capital inflow. In that sense the benefits in question are specific to foreign direct investment.

A first additional benefit, over and above the factor supply effect, is the belief that the entry of foreign firms brings with it superior technology. In terms of Figure 26.5 above, the entry of foreign capital represents not only a movement along the *MVK* schedule, but also an outward shift. The exact extent of the benefits to the host country will depend on whether the technology is form-specific and appropriable by foreign investors, or whether it spreads freely to existing firms.

A second benefit is that foreign direct investment increases competition in the host economy. This point can be thought of in terms of any of a number of models of imperfect competition. The entry of a new firm into a non-traded domestic industry leads to a change in the industry output and the prices charged by individual firms. For example, in a model of duopoly competition on a Salop-style product circle, the entry of a new firm reduces prices and leads to an increase in industry output with favorable welfare effects. The favorable welfare effects are derived from the fact that the imperfectly competitive good is underproduced. Accordingly, an expansion of this sector is welfare improving. We discuss below instances where, because of distortions, foreign capital inflows may reduce welfare.

A third advantage claimed for foreign direct investment, this time in a country's export sectors, is that it gives advantages in terms of foreign market access. These advantages stem from the know-how of foreign firms concerning selling in foreign markets, or from their differential ability to gain market access abroad. This special advantage of foreign firms may come in one of two ways. A first involves scale economies in marketing. A country may obtain larger gains from trade if, rather than operating an export industry on its own, it draws on foreign firms for scale economy. Of course, this argument assumes that the country can, in fact, capture part of the rents stemming from the scale economy advantages enjoyed by the foreign firms. The typical form this would take is either a licensing fee or else an increase in factor prices in the export industry as foreign investors bid up factor costs over and above the level that can be sustained by a smaller scale domestic export industry.

The market access argument is important in the context of trade restrictions in export markets. To the extent that foreign firms, by virtue of their residence, gain access where a developing country cannot, they become a vehicle for gains from trade. Once again the question of the distribution of the rents arises.

3.1.2. The possibility of welfare losses

Even within the classical analysis there is a possibility that capital inflows reduce welfare in a second-best situation. Two particular cases have received attention. In one case capital inflows lead to the expansion of an industry that enjoys some monopoly power in the export sector. As the literature on immiserizing growth has shown, the resulting terms of trade deterioration may lower welfare in the host country. This, of course, is possible only in the absence of an optimum tariff. The second case concerns an economy where there are tariff or tax distortions. It is possible that, through general equilibrium effects, a capital inflow leads to a contraction of an industry that is already producing too little.

In Figure 26.5 above we showed that under perfect competition, with a given price of the country's exportable, a capital inflow raises national income. But assume now that exportables are not in perfectly elastic demand. Then an increase in quantity supplied, due to a capital inflow, must worsen the terms of trade. Accordingly marginal revenue product becomes the relevant measure of the social productivity of capital and it is possible that competitive capital inflows go beyond the optimal point and even turn out to be counterproductive. This must be the case if initially the marginal revenue product of capital falls short of the world rental on capital. Let MRK denote the host country's marginal revenue product of capital and R^* the world rental on capital. The national gain from a marginal capital inflow, dK^*, then is $(MRK - R^*) dK^*$ and can obviously be negative if the industry is competitive. In a multi-sector context the same analysis holds. To the extent that the inflow of capital, taking into account sectoral reallocation of factors, increases export supply, the resulting terms of trade deterioration may reduce national welfare by more than the gain in domestic factor productivity. This effect underlies the Prebisch–Singer criticism of the impact of foreign investment in primary commodity exporting countries which we discuss below.

A different possibility of immiserization was identified by Brecher and Diaz-Alejandro (1977) who consider a small, open economy. Here the focus is on existing domestic distortions such as tariffs or taxes which lead to overproduction and underconsumption of an activity. Specifically, suppose we take a Heckscher–Ohlin model and assume that the import sector is capital intensive. Due to protection, importables are overproduced and underconsumed. A capital inflow, holding constant world and hence domestic relative prices, will, by the Rybczynski effect, expand the production of importable goods and contract, absolutely, the export sector. The reallocation of domestic factors – both capital and labor – toward the import-competing sector transfers them toward lower value added activities and hence potentially reduces welfare.

We now briefly present the demonstration that capital inflows may reduce welfare in a small tariff-protected country. Let $U(C_x, C_m)$ be the utility function and denote the domestic and world relative price of importables by p and p^*, respectively, and let C and Q represent consumption and output. Using maximization and the budget constraint at world prices it can be shown that the marginal welfare effect of a capital inflow is given by:

$$dU/U_x = \left[(dQ_x + p^* dQ_m - R^* dK^*) + (p - p^*) dC_m\right]. \tag{2}$$

The second term, given constant relative prices, represents the welfare effect of changes in consumption of overpriced importables. The sign of dC_m, via the real income effect, is that of dU. Thus, the relevant criterion is the sign of the first term, i.e. the increase in national output at world prices less the rental payment on imported capital. By profit maximization, the increase in output at domestic prices is equal to the rental on capital ($dQ_x + p\,dQ_m = R^*\,dK^*$). By substituting this expression in (2), as well as ($p - p^*$) = tp^* with t the tariff rate, we have:

$$dU/U_x = tp^*[-dQ_m + dC_m]. \tag{2a}$$

By the Rybzynski effect, assuming that importables are capital intensive, the production of importables expands. The first term on the right-hand side of (2a) is negative, and hence welfare must decline.

In the policy discussion on the benefits of foreign investment, the existence of distortions – monopoly in foreign trade or domestic distortions – are important considerations. As the example above shows, foreign capital inflows can easily reduce welfare. The exact details will depend on the production structure and the nature of distortions, but the principle of a potential welfare reduction is apparent. An extensive literature explores many of these possibilities.

3.1.3. Absorptive capacity

The evaluation of the extent of benefits from foreign investment is often assessed in terms of the host country's absorptive capacity, i.e. its ability to use additional investment funds without large declines in the rate of return to these funds. If the capital used in production grows much faster than workers' and administrators' skills, its productivity will fall. While most developing countries struggle against limited capital resources, unlimited capital has its costs. Growth of investment at the rate that occurred in Saudi Arabia in the 1970s, for instance, will reduce rates of return to negligible levels.

Other possibilities come to mind. At one extreme is the early experience of Argentina or the United States. In these land-abundant countries, the inflow of capital, combined with immigration, hardly ran into diminishing returns. The massive capital inflows served to provide infrastructure investment especially in transportation which allowed these countries to be "opened up".

A second possibility arises when there is a dual economy with surplus labor, in the mold of Arthur Lewis. Here, the capital inflow (because of strict complementarity of capital and labor) creates employment opportunities in the advanced sector of an economy, thus raising national income.

In both examples capital inflows are highly productive because the employment of extra capital scarcely runs into economy-wide diminishing returns. But that, of course, need not be the case.

If capital is sufficiently plentiful to exhaust the capacity of an economy to absorb it, some economists suggest that it should be used to import the other missing factors of production. Those countries can also invest abroad, waiting for the day when their economies have matured to the point of having their capital resources repatriated. Much more common though, in countries enjoying big increases in revenues, has been a sharp growth of consumption expenditures. According to Kindleberger, this demonstrates the limits of absorptive capacity all the more clearly.

3.2. Consumption smoothing

The beneficial welfare effects of capital inflows are not derived from their production effects alone. They can also arise in the context of consumption smoothing. Here we want to distinguish between two separate possibilities. One arises in a context of cyclical fluctuations. The ability to borrow in the world capital market allows a country to sustain consumption in the face of transitory shocks. The other varies in a context of growth where foreign saving may be used to initiate a growth process, thus permitting a more stable path of consumption.

3.2.1. Cyclical fluctuations

The case of consumption smoothing in the case of *transitory* disturbances to the terms of trade, output or foreign demand is straightforward. Optimal consumption will fluctuate less than disposable income (or not at all) and hence the possibility to borrow during periods of income shortfalls, with subsequent repayment when income recovers, raises utility. The alternative, a path where consumption varies with real disposable income, involves variations in the marginal utility of income which will be high in states of low income and low when income is high.

The consumption smoothing advantage extends to disturbances that are domestic. Specifically, when government spending is high (for investment or other purposes) the world capital market makes it possible to run current account deficits, thus providing the real resources.

3.2.2. Consumption and growth

Consumption smoothing also arises in a growth context. Growth in per capita income requires an increase in the investment ratio. This can be achieved either by reducing per capita consumption or by drawing on foreign saving. A typical growth path would look as follows. In the first stage, investment is increased and financed by borrowing abroad. The increased rate of investment sustains an increase in per capita income growth. In this initial phase the ratio of debt to income will be rising. But by keeping the growth in per capita consumption

Table 26.14
Korean investment and foreign saving (percent of GDP)

	Investment	Foreign saving	Per capita income growth
1960–69	18.2	9.1	6.4
1970–79	27.6	6.8	7.9
1980–85	30.7	6.7	6.1
1985–86	30.7	0.2	7.3

Source: Dornbusch and Park (1987).

below that of income, the domestic saving rate is raised over time, and increasingly domestic rather than foreign savings finance the investment requirement. In a middle phase the current account deficit vanishes and the debt ratio peaks. In the third phase the saving rate has increased sufficiently so that all investment is financed at home and the ratio of external debt to income starts declining.

The case of Korea, shown in Table 26.14, provides an example of a transition toward a high saving rate, financed by initial large external borrowing.

The extremely large current account deficits – 9.1 and 6.8 percent as averages for the 1960s and 1970s – show how much of the growth was financed by drawing on external resources. As a result of high investment rates per capita, income growth was high. The growing per capita income in turn provided increasingly the resources to finance investment. By 1986–87 the current account had turned toward surplus, and debt started to be retired.

3.3. The distribution of the gains from foreign investment

Much of the policy discussion surrounding foreign investment involves the distribution of the benefits. This distribution question arises in respect to the sharing of gains between foreign capital and the host country's factors of production in the aggregate (as in Figure 26.5 above), but also within the host country between various factors of production. Moreover, in some discussions the question is pursued to the issue of redistribution of political power as a result of foreign capital inflows.

A capital inflow (unaccompanied by immigration) reduces the relative scarcity of capital and thus raises the factor productivity for domestic factors as a group. When capital is accompanied by immigration, as it was, for example, in land-abundant countries like the United States, Canada, Argentina or Australia, the real reward to the immobile factor, land, will rise while the returns to local labor and capital are reduced.[20] The distribution effect may also work on a regional

[20] The result announced here need not necessarily be the outcome. In general the effect on factor prices will depend on technology as well as on the relative increase of the host country's capital stock and labor force.

scale. Since capital inflows in these countries translated into important infrastructure investment in railroads and transport more generally, the result was a shifting economic frontier within each country.

There is no general presumption of how these redistributions affect the development process. But there is no doubt that they have important implications for the political balance between various factor owners as well as for the regional distribution of political power.

The international distribution of the gains from investment has been at the center of a sharp debate throughout the postwar period. In the classical view of trade as an engine of growth, as represented in the writings of Haberler (1984), Nurkse (1952, 1959), Viner (1952) and Myint (1958), economists saw primarily benefits in a policy of openness to world trade in goods and factors. But starting with Singer (1950) the debate centered on the question of whether capital-importing developing countries actually benefited (or benefited relatively more than the capital exporters) from capital import. The basic thesis of this literature is that capital imports are invested in the traditional primary commodity export sector with two consequences. First, the capacity expansion and productivity growth tend to be reflected in terms of trade deterioration, and hence the possibility of net welfare losses. Second, unlike the manufacturing sector, primary commodity production offers little in terms of spill-over effects on the rest of the economy. Thus, foreign investment merely establishes an enclave rather than exerting a pervasive development effort.

To underline the bias in investment in developing countries toward traditional industries, Nurkse (1952) presents the evidence shown in Table 26.15.

Singer (1984, p. 287) summarizes his skeptical view of the gains from trade for developing countries as follows:

> ...the impact of trade of the type prevalent in 1949–50 on developing countries includes not only the "engine of growth" effects emphasized by the classical economists and the theory of comparative advantage, but also potential backwash effects related to a more dynamic concept of comparative advantage.... Such effects on developing countries may under certain conditions offset, or more than offset, any engine of growth effects.

Table 26.15
The structure of U.S. direct investment by country grouping
(percent of total, 1948)

	Developing countries	Developed countries[a]
Extractive industries	59	23
Manufacturing and distribution	22	59
Other	19	18

[a] Canada and Western Europe.
Source: Nurkse (1952).

The view that the distribution of the gains from trade between borrowing and lending countries might not favor the developing country led, on the one hand, to the import substitution policy in Latin America under the auspices of the Economic Commission for Latin America and its forceful advocate, Raul Prebisch [see United Nations (1964)]. On the other hand, an extensive evaluation of the benefits from foreign investment, especially in the context of multinational corporations, has been underway for more than two decades. Some of the issues raised in that discussion will now be reviewed.

3.3.1. Debt versus equity

Much controversy surrounds the question of benefits and costs of capital flows. The orthodox tradition and laissez-faire economists who believe in the efficiency of the free market would stress their benefits: while commercial loans enhance the potential national income over time by increasing investment that cannot be financed with local savings, direct investment pumps up local production. Such direct investment comes with technical assistance and training possibilities, and may well stimulate exports. Nationalists, left-wingers and believers of dependency theory look at capital flows more skeptically and see Multi-National Corporations (MNCs) as unmistakably harmful. In between these two groups there are many economists who claim that capital flows are potentially beneficial but involve some dangers.

Before the debt crisis, criticism concerned mostly the fundamental economic and social meaning of development as it relates to the diverse activities of MNCs. Commercial loans were to be preferred to direct investment, since the problems associated with MNCs activities were numerous.

First, rather than contributing to closing the gap between investment and savings, MNCs might lower domestic savings and investment by stifling competition, by not reinvesting much of their profits, and by generating income for groups with lower propensity to save and higher propensity to import. By importing intermediates from overseas affiliates, rather than buying them from indigenous firms, MNCs would inhibit the expansion of local firms.

Second, rather than contributing to closing the gap between investment and needed foreign exchange, the long-run impact might be to reduce foreign exchange earnings. The current account would deteriorate as a result of substantial importation of intermediates and capital goods, and repatriation of profits, interest, royalties and management fees would add to this deterioration. The smaller the original capital inflows, the larger the local contribution of local bank credit, and the larger the profit repatriation, the greater the pressure on the balance of payments would be.

Third, rather than improving the local government budget by increasing taxable income, MNCs might contribute to the reduction of government revenues because of liberal tax concessions, investment allowances, disguised public subsidies and tariff protection provided by the host government.

Fourth, MNCs might exacerbate income inequalities. They would tend to promote the interest of a small number of well-paid, modern-sector workers against the interest of the non-skilled labor by widening wage differentials. They would divert resources away from needed food production and into the manufacture of sophisticated products catering for the demand of the local elites. They would exaggerate the existing inequality between rural and urban areas by establishing themselves in urban areas.

Fifth, they might bring in to the host country inappropriate products: they would stimulate inappropriate consumption patterns through advertising, and use inappropriate technologies of production given the relative supply of factors of production. As a result local resources would tend to be allocated to socially undesirable projects.

Sixth, management, skills and overseas contacts provided by MNCs might have little impact on local enterprises.

Seventh, the transfer prices used in intrafirm transactions might diverge from equivalent arm's length market prices that would be set in trade between unrelated parties. The opportunities for under- or overinvoicing (in order to shift profits for tax purposes, or to evade foreign trade taxes or exchange controls) are greater for intrafirm trade than for trade between independent producers who are unconcerned with the effect of their actions on the profitability of other affiliates. And finally, it is difficult to fix an exact price for technology transfer, especially if technology is transferred as one element of a package of resources provided by direct investment.

Despite this long list, what may be bad a priori need not emerge as an outcome in a real situation as long as the host government is aware of the a priori possibilities and has enough instruments to avoid or mitigate such possibilities. Few countries are willing to allow MNCs unrestricted access to their territories.[21]

Attitudes towards foreign investment have changed substantially in recent years. Under the circumstances of the debt crisis the argument now was made that foreign direct investment is preferable to bank lending since the former does not create fixed obligations in foreign exchange. In addition, profit outflows are directly related to the success of a project financed with foreign resources.

It has also been claimed that profit outflows tend to decline during recessions and therefore are less of a drain on foreign exchange availabilities than interest payments. A study by the International Monetary Fund[22] reports, however, that

---

[21] Regulations and controls include: limits on profit repatriation, limits on royalty payments, regulated transfer pricing, local partners' requirements, local value added requirements, export requirements, product line and technological appropriateness.

[22] See Goldsbrough (1985).

actually realized profit remittances fluctuate substantially more than foreign investment income. Thus, over the cycle and in response to changing profitability, the portion of investment income that is reinvested tends to fluctuate significantly.

Lessard (1986) asserts that bank loans (as opposed to direct investment) limit a borrower's ability to pay. International financing provides a basis for smoothing national consumption over time through borrowing in periods of low income and replenishing or repaying debt in periods of high income. If a country has existing external obligations, the fixed debt service will magnify the volatility of national income available for consumption.

Finally, since profits are earned only when the investment earns a positive return, part of the risk is borne by the foreign investor. By contrast, bank loans do not require that lenders take responsibility for selection and execution of investment programs. Bank debts fail to shift risks away from particular countries that are unduly exposed. Most commercial bank loans to developing countries involve explicit or implicit government guarantees. Thus, although the funds may be earmarked for a specific project, their payment is not contingent upon that project's outcome. The success or failure of the project is then borne by the guarantor. This is in sharp contrast to direct investment where success is critical to the recovery of funds by the financier, who has a keen interest in assuring that the project is well conceived and executed.

3.3.2. Measuring pros and cons

Praised by some, attacked by others, direct investment flows beg for some empirical measure of their effects. The simplest criterion for evaluating effects of direct investment considers additions to value added. If foreign capital in a single enterprise causes an increase, directly and indirectly, in value added to total output in all sectors greater than the amount appropriated by the investor, then its social returns exceed private returns and its impact is said to be beneficial.

Lall and Streeten (1977) and Reuber (1973) used variations of social cost–benefit analysis to measure the overall effect of foreign investment on national income. The ideological predisposition, the methodology and the data of the two studies differed. Yet, both concluded that 30 percent of proposed import-substituting projects were harmful for the domestic economy. Encarnation and Wells (1986) recently arrived at the same conclusion. They observed that the most important factors affecting the difference between social and private profitability were government policies affecting prices in output markets. The greater the protection from import competition, the lower the social rate of return. Reuber (1973) found that export-oriented projects had lower average production costs than did import-substituting projects protected by tariffs.

The value-added criterion avoids the question of changes in income distribution and assumes an easy transformation between local currency and foreign exchange. Grieco (1986) surveys the empirical findings on the effects of direct investment on growth, distribution of income, technology prices, adequacy of technology, employment and non-economic effects. Results concerning the effects of direct investment on these different variables are highly controversial both on methodological and empirical grounds. As of this writing no conclusions can be drawn from those results with acceptable level of confidence.

3.4. Capital inflows and growth constraints

The World Bank research on growth strategies, in particular Chenery and Bruno (1962) and Chenery and Strout (1966), along with a vast literature taking off from this work, focused on bottlenecks to the growth process. Two bottlenecks, in particular, were identified: the savings gap and the foreign exchange gap.

The two-gap model

The point of departure of the literature is the recognition that growth requires investment. Investment in turn requires savings – domestic and/or foreign. Foreign saving may take the form of private capital inflows, public loans or aid. A first gap arises if domestic saving is inadequate to support the rate of capital accumulation required to achieve a given growth target. A further bottleneck can emerge if the economy does not possess the necessary flexibility to transform domestic into foreign resources. If investment has an import content, then domestic saving is not sufficient to guarantee growth since the saving may not be translatable into foreign exchange earnings with which to acquire imports. This second gap is the foreign exchange gap. The release of the foreign exchange constraint is believed to have accounted for the high productivity of aid under the European Recovery Programme in the late 1940s, when foreign exchange was clearly the factor limiting expansion. A similar situation may occur in developing countries.

Chenery and his associates developed a model of growth and capital flows, the two-gap model, that emphasizes the difference between domestic savings and investment requirements on the one hand, and the difference between needed imports for targeted investment and export revenue,[23] on the other. They stress that in some cases a higher capital inflow can avoid undesirable changes in the

---

[23] Weisskopf (1972a, 1972b) and Blomqvist (1976) test whether the foreign exchange constraint dominated the domestic saving constraint for a set of developing countries. The results generally rejected this hypothesis for most countries.

composition of output and promote growth at higher levels of productivity. Since then, the two-gap approach has become a basic instrument of analysis of the World Bank. When one moves from the description of the policy packages to the analytics of the World Bank programs, one finds a version of the two-gap growth model at the core of most of them.[24]

The basic assumptions of the model are that increased investment will achieve higher rates of GDP growth and that capital imports will increase if investment rises. The usual point of departure is the Harrod growth equation, where the growth rate of output is equal to the savings/GDP ratio, s, times the incremental output–capital ratio, Φ. In the open economy one must add the share of net imports in output to the savings ratio. Assuming that imports are proportional to investment and that this share depends on the ratio between domestic and foreign prices,[25] p, we obtain the expression for the constraint imposed by savings:[26]

$$g = \Phi(s - x(p))/(1 - m(p)), \tag{3}$$

where x is the share of exports in output.

This saving constraint is represented in Figure 26.6 as an upward-sloping schedule.

Where domestic and foreign resources cannot be substituted in capital formation, the inability to acquire foreign exchange by exporting or borrowing will lead to a foreign exchange gap. In the absence of capital inflows, imports must equal exports, and thus the growth rate must be:[27]

$$g = \Phi x(p)/m(p), \tag{4}$$

which is represented by the downward-sloping schedule in Figure 26.6.

The maximum growth rate for this economy is g^*. When the ratio between domestic and foreign prices is equal to p^*, the growth rate is equal to g^* and both constraints are binding.

---

[24] The Bank variant of the two-gap model is defined within the organization as the Revised Minimum Standard Model. See Khan et al. (1986) and World Bank (1980). The two-gap growth model also appears in the bank's analysis of external debt. On this see Selowsky and van der Tak (1986).

[25] Simpler versions of the two-gap approach do not take relative prices into account. Our variant is from Cardoso (1987).

[26] The growth rate of output is $g = \Phi$(investment/output), where Φ is the incremental output/capital ratio. Investment = savings + imports − exports. We assume that: imports = m investment. Combining the three last expressions we obtain (3).

[27] Exports/GDP = import/GDP = m investment/GDP = $(m/\Phi)g$.

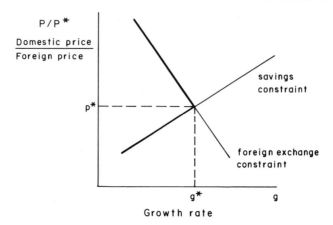

Figure 26.6. Savings and foreign exchange constraints.

If the ratio between domestic and foreign prices is less than p^*, the savings constraint is binding and there is a trade surplus. A real appreciation would reduce net exports, thus augmenting total savings.

If p exceeds p^*, the foreign exchange gap is binding. In that case, potential domestic savings are being frustrated. At least some of the capital goods necessary to undertake desired investment are not produced domestically and cannot be obtained from abroad at going prices. The real exchange rate must depreciate. The real depreciation would generate the exports to finance the importation of capital goods.

One must conclude that a change in relative prices, if feasible, is enough to promote growth when only one constraint is binding.[28] Foreign capital flows for growth are needed in the presence of real price rigidities[29] or costly adjustments of relative prices. In terms of Figure 26.6 above, a capital inflow will shift the downward-sloping schedule to the right. If p exceeds p^*, additional foreign exchange will make more imported capital goods available. It will also supplement domestic savings, filling the gap between domestic savings and investment necessary to achieve a given growth target.[30]

---

[28]On the role of relative prices in the two-gap model, see, too, van Wijnbergen (1986).

[29]Findlay (1971) criticizes the foreign exchange gap theory for the case where there are imports for consumption as well as investment.

[30]Today there is skepticism about the unqualified growth effect of extra foreign resources. Griffin (1970) defends the point of view that aid is essentially a substitute for savings. Mosley (1980) notes that the positive and significant relationship between aid and growth found by Papaneck (1973) for the 1960s have collapsed in the 1970s. He also finds that within the group of high aid receivers, those with less than average growth performance are mainly those in which the tax effort is poor.

If the marginal propensity to save exceeds the average savings/GDP ratio, the gap between the investment/GDP ratio and domestic savings will be closed eventually, and self-sustained growth will be achieved. This exercise fits the Korean experience well.

4. Macroeconomic issues

In this section we discuss several problems posed for macroeconomic policy by capital inflows or outflows. Specifically, we consider problems of stabilization policy posed by excessive capital inflows and those posed by capital flight. The section concludes with a discussion of some policy questions related to capital movements, namely the proper sequencing of liberalization, the scope for multiple exchange rates as a control device, and the possibility of capital controls.

4.1. Overvaluation

At different times during the period 1978–82 a number of countries in Latin America, as well as Israel, had the experience of a strong real appreciation of the currency, followed by balance of payments crises and real depreciation. Figure 26.7 shows the real exchange rate for Argentina and Chile as examples of this process.

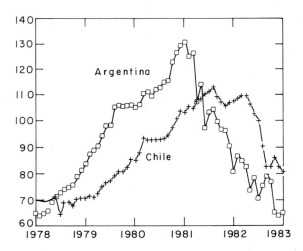

Figure 26.7. Real exchange rates: Argentina and Chile.

Table 26.16
Current accounts in countries with currency overvaluation (percent of GDP)

	1977	1978	1979	1980	1981	1982
Argentina	2.2	2.8	−0.5	−3.1	−3.8	−4.1
Chile	−4.1	−7.1	−5.7	−7.1	−14.5	−9.5
Israel	−2.2	−6.5	−4.8	−3.8	−6.7	−9.5
Mexico	−2.3	−3.1	−4.1	−4.4	−5.8	−3.7

Source: IMF.

The real appreciation experience has been interpreted in two alternative ways. One interpretation highlights the sudden availability of foreign borrowing and the resulting pressure of capital inflows on the real exchange rate. In this view capital flows lead to real appreciation, and in that way bring about an inward transfer of resources. This interpretation has been advanced especially in the case of Chile by Corbo (1985) and Harberger (1986).

The alternative explanation of this experience starts from the recognition that the monetary authorities in all these cases followed a conscious policy of using reduced rates of exchange depreciation or, as in the case of Chile, outright fixing of the exchange rate as a means of achieving disinflation. The combination of reduced depreciation with high nominal interest rates (reflecting the continuing high inflation) attracted capital inflows. The real appreciation in turn led to a current account deterioration. At least in the initial phase, these deficits could be financed by private capital inflows and subsequently by official borrowing abroad.

Table 26.16 shows the current account effects of the overvaluation.[31] The overvaluation experience is accompanied by significant increases in current account deficits. The case of Chile, where trade had been fully liberalized, reflects, in the most striking way, how overvaluation and access to financing can induce a capital import spree. The overvaluation, combined with elimination of tariffs and quotas, led to a massive increase in import spending, especially in the area of durables.

Access to the world capital market is an essential condition for an exchange rate and current account experience, as shown in Figure 26.7 and Table 26.16. But, needless to say, the borrowing experience was thoroughly counterproductive. The large deficits did not reflect high rates of investment.

In fact, especially in the case of Chile, the current account deficit reflected a massive expansion of consumer durable purchases. The sharply increased purchases of durables reflected not only an adjustment to the price reduction, brought about by appreciation and liberalization, but also an expectation that the

---

[31] Of course, the current account also reflects other variables, specifically world interest rates and commodity prices.

low price was unlikely to persist.[32] Moreover, as we shall see presently, the unwinding of overvaluation was accompanied by capital flight, thus adding to the costs of these ill-fated experiments.

The point of the present discussion is that access to the world capital market can be a source of important and costly policy errors. Whether these errors are initiated primarily by spontaneous lending disturbances, or by the ability of governments to finance extravagant exchange rate experiments, remains an open question. The fact that the experiences were exceptionally costly is beyond doubt.

Many of the policy experiments in Latin America, both in respect of liberalization and of stabilization, raise the important issue of credibility. If a policy is both sustainable and credible, then it will be successful. But clearly there are cases where policies can be sustained if they are believed by the public and consequently have the support of stabilizing speculation. By contrast, policies that could survive can break down when lack of credibility leads to speculative attacks which the policy is not sufficiently robust to withstand. Discussion of credibility and commitment often proceeds as if these were objectively verifiable characteristics of policies. In fact they are not. Governments cannot select policies that are 100 percent reliable, and to make policies more credible is invariably costly: high real interest rates or extra low real wages might make a particular stabilization more credible, but they in turn have economic or political costs. The same issues arise in respect of creating conditions for a return of capital flight.

4.2. Capital flight

This subsection discusses the reason for capital flight and offers some analyses of alternative quantitative measures of capital flight. Capital flight from countries with precarious political and financial experience is not new. It occurred in the great political upheavals of Europe in the nineteenth century, it abounded in the 1920s and 1930s from Europe, and it has come to the surface once again in the 1970s and 1980s from Latin America.

There is a preliminary question as to what constitutes capital flight. In some countries, Mexico for example, capital outflows were legal during much of the past ten years. Nonetheless, these capital outflows are routinely characterized as "capital flight" even though they took place through perfectly legal channels. The terminology attributes to these capital flights characteristics different from, say, capital flows from Japan to the United States. Of course, both kinds of flows are dominated by profit considerations and in that sense there is no reason to create special terminology for the outflows from Latin America in those cases where

---

[32] See Dornbusch (1985) and Ramos (1986) for a discussion of the Chilean episode.

Table 26.17
Cross-border bank deposits

By nationals of:	1981	1987	1987 deposits
	(billions of dollars)		(dollars per capita)
Argentina	6.4	8.6	277
Brazil	3.5	11.8	85
Mexico	9.4	18.0	225
Peru	0.6	1.8	89
Venezuela	15.6	12.9	712
Philippines	0.5	1.3	24
Egypt	1.6	3.2	65

Source: IMF, *International Financial Statistics.*

capital flows are legal. But the intent of the terminology is to emphasize the flight from economic and political instability rather than the aspect of illegality, just as in the "flight from money". This suggestive terminology in fact captures well the behavioral aspects of private capital outflows from Latin America.

Table 26.17 reflects the importance of the problem. One point made evident in this table is that capital flight in the form of bank deposits abroad by nationals of developing countries is significant. Clearly, deposit holdings are only part of external assets of developing country residents: holdings of earning assets such as CDs or bonds and of real estate or other physical assets for which data are not available is certainly the larger part, as we will see from the discussion below. But the data in Table 26.17 are already striking. The large amounts of per capita holdings of dollars, for example nearly $300 by Argentineans, and the large increase in the past few years ($78 per head in Argentina), highlight the importance of the topic. External holdings of assets are important in a development context because they represent savings not available for *domestic* capital formation. But the capital flight is also of interest in the context of the debt crisis. Capital flight, in many countries, was an essential ingredient in creating the high level of indebtedness. The size of external asset holdings of Mexico or Argentina, by some estimates, is not very different from the gross external debt.

4.2.1. Reasons for capital flight

Portfolio holders face the choice between overlapping categories of assets: assets located in the developing country and assets located abroad, between assets denominated in home and foreign currencies and claims issued by domestic or foreign borrowers. Which of these particular categories is the most relevant depends on the particular concern. Three broad concerns can be identified: inflation/exchange rate risk, which leads investors to shift from domestic currency to foreign currency assets; political risk, which leads investors to shift assets to a safe haven; and finally tax reasons, which involve taking assets underground or to foreign tax shelters. We discuss below vehicles for capital flight, but we note here that these range from holdings of foreign currency (actual dollar bills) to holding deposits in Miami, Zurich or Panama, real estate in Miami or shares of Fuji held with a Cayman Island depositary.

In principle these are separate motivations. In fact they tend to overlap for any individual country with different considerations being paramount at different points in time. The basic portfolio problem, stated in terms of a choice between domestic and "foreign" (by denomination and possibly location) involves the comparison of rates of return. Let i be the expected after-tax return on a domestic asset, i^* the after-tax return abroad and x the expected rate of depreciation of the home (i.e. developing country) currency. Foreign assets will be more attractive than home assets if the expected return from tax evasion and expected depreciation exceeds the home rate of after-tax return:

$$(1 + i^*)(1 + x) > (1 + i).$$ (5)

Alternatively, looking at real rates of return:

$$(1 + r^*)(1 + \delta) > (1 + r),$$ (5a)

where δ is the expected rate of change of the real exchange rate.

The criterion assumes that investors are risk neutral and evaluate investment by the expected return. If investors are risk averse, then diversification considerations also influence portfolio choices.

Consider now the main two sources of capital flight: real depreciation and taxation. The criterion in (5a) shows that with anticipated real depreciation, capital would move abroad unless home real interest rates exceed those abroad. The expected depreciation consideration is especially important in the context of overvaluation situations such as we discussed above. When it is widely perceived that a maxi depreciation lies ahead, capital flight will turn massive. This is especially the case when capital movements can take place at the official exchange rate. This was, in fact, the case in Argentina and in Mexico during several overvaluation episodes. An attempt to postpone exchange rate adjustment then implies large reserve losses (typically financed by borrowing abroad). The literature on "speculative attacks" on unsustainable exchange rates has grown out of the study of these experiences. Lizondo (1983), in an influential article, showed that the Mexican forward rates, even when the exchange rate was fixed, invariably showed the expectation of a depreciation. The expectation was, of course, borne out by subsequent events. Krugman (1979) and Connolly (1986) are examples of models of speculative attack. In capital markets, maturities for loans

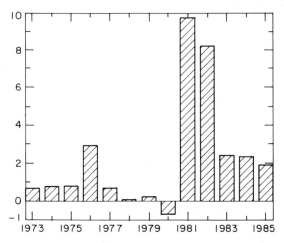

Figure 26.8. Mexican capital flight.

shrink and the high nominal interest rates required to stem capital flight crowd out productive investment and imply a rapid accumulation of domestic debts, often followed by bankruptcy.

Figure 26.8 shows an estimate of Mexican capital flight in the period 1973–85. During periods of major real depreciation – 1976 and the early 1980s – capital flight becomes huge. Table 26.18 shows cumulative sums of capital flight for individual countries.

Clearly major changes in real exchange rates, in the aftermath of massive overvaluation or external shocks, are not the only source of capital flight. Politics is important as, for example, in Brazil and Peru in 1987–88. But taxation is also an issue. Non-resident assets in the United States and many other potential tax havens are untaxed. Thus, over and above exchange rate issues the ability to avoid domestic taxation is an important reason to take capital abroad. The argument goes further when political instability involves occasional levies on assets in developing countries.

Table 26.18
Cumulative capital flight: 1976–82 (billions of dollars)

Argentina	Brazil	Korea	Mexico	Philippines	Venezuela
22.4	5.8	3.3	25.3	4.5	20.7

Source: Cumby and Levich (1987).

4.2.2. Measures of capital flight

Economists disagree on the definition of capital flight.[33] Among the choices are: first, whether capital flight is to be defined in terms of its motivation, or second, in terms of its consequences.

Cumby and Levich (1987) argue that what distinguishes capital flight from other capital flows is that it is a source of national disutility and that capital flight could thus be defined as a capital outflow that is regarded as disadvantageous by the national authorities. Taking this position to its logical end, all private capital outflow from developing countries, be it short-term or long-term, portfolio or equity investment, could be termed capital flight. This is because developing countries are generally capital-poor and capital outflows reduce the resources available to these countries in the development process. Since they represent a loss of potential growth, they could be termed capital flight from the point of view of its consequences.

This concept gives rise to a broad measure of capital flight defined as the identified acquisitions of external assets except official reserves, plus recorded errors and omissions in the balance of payments. Errors and omissions are thus implicitly regarded in their entirety to capital transactions that can be regarded as capital flight. This definition corresponds to that used by Erbe (1985) and Rodriguez (1987), for example. It is measured statistically as a residual – gross capital inflows, less the current account deficit, less the acquisition of official reserves.[34] Estimates for capital flight according to this definition are presented in Table 26.19, under the heading "Broad measure".

Several authors, among them Dooley (1986), Lessard and Williamson (1987) and Deppler and Williamson (1987), argue that capital flight should be distinguished by its motivations, not by its consequences for national welfare. No doubt a definition based on investors' motives for acquiring claims on non-residents involves a good amount of judgement to distinguish capital that is "fleeing" from capital flows in the course of portfolio diversification. Nonetheless, those authors claim that although all capital flows are motivated by endeavors to maximize return on capital, the specific motivation for capital flight is fear of capital loss from risks of expropriation, debt repudiation, or the introduction of new market distortions such as capital controls, taxation and financial repression.

---

[33] The dichotomy between legal and illegal transactions comes immediately to mind. But even if data on illegal transactions were available, the dichotomy would not be useful as a dividing line because illegal transactions need not be motivated by a desire to avoid domestic capital markets. Gulati (1987) and Dornbusch (1987) provide some evidence on countries engaged in overinvoicing import and underinvoicing exports, perhaps to effect capital flight.

[34] The capital flight definition adopted by Morgan Guaranty (1986) also measures capital flight as a residual. In addition to the current account deficit and the increase in official reserves, Morgan's definition also subtracts the increase in short-term foreign assets of the banking system from total capital inflows.

Table 26.19
Capital flight from capital importing developing countries,[a]
1975–85 (billions of dollars)

	1975–78	1979–82	1983–85	Increase from end-1974 to end-1985 in stocks outstanding
		(annual averages)		
Broad measure	15.3	30.0	17.9	235
Derived measure	5.6	26.4	12.5	165

[a] Country classification from International Monetary Fund, *World Economic Outlook*.
Source: Deppler and Williamson (1987, table 1).

To be classified as capital flight, the capital outflow must be a response to losses and risks that are perceived to be large in relation to the moving capital. It is not easy to make operational use of this concept.

Dooley (1986) and Khan and Ul Haque (1985) propose to measure capital flight as that part of a country's stock of foreign assets that does not yield a recorded inflow of investment income credits. The presumption is that only the retention of income abroad is indicative of flight concerns. Capital flight is computed as the difference between total foreign assets and the stock of non-flight capital. This method first estimates gross capital outflows by subtracting from changes in external debt the current account deficit less the part financed by non-debt-creating flows (direct investment flows, changes in international reserves held by the central bank and changes in net foreign assets of domestic banks). The resulting gross capital outflows over a period of time reflect the total stock of external claims of the country. As a second step, non-flight capital is estimated as the capitalized value of recorded investment income credits, using an appropriate interest rate. The difference between this value of nonflight capital and the total stock of external claims is considered capital flight. In Table 26.19 this measure is called "derived measure".

Two other measures that are also commonly used include the private claims measure [Conesa (1986)] and the "hot money" measure [Cuddington (1986)]. Cuddington (1986) adds net short-term capital outflows of the non-bank private sector plus recorded errors and omissions to obtain a measure that views capital flight as similar to "hot money" flows, i.e. funds that respond quickly to changes in expected returns or to changes in risk.

The conceptual differences between the four mentioned measures will naturally lead to different estimates of capital flight. Even though some measures are conceptually broader than others, data problems can be large enough to offset differences in coverage and produce unexpected ordering of estimates.[35]

[35] Deppler and Williamson (1987) offer a detailed discussion of data problems.

Table 26.19 shows recent estimates for capital flight from developing countries.

As the discussion makes clear, measurement of the stock of capital flight is exceptionally difficult at the conceptual level. The situation is exacerbated in dealing with the actual data. The initial flows are uncertain because of such issues as underinvoicing of trade, undisclosed military imports, and the classification of external asset transactions by banks and state enterprises. The stock position is uncertain because there are no detailed statistics (except, to some extent, for bank deposits) on foreign asset holdings by residents of a debtor country. Changes in these stocks over time depend, in part, on flows, on capital gains and interest earnings. Since much of the capital flight that occurred in the late 1970s accumulated interest over the past ten years, assuming a 10 percent rate of return in dollars, each dollar that left in the late 1970s would now be equal to 2.5 dollars in the late 1980s.

4.2.3. Vehicles for capital flight [36]

How do residents of a developing country acquire external assets? There are principally two channels. The most obvious way applies in those instances where the Central Bank allows transfers abroad at the official exchange rate. Because capital controls are cumbersome, and in some countries very ineffective, many governments do in fact authorize, in one form or another, transfers at the official exchange rate. In those instances there can, of course, be massive capital flight in response to a ripe overvaluation.

The second channel, applying when capital cannot be transferred or when underground earnings and assets are involved, takes the form of misinvoicing trade transactions. Overinvoicing of imports and underinvoicing of exports are the means by which foreign assets can be accumulated and then sold in the black market. Evidence from Latin America supports the view that misinvoicing peaks during periods preceding major alignments in exchange rates. It is interesting to note, though, that misinvoicing trade transactions is subject to conflicting temptations. To avoid import taxes there is a tendency to underinvoice imports, exactly the opposite that would be required to effect capital flight. Which of the effects dominate depends on the relative size of the duty and the black market premium.

On the side of exports both capital flight and duty evasion work in the same direction (this is not the case with export subsidies, but GATT rules tend to make these small in the first place). Hence, export underinvoicing tends to be rampant. Estimates of underinvoicing are available from a comparison of import values of

---

[36] See in particular Walter (1985) on the vehicles and outlets of capital flight. Bhagwati, Krueger and Wibulswasdi (1974) discuss the issue of misinvoicing as a vehicle for capital flight. They document that in the presence of import tariffs export underinvoicing rather than overinvoicing of imports be used to move capital abroad. See, too, Dornbusch (1987).

all countries with the export value of a particular exporting country. Using these trade data, Cuddington (1986) reports that in the period 1977–83 the percent of underinvoicing exports showed the following averages: Argentina 19.6 percent, Brazil 12.7 percent, Chile 12.8 percent, Mexico 33.6 percent and Uruguay 27.8 percent.

4.2.4. Costs of capital flight

The costs of capital flight come in three broad forms. First, capital flight destabilizes macroeconomic management. This is very familiar from the discussion of the interwar period. Nurkse argued that capital flight from France destabilized the exchange rate and hence the budget and macroeconomic management. Opponents of that view claimed that poor policy, not speculation, was the cause of instability. The latter view is often correct, but there is an important qualification. Policies are not in fact exogenous. A government, without the threat of capital flight, may be able to pursue certain policies which, with capital flight, become impossible. Thus, if there are multiple equilibria, it is clearly possible that capital flight is an active source of macroeconomic difficulties. With capital flight possibilities, real exchange rates invariably have to be on the defensive side and interest rates need to be sufficiently high to reward asset-holders for the "risk" of holding domestic assets. The political consequence is that the middle and upper classes are having their assets protected at the expense of wage earners. Of course, the argument begs the question of what is the counterfactual experiment. If policies were "credible", or if an effective control of capital flows could be implemented, then such a system would be preferable to one where high real interest rates and a low real wage are required to create the confidence needed to keep asset-holders from shifting into foreign securities.

Capital flight also implies that residents of a country will tend to hold less domestic currency and more foreign currency and assets. To the extent that seigniorage is used as a means of financing budget deficits, reduced seigniorage implies increased inflation, higher taxes or reduced spending.

The second cost of capital flight is that it undermines tax morality. This occurs in several ways. In moving assets abroad, over- or underinvoicing are often an immediate byproduct. But underinvoicing of exports invariably filters down into the tax transactions of exporting firms and is also reflected in reduced tax payments. Once assets are abroad it would be altogether exceptional if taxes were paid on the earnings. Hence, tax revenue is reduced also at this level. Finally, once external assets have become part of the culture they become convenient vehicles for the payment of fraud and bribes.

The third cost can be stated in terms of growth. When a certain percent of GNP is transferred abroad year after year, fewer resources are available for domestic investment. Rather than financing imports of capital goods, for example, export earnings finance (via underinvoicing) the building up of external asset positions. The reduced capital formation implies slower growth and hence a less rapid rate of increase in the standard of living of the immobile factor. The same is true when capital flight is financed at the official exchange rate.

Whichever is the channel through which capital goes abroad, there are only two ways the resources to finance capital flight become available: current account surpluses or external borrowing. In either case less resources are ultimately available for domestic capital formation, and the welfare of labor is thereby reduced. When massive episodes of capital flight occur, in the style of Mexico or Argentina, not only does investment fall, but the level of the standard of living of workers is cut dramatically to provide the financing for the escape.

4.2.5. Policy options

There are few policy options that would be effective in stemming capital flight and at the same time be politically acceptable. The most obvious means is to practice high real interest rates and an undervalued exchange rate. But high real rates of interest will stop investment, and an undervalued exchange rate, besides the inflationary impact of depreciation, also implies a low standard of living for wage earners. Policy-makers therefore search for a means to stop capital flight not at the level of fundamentals, but rather by attempts to segment markets.

Capital controls have been relatively effective in Brazil and Korea and they are considered almost entirely ineffective in Argentina or Mexico. A large part of the difficulty lies in the various geographic conditions of the countries. Mexico, for example, has 3000 miles of border with the United States and has one million people passing across this border each day. Such conditions make controls of any sort extremely difficult. But part of what determines the effectiveness of capital controls involves the government's determination to stop capital flight by effective legal action. It is certainly accepted today that capital controls will not be an answer for many countries.

An alternative to capital controls is a system of dual exchange rates. A fixed (or crawling peg) exchange rate for approved commercial transactions is combined with a free, or at least separate, rate for capital account transactions. Mexico, for example, has practiced such a system. The advantage of a dual rate is that the capital account rate can be moved without an impact on prices and hence real wages. Financial disturbances, therefore, can, in principle, be absorbed in financial markets without feedback on the macro economy. The extent to which this is, in fact, possible, depends on how effectively the markets can be separated and how persistent the disturbances will be. For minor, transitory shocks there is no doubt that the system functions well. But when disturbances are large and persistent there will be an inevitable tendency for under- or overinvoicing to become an issue. The main point would seem to be that a dual rate system is helpful, but that it does not dispense with the need for a realistic commercial exchange rate.

A much larger policy issue involves effective action by industrialized countries to help stop capital flight or, at least, to help developing countries collect some taxes on expatriate asset holdings. For the time being developing countries have gone in the opposite direction in eliminating taxes on non-resident assets, thus providing outright incentives for capital flight.

5. The future of private capital flows

The adjustment process to the debt crisis is no longer on schedule. Favorable conditions in the world economy and the beneficial effects of adjustment programs on the part of debtors were expected to show an improvement in creditworthiness sufficient to warrant a return to voluntary lending. That remains the expectation, but the process is not on schedule. The large discounts in the second-hand market for LDC debts imply that a return to voluntary lending is very remote.

Policy-makers in debtor countries are concerned that ultimately they will bear the costs for prolonging an unreasonable decapitalization of their economies.

5.1. Working out the debt problem

Three facts summarize the lack of success in solving the debt problem so far.

(1) Creditworthiness has been deteriorating. The ratios of debt to exports and debt to GDP of problem debtors have risen since 1982. Seven years of adjustment have made debtor countries look worse rather than better, at least in what concerns their debt burdens.

(2) The large swing in trade surpluses, which finances much of the interest payments today, has a decline in investment as a counterpart. Comparing the 1982–86 period with the preceding five-year period, one observes an increase in Latin America's non-interest current account surplus equal to 5 percent of GDP, and a decline in investment of the same magnitude. A serious imbalance is building up when interest is paid by not investing.

(3) There is no indication of a return to voluntary lending. Loan discounts are very deep for most debtors and even countries with no rescheduling problems (e.g. Colombia) experience difficulties borrowing in the world market.

The basic problem is how to reverse real resource transfer and restore the flow of capital to the debtor countries. Their non-interest surpluses, which today service debt, need to be turned into deficits again to provide a net resource import to supplement domestic saving in financing growth. As long as existing debts are judged to be poor, commercial banks will be reluctant to put up new money to finance at least the interest bill. And they will most definitely not lend over and above the interest bill to finance a net resource transfer. The problem goes further because the existing debt has a prior claim on the debtor countries' resources. It therefore stands in the way of new resources from potential lenders, or investors who have so far not been involved, such as insurance companies. The existing debt also places a burden on debtor countries' policies and thus deteriorates the profitability of direct investment in these depressed or slow-growth economies. Finally, a political backlash in response to the debt collection process may well come one day. At that point there is no assurance of a fine distinction between uncooperative banks holding on to long-dead debts and new investors. In summary, until the problem of old debts is resolved, one way or another, fresh capital resources will be very limited.

5.2. Solutions

Among the many schemes to solve the debt problem we highlight here only four: debt–equity swaps, buy-backs, a facility for interest capitalization or interest recycling.

The prices of LDC debts in the secondary market show large discounts (see Table 26.20). These discounts have focused attention on schemes to pass onto debtor countries some debt principal reduction.

Three quite different schemes of debt reduction center on the secondary market discount. A first one involves debt–equity swaps. In a debt–equity swap, a firm buys a claim from a bank in the secondary market. The claim is then presented to the debtor country's central bank for payment in local currency, at a discount. The proceeds are used for investment in the debtor country. When the transaction is complete, a bank has sold off (at a discount) a claim for dollar

Table 26.20
Prices in the secondary market for bank loans (selling price, cents per dollar face value)

	7/85	1/86	7/86	1/87	5/87	7/87	12/87	1/89
Argentina	60	62	63	62	60	47	45	20
Brazil	75	75	73	74	64	57	47	35
Mexico	80	69	56	54	60	54	50	39
Peru	45	25	18	16	19	11	16	6
Philippines				72	73	68	65	47
Venezuela	81	80	75	77	75	69	61	38

Source: Shearson, Lehman Brothers and Salomon Brothers Inc.

cash. A foreign firm has acquired a real asset in the debtor country. And the central bank has reduced its dollar liabilities, but has an increase in domestic monetary liabilities or in domestic debt. Whether debt–equity swaps are beneficial for the debtor country depends on two considerations. First, whether the investment that takes place is an extra investment, or one that would have taken place anyway. On the latter case the debt–equity swap is costly because the central bank does not receive dollars that could have been used for import liberalization or other uses.

The second consideration is whether the discount at which the central bank redeems its external debt is large enough to offset the extra interest cost incurred on domestic debt issued as a counterpart. By assumption, the debtor is illiquid. The interest cost on new debt will typically exceed the interest on old debt, and hence refinancing raises interest costs unless the discount on conversion is sufficiently large.

In the period 1982–87 debt equity swaps amounted to almost $5 billion. Chile, Brazil, Mexico, Argentina and the Philippines were the main countries allowing some form of debt–equity swap.[37] The impression is widespread that relatively little of the investment that took place was "additional" and invariably the cost of refinancing raised interest burdens. As a result debt–equity swaps are losing momentum. Whatever the merits of swaps, and there may well be some in the form of creating a favorable investment atmosphere, it is clear from the quantitative magnitude of transactions that this cannot be a means to make a major change to the debt problem.

An alternative form in which the secondary market is emerging as a solution is for debtor countries to offer their creditors buy-backs of the debt. This can occur directly in the secondary market, the case of Bolivia being an example. With the help of friendly governments, that country is offering to buy back its external debt at a small fraction of the face value. For major debtors, by contrast, debt conversion would take the form of a new bond offer that involves conversion of existing debt, at a discount, into new bonds. If successful, such a conversion would reduce the face value of debt outstanding and hence interest payments. This is what happened in the 1940s in many debt adjustment plans, as noted earlier. The chief issue in these conversion offers is how to make the new bonds attractive. The new bonds would obviously be attractive, if they had seniority. However, existing creditors have no incentive to part with the seniority of their own claims.

A third possibility, first suggested by Kenen (1983), involves a facility organized by creditor governments. The facility would take over from banks LDC debts at a discount in exchange for debt guaranteed by creditor governments. The claims this acquired would be renegotiated with the debtor countries, passing

---

[37]See Alexander (1987) for an extensive discussion.

on the discount and restructuring the debt in terms of maturity and grace period as well as state contingent payments. The combined operation would leave the fund with claims that yield a present value equal to payments owed to the banks. The only risk is inability or unwillingness of debtors to meet their now reduced and tailored debts.

This proposal for a facility encounters three difficulties. The first is the reluctance of taxpayers in developing countries to assume the guarantee. The second is how to force banks to relinquish their claim rather than benefiting from the debt reduction to exercise their full claim. The third involves moral hazard and priorities. Specifically, countries without debt problems would see an incentive to behave poorly so as to get the benefit of debt reduction. There is also the question whether resources of developed countries (including the World Bank) should be used to solve problems of middle-income countries and banks rather than those of exceptionally poor countries. This issue arises because poor countries have only debts to governments and would not benefit from this mechanism.[38]

An alternative route is to seek relief on interest payments rather than principal. Here two possibilities have been suggested. One is to *automatically* capitalize interest payments. In such a situation payments beyond a certain interest rate, say 5 percent, would be added to the principal of the loan. Such capitalization might also be geared to objective indicators such as export or import prices of key commodities such as oil in the case of Brazil or Mexico, for example.

Another version of interest relief would provide for payment of interest in local currency, available for the creditors to invest in the debtor country's economy. This scheme would avoid the present problem of generating trade surpluses (at the expense of investment) and the associated crowding out of investment and inflationary problems. Creditors would use the interest payments to buy assets or lend, thus allowing investment and growth to resume. The scheme has as its rationale that some countries, specifically Mexico and Brazil, may well be in a position to service their debts in a few years (by surplus or new capital inflows) if they could enjoy a period of reconstruction.

Interest capitalization or recycling of interest are attractive when problems of debt service are temporary. They are not of much help when there is a problem of insolvency. In that case adding to the burden of foreign capital does not improve creditworthiness. Unfortunately, there is no objective criterion for solvency or ability to pay. Sufficiently drastic adjustment would, in virtually all cases, generate the surpluses required to service debts. The difficulty is the social and

---

[38] Buiter and Srinivasan (1987) have emphasized in particular the need to keep a balanced view of the problems of major debtor countries and of those who are much poorer and therefore more deserving of resource transfers. They note: "It is time to think twice before the human and financial resources of the multilateral agencies are concentrated excessively on one relatively small problem area before scarce aid is diverted away from those most in need of it."

political cost. The spreading of moratoria and the insistence of debtor countries that debt is a political problem will no doubt bring 1940s style answers. So far, industrial country governments have discouraged action in this direction, but the disillusionment with the muddling-through process of the past five years, and the associated political and economic instability, is pressuring in the direction of initiatives.

5.3. Non-debt capital flows

Commercial banks are unlikely to provide much development finance in the year to come. Bond markets, likewise, will be closed for countries with a poor debt experience. Efforts to develop private capital flows to debtor countries must therefore focus on other mechanisms.

The immediately obvious candidate is direct foreign investment. It is widely perceived that private investment must play a larger role. Unfortunately, the role of direct investment has never been very large. Moreover, as long as the debt problems persist the debtor countries will show slow growth and unstable financial conditions. As a result, they are unlikely to be highly attractive locations for new investment. Thus, while more direct investment can be expected, and should be encouraged by guarantee schemes and a better investment climate, the quantitative contribution of this source of capital will remain minor.

The second source of private capital is a reflow of flight capital. Conditions for a reflow is that debtor countries offer attractive and stable returns. Just as we observed in respect to direct investment, the solution to the debt problems is probably a sine qua non for a return of flight capital on a major scale.

The third source of capital is equity portfolio investment via organized funds. This mechanism has worked very well in Korea, Thailand and Malaysia, for example, and it is being organized for a number of countries under the auspices of the International Finance Corporation.[39] The scope for investment funds to make an immediate major impact is limited by the size of capital markets in most developing countries. But part of this mechanism would be to push the institutional development of these markets, and thus create the conditions for channelling increasing flows of equity capital, rather than debt, into the developing world. For many of the major problem debtors this should be the soundest strategy to attract financing. Unfortunately, it is quite apparent that the process will be slow, and that the foreseeable future will be overshadowed by the continuing debt crisis.

[39]See van Agtmael (1987).

References

Adler, J. (1967) *Capital movements and economic development*. London: Macmillan.
Alexander, L. (1987) 'Debt conversions: Economic issues for heavily indebted developing countries', International Finance Discussion Papers no. 315, Board of Governors of the Federal Reserve.
Avramovic, D. (1964) *Economic growth and external debt*. Baltimore, MD: The Johns Hopkins Press.
Bernstein, M., ed. (1966) *Foreign investment in Latin America*. New York: Alfred A. Knopf, Inc.
Bhagwati, J., Krueger, A., and Wibulswasdi, C. (1974) 'Capital flight from LDCs: A statistical analysis', in: J. Bhagwati, ed., *Illegal transactions in international trade*. Amsterdam: North-Holland.
Billerbec, K. and Yasugi, Y. (1979) 'Private direct foreign investment in developing countries', World Bank Staff Working Papers no. 348.
Bittermann, H. (1973) *The refunding of international debt*. Durham, NC: Duke University Press.
Blomqvist, A. (1976) 'Empirical evidence on the two-gap hypothesis', *Journal of Development Economics*, July:181–193.
Brau, E.H. (1986) *Export credits*. Washington, DC: International Monetary Fund.
Brau, E., Williams, R.C., et al. (1983) *Recent multilateral debt restructurings with official and bank creditors*. Washington, DC: International Monetary Fund.
Brecher, R. and Diaz-Alejandro (1977) 'Tariffs, foreign capital and immiserizing growth', *Journal of International Economics*, 7:317–322.
Buchanan, N.S. and Lutz, F.A. (1947) *Rebuilding the world economy*. New York: The Twentieth Century Fund.
Buiter, W. and Srinivasan, T.N. (1987) 'Rewarding the profligate and punishing the prudent and poor: Some recent proposals for debt relief,' *World Development*, 15:411–417.
Cardoso, E. (1987) *Inflation, growth and the real exchange rate*. New York: Garland, pp. 86–89.
Cardoso, E. and Dornbusch, R. (1987) 'Brazilian debt: A requiem for muddling through', mimeo, Fletcher School of Law and Diplomacy.
Chenery, H. and Bruno, M. (1962) 'Development alternatives in an open economy: The case of Israel', *Economic Journal*, 72:79–103.
Chenery, H. and Strout, A. (1966) 'Foreign assistance and economic development', *American Economic Review*, 56, no. 4:679–733.
Cohen, B. (1986) *In whose interest? International banking and American foreign policy*. New Haven, CT: Yale University Press.
Conesa, E.R. (1986) 'The causes of capital flight from Latin America, 1970–85', Inter-American Development Bank, unpublished.
Connolly, M. (1986) 'The speculative attack on the peso and the real exchange rate: Argentina 1981', *Journal of International Money and Finance*, 5:5117–5130.
Cooper, R.N. and Truman, T. (1971) 'An analysis of the role of international capital markets in providing funds to developing countries', *Weltwirtschaftliches Archiv*, 106, no. 24:153–183.
Corbo, V. (1985) 'Reforms and macroeconomic adjustment in Chile during 1974–84', *World Development*, 13, no. 8:893–916.
Crawford, V. (1987) *International lending, long-term credit relationships and dynamic contract theory*. Studies in International Finance. Princeton, NJ: Princeton University Press.
Cuddington, J. (1986) *Capital flight: Estimates, issues, and explanations*. Princeton Studies in International Finance 58, Princeton, NJ: Princeton University Press.
Cumby, R. and Levich, R. (1987) 'On the definition and magnitude of recent capital flight', in: D. Lessard and J.J. Williamson, eds., *Capital flight: The problem and policy responses*. Washington, DC: Institute for International Economics.
Deppler, M. and Williamson, M. (1987) 'Capital flight: Concepts, measurement, and issues', in: *Staff studies for the world economic outlook*. Washington, DC: International Monetary Fund.
Dillon, B.K., et al. (1985) *Recent developments in external debt restructuring*. Washington, DC: International Monetary Fund.
Dooley, M. (1986) 'Country-specific risk premiums, capital flight and net investment income payments in selected developing countries', International Monetary Fund, unpublished.
Dornbusch, R. (1981) *Open economy macroeconomics*. New York: Basic Books.

Dornbusch, R. (1985) 'External debt, budget deficits, and disequilibrium exchange rates', in: G. Smith and J. Cuddington, eds., *International debt and the developing countries*. Washington, DC: World Bank.
Dornbusch, R. (1987) 'Overinvoicing and capital flight', mimeo, Massachusetts Institute of Technology.
Dornbusch, R. (1989) 'The world debt problem: Anatomy and solutions', New York: Twentieth Century Fund, forthcoming.
Dornbusch, R. and de Pablo, J.C. (1988) 'Argentina: Debt and macroeconomic instability', mimeo, Massachusetts Institute of Technology.
Dornbusch, R. and Park, Y. (1987) 'Korean growth policy', *Brookings Papers on Economic Activity*, 1.
Dunning, J., ed. (1982) *International investments: Selected readings*. Harmondsworth: Penguin Books.
Dunning, J. and Stopford, J. (1983) *Multinationals: Company performance and global trends*. London: Macmillan.
Eaton, J. (1987a) 'Public capital for economic development', in: H. Chenery and T.N. Srinivasan, eds., *Handbook of economic development*, Vol. II.
Eaton, J. (1987b) 'Public debt guarantees and private capital flight', *World Bank Economic Review*, I, no. 3:377–395.
Eaton, J., Gersovitz, M., and Stiglitz, J. (1986) 'The pure theory of country risk', *European Economic Review*, 3:481–513.
Edelstein, M. (1982) *Overseas investment in the age of high imperialism*. New York: Columbia University Press.
Edwards, S. (1986) 'Order of liberalization of the current and capital account of the balance of payments', in: A. Choksi and D. Papageorgiou, eds., *Economic liberalization in developing countries*. Oxford: Basil Blackwell.
Eichengreen, B. (1987) *Til debt do we part: The U.S. capital market and foreign lending, 1920–1955*. Berkeley, CA and Cambridge: University of California Press, Berkeley and NBER.
Eichengreen, B. and Portes, R. (1986) 'Debt and default in the 1930s: Causes and consequences', *European Economic Review*, 3:599–640.
Encarnation, D. and Wells, L. (1986) 'Evaluating foreign investment', in: T. Moran, ed., *Investing in development: New roles for private capital*. Washington, DC: Overseas Development Council.
Erbe, S. (1985) 'The flight of capital from developing countries', *Intereconomics*, 20:268–275.
Feis, H. (1965) *Europe. The world's banker*. New York: Norton.
Feldstein, M. (1987) 'Muddling through can be just fine', *The Economist*, June.
Feuerlein, W. and Hannan, E. (1940) *Dollars in Latin America*. New York: Council on Foreign Relations.
Findlay, R. (1971) 'The "foreign exchange gap" and growth in developing economies', in: J. Bhagwati, R. Jones, R. Mundell, and J. Vanek, eds., *Trade, balance of payments and growth*. Amsterdam: North-Holland.
Findlay, R. (1984) 'Growth and development in trade models', in: R. Jones and P. Kenen, eds., *Handbook of international economics*, Vol. I. Amsterdam: North-Holland.
Fishlow, A. (1985) 'Lessons from the past: Capital markets during the 19th century and the interwar period', *International Organization*, 39, no. 3:383–439.
Fleming, A. (1981) 'Private capital flows to developing countries and their determination', World Bank Staff Working paper no. 484.
Folkerts-Landau, D. (1985) 'The changing role of international bank lending in development finance', *IMF Staff Papers*, 32, no. 2:317–363.
Foreign Bond Holders Protective Council, various issues, *Report*.
Frieden, J. (1987) *Banking on the world*. New York: Harper and Row.
Gantenbein, J. (1939) *Financial questions in U.S. foreign policy*. New York: Columbia University Press.
Goldsbrough, D. (1985) *Foreign private investment in developing countries*. Washington, DC: International Monetary Fund.
Grieco, J. (1986) 'Foreign investment and development. Theories and evidence', in: T. Moran, ed., *Investing in development: New roles for private capital*. Washington, DC: Overseas Development Council.

Griffin, K. (1970) 'Foreign assistance, domestic savings and economic development', *Bulletin*, 32:99–112.

Gulati (1987) 'A note on trade misinvoicing', in: D. Lessard and J. Williamson, eds., *Capital flight and third world debt*. Washington, DC: Institute for International Economics.

Haberler, G. (1984) 'International trade and economic development', in: Y.C. Koo, ed., *Selected essays of Gottfried Haberler*. Cambridge, MA: MIT Press.

Hale, D.D. (1987) *The economic case for encouraging greater foreign participation in third world equity markets*. Kemper Financial Services, Inc.

Harberger, A. (1986) 'Welfare consequences of capital inflows', in: A.C. Choksi and D. Papageorgiou, eds., *Economic liberalization in developing countries*. Oxford: Basil Blackwell.

Harrod, R. (1963) 'Desirable international movements of capital in relation to growth of borrowers and lenders and growth of markets', in: R. Harrod and D. Hague, eds., *International trade theory in a developing world*. London: Macmillan.

Hirschman, A.O. (1969) *How to divest in Latin America, and why*. Princeton, NJ: International Finance Section, Princeton University Press.

Hobson, C.K. (1914) *The export of capital*. London: Constable and Company Ltd.

Imlah, A. (1958) *Economic elements in the Pax Britannica*. Cambridge, MA: Harvard University Press.

Institute of International Finance (1959) *Statistical analysis of publicly offered foreign dollar bonds*. New York: New York University.

Isze, A. and Ortiz, G. (1987) 'Fiscal rigidities, public debt and capital flight', *IMF Staff Papers*, 34, no. 2:311–332.

Iversen, C. (1967) *International capital movements*. New York: Augustus M. Kelley.

Kenen, P. (1983) 'Third World debt', *The New York Times*, 6 March, Section 3: p. F3.

Kenwood, A. and Lougheed, A. (1983) *The growth of the international economy, 1820–1980*. London: George Allen and Unwin.

Khan, M. and Haque, N.U. (1985) 'Foreign borrowing and capital flight: A formal analysis', *Staff Papers*. International Monetary Fund, 32:606–628.

Khan, M., et al. (1986) *Adjustment with growth: Relating the analytical approaches of the world bank and the IMF*. Development Policy Issues Series, Report no. 8, Washington, DC: World Bank.

Kindleberger, C. (1982) *Economic development*. New York: McGraw-Hill.

Kindleberger, C. (1984) 'The 1929 world depression in Latin America – from outside', in: R. Thorpe, ed., *Latin America in the 1930s*. London: Macmillan.

Kletzer, K. (1986) 'External borrowing by LDC's: A survey of theoretical issues', mimeo, Yale University.

Kraft, J. (1984) *The Mexican rescue*. New York: Group of Thirty.

Krugman, P. (1979) 'A model of balance of payments crises', *Journal of Money, Credit and Banking*, 3:311–325.

Lall, S. (1974) 'Less-developed countries and private foreign investment: A review article', *World Development*, 2:43–48.

Lall, S. and Streeten, P. (1977) *Foreign investment, transnationals and developing countries*. Boulder: Westview Press.

Landes, D. (1979) *Bankers and pashas*. Cambridge, MA: Harvard University Press.

Lary, H.B. (1944) *The United States in the world economy*. Washington, DC: The Government Printing Office.

League of Nations (1932) *World economic survey*. Geneva.

Lessard, D.R. (1986) 'International financing for developing countries', World Bank Staff Working papers no. 783. Washington, DC: The World Bank.

Lessard, D. and Williamson, J. (1987) 'The problem and policy responses', in: D. Lessard and J. Williamson, eds., *Capital flight and third world debt*. Washington, DC: Institute for International Economics.

Lewis, A. (1955) *The theory of economic growth*. London: Allen and Unwin.

Lindert, P.H. and Morton, P.J. (1987) 'How sovereign debt has worked', in: J. Sachs, ed., *Developing country and economic performance*. Chicago: University of Chicago Press, 1989.

Lipson, C. (1985) *Standing guard*. Berkeley, CA: University of California Press.

Livingstone, I., ed. (1971) *Economic policy for development*. Harmondsworth: Penguin Books.

Lizondo, S. (1983) 'Foreign exchange futures prices under fixed exchange rates', *Journal of International Economics*, 14, no. 1–2:69–84.

McDougall, G.D. (1960) 'The benefits and costs of private investment from abroad', *Economic*, March:13–35. Reprinted in: R. Caves and H.G. Johnson, eds., *Readings in international economics*. Homewood, IL: Richard D. Irwin, Inc.

Meier, G. (1963) *International trade and development*. New York: Harper and Row.

Mikesell, R., ed. (1962) *U.S. private and government investment abroad*. Eugene, OR: University of Oregon Books.

Mikesell, R. (1955) *Foreign investment in Latin America*. Washington, DC: Pan American Union.

Mintz, I. (1951) 'Deterioration in the quality of foreign bonds issued in the United States 1920–1930', Report no. 52, National Bureau of Economic Research, New York.

Moran, T., et al. (1986) *Investing in development: New roles for private capital?* Washington, DC: Overseas Development Council.

Morgan Guaranty Trust Company (1986) 'World financial markets', March and September.

Mosley, P. (1980) 'Aid, savings and growth revisited', *Bulletin*, 42:79–95.

Myint, H. (1958) 'The "Classical Theory" of international trade and the underdeveloped countries', *Economic Journal*, 270:317–337.

North, D. (1962) 'International capital movements in historical perspective', in: R. Mikesell, ed., *U.S. private and government investment abroad*. Eugene, OR: University of Oregon Books.

Nowzad, B. and Williams, R.C. (1981) *External indebtedness of developing countries*. Washington, DC: International Monetary Fund.

Nurkse, R. (1952) *Some aspects of capital accumulation in underdeveloped countries*. Cairo: National Bank of Egypt.

Nurkse, R. (1959) *Patterns of trade and development*. Stockholm: Almqvist and Wiksell.

O'Brien, R. (1981) 'Private bank lending to developing countries', Report no. 482, World Bank Staff Working Papers, Washington, DC.

OECD (1987) *International investment and multinational enterprises*. Paris: OECD.

Oman, C. (1984) *New forms of international investment in developing countries*. Paris: OECD.

Papaneck, G. (1973) 'Aid, private foreign investment, savings and growth in less developed countries', *Journal of Political Economy*, 81:120–130.

Portes, R. (1987) 'Debt and the market', mimeo. London: CEPR.

Portes, R. and Swoboda, A. eds. (1987) *Threats to international financial stability*. New York: Cambridge University Press.

Ramos, J. (1986) *Neoconservative economics in the southern cone of Latin America, 1973–1983*. Baltimore, MD: Johns Hopkins University Press.

Reuber, G. (1973) *Private foreign investment in development*. Oxford: Clarendon Press.

Rippy, F. (1977) *British investments in Latin America, 1822–1949*. New York: Arno Press.

Rodriguez, M.A. (1987), 'Consequences of capital flight for Latin America', in: D. Lessard and J. Williamson, eds., *Capital flight and third world debt*. Washington, DC: Institute for International Economics.

Royal Institute of International Affairs (1937) *The problem of international investment*. London: Oxford University Press.

Ruffin, R. (1984) 'International factor movements', in: R. Jones and P. Kenen, eds., *Handbook of international economics*, Vol. I. Amsterdam: North-Holland.

Saini, K.G. (1986) 'Capital market innovations and financial flows to developing countries', Report no. 784, World Bank Staff Working Papers, Washington, DC.

Salter, Sir A. (1951) *Foreign investment*. Princeton, NJ: International Finance Section, Princeton University Press.

Selowsky, M. and van der Tak, H. (1986) 'The debt problem and growth', *World Development*, 14, no. 9:1107–1124.

Singer, H.W. (1950) 'The distribution of gains between investing and borrowing countries', *American Economic Review*, 2:473–485.

Singer, H.W. (1984) 'The terms of trade controversy and the evolution of soft financing: Early years in the U.N.', in: G. Meier and D. Seers, eds., *Pioneers in development*. Oxford: Oxford University Press.

Smith, A. (1984) 'Capital theory and trade theory', in: R. Jones and P. Kenen, eds., *Handbook of international economics*, Vol. I. Amsterdam: North-Holland.

Srinivasan, T.N. (1983) 'International factor movements, commodity trade and commercial policy in a specific factor model', *Journal of International Economics*, 14, no. 3:289–312.

Stallings, B. (1987) *Banker to the third world*. Berkeley, CA: University of California Press.

Taussig, F.W. (1928) *International trade*. New York: Macmillan.

Thomas, B. (1967) 'The historical record of international capital movements to 1913', in: J. Adler, ed., *Capital movements and economic development*. London: Macmillan.

Thorpe, R., ed. (1984) *Latin America in the 1930s*. Oxford: Macmillan.

United Nations (1949) *International capital movements during the interwar period*. New York: United Nations.

United Nations (1954) *The international flow of private capital 1946–52*. New York: United Nations.

United Nations (1964) *Towards a new trade policy for Latin America. Report by the Secretary General of UNCTAD*. New York: United Nations.

United Nations (1965) *External financing in Latin America*. New York: United Nations.

United Nations (1985) *Trends and issues in foreign direct investment and related flows*. New York: U.N. Center on Transnational Corporations.

U.S. Department of Commerce (1984) *International direct investment*. Washington, DC: U.S. Department of Commerce.

van Agtmael, A. (1987) 'Investing in emerging securities markets', mimeo. International Finance Corporation.

van Wijnbergen, S. (1986) 'Macroeconomic aspects of the effectiveness of foreign aid: On the two-gap model, home goods disequilibrium and real exchange rate misalignment', *Journal of International Economics*, 21, no. 1–2:123–136.

Viner, J. (1924) *Canada's balance of international indebtedness 1900–1913*. Cambridge, MA: Harvard University Press.

Viner, J., ed. (1932) *Gold and monetary stabilization*. Chicago, IL: University of Chicago Press.

Viner, J. (1952) *International trade and economic development*. Glencoe, IL: The Free Press.

Wallich, H. (1943) 'The future of Latin American dollar bonds', *American Economic Review*, 43, no. 2:321–335.

Walter, I. (1985) *Secret money*. Lexington, MA: Lexington Books.

Watson, M., et al. (1984) *International capital markets*. Washington, DC: International Monetary Fund.

Watson, M. et al. (1986) *International capital markets*. Washington, DC: International Monetary Fund.

Weiner, M.L. and Dalla-Chiesa, R. (1955) 'International movements of public long-term capital and grants, 1946–1950', *IMF Staff Papers*, IV, no. 1.

Weisskopf, T. (1972a) 'The impact of foreign capital inflow on domestic savings in undeveloped countries', *Journal of International Economics*, 25–38.

Weisskopf, T. (1972b) 'An econometric test of alternative constraints on the growth of underdeveloped countries', *The Review of Economics and Statistics*, 67–78.

Wellons, P. (1986) *Banks and specialized financial intermediaries in development*. Paris: OECD.

Wilson, R. (1931) *Capital imports and the terms of trade*. Melbourne: Melbourne University Press.

Winkler, M. (1933) *Foreign bonds. An autopsy*. Philadelphia, PA: Roland Swain Co.

Woodruff, W. (1966) *The impact of western man*. New York: Macmillan.

World Bank (1980) 'The revised minimum standard model', mimeo, Comparative Analysis and Projections Division.

World Bank (1987) *World debt tables*. Washington, DC: World Bank.

Wright, H., ed. (1961) *The new imperialism*. Lexington, MA: D.C. Heath and Company.

Wynne, W. (1951) *State insolvency and foreign bond holders*. New Haven, CT: Yale University Press.

Chapter 27

TRANSNATIONAL CORPORATIONS AND DIRECT FOREIGN INVESTMENT

G.K. HELLEINER*

University of Toronto

Contents

*I wish to thank the following for comments on an earlier draft, none of whom are to be implicated in the contents of the present version: Manuel Agosin, Sidney Dell, Jonathan Eaton, Sue Horton, Howard Pack, Ed Safarian, T.N. Srinivasan, Paul Streeten, Louis Wells, and Larry Westphal.

Handbook of Development Economics, Volume II, Edited by H. Chenery and T.N. Srinivasan
© *Elsevier Science Publishers B.V., 1989*

1. Introduction

The role of transnational corporations (TNCs)[1] in economic development has long been a matter of intense controversy among social scientists and policymakers in the Third World. What is at issue – in this area, as in many others relating to development – extends well beyond the traditional boundaries of the economics profession. While economists have not hesitated to engage in the broader debates on the transnationals, most would probably agree with Caves' overall assessment:

> Economic analysis has played no great part in resolving disputes between critics and defenders of the MNE's role in development processes... writings on the economic role of MNEs have correspondingly run a high ratio of polemic to documented evidence [Caves (1982, p. 252)].

Criticism of the activities of transnational corporations is frequently, in its essence, criticism of either Western culture, large firms (whether local or foreign), the market system, or all three. The transnational corporation is typically the highest-profile institutional vehicle, as colonial governments once were, for interaction between developing countries and world markets. If international market exchange in a developing country shows signs of disrupting local society, introducing alien tastes, polluting the environment, etc. [Kumar (1980)], the most obvious focus for attack is the profit-seeking foreign institution most visibly involved in the changes associated with such exchange. As Kindleberger has recently put it:

> The most serious charge one can level against the international corporation is that it produces a homogenized world culture, of wall-to-wall carpeting, tasteless meals, Americanized English, traffic jams and gasoline fumes [Kindleberger (1984, p. 31)].

But even this may be somewhat misdirected if new technologies in transport and

---

[1]"Transnational corporation" (TNC) is the term used by the United Nations in its discussions and institutions, and this seems preferable to such alternative usages as "multinational corporation" (MNC) or "multinational enterprise" (MNE), since "the word transnational... better convey(s) the notion that these firms operate from their home bases across national borders" [United Nations (1978, p. 159); definitional issues are discussed on pp. 158–170]. The U.N. Centre on Transnational Corporations employs a broad definition of these corporations, counting all "enterprises which control assets in two or more countries" (p. 158). Political dispute continues as to whether state-owned enterprises should be incorporated within the U.N.'s definition (and therefore the mandate of its Centre and its proposed code of conduct).

communications are independently acting to limit the possibilities for social and cultural variation in a spatially shrinking world.

The frequent prominence of TNCs in developing countries' interaction with the world permits their supporters to be just as vehement in their praise of the TNC role as their critics are in their attacks on them. The TNC is actually just a capitalist firm, albeit typically quite a large one. Pursuit of profit is the basic object of all capitalist enterprise, whether multinational and large, or domestic and small. The TNCs are involved in a highly visible way in extremely sensitive political and social questions in poor foreign countries. Resident social scientists, policymakers and others typically place "developmental" objectives, or indeed their own private ones, well ahead of the pursuit of those of wealthy foreign shareholders. Conflict between TNCs that seek to plan and "rationalize" their global activities within particular industries, and governments (both home and host) that plan on a cross-industry basis within nations is probably inevitable.

The possibility of alternative noncapitalist forms of global economic and political organization is certainly deserving of study, but, in most of the literature of development economics, as opposed to political science or sociology, the current organization of the world economy, TNCs and all, is assumed given. For economic analysts of development the key policy questions relate to the possibilities of more desirable developmental outcomes through alternative means of interacting with the present world, including the TNCs. Can less be paid for that which is useful which they provide? Can detrimental effects of their activities be controlled?

From the standpoint of the host country and the analysis of economic development, then, what is at issue is the acquisition of scarce inputs and complementary services, e.g. export marketing, from external sources on the best possible terms. These external sources may or may not be transnational corporations, strictly defined. The role of foreign buyers (who did not own productive assets outside their home countries) in the development of Korean industrial exports, for example, far exceeded that of transnational corporations; and there can be no presumption that TNCs have everywhere dominated or will continue to dominate individual developing countries' relations with external markets. The attention lavished upon TNC relations with governments of developing countries may thus be disproportionate to the TNC role in overall developing country interaction with the world economy. (Other dimensions of these relationships are discussed in the chapters in this Handbook on trade, technology and capital inflows.) This chapter's focus upon transnational corporations may involve some misplaced concreteness, the product of the existence of a stormy literature on the subject rather than analytical clarity, policy usefulness, or relative importance.

The economics literature on transnational corporations has a major positivist strand, seeking merely to explain the TNC phenomenon and to understand TNC behaviour and its effects. Much of this analysis has been conducted quite independently of the literature of development economics; but it is of crucial significance to any analysis of the interrelationships between TNC activities and development. This literature has focused particularly on the phenomenon of direct foreign investment (DFI).

The debate about the role of transnational corporations in development has also often been conducted as if this was the same issue as that of the role of direct foreign investment in development. This is understandable with reference to the periods when direct foreign investment (usually meaning 100 percent foreign ownership) was overwhelmingly the dominant mode for transnationals' involvement in the developing countries; but in the 1970s and 1980s this has not been the case. Transnational corporations influence development today through a wide range of quasi-DFI or non-DFI activities in the developing countries including those of buying or selling goods, and selling services such as technology, management, marketing or advice. Indeed, among the principal analytical and policy issues today is that of the optimal form of interaction – from the standpoint either of the firms involved or of the home or host governments – between foreign firms, whether transnational corporations, strictly defined, or not, and local economic actors. Since transnational corporations are major economic institutions within today's world market economy this question begins to approximate, from the standpoint of the host government and firms, the apparently much wider one of the optimal modes for interacting with the world market itself.

"New forms" (as they have often been called, though they are not all new)[2] of non-DFI international business activity seem to have become increasingly important in developing countries in recent years – neither wholly or majority-owned investments nor portfolio lending in which there is no direct creditor involvement at all: e.g. joint ventures, licensing agreements, franchising, management contracts, turnkey contracts, production-sharing contracts, international subcontracting [Oman (1984a)]. Both new host government preferences, as expressed in policies toward foreign investment requiring greater local control, and new TNC perceptions of the advantages of alternative forms of involvement – not least for the shedding of risk or increasing leverage on their equity – have contributed to this evolution. These changes have been particularly significant in the petroleum and minerals industries. They have also often been important in the manufacturing sector, particularly where sales are primarily to host country markets; in manufacturing, however, intercountry and interindustry variety has been considerable [United Nations (1983, pp. 40–46) Oman (1984b)].

---

[2] This terminology, now widely employed, is that of Oman (1984a). See below.

It is important to call attention to the limitations of the available data on transnational corporate activity. The statistics that are most readily available relate only to direct foreign investment, which, as has been seen, is only one among many alternative forms of TNC involvement in developing countries. Even those data are highly imperfect and difficult to interpret. The definition of "direct foreign investment" is itself a source of great confusion and difficulty. Although DFI statistics are those most frequently deployed in discussions of transnational corporate activity they are typically subject to wide margins of error, and are highly sensitive to differences (intertemporally or cross-sectionally or both) in these definitions. The most frequently employed data are those of the IMF which defines DFI as "investment made to acquire a lasting interest in a foreign enterprise with the purpose of having an effective voice in its management" [IMF (1985, pp. 28–29)]. In principle it includes all flows, whether direct or through affiliates, from the investor; and includes reinvested earnings, and net borrowings, as well as equity capital.

The DFI data suggest that transnational corporate investments have been concentrated in a relatively few developing countries. In the 1977–81 period, for example, newly industrializing countries and OPEC members received between 60 and 75 percent of all flows of DFI in developing countries [OECD (1983, p. 21)]. Table 27.1 shows the estimated stock of OECD direct foreign investment in developing countries at the end of 1981, with a similar degree of concentration. While the numerous lower-income countries have accounted for small shares of the overall totals, DFI and other transnational corporate activities obviously still loom large in many of these countries' economies.

The DFI data also suggest significant changes in the sectoral composition of TNC investment in developing countries over time. Whereas transnational corporate activity in the less developed countries originally concentrated in the trade and primary sectors, with the bulk of their direct investment in the latter, in recent times its importance in the manufacturing and other service sectors has also been significant. Table 27.2 shows changes in the composition of U.S. DFI in developing countries in the 1970s – with primary production still dominant, manufacturing rising, and services declining.

Evidently, it is difficult to generalize about TNC activities across different countries, time periods, and sectors. Sectoral distinctions are likely to be of analytical significance. For most purposes it is important at least to distinguish DFI and other TNC activities in the resource sector from those in manufacturing. Within the resource sector, oil and mineral resources are usually separated from agricultural ones, and, within the manufacturing sector, export-oriented activity is best kept analytically separate from that catering to local national markets. In the service sector – encompassing banking, insurance, trade, shipping, tourism, advertising, telecommunications, data processing, etc. – generalization is even

Table 27.1
Estimated stock of OECD direct investment in developing countries at end-1981,
by country groups and selected host countries[a]

By group/country	$ billion	Percentage share
Low-income countries:	10.2	7
of which: India	2.7	
Zaire	1.6	
Middle-income countries:	49.1	36
of which: Bermuda[b]	5.5	
Panama[b]	4.9	
Bahamas[b]	3.8	
Neth. Antilles[b]	3.7	
Malaysia	3.5	
Peru	3.0	
Philippines	2.5	
Colombia	2.0	
Chile	2.0	
Liberia[b]	1.7	
Trinidad & Tobago	1.3	
Israel	1.2	
Newly industrializing countries:	55.6	41
of which: Brazil	17.2	
Mexico	10.3	
Spain	6.9	
Argentina	5.6	
Singapore	3.9	
Hong Kong	3.8	
Taiwan	2.3	
Korea (South)	1.6	
Greece	1.0	
OPEC countries:	22.3	16
of which: Indonesia	8.6	
Venezuela	4.3	
Nigeria	1.2	
Libya	1.5	
Total	137.2	100

By continent	$ billion	Percentage share
Europe	11.5	9
Africa	15.5	11
Latin America	71.8	52
Asia	38.4	28
Total	137.2	100

[a] Including unallocated amounts and Japanese official support for private investment. Countries with the book value of stock exceeding $1 billion.
[b] Off-shore Banking Centre.
Source: OECD (1983, p. 25).

Table 27.2
U.S. flows of direct foreign investment to developing countries,
by sector, 1970–72 and 1979–81

	1970–72		1979–81	
	$ billions	%	$ billions	%
Primary	3.1	46	7.9	50
Manufacturing	1.5	22	5.1	32
Services	2.1	32	2.3	15
Other	–	–	0.4	2
Total	6.8	100	15.7	100

Source: United Nations (1983, p. 293).

more impractical. It may therefore be most productive to consider transnational corporate activity as taking place in a variety of different "markets" for it.[3] In a short survey chapter, however, this has not always been feasible.

Another caveat regarding generalizations concerns the possibility that there may be national characteristics, related to home country factor endowments, traditions, etc. associated with the operations of TNCs from different places [Agmon and Kindleberger (1977), Dunning (1981), Kojima (1978, 1985), Lipsey and Kravis (1985)]. Except for brief reference to Third World transnationals this will not be explored here either.

This chapter is organized as follows. Section 2 reviews the historical evolution of transnational corporate activity in the developing countries. In Section 3 alternative theoretical approaches to direct foreign investment are surveyed. Section 4 considers the analysis, and some of the empirical results, of host country benefits and costs from interaction with transnationals. Section 5 reviews the issues in host government/transnational relationships, including bargaining over rent, transfer pricing, and investment incentives. Transnational corporations' roles in technology transfer and export marketing are considered in Section 6. A brief conclusion follows.

2. The changing role of transnational corporations in developing countries

International activities of large private firms have a long history. Merchant capital was engaged in long-distance and international trade long before the

---

[3] In manufacturing, for instance, one empirical investigation sought to distinguish three separate such markets (within each of four industries) – one for investments directed at the market of individual host countries, one for those relating to common markets, and one for those geared to production for export [Guisinger (1985)]. For studies of the TNC role in the services sector, the best sources are the studies of the U.N. Centre on Transnational Corporations. On agriculture, see Glover (1986).

Industrial Revolution in Europe. Later the expansion of European interest and influence to Asia, Africa, and the Americas brought vastly increased commercial exchange, and enormous profit to European firms and governmental Treasuries from trade with these areas as well. The historical association of European firms' activities in the Third World with colonialism has lent further controversy and emotion to what would in any case have been potentially difficult relationships. Equally, U.S. strategic interests in Latin America and the Caribbean, and similar Japanese interests in Asia, have been inextricably intertwined with the history of these home countries' transnational corporate involvements in their respective "spheres of influence". Originally engaging primarily in trading relationships (and such ancillary services as shipping and finance), Northern firms were increasingly involved by the late nineteenth century in direct production in the Third World, notably in mining and estate agriculture. In the interwar period foreign direct investment in the less developed world began to move into import-substituting manufacturing, notably in Latin America and to some extent in India, but overall it was still concentrated in primary production for export.

The 25 years following the Second World War, a period characterized by a worldwide burst of production, trade, and economic activity, brought an unprecedented expansion in the activity of transnational corporations, particularly in the form of direct investment and "international production".[4] Technological change in the spheres of transport, communications, and information processing; liberalization of international transactions; and a buoyant climate of optimism concerning the global economic and political prospect all contributed to this phenomenon. TNCs based in the United States were the original primary movers in this expansion but European, Japanese, and other countries' firms increased their relative importance over time. In the Third World the independence movements altered the political context within which transnational corporations had to find their way and, in many cases, significantly altered the structure of incentives for commercial activity – typically in the direction of import-substituting manufacturing activities. The long "pause" in the activity of international financial markets – the product of the major disruptions of the Depression – also left the opportunities for portfolio investment in the developing countries at this time very limited, requiring that direct investment serve as the primary mode for the utilization of private foreign capital. In consequence of these various influences, direct foreign investment in the Third World expanded rapidly, and most rapidly of all in the manufacturing sector.[5]

---

[4] Dunning has popularized the term "international production" to describe productive operations undertaken by a firm outside its home country [Dunning (1981)].

[5] The best overall accounts of these and subsequent post-Second World War developments may be found in the three general reviews of the U.N. Centre on Transnational Corporations [United Nations (1974, 1978, 1983)].

Table 27.3
Total resource flows to developing countries, by major types of flow,
selected years, 1960–84[a]

	1960–61		1970		1979		1984	
	$ billions	%	$ billions	%	$ billions	%	$ billions	%
Official development assistance	19.5	(56)	22.2	(42)	32.9	(37)	35.8	(42)
Grants by private voluntary agencies	–		2.3	(4)	2.0	(2)	2.5	(3)
Nonconcessional official flows	6.6	(19)	10.4	(20)	18.8	(21)	20.0	(24)
Private:								
Direct investment	6.5	(19)	9.7	(18)	13.8	(16)	9.5	(11)
Bank sector	2.2	(6)	7.9	(15)	20.2	(23)	24.0	(20)[b]
Bond lending	–		0.8	(2)	0.7	(1)	0.5	(1)
Resource flows	34.8	(100)	53.1	(100)	88.4	(100)	92.3	(100)

[a]At 1983 prices and exchange rates.
[b]Includes significant amount of re-scheduled short-term debt.
Source: OECD (1985, pp. 160, 162).

In the 1970s, although direct foreign investment in middle-income developing countries grew at greater rates (in value terms) than in the 1950s or 1960s (and its share of total world DFI actually rose), commercial bank lending to these developing countries grew at much more rapid rates. Table 27.3 shows the consequent relative decline in the importance of DFI in total resource flows to the developing countries. There followed an understandable relative shift of professional and policymaker interest towards the "debt problem". At the same time, and partly because of the new opportunities for alternative sources of finance, there was a relative shift to the so-called "new forms" of transnational corporate involvement in the Third World, so that direct intertemporal comparisons of data on direct investment declined in usefulness as indicators of TNC activity. By the early 1980s, however, severe balance of payments pressures and reaction to the problems of debt servicing in the Third World had led to a relative resurgence of interest in equity investment and more traditional forms of transnational corporate involvement there. As the prospect of continued rapid expansion of commercial bank lending to developing countries faded, an apparent international consensus began to emerge in favour of greatly expanded direct foreign investment, or conversion of existing debt to equity, in the less developed world, and hence liberalized host government policies to support it.

DFI is popularly seen as a source of increased external finance for development which, when in the form of equity, has the major advantage that lenders assume a greater share of the risks than, except for default risk, in the case of bank finance. The DFI phenomenon is at least as much a matter of corporate organization, however, as it is a matter of international capital flow (see Section

3). Apart from some innovative efforts to convert limited amounts of debt to equity it is not evident that much "new" foreign equity capital will materialize from expanded direct foreign investment flows. A survey of 68 direct foreign investment projects in developing countries in the period before the boom in commercial bank financing found that almost half of the new capital raised for them was in the form of debt rather than equity; 40 percent of the equity capital and 54 percent of the debt was obtained in the developing countries themselves [Reuber et al. (1973, p. 67)]. The principal new role of TNCs may therefore be less as suppliers of equity capital than as financial intermediators between nervous banks or other lenders and the developing countries. While TNCs would assume some of the risks with respect to new debt, in such circumstances they would play a role analogous in the financial sphere to that of the World Bank. If debt, rather than equity finance, is likely to be an important source of expanded DFI in developing countries the relevant comparison is between the cost, term to maturity, country distribution, and sectoral distribution of the financial flows one would expect from expanded DFI and those from expanded World Bank or other official intermediation or cofinancing. If increasing finance for developing countries and improved means of sharing risks in international finance are the real object, it would probably be best to consider the virtues of new financial instruments and the possibility of new sources of finance directly [Lessard and Williamson (1985)] rather than developing false hopes regarding DFI. Expectations of the response of TNCs and DFI to policy changes in the developing countries have often been (unrealistically) higher in policy circles in the industrialized world than among analysts of development finance elsewhere. Scepticism concerning the elasticity of direct foreign investment to eased governmental terms in developing countries remains widespread in these countries and among analysts of business behaviour.

Direct investment in the less developed countries has, in any case, been just as erratic in its flow and just as highly concentrated in a relatively few places – indeed in the same countries – as international commercial bank lending. Attempts econometrically to "explain" the intercountry allocation of foreign direct investment in developing countries by various economic and political variables have been somewhat inconclusive; but it seems that economic and political factors work simultaneously. Both economic variables (notably per capita income, balance of payments position, growth rate, inflation rate, wage costs, skill level of the work force) and political variables (political instability, bilateral aid flows from Communist and Western countries and multilateral aid flows) carry statistical significance in an estimated equation "explaining" the country distribution of direct foreign investment in the developing countries [Schneider and Frey (1985)]. Most survey evidence also suggests the general importance of both political stability and a "favourable investment climate", although debate continues to surround the question of governmental investment incentives (see Section

5). What attracts it to particular countries no doubt also depends upon the sector. Natural resources are clearly the prime source of attraction for resource-industry firms. Low labour costs are a prime attraction for international subcontractors. The prospect of large and especially protected local markets are the key to most import-substituting manufacturing firms' foreign activities.

3. Alternative theoretical approaches to direct foreign investment

However much the TNC may be involved in new forms of international business, the literature on TNCs and economic development has been dominated by analyses of direct foreign investment. The theory of the determinants and effects of direct foreign investment upon the host country has gone through several stages in the mainstream literature of economics. Early neoclassical approaches were based upon the premise that direct foreign investment involved international capital arbitrage – a capital flow between nations resulting from differential rates of return. Under the usual simplifying assumptions, particularly concerning the degree of competition, one could deduce the consequent income and distributional effects in comparative static terms; and deploy similar comparative static analysis with variation of assumptions about scale economies, unemployment, tax regimes, terms of trade effects, externalities, the relationship between capital flow and the national stock of capital, concomitant accompanying technical change, and the like [MacDougall (1960)]. Beneficial effects for the host country, in this analysis, are most likely to stem from a larger capital stock, increased tax revenues, increased labour income (or employment), and favourable externalities, particularly from technological diffusion and training.

General equilibrium analysis of the simplified "2 by 2 by 2" type employed by trade theorists has by now been deployed to analyse effects upon host countries of external capital inflows under widely varying assumptions. This analysis, although sometimes characterized, either explicitly or implicitly, as referring to the impact of direct foreign investment, relates more properly to the case of portfolio capital flows. The perfectly competitive product and factor markets typically assumed in these analyses is inconsistent both with the modern theory of direct foreign investment and with empirical observation as to the circumstances in which it is found. It is noteworthy nonetheless that this analysis has uncovered circumstances in which capital inflows may reduce welfare in the capital-importing country – via domestic "distortions" or rigidities that limit income gains to less than the cost of the external capital (or even render them negative), negative terms of trade effects, etc. [e.g. Brecher and Diaz-Alejandro (1977), Bhagwati and Brecher (1980, 1981), Bhagwati and Tironi (1980), Brecher and Findlay (1983)].

The observation that direct investment was typically found in industries characterized by oligopoly and involved a package of other inputs as well as capital flow led to an alternative explanation and analysis of DFI grounded in the theory of industrial organization. A transnational corporation, in this formulation, is basically a multi-plant firm operating in more than one country. Imperfections in markets for intangible assets, intermediate products and information make it more efficient for firms to integrate horizontally or vertically or to diversify rather than interacting with one another as a number of independent single-plant firms. Transactions costs and barriers to entry are key elements in this approach.[6]

In this interpretation foreign firms could only overcome the competition of local firms in local production if they possessed some advantage that was not available to the locals, and that was, in fact, the source of foreign oligopoly power. Unique firm-specific assets – intangibles such as process or product technology, management skills, economies of scale or scope, control over markets or sales and servicing networks, etc. – could explain foreigners' advantages in the kinds of industries in which they clustered, their frequent market concentration and the potential for their earning of quasi-rent in these activities. The location of production could still be explained, in this interpretation, by the traditional tenets of comparative advantage, making allowance for transport costs and other "frictions", and modified, sometimes in a major way, by the policies of governments, particularly, in the case of manufacturing, tariff protection. The question that was still to be resolved was that of why, given the economics of location, and given the advantages of particular firms in production, these firms should not sell their "advantage" to local firms rather than undertaking foreign production themselves. This remaining puzzle was resolved via resort to the traditional theory of the firm, the theory of the choice between hierarchies and markets, the theory of "internalization" [Williamson (1975), Buckley and Casson (1976), Magee (1977)]. In this interpretation, internalization (i.e. direct foreign investment) occurs in consequence of transactions costs, risks and uncertainties in arm's-length markets, and the potential for increased control, improved deployment of market power, reduced uncertainty, scale and scope economies, and advantageous transfer pricing in internalized systems. Internalization is thus seen by some as a means of *overcoming* market imperfections – generated by national boundaries, informational deficiencies, and the like – and, via the creation of "internal markets", as an important contributor to worldwide (Pareto) efficiency [Williamson (1975), Rugman and Eden (1985)]. Far from creating imperfections through its oligopoly power, the TNC is seen as offsetting them.

---

[6] For a good survey of this literature, see Caves (1982).

This "eclectic" theory of direct investment [Dunning (1981)] – drawing on firm-specific attributes, locational advantages, and internalization advantages – is now widely accepted; but it leaves considerable room for disagreement and further analysis concerning the origins of firm-specific advantages and the effects of direct foreign investment upon host (and home) countries. Oligopoly, transfer pricing, and other market imperfections suggest that there may be a degree of indeterminacy about final outcomes, and potential for the deployment of government policy (in particular, for bargaining over DFI terms) in the successful furtherance of national economic welfare.

A related approach to the direct foreign investment phenomenon is associated with host country efforts to "unpackage" it. Analytically one may conceive of independent markets for each of the individual components of whatever the transnational corporation has on offer in its direct investment package. There are also markets for inputs, technologies, etc. which are *not* offered in a particular DFI package. This approach therefore lends itself to the analysis of the potential for extracting the maximum from the entire range of transnational corporate goods and services, indeed from world markets as a whole. Some markets are controlled by foreign oligopolists; others are competitive. Optimal "shopping" among the available markets (both as a buyer and as a seller) – and therefore consideration of the possibility of unpackaging the direct investment package – may therefore, at least in conceptual terms, be the right way of thinking of the relevant buyers–seller or investor–borrower relationships [Vaitsos (1974)]. A full social benefit–cost analysis would require assessment of the transactions and search costs – and indeed the costs of training for the capacity to search effectively – with respect to these various markets. This approach led inevitably to a new focus upon "technology markets" since, as some analysts put it, technology is the transnational corporations' "trump card" [Stopford and Wells (1972, p. 177)].

Structuralist, neo-Marxist and dependence theorists adopt rather broader interpretations of the direct investment phenomenon and transnational corporate influences upon development. While one strand of Marxist thought has always seen capitalist expansion, and thus the expansion of transnational corporate activity to the Third World, as progressive – breaking down obsolete structures and building "productive forces" for the future – radical analysts have more typically denounced the negative effects of transnational corporate activity [e.g. Girvan (1976), Magdoff (1976)].

In radical analyses, direct foreign investment in the Third World arises because of the Northern capitalists' need for new markets and/or new sources of cheap labour and other inputs. Emphasis is usually placed upon the "drain" of surplus out of the host country (the return on capital) rather than upon any positive effects that the capital flow might have engendered in local productive capacity.

Such developmental effects as may be created locally are seen, in these analyses, as likely to distort the local social, political, and economic environment deflecting it from a more desirable and more balanced path by strengthening sectors and interests that are linked to, or controlled by, external forces.

Dependency theorists (and empirical analysts) emphasize the negative domestic impact of the whole range of external relationships among which those involving transnational corporations are obviously prominent. Some posit that growth itself will be hampered in developing countries by transnational corporate activity there, as domestically usable "surplus" is drained away and local entrepreneurial capacity is stifled or co-opted. Others see developing countries' growth as consistent with the overall expansion of the global market (capitalist) system but express concern over the distortions that transnational corporate influence may create over its pattern. Highly unequal income distribution, strengthening of domestic concentrations of economic and political power, inappropriate production technology and taste patterns, stifled national entrepreneurship and indigenous research and development and, generally, locally disintegrated and undesirably externally dependent economic structures are likely, it is argued, to accompany overreliance upon transnational corporations. At the same time disproportionate political influence is likely to be exercised in support of these patterns by transnational corporations, their local allies and their home governments [Biersteker (1978), Moran (1978)].

The analysis of the role of such institutions as the transnational corporation and the state, and the interplay between political, economic, and social forces, are undoubtedly crucially important to an understanding of economic history in most of the Third World. The antiseptic analytics of neoclassical economic theory and economic theories of industrial organization may indeed easily miss that which is of the essence in the role of transnational corporations in development processes. But facile generalizations about their inevitable negative role, frequently based on imperfect and incomplete economic and historical analysis, are not terribly helpful either.

4. Benefits and costs of TNC activities in developing countries

While measurement problems abound, it should nevertheless be possible to conduct a social benefit–cost analysis of any developing country transactions or projects in which there is external participation. Gross benefits in the form of increased access to scarce inputs – typically capital, technology, management or marketing skills – can be assessed at values approximating their marginal (social) productivities including such positive externalities, e.g. training effects, as can be accounted for. Favourable (or unfavourable) impacts upon domestic competition and thus efficiency [e.g. Connor (1977), Lall (1978), Newfarmer (1979),

Newfarmer and Marsh (1981), Dunning (1985)] or government revenue or employment [ILO (1976), Caves (1982, pp. 131–159)] are also often emphasized, but these are usually seen as secondary to or derivative from the provision of extra inputs. It is obviously important therefore to determine how much is actually supplied, and whether it adds to or merely substitutes for domestic inputs. If, for instance, direct foreign investment is financed by borrowing from local banks that might otherwise have lent to local business there may be some change in the price of capital but, barring interest elasticity for which the evidence is weak, there is unlikely to be any national gain in the supply of capital or foreign exchange.[7] Similarly, if foreign firms simply hire skilled local managers or workers away from their existing activities or purchase rights to locally developed innovations, they may generate some redistributional effects, but they do not add to the national stock of management, skill, or available technology. External takeovers frequently add little or nothing in these respects. [The most important effects they create (positive or negative) are sometimes in respect of impacts upon the extent of domestic competition.] Research upon the less direct provision of extra inputs to the host country – through training, the local diffusion of knowledge and technology, etc. – has been fairly limited and anecdotal; such effects are, in any case, virtually impossible to estimate on an ex ante basis. There is therefore an unfortunate but inevitable imprecision concerning the overall supply of extra inputs that TNCs supply in DFI projects or non-DFI external transactions.

Costs of domestic inputs can be assessed at their (social) opportunity costs and those of external inputs at their world prices; again, these costs should incorporate such negative externalities, e.g. pollution, as can be confidently assigned to the transaction or project. Some such social benefit–cost framework is the only coherent means of addressing the continuing controversies over the purported economic advantages and disadvantages of transnational corporate activities for developing countries. This is not the place for a detailed consideration of the merits of alternative methodologies for pricing, the treatment of risk and income

---

[7]The fact that foreign direct investment can be financed from local sources, and thus not add to the national supply of savings, has been a source of analytical confusion. When borrowing is undertaken by foreign firms from local banks and financial institutions, what is happening, analytically speaking, is a capital outflow. If these resources are then invested within the country from which they were obtained, there is an offsetting capital inflow. It should not be surprising that some countries seek to control such local borrowing by foreign firms (capital outflows); equally, the firms can be expected to seek to finance their activities in the cheapest and least risky fashion. Similarly, when retained earnings are employed for the financing of investment they should be thought of analytically as constituting an external payment (foreign earnings) followed by an external inflow of investment. If such investments are freely made they are obviously just as important as any "fresh" capital inflow; earnings on previous foreign investment are as surely foreign as are those from any other payment for an import. If external payments are controlled, as they frequently are, foreign firms may have few options but reinvestment in their own activities (which are usually more attractive than, say, government bonds or bank deposits).

distribution, and the like in social benefit–cost analysis. (For a comprehensive assessment of these issues see Chapter 21 by Squire in this Handbook.) Such an approach obviously does not overcome all of the real empirical and methodological problems associated with the determination of the effects of TNC activities; but the adoption of a clear framework at least highlights the need for and the nature of the most useful specific empirical investigations. It is clear, for instance, within this framework, that benefit–cost analyses would be greatly improved if there were more detailed empirical research on such issues as the effects of TNC activities on local firms' growth, indigenous technical and managerial learning, and domestic market structure.

Such a framework also permits one to place other indicators of the effects of transnational corporate activities or direct foreign investment into their appropriate context. In particular, some writers – particularly those without a background in economics – focus upon the balance of payments effects of direct investment, purporting to find pernicious transnational corporate impact in the fact that external payments may eventually exceed capital inflows. In social benefit–cost terms this is clearly a nonsensical approach. If foreign exchange is particularly "scarce" at the existing official price domestic policies will have to take that into account in all areas, including that of relationships with external suppliers of inputs. In any analysis of balance of payments effects, as in other spheres, one must be clear as to what the counterfactual is. Implicit in that which highlights the negative effects of transnational corporate activity in developing countries there seems to be a counterfactual world in which whatever the transnational has supplied, notably its capital, can be provided domestically instead. The costs and constraints within this counterfactual scenario are unfortunately seldom analysed.[8]

There have been several attempts systematically to estimate the social benefits and costs of foreign direct investment projects in developing countries.[9] Similar

---

[8]As long as a host country is borrowing capital at a positive interest rate it must eventually expect to incur net outflows unless, according to the Domar rule, the rate of growth of the debt (or foreign-owned capital stock) exceeds the rate of return on it (broadly, the rate of interest). As far as the provision of other inputs is concerned, the transnational corporation will presumably be paid at commercial rates in foreign exchange for whatever it provides. Direct foreign investment is therefore likely eventually to generate outflows in the balance of payments, unless it is extremely effective in raising production of tradeable goods (exports or import substitutes). The extent to which external capital or other inputs are deployed to expand foreign exchange earnings or to save on foreign exchange outflows, and thus their overall effect on the balance of payments, will depend on a variety of other matters, including host government policies, few of which are related in an obvious or necessary way to the flow of external capital or other inputs. There is, in any case, no economic rationale for focusing upon (positive or negative) balance of payments effects in particular projects, sectors or spheres of international interaction.

[9]There have also been some crude attempts to find intercountry statistical associations between aggregate foreign direct investment stocks or flows and per capita income and rates of national economic growth. But, apart from the fact of ambiguous results, these can say nothing about the direction of causation or the underlying structural relationships, and are of dubious value in themselves [Reuber (1973), Bornschier (1980), Doland and Tomlin (1980), Jackman (1982)].

analyses of alternative forms of transnational corporate activity have so far tended to be only of a more impressionistic kind. There are inevitably certain arbitrary assumptions required to complete specific benefit–cost analyses [Lal (1975)]. For what they are worth, the results of the analyses of direct foreign investment projects indicate that most have generated positive economic effects. A sizeable minority, however, reduce the host country's national product. One-third of the foreign investment projects in one study [Lall and Streeten (1977)] and between 25 and 45 percent in another [Encarnacion and Wells (1986)] cost the host country more in terms of the opportunity cost of its resources than they earned for it. That is, they lowered national income and welfare in the host country though they earned profit for the private foreign investor. The incidence of bad projects and the social rate of return were systematically associated with higher levels of domestic protection against imports, positively and negatively, respectively. Administratively determined input prices, notably subsidized energy, also played a significant role in these results.

If transactions or projects which are socially injurious to a developing country are found to exist, the question arises as to the responsibility for them and the appropriate policy implications. To the extent that the negative impact is the result of domestic governmental pricing and related policies, the "blame" might best be assigned locally rather than to foreigners, and the first-best remedy would appear to be to correct the relevant domestic policies. Inappropriate national policies may be the product of technical misperception or of the pressure of domestic or foreign interests. In some instances there may be coincidence of interests between ruling groups or bureaucrats and foreign firms, who jointly extract quasi-rent from the national economy. In others, foreign firms can be expected to be at odds with domestic firms with which they compete. In any case, since these policies may themselves be influenced by foreign firms or their allies, the protests of TNC apologists that such effects are "not their fault" are not always convincing. Among the most important issues in this overall literature – although one on which research is difficult and relatively rare [but see, for example, Goodsell (1974), Sklar (1975), Stepan (1978), Evans (1979)] – is the *overall* political-economic role of various transnational corporations in particular developing country contexts. Evidently, protection against imports and domestic subsidies serve many economic and political purposes, and policies in these spheres are not so quickly turned around. It may therefore be productive to develop decisionmaking mechanisms that reduce the likelihood of injurious transactions and projects going forward (see Section 5), rather than to rely exclusively on the prospect of alterations in the whole panoply of domestic policies.

However useful it may be for the assessment of the social desirability of *specific* transactions or projects, benefit–cost analysis, unless extended to possible alternative arrangements in a manner rarely undertaken, does not usually address the possibility of socially superior provisions with respect to the same transaction or project. Rather than asking whether a particular project was socially beneficial, one might well ask instead whether the same project could more beneficially have been launched via domestic investment, the direct investment of another foreign firm, via various "unpackaging" possibilities involving other domestic or foreign actors and other forms of external involvement, via different terms bargained more effectively with the same foreign investor, at a later date, at another location, and so forth. The question of whether a project with foreign involvement has, on balance, been absolutely beneficial or not to the host country, while not without interest, especially in respect of the possibility of screening out socially injurious projects, may be less fruitful to answer than that of whether the best possible terms have been struck. While there are exceptions, as has been seen, there must be a presumption that any addition to a country's overall flow of productive inputs will increase its output, but whether, and by how much, welfare is increased will depend upon the terms on which these extra inputs (if indeed they are extra at all) are acquired. Even where welfare is decreased, it is possible that the project's damage might have been less had it been assembled and financed differently.

5. Relationships between TNCs and developing countries

5.1. Imperfect competition and rent

Many of the transactions between firms or governments in developing countries and transnational corporations take place in a reasonably competitive context, involving little or no opportunity for rental earnings by TNCs. The emphasis upon market imperfection, barriers to entry and oligopoly in the modern theory of transnational corporations and direct investment implies, however, that the prices at which these corporations transact (whether as buyers or as sellers) are frequently not those that would rule in perfectly competitive markets. These circumstances suggest that the overall terms of TNC relations with developing country firms or governments are likely to be the product of bargaining rather than competitive market solutions.

Economic theory's inability to provide determinate answers in the realm of bilateral monopoly, oligopoly, and game-theoretic situations, except via resort to extremely crude behavioural assumptions, perhaps helps to explain the difficulty that economists have had in contributing usefully to the analytical literature of overall TNC–developing country relations. [For an attempt to model bargaining over tax treatment using game-theoretic approaches, however, see Doyle and van Wijnbergen (1984).] Where politics, power, and nonmarket instruments are so important to bargaining relationships it should perhaps not be surprising that noneconomists have been prominent in the relevant literature.

Some theoretical analysts suggest, on the other hand, that, where there is direct foreign investment, outcomes from the "internal markets" of integrated TNCs may more closely approximate efficient competitive solutions than would those of the imperfection-ridden real world in the absence of DFI [Rugman and Eden (1985)]. Indeed, implicit in much of the literature that emphasizes the favourable impact of transnational corporate activity there even seems to be a presumption that, within direct foreign investment arrangements, TNCs offer inputs at less-than-market prices (otherwise why should the host not simply acquire them on more favourable terms in arm's-length markets wherever they are available?), and certainly do not "over-price" them. Where TNCs intermediate between international capital markets and the developing countries there may be good grounds for the latter assumption; but TNC market power makes it dubious in other markets and other dimensions of the DFI package. Whether the actual "price" is above or below a competitive market price is an empirical question and probably not one for which general answers can be given.

Certainly, where firm-specific advantages and market power exist there is potential for rent or quasi-rent in the firms' pricing and earnings. This is particularly evident in respect of the pricing of proprietary technology. Not all developing countries ought to require significant imports of such rent-producing technology. The production technology most useful for developing countries is frequently mature, fairly standardized, and therefore available at minimal cost from the trade literature, contacts with suppliers of equipment, purchasers of output, short-term consultancies, and other informal sources rather than from technology "owners". The demand for "high" technology – of the kind most likely to be proprietary – is confined to a relatively few sectors in most poor countries, and is concentrated in India, China, and the semi-industrialized and middle-income group of developing countries.

Proprietary technology markets are nevertheless important to many firms and governments in developing countries, and they are inherently highly imperfect. Although social optimality conditions would seem to require that, once knowledge is developed, it should be made freely available to all, property rights in knowledge are typically recognized in industry in market economies so as to ensure that there are incentives for its creation. Legally buttressed monopoly is therefore characteristic of markets for commercialized industrial technology. At the same time buyer information is limited in respect of the value of that which is being purchased.

Between the marginal cost of further use of already developed proprietary technology to its owner (which is very small) and the utility of its acquisition to a buyer or the cost of his developing it himself (either of which may be very great) there appears to be a wide range within which its price, when the technology is transferred, may settle. The full cost of technology transfer to new users, for the owner, must include what may be quite considerable teaching and servicing efforts; there may also be risk of damage to other seller interests as its firm-specific assets become more widely spread. Thus, the range within which the price for proprietary technology will settle is a little narrower – between the utility to the purchaser and the total transfer costs to the owner. These transfer costs can vary substantially – with the nature of the technology, the number of previous extra-firm applications, the experience of the buyers, etc. They may also relate to the form of international investment and hence influence decisions in that realm as well [Teece (1977), Caves, Crookell and Killing (1983), Stobaugh and Wells (1984)]. Some claim that subsidiaries can expect to pay less for foreign propri-etary technology than arm's-length transactors; others that technology payments are a major means of extracting excess profit from DFI activities. It has also been argued by some that poor developing countries can expect to pay lower overall prices to price-discriminating sellers than richer purchasers, and by others that their weak bargaining power will instead produce relatively higher purchase prices; the evidence is not as yet in on these issues. Evidently the terms on which technology will be transferred (or sold) are matters on which it is hazardous to generalize.

Moreover, the "terms" must be understood to include a variety of nonprice dimensions such as rights to export, procurement requirements (tie-in provisions), property rights over local adaptations, etc. Some of these nonprice terms may be of strategic importance to the developing country purchaser, e.g. those relating to the development of local technological capacity, export promotion, regional or national economic integration. If they are enforced their costs to the host country may be quite high; in some instances, enforcement costs are high and they may easily be circumvented. About all one can safely say by way of generalization is that the overall terms for proprietary technology transfer are likely to be set in a multidimensional bargaining process rather than in a textbook-style competitive market.

Some governments have attempted to establish formal requirements of technol-ogy import contracts (e.g. upper bounds on royalties expressed as a percentage of sales, prohibition of export restrictions) or vetting procedures for their monitor-ing and control [Lall and Bibile (1977), Chudnovsky (1981)]. It is not entirely clear, however, how successful such policies have generally been in influencing the overall terms of technology transfers. Clearly, it is a good deal easier to prescribe general legal and economic requirements than it is, particularly in the skill-scarce circumstances of most developing countries, effectively to monitor the true terms of transfer or the "quality" of that which is acquired in particular cases.

In the natural resource sector, as well, potential rent arises from the peculiar advantages of resource quality or location (Ricardian rent), in addition to that attributable to such barriers to entry as scale economies and firm-specific knowl-edge. In some parts of the minerals sector, where capital requirements for exploration and development in the developing countries are very large, the evident rent potential and the increasing availability of arm's-length sources of commercial capital, led to host government policies in the 1960s and 1970s, primarily with respect to national ownership, that were designed to redirect rental earnings in a major way towards the hosts. The role of traditional mining companies thus shifted radically during the 1960s. For example, in the copper sector, host government ownership (partial or complete) accounted for only 2.5 percent of total production capacity in the early 1960s but had reached 43 percent by the end of the decade. By 1977 about 60 percent of developing countries' primary copper output was produced in majority-owned government enterprises [Mikesell (1979, p. 17)]. Similar changes occurred in the iron ore and bauxite industries. Elsewhere in the minerals sector changing tax regimes and altered contractual provisions also significantly increased the host countries' share of total revenues. The resulting decline in the foreign private return on minerals investment led to some alarm about the current and future adequacy of exploration and development activities in the developing countries [Radetzki (1982)]. The mining companies' early estimates of declining developing country exploration and development activity were exaggerated; but they added urgency to the search for new forms of international mining company investment that were both stable and equitable to all parties. Since mining development frequently involves few other linkages with the domestic economy [Emerson (1982)], its contribution to government revenues is especially important to analyse carefully.

5.2. Bargaining between TNCs and developing countries

Where there *is* potential for rent or quasi-rent – whether deriving from firm-specific attributes, other sources of market power, or Ricardian considerations – the distribution of the gains from interactions between transnational firms and host country firms or governments is indeterminate within a range of possible outcomes. The outcome is generally attributed to "bargaining" processes which are notoriously difficult to model persuasively [Streeten (1973, 1976), Vaitsos (1976), Doyle and van Wijnbergen (1984)]. Among the determinants of host country (firm or government) bargaining "success" are skill, information, political will, alliances or competitiveness with other hosts, domestic organization, competition among firms, and the like [Fagre and Wells (1982), Encarnacion and Wells (1985)]. More fundamentally, domestic market size is a major element in the strength of the host in bargaining in import-substituting industrial activities, and the attractiveness of the resource (in terms of location and quality) in the minerals sector. At the other extreme, fundamental bargaining strength is at a minimum in activities relating to unskilled labour-intensive manufacturing for export, where there are numerous competitors. The bargaining paradigm for the analysis of host country–transnational interaction tends to assume away, or at least to minimize, the potential for interest group divergences and competition within the host country; in most circumstances the bargains that can be struck by host countries are themselves constrained by internal political factors [Philip (1976)].

In some instances, as has been seen, governmentally created domestic "distortions", such as heavy protection against imports, or subsidized inputs, may generate negative effects from TNC investments for the host country. Even export-oriented DFI projects can waste resources in this way [Encarnacion and Wells (1986)]. Particularly if domestic incentive systems are not easily or quickly altered, this suggests the desirability of offsetting government intervention. Administrative screening and performance requirements may thus be created to attempt to prevent rents resulting from purely domestic arrangements unintentionally flowing abroad. Even where there are inducements to foreign investment they are thus regularly "accompanied by constraints which national governments place on global decision making. Limits on ownership in local subsidiaries, rules on how much they must export or buy locally, whom they must employ and how they must finance their operations apply almost everywhere. These so-called performance requirements are supposed to ensure that the firm provides desired benefits to the host country." Whether the "benefits" from such policies typically exceed their costs remains, in the absence of the necessary empirical research, somewhat uncertain [Encarnacion and Wells (1984, p. 3)].

Bargaining between transnational direct investors and host governments (or firms) is evidently multidimensional. It has to do not only with the broad issues, such as tax and subsidy arrangements and the details of the financing package, but also with such narrower matters as rights regarding the use of expatriates, training and use of local personnel, degree of local input sourcing or export requirements, capital repatriation, "national treatment" vis-à-vis domestic business legislation, the means for the establishment of transfer prices, provisions for arbitration, renegotiation or termination, etc. In principle one may choose to interpret the terms negotiated in each of these dimensions as tradable against an income equivalent, and thereby to translate them all, for the purpose of benefit–cost analysis, into terms of a single numeraire; but such a translation would in practice be extremely difficult to achieve and of dubious credibility, even if achieved. Such translations have, in any case, not been attempted in the literature.

It is also important to recognize that the bargain struck at the entry of a particular transnational corporation to a particular country may be transformed as circumstances change. The developing country scene is strewn with the wreckage of broken agreements – broken both by firms and by governments; "revealed" terms of interaction may be quite different from formally agreed ones, and sanctions against breaches of formal agreements are usually awkward and imperfect. An important strand in the bargaining literature relating to direct foreign investment concerns the stability of bargains over time.

Changes in the underlying determinants of relative bargaining strength, e.g. new resource discoveries, technological change in competing industries, world prices for inputs and outputs, political changes, are bound to undermine the terms of earlier bargains. Some of these determinants, notably sharp political change, are inherently difficult to foresee. On the other hand, in some circumstances one can confidently anticipate an "obsolescing bargain" [Moran (1974), Vernon (1977)]. The host country's bargaining strength is typically at its weakest during the period when it is seeking to attract transnational corporate activity to its country, before foreign firms have sunk any inputs into the country. Particular weakness exists when there is doubt as to whether there will ever be an opportunity for profitable activity there, as, for instance, in the case of attempts to attract mineral exploration activity. Once a foreign firm has sunk its own inputs into a project its capacity to extract concessions from a host government declines – at least until it can offer the possibility of a further burst of fresh inputs again. Over time, the host government or firm can also be expected to learn more about the relevant business so that the previous information balance is also likely to alter in the host's favour. In those cases (a small fraction of the total) in which exploration leads to profitable resource exploitation the resulting apparent "super-profits" (required to finance the unsuccessful exploratory activities) are likely to intensify nationalistic pressures for higher taxation, more controls, or nationalization. An alternative possibility, however, is that host government power may decline over time as the foreign firm builds more domestic alliances [Grieco (1986)]. Anticipation of an obsolescing bargain obviously influences the terms of initial bargains: those who foresee relative deterioration in their bargaining strength will, other things being equal, require better terms at the outset.

In the case of natural resource projects, the problems associated with the allocation of rents and the obsolescence of early bargains have generated schemes for longer-term agreement that allow for future contingencies. The "resource rent" tax (or its otherwise labelled equivalent) prescribes that foreign firms earn at least a "normal" rate of return in return for ascription of increasing shares of any rents above that return to the host country [Garnaut and Ross (1975, 1983), Smith and Wells (1975), Faber and Brown (1980)].

Harder bargaining on the part of host governments with transnational corporations over the disposition of rents (if any), control, and related issues has been varied in its consequences. One recent realistic assessment concludes: "Contrary to the bargaining in natural resources where host governments generally gain in relative power vis-à-vis TNCs, the growth of foreign investment in manufacturing does not appear to have shifted bargaining power in favor of host governments"

[Newfarmer (1984, p. 387)]. This may be attributable, according to this account, to the constant flow of new products and technologies from parent firms or to the character of the domestic political alliances associated with foreign-owned manufacturing production (including as TNC allies such varied groups as managers, labour, middle classes and associated domestic firms). As some technologies and industries mature, other new ones appear, so that while there may be a micro-level obsolescing bargain in manufacturing, in the aggregate, manufacturing transnationals do not appear to run so readily into problems.

Long-term relationships, experience, and "reputation" are likely to be of prime importance to mutually satisfactory host government–transnational interaction. Short-term profit maximization – either by the transnational firm or by the host government – may prove counterproductive. While host governments must depend upon quasi-voluntary compliance with domestic tax and other laws, transnationals must rely on the good faith of host governments in respect of the stability of the terms under which they normally operate. The analysis and practice of bargaining must therefore take fully into account the consistency of shorter-term bargains with longer-run objectives.

It is also important to record the danger that the purported need for screening, bargaining, and control of TNCs in the national interest can breed excessive bureaucracy, inefficiency, and corruption. The likelihood of such outcomes no doubt varies with political and administrative culture, and patterns of organization, in the host countries [Encarnacion and Wells (1985)].

5.3. Transfer pricing

Conflict and bargaining relationships between host governments and TNCs evidently do not stop with an initial contractual agreement and/or foreign direct investment decision. Interactions between the key "players" involve ongoing processes and repeated "games". Particularly sensitive are the *actual* terms on which inputs are sold to host countries or purchases of host country output are made by TNCs within direct foreign investment arrangements. For obvious reasons it is not always possible for those external to the TNC to ascertain what the prices actually being paid for transnational corporate inputs are within direct foreign investment arrangements. Certainly declared rates of profit on overseas activities of home countries' firms are unreliable indicators of actual rates of return on DFI activities. The opportunity for arbitrary pricing of intra-firm transactions of various kinds renders such data of very limited value. There is by now a considerable literature on the theory of transfer pricing, but, for obvious reasons, still rather limited reliable evidence [Murray (1981), Rugman and Eden (1985)].

The manipulation of transfer pricing to evade national taxation or other legislation, and to promote transnational corporate interests that do not coincide with host country interests, has been a source of concern in all countries. Indeed, some of the most intense of recent policy controversies have revolved around the attempts of American state governments to overcome transfer pricing problems by legislating a so-called "unitary" tax which bases corporate income tax on the state's share, as measured by employment or sales, of the worldwide operations of individual firms rather than on profits declared within state boundaries. In the developing countries, however, there has been even greater concern because of the limited capacities of local government tax and monitoring authorities, and the relatively great importance to state revenues of taxes on external transactions and foreign-owned enterprise. In addition to corporate taxes, withholding taxes on foreign factor payments, and trade taxes (import duties and export duties, or sometimes export subsidies), the transnational corporation operating in developing countries frequently also faces foreign exchange controls (limiting external remittances in the form of dividends, royalties, fees, etc.), shared local ownership, and changing political and other risks.

The incentives for transfer price manipulation are many and vary across countries and sectors; besides sheer tax and exchange control avoidance, firms may seek to minimize the income share accruing to local joint owners, maximize the concessions they may obtain from host governments and/or trade unions, minimize their exposure in deteriorating political situations, etc. Underlying the declared profits and dividend remittances are a whole host of arbitrary pricing possibilities relating not only to imported inputs and exported outputs, but also to the terms of interaffiliate loans, royalties, management fees, overhead charges, and the like. While the usual presumption is that transfer price manipulation will cost the developing country hosts (and particularly their governments) real resources, this need not always be the case, as for instance when such countries are offering tax holidays. Empirical evidence on the abuse of transfer pricing is limited but some of it, even if not representative, is quite dramatic, and supportive of developing countries' anxieties [Vaitsos (1974), Murray (1975); see also Kopits (1976)].

The attention devoted by the tax authorities of the industrialized countries [see, for instance, United Nations (1983, pp. 100–101)] to the transfer pricing phenomenon suggests the presence of an important problem. Many developing countries lack even the beginnings of an effective tax audit or foreign exchange control system. With their weak administrative machinery for the policing of transfer prices, the developing countries might be important gainers from a shift to a global system of (unitary) taxation of transnationals; but their gains (if any) would clearly depend upon the nature of the global revenue allocation system. Alternatively, and again depending upon the terms of the relevant agreements, the developing countries could benefit from joint audit arrangements with developed countries such as the latter countries have begun to arrange among themselves. For the present, transfer prices are required by tax (and exchange control) authorities to accord with arm's-length prices or, if they are not available, to be based upon costs or final product selling prices. It is virtually impossible for many developing countries accurately to monitor the full range of transfer prices employed by the foreign firms within their jurisdiction. Ultimately, while some of them may be able to make some impact upon corporate practices by selective and focused audits, particularly where a few large firms dominate the transnational corporate sector and where their home governments cooperate in audits, most developing countries must rely upon the good faith and good citizenship of the transnationals with which they deal.

5.4. National ownership, joint ventures, and "new forms"

Expropriation or nationalization of foreign corporations might seem to be a solution to many of these problems of ongoing conflict, always assuming that those who would thereafter manage the enterprise would have the will and the capacity to do so in the national interest (somehow defined). Unfortunately, the latter crucial assumptions have not always been realized in real-world instances of nationalization, and, as a policy measure, it has frequently been a pis aller [Faundez and Picciotto (1978), Shafer (1983)]. The mere threat of expropriation may nonetheless influence TNC decisionmaking and hence the modes and terms of host country–TNC relationships [Eaton and Gersovitz (1984)].

Governments may alternatively insist upon joint ownership in order to exercise some control or to extract larger shares of rent or simply to acquire more information about the operations of the foreign firm. The relative advantages of alternative forms of interaction with foreign firms for host countries in particular industries have not received the degree of research attention, either in terms of theory [e.g. Bardhan (1982)] or in empirical analysis, that they deserve. (Business schools have been more active in their investigation of their relative advantages for firms.)

The new unpackaged forms of international business favoured by many developing countries over DFI in recent years have not always been disadvantageous to TNCs. It is true that they usually involve higher transactions costs and enforcement costs for transnational corporations, as well as greater risk of the dissipation of some of their firm-specific advantages than in the case of traditional DFI. But some of these relative advantages of DFI for the TNC have been changing as indigenous managerial capacities increase, new systems of international communication are put into place, and governments seek to renegotiate the terms of DFI and impose performance requirements upon it [Oman (1984a)]. There may also be a natural evolution in the forms of international business at the industry level, with different industries at different stages at any point in time. As new technology "matures" – with less need for rapid information transmission on current technology development and less opportunity for rent-earning for those on the frontier – and as worldwide distribution and finance become more important relative to sheer production technology, one would expect the relative role of DFI in a particular industry to decline. Increased and globalized oligopolistic interfirm rivalry in an overall environment of increased economic uncertainty may also have contributed to the increased use of new forms of international business in the 1970s; new firms have used the new forms to overcome entry barriers in particular markets, and both new and old firms have sought to reduce risk and uncertainty with shorter planning horizons and more portfolio-type investment [Oman (1984a, pp. 84–89)].

Joint ventures are less attractive to the TNC when it possesses intangible assets from which rent is earned and it does not want to share this income unnecessarily or risk losing full control over the assets. Where the pricing of intracorporate transfer is important, e.g. where a high proportion of input and output is traded, it may also be reluctant to risk giving up full control over these prices. On the other hand, it is more likely to welcome others' participation if risks are perceived as high, if minimum efficient scale is large, or if such participation brings needed inputs (such as local expertise and contacts), or reduces the risk of unfriendly host country policy [Svejnar and Smith (1984)]. Other things being equal, one would therefore expect joint ventures to be more common in some sectors than in others, and to be found more frequently with smaller and less experienced transnational firms; there is some empirical support for these general propositions [Caves (1982, pp. 85–91)], as well as (unexplained) evidence that the national origin of the firms makes a difference. Japanese firms seem generally more likely and U.S. firms less likely to engage in joint ventures, although some of this difference may be attributable to differences in sectoral composition and in the degree of experience.

5.5. *Host and home government incentives*

It should not be thought that all of the conditions established by host developing countries for potential foreign investors generate benefits for the former and costs for the latter. On the contrary, an important issue in the analysis of relationships between host governments and transnational corporations concerns the efficacy and role of governmentally created "investment incentives" for transnationals [Balasubramanyan (1984)]. Generally, governmental investment incentives are believed to have played a very limited role in TNCs' intercountry investment decisionmaking. A recent OECD survey notes, for instance, that "Experience has shown that measures undertaken by home and host governments to improve the flow of foreign direct investment or to direct it to specific sectors and locations influence investment decisions only marginally" [OECD (1983, p. 8)]. Tax holidays and other incentives offered by developing countries appear to have largely offset one another (where they have not been nullified by home government policies or other influences), leaving the overall flow and pattern of DFI basically unchanged. On the other hand, overall incentives and disincentives – created by a combination of factors, of which one set must be governmental policies (notably those on trade, and not necessarily those described as "investment incentives") – clearly do influence profit-seeking firms [Guisinger (1985)]. The differential effects upon TNC investment and other behaviour of various degrees and types of governmental incentive or performance requirement have not received as much analytical or empirical investigation as these policy issues deserve. Can one say, for instance, that lowering input costs has the same overall effect upon firm behaviour and the host economy as protecting output markets?

Transnational corporate decisions, and relationships between developing country governments and TNCs, may also be influenced by government policies in the TNCs' home countries. Governments of the home countries in which transnationals are based clearly take an interest in their activities. Generally, these governments seek to protect their TNCs' interests even if their objectives do not wholly coincide with those of the firms [Lipson (1985)]. Most home governments offer encouragements to foreign direct investment, technology sales, and various "new forms" of investment in developing countries through investment insurance programmes, and tax credit or sparing provisions to reduce the risk of double taxation and/or increase the efficacy of host government incentive arrangements. Home governments prefer to offer insurance only in countries with which an intergovernmental agreement on the protection of foreign investment has been signed; but such agreements – typically guaranteeing national or most favoured nation treatment to foreign owners of capital, fair and prompt compensation upon nationalization, assured convertibility of earnings and repatriation of invested capital, etc. – are not acceptable to some developing countries. Moreover, other conditions restrict coverage to investments that do not compete with other home country investments. The limitations in these insurance schemes' coverage have limited TNC usage to under 10 percent of the outstanding stock of direct investment in developing countries [OECD (1983, pp. 30–33)]. Home governments may, in some circumstances, seek to discourage overseas investments that threaten to involve the "export of jobs"; and pressures for such protectionist measures may increase. All things considered, home countries' incentives and disincentives are not believed to play a major role in TNC investment or other decisions.

A more stable and effective "regime" for TNCs in the international economy, based on a clear delineation of the rights and obligations of both TNCs and governments, continues to be an objective of negotiations within the U.N. Centre on Transnational Corporations. The prospect of its significant influence on either TNC or governmental behaviour in the foreseeable future, however, seems slight. The coverage, terms, and legal status of the proposed code for TNCs all remain in dispute.

6. The TNC role in technology transfer and export marketing

The developing countries' needs for imported technology and for export markets have led to particular interest in the TNC role in their supply. As has been seen, the terms of TNC relationships with firms and governments in developing countries are generally subject to a wide range of influences. Beyond the question of terms, issues arising in the transfer of technology and export marketing are sufficiently controversial and important that they merit separate attention. This section also considers the potential special role of smaller firms and Third World TNCs in these spheres.

6.1. TNCs and technology transfer

The degree of reliance upon foreign technology in the development process obviously depends upon the specific circumstances of individual host firms, industries, and countries. The ways in which various pieces of knowledge regarding the design and operation of products, processes, and organizations are transferred internationally are themselves manifold. Direct foreign investment offers one possibility. Arm's-length technology transfers can also be achieved via licensing, turnkey plants, and the like, or even as technical assistance from foreign sellers of equipment or inputs and overseas buyers of output [Baranson (1970), Casson (1979)]. In South Korea, where there was a high degree of reliance upon imported technology and where by the 1970s there was already considerable indigenous technical capacity, such sellers and buyers were apparently the most important source of technology for the burgeoning and increasingly outward-oriented industrial sector [Rhee, Ross-Larson and Pursell (1984, pp. 39–49)].

Indigenous technological mastery is not acquired simply by "passively" importing technology. Local efforts (and inputs) to assimilate, adapt, and make best use of technology transfers from abroad are critically important to the attainment of the highest attainable returns from them. Korean government policy, for instance, actively encouraged the development of local technological capacity (particularly production technology) and, in many industries, limited the degree to which foreign proprietary technology could be imported. Korean entrepreneurs were thus encouraged to unbundle foreign packages of inputs, taking only those elements they required, and to adapt and absorb them for their own uses as quickly as possible. Direct foreign investment and licensing were used to start local technology-building efforts only in selected industries, and, of course, in the higher-technology industries where they had no alternatives, e.g. electronics and certain chemicals. Korea's highly selective technology-importing policy was effected under the rubric of "a stated policy... that was liberal but also very vague, so that discretion could reign" [Rhee, Ross-Larson and Pursell (1984, p. 45)]. Unfortunately, other governments, such as that of India, with similar aspirations and policies have been far less successful.

The circumstances in which technical learning best thrives is a matter on which research has not as yet generated conclusive results. As far as international inputs are concerned, it is clear that such learning can take place in developing countries both through informal and noncommercial contacts and through market processes in which TNCs, strictly defined, are not involved. Where TNCs *are* contributors to domestic technical learning, the advantages that their subsidiaries may enjoy – in terms of access to a wider network of expertise and experience [emphasized by Pack (1978)] – may be offset by the reduced incentives that these "advantages" leave for the development of local adaptive and developmental capacities. There is even some evidence for the proposition that in some industries and countries local firms that acquire technology at arm's-length rather than within direct foreign investment relationships perform better in respect of technical adaptation and innovation [Mytelka (1978, 1979)]; generalizations in this sphere, however, remain difficult to sustain [Germidis (1977)].[10]

There has been much argument about and many explanations for TNCs' purported penchant for the use of "inappropriate" technique. The need for private firms to appropriate the fruits of their investment in research and development suggests that, generally, they will concentrate on developing technique that cannot easily be replicated [Magee (1977)]. Unskilled labour-intensive processes and cheap, simple consumer and capital goods are therefore inherently unlikely to motivate much commercial R&D effort. Accordingly, and in the spirit of the above industrial organization analysis of TNCs, TNCs might be expected to cluster in industries – activities and products – in which scale is important, whether for reasons of production cost or for risk-spreading, skill and capital are

---

[10]There may be technical limits to factor substitution in production in some industries and processes, although there is almost always room for some maneouvre in respect of ancillary processes, e.g. transport, handling, administration. Adaptation in a labour-intensive direction is also often possible via increased utilization of plant capacity through more shifts and faster machine speeds, and via the use of lower quality inputs or older machinery, relaxation of output standards, subcontracting, etc. Another frequent source of technical adaptation to developing countries' situations is the use of smaller-scale plants; and this, in itself, is typically associated with greater labour intensity.

necessary inputs, and barriers to entry prevail. Even within industries, TNCs' access to cheaper capital and frequent payment of higher wages than domestic firms would suggest that, other things being equal, TNC subsidiaries would employ less appropriate, and particularly more import-intensive, techniques [Natke and Newfarmer (1985)].

The overall evidence as to the appropriateness of TNC production technique, however, does not support these propositions. The "appropriateness" of technique is typically assessed by comparing activity within TNC subsidiaries either with that of local firms or with that of the same TNC's activity in industrialized countries. When other characteristics like industry, firm size, etc. are controlled the technology employed by TNCs proves no more inappropriate than that of local firms [Helleiner (1975), Morley and Smith (1977), Moxon (1979)]. Indeed, the wider experience and superior information of foreign firms have led some to expect them to be *more* adaptive to local requirements than local firms can be, rather than less, and there is evidence in support of this proposition in Kenya and Thailand where such gaps in knowledge are presumably fairly wide [Pack (1976), Lecraw (1977)]. In some instances, TNCs actually seek to resist local pressure for more "modern", and less appropriate, technology. Perhaps the most important developmental effects of technologies introduced by TNCs are, in any case, less direct, more "dynamic" ones – relating to such issues as the degree of product differentiation, typical production scale, the degree of local competition, the generation of new technology, etc. [Newfarmer (1984, pp. 44–45)].

The transfer of consumption technology – the particular array of products into which product characteristics are congealed at any point in time and location – has generated widespread concern as well. Whereas new products typically expand consumption possibilities and thus increase the importing countries' welfare, there are some notorious cases, notably the marketing of infant formula in countries where breast-feeding is normally safer and more nutritious, and the sale of hazardous chemicals and drugs, where this is not the case. The nonexistence or weakness of consumer protection laws and services and/or the relatively limited experience with modern advertising techniques may render consumers in developing countries, particularly in the poorest societies, particularly vulnerable to misinformation and manipulation at the hands of sophisticated foreign (or local) firms. More broadly, what is at issue is the "appropriateness" of the product-mix available in developing countries, and the role of TNCs and the state in determining what it is. This is a matter raising difficult philosophical issues relating to freedom of choice. If there exists such a concept and objective as a socially optimal or desirable degree of product differentiation and a socially desirable consumption technology a government pursuing them is bound to run into conflict with private firms, both domestic and foreign, over the introduction of particular new products [James and Stewart (1981)]. It is not obvious, however, why TNCs should generate more difficulties in this respect than other profit-motivated domestic or foreign firms.

6.2. TNCs and export marketing

Apart from supplying technology the most important role of transnational corporations in developing countries has frequently been seen as overseas marketing (including the securing of market access where there are official or private barriers to entry). TNC involvement in manufacturing for export from developing countries is varied in its origins. Some involves a logical extension, often stimulated by local government incentives or performance requirements, of prior activities there – as in the further local processing of materials previously exported in their raw state, or the diversion or evolution of previously purely import-substituting activity to successful exporting. "Fresh" export activity is likely to involve either the international relocation of production of unskilled labour-intensive and mature-technology final products; or international subcontracting or production of components and processes usually of similar technological characteristics within vertically integrated or otherwise tightly organized international production systems [Sharpston (1975)]. Protectionism in the industrialized countries has somewhat held back expansion of the former kind, in which local firms have, in any case, usually been relatively more prominent; special tariff and other incentives, on the other hand, have encouraged the rapid growth of the latter "outward processing" or "offshore assembly" type. Where foreign capital is invested in this type of activity, the amounts are usually small and its behaviour is volatile [Flamm (1984)]. The relative importance of foreign direct investment in these activities has varied greatly as between developing countries [Helleiner (1973), Nayyar (1978)].

It is striking, nonetheless, that in the East Asian "success" stories of the 1960s and 1970s, whatever the role of foreign direct investment (which varied with the country) manufactured export marketing was undertaken primarily by foreign firms. In Singapore this was undertaken by TNCs for the output of wholly-owned or majority-owned subsidiaries. In other countries TNCs have been much less prominent, and developed country importers (or, in some cases, retail and department stores, wholesalers or trading companies) have performed these functions. The Korean experience suggests that in the early stages of development, marketing in an export promotion effort can be left largely to (non-TNC) foreign buyers and gradually turned over to local firms as experience and expertise are accumulated. As has been seen, contact with foreign buyers also generated significant technology transfer to Korean firms in the form of "guidance about styles, designs, and production and management techniques" [Rhee,

Ross-Larson and Pursell (1984, p. 65)]. The TNC role (and the role of DFI) in export marketing may be useful, but it is not apparently necessary.

6.3. Small, medium-sized, and Third World TNCs

Some interest and hope resides with the potential for smaller and medium-sized TNCs, some of them with small country and/or Third World homes [Agmon and Kindleberger (1977)], to play larger and more development-sensitive roles in the development process than the large OECD-based TNCs to which most of the TNC debates relate. To the extent that firm-specific intangibles and not sheer scale economies[11] are the basis of firms' advantage there is no reason why small firms should not "go transnational" at relatively early stages in their growth. The appearance of more small and medium-sized transnationals might increase world-wide competition at the individual industry level, particularly "loosening up" buyers' markets for technology and information, and make appropriate (especially smaller-scale) technologies more readily available, thus improving the prospects for developing country importers of TNC services via the new forms of international business. They might also offset tendencies toward concentration in markets for developing countries' manufactured (and other) exports [Tello (1986)].

Particular interest has surrounded the phenomenon of Third World transnationals [Kumar and McLeod (1981), Lall et al. (1983), Wells (1983)]. Third World transnationals have found niches of opportunity in which they possess comparative advantage – notably in more labour-intensive and standardized products, smaller-scale operations, and activities benefiting from cheap local materials or Third World experience; but they have also been successful, without necessarily undertaking direct foreign investment, in construction, consultancy, and a wide range of consumer and capital goods of a more capital-intensive and sometimes technologically more sophisticated type [Lall et al. (1983, pp. 16–17, 259–262)].

Smaller and medium-sized transnationals are unlikely to take over major shares of global activity in the near future. Management, finance, information, and marketing at the global level still benefit from the advantages of size and "the larger firms will continue to occupy the commanding heights of North–South investment" [Oman (1984a, p. 99)]. No doubt the lists of the world's largest firms will continue to include the names of more and more TNCs based in the developing countries as Brazilian, Indian, Korean and other countries' TNCs continue to expand. At the same time, however, in more specialized service activities and forms of production, small and medium-sized firms, both Northern

---

[11] It is possible that there may be scale economies in respect of the costs of international technology transfer that would require modification of this statement.

and Southern, both TNC and national, are likely gradually to increase in importance – to the benefit of the developing countries among others.

7. Conclusion

Economic analysis of transnational corporate activity has made major strides in recent years. From crude and oversimplified models of international capital flow the theoretical literature has shifted to approaches based upon industrial organization theory. Competitive assumptions are typically now supplanted by oligopoly models and attempts to analyse bargaining phenomena. Transactions costs vie with market imperfections as prime objects of attention in current analyses of TNCs. These developments characterize the literature on transnationals in the context of developing countries as well. In terms of relevant theory, the frontier at present seems to lie in the application of game-theoretic approaches to the analysis of host and home government–TNC relationships, and the application of industrial organization approaches to the modelling of the global markets in which the developing countries are most interested.

The most underworked empirical research frontier is thus that which takes as its starting point an industrial organization approach to global industries in which transnational corporations are important.[12] The actual effects of market concentration and internalization of international trade upon the gains from trade for developing countries are still only imperfectly understood. The economic role that TNCs play in individual developing countries is likely to be a product, in large part, of particular industry, firm and host country characteristics. The sources of firms' oligopolistic advantages, the precise nature of the key barriers to entry, and the overall structure of the global industry all are bound to influence their performance in particular countries; these factors also inevitably constrain the host countries' range of possible alternative policies and development paths.

There remains a major need to improve analytical understanding and collect empirical evidence on the determinants and effects (particularly on host countries' development) of the wide variety of alternative institutional forms of TNC (and other firms') involvement in developing countries. The rapid development of "new forms" of "international business" in recent years suggests that there are advantages perceived for some (perhaps all) parties in these alternative modes of interaction. Detailed theoretical and empirical analysis of the interaction of various external agents – whether in collusion or in competition – and consequent impacts upon home and host countries is now long overdue. The impact of

---

[12] See, however, Labys (1980), Stuckey (1982), Gereffi (1983), Grieco (1984), Newfarmer (1984), Grunwald and Flamm (1985).

alternative host governmental policies on the degree and form of TNC involvement in developing countries is another clear area for intensified research; similarly, the differential impact of alternative home government and international policies more generally on TNC activity in developing countries merits more research attention.

Much of the research that most needs doing is specific to particular types of developing country – according to such categories as level of development, creditworthiness, economic structure, etc. – and particular sectors and industries. Relevant theory must build upon improved information at a more disaggregated country and industry level than is frequently available. For the present the most productive research will probably be that which combines the insights of the new theories of TNC activity with micro-level case studies of particular industries and countries. At the same time further interdisciplinary effort to improve understanding of the political dimensions of relationships between TNCs, governments and interest groups in both host and home countries should also prove rewarding.

References

Agmon, T. and Kindleberger, C.P. eds. (1977) *Multinationals from small countries*. Cambridge, MA: M.I.T. Press.

Apter, D.E. and Goodman, L.W. eds. (1976) *The multinational corporation and social change*. New York: Praeger.

Balasubramanyan, V. (1984) 'Incentives and disincentives for foreign direct investment in less developed countries', *Weltwirtschaftliches Archiv*, 120:720–735.

Baranson, J. (1970) 'Technology transfer through the international firm', *American Economic Review*, 60:435–440.

Bardhan, P.K. (1982) 'Imports, domestic production, and transnational vertical integration: A theoretical note', *Journal of Political Economy*, 90:1020–1034.

Bhagwati, J. and Brecher, R.A. (1980) 'National welfare in an open economy in the presence of foreign owned factors of production', *Journal of International Economics*, 19:103–115.

Bhagwati, J. and Brecher, R.A. (1981) 'Foreign ownership and the theory of trade and welfare', *Journal of Political Economy*, 89:497–511.

Bhagwati, J. and Tironi, E. (1980) 'Tariff change, foreign capital and immiserization: A theoretical analysis', *Journal of Development Economics*, 7:71–83.

Biersteker, T.J. (1978) *Distortion or development: Contending perspectives on the multinational corporation*. Cambridge, MA: M.I.T. Press.

Bornschier, V. (1980) 'Multinational corporations and economic growth: A cross-national test of the decapitalization thesis', *Journal of Development Economics*, 7:191–210.

Brecher, R.A. and Diaz-Alejandro, C.F. (1977) 'Tariffs, foreign capital and immiserizing growth', *Journal of International Economics*, 7:317–322.

Brecher, R.A. and Findlay, R. (1983) 'Tariffs, foreign capital and national advantage with sector-specific factors', *Journal of International Economics*, 14:277–288.

Buckley, P.J. and Casson, M. (1976) *The future of the multinational enterprise*. London: Macmillan.

Casson, M. (1979) *Alternatives to the multinational enterprise*. London: Macmillan.

Caves, R.E. (1982) *Multinational enterprise and economic analysis*. Cambridge, MA: Cambridge University Press.

Caves, R., Crookell, H., and Killing, P. (1983) *The imperfect market for technology licenses*. Oxford: Oxford Bulletin of Economics and Statistics.

1476   *G.K. Helleiner*

Chudnovsky, D. (1981) 'Regulating technology imports in some developing countries', *Trade and Development*, 3:133–150.
Connor, J.M. (1977) *The market power of multinationals: A quantitative analysis of U.S. corporations in Brazil and Mexico*. New York: Praeger.
Diaz-Alejandro, C.F. (1979) 'International markets for exhaustible resources, less developed countries, and multinational corporations', in: R.G. Hawkins, ed., *Research in international business and finance: An annual compilation of research*, Vol. I. The economic effects of multinational corporations. Greenwich, CT: JAI Press.
Diaz-Alejandro, C.F. (1981) 'The less developed countries and transnational enterprises', in: S. Grassman and E. Lundberg, eds., *The world economic order: Past and prospects*. London: Macmillan.
Dolan, M.B. and Tomlin, B (1980) 'First World–Third World linkages: External relations and economic development', *International Organization*, 34:41–63.
Doyle, C. and van Wijnbergen, S. (1984) 'Taxation of foreign multinationals: A sequential bargaining approach to tax holidays', Discussion Paper no. 25, London: Centre for Economic Policy Research.
Dunning, J.H. (1981) *International production and the multinational enterprise*. London: George Allen and Unwin.
Dunning, J.H., ed. (1985) *Multinational enterprises, economic structure and international competitiveness*. New York: Wiley.
Eaton, J. and Gersovitz, M. (1984) 'A theory of expropriation and deviations from perfect capital mobility', *Economic Journal*, 94:16–40.
Emerson, C. (1982) 'Mining enclaves and taxation', *World Development*, 10:561–571.
Encarnacion, J. and Wells, T. (1984) 'Competitive strategies in global industries: A view from the host country', mimeo, Harvard business school colloquium on competition in global industries.
Encarnacion, J. and Wells, T. (1985) 'Sovereignty en garde: Negotiating with foreign investors', *International Organization*, 39:47–78.
Encarnacion, J. and Wells, T. (1986) 'Evaluating foreign investment', in: T.H. Moran et al., eds., *Investing in development: New roles for private capital?* Washington, DC: Overseas Development Council, 61–86.
Evans, P. (1979) *Dependent development: The alliance of multinational, state and local capital in Brazil*. Princeton, NJ: Princeton University Press.
Faber, M. and Brown, R. (1980) Changing the rules of the game: Political risk, instability and fair play in mineral concession contracts, *Third World Quarterly*, 2.
Fagre, N. and Wells, L.T., Jr. (1982) 'Bargaining power of multinationals and host countries', *Journal of International Business*, 13:9–23.
Faundez, J. and Picciotto, S., eds. (1978) *The nationalization of multinationals in peripheral economies*. London: Macmillan.
Flamm, K. (1984) 'The volatility of offshore investment', *Journal of Development Economics*, 16:231–248.
Frank, R.T. and Freeman, R.T. (1978) *Distributional consequences of direct foreign investment*. New York: Academic Press.
Garnaut, R. and Clunies-Ross, A. (1975) 'Uncertainty, risk aversion and the taxation of natural resource projects', *Economic Journal*, 85:273–289.
Garnaut, R. and Clunies-Ross, A. (1983) *Taxation of mineral rent*. Oxford.
Gereffi, G. (1983) *The pharmaceutical industry and dependency in the Third World*. Princeton, NJ: Princeton University Press.
Germidis, D., ed. (1977) *Transfer of technology by multinational corporations*, Vols. I and II. Paris: OECD.
Girvan, N. (1976) *Corporate imperialism: Conflict and expropriation*. White Plains, NY: M.E. Sharpe.
Glover, D. (1986) 'Transnational corporations and Third World agriculture', in: T.H. Moran et al., eds., *Investing in development: New roles for private capital?* Washington, DC: Overseas Development Council.
Goodsell, C.T. (1974) *American corporations and Peruvian politics*. Cambridge, MA: Harvard University Press.
Grieco, J.M. (1984) *Between dependency and autonomy: India's experience with the international computer industry*. Berkeley, CA: University of California Press.

Grieco, J.M. (1986) 'Foreign investment and development: Theories and evidence', in: T.H. Moran et al., eds., *Investing in development: New roles for private capital?* Washington, DC: Overseas Development Council, 35–60.

Grossman, G. (1984) 'International trade, foreign investment, and the formation of the entrepreneurial class', *American Economic Review*, 74:605–614.

Grunwald, J. and Flamm, K. (1985) *The global factory, foreign assembly in international trade.* Washington, DC: Brookings Institution.

Guisinger, S. (1985) *Investment incentives and performance requirements: A comparative analysis of country foreign investment policies.* Washington, DC: World Bank.

Helleiner, G.K. (1973) 'Manufactured exports from less developed countries and multinational firms', *Economic Journal*, 83:21–47.

Helleiner, G.K. (1975) 'The role of multinational corporations in the less developed countries' trade in technology', *World Development*, 3:161–189.

Helleiner, G.K. (1977) 'International technology issues: Southern needs and northern responses', in: J.N. Bhagwati, ed., *The new international economic order: The North-South debate.* Cambridge, MA: M.I.T. Press, 295–316.

Helleiner, G.K. (1981) *Intra-firm trade and the developing countries.* London: Macmillan.

Hirschman, A.O. (1969) *How to divest in Latin America, and why: Essays in international finance.* Princeton, NJ: Princeton University, 76.

Horst, T. (1971) 'The theory of the multinational firm: Optimal behavior under different tariff and tax rules', *Journal of Political Economy*, 79: 1059–1072.

Hufbauer, G.C. (1975) 'The multinational corporation and direct investment', in: P.B. Kenen, ed., *International trade and finance: Frontiers for research.* Cambridge, MA: Cambridge University Press, 253–319.

Hughes, H. (1975) 'Economic rents, the distribution of gains from mineral exploitation, and mineral development policy', *World Development*, 3:11–12 and 811–825.

Hymer, S.H. (1976) *The international operations of national firms: A study of direct foreign investment.* Cambridge, MA: M.I.T. Press.

ILO (International Labour Office) (1976) *The impact of multinational enterprises on employment and training.* Geneva.

IMF (1985) 'Foreign private investment in developing countries', Occasional Paper no. 33, Washington.

Jackman, R.W. (1982) 'Dependence on foreign investment and economic growth in the Third World', *World Politics*, 34: 175–196.

James, J. and Stewart, F. (1981) 'New products: a discussion of the welfare effects of the introduction of new products in developing countries', *Oxford Economic Papers*, 33, 1, March: 81–107.

Jenkins, R. (1984) *Transnational corporations and industrial transformation in Latin America.* London: Macmillan.

Jodice, D.A. (1980) 'Sources of change in Third World regimes for foreign direct investment, 1968–76', *International Organization*, 34:177–206.

Johnson, H.G. (1970) 'The efficiency and welfare implications of the multinational corporation', in: C.P. Kindleberger, ed., *The international corporation: A symposium.* Cambridge, MA: M.I.T. Press.

Keohane, R.O. and Ooms, V.D. (1975) 'The multinational firm and international regulation', in: C.F. Bergsten and L.B. Krause, eds., *World politics and international economics.* Washington, DC: Brookings Institution.

Kindleberger, C.P. (1984) *Multinational excursions.* Cambridge, MA: M.I.T. Press.

Kindleberger, C.P. and Audretsch, D., eds. (1983) *The multinational corporation in the 1980s.* Cambridge, MA: M.I.T. Press.

Kobrin, S.J. (1980) 'Foreign enterprise and forced divestment in LDCs', *International Organization*, 34:65–88.

Kojima, K. (1978) *Direct foreign investment: A Japanese model of multinational business operations.* New York: Praeger.

Kojima, K. (1985) 'Japanese and American direct investment in Asia: A comparative analysis', *Hitotsubashi Journal of Economics*, 26:1–35.

Kopits, G.F. (1976) 'Taxation and multinational firm behavior: A critical survey', *IMF Staff Papers*, 23:624–673.

Krugman, P. (1979) 'A model of innovation, technology transfer, and the world distribution of income', *Journal of Political Economy*, 87:253–266.

Kumar, K., ed. (1980) *Transnational enterprises: Their impact on Third World societies and cultures*. Boulder, CO: Westview.

Kumar, K. and McLeod, M.G., eds. (1981) *Multinationals from developing countries*. Lexington, MA: Lexington Books, D.C. Heath.

Labys, W.C. (1980) *Market structure, bargaining power, and resource price formation*. Lexington, MA: Lexington Books, D.C. Heath.

Lal, D. (1975) *Appraising foreign investment in developing countries*. London: Heinemann.

Lall, S. (1973) 'Transfer pricing by multinational manufacturing firms', *Oxford Bulletin of Economics and Statistics*, 35:179–195.

Lall, S. (1978) 'Transnationals, domestic enterprises, and industrial structure in host LDCs: A survey', *Oxford Economic Papers*, 30:217–248.

Lall, S. and Bibile, S. (1977) 'The political economy of controlling transnationals: The pharmaceutical industry in Sri Lanka, 1972–76', *World Development*, 5:677–698.

Lall, S. and Streeten, P. (1977) *Foreign investment, transnationals and developing countries*. London: Macmillan.

Lall, S., et al. (1983) *The new multinationals, the spread of Third World enterprises*. Wiley.

Lecraw, D. (1977) 'Direct investment by firms from less developed countries', *Oxford Economic Papers*.

Lessard, D.R. and Williamson, J. (1985) 'Financial intermediation beyond the debt crisis', *Policy analyses in international economics*, Vol. 12. Washington, DC: Institute for International Economics.

Lipsey, R.E. and Kravis, I.B. (1985) 'The competitive position of U.S. manufacturing firms', *Banca Nazionale del Lavoro quarterly review*, 153:127–154.

Lipson, C. (1985) *Standing guard, protecting foreign capital in the nineteenth and twentieth centuries*. Berkeley, CA: University of California Press.

Lombard, F.J. (1979) *The foreign investment screening process in LDCs: The case of Colombia*. Boulder, CO: Westview.

MacDougall, G.D.A. (1960) 'The benefits and costs of private investment from abroad: A theoretical approach', *Economic Record*, 36:13–35.

Magdoff, H. (1976) 'The multinational corporation and development - a contradiction?', in: D. Apter and L. Goodman, eds., *The multinational corporation and social change*. New York: Praeger.

Magee, S.P. (1977) 'Information and multinational corporations: An appropriability theory of direct foreign investment', in: J. Bhagwati, ed., *The new international economic order*. Cambridge, MA: M.I.T. Press, 317–340.

Mattelart, A. (1983) *Transnationals and the Third World: The struggle for culture*. South Hadley, MA.

Mikesell, R.F. (1971) *Foreign investment in petroleum and mineral industries: Case studies of investor-host country relations*. Baltimore, MD: Johns Hopkins Press for Resources for the Future.

Mikesell, R.F. (1979) *New patterns of world mineral development*. British–North America Committee.

Moran, T.H. (1974) *Multinational corporations and the politics of dependence: Copper in Chile*. Princeton, NJ: Princeton University Press.

Moran, T.H. (1978) 'Multinational corporations and dependency: A dialogue for dependistas and non-dependistas', *International Organization*, 32.

Morley, S.A. and Smith, G.W. (1977) 'Limited search and the technology choices of multinational firms in Brazil', *Quarterly Journal of Economics*, 91:263–288.

Moxon, R.W. (1979) 'The cost, conditions, and adaptations of MNC technology in developing countries', in: R.G. Hawkins, ed., *Research in international business and finance: An annual compilation of research*, *The economic effects of multinational corporations*, Vol. I. Greenwich, CT: JAI Press.

Murray, R., ed. (1981) *Multinationals beyond the market, intra-firm trade and the control of transfer pricing*. Brighton: Harvester Press.

Mytelka, L. (1978) 'Licensing and technology dependence in the Andean Group', *World Development*, 6:447–460.

Mytelka, L. (1979) *Regional development in a global economy: The multinational corporation, technology and Andean integration.* New Haven, CT: Yale University Press.

Natke, P. and Newfarmer, R.S. (1985) 'Transnational corporations, trade propensities and transfer pricing', *Transnational corporations and international trade: Selected issues.* New York: United Nations Centre on Transnational Corporations.

Nayyar, D. (1978) 'Transnational corporations and manufactured exports from poor countries', *Economic Journal,* 88:59–84.

Newfarmer, R. (1979) 'TNC takeovers in Brazil, the uneven distribution of benefits in the market for firms', *World Development,* 7:25–43.

Newfarmer, R., ed. (1984) *Profits, progress and poverty: Case studies of international industry.* South Bend, IN: University of Notre Dame Press.

Newfarmer, R. and Marsh, L. (1981) 'Foreign ownership, market structure and industrial performance: Brazil's electrical industry', *Journal of Development Economics,* 8:47–75.

OECD (1983) *Investing in developing countries.* Paris.

OECD (1985) *Twenty-five years of development co-operation, a review. Efforts and policies of the members of the Development Assistance Committee, 1985 Report.* Paris.

Oman, C. (1984a) *New forms of international investment in developing countries.* Paris: OECD.

Oman, C., ed. (1984b) *New forms of international investment in developing countries, the national perspective.* Paris: OECD.

Ozawa, T. (1979) *Multinationalism, Japanese style: The political economy of outward dependency.* Princeton, NJ: Princeton University Press.

Pack, H. (1976) 'The substitution of labour for capital in Kenyan manufacturing', *Economic Journal,* 86:45–58.

Pack, H. (1979) 'Technology and employment: Constraints on optimal performance', in: S. Rosenblatt, ed., *Technology and economic development: A realistic appraisal.* Boulder, CO: Westview.

Penrose, E. (1976) '"Ownership and control", multinational firms in less developed countries', in: G.K. Helleiner, ed., *A world divided, the less developed countries in the international economy.* New York: Cambridge University Press, 147–174.

Philip, G. (1976) 'The limitations of bargaining theory: a case study of the International Petroleum Company in Peru', *World Development,* 4:231–239.

Radetzki, M. (1982) 'Has political risk scared mineral investment away from the deposits in developing countries?', *World Development,* 10:1.

Radetzki, M. and Zorn, S. (1979) *Financing mining projects in developing countries.* London.

Reuber, G.L., et al. (1973) *Private foreign investment in development.* Oxford: Clarendon Press.

Rhee, Y.W., Ross-Larson, B., and Pursell, G. (1984) 'Korea's competitive edge', *Managing the entry into world markets.* Baltimore, MD: Johns Hopkins University Press.

Rugman, A.M. and Eden, L., eds. (1985) *Multinationals and transfer pricing.* London: Croom Helm.

Schneider, F. and Frey, B.S. (1985) 'Economic and political determinants of foreign direct investment', *World Development,* 13:161–175.

Shafer, M. (1983) 'Capturing the mineral multinationals: Advantage or disadvantage?', *International Organization,* 37(1):93–119.

Sharpston, M. (1975) 'International subcontracting', *Oxford Economic Papers,* 27:94–135.

Sklar, R.L. (1975) *Corporate power in an African state: The political impact of multinational mining companies in Zambia.* Berkeley, CA: University of California Press.

Smith, D.N. and Wells, L.T., Jr. (1975) *Negotiating Third World mineral agreements.* Cambridge, MA: Ballinger.

Stepan, A. (1978) *The state and society.* Princeton, NJ: Princeton University Press.

Stobaugh, R. and Wells, L.T., Jr., eds. (1984) *Technology crossing borders.* Boston, MA: Harvard Business School Press.

Stopford, J.M. and Wells, L.T., Jr. (1972) *Managing the multinational enterprise.* New York: Basic Books.

Streeten, P. (1973) 'The multinational enterprise and the theory of development policy', *World Development,* 1:1–14.

Streeten, P. (1976) 'Bargaining with multinationals', *World Development,* 4:225–229.

Stuckey, J.A. (1982) *Vertical integration and joint ventures in the aluminum industry.* Cambridge, MA: Harvard University Press.

Svejnar, J. and Smith, S. (1984) 'The economics of joint ventures in less developed countries', *Quarterly Journal of Economics*, 99:149–167.

Teece, D.J. (1977) 'Technology transfer by multinational firms: The resource cost of transferring technological knowhow', *Economic Journal*, 87:242–261.

Tello, M. (1986) 'Imperfect international competition, multinational enterprises and manufactured exports from developing countries', Ph.D. thesis, University of Toronto, unpublished.

UNESCO (United Nations Educational, Scientific and Cultural Organization) (1982) *Transnational corporations and endogenous development: Effects on culture, communications, education, science and technology*. Paris: UNESCO.

United Nations (1974) *Multinational corporations in world development*. New York: United Nations.

United Nations (1978) *Transnational corporations in world development: A re-examination*. New York: United Nations.

United Nations (1979) *Transnational corporations in advertising*. New York: United Nations.

United Nations (1982) *Transnational corporations in international tourism*. New York: United Nations.

United Nations (1983) *Transnational corporations in world development, third survey*. New York: United Nations.

Vaitsos, C.V. (1974) *Intercountry income distribution and transnational enterprises*. Oxford: Clarendon Press.

Vaitsos, C.V. (1976) 'Power, knowledge and development policy: Relations between transnational enterprises and developing countries', in: G.K. Helleiner, ed., *A world divided, the less developed countries in the international economy*. New York: Cambridge University Press, 113–146.

Vernon, R. (1977) *Storm over the multinationals: The real issues*. Cambridge, MA: Harvard University Press.

Wells, L.T. (1983) *Third World multinationals, the rise of foreign investment from developing countries*. Cambridge, MA: M.I.T. Press.

Williamson, O.E. (1975) *Markets and hierarchies: Analysis and anti-trust implications*. New York: Free Press.

Chapter 28

DISEQUILIBRIUM AND STRUCTURAL ADJUSTMENT

SEBASTIAN EDWARDS

*University of California, Los Angeles
and National Bureau of Economic Research*

SWEDER VAN WIJNBERGEN*

*World Bank
and National Bureau of Economic Research*

Contents

*We would like to thank Vittorio Corbo, Jon Eaton, and in particular T.N. Srinivasan for helpful comments on earlier drafts of this chapter. Edwards gratefully acknowledges financial support from the National Science Foundation, Grant SES-8419932.

Handbook of Development Economics, Volume II, Edited by H. Chenery and T.N. Srinivasan
© *Elsevier Science Publishers B.V., 1989*

1. Introduction

Starting in the early 1980s countries all across the development spectrum had to adopt a series of policy measures aimed at coping with the severe international economic crisis. Although world relative prices (i.e. terms of trade) went into convulsions much earlier (i.e. 1970s), the easy access to international capital markets in the aftermath of the oil price shocks of 1973 allowed many countries to postpone or spread out adjustment to adverse terms of trade and interest rate developments in the world economy. The debt crisis that developed in mid-1982 effectively put an end to that policy option. An increasing number of countries had to go through severe adjustments of their economies, either because absence of further capital inflows left no other option, or because this type of adjustment was made a precondition by the private banks and the multilateral agencies before new money would be released. These programs have become known as "structural adjustment" programs.

A structural adjustment program can be defined as a set of policy measures that attempts to permanently change relative prices of tradable to nontradable goods in the economy, in order to reallocate, or help along reallocation of, production factors in accordance with the new set of external and domestic economic conditions. These new economic conditions many times are the result of external disturbances, such as terms of trade shocks, that tend to create a crisis situation in the country in question. Other times structural adjustment programs are implemented after inconsistent domestic macroeconomic policies provoke serious disequilibria that are not sustainable in the long run.

Structural adjustment programs can be divided into two broad groups: (1) those implemented as a result of exogenous or international shocks that generate serious macroeconomic disequilibria; and (2) those programs enacted as a response to domestic policies that become unsustainable (or undesirable) in the long run.

We first concentrate on foreign-disturbances-induced programs. The most common type of exogenous shock is related to terms of trade changes. For example, the oil shocks of the 1970s forced many oil importing countries (both developed and underdeveloped) to implement adjustment programs aimed at reducing oil consumption and reallocating investment. Naturally, the response to this crisis was not uniform across countries. While some decided to slow down the rate of growth of consumption, others resorted to foreign borrowing to finance new investment programs and to maintain the consumption pattern. The drastic hike in world interest rates in the late 1970s and early 1980s is another recent example of a major exogenous shock. These developments forced many countries to adapt their development strategies to the new international environment. In some cases this shock was so overwhelming – as in most Latin American nations – that some countries had to enter into broad negotiation processes with their creditors to reschedule their foreign debts.

Although many structural adjustment programs respond to adverse terms of trade shocks, there are a number of cases where *positive* terms of trade disturbances or (what is almost equivalent) natural resource discoveries have led to major adjustment processes. The economic consequences of these positive developments in natural resources based exportable sectors have become known as the "Dutch Disease" problem. In Section 2 of this chapter we deal with some of the more important policy issues of the Dutch Disease.

The second broad group of structural adjustment programs is a response to domestic policies – either macro or micro – that become unsustainable in the long run. Within this broad category it is possible to further distinguish between those adjustment programs stemming from balance of payments crises, and those that seek to reduce the extent of microeconomic distortions (i.e. impediments to trade), independently of the macroeconomic and balance of payments situations. Although the latter type of program is not too common, from an analytical point of view it is crucial to investigate the ramifications of this kind of structural adjustment processes. For example, it is perfectly possible to think that due to political or other reasons a country such as India – that has traditionally maintained relative macroeconomic stability – decides to get rid of some of its many atavistic microeconomic distortions, including price controls, subsidies, licensing schemes, trade restrictions and so on. In Section 4 of this chapter we discuss in detail the implications of this type of structural adjustment program, where an opening up of the economy is assumed to take place in an environment with no balance of payments crises.

Structural adjustment programs that stem from severe macroeconomic and balance of payments disequilibria have been a recurrent phenomenon in Latin America. By now it is possible to identify a common pattern that fits, from a historical point of view, most (but not all) of the Latin American balance of payments crises [see Edwards (1987)]. At some point, responding to political or other pressures, the country's macroeconomic (and in particular fiscal) policies become inconsistent with the chosen nominal exchange rate regime. As a result the Central Bank begins to lose international reserves and the real exchange rate begins to become increasingly overvalued. The authorities, in an effort to stop the drainage of reserves, impose new forms of trade and exchange controls. In the absence of corrective measures that attack the source of the disequilibrium – the inconsistent macroeconomic policies – these exchange controls can only delay the final outcome of the crisis. As a side-effect pervasive black markets for foreign exchange develop, which further magnify the distortions introduced during the process. After some time these policies become clearly unsustainable, and a stabilization cum structural adjustment package, that usually includes a massive devaluation and a liberalization component, is implemented. Section 6 of this chapter deals with some of the most important aspects of this type of program.

The purpose of this chapter is to provide a *selective* survey of several important analytical and empirical issues related to structural adjustment programs, placing special emphasis on the interaction between disequilibrium situations, relative price changes and structural adjustment programs. Since, as pointed out above, structural adjustment programs may take many forms, as do the macro problems associated with them, there is little to be gained from attempts to provide a very general treatment. Instead, we will present a series of models that can handle in a useful way those external and domestic shocks or policy changes that most often require structural adjustment programs. Specifically, in the first part of this survey we cover: (a) changes that influence the sustainable level of aggregate demand and thus the real exchange rate; for example changes in aid flows, an oil discovery, or exogenous changes in debt services burden; (b) changes in the international terms of trade and changes in domestic trade policies; and (c) changes in capital market intervention, for example through a liberalization of the capital account of the balance of payments. This covers what are probably the most important causes of adjustment problems, trade reform and terms of trade shocks.[1] We also discuss the important problem of gradualism versus shock treatment in external sector reforms.

In the second part of the chapter (Section 6) we look at the one macroeconomic policy instrument that has the most direct impact on relative prices, i.e. the nominal exchange rate. We assess its impact on relative prices and labor and commodity market equilibrium. This allows evaluation of the extent to which exchange rate policy can help or jeopardize structural adjustment packages.

2. Natural resource income, aid flows, and the real exchange rate

2.1. Introduction

In recent years a great deal of attention has been devoted to the allegedly harmful consequences of natural resource discoveries. Whether it is natural gas in the Netherlands or oil in Mexico, such discoveries have caused *structural* problems that have required that the economy embarks in major adjustment processes. These structural problems have often been almost as severe as the problems that the absence of indigenous resources has undoubtedly caused in less fortunate countries. These problems have been given a name, the "Dutch Disease", which prompted *The Economist* to comment that "to refer to a vast

---

[1]The oil price increase covered in the preceding section is of course also a terms-of-trade shock, but a rather special one in that it involves intermediate goods imports.

valuable energy resource as the source of a disease is surely ungrateful".

There is a sizeable literature dealing with the Dutch disease. Existing models from international trade, open economy macroeconomics, and natural resource depletion have been extended to study the intersectoral shifts induced by a resource boom and to examine the possible rationale for government intervention. At a more applied level many case studies have examined the necessary steps in the adjustment to the exploitation of oil, gas or coal discoveries in individual countries.

The large-scale exploitation of natural resource discoveries is a real rather than a monetary shock to an economy since its primary impact falls on the level of real income and on the intersectoral allocation of factors of production. Hence, it is natural to analyze the consequences of such discoveries with a real model that abstracts from monetary considerations. Further simplification is possible if we focus on the static effects of a resource boom. This is done in the following subsection using a simple static framework to examine the consequences of this type of shock on relative prices, the size of the exposed trade sector and the level of unemployment. In the third and final subsection, we introduce a two-period model, and examine the effects of a boom on the intertemporal allocation of resources.

Three points should be made before we proceed. The first is that, although the initiating disturbance in all the·models we consider is the discovery and exploitation of natural resources, we ignore issues of optimal depletion rates.

A second issue which should be clarified at the outset relates to the use of the term "Dutch Disease". In fact, there is no presumption that the consequences of a natural resource discovery are harmful. On the contrary, its initial impact is beneficial and amounts to a Pareto improvement for the economy as a whole. Of course, legitimate grounds for concern may arise over the distribution of the gains, over the issue of whether transitional assistance should be offered to declining sectors, and over the issue of the appropriate response to various market failures which may impede the smooth adjustment of the economy to its new equilibrium. However, as we shall point out on a number of occasions, the case for treatment of the "disease" must be considered on its merits in each individual case.

The third point is the similarity, from a structural adjustment and macroeconomic point of view, between increased income from natural resources and aid inflows. Both provide an increase in foreign exchange availability at little or no additional use of domestic factors of production; moreover, both are almost certainly temporary. Finally, both come in the form of additional foreign exchange, but will, at least partially, be spent on nontraded goods, thus putting upward pressure on the real exchange rate.

The resource allocation consequences of a resource-based export boom (or of increased foreign aid) are a shift of labor out of manufacturing and agricultural sectors and into (often) urban services, upward pressure on real wages in terms of tradable goods, and a decline in external competitiveness. A decline in export performance is then unavoidable unless specific policy measures are taken to counteract it. In the particular case of foreign aid this a reason for concern, since one of the main purposes of development aid has always been the promotion of a viable export sector, in the hope that future export revenues so generated would over time do away with the external sector constraint. The conflict between substantial volumes of aid and export promotion is a dilemma policymakers will need to face.

In the next subsection we discuss the short- and long-run adjustment problems that may arise after increases in natural resource income due to either new discoveries or price increases, and after increases in aid inflows; we will for brevity's sake often refer to aid only, in the understanding that the effects are the same as with increased natural resource income.

2.2. Unemployment problems

2.2.1. Unemployment, real wage indexation, and the real exchange rate

The simplest general-equilibrium model within which the static effects of increased aid inflows (or higher resource income) can be analyzed is one which distinguishes between two sectors; one produces a single nontraded good whose price is determined endogenously by the interaction of domestic supply and demand, and the other produces a composite traded good whose price is fixed exogenously. We shall denote the output levels of these two sectors by x_N and x_M ("M" for "manufacturing"), respectively. Hence, when we think of natural resource revenues rather than aid, we assume that the natural resource sector does not directly compete with other sectors for factors of production. As a consequence, the resource boom operates in exactly the same manner as an exogenous increase in aid. Subsection 2.2.1.1 analyzes a market-clearing version of the model; Subsection 2.2.1.2 considers the case where domestic wages and prices do not adjust instantaneously.

2.2.1.1. The spending effect of higher aid inflows. Equilibrium in this economy can be characterized solely in terms of the market-clearing condition for the non-traded good. In obvious notation, this may be written as:

$$x_N(q) = c_N(q, y).$$

$$(2.1)$$

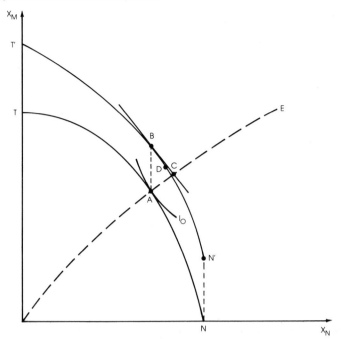

Figure 28.1

Here, x_N and c_N denote domestic production and consumption of the nontraded good, respectively, and equilibrium in the market is brought about by adjustment of the relative price of nontraded to traded goods, q. This price is thus a key variable in this economy: its inverse is often referred to as the *real exchange rate*. While output of the nontraded good depends solely on the real exchange rate, demand depends also on the level of real income, denoted by $y = qx_N + x_T + v$, where v is the value of the aid inflow. Aid raises real income in a once-and-for-all fashion, and the resulting excess demand for the nontraded good raises q, an outcome which we will refer to as a "real appreciation".

The implication of this disturbance for the pattern of output in the economy may be illustrated using the Salter (1959) diagram in Figure 28.1. Nontraded goods output is measured along the horizontal axis and traded goods output (including both manufacturing output and aid) along the vertical axis. The curve *TN* is the economy's initial production possibilities frontier, depending on domestic technology and factor endowments. Before the boom, equilibrium is determined by the intersection of this curve with the highest attainable social indifference curve, I_0, at point *A* [see Neary and van Wijnbergen (1986)]. The effect of aid is to shift the production possibilities curve vertically upwards to $T'N'N$, as shown.

The initial equilibrium relative price equals the slope of the common tangent to the two curves at point A. If this were to remain unchanged, the production point would shift vertically upwards to point B: domestic output of both manufactures and nontraded goods remains unchanged but total domestic availability of traded goods is augmented by the extent of the additional resource output. With production and therefore domestic real income determined at B, desired consumption must lie along the price line tangential to B. Moreover, since relative prices are unchanged, it must take place at the point C, where the price line intersects the income-consumption through A, OAE. The resulting excess demand for nontradables drives up their relative price until the new equilibrium at a point such as D is attained.

The characteristics of this new equilibrium are obvious: domestic welfare has risen, but at the expense of a reallocation of production – the output of the nontraded good has risen, whereas that of manufacturing has *fallen*: the spending effect of higher aid thus unambiguously gives rise to *both* deindustrialization and a real appreciation.

2.2.1.2. The effects of wage and price rigidities. In the preceding discussion we have assumed that the wage rate and the price of the nontraded good are perfectly flexible, so that the economy moves instantaneously to the new equilibrium. If this is not the case, then the adjustment process may be costly; in the short run agents on the long side of either market will be rationed in the manner familiar from the "disequilibrium" or "fix-price" macroeconomic literature [see Malinvaud (1977), Neary (1980) and Neary and van Wijnbergen (1986)]. It might be thought that the only disequilibrium regime to which higher aid can give rise is one of labor shortage. However, as we shall see, this turns out to hinge crucially on the wage setting mechanism. To examine the consequences of wage–price rigidities for the adjustment process, we first show how different exogenous values of the wage and the price of the nontraded good give rise to different disequilibrium regimes. To illustrate this we first locate the equilibrium conditions for the nontraded and labor markets in the (w, q) space, where w is the wage rate measured in terms of traded goods, and then we divide that space into different disequilibrium regions (see Figure 28.2).

Let us consider first the labor market equilibrium locus. Since labor supply is exogenous, the notional locus is unaffected if households are rationed in the nontraded good market. (We assume throughout that no agents are ever rationed in the market for traded goods.) The labor market is then captured by the following equation:

$$l_N(q/w) + l_M(w) = L, \qquad (2.2)$$

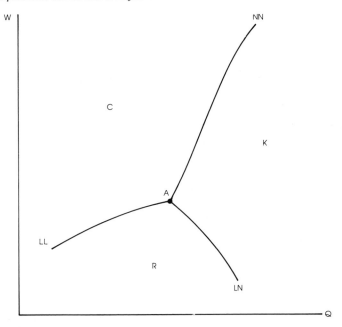

Figure 28.2

where L is the total available labor supply, assumed to be fixed, while l_N and l_M are the labor demand functions in the nontraded and traded sectors. Notice that in the traded sector this demand depends negatively on w, while in the nontraded sector it depends positively on q/w. This locus is then labelled LL, an upward sloping curve that extends to the left of point A in Figure 28.2. To the right of that point, however, there is excess supply of the nontraded good. Domestic producers are rationed therefore, and scale down their labor demand in the face of the sales constraint they face. Thus, the labor market equilibrium locus in this region is given not by (2.2) but by:

$$l_N^c[c_N(q, y)] + l_M(w) = L, \tag{2.3}$$

where both the level of real income, $y(= qx_N + x_M + v)$, and the production of nontraded goods, x_N, are demand-determined. l_N^c is the output-constrained labor demand function in the nontraded sector. The key feature of this locus is that, because employment in the nontraded good sector is now demand-determined, it depends negatively rather than positively on the relative price of the nontraded good, q. The locus is therefore downward- rather than upward-sloping in (w, q) space, and is denoted by the line LN in Figure 28.2.

Consider next the equilibrium locus for the nontraded good market. We may confine attention to the case where unemployment prevails, since under excess demand for labor the effective nontraded good market equilibrium locus coincides with the *LN* curve just derived [see Neary (1980) and van Wijnbergen (1984b)]. With unemployment, the locus is formally identical to the standard case, except that the level of income is no longer at its full employment level but is determined endogenously:

$$y = qx_{\mathrm{N}}(q, w) + x_{\mathrm{M}}(w) + v, \tag{2.4}$$

where v is the value of the aid inflow. This locus is labelled *NN* in Figure 28.2. It may be checked that it is upward-sloping and more steeply sloped than the corresponding notional locus.

As a result of taking account of the spillovers between markets arising from wage and price rigidities, the diagram is partitioned into three regions, each corresponding to a different disequilibrium regime. Following Malinvaud (1977), these are labelled *C* for Classical unemployment, *K* for Keynesian unemployment and *R* for repressed inflation. The next step is investigate the effects of increased aid, v, on the loci. It is clear from equation (2.2) that the *LL* locus is not affected. However, the same is not true of the *NN* and *LN* loci. The increase in aid leads to a greater demand for the nontraded good and, in Figure 28.3, the Walrasian equilibrium shifts from *A* to point *D*. An important feature of the adjustment process is that, contrary to the case of full wage flexibility, the economy does not immediately jump to *D* but instead remains in the short run at point *A*. Relative to the new equilibrium, this point is on the *LL* locus but to the right of the *NN* and *LN* loci. Hence, the initial effect of the resource boom is to leave the labor market in equilibrium and to induce excess demand for the nontraded good.

The principal question of interest is how the economy will move from *A* to *D*, and, in particular, whether any unemployment will emerge during the adjustment period. Without specifying the dynamics of adjustment in detail, we may presume that the relative price of the nontraded good will rise in response to excess demand. However, the behavior of the wage rate is more complex and depends on the wage indexation rule which is adopted. Following van Wijnbergen (1984b), we assume that real consumption wages can be reduced only by temporary unemployment. The crucial issue is therefore whether the real consumption wage at *D* is higher or lower than it is at *A*.

To answer this question, we add a further locus to the diagram, the Wage Indexation locus, labelled *WI*. Along this locus, the real consumption wage $W/\pi(1, q)$, where π is the cost of living index, is constant. Differentiating $W/\pi = \alpha$ gives the slope of *WI* in $w = W/p$ and q space:

$$\hat{w} = \psi \hat{q}. \tag{2.5}$$

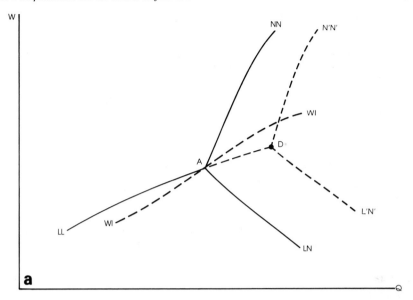

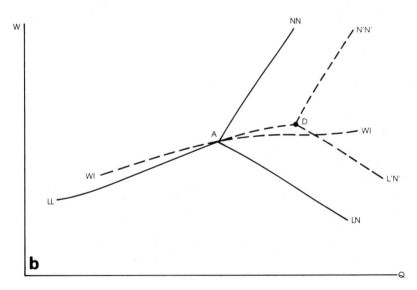

Figure 28.3

Hence, its slope is greater, the larger ψ, the share of nontraded goods in wage earners' consumption basket. Equation (2.5) defines the WI curve. Figure 28.3(a) illustrates the case where it is more steeply sloped than the LL locus so that the movement from A to D requires a fall in the real consumption wage and transitional unemployment must result. It may be checked that this requires that the nontraded sector be "more important" in demand than supply, in the sense that the share of its output in the consumption of wage earnings must exceed its contribution to a weighted average of the supply elasticities of the two sectors [van Wijnbergen (1984b)]. Conversely, if the nontraded good sector is less important in demand than in supply in this sense, the boom will raise the real consumption wage over time, and the economy enters a period of generalized labor shortage as it moves into the R region [see Figure 28.3(b)].

These results seem to accord well with some of the stylized facts of how different countries have responded to increases in foreign aid, natural resource discoveries and increases in the prices of resources. Thus, the countries of the Persian Gulf, many of which import virtually all their consumption goods, experienced excess demand for labor after the oil price shocks. On the other hand, Latin American oil producers, with a long history of prohibitive tariff barriers making many of their consumer goods virtually nontraded, saw no employment benefits and in some cases (such as Mexico and Venezuela) increases in unemployment after the oil boom; a similar phenomenon occurred in some African countries that experienced an increase in aid inflows.

2.2.2. Unemployment, the real exchange rate, and the welfare effects of foreign aid: The two-gap model revisited

The framework of the preceding subsection also allows us to shed light on an issue about which much confusion persists. What we have in mind is the two-gap model and its use by Chenery and others [see, for example, Chenery and Strout (1966)] in their analysis of the important issue of the benefits of development aid. The two-gap model has been (and still is) applied to more countries than any other model. It nevertheless has always been under a cloud because the model's dependence on seemingly ad hoc building blocks has prevented its use for explicit welfare statements. Moreover, the formulation typically used in applications was in the international-macro tradition of the time by completely ignoring relative prices, thereby turning the focus away from the real exchange rate as the crucial variable influencing the effectiveness of aid.[2]

Findlay (1983) criticized the two-gap literature for its neglect of relative prices. That point is, of course, well taken if the two-gap approach is used in a medium

---

[2] The two-gap model is developed and refined in a series of papers by Chenery and associates. See, for example Chenery and Strout (1966). For a more recent treatment, see Taylor (1983), Bacha (1982), and Arida and Bacha (1983). This section draws on van Wijnbergen (1986b).

or long-term growth context, as is almost always done; it is hard to believe in fixed relative prices as long-run phenomena. On the other hand, *short-run* wage–price rigidities are at the core of many macroeconomic problems, especially in developing countries.

In what follows, we address the issue of macroeconomic aspects of effectiveness of aid, highlighting the role of real exchange rate misalignment (a precise definition of which is provided in the context of a disequilibrium model). We demonstrate, in a reinterpretation of the two-gap model, that an ex ante wedge between the savings gap (income minus expenditure) and the trade gap (current account), using Chenery's terminology, implies an ex ante home goods market disequilibrium. A binding trade gap corresponds to excess supply of home goods and, therefore, Keynesian unemployment; a binding savings gap to excess demand for home goods and, therefore, to classical unemployment.

That interpretation suggests a second-best type interpretation of the differential welfare effects of aid: those effects equal the benefits that would be obtained in a market-clearing world, plus a term measuring the impact of aid on the social cost of the wage–price rigidities/distortions. That extra term is positive in the trade gap–Keynesian unemployment regime, but negative in the savings gap–classical unemployment regime.

To bring out the role of real exchange rate misalignment, we slightly reformulate the model of the preceding subsection, using the Neary and Roberts (1980) concept of virtual prices and the theory of duality as applied by Dixit and Norman (1980). In the Keynesian, trade-gap constrained regime, the nontraded goods market is in disequilibrium and the output of nontraded goods is demand-determined. In this regime, we can therefore define the (inverse of) the virtual real exchange rate $\tilde{Q}_K$ as the rate at which producers would willingly produce the amount of nontraded goods demanded at the *actual* price Q:

$$X_{\mathrm{N}}(\tilde{Q}_K, W) = E_Q(Q, 1, U),\tag{2.6}$$

where E_Q is the derivative of the expenditure function with respect to the relative price of nontraded goods. Clearly, if $\tilde{Q}_K < Q$: Keynesian unemployment is associated with an overvalued real exchange rate. The resulting welfare effect of increased development aid (A) can then be written as [van Wijnbergen (1986b)]:

$$\frac{\mathrm{d}U}{\mathrm{d}A} = E_U^{-1}(Q, 1; U) + \phi_K(Q - \tilde{Q}_K) > E_U^{-1},$$

$$\phi_K = E_U^{-1}C_{\mathrm{N}}\big/\big(1 - C_{\mathrm{N}}(Q - \tilde{Q}_K)\big) > 0.\tag{2.7a}$$

In the Keynesian regime, the welfare effects of aid exceed the corresponding Walrasian welfare effect E_U^{-1} by a factor proportional to the degree of overvaluation of the exchange rate (ϕ_K). This is intuitive once one realizes that aid reduces excess supply of nontraded goods and so lowers the gap between $\tilde{Q}_K$ and Q. Since the welfare costs of the relative price rigidity are proportional to $(Q - \tilde{Q}_K)^2$, those welfare costs are reduced by higher aid, hence the additional welfare effect over what is obtained in Walrasian equilibrium.

In the other regime, the classical one, demand for nontraded goods exceeds supply. This regime corresponds to the one where the savings gap is binding. Clearly, $\tilde{Q}_C > Q$, since consumers are rationed in this regime. In this regime, Q_C is the rate at which consumers would willingly consume the amount of nontraded goods supplied at the *actual* relative price of nontraded goods:

$$X_N(Q, w) = E_Q(Q_C, 1; U).\tag{2.8}$$

Simple differentiation of the budget constraint shows that in this macroeconomic regime the effectiveness of aid also differs from the Walrasian term E_U^{-1}:

$$\left.\frac{\mathrm{d}U}{\mathrm{d}A}\right|_C = E_U^{-1}(Q, 1, \tilde{U}) + \phi_C(Q - \tilde{Q}_C) < E_U^{-1},\tag{2.7b}$$

where $\phi_C = E_U^{-1}E_{QU} > 0$. Here the welfare effects fall short of the Walrasian effects, as Chenery et al. (1974) also argued. The reason is clear if one recognizes the effect on the real exchange rate. This is once again positive, but now it *increases* rather than reduces the distortionary costs of the price rigidity, since Q_C was already too high to begin with. Hence, in the savings gap-constrained classical unemployment regime, the welfare effects of aid fall short of the effects that would be obtained in pure Walrasian equilibrium.

2.3. Intertemporal adjustment and public policy

In the previous subsections we showed how increased aid exerts upward pressure on the real exchange rate, causes high real wages, and leads to a loss of external competitiveness and worsened export performance. Although all this sounds dramatic, it is in fact not enough to warrant explicit policy intervention: after all, aid lessens the need for foreign exchange from other sources and, thus, should lead to lower exports.

That, however, glosses over some important intertemporal aspects. First, aid is almost certainly *temporary*, which means that foreign exchange, while relatively cheap now, will be expensive in the future. That would not be a problem in a world with perfect capital markets, since rational firms in the export sector would borrow and invest now so as to have the capital in place when the decline in aid will lead to increased external competitiveness. However, capital markets in developing countries are a far cry from perfect. This in turn means that a temporary appreciation will cause suboptimal investment in the traded goods sector.

A second point is more subtle. There is widespread evidence that productivity growth has been faster in trade-oriented economies than in more inward-looking countries. Moreover, if one believes, à la Arrow (1962), that such productivity gains, rather than taking place exogenously with the passage of time, are a function of accumulated experience, active promotion of the traded sector is called for to capture these dynamic gains from trade. In such a world, an aid-induced temporary real appreciation leads not only to lower exports today, but to lower productivity in the traded sector in the future, even if capital accumulation in that sector does not suffer. In the remainder of this subsection we present a model that incorporates both points and derive policy conclusions.

Consider a two-period extension of the model of the previous subsection: period 1 ("today," with aid) and period 2 ("tomorrow," without aid). Capital letters indicate period 1 variables and lower case letters indicate period 2 variables. We will run ahead of our story to some extent by already incorporating the optimal policy intervention, a subsidy to traded goods producers, S. The domestic producer price of traded goods is therefore $1 + S$. Under the realistic assumption of external balance constraints, first-period expenditure needs to equal first-period income (measured at world prices) plus the flow of aid received in that period.

$R(Q, 1 + S)$ is a revenue function that represents domestic income at domestic prices. The cost of the subsidy needs to be subtracted to arrive at domestic income measured at world prices. R_p (the derivative of R with respect to the traded goods' price $P = 1 + S$) equals output of traded goods. SR_p represents the cost of the subsidy. Domestic income at world prices therefore equals $R(Q, 1 + S) - SR_p$. The first-period budget constraint equals:

$$R(Q, 1 + S) - SR_P + A = E(Q, 1; U), \qquad (2.9)$$

where A is the flow of foreign aid and E is an expenditure function giving the minimum expenditure necessary to achieve (home) welfare U in a given period, given the relative prices [see Dixit and Norman (1980)]. A similar expression holds for period 2, although there will be no aid and, thus, no need for further subsidies:

$$r(q, 1; R_P) = e(q, 1; u). \qquad (2.10)$$

The argument R_P in r (R_P is first-period output of traded goods) captures the dynamic gains from traded goods production. We assume that more traded goods output in period 1 increases productivity in that sector in period 2 ($\partial r_p / \partial R_P > 0$, $\partial r_q / \partial R_P < 0$). We assume, for convenience, that $\partial^2 r / \partial R_P^2 = 0$. Additionally, in both periods, the real exchange rate needs to clear the nontraded goods market:

$$R_Q = E_Q; \qquad r_q = e_q. \tag{2.11}$$

If the dynamic gains from trade are not internalized, either because entrepreneurs are not aware of them or because imperfect capital markets do not allow their exploitation, the optimal policy intervention is a first-period subsidy to traded goods producers ("export promotion").[3] To determine the optimal subsidy (S^*) level, one needs to maximize intertemporal welfare $V = V(U, u)$ subject to the constraints set up so far. Note that tariff protection is *not* called for, since a tariff would add an unnecessary consumer tax to the optimal subsidy.

Differentiating V with respect to S using the budget constraints (2.9) and (2.10) yields:

$$-\frac{\partial V}{\partial U} E_U^{-1} S + \frac{\partial V}{\partial u} e_u^{-1} \frac{\partial r}{\partial R_P} = 0 \tag{2.12}$$

or

$$S^* = \lambda \frac{\partial r}{\partial R_P}; \qquad \lambda = \frac{\Pi \, \partial V/\partial u}{\pi \, \partial V/\partial U},$$

where λ is the ratio of marginal utility of expenditure tomorrow over the marginal utility of expenditure today and Π and π are exact price indexes for each period [see Svensson and Razin (1983)]. In a perfect capital market, λ would equal one over one plus the world interest rate. That is clearly not relevant for most developing countries. The formula for the optimal subsidy has a nice intuitive interpretation. If private producers of traded goods receive the benefits generated on the margin by the dynamic externality, $\lambda \, \partial r / \partial R_P$, they will produce the socially optimal level of traded goods in period 1.

But we are not concerned with the need for traded sector promotion per se. Instead, we wish to know whether increased aid strengthens the case for policies oriented towards the trade sector and whether it raises the cost of the anti-export bias embedded in the trade policies of so many aid recipients.

The workings of the model can be demonstrated using the diagram in Figure 28.4.[4] The locus $NT1$ in the first quadrant depicts nontraded goods market equilibrium in period 1. Increased export promotion (higher S, we use export

---

[3]Since we use a model with only one traded good, we can of course not distinguish meaningfully between export promotion and import substitution.

[4]The analysis of this section follows van Wijnbergen (1984b). The diagrammatic presentation given here involves a short cut: most equilibrium relations and also the OS schedule depend on q, Q, and S, precluding the use of two-dimensional diagrams. van Wijnbergen (1984b) gives the full algebraic analysis, which confirms the results derived here diagrammatically.

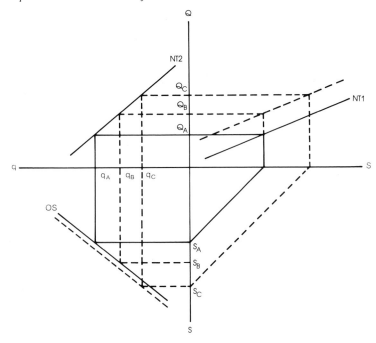

Figure 28.4. Optimal export promotion, increased aid flows and the real exchange rate.

promotion as shorthand for the more exact phrase "promotion of the traded sector") draws resources out of the nontraded sector into the traded sector, putting upward pressure on the relative price Q ($NT1$ slopes up). This is an unavoidable by-product of export promotion. The locus $NT2$ in quadrant 2 describes nontraded goods market equilibrium in period 2. A higher first-period real exchange rate Q draws resources out of the traded sector, thereby reducing dynamic productivity gain in that sector. In the second period, therefore, traded goods production takes place with lowered productivity. This in turn means the private sector will devote less resources to it and produce more nontraded goods instead in period 2. A fall in the period 2 price of nontraded goods follows ($NT2$ has a negative slope).

The third quadrant gives the link between the future relative price of NT, q, and the optimal level of export promotion in the current period (the locus OS). An anticipated future depreciation (a fall in q) increases the value of traded goods in that period and therefore increases the value of future productivity increases in that sector. Therefore an anticipated future depreciation strengthens the need for export promotion: S goes up and the OS schedule has a negative slope.

Let us consider now the exchange rate effects of a temporary aid program. Some of the aid gets spent on NT goods necessitating a higher real exchange rate and a diversion of resources out of the traded goods sector (Q goes up and $NT1$ shifts upward; see dotted line in quadrant 1). This is the conflict between aid and export promotion we encountered in the previous subsection. However, now we also have intertemporal effects. Reduced first-period export performance reduces the dynamic gains from trade and therefore reduces future productivity in traded goods production. Accordingly, resources will be diverted away from the traded goods sector into the NT sector, leading to reduced export performance. *Aid, even when temporary, permanently worsens export performance*, unless proper policy measures are taken.

This brings us to the third quadrant and our main interest, the policy implications of the effects on the exchange rate and export performance of temporary foreign aid. The first effect comes through the anticipated future depreciation once the aid flows will stop (i.e. q falls from q_A to q_B). This means that traded goods will be more valuable in the future and so are, therefore, the dynamic productivity gains that come with more traded goods production today. This effect is measured by the slope of the OS schedule in quadrant three: export promotion should increase from S_A to S_B along OS.

There is, moreover, a second effect at play. Temporary aid increases income today and therefore decreases its marginal utility in the present period. This raises the social discount factor and shifts the tradeoff between current costs and future benefits that determines the optimal level of export promotion in favor of tomorrow and so in favor of more export promotion. In terms of our diagram, the OS schedule shifts out and the optimal level of export promotion goes up further, from S_B to S_C. This second effect of course only matters in imperfect capital markets, since with perfect markets there will be no wedge between the social discount factor and the discount factor prevailing in international capital markets; however, as mentioned before, the assumption of perfect capital markets has little relevance for most aid recipients.

3. Oil prices, structural adjustment, and disequilibrium

In the preceding section we viewed a natural resource shock, and the structural adjustment that follows, from the perspective of the transfer problem. This is appropriate for resource discoveries, and captures an important element of the effects of resource *price* increases. However, resources (oil, for short) price increases, especially when permanent, also have an impact on the aggregate supply side of an economy that was not captured in the preceding analysis. Since oil is a factor of production, such aggregate supply effects lead to structural adjustment problems rather different from those covered until now. Moreover, the aggregate supply-side effects of oil shocks often create a clash between the requirements of microeconomic efficiency and macroeconomic stability, unless proper adjustment measures are taken. Such a conflict is behind many of the discussions over energy pricing. However, many of these discussions are misguided in that they often ignore that other macroeconomic policy instruments can be brought to bear on issues of macroeconomic stability. Countries like Korea show that an efficient pricing strategy does not rule out macroeconomic success.

The intersectoral issues after an oil price shock are straightforward: energy-intensive sectors will need to decline with respect to less energy-intensive sectors, and technology will need to become less energy-intensive across the board. We will not elaborate on this any further. Instead, we focus on the macroeconomic problems to be expected after an oil price shock, particularly on the disequilibrium problems due to wage–price rigidities.

Such macro issues deserve discussion here because they present a major stumbling block for effective structural adjustment. The interaction takes place through two channels at least. The first one is related to the putty–clay nature of capital equipment and is often ignored. Changing over to less energy-intensive production techniques in many sectors is only possible when new capital equipment replaces old machinery. If capital equipment is of a putty–clay nature, factor intensities can only be altered in the design stage. Hence, structural adjustment will take place much faster when the economy manages to avoid a slump and investment rates are high. Macro policies that slow down aggregate capital formation, such as monetary anti-inflation packages, are therefore in direct conflict with rapid structural adjustment.

The second channel runs through external balance, and played a much greater role after the second series of oil price shocks (in 1979/1980) than after the first one (1973/1974). If oil shocks lead to a deteriorating balance of payments situations, external pressure or simply aversion of higher external debt may lead to expenditure reduction. There is evidence that such externally imposed expenditure cuts fall unduly on investment. This would again slow down structural adjustment. In what follows, we discuss such macroeconomic disequilibrium problems in more detail.

Consider, for that purpose, a version of our core model that is at once simpler and more complex than the one of Subsection 2.2. It is simpler because we suppress static resource allocational issues; more complex because oil is introduced as a factor of production. [The model is discussed in more detail in van Wijnbergen (1985c).] Resource allocational aspects are suppressed by assuming the home country produces only one good, using labor, capital and oil as inputs. This leads to a revenue function R for period 1 and r for period 2 of the forms:

$$R = R\big(P, P_0; K, L(W/P, P_0/P)\big) \tag{3.1}$$

and

$$r = r(p, p_0; k, 1),$$ (3.2)

where P is the price of home goods in terms of foreign final goods, P_0 is the price of oil, also in terms of foreign final goods, W is the home wage, expressed in the same numeraire and the lower case letters represent period 2 variables, additionally. $k = K + I$, first-period capital plus investment, equals second-period capital (depreciation is ignored). Consumer behavior can similarly be summarized through an expenditure function E with current and future prices of home and foreign final goods as arguments, in addition to home welfare U. The intertemporal budget constraint then becomes:

$$R + \delta r - PI = E(\Pi(P,1), \delta\pi(p,1), U).$$ (3.3)

Home goods market equilibrium in period 1 and 2 requires:

$$R_P = E_P + I\left(\frac{\delta p}{P}, \frac{\delta p_0}{P}\right); \qquad r_p = E_p,$$ (3.4)

and labor market equilibrium in period 1 implies:

$$L(W/P, P_0/P) = \bar{L}.$$ (3.5)

A similar expression is obtained for period 2 labor market, which we use to substitute out the period 2 wage; in the second period, all markets are always assumed to clear.

The second-period goods market equilibrium can be represented by a positive curve in $P-p$ space (Figure 28.5). Higher first-period terms of trade P have positive income effects, which will, among other things, lead to higher demand for period 2 home goods. Similarly, an increase in P increases the relative price of current consumption in terms of future consumption. That leads to pure substitution effects which also shift demand for future home goods out. To restore equilibrium, p needs to go up.

First-period labor market equilibrium represents an upward-sloping curve in $W/P-P$ space (locus LL in Figure 28.5): higher real (home) product wages W/P reduce labor demand, but a terms of trade improvement increases it for given real product wage. This is because it implies a lower real (home) product price of oil $(d(P_0/P)/dP = -P_0/P^2 dP)$:

$$L_W \, d(W/P)L + P_0 \frac{P_0}{P} \frac{dP}{P} = 0.$$

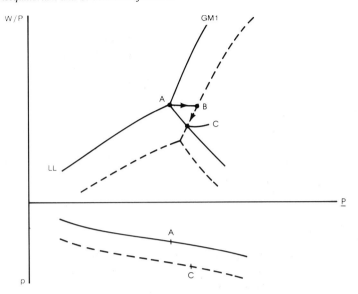

Figure 28.5. An oil price shock with supply element dominant.

The first-period goods market equilibrium curve ($GM1$) is upward-sloping in (W/P–P) space: higher real product wages reduce output and thus increase excess demand. A higher relative price of home goods obviously reduces excess demand for home goods and so restores equilibrium.

Out of equilibrium, behavior depends on which regime prevails. To the right of $GM1$, excess supply persists and unemployment is Keynesian by nature; the real exchange rate (or, more accurately, the terms of trade) is overvalued. In the Keynesian regime, actual first-period output falls short of what firms would be willing to supply. In the classical regime output is supply determined. In both regimes, labor demand falls short of labor supply. Note that our "classical unemployment" regime is *not* characterized by goods market rationing, since we assume *upward* price flexibility [see van Wijnbergen (1986c) for a similar disequilibrium model]. Hence, the C region is on the $GM1$ locus, with commodity markets clearing, but labor in excess supply.

Consider now the impact of an oil price shock, $dP_0 = dp_0 > 0$. First of all, the LL curve will shift down if at least oil and labor are cooperative in production. [See Svensson (1985) for this point; cooperative is not the same as complementary, since the latter controls for output levels.] The latter condition implies that the marginal productivity of labor declines after a decline in energy use; this condition has clear empirical support [Berndt and Wood (1975)]. This implies that real wages need to fall if full employment is to be restored.

What happens to goods market equilibrium is more complicated and depends on the structure of the economy. It, moreover, has important implications for the type of macroeconomic policy that should back up any structural adjustment program in response to an oil price shock. Differentiating the equation describing home goods market equilibrium in period 1 yields:

$$\frac{\partial P}{\partial P_0} = \left(-\left(R_{PP_0} + R_{PL}L_{P_0}\right) - C_{IE}Z\right)/\Delta$$

$$\underset{\substack{\text{supply shock} \\ \text{element } (+)}}{\qquad\qquad} \underset{\substack{\text{transfer} \\ \text{element } (-)}}{\qquad\qquad}$$

The supply shock element shows that the rise in production costs shifts the aggregate supply curve backwards. This causes upward pressure on the price of home goods (works towards an appreciating real exchange rate) and so shifts $GM1$ to the right. The second element operates through the demand side: for given oil use, higher oil prices imply a larger transfer of resources towards the oil-exporting countries. This depresses aggregate demand and shifts the $GM1$ curve to the left. In the configuration of Figure 28.5, the supply element dominates; in Figure 28.6, the demand driven transfer element dominates, so that the economy finds itself in Keynesian unemployment. Consider the classical case first. The backward shift in the AS curve (rightward shift of $GM1$) causes upward

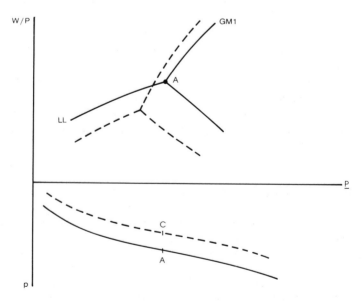

Figure 28.6. An oil price shock with dominant transfer element.

pressure on the final good terms of trade (the economy moves from A to B). This real appreciation will allow a fall in real product wages even if real consumption wages are downward rigid: a move from B to C.

Whether the supply shock goes largely into prices, with high real wages preventing a partially offsetting gross output response, or whether such an output response *is* forthcoming, with associated mitigating effect on P, depends on the slope of the wage indexation line. A more open economy has a steeper line; hence, a more open economy will see a smaller fall in output in this regime. This *contradicts* the often claimed view that openness makes an economy more vulnerable to external shocks. Here, openness reduces macroeconomic problems after an oil price shock.

A final policy implication is that structural adjustment to new oil prices should not be supported by an expansionary macro policy in this regime, the transitional unemployment notwithstanding. This is so because the economy is supply constrained; adding expansionary demand policies would hence lead mostly to price increases, not to extra output and unemployment.

If the transfer element of the shock dominates (Figure 28.6), the results are different. The economy will then be shifted into a deficient effective demand constraint, creating room for expansionary macroeconomic policy. The dominance of the transfer element is the more likely, the higher the substitution elasticity in production, and the larger the share of imported oil in gross output. In this case, an expansionary macro policy is called for. Furthermore, openness plays a different role; since the output multiplier of fiscal policy in the Keynesian regime declines with rising marginal import shares, a macro policy is less effective, the more open the economy is.

The investment response in either regime depends on both the regime and on the nature of technology [van Wijnbergen (1985b)]. Adjustment to new oil prices requires less energy-intensive production technology. If capital is "putty–clay", i.e. changes in technology can only be made in the design state, investment will accelerate even if the optimal size of the new capital stock is lower than the old one, to replace the now-obsolete old machinery. If, however, changes in technology can in fact be made after machines have been installed, investment will fall [van Wijnbergen (1985b)].[5]

4. Trade reform, relative prices, and structural adjustment

Major changes to relative prices – brought about by an exogenous movement in world relative prices or by a change in trade policy – usually require that the country goes through an extended period of structural adjustment. For example,

---

[5]Assuming that energy and capital are technologically "cooperative" [Svensson (1985)]. The argument presented also assumes that the size of the oil price increase is large enough to drive the rent on old capital goods to zero.

changes in the international terms of trade of the type discussed in Section 3 will generally result in resource reallocation, changes in production and income distribution. Also, changes in tariffs will require a significant reallocation of factors of production.

Although in the longer run the opening up of international trade will almost always be beneficial, this kind of policy may generate important short-run adjustment costs. For this reason, it is fundamentally important to distinguish clearly the short- and long-run effects of such a policy. This is done in this section where we analyze in detail the effects of relative price changes on a small open country's economic structure. The analysis is carried out for the specific case of a trade reform, where the economic authorities decide to reduce the level of the existing import tariffs. However, as will be discussed below, this analytical structure can be applied readily to the case of exogenous changes in the world terms of trade.

The analysis presented here is mostly positive and develops an equilibrium model of a simplified economy, with three goods and two factors. The discussion traces in detail the effects of a tariff reduction that will have an impact on relative prices, resource movements, production and income distribution, in the short and medium run. Models of this kind have been previously developed by Edwards (1984a, 1986c), and Edwards and van Wijnbergen (1986a, 1986b). The analysis is largely based on the extension of the Viner–Ricardo model for the case of three goods. In order to simplify the presentation, some long-run issues such as capital accumulation are ignored.[6]

4.1. A stylized model

Assume the case of a small country that produces three goods: exportables (X), importables (M), and nontraded (N). Production is carried out using capital and labor. Production functions have the conventional properties and it is assumed that in the short-run capital is sector-specific, with labor being perfectly mobile between the three sectors. On sector-specific models see, for example, Jones (1971), Mayer (1974), Mussa (1974, 1978, 1982), Neary (1978a, 1978b, 1982), and Edwards (1984a, 1986c). However, we assume that in the medium and longer runs, both capital and labor can move freely across sectors. The nominal exchange rate is assumed to be fixed and equal to one.

Imports are initially subject to a tariff, and external borrowing is not allowed. With respect to the labor market, it will initially be assumed that it is free of distortions. However, the consequences of assuming the existence of an

---

[6] van Wijnbergen (1985c) discusses the macro aspects of trade reform in an intertemporal framework that allows discussion of investment and external deficits.

economy-wide minimum wage, which is binding in the short run, will also be investigated. The domestic capital market is initially assumed to be free of distortions, with the real return on capital being equalized in the long run, across sectors. Regarding factor intensity, it will be assumed that importables have the higher capital/labor ratio, nontraded have the next highest ratio, and exportables are labor-intensive. [This ranking of capital/labor intensities is not only realistic for the LDCs, but is also required for stability; see Neary (1978b).] Tariff proceeds are returned to consumers in a nondistorting lump-sum fashion.

The analysis presented here also ignores initial, pre-reform macroeconomic problems. This represents a simplification of the real world characteristics of most countries that have embarked in tariff reform attempts since, as has been pointed out by Krueger (1981, 1983) and Little (1982), among others, a large number of structural reforms involving tariff reductions have started from crises situations with high inflation.[7] However, by ignoring inflation and other related problems in the present section, it is possible to focus on issues related to structural adjustment, abstracting from those of stabilization. On the relationship between stabilization and liberalization, however, see Krueger (1981), Edwards (1984a), McKinnon (1982), and Mussa (1984).

4.2. Trade reform

4.2.1. Medium-run effects of tariff reform

In this class of models of a small economy with three goods (importables, exportables and nontraded), two factors (capital and labor), and the usual competitive assumptions, long-run domestic prices are fully determined (under nonspecialization) by world prices, technology and tariffs. We assume that all three goods are indeed produced.[8] Equilibrium can then be described in the following way: world prices of exportables and importables (plus the tariff) determine the rewards to both factors of production; these rewards, in turn and under the assumption of competition, determine the price of nontraded. Demand considerations for nontraded determine total output of nontraded and total factors used in their production. This leaves a certain amount of factors that is

---

[7] There have been, however, important exceptions to his rule, including Korea and Indonesia.

[8] This is not an unusually restrictive assumption, because the third commodity is nontraded. Introducing trade in the third good would create a knife-edge equilibrium, with a strong presumption towards specialization. This feature disappears when there are barriers to trade in at least as many goods as there are more goods (or traded factors) than nontraded factors [Neary (1985)]. Incomplete specialization requires that the aggregate capital–labor ratio *net* of capital and labor employed in the *NT* sector, falls between the capital–labor ratios in each traded sector; that guarantees zero profits at positive activity levels for given world traded goods prices.

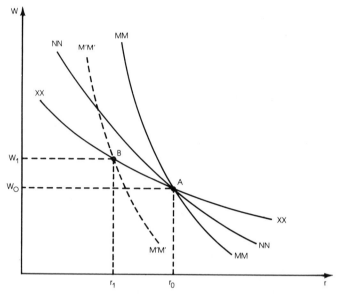

Figure 28.7

used in the production of exportables and importables in a traditional Heckscher–Ohlin (H–O) fashion.

Consider now the effect of a reduction (elimination) of the level of import tariff on the relative prices of final goods and on factors rewards. (Assume that the price of exportables is the numeraire.) This can be analyzed using Figure 28.7, which is the dual to the well-known Lerner–Pearce diagram. The initial equilibrium is given by the intersection of the three isocosts MM, XX and NN, that present the combinations of wages and real returns to capital that result in a constant cost of producing these goods at the existing technology [see Mussa (1979)]. The slopes of these curves are equal to the capital–labor ratio, and as may be seen in Figure 28.7, correspond to our assumptions of relative capital intensities. Initially equilibrium is obtained at A with a wage rate (relative to exports) equal to W_0 and a real return to capital equal to r_0.

The reduction of the imports tariff will result in a leftward shift of the MM curve towards $M'M'$. This is because now, in order to maintain equilibrium between domestic costs and the world price of importables plus the tariff, lower combinations of wages and rental rates will be required. New long-run equilibrium will be obtained at B where the new $M'M'$ curve intersects the XX curve. A new isocost for nontraded goods (not drawn) has to pass through this point after the adjustment has taken place. As the Stolper–Samuelson theorem indicates, the

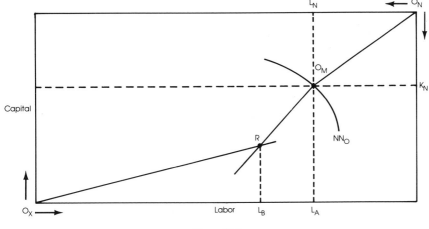

Figure 28.8

reduction of the import tariff in an economy where exportables are labor-intensive will result in higher wage and lower rental rates (i.e. $W_1 > W_0$, and $r_1 < r_0$). The new equilibrium point B is below the NN isocost, indicating that as a consequence of the tariff reduction, the price of nontraded goods in terms of exportables *will have to fall*.

While the relative price of nontraded goods is completely determined by technological considerations, the amount produced of this type of goods will depend on the demand side. In particular, production of N will be such that, at the prevailing prices, the nontraded goods market clears. The production side of the model can be analyzed using a three-goods Edgeworth–Bowley box, as developed by Melvin (1968). Figure 28.8 illustrates the case discussed here where exportables are the most labor-intensive good. In this diagram nontraded goods isoquants are drawn from origin O_N. At the initial prices the nontraded goods market clears at a level of production given by isoquant NN_O. The capital–labor ratio in nontraded goods production is given by the slope of $O_N O_M$. Production of exportables is measured from O_X, and that of importables by distance $O_M R$. In equilibrium the slope of NN_O isoquant at O_M equals the slopes of the corresponding isoquants for exportables and importables, which are tangent at R.

Since as a result of the tariff the wage rate will increase relative to the real return to capital, all three sectors will now become more capital intensive. This is shown in Figure 28.9, where the dashed ray depict the new (after tariff reduction) capital/labor ratios. However, in order to determine the new equilibrium it is necessary to know what will happen to the demand of nontraded goods, as a consequence of the tariff reduction. Assume, as a first step to organize the

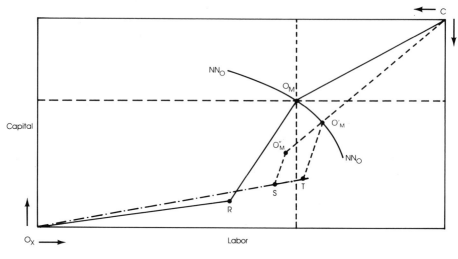

Figure 28.9

discussion, that the quantity demanded for nontraded goods does not change after the imports tariffs are reduced. Then the new equilibrium point in production of nontraded goods will be obtained at the intersection of the new (higher) capital–labor ratio and the initial NN_O isoquant, at point O'_M. Production of importables will be reduced to $O'_M T$, and production of exportables will increase to $M_X T$. This result was obtained under the simplifying assumption that the quantity demanded of nontraded goods was not affected by the reduction of tariffs. In general, of course, this will not be the case. Moreover, since as a consequence of the liberalization of trade the (relative) price of nontraded goods will decline and a positive income effect will take place, there will be an increase in the quantity demanded of N. In Figure 28.9 the new equilibrium will be on the new capital–labor ratio ray to the left of the NN isocost, on a point such as O''_M.

In summary, under our assumptions on capital intensities, when both capital and labor can move across sectors, as a result of the tariff reform (i) prices of nontraded goods, relative to exportables will fall; (ii) wages, relative to all goods, will increase; (iii) the real return on capital, relative to all goods, will decrease; (iv) production of exportables will expand; (v) production of nontraded goods will increase; and (vi) production of importables will decline.

These equilibrium price movements give us information on potential adjustment problems emerging from the trade reform. If, for example, nominal prices on nontraded goods are rigid downward we may have a problem under fixed nominal rates. This is because according to (i) P_N/P_X (the prices of nontraded in terms of exportables) will have to decline in order to maintain equilibrium. Since

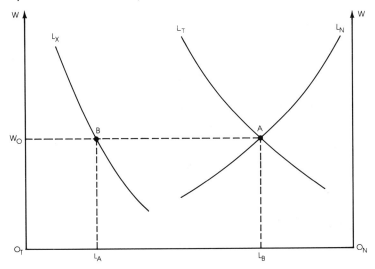

Figure 28.10

under the small country case P_X^* is given, the *nominal* price of nontraded goods would have to decline to attain equilibrium. Notice, however, that if real wages are rigid downward, no disequilibrium situation will emerge in the long run. This is, of course, because according to (ii) real wages will increase in terms of all goods. This, however, will not be the case in the short run, as will be shown below.

4.2.2. Short-run effects

This subsection investigates the short-run effects of a structural tariff reform under the assumption that in the short run capital is sector-specific, while labor can still move freely across sections.[9]

The initial equilibrium situation can be illustrated using Figure 28.10, which is adapted from Mussa (1974) for the case of the three goods. In this figure, the horizontal axis measures total labor available in the economy, while the vertical axis depicts the wage rate in terms of exportables. L_T is the demand for labor by the traded goods sectors and is equal to the (horizontal) sum of the demand for labor by the exportable sector (which is given by L_X in this figure) and the demand for labor of the importable sector. L_N, on the other hand, is the demand for labor of the nontraded goods sector. The initial equilibrium is characterized

---

[9]The representation used in this model, then, is an adaptation for a three goods case of the Viner–Ricardo models of Jones (1971), Mayer (1974) and Mussa (1974).

by a wage rate equal to W_0, with $O_T L_A$ labor used in the production of exportables, $L_A L_B$ labor used in the production of importables and OL_B used in the production of nontraded goods.

There are several differences between this short-run model and the long-run model discussed in the previous subsection. First, since capital is now sector-specific, the direct link between tradable goods prices and factors rewards is broken. The Stolper–Samuelson theorem does not hold (in the short run), and the price of nontraded goods will be determined by the intersection of the demand and supply schedules for these kinds of goods.

In the short run, the reduction of the tariff, under the assumption of sector-specific factors, will generate changes both in the (relative) price of importables and nontraded goods [see, for example, Dornbusch (1974, 1980) and Edwards and van Wijnbergen (1986b)]. While the price of importables will unambiguously fall as the import tariff is reduced, the behavior of the price of nontraded goods will depend on the assumption regarding substitutability and on the magnitude of income effects [Edwards (1986c)]. Assuming that the three goods are gross substitutes in consumption and production, and that the income effect does not exceed the substitution effect, it can be shown that as a result of the reduction of the tariff the price of nontraded goods will fall relative to that of exportables and increase relative to that of importables [Edwards and van Wijnbergen (1986b)].

The lower domestic price of importables will generate a downward shift of the L_T curve (with the L_X curve constant). In Figure 28.11 the new L_T curve will intersect the L_N curve at R. However, this is not a final equilibrium situation, since the tariff reduction will also result in a *decline* in the price of nontraded goods (relative to exports). As a consequence, around the equilibrium, L_N will shift downward (by *less* than L_T) and final *short-run* equilibrium will be achieved at S. In this new equilibrium, production of exportables has increased – with labor used by this sector increasing by $L_A L_Q$. The production of nontraded goods may either increase or decrease, and production of importables will fall. In the case depicted in Figure 28.11 labor has moved out of the importables goods sector, into the exportables and nontraded goods sectors.

What has happened to factors rewards in the short run? Wages have declined in terms of the exportable good (from W_0 to W_1 in Figure 28.11). Also, wages decline in terms of the nontraded good, since the vertical distance between the L_N and L_N^1 curves is smaller than the reduction of W from W_0 to W_1. However, wages increase relative to the importable good, since the domestic price of importables has fallen by more than wages. In the exportables sector, the real return to capital has increased; the rental rates of the capital specific to the importables and nontraded sector could either increase or decrease.[10]

---

[10] Formally, the real return to capital specific to the importable sector will decrease in terms of importables, and could either increase or decrease in terms of the other two goods. With respect to capital specific to the nontraded sector, its rental rate will increase in terms of nontraded goods, and could either increase or decrease in terms of the other two goods.

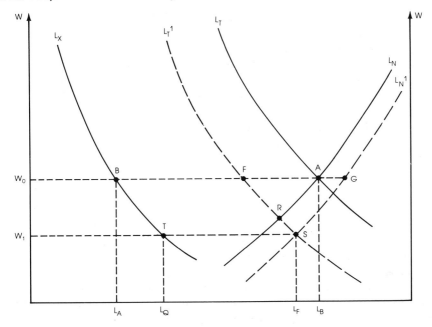

Figure 28.11

The above discussion has assumed that all prices (of goods and factors) are fully flexible. However, this need not be the case. In a number of countries the labor market is usually characterized by the existence of (real) minimum wages. It is easy to see from Figure 28.11 that if economy-wide wages, expressed in terms of exportables, are inflexibly downward, unemployment will result as a consequence of the shock on relative prices of M to X; the magnitude of this unemployment being equal to distance FG. This is basically a short-run adjustment cost, which will tend to disappear as capital moves between sectors in the medium and long run.[11] In general, in the presence of sector-specific capital and wage rigidity, a short-run disequilibrium situation will emerge as a result of the reform and there will be a second-best argument for slow trade liberalization and adjustment assistance. (See Section 5 for more on gradualism.) If, however, the wages are inflexible in terms of the importable, no unemployment will result. If,

---

[11] Naturally, the first-best solution is to eliminate the sources of real wage rigidity (i.e. minimum wage legislation, indexing). In reality, however, countries usually operate under political constraints that may make this type of policy somewhat difficult. See Neary (1982) and Edwards (1982) for discussions regarding trade liberalization, sticky wages and unemployment. It is interesting to note that an effect of this type can be used to analytically derive short-run output losses following a trade liberalization process, as is done by Khan and Zahler (1983).

on the other hand, real wages are inflexible measured in terms of the consumer price index, unemployment may result if the weight of importables in the price index is sufficiently small. Alternatively, it is possible to think of a situation where wage inflexibility affects one sector only. In this case, if workers equalize the expected value of earnings, a mechanism similar to that developed by Harris and Todaro will operate to equilibrate the labor market. Edwards (1986c) shows that in this setting it is not possible to know whether a tariff reduction will increase or decrease the level of unemployment.

Under the assumption of wage flexibility, the tariff reduction will result, in the short run, in an increase in the use of labor (and thus in production, for given amounts of capital) in the exportables and importables sectors. Both the exportable and nontraded goods sectors become relatively more labor-intensive, while the importables sector has become more capital-intensive.

In summary, for the general case with wage flexibility, the short-run effects of a tariff reduction on production, prices, and factors rewards are the following: (i) production of exportables increases; (ii) production of importables is reduced; (iii) production of nontraded goods increases; (iv) wages increase in terms of importables, and decline in terms of exportables and nontraded goods; (v) the rental rate of capital in the exportable sector increases relative to all goods; (vi) the rental rate of capital in the importables sector will decrease relative to the importable good – it could increase or decrease relative to the other goods; and (vii) the rental rate of capital in the nontraded goods sector will increase relative to nontraded goods, and could either increase or decrease relative to the other two goods.

4.2.3. The transition period after a trade reform

The model used in this subsection assumes that the main differences between short-, medium- or long-run effects of a trade liberalization is that in the short run capital is locked into its sector of origin. As time passes, however, capital will move between sectors. In the present model, and in order to simplify the exposition, we assume that the movement of capital does not require the use of resources. However, the analysis could be modified by introducing a "moving industry", which uses labor and some specific factor, as in Mussa (1978). In the final long-run equilibrium all sectors will be more capital-intensive, with the exportable sector using more capital, in absolute terms; and with the importable sector using less capital in absolute terms than prior to the trade reform. The nontraded goods sector could use either a larger or smaller absolute amount of capital than before the tariff reduction.

Although the diagrammatical approach used here cannot capture fully the rich complexities of the dynamic process during the transition, it is possible to use Figure 28.12 to illustrate the type of adjustment to which this economy will be

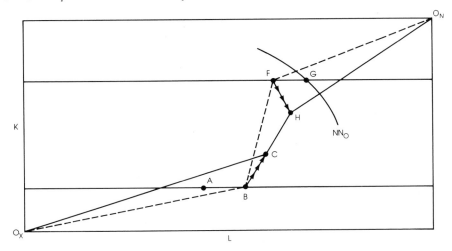

Figure 28.12

subject. As mentioned, initial (i.e. preliberalization) equilibrium is given by points *A* and *G*. Short-run equilibrium is given by points *B* and *F*; while long-run equilibrium will be attained at points *H* and *C*. The arrows between points *B* and *C*, and *F* and *H*, respectively, show the way resources will move during the transition. For the particular case considered here, the transition will be characterized by: (i) capital *and* labor moving out of the importable goods sector; (ii) capital and labor moving into the exportable goods sector; and (iii) capital moving into the nontraded goods sector, and labor moving *out* of the nontraded goods sector.

The preceding discussion has clearly pointed out the existence of potential sources of disequilibria and adjustment costs following a tariff change. Generally speaking, maintaining equilibrium will require that labor moves into the non-traded goods sector in the short run and out of it in the longer run. Factor prices provide a mirror image: real nontraded product wages need to fall in the short run but increase in the long run. A sufficiently high share of nontraded goods in the CPI could, therefore, lead to short-run adjustment problems and transitory unemployment if the real consumption wage is downward rigid. If, moreover, it is costly to move factors around, this movement of labor in and then out of the importable sector may lead to further adjustment problems.

The previous analysis has focused on the effects of changes of tariffs on production, income distribution and resource allocation. Of course, the framework used above can be used to investigate the way in which exogenous changes on world terms of trade affect the domestic economy.

Changes in both import tariffs and international terms of trade will affect the equilibrium value of the real exchange rate (or relative price of tradables to nontradables), giving rise to possible disequilibrium situations of real exchange rate over or under valuation, of the type discussed in Subsection 2.2.2 above. Algebraic versions of the short- and medium-run models developed above can be manipulated to find out the way in which the equilibrium value of the real exchange rate will respond to tariff changes and international terms of trade shocks. Edwards and van Wijnbergen (1987) have shown that, generally speaking, it is not possible to know (at a theoretical level) if a trade reform will result in an equilibrium real appreciation or real depreciation of the exchange rate.

5. Structural reform, adjustment, and gradualism

From a policy perspective, a crucial question is related to whether reforms aimed at altering the economy's structure should be implemented gradually or in an abrupt fashion. In a textbook world with no rigidities, externalities or political constraints, the answer to this question is quite trivial. All existing distortions, like import tariffs, subsidies, quotas and taxes, should be removed simultaneously and instantaneously.[12] In the real world, however, there are a number of rigidities that can make the textbook strategy either unfeasible or inadequate. In this section we discuss the gradualism vs. abrupt reform issue using a simple intertemporal model of a small economy.

The existing literature on the appropriate speed of economic reform is brief and sparse. Most discussions on the subject can be found semi-buried in pieces devoted to general discussions on economic policy in the developing countries. Of course, almost all participants in this debate have pointed out that in an ideal world the first-best policies for a small economy consist of a fast liberalization.

Some authors [Stockman (1982), Krueger (1983), Bruno (1985)] have argued that in order to enhance the credibility of the reform policies, existing distortions and controls should be dismantled fast. This line of reasoning argues that slow preannounced reforms allow resistance to build up, hence lack credibility, and that, as a result, they fail to achieve their objectives of reducing inefficiencies and reallocating resources. On the other hand, other authors have pointed out that from a political economy perspective gradual reforms are more appropriate [Little, Scitovsky and Scott (1970), Clark (1982)]. This idea is also based on the likelihood of the reforms generating political opposition by those groups negatively affected. According to this view, however, a more gradual reform will have

---

[12] This section draws on Edwards and van Wijnbergen (1986a). Of course, if the country in question is large, an optimal export tax should be maintained.

a smaller negative impact on losers during the initial period, and consequently, they will be less prone to lobbying against the reform. A strong argument in exactly the opposite direction, also on political grounds, is made by Bruno (1985), who argues that in the crisis atmosphere that often surrounds the start of a liberalization, reforms should be pushed as far as possible; a second change may not arise once the opposition is organized.

Leamer (1980) has pointed out that income distribution considerations may suggest that a gradual reform is more adequate. This point has also been made by Michaely (1982) who has argued that the dynamic path of reform should take into account the effects of unemployment and the distribution of income. Neary (1982) and Edwards (1982) have pointed out that if capital is sector-specific in the short run and there are labor market distortions in the form of a minimum wage in real terms, the optimal (second-best) strategy will consist of gradually reducing tariffs.

A number of authors have looked at the role of distortions during the adjustment period [Lapan (1976), Neary (1982), Pindyck (1982), Mussa (1984), Edwards and van Wijnbergen (1986a), Rodrik (1985)], and have pointed out that if there are distortions affecting either factor markets or other sectors, it is possible that, from a pure welfare perspective, the optimal (second-best) strategy involves gradualism.

A simple intertemporal model

The welfare costs of intervention in international trade are firmly established theoretically and increasingly well documented empirically. Trading at world prices, both at a point in time in commodity markets and intertemporally via capital markets, maximizes the gain from trade for countries too small to influence the terms at which trade takes place in the world. However, demonstrating the superiority of free trade equilibrium provides little guidance on the problems likely to be encounted *during* an attempt to liberalize the external sector in a particular country. In practice, many times such attempts have been frustrated at different stages, with the countries involved reverting to inward-looking development strategies. The characteristics of the transition between a repressed and a liberalized economy are not well understood, and serious research efforts in this area have started only recently. Among these dynamic aspects those related to the speed and order of liberalization are particularly important. With respect to the former, the main question is how fast an economy should be liberalized, i.e. "cold turkey" vs. gradual approaches.

We consider a two-period model. Under this assumption, an abrupt liberalization implies that import tariffs are zero both in periods 1 and 2. Gradual liberalization, on the other hand, means that there will be a positive tariff in period 1 and a zero tariff in period 2. Consequently, the differential welfare effects of these two trade liberalization strategies can be obtained by evaluating the welfare effect of a positive tariff in period 1 under the assumption of a zero tariff in the second period.

We assume that our two-period economy produces two goods (x and y) using capital and labor with usual technology. Good y is assumed to be the importable good, and to be capital-intensive. It is also assumed that only in period 1 there is a tariff on imports of good y. Investment takes place in period 1. Foreign borrowing also takes place in the first period, but is assumed to be restricted to a maximum amount $\bar{T}$. This borrowing constraint is assumed to fall fully on investment; it is in fact this distortion that gives our analysis a second-best nature. This assumption is empirically the case in most developing countries [see, for example, Hicks and Kubisch (1984) and Haffez (1984)].

We assume a weakly separable intertemporal welfare function with each period's subutility being homothetic. Making use of duality theory, once again, this model can be fully represented by equations (5.1)–(5.4):

$$R^1(1, p_1; K) + \delta * R^2(1, p_2; K + I(\delta)) - I(\delta) + \tau\left(E_{p_1} - R^1_{p_1}\right)$$

$$= E\left(\Pi_1(1, p_1), \delta * \Pi_2(1, p_2); W\right), \tag{5.1}$$

$$\delta * \left[R^2(1, p_2; K + I(\delta)) - \Pi_2 E_{\Pi_2}\left[(\Pi_1(1, p_1), \delta \Pi_2(1, p_2); W)\right]\right] = \bar{T}, \tag{5.2}$$

$$\delta R^2_K = 1, \tag{5.3}$$

$$p_1 = p_1^* + \tau; \qquad p_2 = p_2^*, \tag{5.4}$$

where R^i, $i = 1, 2$, are the revenue functions in each period; p_i, $i = 1, 2$, is the relative price of good y in each period; K is the stock of capital in period 1; I is investment in period 1, with $K + I$ being the stock of capital in the second period; $\delta * = (1 + r^*)^{-1}$ is the world discount factor; $\delta = (1 + r)^{-1}$ is the domestic discount factor; and $\delta * > \delta$. $\tau(E_{p1} - R^1_{p1})$ is the tariff revenue in period 1; E is the present value of expenditure; Π_i, $i = 1, 2$, are exact price indexes for each period; and W is the level of welfare.[13]

---

[13]On exact price indexes, see Svensson and Razin (1983), van Wijnbergen (1984a, 1984b) and Edwards and van Wijnbergen (1983).

Equation (5.1) is the intertemporal budget constraint, which specifies that the present value of revenue has to equal the present value of expenditure. Notice that, given our assumption that the borrowing constraint falls entirely on investment, intertemporal consumption decisions depend on the world discount factor, δ^*, whereas investment depends on the domestic discount factor, δ. Equation (5.2) specifies the borrowing constraint, and states that period 2's current account surplus (i.e. the excess of period 2's revenues over period 2's expenditure) discounted at the world discount factor has to be equal to the maximum of foreign borrowing allowed in period 1 ($\overline{T}$); δ takes the value required for this foreign borrowing constraint to be fulfilled. Equation (5.3) states that investment in this economy will take place until period 2 marginal productivity of capital, discounted by the domestic discount factor, equals 1. From this equation it can be established that investment will be a positive function of δ (negative function of r). Finally, (5.4) specifies that we are only considering a temporary tariff in period 1.

Consider the effects of varying the first-period tariff, τ. Differentiating (5.1) and (5.2) and using (5.3) we obtain the effect of changes in τ on the domestic discount factor δ:

$$\gamma \frac{\mathrm{d}\delta}{\mathrm{d}\tau} = \left[\left(1 - \tau C_y^1\right) \Pi_2 \Pi_{1p_1} \delta^* E_{\Pi_2 \Pi_1} \right] + \left[C_{2E}\tau \left(E_{p_1 p_1} - R^1_{p_1 p_1} \right) \right], \qquad (5.5)$$

$$\quad (A) \qquad\qquad\qquad (B)$$

where γ is a positive constant [see Edwards and van Wijnbergen (1983)], and $C_{2E} = E_{\Pi_2 W} E_W^{-1}$ is the marginal propensity to spend (on all goods) in period 2. Equation (5.5) tells us that a small tariff may *increase* δ, or *lower* the interest rate that has to be charged to investors in order to meet the capital market constraint. The mechanism is clear: a small tariff in the first period *decreases* the consumption discount factor $\delta^* \Pi_2 / \Pi_1$ or, equivalently *increases* the Consumption Rate of Interest (CRI). This leads to higher private savings, leaving more room for investment given the current account constraint. Accordingly, δ can go up, i.e. rise in the direction of the world market discount factor δ^*. This effect corresponds to term (A) in (5.5). If, however, the tariff is too large, term (B), which is proportional to τ, will dominate and reverse the result. The reason is once again clear: a large first-period tariff will inflict a large first-period, real-income loss; consumption smoothing will then lead to downward pressure on the first-period current account. If the real income loss is large enough, this effect will offset the positive effect via the CRI.

An important direct implication of the above discussion is that, in the present context, a small temporary tariff may result in welfare gains. The reason for this is that a (small) temporary tariff in period 1 makes present consumption more expensive, and results in the postponement of consumption. More funds are then available for savings and, consequently, investment in period 1 increases. Since investment was below the undistorted optimal level, this increase in investment is welfare-improving. Obviously, in addition to this positive welfare effect of the temporary tariff there is a traditional static welfare loss in period 1. For a small enough tariff, however, the positive welfare effect dominates. This can be found formally by differentiating (5.1) and (5.2) and using (5.3):

$$\gamma_1 \frac{dW}{d\tau} = \Pi_{1p_1}\Pi_2 E_{\Pi_2\Pi_1}(\delta^* - \delta) + \tau\left(E_{p_1 p_1} - R^1_{p_1 p_1}\right), \qquad (5.6)$$
$$(+;C) \qquad\qquad\qquad (-;D)$$

where $\gamma_1 > 0$ [see Edwards and van Wijnbergen (1986a)]. The first term, (C), is proportional to the size of the capital market distortion $(\delta^* - \delta)$ and to the compensated sensitivity of savings with respect to the rate of interest ($E_{\Pi_2\Pi_1}$) and is positive. A temporary tariff will raise the consumption rate of interest, increasing private savings, therefore leaving more room for private investment and so will reduce the distortionary costs of the external balance constraint cum investment rationing.[14] If the first-period tariff is too large, however, the second term, D, will dominate since it is proportional to τ. In that case the first-period relative price distortion will offset the dynamic gains via the CRI.

Setting the marginal net welfare gain of a first-period tariff equal to zero in equation (5.6) implicitly defines the (second-best) optimal first period tariff:

$$\tau^{**} = -\Pi_2\Pi_{1p_1}E_{\Pi_2\Pi_1}\left(\delta^* - \delta\right)\bigg/\left(E_{p_1 p_1} - R^1_{p_1 p_1}\right) > 0. \qquad (5.7)$$

This example establishes the superiority of gradualism over cold turkey liberalization under the external balance constraint cum investment rationing.[15] It should be emphasized, however, that this result is conditional upon investment taking a disproportionate share of the adjustment burden arising from the external constraint; if a market-clearing real interest rate above world levels can be charged to consumers and investors alike, it can be shown that the argument for additional first-period relative price distortions via temporary tariffs disappears, the favorable CRI effects notwithstanding. However, since as discussed

---

[14]Of course this (positive) intertemporal effect on domestic savings on welfare can also be obtained through the imposition of a temporary tax on consumption in period 1. It should be recognized, however, that in many developing countries it is administratively very difficult to impose consumption taxes.

[15]An interesting extension of the present model refers to the multiperiod case. In this case, gradualism will still be superior to cold turkey liberalization. However, in that setting, the second-period tariff will not necessarily be equal to zero.

above, in most LDCs such a first-best rationing device is typically unavailable, our argument for gradualism stands.

6. Devaluation, structural adjustment, and aggregate output

Nominal devaluations are usually major components of structural adjustment programs – especially of those sponsored by the IMF and/or the World Bank. In the case of developing countries that do not have a floating exchange rate system, this usually means that the value of the exchange rate is abruptly changed. In a vast majority of cases devaluations are implemented under "crisis" conditions, where prior to the devaluation the country in question has entered a deep disequilibrium in the external sector. This disequilibrium situation is usually the result of macroeconomic policies that are inconsistent with the nominal exchange rate regime chosen by the country. The inconsistent macroeconomic policies result in an erosion of the stock of international reserves and in a steady real exchange rate appreciation. The authorities usually try to stop the loss in reserves by imposing all sorts of exchange controls. These policies, however, cannot succeed as long as the source of the disequilibrium – the inconsistent macro policies – is not corrected. At some point the Central Bank "runs out" of international reserves and a *nominal* devaluation – which is usually only one component of a broader adjustment package – is implemented. Usually, at this point the authorities dismantle some of the exchange controls. In principle, the policy objectives of this devaluation are (a) to generate a real devaluation (increase in the relative price of tradables to nontraded goods) or improvement in the international competitiveness of the country; and (b), through the real devaluation, to provoke an improvement in its external position, by improving the current account and the balance of payments. A number of cross-country empirical studies have found that, to the extent that nominal devaluations are accompanied by demand management policies, they are in fact fairly successful in the short and medium run [Cooper (1971a, 1971b), Connolly and Taylor (1976), Krueger (1978), Bird (1983) and Edwards (1987, 1989)]. If, on the other hand, macroeconomic policies remain inconsistent, the devaluation will fail to achieve its objectives.

Recently, a number of authors have questioned the effectiveness of nominal devaluations as policy tools. It has been argued that although devaluations may achieve their goals of generating relative price adjustments, they do so at a high cost. In particular, it has been pointed out that one such (indirect) cost is the decline in total output and employment generated by the devaluation. This critique has come to be known as the *contractionary devaluation* problem.[16]

---

[16] Devaluations traditionally have also had important political connotations [Cooper (1971a, 1971b).

In this section we tackle two main issues related to the role of nominal devaluations as policy tools in the adjustment process. First we look at the effects of devaluations on relative prices and the external sector; and second we analyze the contractionary devaluation issue, investigating the way in which devaluations affect aggregate output and employment.

6.1. Alternative theories of devaluation

Different models of the open economy have different implications for the effectiveness of devaluations as policy tools. Most of the traditional models, however, do not emphasize sufficiently the fact that – at least in most developing nations – devaluations are usually implemented under conditions of disequilibrium characterized by serious foreign exchange shortages and by the existence of generalized exchange controls.

In the simplest elasticities approach framework, a devaluation will be effective – in the sense that it will improve the balance of trade – as long as the Marshall–Lerner condition holds. This condition states that for a small country that specializes in the production of its domestic good the sum of the demand elasticities for domestic exports and demand elasticities for the country's imports exceeds unity.[17] Rigorously, in this simple partial equilibrium framework there is no real exchange rate, so issues of real vs. nominal devaluations cannot be tackled formally.

The absorption approach is general equilibrium in nature and in principle allows for the existence of nontradable goods. This approach establishes the important fact that the current account surplus is equal to the excess of income over expenditure. Thus, in order for a devaluation to have an effect on the current account it has to have an impact either on real income, on real expenditure, or on both. Perhaps the most important insight of the absorption approach is that it distinguishes two basic ways in which domestic policies can affect the current account. The first, *expenditure reducing*, requires that expenditure falls relative to real income. The second, *expenditure switching*, requires that the composition of expenditure moves from foreign to domestic goods. In this case if there are unutilized resources the switching of expenditure will generate an increase in real income (via higher output) and, thus, an improvement of the current account. Whether a devaluation is actually effective, then, depends on its ability to generate expenditure switching and/or reducing effects. The first will be the case if, as in the elasticities approach, the elasticities are "sufficiently high". A devaluation can also generate expenditure reducing effects, mainly via

---

[17]If the initial situation is one of external disequilibrium then the Marshall–Lerner condition has to be modified.

the holdings of real balances. Regarding the effect of nominal devaluations on the real exchange rate the absorption approach is quite general, without specifying a rigid result. If a devaluation works via the expenditure switching channel, it will have to affect relative prices and thus the real exchange rate. Regarding aggregate output, a devaluation that has a positive effect on relative prices and generates an expenditure switching will have a positive impact on the economy's aggregate level of activity.

Although the elasticities approach is fundamentally partial equilibrium in nature, Dornbusch (1975) has shown that it can easily be integrated with the absorption approach. In this integrated view a devaluation will still be effective as long as the elasticities involved are sufficiently high, and the devaluation is accompanied by the appropriate macro policies. In this setting, if devaluations are implemented side-by-side with expansionary monetary or fiscal policies, they will fail to generate an improvement in the balance of trade. Due to the partial equilibrium nature of this approach there is no formal connection between devaluation and the real output or unemployment.

Simple Keynesian models of the open economy can also be integrated with the elasticities approach, in order to investigate the effectiveness of devaluations as policy tools. In this case, again, as long as the Marshall–Lerner condition holds, a nominal devaluation will be very effective: the balance of trade will improve, output will go up, and a real devaluation will take place as a result of a nominal exchange rate adjustment.

Another popular class of model used to analyze the effects of devaluations is the Monetary Approach to the Balance of Payments (MABP) [Frenkel and Johnson (1976)]. In its simplest incarnation this approach is nothing but an open economy version of the quantity theory of money. As such, it is characterized by neutrality and dichotomy. As is indicated by its name, the monetary approach focuses on the interaction between the external sector and the monetary side of the economy. In its textbook version the MABP assumes that the absolute variant of the Purchasing Power Parity (PPP) theory holds, and that uncovered interest arbitrage holds permanently. Under these assumptions a nominal devaluation will have no effect on relative prices or on the real exchange rate. This is because under PPP, $P = EP^*$ (for P domestic price level, E nominal exchange rate, and P^* foreign price level) and consequently a nominal devaluation has a one-to-one effect on domestic prices:

In this setting, however, a devaluation will generate a negative real balance effect and, if domestic credit is kept constant, it will result in a *temporary* improvement in the balance of payments. This positive effect will disappear once monetary equilibrium is re-established. Most versions of the MABP are silent regarding the dynamics of the process, and thus do not specify the speed at which this monetary equilibrium will take place. In general, however, it will be expected that the speed of adjustment will depend on the degree of openness of the capital and current accounts of the balance of payments. According to the simplest version of the MABP a devaluation will have no effect either in the short or long run on real output. The reason for this, of course, is that in the textbook version of the MABP the classical dichotomy holds.

In a sense, the simple Keynesian model and the MABP provide two extremes regarding the role of devaluations in the adjustment process. However, most recent work on open macroeconomics has moved away from these extremes, adopting what we shall call the synthesis approach.[18] This synthesis view combines characteristics of both the MABP and the Keynesian model with some features from other models, in order to derive a framework that is able to track more closely the developments observed in the real world. The synthesis model assumes, up to a certain point, an upward-sloping aggregate supply curve; prices and wages are sticky in the short run; domestic and foreign assets are imperfect substitutes; the Purchasing Power Parity relation does not hold in the short run; and the equilibrium real exchange rate responds to a series of real fundamental determinants.

6.2. Devaluation, output, and the trade balance: A simple framework

The impact that a discrete devaluation has on output, employment, and other real variables will depend in a critical way on the state of the economy. If prices are slow to adjust, the impact effects will depend very much on whether the business cycle has moved market-clearing prices above or below their actual values. We briefly sketch a formal argument to this extent, before reviewing the empirical evidence on the relation between devaluation and aggregate output.

Let us assume that output is produced using labor, intermediate imports ("oil") and capital. The latter is fixed in the short run. This leads to an aggregate supply function that depends negatively on the real product price of labor and oil, W/P and P_0^*E/P, respectively:

$$y^s = y^s(W/P, P_0^*E/P; K).$$ (6.1)

If we define w as the real wage in terms of imports, $w = W/(EP^*)$, p_0^* as the price of oil, deflated similarly and the terms of trade as $q = P/(EP^*)$, with P^* the foreign price of final goods imports; and assume short-run real consumption wage rigidity, w will be a negative function of q:

$$\hat{W} = \psi\hat{P} + (1 - \psi)(\hat{E} + \hat{P}^*) \gg \hat{W} - \hat{P} = -(1 - \psi)\hat{q},$$ (6.2)

[18]See Frenkel et al. (1980) for an attempt to develop such a synthesis.

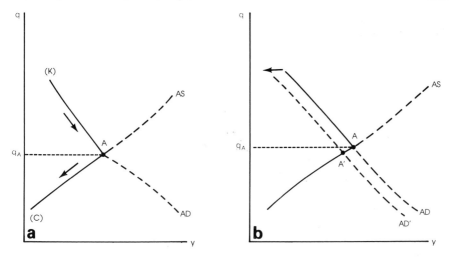

Figure 28.13

where ψ is the share of home goods in the consumption basket, and is smaller than one. From this expression we can represent the aggregate supply as:

$$y^s = y(q; p_0^*, K), \qquad (6.2')$$

with $y_q^s > 0$ (see the Aggregate Supply locus, *AS*, in Figure 28.13). A discrete devaluation that succeeds in lowering q (i.e. bringing about a real depreciation), will reduce aggregate supply [van Wijnbergen (1986a)].

Consider next aggregate demand. That consists of home spending on home goods, c_d, exports $E(q)$, and the component of investment and government expenditure that falls on home goods (I and G):

$$y^\Delta = c_d(q, y - T, MR + K) + I(i - \hat{p}, e/q, K) + E(q) + G, \qquad (6.3)$$

where MR are real money balances, $MR + K$ is total real wealth, T are taxes and $(i - \hat{p})$ is the real interest rate. We can substitute out interest rates by using a money market-clearing condition [where $f(\cdot)$ is the demand function for real cash balances]:

$$MR = f(i, y - T, MR + K). \qquad (6.4)$$

As long as there is less than perfect capital mobility, domestic policies will be able to influence interest rates [Edwards (1985b), Edwards and Khan (1985)]. This leads to an aggregate demand curve y^d (locus AD in Figure 28.13)):

$$y^d = y^d(q, MR, \ldots).$$ (6.5)

Under perfect capital mobility, $(\partial y^d/\partial MR)(\partial MR/\partial E) = 0$. However, if capital mobility is imperfect, we get $(\partial y^d/\partial MR)(\partial MR/\partial E) < 0$.

Consider first the perfect capital mobility case [Figure 28.13(a)]. In this case there is no real balance effect through MR and hence the Walrasian equilibrium A does not shift in response to a discrete devaluation. If all prices are flexible, the initial condition is one of full equilibrium and there is no real balance effect, a nominal devaluation has no real effects. What will happen when prices are rigid and possibly different from their Walrasian market clearing level q_A [see Figure 28.13(a, b)]? If $q > q_A$, there is excess supply of home goods and aggregate demand will determine output levels: segment K of the AD curve in Figure 28.13. This corresponds to Keynesian unemployment [van Wijnbergen (1986b)]. If $q < q_A$, there is excess demand for home goods and aggregate supply determines output: segment C of the AS curve in Figure 28.13. This corresponds to classical unemployment.

Both regimes are characterized by unemployment, since we assume real wages to be above levels where a "repressed inflation"–full employment regime could emerge. The overvaluation ($q > q_A$) K region then corresponds to Keynesian unemployment and the "undervaluation" C region to classical unemployment [van Wijnbergen (1986b)].

The arrows indicate in which directions output will move in different regimes after a nominal devaluation in a sticky price world: a successful nominal devaluation should lead to an *expansion* of output under Keynesian unemployment. The expenditure switching effect of a successful devaluation would shift demand towards "our" goods, increasing effective demand; this in turn leads to higher output since in this regime output is demand determined.

However, output effects are very different in the supply constrained regime. Here increases in effective demand have no actual impact on output, since that is supply constrained; moreover, an effective devaluation (one that actually reduces q) will raise the price of intermediate imports in terms of home goods, P_0^*/q. Also, if real consumption wages are rigid, a real depreciation will lead to higher real wages expressed in home goods to make up for the fall in the real wage in terms of imported goods. Both effects imply higher variable cost of production and hence a reduction in aggregate supply. Thus a devaluation is contractionary when unemployment is classical, but expansionary when unemployment is Keynesian.

The difference in output response also leads to different trade balance effects. In the Keynesian case, one expects a more favorable trade balance response than in the classical regime, because income falls temporarily in the latter but rises temporarily in the Keynesian case [Edwards and van Wijnbergen (1986b)]. In what follows, we look at how these theoretical predictions fare when confronted with empirical evidence.

6.3. Nominal devaluations and the real exchange rate: The empirical evidence

As discussed above, one of the critical questions when evaluating the effectiveness of nominal devaluations as policy tools is whether they are able to generate a real devaluation. In fact, a number of developing countries' governments have refused to follow the IMF advice of devaluing their currencies by arguing that nominal devaluations are associated with equiproportional increases in domestic prices and, consequently, do not affect the real exchange rate.

Some studies have empirically analyzed, over the last few years, whether in fact major devaluations in the LDCs have been associated with relative price changes. Cooper (1971a, 1971b), for example, analyzed 24 devaluations in the developing nations. He found that in most cases nominal devaluations were indeed associated with real devaluations. He also pointed out that in most instances major discrete devaluations had been accompanied by some sort of trade reforms, where quantitative restrictions were lifted, and tariffs were lowered. This finding has also been reported by Krueger (1978) and Edwards (1987).

Connolly and Taylor (1976, 1979) conducted a comprehensive study on the effects of devaluation on the external sector, and found that nominal devaluations were translated into relative price changes, or real devaluations, in the short to medium run. For example, the evidence presented in their 1979 paper suggests that on impact nominal devaluations had an important effect on relative prices; this erodes slowly until 9 quarters after the devaluation the real exchange rate is back to its value of 2 years before the devaluation. An important point made by Connolly and Taylor (1979) is that the effect of devaluation will critically depend on the macro policies that accompany the devaluation.

Other studies by Donovan (1981), Bautista (1982), and Morgan and Davis (1982) also indicate, using different data sets and time periods, that nominal devaluations have an initial positive effect on relative prices. This effect, however, is slowly eroded through time. The results obtained in these studies differ, however, in terms of the speed and the extent of the real erosions of the real exchange rate. More recently, Chuhan (1985) has analyzed the case of 32 discrete devaluations between 1961 and 1978. As most of the other studies analyzed above Chuhan used a "before" and "after" approach, where the value of the real exchange rate index before the devaluation was compared with its value some time after the devaluation. Along the lines of the previous studies, it was found that by and large nominal devaluations have had a positive effect on the real exchange rate, and that this effect was eroded as time went by. The rate of erosion varied across countries and in some cases the effect of the nominal devaluation had completely disappeared after two years.

In a recent study Edwards (1987, 1989) has analyzed several aspects of nominal devaluations in developing countries. Using a data set of 18, (38), major discrete devaluation episodes between 1962 and 1982, Edwards investigates in detail both the period preceding the devaluation and the period immediately following them. In his discussion Edwards concentrates on the role of exchange controls, multiple rates and black markets in the period preceding the devaluation as well as in the period following it. In his analysis of the behavior of the real exchange rate in the period following nominal devaluations, Edwards (1987, 1989) found that on impact the nominal devaluation resulted in a relatively high real devaluation. However, in all cases this positive effect suffered some erosion during the next 16 quarters. Moreover, in some cases the erosion was more than complete, and the nominal exchange rate adjustment was ineffective – Argentina 1970, Bolivia 1979, Nicaragua 1979 are particularly striking examples of this phenomena. Usually in these cases the authorities were forced to further devalue some time down the road. In fact, Edwards shows that the countries that had a high (or complete) erosion of the effect of nominal devaluation in a period of four years, were those that accompanied the exchange rate adjustment with inconsistent macro policies, and/or had wage indexation schemes. In particular, those countries that failed to correct their expansive fiscal policies invariably suffered relapses, and were soon back in a crisis situation. On the other hand, those countries that experienced a small degree of erosion usually implemented consistent demand management policies.

Summarizing, then, the literature reviewed in this section shows that typically abrupt nominal devaluations have been the consequence of crisis situations, resulting from unsustainable expansive monetary and fiscal policies. In most cases the devaluation crises have been preceded by periods of steep declines in the level of international reserves, rapidly increasing real wages, continuous real appreciations, the imposition of tariffs, import licenses and exchange controls, and the proliferation of multiple exchange rates. The empirical analysis reviewed also indicates that nominal devaluations can be helpful to restore real exchange rate equilibrium. The degree of success of nominal devaluations to generate real devaluations will basically depend on the accompanying macro policies and on the initial conditions.

As discussed above, there are several theoretical reasons why, contrary to the traditional views, a devaluation can be contractionary, and generate a decline in aggregate real activity, including employment. In spite of the renewed theoretical interest in the possible contractionary effects of devaluations, the empirical analysis has been sketchy, to say the least. A number of studies have used cross-country data to simulate the effects of devaluations on real output.

Gylfason and Schmid (1983) have constructed a small macro model with intermediate goods, where a devaluation has two conflicting effects: on the one hand, it generates an expansion through aggregate demand; on the other hand, a devaluation results, through its effect on the cost of imported intermediate inputs, in a backward shift in the aggregate supply schedule. The final effect of a devaluation can be either expansionary or contractionary.

Gylfason and Schmid empirically analyze the implications of their model by imputing plausible values to the corresponding parameters for a group of five developed countries and five developing countries. With the exceptions of the United Kingdom and Brazil their results suggest that, as postulated by the more traditional views, devaluations have a positive overall effect on aggregate output.

Connolly (1983) considered a group of 22 countries and regressed for the cross-country data set the change in the rate of real growth on the change in the nominal exchange rate. The coefficient obtained was positive and marginally significant, providing some support for the hypothesis of expansionary devaluations. However, Connolly argues that his results are subject to a selectivity bias, since typically countries that devalue do so after having entered into a recession.

Gylfason and Risager (1984) developed a model for a small country, which stresses the effect of devaluations on interest payments on the foreign debt. Using imputed parameter data they find that while devaluations are generally expansionary in developed countries, in developing countries they are likely to be contractionary. However, a problem with this type of approach is that the parameters used in the simulation are obtained from very different sources, and are likely to be inconsistent among themselves.

Gylfason and Radetzki (1985) developed a small macro model to investigate the effects of devaluations on real output, the current account and real wages. They show that in a world with no capital movements, in order for a devaluation to result in higher real output, real wages necessarily have to fall. They then show that if a devaluation is accompanied by an inflow of foreign funds, it is possible for real output to increase with unchanged real wages. Gylfason and Radetzki use a group of 12 developing countries to simulate their model. As in other papers, in the simulation analysis they use imputed values for the parameters. Their results suggest that, for their group of countries, with nominal wages constant and no capital inflows, a 10 percent devaluation will result in a decline of real GNP of 0.5 percent.

Other authors have constructed country-specific simulation models to analyze the effectiveness of devaluations as stabilization policy tools. Branson (1986), for example, has recently constructed a small simulation model for Kenya to investigate these issues. His results suggest that, contrary to the traditional view, a devaluation will have important contractionary effects in the Kenyan economy. Taylor and Rosensweig (1984), on the other hand, built a fairly large computable general equilibrium model for Thailand, and simulated the effects of a number of policy measures, including a devaluation. Their results indicate that a devaluation of the baht of 10 percent will have an expansionary effect and will generate an *increase* in real GDP of 3.3 percent.

Other studies have discussed the output effects of devaluations in a less formal way. Cooper (1971a), in his well-known study, analyzed 24 devaluations that took place between 1953 and 1966. After looking at the behavior of the principal components of aggregate demand he concluded that "devaluation itself often initially tends to depress economic activity in the devaluing country, contrary to what has normally been expected" (p. 504). Krueger (1978) analyzed output behavior during the periods surrounding major devaluation episodes in the countries considered in the NBER project on trade liberalization. She found that in most cases devaluations had been associated with expansions in the level of real activity. Also, the numerous studies that have investigated the effects of IMF stabilization programs on output have looked at real activity behavior before and after major devaluations. Most of these studies have used a "before" and "after" approach and found that nominal devaluations had not been accompanied, or followed, by major declines in real activity [Gylfason (1983), Khan and Knight (1985)]. All these studies suffer either from the fact that they are based on made-up numbers, or that they do not control for changes in macroeconomic policy instruments that took place simultaneously.

In his general empirical analysis of devaluation, Edwards (1989) looked in detail at the contractionary devaluation issue. This was done in two ways. First, the real activity aspects of the 39 devaluations episodes used in his analysis were closely scrutinized. The behavior of a number of key variables in the period elapsed between three years before the devaluation and three years after the devaluation was analyzed for all 39 devaluation episodes. The emphasis was placed on real aggregate output, aggregate gross investment and real growth. It was found that, by and large, the evidence was mixed, and depending on which variable one looked at, some countries experienced a fall in real activity and others experienced an increase in the level of real activity.

Of course, as with the other papers, a problem of this type of analysis is that it concentrates on the behavior of the key variables "before" and "after" the devaluation, without taking into account the possible role of other policies or external events. This problem was avoided by the second approach taken in this study: an equation for aggregate output in an open economy was estimated for a group of 12 countries, using instrumental variables techniques on pooled data. In addition to the possible effect of the exchange rate on output, this equation incorporates the role of monetary policy, fiscal policy and exogenous terms of trade changes. From this regression analysis it was found that, keeping other things constant, devaluations have a contractionary effect in the short run. In the long run, however, devaluations appear to be neutral, and do not affect the level of aggregate real activity. The result actually obtained was the following [see Edwards (1986b, 1989)]:

$$\log y_{tm} = \begin{array}{c} 0.102[\Delta \log M_t - \Delta \log M_t^*] + 0.210[\Delta \log M_{t-1} - \Delta \log M_{t-1}^*] \\ (1.146) \qquad\qquad\qquad\qquad (2.331) \end{array}$$

$$+ 0.112 \log(GE/Y)_t - 0.083 \log e_t + 0.069 \log e_{t-1}$$
$$(3.023) \qquad\qquad (2.103) \qquad\quad (2.086)$$

$$+ 0.044 \log \theta_t - 0.008 \log \tau_{t-1}, \quad \bar{R}^2 = 0.998, \; SEE = 0.038,$$
$$(1.431) \qquad (-0.265)$$

where y is real output, $[\Delta \log M - \Delta \log M^*]$ is the unexpected rate of growth of money, (GE/Y) is the ratio of government expenditure to GNP, e is the real exchange rate and τ are the terms of trade.

In the short run, a devaluation will lead to a significant fall in output, to the extent that it actually brings about a real devaluation. The amount of the decline is substantial: a 10 percent depreciation leads to a once-off loss of almost 1 percent of GNP. In the second year, however, the economy returns to its trend growth rate.

References

Arida, P. and E. Bacha (1983) Balance of payments: A disequilibrium analysis for semi-industrialized economies", Catholic University of Rio de Janeiro, mimeo.

Arrow, K. (1962) The economic implications of learning by doing", *Review of Economic Studies*, 9:155–173.

Bacha, E. (1982) "Growth with limited supplies of foreign exchange: A reappraisal of the two-gap model", Discussion paper no. 26, Economics Dept., Rio de Janeiro: PUC.

Balassa, B. (1982) *Development strategies in semi-industrial economies*. Oxford: Oxford University Press.

Bautista, R.M. (1982) Exchange rate variations and export competitiveness in less developed countries under generalized floating, *Journal of Development Studies*, April.

Berndt, E. and Wood, D. (1975) Technology, prices and the derived demand for energy, *Review of Economics and Statistics*, 57:259–268.

Bird, G. (1983) 'Should developing countries use currency depreciation as a tool of balance of payments adjustment? A Review of the Theory and Evidence, and a Guide for the Policy Maker', *Journal of Development Studies*, 19:July.

Branson, W.H. (1986) 'Stabilization, stagflation and investment incentives: The case of Kenya 1975–80', in: S. Edwards and L. Ahamed, eds., *Economic adjustment and exchange rates in developing countries*.

Bruno, M. (1985) 'Introduction', *World Development*, August.

Chenery, H.B., et al. (1974) *Redistribution with growth*. London: Oxford University Press.

Chenery, H.B. and Strout, A.M. (1966) 'Foreign assistance and economic development', *American Economic Review*, September.

Chuhan, P. (1985) 'Effect of devaluation', World Bank Working Paper.

Clark, Paul (1982) 'Step-by-step liberalization of a controlled economy: Experience in Egypt', unpublished.

Connolly, M. (1983) 'Exchange rate, real economic activity and the balance of payment', in: E. Classen and P. Salin, eds., *Recent issues in the theory of flexible exchange rates*. Amsterdam: North-Holland.

Connolly, M. and Taylor, D. (1976) 'Adjustment to devaluation with money and nontraded goods', *Journal of International Economics*, 6:289–298.

Connolly, M. and Taylor, D. (1979) 'Exchange rate changes and neutralization: A test of the monetary approach applied to developed and developing countries', *Economica*, August.

Cooper, R. (1971a) 'Currency devaluation in developing countries', in: G. Ranis, ed., *Government and economic development*, New Haven, CT: Yale University Press.

Cooper, R. (1971b) 'Currency depreciation in developing countries', *Princeton Essays in International Finance*, 86.

Dixit, A. and Norman, V. (1980) *Theory of international trade*. Cambridge, MA: Cambridge University Press.

Donovan, D.J. (1981) 'Real responses associated with exchange rate action in selected upper credit tranche stabilization programs', *IMF Staff Papers*, December.

Dornbusch, R. (1974) 'Tariffs and Non-Traded Goods', *Journal of International Economics*, 4:117–185.

Dornbusch, R. (1975) 'Exchange rates and fiscal policy in a popular model of international trade', *American Economic Review*, December.

Dornbusch, R. (1980) *Open Economy Macroeconomics*. New York: Basic Books.

Edwards, S. (1982) 'Minimum wages and trade liberalization: Some reflections based on the Chilean experience', Working Paper no. 230, Dept. of Economics, Los Angeles, CA: UCLA Press.

Edwards, S. (1984a) 'The order of liberalization of the external sector in developing countries', *Princeton Essays in International Finance*, no. 156, Princeton, NJ: Princeton University Press.

Edwards, S. (1984b) 'LDC's foreign borrowing and default risk: An empirical investigation 1976–1980', *American Economic Review*, September.

Edwards, S. (1985a), 'Stabilization with liberalization: An evaluation of ten years of Chile's experiment with free market policies', *Economic Development and Cultural Change*, 33:223–254.

Edwards, S. (1985b) 'Money, the rate of devaluation and interest rate in a semi-open economy', *Journal of Money, Credit and Banking*, February.

Edwards, S. (1986a) 'Commodity export prices and the real exchange rate: Coffee in Colombia', in: S. Edwards and L. Ahamed, eds., *Economic adjustment and exchange rates in developing countries*. Chicago, IL: University of Chicago Press for the National Bureau of Economic Research.

Edwards, S. (1986b) 'Are devaluations contractionary?, *Review of Economics and Statistics*, August.

Edwards, S. (1986c) 'The liberalization of the current and capital accounts of the balance of payments', in: A. Choski and D. Papageorgiou, eds., *Economic liberalization in developing countries*. Oxford: Blackwell.

Edwards, S. (1987) 'Exchange controls, nominal devaluations and the real exchange rate: The Latin American experience', presented at the Banco de la Republica de Colombia Conference on Exchange Controls, Bogota, Colombia, June.

Edwards, S. (1989) *Real exchange rates, devaluation and adjustment: Exchange rate policy in developing countries*, Cambridge, MA: MIT Press, forthcoming.

Edwards, S. and Ahamed, L. eds. (1986) *Economic adjustment and exchange rates in developing countries*. Chicago, IL: University of Chicago Press for the National Bureau of Economic Research.

Edwards, S. and Cox-Edwards, A. (1987) *Monetarism and liberalization: The Chilean experiment*. New York: Ballinger.

Edwards, S. and Khan, M.S. (1985) 'Interest rate determination in developing countries: A conceptual framework', *IMF Staff Papers*.

Edwards S. and van Wijnbergen, S. (1983) 'The welfare effects of trade and capital market liberalization: Consequences of different sequencing scenarios', National Bureau of Economic Research Working Paper.

Edwards, S. and van Wijnbergen, S. (1986a) 'Welfare effects of trade and capital market liberalization: Consequences of different sequencing scenarios', *International Economic Review*, February.

Edwards, S. and van Wijnbergen, S. (1986b) 'On the appropriate timing of trade and financial liberalization', in: M. Connolly, ed., *Trade and financial liberalization in Latin America*. New York: Praeger.

Edwards, S. and van Wijnbergen, S. (1987) 'On the quasi-inconsistency of two popular propositions in international economics', in: *Oxford Economic Papers*, 39:458–464.

Findlay, R. (1983) *International trade and development theory*. New York: Columbia University Press.

Frenkel, J. and Johnson, H. (1976) *The monetary approach to the balance of payments*. London: Allen & Unwin.

Frenkel, J., et al. (1980) 'A synthesis of monetary and Keynesian approaches to short run balance-of-payments theory', *Economic Journal*, 90:582–592.

Gylfason, T. (1983) 'Credit policy and economic activity in developing countries: An evaluation of stabilization programs supported by the IMF 1977–79', IIES Seminar Paper no. 268, Stockholm: University of Stockholm.

Gylfason, T. and Risager, O. (1984) 'Does devaluation improve the current account?, *European Economic Review*, 25:June.

Gylfason, T. and Radetski, M. (1985) Does devaluation make sense in the least developed countries?, IIES Seminar Paper no. 314, Stockholm: University of Stockholm.

Gylfason, T. and Schmid, M. (1983) 'Does devaluation cause stagflation?, *Canadian Journal of Economics*, 21:November.

Haffez, S. (1984) 'Patterns of reduction in sectoral government expenditure in less developed countries: A preliminary investigation', CDP, Washington, DC: The World Bank.

Hicks, N. and Kubisch, A. (1984) 'Cutting government expenditure in LDCs', *Finance and Development*, 21:37–39.

Jones, R.W. (1971) 'A three factor model in theory, trade and history', in: J. Bhagwati, ed., *Trade, balance of payments growth*. Amsterdam: North-Holland.

Khan, M.S. and Knight, M.D. (1985) 'Fund-supported adjustment programs and economic growth', Occasional Paper no. 41, Washington, DC: IMF.

Khan, M.S. and Zahler, R. (1983) 'The macroeconomic effects of changes in barriers to trade and capital flows: A simulation analysis', *IMF Staff Papers*, June:223–282.

Krueger, A.O. (1978) *Foreign trade regimes and economic development: Liberalization attempts and consequences*. Cambridge, MA.

Krueger, A.O. (1981) 'Interactions between inflation and trade objectives in stabilization programs', in: W.R. Cline and S. Weintraub, eds., *Economic stabilization in developing countries*, Washington, DC: Brookings Institution.

Krueger, A.O. (1983) 'The problems of liberalization', The World Bank, unpublished.

Krugman, P. and Taylor, L. (1978) 'Contractionary effects of devaluation', *Journal of International Economics*, 8:445–456.

Lapan, H.E. (1976) 'International trade, factor market distortions, and the optimal dynamic subsidy', *American Economic Review*, June.

Leamer, E.E. (1980) 'Welfare computations and the optimal staging of tariff reductions in models with adjustment costs', *Journal of International Economics*, 10:21–36.

Little, I. (1982) *Economic development*. New York: Basic Books.

Little, I., Scitovsky, T., and Scott, M. (1970) *Industry and trade in some developing countries*. Oxford: Oxford University Press.

Malinvaud, E. (1977) *The theory of unemployment reconsidered*. Oxford: Basil Blackwell.

Mayer, W. (1974) 'Short run and long run equilibrium for a small open economy', *Journal of Political Economy*, 82:955–967.

McKinnon, R.J. (1982) 'The order of economic liberalization: Lessons from Chile and Argentina', in: K. Brunner and A. Meltzer, eds., *Economic policy in a world of change*. Amsterdam: North-Holland.

Melvin, J. (1968) 'Production and trade with two factors and three goods', *American Economic Review*, 1249–1268.

Michaely, M. (1982) 'The sequencing of a liberalization policy: A preliminary statement of issues', unpublished.

Morgan, and Davis (1982) 'On the concomitant effects of exchange rate devaluation', *Economic Development and Cultural Change*, 31:101–130.

Mussa, M. (1974) 'Tariffs and the distribution of income: The "importance of factor specificity, substitutability and intensity in the short and long run"', *Journal of Political Economy*, 82:1191–1203.

Mussa, M. (1978) 'Dynamic adjustment in the Heckscher–Ohlin–Samuelson model, *Journal of Political Economy*, 1191–1203.

Mussa, M. (1979) 'The two sectors model in terms of its dual: A geometric exposition', *Journal of International Economics*, 9:513–526.

Mussa, M. (1982) 'Government policy and the adjustment process', in: J. Bhagwati, ed., *Import competition and response*. Chicago, IL: University of Chicago Press, 73–120.

Mussa, M. (1984) 'The adjustment process and the timing of trade liberalization', The World Bank, unpublished.

Neary, J.P. (1978a) 'Short-run capital specificity and the pure theory of international trade', *Economic Journal*, 88:448–510.

Neary, J.P. (1978b) 'Dynamic stability and the theory of factor-market distortions', *American Economic Review*, 671–682.

Neary, J.P. (1980) 'Non-traded goods and the balance of trade in a neo-Keynesian temporary equilibrium', *Quarterly Journal of Economics*, 95:403–429.

Neary, J.P. (1982) 'Capital mobility, wage stickiness and the case for adjustment assistance', in: J. Bhagwati, ed., *Import competition and response*. Chicago, IL: University of Chicago Press.

Neary, J.P. (1985) 'International factor mobility, minimum wage rates and factor price equalization: A synthesis', *Quarterly Journal of Economics*, 551–570.

Neary, J.P. and Roberts, K. (1980) 'The theory of household behaviour under rationing', *European Economic Review*, 13.

Neary, J.P. and van Wijnbergen, S. eds. (1986) *Natural resources and the macroeconomy*. Cambridge, MA: MIT Press.

Park, Y.C. (1985) 'Korea's experience with external debt management', Working Paper, Korea University.

Pindyck, R.S. (1982) 'The optimal phasing of phased deregulation', *Journal of Economic Dynamics and Control*, 4:281–294.

Rodrik, D. (1985) 'Trade and capital-account liberalization in a Keynesian economy', Discussion Paper Series no. 136D, J.F. Kennedy School of Government, Harvard University.

Salter, W.E.G. (1959) 'Internal and external balance: The role of price and expenditure effects', *Economic Record*, 35:226–238.

Stockman, A.C. (1982) 'The order of economic liberalization: Comment', in: K. Brunner and A.H. Meltzer, eds., *Economic policy in a world of change*. Amsterdam: North-Holland.

Svensson, L. (1985) 'Oil prices and a small country's welfare and trade balance: An intertemporal approach', *Quarterly Journal of Economics*.

Svensson, L. and Razin, A. (1983) 'The terms of trade and the current account: The Harberger–Laursen–Metzler effect', *Journal of Political Economy*, 91:97–125.

Taylor, L. (1983) *Structuralist macroeconomics*. New York: Basic Books.

Taylor, L. and Rosensweig, J. (1984) 'Devaluation, capital flows and crowding out: A CGE model with portfolio choice for Thailand', Working Paper, The World Bank.

van Wijnbergen, S. (1982) 'Stagflationary effects of monetary stabilization policies: A quantitative analysis of South Korea', *Journal of Development Economics*, 10:133–169.

van Wijnbergen, S. (1983a) 'Credit policy, inflation and growth in financially repressed economies', *Journal of Development Economics*, 13:45–65.

van Wijnbergen, S. (1983b) 'Interest rate management in LCS's, *Journal of Monetary Economics*, 12:433–452.

van Wijnbergen, S. (1984a) 'Tariffs, employment and the current account: The macroeconomics of real wage resistance', Center for Economic Policy Research Discussion Paper no. 30, London, *International Economic Review*, forthcoming.

van Wijnbergen, S. (1984b) 'The Dutch disease: A disease after all?' *Economic Journal*, 94:41–55.

van Wijnbergen, S. (1984c) 'Inflation, employment and the Dutch disease in oil exporting countries: A short run disequilibrium analysis', *Quarterly Journal of Economics*, May.

van Wijnbergen, S. (1985a) 'Oil discoveries, intertemporal adjustment and public policy', in: O. Bjerkholt and E. Offerdal, eds., *Macroeconomic prospects for a small oil exporting country*. Dordrecht, Holland: Nijhoff.

van Wijnbergen, S. (1985b) 'The optimal investment and current account response to oil price shocks under putty-clay technology', *Journal of International Economics*, 17:139–147.

van Wijnbergen, S. (1985c) 'Oil price shocks, unemployment and the current account: An intertemporal disequilibrium analysis', *Review of Economic Studies*, 52:627–645.

van Wijnbergen, S. (1985d) 'Trade reform, aggregate investment and capital flight: On credibility and the value of information, *Economic Letters*, 19:369–372.

van Wijnbergen, S. (1986a) 'Exchange rate management and stabilization policy in developing countries', in: S. Edwards and L. Ahmed, eds., *Exchange rate policy and structural adjustment in developing countries*. Chicago, IL: NBER and the University of Chicago Press.

van Wijnbergen, S. (1986b) 'Macroeconomic aspects of the effectiveness of foreign aid: On the two-gap model, home goods disequilibrium and real exchange rate misalignment', *Journal of International Economics*, 21:123–136.

van Wijnbergen, S. (1986c) 'Fiscal policy, private investment and the current account: An intertemporal disequilibrium analysis', Center for Economic Policy Research.

PART 6

COUNTRY EXPERIENCE
WITH DEVELOPMENT

INTRODUCTION TO PART 6

HOLLIS B. CHENERY

Harvard University

The rapid increase in both the number of developing countries and the range of available data has made comparative analysis one of the most popular forms of development research. It produced a great expansion of statistical studies of the "development patterns" type, as illustrated in Part 2 on the structural transformation. Identification of the stylized facts of development then led to analyses of the typical effects of development policies and a search for superior strategies.

This concluding part of the Handbook illustrates some of the findings of these comparative-historical studies. The editors have resisted the temptation to enforce a uniform approach on the five authors, although we have tried to get them to address a common set of questions. Since there has been a shift in interest from differences in internal to external development policies, it was not difficult to reach agreement on "Primary Exporting Countries" (Chapter 29), "Import Substitution" (Chapter 30) and "Outward Orientation" (Chapter 31) as alternative strategies that cover a wide range of country experiences.

In some form these three categories are found in almost all typologies of development experience. As Syrquin shows in Chapter 7 of Part 2, controlling for these differences in external policies leads to more homogeneous categories for structural analysis. The choice of internal criteria for this purpose is less clear, since the most obvious candidate – the level of investment – has shown less explanatory power in recent years. Perkins and Syrquin have therefore chosen to investigate the relations between population size and development performance (Chapter 32), using both historical and econometric tests. Although there is no clear-cut theoretical basis for this relationship, it is obvious that China, India, and Brazil face some quite different choices from their smaller counterparts.

Comparing development strategies

A development strategy can be defined in terms of two sets of factors:

(1) *initial conditions*: structural features such as natural resources, and other elements that are usually treated as "endowments"; and

(2) *policy choices*: social preferences (growth vs. equity), trade policies (outward vs. inward), the levels of investment, etc.

Handbook of Development Economics, Volume II, Edited by H. Chenery and T.N. Srinivasan
© *Elsevier Science Publishers B.V., 1989*

Earlier studies of development experience usually considered each of these factors separately, but the more recent trend is to identify representative country types on the basis of two or three dominant features. The authors in Part 6 have all used some form of this typological approach.

Although all four chapters try to identify common elements of postwar experience, their authors have adopted quite different approaches to this task. For example, Stephen Lewis focuses on the characteristic problems of primary exporters. He controls for their differences by comparing pairs of countries that have similar initial conditions. In a typical case, Australia is shown to have achieved better results than Argentina by choosing policies more in keeping with its comparative advantage.

Perkins and Syrquin also compare countries that have similar initial conditions but follow different policies. Their objective is to identify the effects of scale on the choice of strategy and country performance. Using population as a measure of economic size, they are able to test hypotheses about the relation of scale to trade patterns and other structural characteristics.

The two remaining chapters on outward and inward strategies focus on differences in policy choices rather than on initial conditions. In advocating an outward-oriented strategy, Balassa provides statistical evidence of the correlation between the growth of exports and factor productivity and argues that outward orientation contributes to this result. He supports this conclusion by a comparative analysis of outward-oriented and inward-oriented countries in the pre- as well as the post-oil shock periods. Bruton, on the other hand, adopts a broad definition of import substitution as a general strategy for transforming the economy. He thus expands the list of potential benefits of inward orientation that can be achieved over longer periods of time.

Lessons from experience

Despite these differences in approach, all the authors in Part 6 are looking for typical relationships between initial conditions and policy choices. At a minimum this type of analysis leads to the identification of feasible strategies, such as how to manage the deindustrialization that is induced by the expansion of primary exports (Dutch Disease). A more ambitious objective is to establish the properties of strategies that are optimal under a range of conditions, which Balassa asserts to be the case for outward-oriented trade policies.

A statistical background for typological approaches to development has been given by Syrquin (Chapter 7, p. 249), who classifies 106 countries according to three characteristics of their development strategies: size, openness, and trade orientation. He is then able to measure the typical relations between differences in each factor and the aggregate growth rates for the period 1950–1983.

When each of these characteristics is considered separately, Table 7.5 shows that large countries have grown more rapidly than small, that specialization in manufacturing has been more productive than in primary products, and that Balassa's argument for the advantages of outward orientation was supported in the postwar period, regardless of the initial conditions. By contrast the higher growth rate of large countries is concentrated in the subgroup of primary exporters, and the virtues of manufacturing specialization only appear in the subgroup of small countries.

The popularity of comparative analysis has led to a re-examination of the categorization of countries on which it is based. One of the most controversial is the evaluation of the performance of India vs. South Korea, in which most economists favor the latter because of its much higher growth in total factor productivity. Bruton's advocacy of the opposing view (Chapter 31) demonstrates the effect of a basic difference in the underlying assumptions about development processes.

The choice of strategy

The several surveys of country experiences in Part 6 provide little support for the idea that there is a single optimal strategy for all situations. A more realistic goal for comparative studies is to establish some of the properties of strategies and policy instruments that have been relatively effective. This view is in keeping with theoretical findings about second-best policies, which are likely to vary with the initial conditions.

In sum, the main objectives of Part 6 are to identify typical strategies, and to examine how they have worked under different conditions. Typological comparisons indicate that there have been examples of successful country performance starting from a wide variety of initial conditions. While it may not be possible to determine the best set of policies for each type of country, a beginning has been made in studying the relations between policy and performance under different sets of constraints. The four chapters in Part 6 provide examples of success under a wide range of conditions, together with some working hypotheses as to the major factors involved.

Chapter 29

PRIMARY EXPORTING COUNTRIES

STEPHEN R. LEWIS, JR.*

Carleton College

Contents

*This chapter was written largely while I was a Visiting Fellow at the Institute of Development Studies at the University of Sussex. I was also supported by a sabbatical leave from Williams College. Helpful comments on a draft were given by H.B. Chenery, D. Evans, C. Harvey, G.K. Helleiner, M. Lipton, H. Pack, M. Syrquin and P. Timmer, and I also received useful feedback from seminars on the paper at Harvard and at Sussex. Julia Cross prepared the final manuscript for publication. I am grateful to all those mentioned, but I retain responsibility for errors and for views expressed.

Handbook of Development Economics, Volume II, Edited by H. Chenery and T.N. Srinivasan
© *Elsevier Science Publishers B.V., 1989*

1. Introduction

Modern economic growth is associated with large systematic changes in the structure of production, trade, factor use, product use, location of economic activities, size distribution of productive units, vital rates and other key economic and demographic variables [see, for example, Kuznets (1964) and Chenery (1960, 1979)]. Among the most dramatic changes in economic structure is the decline in the share of the primary producing sectors (principally agriculture, but also forestry, fishing and mining) and a rise in the share of industry, particularly manufacturing industry, in output, exports and employment.[1] Of particular importance is that overall performance and changing economic structure are inter-linked: changes in structure seem to be necessary to sustain further growth.

A number of "successful" primary exporting countries have been identified by Kuznets (1967), Chenery (1979) and Chenery and Syrquin (1975, 1986b). Such countries achieved both sustained development and substantial changes in economic structure (which both accompanied and facilitated that development) while maintaining "abnormally" high shares of primary exports. The issue addressed in this chapter is: What are the key elements in the conditions and the policies of governments that have enabled some primary exporting countries to achieve successful structural transformation and long-term development while others have been arrested, achieving neither sustained development nor structural change, despite stated policy objectives to do both?

Primary exports depend in part on unique characteristics of local, immobile, resources: minerals, soil types, climate, geographic location. These unique characteristics lead to the presence of economic rents which are a crucial element of the economics of primary production, whether from agriculture, fishing, forestry or mining. The search for such rents led to the surplus to be "vented" [Myint (1958)], to the production of the "staples" for export [Watkins (1963)], and to the migration of capital and labor to develop mines and plantations of the "export economies" [Levin (1960)] that figure prominently in discussion of the primary exporters. Many issues involving the success and failure of primary exporting countries can be thought of as problems of managing the economic rents arising from primary production. Four groups of questions seem important in analyzing the experience of the primary exporters. They all relate to choices of economic policy.

---

[1]Unless otherwise noted, product and output will be taken as equivalent to Gross Domestic Product. The differences between GDP and GNP, which constitute net factor payments abroad, are of substantial importance in many primary exporting countries, as referred to below.

First, how much of the economic rents arising from primary production should be captured for use by the country which owns the resource and by the government of the country? A corollary issue is: By what methods should the rents be captured? Both the level and the method of rent extraction help determine the size of rents both in the present and in the future.

Second, how should the rents, once captured, be used? If rents finance investment, how should the capital formation be divided between further growth of the primary sectors and the diversification of the economy? How much should be undertaken by governments, and how much left to the private sector, including the primary producers themselves? If rents are consumed, will it be public or private consumption, by which groups in society, and with what effect on wages paid to all sectors?

Third, how can linkages (other than through the government budget) from the rent-generating primary exporting activities to the rest of the economy be exploited to encourage broader-based growth? This is largely a question of how, and by how much, to divert export revenue to domestic spending. The methods used will effect the extent to which the diversion of demand generates further income or is self-limiting.

Fourth, how should cyclical fluctuations be managed – in both booms and busts? This is partly a question of managing the rents, particularly for non-renewable resources, and it is partly a question of general stabilization policy. The time phasing of investment and consumption expenditures in relation to the variable flows of export earnings and rent-related government revenues seems critical.

The chapter begins with a review of the literature on structural change in development and the identification of countries that are primary export specialists. Section 3 contains a brief discussion of some theoretical issues involved in analyzing the primary exporters and of the terms of trade for primary products and the instability of export earnings. Since mineral exporting countries have some distinctly different characteristics from agricultural exporters, Sections 4 and 5 discuss the special problems of each. Government policy interventions used in achieving, or frustrating, successful structural transformation and sustained development are reviewed in Section 6. Section 7 provides some comparisons among a selection of nine countries that have been more, and less, successful in achieving sustained economic development while remaining relatively specialized in primary exports. Finally, Section 8 provides some concluding comments on the key lessons and what seem to be the open issues.

2. Successful structural transformation

The focus of this chapter must be on *sustained* changes during economic development. Kuznets' (1966) pioneering work on measurement of economic growth continually stressed the need to examine long periods of time when making any judgments about growth and structural change; periods of several decades were a common unit of measurement in his work. He stressed that the cycles common to countries experiencing modern economic growth could easily result in declines of 20 percent in real output in a short period of time; unless there was sustained underlying growth, a sharp cyclical decline could wipe out past gains and return the economy to its original economic level. This seems particularly important in analyzing the experience of the primary exporting countries. If any reminder of the need to look at long periods was needed, the dramatic fall in the price of oil from 1980 to 1986 and the changed fortunes of the oil exporting countries should provide it.[2]

In addition to the experience of countries over time, it is possible to gain some insight into the development process by examining countries at different levels of income at a particular time, as well as by pooling cross-section and time-series data. Studies by Kuznets (1966) and by Chenery both have used cross-section comparisons, and Chenery's work, including collaborative studies of Chenery and Syrquin (1975, 1986b) and Chenery and Taylor (1968) have led to significant insights into the development process by using pooling techniques. The basic structural changes during a long period of development from the lowest to the highest levels of income per capita typically involve the following shifts: a decline in the share of primary sectors from over 70 percent of the labor force, over half of GDP, and over 90 percent of commodity exports in countries with the lowest level of per capita income, to primary shares in the Western industrial countries of around 15 percent of the labor force, 12 percent of GDP, and 33 percent of commodity exports [Chenery and Syrquin (1975, pp. 20–21)].[3]

The time-series data compiled by Kuznets (1967) for the industrialized countries reveal earlier changes in the structure of production and the labor force than in the structure of foreign trade. Chenery and Syrquin (1975, 1986b) estimated the income levels at which half of each major structural shift had taken place. They found that half the decline in the primary share in production occurred much earlier ($700 per capita, 1980 dollars) than that in the labor force ($1300 per capita). Both changes took place at much lower incomes, or earlier in the development process, than the declining share of primary exports in visible exports (around $3500 per capita). The income level at which half the shift in primary export share in GDP has been reached ($515 per capita) was the highest of any of the 22 structural variables for which Chenery and Syrquin (1986b) made calculations, later even than the $2000 per capita level at which half of the expansion of manufactured exports as a share of GDP was achieved. Thus, while

---

[2] See Kuznets (1966, pp. 26–27) for a discussion of the time periods and the importance of economic cycles. In particular he notes that "a substantial movement over a period long enough to have revealed a variety of short-term disturbances can be taken as an indication of economic growth".

[3] In their comprehensive update, Chenery and Syrquin (1986b) give slightly different numbers but similar overall results.

the structural changes away from the primary sectors are all large, most of the change in the structure of production and employment – indeed, in *all* other major structural variables – takes place well before primary exports decline substantially in relative importance. Chenery and Syrquin's figures also show a monotonic increase in the ratio of primary exports to value added in primary sectors from 0.265 to 0.875 as incomes rose from less than $300 to over $515 per capita (in 1980 dollars). Not only does the share of primary exports in total GDP retain its importance well through the development process, but its importance relative to GDP originating in the primary sectors rises during development. These all re-confirm for a large sample of countries and longer time periods the same results from Chenery and Syrquin (1975).

The size of countries plays a major role in determining both the overall degree of openness and the extent to which primary exports continue to play a major role once the development process has begun. Chapter 32 by Perkins and Syrquin in this Handbook examines the very large countries precisely because they have distinctive characteristics. Large populations and large national incomes generate relatively large domestic markets, making possible gains from economies of scale in serving domestic markets; large geographic area is more likely to be associated with diversified natural resources. Consequently, the potential gains from specialization and trade are more limited. The inverse relationship between population and the ratio of foreign trade to GDP is strong and well established for cross-section studies [e.g. Chenery (1960) and Kuznets (1966)]. One would also expect the role of specialization, in either primary exports or manufactured exports, to be greater for smaller countries than for larger countries, a result confirmed by Chenery and Syrquin (1975, 1986b).

Countries differ in resource endowments, past accumulation of reproducible capital (both human and physical), and other attributes that contribute to different patterns of production and trade at given levels of development. But, countries also differ in their policies toward foreign trade and domestic markets. At any time, the differences in economic structure would be due to both past policies and resource endowments. Chenery and Syrquin (1975, 1986b) developed a classification system for the "orientation" of countries in both their production and their trade structures that assists in disentangling the issues. The "trade orientation" of countries is defined by Chenery and Syrquin as the extent to which the relative importance of primary and manufactured exports is greater or less than would be predicted on the basis of the standard pattern of production or trade in primary and manufactured goods as determined from econometric estimates.[4]

---

[4] Trade orientation was defined by Chenery and Syrquin (1975) as the deviation of the observed "trade bias" in a country from the predicted trade bias for a typical country of similar size and income level. Trade bias is $(EP - EM)/E$, where EP and EM are primary and manufactured exports, respectively, and E is their sum. Predicted trade bias is calculated by using predicted EP

Trade orientation as so measured is the result of both "natural" factors and policy influences. Chenery and Syrquin have further analyzed country experiences, particularly by separating the countries into large and small country groups to reflect the importance of size in determining economic structure. Both large and small countries exhibit the effects of natural resource endowments in their trade structures. The two groups of countries have different development patterns, with changes in the composition of production and trade occurring later in the development process for small countries with a primary orientation and earlier for small countries with an industry orientation. The large countries tend more toward the average pattern of transformation. The Chenery–Syrquin classification allows identification of countries with a significant primary orientation in their trade structure for further detailed analysis. The countries considered in Section 7 were selected using this criterion: three at relatively high income levels (Australia, Argentina and Canada) with long histories of primary export orientation; Malaysia and the Ivory Coast as recent examples of relatively sustained growth with primary-led exports but structural change; Zambia and Chile as examples of primary exporters which have not been able to make the structural transformations or sustain development; and two special cases, Botswana, which had the highest recorded growth of any country over the past two decades, and South Africa, a case with some possible lessons despite its unique social/political structure.

3. Some issues of history, theory, and ideology

The questions of economic development strategy and its relation to exports of primary products have long been seen as issues combining economics, politics, sociology, history and ideology. The simple fact that low-income societies tend to be agricultural and high-income countries industrial naturally led to conclusions that development meant not only the growth of industry but also the decline of agriculture. The colonial pattern of trade and investment was one in which capital from the imperial powers, often with labor imported from low-wage areas of the world and capital from high-income countries, developed export activities in mining and agriculture which were not linked to the economies of the colonies, which transferred resources and repatriated profits to the high-income areas, and

---

and *EM* for a typical country of similar size and income level. Trade Orientation is:

$$TO = \frac{EP - EM}{E} - \frac{\widehat{EP} - \widehat{EM}}{\widehat{E}},$$

where the variables with the hats are predicted variables. Chenery and Syrquin classify a country as primary oriented when *TO* is substantially positive, as industry oriented when *TO* is substantially negative, and as "balanced" when the values of *TO* are near zero.

which imported the necessary manufactured goods from abroad [see, inter alia, Baran (1957), Levin (1960) and Beckford (1972)]. By the time economic development strategies were being discussed and developed after World War II, the accumulation of artifacts was a powerful source of the idea that the developing countries should avoid being hewers of wood and drawers of water for the industrial West.

The discussion of the following three subsections involves two separate kinds of effects on the development of the primary exporting countries. One effect is environmental: the nature of underlying resource endowments within countries, the international markets for goods and for factors and the existing technology of export activities. These environmental factors provide the constraints (or opportunities) within which decisions in the public and private sectors are made; a description of them would be broadly shared among analysts of varying political or policy persuasions. The other effect is that of government policy in the face of, or in response to, the environmental characteristics. Crudely put, the problem of the colonial export economies arose in part because government policy did not intervene to offset the effects of the environmental variables, either to capture the rents, to direct demand to the domestic market, to manage cyclical instability, or to invest in diversification of the economy.

3.1. Terms of trade for primary products

Support for the view that the developing countries had to develop a strategy that involved industrialization and, in particular, a reduced role of primary exports came initially from Singer (1950) and Prebisch (1950). The combination of low income and price elasticities of demand for primary products, along with different structures of the product and factor markets in high- and low-income countries, were thought to be the keys to a persistent and secular decline in the terms of trade for the developing world, a key factor affecting the environment within which development policy would be framed. Increased production of primary goods would depress total revenue from primary products at any particular time; and over time the growth of demand for primary products could not be expected to keep up with the growth of incomes in the industrial countries.

There is a long and continuing literature on the secular trend in the terms of trade, most of which is reviewed in Chapter 31 by Balassa in this Handbook [but see also Spraos (1980, 1983), Krueger (1984), World Bank (1986) and Evans (1987)]. Studies have used different time periods, different commodity groups, and different country groupings. The results have differed depending on specifications of the time periods, commodities, units of measurement (prices or unit values, corrected or uncorrected for quality changes), or countries, leaving one without conclusive evidence on the issue of secular changes. One can show clear deterioration for low-income countries, or for primary products generally, for some long periods (including those ending in the mid-1980s), and one can show clear movements in favor of primary products and against high-income countries for other long periods. Despite the appeal of the Singer–Prebisch thesis, the evidence over the longer term has not been supportive of the basic idea of a consistent secular deterioration of either primary product prices as a whole or low-income countries as a group.

However, despite the lack of a strong finding on universal secular change in the net barter terms of trade for all primary commodities or all developing countries, there can be, and have been, sustained movements of long duration for individual commodities or countries. The point is that the empirical results do not provide support for a blanket set of assertions about the virtues, or vices, of primary specialization based on secular strength or weakness of primary prices in general.

The terms of trade controversies have often suffered from a failure to distinguish exactly what is being measured. The net barter terms of trade (prices of exports relative to prices of imports) are the most commonly used variant of the terms of trade, but they are far from the only measure that is of economic significance. The income terms of trade (net barter terms of trade times export volume), or what can also be referred to as the purchasing power of exports, are arguably a relevant measure, since they take account of both the changes in prices and the changes in production (including that arising from productivity growth) and local consumption of exportables. During the period of African economic stagnation of the 1970s, for example, Africa's net barter terms of trade fared no worse than those of the rest of the low-income countries of the world, but the purchasing power of Africa's exports failed to match that of other low-income countries by a substantial amount [Lewis (1986)].

The other important definition of the terms of trade is the factoral terms of trade. The double factoral terms of trade measures the relative earnings of factors in one country as compared with those in another. Their movement depends on both the relative prices of the two goods and the relative productivities of factors in the two countries. If productivity in an export activity increases and increased quantities are produced, the gain is shared between the producer and the purchaser in the other country. If productivity in an import competing activity is raised, the factors in the exporting country may be harmed. These results were important to the Singer–Prebisch thesis as well as to the argument developed by Hicks (1953) in discussion the importance of productivity growth to the gains from trade among the developed countries. The single-factoral terms of trade, which look simply at the barter terms of trade adjusted for productivity growth in the exporting country is, of course, relevant to real factor incomes in the exporting country; productivity growth can offset declines or multiply the gains from movements in the barter terms of trade.

The Singer–Prebisch thesis and its descendants relied largely on the differences between price and income elasticities of demand for manufactured and primary products as two distinct groups, though different structure of product markets for commodities and factor markets in the rich and poor countries also played a role. Other important analyses deal with subgroups of primary commodities and suggest reasons for long-term trends for those groups separately.

In the early 1970s there was a flurry of interest in the decline of non-renewable resources, particularly petroleum, but also hard minerals. The simple notion was a Ricardian one that, with fixed supplies of non-renewable resources and growing world demand, relative prices of the non-renewable resources would rise inexorably, limiting growth in the world. In this context, the characteristics of petroleum were thought to be so special that economists and international institutions divided the world into oil importing and oil exporting countries for many if not most analytical purposes. Long-term projections showed continuing increases in the price of petroleum and other energy sources. At least for the subgroups of countries importing or exporting oil in large quantities, the future of the terms of trade seemed clear. While it is still too early (as Kuznets surely would have told us) to examine a "secular" trend in oil prices, the behavior of petroleum markets and prices in the 1980s suggests that oil may have become just another commodity, albeit an extremely important one, subject to the same cyclical disturbances and contrasting pressures on long-term trends as other non-renewable resources.

The second subgroup of commodities to which some attention has been given is hard minerals. The argument, largely from the international mining companies, runs that changes in ownership and in tax regimes in the developing world over the past two or three decades have shifted decisions about production levels (especially in response to short-term decreases in international prices) to governments and away from mining companies. The depression in hard mineral prices in the late 1970s and especially the early 1980s was the worst since the mid-1930s. In contrast to the period a half century earlier, governments have resisted reductions in production (and in employment and exports) more systematically than did companies in the earlier periods. The difference in response is clearly related to the difference in the variables to be maximized by the owners of the resource. Private owners are concerned about maximizing net profits, including rents, from the natural resource over time, while country governments wish to maximize national income, including the wages of citizen workers. A consequence of maintaining production is a continued depression in world prices of hard minerals. Unlike most models of natural resource production and trade with costless resource mobility, real world circumstances involve the generation of national income using relatively immobile resources along with the draw-down of natural resource stocks [Lewis (1984)]. Under such conditions, the shift of ownership of mineral rights to governments (not necessarily developing country governments) would lead to lower real prices for hard minerals than had been the case in the past. As with oil, it is too soon to see whether the changes of recent years are a manifestation of a sharp cyclical disturbance or whether there is a fundamental shift in the nature of hard mineral markets of the sort that has been alleged.

Tropical products constitute the third commodity group subject to specific theorizing on the secular terms of trade. Sir Arthur Lewis (1978a) is the principal source of this contribution, which is an extension of his earlier work on the dual economy (1954). Lewis argued that the international prices of tropical products were determined by their opportunity cost in producing food in the tropical countries. To the extent that productivity of labor and land in producing food was low in the tropical countries, the real costs of producing tropical products would also be low; gains from productivity growth in export crops would be captured by the importing countries in the form of lower import prices arising from increased supplies in international markets. The only way for the tropical exporting countries to improve the returns to producers is to raise the productivity of land and labor in production of food. In Lewis's example, the Nigerian producing peanuts earns less than the Australian producing wool not because of differences in productivity in the production of wool and peanuts but because of "the respective amounts of food that their cousins could produce on family farms" [Lewis (1978a, p. 19)].

Lewis extended his argument from tropical crops to minerals as well; historically, the flow of labor to mining projects came from the overpopulated, low-productivity parts of Asia to other developing areas. Lewis argued that the end of the colonial era was marked by "the struggle of the newly independent nations to recapture for the domestic revenue the true value of minerals in the ground".

Lewis's earlier point about the opportunity cost of labor in the domestic food-producing sectors can be extended to the post-colonial period. One reason why the mines used imported labor in the colonial period was that, when production was cut back or mines were closed during periods of slack demand or decreasing ore quality, the labor could be sent home or otherwise dismissed. If, however, an independent country does not have relatively high-productivity jobs to which citizen mine workers can go at the time of a cutback in production, the country government will wish to maintain the level of output and employment – even if this means reducing the value of mining rents (or "domestic revenue" in Lewis's terms) both immediately and over time. Thus, unless there is growth in the productivity of factors in other domestic sectors, especially agriculture, political independence and control of ownership of resources will not necessarily improve the net returns for mining activities.

The implications of the secular terms of trade for development strategy and investment allocation are related to the productivity of factors in producing for the domestic market, whether in manufacturing or in agriculture. The Singer–

Prebisch emphasis on production for the domestic instead of international markets only makes sense if the productivity in import-substituting activities exceeds that in export of primary products when adjusted for changes in the terms of trade. Sir Arthur Lewis's emphasis on improving the terms of trade for tropical products turns on the productivity of factors in food production. The reliance of mineral exporters on continued uneconomic production in the face of declines in either export prices or ore grades can only be overcome if there are higher productivity activities in other sectors – which in lower-income countries must be mainly in agriculture. The theme of productivity growth in all sectors, especially in food production, seems critical.

3.2. Instability of primary product markets

In addition to the issue of secular changes in the terms of trade for primary commodities, the instability of primary product prices was an important issue both for post-war development economists and for international organizations. Instability in primary product markets is another environmental factor facing the primary exporters, and numerous studies have been made of the variability of export earnings and of commodity prices [see MacBean (1966), Behrman (1978), Chu and Morrison (1984), Krueger (1984) and Helleiner (1986a)]. These studies have been somewhat more successful in defining general results independent of the selection of time periods, commodities or countries than have terms of trade studies. However, there have always been differences of views as to whether export prices, total export earnings, or purchasing power (either of prices or of earnings) should be the target to be studied.

From a *national* economic management point of view, since most countries are price-takers, an important element of their environment is the level of stability of the price they face in world markets since, ceteris paribus, fluctuations in prices would lead to comparable fluctuations in earnings. Earnings fluctuations may be greater or less than price fluctuations, of course, depending on whether domestic output moves with or against international market prices in the very short term.

While there have been differences in results among some studies, in the main the conclusions of the studies of instability of export earnings indicate that (i) developing countries have generally had larger fluctuations than the developed countries, (ii) fluctuations have been substantial in both manufactured and primary product earnings, (iii) greater commodity concentration of export earnings leads to greater earnings instability, and (iv) quantity fluctuations have generally been the dominant source of instability in export earnings. The poorest countries with the highest commodity concentrations are the most vulnerable to the effects of fluctuations in earnings. Evidence from Africa cited by Lewis (1986), as well as studies by Helleiner (1986b) based on the African experience, suggest that the lowest income, least diversified economies suffer substantially more than the developing countries as a group. Patterns of development that lead to increased diversification of exports would be desirable if one wished to reduce fluctuations in export earnings, while policies that encouraged commodity concentration in exports would lead to greater variability.

Are fluctuations inherently bad? The evidence for developing countries as a group is not clear. Most studies suggest that fluctuations in export earnings are not associated with the retardation of economic growth. However, as Krueger (1984) has pointed out, given the multitude of other factors that affect the rate of growth, the impact of instability of export earnings alone may be hard to distinguish. Without detailed analysis of the alternatives faced and those chosen, the historical record reflects any counter-cyclical policies adopted by the government.

For the colonial export economies, Levin (1960) noted that fluctuations in export earnings were often absorbed largely by the incomes of foreign factors of production and the associated luxury importers of the regions, with little adverse effect on the local economy. It is only in the era since governments have exercised more effective control over the rents accruing to their natural resources that the fluctuations have begun having severe implications for the local level of income. As noted at several points in Section 7, better or worse policies to manage cyclical fluctuations were an important element in determining how well the primary exporting countries managed successful structural change.

3.3. Theories of development of primary exporters

The theories related to the development of the primary exporting countries fall into several categories and share many common features, particularly those which describe the nature of resource endowments and the conditions of their exploitation. Those briefly reviewed here include the classical "vent for surplus" approach, the "staple theory" of the contribution of primary or resource based exports, the dual economy models following from Sir Arthur Lewis, and the "underdevelopment" theorists (who are principally concerned with why primary exports will not lead to development). Levin (1960) captured many of the main themes about "the export economies" that are still important in the discussion of primary exporters today. The theories suggest various possible roles for government policy within the (broadly agreed) environment faced by primary exporting countries.

3.3.1. Vent for surplus

The vent for surplus theory has its origins with Adam Smith but was developed more fully by Myint (1959, 1965). The expansion of international trade, particularly in the colonial era, exposed the resources of regions to a new set of international prices and opportunities. For the so-called "empty countries" or "regions of recent settlement" in the Americas and Australia, existing land was combined with immigrant labor, management and capital. In peasant economies [e.g. Nigeria with a variety of commodities documented by Helleiner (1966)] natural conditions for a new activity presented opportunities for combinations of peasant labor and land in producing a crop with high value relative to leisure (or, in some cases, to food production). Plantation agriculture or mining during the colonial era often involved using foreign capital and foreign labor and only local land and natural resources, including the climate. The basic mechanism involved production of something valuable internationally that was not consumed at home, using local resources that had low opportunity costs and, therefore, that generated rents for the economy as a whole and for the producers.

The link to the international economy in peasant societies [Myint (1965) refers to Ghana and Burma in some detail while Helleiner (1966) documents Nigeria exhaustively] came through foreign marketing firms, while in mines and plantations the owners made the links directly. In the economies experiencing this process during the nineteenth and early twentieth centuries, growth of domestic production was closely related to growing exports. A key issue, however, was the extent to which the benefits of the export activity remained in the countries (or colonies) – a theme in many approaches to the primary exporters.

The vent for surplus notion is not just a remnant of the colonial era; elements are still present in the development of resource-based activities in many countries. The petroleum industry is a particularly marked example of the movement of labor and capital internationally to exploit a natural resource whose principal market is international, not domestic; and the post-World War II shift of tropical agricultural export products such as coffee, tea, oil palm, and cocoa to countries where they had not been grown before can also be thought of in terms of the vent for surplus concept.

3.3.2. Staple theory

Will primary exports that arise initially as a vent for surplus lead the economy to further growth and development? This question leads to the "stable theory" of the development of primary exporting countries, associated with the names of Watkins (1963) and Innis (1915) and Canadian development. Staple theory examines the issues in terms of various characteristics of the "staple", or natural resource-based, export. The impact of the staple exports on the rest of the economy depends on the technology of the export industry (e.g. the labor or capital intensity), the linkages of the industry to the rest of the economy through demand for intermediate goods and infrastructure (such as railroads), the impact on the government budget through taxes, and the relative involvement of foreign and local factors of production. The greater are local linkages, the greater will be the effect of staple exports on the development of the rest of the economy.

A major concern about whether staple exports would effectively lead to development was that the linkages were inherently low. Hirschman's statement (1958, pp. 109–110) is often quoted in support of this view: "agriculture certainly stands convicted on the count of its lack of direct stimulus to the setting up of new activities through its linkage effects; the superiority of manufacturing in this respect is crushing". Seers (1964) looked at the low linkage effects of the petroleum industry in small countries, while Baldwin's classic study (1966) of Northern Rhodesia (now Zambia) detailed the low linkages of copper mining in that colony.

The historical linkages, both in peasant economies and in the plantations and mines, often were low. But, how much in this inherent in the nature of the industries and how much is it subject to influence by policy changes? One of the major reactions of governments of developing countries in the post-World War II era was to dismantle various aspects of the old export system for primary products. New approaches were taken to the distribution of rents both between foreign factors and the domestic economy and between domestic factors and government; and, linkages between the export sector and the domestic economy were promoted in a variety of ways. Policies adopted to replace the former arrangements (discussed in Section 6) have been major determinants of subsequent development experience, as illustrated by the cases discussed in Section 7.

3.3.3. The dual economy

Another fundamental factor in the development even of staple exporters, however, is that secularly rising incomes can come about only through increased productivity of all resources devoted to the development process. Myint (1965) points out that while the stagnation in many countries is due to a combination of low productivity and lack of technical progress in primary production, the problem is not with primary exports per se. Low and stagnant productivity in manufacturing would lead to the same overall stagnation of incomes; only when real productivity (measured at scarcity prices) is considerably higher in manufacturing than in agriculture could incomes rise substantially due solely to switching of factors from agriculture to manufacturing.

This brings us to the dual economy models, developed first by Sir Arthur Lewis (1954, 1958) and formalized by Fei and Ranis (1964), as well as the parallel literature on the role of agriculture in the development process pioneered by Mellor and Johnston (1961), and brought back to the primary export question by Lewis (1978a) in his Janeway Lectures. I refer to these collectively as the dual economy model.

Agriculture plays a key role in the dual economy in a variety of ways. The mechanism for development is a shift of labor from low-productivity subsistence activities to high-productivity modern sector activities. Saving comes from the profits of modern sector, and increased saving arises because of the growth of that sector. Agricultural productivity must grow in the dual economy model either to provide food for the workers in the modern sector or to provide exports. In the absence of such agricultural growth, the modern sector growth grinds to a halt because it faces deteriorating terms of trade. Implicitly in some versions of the model, explicitly in others, the agricultural sector is a market for the expanding output of the modern sector. Growth of productivity in agriculture is critical if development is to occur in the dual economy.

As already noted, the growth of productivity in the traditional agricultural sector is important in several respects for the primary exporting countries. Since most people rely on agriculture for their principal livelihood for a long period, an improvement in the living standard for the majority is dependent on increased productivity in agriculture, particularly in food production. Second, improved productivity in the production of primary exports is necessary if these products are to grow and continue to complete in world markets. As Myint (1965) points out, the gains from trade depend on relative costs, not relative prices, and regardless of the movement of international prices exporting countries will gain from lowering the real costs of producing any given level of exports. Finally, as Lewis (1978a) has stressed, the gains from trade in tropical products will shift in favor of the exporting countries only when they have improved the productivity of resources engaged in growing food. Thus, the successful transformation of an economy from a low-income dual economic structure to a higher-income, diversified, and less dualistic one depends to a large extent on the growth of productivity in the agricultural sectors – a factor stressed by Kuznets (1966) as well, based not on theorizing but on the record of the high-income countries. The literature cited by Timmer in Chapter 8 of this Handbook develops the point more fully.

3.3.4. Underdevelopment

This review would not be complete without reference to serious dissents from what has been the mainstream approach to development theorizing in North America and much of Europe. I include here approaches referred to variously as dependency theory, radical theory, Marxist or neo-Marxist approaches, and underdevelopment [see, for example, Baran (1957), Frank (1967), Griffin (1969), Beckford (1972), Lall (1975), Cardoso and Faletto (1979), and Griffin and Gurley (1986)]. Despite many differences in themes, the different schools have more in common with one another than with the Western mainstream approach, especially in their inclusion of a variety of non-market factors as well as elements of politics, history and sociology in the analysis. Griffin (1969, p. 37) notes that "the concept of 'underdevelopment'... refers to a society's political organization, economic characteristics and social institutions". It is "a product of history..., it is a part of the same process that produced development" (p. 48). One cannot understand the economics of these societies without understanding the institutions, the history, and the political process. Since the underdevelopment theorists paint on the same historical canvas, however, it is not surprising that many of them quote with approval some of the modelling referred to earlier that is based on historical cases. Beckford (1972, pp. 51–52), for example, cites the "quite useful" work of Watkins, Levin, and Seers, and the "significant contributions" of Baldwin and Myint.

While a brief summary may do even more violence to the richness of this literature than to some other branches of analysis, I focus here on why the problems identified by writers in the vent for surplus or staple theory schools have not always been overcome successfully by independent countries. The key reasons lie in the social relations of production, the nature of capital and wage labor, and particularly the links between local elites and international capitalist forces. The argument runs as follows.

The characteristics of capitalist development are even more strongly felt in peripheral capitalist states than in the center; the imperatives of international trade and investment in seeking to extract surplus in the periphery and return it to the center lead to a continuation of the enclave nature of investment and extreme specialization in trade [described, inter alia, by Levin (1960), Seers (1964) or Baldwin (1966)]; developing linkages to domestic supplying industries is not in the interests of international investors; the consumption patterns of the local elites emulate those of the elites in the advanced capitalist countries leading to high import content in consumption; there is a common interest between local capitalists and international capital in maintaining cheap wages and, therefore, low productivity in peasant agriculture; and, despite nominal political independence, the continued dependent relationship (economically and psychologically) on the world capitalist system keeps peripheral elites from making fundamental changes in economic policy, since such changes would put at risk the basic elements of the political, economic, and social structures in the peripheral countries.

Even the attempts by peripheral capitalist economies to diversify their economies away from primary product exports involve continued participation in the world capitalist system. Multinational companies invest in the manufacturing sector, with or without local participation, but usually only with special concessions. Capitalist modes of production, trade links through investment goods and intermediate goods often purchased from sister multinationals abroad, and continued extraction of surplus from the local economy for the benefit of international capital continue. The economy appears to become more diversified in productive structure, but exports remain concentrated in primary products, manufacturing is dependent on international markets to supply its intermediate goods and technology, profits flow abroad (whether legally or through transfer pricing), and neither the local elites nor internationally capital has any interest in the growth of productivity and incomes for the poorest.

In such circumstances, in order to achieve economic, social, and political development, a fundamental change must take place in the nature of all relationships in the society, including: a rejection of the capitalist mode of production, and severance of links with the international capitalist system of investment and trade, nationalization or expulsion of multinational companies, and a focus on self-reliance including the reduction of the extent of dependence on international trade [for an exceptionally clear analysis of de-linking, see Diaz-Alejandro (1978)]. The failure to recognize the basic interrelationships between economic, political, and social factors in a historical context leads mainstream Western economists to neglect the key elements that would permit economic development to take place. The notion that policies could be changed to encourage a different economic structure without a fundamental change in the nature of society – a notion that I would accept for most countries – would not be one with which the underdevelopment theorists would agree.

3.4. An approach to the analysis

The four types of approaches outlined – vent for surplus, staple theory, dual economy models and underdevelopment – share a number of features but differ in some important respects. They may also be seen in some respects as part of a sequence. The vent for surplus theory says that export markets make possible greater output by permitting the greater utilization of some previously under-used resource. In the process, rents are generated by the unique characteristics of that resource. Staple theory begins at the stage where export production has started; it says that the further development of the economy depends on the characteristics of the staple export, including whether there are (or can be) linkages with other domestic sectors. The insights of the dual economy models, and some extensions of the earlier two, involved the interaction of the food-producing traditional or subsistence sectors and the primary exporting sectors – whether mining, plantation agriculture, or peasant agriculture. The dual economy models stress the importance of productivity growth in the traditional food-producing sectors and in the export sectors, even though one basic mechanism of growth in the dual economy models is the inter-sectoral shift of resources from low- to high-productivity uses. Finally, while each of the first three models suggests a role for government in promoting development and structural change, the underdevelopment theorists, working from a similar set of assumptions about international product markets and the nature of primary production at home, conclude that other elements of the primary export economies, particularly political and social factors, will keep governments from adopting appropriate policies.

Before discussing what constitute appropriate policies both to exploit cost advantages inherent in the primary exporting countries and to encourage growth and structural change, I first review the features which seem to be peculiar to the mineral exporting countries and the agricultural exporters. The framework for discussion revolves around the four groups of questions raised in Section 1: how much of the primary sector's rents to capture and by what methods; how to allocate the captured rents between consumption and investment, and among sectors; how to divert spending from export industries to local markets; and how to manage cyclical fluctuations.

4. The mineral exporters[5]

The impact of mining activities, including petroleum extraction, on the economy of developing countries could be approached from many viewpoints. Following the framework of the previous section, I first discuss the division of the sales proceeds from mineral production into economic rents accruing to the owners of the mineral deposit and the costs of extraction and marketing. The division of rents between the country and the rest of the world and the spending of rents for current consumption or investment purposes are key issues. Another issue is that of the optimal depletion path of the mineral resource. With regard to the costs of extraction and marketing, one must examine how to optimize the linkages and the development spin-offs from mining developments. Furthermore, I explore the internal dynamics of mining countries to understand why mineral-led economies have not been particularly successful in transforming their economies or sustaining economic development. Finally, I turn to the question of managing cyclical disturbances.

If and when mineral rights are privately owned, the owners will wish to maximize the value[6] of rents accruing to them and to minimize the costs (both capital and operating) incurred in "winning" the mineral from nature and selling it. The stage of processing at which title to the mineral passes from the owner of the rights, and the extent to which all rents associated with the mineral have been captured, are issues of importance to governments as well as private owners. From a national viewpoint – and virtually all developing countries now recognized in law that the rights to minerals reside in the state, not in private hands – the objective is not necessarily to maximize the value of rents (properly

---

[5] This section draws heavily on Lewis (1984).

[6] I leave aside for a moment the issue of discounting the flow of net rents and assume that one is talking of maximizing the net present value of the expected future flow of rents to the resource using the appropriate discount rate.

discounted) but to maximize national income or national consumption (again properly discounted), or even some more complex objective function taking account of income distribution. From a national planning viewpoint, then, one can separate the discussion conceptually into two parts: maximizing the value of rents received by the nation, and assuring that an optimal amount of the costs of extraction and marketing are incurred in a form that generates further domestic income.

A major criticism of the colonial "export economies" was the extent to which they vested mineral rights in foreign companies, with the result that a large share of the economic rents from the resource accrued to foreign factors. Post-colonial governments increasingly acquired ownership of the rights and of mining companies, by expropriation, by increased taxation, or by negotiation of new and more favorable agreements. It became the rule rather than the exception for new concession agreements to attempt to provide the minimum return to foreign investors consistent with attracting them to develop deposits; in some cases foreign equity finance was minimized and the use of any required foreign expertise was purchased through management agreements or similar devices. The problem of designing tax, royalty, and financial regimes that extract just enough, but not too much, of the returns to foreign factors is a rich subject by itself, and much progress has been made in designing such regimes [see, for example, Garnaut and Ross (1975, 1983)].[7]

The capture of the mineral rents for the developing countries is, in many respects, the easiest problem. The management of rents is much more problematic. Mining projects are "lumpy" projects, with heavy capital investment for several years and then, typically, a sudden increase in government revenues and export earnings from the mining project. Hard minerals tend to have a relatively flat time profile of revenue once capacity production has been reached; and even for many oil fields a similar phenomenon occurs. Such a profile means that mining revenues will typically not grow (unless there are new projects) with the rest of GDP, which raises difficult issues of fiscal management for the government. Cyclical fluctuations, dealt with below, also complicate macroeconomic management.

---

[7] While ownership of the rights became vested in the state and concessions were granted with explicit revenue and performance undertakings by any foreign companies involved, concern still was expressed about the extent of transfer pricing by multinational companies (principally invoicing of exports at prices below the arms length value of the commodities). A variety of devices have been designed by governments to monitor such practices, and the presence of international markets in many homogeneous commodities has eased the problem of valuation, though it still remains a difficulty in some specialty products such as nickel, in commodities where differences in spot and long-term contract markets make it difficult to place unambiguous values on exports of a commodity at a particular time, or where the product exported is a partially-refined concentrate with a narrower market than a fully-refined commodity. In general, mineral exports are easier to check for transfer pricing than other goods.

Conceptually the choices open to a government in utilizing mining rents are to spend on consumption (private, through subsidies, transfers or reductions in other taxes, or public) or to acquire assets – human or physical capital domestically or financial assets at home or abroad. The theoretical statement of the problem is relatively easy: if one is maximizing the net present value of future streams of income or consumption one allocates the spending according to valuations of consumption today and consumption tomorrow evaluated at the appropriate discount rate, and one would invest in human, physical, and financial assets until their returns were driven down to the discount rate.

Practically speaking, the pressures on governments to spend on domestic consumption reflect very high discount rates on the consumption side, but the pressure to spend on anything that creates employment through the government budget, regardless of the economic return to projects, suggests very low discount rates on the investment side. Few governments have been able to manage the economic rents in a manner which, ex post, seems consistent with the long-run objectives those governments set for themselves (for reasons discussed below). In particular, governments have often invested in projects with very low rates of return in investment booms when it would have appeared more rational to have held international financial assets and invested in domestic projects over a longer period [see Gelb (1986), examples from the oil boom of the 1970s]. Indeed, Harberger (1984) suggests that the experience of Indonesia in accumulating substantial foreign financial assets for later spending after the second oil shock of the 1970s was unique among mineral-rich countries with large populations.

A further problem is the determination of the optimal path of mineral depletion. Again, theory has guides (deplete at a rate at which the value of the deposit, after extraction costs, rises at a rate equal to the relevant world real interest rate on the relevant risk class of assets), but the guides are most difficult to follow in practice. From a national viewpoint, when resources engaged in mining are not costlessly transferable into or out of other productive activity, decisions about the optimal depletion rate intersect with decisions about investment and employment in other sectors of the economy. These problems are seen most seriously in response to short-term disturbances in prices, as noted below. Furthermore, even apart from the complementary employment effects, the high discount rates of consumers (and voters) puts pressure on governments to deplete quickly and spend today, decreasing the stock of both reproducible and non-reproducible capital that will be handed on to future generations.

Governments in the post-colonial period also sought to increase the share of the international value of resources that were retained in the country in the form of direct and indirect factor payments. In the old "export economies" both capital and labor, as well as many of the intermediate products used in extraction, the consumption goods of foreign and sometimes even domestic laborers, and the capital goods used in construction of the projects, were supplied from abroad, generating jobs and income elsewhere. While staple theory attributed the impact of mining projects to their technological characteristics, many decisions about what to import and what to produce domestically are subject to policy choice, either through incentives or through regulation. As Myint (1965, p. 68) put it; "it is not so much the inherent limitation of primary export production as such, but lack of the conditions necessary for long term policies which seems to have prevented the foreign-owned mines and plantations from making their full contributions to the economic growth of developing countries". Decisions to reinvest in the local economy, even by foreign investors who first came to exploit minerals, depend on the domestic policy environment.

Policies to increase value retained in the domestic economy have taken a variety of forms. The improved tax and financial regimes have been mentioned. Mineral projects often were permitted duty-free importation of virtually all capital and intermediate goods, and sometimes even duty-free importation of consumer goods for employees, especially in petroleum ventures. In the presence of normal tariff patterns for other commodities, and the relatively high value of local currencies in mineral-rich countries (discussed below), duty-free importation effectively subsidized imports and discriminated against local production of intermediate and capital goods produced for what, in many countries, was the largest single market. Duties on intermediate and capital goods would shift incentives in favor of local procurement and increase the income retained domestically.

Attitudes of both governments and mining companies toward new relationships between mineral exploitation and economic development have shifted, and in most developing countries by the mid-1980s, they are very different from those of even twenty years earlier. The change was part of a long evolution that began in the early post-war years, but it accelerated due to the experience of the oil exporting countries in the 1970s, which unilaterally changed not only the terms on which they sold oil, but also the terms on which they did business with foreign companies. Provisions for local control, for tax rates that two decades earlier would have been regarded as confiscatory, for training of citizens, for local procurement of inputs, for government participation in financing and management, for reporting and controls on marketing arrangements, that would have been unheard of in the early 1960s were commonplace in draft agreements proposed by multinational companies themselves by the 1980s.

Despite the changes that have taken place in fiscal arrangements and the increased government control over natural resource projects and the income generated by them, the performance of the mineral-rich countries as a group has been extremely disappointing [e.g. World Bank (1979) and Nankani (1979)]. Indeed, in his study of factors affecting African economic performance over the post-Independence period, Wheeler (1984) found the presence of minerals a negative factor affecting economic performance among African countries. Gelb's

(1986) analysis of six oil exporting countries' experience from 1974 to 1984 points to their failure to diversify their economies despite large windfall incomes and a stated policy of diversification. All these studies raise interesting questions about the nature of mining developments that might contribute to poor results. In many important respects the world has moved out of the colonial era of the "export economies", but the performance is still disappointing. Is there something at work which makes it difficult for mineral-rich countries to manage development?

4.1. An automatic adjustment mechanism

In an earlier analysis [Lewis (1984)] I suggested that an "automatic adjustment mechanism" in mineral-rich countries equilibrates the balance of payments after such countries temporarily experience a surplus in external payments (and in government budgets) due to mineral projects. The new equilibrium leaves countries with higher measured real GDP per capita; a higher share of government revenue in GDP; higher real modern sector wage rates relative to GDP per capita than had been the case previously; diminished incentives to invest in activities outside mining; a greater share of foreign factor income in GDP; increased inequality in the distribution of income; and increased migration to urban areas. As a consequence, the economy will also be more difficult to manage in cyclical terms.

The elements in the adjustment mechanism start with the "Dutch Disease" (named for the effect on Dutch industry in the 1970s, when the increases in natural gas prices and associated balance of payments surpluses resulted in appreciation of the guilder). The effects of a natural resource boom start even during the construction phase whenever there is foreign financing of the project, which is almost universal for large natural resource projects. First foreign investment and then natural resource exports make it possible to achieve balance of payments equilibrium at a lower price of foreign exchange. The non-traded sectors absorb resources as their prices are bid up relative to traded goods, and the output of the non-mining traded sectors falls. The changed relative prices encourage imports and penalize import competing industries and all exports; however, the high rents in the natural resource export allow those exports to continue.

A second major effect of a resource boom is on wage rates. The first effect is on mining wages, but there is often a spill-over to the government sector due to the effect of a resource boom on government revenue. The combined effect of high wages in mining and government, along with the increased demand for non-traded goods, pushes up other modern sector wages in nominal terms, further decreasing the profitability of import-competing and industries and non-mining exports. [These first two effects are analyzed rigorously by Corden and Neary (1982).]

Third, unless the government and the central bank take corrective action, the monetary effects of a resource boom are inflationary. Balance of payments surpluses will have their counterpart in excess liquidity of the banking system and money and credit levels are likely to increase faster that real GDP.

Fourth, with the government budget in substantial surplus, government spending and net lending are likely to increase at rates that exceed the growth of domestic non-mining incomes [see Morgan (1979)]. This adds to domestic inflationary pressure (and is also likely to weaken both audit control and project management procedures). The country spends more resources, properly discounted, to get fewer benefits, also properly discounted, than had projects and spending been stretched out.

Fifth, the desire to spend and to complete projects, including mining projects, quickly have led to international flows of capital and labor to new mining areas that are somewhat reminiscent of the nineteenth century, especially in the Mid-East oil producing countries. The share of foreign factors in the labor force and in GDP will go up as countries try to break bottlenecks in project completion.

The pressures from monetary policy, fiscal policy, and wage push result in domestic inflation in costs and prices. In the face of the inflation, countries do not devalue to maintain competitiveness; indeed, they have often cut tariffs and revalued currencies to reduce "inflationary" pressure, despite the fact that the principal bottleneck is in non-traded goods and services (e.g. port congestion). The result is more discrimination against the production of non-mineral tradable goods.

Thus, while many policy changes have resulted in improvements in the basic relationships between mineral projects and the countries in which they they are situated, some of the same problems (a tendency toward concentration in primary products, an isolation of the mining projects from the rest of the economy, extensive use of foreign factors of production) have reappeared for the somewhat different reasons outlined in my "automatic adjustment mechanism". In terms of the framework outlined above, countries have been successful at capturing rents, especially in diverting them to the public sector, but the allocation of spending between consumption and investment, the adoption of policies that effectively divert demand to support structural change in production, and the choice of productive investment projects have not been as successful. Indeed, agriculture, which may support the largest share of the population, may be very hard hit by the processes of a mineral boom, as well documented for Nigeria by Oyejide (1986).

The final problem is the management of a mineral-rich country over the economic cycle. The difficulties encountered in managing the up-swing of a cyclical resource boom are similar to those already outlined in the case of a new resource project – the Dutch Disease, inflation, currency appreciation, spending ahead of implementation capacity. The down-swings present an even more difficult problem. In the colonial era, cyclical changes in the mining industry had relatively little effect on the local economy because of the enclave nature of the export economies. Moderate reductions in prices were felt by the foreign owners of capital, and more serious reductions were passed on to foreign workers by lay-offs and reductions in real wages. With few links to the domestic economy, even reductions in production had few effects outside the services sectors, since few industries supplied the mining sectors. With the change in fiscal regimes and with increased integration of mining into the rest of the economy, down-turns in the mining industry become much more serious. Decreases in prices lead to decreases in government revenue and consequent reductions in both development budgets and the growth of recurrent budgets. The better deal the government struck over profit-sharing, the greater will be the loss of government revenue as overall profits drop. On the mining side, to the extent that the industry has become more fully integrated into the local economy and more heavily involved in employing citizens, serious reductions in price that would have led, in earlier days, to reductions in output and to layoffs will be resisted.

The difficulties of managing the down side of the cycle could be mitigated in a straightfoward way by maintaining foreign exchange reserves (the counterpart of government budget surpluses from mineral rents) at higher levels during boom periods, or by borrowing short term during the down-swings. However, the same pressures that lead to "overspending" as described in the automatic adjustment mechanism generally prevent countries from accumulating sufficient reserves, and even have pushed many countries (e.g. Mexico, Nigeria, and Venezuela) into using their resource-based borrowing capacity in incur heavy short-term debt during the boom phases. As a result, many mineral-rich countries, including oil exporters, have had to make very substantial cutbacks in spending and in real output in periods of price weakness.

5. Agricultural exporters

The economics of agricultural development are surveyed by Timmer in Chapter 8 of this Handbook, and the comments here focus on the characteristics of agriculture that are particularly relevant to the issues of agricultural exports, especially since Timmer concentrates largely on food production. A touchstone for all discussions of agriculture and development, the classic article of Johnston and Mellor (1961), defined five roles for agriculture in the development process: providing food for domestic consumption, labor for modern sector employment, saving to finance investment (in all sectors), foreign exchange, and a market for domestic manufacturing goods. In the agricultural exporting countries the last three may seem of most obvious importance, though the importance of the agricultural sector as a source of income and employment must imply that productivity in food production is of considerable importance, as pointed out in the discussion of dual economy models.

Many of the agricultural "export economies" were plantation economies, and as such had a number of characteristics in common with the mineral-rich countries: the importance of foreign factors, rents accruing to either governments through taxation or a few owners (domestic or foreign), enclave economies with low linkages to the domestic economy, and even, in the colonial era, the use of imported labor. In the post-colonial period, the plantation sectors have changed in some respects: tax regimes, increased linkages with the domestic economy, increased domestic ownership, and increased use of smallholder production in addition to estate-owned production. As in the case of mining, some of the former problems of the "export economies" are no longer of such pressing interest.

However, while an ore body or a reservoir of petroleum can be used to produce only what it specifically contains, the land in plantations can be shifted to other commodities. Furthermore, since increased productivity of both land and labor engaged in agriculture is a key element in the development process, activities which raise productivity on plantations would necessarily be an important part of any development effort. The importance of alternative uses of land and labor, the crucial nature of technological change, and the other unique features of agricultural production noted by Timmer, given plantation and other forms of agriculture important common features for purposes of this analysis.

Export economies based on peasant agriculture differ from plantation export economies for the reasons one would expect from staple theory [see, for example, Myint (1965) or Helleiner (1966)], since the technology is different. Peasant export economies generally have higher unskilled labor coefficients and correspondingly low coefficients for skilled labor and reproducible capital. Dispersion of production results in a greater dispersion of infrastructure services, such as transportation, associated with export marketing. Incomes, too, are more widely dispersed. Commodity price fluctuations are passed directly to large numbers of households, rather than initially affecting only government revenues and corporate profits. There are greater linkages of export incomes to domestic consumption and production [though, as Helleiner (1966) notes, in the colonial periods traders in export goods were interested in promoting consumption of the imported goods which they also marketed]. Finally, in peasant agriculture the individual producers face choices among export crops and between export and domestic crops on a continuous basis (though tree crops present special cases). Sir Arthur Lewis's (1978a) remark, cited earlier about relative productivity in food and cash crops, is particularly relevant.

For primary export agriculture to play a major successful role in overall development a number of factors seem to be required.

First, since technological change is critical to agricultural development, investment in research and extension is an important element in a sustained role for export agriculture.

Second, since technological change in agriculture has generally been associated with the use of modern inputs (fertilizers, pesticides), with water control systems, and other aspects of environmental management, development of export agriculture will depend on both the financial resources (from current income or credit) to acquire the inputs and the physical access to the goods (or services). [Chenery and Syrquin (1986a) point to the quantitative importance of increased intermediate purchases by agriculture in the development process.]

Third, given the widespread evidence on the responsiveness of large and small farmers to changes in relative prices, the marketing regime (exchange rates, marketing institutions, export taxes or their equivalents) for export agriculture is important. Marketing regimes or policies which remove the profitability of investment in the expansion or improvement of export crops (or livestock) by extracting more than the rents arising in agriculture inhibit the role that export agriculture can play.

Fourth, export agriculture, particularly peasant agriculture, in a primary-oriented country is by definition a significant potential market. Policies which divert purchasing power (for capital, intermediate and consumer goods) of the agricultural export sector to the domestic economy could be a part of the strategy of using export agriculture as a major source of domestic development in the manufacturing sector. However, if the mechanisms used to accomplish this diversion penalized profitability and interfered with physical availability too severely, they could adversely affect the short- and long-term output of agriculture, and, with that, the source of a growing domestic market.

Fifth, since export agriculture depends on access to international markets, transportation and other infrastructure are required to move goods to market and inputs and capital goods back to the farm. Transport has been key feature in many case of "vent for surplus" exports, and as Helleiner (1966) argues, its widespread effects on other sectors may provide greater benefits in the case of peasant than in plantation agriculture.

In addition to these elements related to short-run production and to investment decisions, the issue of managing cyclical fluctuations is of importance in agricultural exporting countries. Mining and plantation economies have some features in common which differ substantially from agriculture based on smallholders. In boom periods, increased rents in mining and plantation agriculture accrue to a small number of private-sector actors (individuals or companies) and to governments. In small-holder peasant agriculture increased rents during a boom are widely spread in the private sector, and the extent to which they are captured by the government depends on the nature of the export and income tax system. While mining economies have difficulties in booms because of the pressure to spend revenues "imprudently", peasant agricultural economies sometimes have difficulties because the fiscal instruments do not permit a capture of the increased rents from producers. Furthermore, if governments do not capture and neutralize a significant part of the rents, the monetary effects of a commodity boom can be potentially very inflationary; increased foreign exchange reserves add to base money and inject liquidity into the domestic banking system. While some pressure is removed by spending on increased imports, added demand for nontradables is likely to be inflationary and to shift resources out of tradable production. Managing the boom periods in an agricultural export economy can in some ways be more difficult than in a mining economy.

In periods of major price recessions, mining economies face wage bills and input costs that do not fall in nominal terms. Major conflicts can arise surrounding decisions as to whether to reduce production, which also means reducing employment and purchases from local industries. Smallholder agriculture, with most of its income a mix of labor and capital income, absorbs the decreases (not without pain) and individuals make decisions about adjustments to lower prices in succeeding seasons (shifting land or labor to alternative crops, for example). If the cycle in an export economy centered on smallholder agriculture is harder to manage at the peak, it may be easier to manage at the bottom.

An important cyclical management issue for agricultural exporters is the extent to which they try to stabilize prices being paid to producers over the course of the cycle. While there can be many reasons for attempting such domestic price stabilization, the dangers are that the measures used will either over-tax or over-subsidize the producers, that the levels around which prices are stabilized will be significantly different from international market trends, or that governments will use the resources for spending that is destabilizing in the rest of the economy. And, since export agriculture is, by definition, dependent upon international markets, the information from those markets is of critical importance if domestic decision-makers are to make sensible short- and long-run production decisions.

6. Government policy and primary export sectors

This section focuses primarily on the range of policy measures that governments have used to extract rents from primary export production, to divert the incomes of primary export producers to the domestic market, and to stabilize incomes, as well as some consequences of those measures. Discussion of less discriminatory and even promotional policies is included for both the mineral and the agricultural exporters. One of the ironical results is that some of the policies chosen to divert demand to domestic sectors in order to diversify the economy have led to a frustration of structural change and a continued high share of primary exports in the total.

6.1. Trade policy issues

A key generic issue for the primary producing sectors has been the terms of trade they receive domestically as compared with the terms of trade they might receive on international markets were it not for government policy measures. In the days of the colonial export economies, mines and plantation agriculture often enjoyed free rein in dealing internationally in both factor and product markets, which increased the likelihood that their linkages would remain abroad rather than with the domestic economies. In the past-colonial period, however, and even during the late colonial era in many parts of the world, governments increasingly intervened to turn the primary sectors toward greater participation in the domestic economy. In almost all cases this resulted in net barter terms of trade for primary producers that were worse in domestic than in international markets.

The principal instruments for turning the terms of trade against primary production can be divided into those which divert income to governments and those which transfer income among sectors of the economy, though many instruments do both. Export taxes and tariffs on imports raise revenue for the government but also provide subsidies for the domestic use of exportables (in the case of export taxes) and protection for the domestic production of import substitutes (in the case of tariffs). Historically, the imposition of export and import taxes often started with the desire for revenue. The choice of import or export taxes was often a convenience, chosen as an alternative to income or profit taxes. And, in some cases in the post-war years, the use of such indirect taxes was meant to supplement income taxes, especially to prevent export sectors from receiving windfall gains from export price booms or devaluations.

Despite initial intentions, the protective effects of indirect taxes came to dominate the setting of rates in many countries. As is well known, the use of increasingly differentiated tariff structures has often resulted in very high rates of protection to import-competing industries and the creation of domestic industries with cost structures that could not compete in international markets [e.g. Little, Scitovsky and Scott (1970), Balassa and associates (1971), and Krueger (1984)].

In a large number of agricultural exporting colonies (and, later, countries), statutory marketing boards often acted as taxing authorities, even when their initial intentions had been to conduct price stabilization activities or to replace private middlemen. When used as a taxing device these marketing monopolies were similar to an export tax, sometimes using accumulated surpluses for development-related projects or returning portions to the government. West Africa has been the most widely studied area for marketing board activities [see

Helleiner (1966) for a survey], but others have also been documented. In the 1970s, some marketing monopolies in Sub-Saharan Africa acted as taxing devices on farmers, but were run so inefficiently that they absorbed public-sector resources as well [World Bank (1981)].

In a famous article, Lerner (1936) demonstrated the symmetry between import and export taxes. Through the adjustment of the exchange rate, attempts to tax imports resulted in a shift of some of the tax to exporters, while attempts to tax exports would, through an adjustment in the exchange rate, shift some of the tax to importers. In the post-war period a number of countries, especially in Latin America, used multiple exchange rate systems largely in an attempt to tax primary exports by giving less favorable rates to such export commodities. Studies of protection and import substitution of the past fifteen to twenty years [see Krueger (1984) and Chapter 31 by Balassa in this Handbook for surveys of results] emphasized exchange rate policy as a key taxing or subsidizing tool of economic policy, especially when combined with highly differentiated tariff structures and with quantitative restrictions on imports.

Quantitative restrictions, often imposed initially to keep international payments in line with international receipts, have frequently been a major instrument for directing resources to more and less preferred sectors of the economy. A highly over-valued currency may not discriminate too heavily against the export sector if access by primary exporters to capital and intermediate products at the official exchange rate is unhampered by quantitative restrictions *and* if imports are an important component of operating costs – a situation applying in many oil exporting countries. On the other hand, if the quantitative licensing system not only permits substantial currency over-valuation but also starves the primary sectors of inputs and capital goods, the penalty on exporting the main primary commodities can be very great indeed [see World Bank (1981) for examples].

The effects of taxes, tariffs, quantitative restrictions, and exchange rates on different sectors of the economy can be expressed in the form of rates of protection (or as their exchange rate equivalents), either as nominal rates or effective rates. Effective rates measure the extent to which the value added in the activity is changed by the combination of taxes or subsidies to output and to inputs. Studies of effective rates of protection or subsidy necessarily find some sectors favored and others discriminated against. The universal result of studies shows that the export sectors are penalized and import-competing sectors are benefited by systems of trade restriction [see Krueger (1984) and Chapter 31 by Balassa in this Handbook]. However, the extent of penalty varies a great deal among different export sectors: those that use small amounts of protected local inputs having less discrimination while those which have substantial inter-industry links to protected sectors being more heavily penalized.

Studies of effective protection focus on a particular productive activity and the prices it pays for inputs and receives for output. In thinking about broader

sectors of the economy, one needs also to think in terms of the prices faced by
the factors of production in the different sectors for consumption and investment
goods. Combining the effects on all prices received and all prices paid, whether
for intermediate or for final goods, one can estimate the full extent of the terms
of trade shift for or against different sectors of the economy. Such calculations
also give an indication of the extent to which income is transferred from one
sector to other sectors by the regime of taxes, exchange rates, and quantitative
restrictions in place. The size of inter-sectoral transfers of income have in some
countries been extremely large, amounting to several percentage points of GDP,
and much larger fractions of income originating in agriculture (always a loser)
and manufacturing (always a winner). [See Little, Scitovsky and Scott (1970) and
Lewis (1973) for summaries of several studies.]

While many attempts at promoting local manufacturing and diversifying the
local economy were initially conceived to promote manufacturing at the expense
of primary sectors, the result usually has been to promote import substitution at
the expense of all exports. As protection systems grew and became more highly
protected, the only sectors that could compete in international markets at the
exchange rate prevailing and at the domestic cost structure that developed were
those in which countries had substantial comparative cost advantages – the
primary producing sectors. Thus, it is not surprising that in several primary
oriented countries (as identified in the Chenery and Syrquin classification) with
restrictive or highly protective trade regimes, the degree of dependence on
primary products for exports has remained high, or has even increased over time.
The policies adopted to divert demand to domestic production and thereby
promote one element of structural change (the rise in the industry share of
production) have frustrated the achievement of another element of structural
change (the rise in the share of manufacturing in exports).

How serious an issue this is in any given country depends on many things.
However, it may be useful to examine the issue in the context of income transfers
and the importance of productivity growth to economic development. Protection
for one domestic sector must come at the expense of some other sector.[8]
Furthermore, since protection means paying some domestic factors more than the
value of foreign exchange they save, other domestic factors paying the subsidy
must earn (or save) a greater value of foreign exchange than they are paid. As a
protected sector grows, so does its need for subsidy from another sector of the
economy. In the absence of growth of the sectors paying the subsidy, unless
the share of factor incomes paid by the subsidizing sectors continuously rises, the
need for subsidy will outrun the capacity to pay it. In these circumstances there

---

[8]Market power of the county in international trade would enable the country to improve its terms
of trade and shift some burden of trade-restricting policies to its trading partners, but the other
domestic sectors would bear part of the costs even then.

will be a balance of payments crisis, since total domestic factor payments to producers of tradable goods will exceed the net earning or saving of foreign exchange by those producers [Lewis (1972)]. Only the growth of productivity in the protected sectors, which would reduce protection and subsidies, can provide a way out.

In some respects this problem is similar to that of a dual economy in which the growth of wage payments exceeds the growth of wage good production, or to the problem of agriculture not growing fast enough to provide the foreign exchange for the industrial sector. But, it is a slightly more general problem: it has to do with relative rates of growth between protected and subsidizing sectors, and the extent to which the sectors initially protected can achieve enough productivity growth to diminish their need for subsidy per unit of domestic value added. The primary exporting countries have been able to provide larger subsidies and for longer periods of time than those countries with fewer natural resources, since the incomes of the primary sectors in the resource-rich countries contain substantial elements of economic rents. Penalties through the internal terms of trade shift income from one sector to another, but, until they become extreme they have less effect in reducing output or, unless the products are consumed at home, export levels. The extent to which some more, and less, successful primary exporting countries exploited that advantage is discussed below.

Exchange rate policy is also an important part of the package. Arguments against the use of devaluation as a policy instrument for either counter-cyclical or general development policy often have turned on the desire to avoid windfall gains to exporters which would not be fully captured by the tax regime. Similar arguments have been made for the use of export taxes and the pricing policies of marketing monopolies at times of export price booms. Even where countries have been successful in imposing profit taxes on mining companies, for example, devaluations have been opposed because of concerns that short-run supply elasticities are low and exporters would receive windfall gains.

The process of "rent-seeking" behavior in the choice of government policy instruments is well known [Krueger (1974)]. There may also be a process of "rent-denying" on the part of government policy-makers, especially when governments decide on measures for short-term stabilization purposes. Indirect tax instruments, or their equivalents, often were chosen because of their supposed superiority in capturing rents that might accrue to a sector from export price movements or currency changes. The assumptions about low supply elasticities of primary exports are sometimes explicit, sometimes implicit, but the view that rents should be denied seems to have been an important element in choosing policies that implicitly tax the export sectors by reducing their selling prices rather than by taxing their incomes. Primary exporting countries, including mineral exporters, that have been willing to tolerate some windfalls due to external shocks or internal policy changes, seem to have been better able to manage both long-term development and short-term cyclical fluctuations than those which sought full "rent-denial", since the policies of the former have encouraged more adjustment to changed external economic circumstances than did those of the latter.

6.2. Other policies

In addition to government policies affecting foreign trade a range of other government actions have an adverse impact on the primary exporting sectors. A number of these factors can be included under the heading of "urban bias" [see Lipton (1977)]. As indicated in the section on mineral exporters, wage policies are an important issue for the mining countries and, as African experience has indicated, in agricultural exporting countries as well. The growth of modern sectors and government wage rates in many countries has generated both problems of cost competitiveness for modern sector activities and budgetary problems for governments. Primary producing sectors bear the burden of these problems either directly through heavier taxation or indirectly through the terms of trade effects of over-valued currencies brought on by domestic inflation and protection policies that permit the high manufacturing sector wages to be paid.

Another element of urban bias that can adversely affect the primary exporting sectors, particularly in agriculture, is the skewing of provision of government services and infrastructure away from the agricultural areas toward the urban areas. To the extent that growth of primary exports uses substantial amounts of infrastructure, the inadequate infrastructure will penalize export growth. Provision of such infrastructure has been an important element in promoting, or permitting, primary export development in a large number of exporting countries. Indeed, one key element in the "vent for surplus" notion of primary export production is the effect of changed transport costs that made activities profitable which previously were not. And, the transport links of primary exports with world markets are an important element in the characteristics of "staple" exports which do, or do not, lead to further development. Several of the cases below indicate the importance of transportation development to the success of continued growth through primary exports.

With regard to government services, one of the most important issues for the agricultural exporters, in particular, is agricultural research and extension activities. The importance of productivity growth in agriculture is well established. It is also clear from the experience of more successful primary exporting countries (see Section 7 below) that the support of research activities has been of substantial importance in allowing the agricultural sectors to play their role by increasing productivity of resources engaged in agriculture (not just export agriculture) and by permitting or encouraging the shifting of land use patterns as international market conditions or other domestic cost factors have changed. A contrary case has been made for the failure of agricultural production to rise as fast as per capita incomes in Africa over the past twenty years: the neglect of agricultural research and extension services, both for export crops and for local food crops, has reduced the ability of the continent as a whole to grow either food for local consumption or added agricultural cash crops for exports. The African success stories in agricultural exports have been limited to those few in which government research and extension was seriously pursued [see Eicher (1986) and Spencer (1986)].

7. Some country experiences

The longer-term experience of nine countries which exhibit the "primary specialization" trade bias that Chenery and Syrquin have identified may serve to illustrate some of the points raised in the previous sections. I have chosen the nine because of their variety, what I regard as their intrinsic interest (especially in

Table 29.1
Basic data on some primary exporting countries

	Mid-1985 population	1985 US$ GNP per capita	Trade orientation			Primary export share in 1985
			Chenery–Syrquin (1975) 1965	Chenery–Syrquin (1986b) 1965	1980	
Argentina	30.5	2130	0.73	0.33	0.29	82
Australia	15.8	10830	0.75	0.49	0.27	80
Canada	25.4	13680	0.32	0.17	0.47	39
Malaysia	15.6	215	0.32	0.17	0.02	73
Ivory Coast	10.1	660	− 0.04[a]	0.32	0.31	90
Chile	12.1	1430	0.32	0.46	0.40	93
Zambia	6.7	390	0.39	0.39	0.47	98
South Africa	32.4	2010	0.11	[b]	[b]	75
Botswana	1.1	840	n.a.	n.a.	n.a.	92

[a] Trade Orientation shows essentially no deviation from a neutral pattern.

[b] South African data must be adjusted for the treatment of gold, which in the mid-1980s was over 40% of visible exports. Chenery and Syrquin (1986) classified South Africa as manufacturing oriented because gold and some other mineral exports are, in some statistics, classified as manufactured because they are exported in smelted form.

Sources: Population, GNP per capita, and primary export share are from World Bank (1987). Primary export share for Botswana is taken from Bank of Botswana (1987).

Trade Orientation coefficients are from Chenery and Syrquin (1975, Tables 10 and 11), and (1986b, Table 7).

relation to the issues of this survey), and the availability of literature and information. My review of their development experience focuses on the various policy issues outlined in Section 6, the characteristics of primary exporters noted in Sections 3 through 5, and the four general areas of management that were outlined in Section 1: what level, and by what means, to capture rents for the local economy; how to divide the rents between consumption and investment and among sectors; how and to what extent to divert purchases by primary exporters to the domestic economy; and how to manage cyclical booms and busts.

Some basic comparative data for the nine countries are given in Table 29.1. While not chosen at random, the countries do represent a range of experience of countries that (except for Zambia, which slid back over five years) had passed at least into the World Bank's "Lower Middle Income" category of countries by 1985. Only Botswana is a very small country, and none is a particularly large country, though Argentina, Canada, and South Africa were classified as "Large Countries" by Chenery and Syrquin (1975, 1986b). In any brief review of a country, one is bound to be somewhat superficial, but I have tried to focus on generalizations which seem to be reasonably well supported in the literature.

7.1. Three early starters: Argentina, Australia, Canada

The comparison of Argentina, Australia, and Canada has been of interest to economists for many years [e.g. Smithies (1965), Diaz-Alejandro (1970)], in large part due to the initial similarities of the three countries. All were substantial natural resource exporters in the nineteenth and early twentieth centuries and have remained so through the most recent decades; all experienced substantial

Table 29.2
Comparative figures for three "newly settled" regions

	Argentina	Australia	Canada
Income per capita:			
1929 (1964 $)	$700	$1000	$1300
1985 (1985 $)	$2130	$10830	$13680
Exports per capita:			
1929 (1964 $)	$90	$105	$125
1985 (1985 $)	$275	$1440	$3445
Primary exports as % *of visible exports*			
1929	94%	90%	63%
1985	82%	80%	39%

Sources: 1929 figures from Diaz-Alejandro (1970, pp. 55–56); 1985 figures from World Bank (1987).

immigration; all were large importers of capital; all were among the relatively high-income countries by the 1920s. By the most recent half century has seen a considerable gap open between Argentina and the other two, as shown clearly in Table 29.2. The story of policy and performance in the three is of interest when asking: What makes for successful structural transformation?

7.1.1. Canada

Canadian experience provided the basis for the "staple theory" of development advanced by Innis (1915). A long sweep of Canadian history saw the prominence of a succession of natural-resource-based exports, ranging from fish and furs to timber, foodstuffs (principally wheat), and minerals, including base and precious metals and petroleum. Caves and Holton (1961), and other analysts point to the changing mix of exogenous factors – international demand as influenced both by fad and fashion and by productivity in other competing countries, technological change in the production, processing and transportation to international markets of natural-resource-based products, both agricultural and mineral – that led Canada through a succession of staple export booms, and occasional busts, and that brought with them overall rates of economic growth that have produced one of the world's highest per capita income levels.

Canadian development policies have been hotly debated over the decades in some of the same terms that have been used in developing countries since World War II. In submitting a bill with high protective tariffs to support industrialization, the Minister of France in 1879 "insisted that 'the time has arrived when we are to decide whether we will simply be hewers of wood and drawers of water...'" [Deutsch et al. (1965)]. The role of tariff policy, investments in transportation infrastructure, and (of importance in a country Canada's size) regional development policies were all important issues for more than a century.

Trade policies in Canada clearly were aimed at protecting the industrial sector at the expense of exports. However, the Canadian tariff, even in the relatively high tariff era of the late nineteenth century, was moderate in its effect by post-World War II standards. Most consumer goods were subject to tariffs in the 30 percent range, while intermediate goods and capital goods ranged from 10 to 25 percent [Deutsch et al. (1965, pp. 469–470)]. Consequently, the extreme ranges of effective tariff rates were largely avoided. And, the tariff levels were moderated towards the end of the century and in succeeding decades. Caves and Holton (1961, p. 236) are even skeptical that the tariff had major effects on the rate of industrial development. Nor were quantitative restrictions and exchange controls a part of Canadian policy. As a result, while Canadian trade policy provided clear and deliberate discrimination against exports and in favor of industrial import substitutes, the policy extracted resources from the staple exporting sectors without either removing all incentive for continued investment in the staple sector or starving it for resources. Furthermore, it is clear that there has been some balance between the interests of the export sectors in lower tariffs and those of the industrial sectors in higher protection.

The effects of the policies, in both political and economic terms, varied as the state of the staple exports changed. The booming wheat economy of the late nineteenth and early twentieth centuries created a demand for farm machinery and other up-stream activities, leading to extremely rapid growth in the manufacturing sector in the decades before World War I. In the inter-war years, the growth of the mining industry generated substantial development down-stream "in the industries smelting, refining and fabricating Canada's primary nonferrous metals output" and in the post-war years the processing of petroleum and natural gas has been a major source of industrial growth [Caves and Holton (1961, p. 45)].

And, throughout Canadian economic history, even before Confederation of the provinces in 1867, public policy has generally favored the provision of infrastructure investments and research and training institutes to support the development of the staple export sectors.

The relations with the United States are of major importance in Canadian economic and political history, and are clearly linked with the central issues of economic development policy [see, for example, Aitken et al. (1959)]. The protective tariff was seen not only as a device for diversifying the economy but also as a means of ensuring that emigration to the United States did not occur – especially since many of the staple exports were not very labor-intensive and could not provide the magnate for population that Canadian nationalists wished.

Access to the markets of the United States and the availability of relatively cheap water transportation to world markets have been major advantages to both the industrial and the primary export sectors in Canada. Large-scale exploitation of natural resources became economic because of the availability of transportation; and, as Caves and Holton (1961, pp. 388–389) conclude, "she has been able to use her factors of production so much more efficiently than if she produced only for the domestic market that any concerted effort to achieve autonomy would be expensive indeed".

The Canadian record reveals findings of some interest in relation to conditions of successful structural transformation under a primary export orientation. First, government investment has supported the staple export sectors, especially in the area of transportation infrastructure. Second, the succession of different products is impressive; government policy did not attempt to prevent the decline of industries that were becoming uneconomic in terms of international market competition. Third, tariff and related trade policies (exchange rates and exchange controls) did protect the domestic manufacturing market, but the nature and the extent of the protection was not so great as to either produce a manufacturing sector that was a major drain on the rest of the economy or too greatly dampen the incentives for investment in staple exports. As a corollary, the successful transformation in productive structure has been accompanied by a shift to exports of manufactured goods, something that could not be accomplished if domestic manufacturing was permanently high-cost. During investment booms connected directly or indirectly with the staple export sectors, the manufacturing sectors grew to supply a rising share of goods, even though imports rose as well.

The staple export sectors financed the development of the rest of the economy, directly and (through both protection and inducing capital inflows from abroad) indirectly; but equally clearly, the staple sectors were not so discriminated against that their expansion was discouraged. Profits generated in Canadian export activities were reinvested in other domestic ventures (both in staples and in manufacturing). Over time the share of total investment financed domestically steadily increased, though foreign capital retained some importance. Furthermore, as Caves and Holton (1961, p. 118) point out, there are no "conspicuous cases of capital shortages hampering investment for any more than very short periods". Potentially profitable investments found financing either at home or abroad: the lack of serious discrimination against the staple sectors in terms of pricing, and commitment of government resources to infrastructure, made economically viable propositions also financially viable. Finally, both agricultural and mineral exports generated domestic industrial activity both as supplying industries and as down-stream processing operations.

7.1.2. Australia

Australia's experience has some parallels to Canada's but also presents some contrasts. Like Canada, Australia experienced a succession of different staple exports over the past century or more: whale products, gold, wool, dairy products, meat, wheat, coal, base metals, and, most recently, diamonds. Australia's per capita income levels in the last half of the nineteenth century were the highest in the world, due first to the gold boom, but later to other primary exports. As in Canada, some export products have come and gone, others have remained as important contributors over long periods of time. As in Canada, Australia has invested in infrastructure to support the development of the staple exports. As in Canada, there was an overwhelming importance of external financing in early years (one-third of fixed capital formation financed from abroad between 1860 and 1900, 20 percent between 1900 and 1930), but it gave way to a much more moderate role as domestic savings rose and were reinvested in both manufacturing and primary sectors.

However, Australia has significantly different transport costs to and from world markets; it has nothing comparable to Canada's U.S. market, and the total size of the Australian domestic market is much smaller than that of Canada. These differences have resulted in greater prominence of two significant issues in Australian development: tariff policy and the effects of natural resource booms on other sectors of the economy.

The Australian manufacturing sector is "protected" by the large transport costs in reaching the Australian market. Nonetheless, the tariff has been a major instrument for promotion of manufacturing industry in Australia. In the 1960s it was estimated that some two-thirds of Australian manufacturing was a beneficiary of tariff protection [Boehm (1971, p. 142)]. Protection appears to have resulted in greater efficiency losses than in Canada; the geographically dispersed Australian market, its small total size, and aggressive "recruiting" of firms by State governments has resulted in losses of scale efficiency as well as problems of concentration of market power in Australian manufacturing [Caves, in Caves and Krause (1984, pp. 346–347)].

While state governments experimented with tariffs to compete for labor during the 1850s gold booms, the tariff was first seen as an important instrument of federal policy to promote domestic industry in 1908. Federal tariffs developed in the 1920s (to protect industries that had emerged during World War I) and especially in the 1930s, in response to the depression in primary product markets. Australia devalued against Sterling in 1931, and this devaluation was taken into account in determining subsequent tariff adjustments. After World War II, Australia used import licensing as a protective measure but also devalued against the U.S. dollar at the time of the Sterling devaluation in 1949. The use of tariff and other trade policies is, therefore, somewhat more complex in Australia than in Canada: tariffs were supplemented by import licensing, wartime unavailability of imports provided a boost to local manufacturing, and more neutral measures such as devaluation were used in both the 1930s and 1940s. Australia's relative concentration on primary exports as late as the 1980s may be in part a tariff-related failure to develop a competitive manufacturing industry.

Australia is one of three high-income countries (New Zealand and Norway are the others) to have more than 60 percent of exports concentrated in primary export activities, but it has also managed its affairs in such a way as to promote manufacturing to a substantial degree. Its rate of growth of total income has been among the highest over nearly a century. Policies to support manufacturing growth have included a mix of tariffs, for some period of time import licensing, and changes in exchange rates. The effects of the trade and other policies on the incentive to invest in new natural resource projects have not been so adverse as to reduce the growth of mineral exports, and government investment has supported the primary export sectors. A major concern in the past twenty years (reflected in the contributions of Australian economists to the mining boom literature) has been the difficulties caused for both manufacturing and for agriculture by the effects of mineral projects, which reduce the competitive position of both the other sectors. While studies indicate losses from inefficient protected manufacturing industries, these have been small relative to the ability of the primary export sectors to support them. Manufactured exports have developed, albeit largely in industries which are relatively natural-resource-intensive [Krause, in Caves and Krause (1984, pp. 282–284)].

7.1.3. Argentina

Argentina presents a fairly stark contrast to the experience of Australia and Canada, despite considerable similarity to them as late as the 1920s. As shown in Table 29.2, between 1929 and 1985, Argentina dropped from 70 to 20 percent of Australian per capita income and from 54 to 16 percent of Canadian per capita income. In per capita exports, Argentina declined from 86 to 19 percent of Australia's level, and from 72 to 8 percent of Canada's level. Argentina remained the most dependent on primary exports of the three by 1985. What contrasts in Argentine policy and experience explain the difference in performance?

The most comprehensive review of Argentine economic policy and growth is given by Diaz-Alejandro (1970). As early as the 1930s Argentine economic policies were turning against exports, particularly, but not exclusively, those of the primary sectors. Emphasis on production of what Diaz-Alejandro calls "home goods" shifted resources from the production of tradables to the production of domestic goods. While the short-run effects of economic management in the 1930s enabled Argentina to weather the Great Depression relatively well, the policies developed at the end of World War II further turned the terms of trade against primary sectors. At the worst point in 1947–49 about half of potential value added in rural sectors was being "taxed" through adverse terms of trade (a combination of currency over-valuation, tariffs, exchange controls) and transferred to the rest of the economy. In addition, the import licensing system made it extremely difficult for the rural sector to get physical access to imported modern inputs. As a result, Argentine shares of world markets in its traditional exports (meat, grains, and linseed) declined almost monotonically from the mid-1930s through the early 1950s, as Argentine export quantities fell.

The protection regime involved duty-free importation of intermediate goods, so levels of effective protection were substantially above those of nominal protection in manufacturing industries, imposing relatively high real costs on the other tradable producing sectors. The tariff levels, which understated nominal protection due to import licensing and exchange controls, were much higher than in Australia and Canada, by one calculation averaging over 150 percent in 1959 [Diaz-Alejandro (1970, p. 272)]. As Diaz-Alejandro notes, "many manufactured goods in Argentina passed from the category of importable to that of quasi-home goods due to the nature of the system of protection" (p. 79) which broke the link between domestic and international prices. At times "the main preoccupation was defending industries that had arisen during the war, regardless of their efficiency" (p. 113).

In addition to the choice of foreign trade and protection policies, Argentina presents a contrast to the other two countries in at least three other dimensions. First, public-sector spending for infrastructure and for other activities supportive of the rural export sectors did not receive much priority in Argentina in the period after 1930, and particularly after World War II. Second, the attitude toward foreign investment, always a subject of controversy in all three countries, became notably more hostile in Argentina than in Australia and Canada after World War II. The effect on foreign investment was exacerbated by changes in policy regimes during the post-war period, which were much more frequent in Argentina. Third, fiscal and monetary policies in Argentina were generally inflationary (with occasional periods of retrenchment) which, in the presence of fixed exchange rates, exaggerated the adverse effects of foreign trade policy on the rural and nascent manufacturing export sectors and unsettled the policy environment for investors, foreign and domestic. Policies that originated, in part, due to hostility to foreign investment resulted in discouragement to domestic saving and investment as well. More than just the rents were extracted from Argentine agriculture, and resources were not channelled back through public-sector investment.

Might Argentina have chosen its policies differently? At the beginning of the Great Depression Argentina had large foreign balances; and the blockage of Sterling deposits in London during World War II meant that there were substantial reserves at the end of the war. Argentina had suffered (and Australia and Canada had gained) from the adoption of Imperial Preferences by Great Britain, and, to a greater extent than the other two, English-speaking foreign investors were resented for political and social reasons. There were substantial domestic pressures at the end of World War II to de-link from the international economy, and the availability of Sterling balances made it seem attractive to do so. Argentina was not in the position of many countries in which a foreign exchange crisis induced policy choices that were even at the time regarded as second or third best. The policy choice for extreme emphasis on import substitution "was not an integrated and thought-out plan. Rather, it proceeded from one improvisation to another, reacting to short-run economic and political pressures" [Diaz-Alejandro (1970, p. 113)]. Unstable fiscal and monetary policies were not endemic to Argentina as they were in some other countries; they were a new feature of Argentine life after World War II. Other choices might have been made. The choices that were made converted Argentina from a front-rank country in world development to a country still heavily dependent upon a relatively stagnant level of primary exports, without having substituted a dynamic manufacturing sector to provide a source of growth for exports, income, and employment.

7.2. Malaysia and the Ivory Coast: Two tentative "successes"?

Malaysia and the Ivory Coast have much shorter periods of economic development experience, but there are some potential lessons from their experience, too. Both achieved above-average development records in the years since World War II, beginning even before their political independence. Neither is without difficulties – in the Ivory coast especially serious structural problems arose in the early 1980s – but some generalizations may be possible within the framework of analysis developed here.

7.2.1. Malaysia

Malaysia has had one of the better records of income and export growth over the past twenty to thirty years [e.g. among the top 15 of 103 countries ranked by per capita GNP growth 1965–85; World Bank (1987)]. Like Canada and Australia, its primary exports encompass both mineral and agricultural products – rubber, palm oil, tin, and tropical hardwoods. In trade policy, Malaysia maintained relatively moderate levels of protection to manufacturing industry and has simultaneously had modest and selective export taxes on major exports [see Power (1971) and Lim (1973)]. Thus, there has been discrimination against the primary export sectors, but it has not been high by international standards. Estimates place average effective protection in the 30–40 percent range. "Pioneer industry" status involved tax holidays, rather than more extensive use of devices to raise pre-tax profits. There has been relatively little use of exchange controls and import licensing, as compared with other countries, and the currency has not been seriously over-valued. Fiscal policy has been relatively conservative, and inflation has remained low by international standards, thus contributing to the lack of currency over-valuation. By maintaining a realistic currency value, profitable investments arose in many activities, not just import substitutes, and exports were encouraged from all sectors. The share of exports in GDP in the mid-1960s was estimated by Chenery and Syrquin (1975) at more than twice the "normal" levels, reflecting both relatively large export production and a relatively high value for foreign exchange. Counter-cyclical fiscal policy has resulted in relatively high average levels of foreign exchange reserves and a corresponding ability to maintain steadier growth rates of domestic income than of export earnings. The government has not only been supportive both of the infrastructure demands of the primary exporting sectors, but it has also invested heavily in research to raise productivity in the agricultural sectors. Major research and re-planting programs in rubber and oil palm have been undertaken.

Malaysia has experienced a considerable degree of structural change in GDP, employment, and exports during the past three to four decades. There have been new exports in both minerals and agriculture. Productivity has risen in rubber and oil palm production. In rubber, the rise in productivity was crucial in off-setting the decline in rubber prices, and allowed Malaysia both to retain market shares and to maintain profitability of a key export-earning activity. Manufacturing growth was sufficiently rapid that manufacturing share of GDP rose from 10 percent in 1965 to 19 percent in 1983. And, following initial periods of growth led primarily by import substitution, manufactured exports became an increasingly important source of industrial growth. By 1985, manufactured exports constituted 27 percent of export earnings and were over $265 per capita (as compared, for example, with Brazil's level of about $80 per capita).

Malaysia appears to be a case in which many of the transitions from the old export economy to a "successful" primary exporter have taken place. Rents were extracted, but investment in infrastructure and research maintained profitability and encouraged productivity growth in both cash crop and food crop agriculture. Manufacturing was encouraged and import replacement took place, but not in permanently uncompetitive industries. Significant structural change in both exports and production took place while the primary sector both grew and remained relatively profitable.

7.2.2. The Ivory Coast

The experience of the Ivory Coast presents a somewhat more mixed picture than Malaysia, and the length of its documented experience is considerably shorter. However, the Ivory Coast maintained economic growth rates that were well above average for Sub-Saharan Africa and above average for lower middle-income countries in the two decades ending in the early 1980s, though the most recent years were colored by serious debt service problems. As in Malaysia, the Ivory Coast has managed to shift its agricultural production to newer products as partial substitutes for coffee and cocoa (the two principal exports at independence): cotton in the north, pineapples and bananas in the south, and rubber, coconut, and palm oil in forested regions. In part this was accomplished under projects run by autonomous agencies "placed under the supervision of the technical ministries... [and] in most cases closely connected with specialized agricultural research institutes" [den Tuinder (1978, p. 41)].

Pricing policy was recognized as important in light of the responsiveness of producers to price changes. However, producer prices for coffee and cocoa were generally well below the fob export levels as part of the conscious effort to induce diversification to other products. The two major products, however, were beneficiaries of government investment programs aimed at providing research results, infrastructure, and extension to the primary export sectors. Starting in the late 1960s, manufacturing industry became increasingly involved with processing of primary products for export, and such agro-processing was for a number of years the leading sector within manufacturing.

The industrial sector in the Ivory Coast was nurtured by a combination of tariff protection and import restrictions, and, for some export processing industries, export taxes on the raw products and complex quotas for processed and unprocessed materials (which encouraged local processing). Nominal tariffs were not particularly high [den Tuinder (1978, p. 99) reports rates as high as 30–45 percent] and tariffs alone would have provided modest levels of effective protection [20–40 percent by World Bank estimates reported in den Tuinder (1978, p. 48)]. However, the combination of quantitative restrictions on imports and duty-free access to intermediate inputs and raw materials (provided under the 1959 investment code) raised the rates of effective protection considerably. In addition, since there was relatively little indigenous entrepreneurial capacity in the manufacturing sectors, much of the management and equity capital came from foreign sources. Thus, once the costs of imported factors was taken into account, the effective cost of saving foreign exchange through import substitution would be substantially higher than those calculated by normal measures of effective protection. The 1973 revisions to the tariff schedule provided for automatic adjustments "to meet the protective requirements of firms whose priority agreements would expire in the future" [den Tuinder (1978, p. 49)] since manufacturers argued that their costs had not come down quickly enough for them to become competitive. As indicated in Section 6, the continued growth of a protected sector requires the continued growth of subsidies from the exporting sectors. This led to an exacerbation of the balance of payments difficulties facing the Ivory Coast when debt and the terms of trade became serious problems in the early 1980s.

The macroeconomic management of the economy was relatively prudent through the early 1970s, but commercial debt was increasingly contracted in the late 1970s and early 1980s. As a result debt service payments rose from 7 to 21 percent of export earnings in the years 1970–1984. The vulnerability of the economy to changes in the terms of trade for major exports was reduced but by no means eliminated by the diversification of export earnings. Substantial new fixed obligations without either sufficient reserves or additional borrowing capacity led to the need for major corrective actions when the terms of trade deteriorated in the 1980s. This substantially reduced the short-term potential for continued growth. The problem of adjustment was worsened by the increased size of the high-cost, import-substituting industrial sector.

The experience in the Ivory Coast suggests that, despite considerable diversification and investment in the expansion of the primary export sectors, the other ingredients of "success" in primary led growth, particularly counter-cyclical macroeconomic policy and the nature and extent of protection to industry, were lacking. The transition, which seems to depend on the collection of key policies already referred to, was de-railed at least temporarily and nullified some of the earlier successes.

7.3. Two troubled copper countries: Chile and Zambia

The choice of Chile and Zambia as examples of primary exporters might be criticized in the mid-1980s because of the disastrous state of world copper markets, especially since 1973, as copper prices had fallen substantially more than those of almost any other primary commodity. Nonetheless, their experience may be of relevance in searching for lessons from the experience of primary exporters generally.

7.3.1. Chile

Chile has a long history of development, with reasonably well-documented experience stretching back into the mid-nineteenth century [see Mamalakis and Reynolds (1965) and Mamalakis (1976)]. Chile had a major resource boom in the nitrate industry from 1880 to 1930, which provided more than half of government revenue between 1900 and 1930 through an export tax. Chile was the world's largest copper producer up to 1880, and after a long period of decline, it began to re-emerge as a major producer just before World War I, with output rising ten-fold between 1906 and 1929. Chile represented a prototypical case of the "export economy" of Levin (1960), with extensive use of foreign factors of production and a lack of linkages between mining and the domestic economy. Indeed, the rebuilding of the copper industry in the first quarter of the twentieth century was "not financed out of the abundant nitrate surpluses but by the New York capital markets" [Mamalakis (1976, p. 81)]. The continued reliance on foreign financing, despite considerable domestic rents that could have been tapped, resulted in an outflow of dividend and profit remittances whenever the copper mines were profitable. In addition, rather than using the nitrate and copper revenues (the latter considerably smaller relative to national income than the former) to finance further domestic capital formation, the government used them to reduce taxes on other domestic sectors while maintaining government consumption levels and imports [Mamalakis (1976, p. 156)]. While it is quite clear that sizeable nitrate rents went abroad, there is considerable controversy about the extent to which copper rents were adequately captured in the second period of copper expansion. To the extent that the tax regime did capture mining rents for government, however, the rents were not invested in increasing the domestic capital stock.

The pattern of government investment for long periods in Chile did not provide the kinds of support for the export sectors that was found in Canada and Australia. Nor was there investment in education or research that would support either the mining sector or agriculture. Chile continued to rely heavily on foreign technology and skills in mining, and the agricultural sector never received the support that would have enabled it to provide an alternative source of higher income employment or a significant market for domestically produced manufactured goods.

Macroeconomic policies in Chile over an extended period were characterized by inflation, instability, and uncertainty, which produced a number of side-effects. On the one hand, there was an adverse impact on the willingness to invest in domestic assets including, to some extent, those directly associated with copper and nitrate exports. While the economy was generating relatively large rents from the two main exports, it did not provide a climate that encouraged reinvestment of those surpluses (nor, as noted, did the government adequately invest its share of the rents). Indeed, Chileans were expatriating their savings rather than investing them at home. Rather than a counter-cyclical policy of building up reserves in good periods to allow steady expansion during down-turns. Chilean public expenditures fluctuated with revenues to a considerable extent.

Along with macroeconomic policies which produced a fairly long history of an over-valued currency, industrial growth was encouraged through a highly protective tariff. These policies together heavily taxed all export sectors. While copper and the nitrate sector could stand such income transfers and remain profitable, the combination of over-valued currency and high tariffs discouraged the diversification of exports into either other primary products or manufactures. Nor did the mining sector engage in much down-stream processing or fabrication. Reynolds and Mamalakis argue that this was in part due to the adversarial relationship which the government developed between itself and industry on the one hand, and the mining sector on the other. It was not until 1956 that the Copper Department began to encourage a "buy Chilean" policy [Mamalakis (1976, p. 156)]. The manufacture of domestic consumer goods was heavily protected. So, while the manufacturing sector contributed an abnormally high share to measured GDP in Chile [Chenery and Syrquin (1975)], a considerable share of the value added was due to protection, not "real" adding of value. Further growth in the manufactured sector would have to come through improved productivity which would both reduce the drain on the primary export sectors and make it possible for Chile to compete in international markets.

In the Chenery and Syrquin (1975) analysis, Chile shows up as a country with an abnormally large share of manufacturing output, a small share (60 percent of normal) of total exports in GDP, and primary orientation bias in its foreign trade [similar results are shown by Chenery and Syrquin (1986b)]. The failure to invest in both physical and human capital to support export activities is partially responsible for the low export share. Exchange rate policy and policy on industrial protection provide added reasons for both the low level of exports and the abnormally high level of manufactured output destined for the domestic market. In first failing to retain rents in the domestic economy, and later failing to provide incentives for the primary sectors by trying to divert by inefficient methods too large a share of purchases to the domestic market, Chile swung from a prototypical "export economy" to one in which the relative concentration on primary exports was still exceptionally high and the diversification investments were clearly unproductive.

The social and political convulsions which have plagued Chile in recent years have coincided with the prolonged slump in the copper markets; in some respects this suggests that Chile might best be neglected in a review of primary exporters. However, the phenomena that are described above which resulted in an unsuccessful attempt to achieve sustained growth and structural transformation were long-term factors, not recent events. An examination of the situation in the early 1970s would lead to similar conclusions about the essential features which frustrated successful transformation. The package of macroeconomic, foreign trade, exchange rate, and government investment policies would be expected to produce an economy with relatively low levels of exports and relatively high shares of traditional primary exports.

7.3.2. Zambia

Zambia's experience is much shorter than Chile's. Though the rise of copper in (then) Northern Rhodesia began in the 1930s, Zambia did not achieve independence until 1964. Until independence, Zambia resembled a classical "export economy" of the sort described by Levin (1960): skilled labor and management were drawn from abroad, unskilled labor came from other parts of the country, transportation systems were arranged solely for the purpose of the copper industry, and linkages to the rest of the economy were weak. Baldwin's (1966) exceptionally thorough study estimates that "no more than 15 and 20% ... spent on operational stores in 1960 went for commodities processed in the manufacturing or mining sector of the economy" (p. 37). Even this level was accompanied by a 5 percent price preference introduced in the 1950s for goods manufactured in Northern Rhodesia. And, despite the high share of the copper industry in the provision of government revenue, the returns to foreign investors included a fair degree of economic rent that could have been captured for the domestic economy.

The copper industry's principal links to the rest of the economy were in the form of payments for electricity and railway services and government taxes, where the mines provided 60–65 percent of the totals for the country in the late 1950s [Baldwin (1966, pp. 38–39)]. A dual economic structure was evident in wage rates and educational opportunities for Europeans and Africans, as well as in the structure of production. Baldwin's study made much of the technological characteristics of the export industry – in the case of Zambia and copper, capital- and skill-intensive – in explaining the limited extent to which it can pull the rest of the economy forward. Even in agriculture, the presence of white farmers who secured land along the rail line to the Copperbelt led to dualistic development.

After World War II, advancement of Africans to some jobs previously held by Europeans was negotiated with the white mineworkers unions. At about the same time, African wages were increased. The spending patterns of the much more highly paid whites were skewed toward imports, which limited the market for domestically produced consumer goods, while the increased wages for Africans, which could be afforded by the copper mines, put import-competing manufactures at a serious cost disadvantage. Furthermore, the practice of reserving jobs for the whites restricted the training that would otherwise have taken place, limiting the skill levels of the indigenous workforce. Discrimination against African farmers relative to Europeans (except in maize) meant that the livelihoods of the vast majority of Zambians were left unaffected by government efforts in the development of institutions or services. Thus, well before independence, some patterns were established which would present problems for the structural transformation and continued development.

At independence, Zambia had significant assets with which to combat the problems, particularly the fact that its financial and balance of payments position was enviable by the standards of most developing countries. The fortunes of the copper industry were favorable for the first eight or nine years of independence, though the drop in the copper price in the past decade has been nothing short of catastrophic. As suggested in Section 4, managing a mineral economy in good times is difficult, and Zambia had substantial financial resources at and shortly after independence with no experience of independent macroeconomic management. And, Zambia was faced with civil wars in its neighbors and the Unilateral Declaration of Independence by Southern Rhodesia almost from the time independence was achieved. These added to both transportation and security problems. Nonetheless, particular choices of policy in the post-independence period seem to have aggravated rather than eased the transition to life at a lower copper price.

Agriculture was neglected in Zambia after independence, and GDP originating in agriculture has fallen in per capita terms consistently over the past twenty years. The responses to terms of trade shocks from the decline in the copper price, and also to the illegal Unilateral Declaration of Independence did not include any shift in the exchange rate. Adjustment was based on production for domestic markets alone. As a result, the Kwatcha was seriously over-valued for much of the post-independence period, discouraging agricultural output, encouraging the import-intensity of local manufactured goods, penalizing new exports, and, in particularly bad periods for the copper industry, generating operating losses for the copper mines as well. Apart from a sizeable, necessary and long-overdue investment in education, government spending produced a relatively high-paid elite in the cities which, as Baldwin had predicted, made it difficult for new manufacturing enterprises to meet international competition. The tariff structure, built up during succeeding post-independence budgets had the usual characteristics: high duties on luxuries, somewhat lower duties on other consumer goods, and lowest on intermediates and capital goods. Import licensing by "essentiality" took on similar characteristics.

During the early years of independence, rents from mining were devoted to private consumption through financing wage increases for the modern sectors. The lack of investment to support agricultural output meant that not only were there no new agricultural exports, but food imports rose, and a broad-based domestic market for manufacturing failed to develop. Foreign equity holders in the copper mines were bought out with bonds, and fiscal policy during the late 1970s involved an increasing use of foreign commercial borrowing, imposing fixed obligations on an economy 90 percent dependent on a commodity with a highly fluctuating price.

In the brief years since independence it is doubtful whether Zambia could have restructured its economy to avoid the consequences of its long history as an "export economy" combined with the decline in its terms of trade in the 1970s and 1980s. However, the choice of policies both in the immediate post-independence period (on allocation of investment, wages, and capital structure of the mining industry) and in the periods when the external balance of payments began to be under serious pressure (on the exchange rate, import licensing, and tariff protection) have made the structural transformation problems more difficult, rather than easier, to cope with. As in the case of Argentina and Chile, Zambia had the resources available for the first decade of independence that would have made other choices of policy possible.

7.4. Two special cases: South Africa and Botswana

Southern Africa has diverse mineral potential and has produced two rather special cases of primary export-led development: South Africa, better known for its racial policies, had quite rapid growth over a long period and is both a major mineral exporter and an agricultural exporter of some size. Botswana is a very recent Cinderella story, having had the fastest growth rate of GDP in the world from 1965 to 1985 [World Bank (1987)] and by the mid-1980s was one of the worlds leading diamond producers.

7.4.1. South Africa[9]

The discoveries of diamonds at Kimberley and gold near Johannesburg in the late nineteenth century produced what was, at first, a classic case of a colonial export economy. Capital and skilled labor came from Europe and the United States, infrastructure was developed to serve the mining community, and unskilled labor came at some distance, including for periods of time from Asia, on term contracts. The extreme forms of racial discrimination and the eventual attempt to construct separate political structures for the black population in South Africa are somewhat linked to the nature of the economy, but some key elements of economic policy can be analyzed without extensive reference to this unique feature of South African political economy.

South African economic growth through the outbreak of World War I was heavily oriented to the production of gold and diamonds for export. While manufactured goods continued to come largely from abroad, distance provided a protective factor in South Africa as it did in Australia. As in many countries, World War I provided a stimulus to local manufacturing. The economic structure began to change in the 1920s, with both the increasing importance of racial issues related to economics (the so-called "Civilized Labor Policy" involved higher wages for whites than blacks on the same job as well as reservation of certain jobs for whites) and the growth of government attention to economic diversification. A clear policy of industrial protection was first adopted in 1925, and from that point onward the manufacturing sector was nurtured by an increasingly detailed and complex set of tariff rates tailored to the needs of each industry requesting protection.

In the Great Depression there was an initial decrease of output and employment in manufacturing, but the drop was not as great in South Africa as in the industrial countries. South Africa went off the gold standard in 1933, which raised the local gold price and provided a major stimulus for the economy for the rest of the decade. Manufacturing employment in 1938/39 was 66 percent higher than a decade earlier (69 percent for whites and 64 percent for blacks) [Houghton (1964, p. 125)]. World War II gave a further stimulus to manufacturing, despite shortages of skilled labor and the supply of various inputs and capital goods, and it helped lay the base for more sophisticated industries. It also provided a much larger increase in employment for blacks than for whites (74 and 20 percent, respectively) between 1938/39 and 1944/45 [Houghton (1964, p. 127)]. Manufacturing also surpassed mining as a share of GDP during World War II.

The post-war period saw a continued development of manufacturing on the basis of protected import substitution, including detailed controls on the number

---

[9]This subsection draws heavily on Lewis (1989).

of firms and differentiation of products within protected industries, in an effort to reduce the costs of protection and to gain some advantages from scale economies. From 1946 to 1970 manufacturing GDP at constant prices grew by over 6 percent per annum – an unusually fast rate by international standards. Locational advantages and the development of the transport system provided a regional market so that a substantial amount of manufacturing exports developed based to a fairly large extent on the markets of southern Africa.

Nor was agriculture neglected: a key element in the ruling party's coalition was the white farming community, and the agricultural sector received substantial support through research and infrastructure development, subsidized credit and rail rates, and protection from foreign competition.

The financing for the developments since World War I came from three sources: minerals (particularly gold and diamond profits), foreign capital inflows, and the maintenance of artificially low wages for black workers, particularly in the mining industry, due to the system of control on movement and centralized recruitment. It was not until after the gold price was de-linked from the dollar that black wages began to catch up with white wages. Foreign capital was the critical source of finance in the late nineteenth century, but with the development of a manufacturing industry and of local capital markets, there was increasing reinvestment of profits owned by South African companies and individuals. But it was gold and diamonds that provided the major source of finance, both direct and indirect, for the other sectors of the economy; and gold, in particular, contributed to a long period of relatively conservative fiscal policy by successive South African governments. Houghton (1964, p. 113) notes successive governments' fears that increased domestic costs brought on by inflation would render gold mining unprofitable. A concern for the international competitiveness of the most important activity in the country was a healthy guide to some other economic policies, though it also contributed to the desire to maintain low real wages for blacks. Gold also provided a stabilizing influence on the overall financial position of the economy and government. Prior to the 1970s, gold was not subject to the cyclical fluctuations of other primary commodities. Gold often provided 40–50 percent of exports and always accounted for more than one-third of export earnings, even at its lowest relative contribution in the 1950s. Consequently, major cyclical fluctuations in export earnings were reduced.

Gold and diamonds provided substantial rents to the South African economy, but despite significant foreign investment, the rents were largely used within South Africa. The Anglo American/DeBeers group (incorporated in South African though with significant foreign shareholding) was a major financier of industrial development, mining diversification, and continued expansion of gold mining, reinvesting profits from gold and diamonds. Taxes on the mining sector financed infrastructure and research as well as the subsidy programs to the agricultural sectors. Gold mining taxation is based on a formula in which the tax rates rise with increasing profits/sales ratios, which to some extent taxes the rent element without providing a disincentive to production. In indirect terms the gold and diamond sectors also contributed to diversification. The subsidy paid to import-substituting manufacturing through tariff and other forms of protection implicitly taxed the mining sectors as the main source of export earnings. And, mining carried the initial costs of providing rail transport and other infrastructure due to the system of rate setting.

South African economic growth was substantial for almost a century between the initial discovery of diamonds and the demonetization of gold. To a significant extent the long period of high growth and structural change in the economy was based on a mix of policies that continued to provide incentives in the development of the primary sectors while at the same time promoting manufacturing. Rents were reinvested in the economy, and, while foreign investment continued to be important, its relative significance declined as the economy grew and diversified. There are several significant open questions: whether the performance could have been maintained with a wage structure that did not depend on migrant labor recruited under monopsonistic conditions; whether it could have continued into the 1970s without the substantial rise in the gold price that took place, given the mining-based subsidies to large segments of both the agricultural and manufacturing sectors; and whether the significant deceleration in growth since 1970 is due to the nature of apartheid or to the more generic features of a mineral led economy that protects too much.

7.4.2. Botswana[10]

When Botswana became independent in 1966 it was among the poorest countries in the world. It had no infrastructure (about 5 kilometers of paved road in a country the size of France), virtually no manufacturing except an abattoir for cattle, a recurrent budget deficit that was financed by the United Kingdom, and it was just ending a drought that killed one-third of the national cattle herd – then the only national asset. From 1965 to 1985, GDP rose at a compound rate of over 12 percent per year, and GNP per capita grew at 8.3 percent – both rates at the top of the World Bank (1987) league tables over that period. While two decades is too short for strong conclusions, some features of economic policy are worth mentioning, if only because Botswana's record presents some contrast to other countries which have struck a mineral bonanza.

Much of the growth of GDP came about because of a series of clearly identifiable events or actions: the renegotiation of the terms of a customs union with South Africa, Lesotho and Swaziland, that made revenue dependent on the

---

[10] This subsection is based largely on the analysis in Harvey and Lewis (1989) and Lewis and Sharpley (1988).

level of imports into Botswana from all sources regardless of the tariff rates on the goods; three diamond mines developed between 1970 and 1982 that moved Botswana into the front ranks of world producers; a copper–nickel mining project with a capital expenditure equal to 150 percent of GDP at the time it was constructed in the early 1970s; entry of the United Kingdom into the EEC and a successful negotiation of a 90 percent abatement of the variable import levy on beef exports from Botswana; careful attention to donor relations which produced one of the highest levels of development assistance per capita of any developing country. Several aspects of policy are of particular interest in relation to the topic of this chapter.

While the discovery of minerals was not the result of government policy, the terms under which they were developed were the result of careful negotiation. Foreign capital provided virtually all the investment in the mining sector, under terms that sought both to limit rents going to foreign investors and to protect the relatively small economy from down-side risks. The diamond agreements were renegotiated to increase the government's share of the profits at the time the second mine was developed. The copper–nickel project, which was a financial disaster for its shareholders, placed almost all the risk abroad: virtually all the project's debt (including interest) either was repayable on an income-contingent basis or was guaranteed by foreign shareholders.

Revenues from minerals, customs union payments, and donor funds were devoted largely to investments in infrastructure and public services aimed at improving access to basic needs: water, health, and primary education. Expenditure policies were based on long-term trends in revenue, and year-to-year fluctuations were absorbed by changing levels of foreign exchange reserves (once budgetary independence was achieved and a national currency introduced). The exchange rate has been managed actively, with a number of both revaluations and devaluations, sometimes to maintain competitiveness with trading partners and sometimes to minimize imported inflation and its effect on nominal wages. The real effective exchange rate with major trading partners has not been allowed to appreciate. And, while unskilled wages in the government sector have risen faster than inflation (and relative to rural incomes), an incomes policy has generally prevented mining rents from flowing directly into increased private consumption for the already employed. However, since the major growth in job opportunities has been in the high-income modern sectors, those able to find jobs have gained a much greater share of growing GNP than those in the rural sectors.

What about economic diversification? The cattle sector, still of major importance to the majority of citizens, was the object of major investment projects and operating subsidies. The main failure in terms of government diversification efforts has been in arable agriculture, though endemic drought (in five years in the mid-1980s output never reached 20 percent of a normal year) provides extremely difficult conditions. Manufacturing has grown (albeit from a small base) by about 10 percent per year in terms of both value added and employment for more than 15 years, the highest growth rate on the African continent. The largest single subsector is still the abattoir, but firms produce for both domestic and export markets in a variety of light manufacturing activities. Manufactured exports (other than processed beef) by the mid-1980s had surpassed the export value of beef and beef products which, at independence, provided virtually all export earnings. And, import substitution was a more important factor in Botswana's manufacturing growth than in Kenya and was about as large as in Rhodesia during the UDI industrialization boom [Lewis and Sharpley (1988)]. The modest use of import restrictions to promote both manufactured and horticultural production made such protection conditioned on production at import-equivalent prices. Total non-government employment in the formal sector grew by 8 percent per year from 1972 to 1984 and, though data are scanty, probably by a faster rate in the years prior to 1972.

While it is too soon to determine if the record will continue, the results of two decades again suggest that a combination of trade and fiscal policies that stabilize growth of domestic expenditures, that provide modest encouragement to the newer sectors without rendering primary export sectors unprofitable, and that provide infrastructure investments which support the activities of the primary and diversification sectors, are consistent with the observed spread of growth from mining to other sectors in Botswana.

8. Concluding observations

Without attempting to summarize the main points of this chapter, it may be useful to draw out what seem to be the key elements of "successful" primary oriented countries: those that have managed key aspects of structural change in production, employment, trade, and other variables while maintaining a relatively high concentration on the export of primary products and achieving sustained rates of overall economic growth. Similarly, having looked at some instances where structural transformation has been frustrated, or where sustained development has been seriously interrupted, one might usefully try to identify some of the "mistakes", or adverse changes in circumstances, that frustrate the development of countries with a primary export bias in the structure of their trade.

8.1. Elements of "successful transformation"

Successful countries have captured a significant amount of the rents accruing from the unique characteristics of their primary products and have reinvested them in the economy.

The capture of significant rents for the domestic economy is not necessarily inconsistent with a role for foreign factors of production. A climate of incentives in which foreign factors wish to reinvest earnings in the domestic economy is consistent with the reinvestment by citizens and governments in the domestic economy.

The devices used to capture rents from primary production in successful cases have not destroyed the incentives to continue investing in the primary sectors of the economy: not only was continued short-run production not discouraged, but the profitability of investment was not unduly reduced.

In successful countries, government investment in infrastructure, training, research, and services to support the primary export sector (whether mining or agriculture) has been provided. Some portion of the rents transferred from the primary export sectors was returned in the form of services. Provision of research to support productivity growth seems especially important.

The successful countries often have experienced a succession of different primary exports over time. Not only have new exports been promoted but old industries have been allowed to contract. A significant feature of the successful primary exporting countries tends to be their diversification *within* the primary export sectors.

In exchange rate policy, countries that have been relatively successful have not allowed their domestic currencies to become substantially over-valued, and in a number of cases devaluation was actively used as a policy instrument at times of recession in international markets. While they were willing to tax the rents of the primary sectors as a general rule, they were also willing to allow increased incomes through devaluations when changes in the exchange rate seemed appropriate for overall economic management.

Successful countries have followed counter-cyclical policies that might be described as prudent or conservative: they were willing to accumulate reserves and to stabilize the growth of domestic expenditures.

Lest this sound like the "old time religion", it should be made clear that the successful countries did *not* follow a policy of neutrality with respect to prices, protection, and exchange rates; nor did they allow foreign investors free rein. In addition to promoting the primary sectors through budgetary support of research and infrastructure investments, government policies provided tariff protection, protection through quantitative restrictions, and, on occasion, export taxation of primary goods, which provided incentives to manufacturing industry.

When providing protection to manufacturing, however, the successful countries were generally modest in the levels of protection provided, tended to make relatively less use of quantitative restrictions, and kept effective rates of protection closer to nominal rates. This made it more likely that the newly developed industries would eventually become competitive and cease to be a burden on the export industries that, necessarily, provided the subsidy to them. In following this mix of policies, the more successful countries were able to achieve sustained growth of GDP, structural change in production, and increased exports of manufactured goods, albeit remaining relatively more concentrated in primary exports than would be a typical country.

8.2. Policies that spell trouble

The classical "export economy" that was completely open to foreign factors and foreign trade, and that made little or no effort to capture economic rents from primary exports for use in the domestic economy, was a non-starter from the point of view of economic development. A failure to divert incomes, including rents, to be spent in the domestic economy (whether on capital, intermediate, or consumer goods) led to the failure of some primary exporting countries (or colonies) to achieve growth and structural change.

Equally true, policies which attempt to tax the primary sectors in excess of the economic rents generated in them will discourage both short-run production as well as investment in increased output even in a sector in which the country has relatively low costs internationally. Similarly, a failure to provide the supporting investments (infrastructure, research, training, and education) will inhibit the continued expansion of the primary export sectors and frustrate both income growth and structural change.

A mix of policies aimed at penalizing the primary export sectors by a substantial over-valuation of the domestic currency, including an unwillingness to allow devaluations (which would increase rents in primary export sectors) at the time of adverse international market conditions, has led not only to stunted growth of primary exports but also to frustration of new manufactured exports. The ironic result is that the concentration on primary exports remains higher in unsuccessful countries (which, in effect, tried "too hard" to diversify) than in successful ones.

A level and type of protection to manufacturing industry that allows very high rates of both nominal and effective protection, and particularly isolation of domestic markets from international prices through quantitative restrictions, leads to growth of measured value added in manufacturing but will result in dead-end development of that sector because there are no penalties associated with failing to increase productivity and competitiveness. As a result, the manufacturing sector can become a permanent drain on the resources of the primary export sector; rents from the latter are used simply to provide operating subsidies for the former. Sustained growth in aggregate real incomes is then impossible.

By definition, the primary exporting countries will generate significant rents from time to time in international commodity cycles. These boom periods provide opportunities for choice about economic strategy. Failure to manage the periodic booms prudently, either by permitting large consumption of the rents (through wage policy, currency appreciation, or tax cutting on other sectors) or by spending on projects with low rates of return in either the public or private sectors, or by accumulating debts that can be serviced only when prices are at the top of the commodity cycle, are features of the unsuccessful transitions. Similarly, failure in the low phase of cycles to make adjustments in spending, tax, monetary and exchange rate policies have led to exacerbated adjustment problems in the unsuccessful countries, including in more recent years the accumulation of unsustainable levels of commercial debt.

8.3. A cautionary note, and some questions

While the evidence is clear that it is possible to achieve high levels of economic development and diversification while remaining well above "normal" in dependence on primary exports, it is also clear that successful countries actively promoted the diversification of their economies, in both the primary and the manufacturing sectors. Furthermore, there are not cases of relatively high-income countries that have reached that stage by continued emphasis on only one primary export. Finally, one must remember that there are many primary commodities, and that there are significant changes over long periods of time in the relative prices of such commodities. The fact that a number of countries have made substantial progress while emphasizing the development of some primary commodities does not mean that a primary commodity emphasis will work for all countries, all commodities, or all time periods.

While the general direction of the lessons appear clear, the generalizations have left open a good many questions, particularly quantitative ones. Fruitful areas of investigation would appear to be those which would give some order-of-magnitude guidance in addressing questions of how much is too much, or too little, with regard to key issues facing policy-makers in countries rich in primary resources: the levels of rents that can be extracted, the levels of investment in research on the primary sectors which are associated with successful growth, the rates of protection behind which subsidized industries do not ever become competitive, the values for foreign exchange or the discount rate that should be used when making investment decisions during primary commodity booms, the extent to which wage rates or exchange rates can be allowed to stray from shadow rates without digging the economy into an uncompetitive hole. All policy questions must be answered in the context of a particular country at a particular time. But for many, if not most, developing countries decisions are generally not made against a background of detailed quantitative analysis. Guidance based on the experience of other countries could be extremely useful.

References

Adams, F.G. and Behrman, J.R. (1978) *Econometric modeling of world commodity policy*. Lexington, MA and Toronto: Lexington Books, D.C. Heath.

Aitken, H.G.J., Deutsch, J.J., Mackintosh, W.A., Barber, C.L., Lamontagne, M., Brecher, I., and Forsey, E. (1959) *The American economic impact on Canada*. Durham, NC: Duke University Press.

Balassa, B. (1980) *The process of industrial development and alternative development strategies.* Princeton, NJ: Princeton University Press.

Balassa, B. and Associates (1971) *The structure of protection in developing countries.* Baltimore, MD: Johns Hopkins University Press.

Baldwin, R.E. (1963) 'Export technology and development from a subsistence level', *Economic Journal*, 73:80–92.

Baldwin, R.E. (1966) *Economic development and export growth: A study of northern Rhodesia, 1920–1960.* Berkeley and Los Angeles, CA: University of California Press.

Bank of Botswana (1987) *Annual report, 1986.* Gaborone.

Baran, P.A. (1957) *The political economy of growth.* New York: Monthly Review Press.

Beckford, G.L. (1972) *Persistent poverty.* New York: Oxford University Press.

Behrman, J.R. (1978) *Development, the international economic order, and commodity agreements.* Reading, MA: Addison-Wesley.

Beveridge, A.A. and Oberschall, A.R. (1979) *African businessmen and development in Zambia.* Princeton, NJ: Princeton University Press.

Bhagwati, J.N. (1973) *Foreign trade regimes and economic development: Anatomy and consequences of exchange control regimes.* Cambridge, MA: Ballinger.

Boehm, E.A. (1971) *20th century economic development in Australia.* Longman Australia Pty. Limited.

Cardoso, F.H. and Faletto, E. (1979) *Dependency and development in Latin America.* Los Angeles, CA: University of California Press.

Caves, R.E. and Holton, R.H. (1961) *The Canadian economy.* Cambridge, MA: Harvard University Press.

Caves, R.E. and Krause, L.B., eds. (1984) *The Australian economy: A view from the north.* Washington, DC: Brookings Institution.

Chenery, H.B. (1960) 'Patterns of industrial growth', *American Economic Review*, 50(3).

Chenery, H.B. (1979) *Structural change and development policy.* New York: Oxford University Press.

Chenery, H.B. and Syrquin, M. (1975) *Patterns of development, 1950–70.* New York: Oxford University Press.

Chenery, H.B. and Syrquin, M. (1986a) 'The semi-industrial countries', in: H.B. Chenery, S. Robinson, and M. Syrquin, eds., *Industrialization and growth: A comparative study.* New York: Oxford University Press.

Chenery, H.B. and Syrquin, M. (1986b) *Patterns of development: 1950 to 1983.* Washington, DC: World Bank.

Chenery, H.B. and Taylor, L. (1968) 'Development patterns: Among countries and overtime', *Review of Economics and Statistics*, 50:391–416.

Chu, K.Y. and Morrison, T.K. (1984) 'The 1981–82 recession and non-oil primary commodity prices', *IMF Staff Papers*.

Corden, W.M. and Neary, P.J. (1982) 'Booming sector and de-industrialization in a small open economy', *Economic Journal*, 92:825–848.

Denoon, D. (1983) *Settler capitalism: The dynamics of development in the southern hemisphere.* Oxford: Clarendon Press.

Den Tuinder, B.A. (1978) *Ivory coast: The challenge of success.* Baltimore, MD and London: Johns Hopkins University Press.

Deutsch, J.J., Kierstead, B.S., Levitt, K. and Will, R.M., eds., (1965) *The Canadian economy: Selected readings.* The Macmillan Company of Canada Limited.

Diaz-Alejandro, C.F. (1970) *Essays on the economic history of the Argentine republic.* New Haven, CT: Yale University Press.

Diaz-Alejandro, C.F. (1978) 'Delinking north and south: Unshackled or unhinged', in: A. Fishlow, C.F. Diaz-Alejandro, R.R. Fagen, and R.D. Hansen, eds., *Rich and poor nations in the world economy.* New York: McGraw-Hill, 87–162.

Eckaus, R.S. and Rosenstein-Rodan, P.N. (1973) *Analysis of development problems: Studies of the Chilean economy.* Amsterdam: North-Holland.

Eicher, C.K. (1986) 'Strategic issues in combating hunger and poverty in Africa', in: R.J. Berg and J.S. Whitaker, eds., *Strategies for African development.* Berkeley, CA: University of California Press.

Eicher, C.K. and Staatz, J.M., eds. (1984) *Agricultural development in the Third World*. Baltimore, MD: Johns Hopkins University Press.

Elliot, C. ed. (1971) *Constraints on the economic development of Zambia*. Oxford: Oxford University Press.

Ellsworth, P.T. (1945) *Chile: An economy in transition*. New York: Macmillan.

Evans, D. (1987) 'The long-run determinants of north-south terms of trade and some recent empirical evidence', *World Development*, 15:657–671.

Fei, J.C.H. and Ranis, G. (1964) *Development of the labor surplus economy: Theory and policy*. Homewood, IL: Richard D. Irwin.

Findlay, R. (1984) 'Growth and development in trade models', in: W. Jones and B. Kenen, eds., *Handbook of international economics*, Vol. I. Amsterdam: North-Holland, 185–236.

Frank, A.G. (1967) *Capitalism and underdevelopment in Latin America: Historical studies of Chile and Brazil*. New York: Monthly Review Press.

Garnaut, R. and Ross, A.C. (1975) 'Uncertainty, risk aversion and the taxing of natural resource projects', *Economic Journal*, 85:272–287.

Garnaut, R. and Ross, A.C. (1983) *Taxation of mineral rents*. Oxford: Clarendon Press.

Gelb, A.H. (1986) 'Adjustment to windfall gains: A comparative analysis of oil exporting countries', in: P. Neary and S. van Wijnberger, eds., *National resources and the macroeconomy*. London: Center for Policy Research.

Gillis, M., Perkins, D.H., Roemer, M., and Snodgrass, D.R. (1983) *Economics of development*. New York and London: W.W. Norton & Company.

Goode, R. (1985) *Economic assistance to developing countries through the IMF*. Washington, DC: Brookings Institution.

Gravil, R. (1985) *The Anglo-Argentine connection, 1900–1939*. Boulder, CO: Westview Press.

Griffin, K. (1969) *Underdevelopment in Spanish America*. London: George Allen and Unwin.

Griffin, K. and Gurley, J.G. (1985) 'Radical analyses of imperialism, the Third World, and the transition to socialism: A survey', *Journal of Economic Literature*, 23:1089–1144.

Harberger, A.C., ed. (1984) *World economic growth*. San Francisco, CA: Institute for Contemporary Studies.

Harvey, C. and Lewis, S.R., Jr. (1989) *Policy choice and development performance in Botswana*. London: Macmillan, for OECD Development Center.

Helleiner, G.K. (1966) *Peasant agriculture, government, and economic growth in Nigeria*. Homewood, IL: Richard D. Irwin.

Helleiner, G.K. (1986a) 'Primary commodity markets: Recent trends and research requirements', mimeo.

Helleiner, G.K. (1986b) 'Outward orientation, import instability and African economic growth: An empirical investigation', in: S. Lall and F. Stewart, eds., *Theory and reality in economic development*. London: Macmillan.

Hicks, J.P. (1953) 'An inaugural lecture', *Oxford Economic Papers*.

Hirschman, A.O. (1958) *The strategy of economic development*. New Haven, CT: Yale University Press.

Horwitz, R. (1967) *The political economy of South Africa*. New York: Praeger.

Hotelling, H. (1931) 'The economics of exhaustible resources', *Journal of Political Economy*, 39:137–175.

Houghton, D.H. (1964) *The South Africa economy*. Oxford: Oxford University Press.

Innis, H. (1915) *Essays in Canadian economic history*. Toronto.

Johnston, B.F. and Mellor, J.W. (1961) 'The role of agriculture in economic development', *American Economic Review*, 51:566–593.

Jones, R.W. and Kenen, P.B., eds. (1984) *Handbook of international economics*. Amsterdam: Elsevier.

Kindleberger, C.P. (1956) *Terms of trade, A European case study*. London: Chapman and Hall.

Krueger, A.O. (1974) 'The political economy of the rent-seeking society', *American Economic Review*, 64:291–303.

Krueger, A.O. (1984) 'Trade policies in developing countries', in: R.W. Jones and P.B. Kenen, eds., *Handbook of international economics*, Vol. I. Amsterdam: North-Holland, 519–569.

Kuznets, S. (1964) 'Quantitative aspects of the economic growth of nations: Level and structure of foreign trade: Comparisons for recent years', *Economic Development and Cultural Change*, 13:Part 2.

Kuznets, S. (1966) *Modern economic growth: Rate, structure, and spread.* New Haven, CT: Yale University Press.

Kuznets, S. (1967) 'Quantitative aspects of the economic growth of nations: Level and structure of foreign trade: Long-term trends', *Economic Development and Cultural Change*, 15:Part 2.

Lall, S. (1975) 'Is dependence a useful concept in analyzing underdevelopment?', *World Development*, 29:799–810.

Lerner, A.P. (1936) 'The symmetry between import taxes and export taxes', *Economica*, 3.

Levin, J.V. (1960) *The export economies: Their pattern of development in historical perspective.* Cambridge, MA: Harvard University Press.

Lewis, S.R., Jr. (1967) 'Agricultural taxation in a developing economy', in: B.F. Johnston and H.W. Southworth, eds., *Agricultural development and economic growth.* Ithaca, New York: Cornell University Press.

Lewis, S.R., Jr. (1972) 'The effects of protection on the growth rate and on the need for external assistance', Research Memorandum no. 49, Williamstown, MA: Williams College.

Lewis, S.R., Jr. (1973) *Agricultural taxation and intersectoral resource transfers*, Food Research Institute Studies.

Lewis, S.R., Jr. (1981) 'The potential problems of diamond-dependent development', in: Charles Harvey, ed., *Papers on the economy of Botswana.* London: Heinemann.

Lewis, S.R., Jr. (1984) 'Development problems of the mineral-rich countries', in: M. Syrquin, L. Taylor, and L.E. Westphal, eds., *Economic structure and performance, essays in honor of Hollis B. Chenery.* New York: Academic.

Lewis, S.R., Jr. (1986) 'Africa's trade and the world economy', in: R.J. Berg and J.S. Whitaker, eds., *Strategies for African development.* Berkeley, CA: University of California Press.

Lewis, S.R., Jr. (1989) *Economics and apartheid.* New York: Council on Foreign Relations.

Lewis, S.R., Jr. and Sharpley, J. (1988) 'Botswana's industrialisation', Discussion paper 245, Brighton: Institute of Development Studies.

Lewis, W.A. (1954) 'Economic development with unlimited supplies of labour', *Manchester School of Economic and Social Studies*, 22:139–191.

Lewis, W.A. (1958) 'Unlimited labour: Further notes', *Manchester School of Economic and Social Studies*, 26.

Lewis, W.A. (1978a) *The evolution of the international economic order.* Princeton, NJ: Princeton University Press.

Lewis, W.A. (1978b) *Growth and fluctuations 1970–1913.* London: George Allen & Unwin.

Lim, D. (1973) *Economic growth and development in West Malaysia 1947–1970.* New York: Oxford University Press.

Lipton, M. (1977) *Why poor people stay poor: Urban bias in world development.* London: Temple Smith.

Little, I.M.D. (1982) *Economic development: Theory, policy, and international relations.* New York: Basic Books.

Little, I.M.D., Scitovsky, T., and Scott, M. (1970) *Industry and trade in some developing countries.* New York: Oxford University Press.

MacBean, Alasdair I. (1966) *Export instability and economic development.* Cambridge, MA: Harvard University Press.

Mamalakis, M.J. (1976) *The growth and structure of the Chilean economy.* New Haven, CT: Yale University Press.

Mamalakis, M. and Reynolds, C.W. (1965) *Essays on the Chilean economy.* Homewood, IL: Richard D. Irwin.

Marr, W.L. and Patterson, D.G. (1980) *Canada: An economic history.* Toronto: Gage Publishing Limited.

Meier, G.M. (1984) *Emerging from poverty: The economics that really matters.* New York: Oxford University Press.

Meier, G.M. and Seers, D., eds. (1984) *Pioneers in development.* New York: Oxford University Press.

Mellor, John W. and Johnston, Bruce F. (1961) 'The role of agriculture in economic development', *American Economic Review*, 51(3).

Monteon, M. (1982) *Chile in the nitrate era: The evolution of economic dependence, 1880–1930.* Madison, WI: University of Wisconsin Press.

Morgan, D.R. (1979) 'Fiscal policy in oil exporting countries, 1972–1978', *Staff Papers*, 26:55–86.

Myint, H. (1958) 'The classical theory of trade and underdeveloped countries', *Economic Journal*.

Myint, H. (1965) *The economics of the developing countries.* New York: Praeger.

Nankani, G. (1979) 'Development problems of mineral exporting countries', World Bank staff working paper no. 354. Washington, DC: World Bank.

Newbery, D.M.G. and Stiglitz, J.E. (1981) *The theory of commodity price stabilization: A study in the economics of risk.* London: Oxford University Press.

Nurkse, R. (1961) 'Equilibrium and growth in the world economy', Cambridge, MA: Harvard University Press.

Oyejide, T.A. (1986) 'The effects of trade and exchange rate policies on agriculture in Nigeria', Research Report no. 55. Washington, DC: International Food Policy Research Institute.

Pearson, S.R. and Cownie, J. (1974) *Commodity exports and African economic development.* Lexington, MA and Toronto: D.C. Heath.

Power, J.H. (1971) 'The structure of protection in West Malaysia', in: B. Balassa and Associates (1971) *The structure of protection in developing countries.* Baltimore, MD: Johns Hopkins University Press.

Prebisch, R. (1950) *The economic development of Latin America.* New York: United Nations.

Schumann, C.G.W. (1938) *Structural changes and business cycles in South Africa, 1806–1936.* London: P.S. King & Son, Ltd.

Seers, D. (1964) 'The mechanism of an open petroleum economy', *Social and Economic Studies*, 13:233–242.

Seidman, A. and Seidman, N. (1977) *South Africa and U.S. multinational corporations.* Westport, CT: Lawrence Hill & Co.

Singer, H.W. (1950) 'The distribution of gains between investing and borrowing countries', *American Economic Review*, Papers and Proceedings.

Smithies, A. (1965) 'Argentina and Australia', *American Economic Review*, 55:17–22.

Solow, R.M. (1974) 'The economics of resources or the resources of economics', *American Economic Review*, 64:1–14.

Spencer, D.S.C. (1986) 'Agricultural research: Lessons of the past, strategies for the future', in: R.J. Berg and J.S. Whitaker, eds., *Strategies for African development.* Berkeley, CA: University of California Press.

Spraos, J. (1980) 'The statistical debate on the net barter terms of trade between primary commodities and manufactures', *Economic Journal*, 90:107–128.

Spraos, J. (1983) *Inequalising trade: A study of traditional north south specialisation in the context of terms of trade concepts.* Oxford: Clarendon Press.

Stallings, B. (1978) *Class conflict and economic development in Chile, 1958–1973.* Stanford, CA: Stanford University Press.

Watkins, M. (1963) 'A staple theory of economic growth', *Canadian Journal of Economics and Political Science*, 29:141–158.

Wheeler, David (1984) 'Sources of stagnation in Sub-Saharan Africa', *World Development*, 12(1) (January):1–23.

White, D.A. (1967) *Business cycles in Canada.* Economic Council of Canada.

Williams, J.H. (1920) *Argentine international trade under inconvertible paper money 1880–1900.* Cambridge, MA: Harvard University Press.

World Bank (1979) *World development report 1979.* Washington, DC: World Bank.

World Bank (1981) *Accelerated development in sub-saharan Africa.* Washington, DC: World Bank.

World Bank (1984) *Toward sustained development in sub-saharan Africa.* Washington, DC: World Bank.

World Bank (1985) *World development report 1985.* Washington, DC: World Bank.

World Bank (1986) *World development report 1986.* Washington DC: World Bank.

World Bank (1987) *World development report 1987.* Washington DC: World Bank.

Young, K., Bussink, W.C.F., and Hasan, P. (1980) *Malaysia: Growth and equity in a multiracial society.* Washington, DC: World Bank.

Chapter 30

IMPORT SUBSTITUTION

HENRY BRUTON*

Williams College

Contents

*I am greatly obliged to Bela Balassa, Earl McFarland, Brian Levy, Michael McPherson, Gustav Ranis, Michael Roemer, John Sheahan, Paul Streeten and the editors for comments and suggestions on earlier drafts of this chapter. The usual disclaimers, of course, apply.

Handbook of Development Economics, Volume II, Edited by H. Chenery and T.N. Srinivasan
© *Elsevier Science Publishers B.V., 1989*

1. Introduction

During the past 100 to 200 years, the countries of Western Europe, northern North America, and Japan have experienced more or less sustained increases in measured GDP per capita; while in the countries of Asia (except Japan), Latin America, and Africa the output of goods and services did not increase in this steady, regular fashion. In the late 1940s, after the dust of World War II had settled, the world became acutely conscious of the fact that a relatively small number of countries and a small proportion of the world's population had access to a vastly larger quantity of goods and services per person than was the case in most other countries of the world. Even more fundamental was the fact that in most countries, a large proportion of the population lived in severe poverty. The obvious question was then and remains now: Why does this difference in per capita output prevail? And its corollary: Can the GDP-poor countries so modify their economies that output, and welfare, increase as a consequence of the routine functioning of the economy?

One answer to the latter question was at once evident: make over the GDP-poor countries in the image of the GDP-rich countries. The rich countries, therefore, offered an example to be followed or, more specifically, to be learned from. The existence of rich countries offered something else: they created a world environment significantly different from that which prevailed while they were getting rich. Earlier, there were no equivalent rich countries that could be copied or that created a volatile world environment in which the then developing countries had to find their way. The modern developing countries, however, must achieve the metamorphosis of their economies – from non-growth to growth – in a world dominated by a relatively small number of already rich and still growing economies. The developing country must recognize this fact, it must seek to learn from the already rich countries, even while protecting itself from a number of problems that the existence of rich countries creates. Import substitution may be described as a development strategy that seeks to accomplish both of these objectives: to learn from, and in general gain from, the rich countries, and, at the same time, to so protect the domestic economy that the society can find its own way, can create its own form of development, and can redo its economy so that it can function on equal terms in the community of nations.

The idea is not so much a matter of the less developed countries catching up with the rich, although some catching up is part of the story. Rather, it is a matter of creating an economy that is sufficiently flexible, diversified, and responsive that it can weather shocks, can respond to and indeed create opportunities for growth, and can, on its own, generate continually increasing welfare for its people. The basic rationale of the import substitution strategy is that in order for the modern, less developed country to make over its economy in the image just described, it needs protection, for a while at least, from the might of the GDP-rich countries. This chapter is about that protection, its content and the instruments by which it is effected, and, of equal importance, what happens in the country while it is experiencing this protection. Finally, attention must be given to how import substitution ends or can be ended, once the country has accomplished the objectives that the protection was to make possible.

Import substitution is then a matter of two transitions. The first transition is that from a system characterized by lack of growth to a flexible, responsive system in which social welfare is continually rising. This takes place behind some form of protection. The second is the transition from protection to participation on a more equal footing in the world economy. Between these two transitions lies the process by which the economy achieves its metamorphosis.

The notion of import substitution in this chapter is wider than in most of the literature. It considers the major, overriding issue to be the rationale of protection in making over the non-growing economy into a growing one. This question has links with virtually all aspects of development. In focusing on this broad issue, some important specific points have to be neglected, at least to some degree. At the same time, I would argue that the issue to which the chapter directs primary attention is *the* basic issue of the import substitution strategy of development. The more conventional issues of import substitution – tariff and exchange rate policy, use of direct controls, etc. – are examined but they, it is argued, are not the basic content of the strategy.

It may be helpful to compare the import substitution strategy with the most obvious alternative, an outward looking or export oriented strategy. There are no examples of an unambiguously successful application of the import substitution strategy. Protection in one form or another, however, has characterized most developing countries, including those (e.g. Korea and Taiwan) whose development is usually classified as a success story. India has perhaps been more committed to import substitution than has any other large country, and, as discussed in the following pages, there is no doubt that the costs of this commitment have been high. At the same time there is also convincing evidence that India has achieved a technological maturity that exceeds that of any other developing country. The failure of India's strategy, it will be argued, has been due to its method of implementation, not with the strategy itself.

Bela Balassa, Anne Krueger, and many others have accumulated a great deal of statistical and qualitative evidence that show many advantages to an outward looking, export oriented strategy. Balassa reports on their studies in Chapter 31 of this Handbook. Although the evidence that is offered in Balassa's chapter (and elsewhere) is impressive, it cannot be considered conclusive. There is considerable ambiguity with respect to a number of key variables, e.g. "appropriate" exchange rates, export promotion, and terms of trade. In addition, the outward looking strategy gives little attention to the difficulties of decision-making and policy-changing in most developing countries. It may also be noted that world trade in the 1950–1980 period grew at rates unmatched in history, and this too contributed greatly to the apparent success of export oriented policies. The point here is not that outward looking has, in fact, failed, but rather that the evidence remains as yet inconclusive. Hence, the study of import substitution, as defined in this chapter, is an important component of development economics.

It may be noted, as well, that the two strategies have much in common. Both are intended to induce learning and productivity growth, and both emphasize that economic strength requires resilience and the capacity to carry through continuous adjustments in response to changing circumstances. Most (not all) proponents of both strategies also acknowledge that our understanding of productivity growth is still quite primitive. This matter of similarity is referred to again in the final section of this chapter, the section on policies.

2. Import substitution and its critics

In this section I first examine the rationale for an import substitution strategy in some detail. Then, I examine the process by which a country, behind its protection, prepares to face the world. Finally, I comment briefly on arguments that dispute the validity of the whole notion.

2.1. In defense of import substitution

Import substitution is often "measured" by a change in the ratio of imports to the total availability (imports plus domestic output) of a single product or category of products. If this ratio falls over time, then import substitution is said to take place in that particular sector. This has happened, of course, for many activities in many countries, and at the same time aggregate imports as a proportion of total GDP have not declined and often have even risen. This means that the structure, defined as the composition of output, of the economy is changing because some products that were previously imported are no longer imported in the same amount, while total demand for imports as a proportion of income is generally unchanged. The idea is that by replacing the imports of certain commodities by domestic production, the economy will be so modified that it will begin to be more independent, more resilient, more diversified, and better able to generate increasing welfare as a matter of routine. Replacing the imports of certain individual products by their domestic production is, therefore, a means to an end, not an end itself. Three additional points may be noted.

(1) Many developing countries have levied tariffs, quotas, and other protective devices to meet balance of payment difficulties. The objective in this situation is simply to curtail imports to bring the balance of payments under control and is, therefore, sure to be different in effect from an import substitution policy that is carefully and explicitly worked out. It will be argued later that one of the important reasons why import substitution has often seemed to be the source of grave problems is the fact that policy-making has so frequently been ad hoc, and that various parts of the set of policies have been inconsistent with each other. The policy-making process in a particular country is, therefore, relevant to understanding how and why countries pursue the policies that they do.

(2) The import substitution rationale is also distinct from the traditional infant industry argument for the protection of a particular activity. That argument rests on the assumption that an activity can be identified which, if given some initial period of protection, will later become able to compete in an unprotected market. In the case of import substitution one might speak of an infant economy that needs protection while it develops those characteristics it must have to produce rising welfare.

(3) Import substitution should also be distinguished from "delinking". This latter notion examined with great insight by Diaz-Alejandro (1973) refers to a permanent cutoff of a country in all or some respects from the rest of the world in order for truly indigenous development to occur. Delinking does not represent a time during which the economy is restructured and reorganized in order for it to take its place in the world economy.

The basic characteristics of a strong economy are flexibility and the capacity to transform resources into a wide range of products, and the capacity to determine its own economic destiny. There are several reasons why a non-growing economy needs protection to develop these characteristics.

The main reason is that the proximate source of long-term growth is the increased productivity of labor that is produced by more physical capital and by new knowledge. The new knowledge is either built into the physical capital or is acquired by (built into) the labor itself. Conventionally, saving (or foreign aid or loans) is the source of new capital, but knowledge is, of course, necessary to build new capital, and indeed one can say that new knowledge is always necessary. So then development is essentially and ultimately a matter of learning and searching, of trial and error, in a context of continuous change [Nelson, Schultz and Slighton (1971), Sheahan (1972), Bruton (1985)]. Learning applies to a variety of activities, most obviously to production, but also to consumption, and to life styles in general. In this context protection is intended to extend the opportunities for this learning process.

Protection then is a means of inducing diversification and the learning upon which development is based. More accurately, perhaps, it is a means of creating a process of development that builds on search and learning. The goal is to create an economy with the capacity to move in various directions as opportunities are provided and new knowledge is accumulated.[1] When such capacity exists, the economy can *then* seek to concentrate or specialize, because with such capacity it can more readily opt out of a declining sector into one that is recognized to be expanding. If that capacity is lacking, rapid, unanticipated changes are likely to impose major costs on the community. For example, an abrupt change in the terms of trade will result in reduced availabilities rather than in a switch to new activities or other adjustments. In a world of continuous change in technology, tastes, political affiliations, and ideas of the good life, development is necessarily a matter of trial and error, of moving in one direction today and another tomorrow. The capacity to do this at relatively low costs is an essential characteristic of a growing economy. Import substitution seeks to create this characteristic.

2.2. What kind of import substitution?

If protection in the early stages of development is appropriate, one must then ask about the details of that protection. As is often the case, stating general principles is fairly easy, but the formulation of explicit policies is far from simple. Therefore, I begin with the general principles.

If the accepted rationale of import substitution is to protect an infant economy while it matures to the point that it can perform satisfactorily in the world economy, then the society must, while protected, learn. So import substitution must create an environment in which learning occurs. There must then be strong inducements, to search, to experiment, to test – to learn. Protection that simply assures potential producers of a known market may move investments in new directions, but it may also induce the quiet life for the protected monopolist, while large parts of the society remain in severe and continuing poverty. In this situation nothing really happens, and the whole process yields only costs, no returns. Protection may also create distortion, which in this context means that the new activities are inconsistent with the economy's factor endowment. Distortions may add to the cost of the protection by creating bottlenecks that force the economy to reduce its output in order to live with or correct the bottlenecks. There must be accurate signals to induce economic agents to take advantage of the economy's factor endowment. Much of the criticism of import substitution

---

[1] I.M.D. Little, generally a strong critic of import substitution, expresses a similar idea in his discussion of India. He writes at one point: "Moreover it is very early for India to be able to guess where her comparative advantage *will* lie." In the same article, a few pages later, he writes: "In a country as large as India with a wide complement of natural resources, it would be surprising if it *did not turn out* to be economical for India to produce a little of everything" [Little (1960, p. 25), italics added]. In both these statements Little is saying that in some future *after* India has changed her structure into some other state, *then* she will allocate resources in a manner to maximize in the conventional fashion.

has concentrated on the distortions created by policies aimed at protection. It is important to the argument of this chapter that the protection it studies does not impose major distortions. The argument for import substitution is not an argument for distortions or that distortions are not important.

It is recognized that protection generally imposes short-run costs on the economy. Availability of goods and services is expected to be less at the outset of the import substitution strategy than would have been the case with free trade. This reduced availability is then a cost of the protection, a cost of the import substitution strategy. There is the further question of who in the society bears these costs. The reduction in welfare associated with a particular policy may depend on which group in the society bears the major part of the cost. Another way of looking at this cost is possible: the reduced availability of goods and services can be considered an investment. The return on this investment is a more flexible, more responsive economy whose operation can lead to increased welfare. The shorter the period of import substitution as a development strategy, therefore, the less its cost and the higher the return on the investment. This obvious consideration means that the ending or phasing out of import substitutes is an essential part of the strategy itself. As later discussion will show, the ending of an explicit import substitution policy is often an economically difficult and politically dangerous undertaking; hence, there is a strong temptation to delay it.

The other main element of the cost of the investment is that associated with the new activities. Earlier arguments emphasized the importance of diversification, of the creation of new activities, possibly at the expense of the specialization that comparative advantage dictates. The greater the violation of the dictates of comparative advantage, the greater the costs of the policy. So unless a large violation of comparative advantage is expected to yield a "large amount" of learning, the presumption is that these costs are to be kept low. To put it a bit differently: the less comparative advantage is violated, the lower is the cost of the investment. One must remember, of course, it is the cost of creating a new economy, i.e. it is the benefits relative to costs that matter. Even so, the argument here makes clear that an effective import substitution policy does not ignore the conventional message of the static allocation theory of international production known as comparative costs.

The other side of the allocation question is even more important. Extreme violations of the conventional criteria can bring the growth process to a complete halt or slow it down markedly. A stop–go economic performance is especially damaging to learning and to productivity growth. It will be argued later that the primary objective of conventional allocation considerations is to enable growth to continue without interruptions to correct bottlenecks; it is not to achieve the maximum output from given resources in the short run.

To summarize: an import substitution strategy can be defended in terms of the need for protection while a non-growing economy establishes the conditions and characteristics necessary for its routine operations to result in rising social welfare. The main consideration has to do with searching and learning – on the part of all economic agents. Since import substitution imposes a cost on the society, it may be identified as an investment. Two specific sources of costs are especially important: the length of time that the import substitution strategy is in effect and the possibility that it will create distortions of a particularly damaging kind. It was also noted that costs may be affected by unproductive violations of comparative advantage; that is, effective import substitution does not ignore traditional static allocation issues.

Protection can and does take many forms. Impediments to imports are among the most frequently discussed and the best understood, but there are many other forms. Restricting of foreign investments may be an important means of protection, and attitudes toward foreign investment represent an important distinction among developing countries. At the same time foreign investment may also be a source of learning and knowledge transfer. Our understanding of the role of foreign investment in these latter terms is very incomplete, and actual decisions by developing countries are frequently made on the basis of misleading information and irrelevant argument. Controlling the inflow of labor, including foreign consultants and advisers, is yet another form. Tourism may be made easy or difficult, and a government may discourage its own nationals from foreign travel, for reasons independent of foreign exchange consideration. An exchange rate policy can provide protection. In these times of rapid capital movements, financial and product aid, huge earnings from a single mineral, etc. the definition of the "correct" exchange rate is exceedingly difficult. A society may choose to protect its values and life styles by keeping out certain publications, television shows, missionaries, etc. Certain forms or levels of conventional protection may have different effects in one country from those they have in another because various traditions and institutions themselves may provide differing degrees of protection. As our understanding of development and welfare deepens, it becomes necessary to recognize these wider considerations, and to introduce them into our analysis.

These kinds of issues make it difficult to determine how "open" a particular economy really is, and especially how open one society is compared to another. Most observers would probably agree that the Republic of Korea is more open than the Democratic People's Republic of Korea, but one would be less confident in asserting that the Korean economy was more open in the first half of the 1960s than was the Brazilian economy. While import substitution in the literature has been discussed largely in very narrow terms that apply to specific sectors of the economy, it is doubtful if policy-makers have thought in such narrow terms. These issues arise in large part because, as noted earlier, contemporary developing countries pursue their development objectives in a world dominated by the rich and the mighty. The difficult task is to learn from the rich and the mighty without simply imitating them or allowing them to stand in the way of the country finding its own path.

2.3. Searching and learning

To this argument we now need to add a theory of search and a theory of learning. There does not seem now to be a conventional wisdom on learning that can be plugged into the arguments summarized above. There are, however, important insights and hypotheses available, and it is helpful to discuss some of these briefly.

The notion that import substitution induces learning rests on the hypothesis that the exposure of individuals to new phenomena, new ideas, and new things produces learning. Repeated routines develop dexterity (in the Adam Smith pin factory, for example), but little learning. At the same time, the "new" to which exposure is made must be "near" that which is familiar. It must be linked in some way to the familiar to be recognized and acknowledged, yet novel enough to provoke new understandings and new insight.

Hirschman (1968) illustrates this point in noting that "industrialization via import substitution becomes a highly sequential, or tightly staged affair...it is the basic reason for which the import substitution industrialization process is far smoother, less disruptive, but also far less learning intensive than had been the case for industrialization in Europe, North America, and Japan" (p. 6). Hirschman goes on to argue that industrialization that is wholly a matter of imitation and importation of a tried and true process eliminates the travail that produces learning. The importation of a ready-made process is based on the notion that simply "having" a new factory or machine produces the diversification and responsiveness that enable an economy to provide increasing welfare for its people. Hirschman's argument tells us that this presumption is misleading. He emphasizes that the early industrialization in Western Europe and the United States was not limited to the production of light consumer goods, but from the beginning included the production of capital goods. There were no capital goods being produced elsewhere that could be imported. The modern less developed country that imports foreign-made capital goods to produce the consumer good then eliminates a significant source of learning. In particular this creates great difficulties for the importing country to adapt, in any fundamental way, the imported machine to fit local conditions. Given this situation, Hirschman argues, factor-price distortions may not be especially important in explaining what happens to the economy.

A diagram may be used to develop the argument further. Figure 30.1 is adapted from Nelson et al. (1971, p. 96) who use it for a somewhat different purpose. The curve *AB* traces the productivity of labor, given the assumption of

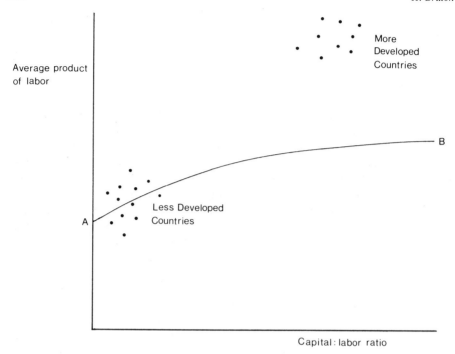

Figure 30.1

no change in the quality of the inputs and no change in the availability of technical knowledge. The curve tells us that if nothing else happens in the less developed country except that capital per worker increases, productivity in the LDC will never reach the level that obtains in the GNP-rich countries. The difference, in broadest terms, is accounted for by technical knowledge and the quality of the labor.

The main message of the diagram for the present argument is a bit different. The rich countries have, over historical time, moved gradually from low capital/labor ratios and low labor productivity, to the position shown in the diagram. One may possibly think in terms of a ladder on which the economies climbed, step by step, to reach the high position on which they now reside. Each step provided the basis, the learning from which the next step could be reached. Each higher step had something in common with the lower step. The movement up this ladder constituted a series of short steps, each related or linked in some way to the preceding ones. For ease in the drawing of the diagram, the argument here is in terms of labor productivity. The more appropriate concept is total factor productivity and this is the concept employed in later sections in discussion of the empirical evidence.

For producers in less developed countries to jump, or seek to jump, from their area to the area of the more developed countries in one mighty leap by importing new machines with the much more productive technology violates this fundamental notion of the learning process – that the new must have some links with the old. If such a big leap is tried, all that can be expected would be an imitation, a copy of that done elsewhere. Some learning doubtless would occur, but in general very little could take place. In particular, one may argue that simply imitating, without having climbed the ladder, will make further productivity growth and further changes difficult indeed, and thereby may make the economy even more vulnerable. Nor will productivity be as high, even where imitation looks complete. Even if skills become available to operate the new machines or new activities, this availability will not contribute to making the economy more flexible and more compatible with the new knowledge. The newly acquired skills are limited to the particular task, and when unexpected problems occur managers are often helpless. Indeed, one of the reasons why repair and maintenance are often so unsatisfactory in newly industrialized countries is that those who use the new technologies and the new machinery are so unacquainted with the underlying principles of how they work.[2]

This argument does not mean that the present-day developing countries cannot speed up their development beyond that achieved by Western Europe and Northern North America. This learning argument does mean that imitation is not development. It also lends considerable legitimacy to the argument for import substitution summarized above, protection is necessary to help an economy with its learning. More specifically, this notion of learning tells us that the developing country must climb its own ladder, but it can climb at a more rapid rate. It can push the various steps closer together in time.

This notion may be illustrated by four brief examples.

(1) Carlos Diaz-Alejandro has emphasized in several places [e.g. (1970, pp. 260 ff), (1984)] that considerable import substitution took place in Latin American countries in the early part of the twentieth century without all of the complex policies that were followed later in the 1950s and 1960s. There were tariffs, but the main kind of "natural" protection was to be found in the world economy and in the prevailing technology. During the depression of the 1930s, though every country was interested in exporting, international trade was modest and declining. Interruption of shipping and non-military production during World War II

---

[2] One may, quite legitimately, raise the question of the operational significance of the argument of these last several paragraphs. There is no specific, universal answer to this question because so much depends on the circumstances in the particular country. The examples and arguments in the text help to give the argument some empirical content, and to identify relevant questions to ask at a specific time and how to go about determining whether the conditions stated in the text are being violated. The most obvious point has to do with the role of foreign investment, foreign aid, and foreign technicians, all which can, and indeed may, bring, or seek to bring, that which violates the learning argument in the text. More on the role of foreign investment as we go along.

not only raised prices of imported goods, but frequently meant that imports simply were not available [Baer (1972)]. Similarly, technology and the nature of new products changed more slowly so that adjustments had more time to take place. As a consequence, many Latin American countries concentrated their import replacement on simple commodities (textiles, cement, milk processing, toiletries, etc.) whose technology had not changed much over extended periods of time. There seemed also to be greater consistency of protectionist policies in the 1930s, e.g. tariffs were imposed along with devaluations, and agriculture was generally not penalized, or not penalized heavily. This picture is quite different from the kind of import substitution observed in the 1950s and 1960s.

(2) World War II also provided "natural" protection. During the war period, imports fell sharply, especially those classified as capital goods, but intermediate goods as well. Yet foreign and domestic demand was strong. There was then a powerful incentive to find ways to increase productivity and output. Indeed, the calculations in Bruton (1967) show that productivity growth during the war years in several Latin American countries was markedly higher than it was in later years. (Data for some other countries, e.g. Egypt and Sri Lanka, suggest a similar picture.) In these years, producers searched for ways to increase the output from the resources available within the country. In the 1950s and 1960s as imports increased and the imitation of the West became a guiding star, productivity growth declined, unemployment and inequality increased, and the rate of growth of measured GNP was more unstable. The message seems to be that evident profit opportunities plus non-distorting protection from the lure of foreign imitation produces the inducements for an economy to find ways to exploit its resources with ever-increasing effectiveness.

(3) A third example that illustrates the protection and learning argument refers to the technological development of the Republic of Korea. This country seems to have made it an essential point in its technological policy to work its way up the kind of ladder described above. There was (until recently) very little direct foreign investment. Thus, the Koreans undertook to do only what they themselves could do, and with strong demand (facilitated by the export biases of policy) the Korean entrepreneurs also had a strong incentive to push hard to find ways to increase output. They learned step by step. There are other factors that must be considered of course (e.g. learning from Japan), but the main point here is simply to illustrate the notion of learning and the corresponding distinction between simply seeking to imitate the rich countries in one great leap and in climbing step by step up an increasing productivity slope.

In these stories, strong and uninterrupted demand that creates obvious profit opportunities plays a key role. Traditional allocation issues matter, not primarily in terms of maximizing output from a given quantity and quality of resources, but in terms of preventing interruptions in growth. Thus, the misallocations that create bottlenecks and force a reduction in demand or in demand growth – the difficulties that create a stop–go situation – do defeat the growth effort. Good export performance helps prevent balance of payments bottlenecks from forcing a slowing or stopping of growth. Exporting may also indicate learning and responsiveness to incentives that are equally important in preventing the stop–go situations from materializing or continuing. Ranis and Orrock (1985, p. 62) note that "once a country has reached the stage where it is able to compete successfully in international markets, it is likely to have acquired sufficient skill and flexibility to overcome many obstacles (to exporting), including the defensive measures resorted to by the advanced industrial countries". This illustrates the main theme of this chapter, and the fundamental notion of development that is its point of departure.

(4) The importance of learning and knowledge accumulation may be further emphasized by reference to the policy-making process. It has often been noted that Singapore and Hong Kong have no policy options other than an all-out effort to export manufactured commodities. Korea and Taiwan have little in the way of natural resources. Their only asset is their labor, their people. They, therefore, had to search for ways to make their labor more productive. They had no policy option but to learn. The fact that there are no natural resources upon which to build a country's exports also eliminates the difficult task of managing rents, a task that many countries have found virtually impossible. (See Chapter 29 by Stephen R. Lewis, Jr. in this Handbook.) Countries rich in natural resources find it much easier to rely on such resources, to export them, import capital goods from the West, and put them in place in their country. The experiences of the oil-rich countries teach how difficult it is to use foreign exchange acquired in this way to create a viable, responsive, and equitable economy. One must note, of course, that *not* having natural resources is hardly a sufficient condition for development.

2.4. The critics of import substitution

The import substitution approach to development has not been without its critics, and criticisms have greatly intensified in recent years. This subsection seeks to examine some aspects of the more widespread criticism.

(1) The most common point is that import substitution penalizes exports. Exports were deemed important in early arguments because they enabled the importation of the capital goods necessary for investment, and prevented balance of payments problems which seem to plague many developing countries. This criticism became common after it was evident that world trade in the 1950s was quite different from the world trade of the 1930s. Most observers had projected a depressed world trade after World War II, and the bias against exports – to the extent that it was recognized – was not considered a major shortcoming. Had

world trade in the 1950s and 1960s in fact been a repeat of that of the 1930s, then the bias against exports would, of course, have appeared much less damaging.

(2) The development of the notions of Effective Rates of Protection (ERP) and Domestic Resource Cost (DRC) made it possible to measure some of the effects of trade restrictions. Although there are major problems with these concepts and their empirical application, the results obtained did convince many members of the profession that the costs of the trade restrictions were often very high indeed. These calculations also showed that the protection of specific activities was much higher than nominal tariff rates indicated, and, equally important, that rates of protection varied widely among activities in a given country. The cost of restrictions was very high in many cases, and the wide variation in rates contributed greatly to distorting the economy further. The cost also fell unequally on the population, thus exacerbating the income distribution problem. Little (1982, p. 136 ff) has a succinct summary of these general results and many references to the literature.

The cost of distortions in terms of output forgone are generally estimated to be quite low, so it is not clear how much loss is involved as a consequence of distortions introduced by the trade restrictions. It is probably correct to argue, as several people have [e.g. Balassa (1975)], that the cost of distortions is greater in developing countries than in the GDP-rich countries. It is also probably correct to argue that the cost of distortions is greater than conventional estimates make it. Even so, it is less convincing that the distortions per se are an important explanation of observed differences in rates of growth of measured GDP among developing countries. In particular, it is not clear from the literature on this issue exactly how a distortion-free economy grows.

(3) Much has been made of the capital intensity of the investment that has taken place behind the high protection. This capital intensity is usually explained in terms of low real interest rates and an exchange rate/import control policy that made capital artificially cheap. The result has been low rates of growth of employment and increased income inequality. Again, these phenomena have occurred in many countries. The practices leading to these particular consequences, however, do not appear to be a necessary part of an import substitution strategy of development.[3] To a significant extent, they are the consequence of the view that prevailed in the 1950s of how growth of output took place, in particular the emphasis on the strategic role of capital formation and the

---

[3] In much of the literature the notion of import substitution includes a range of policies that result in considerable distortion being imposed on the economy. Of course, many countries have in fact done this, but it does not seem to be a necessary part of protection itself. It is argued that the main consequence of distortions is to force the economy to stop to correct a problem – balance of payments, inflation, etc. If no such stoppage is necessary, distortions are generally not very important, except possibly in the case where the stops are prevented simply by large-scale inflows of foreign exchange unrelated to production. This general issue is referred to in several places in the text, and in detail in Section 4.

acceptance of the capital–output ratio as fixed. If production coefficients are fixed and if capital formation is the principal (maybe exclusive) source of growth, then the cheap capital approach makes a great deal of sense. The point here is that the import substitution approach, as such, did not include as an essential ingredient excessive capital intensity, but that such excessiveness emerged from prevailing views on development.

(4) The terms of trade of the developing countries have figured prominently in debates about import substitution. Hans Singer's early article [Singer (1950)] was followed by numerous other studies on what had, in fact, happened to the terms of trade of the developing countries. If it were the case that over an extended period a deterioration in the external terms of trade of the latter countries had taken place, this would constitute a strong argument for sharp changes in the composition of their output. Essentially, this would mean that the terms of trade were moving against agricultural products and minerals and in favor of manufac-turing and certain services. Later work on this issue has made it reasonably clear that the terms of grade have not moved consistently against developing (or agricultural or mineral producing) countries as a group, and indeed that, in general, they fluctuate in several ways. A recent renewal of the debate on this issue is between Singer and Balassa [Meier and Seers (1984, pp. 273–312); see also Spraos (1980)]. There is little doubt, however, that the Singer argument combined with similar arguments from the United Nations Commission for Latin America influenced policy toward import substitution especially in Latin Amer-ica. The conclusion remains that in a flexible, adapting economy the terms of trade are of little interest, except in a very short run. They perform the same role that relative prices perform in any economy; they are meant to provide informa-tion on how resources, especially investment resources, are to be allocated.[4]

(5) A final criticism refers to some new thinking and evidence on the role of exports in development. As already noted, most import substitution policies discriminate against exports. The consequences of this in earlier arguments was that it led to balance of payments problems and slowed down the imports of the capital goods which were deemed to be the basis of the growth process. As the emphasis on the role of capital formation in development has waned, this

---

[4]The "vent-for-surplus" theory of international trade is of some interest in the present context. That theory rests on the assumption that, because of great internal immobility and specificity of resources, a non-trading country is not able to use fully all of its productive capacity. The opening up foreign trade – or the decline in international transportation costs – may then result in an increase in the demand for those products for which the country in question has excess productive capacity. So output and possibly employment may rise as trade begins for this reason. This argument, not widely discussed in recent years, depends greatly on the inflexibility of the productive capacity. Evidently, where such is the case the reduction in trade could cause reduced output and reduced employment. Trade in this case (as in most cases) would yield immediate benefits, but over a longer run the inflexibility and unadaptability of resources will surely defeat any sustained development effort. On the vent-for-surplus notion, see Myint (1958).

argument has lost some of its power. With increasing attention given to technological change specifically and to productivity growth in general as the key to growth, recent hypotheses suggest that exports are an important means of inducing productivity growth. Exporting then is relevant, not primarily to enable the importing of capital goods, but as a means of increasing the productivity of available resources.

This is an important argument because it links up directly with the fundamental source of output growth. In Section 3 we examine some empirical efforts to test the hypothesis that exports and productivity growth are positively related. The hypothesis makes greatest sense when applied to manufacturing exports. It is unlikely that large-scale exports of oil or other natural resources will have an effect on productivity growth.

It may also be noted that much of the criticism aimed at import substitution is, in effect, criticizing the policy-making process in developing countries; more specifically, it is aimed at the often uncoordinated, unstudied way in which policies are made in many less developed countries. Thus, trade restrictions often appear in response to an urgent balance of payments crisis and restrictive monetary and fiscal policies are imposed after inflation is well established. Similarly, decisions are made to establish a particular industrial activity and then a trade restriction is imposed to enable that activity to exist or an export promotion drive is undertaken at the same time that the domestic currency is greatly overvalued. And on and on. A coherent, well-designed, consistent policy package rarely appears anywhere, whether the general picture is one of import substitution, export promotion, or whatever.

All of these criticisms of import substitution are themselves open to criticism, but they are nonetheless of great importance. Indeed, the particular formulation outlined above of an import substitution strategy recognized these criticisms and tried, at least, to take them into account. It is fair to say that the major limitation of these criticisms is that they neither define a theory of growth nor do they offer an explanation of how and why growth takes place. "Correct" allocation of resources does not assure growth, nor does a high rate of exports. Neither does free trade. At the same time no one doubts that widespread misallocation imposes costs, possibly high costs, on a country. Such costs are much more nearly certain than are the long-run gains from protection. Our understanding of the nature, the content, of productivity growth is still exceedingly primitive, and relevant empirical evidence is just beginning to be accumulated. It is this ignorance of the origins, the real origins, of productivity growth and transformation capacity that, it is argued here, is the basis of the dispute between those who push import substitution and those who advocate openness and outward looking. This says, in effect, that until we have a satisfactory theory of development, a "final" criticism or defense of import substitution is not possible.

3. Some empirical problems and evidence

In this section I examine a variety of experiences of countries which have followed, since the 1950s, at least some aspects of an import substitution approach to development.

3.1. Points of departure

When one examines the import substitution experience of a given country, it is convenient to identify three specific characteristics or issues: these may be identified as (1) the initial conditions; (2) the objectives of the government; and (3) the policy-making process. A brief comment on each of these is in order.

3.1.1. Initial conditions

As policy-makers looked at their country in the early 1950s – when economic development caught everyone's attention – they were able to identify various characteristics. The most obvious were, of course, the resource endowment of the country, the labor and management skills, physical capital, technical knowledge, etc. Nevertheless, other characteristics were equally important. The prevailing economic and social organizations, the understanding and interpretation of the country's history, the prevailing economic and social links (e.g. markets, sources of imports, and source of any expatriates), and the dominant interest groups of the society are among the relevant aspects. Especially relevant were prevailing views about how the economic agents will respond to certain inducements. For example, it seems clear that in the early 1950s most policy-makers and most development economists working on and in developing countries believed that economic agents in these countries could not or would not respond simply to price signals, hence physical planning was necessary. In many countries, as well, policy-makers and others were convinced that the operations of the market were a major source of their difficulties. Similarly, many observers believed that world trade in the ensuing years would be very much like that that prevailed in the 1930s. Such views were an important fact of "initial conditions", and helped to determine the approach to development that the countries followed.

3.1.2. Objectives of the government

Governments have many diverse and inconsistent objectives, but it seems fair to say that the most general objective of most countries at this time – or the point they became politically independent – was to be like the West. This meant not only a high GNP per capita, but it also meant new industrial activities, new international economic relationships, and greater independence in policy-making. At the same time, it was also an objective of the government to maintain the society's prevailing ethos, the customs, ideas of morality and the good life, that defined its culture and gave society an identity. Some countries (an extreme example is the Democratic People's Republic of Korea) put so much weight on this last objective (and on certain political issues as well) that they isolated themselves behind so much protection that they had virtually no contact with the rest of the world. These objectives are, of course, vague and do not lead to any specific policy or set of policies. It is doubtful if any government or any economic advisor at this time thought seriously in terms of employment, income distribution, regional equity, basic needs, etc. Governments did, however, see their countries as poor relations, and they wanted to change that. Ambiguity of objectives, except at the very general level, was surely an important explanation of the frequently observed inconsistency of policies and the ad hoc nature of many important decisions.

3.1.3. The policy-making process

The most formal policy instrument was the national plan, and many countries spent substantial resources in drawing up a comprehensive plan. Plans varied widely in design and execution, and in impact on economic performance. Plan documents reflected the initial conditions and government objectives just described. In particular, plans concentrated heavily on manufacturing and other new activities and on the idea of the modernization of the economy. Plan-making and plan-implementing demand highly skilled, experienced labor resources, unambiguously rare in the developing countries in the 1950s. In this situation, such assumptions as fixed capital–output ratios, fixed production coefficients in general, and low saving rates, little entrepreneurial capacity, etc. were very appealing indeed, and justified a large role for the government. Of greater importance, however, was the absence of any sort of explicit policy-making procedures. The result in many countries was a melange of policies that added up to confusion and unclear signals, and that reflected the unspecific objectives.

In the particular context of this chapter, it is important to note that much of the criticism of an "import substitution" strategy refers to things other than protection. Wage and price policies, interest rates and other policies relating to the allocation of investment, neglect or explicit penalization of agriculture, and a variety of other instruments were frequently included in the import substitution package. Added to this is the fact that one ministry or agency of a government could often proceed quite independently of others, thereby producing bottlenecks or excess capacity. Finally, one must mention the role of aid donors in the policy process. There is evidence that certain policies were followed, or at least agreed to, because the aid recipient was under pressure to do so from aid donors. Thus, as we look back at a country's experience, it is tempting to define it as the result of import substitution or export promotion or whatever. Given the way policies got designed and implemented, however, it was a rare country that had as a guiding star any well-articulated, well-defined strategy. Consistency of policy is rarely a characteristic of developing countries, and, as will be argued later, policy inconsistency is a major reason for the emergence of certain difficulties.

3.2. Country experiences

Over the last 10–20 years there have been a great number of detailed country studies that have helped to illuminate many of the issues that are part of the import substitution strategy of development. There have also been a series of studies about trade liberalization that have examined mainly the implications of a movement away from trade controls and other protective devices to a more open, outward looking economy. Anyone seeking to understand import substitution and how it has worked in a particular country or to gain some general view of it as a development strategy must read and reflect on these works.[5] Much of the material in these studies is concerned with incentive structures, especially with respect to how they affect the profitability of producing for the domestic market versus exporting, and for investing in urban manufacturing activities, rather than in rural areas in general and agriculture in particular. Considerable attention has also been given to the costs of rent-seeking and the costs of the absence of a mechanism to compete rents away.

Rather than reviewing this familiar and readily available material, I will tell three stories to see what can be learned about the empirical relevance of the arguments discussed in Section 2. These stories are a comparison of India and Korea, then of India, Korea, and Brazil, and finally a review of total factor productivity in several countries.

3.2.1. Mainly India and Korea

When India began to plan its national development soon after independence, it opted for an import substitution strategy. That strategy was especially evident in the last half of the 1950s when protection from imports was afforded to virtually

---

[5]Studies referred to include the following: Balassa and Associates (1971, 1982); Little, Scitovsky and Scott (1970) which is the comparative review of the multivolume series sponsored by the Organization for Economic Cooperation and Development; the 12-volume study on *Foreign Trade Regimes and Economic Development*, directed by Jagdish Bhagwati and Anne Krueger, sponsored by the National Bureau of Economic Research; a series of books and articles sponsored by Kiel Institute for World Economics and effectively summarized in Donges (1976). There are many others of course.

all manufacturing activities. The protection was of varied forms and was accompanied by other direct controls on the allocation of investment in terms of both its composition and its geographic location. The result was the appearance of a wide range of very high-cost manufacturing activities and the squeezing of agriculture. These policies effectively eliminated the threat of both foreign and domestic competition. Presumably, the expectation was that some inducements other than competition from imports would produce the decline in costs – the increase in productivity – that would enable the country to support this approach. Had productivity growth been rapid, for example, costs would have fallen quickly and the difficulties would have been greatly eased.

A recent book by Ahluwalia (1985) provides a wealth of data on India's experiences since 1960. The data for manufacturing industries show that import availability ratios (defined as imports over imports plus domestic production minus any exports) declined generally and rapidly with few exceptions from 1960 to 1965. Were data available for earlier years, they would doubtlessly show that import substitution, measured in terms of declines in import availability ratios had begun well before 1960. In current prices the ratio of total imports to GNP was 8.2 in 1960 and 10.8 in 1980. In constant prices the ratio is somewhat lower, but changes over the period are about the same. Around the mid-1960s, the rate of import substitution declined in many of these sectors, and by 1980 a majority of the two-digit industries had import availability ratios greater than those that prevailed in 1965. Similarly, the contribution of import substitution to growth declined markedly after 1965 compared to its contribution in prior years.[6] The evidence seems clear enough that around the middle of the 1960s, India began to move away from the previous heavy reliance on import substitution to a different strategy [Ahluwalia (1985, pp. 118 ff)].

The new policy gave increased attention to exports and backed off slightly from full support of import substitution. The shift was not extreme, however, and did not continue very long but did have some effect on the rate of growth of manufactured exports. Data in Wolf (1982, p. 179) show that the average annual rate of growth of manufactured exports in the final half of the 1960s was less than 5 percent, while in the decade 1967/68 to 1977/78 it was about 15 percent

---

[6] The contributions of import substitution to growth is measured by Ahluwalia as the difference between actual growth and that which would have taken place if the import availability ratios had remained unchanged at the values obtained at the beginning of the period. It is also useful to note that measures are frequently ambiguous, and vary with the formula used, the time period chosen, weights applied, etc. Perhaps the simplest is the best; the ratio of imports to total availability of a given product, although this measure, as usually calculated, does not take into account inter-industry relationships. Another simple measure is the allocation of total imports between producer and consumer goods. This measure implies a specific notion about which country produces capital goods and the role of the latter in development. For a full discussion, see Bhagwati and Desai (1970, pp. 84–108).

per annum. The policy change, though apparently modest, then had some effect. As will be emphasized below, the effect on export growth of the policy change in India was considerably less than in a number of other countries.

We now consider, even more briefly, Korea's story in these same terms. The general picture is that Korea followed an import substitution strategy throughout the 1950s, but shifted strongly and unambiguously to a much more export-oriented policy in the very early 1960s. The 1950s were indeed unfortunate for Korea. The rate of growth of GDP averaged about 5 percent per year. The rate of growth of manufacturing was considerably higher, but began from an exceedingly modest level. The total absolute increase in manufacturing output, therefore, was relatively small. This point is relevant to the story because it meant that in 1961 or so there was a less well established manufacturing sector that could object to a significant reorientation in policy. Policy change was easier than it would have been with a large, entrenched sector that depended on protection for its good life.

Frank, Kim and Westphal (1975, pp. 92 ff) estimated that in the last half of the 1950s export expansion contributed 5.1 percent to growth of manufactured output, and import substitution 24.2 percent with domestic demand contributing the remainder. In the 1963–70 period, import substitution fell to below 1 percent and in 1970–73 it was negative [Nishimizu and Robinson (1984, p. 193)], while the role of export expansion increased to 38.1 percent. Even in the 1950s, the ratio of imports to domestic use for individual sectors declined very little, and indeed seemed to rise as often as it fell [Krueger (1979, p. 63)]. The ratio of total imports to GDP, of course, rose spectacularly after 1960 as did the ratio of exports to GDP. In 1955, imports were about 10 percent of GDP and in 1980 they were over 40 percent, having risen more or less steadily. Exports, an been smaller percentage of GDP in the 1950s, reached one-third or so by the 1970s. Manufacturing exports performed in an even more impressive way, achieving growth rates that have seldom been matched in the world. From 1973 to 1980, Korean manufactured export growth (in U.S. dollars) averaged over 40 percent per year. Also, of course, GDP growth averaged almost 10 percent per year after the early 1960s. Of equal significance is the fact that Korea weathered the oil shocks of the 1970s better than most countries. The shift in policy in the early 1960s, therefore, had a marked and immediate effect as the economy responded with great power.

Many observers have placed great – some even exclusive – emphasis on the change in foreign trade policy to account for Korea's phenomenal development over the 1960s and 1970s. There seems little doubt that the sharp change in policy mattered greatly, but there are other issues that are of equal, possibly even greater, relevance. The first point refers to magnitudes and explanations. Given our understanding of how export expansion can generate growth, it is difficult to believe that Korea grew as it did simply because it followed an outward looking, export expansion policy. Therefore, one should be cautious about arguing that if all countries pushed exports as hard as did Korea, then all countries would grow as Korea has grown.

A second point follows from the discussion in Section 2 of this chapter: even were one to accept the argument that export expansion is the heart of the matter, one still must ask why Korea was able to take those steps that did, in fact, push exports. This question cannot be dodged by the economist on the grounds that it is a political or some other kind of issue. As Weintraub (1981) asks: "Why did not Chile, which had an educated population and received large amounts of aid in the 1960s, promote exports as effectively and uncompromisingly as did Korea?" A third point refers to the decision-making process in Korea. Jones and Sakong (1980), in a careful and probing study, concluded that the export spurt in Korea was not mainly a matter of devaluation and export incentives. They argue (pp. 98–99) that total wôn return to exporters was similar in periods of stagnation and of rapid growth. It is essential, they continue, to "look at non-price interventions to comprehend the dynamics of Korean development". They further emphasize the pragmatic approach, the absence of ideology, in the making of economic policy in Korea. There was a willingness to change policies that did not work, an attitude of trial and error. One result is that there is a mixture (Jones and Sakong say "balance") between market forces and direct government intervention, between public and private ownership of productive activity. Finally, of course, there was President Park Chung Hee's full commitment to economic growth without much concern for democracy or decentralization. Evidently, all this is quite different from India, and is, in some sense, more fundamental to understanding Korea's apparent successes and India's alleged failures than are the usual measures of import substitution and outward orientation.

Despite the evidence on sources of growth, there was considerable import substitution taking place in Korea in the 1970s. Data from Frank, Kim and Westphal (1975) for 1970 show that of 1312 major import items, 70 were banned completely and 524 were limited in one way or another. In 1976, 60 items were banned and over 600 restricted in one way or another. Similar data apply to the early 1980s. Korea also has used quantitative restrictions to protect many of its activities, and the familiar escalation of effective rates of protection from lower to higher stages of manufacturing is evident. This evidence suggests that the policy change in the early 1960s was not so much a switch away from import substitution as it was a strong, determined move toward the promotion of exports.

The most powerful evidence in a comparison of Korea and India is that of total factor productivity growth (TFPG). The estimates in Table 30.1 below show unambiguously how far India lagged behind Korea. Not only is TFPG in each Indian industry much lower than in the corresponding Korean industry, but for 14 of the 20 Indian industries. TFPG is negative, as it is for the manufacturing sector as a whole. The data for Korea tell a distinctly different story. The TFPG

Table 30.1
Total factor productivity growth

	India 1960–80	Korea 1960–77	Turkey 1963–76	Yugoslavia 1965–78	Japan 1955–73
Food processing	− 3.6	5.3	1.9	− 0.6	2.2
Beverages	− 3.1				
Tobacco	− 3.6			− 1.7	
Textiles	1.0	4.5	1.4		1.7
Apparel		1.6	2.7	− 0.2	1.9
Footwear	0.7				
Wood products	− 3.0	5.6	− 1.2	− 0.6	1.1
Furniture	2.1	4.9	3.2		− 0.1
Paper	0.1	4.5	1.4	0.1	1.6
Printing and publishing	0.5				
Leather	− 2.4	2.8	− 1.0	− 0.1	0.9
Rubber	− 5.5	5.9	5.8	2.3	− 1.2
Chemicals	− 1.3	4.5	1.6	0.1	2.5
Petroleum	− 5.6	0.7	0.4	0.2	− 0.4
Non-metallic minerals	− 1.2			1.7	
Basic metals	− 0.9	1.9	0.9	− 0.6	1.0
Metal products	− 2.2	6.0	1.5	− 0.6	0.8
Non-electrical machinery	− 1.1	5.7	1.3		3.1
Electrical machinery	− 0.2	7.2	1.8	− 0.25	4.4
Transport equipment	0.1	5.1	3.3		2.5
Miscellaneous	− 4.9				
Manufacturing total	− 0.6	3.7	1.3	0.5	2.0

Sources: India, Ahluwalia (1985). Ahluwalia has several sets of estimates, all of which are similar. The one used here is identified as the Translog estimate, p. 131. Japan, Korea, Turkey, and Yugoslavia, Nishimizu and Robinson (1984).

for each sector is positive and only in apparel, petroleum, and basic metals is less than 2 percent. For several activities, the rate is extraordinarily high, 5–7 percent. Some further implications of these data are discussed below. The point here is that TFPG, a crucial indicator of success, showed India at a large disadvantage relative to Korea.

3.2.2. Mainly Brazil

Brazil's experience introduces two further issues: large-scale, private, direct foreign investment and a rather sharp return to an import substitution strategy after the mid-1970s. Import substitution had begun in Brazil before World War I.

In 1910, import availability ratios for shoes, clothing, furniture, and wood products were all below 10 percent. So import replacement activities were nothing new to Brazil in the postwar period. Finally, Brazil's rapid industrialization has depended heavily on domestic demand, despite the rapid growth of manufactured exports. There are other differences as well, but these are the most relevant to our story.

Until the middle of the 1960s, Brazil pursued an import substitution strategy with considerable enthusiasm and single mindedness. From about 1965 it backed away from full reliance on import substitution for about a decade, and then resumed, more or less, an import substitution approach. For the 1949–64 interval, import substitution accounted for almost one-quarter (23 percent) of the growth of manufacturing demand and export expansion was essentially zero [Tyler (1976, p. 74)]. From 1964 to 1974 the role of import substitution was negative. It was negative for manufacturing as a whole and for almost every two and four level classifications of activity. For 1974–79 import substitution demand for manufacturing as a whole equalled 10 percent, but for the capital goods sector it was 16 percent and almost 15 percent for intermediate goods, and for consumer goods a low 2.5 percent [World Bank (1983, p. 39)]. In the 1970s, Brazil was obviously beginning to push hard into the domestic production of capital goods. In all intervals, domestic demand was far and away the most important source of demand growth. The ratio of manufactured imports to total available domestic supply was 14 percent in 1949, fell to 6 or 7 percent in the late 1960s, but in 1974 it was 12 percent, and by the end of the 1970s it was back to about 7 percent. The decline in the 1970s was largely due to sharp falls in the import ratios for capital goods [Tyler (1976, p. 68) and World Bank (1983, p. 35)]. Finally, as is well known, Brazil's manufactured exports grew rapidly throughout the 1960s and 1970s. In the period 1965–74, the growth rate reached 37 percent (in U.S. dollars), after Korea, the highest in the world. Growth dropped sharply in the 1974–81 period, to about 25 percent, still a respectable figure. In 1982, Brazil's manufactured exports (as well as total exports) declined by over 12 percent compared to 1981. From 1949 to 1964 data from Tyler (1976, p. 141) show that manufactured exports grew at an annual rate of 3.6 percent. Except for processed food products, exports have always been a very small proportion of total output, and even the ratio of food product export to total output about halved from 1965 to 1980. The average ratio is rising over time, so that the ratio of increments of exports over increments of output exceeds the average.

What does this brief survey add to our story? Brazil has long welcomed direct foreign investment, more so after 1964, and, perhaps more than any other large country, it set its objective simply in terms of imitating the United States as quickly as possible. Direct foreign investment seemed an effective instrument to pursue this objective. The main question of interest in the present context is the extent to which the large role of foreign investors affects the extent to which the import substitution strategy accomplishes the objective previously outlined.

The data show clearly that a large share of Brazil's manufactured exports is accomplished by multinational enterprises. Estimates given in Tyler (1976, p. 149) show that 34 percent of Brazilian manufactured exports were produced by multinational firms in 1967, and in 1969 the figure had reached 43 percent. Tyler emphasizes that there are doubts about these estimates, but they do indicate approximate orders of magnitude. For the 1970s, data from World Bank (1983, p. 112 ff) and Bacha (1977) show that exports of products requiring relatively sophisticated technology were produced by multinationals to a very large degree. Some small Brazilian firms, however, did export, as did a number of larger Brazilian firms. It seems fair to conclude that the change in policy in the mid-1960s did induce some Brazilian firms to export. Apparently also some of the multinationals that came to Brazil initially expecting to concentrate mainly or even exclusively on the domestic market also responded to policies aimed at increasing exports.

There are several points to make about Brazil's experience. The hypothesis that the presence of multinationals dampened the evolution of a more indigenous technology and of more learning merits attention. In terms of the argument and Figure 30.1 of Section 2 of this chapter, the Brazilians tried to leap from where they were in the less developed country area of the curve *AB* to the most developed country area of the very much higher curve in the diagram without moving step by step along the climb. They tried to do things that they could not do, and so had to import the skills and knowledge from which little domestic learning seemed possible. Contrast this with Korea, which depended much less on foreign direct investment, and hence did not seek to have what they could not themselves construct and manage. Brazil's new activities were more often (than in Korea) in more advanced, more volatile activities where technology was changing rapidly because of the dominance of the multinationals. This too seems to impede learning, to impede beginning with an established technology and having time to master it before change occurs in some other country of the world. Similarly, several observers have noted the pressure to learn and to respond created by arm's-length transactions appears greater than any that exists in transactions within an enterprise or on a subcontracting arrangement [Westphal et al. (1981)]. This suggests in turn that Brazil may not have learned from its import substitution activities in a way that enabled managers and workers to build from that learning in other and different activities when new opportunities appear.

Of course there are exceptions and the argument in the preceding paragraph does not apply in every instance. The automobile industry in Brazil, for example, heavily dominated by foreign firms, did produce some domestic learning in the production of component parts. The same holds true for some of the new capital goods producers in Brazil. Still, the point in the previous paragraph seems generally valid, and of great importance in understanding Brazil's story.

The best test of this sort of argument would be data on rates of growth of the productivity of capital and labor in the various activities of the manufacturing sector separated into foreign and domestic enterprises. There are no available data that provide this information. The only productivity growth rate that seems available is for total GDP. Elias (1977) estimates TFPG for several five-year intervals from 1950 to 1974. For the decade of the fifties, TFPG averages a bit less than 4 percent per year, in 1960–65 it drops drastically to 0.58 percent, and in 1965–74 the average is about 3.2 percent per year. Estimates in Bruton (1967) show a much lower TFPG for comparable periods, except for the early 1960s. The Bruton data also show that TFPG seems to have declined through the first years of the 1960s, the last period for which estimates are available. Syrquin (1985) has estimates for Latin America, but not for individual countries. His general conclusion (p. 24) on Latin America is that after 1973 "the growth of output becomes increasingly dependent on the growth of investment and exports through their effect on aggregate demand to prevent idle capacity, rather than by their embodying new technology or enhancing the efficiency of the country". This statement was doubtless applicable to the Brazilian economy in general and to the manufacturing sector as well. These estimates, however, do not tell us very much about what we need to know about learning in domestic manufacturing activities. It may be noted that labor productivity data alone can be misleading since they neglect the role of the input of capital services. For example, the rates of growth of labor productivity in the Indian manufacturing activities previously discussed are, with two exceptions, positive. For manufacturing as a whole the growth rate of labor productivity was 2.5 percent per annum, compared to -0.6 percent for all factors.

There are additional questions in the Brazilian case. The movement toward increasing openness during the "miracle years" was slowed down and essentially reversed because of balance of payments problems. In 1972 and 1973 the current account deficit averaged about 1.5 billion dollars and in 1974 it was 7.1 billion. Part of this was due to the jump in the price of oil, but a large part seems to be due to the failure of exports in the miracle years to support the growing demand for imports. A growth rate of total exports of about 20 percent apparently could not support the more outward looking strategy. There is also evidence that in the last half of the 1960s and into 1970, the Brazilian economy was operating well below potential output [Bacha (1977)]. Slack domestic demand in these years not only dampened import growth, but also added pressure on firms, especially multinationals, to find foreign markets. This set of circumstances has led some observers to conclude that the miracle years were not miraculous after all, and that openness was sure to fail. All that it did was to increase Brazil's vulnerability to external shocks.

After 1973, the resumption of the import substitution policy was marked by many of the unfortunate characteristics that marked the 1950s and early 1960s. There is wide variation in effective protection across activities, and many of these rates exceed 100 percent. In addition, a variety of non-tariff barriers to importing were put into place. High protection is especially apparent in activities where technology is changing rapidly [World Bank (1984, p. 17)].

An interesting feature of this package is that it suggests that Brazil's policy-makers had learned very little from their previous bouts with import substitution or from observing the experience of other countries. Even if one were to grant the validity of the move back to a general import substitution strategy, still one may argue that the implementation of that strategy reflected very little learning on the part of the Brazilian policy-makers as to the effects of such a hodgepodge of policies. Recall the attention given above to the role of the policy-making process and the extent to which the country learned from its own experience. It seems that Brazil did not, or could not, learn in the way that Korea did. In the 1950s and early 1960s, the methods of implementing the import substitution approach were generally not at odds with the conventional wisdom of economists; in 1974 they were.

Several observers, especially Jones and Sakong (1980), have emphasized the pragmatic, trial-and-error approach to policy-making in Korea. The Koreans seem to react quickly to a situation that was closely monitored and to choose a new policy if one was failing to produce growth, the overriding objective. They have, in a way, discovered what appears to work. This is indeed what learning means, and how it is accomplished. In the case of India, the dominating objective was an economic independence that seemed to lead to avoiding international trade, and certainly foreign investments, to the extent possible. Brazil's ideology seemed to be to become like the United States overnight. The large amount of direct private foreign investment, as argued above, impeded learning in the manufacturing sector and the government policy-makers in the 1970s seemed not to have learned from the experiences of the 1950–65 period. Or if there was learning, the policy-making process prevented it being brought to bear on actual policy-making.

The final point on Brazil refers to the cost of the export expansion policies. Again, there are no data to which one can refer to help our understanding, but some qualitative observations do appear legitimate. It is evident, of course, that subsidization of exports can be just as much a misallocation of resources as protection and other impediments to imports. With an array of subsidies, the mere fact that an activity is exporting is not unambiguous evidence that it is efficient. There has, however, been much less attention given to possible distortions and costs from pushing exports than to those associated with keeping imports out. It is appropriate to raise this issue here because a number of observers have suggested that Brazil's incentives to export were such as to impose a major cost on it, while this was not the case in Korea. Since India did not go all out on its export expansion policy, the issue is less relevant for it. Even so, some evidence indicates that export subsidies often did not produce sufficient foreign exchange earnings to justify their costs [Bardhan (1984)].

In the case of Korea, Westphal and Kim (1982, p. 272) conclude that the "structural changes induced by the shift to the outward looking policy regime resulted in a more efficient allocation of resources as exports of labor-intensive manufactured products expanded to finance rapidly growing imports of food grains and capital- and skill-intensive manufactured products". In Brazil, on the other hand, Tyler (1981), Weisskoff (1980) and others are less sure. In Brazil, the export incentives, especially those associated with fiscal policy, varied from product to product, and therefore had a misallocating effect in the same way that widely differing effective rates of protection had under import substitution. Thus, certain groups benefited and others were penalized, and the economy distorted. There does not seem to be evidence, however, to the effect that it was increasing misallocations arising from the export promotion policies that accounts for the failure of export promotion to prevent that balance of payments and other problems that led to its modifications in the mid-1970s. Still, it seems clear that problems of this sort were experienced.

In Korea, as well, some observers [e.g. Koo (1984)] have found that the heavy emphasis on exports has begun to create increasing income (and other) inequalities. The strong government support of successful exporters has enabled them to grow rapidly, and to exercise considerable and increasing monopolistic power. Jones and Sakong (1980, p. 192) note that in Korea the new entrepreneur is strictly on his own in a new effort, and consequently most new ventures fail. Those which succeed then receive favored treatment – financial, tax, etc. – and then continue to grow. So bigness is subsidized. Such a policy rests on the assumption – doubtless appropriate in the case of Korea – that the supply and quality of entrepreneurship is strong indeed. Also, a strong government is required. Similarly, employment growth in primary and secondary activities in recent years has declined relative to that in service sectors. If this continues, it will almost certainly produce a decline in the rate of growth of productivity in the future. There also appears increasing inequality in wage rates as the demand for highly skilled people increases much more rapidly than does the demand for the unskilled and semi-skilled [Fei and Ranis (1975), Scitovsky (1985)].

Korea has, over the years, paid relatively little attention to distribution. Cole and Lyman (1971, p. 167) note that this probably reflects the fact that Korea entered the postwar period with very little inequality. During the colonial period, the Japanese held most positions of economic power and the Korean aristocracy was effectively destroyed. The land reform in the late 1940s and the destruction during the war further eliminated any significant sources of great wealth. The remarkable growth in output and exports in the 1960s and 1970s could proceed therefore with little protest from entrenched interests and, as it absorbed labor rapidly, equality was served, more or less incidentally. The policy that produced the great export boom has also apparently begun to produce significant inequalities and class divisions that at least some observers find disquieting.

This story helps to call attention to the role of initial conditions. In the late 1940s, Brazil had an inequality problem and it had entrenched interests that the state could not ignore; therefore, economic policy-making was more difficult to accomplish, irrespective of the guiding strategy, than was the case in Korea. There are, of course, countless reasons for the appearance of a strong state in Korea, but an important one surely is to be found in the "initial conditions" just described that resulted in such a power vacuum at the end of World War II. Neither India nor Brazil had this particular advantage, and policy formulation and implementation were made more complex. Bardhan (1984) notes that an "overdeveloped state relative to the size and structure of the economy has characterized India since pre-colonial days". He argues later (p. 58) that the "Brahminical cultural environment... is highly suspicious of private capital accumulation and often identifies money making in trade and industry with greed and dishonesty...". Any entrenched hierarchical system, as the Indian cast system certainly was, makes difficult the design of an economic policy that rests on decentralization and on the assumption that individual economic agents can do much on their own. India's initial condition (at independence) therefore not only constrained what the policy-maker could do, but what policies were, in fact, considered.

3.2.3. Capital goods production and technological maturity in Brazil, India, and Korea

The final part of the India/Korea/Brazil story refers to even more nebulous matters, something usually identified as "technological maturity". In almost all developing countries, import substitution began with consumer goods, generally consumer durables. The rationale for this is quite simple. Such goods were being imported, so there was an obvious existing market, and it was a relatively simple matter to keep out the imports of these products by tariffs, quotas, or whatever. Then with the foreign exchange saved by not importing these consumer goods, capital goods would be imported. It was also generally believed that the cost disadvantage in the production of consumer goods would be less than it would be for capital goods. Consumer goods, especially durables, were also deemed less essential for development than were capital goods. Given all these arguments heavy protection was given to a wide range of consumer goods, while little or no protection was given to raw materials and capital goods. In addition, in many countries the importation of capital goods was further encouraged by advantageous exchange rates, easy access to import permits. and to credit. This policy meant that the protection of value added in the production of consumer goods was much higher and much more variable than a survey of nominal rates of protection would indicate. The rationale for subsidizing capital goods seemed to rest primarily on the assumption that capital formation was at the heart of the development process and that there was very little flexibility in the productive system.

This "consumer goods production phase", often referred to as the easy phase, could continue only as long as the domestic market could absorb new consumer goods and increasing quantities of old ones. If import substitution were to continue, then intermediate and capital goods production had to be protected and this would raise the cost of the policy. To avoid this result, the country could seek to export its newly-produced consumer goods. Great attention should be given therefore to manufactured exports. The evidence that countries that did export quickly did not get bogged down by the import substitution strategy supports this point. There were other aspects of this original strategy [see Bruton (1970) and Sheahan (1972)], but in the present context these are the main points.[7]

The original form of the argument emphasized the high relative costs of the domestic production of capital goods and the apparent violation of the dictates of static comparative advantage. It was soon evident, however, that there is no a priori reason to believe that capital goods are more costly to produce in the developing countries than are consumer durables. This consideration in turn led to the conclusion that protection should be very similar across the board. In providing greatly divergent rates of protection for various products, the policy-maker was implying that knowledge about costs, economies of scale, externalities, productivity growth, etc. were in fact unknown. Hence the argument that protection, if any, should be uniform.

More recently another argument has been developed about the role of capital goods in the learning and knowledge accumulating process. As noted in Section 2, Hirschman (1968) long ago called our attention to the role of capital goods in the learning process but only recently has it attracted a great deal of attention. The main issue is not the production of capital goods themselves, rather it is the creation of technological capacity – the capacity to develop a more or less continuous flow of new technical knowledge. Brazil, Korea, and India offer convenient examples for the discussion of this issue. All three countries have begun to produce and export capital goods and technical knowledge, and their

---

[7]One of the other aspects has to do with the composition of capital goods. Capital goods are not a simple malleable glob of productive power, but of course come in many shapes and forms. A study of a disaggregated capital goods sector would be useful, but cannot be undertaken here.

experiences illuminate the role that capital goods production plays or can play in import substitution and development. In the narrow sense, the question is whether a country should seek to create a capital goods capacity, a knowledge-creating capacity, behind some form of protection.

The accumulation of relevant empirical data has been underway for only a few years. Exactly what data provide reasonable measures of technical knowledge-creating capacity is complex, as is the question what constitutes protection of these learning activities. Despite these difficulties and ambiguities the available evidence provides enough information to suggest hypotheses and arguments of great importance to our understanding of development and of economic strength.

Lall (1984a, p. 477), for example, identifies four items as technology imports: the purchase of turnkey projects from foreign engineering companies, the inflow of direct foreign investment from abroad, the licensing of foreign technology, and the importation of foreign capital goods or the purchase of foreign components for the local production of capital goods. On the basis of this classification and the data that he accumulated, Lall concludes that India imported far less technology than did Brazil, Korea, or other newly-industrialized countries. In the fifteen years between 1967 and 1982, India employed no foreign engineering firms as prime contractors. In the 1968–82 period, net inflows of direct foreign investments into India were negative. During the same period, Brazil had a net inflow of $14 billion and Korea $648 million, Mexico $7 billion, Argentina $1.5 billion, Hong Kong $3 billion, and so on. A similar result emerges when one normalizes by size of country. Estimates of licensing payments abroad as a ratio of the value added in manufacturing in 1979 were approximately 0.8 percent for India, 1.9 percent for Brazil, and 1.1 percent for Korea. Finally, India's imports of capital goods as a proportion of manufacturing value added was 8.2 percent compared to 8.6 and 41.2 percent for Brazil and Korea, respectively, in the late 1970s. Import content of domestic capital goods production was less than 10 percent for India, about 20 percent for Brazil, and 45 percent for Korea. [All data are from Lall (1984a, p. 477).] Clearly, India was relying much less on the importation of technology and technical knowledge than Brazil and Korea, and indeed all other countries, for its new industrial activities.

The story of technology exports is equally interesting. The cleanest form of the export of technical knowledge would appear to be licensing, consultancy, and technical services supplied in industrial activities. Sanjaya Lall's study (based on his own data and that accumulated by others) show that as of 1981–82, India had some $500 million in contracts for such services, Korea $472 million, and Brazil $357 million. Another indicator of technology export is the export of industrial projects, and here India is far ahead of the other two countries. Lall's data show contract values for India of between $2.2 and $2.5 billion, for Korea $802 million (which he emphasizes is an overestimate), and for Brazil some $285 million (probably an underestimate). In civil construction project exports, Korea is vastly larger than the other two because of its extensive contracts in the oil producing countries of the Middle East. Several observers have noted that Korea's great capacity in these construction activities was learned in on-the-job training carrying out many contracts in conjunction with U.S. military activity in Korea.

Despite the arbitrariness of these measures and the roughness of the estimates, one is entitled to conclude from them that India has created a much broader and deeper technological base than is present in either Brazil or Korea, or indeed any other developing country. It has accomplished this largely on its own, and its accomplishment has required a great deal of protection especially with respect to capital goods production. India has achieved substantial "know-why" (Lall's term), and has thereby created a capacity for continuing technological development and responsiveness in new fields and in new activities. Bardhan (1984), who is generally very critical of India's development strategy, notes that "the overall dynamic impact of import substitution in fostering skill-formation and learning-by-doing in a whole range of sophisticated manufacturing industries (producing engineering, machinery, chemical and other products) may not have been negligible, although produced at a very high immediate cost to consumers and industrial users of domestic intermediate and capital goods" (pp. 28–29). Since the only way to ensure learning is to protect the productive activity that produces it, one may argue that India's relative success in generating a truly indigenous technological capacity depended on, even required, the inward looking import substitution oriented policies that have characterized Indian development strategy.

Brazil and Korea present a different picture. As noted, neither country demonstrates the breadth and depth of technology capacity that India does, but there are other differences as well. Westphal and his various colleagues in several articles emphasize that Korea's technological capacity is much more advanced and much more secure in plant operation and production than it is in the design and development of new products and new processes. They go further to say that most of Korea's exports of capital goods do not represent exports of technology. The significant Korean construction activity in the Middle East was primarily a matter of supplying an established product and service at prices that were lower than those of other bidders.

Sung-Hwan Jo argues [in Kumar and McLeod (1981)] that most of Korea's direct investment abroad has been designed to facilitate their own exports and to acquire and develop foreign sources of raw materials. Similarly, the establishment of foreign branches and subsidiaries of Korea's trading companies and banks were largely motivated by the determination to keep exports growing. Korea's capital goods industries – all large producers with considerable monopoly power and access to subsidized credit – exported virtually from the beginning of production. About two-thirds of Korea's exports of machinery and transport equipment went to developed market economies [Chudnovsky and Nagao (1983, p. 101)], a fact which further suggests that there was little in the way of technology being exported. Brazil and India's capital goods exports, on the other hand, went largely to other developing countries. Some rough estimates of R&D expenditure by a sample of Korean and Indian firms in Chudnovsky and Nagao (1983, p. 132) show that Indian firms did much more R&D than did Korean firms in 1980. Their sample is divided into machine tools, equipment for process industries, and electrical equipment. Each of these is also broken down by ownership. In all categories, Indian firms spent more in absolute terms and as a percentage of output (for India) or sales (for Korea). India's percentages were, with one exception, several times those of Korea. The one exception is the wholly domestic firms in the machine tool sector, where Korean firms spent 4.2 percent of sales on R&D and Indian domestic firms 3.4 percent of their output. All of this evidence is consistent with the argument that India's technological capacity rests on stronger and wider foundations.

Brazilian manufactured exports exceeded India's by a factor of three in 1980, yet India's exports of technology were surely much larger than those of Brazil, and included a much wider range of technologies. Also, of course, Brazil was the only one of the three countries in which foreign-owned and managed firms played a significant role. Another piece of evidence that emerged from a sample survey of Brazilian technology exporters tells us something about the role of price. These respondents stated that "technical factors, more suitable know-how, and better acquaintance with recipient's problems" were much more important than price advantage. On the other hand, high prices were often cited as a reason for failure to win a contract. Thus, low prices will not prevail if quality and appropriateness are not present, but high prices will deter buyers even if quality is evident [Sercovich (1984, p. 593)]. As with all the empirical work on the issues considered here, this result must be treated cautiously. Teubal (1984) found that Brazilian firms put great weight on reputation in their marketing efforts, and that their reputation was enhanced as they supplied products that met increasingly demanding specifications.

What does all this add up to? India has, it seems, carried out an exceptionally successful import substitution policy in the sense that it has led to the creation of an impressive indigenous technological capacity. At the same time, as shown earlier, her output and productivity growth record is extremely unfortunate relative to that of Korea and probably Brazil. Korea's record on output and productivity growth are impressive, but it seems clear that its command of technological know-why is markedly below that of India. Similarly, Brazil, with a much larger rate of manufactured output and exports than India, still lags behind that country in technology exports and in the range and sophistication of its technological capacity. There is, therefore, no simple criterion one may apply to determine which country is more successful and which less.

3.2.4. Import substitution and total factor productivity growth

It was urged earlier that productivity is not only the heart of the explanation of increasing output, but is also an important criterion of successful import substitution. Data on productivity growth are less readily available than output data, but there are some series becoming available. Ahluwlia's (1985) book has considerable detailed data on India's productivity growth and a recent article by Nishimizu and Robinson (1984) provides an illuminating study of productivity growth in Korea, Turkey, Yugoslavia, and Japan. A brief discussion of this evidence is helpful to our study. Table 30.1 shows estimates of total factor productivity growth for industries in India, Korea, Turkey, and Yugoslavia. These estimates must be cautiously interpreted since they are not for the same time interval, are not all calculated in the same way, and the whole notion of total factor productivity can be questioned.[8] In particular, the estimates for Korea and Turkey are probably understated relative to those for India. Despite all these qualifications, the data reveal such a consistent picture that one can conclude that they have some considerable link with reality.

Howard Pack in Chapter 9 of this Handbook reviews some of the more general issues of the Nishimizu/Robinson piece. Concern here is limited to the light that their results shed on the relationship between import substitution and export growth on the one hand and TFPG on the other. They estimate an equation of the form:

$$\text{TFPG} = B_0 + B_{ee} X_{ee} + B_{is} X_{is} + E.$$

In this equation X_{ee} is output growth allocated to export expansion, X_{is} is that allocated to import substitution, and E is the error term. Regressions are estimated from time-series data for each of 13 common sectors for the four countries. (They do not include India in their study.) There are thus 52 estimates of each of the two regression coefficients. Of the estimates of B_{ee}, 26 are significant and positive and two are significant and negative. The remaining 24 are not significant. Thirteen of the estimates of B_{is} are significant and negative, and seven significant and positive. The results therefore provide considerable support for the view that demand created by export expansion is more likely to contribute to TFPG than is demand created by import substitution. In addition

---

[8] The concept of TFPG, and especially its measurement, are open to so many questions that one worries a great deal about building an argument around it. One worries, but one goes ahead and does it. It seems to me that conceptually the notion is useful (as are other, possibly incompatible notions) and is clear. We know so little on these matters that it seems justifiable to try to learn, what the TFPG approach can teach us, and to check it against other data and arguments. One recognizes that it may well be a weak reed, but economists have learned often from weak reeds. Nelson (1981) and Nadiri (1970) are fine surveys of these matters.

to statistical questions that might be noted – and which the authors emphasize – two other points are relevant to the present story.

(1) Japan apparently is different. Only three of Japan's 26 regression coefficients were significantly different from zero. Similarly, the R^2's for Japan are markedly lower than those for the other three countries. The statistically significant B_0's are positive for Japan and negative for the other three countries. Even more impressive is the fact that for Korea 10 of the 13 B_0's are negative, for Yugoslavia and Turkey 12 of the 13 are negative, and for Japan only 6 of 13 are negative.

A negative B_0 implies that total factor productivity will decline if it is not offset by positive contributions for growth of demand from exports or import substitution. This result suggests additional questions, since negative productivity growth is not easy to explain. The most obvious explanation is the appearance of underutilization of capacity as output or its rate of increase falls, because of slack demand, and inputs are not immediately reduced. Similarly, increasing distortions in the economy may prevent continued full utilization because of production bottlenecks. In the latter case, increased imports of intermediate goods may break the bottlenecks and allow output and measured productivity to rise. In the former case, it is not clear why the source of demand matters, since any source would serve the purpose. In neither case would it appear that exports qua exports are the key factor in explaining TFPG. A third explanation is also possible. The investment that occurs and the new activities that are created are in increasingly high cost areas, and there are no gains in productivity in existing industries to offset the higher costs in the new activities. Given the ubiquity of negative TFPG in Indian industries previously noted, and of the negative B_0's in Korea, Turkey, and Yugoslavia, this explanation seems doubtful.

Consider another possible interpretation of Japan's results. The rate of growth of total factor productivity in Japan is built into the way the economic system functions. It is a consequence of the continuous search and learning efforts that have taken place for over a century, and that have made the Japanese so adaptable and responsive to opportunities. Japan's great export power – its great production power – is fundamentally due to this characteristic of the economy. Exports occurred because of this characteristic which in turn produces TFPG, rather than exports creating TFPG. It may be noted that TFPG measures do not usually capture quality changes. Such changes are often of great importance, and the limited information available suggests that they were in these years for Korea and Japan, and in some sectors for India. This brief Japanese story illustrates the basic objective of import substitution: to create an economy in which there is a continuous search and learning process that produces sustained increases in the productivity of resources. The regressions seem to suggest that Japan has reached this stage, while none of the other countries has. This, it seems, is the principal result of these regressions.

(2) There are numerous articles that examine the relationship between growth of total exports and growth of GDP [Balassa (1978, 1985), Feder (1983); these articles all have many additional references]. Attention here has been devoted to the Nishimizu/Robinson article because it concentrates on manufacturing and on the role of TFPG and export expansion and import substitution, and this, as argued earlier, is the heart of the issue considered in this chapter. The relationship between growth of GDP and of exports is of course related to the manufacturing TFPG and manufacturing exports. Jung and Marshall (1985) have examined the former relationships (growth of exports and of GDP) in some 37 countries to determine the direction of causation, i.e. does the growth of exports "cause" the growth of GDP or is it the other way around or is there some other force that acts on the two together: Their test of the direction of causation is that proposed by Granger (1969), which involves essentially a matter of the lagging of the explanatory variable behind the one to be explained: X is said to cause Y if current Y can be predicted more accurately by using past values of X than by not using them. Jung and Marshall have regressed the growth of output on past values of itself, on past values of the growth of exports, and on a constant. Similarly, the export growth rate is regressed on the same variables. Constant price data are used. Of these 37 equations, only four (Indonesia, Egypt, Costa Rica, and Ecuador) are consistent with the hypothesis that export growth causes output growth. For six of the countries the equations show that export promotion reduces growth of GDP. One of these six is Korea, and neither Taiwan nor Brazil offer support for the causal role of exports.

One must conclude from all this that the statistical results are inconclusive. Such efforts have been helpful, of course, but have not led us to a common position. Perhaps, as much has been accomplished by regressions and correlations as can be expected, at least as these regressions are presently designed. The main difficulty, however, seems not be statistical, but conceptual. We still understand so little about searching and learning and productivity growth, and, therefore, about the relationship between these and anything else.

4. Some policy and other conclusions

One might, with considerable profit, review other country and cross-country studies. From such studies come additional insights and bits and pieces of evidence that add to our knowledge and, equally often, reveal, in a particularly illuminating way, our ignorance. Thus, generalizations are exceptionally precarious and policy recommendations always subject to review. Ignorance must be taken seriously. Even so, some policy (and other) conclusions are useful and also help to make some of the arguments of Sections 2 and 3 somewhat clearer.

4.1. General conclusions

In recent years a large number of economists have found it the fun thing to do to lambast the import substitution strategy of development. I have avoided doing this, because I think much of the lambasting is unjustified, and frequently concentrates on the wrong issues, and because the purpose of this chapter is to study import substitution. If it were complete nonsense, no chapter would be necessary. That the strategy has frequently caused problems is not disputed by anyone, although it is not always clear that the problems were due to import substitution as such. The basic idea of the import substitution strategy is that protection is necessary for most contemporary developing countries at some point in their history in order to establish an internal routine that generates increasing welfare. More specifically, the objective is to establish a flexible, responsive economy that can take advantage of opportunities generated in the world at large and, more importantly, that can generate its own opportunities. Behind this protection, new activities are created that modify the structure of the economy and that induce learning. The achievement of both these objectives is necessary if import substitution is to accomplish the intended objectives. Learning is reflected most clearly in total factor productivity growth and in the emergence of an indigenous technological capacity. This latter notion is admittedly fuzzy and TFPG is also open to severe measurement and conceptual problems. At some point when the new routines are established and productivity is growing steadily and transformation capacity has greatly increased so that the economy can move smoothly and quickly into new activities, then protection has accomplished its purpose. If an economy can produce only one or two products (or services) and can move into new activities only at great cost, arguments built around comparative advantage are not very convincing. Protection then is a form of investment the return on which is a more productive, more independent economy.

The empirical evidence to support any development strategy is, of course, open to many doubts. The India story is especially illuminating. India has perhaps pursued the most consistent policy of import substitution of any of the developing countries. The evidence on TFPG in India is dismal indeed, but the evidence of a technological maturing, her genuine know-why, is surely impressive. Certainly, India's strategy has imposed heavy costs on the society, whether these costs are or will be justified is, of course, impossible to tell. The one unambiguous result of the Indian experience is the demonstration of the importance of the policy-making process. The import substitution strategy as followed in India has created an entrenched interest group that makes any moves toward a new policy – e.g. toward a liberalization and opening up – exceedingly difficult and time consuming. It is, however, to be emphasized that it is the policy-making process that is at issue, not import substitution as such that is the source of the problem. Any package of policies helps some groups, and these groups will, if they can, prevent its change.

Korea's story looks much more convincing, but the evidence is far from overwhelming, and its success in the technological maturing race doubtlessly lags behind that of India. Korea's initial conditions, described so effectively by Cole and Lyman (1971), and her effective decision-making machinery seem to emerge as more relevant to the explanation of her success than does a given development strategy. Korea's protection has been marked in a variety of ways and the openness of the economy seems more apparent than real. The strong export incentive and record induce learning and prevent bottlenecks from stopping the economy. So the source of her growth remains ambiguous. In Brazil the frequent policy changes and the large role of multinationals makes her story unclear as well. The evidence on TFPG and technological maturing in Brazil is less clear-cut than for either India or Korea, but consistency of policy and a greater reliance on domestic firms might reveal a now hidden strength. Finally, the many regressions are interesting, informative, and, as we are increasingly recognizing, probably not very powerful.

4.2. Some more specific conclusions

So any conclusion as to the power of import substitution (or any other strategy) remains inconclusive. Despite this agnosticism, there are important policy ideas and conclusions in the analysis presented in the preceding pages. I turn now to a brief review of those that seem to bear most directly on policy matters.

(1) The attention given to productivity growth, and its principal source, learning – learning by doing, by accumulating experience, by trial and error – emphasized three points:

(a) simply the building and operating of modern factories by foreign investors will rarely create much indigenous learning nor will it lead to a dissemination of the learning that does take place;

(b) the new ideas and technologies to which managers and labor are exposed must have some link, some overlap, with the ideas and technologies that they presently know and employ; and

(c) some kind of a capital goods sector is, generally, an important source of learning and facilitates the evolution of an indigenous technological capacity.

(2) Much of the literature tends to include, under the import substitution heading, a range of specific policies that are recognizably distortional in their effects. Many countries have in fact adopted policies that severely distorted their economy, and surely penalized learning in a variety of ways, but such policies are in no sense necessary for the implementation of an import substitution development policy. To repeat a statement made earlier: the purpose of import substitution is not to distort the economy. It was also emphasized that protection takes

many forms, and a particular policy that protects one country at one time may not do so at another time or in another country. Protection is not simply tariffs and quotas. Forbidding direct foreign investment is protection, as is the discouraging of foreign tourists, of foreign advisors, of foreign training. The exchange rate can be used as a source of protection, as can wage policy. Countries with a high personal saving rate and a strong capital goods sector are more protected than are countries with a very high marginal propensity to consume or no capital goods sector. And so on. So when comparisons are made of the openness of several economies, great care is necessary. Similarly, the effectiveness of other policies may be expected to be different because of these considerations. Generalizations across countries about appropriate policies to effect import substitution can, therefore, be done only at a very high level of abstraction.

(3) The role that protection can play is especially illuminated by the experiences of a number of countries during World War II and, to some extent, during the Great Depression of the 1930s. This natural, non-distorting protection, combined with the war, created unambiguously genuine profit opportunities at a time when importing was virtually impossible. Economic agents responded well, ways were found to adjust, adapt, and modify, in order to take advantage of these opportunities. The results in terms of TFPG and the range of outputs were often impressive. This experience suggests that importance of a recognized reliable demand as a means of eliciting an increasing supply through productivity growth and saving induced by anticipated investment opportunities, rather than by income. Such an argument does not mean that there is unlimited supply capacity available waiting to be found, and at some point a more fundamental consideration of supply is necessary [Bruton (1985)]. The natural protection and war-time evidence is impressive, however, of the capacity of the economies to respond when subjected to the appropriate kind of demand pressure.

This experience also suggests that a policy package that seeks to replicate natural protection may be a useful guide. An across-the-board common nominal tariff is now generally recognized as the most appropriate tariff that is administratively feasible. Given the common tariff schedules, an exchange rate that "undervalues" domestic currency affords additional protection of a general sort.[9] Undervaluation would, by definition, lead to an accumulation of foreign exchange, an advantage in itself in the fight against a stop–go situation. Mainly, however, the undervaluation helps to create profitable opportunities that are evident to the community at large. The undervaluation plus the common tariff helps to direct attention away from imports of physical capital goods that do not lend themselves to using available resources with ever-increasing productivity. The general argument here, and the evidence from several countries, also suggests

---

[9]To repeat a point made earlier, in a world of large and rapid capital movements, large-scale aid, and foreign investment the determination of the "correct" exchange rate, even conceptually, is no small matter. The point in the text is to call attention to the advantages of keeping foreign currency expensive as a means of inducing search.

that the widespread practice of subsidizing inputs is not nearly as effective as guaranteed prices – at a favorable level – as a means of eliciting productivity growth. Finally, natural protection doubtless encouraged saving, or at least made consumption less enticing, and high saving rates offer many advantages.

(4) The potential role of a capital goods sector is especially interesting and especially relevant. The protection of the capital goods activities is different in purpose from that for consumer durables or other standardized products. Observers vary in the strength of their convictions on the role of the capital goods sector, but there is no doubt that an increasing number of economists are convinced that such a sector is crucial to the creation of a growing economy. For such activities to evolve, to begin to evolve, requires protection of some form or other. Thus, import substitution is involved and hence imported technical knowledge is to be used sparingly and selectively. The capital goods sector is thus the main source of the emergence of the indigenous technological capacity that is essential to independent and sustained development.

(5) The evidence suggests that the developing country is most likely to succeed in the capital goods sector if it can curve out a special niche, rather than try to compete in the large-scale, mass-produced standardized products. Thus, the most convincing success stories refer to the design and production of a specific product or service that solves a well-defined problem. Output in these new capital goods sectors is likely to be both more heterogeneous and more discrete than in the more developed countries. This is a major reason why know-why is so important. Know-how is not enough. Automobiles, for example, appear to be the wrong kind of activity, and yet the developing world is full of automobile assembly plants, may of which are white elephants.

(6) Numerous case studies also indicate that activities that are engineering based, as opposed to science based, are more suitable and more likely to provide the kind of experience and learning that can be effective in the developing country. A similar point is that activities in which the basic technology is changing rapidly are probably a bad bet. This is surely the case at the early stages of capital goods activity. Where the basic technology is changing rapidly, learning time is squeezed so much that few countries would be able to achieve mastery of the fundamental materials.

(7) It is difficult to believe that exports qua exports are especially significant. Perhaps their most important role is as a means of importing technical knowledge in a directly effective way. This possibility has been mentioned by a number of people, but a thorough investigation does not seem to be available. The role of foreign investment is equally ambiguous, and here so much depends on the capacity of the host country to limit and direct the foreign investor that even abstract generalizations are risky.

(8) The country studies show a great range of experiences. Some governments learn, others do not. Some are able to design effective policies and manage them well and keep rent-seeking under control, and others are not. Corruption is out of

hand in some and is downright productive in others. The objectives of governments and societies differ, as do initial conditions and resource endowments. All of this means that the design of policies and the explanation of events must be very country specific, and a general theory can, at best, help determine the issues to address and the questions to ask.

(9) A more general point refers again to initial conditions and to history and to the general social environment. Mason (1984) suggests that Korea has "perhaps grown so rapidly because it was occupied by Koreans" (p. 19). Similarly, Frances Stewart [in Fransman and King (1984)] notes that "in trying to explain why some societies innovate effectively and others do not, the fundamental and underlying explanation often seems to lie in the realm of history and interests, rather than in particular policies" (p. 88). Such statements remind us of our ignorance, on the one hand, and the great difficulties of policy-making, on the other. The policy-maker is never looking at a blank sheet on which he can put down what an objective, highly competent, but extremely narrow analysis tells him is the right policy. This is especially the case when it comes down to designing a specific policy in a specific country at a specific time.

(10) The "right" policy or "right" broad strategy depends then on many things. This conclusion is especially relevant when, as just noted, one recognizes that all policies are not equally doable. What the policy analyst must then be equipped to do is not to parrot, import substitution or outward looking, but to be able to so examine the economy as it is at the moment and determine what policy instruments are likely to be most effective at the moment. Perhaps this is the main thing that we have learned.

It is essential, however, to emphasize the conclusion that, while we must continue to take ignorance seriously, we have, as well, learned a great deal about import substitution since the 1950s. The idea that some form of protection is in order to enable a country to establish its place in the world economy, in order to establish an economy that is flexible and resilient, is a fundamental idea. To get the form of this protection right and to get the changes that take place behind this protection to produce this kind of economy, is what import substitution is all about.

References[10]

Ahluwalia, I.J. (1985) *Industrial growth in India*. Delhi: Oxford University Press.
Bacha, E.L. (1977) 'Issues and evidence on recent Brazilian economic growth', *World Development*, 5:47–67.
Baer, W. (1972) 'Import substitution and industrialization in Latin America: Experiences and interpretations', *Latin American Research Review*, 7:95–122.

[10] This list includes works that deal with the general issues of the chapter but not specifically cited in the text.

Balassa, B. (1975) 'Trade, protection and domestic production: A comment', in: P.B. Kenen, ed., *International trade and finance*. Cambridge, MA and New York: Cambridge University Press.

Balassa, B. (1978) 'Exports and economic growth: Further evidence', *Journal of Development Economics*, 11:181–189.

Balassa, B. (1985) 'Exports, policy choices and economic growth in developing countries', *Journal of Development Economics*, 18:23–35.

Balassa, B. and Associates (1971) *The structure of protection in developing countries*. Baltimore: The Johns Hopkins University Press.

Balassa, B. and Associates (1982) *Development strategies in semi-industrial economies*. Washington, DC: World Bank.

Bardhan, P. (1984) *The political economy of development in India*. Oxford: Basil Blackwell.

Bell, M., Ross-Larson, B., and Westphal, L. (1984) 'Assessing the performance of infant industries', World Bank Staff Working Papers, no. 666, World Bank.

Bhagwati, J. and Desai, P. (1970) *India planning for industrialization*. London: Oxford University Press.

Bruton, H.J. (1967) 'Productivity growth in Latin America', *The American Economic Review*, 57:1099–1116.

Bruton, H.J. (1968) 'Import substitution and productivity growth', *Journal of Development Studies*, 4:306–326.

Bruton, H.J. (1970) 'The import substitution strategy of economic development: A survey', *The Pakistan Development Review*, 10:123–146.

Bruton, H.J. (1983) 'Egypt's development in the seventies'. *Economic Development and Cultural Change*, 31:679–704.

Bruton, H.J. (1985) 'The search for a development economics', *World Development*, 13:1099–1124.

Chenery, H.B. (1960) 'Patterns of industrial growth', *American Economic Review*, 50:624–654.

Chudnovsky, D. and Nagao, M. (1983) *Capital goods production in the Third World*. New York: St. Martin's Press.

Cline, W.R. (1982) 'Can the East Asian model of development be generalized?, *World Development*, 10:81–90.

Cole, D.C. and Lyman, P.N. (1971) *Korean development: The interplay of politics and economics*, Cambridge, MA: Harvard University Press.

Diaz-Alejandro, C.F. (1970) *Essays on the economic history of the Argentine republic*. New Haven, CT: Yale University Press.

Diaz-Alejandro, C.F. (1973) 'Delinking North and South: Unshackled or unhinged', in: *Rich and poor nations in the world economy*. New York: McGraw-Hill.

Diaz-Alejandro, C.F. (1984) 'Latin America in the 1930s', in: Rosemary Thorp, ed., *Latin America in the 1930s*. New York: St. Martin's Press.

Donges, J.B. (1976) 'A comparative survey of industrialization policies in fifteen semi-industrial countries', *Weltwirtschaftliches Archiv*, 112:626–657.

Donges, J.B. and Riedel, J. (1977) 'The expansion of manufactured exports in developing countries: An empirical assessment of supply and demand issues', *Weltwirtschaftliches Archiv*, 113:58–87.

Dudley, L. (1972) 'Learning and productivity change in metal products', *American Economic Review*, 62:662–669.

Elias, V.J. (1977) 'Sources of economic growth in Latin American countries', Harvard Institute for International Development, 18, Harvard University.

Fane, G. (1973) 'Consistent measures of import substitution', *Oxford Economic Paper*, 25:251–261.

Feder, G. (1983) 'On exports and economic growth', *Journal of Development Economics*, 16:59–74.

Fei, J.C.H. and Ranis, G. (1975) 'A model of growth and employment in the open dualistic economy: The cases of Korea and Taiwan', *The Journal of Development Studies*, 11:32–64.

Frank, C.R., Jr., Kim, S.K., and Westphal, L. (1975) '*Foreign trade regimes and economic development: South Korea*'. New York: Columbia University Press.

Fransman, M. (1982) 'Learning and the capital goods sector under free trade: The case of Hong Kong', *World Development*, 10:991–1015.

Fransman, M. and King, K. (1984) *Technological capability in the Third World*. New York: St. Martin's Press.

Granger, C. (1969) 'Investigating causal relations by econometric models and cross spectral methods', *Econometrica*, 37:424–438.

Hirschman, A.O. (1968) 'The political economy of import substituting industrialization in Latin America', *Quarterly Journal of Economics*, 82:1–32.

Hirschman, A.O. (1977) 'A generalized linkage approach to development, with special reference to staples', *Economic Development and Cultural Change*, 25:67–98.

Hirschman, A.O. (1982) *Shifting involvements*. Princeton, NJ: Princeton University Press.

International Labour Office (1972) *Employment, incomes and equality*. Geneva, ILO.

Jones, L.P. and Sakong, I. (1980) *Government, business and enterpreneurship in economic development: The Korean case*. Cambridge, MA: Harvard University Press.

Jung, W.S. and Marshall, P.J. (1985) 'Export growth and casuality in developing countries', *Journal of Development Economics*, 18:1–12.

Katz, J. (1982) 'Technology and economic development: An overview of research findings', in: M. Syrquin and S. Tietel, eds., *Trade stability, technology, and equity in Latin America*. New York: Academic.

Katz, J. (1984) 'Technological innovation, industrial organization and comparative advantages of Latin American metalworking industries', in: M. Fransman and K. King, eds., *Technological capability in the Third World*. New York: St. Martin's Press.

Kim, K. and Park, J. (1985) *Sources of economic growth in Korea: 1963–1982*. Seoul: Korean Development Institute.

King, K. (1977) *The African artisan: Education and the informal sector*. London: Heinemann.

Knight, P.T. (1981) 'Brazilian socio-economic development: Issues for the eighties', *World Development*, 9:1063–1082.

Koo, H. (1984) The political economy of income distribution in South Korea: The impact of the state's industrialization policies, *World Development*, 12:1029–1037.

Krueger, A.O. (1979) *The development role of the foreign sector and aid*. Cambridge, MA: Harvard University Press.

Kumar, K. and McLeod, M.G. (1981) *Multinationals from developing countries*. Lexington, MA: Lexington Books.

Lall, S. (1981) 'Indian technology exports and technological development', *The Annals*, 458:151–162.

Lall, S. (1982) 'Technological learning in the Third World: Some implications of technology exports', in: F. Stewart and J. James, eds., *The economics of new technology in developing countries*. London: Frances Pinter.

Lall, S. (1984a) 'Exports of technology by newly-industrializing countries: An overview', *World Development*, 12:471–480.

Lall, S. (1984b) 'India', *World Development*, 12:535–565.

Lall, S. and Kumar, R. (1981) 'Firm-level export performance in an inwardlooking economy: The Indian engineering industry', *World Development*, 9:453–463.

Lall, S. and Mohammad, S. (1983) Technological effort and disembodied technology exports: An econometric analysis of inter-industry variations in India, *World Development*, 11:527–535.

Lewis, S.R., Jr., and Soligo, R. (1965) Growth and structural change in Pakistan's manufacturing industry, *Pakistan Development Review*.

Little, I.M.D. (1960) 'The strategy of Indian development', *National Institute Economic Review*, 9:20–29.

Little, I.M.D. (1982) *Economic development: Theory, policy and international relations*. New York: Basic Books.

Little, I., Scitovsky, T., and Scott, M. (1970) *Industry and trade in some developing countries*. London: Oxford University Press.

Mason, E.S. (1984) 'The Chenery analysis and some other considerations', in: M. Syrquin, L. Taylor, and L. Westphal, eds., *Economic structure and performance*. New York: Academic.

Meier, G.M. and Seers, D. (1984) *Pioneers in development* New York and London: Oxford University Press, for the World Bank.

Morley, S.A. and Smith, G.W. (1970) 'On the measurement of import substitution', *American Economic Review*, 60:728–735.

Myint, H. (1958) 'The classical theory of international trade and the underdeveloped countries', *The Economic Journal*, 68:317–327.

Nadiri, M.I. (1970) 'Some approaches to the theory and measurement of total factor productivity: A survey', *Journal of Economic Literature*, 8:1137–1178.

Nelson, R.R. (1981) 'Research on productivity growth and productivity differences: Dead ends and new departures', *The Journal of Economic Literature*, 19:1029–1064.

Nelson, R.R., and Winter, S.G. (1982) *An evolutionary theory of economic change*. Cambridge, MA: Harvard University Press.

Nelson, R.R., Schultz, T.P., and Slighton, R.L. (1971) *Structural change in a developing economy*. Princeton, NJ: Princeton University Press.

Nishimizu, M. and Robinson, S. (1984) 'Trade policies and productivity change in semi-industrialized countries', *Journal of Development Economics*, 16:177–206.

Pack, H. (1981) 'Fostering the capital goods sector in LDCs', *World Development*, 9:227–250.

Psacharopoulos, G. (1981) 'Education, employment and inequality in LDCs', *World Development*, 9:37–54.

Ranis, G. and Orrock, L. (1985) 'Latin American and East Asian NICs: Development strategies compared', in: Esperanza Duran, ed., *Latin America and the world recession*. Cambridge, MA: Cambridge University Press.

Scitovsky, T. (1985) 'Economic development in Taiwan and South Korea: 1965–81', *Food Research Institute Studies*, 19:215–264.

Sercovich, F.C. (1984) 'Brazil', *World Development*, 12:575–599.

Sheahan, J. (1972) 'Import substitution and economic policy: A second review', Research Memorandum no. 50, Center for Development Economics, Williams College.

Singer, H.W. (1950) 'The distribution of gains between investing and borrowing countries', *The American Economic Review*, 40:473–485.

Spraos, J. (1980) 'The statistical debate on the net barter terms of trade between primary commodities and manufacturers', *The Economic Journal*, 90:107–128.

Stewart, F. and James, J., eds., (1982) *'The economics of the new technology in developing countries'*. London: Frances Pinter.

Strassman, W.P. (1968) *Technological change and economic development*. Ithaca, NY: Cornell University Press.

Syrquin, M. (1985) 'Growth and structural change in Latin America since 1960', Development Discussion Paper no. 208, Harvard Institute for International Development, Harvard University.

Syrquin, M. and Teitel, S., eds. (1982) *Trade stability, technology and equity in Latin America*. New York: Academic.

Syrquin, M., Taylor, L., and Westphal, L., eds. (1984) *Economic structure and performance*. New York: Academic.

Teitel, S. (1981) 'Creation of technology within Latin America', *Annals*, 458:136–150.

Teubal, M. (1984) The role of technological learning in the exports of manufactured goods: The case of selected capital goods in Brazil', *World Development*, 12:849–865.

Tyler, W.G. (1976) *Manufactured export expansion and industrialization in Brazil*. J.C.B. Tubinger and P.S. Mohr, eds.

Tyler, W.G. (1981) 'Growth and export expansion in developing countries: Some empirical evidence', *Journal of Development Economics*, 14:121–130.

Weintraub, S. (1981) 'Review of Krueger 1979', *Journal of Economic Literature*, 19:596–598.

Weisskoff, R. (1980) 'The growth and decline of import substitution in Brazil', *World Development*, 8:647–675.

Wells, L.T., Jr. (1983) *Third world multinationals*. Cambridge, MA: MIT Press.

Westphal, L.E. (1982) 'Fostering technological mastery by means of selective infant-industry protection', in: M. Syrquin and S. Tietel, eds., *Trade, stability, technology, and equity in Latin America*. New York: Academic.

Westphal, L. and Kim, K.S. (1982) 'Korea', in: *Development strategies in semi-industrial economies*. Bela Balassa and Associates, eds., Baltimore, MD: Johns Hopkins University Press, Ch. 8.

Westphal, L.E., Rhee, Y.W., and Pursell, G. (1981) 'Korean industrial competence: Where it came from', World Bank Staff Working Paper no. 469, World Bank.

Westphal, L.E., Rhee, Y.W., Kim, L., and Amsden, A.H. (1984) 'Republic of Korea', *World Development*, 12:505–533.

Wolf, M. (1982) *India's exports*. New York: Oxford University Press.

World Bank (1983) 'Brazil', *Industrial policies and manufactured exports*. Washington, DC: World Bank.

World Bank (1984) *Brazil, economic memorandum*. A World Bank Country Study, World Bank.

Chapter 31

OUTWARD ORIENTATION

BELA BALASSA*

Johns Hopkins University

Contents

*The author is Professor of Political Economy at the Johns Hopkins University and Consultant at the World Bank. He is indebted for valuable comments to Hollis Chenery, Stephen Lewis, and T.N. Srinivasan. He alone is responsible for the contents of the chapter that should not be considered to reflect the views of the World Bank.

Handbook of Development Economics, Volume II, Edited by H. Chenery and T.N. Srinivasan
© *Elsevier Science Publishers B.V., 1989*

1. Introduction

In the early postwar period, pessimistic predictions were made as to the prospects for the transmission of economic growth from developed to developing countries. These predictions were translated into policy recommendations for import protection and the recommendations were followed by a number of developing countries during the period.

The experience of subsequent years provided evidence on the inappropriateness of the predictions that represented a form of historical determinism as far as the exports of the developing countries are concerned. Rather, it became apparent that the country's own policies play a crucial role in affecting export expansion and the prospects for economic growth.

Broadly speaking, one may distinguish between outward-oriented and inward-oriented strategies, when the former provides similar incentives to sales in domestic and in foreign markets and the latter discriminates in favor of import substitution and against exports. With the manufacturing sector being protected, inward orientation also involves a bias against primary production that is not found under outward orientation.

Section 2 of this chapter examines the propositions that have been put forward in regard to the role of external conditions in regard to export expansion and economic growth in developing countries. Subsection 2.1 analyzes the trade–growth nexus; Subsection 2.2 reviews empirical evidence on trends in the terms of trade; and Subsection 2.3 provides an appraisal of proposals made for joint action on the part of the developing countries.

Section 3 of the chapter focuses on individual country experiences. It examines the effects of alternative policies on exports and economic growth, with further consideration given to their impact on employment and income distribution. Subsection 3.1 concerns the early postwar period (1945–60), Subsection 3.2 the period of rapid world economic growth (1960–73), and Subsection 3.3 the decade of external shocks (1973–83).

The topics covered in this chapter represent various facets of the outward orientation–inward orientation controversy. At the same time, it has been attempted to minimize overlapping with Ronald Findlay's "Growth and development in trade models" and Anne Krueger's "Trade policies in developing countries", both of which appeared in the *Handbook of International Economics*, Volume I (1984), and with Henry Bruton's "Import Substitution", Chapter 30 in this Handbook.

2. International trade and economic growth

2.1. The export–growth nexus

2.1.1. Predictions on developing country exports

In borrowing an expression introduced by Sir Dennis Robertson, Ragnar Nurkse suggested that trade was the engine of growth during the nineteenth century as economic expansion from Western Europe, in particular the United Kingdom, was transmitted to countries on other continents through international exchange. He cited as evidence the fact that trade was increasing at a rate exceeding the growth of world production by a considerable margin.

Nurkse added that in the twentieth century, and especially after 1928, a marked slackening occurred in the expansion of world trade, with its growth rate falling behind that of world production. Thus, in the first Wicksell lecture, delivered in Stockholm in April 1959, he expressed the view that the "center [the industrial countries], in terms of real income per head, is advancing vigorously, but is not transmitting its own rate of growth to the rest of the world through a proportional increase in its demand for primary products" [Nurkse (1961, p. 294)].

The discussion was conducted in terms of demand for primary products; Nurkse tended to dismiss the possibilities for the developing countries to export manufactured goods by reference to an alleged discontinuity in the comparative cost scale, lack of skills in the developing countries, as well as the danger of protection in the industrial countries. Rather, he called for the parallel expansion of industries to provide for increases in domestic demand in the developing countries.

But, apart from temporary protection on infant industry grounds, Nurkse did not endorse industrial protection or other forms of interference with the process of international trade. In his view, "output expansion for domestic consumption can go ahead side by side with international specialization. It need not be a substitute for international specialization. It is a substitute rather for the growth transmission mechanism which for reasons indicated may not be as powerful today as it was in the nineteenth century" (1961, p. 257).

The alleged slow growth of demand for the developing countries' (the "periphery") primary exports on the part of the industrial countries (the "center") was also given emphasis in early work by Prebisch (1950), who applied to the developing countries the dollar shortage hypothesis that found its full expression in Hicks (1953). While the dollar shortage explanation was subsequently dropped and the thesis of the secular deterioration of the terms of trade (see Subsection 2.2) assumed importance in Prebisch's writings, he formulated the view that, at identical rates of economic growth, the periphery would develop a balance-of-payments deficit vis-à-vis the center, because its income elasticity of import demand is lower than that of the center [Prebisch (1959)].

As noted by Flanders (1964), Prebisch considered the policy choice for the developing countries was said to be growing less rapidly than the developed countries or taking measures to improve their balance of payments. Among possible measures, Prebisch rejected a devaluation on the grounds that foreign demand for the periphery's exports is price-inelastic and recommended import protection (export taxes) instead.[1] The call for protection was also echoed by Myrdal (1957), in whose view the income elasticity of import demand in the developing countries is further increased by the "demonstration effect" on their pattern of consumption emanating from the developed countries.

2.1.2. The role of policies in export growth

Under the assumption of complete specialization, with the developing countries exporting primary products and importing manufactured goods, Prebisch expected the export earnings of these countries to increase as their import protection drew away resources from the primary sector whose exports were said to face price-inelastic demand. Yet, Prebisch's own country, Argentina, is a par excellence case where a reduction in export volume led to losses in export market shares rather than to an increase in export earnings. Thus, as Nurkse (1966, p. 256) noted somewhat facetiously, "we are all indebted to Colonel Perón for an excellent demonstration of the loss which a country can suffer by sacrificing its traditional exports and hence its import capacity also".

As indicated in Subsection 2.3, with the principal exception of tropical beverages, this conclusion applies generally to primary commodities, exported by the developing countries, which compete with production in the developed countries and face price-elastic rather than price-inelastic demand. Yet, models of complete specialization are again in vogue as evidenced by the work of Bacha (1978), Findlay (1980), Chichilnisky (1981), Taylor (1981), and Vines (1984).

The policies advocated by Prebisch and Myrdal came to be widely applied by developing countries in the early postwar period, through the imposition of import protection on manufactured goods and export taxes on primary products.

---

[1] This argumentation neglects the elasticity of demand for the products of the center in the periphery. For a formalization of the argument in a model of complete specialization, see Johnson (1954).

The adverse effects of these measures on the export performance of the developing countries are indicated by aggregated as well as by disaggregated estimates.

Kravis (1970) showed that, after gaining export market shares in previous periods, developing countries lost market shares in both primary and in manufactured exports between 1953 and 1966. The losses were particularly large in primary exports that suffered the largest discrimination under the policies applied. Excluding fuels, the primary exports of the developing countries increased by 1.8 percent a year as against a rise of 5.7 percent a year for the developed countries during the period.

Among primary products, the losses in market shares were the largest in agricultural exports (cereals, meat, and oilseeds) between 1934–38 and 1959–60 [Porter (1970)]. These losses continued between 1959–61 and 1967–68, while developing countries achieved gains in nonagricultural raw materials, where domestic supply limitations led to a divergence between the growth of domestic demand and that of import demand in the developed countries, as well as in manufactured goods, where the adoption of outward-oriented policies in several developing countries led to increases in export market shares [Cohen and Sisler (1971)].

Kravis (1970) added that differential export performance among developing countries was linked to their success in increasing export market shares and diversifying exports which, in turn, were explained by the policies followed. Adams (1973), however, claimed that the intercountry pattern of changes in export market shares was due to differences in initial market shares, the commodity concentration of exports, their geographical concentration, and the rate of inflation, which are structurally given in the short-to-medium term rather than to differences in policies. Crafts (1973) also asserted that initial trade position importantly affects changes in export market shares and emphasized the role of foreign demand – as against domestic supply – in determining export performance.

In his reply, Kravis noted that none of the above variables is structurally given. He further showed that, in the first half of the 1960s, the introduction of initial trade position and export concentration variables does not add to the explanatory power of the regressions, which include the growth of external markets, changes in export market shares, and export diversification as variables explaining inter-country differences in export and GNP growth rates [Kravis (1973a, 1973b)]. His conclusion that the countries' own policies, rather than external factors, determine inter-country differences in export and economic performance was reconfirmed by subsequent work.

Thus, time series analysis of data for 27 developing countries in the period led to the conclusion that the country's own policies rather than external factors, dominated export growth in the developing countries. In particular, "the results are consistent with [the] hypothesis that export success is related to favorable internal factors influencing countries' abilities to compete and diversify" [Love (1984, p. 289)]. Further evidence on the issue is provided by data on individual countries reported in Subsection 3.2.

2.1.3. Prospects for the future

In examining the prospects of the developing countries for the future, in his Nobel Prize lecture Sir Arthur Lewis (1980) restated the pessimistic predictions put forward in the early postwar period. He suggested that while a 6 percent rate of economic growth in the developing countries would require a 6 percent rate of export growth, the imports of the developed countries would rise only 4 percent a year. Apart from the slowdown of economic growth in the developed countries after 1973, Lewis attributed the latter result to the historical relationship he claimed to have established between the growth of industrial production in the developed countries and world exports of primary products, in the form of an elasticity of 0.87.

Lewis further suggested that price inelastic demand on the part of the developed countries would lead to declines in the export earnings of the developing countries in the event of increases in export volumes, applies only to these products. However, as Riedel (1984) noted, this assumption applies best to traditional noncompeting tropical commodities (largely tropical beverages) that constitute a relatively small and declining share of developing country exports. For all other primary commodities, the developing countries are competing with the developed countries and, rather than there being a strict relationship between exports and developed country output, the outcome will depend on their own policies.

Riedel further considered the possibilities for expanding manufactured exports. This contrasts with Lewis's view, according to whom the main link between the two groups of countries has been through trade in primary products and, with a slowdown of industrial growth, the developed countries are more likely to take less rather than more manufactured goods from the developing countries.

A pessimistic view about the prospects for the exports of manufactured goods was also expressed by Cline (1982) in a paper with the provocative title: "Can the East Asian export model be generalized?". Cline gave a negative answer to the question he posed on the grounds that the corresponding expansion of manufactured exports would not be acceptable to the developed countries. According to his estimates, based on earlier analysis by Chenery and Syrquin, the manufactured exports of all other developing countries would have to increase sevenfold in order to match the East Asian ratio of manufactured exports to GNP, with allowance made for differences in population size and per capita incomes. Attaining this ratio, in turn, would necessitate raising the share of the developing countries in the manufactured imports of the seven major developed countries from 17 to 61 percent.

The prospects are less forbidding if one considers instead the share of the developing countries in the developed countries' consumption of manufactured goods. This share was approximately 1.3 percent in 1976, the year Cline's estimate refers to, in the developed countries, on the average [Balassa (1985b)]. The assumed increase in the manufactured exports of the developing countries would raise the ratio to 9.1 percent on the assumption that the consumption of manufactured goods in the developed countries remained unchanged. Yet, the introduction of lower-priced goods imported from the developing countries would tend to increase manufacturing consumption.

Rather than considering changes in market penetration ratios for all of manufacturing, Cline presents results for four-digit sectors established according to the International Standard Industrial Classification in cases when the developing countries would provide more than 15 percent of domestic consumption in the developed countries under the assumptions made. This calculation, however, neglects the fact that differences in factor endowments among developing countries lead to differences in the composition of their manufactured exports.

Nor can it be assumed that countries at varying levels of development, ranging from Mali to Israel, would attain the manufactured export norm of the four East Asian countries within a time period that has practical relevance for the problem at hand. Cline himself makes calculations for a limited group of seven countries (Argentina, Brazil, Colombia, Mexico, Indonesia, Israel, and Malaysia) he calls newly-industrializing, and obtains a fourfold increase in manufactured exports from the developing countries.

But the group includes Indonesia, which cannot be considered a newly-industrializing country, and whose petroleum and other natural resources should not lead to manufacturing export ratios even remotely resembling those of East Asian economies should it in fact reach such a status. More generally, there is no reason to assume that the adoption of outward-oriented policies would lead to identical shares of manufactured exports in all developing countries, for a given population size and per capita incomes. Thus, the East Asian economies are poor in natural resources and one can expect them to have a higher ratio of exports, in particular manufactured exports, to GNP than most other newly-industrializing developing countries.

An alternative approach involves considering the import requirements of economic growth in the developing countries. Following Lewis, assume for these countries a 6 percent target growth rate, an income elasticity of import demand of 1, and a 4 percent growth rate of primary exports to developed countries. Limiting attention to the non-OPEC developing countries, in whose exports manufactured goods had a share of 40 percent in 1983, a simple calculation will show that the import requirements of these countries postulated by Lewis will be met if their manufactured exports were to rise 9 percent a year.

This figure is substantially below the 13 percent rate of growth of manufactured exports from the developing to the developed countries during the 1973–83 period that was characterized by low growth in the latter group of countries. It would also give rise to much lower market penetration ratios than implied by Cline's estimate. Assuming that the consumption of manufactured goods in the developed countries grew at an average annual rate of 4 percent over a ten-year period, the market shares of the developing economies in their manufacturing consumption would increase from 2.3 percent in 1983 to 3.7 percent in 1993. And, even if the exports of manufactured goods from the developing countries to the developed countries rose by 12 percent a year, their market share in the latter's consumption of manufactured goods would not reach 5 percent after a decade.

At the same time, developing countries would use the additional foreign exchange generated through exports to increase their imports, thereby creating demand for the manufactured exports of the developed countries. If the balance of trade in manufactured goods did not change, industrial activity in the developed countries would not be affected in toto, while a reallocation would occur from relatively low-skill to high-skill industries where their comparative advantage lies.

Such a reallocation would take place over a long period, since policy changes in the developing countries, which are a precondition for the acceleration of their economic growth, would have an impact over time. Also, experience indicates that a growing part of the expansion of trade in manufactured goods between the developed countries and the newly-industrializing developing countries involves intra-industry rather than inter-industry specialization, in which case changes will occur in the product composition of the firm rather than in the industrial structure of the economy. This tendency is expected to accelerate in the future as developing countries attain higher levels of industrialization.

Cline's estimates further assume that developing countries would increase their exports of manufactured goods to other developing countries at the same rate as to the developed countries. But, apart from the period immediately following the Mexican financial crisis of August 1982, developing country exports of manufactured goods to developing country markets have been rising more rapidly than to the developed countries. The continuation of this trend may be expected in the future. For one thing, higher economic growth rates in the developing countries will lead to more rapid increases in their demand for manufactured imports than in the developed countries. For another thing, with their increased degree of economic sophistication, the newly-industrializing countries can supply the needs of countries at lower levels of development in an increasing array of commodities.

2.2. The terms of trade issue

2.2.1. The secular deterioration of the terms of trade thesis

Prebisch (1950) and Singer (1950) simultaneously put forward the view that the (commodity) terms of trade of the developing countries have the tendency to deteriorate over time.[2] This secular deterioration was attributed to differences in the process of adjustment to technical progress. While in the developed countries productivity improvements were said to be translated into higher wages, in the developing countries labor supply pressure was said to keep wages unchanged, thus leading to lower prices. Correspondingly, Prebisch claimed that "the great industrial centers not only kept for themselves the benefit of the use of new techniques in their own economy, but are in a favorable position to obtain a share of that deriving from the technical progress of the periphery" (1950, p. 14).

In support of this proposition, Prebisch (1950) presented calculations on the British terms of trade for the 1876–80 to 1946–47 period. He interpreted the apparent improvement in the terms of trade of the United Kingdom, an exporter of manufactured goods and importer of primary products, as implying the secular deterioration of the terms of trade of the developing countries.

In a retrospective evaluation, Singer asserted that "treated as a projection, one can certainly claim that [the secular deterioration of the terms of trade thesis] has passed the test better than most other economic projections" [Singer (1984, p. 282)]. In support of this proposition, Singer cited data for the post-1950 period, with the exclusion of petroleum after 1973.

The results for a relatively short period are, however, affected to a considerable extent by the choice of the initial and the terminal years. Thus, the results cited by Singer were much affected by the fact that 1950 was a year of very high primary product prices following the onset of the Korean war[3] while increases in petroleum prices in 1973–74 contributed to the decline in the prices of nonfuel primary products through their adverse effects on world economic activity.

At any rate, just as Prebisch had done, in his 1950 paper Singer considered long-term tendencies; hence, in judging the validity of his and Prebisch's proposition, data for a longer period are needed. In the 1984 paper, Singer cited

---

[2] From the welfare point of view, it is double-factoral terms of trade (i.e. the commodity terms of trade adjusted for changes in productivity in the production of traded goods) rather than the commodity terms of trade that is relevant. However, in keeping with the Prebisch–Singer analysis, this chapter will not consider the double-factoral terms of trade for which statistical information is not available in any case.

[3] In an earlier defense of the secular deterioration of the terms of trade thesis, Baer (1962) provided data on changes in the terms of trade of primary products until 1947–48 and from 1950 onwards without, however, taking note of the rapid rise of primary product prices that occurred between the two dates.

estimates made by Spraos (1980) for the 1900–70 period.[4] He claimed that, "even if the individual trends [Spraos] calculates are statistically insignificant when taken one by one, the fact that they all point in the same direction surely adds significance" [Singer (1984, p. 291)].

However, the individual results do not point in the same direction. The trend coefficient derived by the use of the U.N. index is positive, representing a terms of trade improvement for the developing countries; a negative result is obtained only if the U.N. index is spliced to the World Bank's index for the postwar period. We thus have a positive and a negative result, neither of them statistically significant, which hardly establishes a trend.[5]

Spraos further presented estimates on the terms of trade of primary products vis-à-vis manufactured goods for the 1871–1938 period. These estimates show a deterioration in the terms of trade for primary products, albeit the extent of the deterioration is only about one-half of that shown by the terms of trade index Prebisch utilized. And, the extent of the deterioration decreases again by nearly one-half if 1929 is taken as the terminal year, with an average annual rate of decline of 0.3 percent estimated by Sir Arthur Lewis (1952) whose results Spraos considers more reliable than competing estimates.

The results indicate the importance of the choice of the benchmark years. The extent of deterioration is smaller if 1929 rather than 1938 is taken as the terminal year since, due to the world depression, primary product prices were particularly low in the latter year. In turn, the early 1870s represented a relatively favorable stage of the business cycle. At the same time, apart from the choice of the benchmark years, several questions arise regard to the validity of the estimates for judging trends in the terms of trade of the developing countries.

2.2.2. The terms of trade controversy

All the reported estimates pertain to the terms of trade of primary commodities vs. manufactured goods. The question has been raised if these calculations are indicative of the terms of trade of the developing vs. the developed countries, when both countries export primary as well as manufactured products.

Spraos (1980) cited calculations made by Lipsey (1963) on improvements in the U.S. terms of trade and by Kindleberger (1956) on the relative decline of the

---

[4]Apart from adding a reference to Kravis and Lipsey (1971), the article was reproduced in a virtually unchanged form in Spraos's later book (1983).

[5]Spraos noted that combining the U.N. index with the one constructed by Yates (1959) for the 1913–53 period would give rise to an upward adjustment in the prices of manufactured goods. He added, however, that Yates considered his unit value index for manufactured goods to be of low reliability and that utilizing the index developed by Maizels (1963) would involve an adjustment of identical magnitude in the opposite direction.

prices of primary products imported by European countries as indirect evidence of adverse changes in the terms of trade of the developing countries, adding however that the estimates are subject to considerable error. He also cited Maizels' (1963) results, according to which trends in primary product prices had been practically identical for the exports of both developing and developed countries in the 1899–1937 period.

Subsection 2.2.3 presents more recent estimates which also include manufactured goods that were neglected in earlier work. Prior to that, two too much-debated issues require attention: the implications for the results of changes in transportation costs and in the quality and composition of manufactured exports.

The estimate cited by Prebisch utilized the U.K. import unit value index to represent the prices of primary products and the U.K. export index to represent the prices of manufactured goods. This procedure has been criticized on the grounds that it fails to consider decreases in transportation costs. Thus, with the terms of trade being measured as the ratio of fob export unit values to cif import unit values, reductions in the cost of transportation may lead to improvements in the so measured terms of trade of all the trading partners. In fact, Ellsworth (1956) provided evidence that the entire improvement in the terms of trade of the United Kingdom between 1876 and 1905 is explained by the decline in the transportation costs of primary products, and the terms of trade of primary producing countries may have even slightly improved during this period. At the same time, improvements in the productivity of transportation services originated in the developed countries.

These observations also apply to the estimates of other authors who relied on fob export and cif import unit value indices. Spraos, however, argued that the resulting bias in the results might have been cancelled by subsequent increases in transportation costs. But while Isserlis's (1938) estimates of tramp shipping freight support Spraos's contention, Kindleberger's (1956) freight index, constructed subsequently and representing more reliable estimates, show that increases in transportation costs in the later period made up only one-half of the earlier decline.

Subsequently, Bairoch (1975) suggested that the decline in the difference between the cif value of the world imports of primary products and the fob value of the world exports of these products from 23 percent in 1976–80 to 10 percent in 1926–29 indicates the existence of a valuation bias in the terms of trade indices due to decreases in transportation costs. The conclusion was queried by Spraos on the grounds that the cif–fob differential covers also factors other than freight and insurance costs, in particular the underestimation of exports. But, this point would be relevant only if it could be established that the underestimation of exports declined over time, an issue Spraos failed to consider.

Data on transport costs for a longer period are available for pig iron. It has been estimated that while in the second half of the eighteenth century the cost of transporting pig iron across the Atlantic was 18–29 percent of the fob export price in New York, the ratio declined to 11 percent by the mid-1970s [Balassa (1977)]. These comparisons are of particular interest as they relate to a standardized commodity, and hence are not affected by changes in the composition of trade. And, although transportation costs may vary to a considerable extent, depending on the direction of trade, this will not affect the conclusion as to the decline in transportation costs over time.

The view has further been expressed that quality improvements and the introduction of new products result in an upward bias of the unit value index for manufactured goods, which does not exist in regard to primary commodities. As Haberler (1961, p. 282) put it: "copper remains copper, cotton remains cotton, and wheat remains wheat, while an automobile, a rubber tire, a radio, an antibiotic, either did not exist at all or was entirely different, less durable, and infinitely less serviceable commodity in earlier periods".

While accepting the view that improvements in quality rarely occur in the case of primary products, Spraos suggested that their export composition will change over time, with higher-quality varieties replacing the lower quality ones. "Perhaps more important [he added] than any of these is the processing of primary products before shipment (for instance, cocoa beans turned into cocoa butter and cocoa paste) which has been increasing all the time, though in developing countries it had gained great momentum only in the last twenty years" [Spraos (1980, pp. 117–118)].

Spraos further suggested that quality deterioration may occur in manufactured goods and that quality improvements in these products may be related to improvements in their primary inputs. He also cited evidence from German and U.S. studies as to the lack of differences between unit value and genuine price indices for manufactured goods in the 1968–74 and 1965–70 periods, respectively.

All in all, Spraos reached the agnostic conclusion that "if quality improvements are liable to be under-allowed on both sides, no presumption can be established in the abstract regarding a systematic bias in terms of trade from this source" (1980, p. 118). Subsequently, Singer claimed that Spraos "has shown convincingly that these difficulties of measurement do not go to the heart of the matter, even empirically" [Singer (1984, p. 286)].

However, the processing of primary commodities is irrelevant for the problem at hand, since unit value indices of primary commodities include unprocessed but not processed goods. At any rate, as Spraos himself noted, the exportation of processed commodities by developing countries is a recent phenomenon. The same comment applies to the upgrading of primary commodities; in fact, all Spraos's examples pertain to the post-Second World War period. At the same time, as noted in Subsection 2.2.3 below, for this period a genuine price index for primary products is available that has been constructed by using prices for specific grades of commodities.

In turn, the unit value index for manufactured goods is customarily derived as a ratio of value to weight. Now, apart from quality improvements and changes in product composition referred to earlier, a bias is introduced due to the shift over time from heavier to lighter materials. This shift is unrelated to changes in the quality of primary inputs since it is due to substitution among such inputs.

These considerations are particularly relevant to machinery and transport equipment where increased sophistication as well as the shift from steel to aluminum and, again, to plastics raised the ratio of value to weight. Confirmation of this tendency was provided by Kravis and Lipsey (1971) whose monumental work was overlooked by Singer. Supplementing data for Germany and the United States referred to above by data for the United Kingdom and Japan, Kravis and Lipsey established that the average price index for machinery and equipment exported by these countries increased by 13 percent between 1953 and 1964, compared with a 24 percent rise in the U.N. unit value index for these commodities indicating the upward bias of the unit value indices.

2.2.3. Recent evidence on the terms of trade

Kravis and Lipsey subsequently extended the country, commodity, and time coverage of their earlier investigation and estimated a price index for manufactured goods exported by the developed countries to the developing countries. The index shows a 127 percent increase between 1953 and 1977, the time period covered by the estimates, compared with a rise of 162 percent in the U.N. unit value index for these exports. Deflating by the U.N. price index for the world exports of primary products other than petroleum, the authors found that the terms of trade of manufactured goods exported by the developed to the developing countries, relative to the prices of nonfuel primary products, declined by 6 percent during the period. This contrasts with an increase of 13 percent estimated from the U.N. unit value indices for manufactured goods and for food and raw materials.

Balassa (1984c) adjusted the Kravis–Lipsey estimates by replacing the U.N. price index for the world exports of primary commodities other than petroleum by the price index estimated by the World Bank for thirty-three nonfuel primary commodities, weighted by the exports of the developing countries. The index shows an average price increase of 154 percent for these primary products between 1953 and 1977, compared with an increase of 145 percent in the U.N. index.

Utilizing the World Bank's index, we observe a decline of 10 percent in the terms of trade of the developed countries in their exchange of manufactured goods for primary products other than fuels with the developing countries during the 1953–77 period. An even larger decline is shown if adjustment is made for quality changes that are not reflected in the cited price index. In the case of the United States, for which Kravis and Lipsey made such estimates, a 105 percent rise in the unadjusted price index for machinery and transport equipment in 1953–77 gives place to a 77 percent increase in the adjusted index. If this result applied to all manufactured goods exported by the developed countries the decline in their terms of trade would be 22 rather than 10 percent.

Changes in relative prices between 1977 and 1985 may have offset the improvements in the terms of trade of the developing countries that occurred during the previous quarter of a century.[6] But, the results are again affected by the choice of the terminal years.

The comparison of the U.N. and the World Bank indices points to the conclusion that the prices of nonfuel primary products exported by the developing countries rose more rapidly than average world primary product prices during the period under consideration. This conclusion was confirmed by Michaely's (1985) estimates that showed unit value indices for primary products exported by low-income countries to have risen by 27 percent between 1952 and 1970, compared with an increase of 10 percent for primary products exported by high-income countries. Michaely's results further showed a 27 percent improvement in the terms of trade for primary products in the case of low-income countries, compared with a 23 percent deterioration for high-income countries, during this period.[7]

The unit values of manufactured goods exported by low-income countries also increased more rapidly (45 percent) than those exported by high-income countries (19 percent) between 1952 and 1970. In the same period, the terms of trade for manufactured goods improved by 14 percent in low-income countries and deteriorated by 12 percent in high-income countries.

For all merchandise trade, taken together, Michaely observed an improvement of 19 percent in the terms of trade for the low-income countries, and a deterioration of 15 percent for the high-income countries, during the 1952–70 period. He further established that terms of trade changes were negatively

---

[6] Between 1977 and 1985, the U.N. unit value index for manufactured goods exported by the developed countries increased by 23 percent. Assuming that the extent of the bias in the unit value index was the same as in the 1953–77 period, the increase in the prices of manufactured goods exported by the developed countries would be estimated at 11 percent, with a further downward adjustment needed for quality changes. In turn, the World Bank's price index for the nonfuel primary exports of developing countries declined by 12 percent. At the same time, the U.N. unit value index of manufactured goods exported by the developing countries, which came to exceed their nonfuel exports, rose by 22 percent.

[7] More exactly, the calculations pertain to price changes for goods classified by income level, when the income level of exports (imports) is derived as an income-weighted average of exports by individual countries. The cited results refer to data for the lower half and the upper half of the distribution. The relevant formulas are provided in Michaely (1985).

correlated with income levels in a fivefold classification scheme; the changes between 1952 and 1970 were -26, -11, -8, $+11$, and $+47$ percent as one moves from the top to the bottom quintile.

Michaely's results thus reinforce the findings of Kravis and Lipsey, indicating that the developing countries improved their terms of trade relative to the developed countries in the post-Korean war period. It is further observed that primary and manufactured commodities exported by the developing countries increased more in price than goods in the same categories exported by the developed countries and that improvements in the terms of trade were inversely correlated with the level of economic development.

These results pertain to the post-Korean war period, which begins with high primary product prices as noted above. Kravis and Lipsey (1984) further calculated changes in the terms of trade between "Industrial Europe" and the developing countries for the 1872–1953 period, by replacing the world export unit value indices of the United Nations with unit value indices for the manufactured exports of Industrial Europe to the developing countries. The results show no change in the terms of trade of Industrial Europe relative to the developing countries between 1872 and 1953. In view of the upward bias of the unit value for manufactured goods, it follows that the use of price indices would show a deterioration in the terms of trade of Industrial Europe, and an improvement in the terms of trade of the developing countries, during this period.

The reported findings disprove the contentions of Prebisch and Singer as to the alleged secular deterioration of the terms of trade of the developing countries. This conclusion is strengthened if account is taken of the growth of manufactured exports by the developing countries and of primary exports by the developed countries that is neglected in conventional calculations of the terms of trade between the two groups of countries. At the same time, the terms of trade may fluctuate to a considerable extent in shorter periods, reflecting the effects of changes in business cycles and other influences, such as major wars.

2.3. The developing countries in the world economy

2.3.1. Possibilities for joint action

Prebisch and Singer used the alleged tendency for the secular deterioration of the terms of trade of the developing countries as an argument for monopolistic action by these countries. The lack of such a tendency does not exclude, however, the exploitation of the monopoly power developing countries may possess in regard to particular commodities which face inelastic demand in the developed countries.

Following the quadrupling of petroleum prices by OPEC, Bergsten (1974) expressed the view that this should not represent a unique case, and that developing countries could form cartels in regard to other commodities as well. Apart from a number of minor commodities, he considered copper, tin, bauxite, phosphates, rubber, tropical timber, coffee, tea, cocoa, and bananas as prime candidates for cartellization. Mikesell (1974), however, raised doubts about the possibilities for developing countries to establish effective cartels for metals, with the conceivable exception of bauxite.

According to Johnson (1968), developing countries that have monopoly power in particular export markets may pursue the following objectives: maximizing export revenue, maximizing profits, maximizing national gain, and maximizing consumption. The first two of these objectives were considered by Radetzki (1975) in the case of copper.

On the bias of assumptions made in regard to demand and supply elasticities in developing and in developed countries, Radetzki concluded that in raising prices by 10 percent through joint production cuts, developing countries would find their combined export revenue lowered by ever-increasing amounts while the rise of profit rates in the first three years would be offset by subsequent losses. These conclusions are said to follow because of the importance of scrap and the availability of highly-competitive substitutes for copper.

Correspondingly, according to Radetzki (1975, p. 53): "the best longer-term policy for copper exporting developing countries would be to accept lower prices and to increase their market share through an aggressive policy of capacity expansion, which would push high cost producers out of business". He subsequently confirmed this conclusion by showing that, during the 1960–74 period, the profits accruing to developing country copper producers would have increased substantially if these countries doubled the rate of growth of output [Radetski (1977)].

Radetski's estimate did not allow for the depletion of an exhaustible resource. This was introduced by Pindyck (1978) who estimated that, acting as a collective monopoly, the copper-exporting developing countries could increase the discounted value of their profits by 8 or 30 percent, depending on the discount rate used. However, this outcome would require large fluctuations in the monopolistically-determined price that consuming countries could anticipate and counteract through stockpiling. Pindyck accordingly concluded that there was little incentive for the copper-exporting developing countries to follow a unified policy of pricing and production.

The negative conclusions reached by Pindyck on the desirability of monopolistic action on the part of the copper-exporting developing countries is strengthened if we consider that he only took account of proven reserves while new reserves are continuously being found. Also, Pindyck appears to have underestimated the possibilities for expansion by competing suppliers and the substitution of other materials for copper.

In the case of bauxite, too, Pindyck used proven rather than potential reserves in his calculations. At the same time, it is of interest to observe that the actual price of bauxite differs little from the estimated monopoly price. Yet, despite Pindyck's reference to cartel-type action, there is no evidence of the operation of a bauxite cartel.

Pindyck further estimated that monopolistic action by OPEC may raise the discounted value of profits by 50–100 percent. For various reasons, this estimate is subject to a serious upward bias. It is again based on estimates of proven rather than potential reserves; it assumes long-term price elasticities of 0.35 under the competitive price of $6 per barrel in constant 1975 dollars and 0.52 if the price is doubled, which are much lower than estimate elasticities for the post-1973 period; and it does not sufficiently allow for the emergence of new suppliers.

In fact, OPEC's share in world petroleum production declined from 68 percent in 1973 to 40 percent in 1985. Also, the price per barrel fell from its peak of $34 in 1980 to $13 in February 1986 under the pressure of competition from other suppliers and the desire on the part of each OPEC country to increase its petroleum earnings with only a small increase to $15 per barrel by the end of the year.

The last point leads to the conditions that need to be fulfilled for collusive behavior to be effective. According to Stern and Tims (1975), the principal such conditions include the domination of the markets by a small number of suppliers, the existence of common interest among them, the essentiality of the commodity, the lack of competing suppliers in the developed countries, and limited possibilities for substitution.

Essentiality is an important characteristic of strategic metals, including chromium, cobalt, manganese, niobium, tungsten, and vanadium, all of which face inelastic demand when taken individually and whose output is dominated by a few producers. However, there is substitution among these metals and the benefits of a cartel encompassing all of them would be small while the problems of coordination would be considerable since twelve countries would need to participate [Radetzki (1984)].

Among the commodities listed by Bergsten, which were not considered so far, tin and rubber have good substitutes and phosphates are produced in the developed countries as well. There remain coffee, tea, and cocoa, tropical timber, and bananas, where developing country producers are the only suppliers. And while coffee and tea face very low demand elasticities, cocoa has substitutes in chocolate manufacturing, bananas compete with other fruits, and tropical timber competes with timber from temperate zone forests.

Thus far, there have been no successful cartels in these commodities although the International Coffee Agreement, designed to stabilize coffee prices, may have raised prices somewhat as the two largest producers, Brazil and Colombia, were willing to reduce their output share. Such reductions were not accepted by India and Sri Lanka, the two largest producers of tea, where six producers account for

70 percent of world exports. Nor has agreement on production quotas been reached in the case of cocoa, bananas, and tropical timber where 4, 9, and 6 developing country producers account for 70 percent of world exports, respectively.

2.3.2. Delinking

The discussion in Subsection 2.3.1 indicated the limitations of monopolistic action on the part of developing countries. At the same time, in cases when the conditions for cartellization are fulfilled, developing countries may increase welfare by imposing optimal export taxes to limit production and exports without otherwise interfering with the system of incentives [Balassa (1978a)].

While monopolistic action represents the exploitation of possibilities offered by the world trading system, delinking means reducing or, in an extreme case, severing links with this system. The idea of delinking first gained currency in the Soviet Union, where it was considered to be a condition for full independence and for eliminating the repercussions of business cycles emanating from the capitalist countries.

In fact, complete delinking was never attained by the Soviet Union which wished to exploit the benefits of trade with the developed capitalist countries. Also, having reduced to a considerable extent trade with the West in the years immediately following the Second World War, the countries of Eastern Europe have since endeavored again to increase such ties. In particular, the Minister of Planning and Deputy Prime Minister of Hungary indicated that increasing exports to the developed capitalist countries is the principal objective of medium-term economic policy [Faluvégi (1984)].

In the literature on developing countries, the advocates of complete delinking considered this to be the logical conclusion of the alleged impossibility of economic development in the capitalist world-system and suggest it as a permanent [Amin (1977)] or a temporary [Senghaas (1980)] solution. Others advocated partial delinking through the imposition of extensive import controls.

In searching for actual cases of delinking, the proponents of such a policy tend to refer to China, Cambodia, Cuba, North Vietnam, and Tanzania. But the experience of these countries hardly supports a policy of delinking. To begin with, its high economic costs have led the Chinese government to reject this policy and importantly to increase international exchange. And, while the consequences of delinking and of political oppression are difficult to separate in the case of Cambodia, political oppression is a pre-condition for making delinking effective. Also, exchanging links with capitalist countries for links with socialist countries has meant that Cuba has been unable to exploit the advantages offered by its educated labor force [Balassa (1986b)].

Virtual delinking from developed capitalist countries appears to have been largely responsible for North Korea increasingly losing ground in competition with South Korea. Thus, while in 1960 per capita incomes in the North were one-half higher than in the South, two decades later South Korea surpassed North Korea's income level by a considerable margin [World Bank (1981)].

Finally, Tanzania has practiced selective delinking through import controls, with unfavorable economic results [Balassa (1985b)]. More generally, socialist countries in sub-Saharan Africa that have, to a greater or lesser extent, engaged in selective delinking had greatly inferior performance than countries of the area that continued to participate in the international division of labor [Balassa (1984b)].

2.3.3. Trade among developing countries

On the whole, one may agree with Diaz-Alejandro (1978, p. 88) that "the case for delinking is primarily political and sociological rather than economic...". The statement made by the same author that "a global international economic order allowing for selective delinking should reduce friction between South and North..." (1978, p. 158), in turn, leads to the question of preferential trade among developing countries.

One form of preferential trade arrangements, sanctioned by GATT, is the establishment of regional common markets and free trade areas. While such arrangements have been successful in the developed countries, this has not been the case in the developing countries. Lewis (1980) gives several reasons for this outcome.

First, the region is not a homogeneous area and there may be considerable differences in the level of industrial development among the countries concerned. Countries at higher levels of development may then attract more industries than less advanced countries that feel exploited by the former. Such differences have largely been responsible for the demise of the East African Common Market, and real or assumed disparities in the allocation of benefits from integration have also contributed to the regression of the Central American Common Market.

Second, countries objected competition from partner countries in the fear that this may adversely affect their own industries. Such may be the case, in particular, for relatively simple industries that each developing country wishes to retain. Third, decreases in transportation costs have reduced the attractiveness of trading with neighboring countries.

The above considerations have led Lewis to advocate trade among developing countries in a world-wide context. The question is, then, as to how such trade may be promoted. Under the heading of collective self-reliance, proposals have been made for the developing countries to extend mutual preferences among themselves.

One may consider the delinking of developing countries from the developed economies as an extreme form of collective self-reliance. In fact, Amin suggested the need for the developing countries to establish a new world system, independent from the capitalist one. He further claimed that such a new world system cannot be based on the market, but would rather require planning [Amin (1974, p. 33)].

As it is difficult to imagine planning on the world level, the proponents of collective self-reliance generally posited the need for a scheme of preferences among developing countries [Haq (1976)]. However, for various reasons, these propositions have not been followed up in practice.

To begin with, a world-wide preference scheme among developing countries would bring together countries whose level of industrialization varies greatly. Correspondingly, the fears as to the consequences of economic disparities among the partner countries may be even greater than in the regional context.

The lack of information on faraway countries adds to these fears. Thus, while countries will have information on the economic potential of their neighbors, they will rarely possess such information on countries in other regions, thereby augmenting uncertainty as to possible adverse effects for their industries.

Finally, developing countries are reluctant to offer preferences to other developing countries that would involve buying commodities at higher prices than the prices of commodities imported from the developed countries. At the same time, in view of the relatively small markets of the developing countries, the preferences received may be considered to have less value to them than exporting to the larger markets of the developed countries.

These considerations support Lewis's proposition that the route towards increased trade among the developing countries is through offering goods to each other on a competitive basis. This recommendation, in turn, leads to the choice of appropriate policies in a national context that is the subject of Section 3 of this chapter.

3. Country experiences with outward orientation

3.1. The experience of the early postwar period (1945–60)

3.1.1. From the staple theory of export-led growth to the exportable surplus approach

As cited in Subsection 2.1.1, Nurkse considered the nineteenth century to have been a period of export-led growth in the newly-developing areas. This explanation was questioned by Kravis (1970) who found little evidence for the existence of a positive relationship between exports and economic growth in the United States. However, Kravis's data begin in 1834 and, for earlier periods, North (1961) provided evidence on the importance of exports for U.S. economic growth.

Also, Caves (1965, p. 426) concluded that "statistical and descriptive analysis of several 'regions of recent settlement' such as Canada, Australia, New Zealand, and South Africa make it clear that through much of their history the export sector has provided the primary source of disturbances to the economy". Economic growth, in turn, was much affected by the magnitude and the direction of the "disturbances".

Although Nurkse reached similar conclusions as far as these temperate zone areas are concerned, he expressed the view that the tropical countries remained outsiders, "being relatively neglected in the process of transmission of economic growth" [Nurkse (1961, p. 289)]. Arthur Lewis, however, suggested that, through growing trade, "the tropics were transformed during the period 1880 to 1913" [Lewis (1969, p. 12)]. This conclusion is supported by Leff's (1973) analysis of the experience of Brazil, one of the largest tropical countries, which had earlier been cited as a classic instance of the failure of export expansion to lead to economic development [Kindleberger (1953, p. 375)].

Leff noted that the growth in export receipts "was perhaps the major source of income growth in an otherwise relatively stagnant economy" [Leff (1973, p. 691)]. Increases in exports raised incomes directly as well as indirectly, with incomes generated in the export sector creating demand for domestically-produced manufactured goods and primary products. Also, railway construction associated with export expansion stimulated growth in the domestic agricultural sector. However, the size of the overall benefits to the Brazilian economy was limited by the relatively low share of exports in domestic output, characteristic of large countries and by the relatively slow growth of exports, owing to the emergence of new competitors in cotton and sugar.

In Brazil, a land-abundant country, immigration contributed to the growth of exports. In India, another large tropical country, abundant labor supplies became an important source of exports. The latter case was generalized by Myint (1955) in an application of the vent-for-surplus theory, which puts emphasis on the utilization of a country's labor surplus through exports, and its contribution to economic growth.

The growth effects of primary exports were categorized by Watkins (1963), who applied Hirschman's (1958) terminology to the "staple theory" of economic growth initiated by Innis (1957), when staples refer to resource-intensive exports. First, export expansion engenders backward linkages by creating demand for transportation facilities and for domestically-produced inputs. Second, an impetus is provided for the establishment of processing activities. Third, there is a final demand linkage as increased incomes in the export sector create demand for domestically-produced consumer goods.

The extent of the transmission of economic growth from the export sector to the rest of the economy will vary positively with size of the export sector and the rate of growth of exports and negatively with the relative importance of foreign ownership in production for export. Other factors that bear on this relationship include the use of skilled vs. unskilled labor, the capital intensity of the production process, and economies of scale in export production; the transportation requirements of exports; the availability of underutilized factors in the rest of the economy; the level of entrepreneurial skills; and the distribution of incomes [Caves (1965, pp. 433–437)].

While students of nineteenth-century economic history have come to emphasize the effects of exports on economic growth, in earlier periods exports had often been considered undesirable on account of the ensuing decline in the availability of goods for domestic consumption [Schumpeter (1954, pp. 369–374)]. This idea rarely made its appearance in subsequent periods in the present-day developed countries, except in war-time and in cases of short-term shortages (e.g. the limitations imposed on soybean exports by the United States in the mid-1970s). It was, however, espoused in several developing countries during the early postwar years.

According to Leff, in the years following the Second World War, the Brazilian government applied the "exportable surplus" approach to international trade, under which "a country exports only the 'surplus' which is 'left over' after the domestic market has been 'adequately' supplied" [Leff (1967, p. 289)]. This approach is also said to have been utilized in India [Cohen (1964)] and, for particular commodities, such as rice, in Egypt and Thailand [Leff (1969, pp. 346–347)].

The exportable surplus approach neglects the adverse effects of export limitations on import capacity and fails to consider the advantages a country can derive from resource allocation according to comparative advantage. It reflects the assumption that the supply of exportable products is price-inelastic, so that increases in exports would reduce the availability, and increase the price, of products for domestic use.

While starting out from different premises, this approach rejoins that of Prebisch and Myrdal on the desirability of limiting exports in developing countries. But, whereas Prebisch and Myrdal focused on the case when the commodity is exported but it is not consumed domestically, the exportable surplus theory pertains to the case of commodities that are both exported and consumed domestically.

Interpreted in a more general sense, the "exportable surplus" theory also includes the case when countries keep prices low in order to benefit consumers, thereby discouraging domestic production and encouraging the shift of resources from export activities to production for domestic needs. In recent years, several developing countries have taken such action.

These policies may be considered as part of an inward-oriented development strategy that discriminates in favor of import substitution and against export industries and, within individual industries, in favor of import substitution and against exports (in short, an anti-export bias). In Balassa and Associates (1971), this bias was interpreted to mean negative effective protection of value added in export activities. In turn, outward orientation was defined as neutrality in the system of incentives, with effective rates of protection being, on the average, approximately equal in import substituting and in export activities. The asymmetry in the definition corresponds to a real life situation as a considerable number of developing counties bias their system of incentives against exports whereas others tend to approximate neutrality without there being cases of the opposite bias.

3.1.2. Policies in free market and socialist economies[8]

Responding to the ideas of Prebisch and Myrdal, an inward-oriented development strategy found application in several developing countries during the early postwar period. Such a strategy was also applied in socialist countries in Central and Eastern Europe that followed the example of the Soviet Union in attempting to reduce reliance on the outside world. Although the measures applied may have differed between the two groups of countries, their overall policy orientation was similar; they contrast with the case of several Northern European countries that adopted an outward-oriented development strategy at the time.

To begin with, inward-oriented countries protected their industries against foreign competition. In market economies, this was done by using a mixture of tariffs and import controls, whereas socialist countries relied on import prohibitions. At the same time, while the infant industry argument calls for temporary protection until industries become internationally competitive, in both groups of countries protection was regarded as permanent and there was a tendency towards what has been described as "import substitution at any cost" by Prebisch.

Furthermore, in all the countries concerned, there were considerable variations in rates of explicit and implicit protection among industrial activities. This was the case, first of all, as continued import substitution involved undertaking activities with increasingly high domestic resource costs per unit of foreign exchange saved. In market economies, the generally uncritical acceptance of demands for protection contributed to this result and, in the absence of international price comparisons, the protective effects of quantitative restrictions could

---

[8] This section draws on Balassa (1970), where appropriate references are provided.

not even be established. In socialist countries the aim was to limit imports to commodities that could not be produced domestically, or were not available in sufficient quantities, and no attempt was made to gauge the extent and the cost of protection the pursuit of this objective entailed.

In both groups of countries the neglect of inter-industry relationships further increased the dispersion of protection rates on value added in processing, or effective protection, with adverse effects on economic efficiency. In Argentina, for example, high tariffs imposed on caustic soda at the request of a would-be producer made the theretofore thriving soap exports unprofitable. In Hungary, the high cost of domestic steel, produced largely from imported iron ore and coking coal, raised costs for steel-using industries while the large investments made in the steel industry delayed the substitution of aluminum for steel, although Hungary possesses considerable bauxite reserves.

Countries applying inward-oriented development strategies were further characterized by the prevalence of sellers' markets. In market economies, the size of national markets limited the possibilities for domestic competition while import competition was virtually excluded by high protection. In socialist countries, the system of central planning applied did not permit competition among domestic firms, or from imports, and buyers had no choice among domestic producers, or access to imported commodities.

The existence of sellers' markets provided little incentive for catering to the users' needs. In the case of industrial users, it led to backward integration as producers undertook the manufacture of parts, components, and accessories in order to minimize supply difficulties. This outcome, observed in market as well as in socialist economies, increased production costs, since economies of scale in the production of these inputs were forgone.

Also, in sellers' markets, firms had little incentive to improve productivity. In market economies, monopolies and oligopolies assumed importance, and the oligopolists often aimed at maintaining market shares while refraining from actions that would invoke retaliation. In socialist countries, the existence of assured outlets and the emphasis on short-term objectives on the part of managers discouraged technological change.

The managers' emphasis on short-term objectives in socialist countries had to do with uncertainty as to the planners' future intentions and the length of their own tenure. In market economies, fluctuations in real exchange rates (nominal exchange rates, adjusted for changes in inflation rates at home and abroad) creased uncertainty for business decisions. These fluctuations, resulting from intermittent devaluations in the face of domestic inflation, reinforced the adverse effects of the bias against exports as the domestic currency equivalent of export earnings varied with the devaluations, the timing of which was uncertain.

In inward-oriented countries, distortions were often apparent in the valuation of time. In market economies, negative real interest rates adversely affected domestic savings, encouraged self-investment, including inventory accumulation, at low returns, and provided inducements for the transfer of funds abroad (McKinnon). Negative real interest rates also led to credit rationing that generally favored import-substituting investments, irrespective of whether rationing was done by the banks or by the government. In the first case, the lower risk of investments in production for domestic, as compared to export, markets gave rise to such a result; in the second case, it reflected government priorities. In turn, in socialist countries, ideological considerations led to the exclusion of interest rates as a charge for capital and as an element in the evaluation of investment projects.

There was also a tendency to underprice public utilities in countries following an inward-oriented strategy, either because of low interest charges in these capital-intensive activities or as a result of conscious decisions. The underpricing of utilities benefited especially energy-intensive industries and promoted the use of capital.

In general, countries applying inward-oriented development strategies de-emphasized the role of prices in the allocation process. In socialist countries, resources were in large part allocated centrally in physical terms; in market economies, output and input prices were distorted and reliance was placed on nonprice measures of import restrictions and credit allocation. A possible explanation is that while price distortions would interfere with the exploitation of the possibilities available in international markets if an outward-oriented strategy is applied, such is not the case under inward orientation.

The described policies were exemplified by the experience of Argentina and Chile among market economies and that of Czechoslovakia and Hungary among socialist countries. In turn, Denmark and Norway provided examples of outward orientation in the early postwar period. The latter two countries not only eliminated quantitative import restrictions but reduced tariffs below the levels observed in the developed countries, with little inter-industry differences in tariff rates. They also adopted realistic exchange rates and interest rates.

3.1.3. Effects on exports and economic growth

Discrimination against exports did not permit the development of manufactured exports in countries that adopted an inward-oriented development strategy. There were also adverse developments in primary exports as low prices for producers and consumers reduced the exportable surplus by discouraging production and encouraging consumption.

In fact, rather than improvements in the external terms of trade as assumed by Prebisch and Myrdal, turning the internal terms of trade against primary activities led to declines in export market shares in the countries concerned. Losses in market shares were especially pronounced in temperate zone agricultural products and metals, benefiting developed countries, in particular the United States, Canada, and Australia.

Among the countries under consideration, the volume of Argentina's principal primary exports, beef and wheat, remained, on the average, unchanged between the mid-1930s and the early 1960s, while the world exports of these commodities doubled. In the same period, Chile's share fell from 28 to 22 percent in the world exports of copper, which accounted for three-fifths of the country's export earnings. Notwithstanding its climatic advantages, the economic policies followed also forestalled the development of Chilean agriculture, thereby impeding the expansion of exports and contributing to increased food imports.

Similar developments occurred in socialist countries. In Hungary, for example, the exports of several agricultural commodities, such as goose liver, fodder seeds, and beans, declined in absolute terms and slow increases in production necessitated the importation of cereals and meat that had earlier been major export products.

In the same period, Denmark nearly doubled its market shares in major agricultural exports and Norway also experienced increases in market shares. And whereas countries following an inward-oriented development strategy failed to expand industrial exports, manufacturing industries in Denmark and Norway became increasingly export oriented, with the share of manufactured goods in total exports increasing to a considerable extent.

The conclusions obtained for the six countries under consideration were confirmed in a study of 29 developing countries by De Vries (1967). The study showed that outward-oriented countries were much more successful in maintaining and improving their market position in primary exports, and developing manufactured exports, than inward-oriented countries.

The slowdown in the growth of primary exports and the lack of emergence of manufactured exports did not provide the foreign exchange necessary for rapid economic growth in countries pursuing inward-oriented development strategies. The situation was aggravated as net import savings declined because of the increased need for foreign materials, machinery, and technological know-how [Bruton (1970)]. Correspondingly, economic growth was increasingly constrained by limitations in the availability of foreign exchange, and intermittent foreign exchange crises occurred as attempts were made to expand the economy at rates exceeding that permitted by the growth of export earnings [Berlinski and Schydlowsky (1982)].

Also, high-cost, capital-intensive production raised incremental capital–output ratios under continuing import substitution, requiring ever-increasing savings ratios to maintain rates of economic growth at earlier levels. At the same time, the loss of incomes due to the high cost of protection reduced the volume of available savings, resulting in a decline in GNP growth rates.

In several developing countries pursuing an inward-oriented development strategy, the cost of protection is estimated to have exceeded 5 percent of the gross national product [Balassa and Associates (1971)]. And while it had been suggested that the high cost of inward-oriented policies will remain temporary [De Vries (1967, pp. 62–69)], this did not prove the case.

Thus, in the highly protected Latin American countries productivity growth slowed down once the first stage of import substitution, involving the replacement by domestic production of the importation of nondurable consumer goods and their inputs, had been completed [Bruton (1967), Elias (1978)]. And, according to a summary of the findings of studies on a number of developing countries, "the misallocation produced by conventional IS [import substituting] policies not only reduces total output below the level that it might have otherwise reached, but it also reduces the growth rate, principally through its effect on productivity growth and the flexibility of the economy" [Bruton (1970, p. 140)].

These results may be explained by reference to changes in product requirements as a country undertakes the production of intermediate commodities and durable goods in proceeding to the second stage of import substitution. Whereas the production of nondurable consumer goods and their inputs requires mainly unskilled labor, uses relatively simple technology, and the efficient scale of production is low, with costs rising little at lower levels of output, at the second stage of import substitution production tends to be capital and/or skill intensive, requires sophisticated technology, as well as large-scale production for efficient operation, with costs rising rapidly at lower output levels [Balassa (1980)].

Thus, at a higher stage of import substitution, developing countries increasingly embarked on the production of commodities, which did not correspond to their production conditions. This, in turn, necessitated high protection in order to establish the industries in question. Yet, as Johnson (1967) showed, in a country that faces world market prices and protects its capital-intensive sector, increases in the capital stock may lead to a fall in real incomes, measured in world market prices, owing to the transfer of labor from the labor-intensive to the capital-intensive sector. Subsequently, Martin (1977) demonstrated that this will be the case if one plus the rate of protection of the capital-intensive sector exceeds the ratio of labor's share in the labor-intensive sector to that in the capital-intensive sector.

While these models are based on restrictive assumptions since they assume factor-price equalization in a two-sector economy, the observed results indicate the potential adverse effects of protection on the long-term growth of the economy. This is confirmed by the cited evidence, which points to the conclusion that, rather than reducing the economic distance vis-à-vis the industrial countries infant industry protection was supposed to achieve, in highly protected developing countries there was a tendency for this lag to increase over time.

Similar developments were observed in Czechoslovakia and Hungary, where the slowdown of export growth and increases in incremental capital–output ratios led to declines in the rate of economic growth. By contrast, the rapid expansion of exports provided the foreign exchange necessary for economic growth in Denmark and Norway, and resource allocation according to comparative advantage permitted reducing incremental capital–output ratios, resulting in the acceleration of economic growth.

3.2. The period of rapid world economic growth (1960–73)

3.2.1. Alternative policy choices [9]

The slowdown in economic growth that eventually resulted from the continued pursuit of an inward-oriented development strategy led to policy reforms in several of the countries applying such a strategy. Among market economies, policy reforms were undertaken in the mid-1960s in Brazil and, to a lesser extent, in Argentina and Mexico. The reforms generally involved providing subsidies to manufactured exports, reducing import protection, applying a system of crawling peg, adopting positive real interest rates, and introducing greater realism in the pricing of public utilities.

Among socialist countries, central resource allocation and price determination gave place to the decentralization of decision-making in Hungary. This involved introducing market relations among firms and increasingly linking domestic prices to world market prices through the exchange rate, with adjustment made for import tariffs and for export subsidies.

The policy reforms undertaken by countries that engaged in second-stage import substitution thus involved making increased use of the price mechanism and reducing price distortions, in particular in foreign trade. The incentive systems that emerged as a result of the reforms in the period preceding the 1973 oil crisis may be compared with the incentive systems applied in countries that adopted an outward-oriented industrial development strategy in the early 1960s, immediately following the completion of first-stage import substitution. The countries in question are Korea, Singapore, and Taiwan.

In comparing the incentive systems applied by the three Far Eastern countries and those adopted in the three Latin American countries following second-stage import substitution, several features deserve attention. These relate to the treatment of the export sector, relative incentives to exports and to import substitution, the variability of incentive rates among particular activities, relative incentives to manufacturing and to primary production, and the automaticity and stability of the incentive system.

In the three Far Eastern countries, a free trade regime was applied to exports. Exporters were free to choose between domestic and imported inputs; they were exempted from indirect taxes on their output and inputs; and they paid no duty

---

[9] This section relies on Balassa (1980), where appropriate references are provided.

on imported inputs. The same privileges were extended to the producers of domestic inputs used in export production.

The application of these procedures provided virtually equal treatment to all exports. And while some additional export incentives were granted, they did not introduce much differentiation among individual export commodities. At the same time, these incentives ensured that in the manufacturing sector, on average, exports received similar treatment as import substitution. Furthermore, there was little discrimination against primary exports and against primary activities in general; incentives were on the whole provided automatically; and the incentive system underwent few modifications over time.

The three Latin American countries that reformed their incentive system after engaging in second-stage import substitution granted subsidies to their nontraditional exports and reduced the extent of import protection. These countries did not, however, provide exporters with a free choice between domestic and imported inputs. Rather, in order to safeguard existing industries, exporters were required to use domestic inputs produced under protection. To compensate exporters for the resulting excess cost, as well as for the effects of import protection on the exchange rate, the countries in question granted explicit export subsidies.

These subsidies did not suffice, however, to provide exporters with incentives comparable to the protection of domestic markets. Thus, there continued to be a bias in favor of import substitution and against exports, albeit at a reduced rate. The extent of discrimination was especially pronounced against traditional primary exports that did not receive export subsidies and, in some instances, continued to be subject to export taxes.

Furthermore, with export subsidies and the protection of inputs used in export industries differing among industries, there was considerable variation in the extent of export subsidies to value added in the production process. Considerable inter-commodity variations were observed also in regard to effective rates of protection on sales in domestic markets. At the same time, some of the incentives were subject to discretionary decision-making.

Nevertheless, with the adoption of the crawling peg, the policy reforms undertaken in the three Latin American countries imparted considerable stability to the incentive system. Also, discrimination against exports and against primary activities was reduced while such discrimination persisted in countries that continued to apply policies of import substitution during the period. Such was the case in India, Chile, and Uruguay during the 1960–73 period.

In India, the introduction of selected export subsidies in the mid-1960s was far overshadowed by the continued use of import prohibitions and the controls imposed on investment; subsidies were also subject to complex regulations and discretionary decision-making. Chile traditionally had the highest level of import protection in Latin America and, after brief experimentation with import liberalization, import restrictions were reimposed in the early 1970s. Protection levels were also high in Uruguay and little effort was made to promote exports.

3.2.2. Incentives and export performance

The incentives applied greatly influenced export performance in the three groups of countries. This may be indicated by reference to the rate of growth of exports and changes in export–output ratios. While export growth rates are affected by a country's initial position, the use of the two measures gave broadly similar results in the present case.

Increases in manufactured exports and in export–output ratios during the 1960–66 period were the most rapid in the three Far Eastern countries, which adopted an outward-oriented strategy in the early 1960s. These countries further improved their export performance in the 1966–73 period, when they intensified their export promotion efforts. As a result, the share of exports in manufactured output rose from 1 percent in 1960 to 14 percent in 1966 and to 41 percent in 1973 in Korea; from 11 percent to 20 percent and to 43 percent in Singapore; and from 9 percent to 19 percent and to 50 percent in Taiwan. Notwithstanding their poor natural resource endowment, the three countries also had the highest growth rates of primary exports, and hence of total exports, among the nine countries under consideration [Balassa (1978a)].

Between 1966 and 1973, the growth of manufactured exports accelerated in the three Latin American countries that reformed their system of incentives during this period. As a result, the share of exports in manufactured output rose from 1 percent in 1966 to 4 percent in 1973 in both Argentina and Brazil. Still, this share remained much lower than in the Far East and the Latin American countries experienced a continued erosion in their traditional primary exports, although they made gains in nontraditional primary exports that received subsidies. Correspondingly, while the countries in question experienced an acceleration in the rate of growth of their total exports, they were far surpassed by the three Far Eastern countries.

India, Chile, and Uruguay, which continued with an inward-looking development strategy, did poorly in primary as well as in manufactured exports and showed a decline in the share of exports in manufactured output between 1960 and 1973. India lost ground in textiles, its traditional export, and was slow to develop new manufactured exports. As a result, its share in the combined exports of manufactured goods of the nine countries declined from 70 percent in 1960 to 13 percent in 1973. In the same period, Chile's share fell from 3 percent to below 1 percent and Uruguay's share from 1 percent to practically zero.

These results relate export incentives to export performance in a comparative framework. In turn, several authors estimated for individual countries the effects on manufactured exports of changes in domestic relative prices, which are affected by changes in export incentives. A review of estimates showed that the price elasticities of export supply, which were statistically significant at least at the 5 percent level, ranged from 0.3 in Pakistan to 3.0 in Egypt, with a median of 0.6–0.7 [Donges and Riedel (1977)].

The estimates were obtained by utilizing the ordinary least squares (OLS) method that is known to have a downward bias. Evidence of this bias is provided in a study of Greek and Korean exports, in a simultaneous equation framework. In the case of Greece, the price elasticity of supply of total exports was estimated at 1.2 by ordinary least squares and 1.6 utilizing two-stage least squares (TSLS); both estimates are statistically significant at the 1 percent level. For the same country, the price elasticity of supply of manufactured exports was estimated at 1.3 using OLS and 2.1 using TSLS; the former is significant at the 5 percent, the latter at the 1 percent level. In turn, the estimated price elasticity of supply of total exports for Korea was 1.5 under OLS and 1.9–2.4 under TSLS estimation, depending on the relative price variable employed. All the elasticities are statistically significant at the 1 percent level [Balassa, Voloudakis, Fylaktos and Suh (1986)].

Yet, the econometric results show the short-term effects of changes in relative prices. The long-term effects may be substantially greater, in part because adjustment takes time and in part because producers and consumers may not react to changes they consider temporary. The latter point is supported by the export supply equations estimated for Korea, where the exchange rate cum export incentives variable was separated from the domestic and foreign price variables. While the elasticity of export supply ranges between 1.9 and 2.5 in regard to the former, it is between 1.0 and 1.5 for the latter, conforming to expectations that businessmen consider changes in the exchange rate and in export incentives as permanent and changes in domestic and foreign prices as temporary.

As far as the effects of exchange rate changes are concerned, the locus classicus is "Currency devaluation in developing countries" [Cooper (1971)]. Having reviewed some three dozen devaluations occurring over the 1953–66 period, Cooper concluded that devaluation appears to improve both the trade balance and the balance of payments after the first year. Subsequently, in a study of twelve developing countries, which adopted stabilization programs in the 1970–76 period, Donovan (1981) concluded that export performance exhibited a striking improvement following the devaluation of the currency. Thus, while exports in these countries declined on the average by 1.3 percent in the year prior to the depreciation, they increased by 9.2 percent in the first post-depreciation year, although the rate of expansion of world exports hardly changed.

The effects of exchange rate changes on exports were examined by Balassa (1986c), utilizing an econometric model that combined time-series data for 52 developing countries. The author found that a 1 percent change in the real exchange rate was accompanied by a 0.5 percentage point change in the ratio of exports to output. The corresponding result for agricultural exports alone was 0.6.

3.2.3. Effects on economic growth, employment, and income distribution

Continued import substitution behind high protection in narrow domestic markets involves "travelling up the staircase" by undertaking the production of commodities that involve increasingly higher domestic costs per unit of foreign exchange saved. By contrast, exporting involves "extending a lower step on the staircase" by increasing the production of commodities in which the country has a comparative advantage, with low domestic resource costs per unit of foreign exchange. Exporting further permits full use of capacity and allows reductions in unit costs through the exploitation of economies of scale, contributing thereby to efficient import substitution. Finally, exposure to foreign competition provides stimulus for technological change.

Resource allocation according to comparative advantage, higher capacity utilization, and the exploitation of economies of scale under an outward-oriented development strategy improve investment efficiency, when the resulting savings in capital may be used to increase output and employment elsewhere in the economy in countries where labor is not fully employed. This will occur through the indirect effects of export expansion that create demand for domestic inputs and generate higher incomes which are in part spent on domestic goods.

Data on the three groups of countries analyzed in Subsection 3.2.2 show considerable differences in regard to the efficiency of investment. For the 1960–73 period as a whole, incremental capital–output ratios were 1.8 in Singapore, 2.1 in Korea, and 2.4 in Taiwan. At the other extreme, these ratios were 5.5 in Chile, 9.1 in Uruguay, and 5.7 in India. Incremental capital–output ratios fell in the three Latin American countries that undertook policy reforms in the mid-1960s, the decline being the largest in Brazil (from 3.8 in 1960–66 to 2.1 in 1966–73), where the policy changes were the most pronounced and excess capacity could be utilized in exporting [Balassa (1978a)].

At the same time, domestic savings will rise as higher incomes are attained under outward orientation. Domestic savings would increase further if a higher than average share of incomes generated by exports were saved. This proposition received support from a cross-section study of 14 developing economies by Weisskopf (1972), who found a positive correlation between exports and domestic savings. Weisskopf's results were confirmed by Papanek (1973) in a cross-sectional analysis of 34 developing economies for the 1950s, and 51 developing countries for the 1960s.

A positive correlation between exports and domestic savings has also been found in a time-series analysis of four developed and eight developing economies by Maizels (1968, ch. 4) for the early post-Second World War period extending to 1962. Maizels' sample includes India; for the same country Bhagwati and Srinivasan (1975, ch. 16) obtained inconclusive results in a comparative study of ten industries for the 1950s and 1960s. Given India's orientation toward import substitution during the entire period, however, the lack of clear-cut results in an inter-industry framework may not modify the cross-sectional and time-series results obtained for the developing economies cited above.[10]

Lower incremental capital–output ratios and higher investment shares resulting from increased domestic and foreign savings contribute to economic growth under outward orientation as compared to inward orientation. This is shown by observed differences in rates of economic growth, ranging from 9–10 percent in Korea, Singapore, and Taiwan, to 2–3 percent in India, Chile, and Uruguay, with Argentina, Brazil, and Mexico occupying the middle ground following the acceleration of their economic growth in the wake of the reforms introduced in the mid-1960s.[11]

One may further examine the relationship between alternative policy choices and economic growth by establishing a correlation between the rate of growth of exports and that of output, when export expansion is taken to reflect the extent of outward orientation. Michaely (1977) suggested, however, that this correlation does not provide an appropriate test for the above hypothesis, since exports are part of output and hence multicollinearity is present. In turn, Heller and Porter (1978) noted that Michaely's own procedure of correlating the growth rate of the export share of output with the output growth rate is subject to the same criticism, and they proposed replacing the latter variable by the growth of output net of exports. The authors obtained a high positive correlation between the two variables in a cross-section investigation of 41 developing countries. Their result was reconfirmed by Balassa (1978b) who correlated export growth with the growth of output net of exports by combining data for the 1960–66 and 1966–73 periods for the nine countries referred to above.

These procedures abstract from the fact that exports and output are affected simultaneously by other variables, such as increases in the capital stock and in the labor force. Michalopoulos and Jay (1973) attempted to remedy this deficiency by introducing domestic and foreign investment and labor as explanatory variables, together with exports, to explain inter-country differences in GNP growth rates for 39 developing countries in the 1960–66 period. The inclusion of

---

[10]At the same time, one may agree with Bhagwati (1978, p. 147) that "while there is much empirical evidence in support of a statistical association between exports and saving, there is little evidence so far for some of the hypotheses that could provide a *rationale* for such an association implying a causal relationship running from exports to savings".

[11]This is not to imply that economic growth rates provide an appropriate success indicator. A more appropriate choice is the rise of factor productivity, to be discussed below.

exports in a production function-type relationship was designed to test for the favorable effect of export expansion on output growth.

While inter-country differences in domestic and foreign investment and in the growth of the labor force explained 53 percent of the inter-country variation in GNP growth rates, adding the export variable raised the coefficient of determination to 0.71. Applying the same procedure to pooled data of nine semi-industrial countries for the 1960–66 and 1966–73 periods, Balassa (1978b) found that adding the export variable increased the explanatory power of the regression equation from 58 to 77 percent. Subsequently, Feder (1983) separated the effects of exports on economic growth into two parts, productivity differentials between export and nonexport activities and externalities generated by exports; he obtained highly significant results in regard to both variables for broadly as well as for narrowly defined semi-industrial countries for the 1964–77 period.

As long as labor is not fully employed, the rapid growth of output under an outward-oriented strategy benefits employment, when additional gains are obtained to the extent that exports are more labor-intensive than import substitution. However, these gains are reduced in the event that outward orientation leads to more rapid increases in labor productivity than would otherwise be the case.

Banerji and Riedel (1980) analyzed the effects of these factors on industrial employment in India and in Taiwan. Their results indicate that the favorable effects of rapid output growth on employment were enhanced by the shift towards labor-intensive export activities in Taiwan while output grew at a slower rate and a shift occurred towards relatively capital-intensive import-substituting activities in India. With higher productivity growth in Taiwan than in India, industrial employment grew at an average annual rate of 10 percent in the first case and 3 percent in the second during the 1960s.

Furthermore, in a comparative study of eight developing countries, Krueger (1983) found that considerable employment gains may be obtained through a shift from import substitution to export orientation. These gains, calculated by the use of labor input coefficients for individual sectors, varied between 21 and 107 percent, with results for Indonesia and Thailand exceeding 100 percent.[12]

Fields (1984) examined the employment effects of outward orientation in Far Eastern countries. He found that between the early 1960s and the early 1970s unemployment rates declined from 8 to 4 percent in Korea, from 9 to 7 percent in Singapore, and from 6 to 2 percent in Taiwan. Also, Carvalho and Haddad (1981, table 2.15) showed that greater outward-orientation in Brazil after the

---

[12]An apparent exception is Chile but this was due to the capital-intensity of its intra-Latin American exports under the policies applied; the labor-intensity of exports in trade with developed countries much exceeded that for import substitution [Krueger (1983, table 6.2)].

mid-1960s led to a 27 percent increase in the labor-intensity of exports relative to import substitution in Brazil.

Apart from its impact on economic growth and on the inter-industry allocation of the factors of production, trade orientation will affect employment through changes in factor prices. Under inward orientation capital goods are underpriced, both because the exchange rate is overvalued and because tariffs on capital goods tend to be low or nonexistent.

Among countries for which estimates have been made in the framework of the Krueger study, the elimination of protection would involve reducing capital costs by 30–40 percent in Chile, Pakistan, and Turkey and by 8 percent in Argentina [Krueger (1983, table 7.1)]. Since a 1 percent change in the relative prices of capital and labor has been shown to be associated with a 1 percent change in the use of labor relative to capital [Behrman (1982, p. 186)], eliminating this distortion would lead to increases in employment commensurate with the rise in the relative cost of capital.

With the growth of employment, real wages increased considerably in outward-oriented economies where exports expanded rapidly. This increase reflects the fact that the rate of growth of the demand for labor on the part of the manufacturing sector exceeded the rate of growth of the supply of labor to this sector. As a result, between 1966 and 1973, real wages in manufacturing doubled in Korea and increased by nearly three-fifths in Taiwan. Also, real wages in manufacturing rose by three-tenths in Brazil after its shift towards increased outward orientation. In turn, real wages decline by one-tenth in India between 1966 and 1973, which continued with inward-oriented policies during this period.

Fields (1984) compared the experience of the three Far Eastern countries with that of three Caribbean countries (Barbados, Jamaica, and Trinidad & Tobago) he considered as open economies albeit, given their high level of protection, they may better be classified as inward oriented. And whereas he attributed the high level of unemployment in these countries to the application of a "lenient" wage policy as against the "strict" wage policies allegedly followed by the Far Eastern countries, this assertion conflicts with the fact that real wages rose much more rapidly in the Far East than in the Caribbean countries, with an absolute decline observed in Jamaica. These differences may be explained by reference to the fact that rapid export expansion "pulled up" wages in the Far Eastern countries that did not occur in the Caribbean where raising wages above productivity levels through labor legislation discouraged exports, thereby adding to unemployment.

Finally, a survey of countries following an inward-oriented strategy showed that this policy produces low employment growth and inequality of incomes [Bruton (1974)]. The results reflect slow growth of employment and wages in the manufacturing sector as well as the deterioration of the domestic terms of trade through agricultural protection. Subsequently, in an econometric study of developing countries for the postwar period, Morrison (1985) found that the expansion of the exports of manufactured goods and exports derived from small-scale agriculture tended to substantially improve the distribution of incomes while exports originating in mines and latifundia had the opposite effect.

3.3. The decade of external shocks (1973–83)

3.3.1. Alternative adjustment policies

Developing countries experienced substantial external shocks between 1973 and 1983. In the first half of the period, the quadrupling of oil prices was accompanied by a world recession, followed by a slow recovery; in the second half, oil prices increased two-and-a-half times, the developed countries again experienced a recession, and interest rates rose to a considerable extent. At the same time, policy responses to these shocks varied greatly. This is discussed in the following in regard to twelve newly-industrializing and twelve less developed countries, drawing on estimates for the periods 1974–78 and 1978–83, reported in Balassa (1984a, 1986a).

Among newly-industrializing developing economies, defined as having per capita incomes between $1100 and $3500 in 1978 and a manufacturing share in GDP of 20 percent in 1977, Korea, Singapore, and Taiwan continued with their outward-oriented development strategy and were joined by Chile and Uruguay. In turn, after earlier efforts to reduce the bias of the incentive system against exports, Argentina, Israel, Mexico, Portugal, Turkey, and Yugoslavia again increased the degree of inward orientation.

Less developed countries span the range between newly-industrializing developing economies and the least developed countries. Within this group, Kenya, Mauritius, Thailand, and Tunisia applied relatively outward-oriented strategies. Conversely, inward orientation predominated in Egypt, India, Jamaica, Morocco, Peru, the Philippines, Tanzania, and Zambia.

The classification scheme has been established on the basis of the policies applied in the 1974–78 period. Policy changes have occurred in several countries since. Among newly-industrializing economies, Portugal applied a stabilization programme in 1978, followed by reductions in import protection. Turkey undertook a far-reaching policy reform in January 1980, while Chile and Uruguay introduced considerable distortions in the system of incentives by fixing their exchange rates in 1980–81. Among less developed countries, Kenya and Tunisia moved in the direction of inward orientation while Jamaica carried out partial reforms. Nevertheless, in order to ensure comparability in the results, the same classification scheme has been used for the second period as well.

In the process of estimation, external shocks have been defined to include terms-of-trade effects, associated in large part with increases in oil prices; export volume effects, resulting from the recession-induced slowdown in world trade; and, in the second period, interest rate effects, due to the rise of interest rates in world financial markets. In turn, policy responses to external shocks have included additional net external financing, defined as increased reliance on foreign capital compared to past trends; export promotion, reflected by increases in export market shares; import substitution, measured as decreases in the income elasticity of import demand; and deflationary macroeconomic policies, expressed by decreases in economic growth rates.

3.3.2. Effects on foreign trade and economic growth

In the 1974–78 period, outward-oriented developing countries suffered considerably larger external shocks than inward-oriented countries (7.5 vs. 3.9 percent of GNP), owing to the fact that they had a much larger export share. However, differences in economic growth rates increased over time and offset differences in the size of external shocks several times. Thus, while outward-oriented countries maintained their rate of economic growth between 1963–73 and 1973–79 at 7.1 percent, on the average, average growth rates declined from 5.7 to 5.0 percent in inward-oriented countries. Differences in economic growth rates, in turn, find their origin in differences in the policies applied that affected investment efficiency as well as domestic savings rates.

Following the quadrupling of oil prices of 1973–74 and the world recession of 1974–75, outward-oriented countries adopted output-increasing policies of export expansion and import substitution that fully offset the adverse balance-of-payments effects of external shocks during the 1974–78 period. By contrast, inward-oriented countries lost export market shares, experienced little import substitution, and financed the balance-of-payments effects of external shocks almost entirely by borrowing abroad.

Apart from the development strategies applied, differences in export performance are explained by the fact that outward-oriented economies maintained realistic exchange rates while inward-oriented countries supported overvalued exchange rates by foreign borrowing. At the same time, a variety of factors contributed to the result that outward-oriented economies experienced substantially more import substitution than their inward-oriented counterparts.

To begin with, the maintenance of realistic exchange rates furthered import substitution in outward-oriented as compared to inward-oriented countries. Furthermore, the lack of discrimination against primary activities and the adoption of realistic energy prices gave rise to import substitution in foodstuffs and petroleum in the first group of countries. Finally, cost reductions through the exploitation of economies of scale in exporting contributed to import substitution in manufactured goods in outward-oriented economies, whereas increasing costs were incurred behind high protective barriers and net foreign exchange savings declined under inward orientation.

At the same time, high and rising protection adversely affected investment efficiency in inward-oriented countries, and the situation was aggravated by the lack of sufficient attention given to economic considerations in their large public investment programs. In turn, apart from the neutrality of the system of incentives, outward-oriented countries had smaller public investment programs and gave greater attention to economic factors in carrying out these programs.

Higher levels of investment efficiency in outward-oriented countries were accompanied by superior savings performance, with average domestic savings ratios rising from 18.0 percent in 1963–73 to 24.4 percent in 1973–79. For one thing, private savings were encouraged through the adoption of realistic interest rates; for another thing, public dissavings were limited through reductions in government budget deficits. In turn, domestic savings ratios rose only from 19.3 to 21.0 percent in inward-oriented countries that generally maintained negative real interest rates and high budget deficits.

As noted above, inward-oriented countries relied to a considerable extent on foreign borrowing. As a result, the debt-service ratios of these countries nearly doubled between 1973 and 1978, reaching 43 percent of export value, while the ratio remained at 12 percent in outward-oriented countries.

Their high indebtedness did not permit inward-oriented countries to continue relying exclusively on foreign borrowing to finance the balance-of-payments effects of external shocks in the 1978–83 period. Nor did they adopt output-increasing policies of export promotion and import substitution. Thus, apart from external borrowing, the countries in question applied deflationary measures to offset the effects of external shocks.

Outward-oriented countries, too, had to rely in part on deflationary policies to cope with the external shocks they suffered during the period. Nevertheless, output-increasing policies remained their principal policy response to external shocks as they continued to gain export market shares and to replace imports by domestic production.

Correspondingly, outward-oriented countries maintained higher economic growth rates than their inward-oriented counterparts between 1979 and 1982. At the same time, the slowdown owing to the imposition of deflationary measures remained temporary, and outward-oriented countries averaged GNP growth rates of 5 percent in 1983. By contrast, inward-oriented countries had to reinforce the application of deflationary measures as interest rates rose on their large external debt, leading to the stagnation of their national economies in 1983.

3.3.3. Policies and performance in a cross-section framework

The above results have been obtained by classifying developing countries as outward-oriented and inward-oriented. While such a binary classification necessarily involves a certain degree of arbitrariness, the results have been reconfirmed in an econometric study of 43 developing countries, in which initial trade orientation and policy responses to external shocks have been separately introduced [Balassa (1985a)].

The extent of trade orientation has been estimated as deviations of actual from hypothetical values of per capita exports, the latter having been derived in a regression equation that includes the ratio of mineral exports to the gross national product in addition to per capita incomes and population, first used by Chenery (1960) as explanatory variables. In turn, alternative policy responses have been represented by relating the balance-of-payments effects of export promotion, import substitution, and additional net external financing to the balance-of-payments effects of external shocks.

The impact of trade orientation on economic growth has been indicated by estimating differences in GNP growth rates between a country in the upper quartile of the distribution in terms of trade orientation, representing the median among outward-oriented countries, and the neutral case where the trade orientation variable takes a zero value. The results show a gain of 0.5 of a percentage point for the country concerned. In turn, a country in the lower quartile of the distribution, representing the median among inward-oriented countries, is shown to experience a shortfall of 0.5 of a percentage point in its GNP growth rate. Ceteris paribus, there is thus a difference in GNP growth rates of 1.0 percentage point between the median outward-oriented and the median inward-oriented country.

In turn, the regression coefficient of the export promotion variable exceeds that of the import substitution and the additional net external financing variables two to two-and-a-half times, indicating that greater reliance on export promotion in response to external shocks permits reaching higher GNP growth rates. Correspondingly, increasing export promotion by 10 percentage points at the expense of import substitution and additional net external financing would add 0.3 of a percentage point to the rate of economic growth. The gain is 0.7 of a percentage point if comparison is made between the upper quartile and the median in terms of reliance on export promotion, and a loss of 0.4 of a percentage point in GNP growth is shown if a country at the lower quartile of the distribution is compared to the median. Comparing the two quartiles, then, a gain of 1.2 percentage points is obtained.

The results are cumulative, indicating that both initial trade orientation and the choice of adjustment policies in response to external shocks importantly contributed to economic growth during the period under review. In fact, these factors explain a large proportion of inter-country differences in GNP growth rates that averaged 5.0 percent in the 43 developing countries under consideration during the 1973–79 period, with an upper quartile of 6.5 percent and a lower quartile of 3.3 percent.

4. Conclusions

Following a review of the world environment in which these policies operate, the present chapter examined the experience of developing countries with outward- and inward-oriented development strategies. While under outward orientation similar incentives are provided to exports and to import substitution, inward orientation involves biasing the system of incentives in favor of import substitution and against exports. With agriculture being the principal export sector in most developing countries, inward orientation also entails discriminating against primary, in particular agricultural, products, whereas agriculture and industry receive similar incentives under outward orientation.

This chapter has provided evidence on the adverse effects of continued inward orientation in developing countries. Such a policy may initially permit rapid economic expansion, but it will eventually run into difficulties as the limitation of domestic markets leads to shifts into new activities that do not conform to the country's resource endowment and circumscribe the possibilities for the exploitation of economies of scale, and do not provide scope for sufficient competition.

In fact, while according to the infant industry argument the short-run costs of import protection would be eventually offset by long-term benefits through increased productivity, available evidence indicates a decline in productivity growth under continued inward orientation.[13] Thus, the growth of total factor productivity, derived as a ratio of the growth of output to that of factor inputs combined, turned negative in India which long persisted in pursuing an inward-oriented development strategy [Ahluwalia (1986)] as well as in Mexico which turned increasingly inward [Balassa (1986c)].

Also, a survey of estimates for 20 developing countries showed that total factor productivity increased at annual rates of over 3 percent in outward-oriented economies[14] while increases were less than 1 percent or even negative in countries with an especially pronounced inward orientation [Chenery (1986, table 2-2)].[15] These results may be explained by reference to the fact that outward orientation leads to the efficient use not only of existing resources but also of increments in

[13]It should be noted, however, that infant-industry objectives can be more efficiently pursued by production subsidies than by import protection.

[14]Hong Kong, Korea, and Taiwan, in earlier periods, Israel, Spain, and Singapore, however, provide an exception.

[15]Argentina, Chile (prior to 1974) India, and Venezuela.

resources, permits the exploitation of economies of scale, and provides the stick and carrot of competition that gives inducement for technological change.

It has been suggested, however, that foreign market limitations would not permit the adoption of outward-oriented policies by an increasing number of developing countries. The proponents of this view neglect the possibilities existing in developed country markets for the manufactured products of the developing countries that still have a small share in these markets; disregard the fact that increased exports by the developing countries lead to their increased imports from the developed countries, in particular of manufactured goods; and fail to recognize the potential for trade among developing countries.

Also, outward orientation should not be confused with export promotion. The adoption of a neutral incentive scheme will promote efficient import substitution in industries that are discriminated against under inward orientation. Apart from primary products, in most developing countries this is the case for capital goods that enter duty free or are subject to low tariffs.

It should further be emphasized that the success of outward orientation will depend on the removal of policy-imposed distortions on capital and in labor markets. Such distortions tend to raise the price of labor relative to the price of capital [Krueger (1983)], thereby hindering the exploitation of comparative advantage. Also, the availability of financial resources is necessary to undertake investments that permit the practical implementation of a strategy of outward orientation.

This chapter has emphasized differences between two archetypes of development strategies: outward and inward orientation. A more complete treatment would also consider intermediate cases that may combine the characteristics of the two. And, very importantly, consideration would need to be given to problems of transition: the path of reform that may lead from inward to outward orientation.

References

Adams, N.A. (1973) 'A note on "Trade as a handmaiden of growth"', *Economic Journal*, 83:210–212.

Ahluwalia, I.S. (1986) 'Industrial growth in India: Performance and prospects', *Journal of Development Economics*, 23:1–18.

Amin, J. (1974) *Accumulation on a world scale: A critique of the theory of underdevelopment*, Vol. 1. New York: Monthly Review Press.

Amin, J. (1977) 'Self-reliance and the new international economic order', *Monthly Review*, 29:1–21.

Bacha, E. (1978) 'An interpretation of unequal exchange from Prebisch–Singer to Emmanuel,' *Journal of Development Economics*, 5:319–330.

Baer, W. (1962) 'The economics of Prebisch and ECLA', *Economic Development and Cultural Change*, 10:169–182.

Bairoch, P. (1975) *The economic development of the Third World since 1900*. London: Methuen.

Balassa, B. (1970) 'Growth strategies in semi-industrial countries', *Quarterly Journal of Economics*, 84:24–47.

Balassa, B. (1977) 'The effects of commercial policy on international trade, the location of production, and factor movements', in: B. Ohlin, P.-O. Hesselborn, and P. M. Wijkman, eds., *The international allocation of economic activity*. London: Macmillan.

Balassa, B. (1978a) 'Export incentives and export performance in developing countries: A comparative analysis', *Weltwirtschaftliches Archiv*, 114:24–61.

Balassa, B. (1978b) 'Exports and economic growth: Further evidence', *Journal of Development Economics*, 5:181–189.

Balassa, B. (1980) 'The process of industrial development and alternative development strategies', *Essays in International Finance*, 141.

Balassa, B. (1984a) 'Adjustment to external shocks in developing countries', in: B. Csikós-Nagy, D. Hague, and G. Hall, eds., *The economics of relative prices*. London: Macmillan.

Balassa, B. (1984b) 'Adjustment policies and development strategies in Sub-Saharan Africa', in: M. Syrquin, L. Taylor, and L.E. Westphal, eds., *Economic structure and performance. Essays in honor of Hollis B. Chenery*. Orlando: Academic Press.

Balassa, B. (1984c) 'The terms of trade controversy and the evolution of soft financing: Early years in the U.N. – Comment', in: G.M. Meier and D. Seers, ed.s, *Pioneers in development*. Oxford: Oxford University Press.

Balassa, B. (1985a) 'Exports, policy choices and economic growth in developing countries after the 1973 oil shock', *Journal of Development Economics*, 18:23–36.

Balassa, B. (1985b) 'The Cambridge group and the developing countries', *The World Economy*, 8:201–218.

Balassa, B. (1986a) 'Policy responses to exogenous shocks in developing countries', *American Economic Review*, Papers and Proceedings, 76:75–78.

Balassa, B. (1986b) 'Dependency and trade orientation', *The World Economy*, 9:259–273.

Balassa, B. (1986c) 'Economic incentives and agricultural performance', paper presented at the Eighth Congress of the International Economic Association held in December 1986, in New Delhi, India, mimeo.

Balassa, B. and Associates (1971) *The structure of protection in developing countries*. Baltimore, MD: The Johns Hopkins University Press.

Balassa, B., Voloudakis, E., Fylaktos, P., and Suh, S.T. (1986) 'Export incentives and export expansion in developing countries: An econometric investigation', World Bank Development Research Department, Discussion Paper no. 159.

Banerji, R. and Riedel, J. (1980) 'Industrial employment expansion under alternative trade strategies: Case of India and Taiwan: 1950–1970', *Journal of Development Economics*, 7:567–577.

Behrman, J.B. (1982) 'Country and sectoral variations in manufacturing elasticities of substitution between capital and labor', in: A.O. Krueger, ed., *Trade and employment in developing countries 2. Factor supply and substitution*. Chicago, IL. Chicago University Press.

Bergsten, C.F. (1974) 'The new era in world commodity markets', *Challenge*, 17:34–42.

Berlinski, J. and Schydlowsky, D.M. (1982) 'Argentina', in: B. Balassa and Associates, *Development strategies in semi-industrial economies*. Baltimore, MD: The Johns Hopkins University Press.

Bhagwati, J.N. (1978) *Foreign trade regimes and economic development: Anatomy and consequences of exchange control regimes*. Cambridge, MA: Ballinger.

Bhagwati, J.N. and Srinivasan, T.N. (1975) *Foreign trade regimes and economic development: India*. New York: Columbia University Press.

Bruton, H.J. (1967) 'Productivity growth in Latin America', *American Economic Review*, 57:1099–1107.

Bruton, H.J. (1970) 'The import substitution strategy of economic development: A survey', *Pakistan Development Review*, 10:124–146.

Bruton, H.J. (1974) 'Industrialization policy and income distribution', Research Memorandum 69, mimeo. Williams College.

Carvalho, J.L. and Haddad, C.L.S. (1981) 'Foreign trade strategies and employment in Brazil', in: A.O. Krueger, M.B. Lary, T. Monson, and N. Akrasanee, eds., *Trade and employment in developing countries 1. Individual studies*. Chicago, IL: Chicago University Press.

Caves, R.E. (1965) 'Export-led growth and the new economic history', in: J.N. Bhagwati, et al., eds., *Trade, balance and payments, and growth*. Amsterdam: North-Holland.

Chenery, H.B. (1960) 'Patterns of industrial growth', *American Economic Review*, 50:624–654.

Chenery, H.B. (1986) 'Growth and transformation', in: H.B. Chenery, S. Robinson, and M. Syrquin, eds., *Industrialization and growth: A comparative study*. Oxford: Oxford University Press, Ch. 2.

Chenery, H.B. and Syrquin, M. (1975) *Patterns of development 1950–1970*. Oxford: Oxford University Press.

Chichilnisky, G. (1981) 'Terms of trade and domestic distribution: Export-led growth with abundant labor', *Journal of Development Economics*, 8:163–192.

Cline, W.R. (1982) 'Can the East Asian experience be generalized?', *World Development*, 10:81–90.

Cohen, B.I. (1964) 'The stagnation of Indian exports', *Quarterly Journal of Economics*, 78:604–620.

Cohen, B.I. and Sisler, D.G. (1971) 'Exports of developing countries in the 1960s', *Review of Economics and Statistics*, 53:354–361.

Cooper, R.N. (1971) 'Currency devaluation in developing countries', *Essays in International Finance*, 86.

Crafts, N.F.R. (1973) 'Trade as a handmaiden of growth: an alternative view', *Economic Journal*, 83:875–884.

De Vries, B.A. (1967) 'The export experience of developing countries', World Bank Staff Occasional Papers no. 3, The Johns Hopkins University Press.

Diaz-Alejandro, C.F. (1978) 'Delinking North and South: Unshackled or unhinged', in: A. Fishlow, C.F. Diaz-Alejandro, R.R. Fagen, and R.D. Hansen, eds., *Rich and poor nations in the world economy*. New York: McGraw Hill.

Donges, J.B. and Riedel, J. (1977) 'The expansion of manufactured exports in developing countries: An empirical assessment of supply and demand issues', *Weltwirtschaftliches Archiv*, 113:58–87.

Donovan, D.J. (1981) 'Real responses associated with exchange rate action in selected upper credit tranche stabilization programs', *International Monetary Fund Staff Papers*, 28:698–727.

Elias, V.J. (1978) 'Sources of economic growth in Latin American countries', *Review of Economics and Statistics*, 60:362–370.

Ellsworth, P.T. (1956) 'The terms of trade between primary producing and industrial countries', *Inter-American Economic Affairs*, 10:47–65.

Faluvégi, L. (1984) 'Gazdasági hatékonyság – gazdaságirányítás', (Economic efficiency – economic management), *Közgazdasági Szemle*, 31:1025–1043.

Feder, G. (1983) 'On exports and economic growth', *Journal of Development Economics*, 12:59–73.

Fields, G.S. (1984) 'Employment, income distribution and economic growth in seven small open economies', *Economic Journal*, 94:74–83.

Findlay, R. (1980) 'The terms of trade and equilibrium growth in the world economy', *American Economic Review*, 70:291–299.

Findlay, R. (1984) 'Growth and development in trade models', in: W. Jones and B. Kenen, eds., *Handbook of international economics*, Vol. I. Amsterdam: North-Holland.

Flanders, M.J. (1964) 'Prebisch on protectionism: An evaluation', *Economic Journal*, 74:305–326.

Grinols, E. and Bhagwati, J.N. (1976) 'Foreign capital, savings and dependence', *Review of Economics and Statistics*, 58:416–424.

Haberler, G. (1961) 'Terms of trade and economic development', in: H. Ellis, ed., *Economic development of Latin America*. New York: St. Martin's Press.

Haq, M.U. (1976), *The poverty curtain: Choices for the Third World*. New York: Columbia University Press.

Heller, P.S. and Porter, R.C. (1978) 'Exports and growth: An empirical re-investigation', *Journal of Development Economics*, 5:191–193.

Hicks, J.P. (1953) 'An inaugural lecture', *Oxford Economic Papers*.

Hirschman, A.O. (1958) *The strategy of economic development*. New Haven, CT: Yale University Press.

Innis, H. (1957) *Essays in Canadian economic history*. Toronto: University of Toronto Press.

Isserlis, L. (1938) 'Tramp shipping cargoes and freights', *Journal of the Royal Statistical Society*, 101:53–164.

Johnson, H.G. (1954) 'Increasing productivity, income-price trends and the trade balance', *Economic Journal*, 64:462–485.

Johnson, H.G. (1967) 'The possibility of income losses from increased efficiency factor accumulation in the presence of tariffs', *Economic Journal*, 17:151–154.

Johnson, H.G. (1968) 'Alternative maximization policies for developing country exporters of primary products', *Journal of Political Economy*, 78:489–493.

Kindleberger, C.P. (1953) *International economics*. Homewood: R.D. Irwin.

Kindleberger, C.P. (1956) *Terms of trade, a European case study*. London: Chapman Hill.

Kravis, I.B. (1970) 'Trade as a handmaiden of growth: Similarities between the nineteenth and the twentieth centuries', *Economic Journal*, 80:850–872.

Kravis, I.B. (1973a) 'A reply to Mr. Adams', *Economic Journal*, 83:212–217.

Kravis, I.B. (1973b) 'A reply to Mr. Crafts' note', *Economic Journal*, 83:885–889.

Kravis, I.B. and Lipsey, R.E. (1971) *Price competitiveness in world trade*. New York: National Bureau of Economic Research.

Kravis, I.B. and Lipsey, R.E. (1984) 'Prices and terms of trade for developed country exports of manufactured goods', in: B. Csikós-Nagy, D. Hague, and G. Hall, eds., *The economics of relative prices*. London: Macmillan.

Krueger, A.O. (1983) *Trade and employment in developing countries 3. Synthesis and conclusions*. Chicago, IL: University of Chicago Press.

Krueger, A.O. (1984) 'Trade policies in developing countries', in: R.W. Jones and P.B. Kenen, eds., *Handbook of international economics*, Vol. I. Amsterdam: North-Holland.

Leff, N.H. (1967) 'Export stagnation and autarkic development in Brazil, 1947–1962', *Quarterly Journal of Economics*, 81:286–301.

Leff, N.H. (1969) 'The "exportable surplus" approach to foreign trade in underdeveloped countries', *Economic Development and Cultural Change*, 17:346–355.

Leff, N.H. (1973) 'Tropical trade and development in the nineteenth century: The Brazilian experience', *Journal of Political Economy*, 81:678–696.

Lewis, W.A. (1952) 'World production, prices and trade, 1870–1960', *Manchester School of Economic and Social Studies*, 21:139–191.

Lewis, W.A. (1969) *Aspects of tropical trade, 1883–1967*. Uppsala: Wiksell.

Lewis, W.A. (1980) 'The slowing down of the engine of growth', *American Economic Review*, 70:555–564.

Lipsey, R.E. (1963) *Price and quantity trends in the foreign trade of the United States*. Princeton, NJ: Princeton University Press.

Love, J. (1984) 'External market conditions, competitiveness, diversification, and LDC exports', *Journal of Development Economics*, 16:279–291.

Martin, R. (1977) 'Immiserizing growth for a tariff-distorted, small economy Further analysis', *Journal of International Economics*, 7:223–228.

Maizels, A. (1963) *Industrial growth and world trade*. Cambridge: Cambridge University Press.

Maizels, A. (1968) *Exports and economic growth in developing countries*. Cambridge, MA: Cambridge University Press.

McKinnon, R.I. (1973) *Money and capital in economic development*. Washington, DC: The Brookings Institution.

Michaely, M. (1977) 'Exports and growth: An empirical investigation', *Journal of Development Economics*, 4:49–54.

Michaely, M. (1985) *Trade, income levels, and dependence*. Amsterdam: North Holland.

Michalopoulos, C. and Jay, K. (1973) 'Growth of exports and income in the developing world: A neoclassical view', U.S. Agency for International Development, Discussion Paper, no. 28, mimeo.

Mikesell, R.F. (1974) 'More Third World cartels ahead?' *Challenge*, 17:24–31.

Morrisson, C. (1985) 'Domestic income distribution and the structure of foreign trade', OECD Development Centre, mimeo.

Myint, H. (1955) 'The gains from trade and the backward countries', *Review of Economic Studies*, 22:129–42.

Myint, H. (1985) 'Growth policies and income distribution', World Bank Development Policy Issues Series, Discussion Paper no. VPERS1, mimeo.

Myrdal, G. (1957) *Economic theory and underdeveloped regions*. London: Duckworth.

North, D.C. (1961) *The economic growth of the United States, 1790–1860*. Englewood Cliffs, NJ: Prentice Hall.

Nurkse, R. (1961) *Equilibrium and growth in the world economy*. Cambridge, MA: Harvard University Press.

Nurkse, R. (1966) 'International trade policy and development policy', in: H.S. Ellis and H.C. Wallich, eds., *Economic development for Latin America*. London: Macmillan.

Papanek, G. (1973) 'Aid, foreign private investment, savings, and growth in less developed countries', *Journal of Political Economy*, 81:120–130.

Pindyck, R.S. (1978) 'Gains to producers from the cartellization of exhaustible resources', *Review of Economics and Statistics*, 60:238–251.

Porter, R.C. (1970) 'Some implications of postwar primary-product trends', *Journal of Political Economy*, 78:586–597.

Prebisch, R. (1950) *The economic development of Latin America*. Lake Success: United Nations.

Prebisch, R. (1959) 'Commercial policy in underdeveloped countries', *American Economic Review*, Papers and Proceedings, 44:251–273.

Radetzki, M. (1975) 'The potential for monopolistic commodity pricing by developing countries', in: G.K. Helleiner, ed., *A world divided: The less developed countries in the international economy*. Cambridge, MA: Cambridge University Press.

Radetzki, M. (1977) 'Long-term copper production options of the developing countries', *Natural Resource Forum*, 1:145–155.

Radetzki, M. (1984) 'Strategic metal markets. Prospects for producer cartels', *Resource Policy*, 10:227–240.

Riedel, J. (1984) 'Trade as the engine of growth in developing countries, revisited', *Economic Journal*, 94:56–73.

Schumpeter, J.A. (1954) *History of economic analysis*. New York: Oxford University Press.

Senghaas, D. (1980) 'The case for autarchy', *Development*, 2:17–22.

Singer, H. (1950) 'The distribution of gains between investing and borrowing countries', *American Economic Review*, Papers and Proceedings.

Singer, H. (1984) 'The terms of trade: Controversy and the evolution of soft financing: Early years in the U.N.', in: G.M. Meier and D. Seers, eds., *Pioneers in development*. Oxford: Oxford University Press.

Spraos, J. (1980) 'The statistical debate on the net barter terms of trade between primary commodities and manufactures', *Economic Journal*, 90:107–128.

Spraos, J. (1983) *Inequalizing trade?* Oxford: Clarendon Press.

Stern, E. and Tims, W. (1975) 'The relative bargaining strengths of the developing countries', *American Journal of Agricultural Economics*, 57:225–236.

Taylor, L. (1981) 'South-South trade and southern growth: Bleak prospects from the structuralist point of view', *Journal of International Economics*, 11:589–602.

Vines, D. (1984) 'A North-South growth model along Kaldorian lines', Centre for Economic Policy Research, Discussion Paper Series no. 26, mimeo.

Watkins, M.H. (1963) 'A staple theory of economic growth', *Canadian Journal of Economics and Political Science*, 29:141–158.

Weisskopf, T.E. (1972) 'The impact of foreign capital inflow on domestic savings in underdeveloped countries', *Journal of International Economics*, 2:25–38.

World Bank (1981) *World development report 1981*. World Bank.

Yates, P.L. (1959) *Forty years of foreign trade*. London: Allen & Unwin.

Chapter 32

LARGE COUNTRIES: THE INFLUENCE OF SIZE

DWIGHT H. PERKINS

Harvard University

MOSHE SYRQUIN*

Bar-Ilan University

Contents

*In preparing this chapter, the authors are deeply indebted to Yosi Deutsch and Delfin Go for their help with management and analysis of the large amounts of data required by this topic. For useful comments on drafts of this chapter, we wish to thank Hollis Chenery, T.N. Srinivasin, and C. Peter Timmer.

Handbook of Development Economics, Volume II, Edited by H. Chenery and T.N. Srinivasan
© *Elsevier Science Publishers B.V., 1989*

1. Introduction

Nations differ along many dimensions. Their citizens speak different languages and have developed widely varying cultures. Some are located in the tropics, others in the northern or southern temperate zones. There are rich nations and poor nations. And of central concern to this chapter, there are large nations and small ones.

Size, when measured in terms of population, clearly makes a difference to a nation's role and performance. The great powers of the world are all large nations, although there are large nations which are not great powers. Large nations are of greater interest to the world community than small ones if for no other reason than that most of the world's people live in the fifteen largest countries, which are the main focus of this chapter. Over three-quarters of all people on the globe reside in the fifteen nations whose population in 1980 was greater than 50 million persons. The other 120 or so countries house the remaining 20 percent.

But how important is size in affecting a nation's economic structure and performance? The view that there is a relationship between size and economic development goes back at least to Adam Smith.[1] More recently, several decades ago, Simon Kuznets showed that there was an inverse relationship between a nation's size, as measured by its population, and the share of foreign trade in that country's gross national product.[2] Subsequent research has shown that a nation's size is also correlated with a number of other variables.[3]

In addition to these statistical relationships, there has been speculation about why larger country size might lead to better or worse economic performance. On the one hand, it has been argued that the United States benefited economically from the large size of its internal market. On the other hand, China's and India's economies, it has been suggested, suffered because of their large size. Governing such huge and diverse nations was difficult, the argument goes, and problems of governance interfered with appropriate economic policies and institutions.

Few analysts, however, have attempted to combine theoretical speculation about how size might affect economic performance with international comparative data that could be used to test the hypotheses put forward. The analysis in this chapter is an effort to fill that gap. In making this effort, we hope to establish

---

[1] Adam Smith (1776, p. 381). See also Young (1928).

[2] The influence of country size as measured by population or total output on a nation's foreign trade ratio is a theme found in much of Simon Kuznets' work. See, for example, Kuznets (1959, 1960, 1964).

[3] Because of the influence of size and its interaction with per capita income, Chenery and Syrquin (1975) separate out large countries from small ones before running their regressions relating various structural variables to national income. Recent studies that focus on the relation of size to economic structure include Chenery (1982) and Wood (1986).

whether and where country size makes a contribution to the structure and performance of large economies.

Any analysis of size must begin by defining what is meant by country size and why one picks the nation state as the unit of analysis. Many analysts have used national population as the appropriate measure of size, but why is population a better measure than geographic size, the amount of arable land, or the magnitude of a nation's gross domestic product? And why is the nation state a superior unit for analytical purposes to the continent, the area of common culture, or subregions with common characteristics within a particular country? Was the creation of the nation state influenced to a large degree by economic forces? If it was, that fact alone would provide a strong reason for believing that the economic forces that made a large nation possible, would also have a profound influence on that nation's subsequent economic structure and performance. These and related issues take up the first part of this chapter.

The remainder of the chapter is concerned with how country size affects economic structure and performance. The analysis of structure begins from Kuznets' observation that trade ratios, defined as exports plus imports divided by GDP, fall as a country's size increases. Do lower trade ratios limit the options open to large nations, or are low trade ratios the result of deliberate choices among options that also include high trade ratios? Smaller nations with high trade ratios can specialize in a few products and import the rest, but do they do this by choice or because domestic markets are too small to support a more diversified structure? Large nations, whether by choice or necessity, produce domestically most of what they consume or invest. If nations at a particular stage of development consume and invest much the same goods, the economic structure of large nations with a similar level of per capita income should be much alike. China and India, for example, should have much the same economic structure despite the many differences in their economic and political systems. The structure of small countries should vary more and there is no reason to think that the typical structures of small nations would be the same as those of the large. Whether or not these differences between the large and the small can be established with cross-country comparative data is the main subject of the central portion of this chapter. The information analyzed refers to the post-war period; the findings may or may not be applicable to earlier periods. An important related issue is whether international data are collected in a form that allows one to draw conclusions about the relationship of size to structure. Differences in relative prices between nations, for example, could obscure underlying similarities in the "real" structure of the economy.

The relationship between country size and economic performance is concerned with the standard issues of efficiency and equity. Do large countries grow faster than small ones? Is their growth determined more by increases in productivity or by increases in inputs? Is inequality to some degree a function of size? If inequality between regions within a country is a major source of inequality between households, then one would expect large countries to have greater regional diversity and hence higher levels of inequality. These issues are the subject of the final part of this chapter.

2. Measuring size

There are several dimensions to country size. Australia and Canada are often considered to be large nations because of the extent of their territory. Others suggest that it is the size of the domestic market or a nation's gross national product that really matters for economic structure. And the empirical work of Kuznets, Chenery and Syrquin, and others all suggest that it is population size that influences structure. At the outset, therefore, one must clarify what one means by size.

Size is a relative concept and varies over time. The dividing line between what is considered large and what is small will also vary over time. In terms of population, Kuznets (1960) set the dividing line between large and small at 10 million; while Chenery and Syrquin (1975) set it at 15 million for 1960. In this chapter, primary attention is given to nations with 50 million or more people in 1980. In the year 1700, only two countries (China and India) had a population greater than 50 million. By 1980 there were fifteen (sixteen if Vietnam is included).

Size varies over time, particularly when the concern is with market size. Colonies, for example, were integrated to varying degrees with the markets of the colonizing country, but this integration declined with independence.[4] Transport costs also influence market size, and transport costs have fallen sharply over time with the invention of the steamship, the railroad, and the airplane.

The focus in this chapter, as in most work on this subject, is on population as the prime measure of country size. But as one digs deeper into why structure varies with population size, it is clear that there is more at work than just the number of people. Geography, for example, also makes a difference. In fact, some of the structural differences attributed to population size may be equally or more the result of a nation's geographic size. Separating the influences of population and geography is especially difficult because the two variables are themselves correlated with each other. But, as the data in Table 32.1 and the correlation coefficients in Table 32.2 make clear, the correlation is far from perfect. The United States, China, India, and the Soviet Union are large on both counts. But Japan, in contrast, has a population of over 100 million, the seventh largest in the world, crammed into an area only 4 percent as large as that of the United States. For Japan, as we shall see, this difference has a profound impact on the structure of its foreign trade.

---

[4]The decline was not abrupt, particularly in the case of France and her former colonies. See Kleiman (1976).

Table 32.1
Nations classified by area and population, 1952, 1980

Area (millions of square km)	1952 Population (millions)		
	> 100	40–100	20–40
> 2	U.S.S.R. U.S.A. India China	Brazil	
1–2		Pakistan[a] Indonesia	Mexico Egypt Iran South Africa
0.5–1		France	Spain Turkey Burma Thailand
< 0.5		Japan W. Germany U.K. Italy	Korea[b] Poland Philippines

Area (millions of square km)	1980 Population (millions)			
	> 200	100–200	60–100	40–60
> 2	U.S.S.R. U.S.A. India China	Brazil		
1–2 0.5–1		Indonesia	Mexico Nigeria Pakistan	Egypt France Turkey Thailand
< 0.5		Japan	Bangladesh W. Germany	Italy Philippines Vietnam U.K.

[a] Includes Bangladesh.
[b] Includes South and North.
Sources: 1952 – Woytinsky and Woytinsky (1955, p. 566). 1980 – World Bank (1984).

Geographic size is important because minerals and other natural resources are more apt to be present in larger quantities and greater variety in a large territory than in a small one. It is possible to have a huge expanse of territory and few petroleum reserves, but the odds are against it. In a similar way, climate is likely to vary more across regions in a large country and hence to support greater agricultural diversity.

Table 32.2

The relationship between different measures of country size (correlation matrix for 1970: $n = 97$)

	(1) Per capita income	(2) Population	(3) GNP	(4) Arable land	(5) Total area	(6) Density	(7) Trade ratio
(1) Per capita income	1.00	–	–	–	–	–	–
(2) Population	– 0.026	1.00	–	–	–	–	–
(3) GNP	0.463	0.270	1.00	–	–	–	–
(4) Arable land	0.125	0.720	0.641	1.00	–	–	–
(5) Total area	0.141	0.546	0.437	0.733	1.00	–	–
(6) Density[a]	0.240	0.141	0.154	– 0.004	– 0.193	1.00	–
(7) Trade ratio[b]	0.131	– 0.387	– 0.249	– 0.435	– 0.361	– 0.031	1.00

[a] Density is the number of people per square kilometer of total land area.
[b] The trade ratio is exports plus imports divided by gross domestic product (GDP).
Source: World Bank data.

Geographic size is also important because of the impact of transport costs. In the interior of large countries, for example, transport costs alone can be high enough to make the import of certain commodities from abroad or from the coastal region of the country itself prohibitively expensive.

For some purposes, however, it is not the nation's total area that matters but the nature of its climate and the quality of its soil. The deserts of Central Asia, the Middle East, and Africa may be full of minerals, but they have little capacity to feed people. Because of the obvious relationship between food and population, it is no surprise that the correlation coefficient between arable land and population is high (see Table 32.2). The correlation, however, is not perfect. Various studies have shown that a limited land area is not necessarily a barrier to large increases in population.[5] Nevertheless, the theory of comparative advantage, among others, suggests that there ought to at least be some relationship between the amount of arable land per capita and the composition of foreign trade.

The relationship between total land area and population is also of interest. Population density through its impact on domestic demand, for example, may have a great deal to do with whether mineral resources within a nation's territory are used domestically or exported.

The one "size" variable that appears to have little relationship with the others is gross national product. The correlation between population and GNP in particular is less than 0.3. If population size and economic structure vary systematically, therefore, one likely outcome is that GNP size and economic structure do not vary systematically with each other. But how does one reconcile this conclusion with the frequently drawn connection between the size of the market and economies of scale? A partial answer presumably lies in the fact that, where international trade exists, the size of the market for a given industry in a single country is not determined solely or even primarily by the size of the market within that one country. Another part of the answer is that econometrically one cannot easily distinguish the effects of population size and GNP size on economic structure. GNP size, therefore, may in fact influence economic structure significantly. We shall return to this latter point below.

3. The nation as the unit of analysis

The distinction between a foreign and a domestic market is first of all a legal one. If the market in question is on the opposite side of an international boundary, it

---

[5] There is now a considerable literature challenging the essentially Malthusian notion that population growth is constrained by the availability of arable land and by autonomous technological innovations that make increases in the productivity of that land possible. In fact, population growth itself induces many increases in land productivity. See, for example, Boserup (1965), Perkins (1969), and Geertz (1963).

is by definition foreign. Legal distinctions, however, are not the major reason for choosing the nation state as the unit of analysis. Economic development is best understood as a process that involves the interaction of millions of households and firms within a framework determined to a large degree by the sovereign governments that rule those households and firms. By looking only at households and firms, one misses many relationships and similarities that are common to all of the particular subgroups precisely because they are part of a single nation state. Similarly, at the opposite end of the spectrum, it is difficult to analyze development at a supra-national level because so many of the decisions governing growth are made at the national level. It is national governments, for the most part, that place custom houses on their borders and manipulate tariffs, quotas, and exchange rates. The results of these manipulations are prices and market structures within the territory of a given nation state that differ significantly from those outside the boundaries of that country. Thus, the discontinuities between states due to differences in language and culture are reinforced by trade policies.[6] And trade barriers are only one subset of tools among many available to governments in shaping their domestic economies. The contrast between the centrally-planned system of the Soviet Union and the laissez-faire system of nineteenth-century Great Britain illustrates the point. State interventions are an integral and essential part of modern economic growth.[7]

There is also, of course, a practical reason for using the nation state as a unit of analysis. Data, for the most part, are collected on a national basis and it would be both difficult and expensive to attempt to pull together data for some other larger or smaller unit of analysis. Data are collected on a national basis to aid governments of those nations in their efforts to manage and develop their societies. As Kuznets pointed out, the very word "statistics" is a derivative of "state".[8]

For some purposes, however, the use of alternative units of analysis such as the European Economic Community can be enlightening. Customs unions may allow a small nation to enjoy some of the key economic benefits of larger size. The existence of multinational corporations and international capital markets may have reduced discontinuities between nation states, but one should not overstate the case. Investment by nations in their domestic economy, for example, is highly correlated with domestic savings despite the existence of an international pool of capital.[9]

The case for using the nation state as the primary unit of analysis would be even more compelling if nations were created and their size determined to a large degree by economic forces. Wittfogel, for example, argued that the hydraulic

[6]Svennilson (1960).
[7]Kuznets (1966).
[8]Kuznets (1951).
[9]Feldstein and Horioka (1980).

systems of pre-modern Asia required centralized bureaucracies capable of governing large expanses of territory, encompassing in some cases entire river systems.[10] Conceivably, modern industrial technology could have had something to do with the creation or sustenance of large nations in the nineteenth and twentieth centuries. If the forces of modern economic growth had much to do with why nations became or remained large, it would seem likely that those same forces would have a profound impact on the structure of large nations' economies.

In fact, as will be argued below, modern economic growth had relatively little to do with why some nations became large while others remained small. With few common economic or technological threads to the origins or continued existence of large nations, there is little reason on these grounds to think that large nations would have a common and distinctive economic structure.

3.1. A brief historical review

What is the evidence that economics and technology in general and modern economic growth in particular had little to do with why some countries became very large? A brief review of the histories of a few of these giants will be sufficient to establish the main point being made.

China and India are by far the largest nations in the world in terms of population. China's unity over such a wide territory and large population, for example, was primarily the product of two interrelated influences.[11] To begin with, there was China's written language and culture that provided the population with a shared set of values and a means of communicating those values to the people, particularly the ruling elites. The high culture of most of China's immediate neighbors was less developed so that they were either absorbed into Chinese culture as they came in contact with it, or retreated to the south. To rule this area of common culture and written language, the Chinese developed the Confucian bureaucratic state governed not by alliances of victorious generals, but by an elite highly educated in Confucian values and selected by examination. As a result, China ruled over a territory much like what it is today for well over a millennium, long before the era of modern economic growth began even in Europe. Geography played a role in setting the boundaries of this unified bureaucratic state. China's culture and people could not penetrate through to the other side of the Himalayas or the great Central Asian deserts. And the southward drift of China's population was slowed as the southern center of

---

[10] Wittfogel (1957). See also Carneiro (1970) for a critique of various theories of state origins.
[11] For a view of some of the earlier explanations of China's size and unity by one of the authors of this chapter, see Perkins (1969, ch. VIII).

population moved further away from the capital in the north and met increasingly effective resistance from peoples to the south.[12]

India's history is different from that of China, but there are some common threads. India's high Hindu culture provided an important set of shared values across a large population, and early India had a common written elite language (Sanskrit) which served as a base for a number of the country's living regional languages. India's more recent history was dominated by the interaction of these Hindu populations with the Mogul (Moslem) conquests. The Mogul conquest was followed by that of the British, achieved in part by military means and in part by negotiation with the princely states. But the unity of the Mogul and British empires could not be sustained at independence and the country broke into two nations at the time of independence and then into three with the creation of Bangladesh. Islam was not a force for unity sufficient to overcome the distance, both cultural and geographic, between Punjabis and Bengalis of West and East Pakistan. Geography, the Indian Ocean and the Himalayas, plus religion, thus account for the modern borders of India, but culture and colonial and pre-colonial history account for why such a large territory remained unified after 1948.

The creation of the continent-wide nations of the Soviet Union and the United States also cannot be described as being shaped by primarily economic considerations. Economic forces, of course, were present, particularly when viewed from the perspective of individuals, but they played more of a supporting role than a primary one when it came to determining where boundaries were to be drawn. The current boundaries of both nations were achieved to a large degree by military conquest, reinforced in the case of the United States by large-scale migration of the dominant population which was of British and northern European origin. The continued expansion of the United States was stopped by the Pacific Ocean and a combination of essentially political considerations that made the annexation of either Canada or Mexico seem unattractive. Russian conquest was also stopped by the Pacific Ocean and the inability of the Russians to conquer the large population centers ruled by hostile empires to the east and south and by more advanced and militarily powerful nations to the west.

In China, India, and the Soviet Union, we find vast territories and people that remained under unified rule, while in Spanish America the situation is exactly the opposite. A population in a large territory with geographical continuity, sharing mostly a common language and religion, a similar colonial background, and

---

[12] The literature on what determined the nature of the Chinese state and its ability to govern such a large territory is far too voluminous to be cited in this chapter. Essentially the same point can be made about the other large countries discussed here. In reaching these conclusions the authors have relied on their own knowledge derived from the reading of history and from consultation with those who know the history of particular countries far better than we do.

administrative structure, nevertheless gave rise to almost 20 separate nations. The observed fragmentation in Spanish America reflected the administrative framework already in place at the time of independence (around 1820). Independent nations arose in those places which had had the status of viceroyalty, presidency, or captaincy-general. Captains-general and presidents were directly appointed by the king of Spain, and although they were nominally subordinate to the viceroyalty, in practice the great distances allowed them significant autonomy. With the exception of Central America, which did split into five units, all Latin American nations existing by the 1820s still exist today and no new ones were formed, although there were some unsuccessful secessionist movements (in Yucatan, West Argentina, and Rio Grande do Sul).

Brazil, the largest country in Latin America, became independent from Portugal much later and under the best possible conditions for continuity. The king of Portugal, John VI, fled to Brazil after the Napoleonic invasion and established the United Kingdom of Portugal, Brazil, and the Algarves. When pressures arose in Portugal to re-establish a colonial status for Brazil, his son, Dom Pedro II, declared independence. In the first half of the nineteenth century, most of Brazil's population was concentrated along a narrow coastal plain. At that time, Brazil was smaller than the modern nation. The Amazon Valley was uncharted and Brazil was to acquire additional territory through favorable boundary settlements.

Despite a shared language and many shared values, and a reasonably effective central government, the United States almost broke in two in the 1860s, although there was never a threat of fragmentation comparable to what happened in Spanish Latin America. India, as already mentioned, did break into two and then three parts. Nigeria had to overcome the Biafran civil war to maintain its unity and, at an earlier time, Brazil had to overcome separatist forces in the northeast. Nigeria's borders, like most of those in Africa, were drawn for the administrative convenience of the European colonial powers and had little other rationale.[13]

Even a casual reading of European history makes it clear that a large territory unified under one government, sharing some common elements of culture, and with few major internal geographic divisions, could still fall apart. The empires of Rome and Charlemagne broke apart long ago, but Austro-Hungary fell apart after World War I. European unity, where it existed, largely followed linguistic lines. And where groups with a common language were divided, as in nineteenth-century Germany and Italy, they eventually found a way to come together.

Language, culture, political organization, and superior military fire power, therefore, are what built the large nations of today. Economic power does have

---

[13]A useful presentation of this view and its connection with the current politics of West Africa can be found in Hart (1982).

something to do with military power, but the limits of conquest were set more by geography, the weakness of the opposition, and other political considerations. As opposition increased, so did the costs of further expansion measured both in economic and political terms. Political leaders, however, did not sit down and calculate what would make an optimum-size nation from an economic point of view and then set out to conquer it. One motive for the conquest of territory was the desire to gain control over natural resources (Japan in World War II, for example), but few national boundaries were shaped primarily by such efforts.

The case cannot be made, therefore, that the size of large countries was determined primarily or to a large degree by underlying economic forces that in turn shaped the structure of those nations' economies. Such economic forces as did exist, for the most part exerted their influence prior to the rise of the modern industrial system except perhaps in Germany and Italy.

3.2. Alternative units of analysis

If the large nation state was not created primarily by economic forces, it may be useful to look at units other than the nation state when analyzing why economic structures vary from one part of the globe to another. It would be particularly useful to separate out those elements of economic structure that are not simply the result of the way international boundaries were drawn.

Data for trade within the European Economic Community and between that community and the rest of the world, for example, can be used to show that certain elements of national economic structure may not result from underlying economic forces such as factor endowment or economies of scale so much as from the political and cultural influences that drew boundaries dividing one region from another. The relevance of these influences is most apparent when one analyzes the reasons why trade shares are low in large countries relative to trade shares in small countries.

The European Economic Community (EEC) data used to make this point are for the original members of the Community only and are presented in Table 32.3. The years chosen are those immediately following formation of the Community. If the intra- and extra-EEC trade figures are combined for each of the five countries, the expected relationship between country size and the share of foreign trade emerges clearly. In 1971, for example, the trade shares of Belgium and the Netherlands ([exports + imports] $\times$ 100 $\div$ national income) were 107.3 and 94.8 percent, respectively. For the much larger nations of Germany, Italy, and France, the comparable figures were 54.5, 46.5, and 42.9 percent, respectively. And even these latter figures were high in comparison with those of the then largest countries in the world whose trade ratios only rarely exceed 20 percent.

Table 32.3

Share of exports and imports in national income: 1960–71

	Exports					Imports				
	Germany	France	Italy	Netherlands	Belgium	Germany	France	Italy	Netherlands	Belgium
Intra EEC										
1960	7.0	5.6	5.1	21.1	–	7.1	4.8	5.2	22.9	–
1965	7.9	6.8	7.6	23.6	26.8	9.0	6.6	5.3	25.7	24.3
1971	10.2	9.5	9.6	29.5	35.3	11.2	9.6	8.9	28.0	31.3
Other										
1960	18.6	14.0	13.1	24.2	–	15.2	12.4	13.4	23.9	–
1965	16.8	11.5	13.2	18.1	18.4	15.3	10.6	12.2	19.8	20.7
1971	18.0	12.4	14.3	17.1	19.8	15.1	11.4	13.7	20.2	20.9

[a]Goods only.
Source: Halevi (1976, p. 338).

If the EEC is looked at as a whole and treated as a single country, however, an interesting change occurs. The five EEC nations treated as a single entity had a combined population of 190 million in the early 1970s, nearly the same number as in the United States. To obtain the foreign trade ratio of the EEC as a unit, one must eliminate all intra-EEC trade. As the data in Table 32.3 suggest, the resulting ratio would be around 30 percent or a bit less, still above the shares of other very large countries, but not by such a wide margin as they are when the EEC countries are looked at individually.

Another interesting feature of the EEC experience is the rapid rise in the intra-EEC trade share each of the five countries achieved after integration as contrasted with the steady share of trade between those countries and the nations outside of the EEC. Clearly, policy choices that lead to the creation or dismantling of barriers to international commerce make a difference.[14] Trade shares are not determined by nature or the size of a country alone.

These EEC data, therefore, support the view that some of the influences of size on a nation's economic structure result from little more than the fact that big geographic regions and populations will have more international trade if they are broken up into smaller rather than larger political units. A significant part of the lower trade ratio of large nations, however, cannot be explained in this way. The use of the nation state as the primary unit of analysis is thus rooted in considerations more profound than simply that data are more available for nations than for larger or smaller units.

Similar reasoning applies to why the nation state rather than subregions within nations are the preferred units of analysis. It was argued above that a nation can be distinguished from larger units by various discontinuities related to political authority, language, religion, and institutions. The reason for preferring the nation as the unit of analysis over a smaller unit is the assumption that within a nation there is a high degree of political, cultural, and economic continuity. To this we can add the usual assumption in trade theory of factor mobility within, but not among, countries, and the fact that many decisions related to growth are made at the national level. However, it is often true, particularly at the early stages of development, that there is a high degree of regional fragmentation and regional barriers to factor flows. The fragmentation had led, in some cases, to civil war and to a break-up of nations into smaller units. In extreme cases it may be more useful to study the regions rather than the nation. In general, however, the reasons for preferring the nation seem more weighty. Regional inequalities are briefly considered in Section 6.

---

[14]At the time the EEC was set up, there was a large literature on whether that move would be "trade creating" or "trade diverting". That subject is clearly related to the question of the degree to which trade shares in GNP are determined by country size as contrasted to other influences.

4. Country size and economic structure

How then does country size affect a nation's economic structure? The analysis in this part of the chapter is concerned with both how the structures of large countries differ from small ones and why those structures differ. And this chapter is particularly concerned with the world's fifteen largest nations, a number small enough to allow one to bring individual country experience to bear on the question of why large country structures vary from those of small countries. This analysis of the relationship between country size and economic structure starts from the one proposition that is beyond dispute: the larger a nation's population, the lower is the share of foreign trade in that nation's GDP.

4.1. The share of foreign trade in GDP

What accounts for the declining share of foreign trade in GDP as population size increases? First, it is important to establish clearly that these ratios do fall as size increases. The relevant data are presented in Tables 32.4 and 32.5. These data and others used throughout this chapter are based on a sample of countries that varies somewhat depending on the variable being analyzed. Most of the estimates in tables in the text are simple averages of the variables being considered, but in Appendix A we have estimated the impact of size on these same variables in the context of a regression equation in which size is handled as two dummy variables. In the figures used here and in many of the other tables as well, the sample consists of 75 small countries, 14 very large countries, and 15 other large countries. The Soviet Union is included in some tables, but is not included in the sample from which country averages by size are derived. When nations are divided into those with populations above 50 million people, those between 15 and 50 million, and those below 15 million, the very large nation category has a foreign trade ratio of 20.1 percent ([exports + imports] $\times$ 100 $\div$ GDP) in 1970–72, while the small group has a ratio of 41.5 percent in the same years. The figures for the world's fifteen largest nations for 1970–72 are presented in Table 32.5. In 1970–72 three of the four most heavily populated nations (China, India, and the United States) had trade ratios below 10 percent and only Indonesia among the top seven nations had a ratio above 20 percent in those years.

While the trade ratios for large countries are consistently low, they are not particularly stable over time nor within the very large country sub-sample does one country always have a lower trade ratio than all nations with smaller populations. China and India, the two largest nations, for example, have higher trade ratios in most years than those of the Soviet Union. Indonesia, the world's fifth largest nation, has a substantially higher ratio than Brazil and Japan, the

Table 32.4
Foreign trade shares by country size (foreign trade/GDP in %)

	1962–64			1970–72			1979–81		
	Total	Manufactured	Primary	Total	Manufactured	Primary	Total	Manufactured	Primary
						Merchandise exports			
Very large countries	9.1	5.0	4.1	10.3	6.0	4.3	14.8	8.6	6.2
Other large countries	14.4	1.9	12.5	13.2	3.6	9.6	15.9	7.6	8.3
Small countries	19.0	3.7	15.3	19.7	9.6	14.8	23.5	7.8	15.7
						Merchandise imports			
Very large countries	9.4	4.9	4.5	9.8	6.0	3.8	16.1	8.7	7.4
Other large countries	13.9	9.4	4.5	14.5	10.4	4.1	19.6	12.0	7.6
Small countries	20.6	14.0	6.6	21.8	15.3	6.5	29.8	18.8	11.0

Source: World Bank data.

Table 32.5

Foreign trade shares of very large countries in 1970–72 (percent of GDP)

	Merchandise exports			Merchandise imports			Exports + imports total
	Total	Manufactured	Primary	Total	Manufactured	Primary	
China[a]	2.9	1.4	1.6	2.4	n.a.	n.a.	5.3
India	3.8	2.1	1.8	3.6	2.1	1.5	7.4
U.S.S.R.	6.1	n.a.	n.a.	9.1	n.a.	n.a.	15.2
U.S.A.	4.6	3.3	1.3	4.3	2.9	1.4	8.9
Indonesia	14.3	0.2	14.1	12.9	10.7	2.2	27.2
Brazil	6.2	1.1	5.1	6.3	4.4	1.9	12.5
Japan	9.5	8.9	0.6	6.8	1.7	5.1	16.3
Bangladesh[a]	6.2	4.2	2.0	17.4	10.2	7.2	23.6
Nigeria	14.0	0.2	13.2	9.9	8.6	1.3	23.9
Pakistan	6.7	3.8	2.9	10.4	6.5	3.9	17.1
Mexico	3.8	1.3	2.4	5.9	4.8	1.1	9.7
W. Germany	17.4	15.5	1.9	14.4	8.2	6.2	31.8
Italy	13.9	11.6	2.3	14.0	6.4	7.6	27.9
U.K.	16.3	13.7	2.6	16.5	7.9	8.6	32.8
France	13.1	9.7	3.4	12.7	7.6	5.1	25.8

[a] Figures are for 1980 for Bangladesh. Chinese GDP was estimated by adding 15 percent to Net Material Product.

Note: Countries are ranked by population size.

Sources: World Bank data except for China, which are derived from State Statistical Bureau (1986, pp. 41, 481) and Ministry of Foreign Economic Relations and Trade Compilation Committee (1984, p. IV-9); and the Soviet Union, which were estimated by Treml (1980, pp. 187–188). The Soviet figures are expressed as a percentage of national income after converting Soviet trade data from foreign trade prices to domestic prices.

sixth and seventh most populous countries.[15] Thus, while the downward slope of the regression line relating the foreign trade ratio and country size is clear enough, there is considerable variance around the regression line, enough to suggest caution in attempting to predict any given nation's ratio from the general tendency of all nations.

What causes the foreign trade ratios of large nations to be low? There are four possible explanations, all of which have some role in this outcome.[16]

(1) Location considerations closely linked to transport costs favor domestic producers in large countries over their foreign competitors for a wider range of products than is the case in small countries.

(2) Low foreign trade ratios are also the product of deliberate policy choices of governments favoring import substitution and a more closed economic development strategy.

(3) These ratios reflect the advantage of economies of scale enjoyed by large nations. In a world of free trade, the absence of uncertainty, and completely open economies, large nations would be in no better position to take advantage of economies of scale, at least for traded goods, than small nations. But for sustained periods in the real world, the 1930s and 1940s, for example, economies have not been open to free trade and the size of the domestic market becomes critical for achieving scale economies.

(4) Mineral resources are distributed across the globe in ways such that small nations typically end up with larger quantities of a few minerals than they can possibly use at home. Larger nations typically have a closer match between the domestic supply of key minerals and their demand for those minerals.

All four of these points are in effect explanations of why a nation's structure of production differs from that same nation's structure of demand. Trade is the residual (positive or negative) that results from disparities in these two structures. On the demand side, numerous studies have shown that the structure of demand varies with per capita income, but is otherwise quite similar across countries of varying cultures and size [Houthakker (1957), Lluch, Powell and Williams (1977)]. It is variation on the production or supply side, therefore, that accounts for much of the difference between demand and production structures that results in international trade. All four of the explanations of high or low foreign trade ratios explored here are, in essence, explanations of why large country production structures differ from those of small countries.

---

[15] The standard deviation of the export ratio divided by the mean for the small country subsample is 0.694, whereas for the large country subsample it is 0.715, essentially the same.

[16] There is a purely formal aspect of the relation between size, as measured by GDP, and trade proportions. With only two countries and balanced trade, the trade proportions in the two countries will necessarily be inversely related to the ratio of their GDPs [Kuznets (1964, p. 15)]. A similar point was also made by Machlup (1977, p. 77). Imagine three countries of equal size and trade. If two of them merge, the foreign trade ratio in the now large country will be reduced to one-half.

4.1.1. Transport costs and trade shares

The first explanation is closely linked to the point made earlier using data from the European Economic Community. If trade were spread evenly across the globe, trade ratios could rise as the global political system became more fragmented. At one extreme, if all nations were combined into one, foreign trade would, by definition, disappear. At the other extreme, trade ratios might rise to even higher levels as the political makeup of the globe broke down first into a few large nations, then into several hundred, and then into tens of thousands or more as every country or even every household declared its independence and national sovereignty. Given the political boundaries of the world as they are today, foreign trade ratios would be determined largely by whether, when transport costs and the uncertainty involved in relying on shipments from outside the country were taken into account, it was cheaper to produce a good within one's own borders than to ship it in from outside.

Clearly, geography and transport costs do have something to do with whether trade in a given situation will be classified as domestic or foreign, particularly when per capita incomes and factor endowments across a given region are similar, as is the case with the European Economic Community. The foreign trade ratios of Europe rise from 30 percent for the Community as a whole to 40–50 percent for France and Germany and might rise to 100 percent and more if the European Community were broken up into nations the size of Belgium.[17]

Support for the view that there is more to foreign trade ratios than geography and transport costs can be derived from the fact that population size and geographic size are not perfectly correlated, as mentioned above. Two of the very large countries in particular, Japan and Bangladesh, are quite small in area. Furthermore, most regions in both countries have ready access to water transport which, potentially at least, is relatively cheap. Almost all populated parts of Japan have easy access to the sea, and Bangladesh is laced with the many rivers that make up the Ganges delta. Other things being equal, therefore, if it is geography that matters most, Japan and Bangladesh should have trade ratios considerably higher than those of other nations with roughly comparable numbers of people. In fact, Japan's trade ratio in the 1970s was half that of France, a nation that was larger in area, but had less than half of Japan's population. Bangladesh's trade ratio in 1970–72 was 23.6 percent, a figure less than that of Spain despite the fact that Spain had a territory nearly four times as large as Bangladesh. Despite these exceptions, if one estimates the correlation of the foreign trade ratio with country area instead of population, there is still a clear negative relationship, as one would expect given the correlation between country population and area. The fit is slightly, but only slightly, poorer as evidenced by

[17]See Table 32.3.

the fall in the correlation coefficient from 0.39 to 0.36 (see Table 32.2). Thus, geography does appear to play an important role in determining the trade shares of nations of varying size.

4.1.2. Policy and trade shares

A second view of how trade shares are determined, stated baldly, is that foreign trade shares result mainly from the deliberate policy choices of governments. If a nation has a low trade ratio, it is because that nation's government deliberately set out to reduce the role of trade by pushing import substitution and ignoring or even putting barriers in the way of exports.

Clearly, policy choices do have an influence on the level of foreign trade.[18] In the large countries of Latin America trade shares were significantly reduced in the immediate post-war period largely as a result of import substitution policies. Between 1950 and 1965 the shares of exports in GDP fell from 9.4 to 7.6 percent in Argentina; from 8.2 to 7.4 in Brazil; and from 14.1 to 9.3 percent in Mexico [World Bank (1980)]. By 1970–72 China's trade ratio had fallen to 5.2 percent from 10.4 percent only fifteen years earlier. Any reading of Chinese history for this period leaves little doubt that this fall was a direct result of the failures of the Great Leap Forward (1958–60) and the anti-foreignism of the early years of the Cultural Revolution (1966–69 were the peak years of Cultural Revolution politics). The extremely low ratios of the Soviet Union in the 1930s and 1950s had similar political origins. No country can afford to do without trade altogether, but the Soviet Union in the late 1930s came close, with ([exports + imports] ÷ GNP in current prices) falling from 3.1 percent in 1933–37 to 0.6 percent in 1940.[19]

Nations can also deliberately set out to expand their share of international trade. South Korea's export drive that raised that country's trade ratio from 11.8 percent in 1955 to 83.9 percent in 1981 is one of the best-known cases.[20] Of greater world wide impact was the ability of the Organization of Petroleum Exporting Countries (OPEC) to form a cartel and raise oil prices dramatically, first in 1973 and then again in 1979. The rise in oil prices itself led to a rise in the trade shares of oil exporting nations and in the trade shares of the rest of the world, but the increase in trade was not solely a price phenomenon. The OPEC nations quickly began increasing their own imports in real terms. The mirror image of this rise in OPEC imports was a real rise in exports from those countries

---

[18] Policy here is distinguished from market forces that operate independently of government actions. These policies may improve on or worsen economic performance. Their key feature is that they are implemented in order to divert the economy from the path set by unfettered market forces and underlying economic conditions.

[19] Kuznets (1963, p. 365).

[20] Foreign trade share data are from World Bank (1983, pp. 504–507).

that were major importers of oil. The trade ratios of developing countries as a whole, which were 33.5 percent in 1970, had risen to 54.1 percent in 1981. For industrial market economies the rise was from 26.3 to 39.9 percent.[21]

In short, policy decisions by governments do matter, but the policy decisions that matter most may not always be those made by one's own government. The OPEC decision is one case in point. The free trade policy of the American government in the 1950s and 1960s that facilitated export growth in East Asia, among other places, is another important example. Policy decisions made by the countries themselves, however, have also been important. Within the very large country group, for example, the low trade ratios of Mexico, Brazil, China, India, and the Soviet Union were all the result of policy decisions made by the governments of those nations. These import substitution policies are discussed at length by Bruton in Chapter 30 and by Balassa in Chapter 31 of this Handbook.

If policy decisions do matter, it is also clear that there are limits to the scope for policy choice. Japan is usually seen as a nation whose government was geared to pushing exports and an expanding Japanese position in world trade. There is an element of truth in this view, even if the popular perception of Japan as an exporting machine is exaggerated. Japan's foreign trade did grow rapidly, yet because Japanese GDP was growing equally rapidly, Japan's trade ratio remained nearly constant at a modest 20 percent or less from the 1950s well into the 1970s. In the late 1970s and early 1980s this ratio did rise, but by no more than was generally the case for all industrial market economies.

Policy-makers could call for drastic change in the role of foreign trade and they could take steps to implement what their rhetoric called for, as Bruton and Balassa point out in Chapters 30 and 31 of this Handbook, but in most cases there were forces at work that limited the degree of change actually achieved. Efforts to reduce the role of trade ran up against the need to import essential inputs that could not be efficiently produced within the nation. Export promotion drives were slowed by protectionist policies in the receiving market or by the greater attractiveness of their own market for domestic entrepreneurs.

4.1.3. Economies of scale

While many economic conditions affect the role of foreign trade in particular countries, which of these is central to an understanding of the low trade ratio of large nations? The economic influence most commonly referred to in this context is economies of scale. In fact, economies of scale are typically seen as the principal reason that large countries have low foreign trade ratios.[22] The logic of this position is relatively straightforward. Large nations have large markets which

---

[21] World Bank (1983, pp. 504–507).
[22] Kuznets (1960).

enable a producer in an industry with economies of scale to build a plant of a sufficient size to take advantage of these economies. Small nations have domestic markets of insufficient size so that enterprises with scale economies must either locate elsewhere or produce to a large degree for export. A small country, therefore, will either avoid industries with marked economies of scale or will specialize in a few such sectors where it has special advantages. Either way the small country will import large amounts of the product of those industries it chooses not to develop. A large country can develop all sectors and, for reasons of economies of scale at least, has little need to import anything.

There is something to the notion of a relationship between scale economies and foreign trade ratios, but the relationship is not so straightforward as the above argument would suggest. To begin with, the size of a nation's domestic market is related more to the size of its GNP than it is to the number of people who live there. And yet it is population size that is usually correlated with foreign trade ratios. As Kuznets showed several decades ago, there is little correlation between a nation's per capita national product and its foreign trade ratio.[23] This argument, however, may not be as damaging to the role of scale economies as it at first appears. If both per capita income and GNP are used as explanatory variables for the foreign trade ratio, then the fit is identical to the fit achieved if per capita income and population size are the explanatory variables.[24] It is the

---

[23] Kuznets (1963).

[24] That is:

$$x = a + b \ln y + c \ln N, \tag{1}$$

gives the same result for c as the regression equation

$$x = a' + b' \ln y + c \ln \text{GDP}, \tag{2}$$

where

x = foreign trade ration,
y = per capita income,
N = total population,
GDP = absolute size of GDP.

The identity of the estimate of c in the two equations results from the fact that, by holding per capita income constant, an increase in population implies an equiproportional increase in GDP. Thus, this formulation of the relationship between trade ratios and size does not provide a basis for choosing between population and GDP as the appropriate measure of size. But the formulation in equation (2) does indicate that there is a plausible way of demonstrating a relationship between trade shares and market size as measured by GDP. The inclusion of the per capita income variable has intuitive appeal in a number of ways, including one that relates to economies of scale. Countries with low per capita income tend to have fragmented domestic markets because of poorly developed transport and related infrastructure. The size of these poorer countries' GDP, therefore, tends to exaggerate the size of the market as it relates to the issue of economies of scale. The inclusion of the per capita income variable, absolute size of the GNP, not per capita GNP, that influences the size of the market and there is some negative correlation between trade shares and the absolute size of GNP,[25] although the fit is not as good as when population size is the independent variable.

It is possible, therefore, to show statistically that there is a relationship between trade shares and a measure of market size (GNP and GNP per capita) that has a more plausible connection with economies of scale than does population size. But what kind of scale economies are we referring to? A review of the literature on the subject indicates that some definitions of scale economies have little to do with the size of the market. Denison, for example, includes a measure of the contribution of economies of scale in his growth accounting exercise.[26] But Denison's definition is based on the view that efficiency gains of countries with lower per capita incomes than the United States become greater as those nations' per capita incomes rise, hence consumption patterns become more like those of the United States. The transfer of know-how from the United States to these countries thus becomes easier because the industries in the poorer countries have become more like those in the United States. This concept of economies of scale thus has little to do with the absolute size of the market and hence also has little to say about the relationship between low foreign trade ratios and country size.

Several definitions of economies of scale, however, are relevant to country size and the share of foreign trade.

(1) Certain industries operate much more efficiently at large levels of output, levels that are frequently greater than the total domestic market for that output, particularly in small, poor countries. Automobiles are a prime example since an efficient production run (one that minimizes long-run average cost) is typically several hundred thousand vehicles per year. Even in a fairly large and relatively prosperous country such as Korea, the total annual demand for automobiles in the latter half of the 1970s was only 20 000–30 000. Other industries where economies of scale are also pronounced include aircraft, steel, petroleum refining, many chemicals, ship-building, some consumer durables, and certain heavy electrical and railroad equipment.[27]

---

in effect, captures this limitation on market size. The per capita income variable, however, also captures a number of influences other than market size and economies of scale. If market size was the dominant influence, the coefficient *b* of the per capita income variable would be negative when foreign trade share is the dependent variable. In fact, *b* is slightly positive, although the fit is poor. The implication is that influences other than market size and economies of scale dominate at least to a limited degree. See Chenery (1960).

[25] See the correlation coefficient in Table 32.2.

[26] Denison (1967). This approach is explained and qualified in Matthews (1968).

[27] See, for example, the introduction in Robinson (1960) and Balassa (1965). See also Roemer (1979) for evidence on economies of scale in industries based on natural resources.

(2) As per capita incomes rise, demand tends to become more differentiated. At low levels of income people may be satisfied with cheap standardized clothing and a few basic food items. At higher income levels people will not only want automobiles, some will want small cars, others will want large ones, different styles, or different engine performance. Thus, a nation might have a large enough domestic market to support a production run of 300 000 standardized vehicles a year, but the public might not want more than 50 000 of any one variety. Under such circumstances, therefore, domestic demand would have to reach one or two million vehicles a year before the domestic market alone could support an automobile industry operating at an efficient scale.[28] This concept of economies of scale is relevant to industries as diverse as textiles, certain petrochemicals, and various types of machinery.[29]

(3) Exporting is the classic way around an inadequate domestic market. Relying on foreign trade to exploit economies of scale, however, sounds more convincing today than it did some 30 years ago. In the 1950s, after three decades of disarray in the international network of trade, perceptions were different from what they are today and those views influenced policy at the time. Trade was seen as a precarious escape from small size because of various uncertainties and the need for a large home market to serve as a springboard for exports [Robinson (1960)]. Even today exports may not be an effective way for small countries to realize economies of scale in manufacturing. Most industries in developing countries begin by producing for the domestic market and only later progress to exporting. If the domestic market is too small to sustain a plant of efficient size, a smaller less efficient plant may be built. Worse still, import substitution policies often create incentives to build several plants when the market is not sufficient to sustain even one operating at world prices. Thus, the small country remains dependent on the export of primary products to meet its foreign exchange requirements.

(4) External economies are frequently related to size, not of the individual firm or industry, but to the size of industry in general, either within the country as a whole or within a region of that country. Industries locate in cities because of the advantages of sharing infrastructure such as transport, reliable electric power, and financial institutions. High technology industries tend to locate near major sources of supply of the kinds of skilled labor they find so essential. And there are many other examples.[30]

What relevance do these several kinds of economies of scale have to the share of foreign trade in national product? For countries with a low per capita income and a population of two or three million, the answer is a great deal. Such

[28] Linder (1961).
[29] Balassa and Stoutjesdijk (1975).
[30] Isard (1956).

countries would not have domestic markets sufficient to support any of the kinds of industries listed under (1) or (2) above. Nor would most of them have urban centers large enough to provide the infrastructure and external economies required by many firms. City states like Singapore are able to provide the necessary infrastructure, but the population of most countries of two or three million is partly rural and their urban population is scattered among a number of urban centers and market towns. Some of these nations will be in the early stages of development and will have to import most of their need for manufactures. But even those which have the know-how to build and run manufacturing enterprises will have to specialize in products that do not have economies of scale, or in a limited number with scale economies that can be exported. Either way a substantial portion of the requirement for manufactures will have to be imported.

But at what size of population or GNP can economies of scale be fully realized within the domestic market alone? Are some economies of scale realizable only in nations with trillion dollar GNPs or over 200 million people? Or can most be realized with a GNP of 30 billion dollars and a population of only 20 million? A precise answer to these questions would depend on an industry-by-industry analysis of efficient scales of production and would vary from period to period since technologies change over time. Such an analysis is beyond the scope of this chapter. There is reason to believe, however, that there are relatively few industries that require markets the size of those of the United States, the Soviet Union, or Japan. In 1970, for example, 25 nations in the world had annual steel production of 3 million tons or more annually, a scale that, if produced by one mill, would be sufficient to reap most of the economies of scale of the technology of that time.[31] By way of contrast, there were only ten countries in 1970 that produced over 300 000 motor vehicles each year, and given the variety of motor vehicles required, even 300 000 may not have been an efficient scale.[32]

Thus, there are very few products that require a market the size of the United States or the European Economic Community to reach an efficient scale of production. Automobiles and large commercial aircraft may be among the few exceptions. But in some countries the market might be large enough to support only one plant of an appropriate scale, in which case efficiency might suffer because of a lack of competition.[33] In essence there is a continuum with respect to both country market size and economies of scale. As population and GNP rise, more and more industries face domestic markets large enough to make possible

[31] United Nations (1975, p. 310).

[32] The figures here are for domestic production when what is really wanted are figures for domestic demand, but the production figures give a rough idea of the size of the domestic market when used in this way.

[33] This point is made by Scitovsky (1958). A related point is a finding by Caves that plant size in the United States and Europe increases with the size of the domestic market. Caves argues that the evidence "clearly indicates that the nation is a good first approximation to the geographic span of 'the market' in manufacturing industries" [Caves (1987, p. 13)].

levels of production that take advantage of economies of scale and allow for competition.

If economies of scale were the primary determinant of trade shares in GNP, therefore, one would expect that the share of trade would decline as industrialization took place and markets grew to a size needed to realize most scale economies. In reality, the share of foreign trade world wide, that had been declining through the 1930s and 1940s because of the Great Depression and World War II, began rising steadily after the war and continued to rise into the early 1980s. This rise occurred not only in small countries, but in each of the fifteen very large nations with which this chapter is particularly concerned.

Along with the rise in the share of foreign trade in both large and small countries have come new explanations of what causes international trade to take place. In trade between industrial and developing countries, Heckscher–Ohlin and other theories relating the flow of trade to differences between countries in endowments of capital, labor, and natural resources still explain a lot of what is happening. But new theories stressing product differentiation and the relations between different components of multinational companies have been needed to explain the growing trade among the most advanced industrial nations of the world.

Economies of scale may have an influence on the composition of exports, if not on the overall level relative to GDP. Manufactures are the main repositors of scale economies and the ratio of manufactured exports to GDP does not decline systematically with size (see Table 32.4 above). In fact, in both 1962–64 and 1979–81 the share of manufactured exports in GDP was higher in very large countries than in small ones. Even if one controls for differences in per capita income, there is no unambiguous decline in the share of manufactured exports as country size increases (see Figure 32.2 below).

In short, economies of scale have something to do with why large countries have low trade ratios and in the composition of their exports, but they are certainly not the whole story. As we shall argue below, they are probably not even the most important part of the story.

4.1.4. Trade in primary products

The final reason why small country trade ratios are higher than those of large countries is related to the determinants of foreign trade in primary products. The key difference between large and small nations is on the export side. Primary products, for example, constituted 75 percent of the exports of all small countries taken together, but only 42 percent of the exports of the fifteen largest countries. The difference on the import side is much less pronounced, with primary imports accounting for 30 percent of total small country imports and 39 percent of

Table 32.6
Share of minerals trade in GDP for very large countries in 1970

Country	Area (in 1000 sq. km)	Share in GDP of trade in fuels, minerals, and metals Exports	Imports
Bangladesh	144	n.a.	n.a.
U.K.	230	0.018	0.049
W. Germany	248	0.013	0.038
Italy	301	0.012	0.042
Japan	370	0.002	0.040
France	551	0.010	0.032
Pakistan	804	0.001	0.014
Nigeria	924	0.077	0.007
Indonesia	1492	0.057	0.002
Mexico	1973	0.014	0.007
India	3043	0.006	0.008
Brazil	8512	0.007	0.013
U.S.A.	9363	0.005	0.008
China	9561	0.001	n.a.

Sources: World Bank data except for China, which were derived from data in State Statistical Bureau (1986, p. 40), and Ministry of Foreign Economic Relations and Trade Compilation Committee (1984, p. IV-11).

imports of the fifteen largest nations in 1970–72, and 37 and 46 percent, respectively, in 1979–81.

If one excludes agriculture and looks only at the trade in minerals and fuels, there appear to be three forces at work determining the shares of minerals and fuels in foreign trade. First, large countries in terms of geographic size are likely to have a wider range of mineral deposits within their borders than small countries. Thus, they are less likely to have to import certain minerals or fuels because of their total absence at home. If these nations are also large in terms of national product, however, they will have a substantial domestic demand for these minerals and hence are less apt to have a huge surplus of any particular mineral for export. If a country's total and per capita incomes are both low, on the other hand, domestic demand for minerals may be weak.

The data in Table 32.6, where the very large countries have been arranged in ascending order of size as measured by geographic area, bear out these basic propositions. The major importers of primary products are the high income nations of Western Europe and Japan with large populations occupying relatively small areas. The share of primary imports among the very large developing countries is generally very low, ranging only from 0.2 to 1.4 percent, a rather narrow range given the big differences in per capita income among these countries.

On the export side, a notable feature is the small share in GDP of minerals exports for twelve of the fifteen very large nations. Low levels of primary exports are not necessarily an indication of limited availability of natural resources. Some of the very large countries possess ample amounts of natural resources, but a high proportion is consumed domestically. The proportion that is traded, as a result, represents only a low percentage of the large GDP of these countries. Two exceptions are Nigeria and Indonesia, nations that combine low per capita incomes with substantial deposits of petroleum. Unlike the situation in Saudi Arabia or Kuwait, the petroleum surpluses of Nigeria and Indonesia do not reflect vast reserves so much as they do the limited domestic demand for the reserves that do exist. As these nations industrialize, the share of mineral exports can be expected to fall as a higher and higher proportion is consumed domestically. Both Mexico and China, for example, have petroleum output levels comparable to Indonesia and Nigeria, but a much smaller share of that output is available for export. This relationship between low income and a high primary

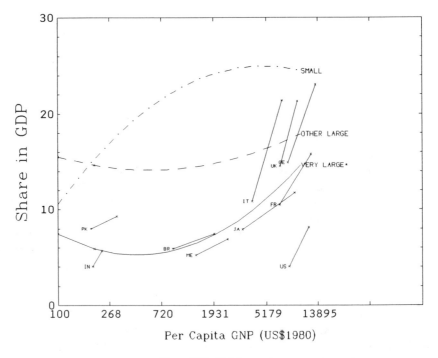

Figure 32.1. Total exports.

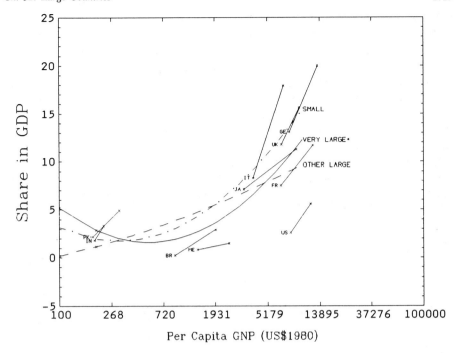

Figure 32.2. Manufactured exports.

export share in large countries with abundant resources has been pointed out in earlier studies as well [Chenery and Syrquin (1975), Syrquin and Chenery (1986)]. In some of the tables appearing later in this chapter, the statistics for very large countries are reported with and without the data for Indonesia and Nigeria. Sometimes the effects of size are better highlighted if these low-income, petroleum-surplus countries are removed from the averages.

These relationships can also be illustrated on a more general level with data on export shares in GDP for 14 very large countries (excluding the Soviet Union), 15 other large countries, and 74 small countries for the years beginning in 1962 and extending through 1982 or 1983. These data are presented in Figures 32.1, 32.2, and 32.3.

As these figures indicate, the export shares of very large and large countries differ in two fundamental ways from the export shares of small countries. First, as already noted, the large country shares are much lower, particularly at higher per capita incomes. Second, large country shares do not rise very much with per

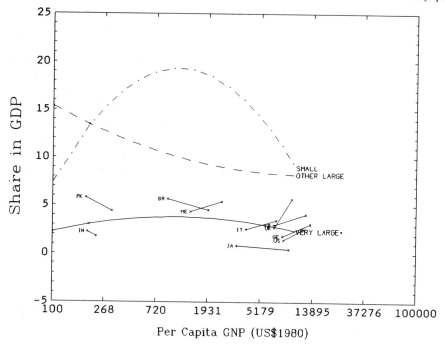

Figure 32.3. Primary exports.

capita income, while the export shares of small countries rise in a very pro-nounced fashion as incomes increase, particularly at incomes below $600 per capita. The reason for this second difference is relevant to the discussion here of the relationship between primary exports and country size.

Manufactured exports as a percentage of GDP rise as incomes increase in nations large and small although the rise is less pronounced in very large countries. Primary exports in both large and very large countries, in contrast, fall particularly after per capita income passes $1000. Presumably what is happening is some version of the Heckscher–Ohlin story where a nation's comparative advantage shifts away from natural-resource-based products to those based on increasingly abundant human and physical capital, namely manufactured goods.

The share of primary exports in small countries also declines, but does not fall below 15 percent of GDP until per capita income surpasses $4000. Manufactured exports, instead of substituting for primary exports, are simply added on top making the overall small country export share rise. The failure of the primary export share to fall except at very high levels of per capita income presumably rests on some kind of "vent for surplus" explanation. Small nations have highly skewed endowments of natural resources. Even at fairly high per capita incomes, therefore, they cannot make use of more than a small fraction of their total output of tin, bauxite, or cacao beans.

Size, therefore, has a major influence on the nature of international trade in minerals. Small countries have excessive amounts of some minerals and little or none of others. They must find a vent for their surplus of the one and must import the others. Large countries have few such surpluses for export. The exceptions are nations in the early stages of development that have limited demand for their own resources and few alternative products available for export. Large nations also have less need to go abroad for key raw materials. The exceptions are those nations like Japan and the United Kingdom that are large in terms of population and income, but not in area.

4.1.5. The reason for low trade ratios

Taken together, which of the above four explanations has the most to do with why large nations have lower foreign trade ratios than small ones? A quantitative analysis of the prime sources of the difference would be desirable, but is not really possible. The most important reason would appear to be the natural protection provided to domestic industries in large countries by the high cost of transport from the border to many points in the interior. Transport costs, for example, appear to be at the heart of the explanation for the difference between the 100 percent trade ratios of Belgium and the Netherlands and the 40–50 percent ratios of France and Germany.

The need to vent the surplus of minerals in small countries also played an important role. If primary products were the same share in total trade in both the small and the fifteen largest countries, holding trade in manufactures constant, the export share in GDP of small countries would fall from 19.7 to 9.2 percent, essentially the same as the 10.3 percent of the largest nations. These figures are for 1970–72, but much the same relationship holds in the other years as well. Manufacturing trade, of course, would probably not remain the same if primary exports fell, but would manufactured exports rise enough to maintain the original trade share of small countries? It seems unlikely.

Policy choices by governments also clearly make a difference. Exports plus imports as a percentage of GDP in all developing countries rose from 33.5 percent in 1970 to 54.1 percent in 1981, and the OPEC price increases clearly had much to do with this rise.[34] The rise in industrial market economies' trade share over the same period from 26.3 to 39.9 percent probably has a similar explana-

---

[34] World Bank (1983).

tion. OPEC's influence, however, was felt by nations both large and small. It is not clear whether deliberate policy choices by nations had a differential impact on large nations as contrasted to small ones.

It is even more difficult to quantify the impact of scale economies on the foreign trade ratios of large countries. Holding per capita income constant, large countries probably import fewer airplanes and automobiles than small nations, but do these and similar industries with substantial scale economies account for much of the overall difference in trade ratios between large and small nations?

4.2. The composition of foreign trade

The analysis to this point has concentrated on the question of how size affects the share of foreign trade in a nation's GDP. But as the discussion of the relationship between exports of primary products and country size indicates, the impact of country size on the composition of foreign trade is as pronounced as the impact of size on the level of foreign trade. Manufactured exports play a more important role in the foreign trade of large countries than small ones, especially at low levels of per capita income. Mineral exports are a much higher share of the foreign trade of small countries than of large ones, especially at high levels of per capita income.

The effect of size on the composition of trade has been noted in various studies [Keesing (1968), Chenery and Syrquin (1975)]. The total effect of size on trade in manufactures (exports up and imports down) has been interpreted as an indication of the necessity of large domestic markets for exporting manufactures because of economies of scale [Balassa (1969)]; and similarly as an indication of prior import substitution for a larger internal market [McCarthy, Taylor and Talati (1987)].

The composition of foreign trade is related to size in other ways as well, but the relevant concepts of size have to do with the relationship between total geographic area or amount of arable land and population. The best measure of this relationship is "density". A nation's density is measured by the ratio of population to total or arable land area. Total land density has important explanatory power with respect to the export of both primary and manufactured exports, but particularly the latter.[35]

The figures in Table 32.7 present the results of a regression designed to measure the impact of density together with a country's population size on both the level and composition of foreign trade. As these estimates indicate, greater density has a positive impact on the share of total trade in GDP and an even

---

[35] The use of density as a way of taking natural resources into account was initially suggested by Keesing and Sherk (1971).

Table 32.7
The impact of population density on foreign trade

Variable	Partial effect of density[a]	t ratio
Merchandise exports		
Total	0.20	4.7
Primary	−0.19	4.6
Manufactured	0.39	21.6
Merchandise imports		
Total	0.38	10.6
Primary	0.26	15.9
Manufactured	0.13	5.2

[a]Coefficient of density in regressions of trade shares in GDP including also per capita income, population size, and a time dummy for years after 1973.

more pronounced positive impact on the share of manufactured exports in GDP. With respect to primary exports, the higher the density, the lower the share of these exports. On the import side, greater density leads to a rise in the shares in GDP of both primary and manufactured goods.

What is reflected in these figures is the familiar story of the workings of comparative advantage. A nation with high density has lots of labor but few natural resources relative to labor. At higher per capita incomes in such countries, manufactured exports, which use labor and capital, make up a larger share of GDP than in countries with a less dense population. Whatever natural resources a country possesses are increasingly required at home and hence are unavailable for export. Instead, the more densely populated a country is, the greater are its imports of primary products.[36]

Japan, for example, is a nation with one of the highest densities in the world. Its exports by the 1970s and 1980s were almost exclusively manufactures (96 percent in 1980). Japan's imports were made up mostly of primary products. The United States, in contrast, despite its high per capita income, earned a third of its export income from the sale of primary products. Brazil, with a lower per capita income and an even lower density of population than the United States, earned 60 percent of its export income from the sale of primary products in 1980 and an even higher share in earlier years.

The world's largest nations in terms of population are also on average the most densely populated. Excluding the Soviet Union, the fourteen largest nations in our sample have on average three times the density of the average small nation.

---

[36]For a similar analysis see Krueger (1977).

Density, therefore, helps explain why very large nations have higher shares of manufactured exports and lower shares of primary exports than do smaller nations at comparable levels of per capita income.

Since density is positively correlated with total foreign trade as well as the composition of that trade, the fact that very large nations have higher densities tends to a limited degree to offset the other impacts of country size on total trade. Those other effects of size tend to reduce the share of foreign trade in large nations, while density tends to increase the role of foreign trade.

Finally, the decline in trade shares with size is more marked for imports than for exports and as a result the share of capital inflows in GDP also declines with size.[37]

The relation to size of one particular source of capital inflow, aid, has been analyzed in various studies [e.g. Isenman (1976) and Edelman and Chenery (1977)]. The principal determinant of aid is the level of per capita income. Holding this factor constant there is a strong negative association between per capita aid and size. Among the reasons mentioned for the larger per capita flows to smaller nations are that nations have independent foreign policies that can be influenced by aid, and that relatively more of the small countries tend to have close ties with one or more donor. In addition, multilateral lenders are virtually obliged to lend to all members, and constraints of minimum project size lead to relatively large per capita commitments in small countries.

4.3. The sectoral structure of GDP

A lower foreign trade share should also have a measurable impact on the overall structure of those nations' gross national or domestic product (GNP or GDP). The principal influence, as indicated in the introduction to this section on size and economic structure, is to push large nations in the direction of a balanced growth strategy. But do available statistical data bear out this supposition?

In essence, the balanced growth hypothesis for large countries implies a lower variance in the economic structures of such countries. Various studies of consumer demand have shown, for example, that demand for particular products at a given level of income per capita is similar across countries irrespective of differences in culture or geography. If the supply or production to meet this demand in a given country comes primarily from domestic sources, as is the case in large countries, then the structure of production should be much like that in

---

[37]The capital inflow share, measured by the trade deficit as a share of GDP, is significantly associated with various indicators of economic structure [Chenery and Syrquin (1975)].

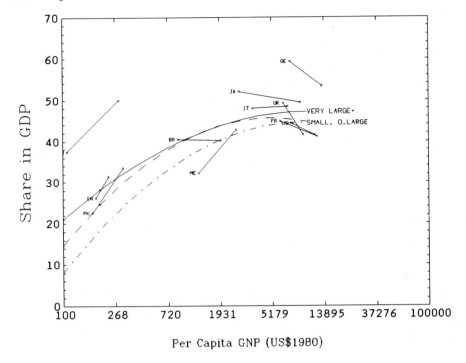

Per Capita GNP (US$1980)

Figure 32.4. Value added of industry.

another large nation which is meeting most of its needs from domestic sources. Hence, the structure of GDP in the two societies will be similar and the variance in the structure of large countries taken as a group will be small.

The structure of GDP will be similar, that is, for countries with similar levels of per capita income. Economic structure, as Kuznets and Chenery have shown, varies systematically with per capita income and hence this variation due to income differences must be removed before comparing the structure of large and small nations.

Figures 32.4–32.9 present the regression lines derived from a 70-country sample of small countries, a 15-country sample of large countries which excludes the 14 largest countries, and a 14-country sample of the largest countries (data for the Soviet Union are not included). Data are for roughly a 24-year period beginning about 1960 and ending in 1982 or 1983.

As the regression lines in these charts indicate, there is little meaningful difference in the mean of the production structures of very large, large, or small countries. What little difference exists probably has little to do with country size.

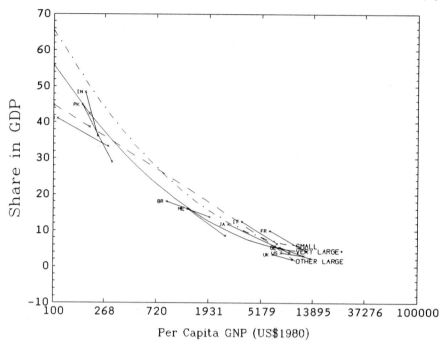

Figure 32.5. Value added of agriculture.

As indicated in Figure 32.8, for example, the share of the labor force in industry is consistently 2 or 3 percentage points higher in large countries than in small countries. The share of the fourteen very large countries, however, is actually below that of small countries when per capita incomes rise above $1000. In a similar vein, agriculture's share in GDP in very large countries is virtually identical to that of small countries for per capita incomes above $600 (Figure 32.5). Given the considerable variation of individual country trends around these regression lines, the similarity of the means of the groupings by country size is remarkable.

If the mean values vary little by country size, that is definitely not true of the variation around those means. The structure of small countries varies more than that of large nations. The most plausible explanation for this phenomenon is that the larger shares of foreign trade in GDP make it possible for small countries to pursue development strategies that differ significantly from each other. Large countries, in contrast, particularly the very large ones, have low trade ratios and

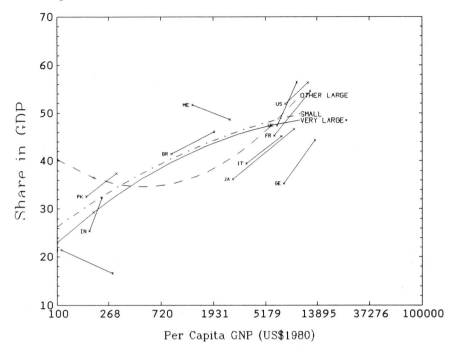

Figure 32.6. Value added of services.

their economic structure must stay fairly close to what is dictated by the structure of demand at particular levels of per capita income.

If the proposition that the economic structure of large countries varies less than for small countries is valid, what are the implications for their economic development strategies? Large countries, it would appear, have fewer choices than small ones. It has been argued, for example, that India and China allocated large resources to the steel and machinery sectors because economic planners in those two countries were particularly enamored by the Soviet strategy of economic development in the 1930s and 1940s. There is no question that Chinese and Indian planners in the 1950s did admire the Soviet model, but they might well have ended up allocating substantial investment to steel and machinery even if they had been unaware of Soviet experience. Shortly after Mao's death in 1976, for example, the Chinese came out with a long-term plan that called for the production of 50 million tons of steel by 1985, up from 24 million tons in 1975. A year later that plan was being roundly denounced as a product of a blind pursuit

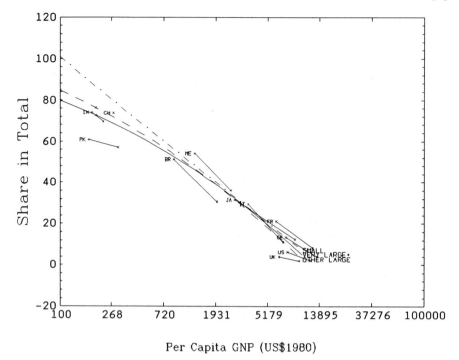

Per Capita GNP (US$1980)

Figure 32.7. Agricultural labor.

of heavy industry at a time when what was needed was more production of consumer goods. Consumer goods advocates won the day politically and introduced major changes in policy. And yet when 1985 rolled around steel production had risen to 46.7 million tons and steel demand had risen well above 50 million tons with the difference made up by imports from Japan. Given the extraordinary changes taking place in so many other ways in China's economy, however, a plausible explanation for the continued development of steel is that the options facing Chinese planners in such a large and rapidly growing economy were not great.

One piece of evidence that economic structure varies less in large countries than in small countries is the residual variation from regressions for size groups presented in Table 32.8. In the case of employment, the standard error for very large countries was well below that of small countries in two of the three sectors. A similar pattern can be observed in the data on foreign trade shares. The

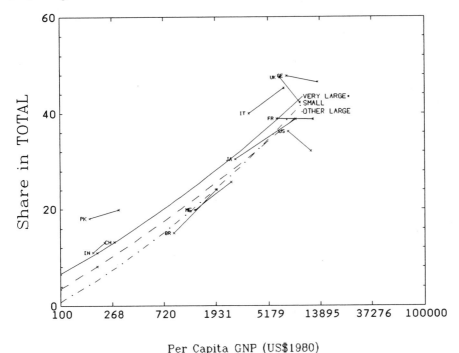

Per Capita GNP (US$1980)

Figure 32.8. Industrial labor.

variation in the share of manufactured exports in GDP for very large countries, for example, is less than that for large nations, which in turn is less than the variation in the manufactured exports of small countries. In effect virtually all very large countries export substantial amounts of manufactures, while some small countries are major exporters of manufactures, while others export mainly primary products. These data are controlled for per capita income so none of these differences in variation can be explained by differences in per capita incomes of countries in the three separate categories. With respect to production shares, the data for the standard error of the estimates of these shares show size effects for mining, construction, and utilities, but a reverse relationship for the critical manufacturing sector.

Given these regression results, is there evidence that the balanced growth argument for large countries also holds for the industrial sector? Lower foreign trade ratios in large countries imply that those nations must produce a wider

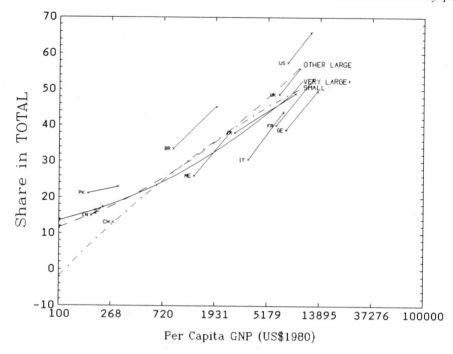

Figure 32.9. Service labor.

range of manufactures at a given level of per capita income than smaller nations. At low per capita incomes, small nations can specialize in manufactured products with simpler more labor-intensive processes. Later they can move on to more complex and capital-intensive industries, but in the interim they can meet their demand for the products of these industries through imports. Large countries, in contrast, may begin development of the more complex capital-intensive industries at an earlier stage because their foreign exchange resources are not sufficient to meet domestic demand for these products through imports. In principle large countries could expand their foreign trade earnings in order to be able to import more, but in practice, as discussed earlier in this chapter, they do not.

Data in Table 32.9 on the shares in GDP of "early", "middle", and "late" industries lend support to the view that there is a relationship between country size and the timing of the development of particular industries.[38] The relationship is even stronger if Indonesia and Nigeria, the two low-income oil exporters, are

[38]Chenery and Taylor (1968).

Table 32.8
Residual variation in labor, trade, and product shares

	Country size		
	Very large countries	Large countries	Small countries
Variation in			
labor force shares			
Agriculture	6.3	11.7	11.9
Industry	5.4	5.1	5.5
Services	5.5	8.9	8.8
Variation in			
foreign trade shares			
Primary exports	5.3	9.9	9.9
Manufactured exports	3.7	4.3	5.1
Variation in			
product shares			
Agriculture	8.4	7.0	9.6
Mining	5.1	6.7	8.5
Manufacturing	7.7	4.5	5.7
Construction	1.4	1.8	2.2
Utilities	1.8	1.9	3.2
Services	6.5	5.9	7.6

Note: Shares were calculated as a percentage of gross domestic product. Figures in the table are for the standard errors of the following regression:

$$\text{share} = a + b_1 \ln y + b_2 (\ln y)^2,$$

where y = GNP per capita.

excluded. The share in GDP of "late" industries at low levels of per capita income in the largest fourteen countries is twice that of small nations (Figure 32.12). The shares of "early" and "middle" industries, in contrast, do not appear to vary systematically with country size (Figures 32.10 and 32.11).

4.4. Relative prices and economic structure

The shares in GDP of manufacturing, agriculture, and the other sectors are very sensitive to the prices used in measuring GDP. And prices, as well as per capita incomes, vary enormously from one country to another. Unfortunately, it is not as easy to correct for variation in prices as it is to control for differences in per capita income.

Table 32.9
Variation in industrial sector shares by income and country size (as percent of GDP)

Industry sector	Income ($ per capita)	300	600	1000	2000	6000
Early industries						
Small		6.4	8.1	8.9	9.2	7.9
Large		9.9	9.2	8.6	7.7	5.9
Very large		6.4	7.0	7.3	7.4	7.1
Very large[a]		7.5	8.6	8.9	8.9	7.5
Middle industries						
Small		2.8	3.7	4.2	4.9	5.6
Large		3.8	4.8	5.3	5.6	5.6
Very large		3.3	4.6	5.3	6.2	7.0
Very large[a]		4.1	5.7	6.6	7.3	7.4
Late industries						
Small		1.7	2.9	4.1	6.1	10.3
Large		2.1	4.1	5.6	7.6	10.9
Very large		4.0	5.9	7.6	10.0	14.4
Very large[a]		5.6	8.2	9.9	12.1	15.0

[a] These figures are for eleven very large countries, excluding Indonesia and Nigeria.

The main effort to eliminate the effect of relative prices on the measurement of economic structure is that of Kravis and his collaborators (1982). Data derived from Kravis's work are presented in Table 32.10. Since Kravis's figures are for the expenditure side they are most useful for analyzing the structure of demand, whereas this study is primarily concerned with the structure of production. While Kravis's figures cannot readily be used to recalculate the production structures of large and small countries, they can be used to illustrate the magnitude of the variation in prices across countries. The relative price of producer durables in India, for example, is two and one-half times the price of similar goods in the United States, while transport costs in India are only 70 percent of those in the United States. There is some relationship between differences in price structure and per capita income levels. This is particularly true in the service sector (represented best by the "Government compensation" sector in Table 32.10), where relative prices rise markedly with per capita income. The reason, of course, is that this sector's costs are made up mainly of workers' wages which rise with the general increase in per capita income. Similarly, the relative prices of producer durables decline systematically as per capita incomes rise, although the reasons for this decline are more complex than in the case of services.

But there are also a number of influences on relative price structures that are not systematically related to per capita income. Tariff policies, for example, have

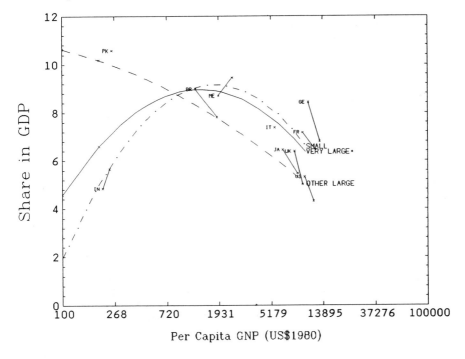

Figure 32.10. Early industries.

an enormous influence on the domestic prices of tradable goods, and tariff policies vary widely across countries. Similarly, some countries subsidize their agricultural sector with high support prices (e.g. Japan and South Korea), while others keep farm prices depressed in order to subsidize the urban population. Until these relative price differences can be removed from our data, conclusions about the differences in structure between large and small economies will rest on a seriously flawed data base. It is one reason, for example, why labor force sectoral shares as a percentage of the total labor force are probably a more reliable basis for analyzing the influence of country size than are sectoral shares of GDP.

5. Size and productivity growth

Is there a relationship between country size and overall economic performance? Do large countries grow faster than small countries or slower? Is the growth of

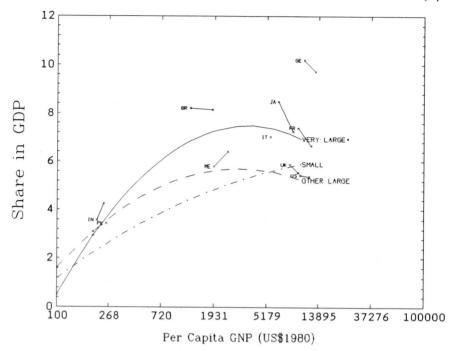

Figure 32.11. Middle industries.

large countries due mainly to increases in inputs of capital and labor or to rising productivity in the use of those inputs?

It is not difficult to come up with plausible arguments that country size should be related to the efficiency with which inputs of capital and labor are used. In a world full of restrictions on international trade, for example, it may be easier to achieve economies of scale in larger than in smaller nations. On the other hand, small countries with high foreign trade ratios are in a better position to specialize by concentrating on a few sectors for which they have special knowledge or particularly suitable natural resources. If large countries with low foreign trade ratios follow a more balanced growth path, they will have to invest in a wide variety of industries drawing on a multiplicity of skills, some of which will be in short supply.

A more politically oriented argument is that large nations may be more difficult to manage. Just holding a large nation together may require compromises that divert resources toward regions that cannot use those resources efficiently. Planning in a large country may be more difficult simply because of the large

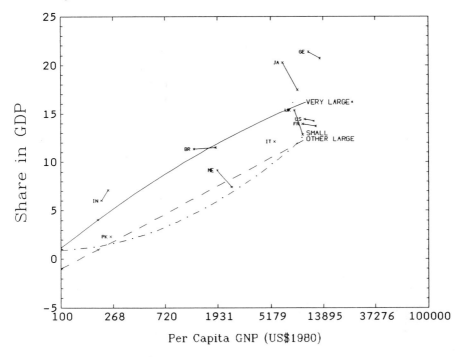

Figure 32.12. Late industries.

numbers of enterprises that must be included in the plan. Import substitution may seem like a more attractive policy in a large country simply because such a policy is more feasible than in a small country, even if it is not as efficient as alternative policies.

What does the experience of nations during the 1960–82 period indicate about the relative growth performance of large countries? The data presented in Tables 32.11 and 32.12 were calculated using the growth accounting framework pioneered by Solow, Denison, and others. This framework distinguishes between growth brought about by higher inputs of labor and capital and increases in the productivity with which those inputs are used, which are calculated as a residual.

The estimates presented here are based on very crude assumptions and data. Furthermore, the concept of productivity used here encompasses many elements that in more detailed studies would be classified as inputs (improvements in the quality of labor and capital, for example). Care should be used in drawing conclusions from these estimates, but the differences between groups of countries are striking enough to suggest some conclusions relevant to this study.

Table 32.10

Relative price structures of large countries

Country or country group	Expenditure category	(1) Consumption goods	(2) Food	(3) Clothing	(4) Transport and communication	(5) Construction	(6) Producer durables	(7) Government compensation
Group I (8 countries)		76	100	96	115	83	235	26
India		67	100	122	70	70	258	24
Pakistan		76	100	80	50	86	261	22
Group II (6 countries)		78	100	87	113	76	154	58
Brazil		97	100	147	163	96	140	43
Group III (6 countries)		86	100	113	138	98	190	62
Mexico		81	100	104	92	68	189	59
Group IV (4 countries)		82	100	121	125	95	144	62
Italy		82	100	97	102	77	116	75
Group V (9 countries)		74	100	112	124	106	113	106
U.K.		102	100	125	160	128	143	78
Japan		83	100	80	94	102	74	84
France		95	100	138	120	95	111	98
W. Germany		94	100	104	122	89	114	108
Group VI = U.S.A.		100	100	100	100	100	100	100

Notes: The methodology used in constructing this table is designed to highlight differences between the relative price structure of individual countries and that of the United States. If the relative price structures of other nations were the same as in the United States, all of the index numbers in the table would be "100". An index number of 250 indicates that the price of goods in that category are 2.5 times higher relative to the price of food than is the case in the United States. The specific formula used to derive each index was,

$$(P_g^* \div P_{2g}) \div (P_{US}^* \div P_{2US}),$$

where

P^* = the price of the * category of goods in country g,
P_{2g}^g = the price of food (category 2) in country g,
P_{US}^* = the price of the * category of goods in the U.S.,
P_{2US} = the price of food (category 2) in the U.S.

Source: Based on Kravis, Heston and Summers (1982).

Table 32.11
Sources of growth by country size (all figures in percent)

Country group	GDP		Input		Factor productivity	
	1960–70	1970–82	1960–70	1970–82	1960–70	1970–82
Very large[a]	5.10	4.23	3.33	3.76	1.77	0.47
Largest 10[a]	5.35	4.95	3.47	4.06	1.88	0.89
Large	5.82	4.37	3.55	4.14	2.26	0.23
Small	4.51	3.54	3.34	3.84	1.17	−0.30

[a] Excluding the Soviet Union.

Notes: The residual was calculated using the following form of the sources of growth equation:

$$G_Y = MPK \cdot I/Y + E_L G_L + \lambda,$$

where

G_Y = growth rate of GDP,
MPK = marginal product of capital,
I/Y = domestic investment as a share of GDP,
E_L = elasticity of output with respect to labor,
G_L = growth rate of labor,
λ = residual or growth of total factor productivity.

Because data are not available for all of these variables and in the right form, a number of assumptions had to be made to fill the gaps:

(1) The labor force growth rate was assumed to be the same as the population growth rate of the previous decade.

(2) The share of labor in national income in growth accounting exercises ranges widely. We have used the value 0.6 which falls within the range of ratios found in such analyses.

(3) The marginal product of capital is assumed to be 0.12.

Two conclusions in particular emerge from these figures. First, the growth rate of large and very large countries in both the 1960–70 and 1970–82 periods was higher than in small countries. However, most of the very fast growers during this period were small or medium-sized countries. The smaller countries, being more specialized, were more subject to the commodity lottery. A small country in a favorable position is likely to show a higher than average performance [Robinson (1960, p. 388)]. Within larger economies there is an internal averaging that masks extreme performance of separate regions; thus, compensatory mechanisms often iron out extreme regional disparities. It is unlikely, for example, for a commodity price boom per se to lead to very high growth rates in large countries. The exceptions are low-income oil exporters such as Indonesia and Nigeria, where the commodity dominates the national economies to such an extent that these countries are best treated separately.

Table 32.12
Sources of growth in very large countries (all figures in percent)

Country	Population growth rate		Gross domestic investment		Input growth		Residual		GDP growth rate	
	1950-60	1960-72	1960-70	1970-82	1960-70	1970-82	1960-70	1970-82	1960-70	1970-82
China	1.80	2.30	23.7	32.5	3.92	5.08	0.08	0.42	4.0	5.5
India	1.70	2.10	18.1	20.5	3.19	3.68	0.37	-0.08	3.6	3.6
U.S.S.R.	1.60	1.20	26.2	31.0	4.10	4.44	1.03	-1.23	5.1	3.2
U.S.	1.80	1.70	18.8	17.6	3.33	3.09	0.88	-0.39	4.2	2.7
Indonesia	1.70	2.50	10.7	21.5	2.30	4.07	1.52	2.93	3.8	7.0
Brazil	2.70	2.30	24.5	27.2	4.56	4.65	0.71	2.05	5.3	6.7
Japan	1.90	1.30	31.3	35.6	4.90	5.08	4.98	-0.58	9.9	4.5
Bangladesh	2.10	2.90	10.0	8.0	2.46	2.74	1.26	1.46	3.7	4.2
Nigeria	1.80	1.80	12.5	25.6	2.58	4.17	2.29	-0.17	4.9	4.0
Pakistan	1.90	2.70	18.5	13.8	3.36	3.30	3.55	2.10	6.9	5.4
Mexico	2.80	3.20	20.2	23.8	4.10	4.74	3.15	1.16	7.3	5.9
W. Germany	0.20	0.80	27.0	24.5	3.36	3.41	0.99	-1.01	4.4	2.4
Italy	-0.10	0.60	23.2	19.8	2.73	2.79	2.62	-0.09	5.4	2.7
U.K.	0.60	0.40	18.2	17.8	2.55	2.37	0.30	-0.87	2.9	2.7
France	0.70	1.00	23.8	23.9	3.27	3.46	2.03	-0.36	5.3	1.5
Average	1.54	1.83	20.0	22.3	3.33	3.77	1.77	0.47	5.10	3.1
Standard deviation	0.84	0.86	5.91	6.84	0.77	0.89	1.37	1.20	1.78	4.24
Coefficient of variation	0.55	0.47	0.30	0.31	0.23	0.24	0.77	2.55	0.35	1.63
										0.38

Sources: World Bank data plus estimates by the authors. Data for the Soviet Union are from Joint Economic Committee (1982).

Table 32.13
Variance of performance by size: 1950–83

Group	Number of countries	Annual growth rate of GDP			Number of cases with growth	
		Mean	Standard deviation	Coefficient of variation	< 2.5%	> 7.0%
Very large	14	4.91	1.49	0.30	0	1
Other large	15	5.03	1.54	0.31	1	2
Small	77	4.48	2.07	0.46	14	8

Source: World Bank data.

The above discussion suggests that among small countries the variance of performance should be higher than among large countries. Table 32.13 gives some evidence supporting that view. Second, and even more striking, the difference in growth rates by country size is accounted for largely by differences in productivity growth (the residual), not differences in the growth rate of inputs.[39] Any successful explanation of why some countries grow faster than others, therefore, must be able to elaborate on why one nation's productivity growth is higher than that of another. Unfortunately, we know much more about why savings rates and labor force growth rates differ than why productivity differs across countries. All we can do in this chapter is point out the significance of productivity growth for the relative performance of countries.

The higher GDP and productivity growth rate for large countries is an historical fact. But was it size that made possible this higher level of performance? Or did large countries share some other common feature that pushed them to this higher level?

Although a definitive answer to this last question is not possible in this limited discussion, the data in Table 32.14 provide some evidence that there is more to the differences in performance than the effects of size. The data in Table 32.14 are arranged by geographic region rather than country size. As was the case in explaining differences in growth rates by size, differences in the rate of growth of capital and labor inputs explain only a small part of why regional GDP growth rates differ. Rates of increase in capital and labor, when averaged within regions, vary only within narrow limits across the world. Rates of increase in productivity,

---

[39]Chenery (1986) showed that during the 1960s the best performers among developing countries and Japan achieved their higher growth rates by both higher factor inputs and higher factor productivity than the typical developing countries. There are only six countries in the high growth category used to reach this conclusion, and only one of these was a very large country (Japan).

in contrast, range from a negative figure for Sub-Saharan Africa and South Asia in the 1970s to around 4 percent a year in East Asia in that same period. These figures tell a now familiar story of economic stagnation in much of Africa and contrasting high growth performance in East Asia.

The immediate relevance of these regional data to the question of size is due to the fact that the small country sample includes over 20 countries from Sub-Saharan Africa, roughly one-third of the small country sample. Only one of the very large countries (Nigeria) or 7 percent of that sample was from Africa. On the other hand, South Asia, another region of slow productivity growth, is over-represented in the very large country sample.

Statistical correlations of this sort can never answer questions of causation. A plausible case can be made that country size did lead to higher rates of GDP and productivity growth, at least during the period covered by the data in these tables. A much more compelling case for the underlying determinants of rapid growth rests on the importance of regional differences. But whether that regional variation rests in turn on differences in historical background, on cultural differences, or on variations in economic policy is the subject for a separate study.

Finally, a brief comment is in order on the quality of these estimates of productivity growth. Economists who estimate the sources of growth use varying methodologies that produce quite different results. Some add variables other than capital and labor. Others use gross rather than net domestic capital formation. The figures in Tables 32.11, 32.12, and 32.14 used a simple methodology explained in the notes to those tables. Even with this simple methodology, large data gaps were filled by assumption. In particular, the shares of labor and capital in national income were estimated not from data of each of the countries, but using plausible assumptions about their likely values based on previous studies. Fortunately, our most important results are not very sensitive to these assumptions. To illustrate the point, quite different assumptions were made about the shares of capital and labor used to construct the estimates in Table 32.15. These assumptions adjust income shares to take account of how these shares change as per capita income rises. The results produce estimates of productivity growth higher than in Tables 32.11 and 32.12. The relative differences between large and small countries, however, remain much the same.

6. Income distribution and size

A similar conclusion arises out of an analysis of the relationship between country size and the distribution of income. Income distribution data are not as readily available as national accounts statistics, and the quality of these data is particu-

Table 32.14
Productivity growth by region

Country	GDP growth rates (%)		Population growth rates (%)		Gross domestic investment (as share of GDP) (%)		Residual			
							(A)		(B)	
	1960–70	1970–81	1950–60	1960–70	1960–70	1970–81	1960–70	1970–81	1960–70	1970–81
Developing countries	5.45	5.2	2.0	2.35	17.2	23.8	2.7	1.6	2.2	0.9
Africa, south of Sahara	5.0	3.3	2.3	2.45	18.4	22.5	1.9	−0.2	1.4	−0.9
Middle East and North Africa	4.8	7.1	2.5	2.65	18.5	26.7	1.6	3.1	1.1	2.3
East Asia	6.85	8.0	1.9	2.25	11.2	25.0	4.6	4.4	4.4	3.7
South Asia	4.6	3.8	1.9	2.4	16.9	20.1	1.9	0.5	1.4	−0.1
Latin America	5.55	5.2	2.8	2.7	20.4	24.0	2.0	1.4	1.4	0.7
Industrial market economies	5.05	3.0	1.2	1.05	22.1	22.4	2.3	0.5	1.7	−0.3

Table 32.15
Productivity growth by country size (II) (residual share in percent per year)

	1960–70		1970–82	
	(A)	(B)	(A)	(B)
All countries	2.7	2.3	1.2	0.7
Very large countries	3.2	3.0	1.8	1.5
Other large countries	3.5	3.1	1.5	1.0
Small countries	2.4	2.0	1.0	0.5
Specific countries (in size order):				
China	1.2	0.2	1.4	0.1
India	1.5	0.7	1.1	0.2
U.S.A.	2.3	2.3	1.0	1.0
Indonesia	2.8	2.5	4.3	3.6
Brazil	1.9	1.6	3.3	2.9
Japan	6.4	6.4	0.8	0.8
Bangladesh	2.4	2.0	2.7	2.3
Nigeria	3.6	3.2	1.1	0.4
Pakistan	4.7	3.9	3.3	2.7
Mexico	4.4	4.1	2.4	2.1
Germany	2.4	2.4	0.4	0.4
Italy	4.1	4.1	1.3	1.3
U.K.	1.7	1.7	0.6	0.6
France	3.4	3.4	1.0	1.0

Method of calculation of residual:

This table uses the same growth accounting equation as in the previous table. The same assumptions are made about the growth of the labor force and the same investment data (as a share of GDP) are used.

However, different assumptions are made about the productivity of capital and the elasticity of labor. These assumptions were made in part to take into account the likelihood that the capital–output ratio, the rate of return on capital, and the depreciation rate and the elasticity of labor vary systematically with income. These assumptions are secondly a way of testing the sensitivity of our results to the assumptions made above.

Notes:

Assumption A: The marginal product of capital is assumed to be constant at 0.12 (12 percent). Capital output ratios and depreciation rates are assumed to vary systematically with income (see table below). Under both this assumption and Assumption B the elasticity of output with respect to labor is assumed to increase with income.

Assumption B: The capital–output ratio is assumed to be constant at 3.0 but the marginal product of capital and the rate of depreciation vary systematically with income (see table below).

Country groups	Elasticity of output with respect to labor (E_L)	Assumption A ($MPK = 0.12$)		Assumption B ($K/Y = 3.0$)	
		Capital–output ratio	Depreciation rate	Marginal product of capital	Depreciation rate
Lower income	0.52	4.0	0.08	0.16	0.06
Lower middle income	0.55	3.75	0.10	0.15	0.08
Upper middle income	0.60	3.33	0.10	0.133	0.09
Industrial	0.64	3.0	0.12	0.12	0.12

Table 32.16
Income distribution in large countries

Country (year)	Share in total income of:		
	Top 20% of population	Middle 40% of population	Bottom 40% of population
Brazil (1972)	66.6	26.4	7.0
Mexico (1977)	57.7	32.4	9.9
India (1975–76)	49.4	34.4	16.2
Indonesia (1976)	49.4	36.2	14.4
Bangladesh (1976–77)	46.9	36.0	17.1
France (1975)	45.8	37.8	16.4
Pakistan (1964)	45.0	37.5	17.5
Italy (1977)	43.9	38.6	17.5
U.S.A. (1980)	39.9	42.9	17.2
U.K. (1979)	39.7	41.8	18.5
Germany (1978)	39.5	40.1	20.4
Japan (1979)	37.5	40.6	21.9

Sources: World Development Report (1986) and Chenery et al. (1974, pp. 8–9).

larly poor. Furthermore, the data that do exist are before taxes and transfers, whereas ideally one would want data for income after taxes and transfers had taken place. Still, the figures presented in Table 32.16 are sufficient to make the main point. The two nations with the highest degree of inequality by a substantial margin are in Latin America. The two with the lowest degree of inequality are those with the highest per capita income. And the two South Asian nations fall in between. If comparable data were available for China and the Soviet Union, they would probably show levels of inequality similar to or slightly below those of Japan and the United States.

Clearly, there is no simple or dominant relationship between inequality and country size. The principal influences determining inequality are per capita income, culture, and the presence or absence of a socialist revolution that eliminates most property incomes. Latin American nations, whatever their size, tend to cluster at the high end of the inequality range. East Asian nations, regardless of size or per capita income, tend to cluster at the low end of that range.

If country size is not the dominant influence on inequality, there are still grounds for arguing that size does influence the degree of inequality. The argument rests on the belief that large countries have greater regional variation in incomes than small countries. Other things being equal, therefore, a large country will have more inequality in income than a small one.

The essential argument can be illustrated with the experience of China. In the early 1950s China completed a revolution that involved the socialization of virtually all urban industry and commerce and the confiscation of all farmland not owned by the tiller of that land. With minor exceptions, property incomes in the cities were eliminated. In the countryside, farmers could earn more income than their neighbors if they worked harder or had more able-bodied adult family members. But farmers also earned more income if they had more and richer land than farmers elsewhere, or if that land were located near a city or a major transport route. Regional inequality in farm incomes, therefore, persisted long after inequality within narrowly defined areas had been eliminated or greatly reduced by collectivization. Surprisingly, crude estimates of income inequality in rural China in the late 1970s and early 1980s suggests that inequality may even have risen over what it had been immediately after land reform but prior to collectivization in 1952.[40] Whether inequality rose or not, the persistence of substantial differentials was due to large pockets of regional poverty in China's southwest and northwest.

There is no mathematical inevitability to the presence of greater regional inequality in large countries. Still, if pockets of poverty and wealth are distributed randomly across the landscape, it is likely that a larger area will encompass more of the full range of variation than a small area. Large size, for example, may be an important part of the explanation of why the distribution of income in rural areas in China is not much different from that of rural areas in South Korea. In both countries, the top 20 percent of the rural population received about 40 percent of total income in the 1970s, while the bottom 40 percent received about 20 percent.[41] Both countries carried out successful land reform programs, but the Chinese made a much greater effort to ensure that the poorest segments of the population received most of the former landlord-owned land. Collectivization in China then eliminated differences in landholdings between individual families within a single village. But regional variations in rural China appear to be much greater than those of rural Korea.

Size may also account for why Pakistan has a slightly lower level of inequality than India. Certainly there is large well-known regional variation within India ranging from the prosperous Punjab to the poverty of Bihar. The contrast in per capita income in Brazil between Sao Paulo and the Northeast is another example of the extremes of regional inequality sometimes found in very large countries. Further work would be required, however, before any such conclusion could be reached with confidence. Income distribution estimates are notoriously unreliable and our knowledge of what determines inequality is still at a rudimentary level.

---

[40] This discussion of China is based on Perkins and Yusuf (1984).
[41] The Korean data are from Ban, Moon and Perkins (1980, p. 307), Perkins and Yusuf (1984), and data from State Statistical Bureau (1985, p. 572).

Regional variation, of course, is not solely a question of country size. As Williamson has shown, regional income distribution, like the size distribution of income, appears to be a function of per capita income.[42] The familiar U-shaped curve, where inequality first increases as per capita income rises and then falls with further rises in per capita income, applies to regional income distribution data as well. Cultural and ethnic diversity such as that found within India and Brazil, but which is much less evident in China, may also increase regional inequality since cultural and ethnic diversity frequently have a regional component.

There are not a sufficient number of estimates of regional inequality to test this hypothesis about its relationship with country size. However, we do have data for 48 countries on the size distribution of income [World Bank (1985)]. If regional income distribution were systematically related to size, a reasonable supposition is that the size distribution of income would also be related to size. After all, regional inequality is one source of the inequality in the distribution by size.

The supposition is a reasonable one, but it finds no support in our 48-country sample. The correlation coefficient between country size (measured in terms of population) and the income share of the bottom 40 percent of the distribution or of the gini coefficient for the whole population is actually negative (but small). A regression equation relating these two measures of inequality to income and country size produces the following results (t ratios in parentheses):

$$X_1 = \underset{(5.42)}{0.7375} - \underset{(4.69)}{0.1734 \ln Y} + \underset{(4.99)}{0.0123 \ln Y^2} - \underset{(0.07)}{0.0002 \ln N} R^2 = 0.42,$$

$$X_2 = -\underset{(2.34)}{0.5929} + \underset{(4.37)}{0.3016 \ln Y} - \underset{(4.77)}{0.0220 \ln Y^2} - \underset{(0.04)}{0.0003 \ln N} R^2 = 0.47,$$

where

X_1 = share of bottom 40 percent in total income,
X_2 = gini coefficient of the income distribution,
Y = per capita income
N = population size.

The coefficients for country size are both very small and statistically insignificant. The data, therefore, lend no support at all to the hypothesized relationship between inequality and country size.

---

[42] Williamson (1965).

7. Conclusion

Large nations became large for reasons that only secondarily involved economics. But while economics had little direct influence on the size of nations, size did have an important influence on the economy. Population size was the dominant influence on economic structure, but geographic size mattered as well.

The principal feature that separates very large and large nations from small ones is the negative relationship between country size and the share of foreign trade in gross national product. The ability of large countries to take greater advantage of economies of scale has something to do with this relationship, but other elements at work are probably more important. These other elements include the influence of transport costs, the need of small countries but not large ones to vent their surpluses of mineral products, and the greater ease with which large nations could pursue import substitution policies.

Other differences in structure between large and small nations follow from the influence of these differences in the foreign trade ratio. One such influence is on the structure of foreign trade itself. Large nations, particularly the very large ones, concentrate more on the export of manufactures. Mineral exports, in contrast, have a proportionately much higher share of the exports of small countries.

Given the differences in the share and composition of foreign trade between large countries and small ones, a surprising conclusion is that there is almost no difference between the shares of industry, agriculture, and services in national product. This conclusion holds particularly for labor force shares which are less subject to distorted relative prices than are value added shares. As one disaggregates further, however, differences in the means of value added shares do appear. Within the manufacturing sector, industries associated with higher per capita incomes – what Chenery and Taylor have called "late industries" – appear earlier in large countries than in small ones. Very large and large countries are pushed by their size and their limited ability to depend on imports to provide for a wider variety of needs from domestic production. In effect the large countries are influenced to follow a more balanced growth strategy and hence for their economic structures to become more alike as a result.

Data on the variance in the shares of value added and labor force lend further support to this hypothesis about the relationship between size and balanced growth. Shares vary more for small countries than for large ones, at least for agriculture and for services.

Size also influences economic performance. The data used in this study lend limited support to the view that large countries perform significantly differently from small ones. A priori there is reason to believe that the distribution of income should be more unequal in large countries, but the data used here lend no support at all to this hypothesis.

Large countries do appear to grow faster than small ones. The difference is not in inputs of capital and labor, which vary little with size, but in productivity growth where there is a full percentage point difference between the large and the small nations of the world. Whether or not large size is a cause of higher productivity growth, however, remains to be demonstrated.

Size, therefore, makes a difference to economic structure and performance. On balance, large countries appear to enjoy some advantages not shared by small nations. There was no compelling a priori reason for expecting these advantages to exist and they may in fact be created by influences only spuriously correlated with size. And the advantages may be transitory applying only to the 1960–82 period from which our data were drawn. Transitory or not, and spurious or not, large countries did grow faster than their small brethren.

It is tempting to conclude that the higher productivity growth of large countries with their low trade ratios implies that there is little relationship between an outward-oriented development strategy with its high trade ratios and rapid growth. But the experience of China in the 1977–85 period where opening up was associated with rapid productivity gains, and of other nations earlier, suggest that one cannot use international cross-section data to predict the productivity performance of individual countries. The issue is not the absolute size of foreign trade relative to gross national product, but whether a nation is getting the most out of the efficient trade opportunities open to it.

Size, therefore, matters for both structure and performance. Large countries have less choice in determining development strategy than small ones, but, as the data presented here indicate, having a wider range of options is not necessarily an advantage in efforts to achieve modern economic growth.

Appendix A: Average effects of size

In the text the effects of size on economic structure were illustrated by comparing income-related patterns of change for various size groups. A simple and concise way of summarizing average effects of size is by means of size dummy variables in pooled regressions of the form:

$$X = a + b_1 \ln y + b_2 (\ln y)^2 + d_1 DL + d_2 DVL,$$

where X is a structural characteristic expressed as a share of GDP or employment, y is per capita income, DL is a dummy variable taking the value of 1 if the observation refers to a large country, and DVL is a dummy variable for very large countries.

The coefficient of DL, d_1, gives the expected difference in X for a typical large or very large country at any income level. The coefficient of the second dummy variable, d_2, gives the incremental effect, in case the country is a very large one, over and above the large country effect represented by d_1. Table A.1 shows the

Table A.1
Average size effects

	Coefficient[a]		*t* ratio	
	Large (d_1)	Very large (d_2)	Large	Very large
Demand				
Consumption	−3.9	3.7	8.5	6.2
Government	−0.6	−2.2	2.4	6.9
Investment	1.3	−1.1	3.9	2.4
Exports	−7.1	−6.8	12.7	9.1
Imports	−10.2	−6.4	16.9	7.8
Merchandise trade				
Primary exports	−5.2	−3.7	8.6	4.5
Manufactured exports	−0.7	−1.0	2.1	2.4
Primary imports	−2.4	−0.5	9.7	1.5
Manufactured imports	−5.1	−4.9	13.6	9.6
Value added				
Agriculture	−3.6	1.8	6.7	2.6
Mining	0.1	−0.6	0.3	1.0
Manufacturing	3.8	2.3	10.8	5.0
Construction	−0.1	−0.0	0.7	0.1
Utilities	0.6	−1.2	3.6	5.6
Services	−0.9	−2.3	2.1	3.9
Manufacturing				
Early	−0.2	−0.3	0.9	1.0
Middle	0.8	0.3	5.2	1.5
Late	1.1	2.4	4.3	7.6
Employment				
Agriculture	−4.3	−0.1	6.9	0.2
Industry	1.7	1.1	5.6	2.7
Services	2.6	−1.0	5.6	1.5

[a] Coefficients from regressions of the form:

$$x = a + b_1 \ln y + b_2 (\ln y)^2 + d_1 DL + d_2 DVL.$$

estimated values of the coefficients of the two dummy variables, from regressions for about 100 countries over the period 1950–83, except for merchandise trade which refers to the post-1962 period.

To explain the meaning of the results we refer to the case of exports. The coefficients in the table imply that, on the average, the export share in a large country is expected to be 7.1 percentage points lower than in a small country. The expected export share in a very large country is even lower by *additional* 6.8 percentage points; that is, when compared to a small country, a very large one has on the average a lower export share by 13.9 percentage points at any income level. Some brief observations on the results in the table are now presented.

(1) In most cases the estimated size effects are statistically significant.

(2) In most cases the two coefficients go in the same direction, implying that for very large countries the overall size effect is stronger than the one for other large countries.

(3) As expected, the largest effect appears in the trade variables. As compared to small countries in very large countries, the export share is expected on the average to be lower by 13.9 percentage points, and the import ratio by 16.8 points. The difference implies that capital inflows as a share of GDP are also lower. Within merchandise trade the effects of size are strongest for primary exports and for manufactures imports.

(4) Except for trade, the size effects on demand are small and not always monotonic.

(5) The main effect on the production structure is on manufacturing and within the sector, on the group of "late" industries.

Appendix B: Summary data table

	Size group	Per capita income (1980 U.S. $)				
		300	600	1000	2000	6000
Demand						
Consumption	VL	76.3	72.3	69.7	66.4	62.0
	VL^1	75.5	71.7	69.1	66.1	62.0
	OL	71.4	69.8	68.1	65.4	59.7
	Sm	77.7	72.6	69.3	65.5	61.0
Government	VL	8.1	8.1	8.7	10.2	14.4
	VL^1	8.1	8.2	8.7	10.3	14.4
	OL	12.8	11.8	11.7	12.2	14.9
	Sm	13.0	13.3	13.6	14.3	15.6
Investment	VL	18.2	20.9	22.2	23.3	23.1
	VL^1	19.5	22.1	23.4	24.2	23.2
	OL	18.1	20.8	22.3	23.7	24.2
	Sm	16.0	19.2	21.1	23.1	24.9

Appendix B:　Continued

	Size group	Per capita income (1980 U.S. $)				
		300	600	1000	2000	6000
Exports	VL	10.0	11.5	12.6	14.0	16.2
	VL[1]	7.2	8.0	9.0	11.0	15.5
	OL	17.9	17.3	17.3	18.0	20.6
	Sm	21.7	24.9	26.9	29.3	31.9
Foreign	VL	2.6	1.3	0.6	−0.1	−0.5
capital	VL[1]	3.1	2.0	1.3	0.5	−0.3
inflow	OL	2.3	2.4	2.1	1.2	−1.2
(imports − exports)	Sm	6.7	5.1	4.1	2.9	1.5
Trade						
Primary	VL	7.4	8.8	9.0	8.2	4.3
exports	VL[1]	3.3	3.7	3.8	3.7	2.9
	OL	12.5	11.0	10.2	9.3	8.4
	Sm	15.8	18.5	19.3	18.5	13.2
Manufactured	VL	1.6	1.1	1.6	3.3	8.8
exports	VL[1]	2.1	1.6	2.1	3.8	8.9
	OL	1.8	3.1	4.1	5.6	8.3
	Sm	1.7	2.3	3.3	5.7	11.7
Manufactured	VL	7.1	6.5	6.3	6.1	6.3
imports	VL[1]	5.3	4.4	4.1	4.2	5.8
	OL	10.7	10.7	10.7	10.9	11.3
	Sm	14.1	15.8	16.8	17.7	18.3
Value added						
Agriculture	VL	40.1	31.0	24.8	17.2	6.9
	VL[1]	34.9	25.2	19.1	12.5	5.8
	OL	35.1	28.8	24.0	17.4	6.7
	Sm	42.0	30.1	22.9	15.1	7.4
Mining	VL	4.1	5.7	6.2	5.9	3.1
	VL[1]	1.5	2.1	2.4	2.5	2.1
	OL	3.8	5.1	5.8	6.4	6.6
	Sm	3.7	6.4	7.4	7.4	4.5
Manufacturing	VL	14.6	17.3	19.5	22.6	28.1
	VL[1]	19.9	23.2	25.2	27.3	29.3
	OL	14.5	18.2	20.2	21.9	22.0
	Sm	9.2	12.6	15.0	18.1	22.6
Construction	VL	4.5	5.2	5.6	6.1	6.7
	VL[1]	4.5	5.1	5.4	5.9	6.6
	OL	4.3	5.0	5.5	6.0	6.7
	Sm	4.3	4.9	5.4	6.1	7.2
Utilities and	VL	36.7	40.8	43.9	48.1	55.2
services	VL[1]	39.2	44.5	47.8	51.7	56.2
	OL	42.3	42.9	44.5	48.3	58.0
	Sm	40.8	46.0	49.4	53.4	58.3
Labor force						
Agriculture	VL	69.1	60.1	52.3	40.0	16.8
	VL[1]	67.7	58.2	50.3	38.3	16.4
	OL	70.8	60.0	51.3	38.2	14.7
	Sm	78.0	63.7	53.3	39.2	17.2

Appendix B: Continued

	Size group	Per capita income (1980 U.S. $)				
		300	600	1000	2000	6000
Industry	VL	12.1	16.8	20.7	26.8	38.2
	VL¹	13.7	18.7	22.7	28.5	38.5
	OL	11.0	16.2	20.2	25.9	35.6
	Sm	8.2	13.7	18.1	24.6	36.2
Services	VL	18.8	23.1	27.0	33.2	45.0
	VL¹	18.6	23.1	27.0	33.2	45.1
	OL	18.2	23.8	28.5	35.9	49.7
	Sm	13.8	22.6	28.6	36.2	46.6
Manufacturing						
Early	VL	6.4	7.0	7.3	7.4	7.1
industries	VL¹	7.5	8.6	8.9	8.9	7.5
	OL	9.9	9.2	8.6	7.7	5.9
	Sm	6.4	8.1	8.9	9.2	7.9
Middle	VL	3.3	4.6	5.3	6.2	7.0
industries	VL¹	4.1	5.7	6.6	7.3	7.4
	OL	3.8	4.8	5.3	5.6	5.6
	Sm	2.8	3.7	4.2	4.9	5.6
Late	VL	4.0	5.9	7.6	10.0	14.4
industries	VL¹	5.6	8.2	9.9	12.1	15.0
	OL	2.1	4.1	5.6	7.6	10.9
	Sm	1.7	2.9	4.1	6.1	10.3

VL = Very large countries (excluding the Soviet Union)
VL¹ = Very large countries (excluding Indonesia and Nigeria)
OL = Other large countries
Sm = Small countries

References

Balassa, B. (1965) *Economic development and integration*. Mexico: CEMLA.

Balassa, B. (1969) 'Country size and trade patterns: Comment', *American Economic Review*, 59:201–204.

Balassa, B. and Stoutjesdijk, A. (1975) 'Economic integration among developing countries', *Journal of Common Market Studies*, 14:37–55.

Ban, S.H., Moon, P.Y., and Perkins, D.H. (1980) *Rural development in Korea*. Cambridge, MA: Harvard Council on East Asian Studies.

Bergson, A. and Kuznets, S., eds. (1963) *Economic trends in the Soviet Union*. Cambridge, MA: Harvard University Press.

Boserup, E. (1965) *The conditions of agricultural growth: The economics of agrarian change under population pressure*. Chicago, IL: Aldine.

Carneiro, R.L. (1970) 'A theory of the origin of the state', *Science*, 169:733–738.

Caves, R. (1987) 'International differences in industrial organization', in: R. Schmalensee and R.C. Willig, eds., *Handbook of Industrial Organization*. Amsterdam: North-Holland, forthcoming.

Chenery, H.B. (1960) 'Patterns of industrial growth', *American Economic Review*, 50:624–654.

Chenery, H.B. (1982) 'Industrialization and growth: The experience of large countries', World Bank Staff Working Paper no. 539.

Chenery, H.B. (1986) 'Growth and transformation', in: H. Chenery, S. Robinson, and M. Syrquin, eds., *Industrialization and growth: A comparative study*. New York: Oxford University Press.

Chenery, H.B. and Syrquin, M. (1975) *Patterns of development, 1950–1970*. London: Oxford University Press.

Chenery, H.B. and Taylor, L. (1968) 'Development patterns: Among countries and over time', *Review of Economics and Statistics*, 50:391–416.

Chenery, H.B., et al. (1974) *Redistribution with growth*. London: Oxford University Press.

Denison, E.F. (1967) *Why economic growth rates differ: Postwar experience in nine western countries*. Washington, DC: Brookings Institution.

Edelman, J.A. and Chenery, H.B. (1977) 'Aid and income distribution', in: J. Bhagwati, ed., *The new international economic order*. Cambridge, MA: MIT Press.

Feldstein, M. and Horioka, C. (1980) 'Domestic saving and international capital flows', *Economic Journal*, 90:314–329.

Geertz, C. (1963) *Agricultural involution: The process of ecological change in Indonesia*. Berkeley, CA: University of California Press.

Halevi, N. (1976) 'Some indexes of trade and factor integration for the EEC: 1960–1971', *Journal of Common Market Studies*, 14:336–343.

Hart, K. (1982) *The political economy of West African agriculture*. London: Cambridge University Press.

Houthakker, H.S. (1957) 'An international comparison of household expenditure patterns: Commemorating the centenary of Engel's law', *Econometrica*, 25:532–551.

Isard, W. (1956) *Location and space-economy*. Cambridge, MA: MIT Press.

Isenman, P. (1976) 'Biases in aid allocations against poorer and larger countries', *World Development*, 4:631–641.

Joint Economic Committee of the U.S. Congress (1982) *USSR: Measures of economic growth and development, 1950–80*. Washington, DC: Government Printing Office.

Keesing, D.B. (1968) 'Population and industrial development: Some evidence from trade patterns', *American Economic Review*, June: 448–455.

Keesing, D.B., and Sherk, D.R. (1971) 'Population density in patterns of trade and development', *American Economic Review*, 61:956–961.

Kleiman, E. (1976) 'Trade and the decline of colonialism', *Economic Journal*, 86:459–480.

Kravis, I.B., Heston, A.W., and Summers, R. (1982) *World product and income: International comparisons of real gross product*. Baltimore, MD: Johns Hopkins University Press.

Krueger, A.O. (1977) 'Growth, distortions, and patterns of trade among many countries', Princeton Studies in International Finance no. 40, Princeton University Press.

Kuznets, S. (1951) 'The state as a unit in the study of economic growth', *Journal of Economic History*, 11:25–41.

Kuznets, S. (1959) *Six lectures on economic growth*.

Kuznets, S. (1960) 'Economic growth of small nations', in: E.A.G. Robinson, ed., *Economic consequences of the size of nations*. London: Macmillan.

Kuznets, S. (1964) 'Quantitative aspects of the economic growth of nations: IX. Level and structure of foreign trade: Comparisons for recent years', *Economic Development and Cultural Change*, 13:1–106.

Kuznets, S. (1966) *Modern economic growth*. New Haven, CT: Yale University Press.

Linder, S.B. (1961) *An essay on trade and transformation*. New York: Wiley.

Lluch, C.A., Powell, A., and Williams, R.A. (1977) *Patterns in household demand and savings*. New York: Oxford University Press.

Machlup, F. (1977) *A history of thought on economic integration*. New York: Columbia University Press.

McCarthy, F.D., Taylor, L., and Talati, C. (1987) 'Trade patterns in developing countries, 1964–82', *Journal of Development Economics*, 40.

Ministry of Foreign Economic Relations and Trade Compilation Committee (1984) *Zhongguo duiwai jingji maoyi nianjian 1984*. Beijing: Ministry of Foreign Economic Relations and Trade.

Perkins, D.H. (1969) *Agricultural development in China, 1368–1968*. Chicago, IL: Aldine.

Perkins, D.H. and Yusuf, S. (1984) *Rural development in China*. Baltimore, MD: Johns Hopkins University Press.

Robinson, E.A.G., ed. (1960) *Economic consequences of the size of nations*. London: Macmillan.

Roemer, M. (1979) 'Resource-based industrialization in the developing countries', *Journal of Development Economics*.

Scitovsky, T. (1958) *Economic theory and Western European integration*. Stanford, CA: Stanford University Press.

Smith, A. *The wealth of nations* (originally published 1776). New York: Modern Library.

Srinivasan, T.N. (1986) 'The costs and benefits of being a small, remote, island, landlocked, or ministate economy', *The World Bank Research Observer*, 1:205–218.

State Statistical Bureau (1985) *Statistical yearbook of China, 1985* (in Chinese). Beijing: Statistical Press.

State Statistical Bureau (1986) *Statistical yearbook of China, 1986*. Hong Kong: Economic Information and Agency.

Svennilson, I. (1960) 'The concept of the nation and its relevance to economic analysis', in: E.A.G. Robinson, ed., *Economic consequences of the size of nations*. London: Macmillan.

Syrquin, M., and Chenery, H.B. (1986) 'Patterns of development: 1950–1983', processed, World Bank.

Treml, V. (1980) 'Foreign trade and the Soviet economy: Changing parameters and interrelations', in: E. Neuberger and L.A. Tyson, eds., *The impact of international economic disturbances on the Soviet Union and Eastern Europe: Transmission and response*. New York: Pergamon.

United Nations (1975) *Statistical yearbook, 1974*. New York: United Nations.

Williamson, J. (1965) 'Regional inequality and the process of national development: A description of the patterns', *Economic Development and Cultural Change*, 13:3–84.

Wittfogel, K.A. (1957) *Oriental despotism*. New Haven, CT: Yale University Press.

Wood, A. (1986) 'Growth and structural change in large low-income countries', World Bank Staff Working Paper no. 763.

World Bank (1980) *World tables: The second edition*. Baltimore, MD and London: Johns Hopkins University Press.

World Bank (1983) *World tables: The third edition*. Washington, DC: The World Bank.

World Bank (1984) 'World development report 1984', Oxford University Press.

World Bank (1985) 'World development report 1984', Oxford University Press.

World Bank (1986) 'World development report 1984', Oxford University Press.

Woytinsky, W.S. and Woytinsky, E.S. (1955) *World commerce and governments*. New York: Twentieth Century Fund.

Young, A.A. (1928) 'Increasing returns and economic progress', *Economic Journal*, 38:117–132.

INDEX